Lecture Notes in Artificial Intelligence 11468

Subseries of Lecture Notes in Computer Science

More information about this series at http://www.springer.com/series/1244

Francesco Calimeri · Nicola Leone ·
Marco Manna (Eds.)

Logics in
Artificial Intelligence

16th European Conference, JELIA 2019
Rende, Italy, May 7–11, 2019
Proceedings

 Springer

Editors
Francesco Calimeri 🆔
University of Calabria
Rende, Italy

Nicola Leone
University of Calabria
Rende, Italy

Marco Manna🆔
University of Calabria
Rende, Italy

ISSN 0302-9743   ISSN 1611-3349 (electronic)
Lecture Notes in Artificial Intelligence
ISBN 978-3-030-19569-4   ISBN 978-3-030-19570-0 (eBook)
https://doi.org/10.1007/978-3-030-19570-0

LNCS Sublibrary: SL7 – Artificial Intelligence

This Springer imprint is published by the registered company Springer Nature Switzerland AG
The registered company address is: Gewerbestrasse 11, 6330 Cham, Switzerland

Preface

This volume contains the papers presented at the 16th European Conference on Logics in Artificial Intelligence (JELIA 2019) held during May 7–11, 2019 in Rende (Cosenza), Italy. This edition was organized by the Artificial Intelligence Group of the Department of Mathematics and Computer Science at the University of Calabria.

The European Conference on Logics in Artificial Intelligence (or Journées Européennes sur la Logique en Intelligence Artificielle – JELIA) began back in 1988, as a workshop, in response to the need for a European forum for the discussion of emerging work in this field. Since then, JELIA has been organized biennially, with proceedings published in the Springer series *Lecture Notes in Artificial Intelligence.* Previous meetings took place in Roscoff, France (1988), Amsterdam, The Netherlands (1990), Berlin, Germany (1992), York, UK (1994), Évora, Portugal (1996), Dagstuhl, Germany (1998), Málaga, Spain (2000), Cosenza, Italy (2002), Lisbon, Portugal (2004), Liverpool, UK (2006), Dresden, Germany (2008), Helsinki, Finland (2010), Toulouse, France (2012), and Larnaca, Cyprus (2016). The aim of JELIA is to bring together active researchers interested in all aspects concerning the use of logics in artificial intelligence to discuss current research, results, problems, and applications of both theoretical and practical nature. JELIA strives to foster links and facilitate cross-fertilization of ideas among researchers from various disciplines, among researchers from academia and industry, and between theoreticians and practitioners. The scientific community has been increasingly showing interest in JELIA, which during the years featured the growing participation of researchers from outside Europe and a very high overall technical quality of contributions; hence, the conference turned into a major biennial forum and a reference for the discussion of approaches, especially logic-based, to artificial intelligence.

JELIA 2019 received 126 submissions in two different formats (long and short papers); throughout the reviewing process, three Program Committee members took care of each work; at the end, the Program Committee decided to accept a final list of 50 papers, consisting of 40 long and 10 short contributions. The accepted papers span a number of areas within logics in AI; eventually, we classified them in the categories that these proceedings are organized in: "Belief Revision and Argumentation," "Causal, Defeasible and Inductive Reasoning," "Conditional, Probabilistic and Propositional Logic," "Description Logics," "Logic Programming," "Modal and Default Logic," and "Temporal Logic." We would like to acknowledge the authors of all the submitted papers, including those not accepted for publication: the quality of the contributions was rather high, and this is the first and essential ingredient for a successful scientific conference.

The JELIA 2019 program was anchored by the invited talks by Georg Gottlob and Henri Prade, who provided the audience with two keynote speeches: "Vadalog: Recent Advances and Applications" and "Possibilistic Logic: From Certainty-Qualified Statements to Two-Tiered Logics – A Prospective Survey," respectively. Two out of all the accepted papers were nominated via a secret ballot among the Program Committee members as the Best Paper (authored by Forkel and Borgwardt: "Closed-World Semantics for Conjunctive Queries with Negation over ELH-bottom Ontologies") and the Best Student Paper (authored by Cabalar, Fandinno, Schaub and Schellhorn: "Lower Bound Founded Logic of Here-and-There"); they received a cash prize of EUR 500 each, kindly offered by Springer. These two contributions were also invited to the IJCAI-19 Sister Conference Best Paper Track in order to represent JELIA 2019. Furthermore, the authors of the top-notch contributions (including both best papers) will be invited to submit long and more elaborate versions of their work for a special issue of *Theory and Practice of Logic Programming* (TPLP).

JELIA 2019 closed by hosting an engaging public event, titled "Intelligenza Artificiale: etica, opportunità, insidie": a disseminative panel discussion (held in Italian) about ethics, opportunities, and threats of AI that was open to the general public, and featured top-notch scientists, journalists, and industry leaders. Among participants, we mention here Nicola Leone, Georg Gottlob, Bruno Siciliano, Gianluigi Greco, Pietro Scarpino, Marco Menichelli, and Maurizio Melis.

Many people and organizations contributed to the success of JELIA 2019; we start from the authors, the members of the Program Committee, and the additional experts who helped during the reviewing process, who diligently worked to produce a fair and thorough evaluation of the submitted papers, thus contributing and ensuring the high scientific quality of JELIA 2019; most importantly, we mention the invited speakers and the authors of the accepted papers, who provided the conference with a state-of-the-art technical program. We thank all of them!

We gratefully acknowledge all members and helpers of the local Organizing Committee of the Department of Mathematics and Computer Science at the University of Calabria, for taking care of all the big and small things needed in order to allow this event to actually take place. Furthermore, we gratefully acknowledge our sponsors and supporters for their generous help; in this respect, a special mention goes to Simona Perri, who did an awesome job playing several key roles: publicity chair, finance chair, member of the team organizing the closing event. Last, but not least, we thank the people of EasyChair for providing resources and a great conference management system.

May 2019

Francesco Calimeri
Nicola Leone
Marco Manna

Organization

Committees

General Chair

Nicola Leone — University of Calabria, Italy

Program Chairs

Francesco Calimeri — University of Calabria, Italy
Marco Manna — University of Calabria, Italy

Program Committee

José Julio Alferes	Universidade Nova de Lisboa, Portugal
Mario Alviano	University of Calabria, Italy
Leila Amgoud	IRIT-CNRS, France
Carlos Areces	Universidad Nacional de Córdoba, Argentina
Franz Baader	TU Dresden, Germany
Pietro Baroni	University of Brescia, Italy
Peter Baumgartner	CSIRO, Australia
Salem Benferhat	CNRS, Université d'Artois, France
Leopoldo Bertossi	Carleton University, RelationalAI Inc., Canada
Meghyn Bienvenu	CNRS, University of Bordeaux, France
Alexander Bochman	Holon Institute of Technology, Israel
Gerhard Brewka	Leipzig University, Germany
Pedro Cabalar	University of Coruna, Spain
Marco Calautti	The University of Edinburgh, UK
David Carral	TU Dresden, Germany
Giovanni Casini	University of Luxembourg, Luxembourg
Cristina Civili	Samsung R&D Institute United Kingdom, UK
Mehdi Dastani	Utrecht University, The Netherlands
James Delgrande	Simon Fraser University, Canada
Didier Dubois	IRIT, Université Paul Sabatier, France
Ulle Endriss	University of Amsterdam, The Netherlands
Wolfgang Faber	Alpen-Adria-Universität Klagenfurt, Austria
Luis Farinas Del Cerro	CNRS, France
Eduardo Fermé	Universidade da Madeira, Portugal
Michael Fisher	University of Liverpool, UK
Michael Gelfond	Texas Tech University, USA
Laura Giordano	Università del Piemonte Orientale, Italy
Valentina Gliozzi	Università di Torino, Italy
Lluis Godo	Artificial Intelligence Research Institute, IIIA-CSIC
Andreas Herzig	IRIT-CNRS, University of Toulouse, France

Tomi Janhunen	Aalto University, Finland
Gabriele Kern-Isberner	Technische Universität Dortmund, Germany
Sébastien Konieczny	CRIL-CNRS, France
Roman Kontchakov	University of London, UK
Jérôme Lang	CNRS, Université Paris-Dauphine, France
Joohyung Lee	Arizona State University, USA
João Leite	Universidade Nova de Lisboa, Portugal
Vladimir Lifschitz	The University of Texas at Austin, USA
Michael Loizos	Open University of Cyprus, Cyprus
Emiliano Lorini	IRIT-CNRS, France
Thomas Lukasiewicz	University of Oxford, UK
Inês Lynce	INESC-ID, Universidade de Lisboa, Portugal
Marco Maratea	University of Genoa, Italy
Jerzy Marcinkowski	Uniwersytetu Wroclawskiego, Poland
Pierre Marquis	CNRS, Université d'Artois, France
Thomas Meyer	University of Cape Town and CAIR, South Africa
Angelo Montanari	University of Udine, Italy
Michael Morak	Vienna University of Technology, Austria
Manuel Ojeda-Aciego	University of Malaga, Spain
Magdalena Ortiz	Vienna University of Technology, Austria
David Pearce	Universidad Politécnica de Madrid, Spain
Rafael Peñaloza	Free University of Bozen-Bolzano, Italy
Luís Moniz Pereira	Universidade Nova de Lisboa, Portugal
Andreas Pieris	The University of Edinburgh, UK
Henri Prade	IRIT-CNRS, France
Christoph Redl	Technische Universität Wien, Austria
Christian Retoré	CNRS, LIRMM University of Montpellier, France
Francesco Ricca	University of Calabria, Italy
Fabrizio Riguzzi	University of Ferrara, Italy
Jussi Rintanen	Aalto University, Finland
Chiaki Sakama	Wakayama University, Japan
Uli Sattler	The University of Manchester, UK
Michael Thielscher	The University of New South Wales, Australia
Mirek Truszczynski	University of Kentucky, USA
Leon van der Torre	University of Luxembourg, Luxembourg
Rineke Verbrugge	University of Groningen, Institute of Artificial Intelligence, The Netherlands
Carlos Viegas Damásio	Universidade Nova de Lisboa, Portugal
Toby Walsh	The University of New South Wales, Australia
Mary-Anne Williams	Innovation and Enterprise Research Lab, UTS
Frank Wolter	University of Liverpool, UK
Stefan Woltran	Vienna University of Technology, Austria

Publicity Chair

Simona Perri   University of Calabria, Italy

Finance Chair

Simona Perri   University of Calabria, Italy

Organization Chairs

Giovanni Amendola   University of Calabria, Italy
Carmine Dodaro   University of Genoa, Italy
Valeria Fionda   University of Calabria, Italy

Organizing Committee

Weronika T. Adrian   University of Calabria, Italy
Pierangela Bruno   University of Calabria, Italy
Francesco Cauteruccio   University of Calabria, Italy
Roberta Costabile   University of Calabria, Italy
Bernardo Cuteri   University of Calabria, Italy
Alessio Fiorentino   University of Calabria, Italy
Stefano Germano   University of Calabria, Italy
Cinzia Marte   University of Calabria, Italy
Aldo Marzullo   University of Calabria, Italy
Francesco Pacenza   University of Calabria, Italy
Jessica Zangari   University of Calabria, Italy

Additional Reviewers

Alberti, Marco
Aravanis, Theofanis
Aït-Kaci, Hassan
Cohen, Andrea
Console, Marco
Cota, Giuseppe
Cramer, Marcos
Delobelle, Jérôme
Dodaro, Carmine
Doder, Dragan
Ferrando, Angelo
Flaminio, Tommaso
Gebser, Martin
Gigante, Nicola
Gonçalves, Ricardo
Hans.Van-Ditmarsch, Hans
Haslum, Patrik
Hustadt, Ullrich
Ioannou, Christodoulos
Jeřábek, Emil
Kieroński, Emanuel
Lisitsa, Alexei
Lorini, Emiliano
Mantadelis, Theofrastos
Martinez, Maria Vanina
Matos, Vinícius
Michaliszyn, Jakub
Molinari, Alberto
Nicolosi-Asmundo, Marianna
Novaro, Arianna
Nuradiansyah, Adrian
Pagnucco, Maurice
Parent, Xavier
Peppas, Pavlos
Ribeiro, Jandson S.
Sallinger, Emanuel
Sciavicco, Guido
Son, Tran Cao
Wallon, Romain
Wang, Yi
Weydert, Emil
Yang, Zhun
Zese, Riccardo

Main Sponsors

- University of Calabria (https://www.mat.unical.it)
- Department of Mathematics and Computer Science, University of Calabria (https://www.mat.unical.it)
- Regione Calabria: Assessorato Istruzione e Attività Culturali, Università e Alta Formazione (http://www.regione.calabria.it)
- EurAI (https://www.eurai.org)
- Springer (https://www.springer.com)
- Altilia S.r.l. (http://www.altiliagroup.com/)
- Integris S.p.a. (http://www.integris.it/home)
- Intellimech (https://www.intellimech.it)
- Magazzini Rossella (http://www.magazzinirossella.it)
- NTT Data (https://it.nttdata.com/)

Under the patronage of

- Città di Rende (https://www.comune.rende.cs.it/)
- Città di Cosenza (http://www.comune.cosenza.it/)

Contents

Logic Programming

Modal and Default Logic

Temporal Logic

Invited Talks

Possibilistic Logic:
From Certainty-Qualified Statements to Two-Tiered Logics – A Prospective Survey

Didier Dubois and Henri Prade[(✉)]

IRIT – CNRS, 118, Route de Narbonne, 31062 Toulouse Cedex 09, France
{dubois,prade}@irit.fr

Abstract. Possibilistic logic (PL) is more than thirty years old. The paper proposes a survey of its main developments and applications in artificial intelligence, together with a short presentation of works in progress. PL amounts to a classical logic handling of certainty-qualified statements. Certainty is estimated in the setting of possibility theory as a lower bound of a necessity set-function. An elementary possibilistic formula is a pair made of a classical logic formula, and a certainty level belonging to a bounded scale. Basic PL handles only conjunctions of such formulas, and PL bases can be viewed as classical logic bases layered in terms of certainty. Semantics is in terms of epistemic states represented by fuzzy sets of interpretations. A PL base is associated with an inconsistency level above which formulas are safe from inconsistency. Applications include reasoning with default rules, belief revision, Bayesian possibilistic networks, information fusion, and preference modeling (in this latter case, certainty is turned into priority). Different extensions of basic PL are briefly reviewed, where levels take values in lattices, are replaced by vectors of levels, or are handled in a purely symbolic manner (without being instantiated). This latter extension may be of interest for explanation purposes. A paraconsistent treatment of inconsistency is also discussed. Still another extension allows for associating possibilistic formulas with sets of agents or sources that support them. In generalized possibilistic logic (GPL), negation and disjunction can be applied as well as conjunction, to possibilistic formulas. It may be viewed as a fragment of modal logic (such as KD45) where modalities cannot be nested. GPL can be still extended to a logic involving both objective and non-nested multimodal formulas. Applications of GPL to the modeling of ignorance, to the representation of answer set programs, to reasoning about other agents' beliefs, and to a logic of argumentation are outlined. Generally speaking, the interest and the strength of PL relies on a sound alliance between classical logic and possibility theory which offers a rich representation setting allowing an accurate modeling of partial ignorance. The paper focuses more on ideas than on technicalities and provides references for details (Invited talk presented by the second author).

© Springer Nature Switzerland AG 2019
F. Calimeri et al. (Eds.): JELIA 2019, LNAI 11468, pp. 3–20, 2019.
https://doi.org/10.1007/978-3-030-19570-0_1

1 Introduction

An important part of the pieces of information one has to deal with are pervaded with uncertainty. In other words, we have to handle statements that are not all fully certain. This does not mean that we are always able to quantify the certainty of a given piece of information in a precise manner. This calls for a setting that may be qualitative. Moreover, the fact that one has no certainty at all in favor of some statement should not entail that we have some certainty about the opposite statement, since one may be fully ignorant about a situation. This rules out probabilities $(\text{Prob}(A) = 0$ entails $\text{Prob}(\text{not}A) = 1)$.

Possibility theory has not this drawback since uncertainty about A is assessed in terms of two dual set functions, called possibility and necessity measures, by $\Pi(A)$ and $N(A) = 1 - \Pi(\text{not}A)$, and $N(A) = 0 = N(\text{not}A)$ in case of total ignorance about A. Moreover, possibility theory may be numerical or qualitative [47]. In the first case, possibility measures and the dual necessity measures can be regarded respectively as upper bounds and lower bounds of ill-known probabilities; they are also particular cases of plausibility and belief functions respectively [41, 72]. In fact, possibility measures and necessity measures constitute the simplest, non trivial, imprecise probabilities system [73]. Second, when qualitative, possibility theory provides a natural approach to the grading of possibility and necessity modalities on finite scales in an ordinal way.

Possibility theory has a logical counterpart, called possibilistic logic (PL) [35,37,48,50], which remains close to classical logic, and propagates certainty in a qualitative manner, retaining the weakest link in a chain of inferences. As this survey is going to show, PL logic turns to be an unexpectedly versatile tool. The paper is organized as follows. We give a short background on possibility theory in Sect. 2. Section 3 is devoted to basic PL, which handles conjunctions of PL formulas, made of a classical logic formula associated with a lower bound of necessity measure. Section 4 provides an overview of various applications of basic PL to default reasoning, belief revision, information fusion, decision under uncertainty, and uncertainty handling in databases; some other applications are briefly mentioned, as well as the close relationship of PL bases with possibilistic networks. Section 5 covers different extensions of PL where classical logic formulas may be associated with values in lattices, with vectors of certainty levels, with purely symbolic (non instantiated) values, with paraconsistent valuations, or still with sets of agents or sources that support them. Section 6 deals with generalized possibilistic logic, a two-tiered logic having a powerful representation ability for modeling uncertain epistemic states, which can capture answer set programming. Section 7 points out potential applications to multiple agent reasoning and to argumentative reasoning.

2 Short Refresher on Possibility Theory

Possibility theory originates in Zadeh's paper [75] and has been more extensively investigated in [40,41]. Zadeh starts from the idea of a possibility distribution to which he associates a possibility measure. A possibility distribution is a mapping

π from a set of states, or universe of discourse, U (it may be an attribute domain, the set of interpretation of a propositional language, etc) to a totally ordered scale $\mathcal{S}$, with top denoted by 1 and bottom by 0. It is assumed that $\mathcal{S}$ is equipped with an order-reversing map denoted by $\lambda \in \mathcal{S} \mapsto 1 - \lambda$. Different types of scales may be used from a finite scale $\mathcal{S} = \{1 = \lambda_1 > \ldots \lambda_n > \lambda_{n+1} = 0\}$ in the qualitative case, to the unit interval in the quantitative case, see [52] for other options. $\pi(u) = 0$ means that state u is rejected as impossible; $\pi(u) = 1$ means that state u is totally possible (= plausible). The larger $\pi(u)$, the more possible the state u is. If the universe U is exhaustive, at least one of the elements in $\mathcal{S}$ should be the actual world, so that $\exists u, \pi(u) = 1$ (normalization). This condition expresses the consistency of the epistemic state described by π.

A possibility distribution π is said to be at least as specific as another π' if and only if for each state of affairs u: $\pi(u) \le \pi'(u)$ [74]. Then, π is at least as restrictive and informative as π', since it rules out at least as many states with at least as much strength. In this setting, extreme forms of partial knowledge can be captured, namely: (i) complete knowledge: for some $u_0, \pi(u_0) = 1$ and $\pi(u) = 0, \forall u \ne u_0$ (only u_0 is possible); (ii) complete ignorance: $\pi(u) = 1, \forall u \in U$ (all states are possible).

Two dual set functions are associated with a possibility distribution, namely a possibility measure Π and a necessity measure N: $\forall A \subseteq U$,

$$\Pi(A) = \sup_{u \in A} \pi(u); \quad N(A) = 1 - \Pi(A^c) = \inf_{s \notin A} 1 - \pi(u),$$

with $A^c = U \setminus A$. $\Pi(A)$ (resp. $N(A)$) evaluates to what extent A is consistent with π (resp. A is certainly implied by π). Generally, $\Pi(U) = N(U) = 1$ and $\Pi(\emptyset) = N(\emptyset) = 0$ (since π is normalized to 1). In the Boolean case, the possibility distribution reduces to a disjunctive (epistemic) set $E \subseteq U$, and possibility and necessity are s.t.: (i) $\Pi(A) = 1$ if $A \cap E \ne \emptyset$, and 0 otherwise; (ii) $N(A) = 1$ if $E \subseteq A$, and 0 otherwise.

Possibility measures satisfy a characteristic "maxitivity" property $\Pi(A \cup B) = \max(\Pi(A), \Pi(B))$, and necessity measures a "minitivity" property $N(A \cap B) = \min(N(A), N(B))$. On infinite spaces, these axioms must hold for infinite families of sets. As a consequence, of the normalization of π, $\min(N(A), N(A^c)) = 0$ and $\max(\Pi(A), \Pi(A^c)) = 1$, or equivalently $\Pi(A) = 1$ whenever $N(A) > 0$, namely that something somewhat certain should be first fully possible, i.e. consistent with the available information. Moreover, one cannot be somewhat certain of both A and A^c, without being inconsistent. But we only have $N(A \cup B) \ge \max(N(A), N(B))$. This goes well with the idea that one may be certain about the event $A \cup B$, without being really certain about more specific events such as A and B.

Human knowledge is often expressed by statements to which belief degrees are attached. Certainty-qualified pieces of uncertain information of the form "A is certain to degree α" can then be modeled by the constraint $N(A) \ge \alpha$. It represents a family of possible epistemic states π that obey this constraint. The least specific possibility distribution among them exists and is defined by [41]: $\pi_{(A,\alpha)}(u) = 1$ if $u \in A, \pi_{(A,\alpha)}(u) = 1 - \alpha$ otherwise. If $\alpha = 1$ we get the characteristic function of A. If $\alpha = 0$, we get total ignorance. It is a key building-block to construct possibility distributions from several pieces of uncertain knowledge. It is instrumental in PL semantics.

There are two other set functions: (i) a measure of *guaranteed possibility* or *strong* possibility [31,47]: $\Delta(A) = \inf_{u \in A} \pi(u)$ which estimates to what extent *all* states in A are possible according to evidence. $\Delta(A)$ can be used as a degree of evidential support for A, and its dual conjugate ∇ such that $\nabla(A) = 1 - \Delta(A^c) = \sup_{u \notin A} 1 - \pi(u)$. $\nabla(A)$ evaluates the degree of potential or *weak* necessity of A, as it is 1 only if some state u out of A is impossible. Thus, the functions Δ and ∇ are *decreasing* wrt set inclusion (in full contrast with Π and N which are increasing). They satisfy the characteristic properties $\Delta(A \cup B) = \min(\Delta(A), \Delta(B))$ and $\nabla(A \cap B) = \max(\nabla(A), \nabla(B))$.

Interestingly enough, the four evaluations of an event A and the four evaluations of its opposite A^c can be organized in a cube of opposition [49] (see below), whose front and back facets are graded extension of the traditional square of opposition [67]. Counterparts of the characteristic properties of the square of opposition do hold. First, the diagonals (in dotted lines) of these facets link dual measures through the involutive order-reversing function $1 - (\cdot)$. The vertical edges of the cube, as well as the diagonals of the side facets, which are bottom-oriented arrows, correspond to entailments here expressed by inequalities. Indeed, provided that π and $1 - \pi$ are both normalized, we have for all A, $\max(N(A), \Delta(A)) \leq \min(\Pi(A), \nabla(A))$. The thick black lines of the top facets express mutual exclusiveness under the form $\min(N(A), N(A^c)) = \min(\Delta(A), \Delta(A^c)) = \min(N(A), \Delta(A^c)) = \min(\Delta(A), N(A^c)) = 0$. Dually, the double lines of the bottom facet correspond to $\max(\Pi(A), \Pi(A^c)) = \max(\nabla(A), \nabla(A^c)) = \max(\Pi(A), \nabla(A^c)) = \max(\nabla(A), \Pi(A^c)) = 1$. Thus, the following cube summarizes the interplay between the different set functions in possibility theory.

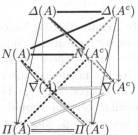

3   Basic Possibilistic Logic

A basic PL formula is a pair (a, α) made of a classical logic formula a associated with a certainty level $\alpha \in (0, 1]$, viewed as a lower bound of a *necessity measure*, i.e., (a, α) is semantically understood as $N(a) \geq \alpha$. Formulas of the form $(a, 0)$, contain no information ($N(a) \geq 0$ always holds), and are not considered. Thanks to the minitivity property of necessity measures for conjunction, i.e., $N(a \wedge b) = \min(N(a), N(b))$, a PL base, i.e., a set of PL formulas, can be always put in an equivalent clausal form.

Syntactic Aspects. Here we only consider the case of (basic) possibilistic *propositional* logic, i.e., PL formulas (a, α) are s.t. a is a formula in a propositional language; for (basic) possibilistic *first order* logic, the reader is referred to [37].

Axioms and Inference Rules. The PL axioms [37] are those of propositional logic, where each axiom schema is now supposed to hold with certainty 1. Its inference rules are:

- if $\beta \leq \alpha$ then $(a, \alpha) \vdash (a, \beta)$ (certainty weakening).
- $(\neg a \lor b, \alpha), (a, \alpha) \vdash (b, \alpha), \forall \alpha \in (0, 1]$ (modus ponens).

We may also use the certainty weakening rule with the following PL-resolution rule:

- $(\neg a \lor b, \alpha), (a \lor c, \alpha) \vdash (b \lor c, \alpha), \forall \alpha \in (0, 1]$ (resolution).

Using certainty weakening, it is easy to see that the following inference rule is valid:

- $(\neg a \lor b, \alpha), (a \lor c, \beta) \vdash (b \lor c, \min(\alpha, \beta))$ (weakest link resolution).

So in a reasoning chain, the certainty level of the conclusion is the smallest of the certainty levels of the formulas involved in the premises. The following inference rule, we call *formula weakening* holds also as a consequence of α-β-resolution.

- if $a \vdash b$ then $(a, \alpha) \vdash (b, \alpha), \forall \alpha \in (0, 1]$ (formula weakening).

Inference and Consistency. Let $\Gamma = \{(a_i, \alpha_i), i = 1, ..., m\}$ be a set of possibilistic formulas. In a way quite similar to propositional logic, proving $\Gamma \vdash (a, \alpha)$ amounts to proving $\Gamma, (\neg a, 1) \vdash (\bot, \alpha)$ by repeated application of the weakest link-resolution rule. Moreover, note that $\Gamma \vdash (a, \alpha)$ if and only if $\Gamma_\alpha \vdash (a, \alpha)$ if and only if $(\Gamma_\alpha)^* \vdash a$, where $\Gamma_\alpha = \{(a_i, \alpha_i) \in \Gamma, \alpha_i \geq \alpha\}$ and $\Gamma^* = \{a_i \mid (a_i, \alpha_i) \in \Gamma\}$. The certainty levels stratify the knowledge base Γ into nested level cuts Γ_α, i.e. $\Gamma_\alpha \subseteq \Gamma_\beta$ if $\beta \leq \alpha$. A consequence (a, α) from Γ can only be obtained from formulas having a certainty level at least equal to α, so from formulas in Γ_α; then a is a classical consequence from the PL knowledge base $(\Gamma_\alpha)^*$, and $\alpha = \max\{\beta | (\Gamma_\beta)^* \vdash a\}$.

The *inconsistency level* of Γ is defined by $inc(\Gamma) = \max\{\alpha | \Gamma \vdash (\bot, \alpha)\}$. The possibilistic formulas in Γ whose level is strictly above $inc(\Gamma)$ are safe from inconsistency, namely $inc(\{(a_i, \alpha_i)|(a_i, \alpha_i) \in \Gamma \text{ and } \alpha_i > inc(\Gamma)\}) = 0$. Indeed, if $\alpha > inc(\Gamma)$, $(\Gamma_\alpha)^*$ is consistent. The classical consistency of Γ^* is equivalent to $inc(\Gamma) = 0$.

Semantic Aspects. The semantics of PL [37] is expressed in terms of possibility distributions, and necessity measures on the set Ω of interpretations of the language. A PL formula (a, α) encodes the statement $N(a) \geq \alpha$. Its semantics is given by the following possibility distribution $\pi_{(a,\alpha)}$ defined in agreement with certainty qualification:

$$\forall \omega \in \Omega, \pi_{(a,\alpha)}(\omega) = 1 \text{ if } \omega \models a \text{ and } \pi_{(a,\alpha)}(\omega) = 1 - \alpha \text{ if } \omega \models \neg a$$

where ω is any interpretation of the considered propositional language. Intuitively, this means that any interpretation that is a counter-model of a, is all the less possible as a is more certain, i.e. as α is higher. It can be easily checked that the associated necessity measure is such that $N_{(a,\alpha)}(a) = \alpha$, and $\pi_{(a,\alpha)}$ is the *least informative* possibility distribution (i.e. maximizing possibility degrees) such that this constraint holds. In fact, any possibility distribution π such that $\forall \omega, \pi(\omega) \leq \pi_{(a,\alpha)}(\omega)$ is such that its associated necessity measure N satisfies $N(a) \geq N_{(a,\alpha)}(a) = \alpha$ (hence is more committed).

The base Γ is semantically associated with the possibility distribution:

$$\pi_\Gamma(\omega) = \min_{i=1,\ldots,m} \pi_{(a_i,\alpha_i)}(\omega) = \min_{i=1,\ldots,m} \max([a_i](\omega), 1 - \alpha_i)$$

where $[a_i]$ is the characteristic function of the models of a_i, namely $[a_i](\omega) = 1$ if $\omega \vDash a_i$ and $[a_i](\omega) = 0$ otherwise. Thus, the least informative induced possibility distribution π_Γ is obtained as the min-based conjunction of the fuzzy sets of interpretations (with membership functions $\pi_{(a_i,\alpha_i)}$), representing each formula. It can be checked that $N_\Gamma(a_i) \geq \alpha_i$ for $i=1,\ldots,m$, where N_Γ is the necessity measure defined from π_Γ. Note that we may only have an inequality here since Γ may, for instance, include two formulas associated to equivalent propositions, but with distinct certainty levels. The semantic entailment is defined by $\Gamma \vDash (a, \alpha)$ if and only if $\forall \omega, \pi_\Gamma(\omega) \leq \pi_{\{(a,\alpha)\}}(\omega)$. PL is sound and complete [37] wrt this semantics: $\Gamma \vdash (a, \alpha)$ if and only if $\Gamma \vDash (a, \alpha)$.

Moreover, we have $inc(\Gamma) = 1 - \max_{\omega \in \Omega} \pi_\Gamma(\omega)$, which acknowledges the fact that the normalization of π_Γ is equivalent to the classical consistency of Γ^*. Thus, an important feature of PL is its ability to deal with inconsistency.

4   Applications of Basic Possibilistic Logic

Before briefly surveying different uses of basic PL, we mention possibilistic networks as another compact representation setting that can be related to PL.

Possibilistic Networks. We first need to define conditioning in possibility theory. Conditional possibility can be defined similarly to probability theory using a Bayesian-like equation of the form [42] $\Pi(B \cap A) = \Pi(B \mid A) \star \Pi(A)$ where $\Pi(A) > 0$ and $\star$ may be the minimum or the product; moreover $N(B \mid A) = 1 - \Pi(B^c \mid A)$. If operation $\star$ is the minimum, the equation $\Pi(B \cap A) = \min(\Pi(B \mid A), \Pi(A))$ fails to characterize $\Pi(B \mid A)$, and we must resort to the minimal specificity principle to define a qualitative conditioning [41]: $\Pi(B \mid A) = 1$ if $\Pi(B \cap A) = \Pi(A) > 0$, $\Pi(B \mid A) = \Pi(B \cap A)$ otherwise. It is clear that $N(B \mid A) > 0$ if and only if $\Pi(B \cap A) > \Pi(B^c \cap A)$. Note also that $N(B \mid A) = N(A^c \cup B)$ if $N(B \mid A) > 0$. In the numerical setting, we must choose $\star$ = product that preserves continuity, so that $\Pi(B \mid A) = \frac{\Pi(B \cap A)}{\Pi(A)}$ which makes possibilistic and probabilistic conditionings very similar, and then gradual positive reinforcement of possibility is allowed.

There are several notions of possibilistic independence between events. Let us just mention two main directions (see [9] for details, discussions and reference):

- *Unrelatedness:* $\Pi(A \cap B) = \min(\Pi(A), \Pi(B))$. When it does not hold, it indicates an epistemic form of mutual exclusion between A and B. It is symmetric but sensitive to negation. When it holds for all pairs made of A, B and their complements, it is an epistemic version of logical independence, useful in default reasoning.
- *Causal independence:* $N(B \mid A) = N(B)$. This notion is different from the former one and stronger. It is a form of directed epistemic independence whereby learning A does not affect the certainty of B. It is neither symmetric not insensitive to negation. A weaker qualitative version is $N(B \mid A) > 0$ and $N(B) > 0$.

Graphical Structures. Like joint probability distributions, joint possibility distributions can be decomposed into a conjunction of conditional possibility distributions (using $\star$ = minimum, or product), once an ordering of the variables is chosen, in a way similar to Bayes nets [13]. A joint possibility distribution associated with ordered variables $X_1, \ldots, X_n$, can be decomposed by the chain rule

$$\pi(X_1, \ldots, X_n) = \pi(X_n \mid X_1, \ldots, X_{n-1}) \star \cdots \star \pi(X_2 \mid X_1) \star \pi(X_1).$$

Since possibilistic nets and PL bases are compact representations of possibility distributions, it should not come as a surprise that possibilistic nets can be directly translated into PL bases and vice-versa, both when conditioning is based on minimum or on product [13]. Hybrid representations formats have been introduced where local PL bases are associated to the nodes of a graphical structure rather than conditional possibility tables [25]. An important feature of the PL setting is the existence of equivalent representation formats: set of prioritized logical formulas, preorders on interpretations (possibility distributions) at the semantical level, possibilistic nets, but also set of conditionals of the form $\Pi(a \wedge b) > \Pi(a \wedge \neg b)$. There are algorithms for translating one format in another [13].

Default Reasoning. PL can be used for describing the normal course of things. A default rule "if a then b, generally" is understood formally as the constraint $\Pi(a \wedge b) > \Pi(a \wedge \neg b)$ on a possibility measure Π describing the semantics of the available knowledge. It expresses that in the context where a is true, there exists situations where having b true is strictly more plausible than any situations where b is false in the same context. Any finite consistent set of constraints of the above form, representing a set of defaults $\mathcal{D} = \{a_i \rightsquigarrow b_i, i = 1, \cdots, n\}$, is compatible with a non-empty family of possibility measures Π, and induces a partially defined ranking on the set of interpretations, that can be completed according to the principle of minimal specificity, e.g. [18]. This principle assigns to each world ω the highest possibility level without violating the constraints. This defines a unique complete preorder. The method then consists in turning each default $a_i \rightsquigarrow b_i$ into a possibilistic clause $(\neg a_i \vee b_i, N(\neg a_i \vee b_i))$, where N is computed from the greatest possibility distribution π induced by the set of constraints corresponding to the default knowledge base, as already explained. We thus obtain a PL base K. This encodes the generic knowledge embedded in the default rules. Then we apply the possibilistic inference for reasoning with the formulas in K encoding the defaults together with the available factual knowledge encoded as fully certain possibilistic formulas in a base F. However, the conclusions that can be obtained from $K \cup F$ with a certainty level strictly greater than the level of inconsistency of this base are safe. Roughly speaking, it turns out that in this approach, the most specific rules w.r.t. a given context remain above the level of inconsistency. Such an approach has been proved to be in full agreement with the Kraus-Lehmann-Magidor postulates-based approach to nonmonotonic reasoning [60]. More precisely, two nonmonotonic entailments can be defined in the possibilistic setting, the one presented above, based on the least specific possibility distribution compatible with the constraints encoding the set of defaults, and another one more cautious, where one considers that b can be deduced in the situation where all we know is $F = \{a\}$ iff the inequality $\Pi(a \wedge b) > \Pi(a \wedge \neg b)$ holds true for *all* the Π compatible with the constraints encoding the set of defaults. The first entailment coincides with the rational closure inference [63], while the later corresponds to the (cautious) preferential entailment [60]; see [15, 45].

PL can be also applied to inductive logic programming (ILP). Indeed having a stratified set of first-order logic rules as an hypothesis in ILP is of interest for learning both rules covering normal cases and more specific rules for exceptional cases [71].

Belief Revision. Since nonmonotonic reasoning and belief revision can be closely related, PL finds application also in belief revision. In fact, comparative necessity relations (which can be encoded by necessity measures) [28] are nothing but the epistemic entrenchment relations [43] that underlie well-behaved belief revision processes [57]. This enables the PL setting to provide syntactic revision operators that apply to possibilistic knowledge bases, including the case of uncertain inputs [21, 46, 70]. Note that in PL, where formulas (a, α) are pieces of belief with certain levels, the epistemic entrenchment of formulas is made explicit through these levels. Besides, in a revision process it is expected that all formulas independent of the validity of the input information should remain in the revised state of belief; this idea may receive a precise meaning using a definition of possibilistic causal independence between events [29].

Updating in a dynamic world obeys other principles than the revision of a belief state by an input information in a static world. It is linked to the idea of Lewis' *imaging*, whose a possibilistic counterpart is proposed in [44]. A PL transposition of Kalman filtering that combines the ideas of updating and revision can be found in [19].

In contrast with static beliefs, expected to be closed under conjunctions, (positive) desires are such that endorsing $a \vee b$ as a desire means to desire a *and* to desire b. However, desiring both a and $\neg a$ does not sound rational; so when a new desire is added to the set of desires of an agent, a revision process is necessary. Just as belief revision relies on an epistemic entrenchment relation (and thus on a necessity measure), well-behaved desire revision relies on a guaranteed possibility function Δ [39].

Information Fusion. The combination of possibility distributions can be equivalently performed in terms of PL bases: The syntactic counterpart of the pointwise combination of two possibility distributions π_1 and π_2 into a distribution $\pi_1 \circledast \pi_2$ by any monotonic combination operator $\circledast$ such that $1 \circledast 1 = 1$, can be computed, following an idea first proposed in [26]. Namely, if the PL base Γ_1 is associated with π_1 and the base Γ_2 with π_2, a PL base $\Gamma_{1 \circledast 2}$ semantically equivalent to $\pi_1 \circledast \pi_2$ is given by [16]:

$$\{(a_i, 1 - (1 - \alpha_i) \circledast 1) \text{ s.t. } (a_i, \alpha_i) \in \Gamma_1\} \cup \{(b_j, 1 - 1 \circledast (1 - \beta_j)) \text{ s.t. } (b_j, \beta_j) \in \Gamma_2\}$$
$$\cup \{(a_i \vee b_j, 1 - (1 - \alpha_i) \circledast (1 - \beta_j)) \text{ s.t. } (a_i, \alpha_i) \in \Gamma_1, (b_j, \beta_j) \in \Gamma_2\}.$$

For $\circledast = \min$, we get $\Gamma_{1 \oplus 2} = \Gamma_1 \cup \Gamma_2$ with $\pi_{\Gamma_1 \cup \Gamma_2} = \min(\pi_1, \pi_2)$ as expected (conjunctive combination). For $\circledast = \max$ (disjunctive combination), we get $\Gamma_{1 \oplus 2} = \{(a_i \vee b_j, \min(\alpha_i, \beta_j)) \text{ s.t. } (a_i, \alpha_i) \in \Gamma_1, \text{ and } (b_j, \beta_j) \in \Gamma_2\}$. With non idempotent $\oplus$ operators, some reinforcement effects may be obtained. See [20,58,69] for further studies on possibilistic logic merging operators. Besides, this approach can be also applied to the syntactic encoding of the merging of *classical* logic bases based on Hamming distance (where distances are computed between each interpretation and the different classical logic bases, thus giving birth to counterparts of possibility distributions) [14].

Decision Under Uncertainty. Possibility theory provides a valuable setting for qualitative decision under uncertainty where a pessimistic and an optimistic decision criterion have been axiomatized [53]. The counterpart of these criteria, when knowledge and preferences are under the form of *two distinct* PL bases, is given by the definitions [38]:

- the pessimistic utility $u_*(d)$ of decision d is the maximal $\alpha \in S$ s.t. $K_\alpha \wedge d \vdash_{PL} P_{\nu(\alpha)}$,
- the optimistic utility $u^*(d)$ of d is the maximal $\nu(\alpha) \in S$ s.t. $K_{\underline{\alpha}} \wedge d \wedge P_{\underline{\alpha}} \not\equiv \perp$,

where S is a finite bounded totally ordered scale, ν the ordered reversing map of this scale; K_α is a set of classical logic formulas gathering the pieces of knowledge that are certain at a level at least α, and where P_β is a set of classical logic formulas made of a set of goals (modeling preferences) whose priority level is *strictly* greater than β. An optimal pessimistic decision leads for sure to the satisfaction of all goals in $P_{\nu(\alpha)}$ with a priority as low as possible, using only a part K_α of knowledge which has high certainty. An optimal optimistic decision maximizes the consistency of all the more or less important goals with all the more or less certain pieces of knowledge.

Other Applications. In a computational perspective, possibilistic logic has also impacted logic programming [1,6,65,66]. Besides, the possibilistic handling of uncertainty in description logic [68,76] has also computational advantages, in particular in the case of the *possibilistic DL-Lite* family [11,12]. Another application is the encoding of control access policies [22]. Lastly, PL has been recently shown to be of interest in database design where the presence of tuples in the database is possible only to some extent, and where functional dependencies are certain only to some extent [59,64].

5   Extensions of Basic Possibilistic Logic

This section surveys various extensions of basic PL where logical formulas are no longer associated with simple levels valued in a linearly ordered scale.

Lattices. A first idea is to use lattices of values instead of a scale. Examples are: (i) a timed PL where logical formulas are associated with *fuzzy* sets of time instants where the formula is known as being certain to some extent. Semantically, it leads to define necessity measures valued in a distributive lattice; (ii) a *logic of supporters* [61], where formulas a are associated with sets of logical arguments in their favor, (iii) an *interval-based PL* [23] where levels are replaced by intervals, modeling imprecise certainty.

Vectors of Certainty Levels. An obvious consequence of the PL resolution rule is that only the smallest weight of the formulas used in a proof is retained. Thus no difference is made between, e.g., getting (b, β) from $(\neg a \vee b, 1)$ and (a, β), or getting it from $(\neg c \vee d, 1)$, $(\neg d \vee b, \alpha)$ and (c, β) assuming $\alpha \geq \beta$, although we may find the first proof stronger. This idea can be captured by a new resolution rule $(\neg a \vee b, \alpha)$; $(a \vee c, \beta) \vdash (b \vee c, \alpha\beta)$ where α and β are lists of weights, and $\alpha\beta$ is the list obtained as the concatenation of α and β. In the above example, the first proof yields $(b, (1, \beta))$, while the second one leads to $(b, (1, \alpha, \beta))$. Assuming a finite scale, we have then to rank-order the proofs according to their strength. This can be done by a refinement of min-based ordering, called *leximin* [48] which amounts to a lexicographic ordering of the vectors once they have been completed with 1's for making them of equal length, and increasingly reordered. This can be equivalently encoded by treating the vectors as multisets, replacing $\alpha\beta$ by the union $\otimes$ of the corresponding multisets, and defining an associative operation $\oplus$ that selects the multiset containing the least possible value with a number of occurrences lower than its occurrence in the other multiset (after discarding the values common in equal number in the two multi sets). See [30] for the semiring structure based on $\oplus$ and $\otimes$. On this basis an extended PL could be fully developed.

Purely Symbolic Levels. Another extension of interest is to consider that the values of certainty levels associated to formulas (still assumed to belong to a totally ordered scale) may be unknown, while the relative ordering between some of them may be known. In such a case, we have to process these levels in a purely symbolic manner, i.e., computing the level from a derived formula as a symbolic expression. For instance, $\Gamma = \{(a, \alpha), (\neg a \vee b, \beta), (b, \gamma)\} \vdash (b, \max(\min(\alpha, \beta), \gamma))$. There still exists a partial order between formulas based on the partial order between symbolic levels (e.g., $\max(\min(\alpha, \beta), \alpha, \gamma) \geq \min(\alpha, \delta)$ for any values of $\alpha, \beta, \gamma, \delta$). See [24] for details and [27] for the proof of completeness.

The use of symbolic levels may serve *explanation* purposes by providing a tool for tracing the impact of the certainty of some pieces of information on a conclusion of interest, as early suggested in [56]. Possibilistic logic formulas with symbolic weights have been used in preference modeling [10]. Then, interpretations (corresponding to the different alternatives) are compared in terms of symbolic vectors acknowledging the satisfaction or the violation of the formulas associated with the different (conditional) preferences, using suitable order relations. Thus, partial orderings of interpretations can be obtained, and may be refined in case some additional information on the relative priority of the preferences is given. Another use may concern access rights: The different contexts of an ontology, like the access rights of a user, the trust level or the level of detail requested by the user, my be expressed by elements of a lattice, leading to a calculus similar to PL with symbolic weights [3].

Paraconsistent Valuations. An extension of the possibilistic inference has been proposed for handling paraconsistent information [17]. The idea is the following. Given a PL base Γ, we build a set Γ° of bi-weighted formulas: for each formula (a, α) in Γ, we compute triples (a, β, γ) where β (resp. γ) is the highest degree with which a (resp. $\neg a$) is supported in Γ (a is said to be *supported* in Γ *at least at degree* β if there is a *consistent* sub-base of $(\Gamma_\beta)^*$ that entails a, with $\Gamma_\beta^* = \{a_i \mid (a_i, \alpha_i) \in \Gamma, \ \alpha_i \geq \beta\}$).

Clearly the set of formulas of the form $(a, \beta, 0)$ in Γ° is not paraconsistent, and thus leads to safe conclusions. However, one may obtain a larger set of consistent conclusions from Γ° as explained now. This requires two evaluations: (i) the *undefeasibility* degree of a consistent set A of formulas: $UD(A) = \min\{\beta \mid (a, \beta, \gamma) \in \Gamma^\circ$ and $a \in A\}$; (ii) the *unsafeness* degree of a consistent set A of formulas: $US(A) = \max\{\gamma \mid (a, \beta, \gamma) \in \Gamma^\circ$ and $a \in A\}$. Then an entailment $\vdash_{SS}$, named *safely supported* consequence relation, is defined by $\Gamma^\circ \vdash_{SS} b$ if and only if $\exists$ a minimal consistent subset A that classically entails b such that $UD(A) > US(A)$. It can be shown that the set $\{b \mid \Gamma^\circ \vdash_{SS} b\}$ is classically consistent [17]. See [32,51] for details, discussions and other approaches to the handling of inconsistency in the PL setting.

Subsets of Agents. Another early proposed idea, in an information fusion perspective, is to associate each formula with a set of distinct explicit sources that support its truth [36]. Then formulas are associated with sets of sources. This has led to the proposal of a "multiple agent" logic (*ma-L*) where formulas are of the form (a, A), where A denotes a subset of agents and the formula means that *at least all* the agents in A believe that a is true. In spite of an obvious formal parallel with PL, (a, A) should not only be seen as another way of expressing the strength of the support in favor of a (the larger A, the stronger the support) [33], but also as a piece of information linking a proposition with a particular subset of agents. *ma-L* has two inference rules: (i) if $B \subseteq A$ then $(a, A) \vdash (a, B)$ (subset weakening); (ii) $(\neg a \vee b, A), (a, A) \vdash (b, A), \forall A \in 2^{ALL} \setminus \emptyset$ (modus ponens). As a consequence, we also have the resolution rule if $A \cap B \neq \emptyset$, then $(\neg a \vee b, A), (a \vee c, B) \vdash (b \vee c, A \cap B)$. If $A \cap B = \emptyset$, the resulting information is trivial: $(a, \emptyset)$ is a formula of no use. An *inconsistent subset* of agents for Γ can be defined as

$$inc\text{-}s(\Gamma) = \bigcup\{A \subseteq All \mid \Gamma \vdash (\bot, A)\} \text{ and } inc\text{-}s(\Gamma) = \emptyset \text{ if } \nexists A \text{ s.t. } \Gamma \vdash (\bot, A).$$

Clearly, $inc\text{-}s(\Gamma) = \emptyset$ does not imply the consistency of $\Gamma^\circ = \{a_i \mid (a_i, A_i) \in \Gamma, i = 1, m\}$. It contrasts with possibilistic logic. Just consider the example

$\Gamma = \{(a, A), (\neg a, \overline{A})\}$, then $inc\text{-}s(\Gamma) = A \cap \overline{A} = \emptyset$ while Γ° is inconsistent. This is compatible with situations where agents contradict each other. Yet, the consistency of Γ° does entail $inc\text{-}s(\Gamma) = \emptyset$. What matters in $ma\text{-}L$ is the collective consistency of *subsets* of agents (while the collection of the beliefs held by the whole set of agents may be inconsistent).

The semantics of $ma\text{-}L$ is expressed in terms of set-valued possibility distributions, and set-valued possibility and necessity measures. Namely, the semantics of formula (a, A) is given by set-valued distribution $\pi_{\{(a,A)\}}$: $\forall \omega \in \Omega$, $\pi_{\{(a,A)\}}(\omega) = All$ if $\omega \models a$, $\pi_{\{(a,A)\}}(\omega) = A^c$ if $\omega \models \neg a$ where $A^c = All \setminus A$, and the formula (a, A) is understood as expressing the constraint $\mathbf{N}(a) \supseteq A$ where $\mathbf{N}$ is a set-valued necessity measure. Soundness and completeness results can be established with respect to this semantics [7].

Basic PL and $ma\text{-}L$ may be combined in a possibilistic multiple agent logic (P$ma\text{-}L$). Formulas are pairs (a, F) where F is a fuzzy subset of All. One may in particular consider the fuzzy sets $F = (\alpha/A)$ s.t. $(\alpha/A)(k) = \alpha$ if $k \in A$, and $(\alpha/A)(k) = 0$ if $k \in A^c$; it encodes the piece of information "at least all agents in A believe a at least at level α". Interpretations are then associated with fuzzy sets of agents. Soundness and completeness of P$ma\text{-}L$ has been established [8].

6 Generalized Possibilistic Logic

In basic possibilistic logic, only conjunctions of possibilistic logic formulas are allowed. But since (a, α) is semantically interpreted as $N(a) \geq \alpha$, a possibilistic formula can be manipulated as a propositional formula that is true (if $N(a) \geq \alpha$) or false (if $N(a) < \alpha$). Then possibilistic formulas can be combined with all propositional connectives, including disjunction and negation. This is *generalized possibilistic logic* (GPL) [34, 55]. GPL is a two-tiered propositional logic, in which propositional formulas are encapsulated by weighted modal operators interpreted in terms of uncertainty measures from possibility theory. Let $\Lambda_k = \{0, \frac{1}{k}, \frac{2}{k}, ..., 1\}$ with $k \in \mathbb{N} \setminus \{0\}$ be a finite set of certainty degrees, and let $\Lambda_k^+ = \Lambda_k \setminus \{0\}$. The language of GPL, $\mathcal{L}_{\mathbf{N}}^k$, with $k + 1$ certainty levels is built on top of the propositional language $\mathcal{L}$ as follows: (i) If $a \in \mathcal{L}$, $\alpha \in \Lambda_k^+$, then $\mathbf{N}_\alpha(a) \in \mathcal{L}_{\mathbf{N}}^k$; (ii) if $\varphi \in \mathcal{L}_{\mathbf{N}}^k$, $\psi \in \mathcal{L}_{\mathbf{N}}^k$, then $\neg \varphi$ and $\varphi \wedge \psi$ are also in $\mathcal{L}_{\mathbf{N}}^k$.

Here we use the notation $\mathbf{N}_\alpha(a)$, instead of (a, α), emphasizing the closeness with modal logic. So, an agent asserting $\mathbf{N}_\alpha(a)$ has an epistemic state π such that $N(a) \geq \alpha > 0$. Hence $\neg\mathbf{N}_\alpha(a)$ stands for $N(a) < \alpha$, which, given the finiteness of the set of considered certainty degrees, means $N(a) \leq \alpha - \frac{1}{k}$ and thus $\Pi(\neg a) \geq 1 - \alpha + \frac{1}{k}$. Let $\nu(\alpha) = 1 - \alpha + \frac{1}{k}$. Then, $\nu(\alpha) \in \Lambda_k^+$ iff $\alpha \in \Lambda_k^+$, and $\nu(\nu(\alpha)) = \alpha, \forall \alpha \in \Lambda_k^+$. Thus, we can write $\mathbf{\Pi}_\alpha(p) \equiv \neg\mathbf{N}_{\nu(\alpha)}(\neg p)$. In particular, $\mathbf{\Pi}_1(a) \equiv \neg\mathbf{N}_{\frac{1}{k}}(\neg a)$ if $k > 1$. So, in GPL, one can distinguish between the absence of sufficient certainty that a is true ($\neg\mathbf{N}_\alpha(a)$) and the stronger statement that a is somewhat certainly false ($\mathbf{N}_\alpha(\neg a)$).

The semantics of GPL is as in PL defined in terms of normalized possibility distributions over propositional interpretations, where possibility degrees are limited to Λ_k. A model of a GPL formula $\mathbf{N}_\alpha(a)$ is any Λ_k-valued possibility distribution π such that $N(a) \geq \alpha$, where N is the necessity measure induced by π, and then the standard definition for $\pi \models \varphi_1 \wedge \varphi_2 \ \pi \models \neg\varphi$. As usual, π is called a model of a set of GPL formulas Γ, written $\pi \models \Gamma$, if π is a model of each formula in Γ. We write $\Gamma \models \phi$, for Γ a set of GPL formulas and ϕ a GPL formula, iff every model of Γ is also a model of ϕ. Note that a formula in GPL will not always have a least specific possibility distribution that satisfies it. For instance, the set of possibility distributions satisfying the disjunction '$\mathbf{N}_\alpha(a) \vee \mathbf{N}_\alpha(b)$' no longer has a unique least informative model as it is the case for conjunction in PL. The soundness and completeness of the following axiomatization of GPL holds with respect to the above semantics [55]:

(**PL**) The Hilbert axioms of classical logic; (**K**) $\mathbf{N}_\alpha(a \to b) \to (\mathbf{N}_\alpha(a) \to \mathbf{N}_\alpha(b))$;
(**N**) $\mathbf{N}_1(\top)$; (**D**) $\mathbf{N}_\alpha(a) \to \mathbf{\Pi}_1(a)$; (**W**) $\mathbf{N}_{\alpha_1}(a) \to \mathbf{N}_{\alpha_2}(a)$, if $\alpha_1 \geq \alpha_2$.

with modus ponens as the only inference rule.
Note that when α is fixed we get a fragment of the modal logic KD. See [5] for a survey of studies of the links between modal logics and possibility theory, and extensions of GPL with objective and non-nested multimodal formulas, as in KD45 and S5.

7   Applications of Generalized Possibilistic Logic

Nonmonotonic Logic Programming. A remarkable application of GPL is its capability to encode answer set programs, using a 3-valued scale $\Lambda_2 = \{0, 1/2, 1\}$. Then, we can discriminate between propositions we are fully certain of and propositions we consider only more plausible than not. It is enough to encode nonmonotonic ASP rules (with negation as failure) within GPL and lay bare their epistemic semantics. For instance, the ASP rule $a \leftarrow b \wedge \operatorname{not} c$ is encoded as $\mathbf{N}_1(b) \wedge \mathbf{\Pi}_1(\neg c) \to \mathbf{N}_1(a)$ in GPL. See [55] for theoretical results, and [54] for the GPL encoding of Pearce equilibrium logic.

Multiple Agent Reasoning. We consider the muddy children problem: Two children come home from garden. The father sees their muddy foreheads. They sit by him. Father declares at least one of them has a muddy forehead. Then he asks them whoever has mud on the forehead to stand up. None does. Then the question is asked again. Both stand up. Why? Informally, the children did not stand up in the first place because they do not see their own forehead and they see the other is muddy, but as the latter did not stand up it means he did not know either it was muddy because he sees the former is muddy.

Since there is no uncertainty, we use a particular case of GPL, where $k = 1$ with value scale Λ_1, known as Meta-Epistemic Logic (MEL) [4]; $\Box a$ is identified with $\mathbf{N}_1(a)$ and $\Diamond a$ with $\mathbf{\Pi}_1(a)$. Moreover $\mathbf{\Pi}_1(a) \equiv \neg\mathbf{N}_1(\neg a)$. For the example, we consider the point of view of one child (say child 1): we say "I". The other is "You". We use a standard propositional language $\mathcal{L}$ with variables

$V = \{m_I, m_Y, s_Y\}$ (for I am muddy, you are muddy, you stand up). We use one MEL modality $\Box_Y$ standing for "I know that You know" Each pure propositional formula $a \in \mathcal{L}$ not in the scope of $\Box_Y$ is interpreted as "I know a" (modality $\Box_I$) is not explicitly used because we exclude for the reference agent ("I") the possibility of declaring ignorance). So "My" knowledge is the following:

1. Father's public announcement: I know one of us is muddy and I know You know it too: $m_I \lor m_Y$; $\Box_Y(m_I \lor m_Y)$;
2. I know that You know whether I am muddy or not (You see me): $\Box_Y m_I \lor \Box_Y \neg m_I$;
3. I know that you ignore if You are muddy or not (like me): $\neg\Box_Y m_Y \land \neg\Box_Y \neg m_Y$;
4. I know that if You knew I was not muddy and that one of us is muddy anyway, then You would know that you are muddy: $\Box_Y \neg m_I \land \Box_Y(m_I \lor m_Y) \to \Box_Y(m_Y)$;
5. I know that if You knew you were muddy You would stand up when invited too: $\Box_Y(m_Y) \to s_Y$; we also have $\Box_Y(m_Y) \to m_Y$.

I see You did not stand up, so I add $\neg s_Y$ to my knowledge base, and I reason as follows: $\frac{\neg s_Y, \Box_Y(m_Y) \to s_Y}{\neg\Box_Y(m_Y)}$. You did not stand up because you did not know if you were muddy (and now I know it). $\frac{\neg\Box_Y(m_Y), \Box_Y(m_I \lor m_Y), \Box_Y \neg m_I \land \Box_Y(m_I \lor m_Y) \to \Box_Y(m_Y)}{\neg\Box_Y \neg m_I}$. As one of us at least is muddy and you have no knowledge to claim you are muddy, it means that I know You cannot claim I am not muddy. $\frac{\neg\Box_Y \neg m_I, \Box_Y m_I \lor \Box_Y \neg m_I}{\Box_Y m_I}$. Since it is wrong that you know I am not muddy, while you know if I am muddy or not, it is because you know I am muddy. $\frac{\Box_Y m_I, \Box_Y m_I \to m_I}{m_I}$. Now I know that You know I am muddy, so, I know I am muddy, and I will stand up next time I am invited to.

Argumentative Reasoning. A logic of arguments similar to GPL has been outlined in [2]. The basic formulas are pairs (x, y) ("y is a reason for x"), which are manipulated as propositional formulas using $\land, \lor, \neg$ connectives. Thus, e.g., we allow the use of negation in three places: $(x, \neg y)$, $(\neg x, y)$, $\neg(x, y)$, making also difference between (x, y) and $(\neg y \lor x, \top)$, and $(\neg x \lor x', y), (x \lor z, y') \vdash (x' \lor z, y \land y')$ is a valid inference rule.

8   Conclusion

This survey has covered old results and works in progress about PL, a simple, but quite powerful approach to the handling of uncertainty that remains as close as possible to classical logic. For complexity issues of PL and GPL the reader is referred to [62] and [55].

References

1. Alsinet, T., Godo, L., Sandri, S.: Two formalisms of extended possibilistic logic programming with context-dependent fuzzy unification: a comparative description. Elec. Notes Theor. Comput. Sci. **66**(5), 1–21 (2002)
2. Amgoud, L., Prade, H.: Towards a logic of argumentation. In: Hüllermeier, E., Link, S., Fober, T., Seeger, B. (eds.) SUM 2012. LNCS (LNAI), vol. 7520, pp. 558–565. Springer, Heidelberg (2012). https://doi.org/10.1007/978-3-642-33362-0_43
3. Baader, F., Knechtel, M., Peñaloza, R.: Context-dependent views to axioms and consequences of semantic web ontologies. J. Web Semant. **12**, 22–40 (2012)
4. Banerjee, M., Dubois, D.: A simple logic for reasoning about incomplete knowledge. Int. J. Approx. Reason. **55**, 639–653 (2014)
5. Banerjee, M., Dubois, D., Godo, L., Prade, H.: On the relation between possibilistic logic and modal logics of belief and knowledge. J. Appl. Non-Class. Log. **27**, 206–224 (2017)
6. Bauters, K., Schockaert, S., De Cock, M., Vermeir, D.: Possible and necessary answer sets of possibilistic answer set programs. In: Proceedings of the 24th IEEE International Conference on Tools for AI (ICTAI), Athens, pp. 836–843 (2012)
7. Belhadi, A., Dubois, D., Khellaf-Haned, F., Prade, H.: Multiple agent possibilistic logic. J. Appl. Non-Class. Logics **23**, 299–320 (2013)
8. Belhadi, A., Dubois, D., Khellaf-Haned, F., Prade, H.: Reasoning with multiple-agent possibilistic logic. In: Schockaert, S., Senellart, P. (eds.) SUM 2016. LNCS (LNAI), vol. 9858, pp. 67–80. Springer, Cham (2016). https://doi.org/10.1007/978-3-319-45856-4_5
9. Ben Amor, N., Benferhat, S., Dubois, D., Mellouli, K., Prade, H.: A theoretical framework for possibilistic independence in a weakly ordered setting. Int. J. Uncertain. Fuzziness Knowl.-Based Syst. **10**, 117–155 (2002)
10. Ben Amor, N., Dubois, D., Gouider, H., Prade, H.: Possibilistic preference networks. Inf. Sci. **460–461**, 401–415 (2018)
11. Benferhat, S., Bouraoui, Z.: Possibilistic DL-Lite. In: Liu, W., Subrahmanian, V.S., Wijsen, J. (eds.) SUM 2013. LNCS (LNAI), vol. 8078, pp. 346–359. Springer, Heidelberg (2013). https://doi.org/10.1007/978-3-642-40381-1_27
12. Benferhat, S., Bouraoui, Z., Loukil, Z.: Min-based fusion of possibilistic DL-Lite knowledge bases. In: Proceedings of the IEEE/WIC/ACM International Conference on Web Intelligence (WI 2013), Atlanta, pp. 23–28 (2013)
13. Benferhat, S., Dubois, D., Garcia, L., Prade, H.: On the transformation between possibilistic logic bases and possibilistic causal networks. Int. J. Approx. Reas. **29**, 135–173 (2002)
14. Benferhat, S., Dubois, D., Kaci, S., Prade, H.: Possibilistic merging and distance-based fusion of propositional information. Ann. Math. Artif. Intellig. **34**, 217–252 (2002)
15. Benferhat, S., Dubois, D., Prade, H.: Nonmonotonic reasoning, conditional objects and possibility theory. Artif. Intell. **92**(1–2), 259–276 (1997)
16. Benferhat, S., Dubois, D., Prade, H.: From semantic to syntactic approaches to information combination in possibilistic logic. In: Bouchon-Meunier, B. (ed.) Aggregation and Fusion of Imperfect Information, pp. 141–161. Physica-Verlag, Heidelberg (1998)
17. Benferhat, S., Dubois, D., Prade, H.: An overview of inconsistency-tolerant inferences in prioritized knowledge bases. In: Fuzzy Sets, Logic and Reasoning about Knowledge, pp. 395–417. Kluwer (1999)

18. Benferhat, S., Dubois, D., Prade, H.: Possibilistic and standard probabilistic semantics of conditional knowledge bases. J. Logic Comput. **9**(6), 873–895 (1999)
19. Benferhat, S., Dubois, D., Prade, H.: Kalman-like filtering in a possibilistic setting. In: Proceedings of the 14th European Conference ECAI 2000, Berlin, pp. 8–12. IOS Press (2000)
20. Benferhat, S., Dubois, D., Prade, H.: A computational model for belief change and fusing ordered belief bases. In: Frontiers in Belief Revision, pp. 109–134. Kluwer (2001)
21. Benferhat, S., Dubois, D., Prade, H., Williams, M.A.: A framework for iterated belief revision using possibilistic counterparts to Jeffrey's rule. Fundam. Inform. **99**, 147–168 (2010)
22. Benferhat, S., El Baida, R., Cuppens, F.: A possibilistic logic encoding of access control. In: Proceedings of the 16th International FLAIRS Conference, St. Augustine, pp. 481–485. AAAI Press (2003)
23. Benferhat, S., Hué, J., Lagrue, S., Rossit, J.: Interval-based possibilistic logic. In: Proceedings of the 22nd IJCAI 2011, Barcelona, pp. 750–755 (2011)
24. Benferhat, S., Prade, H.: Encoding formulas with partially constrained weights in a possibilistic-like many-sorted propositional logic. In: Proceedings of the 9th IJCAI, Edinburgh, pp. 1281–1286 (2005)
25. Benferhat, S., Smaoui, S.: Hybrid possibilistic networks. Int. J. Approx. Reason. **44**(3), 224–243 (2007)
26. Boldrin, L., Sossai, C.: Local possibilistic logic. J. Appl. Non-Class. Log. **7**, 309–333 (1997)
27. Cayrol, C., Dubois, D., Touazi, F.: Symbolic possibilistic logic: completeness and inference methods. J. Log. Comput. **28**(1), 219–244 (2018)
28. Dubois, D.: Belief structures, possibility theory and decomposable measures on finite sets. Comput. AI **5**, 403–416 (1986)
29. Dubois, D., Fariñas del Cerro, L., Herzig, A., Prade, H.: A roadmap of qualitative independence. In: Fuzzy Sets, Logics and Reasoning about Knowledge, pp. 325–350. Kluwer (1999)
30. Dubois, D., Fortemps, P.: Selecting preferred solutions in the minimax approach to dynamic programming problems under flexible constraints. Eur. J. Oper. Res. **160**, 582–598 (2005)
31. Dubois, D., Hajek, P., Prade, H.: Knowledge-driven versus data-driven logics. J. Logic Lang. Inf. **9**, 65–89 (2000)
32. Dubois, D., Prade, H.: Inconsistency management from the standpoint of possibilistic logic. Int. J. Uncertain. Fuzziness Knowl.-Based Syst. **23**(Suppl. 1), 15–30 (2015)
33. Dubois, D., Prade, H.: A set-valued approach to multiple source evidence. In: Benferhat, S., Tabia, K., Ali, M. (eds.) IEA/AIE 2017. LNCS (LNAI), vol. 10351, pp. 113–118. Springer, Cham (2017). https://doi.org/10.1007/978-3-319-60045-1_14
34. Dubois, D., Prade, H.: A crash course on generalized possibilistic logic. In: Ciucci, D., Pasi, G., Vantaggi, B. (eds.) SUM 2018. LNCS (LNAI), vol. 11142, pp. 3–17. Springer, Cham (2018). https://doi.org/10.1007/978-3-030-00461-3_1
35. Dubois, D., Lang, J., Prade, H.: Advances in automated reasoning using possibilistic logic. In: Extended abstracts 1st European Workshop JELIA 1988, Roscoff, pp. 95–99 (1988)
36. Dubois, D., Lang, J., Prade, H.: Dealing with multi-source information in possibilistic logic. In: Proceedings of the 10th European Conference on Artificial Intelligence (ECAI 1992), Vienna, pp. 38–42 (1992)

37. Dubois, D., Lang, J., Prade, H.: Possibilistic logic. In: Gabbay, D.M., et al. (eds.) Handbook of Logic in Artificial Intelligence and Logic Programming, vol. 3, pp. 439–513. Oxford U. P. (1994)

38. Dubois, D., Le Berre, D., Prade, H., Sabbadin, R.: Using possibilistic logic for modeling qualitative decision: ATMS-based algorithms. Fundamenta Informaticae 37, 1–30 (1999)

39. Dubois, D., Lorini, E., Prade, H.: The strength of desires: a logical approach. Minds Mach. 27(1), 199–231 (2017)

40. Dubois, D., Prade, H.: Fuzzy Sets and Systems - Theory and Applications. Academic Press, Cambridge (1980)

41. Dubois, D., Prade, H.: Possibility Theory. Plenum Press, New York and London (1988)

42. Dubois, D., Prade, H.: The logical view of conditioning and its application to possibility and evidence theories. Int. J. Approx. Reason. 4(1), 23–46 (1990)

43. Dubois, D., Prade, H.: Epistemic entrenchment and possibilistic logic. Artif. Intell. 50, 223–239 (1991)

44. Dubois, D., Prade, H.: Belief revision and updates in numerical formalisms: an overview, with new results for the possibilistic framework. In: Proceedings of the 13th IJCAI, Chambéry, pp. 620–625 (1993)

45. Dubois, D., Prade, H.: Conditional objects, possibility theory and default rules. In: Conditionals: From Philosophy to Computer Science, pp. 301–336. Oxford Science Publ. (1995)

46. Dubois, D., Prade, H.: A synthetic view of belief revision with uncertain inputs in the framework of possibility theory. Int. J. Approx. Reason. 17, 295–324 (1997)

47. Dubois, D., Prade, H.: Possibility theory: qualitative and quantitative aspects. In: Gabbay, D.M., Smets, P. (eds.) Quantified Representation of Uncertainty and Imprecision. Handbook of Defeasible Reasoning and Uncertainty Management Systems, vol. 1, pp. 169–226. Kluwer (1998)

48. Dubois, D., Prade, H.: Possibilistic logic: a retrospective and prospective view. Fuzzy Sets Syst. 144, 3–23 (2004)

49. Dubois, D., Prade, H.: From Blanché's hexagonal organization of concepts to formal concept analysis and possibility theory. Logica Universalis 6(1–2), 149–169 (2012)

50. Dubois, D., Prade, H.: Possibilistic logic. An overview. In: Gabbay, D.M., et al. (eds.) Handbook of The History of Logic. Computational Logic, vol. 9, pp. 283–342. North-Holland (2014)

51. Dubois, D., Prade, H.: Being consistent about inconsistency: toward the rational fusing of inconsistent propositional logic bases. In: The Road to Universal Logic, II, pp. 565–571. Birkhäuser (2015)

52. Dubois, D., Prade, H.: Qualitative and semi-quantitative modeling of uncertain knowledge - a discussion. In: Computational Models of Rationality, pp. 280–296. College Publ. (2016)

53. Dubois, D., Prade, H., Sabbadin, R.: Decision-theoretic foundations of qualitative possibility theory. Eur. J. Oper. Res. 128(3), 459–478 (2001)

54. Dubois, D., Prade, H., Schockaert, S.: Stable models in generalized possibilistic logic. In: Proceedings of the 13th International Conference Principles Knowledge Representation and Reasoning (KR 2012), Rome, pp. 519–529 (2012)

55. Dubois, D., Prade, H., Schockaert, S.: Generalized possibilistic logic: foundations and applications to qualitative reasoning about uncertainty. Artif. Intell. 252, 139–174 (2017)

56. Farreny, H., Prade, H.: Positive and negative explanations of uncertain reasoning in the framework of possibility theory. In: Proceedings of the 5th Conference on UAI 1989, Windsor, pp. 95–101 (1989)

57. Gärdenfors, P.: Knowledge in Flux. MIT Press (1988). (2nd edn, College Publications 2008)

58. Kaci, S., Benferhat, S., Dubois, D., Prade, H.: A principled analysis of merging operations in possibilistic logic. In: Proceedings of the 16th Conference Uncertainty in Artificial Intelligence, (UAI 2000), Stanford, pp. 24–31 (2000)

59. Koehler, H., Leck, U., Link, S., Prade, H.: Logical foundations of possibilistic keys. In: Fermé, E., Leite, J. (eds.) JELIA 2014. LNCS (LNAI), vol. 8761, pp. 181–195. Springer, Cham (2014). https://doi.org/10.1007/978-3-319-11558-0_13

60. Kraus, S., Lehmann, D., Magidor, M.: Nonmonotonic reasoning, preferential models and cumulative logics. Artif. Intell. **44**, 167–207 (1990)

61. Lafage, C., Lang, J., Sabbadin, R.: A logic of supporters. In: Bouchon-Meunier, B., Yager, R.R., Zadeh, L.A. (eds.) Information, Uncertainty and Fusion, pp. 381–392. Kluwer (1999)

62. Lang, J.: Possibilistic logic: complexity and algorithms. In: Algorithms for Uncertainty and Defeasible Reasoning, pp. 179–220. Kluwer (2001)

63. Lehmann, D., Magidor, M.: What does a conditional knowledge base entail? AIJ **55**, 1–60 (1992)

64. Link, S., Prade, H.: Relational database schema design for uncertain data. In: Proceedings of the 25th ACM International Conference CIKM 2016, Indianapolis, pp. 1211–1220 (2016)

65. Nicolas, P., Garcia, L., Stéphan, I., Lefèvre, C.: Possibilistic uncertainty handling for answer set programming. Ann. Math. Artif. Intell. **47**(1–2), 139–181 (2006)

66. Nieves, J.C., Osorio, M., Cortés, U.: Semantics for possibilistic disjunctive programs. In: Baral, C., Brewka, G., Schlipf, J. (eds.) LPNMR 2007. LNCS (LNAI), vol. 4483, pp. 315–320. Springer, Heidelberg (2007). https://doi.org/10.1007/978-3-540-72200-7_32

67. Parsons, T.: The traditional square of opposition. In: Zalta, E.N. (ed.) The Stanford Encyclopedia of Philosophy, Spring 2014 edn. Stanford University (1997)

68. Qi, G., Ji, Q., Pan, J.Z., Du, J.: Extending description logics with uncertainty reasoning in possibilistic logic. Int. J. Intell. Syst. **26**(4), 353–381 (2011)

69. Qi, G., Liu, W., Bell, D.: A comparison of merging operators in possibilistic logic. In: Bi, Y., Williams, M.-A. (eds.) KSEM 2010. LNCS (LNAI), vol. 6291, pp. 39–50. Springer, Heidelberg (2010). https://doi.org/10.1007/978-3-642-15280-1_7

70. Qi, G., Wang, K.: Conflict-based belief revision operators in possibilistic logic. In: Proceedings of the 26th AAAI Conference on Artificial Intelligence, Toronto (2012)

71. Serrurier, M., Prade, H.: Introducing possibilistic logic in ILP for dealing with exceptions. Artif. Intell. **171**, 939–950 (2007)

72. Shafer, G.: A Mathematical Theory of Evidence. Princeton Univ. Press, Princeton (1976)

73. Walley, P.: Measures of uncertainty in expert systems. Artif. Intell. **83**, 1–58 (1996)

74. Yager, R.R.: An introduction to applications of possibility theory. Hum. Syst. Manag. **3**, 246–269 (1983)

75. Zadeh, L.: Fuzzy sets as a basis for a theory of possibility. Fuzzy Sets Syst. **1**, 3–28 (1978)

76. Zhu, J., Qi, G., Suntisrivaraporn, B.: Tableaux algorithms for expressive possibilistic description logics. In: Proceedings of the IEEE/ACM International Conference Web Intelligence (WI 2013), Atlanta, pp. 227–232 (2013)

Vadalog: Recent Advances and Applications

Georg Gottlob[1,2](✉), Andreas Pieris[3], and Emanuel Sallinger[1,2]

[1] University of Oxford, Oxford, UK
georg.gottlob@cs.ox.ac.uk
[2] TU Wien, Vienna, Austria
[3] University of Edinburgh, Edinburgh, UK

Abstract. Vadalog is a logic-based reasoning language for modern AI applications, in particular for knowledge graph systems. In this paper, we present recent advances and applications, with a focus on the Vadalog language itself. We first give an easy-to-access self-contained introduction to Warded Datalog+/−, the logical core of Vadalog. We then discuss some recent advances: Datalog rewritability of Warded Datalog+/−, and the piece-wise linear fragment of Warded Datalog+/− that achieves space efficiency. We then proceed with some recent practical applications of the Vadalog language: detection of close links in financial knowledge graphs, as well as the detection of family-owned businesses.

1 Introduction

Modern AI systems have drastically changed the way IT systems are designed and what can be achieved using them. At the same time, the requirements such AI systems impose on their underlying reasoning mechanisms have drastically changed as well. Logic-based reasoning has to harmonically integrate with statistical reasoning (or machine learning). Knowledge graphs systems are a type of modern AI systems where this can be observed particularly well. They must be able to reason using strict rules (e.g., for encoding regulations that an organization has to be compliant to no matter what the circumstances are), and at the same time they need to be able to make statistical or machine-learning based inferences (e.g., for determining whether two entities represented in the graph are likely to be the same).

Apart from this overarching requirement, more fine-grained requirements are imposed on knowledge graph systems: the need for recursive reasoning to be able to traverse graphs; the need for ontological reasoning to express knowledge about the domain the knowledge graph represents; and many more. It is well known, and we shall discuss in more detail in the remainder of this paper, that simply putting together many of these features will lead to high computational complexity, or even undecidability. At the same time, scalability is at the heart of most modern AI applications. It is particularly important for knowledge graphs, where more often than not, we have to deal with billions of nodes and edges.

© Springer Nature Switzerland AG 2019
F. Calimeri et al. (Eds.): JELIA 2019, LNAI 11468, pp. 21–37, 2019.
https://doi.org/10.1007/978-3-030-19570-0_2

This requires a careful balance between expressive power and scalability when designing reasoning languages.

Vadalog. Vadalog is a logic-based reasoning language. It is designed to be used as a reasoning language of modern AI systems such as knowledge graph management systems [7]. Vadalog has been developed as part of the VADA programme [15,20], a joint initiative between the University of Oxford, Manchester and Edinburgh. The Vadalog system [8], an implementation of Vadalog, is currently in use at these universities, as well as more than 20 industrial partners.

Vadalog builds upon a long legacy of KR languages, in particular that of Datalog and ontology languages. The logical core of Vadalog is *Warded Datalog$^\pm$*, an extension of Datalog with existential quantification (the "+" in Datalog$^\pm$). Most reasoning problems under Datalog with existential quantification are undecidable. Therefore, one has to impose certain restrictions on the language (the "$-$" in Datalog$^\pm$) based on the particular design goals of the language. Warded Datalog$^\pm$ has as its design goals to (i) allow unrestricted recursion, i.e., every Datalog program is a Warded Datalog$^\pm$ program, (ii) include existential quantification at least as much as required by OWL 2 QL i.e., every OWL 2 QL ontology can, by minimal syntactical translation, be transformed into a Warded Datalog$^\pm$ program, and (iii) has at most PTIME data complexity.

However, it is clear that Datalog alone, even if it had access to unrestricted existential quantification, is not enough to meet all needs of real practical applications. Additional features need to be available in Vadalog, such as arithmetic, aggregation, access to external functions and systems such as machine learning, access to external data sources, extraction of web data, etc. [7]. It is also clear, and well known, that adding many of these features leads to undecidability of most reasoning tasks. Thus, a second balance has to be struck: adding features of practical significance to extend Warded Datalog$^\pm$, the logical core of Vadalog, which could in principle lead to an explosion of computational complexity, but in the targeted specific applications does not.

This balance provides a particularly interesting field for both theoretical and practical research. On the practical side, which applications remain scalable when using such features, i.e., go beyond Warded Datalog$^\pm$? For which applications is already full Warded Datalog$^\pm$ (with PTIME data complexity) not scalable enough? And on the theory side, which fragments of Warded Datalog$^\pm$ ensure data complexity below PTIME? Can theoretical guarantees be given for Vadalog programs that use particular features (possibly in a limited way), i.e., go beyond Warded Datalog$^\pm$?

Overview. In this paper, we give an overview of recent advances on theoretical and practical aspects of Vadalog. We first give an easy-to-access self-contained introduction to Warded Datalog$^\pm$, the logical core of Vadalog. We then discuss recent advances. As the first one, we discuss Datalog rewritability of Warded Datalog$^\pm$. As the second one, we give an answer to the question of more efficient fragments of Warded Datalog$^\pm$ by introducing the piece-wise linear fragment of Warded Datalog$^\pm$, the space-efficient core of Vadalog. To complement the theoretical part, we then talk about practical applications, and Vadalog features that go beyond Warded Datalog$^\pm$ that are needed to effectively support such applications. As concrete applications, we discuss the detection of close links in financial knowledge graphs, and the detection of family-owned businesses. Both applications are good examples where the employed features lead to the undecidability of reasoning, but the specific applications scale well in practice.

2 Preliminaries

Basics. We consider the disjoint countably infinite sets $\mathbf{C}$, $\mathbf{N}$, and $\mathbf{V}$ of *constants, (labeled) nulls*, and *variables*, respectively. The elements of $(\mathbf{C} \cup \mathbf{N} \cup \mathbf{V})$ are called *terms*. An *atom* is an expression of the form $R(\bar{t})$, where R is an n-ary predicate, and $\bar{t}$ is an n-tuple of terms. We write $\mathsf{var}(\alpha)$ for the set of variables in an atom α; this notation extends to sets of atoms. A *fact* is an atom that contains only constants. We assume the reader is familiar with the fundamental notion of homomorphism.

Relational Databases. A *schema* $\mathbf{S}$ is a finite set of relation symbols (or predicates), each having an associated *arity*. We write R/n to denote that R has arity $n \geq 0$. A *position* $R[i]$ in $\mathbf{S}$, where $R/n \in \mathbf{S}$ and $i \in [n]$, identifies the i-th argument of R. An *instance* over $\mathbf{S}$ is a (possibly infinite) set of atoms over $\mathbf{S}$ that contain constants and nulls, while a *database* over $\mathbf{S}$ is a finite set of facts over $\mathbf{S}$. The *active domain* of an instance I, denoted $\mathsf{dom}(I)$, is the set of all terms occurring in I.

Conjunctive Queries. A *conjunctive query* (CQ) over $\mathbf{S}$ is an expression

$$Q(\bar{x}) \leftarrow R_1(\bar{z}_1), \ldots, R_n(\bar{z}_n),$$

where Q is a predicate used only in the head of CQs, each $R_i(\bar{z}_i)$, for $i \in \{1, \ldots, n\}$, is an atom without nulls over $\mathbf{S}$, and $\bar{x} \subseteq \bar{z}_1 \cup \cdots \cup \bar{z}_n$ are the *output variables* of q. The *evaluation* of $q(\bar{x})$ over an instance I, denoted $q(I)$, is the set of all tuples $h(\bar{x})$ of constants with h being a homomorphism from $\{R_1(\bar{z}_1), \ldots, R_n(\bar{z}_n)\}$ to I.

Tuple-Generating Dependencies. A *tuple-generating dependency* (TGD) σ is a first-order sentence of the form

$$\forall \bar{x} \forall \bar{y} \, (\varphi(\bar{x}, \bar{y}) \to \exists \bar{z} \, \psi(\bar{x}, \bar{z})),$$

where $\bar{x}, \bar{y}, \bar{z}$ are tuples of variables of $\mathbf{V}$, and φ, ψ are conjunctions of atoms without constants and nulls. Note that TGDs are at the heart of Datalog$^\pm$ languages. A Datalog rule extended with existential quantification is essentially a TGD. Therefore, a Datalog$^\pm$ language should be understood as a syntactic class of TGDs. For brevity, we write σ as $\varphi(\bar{x}, \bar{y}) \to \exists \bar{z} \, \psi(\bar{x}, \bar{z})$, and use comma instead of $\wedge$ for joining atoms. We refer to φ and ψ as the *body* and *head* of σ, denoted $\mathsf{body}(\sigma)$ and $\mathsf{head}(\sigma)$, respectively. The *frontier* of the TGD σ, denoted $\mathsf{frontier}(\sigma)$, is the set of variables that appear both in the body and the head of σ.

We also write $\mathsf{var}_\exists(\sigma)$ for the existentially quantified variables of σ. The schema of a set Σ of TGDs, denoted $\mathsf{sch}(\Sigma)$, is the set of predicates occurring in Σ. An instance I satisfies a TGD σ as the one above, written $I \models \sigma$, if the following holds: whenever there exists a homomorphism h such that $h(\varphi(\bar{x}, \bar{y})) \subseteq I$, then there exists $h' \supseteq h_{|\bar{x}}$ such that $h'(\psi(\bar{x}, \bar{z})) \subseteq I$. The instance I satisfies a set Σ of TGDs, written $I \models \Sigma$, if $I \models \sigma$ for each $\sigma \in \Sigma$.

Query Answering under TGDs. The main reasoning task under TGD-based languages is *conjunctive query answering*. Given a database D and a set Σ of TGDs, a *model* of D and Σ is an instance I such that $I \supseteq D$ and $I \models \Sigma$. Let $\mathsf{mods}(D, \Sigma)$ be the set of all models of D and Σ. The *certain answers* to a CQ q w.r.t. D and Σ is

$$ \mathsf{cert}(q, D, \Sigma) \ := \ \bigcap \{ q(I) \mid I \in \mathsf{mods}(D, \Sigma) \}. $$

Our main task is to compute the certain answers to a CQ w.r.t. a database and a set of TGDs from a certain class C of TGDs; concrete classes are discussed below. As usual when studying the complexity of this problem, we focus on its decision version:

PROBLEM : CQAns(C)
INPUT : A database D, a set $\Sigma \in$ C of TGDs, a CQ $q(\bar{x})$, and $\bar{c} \in \mathsf{dom}(D)^{|\bar{x}|}$.
QUESTION : Is it the case that $\bar{c} \in \mathsf{cert}(q, D, \Sigma)$?

We consider the *combined complexity* and *data complexity* of the problem, where the latter assumes that the set of TGDs and the CQ are fixed. A useful tool for tackling the above problem is the well-known *chase procedure* (see, e.g., [11,13,18,21]) that, given a database D and a set Σ of TGDs, builds a *universal model* $\mathsf{chase}(D, \Sigma)$ of D and Σ, i.e., a model that can be homomorphically embedded into every other model of D and Σ. This immediately implies that $\mathsf{cert}(q, D, \Sigma) = q(\mathsf{chase}(D, \Sigma))$.

3 The Logical Core of Vadalog

As discussed in Sect. 1, the Vadalog language is a general-purpose formalism for knowledge representation and reasoning. The logical core of this language is the well-behaved class of warded sets of TGDs that has been proposed in [3,17].

An Informal Description. Wardedness applies a restriction on how certain "dangerous" variables of a set of TGDs are used. These are body variables that can be unified with a null during the chase, and are also propagated to the head. For example, given

$$ P(x) \rightarrow \exists z\, R(x, z) \qquad \text{and} \qquad R(x, y) \rightarrow P(y) $$

the variable y in the body of the second TGD is dangerous. Indeed, once the chase applies the first TGD, an atom of the form $R(\_, \bot)$ is generated, where $\bot$

is a null value, and then the second TGD is triggered with the variable y being unified with $\perp$ that is propagated to the obtained atom $P(\perp)$. The unrestricted use of dangerous variables leads to a prohibitively high computational complexity of reasoning [11]. The main goal of wardedness is to limit the use of dangerous variables with the aim of taming the way that null values are propagated during the execution of the chase procedure. This is achieved by posing the following two conditions: (1) all the dangerous variables should appear together in a single body atom α, called a ward, and (2) α can share only harmless variables with the rest of the body, i.e., variables that unify only with constants. We proceed to formalize the above informal description.

The Formal Definition. We first need some auxiliary terminology. The set of positions of a schema $\mathbf{S}$, denoted $\mathsf{pos}(\mathbf{S})$, is defined as $\{R[i] \mid R/n \in \mathbf{S},\ \text{with}\ n \geq 1\ \text{and}\ i \in \{1, \ldots, n\}\}$. Given a set Σ of TGDs, we write $\mathsf{pos}(\Sigma)$ instead of $\mathsf{pos}(\mathsf{sch}(\Sigma))$. The set of *affected positions* of $\mathsf{sch}(\Sigma)$, denoted $\mathsf{affected}(\Sigma)$, is inductively defined as follows:

- if there exists $\sigma \in \Sigma$ and $x \in \mathsf{var}_\exists(\sigma)$ at position π, then $\pi \in \mathsf{affected}(\Sigma)$, and
- if there exists $\sigma \in \Sigma$ and $x \in \mathsf{frontier}(\sigma)$ in the body of σ only at positions of $\mathsf{affected}(\Sigma)$, and x appears in the head of σ at position π, then $\pi \in \mathsf{affected}(\Sigma)$.

Let $\mathsf{nonaffected}(\Sigma) = \mathsf{pos}(\Sigma) - \mathsf{affected}(\Sigma)$. We can now classify body variables into harmless, harmful, and dangerous. Fix a TGD $\sigma \in \Sigma$ and a variable x in $\mathsf{body}(\sigma)$:

- x is *harmless* if at least one occurrence of it appears in $\mathsf{body}(\sigma)$ at a position of $\mathsf{nonaffected}(\Sigma)$,
- x is *harmful* if it is not harmless, and
- x is *dangerous* if it is harmful and belongs to $\mathsf{frontier}(\sigma)$.

We are now ready to formally introduce wardedness.

Definition 1 (Wardedness). *A set Σ of TGDs is* warded *if, for each TGD $\sigma \in \Sigma$, there are no dangerous variables in $\mathsf{body}(\sigma)$, or there exists an atom $\alpha \in \mathsf{body}(\sigma)$, called a* ward, *such that (1) all the dangerous variables in $\mathsf{body}(\sigma)$ occur in α, and (2) each variable of $\mathsf{var}(\alpha) \cap \mathsf{var}(\mathsf{body}(\sigma) - \{\alpha\})$ is harmless.* ∎

We denote by WARD the class of all (finite) warded sets of TGDs. The problem of CQ answering under warded sets of TGDs has been recently investigated in [3,17]:

Theorem 1. CQAns(WARD) *is complete for* EXPTIME *in combined complexity, and complete for* PTIME *in data complexity.*

4   Query Answering via Proof Trees

Our main technical tool for studying the Datalog rewritability of warded sets of TGDs in Sect. 5, as well as the piece-wise linear fragment of warded sets of

TGDs in Sect. 6, is a new notion of proof tree that has been recently proposed in [9]. The goal of this section is to informally explain, via a simple example, the essence underlying this new notion of proof tree, and how it can be used for query answering purposes.

Unfolding. It is known that given a CQ q and a set Σ of TGDs, we can unfold q using the TGDs of Σ into an infinite union of CQs q_Σ such that, for every database D, $\mathrm{cert}(q, D, \Sigma) = q_\Sigma(D)$; see, e.g., [16,19]. Let us clarify that in our context, an unfolding, which is essentially a resolution step, is more complex than in the context of Datalog due to the existentially quantified variables in the head of TGDs. The purpose of a proof tree is to encode a finite branch of the unfolding of a CQ q with a set Σ of TGDs. Such a branch is a sequence $q_0, \ldots, q_n$ of CQs, where $q = q_0$, while, for each $i \in \{1, \ldots, n\}$, q_i is a obtained from q_{i-1} via an unfolding step. Here is a simple example, which will serve as a running example, that illustrates the notion of unfolding.

Example 1. Consider the set Σ of TGDs consisting of

$$R(x) \to \exists y\, T(y, x) \qquad T(x, y), S(y, z) \to T(x, z) \qquad T(x, y), P(y) \to G()$$

and the CQ $Q \leftarrow G()$, which simply asks whether $G()$ is entailed. Since the unfolding of q with Σ should give the correct answer for *every* input database, and therefore, for databases of the form $\{R(c^{n-1}), S(c^{n-1}, c^{n-2}), \ldots, S(c^2, c^1), P(c^1)\}$, for some $n > 1$, one of its branches should be $q = q_0, q_1, \ldots, q_n$, where

$$q_1 = Q \leftarrow T(x, y^1), P(y^1)$$

obtained by resolving q_0 using the third TGD,

$$q_i = Q \leftarrow T(x, y^i), S(y^i, y^{i-1}), \ldots, S(y^2, y^1), P(y^1),$$

for $i \in \{2, \ldots, n-1\}$, obtained by resolving q_{i-1} using the second TGD, and

$$q_n = Q \leftarrow R(y^{n-1}), S(y^{n-1}, y^{n-2}), \ldots, S(y^2, y^1), P(y^1)$$

obtained by resolving q_{n-1} using the first TGD.   ■

Query Decomposition. One may be tempted to think that the proof tree that encodes the branch $q_0, \ldots, q_n$ of the unfolding of q with Σ is the finite labeled path $v_0, \ldots, v_n$, where each v_i is labeled by q_i. However, another crucial goal of such a proof tree, which is not achieved via the naive path encoding, is to split each resolvent q_i, for $i > 0$, into smaller subqueries $q_i^1, \ldots, q_i^{n_i}$, which are essentially the children of q_i, in such a way that they can be processed independently by resolution. The crux of this encoding is that it provides us with a mechanism for keeping the CQs that must be processed by resolution small. Example 1 shows that by following the naive path encoding, without splitting the resolvents into smaller subqueries, we may get CQs of unbounded size.

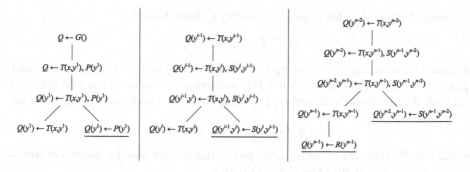

Fig. 1. Partial trees of the proof tree that encodes the branch $q = q_0, \ldots, q_n$ of the unfolding of q with Σ from Example 1.

The key question here is how a CQ q can be decomposed into subqueries that can be processed independently. The subtlety is that, after splitting q, occurrences of the same variable may be separated into different subqueries. Thus, we need a way to ensure that a variable in q, which appears in different subqueries after the splitting, is indeed treated as the same variable, i.e., it has the same meaning. We deal with this issue by restricting the set of variables in q of which occurrences can be separated during the splitting step. In particular, we can only separate occurrences of an output variable. This relies on the convention that output variables correspond to fixed constant values of $\mathbf{C}$, and thus their name is "frozen" and never renamed by subsequent resolution steps. Hence, we can separate occurrences of an output variable into different subqueries, i.e., different branches of the proof tree, without losing the connection between them. Summing up, the idea underlying query decomposition is to split the CQ at hand into smaller subqueries that keep together all the occurrences of a non-output variable, but with the freedom of separating occurrences of an output variable.

Query Specialization. From the above discussion, one expects that a proof tree of a CQ q w.r.t. a set Σ of TGDs can be constructed by starting from q, which is the root, and applying two steps: unfolding and decomposition. However, this is not enough for our purposes as we may run into the following problem: some of the subqueries will mistakenly remain large since we have no way to realize that a non-output variable corresponds to a fixed constant value, which in turn allows us to "freeze" its name and separate different occurrences of it during the decomposition step. This is illustrated by Example 1. Observe that the size of the CQs $\{q_i\}_{i>0}$ grows arbitrarily, while our query decomposition has no effect on them since they are Boolean queries, i.e., queries without output variables, and thus, we cannot split them into smaller subqueries. The above issue can be resolved by having an intermediate step between unfolding and decomposition, the so-called specialization step. A specialization of a CQ is obtained by converting some non-output variables of it into output variables, while keeping their name, or taking the name of an existing output variable.

Example 2. Consider, for example, the CQ q_1 from Example 1

$$Q \leftarrow T(x, y^1), P(y^1)$$

obtained by resolving $q = q_0$ using the third TGD. Query decomposition cannot split it into smaller subqueries since the variable y^1 is a non-output variable, and thus, all its occurrences should be kept together. We can consider the following specialization of q_1

$$Q(y^1) \leftarrow T(x, y^1), P(y^1),$$

which simply converts y^1 into an output variable, and now by query decomposition we can split it into the atomic queries

$$Q(y^1) \leftarrow T(x, y^1) \qquad Q(y^1) \leftarrow P(y^1),$$

which represent the original query q_1. ∎

Proof Trees. We are now ready to explain the high-level idea underlying the new notion of proof tree by exploiting our running example. Consider the set Σ of TGDs and the CQ q from Example 1. The branch $q_0, \ldots, q_n$ of the unfolding of q with Σ given in Example 1 is encoded via a proof tree of the form

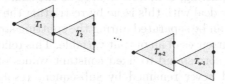

where each T_i, for $i \in \{1, \ldots, n-1\}$, is a rooted tree with only two leaf nodes. The actual trees are depicted in Fig. 1; the left one is T_1, the middle one is T_i for $i \in \{2, \ldots, n-2\}$, while the right one is T_{n-1}. For each $i \in \{1, \ldots, n-1\}$, the child of the root of T_i is obtained via unfolding, then we specialize it by converting the variable y^i into an output variable, and then we decompose the specialized CQ into two subqueries. In the tree T_{n-1}, we also apply an additional unfolding step in order to obtain the leaf node $Q(y^{n-1}) \leftarrow R(y^{n-1})$. The underlined CQs are actually the subqueries that represent the CQ q_n of the unfolding. Indeed, the conjunction of the atoms occurring in the underlined CQs is precisely the CQ q_n.

The next result illustrates how proof trees as described above can be used for query answering purposes. We refer to a proof tree $\mathcal{P}$ obtained from a CQ q and a set Σ of TGDs as a proof tree of q w.r.t. Σ. We also refer to the CQ encoded at its leaf nodes – see the underlined CQs in Fig. 1, which essentially encode the Boolean CQ $Q \leftarrow R(y^{n-1}), S(y^{n-1}, y^{n-2}), \ldots, S(y^2, y^1), P(y^1)$ – as the CQ induced by $\mathcal{P}$; by abuse of notation, we write $\mathcal{P}$ for the CQ induced by $\mathcal{P}$.

Theorem 2. *Consider a database D, a set Σ of TGDs, a CQ $q(\bar{x})$, and $\bar{c} \in \text{dom}(D)^{|\bar{x}|}$. The following are equivalent:*

1. *$\bar{c} \in \text{cert}(q, D, \Sigma)$.*
2. *There exists a proof tree $\mathcal{P}$ of q w.r.t. Σ such that $\bar{c} \in \mathcal{P}(D)$.*

5 Datalog Rewritability

A desirable property of a class C of TGDs is Datalog rewritability. We say that C is *Datalog rewritable* if the following holds: given a set $\Sigma \in C$ of TGDs and a CQ q, we can construct a Datalog query q_Σ such that, for every database D, $\mathsf{cert}(q, D, \Sigma)$ coincides with the evaluation of q_Σ over D. Recall that a Datalog query is essentially a pair (Π, R), where Π is a set of existential-free TGDs with only one head atom, called Datalog program, and R is an n-ary predicate. The answer to such a Datalog query q over a database D, denoted $q(D)$, is defined as the set of tuples $\mathsf{cert}(q_R, D, \Sigma)$, where q_R is the atomic query $R(x_1, \ldots, x_n)$. Datalog rewritability implies that the certain answers to a CQ w.r.t. a database and a set of TGDs from C can be computed by using existing Datalog engines. As it has been observed in [9], by exploiting the notion of the proof tree, we can show that the class of warded sets of TGDs is Datalog rewritable. This relies on the fact that a proof tree can be converted into a Datalog query.

A Proof Tree into a Datalog Query. Consider the set Σ of TGDs given in Example 1, and let $\mathcal{P}$ be the proof tree of q w.r.t. Σ that encodes the branch $q_0, \ldots, q_n$ of the unfolding of q with Σ for $n = 4$. In other words, $\mathcal{P}$ is the tree consisting of the trees T_1, T_{n-2} and T_{n-1} depicted in Fig. 1. Each node of $\mathcal{P}$, together with its children, is converted into a Datalog rule. Assume that the node v has the children u_1, u_2 in $\mathcal{P}$, where v is labeled by $p_0(\bar{x}_0)$ and, for $i \in \{1, 2\}$, u_i is labeled by the CQ $p_i(\bar{x}_i)$ with $\bar{x}_0 \subseteq \bar{x}_i$. In this case, we construct the Datalog rule

$$C_{[p_1]}(\bar{x}_1), C_{[p_2]}(\bar{x}_2) \;\rightarrow\; C_{[p_0]}(\bar{x}_0),$$

where $C_{[p_i]}$ is a predicate that corresponds to the CQ p_i, while $[p_i]$ refers to a *canonical renaming* of p_i. The intention underlying such a canonical renaming is the following: if p_i and p_j are the same up to variable renaming, then $[p_i] = [p_j]$. Moreover, for each leaf node of $\mathcal{P}$ labeled by the atomic query $p(\bar{x})$ of the form $Q(\bar{x}) \leftarrow R(\bar{y})$, where the tuples $\bar{x}$ and $\bar{y}$ mention the same variables, we construct the Datalog rule

$$R(\bar{y}) \;\rightarrow\; C_{[p]}(\bar{x}).$$

From the above description, $\mathcal{P}$ is converted into the following Datalog program $\Pi_{\mathcal{P}}$; note that we do not keep the rules that are already present (up to variable renaming). For brevity, we adopt the following naming convention: $p_{i,j}$ is the CQ that labels the j-th node (from left-to-right) of the i-th level of $\mathcal{P}$. If the i-th level has only one node, we simply write p_i. With this naming convention, the root is labeled with p_0, its child with p_1, etc. The Datalog program $\Pi_{\mathcal{P}}$ obtained from $\mathcal{P}$ follows:

$$
\begin{aligned}
C_{[p_1]} &\rightarrow C_{[p_0]} & C_{[p_{3,1}]}(y^2), C_{[p_{7,2}]}(y^1, y^2) &\rightarrow C_{[p_6]}(y^1, y^2) \\
C_{[p_2]}(y^1) &\rightarrow C_{[p_1]} & C_{[p_{13}]}(y^3) &\rightarrow C_{[p_{3,1}]}(y^3) \\
C_{[p_{3,1}]}(y^1), C_{[p_{3,2}]}(y^1) &\rightarrow C_{[p_2]}(y^1) & P(y^1) &\rightarrow C_{[p_{3,2}]}(y^1) \\
C_{[p_5]}(y^1) &\rightarrow C_{[p_{3,1}]}(y^1) & S(y^2, y^1) &\rightarrow C_{[p_{7,2}]}(y^1, y^2) \\
C_{[p_6]}(y^1, y^2) &\rightarrow C_{[p_5]}(y^1) & R(y^3) &\rightarrow C_{[p_{13}]}(y^3).
\end{aligned}
$$

The Datalog query $q_\mathcal{P}$ is defined as $(\Pi_\mathcal{P}, C_{[p_0]})$. It is clear that, for every database D, $\mathcal{P}(D) = q_\mathcal{P}(D)$; recall that we may write $\mathcal{P}$ for the CQ induced by $\mathcal{P}$.

The Actual Datalog Rewriting. Having the above transformation of a proof tree into a Datalog query, we can easily rewrite every warded set Σ of TGDs and a CQ q into a Datalog query q_Σ. But before doing this, we need a crucial result regarding warded sets of TGDs and proof trees. The *node-width* of a proof tree $\mathcal{P}$, denoted $\mathsf{nwd}(\mathcal{P})$, is the size of the largest CQ over all CQs that label its nodes. In the case of warded sets of TGDs, we can focus on proof trees of node-width at most $f_{\mathsf{WARD}}(|q| + |\Sigma|)$, where $f_{\mathsf{WARD}}(\cdot)$ is a polynomial. More precisely, Theorem 2 can be strengthen as follows:

Theorem 3. *Consider a database D, a set $\Sigma \in \mathsf{WARD}$ of TGDs, a CQ $q(\bar{x})$, and $\bar{c} \in \mathsf{dom}(D)^{|\bar{x}|}$. The following are equivalent:*

1. *$\bar{c} \in \mathsf{cert}(q, D, \Sigma)$.*
2. *There is a proof tree $\mathcal{P}$ of q w.r.t. Σ s.t. $\mathsf{nwd}(\mathcal{P}) \leq f_{\mathsf{WARD}}(|q| + |\Sigma|)$ and $\bar{c} \in \mathcal{P}(D)$.*

The above result suggests that the Datalog rewriting q_Σ can be obtained by exhaustively converting each proof tree $\mathcal{P}$ of q w.r.t. Σ with node-width at most $f_{\mathsf{WARD}}(|q| + |\Sigma|)$ into a Datalog query $q_\mathcal{P}$, and then take the union of all those queries. Since we consider the canonical renaming of the CQs occurring in a proof tree, and since the size of those CQs is bounded by $f_{\mathsf{WARD}}(|q| + |\Sigma|)$, we immediately conclude that we need to explore finitely many CQs. Thus, the above iterative procedure will eventually terminate and construct a finite Datalog query that is equivalent to Q.

Theorem 4. *Consider a set $\Sigma \in \mathsf{WARD}$ of TGDs and a CQ q. We can construct a Datalog query q_Σ such that $\mathsf{cert}(q, D, \Sigma) = q_\Sigma(D)$.*

At this point, we would like to stress that the notion of proof tree can be also used to re-establish the complexity of $\mathsf{CQAns(WARD)}$ (see Theorem 1) in a more transparent way than the algorithm in [3,17]. By Theorem 3, we simply need to search for a proof tree that has bounded node-width that entails the give tuple of constants. This can be done via a space-bounded algorithm that constructs in a level-by-level fashion the branches of the proof tree in parallel universal computations using alternation. Since this alternating algorithm uses polynomial space in general, and logarithmic space when the set of TGDs and the CQ are fixed, we immediately get an EXPTIME upper bound in combined, and a PTIME upper bound in data complexity, which confirms Theorem 1.

6   Limiting Recursion

We now focus our attention on the question whether we can limit the recursion allowed by wardedness in order to obtain a formalism that provides a convenient syntax for expressing useful recursive statements, and at the same time achieves space-efficiency. This question has been recently posed in [9], where it has been observed that most of the examples coming from our industrial partners use recursion in a restrictive way: each TGD has at most one body atom whose predicate is mutually recursive with a predicate occurring in the head of the TGD. Interestingly, this linear-like recursion has been already investigated in the context of Datalog, and it is known as *piece-wise linear*; see, e.g., [2]. It turned out that this type of recursion is the answer to our main question.

To formally define piece-wise linearity, we first need to define when two predicates are mutually recursive, which in turn relies on the well-known notion of the predicate graph. The *predicate graph* of a set Σ of TGDs, denoted $\mathsf{pg}(\Sigma)$, is a directed graph (V, E), where $V = \mathsf{sch}(\Sigma)$, and there exists an edge from a predicate P to a predicate R, i.e., $(P, R) \in E$, iff there exists a TGD $\sigma \in \Sigma$ such that P occurs in $\mathsf{body}(\sigma)$ and R occurs in $\mathsf{head}(\sigma)$. Two predicates $P, R \in \mathsf{sch}(\Sigma)$ are *mutually recursive* (w.r.t. Σ) if there exists a cycle in $\mathsf{pg}(\Sigma)$ that contains both P and R (i.e., R is reachable from P, and vice versa). We are now ready to define piece-wise linearity for TGDs.

Definition 2 (Piece-wise Linearity). *A set Σ of TGDs is* piece-wise linear *if, for each TGD $\sigma \in \Sigma$, there exists at most one atom in $\mathsf{body}(\sigma)$ whose predicate is mutually recursive with a predicate in $\mathsf{head}(\sigma)$.* ∎

Let PWL be the class of piece-wise linear sets of TGDs. The next result shows that indeed the piece-wise linear fragment of warded sets of TGDs ensures space-efficiency:

Theorem 5. $\mathsf{CQAns}(\mathsf{WARD} \cap \mathsf{PWL})$ *is* PSPACE-*complete in combined complexity, and* NLOGSPACE-*complete in data complexity.*

The lower bounds are inherited from linear Datalog, that is, the fragment of Datalog where only one intensional predicate can appear in the body of a rule. Interestingly, the upper bounds heavily rely on the notion of proof tree discussed above. For piece-wise linear warded sets of TGDs, we can strengthen Theorem 2 by focussing on proof trees that enjoy two syntactic properties: (i) their node-width is bounded by $f_{\mathsf{WARD} \cap \mathsf{PWL}}(|q| + |\Sigma|)$, where $f_{\mathsf{WARD} \cap \mathsf{PWL}}(\cdot)$ is a polynomial (different than f_{WARD}), and (ii) they have a path-like structure, i.e., each node has at most one child that is not a leaf – such proof trees are called *linear*. Theorem 2 can be strengthen as follows:

Theorem 6. *Consider a database D, a set $\Sigma \in \mathsf{WARD} \cap \mathsf{PWL}$ of TGDs, a CQ $q(\bar{x})$, and $\bar{c} \in \mathsf{dom}(D)^{|\bar{x}|}$. The following are equivalent:*

1. $\bar{c} \in \mathsf{cert}(q, D, \Sigma)$.
2. *There is a linear proof tree $\mathcal{P}$ of q w.r.t. Σ with $\mathsf{nwd}(\mathcal{P}) \leq f_{\mathsf{WARD} \cap \mathsf{PWL}}(|q| + |\Sigma|)$ such that $\bar{c} \in \mathcal{P}(D)$.*

The above results suggests that for deciding whether $\bar{c} \in \mathsf{cert}(q, D, \Sigma)$, we need to search for a linear proof tree $\mathcal{P}$ that has bounded node-width such that $\bar{c} \in \mathcal{P}(D)$. This can be done via a space-bounded algorithm that non-deterministically constructs in a level-by-level fashion the branches of the proof tree. Notice that we do not need alternation, as in the case of warded sets of TGDs, since we are looking for a linear proof tree. Since this algorithm uses polynomial space in general, and logarithmic space when the set of TGDs and the CQ are fixed, we immediately get the desired upper bounds.

Regarding Datalog rewritability, it is clear that the machinery described in Sect. 5 applies also in the case of piece-wise linear warded sets of TGDs. However, since we can consider only linear proof trees, it is not difficult to verify that the obtained Datalog query is actually piece-wise linear. Furthermore, it is well-known that a piece-wise linear Datalog query can be transformed into a linear Datalog query [2]. Summing up, we get the following interesting result concerning Datalog rewritability:

Theorem 7. *Consider a set* $\Sigma \in$ WARD $\cap$ PWL *of TGDs and a CQ* q. *We can construct a linear Datalog query* q_Σ *such that* $\mathsf{cert}(q, D, \Sigma) = q_\Sigma(D)$.

7   Applications

In this section, we show how the theory of Vadalog discussed so far translates into practice. As discussed in the introduction, it is clear that Datalog alone, even if it had access to unrestricted existential quantification, is not enough to meet all needs of real practical applications. Features need to be available such as arithmetic, aggregation, access to external functions and systems such as machine learning, access to external data sources, extraction of web data, etc. A detailed analysis of the requirements in knowledge graphs can be found in [7], an analysis tailored to the requirements of Enterprise AI in [5]. As mentioned before, adding many of these features leads to undecidability of most reasoning tasks. Thus, for practical applications, a careful balance has to be established. Features of practical significance need to be added that go beyond warded sets of TGDs as much as needed by applications. At the same time, these features need to be carefully chosen and used to allow for practical scalability in the desired applications.

We discuss here two such applications. Our domain will be financial knowledge graphs, that is, knowledge graphs that represent entities in the financial space (such as companies, persons, assets, rights, etc.) and their relationships. Both relate to actual applications of the Vadalog system, in use with our industrial partners. More details on both applications, and further financial applications, can be found in [5]. We will not be able to discuss a number of other applications, such as the use of Vadalog and its tools in data science pipelines [6], and data extraction [14] such as with our partners at DBLP [22]. We are currently working on a number of other applications. A wider area of application is the direct execution of SPARQL queries under standard bag semantics using Vadalog, which uses existential quantifiers to distinguish duplicates [10]. We are also working on applications in the area of large computational social choice scenarios [12] and light-weight consistent query answering [4].

Close Links. The first application is the detection of *close links* between companies. The concept of *close link* is a technical term in the financial industry, and, e.g., specified and used in the *European Central Bank regulations on monetary policy instruments and procedures of the Eurosystem* [1]. Intuitively speaking, it enforces that companies that are in a close relationship with each other (e.g., by one company owning a large part of the other company) cannot be acting as guarantors of loans for each other. This intuitively makes sense; if, e.g., the parent company of a wholly owned subsidiary guarantees a loan, there is a risk that if the company itself cannot repay the loan, the subsidiary cannot do so either. Such situations are thus forbidden by regulations.

Before describing the technical implementation as a financial knowledge graph in Vadalog, let us make the problem statement and context precise. For the context, we are discussing real-world regulatory requirements: most types of financial entities within the Eurosystem have to conform to these regulations. There are two separate entities we are dealing with: the *European Central Bank* (ECB), which releases the guidelines we are discussing here [1] and the *Eurosystem*, which consists of the ECB and the national Central Banks of the countries that adopted the euro, which adhere to and enforce it. With the terms clarified, let us consider the concrete definition of close links [1].

Close links is a situation in which the counterparty is linked to an issuer, debtor, or guarantor of eligible assets by reason of the fact that:

(a) *the counterparty owns directly, or indirectly, through one or more other undertakings, 20% or more of the capital of the issuer/debtor/guarantor;*
(b) *the issuer/debtor/guarantor owns directly, or indirectly through one or more other undertakings, 20% or more of the capital of the counterparty; or*
(c) *a third party owns more than 20% of the capital of the counterparty and more than 20% of the capital of the issuer/debtor/guarantor, either directly or indirectly, through one or more undertakings.*

While the detection of close links forms a clear problem statement, the problem still exists within the context of a larger regulatory framework. Translated to knowledge graphs, it is thus important to note that while one requirement is that the problem is accurately represented in the knowledge graph, another one is that it interfaces naturally with other parts of the knowledge graph. We shall concentrate on illustrating the first aspect here, but want to emphasize that the second one is just as important.

Example 3. Assume that ownership of companies is encoded in a ternary predicate $Own(x, y, u)$, where x is the owning company, y is the owned company, and u is the fraction (between 0 and 1) that x owns of y. Assume that we want to provide close links in the relation $CloseLink(x, y)$ in the knowledge graph, expressing that x is in a close link with y. The Vadalog rules expressing the definition of close link given above are:

1: $Own(x, y, u), w = \text{msum}(u, \langle y \rangle) \rightarrow TotalOwn(x, y, w)$.
2: $TotalOwn(x, z, u), Own(z, y, v), w = \text{msum}(u \cdot v, \langle z \rangle) \rightarrow TotalOwn(x, y, w)$.

3: $\text{TotalOwn}(x, y, w),\ w \geq 0.2 \to \text{CloseLink}(x, y)$.
4: $\text{TotalOwn}(z, x, v),\ \text{TotalOwn}(z, y, w), v \geq 0.2,\ w \geq 0.2 \to \text{CloseLink}(x, y)$.
5: $\text{CloseLink}(x, y) \to \text{CloseLink}(y, x)$.   ∎

There are multiple things to note here. First, before discussing the actual meaning of the rules, there is one Vadalog feature used in these rules that is not part of warded sets of TGDs, the core language we discussed in the theoretical part so far: this is *monotonic aggregation* (or, more specifically, monotonic sum, or msum). Monotonic aggregation has been introduced in the Datalog setting [23]. Intuitively, instead of regular aggregation, where execution is blocked until all values contributing to the aggregation are available, in monotonic aggregation intermediate values are provided. This is particularly important for the use of aggregation within recursion, where collecting all such values may simply not be possible beforehand (as it may be part of the recursion). An additional advantage of monotonic aggregation is streamability, as execution does not become blocked. On the other hand, there is a downside, namely the requirement for monotonicity – both required for giving meaningful semantics within recursion, and for being able to actually use the values in a meaningful way in the remainder of the program. Specifically, monotonicity requires that the result values of the aggregation either monotonically increase (such as, in our case, sum), or decrease. This restriction is the reason that Vadalog, apart from monotonic aggregation also supports regular aggregation, as both are required by applications.

Let us now return to our concrete use of monotonic aggregation. The first rule in our program in Example 3 expresses that if a company x directly owns of company y a fraction u, this fraction should be added to the total ownership that x owns of y. Similarly, the second rule expresses indirect ownership, i.e., if a company x already owns in total of company z a fraction u, and if company z directly owns of company y a fraction v, then a fraction uv should be added to the total ownership that x owns of y.

There are two mechanism that make such rules work. One is directly visible, one is more subtle. The directly visible one is the expressions in angle brackets, namely $\langle y \rangle$ and $\langle z \rangle$. These are subgrouping expressions, introduced in [23] and similar to SQL's subgrouping feature. Intuitively, such subgrouping expression are "keys" for aggregation: each subgroup contributes at most once to the aggregate. This is particularly important in the case of Datalog-based languages, if (e.g., due to optimization) there is no guarantee on how many times a rule is fired, as otherwise the (normally idempotent) repeat firing of a rule would add to the aggregate function. The more subtle one is where the "group by" for the aggregate function comes from, and why the two aggregate expressions in the two separate rules contribute to the same value. Both are determined by the head: "Group by" variables are all variables in the head that are not contained in the aggregate expression itself, and all aggregate functions with the same head predicate contribute to the same aggregate value. In our example, the second rule has x and y as grouping variables and z as a sub-grouping variable – in total ensuring that for each combination of x, y and z, the value is counted at most once towards the aggregate.

Let us note that the fourth rule, which encodes condition (c) in the definition of close links, is computationally the most demanding one requiring in principle to check from arbitrary third companies z whether they satisfy the underlying condition. Of course, optimized execution can avoid some of that expensive computational task.

Family Ownership. While the *close link* problem is a clear, distinct problem, required to be checked by, e.g., Eurozone regulations, it is only one aspect of a typically much larger financial knowledge graph that most institutions have to deal with. Although we cannot go into as much detail as in the previous application, in this last part, we give a glimpse on how such a (slightly) broader knowledge graph looks like.

It is clear that in reality direct ownership of a person or organization of a certain company is not the only way to have control over that company. Multiple distinct members of a family, i.e., multiple distinct persons, may each own a smaller part of the company, but together may control a company. It is thus clear why economic research studies *families* as units of company control. Consider the following setting.

Example 4. Assume that companies c consist of multiple assets a whose value is a fraction v of the companies' share capital, given as $\mathrm{Asset}(a, c, v)$. Assume that an owner o has rights to a fraction h of an asset a, given as $\mathrm{Right}(o, a, h)$. Suppose that a relation $\mathrm{Person}(p, \bar{x})$ provides information about persons p and a vector of their properties $\bar{x}$. Assume that an (incomplete or possibly entirely missing) relation $\mathrm{Family}(f, p)$ encodes that family f contains person p as a member.

1: $\mathrm{Right}(o, a, w)$, $\mathrm{Asset}(a, c, v)$,

$$\mathrm{Right}(c, a', w'), h = \mathrm{msum}((\langle a \rangle, v \cdot w \cdot w') \to \mathrm{Right}(o, a', h)$$

2: $\mathrm{Person}(p, \bar{x}) \to \exists f\ \mathrm{Family}(f, p)$.
3: $\mathrm{Person}(p, \bar{x})$, $\mathrm{Family}(f, p)$, $\mathrm{Person}(p', \bar{x}')$, $\mathrm{Family}(f', p')$,

$$\#\mathrm{FamilyProperty}(\bar{x}, \bar{x}') \to f = f'.$$

4: $\mathrm{Right}(p, a, w)$, $\mathrm{Family}(f, p)$, $v = \mathrm{msum}(\langle p \rangle, w) \to \mathrm{Own}(f, a, w)$. ∎

We see a number of features used in this example. Among them is existential quantification (which we know how to deal with given the earlier sections of this paper), monotonic aggregation (described earlier in this section), equality in the heads (called an *equality-generating dependency* or EGD), as well as a custom predicate #FamilyProperty bound against an external machine-learning based system. It is well known that a naive combination of these features (or even just TGDs and EGDs together) will lead to undecidability. Yet, and here we return to where we started this section, these features are in a carefully chosen balance within this concrete application, allowing the knowledge graph system scale to the volume of data encountered. At the same time, and here we return to the introduction, this is also an interesting starting point for theoretical future work: which fragment of Datalog extended by these features ensures good behavior?

Acknowledgements. This work has been supported by the EPSRC programme grant EP/M025268/1 VADA, the WWTF grant VRG18-013, the EU Horizon 2020 grant 809965, and the EPSRC grant EP/S003800/1 EQUID.

References

1. Guideline (EU) 2018/570 of the ECB. https://www.ecb.europa.eu/ecb/legal/pdf/celex_32018o0003_en_txt.pdf (2018). Accessed 04 Mar 2019
2. Afrati, F.N., Gergatsoulis, M., Toni, F.: Linearisability on datalog programs. Theor. Comput. Sci. **308**(1–3), 199–226 (2003)
3. Arenas, M., Gottlob, G., Pieris, A.: Expressive languages for querying the semantic web. ACM Trans. Database Syst. **43**(3), 13:1–13:45 (2018)
4. Arming, S., Pichler, R., Sallinger, E.: Complexity of repair checking and consistent query answering. In: ICDT, pp. 21:1–21:18 (2016)
5. Bellomarini, L., Fakhoury, D., Gottlob, G., Sallinger, E.: Knowledge graphs and enterprise AI: the promise of an enabling technology. In: ICDE (2019)
6. Bellomarini, L., et al.: Data science with Vadalog: bridging machine learning and reasoning. In: Abdelwahed, E.H., Bellatreche, L., Golfarelli, M., Méry, D., Ordonez, C. (eds.) MEDI 2018. LNCS, vol. 11163, pp. 3–21. Springer, Cham (2018). https://doi.org/10.1007/978-3-030-00856-7_1
7. Bellomarini, L., Gottlob, G., Pieris, A., Sallinger, E.: Swift logic for big data and knowledge graphs. In: IJCAI, pp. 2–10 (2017)
8. Bellomarini, L., Sallinger, E., Gottlob, G.: The Vadalog system: datalog-based reasoning for knowledge graphs. PVLDB **11**(9), 975–987 (2018)
9. Berger, G., Gottlob, G., Pieris, A., Sallinger, E.: The space-efficient core of Vadalog. In: PODS (2019, to appear)
10. Bertossi, L.E., Gottlob, G., Pichler, R.: Datalog: bag semantics via set semantics. In: ICDT (2019, to appear)
11. Calì, A., Gottlob, G., Kifer, M.: Taming the infinite chase: query answering under expressive relational constraints. J. Artif. Intell. Res. **48**, 115–174 (2013)
12. Csar, T., Lackner, M., Pichler, R., Sallinger, E.: Winner determination in huge elections with MapReduce. In: AAAI, pp. 451–458 (2017)
13. Fagin, R., Kolaitis, P.G., Miller, R.J., Popa, L.: Data exchange: semantics and query answering. Theor. Comput. Sci. **336**(1), 89–124 (2005)
14. Fayzrakhmanov, R.R., Sallinger, E., Spencer, B., Furche, T., Gottlob, G.: Browser-less web data extraction: challenges and opportunities. In: WWW, pp. 1095–1104 (2018)
15. Furche, T., Gottlob, G., Neumayr, B., Sallinger, E.: Data wrangling for big data: towards a lingua franca for data wrangling. In: AMW (2016)
16. Gottlob, G., Orsi, G., Pieris, A.: Query rewriting and optimization for ontological databases. ACM Trans. Database Syst. **39**(3), 25:1–25:46 (2014)
17. Gottlob, G., Pieris, A.: Beyond SPARQL under OWL 2 QL entailment regime: rules to the rescue. In: IJCAI, pp. 2999–3007 (2015)
18. Johnson, D.S., Klug, A.C.: Testing containment of conjunctive queries under functional and inclusion dependencies. J. Comput. Syst. Sci. **28**(1), 167–189 (1984)
19. König, M., Leclère, M., Mugnier, M.-L., Thomazo, M.: Sound, complete and minimal ucq-rewriting for existential rules. Semant. Web **6**(5), 451–475 (2015)
20. Konstantinou, N., et al.: The VADA architecture for cost-effective data wrangling. In: SIGMOD, pp. 1599–1602 (2017)

21. Maier, D., Mendelzon, A.O., Sagiv, Y.: Testing implications of data dependencies. ACM Trans. Database Syst. 4(4), 455–469 (1979)
22. Michels, C., Fayzrakhmanov, R.R., Ley, M., Sallinger, E., Schenkel, R.: OXpath-based data acquisition for DBLP. In: JCDL, pp. 319–320 (2017)
23. Shkapsky, A., Yang, M., Zaniolo, C.: Optimizing recursive queries with monotonic aggregates in deals. In: ICDE, pp. 867–878 (2015)

Belief Revision and Argumentation

AGM Meets Abstract Argumentation: Contraction for Dung Frameworks

Ringo Baumann[✉] and Felix Linker

Computer Science Institute, Leipzig University, Leipzig, Germany
baumann@informatik.uni-leipzig.de, linker@studserv.uni-leipzig.de

Abstract. The aim of the paper is to combine two of the most important areas of knowledge representation, namely belief revision and argumentation. We present a first study of AGM-style contraction for abstract argumentation frameworks (AFs). Contraction deals with removing former beliefs from a given knowledge base. Our presented approach is based on a reformulation of the original AGM postulates. In contrast to the AGM setup, where propositional logic is used, we build upon the recently developed Dung-logics. These logics have been introduced to tackle the somehow inverse problem, namely adding new beliefs. Importantly, they satisfy the characterization property that ordinary equivalence in Dung logics coincides with strong equivalence for the respective argumentation semantics. Although using the same setup we prove a negative result regarding the unrestricted existence of contraction operators. This means, an analog to the Harper Identity, which allows to construct a contraction operator from a given revision operator, is not available. However, dropping the somewhat controversial recovery postulate leads to the existence of reasonable operators.

Keywords: Abstract argumentation · Argumentation frameworks · Belief contraction · Belief revision · Knowledge representation

1 Introduction

Argumentation theory has become a vibrant research area in Artificial Intelligence, covering aspects of knowledge representation, multi-agent systems, and also philosophical questions (cf. [2,30] for excellent overviews). The simplicity of Dung's argumentation frameworks (AFs) [18], which are set-theoretically just directed graphs, has considerably contributed to the dominant role of them in the field of abstract argumentation. The latter is primarily concerned with the evaluation of arguments, viewed as abstract entities. The evaluation, i.e. the definition of acceptable sets of arguments, is performed by so-called argumentation semantics which are most commonly based on the attack relation among arguments [3].

Belief revision is concerned with changing the current beliefs of an agent, represented in a suitable representation language, in the light of new information

© Springer Nature Switzerland AG 2019
F. Calimeri et al. (Eds.): JELIA 2019, LNAI 11468, pp. 41–57, 2019.
https://doi.org/10.1007/978-3-030-19570-0_3

(cf. [22,24] for an overview). One central paradigm is that of *minimal change*, i.e. the modification of the current knowledge base has to been done economically. Two main types of belief change are intensively studied, namely *revision* and *contraction*.

Whereas revision potentially replaces information with new knowledge, contraction removes information from a given knowledge base. Both revision and contraction have been studied in depth in the context of propositional logic, with AGM theory [1] certainly being the most influential account. Although, as just mentioned, AFs are widely used, and dynamic aspects obviously play a major role in argumentation, the dynamics of AFs have received an increasing interest over the last few years only. Confer [19] for historical relations between belief revision and argumentation. There are a few works which are dealing with revising AFs [5,14,15,17]. All mentioned works are guided by an axiomatic approach inspired by the AGM postulates. However, several conceptional differences can be observed. For instance, they differ in their underlying equivalence notions, namely strong or ordinary equivalence, respectively as well as in their allowed types of manipulations, e.g. modifying the attack relation only vs. no restrictions at all. To the best of our knowledge the study of AF contraction has been neglected so far. The aim of the paper is to close this gap.

The presented approach builds upon the recently developed Dung-logics which have been introduced to tackle revision [5]. Although here we use the same setup as for revision, we can show a negative result regarding the unrestricted existence of contraction operators. This basically means that an analog to the Harper Identity [25], which allows to construct a contraction operator from a given revision operator, is not available. The main reason for this impossibility is simply that we can not rely on the same expressive power as in propositional logic. More precisely, we do not have an analog to disjunction nor negation in Dung-logics which is essential for the mentioned Harper Identity. It turns out, however, that dropping the somewhat controversial recovery postulate leads to the existence of reasonable operators.

The paper is organized as follows. In Sect. 2 we provide the background relevant for this paper covering abstract argumentation, ordinary and strong equivalence, kernels, Dung logics and AGM-style contraction. Section 3 presents contraction postulates for AFs, proves the non-existence of contraction operators in general and shows possible ways out. Section 4 summarizes the results of the paper and concludes.

2   Background

2.1   Abstract Argumentation

An *argumentation framework (AF)* is set-theoretically just a directed graph $F = (A, R)$ [18]. In the context of abstract argumentation we call an element $a \in A$ an *argument* and in case of $(a, b) \in R$ we say that a *attacks* b or a is *an attacker of* b. Moreover, an argument b is *defended by* a set A if each attacker of b is counterattacked by some $a \in A$. For a set E we use $E^+ = \{b \mid (a, b) \in R, a \in E\}$ and define $E^{\oplus} = E \cup E^{+}$. Throughout the paper we will write $F \sqcup G = (A_F \cup A_G, R_F \cup R_G)$ for the union of two AFs $F = (A_F, R_F)$, $G = (A_G, R_G)$ and $F \sqsubseteq G$ if $A_F \subseteq A_G$ and $R_F \subseteq R_G$. Moreover, for a set S we define the restriction of F to S as $F|_S = (S, R_F \cap (S \times S))$. In this paper we consider finite AFs only (cf. [7,8] for a consideration of infinite AFs). We use $\mathcal{F}$ for the set of all finite AFs.

An *extension-based semantics* σ is a function which assigns to any AF $F = (A, R)$ a set of reasonable positions, so-called σ-*extension*, i.e. $\sigma(F) \subseteq 2^A$. Beside the most basic conflict-free and admissible sets (abbr. *cf* and *ad*) we consider the following mature semantics, namely stable, stage, semi-stable, complete, preferred, grounded, ideal and eager semantics (abbr. *stb, stg, ss, co, pr, gr, id* and *eg* respectively). A very good overview can be found in [3].

Definition 1. *Let $F = (A, R)$ be an AF and $E \subseteq A$.*

1. $E \in cf(F)$ *iff for no* $a, b \in E$, $(a, b) \in R$,
2. $E \in ad(F)$ *iff* $E \in cf(F)$ *and E defends all its elements,*
3. $E \in stb(F)$ *iff* $E \in cf(F)$ *and* $E^{\oplus} = A$,
4. $E \in stg(F)$ *iff* $E \in cf(F)$ *and for no* $I \in cf(F)$, $E^{\oplus} \subset I^{\oplus}$,
5. $E \in ss(F)$ *iff* $E \in ad(F)$ *and for no* $I \in ad(F)$, $E^{\oplus} \subset I^{\oplus}$,
6. $E \in co(F)$ *iff* $E \in ad(F)$ *and for any* $a \in A$ *defended by E, $a \in E$,*
7. $E \in pr(F)$ *iff* $E \in co(F)$ *and for no* $I \in co(F)$, $E \subset I$,
8. $E \in gr(F)$ *iff* $E \in co(F)$ *and for any* $I \in co(F)$, $E \subseteq I$,
9. $E \in id(F)$ *iff* $E \in co(F)$, $E \subseteq \bigcap pr(F)$ *and for no* $I \in co(F)$ *satisfying* $I \subseteq \bigcap pr(F)$ *we have: $E \subset I$,*
10. $E \in eg(F)$ *iff* $E \in co(F)$, $E \subseteq \bigcap ss(F)$ *and for no* $I \in co(F)$ *satisfying* $I \subseteq \bigcap ss(F)$ *we have: $E \subset I$.*

Two AFs can be equivalent in many different ways (cf. [6] for an overview). The simplest form of equivalence is possessing the same extensions known as *ordinary* or *standard equivalence*. A further one is *strong equivalence* which requires semantical indistinguishability even in the light of further information. The latter plays an important role for nonmonotonic formalisms. Consider the following definitions.

Definition 2. *Given a semantics σ. Two AFs F and G are*

1. *ordinarily σ-equivalent if $\sigma(F) = \sigma(G)$ and* $(F \equiv^{\sigma} G)$
2. *strongly σ-equivalent if $\sigma(F \sqcup H) = \sigma(G \sqcup H)$ for any $H \in \mathcal{F}$.* $(F \equiv^{\sigma}_{s} G)$

Clearly, both concepts are semantically defined. Surprisingly, in case of strong equivalence it turned out that deciding this notion is deeply linked to the syntax of AFs [27]. In general, any attack being part of an AF may contribute towards future extensions. However, for each semantics, there are patterns of redundant attacks captured by so-called *kernels*. Formally, a kernel is a function $k : \mathcal{F} \to \mathcal{F}$ where $k(F) = F^k$ is obtained from F by deleting certain redundant attacks. We call an AF F *k-r-free* iff $F = F^k$. The following kernels will be considered.

Definition 3. *Given an AF $F = (A, R)$. The σ-kernel $F^{k(\sigma)} = \left(A, R^{k(\sigma)}\right)$ is defined as follows:*

1. $R^{k(stb)} = R \setminus \{(a, b) \mid a \neq b \wedge (a, a) \in R\}$,
2. $R^{k(ad)} = R \setminus \{(a, b) \mid a \neq b \wedge (a, a) \in R \wedge \{(b, a), (b, b)\} \cap R \neq \varnothing\}$,
3. $R^{k(gr)} = R \setminus \{(a, b) \mid a \neq b \wedge (b, b) \in R \wedge \{(a, a), (b, a)\} \cap R \neq \varnothing\}$ *and*
4. $R^{k(co)} = R \setminus \{(a, b) \mid a \neq b \wedge (a, a), (b, b) \in R\}$.

Please note that for any considered kernel the decision whether an attack (a, b) has to be deleted does not depend on further arguments than a and b. Put differently, the reason of being redundant is *context-free*, i.e. it stems from the arguments themselves [4]. This property will play an essential role in several proofs.

Example 1. Consider the AF F and its associated stable kernel.

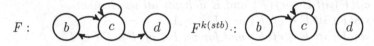

The only stable extension in our example is $\{b, d\}$. In order to compute a stable kernel, all attacks that come from a self-attacking argument must be deleted. In this example, we can see why this does not change extensions. c will have its self-attack remaining therefore it still can't be part of any extension as stable extensions must be conflict-free. Since stable extension must attack c, it does not matter whether c is attacking other arguments as well.

Kernels allow to efficiently decide on strong equivalence since one just needs to compute the respective kernels and compare them for equality. Hence, strong equivalence regarding AFs is a syntactical feature, i.e. it can be decided just be inspecting the syntax of two AFs.

Theorem 1 ([10, 27]). *For two AFs F and G we have,*

1. $F \equiv_s^\sigma G \Leftrightarrow F^{k(\sigma)} = G^{k(\sigma)}$ *for any semantics $\sigma \in \{stb, ad, co, gr\}$,*
2. $F \equiv_s^\tau G \Leftrightarrow F^{k(ad)} = G^{k(ad)}$ *for any semantics $\tau \in \{pr, id, ss, eg\}$ and*
3. $F \equiv_s^{stg} G \Leftrightarrow F^{k(stb)} = G^{k(stb)}$.

2.2 Dung-Logics

In propositional logic ordinary and strong equivalence coincide. Consequently, converting AGM postulates to a certain non-monotonic formalism $\mathcal{L}$ might be studied under two different guidelines, namely respecting ordinary or strong equivalence in $\mathcal{L}$. For Dung-style AFs the latter was firstly done in [5] for belief expansion and revision. In order to do so the authors introduced so-called *Dung-logics* which perform reasoning purely on the level of AFs. The heart of these logics are so-called *k-models*. A *k*-model of an AF F is again an AF which satisfies at least the information of F minus redundancy, but may have more information than encoded by F. Analogously to the relation between the logic of here and there and logic programs we have that Dung-logics are characterization logics for AFs [9, 26]. This means, ordinary equivalence in Dung-logics is necessary and sufficient for strong equivalence regarding argumentation semantics.

Definition 4. *Given a kernel k, two AFs F and G as well as a set of AFs $\mathcal{M}$.*

1. *The set of k-models is defined as: $Mod^k(F) = \{G \in \mathcal{F} \mid F^k \sqsubseteq G^k\}$ and $Mod^k(\mathcal{M}) = \bigcap_{F \in \mathcal{M}} Mod^k(F)$*
2. *The k-consequence relation is given as: $\mathcal{M} \models^k F \Leftrightarrow Mod^k(\mathcal{M}) \subseteq Mod^k(F)$*
3. *The ordinary k-equivalence is defined as: $F \equiv^k G \Leftrightarrow Mod^k(F) = Mod^k(G)$*

In the rest of the paper we will consider AGM-style contraction for single AFs. Therefore, as usual, we will drop braces and write $F \models^k G$ instead of $\{F\} \models^k G$. The following property is not explicitly mentioned in [5] and will be frequently used throughout the paper. It relates consequence relations with subgraph relations.

Lemma 1. *Given a kernel k and two AFs F, G,*

$$F \models^k G \Leftrightarrow G^k \sqsubseteq F^k.$$

Proof.

$$(\Rightarrow) \quad F \models^k G \Leftrightarrow Mod^k(F) \subseteq Mod^k(G) \qquad \text{(Def. 4.2)}$$
$$\Rightarrow F \in Mod^k(G) \Rightarrow G^k \sqsubseteq F^k \qquad \text{(Def. 4.1)}$$

$$(\Leftarrow) \quad G^k \sqsubseteq F^k \Rightarrow (\forall H \in \mathcal{F} : F^k \sqsubseteq H^k \Rightarrow G^k \sqsubseteq H^k) \qquad \text{(Def. } \sqsubseteq)$$
$$\Rightarrow (\forall H \in \mathcal{F} : H \in Mod^k(F) \Rightarrow H \in Mod^k(G)) \qquad \text{(Def.4.1)}$$
$$\Rightarrow Mod^k(F) \subseteq Mod^k(G) \Leftrightarrow F \models^k G \qquad \text{(Def.4.2)}$$

$\square$

In the following we illustrate several definitions (cf. [5] for more details).

Example 2. Consider the AFs F, G and their associated stable kernels.

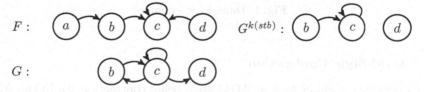

In contrast to G we observe that F is $k(stb)$-r-free since $F = F^{k(stb)}$, i.e. F does not possess any redundant attack w.r.t. stable semantics. Moreover, $G^{k(stb)} \sqsubseteq F^{k(stb)}$ verifies that F is a $k(stb)$-model of G. Loosely speaking, this means that F is a possible future scenario of G. Finally, according to Lemma 1 we deduce

$F \models^{k(stb)} G$, i.e. believing in the information encoded by F justifies assertions encoded by G.

Figure 1 depicts this example and can be interpreted as a Hasse-diagram for the partial order $(\mathcal{F}, \sqsubseteq)$. Remember that this order possesses a least element, namely the uniquely defined tautology $(\varnothing, \varnothing)$ since $(\varnothing, \varnothing) \sqsubseteq H$ for any $H \in \mathcal{F}$. Each of the cones stands for a set of k-models of a specific (redundant-free) AF which is located at the origin of the respective cone. This figure can also be interpreted as an upside down Hasse-diagram for the partial order $(\mathcal{F}, \models^k)$ as we know by Lemma 1 that the $\models^k$ relation is characterized by the $\sqsubseteq$ relation. The diagram then possesses a *greatest* element, namely $(\varnothing, \varnothing)$. Although this figure successfully illustrates the $\sqsubseteq$-relation of AFs and their models, it still is just an illustration and therefore inappropriate in a way. The figure conveys the impression that for any AFs $H, H' \in \mathcal{F}$ there is a non-empty intersection of their models, which is not the case. There are indeed such AFs H and H' that $Mod^k(H) \cap Mod^k(H') = \varnothing$ (cf. Example 3).

We drew G with dashed lines as its place in the $(\mathcal{F}, \models^k)$ order coincides with the place of $G^{k(stb)}$. Remember, that the $\models^k$-relation is determined only by looking at the kernels of AFs. This partial order therefore could also be defined on $\equiv^k$-equivlance classes.

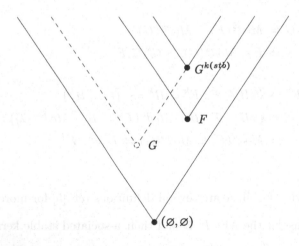

Fig. 1. Dung-logic example

2.3   AGM-Style Contraction

Let us now take a closer look at AGM-style belief contraction [1]. In the AGM paradigm the underlying logic is assumed to be classical logic and the beliefs are modeled by a theory, i.e. a deductively closed set of sentences (a so-called *belief set*). The provided postulates address the problem of how a current belief set K should be changed in the light of removing a former belief p. In the following we list the basic postulates. We use $\models$ for the classical consequence relation, $K \div p$ for the results of contracting a belief p from K and $K + p$ for $\subseteq$-least deductively closed set of formulas containing both K and p. The latter operator is called *expansion* and it simply adds new beliefs without restoring consistency.

$C1$ $K \div p$ is a belief set   *(closure)*
$C2$ $K \div p \subseteq K$ *(inclusion)*
$C3$ $p \notin K \Rightarrow K \div p = K$ *(vacuity)*
$C4$ $\not\models p \Rightarrow p \notin K \div p$ *(success)*
$C5$ $K \subseteq (K \div p) + p$ *(recovery)*
$C6$ $\models p \leftrightarrow q \Rightarrow K \div p = K \div q$ *(extensionality)*

The *closure* axiom $C1$ states that the result of a contraction is a deductively closed theory. The postulate of *inclusion* $C2$ stipulates that when contracting, nothing should be added. The so-called *vacuity* postulate $C3$ complements the former axiom since it determines the precise result of contraction whenever p is not included in the current beliefs. $C4$ encodes the *success* of contraction, i.e. p is no longer believed given that p is not tautological. Postulate $C5$, axiom of *recovery*, states a relation between contraction and expansion. It stipulates that no information is lost if we contract and afterwards expand by the same belief. This axiom is often subject to criticism and is intensively discussed in the literature (see [20, Section 3.1] for more details). The *extensionality* axioms $C6$ encode that the results of belief change are independent of the syntactic form, i.e. results of contraction do not differ if contracting with semantical equivalent formulae.

3   Dung-Style Contraction

Strong equivalence can be seen as the non-monotonic analog of ordinary equivalence in classical logic since it respects the so-called substitution principle (cf. [33] for more details), i.e. for two equivalent sets of formulas Σ and Δ and any set of formulas Γ, $\Gamma \cup \Sigma$ is equivalent to $\Gamma \cup \Delta$. In [5] the authors tackled belief revision for AFs in a way which respects exactly this strong notion of equivalence. In this section we will continue this line of research and consider AGM-style contraction with regard to Dung-logics. We recap the definitions of k-tautology and k-expansion firstly introduced in [5].

Definition 5. *Given a kernel k. An AF F is a k-tautology if $Mod^k(F) = \mathcal{F}$.*

It turns out that the empty framework $F_\varnothing = (\varnothing, \varnothing)$ is the uniquely determined k-tautology. Analogously to classical logic we define expansion semantically, namely as the intersection of the initial models.

Definition 6. *Given a kernel k. For two AFs F, G we define the result of k-expansion as, $Mod^k(F +_k G) = Mod^k(F) \cap Mod^k(G)$.*

48   R. Baumann and F. Linker

In classical logic, the realization of expansion is straightforward from a technical point of view since the intersection of the models can be simply encoded by using conjunctions. It was one main result that even the intersection of k-models is always realizable if considering sets of AFs (cf. [5, Theorem 5, Lemma 6] for more details). In this paper we will require the following result only.

Lemma 2. *Given* $k \in \{k(stb), k(ad), k(gr), k(co)\}$. *For any two AFs* F, G, *s.t.* $Mod^k(F) \cap Mod^k(G) \neq \varnothing$ *we have:* $F +_k G = F^k \sqcup G^k$.

Example 3. Consider the AFs F, G and $k = k(stb)$.

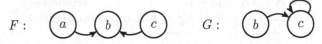

Both AFs are k-r-free, as argument c in G does not have any attacks outgoing. In this case, what does hold regarding $Mod^k(F) \cap Mod^k(G)$? At first glance, one might think that the intersection is not empty, as one would surely find an AF that is an extension of both F and G. However, remember that k-models are not required to include (w.r.t. subgraph relation) the respective AF of which they are a model but to do so modulo redundancy. A k-model of both AFs must include the attacks (b, c), (c, b) and (c, c) which is not possible as (c, b) is a k-redundant attack when (c, c) is given. Therefore we have $Mod^k(F) \cap Mod^k(G) = \varnothing$ leading to $F +_k G$ being undefined.

3.1 Contraction Postulates for Kernel k

The axiom translation is relatively straightforward because we can utilize a full-fledged logic which allows us to translate all axioms in a direct fashion. Note that since belief sets are closed sets we can rephrase any axioms using subset/element relations into postulates using consequence relations. More precisely, for two deductively closed sets of propositional formulas Γ and Δ we find, $\Gamma \subseteq \Delta \Leftrightarrow \Delta \models \Gamma$. For instance, the inclusion axiom $K \div p \subseteq K$ translates to $K \models K \div p$. Now, converting these from classical logic to Dung-logics, i.e. replacing $\models$ with $\models^k$ results in $F \models^k F \div_k G$ which is equivalent to $(F \div_k G)^k \sqsubseteq F^k$ according to Lemma 1. All other axioms can be translated in the same fashion.

$$\begin{aligned}
&\mathbf{C1}^k \ F \div_k G \text{ is an AF} &&\textit{(closure)}\\
&\mathbf{C2}^k \ (F \div_k G)^k \sqsubseteq F^k &&\textit{(inclusion)}\\
&\mathbf{C3}^k \ G^k \not\sqsubseteq F^k \Rightarrow (F \div_k G) \equiv^k F &&\textit{(vacuity)}\\
&\mathbf{C4}^k \ G^k \neq (\varnothing, \varnothing) \Rightarrow G^k \not\sqsubseteq (F \div_k G)^k &&\textit{(success)}\\
&\mathbf{C5}^k \ F^k \sqsubseteq \left((F \div_k G) +_k G\right)^k &&\textit{(recovery)}\\
&\mathbf{C6}^k \ G \equiv^k H \Rightarrow F \div_k G \equiv^k F \div_k H &&\textit{(extensionality)}
\end{aligned}$$

Definition 7. *An operator* $\div_k : \mathcal{F} \times \mathcal{F} \to \mathcal{F}$ *where* $(F, G) \mapsto F \div_k G$ *is called a k-contraction iff axioms* $C1^k$–$C6^k$ *are satisfied.*

Let us start with some reflections on what is required for an operator in order to be a k-contraction. The redundancy-free version of the result $F \div_k G$ is by postulate $\boldsymbol{C2^k}$ upwards bounded by F^k, i.e. $(F \div_k G)^k \sqsubseteq F^k$. Since postulate $\boldsymbol{C1^k}$ ensures that we have to end up with an AF we deduce that any contraction for one of the kernels considered in this paper has to delete single arguments together with their corresponding attacks or attacks only. Note that nothing has to be deleted if F is no k-model of G (axiom $\boldsymbol{C3^k}$). Now, given that G is non-empty the success postulate $\boldsymbol{C4^k}$ requires that at least one argument or one non-redundant attack in G is not contained in $(F \div_k G)^k$. Consider Fig. 2 for illustration purposes. The depicted situation illustrates that $G^k \sqsubseteq F^k$ or equivalently $F \models^k G$.

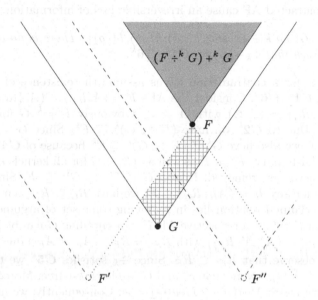

Fig. 2. Dung-logic contraction

What are possible places so far for $F \div_k G$? The AFs F' and F'' show two options. It is possible to move F' and F'' around inside the dotted cone originating from F but it is crucial for them to not lie in the patterned area between F and G since this would lead to $G^k \sqsubseteq (F \div_k G)^k$ and an unsuccessful contraction ($\boldsymbol{C4^k}$). It would however not be possible to move them out of the dotted cone since this would conflict with the inclusion postulate $\boldsymbol{C2^k}$. The postulate $\boldsymbol{C5^k}$ demands the possibility of a recovery of a contracted AF. This means the result of expanding $F \div_k G$ by G has to be located in the grey-drawn space. Unfortunately, we will see that in general this is impossible due to formal reasons.

3.2   Non-existence of Contraction Operators

We now formally prove the non-existence of contraction operators for Dung-logics. Roughly speaking, the reason why there is no suitable operator is that arguments and attacks do not possess the same independency status regarding their own existence. More precisely, in order to reobtain an AF we observe that the deletion of certain arguments necessarily causes the deletion of attacks. In contrast, deleting attacks from an AF results in an AF too. As already discussed, on the one hand, postulates $C2^k$ and $C4^k$ enforce the deletion and prohibit the addition of information and on the other hand, axiom $C5^k$ postulates the possibility of restoring all information. The proof of the following theorem shows that removing arguments that have attacks dependent on them which are not part of the contracted AF cause an irreversible loss of information.

Theorem 2. *Given $k \in \{k(stb), k(ad), k(gr), k(co)\}$. There is no operator $\div_k :$ $\mathcal{F} \times \mathcal{F} \to \mathcal{F}$ such that $\div_k$ satisfies $C1^k$–$C6^k$.*

Proof. Striving for a contradiction let us assume the existence of an operator $\div_k$ satisfying $C1^k$–$C6^k$. Consider the AFs $F = (A, R_F) = (A, \{(a, a) \mid a \in A\})$ and $G = (A, R_G) = (A, \varnothing)$ with $A \neq \varnothing$. Obviously $F \models^k G$ for any kernel k considered. Due to $C2^k$ we have $(F \div_k G)^k \sqsubseteq F^k$. Since $G \neq (\varnothing, \varnothing)$ and therefore $\not\models^k G$ we also have $G^k \not\sqsubseteq (F \div_k G)^k \sqsubseteq F^k$ because of $C4^k$. Note that F and G are k-r-free, i.e. $F^k = F$ as well as $G^k = G$ for all kernels k considered, as self-loops never are removed. Hence, $G \not\sqsubseteq (F \div_k G)^k \sqsubseteq F$. Since $R_G = \varnothing$ and therefore for any $H = (A_H, R_H) \in \mathcal{F}$, we have $R_G \subseteq R_H$, our only chance to satisfy the claimed relation lies in removing some set of arguments A' with $\varnothing \subset A' \subseteq A$ in F. Thus, a respective AF F' not entailing G can be identified by $F' = (A_{F'}, R_{F'}) = (A \setminus A', R_{F'})$ with $R_{F'} = R_F \cap (A_{F'} \times A_{F'})$ due to postulate $C1^k$. Please observe that $R_{F'} \subset R_F$. Since $\div_k$ satisfies $C5^k$ we must end up with $F^k \sqsubseteq (F' +^k G)^k$. Note that F' and G are both k-r-free. Moreover, $G \sqsubseteq F'$ and $G \sqsubseteq G$ witnesses $Mod(F') \cap Mod(G) \neq \varnothing$. Consequently, we may conclude as follows:

$$
\begin{aligned}
F' +^k G = F'^k \sqcup G^k &= F' \sqcup G && \text{(Lem. 2, } k\text{-r-freeness)} \\
&= (A \setminus A', R_{F'}) \sqcup G && \text{(Def. } F') \\
&= ((A \setminus A') \cup A, R_{F'} \cup \varnothing) \\
&= (A, R_{F'}) \\
&\not\sqsupseteq F = (A, R_F) && (R_{F'} \subset R_F).
\end{aligned}
$$

Contradiction! $\square$

Example 4. Given $F, G \in \mathcal{F}$ as considered in the proof of Theorem 2. We illustrate the counterexample in Fig. 3. The result of $(F \div_k G) +^k G$ should be located in the grey shaded area above F as $C5^k$ demands that $F^k \sqsubseteq (F \div_k G) +^k G$ which means that F should be a $\sqsubseteq$-smaller AF than the result of the expansion.

Expanding $F \div_k G$ with G results in an AF that is $\sqsubseteq$-greater than G. But, as we have shown, the contraction of F with G results in an irreversible loss of information, namely any argument removed from F, as G does not posses all information formerly removed from F and therefore $(F \div_k G) +^k G$ will be truly $\sqsubseteq$-smaller than F which conflicts with $C5^k$. Intuitively speaking, when expanding $F \div_k G$ with G, G is not able to "push" the contraction result "above" F. This means that the result of $(F \div_k G) +^k G$ is located somewhere in the area "between" F and G, highlighted by dotted lines. One imaginable result for $(F \div_k G) +^k G$ is depicted by F'.

Remember that one single kernel may serve for different semantics (Theorem 1). This means, the non-existence of a syntactically-based version of contraction applies to any semantics characterizable through one of the considered kernels. Moreover, the proof reveals that only very common properties of kernels are used. This indicates that further semantics might be affected by this negative result. A study of this issue will be part of future work.

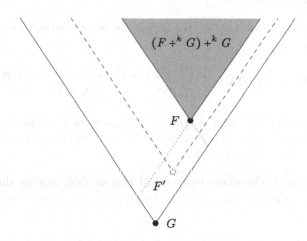

Fig. 3. Counterexample (Theorem 2)

3.3 Brute Contraction

In this section we will show that dropping the somewhat controversial recovery postulate leads to the existence of reasonable operators by introducing the brute contraction operator. In [20, Section 3.1] a good example for why the recovery postulate might lead to counter-intuitive results is given. Suppose you know that Cleopatra has a son but later you find out that Cleopatra doesn't have a child at all so you contract your belief set with the belief "Cleopatra has a child". Obviously, this would lead to forgetting that Cleopatra has a son as well. If you were then to learn that Cleopatra has indeed a child thereby expanding your belief set by "Cleopatra has a child", the recovery postulate would demand the belief "Cleopatra has a son" to be part of your new belief set as well. This counter-example holds in general. Whenever you contract a belief set with a more general belief, all more specific beliefs that imply the contracted one must be removed as well. However, when then expanding the more general belief all more specific ones, although not implied by the more general belief, must be restored.

We coined the name *brute contraction* and we will explain why. As indicated in the proof of Theorem 2, for two AFs F and G with $F \models^k G$ it suffices to remove some non-empty subset of the arguments in G from F when contracting G from F to accomplish success postulate $C4^k$. This leaves us with the problem to decide *which* elements to remove whilst ensuring that there is a deterministic decision procedure to determine the result of a contraction. It seems that no heuristic selecting arguments to be removed can accomplish this without relying on a strict order on the set of arguments in some way. The brute contraction operator avoids this problem by being *brute* in the sense that it removes *any* argument and attack of G from F when contracting F with G. Consider therefore the following definition.

Definition 8. *Given a kernel k. We define the brute contraction operator $-_k$: $\mathcal{F} \times \mathcal{F} \to \mathcal{F}$ as:*

$$(A, R) -_k (A', R') = \begin{cases} ((A, R)|_{A \setminus A'})^k & (A', R')^k \sqsubseteq (A, R)^k \\ (A, R)^k & otherwise. \end{cases}$$

Example 5. Consider the AFs F and G discussed in Example 2 and let $k = k(stb)$. We already observed that $G^k \sqsubseteq F^k$. Hence, the first case of Definition 8 applies, i.e. $F -_k G = (\{a\}, \varnothing)$.

We proceed with the main theorem of this section stating that the brute contraction operator satisfies all contraction postulates apart from the recovery axiom.

Theorem 3. *Given $k \in \{k(stb), k(ad), k(gr), k(co)\}$. The brute contraction operator $-_k$ satisfies $C1^k$–$C4^k$ and $C6^k$ but does not satisfy $C5^k$.*

Proof. Given $k \in \{k(stb), k(ad), k(gr), k(co)\}$ and the brute contraction $-_k$. In the following we consider $F = (A_F, R_F)$, $G = (A_G, R_G)$ and $H = (A_H, R_H)$ as arbitrary but fixed AFs.

$C1^k$ By definition we have that restrictions as well as kernels of AFs are AFs again. Hence, in both cases of Definition 8 we obtain that $F -_k G$ is an AF.
$C2^k$ We have to prove that $(F -_k G)^k \sqsubseteq F^k$.
  Consider the first case of Definition 8. Since any considered kernel k is *context-free* [4, Definition 7] we have that for any AF H and any set A, $(H|_A)^k \sqsubseteq H^k$. Consequently,

$$F -_k G =^{(\text{Def. } 8)} ((A_F, R_F)|_{A_F \setminus A_G})^k \sqsubseteq (A_F, R_F)^k = F^k.$$

Since $F -_k G \sqsubseteq F^k$ we further deduce $(F -_k G)^k \sqsubseteq F^k$ since $\left(F^k\right)^k = F^k$ and thereby, $(F -_k G)^k = F -_k G$ for any considered kernel k.

In the second case we have $F -_k G = F^k$. Again, since $\left(F^k\right)^k = F^k$ we deduce $(F -_k G)^k \sqsubseteq F^k$.

$\mathbf{C3}^k$ We have to show $G^k \not\sqsubseteq F^k \Rightarrow (F -_k G) \equiv^k F$.

Assuming $G^k \not\sqsubseteq F^k$ pushes us to the second case, i.e. $F -_k G = F^k$. We deduce $(F -_k G)^k = \left(F^k\right)^k = F^k$ which means $(F -_k G) \equiv^k F$.

$\mathbf{C4}^k$ We have to prove $G^k \neq (\varnothing, \varnothing) \Rightarrow G^k \not\sqsubseteq (F -_k G)^k$.

For any considered kernel k we have, $G^k \neq (\varnothing, \varnothing)$ if and only if $G \neq (\varnothing, \varnothing)$. Hence, assume $G \neq (\varnothing, \varnothing)$. In the first case we have by definition, $F -_k G = \left((A_F, R_F)|_{A_F \setminus A_G}\right)^k = (A_F \setminus A_G, R_F \cap (A_F \setminus A_G \times A_F \setminus A_G))^k$. Consequently, $G^k \not\sqsubseteq (F -_k G)^k$ since $A_G \not\subseteq A_F \setminus A_G$ because A_G is assumed to be non-empty. In the second case, we may assume $G^k \not\sqsubseteq F^k$. Since $F -_k G = F^k$ by definition and furthermore, $\left(F^k\right)^k = F^k$ for any considered kernel k we immediately verify $G^k \not\sqsubseteq (F -_k G)^k$.

$\mathbf{C5}^k$ Confer Example 6.

$\mathbf{C6}^k$ We have to show $G \equiv^k H \Rightarrow F -_k G \equiv^k F -_k H$.

Assume $G^k = H^k$. Consequently, $G^k \sqsubseteq F^k$ if and only if $H^k \sqsubseteq F^k$. For the second case we have nothing to show since the result F^k neither depend on G, nor on H. Now, for the first case. It is essential to see that $G^k = H^k$ implies $A_G = A_H$ for any considered kernel k. Thus,

$$F -_k G = \left((A_F, R_F)|_{A_F \setminus A_G}\right)^k = \left((A_F, R_F)|_{A_F \setminus A_H}\right)^k = F -_k H$$

Therefore $F -_k G \equiv^k F -_k H$ since they are even identical.   □

The following example shows that brute contraction indeed does not satisfy the recovery postulate $\mathbf{C5}^k$.

Example 6. Consider again the AFs F and G introduced in Example 2 and let $k = k(stb)$. For convenience, we depicted all relevant frameworks below including the running examples F and G.

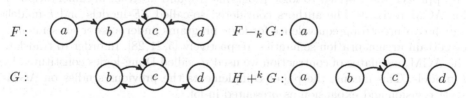

According to Example 5 we have $H = F -_k G$ as depicted above. Since $G^k \sqsubseteq F^k$ as well as $H^k \sqsubseteq F^k$ we have $Mod^k(G) \cap Mod^k(H) \neq \varnothing$. Hence, in consideration of Lemma 2 we infer that $H +^k G = H^k \sqcup G^k$ as displayed above. One can clearly see that the recovery postulate $\mathbf{C5}^k$ is not fulfilled since $F^k \not\sqsubseteq \left((F \div_k G) +_k G\right)^k = H +_k G$. The attack (a, b) in F is irrecoverably contracted.

3.4   Discussion

In [25] it was shown that a contraction operator can be constructed from a given revision operator via the union of sets of models as well as the complement of a set of models which can be implemented with disjunction or negation, respectively, in case of belief bases (cf. [13, Definition 3] for excellent explanations). This raises the question why we cannot construct contraction operators although we are equipped with revision operators for Dung-logics [5, Theorem 9]. The reason for this is simply that we do not have an analog to disjunction or negation in Dung-logics. In other words, not every set of k-models is realizable. In [5, Section 3] a first study was presented and it will be an exciting project to exactly characterize the expressive power of Dung-logic.

A further possible view why contraction is not possible in Dung-logics is as follows: We already mentioned that the syntax of AFs is layered, i.e. one part depends on the other whilst the converse does not. In contrast, the classical AGM-postulates were phrased with propositional logic in mind where such a kind of dependence is not given. Consequently, one possible way out is to rephrase all axioms or single problematic postulates in such a way that they better match a logic whose syntax is layered.

Finally, we want to mention that the recovery postulate $C5^k$ does not carry the sole fault regarding the non-existence of contraction operators. It can be shown that dropping the success postulate $C4^k$ leads to the existence of operators but giving up this axiom would be in conflict with the very idea of contraction.

4   Related Work and Summary

In this paper we presented a first study of AGM-style contraction for abstract argumentation frameworks. Since ordinary and strong equivalence coincide in the underlying formalism of the AGM setup, i.e. propositional logic, one may pursue two in principle different options for converting AGM postulates to a certain non-monotonic logic. In this paper we focus on strong equivalence. Such an approach was applied to logic programs [16] and abstract argumentation [5] for AGM revision. The authors considered so-called SE-models and k-models which capture strong equivalence for logic programs under answer set semantics or certain argumentation semantics, respectively [5,21,28]. In order to translate the AGM postulates of contraction we used so-called Dung-logics constituted by k-models. This means, the paper complements the previous studies on AGM-style revision and expansion as presented in [5].

The general result is a negative one, that is, there are no contraction operators satisfying all 6 translated postulates. This means, an analog to the Harper Identity, which allows to construct a contraction operator from a given revision operator, is not available (cf. discussion part). Interestingly, a similar problem was discovered for contraction in the realm of logic programming [11]. Instead of the problematic recovery postulate the authors considered the alternative *relevance postulate* introduced in [23]. Such a kind of consideration, i.e. a study of further postulates given in the literature, will be part of future work.

As mentioned in the Introduction, we are not aware of any alternative approaches to contraction in the context of abstract argumentation. In [31] argument contraction (as well as revision) for structured argumentation was studied. The authors presented postulates also influenced by the AGM-postulates but adapted to the more involved ASPIC$^+$ system [29]. In contrast to the original setup contraction functions may return several alternative theories and moreover, the resulting theories might be inconsistent. Interestingly, although a straightforward analog to the Harper Identity is not given, the authors showed how to define a meaningful revision in terms of contraction.

There are several directions for future work. In particular, we plan to extend the analysis of revision and contraction to the more general abstract dialectical frameworks (ADFs) [12]. It will be interesting to compare these results with the ones already proposed in [11,16] since there are standard translations such that the semantics of logic programs and ADFs coincide [32].

Acknowledgments. This work was partially supported by a postdoc fellowship of the German Academic Exchange Service (DAAD) 57407370.

References

1. Alchourrón, C.E., Gärdenfors, P., Makinson, D.: On the logic of theory change: partial meet contraction and revision functions. J. Symbolic Logic **50**, 510–530 (1985)
2. Baroni, P., Gabbay, D., Giacomin, M., van der Torre, L.: Handbook of Formal Argumentation. College Publications (2018)
3. Baroni, P., Caminada, M., Giacomin, M.: An introduction to argumentation semantics. Knowl. Eng. Rev. **26**, 365–410 (2011)
4. Baumann, R.: Context-free and context-sensitive kernels: update and deletion equivalence in abstract argumentation. In: ECAI 2014, pp. 63–68 (2014)
5. Baumann, R., Brewka, G.: AGM meets abstract argumentation: expansion and revision for Dung frameworks. In: IJCAI 15, pp. 2734–2740. AAAI Press (2015)
6. Baumann, R., Brewka, G.: The equivalence zoo for Dung-style semantics. J. Logic Comput. **28**(3), 477–498 (2018)
7. Baumann, R., Spanring, C.: Infinite argumentation frameworks. In: Eiter, T., Strass, H., Truszczyński, M., Woltran, S. (eds.) Advances in Knowledge Representation, Logic Programming, and Abstract Argumentation. LNCS (LNAI), vol. 9060, pp. 281–295. Springer, Cham (2015). https://doi.org/10.1007/978-3-319-14726-0_19
8. Baumann, R., Spanring, C.: A study of unrestricted abstract argumentation frameworks. In: IJCAI 2017, pp. 807–813 (2017)
9. Baumann, R., Strass, H.: An abstract logical approach to characterizing strong equivalence in logic-based knowledge representation formalisms. In: KR 2016, pp. 525–528 (2016)
10. Baumann, R., Woltran, S.: The role of self-attacking arguments in characterizations of equivalence notions. J. Logic Comput. **26**(4), 1293–1313 (2016)

11. Binnewies, S., Zhuang, Z., Wang, K.: Partial meet revision and contraction in logic programs. In: AAAI 2015, pp. 1439–1445 (2015)
12. Brewka, G., Strass, H., Ellmauthaler, S., Wallner, J.P., Woltran, S.: Abstract dialectical frameworks revisited. In: IJCAI 2013, pp. 803–809 (2013)
13. Caridroit, T., Konieczny, S., Marquis, P.: Contraction in propositional logic. In: Destercke, S., Denoeux, T. (eds.) ECSQARU 2015. LNCS (LNAI), vol. 9161, pp. 186–196. Springer, Cham (2015). https://doi.org/10.1007/978-3-319-20807-7_17
14. Coste-Marquis, S., Konieczny, S., Mailly, J., Marquis, P.: On the revision of argumentation systems: minimal change of arguments statuses. In: KR 2014 (2014)
15. Coste-Marquis, S., Konieczny, S., Mailly, J.-G., Marquis, P.: A translation-based approach for revision of argumentation frameworks. In: Fermé, E., Leite, J. (eds.) JELIA 2014. LNCS (LNAI), vol. 8761, pp. 397–411. Springer, Cham (2014). https://doi.org/10.1007/978-3-319-11558-0_28
16. Delgrande, J.P., Schaub, T., Tompits, H., Woltran, S.: Belief revision of logic programs under answer set semantics. In: Principles of Knowledge Representation and Reasoning: Proceedings of the Eleventh International Conference, KR 2008, Sydney, Australia, 16–19 September 2008, pp. 411–421 (2008)
17. Diller, M., Haret, A., Linsbichler, T., Rümmele, S., Woltran, S.: An extension-based approach to belief revision in abstract argumentation. Int. J. Approx. Reason. **93**, 395–423 (2018)
18. Dung, P.M.: On the acceptability of arguments and its fundamental role in non-monotonic reasoning, logic programming and n-person games. Artif. Intell. **77**(2), 321–358 (1995)
19. Falappa, M., Garcia, A., Kern-Isberner, G., Simari, G.: On the evolving relation between belief revision and argumentation. Knowl. Eng. Rev. **26**, 35–43 (2011)
20. Fermé, E.L., Hansson, S.O.: AGM 25 years - twenty-five years of research in belief change. J. Philos. Logic **40**(2), 295–331 (2011)
21. Ferraris, P., Lifschitz, V.: Mathematical foundations of answer set programming. In: We Will Show Them! Essays in Honour of Dov Gabbay, pp. 615–664. King's College Publications (2005)
22. Gärdenfors, P.: Belief Revision. Cambridge Tracts in Theoretical Computer Science, Cambridge University Press (1992)
23. Hannson, S.: New operators for theory change. Theoria **55**(2), 114–132 (1989)
24. Hansson, S.O.: A Textbook of Belief Dynamics: Solutions to Exercises. Kluwer Academic Publishers, Norwell (2001)
25. Harper, W.L.: Rational conceptual change. PSA: Proc. Biennial Meet. Philos. Sci. Assoc. **1976**, 462–494 (1976)
26. Lifschitz, V., Pearce, D., Valverde, A.: Strongly equivalent logic programs. ACM Trans. Comput. Logic **2**(4), 526–541 (2001)
27. Oikarinen, E., Woltran, S.: Characterizing strong equivalence for argumentation frameworks. Artif. Intell. **175**(14–15), 1985–2009 (2011)
28. Pearce, D.: A new logical characterisation of stable models and answer sets. In: Dix, J., Pereira, L.M., Przymusinski, T.C. (eds.) NMELP 1996. LNCS, vol. 1216, pp. 57–70. Springer, Heidelberg (1997). https://doi.org/10.1007/BFb0023801
29. Prakken, H.: An abstract framework for argumentation with structured arguments. Argument Comput. **1**(2), 93–124 (2010)
30. Rahwan, I., Simari, G.R.: Argumentation in Artificial Intelligence, 1st edn. Springer, Heidelberg (2009). https://doi.org/10.1007/978-0-387-98197-0

31. Snaith, M., Reed, C.: Argument revision. J. Logic Comput. **27**(7), 2089–2134 (2017)
32. Strass, H.: Approximating operators and semantics for abstract dialectical frameworks. Artif. Intell. **205**, 39–70 (2013)
33. Truszczynski, M.: Strong and uniform equivalence of nonmonotonic theories - an algebraic approach. Ann. Math. Artif. Intell. **48**(3–4), 245–265 (2006)

A Possible World View and a Normal Form for the Constellation Semantics

Stefano Bistarelli and Theofrastos Mantadelis[(✉)]

Department of Mathematics and Computer Science,
Member of the INdAM Research Group GNCS, University of Perugia,
Perugia, Italy
{stefano.bistarelli,theofrastos.mantadelis}@unipg.it

Abstract. After Dung's founding work in Abstract Argumentation Frameworks there has been a growing interest in extending the Dung's semantics in order to describe more complex or real life situations. Several of these approaches take the direction of weighted or probabilistic extensions. One of the most prominent probabilistic approaches is that of constellation Probabilistic Abstract Argumentation Frameworks.

In this paper, we introduce the probabilistic attack normal form for the constellation semantics; and we prove that the probabilistic attack normal form is sufficient to represent any Probabilistic Abstract Argumentation Framework of the constellation semantics.

1 Introduction

Argumentation is an everyday method of humanity to discuss and solve myriad different situations where opinions or point of views conflict. Abstract Argumentation Frameworks [8] (AAFs) aim in modeling everyday situations where information is inconsistent or incomplete. Many different extensions of AAFs from Dung's pioneering work have appeared in order to describe different everyday situations. Sample works includes assumption based argumentation [4], extending AAFs with support [15], introducing labels [16]. Other approaches of extending AAFs have focused on introducing weights in elements of the AAF, such as [2,3]. Such approaches are powerful tools to model voting systems, belief in arguments and argument strength.

Knowledge representation with the use of probabilistic information has been used in many areas of computer science. Probabilistic information, is a powerful medium to represent knowledge. Similarly, many researchers have extended AAFs by adding probabilistic information. These very prominent extensions of AAFs have been categorized in two big groups by Hunter [11]: the **epistemic** approaches and the **constellation** approaches.

The epistemic approaches, such as those presented in [12] describe probabilistic AAFs that the uncertainty does not alter the structure of the AAFs.

This work has been partially supported by: "Argumentation 360" and "RACRA18" (funded by Ricerca di Base 2017/2018).

© Springer Nature Switzerland AG 2019
F. Calimeri et al. (Eds.): JELIA 2019, LNAI 11468, pp. 58–68, 2019.
https://doi.org/10.1007/978-3-030-19570-0_4

Furthermore, the epistemic approaches quantify the existing uncertainty (either of arguments being part of extensions, or augement label) instead of introducing new uncertainty.

The constellation approaches, such as those presented in [6,7,9,13] introduce probabilistic elements in the AAF in such a way that the structure of the AAF becomes uncertain. The constellation approaches generate a set of AAFs with a probabilistic distribution and as such define a probabilistic distribution over the extensions of those AAFs.

In this paper we focus on the constellation approach from Li et al. [13]. [13] introduced probabilistic elements to the structure of AAFs, resulting to a set of AAFs. This allows for a set of arguments to be an (admissible, stable, ground, etc.) extension in some of the AAFs that are represented by the constellation. This simple but yet powerful representation has the ability to represent naturally many different uncertain scenarios.

The works of [11,13] can be considered as the pioneering work on combining probabilities with AAFs. In this paper, we (a) connect induced AAFs with possible worlds; (b) define the probabilistic attack normal forms for PrAAFs; and (c) illustrate how the normal form can represent any general PrAAF.

The rest of the paper is structured as follows. First, we briefly introduce AAFs and PrAAFs. We then present the possible worlds notion, the probabilistic attack normal form for PrAAFs and a transformation of general PrAAFs to probabilistic attack normal form. Finally, we conclude and present future work.

2 Preliminaries

2.1 Abstract Argumentation

An abstract argumentation framework [8] (AAF) is a tuple $AAF = (Args, Atts)$ where $Args$ is a set of arguments and $Atts$ a set of attacks among arguments of the form of a binary relation $Atts \subseteq Args \times Args$. For arguments $a, b \in Args$, we use $a \rightarrow b$ as a shorthand to indicate $(a, b) \in Atts$ and we say that argument a attacks argument b. Figure 1 illustrates an example AAF.

A set of arguments $S \subseteq Args$ is said to be *conflict-free* iff $\nexists a, b \in S$ where $a \rightarrow b \in Atts$. An argument $a \in Args$ is acceptable with respect to set $S \subseteq Args$ if no argument attack a or if $\forall b \in Args$ that $\exists b \rightarrow a \in Atts$ then $\exists c \in S$ where $c \rightarrow b \in Atts$.

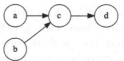

Given the above [8] gives semantics to AAF by the use of extensions over subsets of arguments. Dung first defines the *admissible* semantics. A set $S \subseteq Args$ is admissible iff S is conflict free and each $a \in S$ is acceptable with respect to S. Following our example AAF from Fig. 1, the set $\{a, b, d\}$ is admissible. Over time several different semantics have been discussed such as complete, preferred, grounded, stable [8], semi-stable [5], CF2 [10] etc.

Fig. 1. Example AAF $(\{a, b, c, d\}, \{a \rightarrow c, b \rightarrow c, c \rightarrow d\})$. Arguments are represented as cycles and attacks as arrows. Arguments a, b are attacking argument c which attacks argument d.

2.2 Constellation Based Probabilistic Abstract Argumentation Frameworks

Hunter [11], categorizes probabilistic abstract argumentation frameworks (PrAAFs) in two different categories: the *constellation* and the *epistemic* PrAAFs. For this paper we will focus on the constellation approaches and we base our work in the definition of PrAAFs by [13].

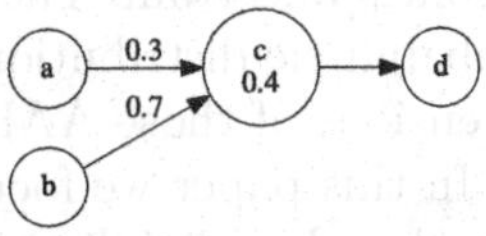

A constellation approach to PrAAFs defines probabilities over the structure of the AAF graph. One can assign probabilities to either the arguments or/and attacks of the AAF. We refer to arguments/attacks with assigned probabilities less than 1 as probabilistic arguments/attacks and we refer as probabilistic elements to either probabilistic arguments or probabilistic attacks.

A probabilistic element e exists in an AAF with probability $P(e)$. These probabilistic elements correspond to random variables, which are assumed to be mutually independent[1]. As such, a PrAAF defines a probability distribution over a set of AAFs.

Fig. 2. Example PrAAF $(\{a, b, c, d\}, \{1, 1, 0.4, 1\}, \{a \rightarrow c, b \rightarrow c, c \rightarrow d\}, \{0.3, 0.7, 1\})$. Arguments are represented as cycles and attacks as arrows.

Definition 1. *Formally, a PrAAF is a tuple $PrAAF = (Args, P_{Args}, Atts, P_{Atts})$ where Args, Atts define an AAF, P_{Args} is a set of probabilities for each $a \in Args$ with $0 < P_{Args}(a) \leq 1$ and P_{Atts} is a set of probabilities for each $\rightarrow \in Atts$ with $0 < P_{Atts}(\rightarrow) \leq 1$.*

Finally, stating an argument or an attack having probability 0 is redundant. A probabilistic argument or attack with 0 probability is an argument or attack that is not part of any AAF that the constellation represents. Figure 2, illustrates an example PrAAF with 3 different probabilistic elements.

2.3 Inducing AAFs by Imposing Restrictions

Li et al. [13] in order to restrict the combinations of probabilistic elements to only those that generate valid AAFs introduced extra restrictions and stated that the probabilities P_{atts} are conditional probabilities instead the likelihood of existence for the attack. These restrictions appear as a separate definition, formally:

Definition 2 (Inducing an AAF from a PrAAF). *An AAF $(Args_{Ind}, Atts_{Ind})$ is said to be induced from a PrAAF $(Args, P_{Args}, Atts, P_{Atts})$ iff all of the following hold:*

1. *$Args_{Ind} \subseteq Args$*
2. *$Atts_{Ind} \subseteq Atts \cap (Args_{Ind} \times Args_{Ind})$*

---

[1] As we are going to present later in the paper, the structure of AAF might impose dependencies among otherwise assumed independent probabilistic elements.

3. $\forall a \in Args$ such that $P_{Args}(a) = 1, a \in Args_{Ind}$
4. $\forall a1 \rightarrow a2 \in Atts$ such that $P_{Atts}(a1 \rightarrow a2) = 1$ and $P_{Args}(a1) = P_{Args}(a2) = 1, a1 \rightarrow a2 \in Atts_{Ind}$

Furthermore, $P_{Att}(a1 \rightarrow a2)$ is stated to be the conditional probability of the attack existing when both attacking and attacked argument exist in the AAF ($P_{Att}(a1 \rightarrow a2 | a1, a2 \in Args_{Ind})$).

Table 1. Induced AAF of our example PrAAF from Fig. 2. Shaded rows, illustrate an Induced AAF that contains multiple possible worlds that would generate an invalid AAF.

AAF	Possible World	Prob.	Admissible Sets
	$(\neg(a \rightarrow c) \wedge \neg(b \rightarrow c) \wedge \neg c) \vee (\neg(a \rightarrow c) \wedge (b \rightarrow c) \wedge \neg c) \vee ((a \rightarrow c) \wedge \neg(b \rightarrow c) \wedge \neg c) \vee ((a \rightarrow c) \wedge (b \rightarrow c) \wedge \neg c)$	0.6	$\{\}, \{a\}, \{b\}, \{d\}, \{a,b\}, \{a,d\}, \{b,d\}, \{a,b,d\}$
	$\neg(a \rightarrow c) \wedge \neg(b \rightarrow c) \wedge c$	0.084	$\{\}, \{a\}, \{b\}, \{c\}, \{a,b\}, \{a,c\}, \{b,c\}, \{a,b,c\}$
	$\neg(a \rightarrow c) \wedge (b \rightarrow c) \wedge c$	0.196	$\{\}, \{a\}, \{b\}, \{a,b\}, \{b,d\}, \{a,b,d\}$
	$(a \rightarrow c) \wedge \neg(b \rightarrow c) \wedge c$	0.036	$\{\}, \{a\}, \{b\}, \{a,b\}, \{a,d\}, \{a,b,d\}$
	$(a \rightarrow c) \wedge (b \rightarrow c) \wedge c$	0.084	$\{\}, \{a\}, \{b\}, \{a,b\}, \{a,d\}, \{b,d\}, \{a,b,d\}$

Table 1 presents the induced AAFs from our example PrAAF[2]. Clearly, there is an exponential number of induced AAFs that a PrAAF represents. We find that the imposed restrictions from Li et al. [13] create a more complex and less intuitive PrAAF definition than what is necessary.

3   Possible Worlds and AAFs

As mentioned a PrAAF defines a probability distribution for all the possible non-probabilistic AAFs it contains. Each single possible set of probabilistic elements (arguments or attacks) of the PrAAF can be called a **possible world**. Table 2 presents all possible worlds for the example PrAAF of Fig. 2. One can

---

[2] For now we ask the reader to ignore the possible world column which is used later in the paper.

Table 2. Possible worlds of our example PrAAF from Fig. 2. Shaded rows, illustrate possible worlds that generate an invalid AAF.

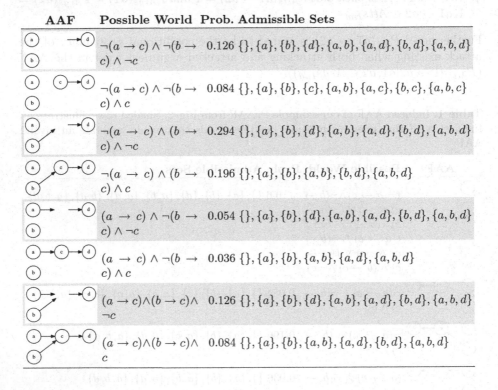

AAF	Possible World	Prob.	Admissible Sets
	$\neg(a \to c) \wedge \neg(b \to c) \wedge \neg c$	0.126	$\{\}, \{a\}, \{b\}, \{d\}, \{a,b\}, \{a,d\}, \{b,d\}, \{a,b,d\}$
	$\neg(a \to c) \wedge \neg(b \to c) \wedge c$	0.084	$\{\}, \{a\}, \{b\}, \{c\}, \{a,b\}, \{a,c\}, \{b,c\}, \{a,b,c\}$
	$\neg(a \to c) \wedge (b \to c) \wedge \neg c$	0.294	$\{\}, \{a\}, \{b\}, \{d\}, \{a,b\}, \{a,d\}, \{b,d\}, \{a,b,d\}$
	$\neg(a \to c) \wedge (b \to c) \wedge c$	0.196	$\{\}, \{a\}, \{b\}, \{a,b\}, \{b,d\}, \{a,b,d\}$
	$(a \to c) \wedge \neg(b \to c) \wedge \neg c$	0.054	$\{\}, \{a\}, \{b\}, \{d\}, \{a,b\}, \{a,d\}, \{b,d\}, \{a,b,d\}$
	$(a \to c) \wedge \neg(b \to c) \wedge c$	0.036	$\{\}, \{a\}, \{b\}, \{a,b\}, \{a,d\}, \{a,b,d\}$
	$(a \to c) \wedge (b \to c) \wedge \neg c$	0.126	$\{\}, \{a\}, \{b\}, \{d\}, \{a,b\}, \{a,d\}, \{b,d\}, \{a,b,d\}$
	$(a \to c) \wedge (b \to c) \wedge c$	0.084	$\{\}, \{a\}, \{b\}, \{a,b\}, \{a,d\}, \{b,d\}, \{a,b,d\}$

notice that having only three different probabilistic elements it generates eight possible worlds. The possible worlds of a PrAAF are exponential in the number of probabilistic elements (2^N where N the number of probabilistic elements).

Definition 3 (Probability of Possible World). *The probability of a possible world equals to the product of the probability of each probabilistic element that is in the possible world with the product of one minus the probability of each probabilistic element that is excluded from the possible world.*

$$P_{world} = \prod_{e_i \in AAF_{world}} P(e_i) \cdot \prod_{e_j \notin AAF_{world}} (1 - P(e_j))$$

While it is natural to use the notion of possible worlds to describe PrAAFs, unfortunately in general PrAAFs[3] not all possible worlds generate a valid AAF. Ideally, we want each possible world to generate a single unique valid AAF.

---

[3] We refer to general PrAAFs, as any constellation PrAAF that uses a definition similar to Definition 1. With the term general PrAAFs we do not include any extra restrictions imposed to the PrAAF definition.

A second pitfall for general PrAAFs, lies in the combination of the independence assumption of PrAAFs probabilistic elements. We earlier stated that we assume each probabilistic element is independent from the other probabilistic elements. When a probabilistic argument is connected with a probabilistic attack and we consider a possible world where the probabilistic argument does not exist we are implicitly also forcing the probabilistic attack not to exist, thus creating an implicit dependency among probabilistic elements.

To better illustrate this pitfall of general PrAAFs, we use the example PrAAF of Fig. 2. Consider the attack $a \rightarrow c$ which has a 0.3 probability of existence for each generated AAFs. If you sum the possible worlds of Table 2 where the edge $a \rightarrow c$ exists you do get a probability of 0.3 but if you sum the possible worlds of Table 2 where the edge $a \rightarrow c$ exists and it is a valid AAF then you get a probability of $0.036 + 0.084 = 0.12$ as it only exists in two possible worlds (rows 6 and 8 of Table 2) instead of the expected four possible worlds (rows 5 to 8 of Table 2).

Notice at Table 1 that the highlighted induced AAF represents the four worlds that argument c is not part of the AAF. Also notice that that the specific induced AAF is not part of any possible world, but is the corrected AAF of the four non valid AAFs that the possible worlds generate.

4   Probabilistic Attack Normal Form

In this section we introduce the Probabilistic Attack Normal Form for PrAAFs. The normal formed PrAAFs definition does not require any added restrictions in order for the PrAAFs to generate possible worlds with only valid AAFs. Also the probabilistic elements of normal formed PrAAFs are mutually independent and the probabilities of probabilistic elements always represents their likelihood of existence. These characteristics of normal formed PrAAFs allow for easier reasoning and also define a clearer probabilistic distribution.

Definition 4 (Probabilistic Attack Normal Form). *A PrAAF P is in its probabilistic attack normal form if it contains no probabilistic arguments ($\forall a \in Args, P(a) = 1$).*

The probabilistic attack normal form definition does not fall to the aforementioned pitfalls and does not require further restrictions like the general PrAAFs definition. The pitfalls in general PrAAFs originate in the interaction of connected probabilistic arguments with probabilistic attacks. By having only probabilistic attacks the two pitfalls do not appear. Furthermore, the probabilistic attack normal form definition for PrAAFs is simpler and allows easier reasoning about PrAAF properties.

Finally, we are going to illustrate that having PrAAFs in the probabilistic attack normal form does not reduce the representation power of PrAAFs and that any probabilistic distribution that can be represented in general PrAAFs it can also be represented in the probabilistic attack normal form for PrAAFs. While this paper will only focus on Probabilistic Attack Normal Form PrAAFs one could similarly illustrate the same properties also for the Probabilistic Argument Normal Form PrAAFs.

4.1 Transforming General PrAAFs to Probabilistic Attack Normal Form PrAAFs

In this section we present a transformation that illustrates that any general PrAAF can be transformed to a Probabilistic Attack Normal Form. Both the original and the transformed PrAAF have the same probabilistic distribution over their extensions. Because of the existence of such a transformation one could use PrAAFs with only Probabilistic Attacks in order to represent any general PrAAF. Or, from a different perspective, one could define Probabilistic Arguments as syntactic sugar using Probabilistic Attacks and definite Arguments.

4.2 Transforming Probabilistic Arguments to Probabilistic Attacks

Before we present the transformation of probabilistic argument to probabilistic attack, we need to define a special argument that we call *ground truth*:

Definition 5 (Ground Truth[4]). *We introduce a special argument called* Ground Truth *and shorthand it with the letter η. We say that η is undeniably true meaning that η is never attacked by any argument and is always included in all extensions regardless the semantics used.*

The η argument modifies the extensions of an AAF for all semantics in such a way that η must always be included. For example, in the admissible semantics of an AAF without η a valid extension is the empty set ($\{\}$), but in an AAF that contains η the empty set is not a valid extension under the admissible semantics and the equivalent extension to the empty set is $\{\eta\}$. Note, that the extensions of the original AAF and the extensions of an AAF with $\{\eta\}$ have a one-on-one correspondence for all semantics.

Definition 6 (Acceptable Extensions). *For AAFs that contain η, an acceptable extension E is one that includes η ($\eta \in E$).*

By using $\{\eta\}$ now we can define a normal expansion transformation for general PrAAFs to Probabilistic Attack Normal Form as follows.

Transformation 1 (General PrAAF to Probabilistic Attack Normal Form). *Any PrAAF P, can be transformed[5] to an equivalent PrAAF P' by removing any probabilistic information attached to an argument $a \in Args$, with $P(a)$ and introducing a probabilistic attack from the ground truth η to argument a with probability $1 - P(a)$.*

---

[4] The η argument is only a construct we use in order to illustrate how Probabilistic Arguments can be transformed to Probabilistic Attacks and the PrAAF to retain the same probabilistic distribution.

[5] Such transformation is categorized as a normal expansion [1] of the original PrAAF.

Definition 7. *We notate $P \equiv^{\sigma}_{|\eta} P'$ the standard equivalence [14] of PrAAF P with PrAAF P' under semantics σ by ignoring the existence of η in the acceptable extensions.*

Theorem 1 (Equivalence of transformed PrAAF). *A transformed PrAAF P' has an equivalent distribution in terms of admissible sets containing η compared with the admissible sets of the original PrAAF P.*

Proof. We split the proof in two parts. First we show that PrAAF P generates AAFs that have the same admissible sets with the generated AAFs from PrAAF P'. We point out that for PrAAF P' acceptable admissible sets are only the ones that contain the ground truth argument which we ignore its existence when comparing admissible sets. For example, the empty admissible set of P is equivalent with the $\{\eta\}$ admissible set of P'. A probabilistic argument pa generates two different sets of AAFs, set S_1 where pa exists and S_2 where pa does not exist.

PrAAF P' generates S'_1 the equivalent sets of S_1 when $\eta \rightarrow pa$ does not exist and the equivalent S'_2 sets of S_2 when $\eta \rightarrow pa$ exists. When comparing an AAF with pa versus an AAF without $\eta \rightarrow pa$ the only difference is the existence of η as we only consider admissible sets that contain it and we ignore its existence in the admissible sets the two graphs are equivalent thus the S'_1 sets are equivalent with the S_1 sets.

For S_2 where pa does not exist, the equivalent S'_2 contains AAFs where the argument pa is been attacked by η and is not defended by any other argument. Clearly, as η is included in every extension that we consider then every attack originating from pa is defended; thus, the AAFs of S_2 generate the same admissible extensions with the AAFs of S'_2.

Next part is to show that the probability of each extension is the same. The probability that a set is an admissible extension is been computed by the summation of the possible worlds where that set is admissible. As S_1, S_2 are equivalent with S'_1, S'_2 and produce equivalent AAFs then the possible worlds are equivalent too. The probability of each possible world is also the same as when pa would exist the possible world probability is multiplied by $P(pa)$. In the equivalent case the attack $\eta \rightarrow pa$ does not exist and the possible world probability is multiplied by $1 - (1 - P(pa)) = pa$. Similarly, for the possible worlds that pa does not exist.

Corollary 1. *PrAAF P' has equivalent acceptable extensions with PrAAF P for all semantics where acceptability of an argument is necessary for the inclusion of the argument in the extension. Such semantics include: complete, preferred, ground and stable semantics. Similarly, as the probabilistic distributions are equivalent then all acceptable extensions of P' will have equal probability with their equivalent extension from P.*

We also want to point out that each general PrAAF can be transformed to a unique Probabilistic Attack Normal Form containing η. Also any Probabilistic Attack Normal Form that contains η is reversible to the general PrAAF. For those reasons we can claim that the transformation is a one-to-one reversible transformation.

Proposition 1 (Reversibility of the transformation). *The general PrAAG to Probabilistic Attack Normal Form transformation is reversible and creates a one-on-one equivalent PrAAF.*

Proof. Any argument a that is attacked by η is transformed to a Probabilistic Argument with $(1 - P(\eta \to a))$ probability. Finally, you can drop η to return to the original general PrAAF.

By using the general PrAAF to Probabilistic Attack Normal Form transformation to the PrAAF of Fig. 2 we get the PrAAF of Fig. 3. Table 3 presents the possible worlds of the PrAAF of Fig. 3. Now, each possible world represents a valid AAF that generates the equivalent acceptable admissible sets like the original PrAAF. Furthermore, the probabilistic distribution is identical.

Table 3. Possible worlds after transforming PrAAF of Fig. 2.

AAF	Possible World	Prob.	Acceptable Admissible Sets
	$\neg(a \to c) \wedge \neg(b \to c) \wedge$ $(\eta \to c) \equiv \neg(a \to c) \wedge$ $\neg(b \to c) \wedge \neg c$	0.126	$\{\eta\}, \{\eta, a\}, \{\eta, b\}, \{\eta, d\}, \{\eta, a, b\},$ $\{\eta, a, d\}, \{\eta, b, d\}, \{\eta, a, b, d\}$
	$\neg(a \to c) \wedge \neg(b \to c) \wedge$ $\neg(\eta \to c) \equiv \neg(a \to$ $c) \wedge \neg(b \to c) \wedge c$	0.084	$\{\eta\}, \{\eta, a\}, \{\eta, b\}, \{\eta, c\}, \{\eta, a, b\},$ $\{\eta, a, c\}, \{\eta, b, c\}, \{\eta, a, b, c\}$
	$\neg(a \to c) \wedge (b \to c) \wedge$ $(\eta \to c) \equiv \neg(a \to c) \wedge$ $(b \to c) \wedge \neg c$	0.294	$\{\eta\}, \{\eta, a\}, \{\eta, b\}, \{\eta, d\}, \{\eta, a, b\},$ $\{\eta, a, d\}, \{\eta, b, d\}, \{\eta, a, b, d\}$
	$\neg(a \to c) \wedge (b \to c) \wedge$ $\neg(\eta \to c) \equiv \neg(a \to$ $c) \wedge (b \to c) \wedge c$	0.196	$\{\eta\}, \{\eta, a\}, \{\eta, b\}, \{\eta, a, b\}, \{\eta, b, d\},$ $\{\eta, a, b, d\}$
	$(a \to c) \wedge \neg(b \to c) \wedge$ $(\eta \to c) \equiv (a \to c) \wedge$ $\neg(b \to c) \wedge \neg c$	0.054	$\{\eta\}, \{\eta, a\}, \{\eta, b\}, \{\eta, d\}, \{\eta, a, b\},$ $\{\eta, a, d\}, \{\eta, b, d\}, \{\eta, a, b, d\}$
	$(a \to c) \wedge \neg(b \to c) \wedge$ $\neg(\eta \to c) \equiv (a \to c) \wedge$ $\neg(b \to c) \wedge c$	0.036	$\{\eta\}, \{\eta, a\}, \{\eta, b\}, \{\eta, a, b\}, \{\eta, a, d\},$ $\{\eta, a, b, d\}$
	$(a \to c) \wedge (b \to c) \wedge$ $(\eta \to c) \equiv (a \to c) \wedge$ $(b \to c) \wedge \neg c$	0.126	$\{\eta\}, \{\eta, a\}, \{\eta, b\}, \{\eta, d\}, \{\eta, a, b\},$ $\{\eta, a, d\}, \{\eta, b, d\}, \{\eta, a, b, d\}$
	$(a \to c) \wedge (b \to c) \wedge$ $\neg(\eta \to c) \equiv (a \to c) \wedge$ $(b \to c) \wedge c$	0.084	$\{\eta\}, \{\eta, a\}, \{\eta, b\}, \{\eta, a, b\}, \{\eta, a, d\},$ $\{\eta, b, d\}, \{\eta, a, b, d\}$

Proposition 2 (Complexity of the Transformation). *The general PrAAF to Probabilistic Attack Normal Form transformation has linear complexity $O(N)$ to the number of probabilistic arguments N that the original PrAAF contains. It grows the size of the original PrAAF by one argument and by N attacks. The transformation does not affect the worst case complexity of computing any extension or the probability that a set is any type of an extension.*

5 Conclusion and Future Work

In this paper, we (a) make the connection of induced AAFs with possible worlds; (b) formally introduce the Probabilistic Attack Normal Form for PrAAFs; and (c) illustrate that the Probabilistic Attack Normal Form is sufficient to represent any general PrAAF as defined by [13].

Our motivation is to provide a simpler but powerful definition for constellation PrAAFs; furthermore, we give an insight in the constellation semantics and its restrictions from the point of view of generating possible worlds. For future work, we want to investigate to what degree the constellation semantics can contain epistemic constructs and what relations are between the two approaches; finally, we are planning to examine how the properties of AAF can be used to simplifying probabilistic inference in PrAAFs.

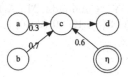

Fig. 3. Example transformed PrAAF ($\{a, b, c, d, \eta\}$, $\{1, 1, 1, 1, 1\}$, $\{a \rightarrow c, b \rightarrow c, c \rightarrow d, \eta \rightarrow c\}$, $\{0.3, 0.7, 1, 0.6\}$).

References

1. Baumann, R., Brewka, G.: Expanding argumentation frameworks: enforcing and monotonicity results. In: Computational Models of Argument (COMMA), pp. 75–86 (2010)
2. Bench-Capon, T.J.M.: Persuasion in practical argument using value-based argumentation frameworks. J. Log. Comput. **13**(3), 429–448 (2003)
3. Bistarelli, S., Rossi, F., Santini, F.: A novel weighted defence and its relaxation in abstract argumentation. Int. J. Approx. Reason. **92**, 66–86 (2018)
4. Bondarenko, A., Toni, F., Kowalski, R.A.: An assumption-based framework for non-monotonic reasoning. In: Logic Programming and Non-monotonic Reasoning, (LPNMR), pp. 171–189 (1993)
5. Caminada, M.W.A., Carnielli, W.A., Dunne, P.E.: Semi-stable semantics. J. Logic Comput. **22**(5), 1207–1254 (2012)
6. Doder, D., Woltran, S.: Probabilistic argumentation frameworks – a logical approach. In: Straccia, U., Calì, A. (eds.) SUM 2014. LNCS (LNAI), vol. 8720, pp. 134–147. Springer, Cham (2014). https://doi.org/10.1007/978-3-319-11508-5_12
7. Dondio, P.: Toward a computational analysis of probabilistic argumentation frameworks. Cybern. Syst. **45**(3), 254–278 (2014)
8. Dung, P.M.: An argumentation-theoretic foundations for logic programming. J. Log. Program. **22**(2), 151–171 (1995)
9. Fazzinga, B., Flesca, S., Parisi, F.: On the complexity of probabilistic abstract argumentation. In: International Joint Conference on Artificial Intelligence (IJCAI), pp. 898–904 (2013)
10. Gaggl, S.A., Woltran, S.: Cf2 semantics revisited. In: Computational Models of Argument (COMMA), pp. 243–254 (2010)
11. Hunter, A.: Some foundations for probabilistic abstract argumentation. In: Computational Models of Argument (COMMA), pp. 117–128 (2012)
12. Hunter, A., Thimm, M.: Probabilistic reasoning with abstract argumentation frameworks. J. Artif. Intell. Res. **59**, 565–611 (2017)

13. Li, H., Oren, N., Norman, T.J.: Probabilistic argumentation frameworks. In: Modgil, S., Oren, N., Toni, F. (eds.) TAFA 2011. LNCS (LNAI), vol. 7132, pp. 1–16. Springer, Heidelberg (2012). https://doi.org/10.1007/978-3-642-29184-5_1
14. Oikarinen, E., Woltran, S.: Characterizing strong equivalence for argumentation frameworks. Artif. Intell. **175**(14), 1985–2009 (2011)
15. Oren, N., Norman, T.J.: Semantics for evidence-based argumentation. In: Computational Models of Argument (COMMA), pp. 276–284 (2008)
16. Wu, Y., Caminada, M.: A labelling-based justification status of arguments. Stud. Logic **3**(4), 12–29 (2010)

Well-Foundedness in Weighted Argumentation Frameworks

Stefano Bistarelli and Francesco Santini[(✉)]

Department of Mathematics and Computer Science,
University of Perugia, Perugia, Italy
{stefano.bistarelli,francesco.santini}@unipg.it

Abstract. We revise classical properties of Abstract Argumentation Frameworks in presence of weights on attacks. We focus on the notion of well-foundedness originally provided by P. M. Dung in his pioneering work. We generalise it by considering sequences of *Set-maximal Attack* sets, instead of a plain sequence of arguments: such sets include all the arguments attacking a previous set in the sequence. By using a parametric framework based on an algebraic structure, we are able to study different proposals of weighted defence in the literature, and consequently relate their well-foundedness. We generalise such a property to any weighted defence, but also to original Dung's defence. Finally, we provide conditions for the uniqueness of the preferred and existence of the stable extensions.

1 Introduction

Defining the properties of Abstract Argumentation semantics [16] amounts to specifying the criteria for deriving a set of subsets of arguments (i.e., *extensions*) from an *Abstract Argumentation Framework* (*AAF*), which is simply defined only by a set of arguments and an attack relationship, i.e., $\langle A, R \rangle$.

Properties of such extension-based semantics are important for the sake of the theoretical approach itself, but also due to practical reasons. For instance, they can be used to improve the performance of solvers [6]: by looking at a framework and immediately derive from its structure that there is no stable-extension, or just only a preferred one, we can quickly return an answer for decision problems as the *enumeration* and *existence* of extensions, or *sceptical/credulous* acceptance of arguments in those semantics. Moreover, such properties can be studied to improve the performance of composed tasks: for instance, in the special track "Dung's Triathlon" at the *International Competition on Computational Models of Argumentation (2017 edition)*[1], solvers were required to enumerate all extensions of all standard Dung-semantics (complete, preferred, stable, grounded) at once. However, in case the considered framework is *well-founded*, there is only one complete extension, which it happens to be also the only grounded, preferred, and stable extension at the same time.

---

[1] ICCMA 2017: http://argumentationcompetition.org/2017/index.html.

© Springer Nature Switzerland AG 2019
F. Calimeri et al. (Eds.): JELIA 2019, LNAI 11468, pp. 69–84, 2019.
https://doi.org/10.1007/978-3-030-19570-0_5

In this paper we turn our attention to *Weighted AAFs* (*WAAF*), by considering AAFs where attacks are associated with a score. In particular, we mainly refer to *semiring-based WAAFs* [4,7,8], which can be described by a tuple $\langle A, R, W, \mathbb{S} \rangle$ that encompasses a weight function W with domain in R, and a c-semiring $\mathbb{S}$ to be parametrically instantiated to a specific metrics of weights (see Sect. 2). In addition, we take into consideration other two proposals of weighted abstract-frameworks, i.e., *Martínez et al.* [18] and *Coste-Marquis et al.* [14]. In [4,7] we have proved that [18] and [14] can be cast in the same semiring-based framework, still in terms of semiring-based operators.

Our goal is to revise well-known properties of classical frameworks [16] in such weighted approaches, thus proposing, the first general study of this kind on WAAFs (as far as we know). We commence by *(i)* revising the notion of well-foundedness. Most of this work is focused on revising the notion of well-foundedness from sequences of arguments to sequences of argument sets, similarly to what generalised in [19]. However, we extend the *synergic* effect of several attacks to a single argument (proposed in [19]), by also considering the combined effect of several attacks from one argument to a set of arguments. Then, *(ii)* we show how well-foundedness can be adapted to WAAFs and it still leads to have a single complete/preferred/stable/grounded extension also in WAAFs. Finally, *(iii)* we show we are able to recover also in WAAFs some classical unicity and existence properties for the (w-)preferred and (w-)stable semantics.

This paper complements and extends the preliminary results in [9]. It is structured as follows: in Sect. 2 we summarise and integrate the formal results obtained in [4,7,8]. Then, in Sect. 3 we revise the notion of well-foundedness in [19], and we provide a new one by showing how it is applicable to WAAFs. We finally generalise the definition of well-foundedness for other possible notions of weighted defence. In Sect. 4 we recover in weighted frameworks some unicity and existence results of classical extension: for instance, if a WAAF is well-founded, the w-grounded extension is also the only w-preferred and w-stable extension in that WAAF. In Sect. 5 we revise the related work on weighted frameworks and properties of them. Finally, Sect. 6 concludes the paper by drawing conclusions and also providing ideas for future work.

2   Background

C-semirings are commutative semirings where $\otimes$ is used to compose values, while an idempotent $\oplus$ is used to represent a partial order among them.

Definition 1 (C-semirings [3]). *A c-semiring is a five-tuple* $\mathbb{S} = \langle S, \oplus, \otimes, \perp, \top \rangle$ *such that S is a set,* $\top, \perp \in S$, *and* $\oplus, \otimes : S \times S \to S$ *are binary operators making the triples* $\langle S, \oplus, \perp \rangle$ *and* $\langle S, \otimes, \top \rangle$ *commutative monoids, satisfying,* (i) *distributivity* $\forall a, b, c \in S . a \otimes (b \oplus c) = (a \otimes b) \oplus (a \otimes c)$, (ii) *annihilator* $\forall a \in A . a \otimes \perp = \perp$, *and* (iii) *absorptivity* $\forall a, b \in S . a \oplus (a \otimes b) = a$.

The idempotency of $\oplus$, which derives from absorptivity, leads to the definition of a partial order $\leq_{\mathbb{S}}$ over S: $a \leq_{\mathbb{S}} b$ iff $a \oplus b = b$, which means

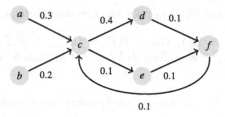

Fig. 1. An example of WAAF; these weights may belong to, for instance, the Weighted, Probabilistic, or Fuzzy c-semiring.

that b is "better" than a.[2] $\oplus$ is the *least upper bound* of the lattice $\langle S, \leq_\mathbb{S} \rangle$. Some c-semiring instances are: *Boolean* $\langle \{F, T\}, \vee, \wedge, F, T \rangle$, *Probabilistic* (or *Viterbi*) $\langle [0, 1], \max, \times, 0, 1 \rangle$ *Fuzzy* $\langle [0, 1], \max, \min, 0, 1 \rangle$, and *Weighted* $\langle \mathbb{R}^+ \cup \{+\infty\}, \min, +, +\infty, 0 \rangle$. In the remainder of the paper we will use "semiring" as a synonym of "c-semiring".

The following definition of WAAFs can be used to represent problems where attacks are weighted with different metrics of values, parametric to a given framework. All the background information in the remainder of this section derives from results in [7,8].

Definition 2 (c-semiring-based WAAF). *A semiring-based Argumentation Framework (WAAF$_\mathbb{S}$) is a quadruple* $\langle \mathscr{A}_{rgs}, R, W, \mathbb{S} \rangle$, *where* $\mathbb{S}$ *is a semiring* $\langle S, \oplus, \otimes, \perp, \top \rangle$, $\mathscr{A}_{rgs}$ *is a set of arguments,* R *the attack binary-relation on* $\mathscr{A}_{rgs}$, *and* $W : \mathscr{A}_{rgs} \times \mathscr{A}_{rgs} \to S$ *is a binary function. Given* $a, b \subset \mathscr{A}_{rgs}$, $\forall (a, b) \subset R$, $W(a, b) = s$ *means that* a *attacks* b *with a weight* $s \in S$. *Moreover, we require that* $R(a, b)$ *iff* $W(a, b) <_\mathbb{S} \top$.

An example of c-semiring-based WAAF is represented in Fig. 1, where we can consider weights either in the Weighted, Probabilistic, or in the Fuzzy semiring.

In [4] the authors define w-defence: a set $\mathscr{B}$ defends an argument b from a if the set-wise $\otimes$ of the attacks from all $c \in \mathscr{B}$ that defend b, i.e., $W(\mathscr{B}, a) = \bigotimes_{c \in \mathscr{B}} W(c, a)$, is worse than (i.e., stronger) or equal to the set-wise $\otimes$ of the attacks from a to b and all the arguments in $\mathscr{B}$, i.e., $W(a, \mathscr{B} \cup b)$ (some set-wise operations can be defined[3]).

Definition 3 (w-defence or $\mathbb{D}_w$). *Given* $WF = \langle \mathscr{A}_{rgs}, R, W, \mathbb{S} \rangle$, $\mathscr{B} \subseteq \mathscr{A}_{rgs}$ w-*defends* $b \in \mathscr{A}_{rgs}$ *from* $a \in \mathscr{A}_{rgs}$ *s.t.* $R(a, b)$, *iff* $W(a, \mathscr{B} \cup \{b\}) \geq_\mathbb{S} W(\mathscr{B}, a)$; $\mathscr{B}$ w-*defends* b *iff it defends* b *from any* a *s.t.* $R(a, b)$.

---

[2] Note that in the following of the paper we will use "worse" or "better" because "greater" or "lesser" would be misleading: for instance, in the weighted semiring we have $7 \leq_\mathbb{S} 3$ ($\leq_\mathbb{S}$ is not $\leq$). Hence, given a WAAF, an attack with value 7 is stronger than one associated with 3.

[3] $W(\mathscr{B}, a) = \bigotimes_{b \in \mathscr{B}} W(b, a)$, $W(a, \mathscr{B}) = \bigotimes_{b \in \mathscr{B}} W(a, b)$, and $W(\mathscr{B}, \mathscr{D}) = \bigotimes_{b \in \mathscr{B}, d \in \mathscr{D}} W(b, d)$.

As defined, w-defence ($\mathbb{D}_w$) implies the classical Dung's defence ($\mathbb{D}_0$).

Proposition 1 ($\mathbb{D}_w \Rightarrow \mathbb{D}_0$). *Given* $WF = \langle \mathscr{A}_{rgs}, R, W, \mathbb{S} \rangle$, *a subset of arguments* $\mathscr{B}$, *and* $b \in \mathscr{A}_{rgs}$, *"$\mathscr{B}$ w-defends b"* $\Rightarrow$ *"$\mathscr{B}$ defends b" in the corresponding not-weighted* $\langle \mathscr{A}_{rgs}, R \rangle$.

We have now all the necessary preliminary information to introduce w-semantics.

Definition 4 (w-semantics). *Given* $WF = \langle \mathscr{A}_{rgs}, R, W, \mathbb{S} \rangle$, $\mathscr{B}$ *is a conflict-free set* [16] *iff* $W(\mathscr{B}, \mathscr{B}) = \top$. $\mathscr{B}$ *can be:*

- *a w-admissible (wadm) extension iff all the arguments in $\mathscr{B}$ are w-defended by $\mathscr{B}$;*
- *w-strongly-admissible (wssa) iff every $b \in \mathscr{B}$ is w-defended by some $\mathscr{B}' \subseteq \mathscr{B} \setminus \{b\}$;*
- *a w-complete (wcom) extension iff each argument $b \in \mathscr{A}_{rgs}$ s.t. $\mathscr{B} \cup \{b\}$ is w-admissible belongs to $\mathscr{B}$;*
- *a w-preferred (wprf) extension iff it is a maximal (w.r.t. set inclusion) w-admissible subset of $\mathscr{A}_{rgs}$;*
- *w-semi-stable (wsst) iff, given the range of $\mathscr{B}$ defined as $\mathscr{B} \cup \mathscr{B}^+$, where $\mathscr{B}^+ = \{a \in \mathscr{A}_{rgs} : W(\mathscr{B}, a) <_{\mathbb{S}} \top\}$, $\mathscr{B}$ is a w-complete extension with maximal (w.r.t. set inclusion) range.*
- *a w-stable extension (wstb) iff $\mathscr{B} \in wadm(WF)$ and $\forall a \notin \mathscr{B}, \exists b \in \mathscr{B}.W(b, a) <_{\mathbb{S}} \top$;*
- *a w-grounded (wgrd) extension, iff $\mathscr{B} \in wadm(WF)$, and $\mathscr{B} \subseteq \bigcap wcom(WF)$, and $\nexists \mathscr{B}' \in wadm(WF)$ satisfying $\mathscr{B}' \subseteq \bigcap wcom(WF)$ s.t. $\mathscr{B} \subsetneq \mathscr{B}'$;*
- *a w-ideal (wide) extension, iff $\mathscr{B}$ is w-admissible and $\forall \mathscr{B}' \in wprf(WF)$, $\mathscr{B} \subseteq \mathscr{B}'$. The w-ideal extension is the maximal (w.r.t. set inclusion) w-ideal set;*
- *a w-eager (weag) extension, iff $\mathscr{B}$ is admissible and $\forall \mathscr{B}' \in wsst(WF)$, $\mathscr{B} \subseteq \mathscr{B}'$. The w-eager extension is the maximal (w.r.t. set inclusion) w-eager set.*

In [8], we report a novel definition of the weighted grounded extension, which is not simply the minimal w.r.t. set inclusion of the complete extensions. Such a definition overcomes the inconvenience that weighted frameworks often return more than one grounded extension, e.g., [14,18]: in fact, it is desirable to have sceptical semantics that always yields exactly one extension (also *wide* and *weag*). Proposition 2 reports some properties of this w-grounded semantics.

Proposition 2 (Properties of w-grounded). *Given the definition of w-grounded semantics in Definition 4, then*

- *A w-grounded extension always exists and it is unique.*
- *The w-grounded extension corresponds to the set of sceptically accepted arguments in $wcom(WF)$: $grd(WF) = \{a \in \mathscr{A}_{rgs} \mid \forall \mathscr{B} \in wcom(WF), a \in \mathscr{B}\}$.*
- *The w-grounded extension is w-strongly-admissible.*

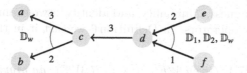

Fig. 2. Using the Weighted semiring, $\{e, f\}$ defends c from d according to $\mathbb{D}_2$ and $\mathbb{D}_w$, since $(2 + 1) \leq_{Weighted} 3$, but not according to $\mathbb{D}_1$, since $2 \not\leq_{Weighted} 3$ and $1 \not\leq_{Weighted} 3$. Moreover, d defends $\{a, b\}$ from c according to $\mathbb{D}_1$ and $\mathbb{D}_2$, but not according to $\mathbb{D}_w$ since $3 \not\leq_{Weighted} (3 + 2)$.

Note that, in general, the w-grounded extension is no longer the supremum of the w-strongly-admissible extensions, as it is in Dung instead [8]. Note also that w-ideal and w-eager are not w-strongly-admissible, as for classical frameworks [11].

For more properties and relations among w-semantics, and between w-semantics and their classical correspondence in unweighted frameworks, please refer to [7].

We conclude this background section by justifying why we have not introduced the framework by Dung before ours. If we use the *Boolean* c-semiring, thus considering $W(a, b) = \bot = false$ whenever $R(a, b)$, we exactly obtain the same semantics in [16]: we encompass it besides being capable of representing weighted systems within the same parametric framework. Hence, for instance, the set of w-stable extensions in *WF* is the same as the set of stable extensions in *F*, that is *F* considered as not weighted.

2.1 Other Weighted Proposals in the Literature

In Definition 2 we have defined a formal parametric framework where it is possible to plug and play with different semirings in a WAAF. Because of the aforementioned characteristics, the same framework can be also used to study different proposals in the literature, and compare different notions of weighted defence to Definition 3: in [4,7] we have rephrased two different proposals, i.e., [18] and [14], by using semiring operators and WAAFs.

In [18] attacks are relatively ordered by their force, i.e., $R(a, b) \gg R(b, a)$ means that the former attack is stronger than the latter (vice-versa, a weaker attack). Equivalent and incomparable classes are considered as well, i.e., respectively $R(a, b) \approx R(b, a)$ and $R(a, b)?R(b, a)$. In Definition 5 we exactly rephrase the defence in [18] by modelling the total order defined by $[\gg, \approx]$ with a c-semiring $\mathbb{S}$:

Definition 5 ($\mathbb{D}_1$ [7]). *Given $WF = \langle \mathscr{A}rgs, R, W, \mathbb{S} \rangle$, $a, b, c \in \mathscr{A}rgs$, $\mathscr{B} \subseteq \mathscr{A}rgs$, then b is defended by $\mathscr{B}$ if for any $R(a, b), \exists c \in \mathscr{B}$ s.t. $W(a, b) \geq_{\mathbb{S}} W(c, a)$.*

In [14] the authors define $\sigma^{\odot}$-extensions, where σ is one of the given semantics (e.g., admissible), and $\odot$ is an *aggregation function*. Such a function needs to satisfy non-decreasingness, minimality, and identity[4]: two examples are the arithmetic sum and max operators. In Definition 6 we cast it in the same semiring-based framework.

Definition 6 ($\mathbb{D}_2$ [7]). *Given $WF = \langle \mathscr{A}_{rgs}, R, W, \mathbb{S} \rangle$, an argument b is defended by a subset of arguments $\mathscr{B}$ if $\forall a \in \mathscr{A}_{rgs}$ s.t. $R(a,b)$, we have that $W(a,b) \geq_{\mathbb{S}} W(\mathscr{B}, a)$.*

In [4] and [7] we have proved some implications between the different notions of defence $\mathbb{D}_0$, $\mathbb{D}_1$, $\mathbb{D}_2$, and $\mathbb{D}_w$.

Theorem 1 (Relations among defences [7]). *Given $\mathbb{D}_w$ in Definition 3, $\mathbb{D}_1$ in Definition 5, $\mathbb{D}_2$ in Definition 6, and $\mathbb{D}_0$ being the classical defence in [16], then:*

1. *$\mathbb{D}_w \Rightarrow \mathbb{D}_0$, $\mathbb{D}_1 \Rightarrow \mathbb{D}_0$, $\mathbb{D}_2 \Rightarrow \mathbb{D}_0$.*
2. *$\mathbb{D}_w \Rightarrow \mathbb{D}_2$.*
3. *$\mathbb{D}_1 \Rightarrow \mathbb{D}_2$.*
4. *If $\mathbb{S} = $ Fuzzy, then $\mathbb{D}_1 \Leftrightarrow \mathbb{D}_2$, and $\mathbb{D}_w \Rightarrow \mathbb{D}_1$.*
5. *If $\mathbb{S} = $ Boolean, then $\mathbb{D}_w \Leftrightarrow \mathbb{D}_0 \Leftrightarrow \mathbb{D}_1 \Leftrightarrow \mathbb{D}_2$.*

Figure 2 visually supports the explanation about the differences among the three weighted defences reported so far. All three of them aggregate weights (in different ways) towards the same argument d to check if $\{e, f\}$ defends c from it: that is, c is defended if $W(\{e, f\}, d) \leq_{\mathbb{S}} W(d, \{c\})$. Only $\mathbb{D}_w$ also aggregates all the weights on the attacks from the same attacker to the set of arguments to be defended: to check if d defends $\{a, b\}$ from c, we need that $W(\{d\}, c) \leq_{\mathbb{S}} W(c, \{a, b\})$.

3   Well-Foundedness in Weighted AAFs

We divide the content in two subsections: the first one (Sect. 3.1) introduces the problems in defining well-founded frameworks in case of a *synergy* among attacks; the second one (Sect. 3.2) proposes a solution that encompasses different proposals in the literature, with the definition of *set-maximal attack* (*SMA*) sequences of sets.

3.1   Motivations

In this section we consider WAAFs in Sects. 2 and 2.1, and we revise the notion of well-foundedness and derived properties, as the uniqueness of complete extensions. We start by recalling the definition of well-founded sets.

Definition 7 (Well-founded set). *A set S is well-founded iff it does not exist any infinite descending sequence of elements of S according to a relation $Rl(x, y)$ ("x precedes y"), where Rl is a binary relation on the elements of S.*

---

[4] Such properties are satisfied by a c-semiring, *e.g.*, minimality corresponds to the absorptivity of $\otimes$ w.r.t. $\bot$.

Dung defines the sufficient conditions behind well-foundedness in AAFs in his pioneering work [16]. S is equivalent to $\mathscr{A}_{rgs}$, and the Rl relation is simply the attack relation R in a framework $\langle \mathscr{A}_{rgs}, R \rangle$. A well-founded AAF is an AAF without an infinite defeating sequence of arguments.

Definition 8 (Well-founded$_{Dung}$ [16]). *An AAF is well-founded iff there exists no infinite sequence* $a_1, a_2, \ldots, a_n, \ldots$ *(with $a_i \in \mathscr{A}_{rgs}$) such that for each i, $R(a_{i+1}, a_i)$.*

However, the notion of w-defence in Definition 3 and the other two notions of weighted defence in Sect. 2.1 take sets of arguments and their synergy into consideration. For this reason, Definition 8 is not enough to capture the aggregation of weights from/to sets, since it is based on plain sequences of arguments. The *synergy* of multiple attacks towards the same argument is in practice not considered in [16]: the "added value" of two attacks towards a single argument, e.g., $R(e, d)$ and $R(f, d)$ in Fig. 2, cannot be modelled by the original formulation.

Extending such a formulation with the purpose to produce an intensification of a combined attack has been already considered in [19]. There, the authors generalise Dung's approach to allow it to handle sets of attacking arguments. However, the aim is to let the framework be capable of dealing with *synergies* among arguments in *and*, thus *without* considering numerical strengths, something that is at the core of this work instead. For instance, "a_1: *Joe does not like Jack*", and "a_2: *There is a nail in Jack's antique coffee table*" do not attack separately "a_3: *Joe did not hammer a nail into Jack's antique coffee table*", but they do it only in conjunction (example taken from [19]).

We report the definition of minimal attack in [19], on which the notion of well-foundedness is then based upon.

Definition 9 (Minimal attack [19]). *Given a Dung's framework, $\mathscr{B} \subseteq \mathscr{A}_{rgs}$ and an argument a such that $\mathscr{B}$ attacks a (that is $\exists c \in \mathscr{B}$ s.t. $R(c, a)$), we say that $\mathscr{B}$ is a* minimal attack *on a if there is no $\mathscr{B}' \subsetneq \mathscr{B}$ such that $\mathscr{B}'$ attacks a.*

In [19], a framework is well-founded if there exists no infinite sequence of $\mathscr{B}_1, \mathscr{B}_2, \ldots$ s.t. set $\mathscr{B}_i$ is a minimal attack on an argument in $\mathscr{B}_{i-1}$.

We believe Definition 9 has two limitations:

(i) firstly, $\mathscr{B}$ is not required to be conflict-free to be a minimal attack on an argument a. Indeed any synergic effect on a cannot be originated by a source that is internally in conflict, even in a qualitative approach as supposed in [19]. Let us rephrase the previous nail-in-the-table example as "a_1': *Since Jack loves coffee more than tea, Joe does not like Jack*", and "a_2': *Even if there is a nail in Jack's antique coffee table, Jack will give precedence to restoring his decorated tea-pot: so Jack loves tea more than coffee*". These two arguments still attack "a_3: *Joe did not hammer a nail into Jack's antique coffee table*" only in conjunction: nevertheless, they are just in conflict, so their combined effect has no sens anymore;

(ii) secondly, the synergy of multiple combined attacks from a single attacker towards a set of arguments (*outcoming*) cannot be modelled with the definition of sets in Definition 9, since minimal attack is towards one single argument in a set (*incoming*). This effect can be represented only by $\mathbb{D}_w$ [4,7], and not by the other weighted defences in Sect. 2.1 (see Fig. 2). We provide a qualitative example, as for the nail-in-the-table case: "a_1: *I have enough money to book one single trip this summer*" does not attack either "a_2: *I will spend June in Norway*" or "a_2: *I will spend July in Greece*". However, a_1 attacks a_2 *and* a_3 when taken together.

All these considerations are also valid in case of a quantitative approach, where weights of attacks can be aggregated together in different ways, as shown in Fig. 2. The next section rephrases well-foundedness with the purpose to address the aforementioned issues.

3.2   Well-Foundedness

Because of the premises advanced in the previous section, in Definition 10 we redefine the notion of *minimal attack* in [19] into *set-maximal attack (SMA)* sets. This is one of the main contributions in the paper, from which all the other ones follow.

Definition 10. (Set-maximal attack (SMA) sets). *Given* $WF = \langle \mathscr{A}_{rgs}, R, W, \mathbb{S} \rangle$ *and* $\mathscr{B}, \mathscr{D} \subseteq \mathscr{A}_{rgs}$, *then* $\mathscr{B}$ *is a set-maximal attack on* $\mathscr{D}$, *iff*

(i) $\mathscr{B}$ is conflict-free;
(ii) $\forall b \in \mathscr{B}, \exists d \in \mathscr{D}$ s.t. $R(b, d)$;
(iii) there exists no $\mathscr{B}'$ s.t. condition (i) and (ii) hold and $\mathscr{B} \subsetneq \mathscr{B}'$.

Note that the above definition differs from [19] because in our statement $\mathscr{B}$ needs to be conflict-free. The reason is that we want to aggregate the weights of arguments with the purpose to provide an aggregated defence: this is not possible if defending arguments attack each other (this defence is not allowed).

Example 1. Figure 3 shows a fragment of an infinite sequence of SMA sets, obtained on the WAAF represented in Fig. 1; we start from the conflict-free set $\{f\}$. The sequence is: $\mathscr{B}_1$-$\mathscr{B}_2$-$\mathscr{B}_3$-$\mathscr{B}_4$-... (it continues as $\mathscr{B}_2$).

We can now provide sufficient conditions for well-foundedness in [4,7], that is using the $\mathbb{D}_w$ notion of defence in Definition 3.

Definition 11 (Well-foundedness for the approach in [7] (wfd_w)). *A* $WF = \langle \mathscr{A}_{rgs}, R, W, \mathbb{S} \rangle$ *is well-founded if there exists no infinite sequence of SMA sets* $\omega = \mathscr{B}_1, \mathscr{B}_2, \ldots$, *and* $\forall \mathscr{B}_{i-1}, \mathscr{B}_i, \mathscr{B}_{i+1} \in \omega$ *and* $\forall b \in \mathscr{B}_i$ *the following holds:*

$$W(\mathscr{B}_{i+1}, b) \leq_{\mathbb{S}} W(b, \mathscr{B}_{i-1})$$

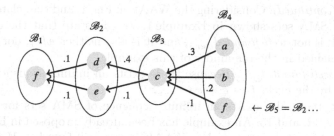

Fig. 3. A fragment of an infinite sequence of SMA sets. $\mathscr{B}_5$ is identical to $\mathscr{B}_2$ and the chain infinitely continues from it. This example shows *incoming* synergic effect (from $\mathscr{B}_4$ to $\mathscr{B}_4$), and *outcoming* synergic effect (from $\mathscr{B}_3$ to $\mathscr{B}_2$).

Similar considerations hold for well-foundedness in the other two weighted defences surveyed in Sect. 2.1, since their defence notion is based on sets either. We start by defining well-foundedness for [18] and then for [14]. Note that well-foundedness is parametrically defined w.r.t. to a given semiring even in these two proposals.

Definition 12 (Well-foundedness for the approach in [18] (wfd_2)). *A $WF = \langle \mathscr{A}_{rgs}, R, W, \mathbb{S} \rangle$ defined in [18] is well-founded if there exists no infinite sequence of SMA sets $\omega = \mathscr{B}_1, \mathscr{B}_2, \ldots$, and $\forall \mathscr{B}_{i-1}, \mathscr{B}_i, \mathscr{B}_{i+1} \in \omega$ and $\forall b \in \mathscr{B}_i, \forall a \in \mathscr{B}_{i-1}, \exists c \in \mathscr{B}_{i+1}$, the following holds:*[5]

$$W(c, b) \leq_{\mathbb{S}} W(b, a)$$

Definition 13 (Well-foundedness for the approach in [14] (wfd_1)). *A $WF = \langle \mathscr{A}_{rgs}, R, W, \mathbb{S} \rangle$ defined in [14] is well-founded if there exists no infinite sequence of SMA sets $\omega = \mathscr{B}_1, \mathscr{B}_2, \ldots$, and $\forall \mathscr{B}_{i-1}, \mathscr{B}_i, \mathscr{B}_{i+1} \in \omega$ and $\forall b \in \mathscr{B}_i, \forall a \in \mathscr{B}_{i-1}$, the following holds:*

$$W(\mathscr{B}_{i+1}, b) \leq_{\mathbb{S}} W(b, a)$$

Remark 1. All these three notions of well-foundedness are similar, in the sense that two different conditions need to be satisfied at the same time: *(i)* one concerning the absence of an infinite sequence of SMA sets on a framework (such a condition does not consider weights), and *(ii)* one stating that each $\mathscr{B}_{i+1}$ in any sequence of SMA sets has to defend $\mathscr{B}_{i-1}$ from $\mathscr{B}_i$, according to each specific definition of defence $\mathbb{D}$ (which is different in the three definitions). With "$\mathscr{B}$ defends $\mathscr{D}$ from $\mathscr{C}$" we mean that $\mathscr{B}$ defends all the $d \in \mathscr{D}$ from any $c \in \mathscr{C}$ (e.g., using Definition 3 in Definition 11).

In the continuation of Example 1 we show that the WAAF presented in Fig. 1 does not satisfy any of the definition of well-foundedness introduced so far, including, the original one given by Dung, i.e., *well-founded$_{Dung}$*.

---

[5] Note that synergy in [18] is represented by $\exists c \in \mathscr{B}_{i+1}$: lower-strength defences are helped by higher-strength ones.

Example 1 (continued). Considering the WAAF in Fig. 1, and the related infinite sequences of SMA sets shown in Example 1, we can state that the c-semiring based WAAF is not *well-founded$_{Dung}$*, and it is also neither *wfd$_1$*, nor *wfd$_2$*, not *wfd$_w$*, as explained in the remainder of this example.

It is not *well-founded$_{Dung}$* because there exists an infinite sequence of arguments given by the cycle $f \leftarrow e \leftarrow c \leftarrow \ldots$.

Moreover, there also exists an infinite sequence of SMA sets for the three Definitions 11, 12, and 13. An example has been already proposed in Example 1. This is enough to state that such a WAAF is not well-founded. However, we check also the condition on the weighted defence to better explain the differences between the aforementioned well-foundedness notions. In the following we consider the *Weighted* semiring.

- $\mathscr{B}_5 = \mathscr{B}_2$ does not defend $\mathscr{B}_3$ from a and b in $\mathscr{B}_4$ (there is no attack at all from $\mathscr{B}_5$ to a and b), according to any possible defence used in this paper (for this item, it is a matter of attacks more than weights);
- The second condition (on weights) in Definition 11 is respected: $\mathscr{B}_4$ defends $\mathscr{B}_2$ from $\mathscr{B}_3$. $W(\mathscr{B}_4, c) \leq_{Weighted} W(c, \mathscr{B}_2)$, that is $0.3 + 0.2 + 0.1 \leq 0.4 + 0.1$. In this case, the synergic effect of the attacks from c to $\mathscr{B}_2$ is compensated by the strength of the defence.
- The second condition (on weights) in Definition 13 is respected: $\mathscr{B}_4$ defends $\mathscr{B}_2$ from $\mathscr{B}_3$. $W(\mathscr{B}_4, c) \leq_{Weighted} W(c, d)$ since $0.3 + 0.2 + 0.1 \leq 0.4$, and $W(\mathscr{B}_4, c) \leq_{Weighted} W(c, e)$ since $0.3 + 0.2 + 0.1 \leq 0.1$. In this case, the synergic attack from c is not considered.
- The second condition (on weights) in Definition 12 is not respected: $\mathscr{B}_4$ cannot defend $\mathscr{B}_2$ from $\mathscr{B}_3$ because there is no attack from $\mathscr{B}_4$ to c (whose values are 0.3, 0.2, 0.1) which is at least as strong as the attack from c to d in $\mathscr{B}_2$ (i.e., 0.4).

Therefore, imposing further conditions on the weights restrains the possibility of having a simple infinite sequence as required in [16]: a framework has less chances to be well-founded when considering weighted defences, since the absence of infinite sequences of SMA sets in not sufficient.

We relate the property of a framework to be well-founded, by considering the three weighted proposals we consider in this paper and *well-founded$_{Dung}$* as well.

Theorem 2 (Implications among definitions). *Given any WAAF (or AAF if considering it without weights), the following implications hold:*

1. *well-founded$_{Dung}$* $\Leftarrow$ *wfd$_w$*, *well-founded$_{Dung}$* $\Leftarrow$ *wfd$_1$*, *well-founded$_{Dung}$* $\Leftarrow$ *wfd$_2$*.
2. *wfd$_2$* $\Leftarrow$ *wfd$_w$*.
3. *wfd$_2$* $\Leftarrow$ *wfd$_1$*.
4. *When using the Fuzzy semiring, wfd$_1$* $\Leftrightarrow$ *wfd$_2$* *wfd$_1$* $\Rightarrow$ *wfd$_w$*.
5. *When using the Boolean semiring, wfd$_w$* $\Leftrightarrow$ *wfd$_1$* $\Leftrightarrow$ *wfd$_2$*.

Proof. Each item in Theorem 2 directly derives from *(i)* the corresponding definitions of well-foundedness, and *(ii)* the relations among the different notions of defence in Theorem 1. Conditions based on weights (see Remark 1) for sequences of SMA sets in Definitions 11, 12, and 13 correspond to $\mathbb{D}_w$, $\mathbb{D}_2$, and $\mathbb{D}_1$.

We notice that checking the well-foundedness property on any weighted framework, and obtaining a positive response, is enough to state that the same framework is also well-founded according to Dung, that is without considering weights (item 1 in Theorem 2). As a further general consideration, we notice that wfd_2 is less selective w.r.t. wfd_1 and wfd_w (items 2 and 3). In case of using the Fuzzy semiring, item 4 in Theorem 2 states that it is easier for a framework to be wfd_w than to be wfd_1 or wfd_2.

We conclude this section with a definition that generalises the definition of well-foundedness on the different notion of (weighted) defence. Therefore, the definition of well-foundedness becomes parametric with respect to the chosen semiring *and* the selected defence. Other weighted defences may directly inherit from the definition to check the conditions under which they allow for a well-founded framework. This represents the second main result of the paper.

Definition 14 (Generalisation of well-foundedness). *Given a framework* $WF = \langle \mathscr{A}_{rgs}, R, W, \mathbb{S} \rangle$, *if there does not exist an infinite sequence* ω *of SMA sets* $\mathscr{B}_1, \mathscr{B}_2, \ldots$, *such that for every* $\mathscr{B}_{i+1}$, $\mathscr{B}_i$, *and* $\mathscr{B}_{i-1}$ *we have that* $\mathscr{B}_{i+1}$ *defends* $\mathscr{B}_{i-1}$ *from each* $a \in \mathscr{B}_i$ *according to a generic defence* $\mathbb{D}$, *then* WF *is well-founded w.r.t.* $\mathbb{D}$.

4   Some Formal Results on Unicity and Existence

The well-foundedness property is interesting because it points to a framework there exists only a set of arguments that it is worth to be considered under any semantics. According to [16], every well-founded AAF has exactly one complete extension, which is also grounded, preferred, and stable.

The same result is preserved also in each the weighted approaches presented in this paper, depending on the specific notion of well-foundedness respectively presented in Definitions 11, 12, and 13. The following theorem formalises this result.

Theorem 3 (Uniqueness of w-complete extension). *Given a notion of defence, any well-founded WAAF where the w-grounded is also w-complete has exactly one w-complete extension, which is also w-grounded, w-preferred, and w-stable.*

Proof. As in [16], the proof is by contradiction. We assume there exists a well-founded WAAF whose w-grounded extension is not a w-stable extension. Let $WF = \langle \mathscr{A}_{rgs}, R, W, \mathbb{S} \rangle$ be a WAAF such that

$$\mathscr{S} = \{\mathscr{B} \mid \mathscr{B} \subseteq (\mathscr{A}_{rgs} \setminus wgrd(WF)) \wedge W(\mathscr{B}, \mathscr{B}) = \top \wedge W(wgrd(WF), \mathscr{B}) = \top\}$$

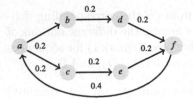
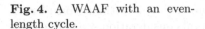

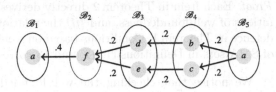

Fig. 4. A WAAF with an even-length cycle.

Fig. 5. An even-length sequence of SMA sets for the WAAF in Fig. 4. It also satisfies $\mathbb{D}_w$.

$\mathscr{S}$ is made of all the conflict-free subsets of arguments not included in the w-grounded extension, and not attacked by it; $\mathscr{S} \neq \{\emptyset\}$ by assumption. Now we want to show that each set $\mathscr{B}_i \in \mathscr{S}$ is attacked by another $\mathscr{B}_j \in \mathscr{S}$. Since $\mathscr{B}_i$ is not acceptable in $wgrd(WF)$, this means there is a conflict-free set $\mathscr{B}_j$ such that $wgrd(WF)$ does not defend $\mathscr{B}_i$ from all the possible arguments $a \in \mathscr{B}_j$ that attacks an argument in $\mathscr{B}_i$. For instance, considering $\mathbb{D}_w$, $W(wgrd(WF), a) \not\leq_S W(a, \mathscr{B}_i)$. Hence also $\mathscr{B}_j$ belongs to $\mathscr{S}$ and the same considerations hold for it either. Now we have an infinite sequence ω of SMA sets $\mathscr{B}_i, \mathscr{B}_j, \ldots$.

Note that the additional condition related to the w-grounded, which needs to be w-complete in Theorem 3, is required by the fact that weighted frameworks may have multiple grounded extensions (Sect. 2.1); we fixed it in [8] by defining a w-grounded that can be not w-complete (see also Sect. 2). Without such a requirement, in the proof of Theorem 3 we cannot exploit the fact that the w-grounded extension includes all the arguments that also defends (according to any weighted defence). The case a framework is well-founded, but the w-grounded is not w-complete, is left as future work (see Sect. 6).

Properties of Weighted Preferred and Stable Semantics. Some of formal results obtained in the original proposal by Dung can be recovered also in weighted frameworks. We first turn our attention to the uniqueness of the w-preferred extension.

In [17] Dunne Bench-Capon gave sufficient conditions for a preferred extension to be unique (the converse does not hold): let $F = \langle \mathscr{A}_{rgs}, R \rangle$. If F has no even-length cycle, then AF has an unique preferred extension. In Theorem 4 we re-obtain the same result for any WAAF using $\mathbb{D}_1$, $\mathbb{D}_2$, and $\mathbb{D}_w$: the following theorem is parametric w.r.t. $\mathbb{D}$. As for Theorem 3, we suppose that the w-grounded extension is a w-complete extension as well.

Theorem 4 (Uniqueness of w-preferred). *Given $WF = \langle \mathscr{A}_{rgs}, R, W, \mathbb{S} \rangle$. If WF has no even-length cycle of SMA sets $\omega = \mathscr{B}_1, \mathscr{B}_2, \ldots$ such that all $\mathscr{B}_{i-1}$ are defended by $\mathscr{B}_{i+1}$ from each $a \in \mathscr{B}_i$ using $\mathbb{D}$, then WF has an unique w-preferred extension.*

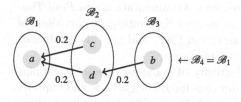

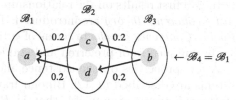

Fig. 6. A WAAF with an odd-length cycle of SMA sets, but $\mathscr{B}_1$ is not defended by $\mathscr{B}_3$ according to, for instance, $\mathbb{D}_w$. There exists $\{b,c\}$ as stable extension.

Fig. 7. A WAAF with an odd-length cycle of SMA sets: $\mathscr{B}_1$ is defended by $\mathscr{B}_3$ according to, for instance, $\mathbb{D}_w$. For this WAAF there exists no stable extension.

Proof (Sketch of). The proof can be provided similarity as in [17], by showing that if a WF has two w-preferred extensions $\mathscr{B}_i$ and $\mathscr{B}_j$, then it has an even-length cycle. In this case, instead of plain sequences of attacks, SMA sets need to be collected for subset of arguments that is in $\mathscr{B}_i \setminus \mathscr{B}_j$ and $\mathscr{B}_j \setminus \mathscr{B}_i$.

Example 2. In Fig. 4 we show a WAAF that has an even-length ω (the length is 4) represented in Fig. 5. Such a sequence of SMA sets also respects $\mathbb{D}_w$, and consequently, according to Theorem 4, this framework may have more than one w-preferred extensions. In fact, it has two of them: $\mathscr{B}_1 \cup \mathscr{B}_3 = \{a,d,e\}$ and $\mathscr{B}_2 \cup \mathscr{B}_3 = \{b,c,f\}$.

A final result concerns the existence of at least one w-stable extension for a given framework F, i.e., the non-emptiness of this set, which can be re-conducted to the solutions set of the stable marriage problem [16] represented by F. If $F = \langle \mathscr{A}_{rgs}, R \rangle$ has no odd-length cycle, then F has at least one stable extension.

Theorem 5 (Existence of w-stable extensions). *If WF has no odd-length cycle of SMA sets $\omega = \mathscr{B}_1, \mathscr{B}_2, \ldots$ such that all $\mathscr{B}_{i-1}$ are defended by $\mathscr{B}_{i+1}$ from each $a \in \mathscr{B}_i$ using $\mathbb{D}$, then WF has at least one w-stable extension.*

Proof (Sketch of). If ω has not an odd-length chain such that all its odd-indexed sets $\mathscr{B}_i$ are defended, then it is not possible to have a conflict-free union of $\mathscr{B}_i$ that attack all the other arguments in $\mathscr{A}_{rgs}$. An example is given in Figs. 6 and 7.

5 Related Work

In [1] the authors define a link between the preference relation in *Preference-based Argumentation Frameworks* (*PAFs*), where a binary relation expresses preferences between arguments, and the notion of well-foundedness. The main aim is to show when a PAF has exactly one complete/preferred/stable/grounded extension.

In [15] first results on the relationship between Argumentation and *Paul Thagard's coherence theory* are introduced. The authors then interpret partitions of *Bipolar Coherence graphs* in terms of extensions in PAF, and provide conditions for the uniqueness of preferred and stable extensions.

A few properties on the existence and unicity of some extensions in bipolar systems are described in [12]. Bipolar frameworks have both attack and support relations between arguments, that is R_{att} and R_{supp}. The paper links these properties to the property for a framework to be *safe*: there does not exist an argument for which a set $\mathscr{B}$ attacks b and either $\mathscr{B}$ also supports it, or b belongs to $\mathscr{B}$.

In [13] the authors study the properties in symmetric AAF, that are frameworks where the attack relation is symmetric. For instance, they prove that no symmetric AAF is well-founded, or that every symmetric AAF is *coherent* (i.e., preferred and stable extensions coincide).

Finally we end this section by detailing the main difference between this work and our previous results in [9]. In that work we proposed a preliminary approach that only considers *(i)* acyclic frameworks and *(ii)* conditions on weights (as in definitions in Sect. 3.2). In this paper we define and use SMA sets instead, inspired by [19], in order to relax this restrictive condition of having acyclic frameworks (i.e., condition *i*).

Proposition 3. *If a weighted framework $WF = \langle \mathscr{A}_{rgs}, R, W, \mathbb{S} \rangle$ is well-founded according to [9], then it is well-founded also as proposed in the different definitions in Sect. 3.2 (i.e., wfd_1, wfd_2, wfd_w), if they respect the same conditions on weights.*

Proof (Sketch of). The proof comes from the fact that if a WAAF is acyclic, then it is not possible to find an infinite sequence of SMA sets as defined in Definition 10 in the same WAAF.

6   Conclusion

The contribution in this paper is two-sided: first, we extend the concept of synergies from what advance in [19] by also considering the effect from on argument to a set of arguments, and we define SMA sets instead of minimal set attacks. The second aspect represents the core of the paper and shows how the definition of well-foundedness can be adapted in case of weighted frameworks. Besides our proposal, we have studied [18] and [14] by casting them in the same framework. Hence, we show that classical results can be obtained for WAAFs as well, and we propose, as far as we know, the first general study on such properties in weighted frameworks.

In the future we want to widen this study by exploring further properties not investigated here for the sake of space: for instance, we would like to better study (weighted) asymmetric frameworks by extending the results in [13]. In addition, we plan to study the same properties recalled in this paper also from the point of view of other weighted proposals in Sect. 5.

We would also like to develop algorithmic procedures and constraints with the purpose to check such properties before the search of solutions (e.g., when enumerating extensions), in order to improve the performance of *ConArg* [5] and *ConArgLib* [10] in case of adopting WAAFs.

We plan to further follow the same approach adopted in [16], and to inspect the relation between the Stable Marriage Problem with weighted preferences [2] and w-semantics.

Finally, we would like to study well-foundedness in case the side condition "w-grounded is also w-complete" is removed from Theorem 3. Its absence, i.e., the fact that sceptically accepted arguments in w-complete extensions do not include all the arguments they defend, impacts on the results usually carried by well-foundedness (no uncertainty), as well as further properties as the uniqueness of w-preferred extensions. In this case, it seems that showing uncertainty in the most certain semantics, that is the w-grounded one (the most sceptical one), affects the lack of uncertainty from the foundations.

Acknowledgements. This work has been supported by the following three projects funded by our Department: *Argumentation 360* ("Ricerca di Base" 2017–2019) and *Rappresentazione della Conoscenza e Apprendimento Automatico (RACRA)* ("Ricerca di base" 2018–2020).

References

1. Amgoud, L., Vesic, S.: On the role of preferences in argumentation frameworks. In: 22nd IEEE International Conference on Tools with Artificial Intelligence, ICTAI, pp. 219–222. IEEE Computer Society (2010)
2. Bistarelli, S., Foley, S., O'Sullivan, B., Santini, F.: From marriages to coalitions: a soft CSP approach. In: Oddi, A., Fages, F., Rossi, F. (eds.) CSCLP 2008. LNCS (LNAI), vol. 5655, pp. 1–15. Springer, Heidelberg (2009) https://doi.org/10.1007/978-3-642-03251-6_1
3. Bistarelli, S., Montanari, U., Rossi, F.: Semiring-based constraint satisfaction and optimization. J. ACM **44**(2), 201–236 (1997)
4. Bistarelli, S., Rossi, F., Santini, F.: A collective defence against grouped attacks for weighted abstract argumentation frameworks. In: Florida Artificial Intelligence Research Society Conference, FLAIRS, pp. 638–643. AAAI (2016)
5. Bistarelli, S., Rossi, F., Santini, F.: ConArg: a tool for classical and weighted argumentation. In: Computational Models of Argument - Proceedings of COMMA. FAIA, vol. 287, pp. 463–464. IOS Press (2016)
6. Bistarelli, S., Rossi, F., Santini, F.: Not only size, but also shape counts: abstract argumentation solvers are benchmark-sensitive. J. Log. Comput. **28**(1), 85–117 (2018)
7. Bistarelli, S., Rossi, F., Santini, F.: A novel weighted defence and its relaxation in abstract argumentation. Int. J. Approx. Reasoning **92**, 66–86 (2018)
8. Bistarelli, S., Santini, F.: A Hasse diagram for weighted sceptical semantics with a unique-status grounded semantics. In: Balduccini, M., Janhunen, T. (eds.) LPNMR 2017. LNCS (LNAI), vol. 10377, pp. 49–56. Springer, Cham (2017). https://doi.org/10.1007/978-3-319-61660-5_6

9. Bistarelli, S., Santini, F.: Some thoughts on well-foundedness in weighted abstract argumentation. In: Principles of Knowledge Representation and Reasoning, KR, pp. 623–624. AAAI Press (2018)
10. Bistarelli, S., Rossi, F., Santini, F.: A ConArg-based library for abstract argumentation. In: 29th IEEE International Conference on Tools with Artificial Intelligence, ICTAI, pp. 374–381. IEEE Computer Society (2017)
11. Caminada, M.: Comparing two unique extension semantics for formal argumentation: ideal and eager. In: Belgian-Dutch Conference on Artificial Intelligence (BNAIC), pp. 81–87 (2007)
12. Cayrol, C., Lagasquie-Schiex, M.: Bipolar abstract argumentation systems. In: Simari, G.R., Rahwan, I. (eds.) Argumentation in Artificial Intelligence, pp. 65–84. Springer, Heidelberg (2009). https://doi.org/10.1007/978-0-387-98197-0_4
13. Coste-Marquis, S., Devred, C., Marquis, P.: Symmetric argumentation frameworks. In: Godo, L. (ed.) ECSQARU 2005. LNCS (LNAI), vol. 3571, pp. 317–328. Springer, Heidelberg (2005). https://doi.org/10.1007/11518655_28
14. Coste-Marquis, S., Konieczny, S., Marquis, P., Ouali, M.A.: Weighted attacks in argumentation frameworks. In: Principles of Knowledge Representation and Reasoning (KR), pp. 593–597. AAAI (2012)
15. Dimopoulos, Y., Moraitis, P., Sierra, C.: Some theoretical results on the relationship between argumentation and coherence theory. In: Criado Pacheco, N., Carrascosa, C., Osman, N., Julián Inglada, V. (eds.) EUMAS/AT -2016. LNCS (LNAI), vol. 10207, pp. 565–579. Springer, Cham (2017). https://doi.org/10.1007/978-3-319-59294-7_45
16. Dung, P.M.: On the acceptability of arguments and its fundamental role in nonmonotonic reasoning, logic programming and n-person games. Artif. Intell. **77**(2), 321–357 (1995)
17. Dunne, P.E., Bench-Capon, T.J.M.: Complexity and combinatorial properties of argument systems. University of Liverpool, Department of Computer Science (ULCS), Technical report (2001)
18. Martínez, D.C., García, A.J., Simari, G.R.: An abstract argumentation framework with varied-strength attacks. In: Principles of Knowledge Representation and Reasoning (KR), pp. 135–144. AAAI (2008)
19. Nielsen, S.H., Parsons, S.: A generalization of Dung's abstract framework for argumentation: arguing with sets of attacking arguments. In: Maudet, N., Parsons, S., Rahwan, I. (eds.) ArgMAS 2006. LNCS (LNAI), vol. 4766, pp. 54–73. Springer, Heidelberg (2007). https://doi.org/10.1007/978-3-540-75526-5_4

Multi-valued GRAPPA

Gerhard Brewka[1]([✉]) [iD], Jörg Pührer[2] [iD], and Stefan Woltran[2] [iD]

[1] Computer Science Department, Leipzig University, Leipzig, Germany
brewka@informatik.uni-leipzig.de
[2] Institute of Logic and Computation, Vienna University of Technology,
Vienna, Austria

Abstract. Abstract dialectical frameworks (ADFs) are generalizations of Dung's argumentation frameworks which allow arbitrary relationships among arguments to be expressed. In particular, arguments can not only attack each other, they also may provide support for other arguments and interact in various complex ways. The ADF approach has recently been extended in two different ways. On the one hand, GRAPPA is a framework that applies the key notions underlying ADFs – in particular their operator-based semantics – directly to arbitrary labelled graphs. This allows users to represent argumentation scenarios in their favourite graphical representations without giving up the firm ground of well-defined semantics. On the other hand, ADFs have been further generalized to the multi-valued case to enable fine-grained acceptance values. In this paper we unify these approaches and develop a multi-valued version of GRAPPA combining the advantages of both extensions.

Keywords: Argumentation · Nonmonotonic reasoning · Multi-valued logics

1 Introduction

Computational models of argumentation are a highly active area of current research. The field has two main subareas, namely logic-based (also called structured) argumentation and abstract argumentation. The former studies the structure of arguments, how they can be constructed from a given formal knowledge base, and how they logically interact with each other. The latter, in contrast, assumes a given set of abstract arguments together with specific relations among them. The focus is on evaluating the arguments based on their interactions with one another. This evaluation typically uses a specific semantics, thus identifying subsets of the available arguments satisfying intended properties so that the chosen set arguably can be viewed as representing a coherent world view.

In the abstract approach, Dung's argumentation frameworks (AFs) [18] and their associated semantics are widely used. In a nutshell, an AF is a directed

This research has been supported by DFG (Research Unit 1513 and project BR 1817/7-2) and FWF (project I2854).

F. Calimeri et al. (Eds.): JELIA 2019, LNAI 11468, pp. 85–101, 2019.
https://doi.org/10.1007/978-3-030-19570-0_6

graph with each vertex being an abstract argument and each directed edge corresponding to an attack from one argument to another. These attacks are then resolved using appropriate semantics. The semantics are typically based on two important concepts, namely conflict-freeness and admissibility. The former states that if there is a conflict between two arguments, i.e. one argument attacks the other, then the two cannot be jointly accepted. The latter specifies that every set of accepted arguments must defend itself against attacks. A variety of semantics has been defined, ranging from Dung's original complete, preferred, stable, and grounded semantics to the more recent ideal and cf2 semantics. The different semantics reflect different intuitions about what "coherent world view" means in this context, see e.g. [5] for an overview.

Despite their popularity, there have been various attempts to generalize AFs as many researchers felt a need to cover additional relevant relationships among arguments (see e.g. the work of [14]). One of the most systematic and flexible outcomes of this research are abstract dialectical frameworks (ADFs) [7,11]. ADFs allow for arbitrary relationships among arguments. In particular, arguments can not only attack each other, they also may provide support for other arguments and interact in various complex ways. This is achieved by adding explicit acceptance conditions to the arguments which are most naturally expressed in terms of a propositional formula (with atoms referring to parent arguments). This way, it is possible to specify individually for a particular argument, say, under what conditions the available supporting arguments outweigh the counterarguments. Meanwhile various applications of ADFs have been presented, for instance in legal reasoning [1–4] and text exploration [13]. Also a mobile argumentation app based on ADF techniques has been developed [19].

The operator-based semantics of ADFs can be traced back to the work of [15–17] on approximation fixpoint theory (AFT), an algebraic framework for studying semantics of knowledge representation formalisms. We refer to the work of [20] for a detailed analysis of the relationship between ADFs and AFT. The presentation of our approach in this paper does not assume specific background knowledge in AFT.

In the meantime, ADFs themselves have been extended in two different ways. GRAPPA [12] allows argumentation scenarios to be represented as arbitrary edge-labelled graphs. Acceptance functions now are defined in terms of the (multi-set of) active labels, that is, labels of incoming links whose source nodes are true in an interpretation. To conveniently express these functions so-called acceptance patterns are used. The definition of the different semantics then is based on similar operators as for ADFs. The GRAPPA approach has several advantages over ADFs, in particular, it is often easier to model relevant argumentation problems in terms of labelled graphs and users commonly illustrate argumentation scenarios using such graphs. GRAPPA thus allows users to stay as close as possible to their graphical representations yet turns them into full-fledged knowledge representation formalisms by providing formal semantics. Moreover, various intuitive acceptance conditions (e.g. "accept if there are more active + labels than active − labels") have the same representation as acceptance pattern for all nodes in the graph, whereas the corresponding acceptance condition for ADFs depends on the node at hand. For a joint discussion of ADFs and GRAPPA, we refer to the recent handbook article [8].

A second extension are the recently proposed weighted ADFs (wADFs) [6, 9, 10][1]. Rather than being based on partial two-valued interpretations, the semantics of wADFs is based on partial V-valued interpretations, where V is some chosen set of acceptance degrees for arguments. This obviously allows for much more fine-grained distinctions among arguments in the semantics. The authors show that the extension to the multi-valued case is surprisingly smooth: the standard ADF operators only need mild reformulations to be able to capture arbitrary acceptance degrees.

The goal of this paper is to combine the two mentioned extensions of ADFs, thus bringing together the best of the two worlds. We are interested here in a formalism that extends GRAPPA the same way as wADFs extend ADFs. The approach we propose, called multi-valued GRAPPA (mvGRAPPA), is thus a knowledge representation formalism on the basis of simple labelled graphs equipped with a variety of multi-valued semantics rooted in argumentation and will be developed in the remainder of the paper.

Our article is organized as follows. The generalization of GRAPPA to the multi-valued case is presented in Sect. 2. The generalization is based on acceptance functions which determine the value of a node in the argument graph based on multi-sets of value/label pairs. We show that our concept of acceptance functions allows for a natural definition of different semantics that enjoy the expected relationships. The challenge how to represent acceptance functions adequately and in a user-friendly way is then addressed Sect. 3, where we propose so-called acceptance programs to specify those functions. Various examples illustrating the flexibility and expressiveness of this approach are discussed in Sect. 4. Section 5 concludes the paper.

2 Multi-valued GRAPPA

In this section we introduce syntax and semantics of multi-valued GRAPPA. We will introduce the generalized definitions right away and point out where they differ from the original definitions in [12]. Our approach allows for arbitrary sets of values in interpretations.

We assume a dedicated undefined truth value $\mathbf{u}$.

Definition 1. *A set V of values (acceptance degrees) is called $\mathbf{u}$-free if $\mathbf{u} \notin V$.*

For every $\mathbf{u}$-free set of values used in this work we assume an underlying information ordering $<_i$ on $V \cup \{\mathbf{u}\}$, where $<_i = \{\langle \mathbf{u}, v \rangle \mid v \in V\}$, i.e., the information content of all values in V is equal and strictly greater than that of $\mathbf{u}$. We write $v \leq_i v'$ whenever $v <_i v'$ or $v = v'$.

---

[1] The approach in [6] differs from [10] and [9] in the treatment of non-flat information orderings. In this paper we only consider flat orderings where $\mathbf{u}$ is the only value considered less informative than others.

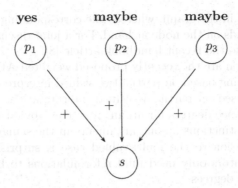

Fig. 1. The {**yes, no, maybe**}-LAG from Example 1 under interpretation v.

Definition 2. *Let L be a set of labels and V be a **u**-free set of values. A V-valued acceptance function over L is a function $c : (V \times L \to \mathbb{N}) \to V$. The set of V-valued acceptance functions over L is denoted by $F^{V,L}$.*

Intuitively, c determines the truth value to be assigned to a node n. This value is an element of V and depends on the truth values assigned to n's parent nodes, but also on the labels of links connecting parent nodes to n. Since the same value/label pair may appear more than once – and since this may be relevant for the value assigned to n – the actual assignment is based on a multi-set. Intuitively, this set counts the number of edges to n with a given label from parent nodes that are assigned a given truth value.

Definition 3. *Let V be a **u**-free set of values. A V-valued labelled argument graph (V-LAG) is a tuple $G = \langle S, E, L, \lambda, \alpha \rangle$ where*

- S *is a set of nodes (statements),*
- $E \subseteq S \times S$ *is a set of edges,*
- L *is a set of labels,*
- $\lambda : E \to L$ *assigns labels to edges, and*
- $\alpha : S \to F^{V,L}$.

This definition is almost identical to the definition of LAGs in [12]. The single exception is α which now assigns an acceptance function over an arbitrary fixed set V, whereas acceptance functions in the earlier paper were only allowed to assign **t** and **f**. In other words, V was fixed to {**t, f**} in [12].

A V-*valued interpretation for S* (or simply *interpretation* when V and S are clear from context) is a function $v : S \to V_{\mathbf{u}}$ with $V_{\mathbf{u}} = V \cup \{\mathbf{u}\}$. Slightly abusing terminology we will also apply $\leq_i$ and $<_i$ to interpretations with the standard pointwise reading. For instance, $v \leq_i v'$ stands for: $v(s) \leq_i v'(s)$ for all $s \in S$. An interpretation v is *total* if it does not assign **u** to any statement. A *completion of v* is any total interpretation w with $v \leq_i w$. We denote the set of completions of v by $[v]_c$.

Definition 4. *Let V be a* **u**-*free set of values, $G = \langle S, E, L, \lambda, \alpha \rangle$ a V-LAG, and v a total V-valued interpretation for S. The multi-set of valued labels of $s \in S$ in G under v, m_s^v, is defined as*

$$m_s^v(\mathbf{x}, l) = |\{(p, s) \in E \mid v(p) = \mathbf{x}, \lambda((p, s)) = l\}|$$

for each $\mathbf{x} \in V$ and each $l \in L$.

Example 1. Let $G = \langle S, E, L, \lambda, \alpha \rangle$ be a V-LAG over values $V = \{\mathbf{yes}, \mathbf{no}, \mathbf{maybe}\}$ and with labels $L = \{+, -\}$. Suppose $s \in S$ is a node in G with three parents p_1, p_2, and p_3 such that the links from p_1, p_2 and p_2 to s are all labelled '+'. G is depicted in Fig. 1.

For an interpretation v with $v(p_1) = \mathbf{yes}$ and $v(p_2) = v(p_3) = \mathbf{maybe}$ we have

$$m_s^v(\langle \mathbf{yes}, + \rangle) = 1,$$
$$m_s^v(\langle \mathbf{no}, + \rangle) = 0,$$
$$m_s^v(\langle \mathbf{maybe}, + \rangle) = 2,$$
$$m_s^v(\langle \mathbf{yes}, - \rangle) = 0,$$
$$m_s^v(\langle \mathbf{no}, - \rangle) = 0, \text{ and}$$
$$m_s^v(\langle \mathbf{maybe}, - \rangle) = 0.$$

Like for GRAPPA and ADFs, our semantics is based on a characteristic operator on interpretations. As mentioned in the introduction, it is inspired from similar operators in AFT.

Definition 5 (Characteristic Operator Γ_G^V). *Let V be a* **u**-*free set of values, $v : S \to V_{\mathbf{u}}$ an interpretation, and $G = \langle S, E, L, \lambda, \alpha \rangle$ a V-LAG. Applying Γ_G^V to v yields a new interpretation (the consensus over $[v]_c$) defined as*

$$\Gamma_G^V(v) : S \to V_{\mathbf{u}} \quad \text{with} \quad s \mapsto \textstyle\prod_i \{\alpha(s)(m_s^{v_c}) \mid v_c \in [v]_c\}$$

where $\prod_i$ denotes the greatest lower bound in $(V_{\mathbf{u}}, \leq_i)$.

Intuitively, $\Gamma_G^V(v)$ maps statements to the greatest truth value (with respect to the information order) that is compatible with all results of evaluating G under some completion of v.

Example 2. Let $G = \langle S, E, L, \lambda, \alpha \rangle$ be defined as in Example 1 and let the acceptance function $\alpha(s)$ of node s be given by

$$\alpha(s)(m) = \begin{cases} \mathbf{yes} & \text{if } \langle \mathbf{no}, + \rangle \notin m, \\ \mathbf{maybe} & \text{if } m(\langle \mathbf{yes}, + \rangle) \geq m(\langle \mathbf{no}, + \rangle), \\ \mathbf{no} & \text{otherwise.} \end{cases}$$

Hence, s is assigned **yes** if there are no '+'-parents assigned **no**.[2] Furthermore, s is assigned **maybe** if there are more or equally many '+'-parents assigned **yes**

---

[2] We call a parent n' of a node n l-parent if the link (n', n) is labelled with l.

than **no**. Consider the interpretation v' with $v'(p_1) = $ **yes** and $v'(p_2) = $ **maybe** and $v'(p_3) = \mathbf{u}$. The set of completions of v' is $[v']_c = \{v, v_y, v_n\}$ where v is given as in Example 1, and v_y and v_n coincide with v' and v except for the assignments $v_y(p_3) = $ **yes** and $v_n(p_3) = $ **no** of p_3.

The multi-sets of valued labels of these completions are given by

$$m_s^v = [\langle \mathbf{yes}, + \rangle, \langle \mathbf{maybe}, + \rangle, \langle \mathbf{maybe}, + \rangle],$$
$$m_s^{v_y} = [\langle \mathbf{yes}, + \rangle, \langle \mathbf{yes}, + \rangle, \langle \mathbf{maybe}, + \rangle], \text{ and}$$
$$m_s^{v_n} = [\langle \mathbf{yes}, + \rangle, \langle \mathbf{no}, + \rangle, \langle \mathbf{maybe}, + \rangle].$$

We have $\alpha(s)(m_s^v) = $ **yes**, $\alpha(s)(m_s^{v_y}) = $ **yes**, and $\alpha(s)(m_s^{v_n}) = $ **maybe**. Consequently, $\Gamma_G^V(v)(s) = \bigcap_i \{\mathbf{yes}, \mathbf{maybe}\} = \mathbf{u}$. Note that in the example we did not use the $-$ label for simplicity.

We are now in the position to define the standard semantics of argumentation on top of V-LAGs in the expected way.

Definition 6. *Let $G = \langle S, E, L, \lambda, \alpha \rangle$ be a V-LAG. An interpretation $v : S \to V_{\mathbf{u}}$ is*

- *a model of G iff $v(s) \neq \mathbf{u}$ for all $s \in S$ and $\Gamma_G^V(v) = v$.*
  Intuition: the value of a node s in v is exactly the one required by the acceptance function of S.
- *grounded for G iff $v = lfp(\Gamma_G^V)$, i.e., v is the least fixpoint of Γ_G^V w.r.t $\leq_i$.*
  Intuition: v collects all the information which is beyond any doubt.
- *admissible for G iff $v \leq_i \Gamma_G^V(v)$.*
  Intuition: v does not contain unjustifiable information.
- *preferred for G iff it is $\leq_i$-maximal admissible for G.*
  Intuition: v has maximal information content without giving up admissibility.
- *complete for G iff $v = \Gamma_G^V(v)$.*
  Intuition: v contains exactly the justifiable information.

For $\sigma \in \{adm, com, prf\}$, $\sigma(G)$ denotes the set of all admissible (resp. complete, preferred) interpretations with respect to G. Moreover, we use $mod(G)$ to denote the models of G.

We still need to show existence of the least fixpoint of Γ_G^V. This is a consequence of the monotonicity of the operator Γ_G^V. The pair $(\{v : S \to V_{\mathbf{u}}\}, \leq_i)$ forms a complete partial order in which the characteristic operator Γ_D of wADFs is monotone.

Proposition 1. *The operator Γ_G^V is $\leq_i$-monotone, that is, $v \leq_i w$ implies $\Gamma_D(v) \leq_i \Gamma_D(w)$ for all interpretations $v, w : S \to V_{\mathbf{u}}$.*

Existence of the least fixpoint of Γ_G^V then follows via the fixpoint theorem for monotone operators in complete partial orders.

Next, we show that the well-known relationships between Dung semantics carry over to our generalizations.

Proposition 2. *Let G be a V-LAG. It holds that*

$$mod(G) \subseteq prf(G) \subseteq com(G) \subseteq adm(G).$$

We now show how stable semantics can be generalized following the approach in [10]. Stable semantics treats truth values asymmetrically. For standard ADFs **f** (false) can be assumed to hold (by default), whereas **t** (true) needs to be justified by a derivation. This is achieved by building the reduct of an ADF and then checking whether the grounded interpretation of the reduct coincides with the original model on the nodes which "survive" in the reduct. Moving from the two-valued to the multi-valued case allows us to choose what the assumed, respectively derived truth values are. Stable semantics thus becomes parametrized by a subset W of the set of values V.

Definition 7. *Let* $G = \langle S, E, L, \lambda, \alpha \rangle$ *be a V-LAG. Let* $v : S \to V$ *be a model of G (that is, v is total). Let* $W \subseteq V$ *be the set of assumed truth values. The* v, W-reduct of G is the V-LAG $G_W^v = (S_W^v, E_W^v, L, \lambda_W^v, \alpha_W^v)$ where

- $S_W^v = \{s \in S \mid v(s) \notin W\}$,
- $E_W^v = E \cap (S_W^v \times S_W^v)$,
- λ_W^v is λ restricted to E_W^v,
- α_W^v is obtained from α as follows: $\alpha_W^v(n)(m) = \alpha(n)(m')$ where, for each value/label pair (x, l), $m'(x, l) = m(x, l) + \mid \{s \in S \setminus S_W^v \mid v(s) = x, \lambda(s, n) = l\} \mid$.

The v, W-reduct can be viewed as the partial evaluation of the original graph which takes values in W for granted. Now stable models can be defined as usual:

Definition 8. *Let* $G = \langle S, E, L, \lambda, \alpha \rangle$ *be a V-LAG and let* $v : S \to V$ *be a model of G. Let* v_g *be the grounded interpretation of the* v, W-reduct of G. v *is a W-stable model of G iff* $v(s) = v_g(s)$ *for each* $s \in S_W^v$.

We conclude this section with the following result:

Proposition 3. *Multi-valued GRAPPA generalizes both GRAPPA [12] and weighted ADFs with flat information ordering [10].*

Proof. Sketch: (a) Weighted ADFs can be modelled by labelling each link with the source node. Acceptance functions of weighted ADFs are functions from value assignments of the parents of a node to values for that node. With nodes as labels these value assignments can be reconstructed from the multi-sets used in multi-valued GRAPPA via the corresponding value/label pairs. This allows us to model the acceptance functions of weighted ADFs. (b) GRAPPA is just the special case of multi-valued GRAPPA with $V = \{\mathbf{f}, \mathbf{t}\}$ and acceptance functions which only depend on the number of parent nodes with value **t**.

From an abstract, mathematical point of view our generalization may seem straightforward. However, it brings with it an important practical issue which needs to be addressed: how to conveniently represent acceptance functions? In original GRAPPA the issue was dealt with by so-called acceptance patterns. An acceptance pattern is basically a condition that evaluates to **t** or **f** and directly determines the value of a node via this evaluation. In our new multi-valued setting this simple approach obviously does not work. To solve this issue we propose a rule-based approach: we use a set of rules; each rule consists of a condition and a value from V; the value assigned is computed from the values of all rules whose conditions evaluate to true.

3   Acceptance Programs

In this section we develop a method to represent multi-valued acceptance functions via so-called acceptance programs. An acceptance program $\mathscr{S} = (AG, R)$ consists of a collection of acceptance rules R and an aggregation function AG. Each rule $r \in R$ is of the form

$$\mathsf{v} : \mathsf{b},$$

where, intuitively, v describes some value in V and b is an expression that evaluates to true or false for any given multi-set m of value/label pairs. This way the rules determine potential values taken from V. The role of the aggregation function $AG : 2^V \to V$ is to determine a unique value to be assigned to the node at hand based on the potential values. For convenience we also consider programs based on non-ground rules. We now formally define syntax and semantics of acceptance programs.

3.1   Syntax

We define the syntax in a bottom up fashion. Acceptance rules are built from three basic types of expressions: label expressions, value expressions, and numeric expressions. On top of these we define Boolean expressions.

Definition 9. *A GRAPPA signature* $\Sigma = (V, L, Var_V, Var_L, F, Rel)$ *consists of a set of values* V, *a set of labels* L, *sets of value and label variables* Var_V *and* Var_L, *respectively, a set of function symbols* F *and a set of binary relation symbols* Rel.

   A label expression (over Σ*)*[3] *is*

– *a label* $l \in L$ *or*
– *a label variable* $X_L \in Var_L$.

   A value expression is recursively defined as

– *a value* $\mathbf{x} \in V$,
– *a value variable* $\mathbf{X} \in Var_V$,
– *a value function term* $f(\overrightarrow{e})$ *where* $f \in F$ $\overrightarrow{e} = \langle e_1, \ldots, e_k \rangle$ *is a vector of label, value, or numeric expressions,*

---

[3] We will often leave Σ implicit in definitions from now on.

- $min_{W, \preceq}(\mathsf{l})$, or
- $max_{W, \preceq}(\mathsf{l})$ where W is a set of value expressions, $\preceq \in Rel$ a binary relation symbol, and l a label expression.

A numeric expression is of the form

- $c \in \mathbb{R}$,
- $\#_W(\mathsf{l})$, where l is a label expression,
- sum_W,
- $count_W$,
- min_W, or
- max_W where W is a set of value expressions, or
- $(\mathsf{n} \oplus \mathsf{n}')$ where n and n' are numeric expressions and $\oplus \in \{+, *\}$.

A Boolean expression is of the form

- $m \sim n$ where m and n are numeric expressions and $\sim \in \{<, \leq, =, \geq, >, \neq\}$,
- $\mathbf{v} \sim \mathbf{w}$ where $\mathbf{v}$ and $\mathbf{w}$ are value expressions and $\sim \in Rel$,
- $\perp$,
- $\top$,
- $\mathsf{b} \otimes \mathsf{b}'$ where b and b' are Boolean expressions and $\otimes \in \{\wedge, \vee, \rightarrow\}$, or
- $\neg a$ where a is a Boolean expression.

We are now in a position to define rules. As mentioned above rules derive potential values based on some Boolean condition:

Definition 10. *An* acceptance rule *is of the form*

$$\mathsf{v} : \mathsf{b},$$

where v *is a value expression and* b *a Boolean expression. An acceptance rule is* ground *if it contains no (label nor value) variables.*

Since rules may identify multiple potential values (or none), acceptance programs need an additional component which computes (or simply picks) one specific value out of the set of candidate values. This is the role of the aggregation function.

Definition 11. *An* acceptance program $\mathscr{S}$ *(over Σ) is a pair* $\langle AG, R \rangle$, *where* $AG : 2^V \rightarrow V$ *is a* value aggregation function *and R is a set of acceptance rules. $\mathscr{S}$ is* ground *if all of its acceptance rules are ground. Π_Σ is the set of acceptance programs over Σ.*

One obvious choice for aggregation functions are functions which, given some total order on V, pick the maximal, respectively the minimal element among the candidates. We will see specific examples in Sect. 4.

Definition 12. *Let V be a u-free set of values. A V-valued GRAPPA instance over Σ is a tuple* $G = \langle S, E, L, \lambda, \pi \rangle$ *where S, E, L and λ are defined as for a V-LAG and π is a function $\pi : S \rightarrow \Pi_\Sigma$ that assigns to each statement $s \in S$ an acceptance program over Σ. G is* ground *if $\pi(s)$ is ground for all $s \in S$.*

In order to handle variables, we use variable substitutions as defined next.

Definition 13. *Let $G = \langle S, E, L, \lambda, \pi \rangle$ be a V-valued GRAPPA instance. A variable substitution for G is a mapping θ that assigns every label variable X_L, respectively every value variable $\mathbf{X}$ that appears in some acceptance program $\pi(s)$ ($s \in S$), a label from L, respectively, a value from V. For an acceptance rule r, $r\theta$ denotes the acceptance rule obtained by replacing every variable v in r by $\theta(v)$. The set of variable substitutions for G is denoted by Θ_G.*

The grounding of G is given by $gr(G) = \langle S, E, L, \lambda, \pi' \rangle$ such that for every $s \in S$, $\pi'(s) = \langle AG, \{r\theta \mid r \in R, \theta \in \Theta_G\} \rangle$, where $\pi(s) = \langle AG, R \rangle$.

3.2 Semantics

In the following, we assume a GRAPPA signature $\Sigma = (V, L, Var_V, Var_L, F, Rel)$ where each $f \in F$ with arity k comes with an associated function $\hat{f} : (L \cup V \cup \mathbb{R})^k \to V$. Similarly, each relation symbol $r \in Rel$ has an associated binary relation $\hat{r}$ on V.

As a first step we need to define the value assigned to a given multi-set by an acceptance program. Since the semantics of non-ground GRAPPA instances is defined in terms of their groundings, we can restrict the following definitions of valuation to the ground case.

Definition 14. *Let m be a multi-set $m : V \times L \to \mathbb{N}$. The valuation of a ground value expression (over Σ) is given by*

- $val^m(\mathbf{x}) = \mathbf{x}$ *for* $\mathbf{x} \in V$
- $val^m(f(\mathbf{e}_1, \ldots, \mathbf{e}_n)) = \hat{f}(val^m(\mathbf{e}_1), \ldots, val^m(\mathbf{e}_n))$
- $val^m(min_{W, \preccurlyeq}(l)) = min_{\preccurlyeq}\{val^m(\mathbf{v}) \mid \mathbf{v} \in W, m(\langle val^m(\mathbf{v}), l \rangle) > 0, l \in L\}$
- $val^m(max_{W, \preccurlyeq}(l)) = max_{\preccurlyeq}\{val^m(\mathbf{v}) \mid \mathbf{v} \in W, m(\langle val^m(\mathbf{v}), l \rangle) > 0, l \in L\}$[4]

Naturally, value constants are interpreted by themselves and function symbols by the application of their associated functions on their evaluated arguments. Intuitively, $min_{W, \preccurlyeq}(l)$ extracts the $\hat{\preccurlyeq}$-minimal value of all l-parents that evaluates to a value from W. The intuition of the max-case is analogous.

Example 3. Let $V = [0; 1]$, $L = \{+, -\}$, and $m = [\langle 0.1, + \rangle, \langle 0.3, + \rangle, \langle 0.4, - \rangle, \langle 0.7, + \rangle)]$. Then, the valuation of the the value expression $max_{[0;0.5], \leq}(+)$, where $\leq$ is the relation symbol for the natural order, is given by $val^m(max_{[0;0.5], \leq}(+)) = max\{0.1, 0.3\} = 0.3$.

Definition 15. *Let m be a multi-set $m : V \times L \to \mathbb{N}$. The valuation of a ground numeric expression (over Σ) is given by*

---

[4] The values $val^m(max_{W, \preccurlyeq}(l))$ and $val^m(min_{W, \preccurlyeq}(l))$ are only defined when $\hat{\preccurlyeq}$ is an order that has a maximal, respectively, minimal, element for every subset of V. The expressions $max_{W, \preccurlyeq}(l)$ and $min_{W, \preccurlyeq}(l)$ may only be used when this is the case.

- $val^m(c) = c$ for $c \in \mathbb{R}$
- $val^m(\#l_W) = \sum_{v \in W} m(\langle val^m(v), l \rangle)$
- $val^m(sum_W) = \sum_{v \in W, l \in L} m(\langle val^m(v), l \rangle)$
- $val^m(count_W) = |\{l \mid v \in W, m(\langle val^m(v), l \rangle) > 0\}|$
- $val^m(min_W) = min\{l \in L \mid m(\langle val^m(v), l \rangle) > 0, v \in W\}$
- $val^m(max_W) = max\{l \in L \mid m(\langle val^m(v), l \rangle) > 0, v \in W\}$[5]
- $val^m(o \oplus p) = val^m(o) \oplus val^m(p)$ where $\oplus \in \{+, *\}$

Notice the semantic differences of the expressions $\#l_W$, sum_W, and $count_W$: $\#l_W$ counts the number of l-parents that evaluate to values from W. In contrast, sum_W and $count_W$ are not dependent on a label. The expression sum_W returns the number of all parents that evaluate to values from W and $count_W$ counts the number of different labels of parents that evaluate to a value from W. The expressions min_W and max_W give the minimal, respectively maximal, label to a parent that evaluates to a value from W.

Definition 16. *Let m be a multi-set $m : V \times L \to \mathbb{N}$, where n and o numeric expressions, $\mathbf{v}$ and $\mathbf{w}$ value expressions, and a and b Boolean expressions. Function val^m maps Boolean expressions to $\mathbf{t}$ or $\mathbf{f}$. In particular, the valuation of a ground Boolean expression (over V and L) is given by*

- $val^m(n \sim o) = \mathbf{t}$ *iff* $val^m(n) \sim val^m(o)$, *where* $\sim \in \{<, \leq, =, \geq, >, \neq\}$
- $val^m(\mathbf{v} \sim \mathbf{w}) = \mathbf{t}$ *iff* $val^m(\mathbf{v}) \tilde{\sim} val^m(\mathbf{w})$ *with* $\sim \in Rel$
- $val^m(\bot) = \mathbf{f}$
- $val^m(\top) = \mathbf{t}$
- $val^m(a \wedge b) = \mathbf{t}$ *iff* $val^m(a) = \mathbf{t}$ *and* $val^m(b) = \mathbf{t}$
- $val^m(a \vee b) = \mathbf{t}$ *iff* $val^m(a) = \mathbf{t}$ *or* $val^m(b) = \mathbf{t}$
- $val^m(a \to b) = \mathbf{t}$ *iff* $val^m(a) = \mathbf{f}$ *or* $val^m(b) = \mathbf{t}$
- $val^m(\neg a) = \mathbf{t}$ *iff* $val^m(a) = \mathbf{f}$

Definition 17. *Let m be a multi-set $m : V \times L \to \mathbb{N}$. For a ground acceptance program $\pi = \langle AG, R \rangle \in \Pi_\Sigma$, its valuation is defined as*

$$val^m(\pi) = AG(\{val^m(\mathbf{v}) \mid \mathbf{v} : b \in R, val^m(b) = \mathbf{t}\}).$$

With these definitions we can reformulate the definition of the characteristic operator taking into account that acceptance functions are represented by acceptance programs:

Definition 18 (Characteristic Operator Γ_G^V). *Let V be a $\mathbf{u}$-free set of values, $v : S \to V_\mathbf{u}$ an interpretation, and G a V-valued GRAPPA instance with $gr(G) = \langle S, E, L, \lambda, \pi \rangle$. Applying Γ_G^V to v yields a new interpretation (the consensus over $[v]_c$) defined as*

$$\Gamma_G^V(v) : S \to V_\mathbf{u} \quad \text{with} \quad s \mapsto \prod_i \{val^{m_s^{v_c}}(\pi(s)) \mid v_c \in [v]_c\}$$

where $\prod_i$ denotes the greatest lower bound in $(V_\mathbf{u}, \leq_i)$.

---

[5] The use of min_W and max_W is restricted to settings where the label domain L is numeric.

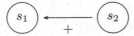

Fig. 2. The GRAPPA instance used in Example 4.

The semantics of a GRAPPA instance is then defined analogously to that of a V-LAG (see Definition 6). For the case of stable semantics, also a v, W-reduct of a GRAPPA instance can be defined in a similar fashion as for a V-LAG, using the same construction of multi-set m' as in Definition 7.

4 Examples

In this section we illustrate our approach with a number of examples. We will make use of aggregation functions of the form provided next. Note that in case the rules provide no candidates at all, a certain default value needs to be picked. For some total order $\trianglelefteq$ on V, we use

- $max_{\triangleleft}(V')$, where $max_{\triangleleft}(V') = \mathbf{v}$ when $\mathbf{v}$ is the $\trianglelefteq$-maximal element of V' if $V' \neq \emptyset$, and the $\trianglelefteq$-minimal element of V, otherwise,
- $min_{\triangleleft}(V')$, where $max_{\triangleleft}(V') = \mathbf{v}$ where $\mathbf{v}$ is the $\trianglelefteq$-minimal element of V' if $V' \neq \emptyset$, and the $\trianglelefteq$-maximal element of V, otherwise, and
- $\Sigma(V')$, where V is numeric and $\Sigma(V') = \Sigma_{v \in V'} v$ returns the sum of elements of V'.

We start with examples where acceptance programs evaluate to statically chosen values. Recall that a parent n' of a node n is an l-parent if the link (n', n) is labelled with l.

Example 4. Let $L = \{+, -\}, V = \{\mathbf{yes}, \mathbf{no}, \mathbf{maybe}\}$ and assume we want to assign **yes** to a node if (a) more '+'-parents have value **yes** than '−'-parents or (b) the same number of '+'- and '−'-parents have value **yes** but more '+'-parents have value **maybe** than '−'-parents. In addition, we assign **maybe** to the node if (a) the same number of '+'- and '−'-parents have value **yes** and the same number of '+'- and '−'-parents have value **maybe**. We assign **no** to the node in all other cases.

Using the aggregation function $AG = min_{(\mathbf{yes} \trianglelefteq \mathbf{maybe} \trianglelefteq \mathbf{no})}$ the following set of rules R produces the intended values:

$$\mathbf{yes} : \big(\#_{\{\mathbf{yes}\}}(+) > \#_{\{\mathbf{yes}\}}(-)\big) \vee$$
$$\big((\#_{\{\mathbf{yes}\}}(+) = \#_{\{\mathbf{yes}\}}(-)) \wedge (\#_{\{\mathbf{maybe}\}}(+) > \#_{\{\mathbf{maybe}\}}(-))\big)$$

$$\mathbf{maybe} : (\#_{\{\mathbf{yes}\}}(+) = \#_{\{\mathbf{yes}\}}(-)) \wedge (\#_{\{\mathbf{maybe}\}}(+) = \#_{\{\mathbf{maybe}\}}(-))$$

$$\mathbf{no} : \top$$

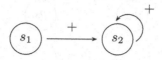

Fig. 3. The GRAPPA instance used in Example 6 that shows how acceptance rules can derive dynamically computed value expressions and demonstrates how different aggregation functions yield different semantics.

Note that **no** is always among the values derived from these rules. The aggregation function guarantees that nevertheless the right value is chosen, in case one of the other rules fire.

Consider the V-valued GRAPPA instance $\langle S, E, L, \lambda, \pi \rangle$, given in Fig. 2, with $S = \{s_1, s_2\}$, $E = \{(s_2, s_1)\}$, $L = \{+, -\}$, $\lambda((s_2, s_1)) = +$, and π assigning above acceptance program (AG, R) to both s_1 and s_2.

Admissible semantics yield interpretations $\{s_1 \mapsto \mathbf{u}, s_2 \mapsto \mathbf{u}\}$, $\{s_1 \mapsto \mathbf{u}, s_2 \mapsto \mathbf{maybe}\}$, $\{s_1 \mapsto \mathbf{yes}, s_2 \mapsto \mathbf{u}\}$, and $\{s_1 \mapsto \mathbf{yes}, s_2 \mapsto \mathbf{maybe}\}$. For the complete, grounded, preferred, and model semantics, we obtain a single interpretation $\{s_1 \mapsto \mathbf{yes}, s_2 \mapsto \mathbf{maybe}\}$: intuitively, s_2 maps to **maybe** because it has no parents and thus the second rule of the program applies. s_1 maps to **yes** because there is neither a '+'-parent nor a '−'-parent with value **yes**, but one '+'-parent (namely s_2) with value **maybe** but no such '−'-parent.

Example 5. In the next example we use the unit interval as set of values $V = [0; 1]$ in order to exemplarily illustrate terms from the value domain of form $max_{W, \leq}(l)$: the term selects the maximal truth value from W (with respect to the natural ordering $\leq$ over reals) appearing in the multi-set for label l.

Moreover, let the labels be $L = \{-, +, ++\}$. We want to express the following conditions (1) Parent nodes with value at least 0.5 and connected via edges with labels $++$ can veto for full acceptance (i. e., assigned value **1**). (2) Nodes with some greater '+'-parent value than '−'-parent values get **0.75**. (3) Nodes with equal maximal '+' and '−'-parent values get **0.6** if there are more nodes with $+$ than $-$ that have this maximal value (here we use $max_{W, \leq}(l)$ for indexing a #-based term). (4) Nodes with equal maximal '+' and '−'-parent values get **0.5** if there are equally many nodes with $+$ and $-$ that have this maximal value. (5) Nodes with equal maximal '+' and '−'-parent values get **0.4** if there are less nodes with $+$ than $-$ that have this maximal value. (6) Otherwise, we assign value **0**. For the aggregation function AG we use $max_{\leq}$ and specify the conditions via the following acceptance rules

$$\mathbf{1} : \#_{[0.5;1]}(++) \geq 1,$$
$$\mathbf{0.75} : max_{[0;1], \leq}(+) > max_{[0;1], \leq}(-)$$
$$\mathbf{0.6} : max_{[0;1], \leq}(+) = max_{[0;1], \leq}(-) \wedge \#_{\{max_{[0;1], \leq}(+)\}}(+) > max_{\{max_{[0;1], \leq}(+)\}}(-)$$
$$\mathbf{0.5} : max_{[0;1], \leq}(+) = max_{[0;1], \leq}(-) \wedge \#_{\{max_{[0;1], \leq}(+)\}}(+) = max_{\{max_{[0;1], \leq}(+)\}}(-)$$
$$\mathbf{0.4} : max_{[0;1], \leq}(+) = max_{[0;1], \leq}(-) \wedge \#_{\{max_{[0;1], \leq}(+)\}}(+) < max_{\{max_{[0;1], \leq}(+)\}}(-)$$
$$\mathbf{0} : \top$$

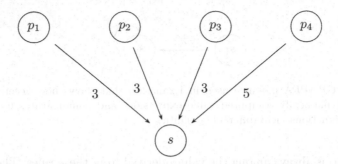

Fig. 4. In Example 7 we show how the numeric labels of this GRAPPA instance can be used as weight factors for computing the value of node s as the weighted sum of the values of nodes p_1 to p_4.

So far, we have provided rules that statically assign truth values (i.e., the rule heads have been given via concrete values). However, our language allows arbitrary value expressions in rule heads. The following example gives a simple application of that.

Example 6. Let $L = \{+\}$, $V = [0; 1]$ and consider an acceptance rule of the form

$$max_{[0;1]}(+) : \#_{[0;1]}(+) \geq 1$$

which simply states that, if there is some parent-node, assign the maximal value of all parents to the current node. Note that in this case, any aggregation function AG that satisfies $AG(\{x\}) = x$ can be chosen; however, the default-value of AG is crucial here for nodes with no parents. Consider a V-valued GRAPPA instance with two nodes $S = \{s_1, s_2\}$ and two edges $E = \{(s_1, s_2), (s_2, s_2)\}$, as illustrated in Fig. 3, including a self-loop for s_2. Both nodes use the acceptance rule shown above.

First assume both nodes use aggregation function $AG_1 = max_{\leq}$. As s_1 has no parent, the rule body will never fire in the evaluation of s_1. As a consequence AG_1 will be applied on the empty set, yielding value $\mathbf{0}$ for s_1 under every interpretation. Node s_2 has two parents, s_1 and itself, therefore the rule will fire and s_2 can take any value from $[0; 1]$.

Now assume both nodes use aggregation function $AG_2 = min_{\leq}$. Also here, AG_2 will be applied on the empty set for node s_1, this time yielding value $\mathbf{1}$ for s_1 under every interpretation. The rule will fire for s_2 and its head will evaluate to the maximal value of each '+'-parent, i.e., to $\mathbf{1}$ as s_1 is assigned $\mathbf{1}$.

Example 7. Our final example shows that acceptance programs can also be used to specify propagation of values throughout a network. To this end, we assume that labels and values are both numbers, i.e. $L = V = \mathbb{N}$. Suppose we want nodes to be assigned the weighted sum of the values of parent nodes, where labels are used as weight factors. We provide an acceptance program $\langle AG, \{r\} \rangle$

with a single non-ground rule

$$r = \#_{\{\mathbf{X}\}}(X_L) * \mathbf{X} * X_L : \top$$

and AG being the summation function Σ. Note that multiplication $*$ here is formally a value function, $\mathbf{X}$ a value variable and X_L a label variable. Let us consider the graph given in Fig. 4 and apply $\langle AG, \{r\}\rangle$ to node s.

Consider interpretation v with $v(p_1) = v(p_2) = \mathbf{1}$, $v(p_3) = \mathbf{2}$, and $v(p_4) = \mathbf{0}$. The relevant parts of the the grounding of r are provided by substituting $\mathbf{X}$ by $\mathbf{1}$, $\mathbf{2}$, and resp. $\mathbf{0}$ and X_L by 3 and 5.

$$\#_{\{\mathbf{1}\}}(3) * \mathbf{1} * 3 : \top$$
$$\#_{\{\mathbf{1}\}}(5) * \mathbf{1} * 5 : \top$$
$$\#_{\{\mathbf{2}\}}(3) * \mathbf{2} * 3 : \top$$
$$\#_{\{\mathbf{2}\}}(5) * \mathbf{2} * 5 : \top$$
$$\#_{\{\mathbf{0}\}}(3) * \mathbf{0} * 3 : \top$$
$$\#_{\{\mathbf{0}\}}(5) * \mathbf{0} * 5 : \top$$

The evaluation of the $\#_W(\cdot)$ value expression under v is obtained via multi-set

$$m_s^v(\mathbf{0}, 5) = |\{(p_4, s)\}| = 1$$
$$m_s^v(\mathbf{1}, 3) = |\{(p_1, s), (p_2, s)\}| = 2$$
$$m_s^v(\mathbf{2}, 3) = |\{(p_3, s)\}| = 1$$
$$m_s^v(\mathbf{x}, l) = 0 \quad \text{for all other } \mathbf{x}, l$$

Thus, the value assigned to s is thus determined by the first and the third rule of the grounding rules shown above (all others have factor 0) which evaluate to the sum of $\mathbf{12}$.

5   Conclusions

In this paper we have successfully combined two recent extensions of ADFs, namely the extension to the multi-valued case where the user can pick the set of truth values which is best-suited for a particular application, and the GRAPPA approach which defines operator-based argumentation semantics directly on top of arbitrary labelled argument graphs. We believe this combination is highly useful for the following reasons. First of all, it is important to come up with knowledge representation formalisms that provide means to express the relevant information in a way that is as user friendly as possible - without giving up precisely defined formal semantics. We believe graphical representation are particularly well-suited to play this role, and our operator-based semantics turns graphs into full-fledged knowledge representation formalisms. On the other hand, it is important to provide enough flexibility for more fine-grained distinctions than possible with only two truth values. Multi-valued GRAPPA combines these features and thus, as we believe, is a useful tool for argumentation.

The challenge posed by the combination aimed for in this paper was not so much the generalization of the relevant definitions underlying the operator-based semantics. It was the identification of an adequate representation of the acceptance functions. We believe acceptance programs are a sufficiently flexible yet manageable means to this end. Acceptance programs may seem at odds with the requirement of user-friendliness discussed above. This is to a large extent due to the generality of our approach which allows us to handle arbitrary sets of values. We expect that for specific sets of values simpler representations - and maybe a small number of useful predefined functions - can be identified. This is a topic of future research.

References

1. Al-Abdulkarim, L., Atkinson, K., Bench-Capon, T.J.M.: Abstract dialectical frameworks for legal reasoning. In: Hoekstra, R. (ed.) Proceedings of the 27th Annual Conference on Legal Knowledge and Information Systems (JURIX 2014), Jagiellonian University, Krakow, Poland, 10–12 December 2014. FAIA, vol. 271, pp. 61–70. IOS Press (2014)
2. Al-Abdulkarim, L., Atkinson, K., Bench-Capon, T.J.M.: A methodology for designing systems to reason with legal cases using abstract dialectical frameworks. Artif. Intell. Law **24**(1), 1–49 (2016). https://doi.org/10.1007/s10506-016-9178-1
3. Al-Abdulkarim, L., Atkinson, K., Bench-Capon, T.J.M., Whittle, S., Williams, R., Wolfenden, C.: Noise induced hearing loss: an application of the angelic methodology. In: Proceedings of the 30th Annual Conference on Legal Knowledge and Information Systems (JURIX 2017), Luxembourg, 13–15 December 2017, pp. 79–88 (2017). https://doi.org/10.3233/978-1-61499-838-9-79
4. Atkinson, K., Bench-Capon, T.J.M.: Relating the ANGELIC methodology and ASPIC+. In: Modgil, S., Budzynska, K., Lawrence, J. (eds.) Proceedings of the 7th International Conference on Computational Models of Argument (COMMA 2018), Warsaw, Poland, 12–14 September 2018, pp. 109–116 (2018). https://doi.org/10.3233/978-1-61499-906-5-109
5. Baroni, P., Caminada, M., Giacomin, M.: An introduction to argumentation semantics. Knowl. Eng. Rev. **26**(4), 365–410 (2011)
6. Bogaerts, B.: Weighted abstract dialectical frameworks through the lens of approximation fixpoint theory. In: Hentenryck, P.V., Zhou, Z.H. (eds.) Proceedings of the 33rd AAAI Conference on Artificial Intelligence (AAAI 2019), Honolulu, Hawaii, USA, 27 January–1 February 2019 (2019)
7. Brewka, G., Ellmauthaler, S., Strass, H., Wallner, J.P., Woltran, S.: Abstract dialectical frameworks revisited. In: Rossi, F. (ed.) Proceedings of the 23rd International Joint Conference on Artificial Intelligence (IJCAI 2013), Beijing, China, 3–9 August 2013, pp. 803–809. AAAI Press/IJCAI (2013). http://ijcai.org/papers13/Papers/IJCAI13-125.pdf
8. Brewka, G., Ellmauthaler, S., Strass, H., Wallner, J.P., Woltran., S.: Abstract dialectical frameworks. In: Baroni, P., Gabbay, D., Giacomin, M., van der Torre, L. (eds.) Handbook of Formal Argumentation, Chap. 5, pp. 237–285. College Publications (2018)
9. Brewka, G., Pührer, J., Strass, H., Wallner, J.P., Woltran, S.: Weighted abstract dialectical frameworks: extended and revised report. CoRR abs/1806.07717 (2018). http://arxiv.org/abs/1806.07717
10. Brewka, G., Strass, H., Wallner, J.P., Woltran, S.: Weighted abstract dialectical frameworks. In: Proceedings of the 32nd AAAI Conference on Artificial Intelligence (AAAI 2018), New Orleans, Louisiana, USA, 2–7 February 2018, pp. 1779–1786 (2018). https://www.aaai.org/ocs/index.php/AAAI/AAAI18/paper/view/16373

11. Brewka, G., Woltran, S.: Abstract dialectical frameworks. In: Lin, F., Sattler, U., Truszczyński, M. (eds.) Proceedings of the 12th International Conference on Principles of Knowledge Representation and Reasoning (KR 2010), Toronto, Ontario, Canada, 9–13 May 2010, pp. 102–111. AAAI Press (2010). http://aaai.org/ocs/index.php/KR/KR2010/paper/view/1294

12. Brewka, G., Woltran, S.: GRAPPA: a semantical framework for graph-based argument processing. In: Schaub, T., Friedrich, G., O'Sullivan, B. (eds.) Proceedings of the 21st European Conference on Artificial Intelligence (ECAI 2014), Prague, Czech Republic, 18–22 August 2014. Frontiers in Artificial Intelligence and Applications, vol. 263, pp. 153–158. IOS Press (2014). https://doi.org/10.3233/978-1-61499-419-0-153

13. Cabrio, E., Villata, S.: Abstract dialectical frameworks for text exploration. In: van den Herik, H.J., Filipe, J. (eds.) Proceedings of the 8th International Conference on Agents and Artificial Intelligence (ICAART 2016), Rome, Italy, 24–26 February 2016, vol. 2, pp. 85–95. SciTePress (2016)

14. Cayrol, C., Lagasquie-Schiex, M.: Bipolar abstract argumentation systems. In: Simari, G., Rahwan, I. (eds.) Argumentation in Artificial Intelligence, pp. 65–84. Springer, Boston (2009). https://doi.org/10.1007/978-0-387-98197-0_4

15. Denecker, M., Marek, V.W., Truszczyński, M.: Uniform semantic treatment of default and autoepistemic logics. Artif. Intell. **143**(1), 79–122 (2003)

16. Denecker, M., Marek, V.W., Truszczyński, M.: Approximations, stable operators, well-founded fixpoints and applications in nonmonotonic reasoning. In: Minker, J. (ed.) Logic-Based Artificial Intelligence, pp. 127–144. Kluwer Academic Publishers, Dordrecht (2000)

17. Denecker, M., Marek, V.W., Truszczyński, M.: Ultimate approximation and its application in nonmonotonic knowledge representation systems. Inf. Comput. **192**(1), 84–121 (2004)

18. Dung, P.M.: On the acceptability of arguments and its fundamental role in nonmonotonic reasoning, logic programming and n-person games. Artif. Intell. **77**(2), 321–357 (1995)

19. Pührer, J.: ArgueApply: abstract argumentation at your fingertips. Künstl. Intell. **32**, 209–212 (2018). https://doi.org/10.1007/s13218-018-0532-1

20. Strass, H.: Approximating operators and semantics for abstract dialectical frameworks. Artif. Intell. **205**, 39–70 (2013). https://doi.org/10.1016/j.artint.2013.09.004

Empirical Study on Human Evaluation of Complex Argumentation Frameworks

Marcos Cramer[1]([✉]) and Mathieu Guillaume[2]

[1] International Center for Computational Logic, TU Dresden,
Dresden, Germany
marcos.cramer@tu-dresden.de
[2] Centre for Research in Cognitive Neuroscience (CRCN),
Université Libre de Bruxelles, Brussels, Belgium
maguilla@ulb.ac.be

Abstract. In abstract argumentation, multiple argumentation semantics have been proposed that allow to select sets of jointly acceptable arguments from a given argumentation framework, i.e. based only on the attack relation between arguments. The existence of multiple argumentation semantics raises the question which of these semantics predicts best how humans evaluate arguments. Previous empirical cognitive studies that have tested how humans evaluate sets of arguments depending on the attack relation between them have been limited to a small set of very simple argumentation frameworks, so that some semantics studied in the literature could not be meaningfully distinguished by these studies. In this paper we report on an empirical cognitive study that overcomes these limitations by taking into consideration twelve argumentation frameworks of three to eight arguments each. These argumentation frameworks were mostly more complex than the argumentation frameworks considered in previous studies. All twelve argumentation framework were systematically instantiated with natural language arguments based on a certain fictional scenario, and participants were shown both the natural language arguments and a graphical depiction of the attack relation between them. Our data shows that grounded and CF2 semantics were the best predictors of human argument evaluation. A detailed analysis revealed that part of the participants chose a cognitively simpler strategy that is predicted very well by grounded semantics, while another part of the participants chose a cognitively more demanding strategy that is mostly predicted well by CF2 semantics.

Keywords: Abstract argumentation · Argumentation semantics · Empirical cognitive study

1 Introduction

The formal study of argumentation is an important field of research within AI [21]. One important methodological approach in the formal study of argumentation is abstract argumentation as introduced by Dung [11], in which one models

© Springer Nature Switzerland AG 2019
F. Calimeri et al. (Eds.): JELIA 2019, LNAI 11468, pp. 102–115, 2019.
https://doi.org/10.1007/978-3-030-19570-0_7

arguments by abstracting away from their internal structure to focus on the relation of attacks between them, i.e. on the relation between a counterargument and the argument that it counters. Multiple *argumentation semantics* have been proposed in the literature as criteria for selecting acceptable arguments based on the structure of the attack relation between the arguments (see [4]). Given that the applicability of abstract argumentation theory to human reasoning is desirable, this situation gives rise to the question which semantics best predicts the judgments that humans make about the acceptability of arguments based on the attack relation between the arguments.

There have been two previous empirical cognitive studies that have tested how humans evaluate sets of arguments depending on the attack relation between them, namely a 2010 study by Rahwan et al. [20] as well as a recent study by the authors of this paper [8]. These previous studies have been limited to small sets of very simple argumentation frameworks, so that some semantics studied in the literature could not be meaningfully distinguished by these studies. The study presented in this paper was designed to overcome this limitation by taking into account a larger number of argumentation frameworks, including some that are more complex than any of the argumentation frameworks used in previous studies.

When studying human evaluation of argumentation frameworks, it is important to fill the arguments with meaning rather than just presenting abstract graphs to humans, as most humans will not be able to properly understand the reasoning task if it is presented in a purely abstract manner (see Chapter 4 of [14]). For this reason, we instantiated the argumentation frameworks with natural language arguments, as was also done by the two previous studies cited above. When instantiating argumentation frameworks with natural language arguments, one needs to be careful in choosing the natural language arguments in such a way that for each pair of arguments, humans judge the existence and directionality of the attack between the two arguments as intended by the designers of the study. In a recent paper [7], we have presented the results of two empirical cognitive studies that tested how humans judge the existence and directionality of attacks between pairs of arguments. Note that designing sets of natural language arguments that – based on our findings in this recent paper – correspond to complex argumentation frameworks is a highly non-trivial task.

In order to approach this task in a systematic way, we carefully designed a fictional scenario in which information from multiple sources is analyzed, and developed a method to instantiate argumentation frameworks of arbitrary complexity with natural language arguments related to this fictional scenario. All attacks between arguments were based on undercutting the trustworthiness of a source, as our recent paper suggests that undercutting the trustworthiness of a source corresponds well to a unidirectional attack [7]. We used this method to design twelve sets of natural language arguments corresponding to twelve argumentation frameworks that had been carefully chosen to highlight the differences between existing argumentation semantics. As the natural language arguments were quite long and complex, we presented to the participants not only the natural language arguments, but also a graphical visualization of the corresponding argumentation framework.

We compared the results of our study to six widely studied argumentation semantics, namely to *grounded, preferred, semi-stable, CF2, stage* and *stage2* semantics. More precisely, we compare them to a three-valued justification status that can be defined with respect to each semantics. Due to certain considerations about these justification statuses, we do not separately consider *complete* and *stable* semantics in this paper.

The results of our study show that grounded and CF2 semantics were the best predictors of human argument evaluation. A detailed analysis revealed that part of the participants chose a cognitively simpler strategy that is predicted very well by grounded semantics, while another part of the participants chose a cognitively more demanding strategy that is mostly predicted well by CF2 semantics. In the discussion of our results, we pay special attention to the observation that the only argumentation framework for which CF2 semantics predicted the outcome of this cognitively more demanding strategy not as well as some other semantics was a framework including a six-cycle.

The rest of this paper is structured as follows: In Sect. 2, we present the formal preliminaries of abstract argumentation theory that are required in this paper. In particular, we define stage, CF2 and stage2 semantics and the three justification statuses used in this paper. In Sect. 3, we present some general background from cognitive science that will help to make our methodological choices and our discussion of the results more understandable. The design of our study is explained in Sect. 4. In Sect. 5, we present and discuss the results of our study. Section 7 concludes the paper and suggests directions for future research.

2   Preliminaries of Abstract Argumentation Theory

We will assume that the reader is familiar with the basics of abstract argumentation theory as introduced by Dung [11] and as explained in its current state-of-the-art form by Baroni et al. [4]. In particular, we will assume that the reader knows the notion of an *argumentation framework* (AF) as well as the *complete, grounded, stable, preferred* and *semi-stable* argumentation semantics, both in their traditional extension-based variant and in their label-based variant [3,4]. In this section we furthermore define stage, CF2 and stage2 semantics as well as the notions of *strong acceptance* and *strong rejection*.

Stage semantics was first defined by Verheij [23]. The idea behind it is that we minimize the set of arguments that are not accepted despite not being attacked by an accepted argument. To formalize this, we first need some auxiliary notions:

Definition 1. *Let $F = \langle Ar, att \rangle$ be an AF and let $S \subset Ar$ be a set of arguments. We say that S is conflict-free iff there are no arguments $b, c \in S$ such that b attacks c (i.e. such that $(b, c) \in att$). We define $S^+ := \{b \in Ar \mid$ for some $a \in S$, $(a, b) \in att\}$*

Now stage extensions are defined as follows:

Definition 2. *Let $F = \langle Ar, att \rangle$ be an AF and let $S \subset Ar$. Then S is a stage extension of F iff S is a conflict-free set such that $S \cup S^+$ is maximal with respect to set inclusion.*

CF2 semantics was first introduced by Baroni *et al.* [5]. The idea behind it is that we partition the AF into *strongly connected components* and recursively evaluate it component by component by choosing maximal conflict-free sets in each component and removing arguments attacked by chosen arguments. We formally define it following the notation of Dvořák and Gaggl [13]. For this we first need some auxiliary notions:

Definition 3. *Let $F = \langle Ar, att \rangle$ be an AF. We define $a \sim b$ iff either $a = b$ or there is an att-pat path from a to b and there is an att-path from b to a. The equivalence classes under the equivalence relation $\sim$ are called* strongly connected components (SCCs) *of F. We denote the set of SCCs of F by $SCCs(F)$. Given $S \subseteq Ar$, we define $D_F(S) := \{b \in Ar \mid \exists a \in S : (a,b) \in att \wedge a \not\sim b\}$.*

We now recursively define CF2 extensions as follows:

Definition 4. *Let $F = \langle Ar, att \rangle$ be an AF, and let $S \subseteq Ar$. Then S is a CF2 extension of F iff either*

- $|SCCs(F)| = 1$ *and S is a maximal conflict-free subset of A, or*
- $|SCCs(F)| > 1$ *and for each $C \in SCCs(F)$, $S \cap C$ is a CF2 extension of $F|_{C - D_F(S)}$.*

Stage2 semantics as introduced by Dvořák and Gaggl [12,13] combines features of stage and CF2 semantics by making use of the SCC-recursive scheme as in the definition of CF2, but using stage semantics rather than maximal conflict-freeness as the criterion to apply within a single SCC:

Definition 5. *Let $F = \langle Ar, att \rangle$ be an AF, and let $S \subseteq Ar$. Then S is a stage2 extension of F iff either*

- $|SCCs(F)| = 1$ *and S is a stage extension of A, or*
- $|SCCs(F)| > 1$ *and for each $C \in SCCs(F)$, $S \cap C$ is a stage2 extension of $F|_{C - D_F(S)}$.*

While the grounded extension of an AF is always unique, an AF with cycles may have multiple preferred, semi-stable, CF2, stage and stage2 extensions. In our experiment, however, participants were asked to make a single judgment about each argument, so we compare their judgments to the *justification status* of arguments according to various semantics (see [4,26]), as the justification status is always unique for each argument. In particular, we focus on the justification statuses *strongly accepted*, *strongly rejected* and *weakly undecided*, which can be defined as follows:

Definition 6. *Let $F = \langle Ar, att \rangle$ be an AF, let σ be an argumentation semantics, and let $a \in A$ be an argument. We say that a is* strongly accepted *with respect* to σ *iff for every σ-extension E of F, $a \in E$. We say that a is* strongly rejected *with respect to σ iff for every σ-extension E of F, some $b \in E$ attacks a. We say that a is* weakly undecided *iff it is neither strongly accepted nor strongly rejected.*

Note that in the labeling approach, strong acceptance of a corresponds to a being labeled in by all labelings, strong rejection of a corresponds to a being labeled out by all labelings, and a weakly undecided status for a of corresponds to a either being labeled undecided by at least one labeling, or a being labeled in by some labeling and out by some other labeling.

When comparing semantics to responses by humans, we will use these three justification statuses as a predictor for the human judgments to *accept* an argument, *reject* it or consider it *undecided*.

For some argumentation frameworks, stable semantics does not provide any extension whatsoever, which leads to the rather unintuitive situation that all arguments are both strongly accepted and strongly rejected. For this reason, we do not consider stable semantics as a potential predictor for human argument evaluation in this paper. The justification status with respect to complete semantics is always identical to the justification status with respect to grounded semantics, so that for the rest of the paper we do not separately consider complete semantics.

We would like to point our three properties that the justification status of an argument a satisfies in all semantics considered in this paper:

- If all arguments attacking a are strongly rejected, then a is strongly accepted.
- If some argument attacking a is strongly accepted, then a is strongly rejected.
- If not all arguments attacking a are strongly rejected, then a is not strongly accepted.

We use this observation to define a notion of *coherence* of a human judgment of the status of an argument with respect to the judgments of the other arguments in the same framework.

Definition 7. *Let $F = \langle Ar, att \rangle$ be an AF, and let $j : Ar \rightarrow \{accept, reject, undecided\}$ be a function that represents three-valued judgments on the arguments in Ar. Given an argument $a \in Ar$, we say that the judgment of j on a is* coherent *iff the following three properties are satisfied:*

- *If $j(b) = reject$ for each argument b that attacks a, then $j(a) = accept$.*
- *If $j(b) = accept$ for some argument b that attacks a, then $j(a) = reject$.*
- *If $j(b) = undecided$ for some argument b that attacks a, then either $j(a) = undecided$ or $j(a) = reject$.*

3 Cognitive Variability of Humans

Given that this paper presents findings of a cognitive empirical study to an audience whose scientific expertise lies mainly in areas outside of cognitive science, we present some general background from cognitive science that will help to make our methodological choices and our discussion of the results more understandable.

Humans are heterogeneous by nature; they differ from each other with respect to their cognitive abilities [1]. Cronbach [10] claimed that human heterogeneity is actually a major disturbance in the conduction of empirical studies. Cognitive variability has thus been mostly considered as an undesirable random noise in cognitive studies. This disturbance is even more problematic in the case of empirical studies that evaluate complex cognitive processes such as logical thinking and reasoning. Indeed, the inherent difficulty of such tasks not only emphasizes human differences relative to pure cognitive abilities (such as intelligence), but also involves motivational aspects that are crucial to obtain a reliable performance from the participant [25]. In order to test the cognitive plausibility of abstract argumentation theory by minimizing unwanted bias purely related to cognition and motivation properties, we set up a methodology that favored rational thinking during the assessment.

Previous results showed that individual performance, which has generally been reported to be quite poor in pure logic and reasoning tasks, could actually be enhanced by cooperative discussion with peers. For instance, faced with the Wason selection task [24], humans solving the task in groups achieved a level of insight that was qualitatively superior to the one achieved by single individuals [2,15]. Additionally, and more generally, discussion with peers was shown to substantially improve motivation to solve a given task [18]. For these reasons, we decided to incorporate in our methodology a cooperative discussion to help participants to elaborate and enrich their thinking. This collective step with peers was designed to obtain an evaluation of the justification status more reliable than a single individual judgment. Such reliability is crucial to test the cognitive plausibility of our predictions.

4   Design of the Study

Sixty-one undergraduate students participated in the empirical study (mean age = 20.8). With the help of a questionnaire, we asked our participants to evaluate the acceptability status of natural language arguments. The argument sets were set in the following fictional context: participants were located on an imaginary island, faced to conflicting information coming from various islanders, and they had to evaluate the arguments provided in order to hopefully find the location(s) of the buried treasure(s). We used such a fictional scenario to avoid as much as possible any unwanted interference from their general knowledge to make a decision about the acceptability of a given argument.

All the attacks between the arguments were based on information that a certain islander is not trustworthy. Consider for example the following set of arguments that we used in the study:

Argument G: Islander Greg says that islander Hans is not trustworthy and that there is a treasure buried in front of the well. So we should not trust what Hans says, and we should dig up the sand in front of the well.

Argument H: Islander Hans says that islander Irina is not trustworthy and that there is a treasure buried behind the bridge. So we should not trust what Irina says, and we should dig up the sand behind the bridge.

Argument I: Islander Irina says that there is a treasure buried near the northern tip of the island. So we should dig up the sand near the northern tip of the island.

Argument J: Islander Jenny says that there is a treasure buried near the southern tip of the island. So we should dig up the sand near the southern tip of the island.

Here argument G attacks argument H, because argument H is based on information from islander Hans, and argument G states that islander Hans is not trustworthy. Similarly, argument H attacks argument I, whereas arguments I and J do not attack any argument because they do not state that someone is not trustworthy. (Note that participants were informed that there might be multiple treasures, so there is no conflict between a treasure being in one place and a treasure being in another.)

As the natural language arguments where quite long and complex, we presented to the participants not only the natural language arguments, but also a graphical visualization of the corresponding AF. For example, Fig. 1 depicts the AF corresponding to the natural language argument set presented above.

$$G \longrightarrow H \longrightarrow I \qquad J$$

Fig. 1. Graphical visualization of the AF corresponding to the natural language arguments G, H, I and J.

Before the start of the questionnaire, we showed to the participants examples of three simple AFs of two arguments each, namely a unilateral attack from an argument to another one, a bilateral attack between two arguments, and two arguments without any attack between them. These examples were presented both as sets of natural language arguments and as graphically depicted AFs, and the correspondence between these two modes of presentation were explained.

Participants were instructed to make a judgment about each argument by ticking a box labeled *accept, undecided* or *reject*. For the purpose of making these judgments, participants were explicitly instructed to follow the principle that they trust an islander as long as they do not have a good reason to believe that this islander is not trustworthy. We explained these three possible judgments on the six arguments from the three simple AFs that we showed as examples. Note that on these simple AFs, the justification status of each argument is the same in each of the six semantics considered in this paper, so that our explanations about these examples did not prime the participants to favor one of the semantics over the others.

Similarly as in our previous study [8], our methodology incorporated a group discussion to stimulate more rational thinking: Participants had to first respond individually to each argument from an argument set, then in a second step they had to collaboratively discuss with their peers about the set under consideration, and finally they had to make a final individual judgment. We formed twenty groups of mostly three participants each (exceptionally two or four participants). The questionnaire had two versions, each consisting in six different AFs, for a total of twelve argument frameworks. The full set of the argument sets used in our study can be found in the technical report of this paper [9].

5 Results and Discussion

Figure 2 summarizes both the theoretical predictions and the final individual response of participants in our study. In the first six columns of the figure, we explicitly represent the justification status of each argument with respect to each of the six semantics considered in this paper. We depict the justification status *strongly accepted* as a white square, *strongly rejected* as a black square, and *undecided* as a gray square. In the next two columns, we have depicted the proportion of different responses made by the participants as well as the majority response. With the exception of argument 59, the arguments had a unique majority response, i.e. a response chosen more often than each of the other two responses, which is depicted by one of the three pure colors defined above. In the case of argument 59, *reject* and *undecided* were equally frequent responses, so the majority response square is depicted half black and half gray.

In a first analysis, we assessed which semantics was the best to predict human evaluation of the acceptability of our natural language arguments. We computed the percentage of agreement between the predictions of each semantics and the final responses made by all participants. Predictions according to grounded semantics were correct in 74.07%, preferred in 68.42%, semi-stable in 62.84%, CF2 in 75.46%, stage in 62.79%, and stage2 in 68.36% of the cases. Exact binomial tests revealed that for all semantics, the proportion of correct predictions were significantly larger than the chance level (i.e., 33%), all $ps < .001$. It is noteworthy that, in many cases, the semantics make the same prediction, so to evaluate the significance of the difference between any two semantics, we should not consider the general predictive accuracy, but rather focus on the instances where the two semantics under consideration differed. We thus conducted exact binomial tests between each pair of semantics, restricting to the arguments where different predictions were provided, and we observed that both grounded and CF2 were systematically better than the other semantics, all $ps < .001$. However, grounded and CF2 did not significantly differ from each other, $p = .212$. In other words, across all our participants, grounded and CF2 semantics were the semantics providing the best predictions.

In order to get a better picture of the cognitive strategies employed by participants to evaluate arguments, we made some additional analysis of the data. We observed that participants mostly responded in a way that is coherent in the sense defined at the end of Sect. 2. More precisely, 86.7% of the responses were coherent, and 49 of the 61 participants (i.e. 80.3% of the participants)

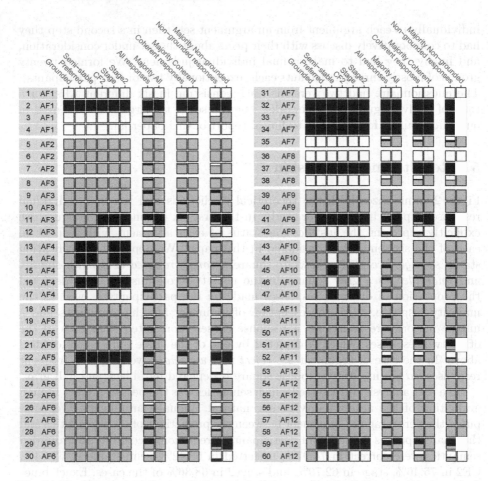

Fig. 2. Visualization of the predictions and of the results. Each line represents one of the 60 arguments in our study. The squares represent theoretical predictions according to the six semantics and as well as final individual responses (average response and majority response) in three categories of participants: all participants, coherent participants and coherent non-grounded participants. White, black and gray stand for *accept*, *reject* and *undecided* respectively. For representing the proportion of different responses, the corresponding square has been filled with white, gray and black area in proportion to the number of *accept*, *reject* and *undecided* judgments made by the participants.

had more than 80% coherent responses. Recall that the notion of coherence was based on properties that are satisfied in all semantics considered in this paper, so these results show that participants were mostly able to use cognitive strategies that are in line with these semantics-independent properties. We hypothesize that those 12 participants who had more than 20% incoherent responses either did non fully understand the task or are outliers with respect to the cognitive strategy they employed. As we were interested in understanding the cognitive strategies employed by the majority of participants, we decided to disregard these 12 participants in the further analysis of our data. We use the expression *coherent participants* to refer to the 49 participants that had more than 80% coherent responses. The average and majority responses of coherent participants are depicted in Fig. 2 in the two columns that are to the right of the columns depicting the responses of all participants.

Within coherent participants, predictions according to grounded semantics were correct in 82.79%, preferred in 75.17%, semi-stable in 68.10%, CF2 in 82.24%, stage in 67.14%, and stage2 in 74.22% of the cases. A paired t-test revealed that the predictions here were significantly better than the predictions across all participants, $t(5) = 12.38, p < .001$. This is in line with our hypothesis that the identified and excluded 12 participants were outliers. Once again, grounded and CF2 were the two best semantics, as confirmed by exact binomial tests restricting to the arguments for which the predictions differed, relevant $ps < .001$, and they did not significantly differ from each other, $p = .187$. Subsequently, within coherent participants, and similarly to our findings within all participants, grounded and CF2 were the best semantics to predict human responses.

Furthermore, we would like to point out that in the grounded semantics, 48 of the 60 arguments in our study were undecided. For this reason, the general strategy of choosing *undecided* whenever there is some reason for doubt was a cognitively simple way to get full or almost full agreement with the prediction of grounded semantics. While it is an interesting observation that a significant number of participants chose this strategy for the task in our study, we were also interested in understanding better the cognitive strategy of those who did not make use of this simplifying general strategy. In order to get some insights about this cognitive strategy, we decided to make some additional analysis of our data restricted to those coherent participants that did not employ this grounded-leaning general strategy. For this purpose, we had to define a criterion for deciding who counts as not having applied the grounded-leaning general strategy. We chose to use the following criterion: If a participant made at least one coherent response that was not the response predicted by the grounded semantics, we considered this participant a *non-grounded participant*. Of the 49 coherent participants, 27 were non-grounded participants according to this criterion, while 22 participants were *grounded participants*. The average and majority responses of coherent non-grounded participants are depicted in the two last columns of Fig. 2.

Within coherent non-grounded participants, predictions according to grounded semantics were correct in 73.09%, preferred in 73.70%, semi-stable in 65.80%, CF2 in 79.75%, stage in 67.04%, and stage2 in 74.94% of the cases. In this case, CF2 alone was the best predictor in comparison to every other semantics, with the largest $p = .001$. This result provides further insights about the cognitive strategies adopted by participants: While grounded and CF2 semantics both provide adequate predictions of the human evaluation of the acceptability of the arguments, this is actually due to heterogeneous behavior from our participants. Our results suggest that 27 non-grounded participants used a more demanding cognitive strategy well predicted by CF2 whereas the other 22 grounded participants used a more straightforward strategy well predicted by grounded semantics.

We would like to point out that the only two arguments in which some semantics other than CF2 predicted the judgments of coherent non-grounded participants better than CF2 were arguments 59 and 60 according to the numbering used in Fig. 2, which were arguments I and J in the AF depicted in Fig. 3. While in CF2 and grounded semantics both of these arguments are weakly undecided, in preferred, semi-stable, stage and stage2 semantics, I is strongly rejected and J is strongly accepted.

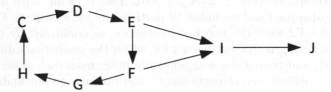

Fig. 3. AF in which other semantics made better prediction than CF2

Note that this AF contains a six-cycle, and the behavior of CF2 on a six-cycle was criticized by Dvořák and Gaggl [13] as unintuitive and used as a motivation for introducing stage2 semantics. We included this AF in our study to test whether this criticism on CF2 semantics is in line with human judgments on such AFs, and our data does indeed support this criticism on CF2. However, all other arguments on which the predictions of CF2 and stage2 differed were judged by most coherent non-grounded participants more in line with CF2 than in line with stage2, so our data does not support stage2 as a good alternative to CF2.

Taken together, this suggests that for the goal of predicting well human argument acceptance, it might be necessary to develop a novel semantics that behaves similarly to CF2 on most argumentation frameworks considered in our study but which treats even cycles of length 6 or more in the way they are treated by preferred, semi-stable, stage and stage2 semantics rather than in the way they are treated by CF2 semantics.

6   Related Work

While there have been multiple empirical studies that have evaluated the correspondence between human reasoning and formalism from abstract, structured and dialogical argumentation (see for example [6,16,19,22]), only two previous studies have aimed at comparing human evaluation of arguments to abstract argumentation semantics: Rahwan *et al.* [20] tested how humans evaluate two simple argumentation frameworks, the *simple reinstatement* framework with three arguments and the *floating reinstatement* framework with four arguments.

In a recent paper [8], the authors of the present study have improved Rahwan et al.'s methodology and applied this improved methodology to three different argumentation frameworks, namely the two AFs already considered by Rahwan as well as the *3-cycle reinstatement* framework with five arguments.

Since the simple reinstatement framework is treated in the same way by all standard semantics, in Rahwan et al.'s study only the floating reinstatement framework was able to distinguish between different semantics. While this allowed Rahwan et al. to conclude that for the floating reinstatement argumentation frameworks the preferred semantics predicts human evaluation of arguments better than the grounded semantics, it did not allow to distinguish preferred semantics from other non-grounded semantics like semi-stable, stage or CF2. By including the 3-cycle reinstatement framework in our previous study, we were able to observe that naive-based semantics like CF2, stage or stage2 are better predictors for human argument evaluation than admissibility-based semantics like preferred or semi-stable (see [8]). However, the AFs used in that study still did not allow to distinguish between the different naive-based semantics, nor did they allow to distinguish preferred from semi-stable semantics. The present study was designed to overcome this limitation.

We now compare the results from the present paper with those from our recent paper [8]. The current study confirmed the result of the previous study that CF2 semantics is a better predictor for human argument evaluation than preferred semantics, and extended this result by also showing that CF2 is a better predictor than semi-stable, stage, stage2 semantics. The previous study had additionally suggested that both preferred and CF2 semantics are better predictors than grounded semantics, whereas the current study suggests that grounded semantics is as good a predictor as CF2 semantics. We believe that the main reason for this apparent mismatch lies in the fact that our present study used more complex argumentation frameworks and instantiated them with a fictional scenario, which made the reasoning task cognitively more challenging and therefore led to more participants making use of the simplifying strategy of choosing *undecided* whenever there is some reason for doubt.

Both Rahwan et al.'s study and our previous study made use of natural language arguments that referred to real-world entities and actions rather than to a purely fictional scenario as in the present study. While this reference to real-world entities and actions reduces the cognitive load for participants, it also allows them to make use of their world knowledge in judging the arguments. But as the goal of these studies was to predict argument evaluation based on the attack relation between arguments rather than based on the content of the argument and the world knowledge of the participants, this interference of world knowledge was undesirable. By making use of a fictional scenario in the present study we avoided this undesirable feature of the previous studies.

7 Conclusion and Future Work

In this paper we have reported on an empirical cognitive study in which we tested how humans judge the acceptability of arguments in complex argumentation frameworks. A detailed analysis of our results revealed that part of the participants chose a cognitively simpler strategy that is predicted very well by grounded semantics, while another part of the participants chose a cognitively more demanding strategy that is mostly predicted well by CF2 semantics.

The present study suggests multiple paths for future research. As for future research within formal argumentation, our study suggests that researchers in this field who are interested in developing formalisms that correspond well to human argumentation should direct their attention more to CF2 and similarly-behaved semantics. More precisely, given that the cognitively more demanding strategy was predicted well by CF2 semantics with the exception of the AF involving a six-cycle, it seems worthwhile to develop and study novel semantics that behave similarly to CF2 on most argumentation frameworks considered in our study but which treat even cycles of length 6 or more in the way they are treated by preferred, semi-stable, stage and stage2 semantics rather than in the way they are treated by CF2 semantics. Furthermore, given that in the context of structured argumentation frameworks like ASPIC+ (see [17]) the rationality postulate of *Closure under Strict Rules* is violated for not admissibility-based semantics like CF2, further research is required to find a method to satisfy this rationality postulate in structured argumentation while using an argumentation semantics that corresponds well to human judgments on argument acceptability.

As for future empirical work related to the work presented in this paper, it would be good to empirically test whether our tentative explanation that we have given in Sect. 6 for explaining the mismatch between the current study and our previous study (see [8]) is correct. Furthermore, it would be good if some future empirical study could overcome a limitation that all existing empirical studies on abstract argumentation theory have, namely the limitation that they can only compare the semantics on the single-outcome justification status, thus ignoring some of the information present in the full set of extensions provided by each semantics. For overcoming this limitation, a novel approach to designing empirical cognitive studies for testing argumentation semantics needs to be developed.

References

1. Anastasi, A.: Differential Psychology: Individual and Group Differences in Behavior. Macmillan, London (1958)
2. Augustinova, M.: Falsification cueing in collective reasoning: example of the Wason selection task. Eur. J. Soc. Psychol. **38**(5), 770–785 (2008)
3. Baroni, P., Caminada, M., Giacomin, M.: An introduction to argumentation semantics. Knowl. Eng. Rev. **26**(4), 365–410 (2011)
4. Baroni, P., Caminada, M., Giacomin, M.: Abstract argumentation frameworks and their semantics. In: Baroni, P., Gabbay, D., Giacomin, M., van der Torre, L. (eds.) Handbook of Formal Argumentation, pp. 159–236. College Publications (2018)
5. Baroni, P., Giacomin, M., Guida, G.: SCC-recursiveness: a general schema for argumentation semantics. Artif. Intell. **168**(1), 162–210 (2005)

6. Cerutti, F., Tintarev, N., Oren, N.: Formal arguments, preferences, and natural language interfaces to humans: an empirical evaluation. In: Schaub, T., Friedrich, G., O'Sullivan, B. (eds.) Proceedings of the 21st ECAI 2014, pp. 207–212 (2014)

7. Cramer, M., Guillaume, M.: Directionality of attacks in natural language argumentation. In: Schon, C. (ed.) Proceedings of the Workshop on Bridging the Gap between Human and Automated Reasoning, vol. 2261, pp. 40–46. RWTH Aachen University, CEUR-WS.org (2018). http://ceur-ws.org/Vol-2261/

8. Cramer, M., Guillaume, M.: Empirical cognitive study on abstract argumentation semantics. Frontiers in Artificial Intelligence and Applications, pp. 413–424 (2018)

9. Cramer, M., Guillaume, M.: Technical report of "Empirical study on human evaluation of complex argumentation frameworks". arXiv:1902.10552, February 2019

10. Cronbach, L.J.: The two disciplines of scientific psychology. Am. Psychol. **12**(11), 671–684 (1957)

11. Dung, P.M.: On the acceptability of arguments and its fundamental role in non-monotonic reasoning, logic programming and n-person games. Artif. Intell. **77**(2), 321–357 (1995)

12. Dvořák, W., Gaggl, S.A.: Incorporating stage semantics in the SCC-recursive schema for argumentation semantics. In: Proceedings of the 14th International Workshop on Non-Monotonic Reasoning (NMR 2012) (2012)

13. Dvořák, W., Gaggl, S.A.: Stage semantics and the SCC-recursive schema for argumentation semantics. J. Log. Comput. **26**(4), 1149–1202 (2016)

14. Evans, J.S.B., Newstead, S.E., Byrne, R.M.: Human Reasoning: The Psychology of Deduction. Psychology Press, London (1993)

15. Geil, D.M.M.: Collaborative reasoning: evidence for collective rationality. Think. Reason. **4**(3), 231–248 (1998)

16. Hunter, A., Polberg, S.: Empirical methods for modelling persuadees in dialogical argumentation. In: 29th International Conference on Tools with Artificial Intelligence (ICTAI), pp. 382–389. IEEE (2017)

17. Modgil, S., Prakken, H.: The ASPIC+ framework for structured argumentation: a tutorial. Argum. Comput. **5**(1), 31–62 (2014)

18. Piaget, J., Smith, L., Brown, T., Campbell, R., Emler, N., Ferrari, D.: Sociological Studies. Routledge, London (1995)

19. Polberg, S., Hunter, A.: Empirical evaluation of abstract argumentation: supporting the need for bipolar and probabilistic approaches. Int. J. Approx. Reason. **93**, 487–543 (2018)

20. Rahwan, I., Madakkatel, M.I., Bonnefon, J.-F., Awan, R.N., Abdallah, S.: Behavioral experiments for assessing the abstract argumentation semantics of reinstatement. Cogn. Sci. **34**(8), 1483–1502 (2010)

21. Rahwan, I., Simari, G.R.: Argumentation in Artificial Intelligence, 1st edn. Springer, Boston (2009). https://doi.org/10.1007/978-0-387-98197-0

22. Rosenfeld, A., Kraus, S.: Providing arguments in discussions on the basis of the prediction of human argumentative behavior. ACM Trans. Interact. Intell. Syst. **6**(4), 30:1–30:33 (2016)

23. Verheij, B.: Two approaches to dialectical argumentation: admissible sets and argumentation stages. Proc. NAIC **96**, 357–368 (1996)

24. Wason, P.C.: Reasoning. In: Foss, B. (ed.) New Horizons in Psychology, pp. 135–151. Penguin Books, Harmondsworth (1966)

25. Weiner, B.: Theories of Motivation: From Mechanism to Cognition. Markham Psychology Series. Markham Publishing Co., Chicago (1972)

26. Wu, Y., Caminada, M.: A labelling-based justification status of arguments. Stud. Log. **3**(4), 12–29 (2010)

Preprocessing Argumentation Frameworks via Replacement Patterns

Wolfgang Dvořák[1](✉)[iD], Matti Järvisalo[2][iD], Thomas Linsbichler[1][iD],
Andreas Niskanen[2][iD], and Stefan Woltran[1][iD]

[1] Institute of Logic and Computation, TU Wien, Vienna, Austria
dvorak@dbai.tuwien.ac.at
[2] HIIT, Department of Computer Science, University of Helsinki, Helsinki, Finland

Abstract. A fast-growing research direction in the study of formal argumentation is the development of practical systems for central reasoning problems underlying argumentation. In particular, numerous systems for abstract argumentation frameworks (AF solvers) are available today, covering several argumentation semantics and reasoning tasks. Instead of proposing another algorithmic approach for AF solving, we introduce in this paper distinct AF preprocessing techniques as a solver-independent approach to obtaining performance improvements of AF solvers. We establish a formal framework of replacement patterns to perform local simplifications that are faithful with respect to standard semantics for AFs. Moreover, we provide a collection of concrete replacement patterns. Towards potential applicability, we employ the patterns in a preliminary empirical evaluation of their influence on AF solver performance.

Keywords: Abstract argumentation · Preprocessing ·
Extension enumeration

1 Introduction

Argumentation is today a vibrant area of modern AI research [4]. In particular, the study of computational aspects of argumentation connects with several AI subfields such as knowledge representation, constraints, and complexity of reasoning. The development of practical systems and algorithmic solutions for central reasoning problems underlying argumentation is motivated by a range of applications [1].

Abstract argumentation offers argumentation frameworks (AFs) as an important graph-based knowledge representation formalism for argumentation [9]. Computational models of argumentation, in particular from the perspective of the development of practical algorithms, have recently received a lot of attention. Several optimized practical AF reasoning systems (AF solvers) are available today [6], covering several argumentation semantics and reasoning tasks such as enumeration and skeptical and credulous query answering. The various state-of-the-art AF solvers, developed by several research groups around the world, are

F. Calimeri et al. (Eds.): JELIA 2019, LNAI 11468, pp. 116–132, 2019.
https://doi.org/10.1007/978-3-030-19570-0_8

evaluated in the biennially organized ICCMA AF solver competitions [13,22], providing further incentives for seeking improvements in AF solver technology.

While both specialized and constraint-based AF solvers have been developed, less attention has been so far put on the development of preprocessing and simplification techniques working directly on AFs. This is despite the fact that polynomial-time preprocessing (rewriting) has been shown to bring great practical performance improvements in various constraint solving paradigms [11,14,17–20]. Notably, preprocessing techniques applied before invoking a solver for the reasoning task at hand are *solver-independent*. Thereby the development of practical preprocessing techniques has the potential of improving the performance of various solvers. As proven to be the case in the area of propositional reasoning [18], applying combinations of relatively simple individual preprocessing techniques can have a surprisingly significant positive effect on solver performance.

In this work, we take first steps in solver-independent preprocessing for AFs. By preprocessing we understand a family of polynomial-time applicable simplification rules which preserve an appropriate form of equivalence. In the domain of AFs this amounts to searching for particular sub-AFs that can be replaced by a smaller and/or simpler AF without changing the semantics of the whole AF. However, the nonmonotonic nature of AF semantics makes the understanding of such replacements non-trivial. In addition, we aim for removing arguments that cannot be accepted and for merging arguments that can only be jointly accepted. Since preprocessing itself should rely on efficient polynomial-time algorithms, we cannot include any semantic treatment of AFs or sub-AFs into the procedures.

To this end, we introduce the concept of *replacement patterns* which contain information about (i) which AFs need to be matched on subgraphs of the AF at hand, and (ii) how to simplify them independently of the surrounding framework. The recently introduced notion of *C-relativized equivalence* [5] provides a suitable tool to prove faithfulness of such simplifications. However, we need to extend this notion properly in order to also capture the concept of merging of arguments in a formally sound way. Our formal results refine equivalence results for AFs with merged arguments and show how these can be used to show faithfulness of our patterns. Consequently, AFs obtained by iterative applications of replacement patterns are equivalent to the original AF one started with, which makes them applicable even for the task of extension enumeration.

An alternative approach to local simplifications of AFs is the S-equivalence of multipoles [2]. However, S-equivalence treats the part of the AF to be replaced as "black-box" and thus allows for changes in the extensions w.r.t. arguments which are not in the IO-interface of the multipole. As our work is focusing on replacements that preserve the extensions of the AF we thus follow and extend the approach of [5].

The preprocessed AFs obtained via applications of replacement patterns can be input to any state-of-the-art AF solver for obtaining solutions to enumeration and reasoning tasks over the original input AF. After obtaining a solution to the preprocessed AF, the only additional tasks to be performed is to reconstruct actual arguments from merged arguments, which is straightforward for our replacement patterns.

We provide a set of concrete polynomial-time checkable replacement patterns which we consider as a first suite of solver-independent AF preprocessing techniques for stable, preferred, and complete semantics. We further study the impact of our preprocessing routine via a preliminary empirical evaluation on both two state-of-the-art native AF solvers [15,21] and a SAT-based AF solver [10,12] on the task of extension enumeration. Our results reveal that in particular the native solvers can highly benefit from preprocessing; also the performance of constraint-based solvers can be improved at times. Hence preprocessing appears promising for further closing the current performance gap [8] between state-of-the-art native and constraint-based solvers, and the first empirical results presented motivate further studies of practical preprocessing techniques for different AF reasoning tasks, including acceptance problems where preprocessing needs not to preserve all extensions, in constrast to extension enumeration.

The paper is organized as follows. We first recall abstract argumentation and the notion of C-relativized equivalence (Sect. 2). Next, we introduce *replacement patterns* as a formal framework for studying faithful simplifications of AFs, and extend the notion of C-relativized equivalence to allow for formally establishing faithfulness of replacement patterns (Sect. 3.1). We then provide concrete replacement patterns for preprocessing AFs (Sect. 3.2). Finally, we present an empirical evaluation of the presented patterns (Sect. 4).

2   Argumentation Frameworks and Equivalence

We recall abstract argumentation frameworks [9], their semantics (see [3] for an overview), and the notion of C-relativized equivalence [5] which we will employ to show the faithfulness of replacements. We fix U as a countably infinite domain of arguments.

Definition 1. *An* argumentation framework (AF) *is a pair* $F = (A, R)$ *where* $A \subseteq U$ *is a finite set of arguments and* $R \subseteq A \times A$ *is the attack relation. The pair* $(a, b) \in R$ *means that a attacks b. We use A_F to refer to A and R_F to refer to R. We say that an AF is given over a set B of arguments if $A_F \subseteq B$.*

Definition 2. *Given an AF F and set $S \subseteq A_F$, we define* $S_F^+ = \{x \mid \exists y \in S : (y, x) \in R_F\}$, $S_F^- = \{x \mid \exists y \in S : (x, y) \in R_F\}$, *and the* range *of S in F as* $S_F^\oplus = S \cup S_F^+$.

The following adaptions of set-theoretic operators to pairs of AFs will be useful in the rest of the paper.

Definition 3. *Given AFs* $F = (A, R)$, $F' = (A', R')$, *we denote the* union *of AFs as* $F \cup F' = (A \cup A', R \cup R')$. *For a set $S \subseteq U$ of arguments, and a set $T \subseteq (A \times A)$ of attacks, we define* $F \setminus S = (A \setminus S, R \cap ((A \setminus S) \times (A \setminus S)))$, $F \setminus T = (A, R \setminus T)$, $F \cap S = (A \cap S, R \cap ((A \cap S) \times (A \cap S)))$, $F \cup S = (A \cup S, R)$, *and* $F \cup T = (A, R \cup T)$. *For mixed sets $S \cup T$ of arguments S and attacks T we define* $F \setminus (S \cup T) = (F \setminus T) \setminus S$.

We next give a formal definition of sub-AFs. In words, a sub-AF is an induced subgraph of the directed graph representation of an AF.

Definition 4. *We call an AF F to be a* sub-AF *of G, in symbols $F \sqsubseteq G$, if $A_F \subseteq A_G$ and $R_F = R_G \cap (A_F \times A_F)$.*

Replacement is a central notion in this work, and intuitively defines substitutions of a sub-AF with another.

Definition 5. *Given AFs F, F', G such that $F \sqsubseteq G$ and $A_{F'} \cap (A_G \setminus A_F) = \emptyset$, let $A = (A_G \setminus A_F) \cup A_{F'}$. The* replacement *of F by F' in G is defined as $G[F/F'] = (A, ((R_G \setminus R_F) \cap (A \times A)) \cup R_{F'})$.*

Semantics for AFs are defined based on the notions of defense and the characteristic function.

Definition 6. *Given an AF $F = (A, R)$, argument $a \in A$ is* defended *(in F) by a set $S \subseteq A$ if $\{a\}_F^- \subseteq S_F^+$. The* characteristic function $\mathcal{F}_F : 2^A \rightarrow 2^A$ *of F is defined as $\mathcal{F}_F(S) = \{a \in A \mid a$ is defended by S in $F\}$.*

Semantics are functions σ which assign to each AF F a set $\sigma(F) \subseteq 2^{A_F}$ of extensions. We consider for σ the functions *stb*, *com*, and *prf*, which stand for stable, complete, and preferred semantics, respectively.

Definition 7. *Let $F = (A, R)$ be an AF. A set $S \subseteq A$ is* conflict-free *(in F), if there are no $a, b \in S$ such that $(a, b) \in R$. $cf(F)$ denotes the collection of conflict-free sets of F. For a conflict-free set $S \in cf(F)$, it holds that*

- *$S \in stb(F)$, if $S_F^\oplus = A$;*
- *$S \in com(F)$, if $S = \mathcal{F}_F(S)$;*
- *$S \in prf(F)$, if $S \in com(F)$ and $\nexists T \supset S$ s.t. $T \in com(F)$.*

Under a standard notion, two AFs are equivalent under a semantics iff they have the same extensions.

Definition 8. *We call two AFs F and G to be* equivalent in semantics σ, *in symbols $F \equiv^\sigma G$, iff $\sigma(F) = \sigma(G)$.*

Baumann et al. [5] have studied the following refined notion of equivalence, which is sensitive to expansions as long as they do not affect a certain core of arguments.

Definition 9. *Given a semantics σ and $C \subseteq U$. Two AFs F and G are C-relativized equivalent w.r.t. σ ($F \equiv_C^\sigma G$) iff $F \cup H \equiv^\sigma G \cup H$ holds for each AF H over $U \setminus C$.*

In order to decide whether two AFs are C-relativized equivalent, C-restricted semantics have been introduced. Those restrict the relevant properties of the original semantics to the core arguments C. We present these concepts in detail for stable semantics, on which we shall focus in the remainder of the paper.

Definition 10. *Let F be an AF, $C \subseteq U$ and $E \subseteq A_F$. We have that $E \in stb_C(F)$ if $E \in cf(F)$ and $A_F \cap C \subseteq E_F^{\oplus}$.*

That is, for C-restricted stable extensions we relax the conditions for stable semantics such that, beside the extension being conflict-free, we only require that all arguments in the core are in the range of the extension.

We have that two AFs F, G can only be C-relativized equivalent w.r.t. a semantics σ if they have exactly the same C-restricted σ extensions. However, this is only a necessary but not a sufficient condition. We additionally require that, except for arguments in the core C, the AFs F, G have the same arguments and for stable semantics that all C-restricted stable extensions have the same range in F and G when ignoring the core arguments C.

Theorem 1 [5]. *Let F, G be AFs and $C \subseteq U$. Then, $F \equiv_C^{stb} G$ iff the following jointly hold:*

1. *if $stb_C(F) \neq \emptyset$, $A_F \setminus C = A_G \setminus C$;*
2. *$stb_C(F) = stb_C(G)$; and*
3. *for all $E \in stb_C(F)$, $E_F^+ \setminus C = E_G^+ \setminus C$.*

3   Replacement Patterns

The idea behind the notion of replacement patterns is to allow for some freedom in the subgraphs we are looking for to apply simplifications. For example, often the existence of certain attacks does not affect the applicability of replacements; a specific replacement pattern defines similar graphs that qualify for replacements. In what follows, we first introduce the formal framework of replacement patterns and show how faithfulness of patterns can be achieved using the notion of C-relativized equivalence. Then we present concrete replacement patterns for preprocessing AFs.

3.1   Main Concepts

A central ingredient of replacement patterns is merging of arguments, resulting in arguments of the form m_S with $S \subseteq U$ being standard arguments. The universe of all such arguments is given by $U_m = \{m_S \mid S \subseteq U, S \text{ is finite}\}$.

Definition 11. *Let $F = (A, R)$ be an AF and $a, b \in A$. The merge $\mathsf{M}(F, a, b)$ of a, b in F is the AF (A', R') given by $A' = A \setminus \{a, b\} \cup \{m_{\{a,b\}}\}^1$ and $R' = R \cap (A' \times A') \cup \{(m_{\{a,b\}}, c) \mid (a, c) \in R \text{ or } (b, c) \in R\} \cup \{(c, m_{\{a,b\}}) \mid (c, a) \in R \text{ or } (c, b) \in R\}$.*

The following two unpacking functions $\mathsf{U}(\cdot)$ map (i) a set of arguments over $U \cup U_m$ to the corresponding set of arguments in U, and (ii) an AF with merged arguments back to an AF over U.

---
[1] However, we keep the set structure flat, i.e., when merging arguments $m_S, m_{S'} \in U_m$ the resulting argument is $m_{S \cup S'}$.

Definition 12. *Let $F = (A, R)$ be an AF with $A \subseteq U \cup U_m$ and $E \subseteq A$. The unpacked set $\mathsf{U}(E)$ of E is given by $(E \cap U) \cup \bigcup_{m_S \in E} S$. The unpacked AF $\mathsf{U}(F)$ of F is the AF (A', R') given by $A' = \mathsf{U}(A)$ and $R' = R \cap (A' \times A') \cup \{(a, c) \mid (m_S, c) \in R, a \in S\} \cup \{(c, a) \mid (c, m_S) \in R, a \in S\} \cup \{(a, c) \mid (m_S, m_{S'}) \in R, a \in S, c \in S'\}$.*

Notice that $\mathsf{U}(F)$ is always an AF over U. In the next step we generalize standard equivalence by taking into account AFs which have resulted from merging of arguments. That is we do not compare extensions directly but consider AFs to be equivalent if their unpacked extensions coincide.

Definition 13. *We call two AFs F and G over $U \cup U_m$ to be equivalent in semantics σ, in symbols $F \equiv^\sigma G$, iff $\{\mathsf{U}(E) \mid E \in \sigma(F)\} = \{\mathsf{U}(E) \mid E \in \sigma(G)\}$.*

We are now ready to give a formal notion of a replacement pattern. In order to define a replacement for a class of (similar) graphs instead of just a single graph in our replacement pattern we have to define a replacement for each of the graphs in the class. That is, a replacement pattern P_C consists of pairs (F, F') that coincide on arguments not in C. When applying such a pattern P_C to a larger AF G some sub-AF M of G that is isomorphic to F is replaced by a graph isomorphic to F'. We first give a formal definition of replacement patterns and then define how to apply such patterns to AFs.

Definition 14 (Replacement pattern). *A replacement pattern P_C for $C \subseteq U$ is a set of pairs (F, F') of AFs F, F' such that $A_F \subseteq U$, $A_{F'} \subseteq U \cup U_m$, and F and F' coincide on the arguments not contained in $C_m = C \cup \{m_S \mid S \subseteq C\}$, i.e., a replacement pattern is of the form*

$$P_C = \{(F, F') \mid F, F' \text{ AFs}, F \setminus C = F' \setminus C_m\},$$

such that for any $(F_1, F'_1), (F_2, F'_2) \in P_C$, $F_1 \neq F_2$.

For preprocessing, we need to detect an instantiation of a pattern P_C as what we call C-encircling sub-AF of an AF G, i.e. a sub-AF F such that C might be connected to F but is not connected to $G \setminus F$, and then apply the pattern in the form of a replacement.

Definition 15 (C-encircling sub-AF). *An AF F is a C-encircling sub-AF of an AF G if (i) $F \sqsubseteq G$ and (ii) $C_G^\oplus \cup C_G^- \subseteq A_F$, i.e., C is not connected to $A_{G \setminus F}$ in G.*

Now a match of a pattern $P_C = \{(F_i, F'_i) \mid 1 \leq i \leq k\}$ on G is a C'-encircling sub-AF I of G that is isomorphic to some F_i where C' is the image of C under the isomorphism from F_i to I.

Definition 16 (Applying P_C). *Given AF G and pattern P_C, a match of P_C on G is a tuple (F, F', I, α), where $(F, F') \in P_C$, I is a C'-encircling sub-AF of G, and I is isomorphic to F via isomorphism $\alpha : A_F \to A_G$ such that $\alpha(C) = C'$. We say a pattern P_C can be applied to G if there exists a match of P_C on G.*

An application $P_C[G]$ of pattern P_C on G then picks a match (F, F', I, α) of P_C on G and returns $G[I/\alpha(F')]$, where α is extended to arguments m_S by mapping them to $m_{\alpha(S)}$.

The following example illustrates these concepts.

Example 1. Consider the replacement pattern $P_{\{a,b,c\}}^Y$ containing the pair (F, F') with $F = (\{a, b, c, d, e\}, \{(d, a), (a, b), (b, c), (c, e), (e, d)\})$ and $F' = \mathsf{M}(F \setminus \{(b, c)\}, a, c) = (\{m_{\{a,c\}}, b, d, e\}, \{(d, m_{\{a,c\}}), (m_{\{a,c\}}, b), (m_{\{a,c\}}, e), (e, d)\})$. Moreover, consider the AF G depicted in in Fig. 1 (left). Now observe that the tuple (F, F', I, α) is a match of $P_{\{a,b,c\}}^Y$ on G with $I = G \cap \{x_1, \dots, x_5\}$ and $\alpha = \{a \mapsto x_1, b \mapsto x_2, c \mapsto x_3, d \mapsto x_5, e \mapsto x_4\}$. Hence $P_{\{a,b,c\}}^Y$ can be applied to G, resulting in the AF $G[I/\alpha(F')] = G'$ depicted in Fig. 1 (center). For stable semantics, we can verify that this replacement is equivalence preserving, since $stb(G) = \{\{x_0, x_1, x_3\}\}$ and $stb(G') = \{\{x_0, m_{\{x_1,x_3\}}\}\}$, meaning that $\{\mathsf{U}(E) \mid E \in stb(G)\} = \{\mathsf{U}(E) \mid E \in stb(G')\} = \{\{x_0, x_1, x_3\}\}$. Note, however, that $\mathsf{U}(G') \neq G$, since $\mathsf{U}(G')$ contains the attacks (x_3, x_2), (x_5, x_3), and (x_1, x_4), which are not present in G. ◇

Naturally, a replacement pattern is faithful only if each of its possible applications is an equivalence-preserving modification.

Definition 17 (Faithful pattern). *A replacement pattern P_C is σ-faithful iff $P_C[G] \equiv^\sigma G$ for all G over $U \cup U_m$.*

Testing whether a replacement pattern is faithful can be reduced to testing C-relativized equivalence of the pairs of AFs covered by the pattern. This applies directly to patterns that do not involve the merging of arguments, and requires unpacking for patterns that do.

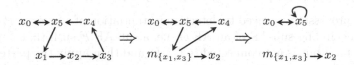

Fig. 1. Applying (i) the 3-path pattern (cf. Example 1) and (ii) the 3-loop pattern (cf. Example 3).

Theorem 2. *For semantics $\sigma \in \{stb, prf, com\}$ and replacement pattern P_C such that for each $(F, F') \in P_C$, $A_{F'} \cap S = \emptyset$ for $m_S \in A_{F'}$ and $S \cap S' = \emptyset$ for $m_S, m_{S'} \in A_{F'}$, the following statements are equivalent.*

1. P_C is σ-faithful.
2. $F \equiv_C^\sigma \mathsf{U}(F')$ for each $(F, F') \in P_C$.

We next continue our example to illustrate how one can use the above theorem in order to prove our pattern to be *stb*-faithful.

Example 2. Again consider the replacement pattern P_C^Y with $C = \{a, b, c\}$ from Example 1 and assume it contains just the pair (F, F'). Now observe that $\mathsf{U}(F') = F \setminus \{(b, c)\} \cup \{(a, e), (d, c), (c, b)\}$. It holds that (1) $A_F \setminus C = A_{\mathsf{U}(F')} \setminus C = \{d, e\}$, (2) $stb_C(F) = stb_C(\mathsf{U}(F')) = \{\{a, c\}, \{b, d\}\}$, and (3) $\{a, c\}_F^+ \setminus C = \{a, c\}_{\mathsf{U}(F')}^+ \setminus C = \{e\}$ and $\{b, d\}_F^+ \setminus C = \{b, d\}_{\mathsf{U}(F')}^+ \setminus C = \emptyset$. It thus holds that $F \equiv_C^{stb} \mathsf{U}(F')$ (cf. Theorem 1) and, by Theorem 2, that P_C^Y is stb-faithful. $\Diamond$

Proof of Theorem 2

In this section we provide a proof of Theorem 2. We call an AF that meets the conditions of Theorem 2 an *arg-unique* AF.

Definition 18. *An AF F over $U \cup U_m$ is called* arg-unique *if $A_F \cap S = \emptyset$ for $m_S \in A_F$ and $S \cap S' = \emptyset$ for $m_S, m_{S'} \in A_{F'}$.*

We first observe that two arg-unique AFs are equivalent iff their unpackings are equivalent. The proof of the lemma exploits the fact that the unpacked extensions of an arg-unique AF F coincide with the extensions of its unpacking $\mathsf{U}(F)$.

Lemma 1. *For semantics $\sigma \in \{stb, prf, com\}$, arg-unique AFs F, G over $U \cup U_m$ we have $F \equiv^\sigma G$ iff $\mathsf{U}(F) \equiv^\sigma \mathsf{U}(G)$.*

Proof. We show that $\sigma(\mathsf{U}(F)) = \{\mathsf{U}(E) \mid E \in \sigma(F)\}$ which implies the lemma.

$\subseteq$: Consider $E \in \sigma(\mathsf{U}(F))$ and an argument $m_S \in A_F \cap U_m$. As all arguments in S have the same attackers in $\mathsf{U}(F)$ we have that either $S \subseteq E$ or $S \cap E = \emptyset$. Now it is easy to verify that for the set $E' = \{a \mid a \in A_F \cap E\} \cup \{m_S \mid m_s \in A_F, S \subseteq E\}$ it holds that $E' \in \sigma(F)$ and $\mathsf{U}(E') = E$.

$\supseteq$: For $E \in \sigma(F)$ it is easy to verify that $\mathsf{U}(E) \in \sigma(\mathsf{U}(F))$. In particular, m_S is defended by E in F iff each $a \in S$ is defended by $\mathsf{U}(E)$ in $\mathsf{U}(F)$. $\square$

We next extend the notion of C-relativized equivalence to AFs over $U \cup U_m$.

Definition 19. *Given a semantics σ and $C \subseteq U \cup U_m$. Two AFs F and G over $U \cup U_m$ are* C-relativized equivalent *w.r.t. σ ($F \equiv_C^\sigma G$) iff $F \cup H \equiv^\sigma G \cup H$ for H over $(U \cup U_m) \setminus C$.*

Notice that if F, G are AFs over U the above notion coincides with the earlier notion of C-relativized equivalence. We next show that a pattern with core C is faithful iff the two AFs in each of the pattern's pairs are C_m-relativized equivalent.

Proposition 1. *For $C \subseteq U$ and $C_m = C \cup \{m_S \mid S \subseteq C\}$ the pattern P_C is σ-faithful iff $F \equiv_{C_m}^\sigma F'$ for each $(F, F') \in P_C$.*

Proof. $2 \Rightarrow (1)$ We have to show $P_C[G] \equiv^\sigma G$, for every G and every possible match. Consider a match (F, F', I, α). First notice that $F \equiv_{C_m}^\sigma F'$ implies $I = \alpha(F) \equiv_{C'}^\sigma \alpha(F') = I'$ (with $C' = \alpha(C)$) as the equivalence does not depend on the names of arguments from U, but only on whether they are in the core C, resp.

C', which is maintained by α. By the definition of $\equiv^\sigma_{C'}$ we have $I \cup H \equiv^\sigma I' \cup H$ for all H that do not contain arguments from C'_m. Finally, by setting $H = G \setminus C'$ we obtain that $P_C[G] \equiv^\sigma G$.

$1 \Rightarrow (2)$ If $F \not\equiv^\sigma_C F'$ for some $(F, F') \in P_C$ there is an AF H over $(U \cup U_m) \setminus (C \cup \{m_S \mid S \subseteq C\}$ such that $F \cup H \not\equiv^\sigma F' \cup H$. Now as there is a match with $P_C[F \cup H] = F' \cup H$ we obtain that P_C is not σ-faithful.   □

Finally, for arg-unique AFs the C-relativized equivalence tests for $(F, F') \in P_C$ can be reduced to C-relativized equivalence tests on AFs over U. That is, to the case already studied and well characterised in [5].

Lemma 2. *For semantics* $\sigma \in \{stb, prf, com\}$, *cores* $C \subseteq U$, $C_m = C \cup \{m_S \mid S \subseteq C\}$, *AF* F *over* U *and arg-unique AF* F' *over* $U \cup U_m$ *such that* $F \setminus C = F' \setminus C_m$, *the following statements are equivalent:*

1. $F \equiv^\sigma_{C_m} F'$.
2. $F \equiv^\sigma_C \mathsf{U}(F')$.

The proof of the lemma is based on the observation that given an AF H over $U \cup U_m$ such that $F \not\equiv^\sigma_{C_m} F'$, by exploiting Lemma 1 we can construct an AF H' over U showing $F \not\equiv^\sigma_C \mathsf{U}(F')$, and vice versa.

Proof. $2 \Rightarrow (1)$ W.l.o.g. assume there are E and H such that $E \in \sigma(F \cup H)$ but $E \notin \sigma(F' \cup H)$. It is easy to verify that $\mathsf{U}(F' \cup H) = \mathsf{U}(F') \cup \mathsf{U}(H)$ (notice that $F'_A \cap H_A \subseteq F_A \subseteq U$). By Lemma 1 we have $\mathsf{U}(F \cup H) \not\equiv^\sigma \mathsf{U}(F' \cup H)$. Thus there is an E' such that $E' \in \sigma(F \cup \mathsf{U}(H))$ but $E' \notin \sigma(\mathsf{U}(F') \cup \mathsf{U}(H))$, i.e., $\mathsf{U}(F) \cup \mathsf{U}(H) \not\equiv^\sigma \mathsf{U}(F') \cup \mathsf{U}(H)$. Moreover, by construction, $\mathsf{U}(H)$ does not contain arguments from $\mathsf{U}(C)$. Hence, $\mathsf{U}(F) \not\equiv^\sigma_{\mathsf{U}(C)} \mathsf{U}(F')$.

$1 \Rightarrow (2)$ W.l.o.g. assume there is a set E and an AF H such that $E \in \sigma(F \cup H)$ but $E \notin \sigma(\mathsf{U}(F') \cup H)$. As $A_F \setminus C = A_{F'} \setminus C_m$ the set $A_{F'} \setminus C_m$ does not contain merged arguments. Thus we have $\mathsf{U}(F') \cup H = \mathsf{U}(F' \cup H)$ and, by Lemma 1, we have $E \in \sigma(F \cup H)$ but $E \notin \sigma(\mathsf{U}(F') \cup H)$, i.e., $F \cup H \not\equiv F' \cup H$. Hence, $F \not\equiv^\sigma_{C_m} F'$.   □

Finally, Theorem 2 is immediate by combining Proposition 1 with Lemma 2.

3.2   Formalizing Concrete Patterns

We will now present our concrete replacement patterns. For this, we will use the concept of a *lagging*. Intuitively, for a given core-AF F a lagging F_L is an AF extending F by new arguments that either attack or are attacked by arguments in F. When defining our patterns we are typically interested in all laggings of a specific core-AF satisfying certain conditions.

Definition 20. *Given an AF* $F = (A, R)$, *a lagging of* F *is any AF* $F_L = (A', R')$ *with* $A \subseteq A'$ *such that* $F_L \cap A = F$ *and* $A^\oplus_{F_L} \cup A^-_{F_L} = A'$. *Given a lagging* F_L, *we sometimes refer to* F *as the core-AF.*

For instance, the AF F in the pattern of Example 1 is a lagging of the. AF $(\{a, b, c\}, \{(a, b), (b, c)\})$.

We have already given a glimpse on one of the patterns in Examples 1 and 2. There, the pattern contained just a single pair of AFs (F, F'), where the core contained the directed path $a \to b \to c$. The insight that, given that b and c are otherwise unattacked, in such cases a and c can be merged as they will appear together in every (stable) extension, is the central concept to the following pattern.

Definition 21. *Let* $F_{3P} = (\{a, b, c\}, \{(a, b), (b, c)\})$ *be the core-AF. The* 3-path pattern *is given by*

$$P_{\{a,b,c\}}^{3P} = \{(F, F') \mid F \text{ is a lagging of } F_{3P},$$

$$\{b, c\}_F^- = \{a, b\}, F' = \mathsf{M}(F \setminus \{(b, c)\}, a, c)\}.$$

In words, the 3-path pattern concerns all AFs which contain a proper 3-path $a \to b \to c$ such that each argument x different from a, b, c is adjacent to this 3-path. In order to contain the 3-path properly, x can only attack a, but it can be attacked by a, b, or c. Each such AF F is replaced by merging a and c, without taking $b \to c$ into account. Loosely speaking we aim to replace in F the path $a \to b \to c$ by $m_{\{a,c\}} \to b$.

Proposition 2. $P_{\{a,b,c\}}^{3P}$ *is a stb-faithful replacement pattern.*

Proof. Due to Theorem 2 it suffices to show that $F =_C^\sigma \mathsf{U}(F')$ holds for each $(F, F') \in P_C^{3P}$, where $C = \{a, b, c\}$. Consider an arbitrary $(F, F') \in P_C^{3P}$. First note that, since $F' = \mathsf{M}(F \setminus \{(b, c)\}, a, c)$, $\mathsf{U}(F') = (A_F, R_F \setminus \{(b, c)\} \cup \{(a, x) \mid (c, x) \in R_F\} \cup \{(c, x) \mid (a, x) \in R_F\} \cup \{(x, c) \mid (x, a) \in R_F\}$. Let $G = \mathsf{U}(F')$.

For $F \equiv_C^\sigma G$ we need to show that (1) if $stb_C(F) \neq \emptyset$ then $A_F \setminus C = A_G \setminus C$, (2) $stb_C(F) = stb_C(G)$, and (3) for all $E \in stb_C(F)$, $E_F^+ \setminus C = E_G^+ \setminus C$.

(1) is immediate by $A_G = A_F$. For (2), consider an arbitrary $E \in stb_C(F)$. By $F \cap C = F_{3P}$ (F is a lagging of F_{3P}) and $\{b, c\}_F^- = \{a, b\}$, we have $\{b\}_F^- = \{a\}$. Hence either (i) $a \in E$ or (ii) $b \in E$. In case of (i) we get, since $\{c\}_F^- = \{b\}$ and a attacks b, that also $c \in E$. As attacks among arguments $A_F \setminus C$ remain unchanged in G, i.e. $R_F \setminus (C \times C) = R_G \setminus (C \times C)$, we get that $E \in cf(G)$. As $(a, b) \in R_G$, also $E \in stb_C(G)$. In case of (ii) there must be some $x \in E$ with $(x, a) \in R_F$. By construction of G, then $(x, a), (x, c) \in R_G$, hence $E_G^+ \supseteq C$. Consequently, $E \in stb_C(G)$. Hence $stb_C(F) \subseteq stb_C(G)$. For the other direction, consider an arbitrary $E \in stb_C(G)$. By the same reason as above, either (i) $a \in E$ or (ii) $b \in E$. For (i) observe that, for each $x \in A_G$, $(x, c) \in R_G$ iff $(x, a) \in R_G$. Hence also $c \in E$. By $R_F \setminus (C \times C) = R_G \setminus (C \times C)$ and $(a, b) \in A_F$, it follows that $E \in stb_C(F)$. In case of (ii) there must be some $x \in E$ with $(x, a) \in R_G$, hence also $(x, a) \in R_F$. Moreover, $(b, c) \in R_F$, hence $E \in stb_C(F)$.

For (3) let $E \in stb_C(F)$. As before, we can distinguish between (i) $a, c \in E$ and (ii) $b \in E$. Now by construction of G it holds that $S_F^+ \setminus C = S_G^+ \setminus C$ for any $S \supseteq \{a, c\}$, in particular for E. Also in case of (ii) we get $E_F^+ \setminus C = E_G^+ \setminus C$ since $a, c \notin E$.

We can conclude that $F \equiv_C^{stb} G$ and P_C^{3P} is *stb*-faithful. $\qquad\square$

Another candidate for simplification are odd-length cycles. More concretely, in every occurrence of a directed cycle of length 3, $a \to b \to c \to a$, where only a is attacked from the outside, one can disregard c as well as the attack (a, b) when adding a self-loop to a. This is formalized in the following replacement pattern.

Definition 22. *Let* $F_{3L} = (\{a, b, c\}, \{(a, b), (b, c), (c, a)\})$ *be the core-AF. The 3-loop pattern is given by*

$$P^{3L}_{\{a,b,c\}} = \{(F, F') \mid F \setminus \{(a, a), (c, c)\} \text{ is a lagging of } F_{3L},$$
$$\{b, c\}^-_F \subseteq \{a, b, c\}, F' = (F \setminus \{c, (a, b)\}) \cup \{(a, a)\}.$$

Example 3. Consider the AF G' in Fig. 1 (center), which we obtained through application of $P^{3P}_{\{a,b,c\}}$ (cf. Example 1). We can now apply $P^{3L}_{\{a,b,c\}}$ on G': the tuple (F, F', I, α) is a match of $P^{3L}_{\{a,b,c\}}$ on G' with $F = F_{3L} \cup (\{a, b, d, e\}, \{(a, d), (d, a), (b, e)\})$ (a lagging of F_{3L}), $F' = F \setminus \{c, (a, b)\} \cup \{(a, a)\}$, $I = G'$, and $\alpha = \{a \mapsto x_5, b \mapsto m_{\{x_1, x_3\}}, c \mapsto x_4, d \mapsto x_0, e \mapsto x_2\}$. One can check that $(F, F') \in P^{3L}_{\{a,b,c\}}$ and I is isomorphic to F via α. The result is the AF G'' depicted in Fig. 1 (right). It holds that $G' \equiv^{stb} G''$ since $\{\mathsf{U}(E) \mid E \in stb(G')\} = \{\mathsf{U}(E) \mid E \in stb(G'')\} = \{\{x_0, x_1, x_3\}\}$.   ◊

Now consider two arguments in arbitrary attack relation, one of them being otherwise unattacked. Then, any stable extension must contain one of the two arguments. Hence, under *stb*, we can safely remove any argument that is attacked by the two without attacking back, together with all incident attacks. The following pattern expresses this simplification.

Definition 23. *Let* $F_{3C} = (\{a_1, a_2, b\}, \{(a_1, b), (a_2, b)\})$ *be the core-AF. The 3-cone pattern is given by*

$$P^{3C}_{\{a_1,a_2,b\}} = \{(F, F') \mid F \setminus \{(a_1, a_2), (a_2, a_1)\} \text{ is a lagging of } F_{3C},$$
$$\{a_2\}^-_F \subseteq \{a_1\}, F' = F \setminus \{b\}\}.$$

The pattern $P^{3C}_{\{a_1,a_2,b\}}$ is illustrated in Fig. 2. Solid edges represent necessary attacks while optional attacks are given by dotted edges.

The next pattern expresses that two arguments which have the same attackers and are not conflicting with each other can be merged to a single argument.

Definition 24. *Let* $F_{2to1} = (\{a, b\}, \emptyset)$ *be the core-AF. The 2-to-1 pattern is given by*

$$P^{2to1}_{\{a,b\}} = \{(F, F') \mid F \text{ is a lagging of } F_{2to1},$$
$$\{a\}^-_F = \{b\}^-_F, F' = \mathsf{M}(F, a, b)\}.$$

The pattern $P^{2to1}_{\{a,b\}}$ is illustrated in Fig. 3.

All patterns presented so far can be generalized. We exemplify this by presenting the patterns 4-path, 4-cone, and 3-to-2, extending 3-path, 3-cone, and 2-to-1, respectively.

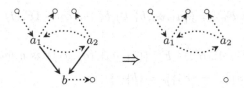

Fig. 2. The pattern $P^{3C}_{\{a_1,a_2,b\}}$.

First, in the 4-path pattern the core-AF is the directed path $a \to b \to c \to d$ and, given that beside (a,d) there are no further attacks among the core arguments, a, c as well as b, d can be merged as they will appear together in every (stable) extension. Loosely speaking we aim to replace in F the 4-path $a \to b \to c \to d$ by the 2-path $m_{\{a,c\}} \to m_{\{b,d\}}$.

Definition 25. Let $F_{4P} = (\{a,b,c,d\}, \{(a,b),(b,c),(c,d)\})$ be the core-AF. The 4-path pattern is given by

$$P^{4P}_{\{a,b,c,d\}} = \{(F,F') \mid F \setminus \{(a,d)\} \text{ is a lagging of } F_{4P},$$
$$\{b,c,d\}^-_F = \{a,b,c\}, F' = \mathsf{M}(\mathsf{M}(F \setminus \{(b,c)\},a,c),b,d)\}.$$

In the 4-cone pattern we consider three arguments in arbitrary attack relation, one of them being otherwise unattacked. Each stable extension contains at least one of the three arguments and we can remove any argument that is attacked by the three without attacking back.

Definition 26. Let $F_{4C} = (\{a_1,a_2,a_3,b\}, \{(a_1,b),(a_2,b),(a_3,b)\})$ be the core-AF. The 4-cone pattern is given by

$$P^{4C}_{\{a_1,a_2,a_3,b\}} = \{(F,F') \mid F \setminus \{(a_i,a_j) \mid i \neq j \in \{1,2,3\}\}$$
$$\text{is a lagging of } F_{4G}, \{a_3\}^-_F \subseteq \{a_1,a_2\}, F' = F \setminus \{b\}\}.$$

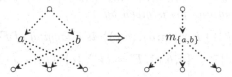

Fig. 3. The pattern $P^{2to1}_{\{a,b\}}$.

Finally, in the 3-to-2 pattern we consider three arguments a_1, a_2, b that are attacked by the same arguments, and only a_1 and a_2 are conflicting. Each stable extension can only accept one of a_1 and a_2 but whenever accepting one of them also accepts b. Thus we can safely replace the three arguments by two merged arguments $m_{\{a_1,b\}}, m_{\{a_2,b\}}$.

Definition 27. *Let* $F_{3to2} = (\{a_1, a_2, b\}, \emptyset)$ *be the core-AF. The* 3-to-2 *pattern is given by*

$$P^{3to2}_{\{a_1,a_2,b\}} = \{(F, (A', R')) \mid F \setminus \{(a_1, a_2), (a_2, a_1)\} \text{ is a lagging of } F_{3to2},$$
$$\{a_1\}_F^- = \{a_2\}_F^- = \{b\}_F^-\},$$

where $A' = (A_G \setminus \{a_1, a_2, b\}) \cup \{m_{\{a_1,b\}}, m_{\{a_2,b\}}\}$ *and*

$$R' = R_G \cap (A' \times A') \cup \{(m_{\{a,b\}}, c) \mid a \in \{a_1, a_2\} \wedge ((a, c) \in R_G \vee (b, c) \in R_G)\} \cup$$
$$\{(c, m_{\{a_1,b\}}), (c, m_{\{a_2,b\}}) \mid c \in \{b\}_F^-\}.$$

Patterns for stb Semantics. This concludes our replacement patterns for stable semantics. For preprocessing AFs, we apply these patterns recursively until no match for any of the patterns can be found. Notice that by the transitivity of the equivalence relation the recursive application of faithful replacement patterns is also equivalence preserving. For instance we simplify a 5-cycle by first applying the 3-path pattern and then the 3-loop pattern (cf. Fig. 1). Notice that, (a) when searching for matches of the pattern we only need to check whether a graph from a finite set of finite graphs appears as sub-AF and (b) with each replacement we delete either arguments or attacks, and thus the preprocessing is indeed in polynomial-time.

Patterns for prf and com Semantics. While the path, 2to1, and 3to2 patterns are also *prf*-preserving and *com*-preserving (cf. Table 1) the remaining patterns, in general, are not. However, by a small modification, we can adapt the 3-loop pattern to work for *prf* as well as *com* as follows. Given an occurrence of a directed cycle of length 3, $a \to b \to c \to a$, where only a is attacked from the outside, we can safely add a self-loop to a. In contrast to stable semantics we have to maintain that attack (a, b), and cannot simply disregard c but rather have to merge a and c, i.e. we still can delete c but for each attack (c, x) in the original AF we have an attack (a, x) in the simplified AF. This is formalized in the following replacement pattern. Notice that we can avoid using a merged argument $m_{\{a,c\}}$ as both a and c cannot appear in any extension.

Definition 28. *Let* $F_{3L} = (\{a, b, c\}, \{(a, b), (b, c), (c, a)\})$ *be the core-AF. The* 3-loop *pattern for com and prf is given by*

$$P^{3L'}_{\{a,b,c\}} = \{(F, F') \mid F \setminus \{(a, a), (c, c)\} \text{ is a lagging of } F_{3L},$$
$$\{b, c\}_F^- \subseteq \{a, b, c\}, F' = (F \setminus \{c\}) \cup \{(a, x) \mid (c, x) \in R_F\}.$$

In order to adapt the 3-cone and 4-cone pattern for *prf*, one additionally requires that one of the arguments a_i defends itself against all attackers. However, there is no such fix for *com* semantics.

Theorem 3. *The presented patterns are* σ-*preserving as depicted in Table 1.*

The proofs except for P^{3to2} exploit Theorem 2 and the results of [5], following the same schema as the proof of Proposition 2. Finally, we note that further generalizations of our patterns are possible, e.g., extending the 3-loop pattern to 5-loop.

Table 1. σ-faithfulness of replacement patterns.

	3-path	3-loop	3-cone	2to1	4-path	4-cone	3to2
stb	✓	✓	✓	✓	✓	✓	✓
prf	✓	(✓)	(✓)	✓	✓	(✓)	✓
com	✓	(✓)	×	✓	✓	×	✓

4 Empirical Evaluation

We overview first empirical results of the potential of replacement patterns as an AF preprocessing approach in the context of *extension enumeration*. Our main goal was to investigate to which extent applying the patterns affects the AF solver running times.

In terms of AF semantics we overview results under stable and preferred semantics. As preprocessing, we applied all the presented patterns (cf. Table 1). For these first experiments, we implemented a software prototype for the application of the replacement patterns in a somewhat brute-force way. In particular, we encoded the search for a set of arguments to which a specific replacement pattern is applicable through an answer set programming (ASP) encoding, and iterated through all considered replacement patterns one-by-one until no applicable set of arguments was reported by the ASP solver Clingo (version 5.3.0). Note that this approach would require the ASP solver to *prove* in the end that a fixpoint is reached, i.e., that no replacements are applicable. To ensure the relatively fast termination of the preprocessing loop, we enforced a time limit of 5 s on each of the ASP solver calls, and terminated preprocessing for a particular pattern as soon as the ASP solver timed out. The experiments were run on Intel Xeon E5-2680 v4 2.4 GHz nodes with 128 GB RAM under CentOS 7. A per-instance timeout of 1800 s was enforced on each solver, with the preprocessing times included.

As benchmarks, we used a total of 440 AFs based on the Watts-Strogatz model with the number of arguments $n \in \{500, 600, \dots, 1500\}$ and parameters $k \in \{\lfloor \log_2(n) \rfloor - 1, \lfloor \log_2(n) \rfloor + 1\}$, $\beta \in \{0.1, 0.3, \dots, 0.9\}$, and *probCycles* $\in \{0.1, 0.3, \dots, 0.7\}$, generated using AFBenchGen2 [7] that was also employed in the 2017 ICCMA argumentation solver competition.

As for size reductions achieved on these instances, on average 11% of arguments and 17% of attacks were removed, with the maximum proportions of deleted arguments and attacks being 72% and 80%, respectively.

Runtime comparisons with and without preprocessing under stable semantics are shown for ArgTools [15], Heureka [21], and CEGARTIX [10] in Fig. 4, with the runtime of the original instance on the x-axis and the runtime of the preprocessed instance on the y-axis (with preprocessing time included). Applying the patterns has a strong effect on the runtimes of the native AF solvers ArgTools (Fig. 4 left) and Heureka (Fig. 4 center): some instances which originally took over 500 s for solving can now be solved in under 10 s. The number of

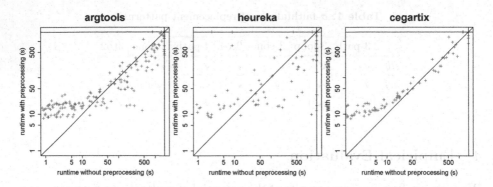

Fig. 4. Effect of preprocessing on runtimes of solvers under stable semantics.

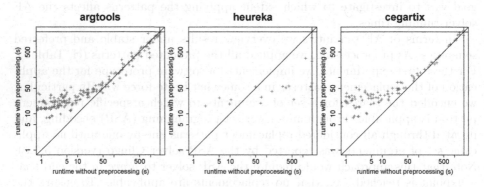

Fig. 5. Effect of preprocessing on runtimes of solvers under preferred semantics.

timeouts also is reduced: from 141 to 134 for ArgTools and from 251 to 243 for Heureka. The contributions of preprocessing to the running times is fairly small even using the somewhat brute-force prototype implementation; the preprocessing overhead is from some seconds to around 20 s at most. This explains the increased running times on the easiest of the benchmark instances. The positive impact of preprocessing is evident on the harder (expectedly more interesting) benchmark instances. These results demonstrate the potential of AF preprocessing for improving the competitiveness of native AF solvers. In contrast, preprocessing appears to have no noticeable impact on the the SAT-based CEGARTIX system (Fig. 4 right).

Results for preferred semantics are shown in Fig. 5. Again, there seems to be no effect on CEGARTIX, and the effect on ArgTools is more modest when compared to the results for stable semantics. However, the effect on Heureka is similar to stable semantics, as it is able to solve instances which originally timed out without preprocessing, although Heureka seems to perform weakly on this particular set of instances under preferred semantics. As for size reductions, on average 6% of arguments and 9% of attacks were removed, with the maximum values being 62% and 72%, respectively.

5   Conclusions

In this paper, we introduced distinct preprocessing techniques for abstract argumentation frameworks which provide a solver-independent approach towards more efficient AF solving. Our formal framework of *replacement patterns* allows for identifying local simplifications that are faithful w.r.t. standard semantics for AFs. We provided a suite of concrete replacement patterns and evaluated their impact with encouraging results especially for native AF solvers. So far we focused on equivalence-preserving preprocessing that allows for an easy reconstruction of all extensions of the original AF. We see even more potential for preprocessing in the context of credulous and skeptical acceptance, where faithfulness is required only in terms of a particular query argument; in that context, also the concept of S-equivalence of input/output AFs [2, 16] deserves attention. Motivated by the first empirical results presented in this work, we are planning on engineering a fully-fledged stand-alone preprocessor, providing optimized implementations of applications of both the replacement patterns presented in this work as well as other forms of native AF preprocessing techniques. Furthermore, preprocessing rules (or restricted forms of them) may also be integrated into solvers for adding reasoning to the core search routine, which is another interesting topic for further work.

Acknowledgments. This work was financially supported by Academy of Finland grants 276412 and 312662 (M.J. and A.N.), the Austrian Science Fund (FWF) grants P30168-N31 and I2854 (W.D. and S.W.), and University of Helsinki Doctoral Programme in Computer Science (A.N.).

References

1. Atkinson, K., et al.: Towards artificial argumentation. AI Mag. **38**(3), 25–36 (2017)
2. Baroni, P., Boella, G., Cerutti, F., Giacomin, M., van der Torre, L., Villata, S.: On the input/output behavior of argumentation frameworks. Artif. Intell. **217**, 144–197 (2014)
3. Baroni, P., Caminada, M., Giacomin, M.: An introduction to argumentation semantics. Knowl. Eng. Rev. **26**(4), 365–410 (2011)
4. Baroni, P., Gabbay, D., Giacomin, M., van der Torre, L. (eds.): Handbook of Formal Argumentation. College Publications (2018)
5. Baumann, R., Dvořák, W., Linsbichler, T., Woltran, S.: A general notion of equivalence for abstract argumentation. In: Proceedings of IJCAI, pp. 800–806. ijcai.org (2017)
6. Cerutti, F., Gaggl, S.A., Thimm, M., Wallner, J.P.: Foundations of implementations for formal argumentation. IfCoLog J. Log. Appl. **4**(8), 2623–2707 (2017)
7. Cerutti, F., Giacomin, M., Vallati, M.: Generating structured argumentation frameworks: AFBenchGen2. In: Proceedings of COMMA. Frontiers in Artificial Intelligence and Applications, vol. 287, pp. 467–468. IOS Press (2016)
8. Cerutti, F., Vallati, M., Giacomin, M.: Where are we now? State of the art and future trends of solvers for hard argumentation problems. In: Proceedings of COMMA. Frontiers in Artificial Intelligence and Applications, vol. 287, pp. 207–218. IOS Press (2016)

9. Dung, P.M.: On the acceptability of arguments and its fundamental role in non-monotonic reasoning, logic programming and n-person games. Artif. Intell. **77**(2), 321–358 (1995)
10. Dvořák, W., Järvisalo, M., Wallner, J.P., Woltran, S.: Complexity-sensitive decision procedures for abstract argumentation. Artif. Intell. **206**, 53–78 (2014)
11. Eén, N., Biere, A.: Effective preprocessing in SAT through variable and clause elimination. In: Bacchus, F., Walsh, T. (eds.) SAT 2005. LNCS, vol. 3569, pp. 61–75. Springer, Heidelberg (2005). https://doi.org/10.1007/11499107_5
12. Egly, U., Gaggl, S.A., Woltran, S.: Answer-set programming encodings for argumentation frameworks. Argum. Comput. **1**(2), 147–177 (2010)
13. Gaggl, S.A., Linsbichler, T., Maratea, M., Woltran, S.: Introducing the second international competition on computational models of argumentation. In: Proceedings of SAFA. CEUR Workshop Proceedings, vol. 1672, pp. 4–9. CEUR-WS.org (2016)
14. Gebser, M., Kaufmann, B., Neumann, A., Schaub, T.: Advanced preprocessing for answer set solving. In: Proceedings of ECAI. Frontiers in Artificial Intelligence and Applications, vol. 178, pp. 15–19. IOS Press (2008)
15. Geilen, N., Thimm, M.: Heureka: a general heuristic backtracking solver for abstract argumentation. In: Black, E., Modgil, S., Oren, N. (eds.) TAFA 2017. LNCS (LNAI), vol. 10757, pp. 143–149. Springer, Cham (2018). https://doi.org/10.1007/978-3-319-75553-3_10
16. Giacomin, M., Linsbichler, T., Woltran, S.: On the functional completeness of argumentation semantics. In: Proceedings of KR, pp. 43–52. AAAI Press (2016)
17. Heule, M., Järvisalo, M., Lonsing, F., Seidl, M., Biere, A.: Clause elimination for SAT and QSAT. J. Artif. Intell. Res. **53**, 127–168 (2015)
18. Järvisalo, M., Heule, M.J.H., Biere, A.: Inprocessing rules. In: Gramlich, B., Miller, D., Sattler, U. (eds.) IJCAR 2012. LNCS (LNAI), vol. 7364, pp. 355–370. Springer, Heidelberg (2012). https://doi.org/10.1007/978-3-642-31365-3_28
19. Korhonen, T., Berg, J., Saikko, P., Järvisalo, M.: MaxPre: an extended MaxSAT preprocessor. In: Gaspers, S., Walsh, T. (eds.) SAT 2017. LNCS, vol. 10491, pp. 449–456. Springer, Cham (2017). https://doi.org/10.1007/978-3-319-66263-3_28
20. Lonsing, F., Bacchus, F., Biere, A., Egly, U., Seidl, M.: Enhancing search-based QBF solving by dynamic blocked clause elimination. In: Davis, M., Fehnker, A., McIver, A., Voronkov, A. (eds.) LPAR 2015. LNCS, vol. 9450, pp. 418–433. Springer, Heidelberg (2015). https://doi.org/10.1007/978-3-662-48899-7_29
21. Nofal, S., Atkinson, K., Dunne, P.E.: Looking-ahead in backtracking algorithms for abstract argumentation. Int. J. Approx. Reason. **78**, 265–282 (2016)
22. Thimm, M., Villata, S.: The first international competition on computational models of argumentation: results and analysis. Artif. Intell. **252**, 267–294 (2017)

Manipulating Skeptical and Credulous Consequences When Merging Beliefs

Adrian Haret[ID] and Johannes P. Wallner[(✉)][ID]

Institute of Logic and Computation, TU Wien, Vienna, Austria
{haret,wallner}@dbai.tuwien.ac.at

Abstract. Automated reasoning techniques for multi-agent scenarios need to address the possibility that procedures for collective decision making may fall prey to manipulation by self-interested agents. In this paper we study manipulation in the context of belief merging, a framework for aggregating agents' positions, or beliefs, with respect to a set of issues represented by propositional atoms. Within this framework agents submit their positions as propositional formulas that are to be aggregated into a single formula. To reach a final decision, we employ well-established acceptance notions and extract the *skeptical* and *credulous* consequences (i.e., atoms true in all and, respectively, at least one model) of the resulting formula. We find that, even in restricted cases, most aggregation procedures are vulnerable to manipulation by an agent acting strategically, i.e., one that is able to submit a formula not representing its true position. Our results apply when the goal of such an agent is either that of (i) affecting an atom's skeptical or credulous acceptance status, or (ii) improving its satisfaction with the result. With respect to latter task, we extend existing work on manipulation with new satisfaction indices, based on skeptical and credulous reasoning. We also study the extent to which an agent can influence the outcome of the aggregation, and show that manipulation can often be achieved by submitting a *complete* formula (i.e., a formula having exactly one model), yet, the complexity of finding such a formula resides, in the general case, on the second level of the polynomial hierarchy.

Keywords: Belief merging · Manipulation · Complexity

1 Introduction

Collective decision making often involves the aggregation of multiple, possibly conflicting viewpoints. Apart from the matter of how to represent and aggregate such viewpoints, a looming concern in any deliberation scenario is that the agents involved may have an incentive to misrepresent their positions, and thus manipulate the aggregation result, if doing so can bring an advantage. Hence, an understanding of the potential for manipulation of any aggregation procedure is a prerequisite to its successful deployment in real world contexts.

© Springer Nature Switzerland AG 2019
F. Calimeri et al. (Eds.): JELIA 2019, LNAI 11468, pp. 133–150, 2019.
https://doi.org/10.1007/978-3-030-19570-0_9

If agents deliberate with respect to a small number of independent alternatives, as is the case in a typical election, aggregation [25] and manipulation [6,13] are well understood due to extensive research in the field of Social Choice. But if agents have to decide on multiple interconnected issues at the same time (as when electing a committee, or choosing a product specification), then the number of possible alternatives can grow too large to expect agents to have explicit preferences over the whole set. The problem, known as *combinatorial voting* in Social Choice [22], acquires a knowledge representation dimension as agents need compact ways to express positions over a large domain, and automatizable procedures to perform reasoning with such preferences.

Here we use belief merging as a framework for aggregating complex positions over all possible assignments of values to a set of propositional atoms [19,21]. Propositional atoms, in this setting, encode the issues deliberated upon, while truth-value assignments to atoms, also called *interpretations*, encode combinations of issues that could make it into the final result, and over which agents can have preferences. In this, propositional logic suggests itself as a natural choice for representing the ways in which issues are interconnected, and lends itself naturally to the modeling of aggregation problems inspired by Social Choice [8,9,11,12,15].

Within the belief merging framework each agent i submits a propositional formula K_i, which stands for i's reported belief about what are the best interpretations with respect to the issues being deliberated upon. A merging operator then aggregates the individual reported beliefs, in the presence of an integrity constraint that must be satisfied. Its result is a set of "winning" interpretations, representable as a propositional formula, that respect the integrity constraint of the merging process.

In general, the set of winning interpretations is not always expected to be the final step in a reasoning process: without further means, such a set of interpretations does not give a direct answer to which atoms (alternatives) are to be ultimately accepted. One can view the winning set as a "tie" between all the interpretations in the set. If the decision procedure needs to be explicit about every issue under consideration, then a further reasoning mechanism is required, amounting to a method of breaking ties. To this end, we employ well established *acceptance notions* from the field of knowledge representation and reasoning: skeptical and credulous consequences [24]. An atom is a skeptical consequence of a set of interpretations if the atom is part of all interpretations, and a credulous consequence if the atom is part of at least one interpretation in the set. With regards to propositional formulas, skeptical reasoning is equivalent to (atomwise) classical logical entailment.

Example 1. A collective of four agents must decide who to give an award to. There are three possible candidates, represented by propositional atoms a, b and c, and the collective is operating under the constraint $\mu = a \vee b \vee c$, i.e., at least one (and possibly more) of the candidates can receive the award. The decision is arrived at by first aggregating the agents' beliefs under a known procedure, called a *belief merging operator* (details of which are reserved for later;

see, e.g., Example 2). This produces a collective belief, potentially satisfiable by more than one interpretation: since this does not lead to an unequivocal decision, an additional tie-breaking step is required. This tie-breaking step can be thought of as a general strategy, or attitude, the collective adopts for dealing with uncertainty. In this case, we assume the collective affects a conservative (or, as we will call it, *skeptical*) approach: if there is any uncertainty with respect to a candidate, the candidate is not given the award.

The beliefs of the agents are represented by propositional formulas, as follows. Agent 1 believes candidate b should get the award, is against candidate a and has no opinion with respect to candidate c: this is represented by the formula $K_1 = \neg a \wedge b$. Agents 2 and 3 are represented by formulas $K_2 = a \wedge (b \leftrightarrow \neg c)$ and $K_3 = b \wedge (a \rightarrow c)$, respectively. We assume that agent 4 is what we will call a *strategic agent*, i.e., it is not itself compelled to submit its true belief. Agent 4's true belief happens to be $K_4^T = a \wedge \neg b \wedge \neg c$ and, were it to actually submit K_4^T, the result under the aggregation procedure would be $b \wedge \neg c$: candidate b surely gets the award, c is ruled out and there is no verdict on a. In other words, this particular aggregation procedure offers up two winning configurations (i.e., the models of the propositional formula $b \wedge \neg c$): one possible world in which a gets the award, another in which a does not get it. Thus, under the conservative tie-breaking procedure mentioned above, the final decision is arrived at by ruling out a: the final verdict is that b is the sole recipient of the award.

Significantly, if agent 4 reports $K_4^F = a \wedge \neg b \wedge c$ instead of K_4^T, the result becomes $a \wedge c$, with the award now going to a and c. Thus, by misreporting its own belief, agent 4 ensures that its most preferred candidate a is among the recipients of the award.

Example 1 features the main ingredients of the framework we are working in: propositional logic as the language in which agents state their beliefs about the best interpretations to be included in the result, and in which the result is expressed; aggregation *via* merging operators; the need for an additional tie-breaking step; and the possibility that one agent acting strategically can influence the result to its advantage. The example also sets up the main aims of the paper: (i) formalizing strategic goals of possibly untruthful agents with respect to skeptical and credulous reasoning, (ii) investigating vulnerabilities of established merging operators to such strategic manipulation, and (iii) ways in which an agent can change (manipulate) the outcome of the aggregation process, to the extent that this is possible. Our main contributions are as follows:

- We propose to approach manipulation of skeptical or credulous consequences in two ways: (a) by considering what we call *constructive* and *destructive* manipulation, where the aim is to usher a desired atom into (or out of) the skeptical or credulous consequences, and (b) by adapting an earlier approach to manipulation [11] that utilizes satisfaction indices to quantify the satisfaction of agents w.r.t. merged outcomes; our contribution here consists in proposing new indices.
- We give the full landscape of (non-)manipulability: concretely, we show that all main aggregation operators are manipulable (even when enforcing restric-

tions that yielded non-manipulability in earlier works [11]); the sole exception is the case when aggregation is done using only so-called *complete* bases (i.e., such that each formula has exactly one model) without integrity constraint and using aggregation operator $\Delta_{\top}^{d_H, \Sigma}$ (defined below), under our new satisfaction indices.

- On the question of how an agent can manipulate, we look at general approaches to influencing the aggregation procedure by promoting or demoting interpretations. Further, we show that manipulation under skeptical consequences can be carried out by the strategic agent submitting a complete base, suggesting that manipulation does not require sophisticated propositional structures to succeed; however, in the same light, we show that deciding the existence of such a complete base is a complex problem, namely a Σ_2^P-complete problem, for destructive manipulation.

This paper improves on an earlier workshop version [17]. Proof details can be found online [18].

2   Belief Merging

Propositional Logic. We assume a finite set $\mathcal{P}$ of propositional atoms, with $\mathcal{L}$ the set of formulas generated from $\mathcal{P}$ using the usual connectives. A *knowledge base* K is a formula from $\mathcal{L}$. The models of a propositional formula μ are the interpretations which satisfy it, and we write $[\mu]$ for the set of models of μ. We typically write interpretations as words where letters are the atoms assigned to true, e.g., $\{\{a,b\},\{b,c\}\}$ is written as $\{ab, bc\}$. If $\varphi_1, \varphi_2 \in \mathcal{L}$, we say that $\varphi_1 \models \varphi_2$ if $[\varphi_1] \subseteq [\varphi_2]$, and that $\varphi_1 \equiv \varphi_2$ if $[\varphi_1] = [\varphi_2]$. A knowledge base K is *complete* if it has exactly one model. A formula φ is *consistent* (*satisfiable*), if $[\varphi] \neq \emptyset$. If v and w are interpretations, $v \triangle w$ is their symmetric difference, defined as $v \triangle w = (v \setminus w) \cup (w \setminus v)$.

Aggregation. A *profile* $P = (K_1, \ldots, K_n)$ is a finite tuple of consistent bases, representing the reported beliefs of n distinct agents. We say that K_i *is agent i's reported belief*. The qualification that the K_i's stand for *reported* beliefs is important, as we want to allow for the possibility of agents participating in the merging process with beliefs other than their truthful ones. We typically write K_i^T for agent i's truthful belief, and K_i^F for an untruthful belief that i reports in the merging scenario.

If P_1 and P_2 are profiles, we write $P_1 + P_2$ for the profile obtained by appending P_2 to P_1. If K is a base and there is no danger of ambiguity, we write $P + K$ instead of $P + (K)$.

A merging operator Δ is a function mapping a profile P of consistent knowledge bases and a propositional formula μ, called *the constraint*, to a propositional formula, written $\Delta_\mu(P)$. We focus on semantic operators $\Delta^{d, f}$ from the framework of logic-based merging [21], the main ingredients of which are a distance d and an aggregation function f. To define these operators we start with a distance d between interpretations. Given a distance d between interpretations, an interpretation w and a propositional formula φ, *the distance $d(w,\varphi)$ from w to φ* is defined as $d(w,\varphi) = \min\{d(w,v) \mid v \in [\varphi]\}$. This makes it possible to order interpretations w.r.t. bases: $w_1 \leq_K^d w_2$ if $d(w_1,K) \leq d(w_2,K)$. For a profile $P = (K_1,\ldots,K_n)$ and an aggregation function f, *the distance d^f from w to P* is $d^f(w,P) = f(d(w,K_1),\ldots,d(w,K_n))$. That is, $d_f(w,P)$ is the result of aggregating, *via* f, the distances between w and each $K_i \in P$.

We assume that distances from interpretations to profiles can be compared using an order $\leq$, such that, for any interpretations w_1 and w_2, we have either $d^f(w_1,P) \leq d^f(w_2,P)$ or $d^f(w_2,P) \leq d^f(w_1,P)$. We say that $w_1 \leq_P^{d,f} w_2$ if $d^f(w_1,P) \leq d^f(w_2,P)$. If d is a distance between interpretations and f is an aggregation function, the *propositional merging operator* $\Delta^{d,f}$ is defined, for any profile P and constraint μ, as $[\Delta_\mu^{d,f}(P)] = \min_{\leq_P^{d,f}}[\mu]$. The result of aggregating the bases in P thus consists of the models of μ, also called *the winning interpretations*, at minimum overall distance to the consistent bases in P, with distances specified via d and aggregation function f.

We will focus on a sample of representative merging operators, constructed using a set of common distance/aggregation functions. If w_1 and w_2 are interpretations, the *drastic* and *Hamming* distances d_D and d_H, respectively, are defined as follows:

$$d_D(w_1,w_2) = \begin{cases} 0, & \text{if } w_1 = w_2, \\ 1, & \text{otherwise,} \end{cases} \qquad d_H(w_1,w_2) = |w_1 \triangle w_2|.$$

Table 1. Example of merging. Gray cells are the permitted models when integrity constraint $\mu = (a \vee b \vee c)$. Column 1 contains all interpretations over the alphabet $\mathcal{P} = \{a,b,c\}$, columns 2–6 show the minimal (Hamming) distances between interpretations and bases (see Example 1 for what the bases are). Columns 7–10 show the aggregated distances under Σ and gmax with respect to the profiles P^T and P^F. Bold numbers indicate models with minimum distance.

	$[K_1]$ $\{b,bc\}$	$[K_2]$ $\{ab,ac\}$	$[K_3]$ $\{b,bc,abc\}$	$[K_4^T]$ $\{a\}$	$[K_4^F]$ $\{ac\}$	$d_H^\Sigma(\cdot,P^T)$	$d_H^\Sigma(\cdot,P^F)$	$d_H^{gmax}(\cdot,P^T)$	$d_H^{gmax}(\cdot,P^F)$
$\emptyset$	1	2	1	1	2	5	6	(2,1,1,1)	(2,2,1,1)
a	2	1	2	0	1	5	6	(2,2,1,0)	(2,2,1,1)
b	0	1	0	2	3	3	4	(2,1,0,0)	(3,1,0,0)
c	1	1	1	2	1	5	4	(2,1,1,1)	(1,1,1,1)
ab	1	0	1	1	2	3	4	**(1,1,1,0)**	(2,1,1,0)
ac	2	0	1	1	0	4	3	(2,1,1,0)	(2,1,0,0)
bc	0	2	0	3	2	5	4	(3,2,0,0)	(2,2,0,0)
abc	1	1	0	2	1	4	3	(2,1,1,0)	**(1,1,1,0)**

If $X = (x_1,\ldots,x_n)$ is an n-tuple of non-negative integers, the Σ, max and gmax aggregation functions are defined as follows:

- $\Sigma(X) = \Sigma_{i=1}^{n} x_i$,
- $\max(X) = \max(\{x_i \mid 1 \le i \le n\})$, and
- $\mathrm{gmax}(X)$ is X in descending order.

For $f \in \{\Sigma, \max\}$ the aggregated value $d^f(w, P)$ is an integer and thus interpretations can be ordered w.r.t. their distance to P. For $f = \mathrm{gmax}$, $d^{\mathrm{gmax}}(v, P)$ is an n-tuple made up of the numbers $d(w, K_1), \ldots, d(w, K_n)$ ordered in descending order. To rank interpretations via gmax we order vectors lexicographically: $(x_1, \ldots, x_n) <_{lex} (y_1, \ldots, y_n)$ if $x_i < y_i$ for the first i where x_i and y_i differ. We recall that if $X = (x_1, \ldots, x_n)$ and $Y = (y_1, \ldots, y_n)$ are n-tuples of non-negative integers, $z \in \mathbb{N}$, π is a permutation of $\{1, \ldots, n\}$ and $f \in \{\Sigma, \max, \mathrm{gmax}\}$ is an aggregation function, the following properties hold [21]: $f(x_1, \ldots, x_n) = f(x_{\pi(1)}, \ldots, x_{\pi(2)})$ (symmetry); and if $x_i \le x_i'$, then $f(x_1, \ldots, x_i, \ldots, x_n) \le f(x_1, \ldots, x_i', \ldots, x_n)$ (monotony).

Example 2. The scenario described in Example 1 features two aggregation tasks: one involving the profile $P^T = (K_1, K_2, K_3, K_4^T)$, containing the true position of agent 4; the other involving the profile $P^F = (K_1, K_2, K_3, K_4^F)$, obtained by agent 4 acting strategically. Both tasks occur under the same constraint $\mu = a \vee b \vee c$. Table 1 illustrates the results of aggregating profiles P^T and P^F under constraint μ with operators $\Delta_\mu^{d_H, \Sigma}$ and $\Delta_\mu^{d_H, \mathrm{gmax}}$. The aggregation result is computed by choosing, from the models of μ, the ones with minimum aggregated distance. For instance, we have $K_2 = a \wedge (b \leftrightarrow \neg c)$. Further, we have $[K_2] = \{ab, ac\}$ and $d_H(ab, K_2) = \min\{d_H(ab, ab), d_H(ab, ac)\} = \min\{0, 2\} = 0$. The following holds: $d_H^\Sigma(ab, P^T) = d_H(ab, K_1) + d_H(ab, K_2) + d_H(ab, K_3) + d_H(ab, K_4^T) = 3$. The orders $\le_{P^T}^{d_H, f}$ and $\le_{P^F}^{d_H, f}$, for $f \in \{\Sigma, \mathrm{gmax}\}$, are obtained by ordering interpretations according to their aggregated distances to P^T and P^F, respectively. Finally, we get that $[\Delta_\mu^{d_H, \Sigma}(P^T)] = \{b, ab\}$, $[\Delta_\mu^{d_H, \Sigma}(P^F)] = \{ac, abc\}$, $[\Delta_\mu^{d_H, \mathrm{gmax}}(P^T)] = \{ab\}$ and $[\Delta_\mu^{d_H, \mathrm{gmax}}(P^F)] = \{abc\}$.

It is worth mentioning that $\Delta_\mu^{d_D, \Sigma}$ and $\Delta_\mu^{d_D, \mathrm{gmax}}$ are equivalent, for any profile P and constraint μ (i.e., $[\Delta_\mu^{d_D, \Sigma}(P)] = [\Delta_\mu^{d_D, \mathrm{gmax}}(P)]$). Further, the operator $\Delta_\mu^{d_D, \max}$ delivers $[\bigwedge P \wedge \mu]$, if consistent, and $[\mu]$ otherwise.

3   Acceptance and Satisfaction Notions

Merging operators output a set of interpretations, all of which can be seen as tied for the winning position. In decision terms, this translates as inconclusiveness with respect to the final verdict (see Example 1). To arrive at a definite opinion on every issue we use well-established notions of *acceptance* with respect to a formula. Further, in order to make sense of the way an agent can manipulate, we need to be able to measure an agent's satisfaction with respect to the result of a merging operator. To this end we introduce a set of *satisfaction indices* that build on the acceptance notions.

Acceptance. An *acceptance function* $\mathrm{Acc}\colon \mathcal{L} \to 2^{\mathcal{P}}$ maps propositional formulas to sets of atoms in $\mathcal{P}$. We say that $\mathrm{Acc}(\varphi)$ *are the accepted atoms of φ*. For a formula φ, we define the following acceptance notions:

$$\texttt{Skept}(\varphi) = \bigcap_{w \in [\varphi]} w, \qquad\qquad \texttt{Cred}(\varphi) = \bigcup_{w \in [\varphi]} w.$$

For a formula φ, an atom is *skeptically accepted* if it is true in all models of φ (i.e., is in $\texttt{Skept}(\varphi)$); an atom is *credulously accepted* if it is true in at least one model of φ (i.e., is in $\texttt{Cred}(\varphi)$).[1] Skeptical acceptance is equivalent to atom-wise logical entailment, and credulous acceptance indicates support of an atom in at least one model.

Example 3. In Example 2 we obtain that $[\Delta_\mu^{d_H, \Sigma}(P^T)] = \{b, ab\}$. For the acceptance notions introduced, we have $\texttt{Skept}(\Delta_\mu^{d_H, \Sigma}(P^T)) = b$ and $\texttt{Cred}(\Delta_\mu^{d_H, \Sigma}(P^T)) = ab$.

These acceptance notions focus on positive literals. Thus, we say that $p \in \texttt{Skept}(\varphi)$ if the atom p is in every model of φ, but we do not treat acceptance of negative literals in a similar fashion: for instance, in Example 3 we do not say something like '$\texttt{Skept}(\Delta_\mu^{d_H, \Sigma}(P^T)) = b\neg c$', even though c is in none of (and hence rejected by) all the models of $\Delta_\mu^{d_H, \Sigma}(P^T)$. This asymmetry is not unusual in a Social Choice context, where rejection of a candidate is often assimilated to non-acceptance, but would be worth looking at in a more extensive treatment of acceptance notions.

Satisfaction. A *satisfaction index* $i \colon \mathcal{L} \times \mathcal{L} \to \mathbb{N}^+$ is a function that maps a pair of formulas to a non-negative integer [11]. If φ and ψ are two propositional formulas and $\texttt{Acc}$ is an acceptance notion, *the satisfaction index* $i_{\texttt{Acc}}$ is defined as $i_{\texttt{Acc}}(\varphi, \psi) = |\texttt{Acc}(\varphi) \triangle \texttt{Acc}(\psi)|$. For the two acceptance notions introduced above, this gives us the satisfaction indices $i_{\texttt{Skept}}$ and $i_{\texttt{Cred}}$.

Example 4. For K_4^T from Example 2 we have $[K_4^T] = \{a\}$ and $[\Delta_\mu^{d_H, \Sigma}(P^T)] = \{b, ab\}$. With the indices we can measure agent 4's satisfaction regarding the truthful aggregation result: we have $i_{\texttt{Skept}}(K_4^T, \Delta_\mu^{d_H, \Sigma}(P^T)) = |\texttt{Skept}(K_4^T) \triangle \texttt{Skept}(\Delta_\mu^{d_H, \Sigma}(P^T))| = |a \triangle b| = 2$. Analogously, $i_{\texttt{Cred}}(K_4^T, \Delta_\mu^{d_H, \Sigma}(P^T)) = |a \triangle ab| = 1$.

For arbitrary formulas the numeric results given by the indices $i_{\texttt{Skept}}$ and $i_{\texttt{Cred}}$ are generally not directly correlated, in that each may be higher or lower than the other. However, there is a duality relation between the indices and aggregation operators defined via skeptical and credulous acceptance. *The dual $\overline{\varphi}$ of a formula* φ is obtained by replacing every literal in φ with its negation. If $P = (K_1, \ldots, K_m)$ is a profile, then *the dual $\overline{P}$ of P* is the profile defined as

---

[1] We note that the notions of *skeptical* (cautious) and *credulous* (brave) consequences are not uniformly used throughout the literature. For instance, skeptical consequences may be defined as those consequences that follow (e.g., by classical logic) from all formulas in a set of formulas, and skeptical acceptance may refer to membership of an object in all sets of a given set of sets. We make use of the latter interpretation.

$\overline{P} = (\overline{K_1}, \ldots, \overline{K_m})$. If w is an interpretation, *the dual $\overline{w}$ of w* is the complement of w, i.e., the interpretation $\mathcal{P} \setminus w$. If W is a set of interpretations, *the dual $\overline{W}$ of W* is the set of interpretations defined as $\overline{W} = \{\overline{w} \mid w \in W\}$. For a propositional formula φ we have $\overline{[\varphi]} = [\overline{\varphi}]$. This transfers to the indices: it holds that $i_{\mathtt{Skept}}(\varphi, \psi) = i_{\mathtt{Cred}}(\overline{\varphi}, \overline{\psi})$. Intuitively, this is because an atom p being in the symmetric difference of the skeptical consequences is equivalent to there being a model of one of the formulas not containing p, with the dual having p in at least one model. Interestingly, a duality also holds with respect to merging operators.

Proposition 1. *If P is a profile, μ is a constraint, $d \in \{d_H, d_D\}$ is a distance function, and $f \in \{\Sigma, \mathtt{max}, \mathtt{gmax}\}$ is an aggregation function, then* $\overline{\mathtt{Skept}(\Delta_\mu^{d,f}(P))} \equiv \mathtt{Cred}(\Delta_{\overline{\mu}}^{d,f}(\overline{P}))$.

Proposition 1 builds on an interesting symmetry exhibited by the merging operators we work with: the result of merging a profile P under a constraint μ and the result of merging $\overline{P}$ under constraint $\overline{\mu}$ turn out to be themselves duals of each other. This allows us, once we have found some instance related to the skeptical index, to automatically adapt it to the credulous index.

Example 5. For the alphabet $\mathcal{P} = \{a, b\}$, take a profile $P = (K_1, K_2)$, with $K_1 = a \to b$, $K_2 = \neg a$ and $\mu = a$. We get $[\Delta_\mu^{d_H, \Sigma}(P)] = \{ab\}$, and $\mathtt{Skept}(\Delta_\mu^{d_H, \Sigma}(P)) = ab$. Taking the duals, we have $\overline{K_1} = \neg a \to \neg b$, $\overline{K_2} = a$ and $\overline{\mu} = \neg a$. Notice that $[K_1] = \{\emptyset, b, ab\}$ and $\overline{[K_1]} = \{ab, a, \emptyset\} = \{\overline{\emptyset}, \overline{b}, \overline{ab}\} = [\overline{K_1}]$, i.e., the models of the dual of K_1 are the duals of the models of K_1. We get that $[\Delta_{\overline{\mu}}^{d_H, \Sigma}(\overline{P})] = \{\emptyset\}$, which is the same as $\overline{[\Delta_\mu^{d_H, \Sigma}(P)]}$ (this equality also holds more generally). Lastly, $\overline{\mathtt{Skept}(\Delta_\mu^{d_H, \Sigma}(P))} = \mathtt{Cred}(\Delta_{\overline{\mu}}^{d_H, \Sigma}(\overline{P}))$.

4 Manipulability and Strategyproofness

Manipulation occurs when an agent, called *the strategic agent*, can influence the merging result in its favor by submitting a base different from its truthful one. Unless otherwise stated, the agent's truthful position is the base K^T, and the base with which it manipulates as K^F. We represent the strategic agent's contribution by appending its submitted base to a pre-existing profile P (e.g., $P + K^T$): intuitively, it is as if the strategic agent joins the aggregation process *after* everyone else has submitted their positions. This is merely a notational choice, meant to improve readability, and no generality is lost in this way: all aggregation functions used here satisfy the symmetry property (see Sect. 2) and the result never depends on the merging order.

A profile P, constraint μ, distance d, aggregation function f and acceptance notion $\mathtt{Acc}$ are assumed in most definitions, but, in the interest of concision, are explicitly referred to only under pain of ambiguity. Unless otherwise stated, d ranges over $\{d_D, d_H\}$ and f over $\{\Sigma, \mathtt{gmax}, \mathtt{max}\}$.

4.1 Constructive and Destructive Manipulation with Respect to an Atom

One of the most basic forms of manipulation is one in which the strategic agent has a specific atom p that it targets for acceptance: the strategic agent may want to see p get accepted (or rejected) in the final result. This sets up the stage for what we call, along the lines of similar concepts from Social Choice [6], *constructive* and *destructive* manipulation. The strategic agent *constructively* Acc-*manipulates* P w.r.t. p *using* K^F if $p \notin \text{Acc}(\Delta_\mu(P + K^T))$ and $p \in \text{Acc}(\Delta_\mu(P + K^F))$, and *destructively* Acc-*manipulates* P w.r.t. p *using* K^F if $p \in \text{Acc}(\Delta_\mu(P + K^T))$ and $p \notin \text{Acc}(\Delta_\mu(P + K^F))$. Intuitively, an agent constructively Acc-manipulates w.r.t. p if it can make p be in the accepted atoms of the aggregation result by submitting K^F instead of K^T; similarly, an agent destructively manipulates w.r.t. p if it can kick p out of the accepted atoms of the result. We say that an operator Δ is Acc-*strategyproof* if there is no profile P, constraint μ, atom p and bases K^T and K^F s.t. the strategic agent, having K^T as its truthful position, Acc-manipulates P, either constructively or destructively, w.r.t. p using K^F.

We first note that, if K^T is the strategic agent's truthful position, any instance of constructive manipulation with respect to p using K^F is also an instance of destructive manipulation with respect to p, obtained by swapping K^T and K^F as the truthful and manipulating bases, respectively. Next, our results regarding duality (see Proposition 1) imply the following duality for manipulation.

Proposition 2. *A strategic agent constructively (destructively)* Skept-*manipulates P with respect to p iff it destructively (constructively)* Cred-*manipulates $\overline{P}$ with respect to p using $\overline{K^F}$, with $\overline{K^T}$ as its truthful position and $\overline{\mu}$ as the constraint.*

In other words, an instance of constructive Skept-manipulation has a direct counterpart, *via* the duals, in an instance of destructive Cred-manipulation, and likewise for destructive Skept-manipulation and constructive Cred-manipulation. This simplifies our study as we can focus on only one acceptance notion, with results for the other notion following by Proposition 2.

Example 6. In Example 2 agent 4 constructively Skept-manipulates the profile $P = (K_1, K_2, K_3)$ w.r.t the atom a (relative to the operator $\Delta^{d_H, \Sigma}$ and constraint $\mu = a \lor b \lor c$), in that $a \notin \text{Skept}(\Delta_\mu^{d_H, \Sigma}(P^T))$ but $a \in \text{Skept}(\Delta_\mu^{d_H, \Sigma}(P^F))$. Consider, now, a merging scenario where every formula is replaced by its dual. Thus, the truthful position of agent 4 is $\overline{K_4^T}$: we get that $[\overline{K_4^T}] = \{bc\}$, the constraint is $\overline{\mu} = \neg a \lor \neg b \lor \neg c$, with $[\overline{\mu}] = \{\emptyset, a, b, c, ab, ac, bc\}$, and the profile is $\overline{P}$. We get that $[\Delta_{\overline{\mu}}^{d_H, \Sigma}(\overline{P^T})] = \{c, ac\}$, and $a \in \text{Cred}(\Delta_{\overline{\mu}}^{d_H, \Sigma}(\overline{P^T}))$. However, if agent 4 now submits $\overline{K_4^F}$, we get that $[\Delta_{\overline{\mu}}^{d_H, \Sigma}(\overline{K_4^F})] = \{\emptyset, b\}$, with $a \notin \text{Cred}(\Delta_{\overline{\mu}}^{d_H, \Sigma}(\overline{K_4^F}))$. Hence, if agent 4's truthful position is $\overline{K_4^T}$, then it destructively Cred-manipulates $\overline{P}$ w.r.t a using $\overline{K_4^F}$.

Examples 2 and 6 already show that $\Delta^{d_H, \Sigma}$ is constructively Skept-manipulable (and destructively Cred-manipulable). Indeed, this extends to all operators introduced so far.

Theorem 1. *For any $n \in \mathbb{N}$ and $p \in \mathcal{P}$, there exists a profile $P = (K_1, \ldots, K_n)$ and bases K^T, K^F such that the strategic agent constructively (and destructively, respectively) Acc-manipulates P w.r.t p using K^F, even if $\mu = \top$ and all K_i, for $i \in \{1, \ldots, n\}$, as well as K^T and K^F, are complete.*

Theorem 1 suggests that the situation with respect to constructive/destructive manipulation is acute, for two reasons. Firstly, restrictions on the size of the profile or on the specificity of the bases (e.g., requiring that all bases are complete), which ensure strategyproofness in other contexts [11], turn out not to have any effect in this case. Second, instances of manipulation exist for *any* size of the profile P: this is best understood by consulting Example 7.

Example 7. To constructively Skept-manipulate a profile of size $n = 4$ w.r.t. the atom a, relative to the constraint $\mu = \top$ and $f \in \{\Sigma, \text{gmax}\}$, take K_i, for $i \in \{1, 2, 3, 4\}$, K^T and K^F as in Table 2. It is straightforward to see that $[\Delta_\mu^{d, f}(P^T)] = \{\emptyset\}$ and $[\Delta_\mu^{d, f}(P^F)] = \{a\}$, for $d \in \{d_D, d_H\}$ and $f \in \{\Sigma, \text{gmax}\}$ (Table 2 shows results for d_H, but the reasoning for d_D is entirely similar). This example easily generalizes to any even n. If n is odd, which we can write as $n = 2p + 1$, for $p \in \mathbb{N}$, we can take $[K_1] = \cdots = [K_p] = \{\emptyset\}$, $[K_{p+1}] = \cdots = [K_n] = \{a\}$, and K^T, K^F as above.

Table 2. Constructive Skept-manipulation of a profile of size 4 w.r.t the atom a

| | $[K_1]$ | $[K_2]$ | $[K_3]$ | $[K_4]$ | $[K^T]$ | $[K^F]$ | $d^\Sigma(\cdot, P^T)$ | $d^{\text{gmax}}(\cdot, P^T)$ | $d^\Sigma(\cdot, P^F)$ | $d^{\text{gmax}}(\cdot, P^F)$ |
	$\{\emptyset\}$	$\{\emptyset\}$	$\{a\}$	$\{a\}$	$\{\emptyset\}$	$\{a\}$				
$\emptyset$	0	0	1	1	0	1	2	$(1,1,0,0,0)$	3	$(1,1,1,0,0)$
a	1	1	0	0	1	0	3	$(1,1,1,0,0)$	2	$(1,1,0,0,0)$
b	1	1	2	2	1	2	7	$(2,2,1,1,1)$	8	$(2,2,2,1,1)$
...	...	...	...	...	...	...	...	...	...	...

If possible for an agent to constructively or destructively manipulate, it is appropriate to ask *how* it can do it: are intricate formulas needed to achieve the goal, or can a 'simple' base work just as well? In Example 7 the strategic agent manipulates using complete bases, suggesting that the answer lies with the second option. Indeed we can show that, if manipulation is possible at all, then it can be done with a complete base.

Theorem 2. *If the strategic agent constructively/destructively Acc-manipulates P w.r.t. p using K^F, for $\text{Acc} \in \{\text{Skept}, \text{Cred}\}$, then there exists a complete base K_*^F such that $K_*^F \models K^F$ and the agent constructively/destructively Skept-manipulates P w.r.t. p using K_*^F.*

We give here the intuition driving the proof for Skept-manipulation, adding as well the fact that the base K_*^F is found in the same way for constructive and destructive manipulation: if manipulation is possible with K^F, then pick a model of K^F that is closest to one of the models of μ crucial for the success of manipulation. In the case of destructive Skept-manipulation, this would be an interpretation v_* that ends up being in $[\Delta_\mu^{d,f}(P + K^F)]$ and is such that $p \notin v_*$: v_* must exist, under the assumption that K^F successfully achieves destructive Skept-manipulation. We can then replace K^F with K_*^F, where $[K_*^F] = \{v_*\}$ and still achieve destructive Skept-manipulation.

There is one thing that mitigates the acuteness of the manipulation results. Note that we have not assumed so far that the strategic agent needs to have p among its accepted atoms, i.e., we do not require the agent to actually *believe* p in order to constructively/destructively manipulate with respect to it. Seeing the merging process as aggregation of agents' *reported* beliefs, stressed in Sect. 2, comes into play, as it allows for agents to participate with bases that can reflect a richer cognitive structure (e.g., the effects of bribery, or influence, motivating an agent to alter its reported beliefs). Thus, here we operate under the assumption that p (its acceptance, or otherwise) figures for the agent as a goal, regardless of whether it is actually part of its beliefs (manipulation furthering the truthful beliefs of the strategic agent is treated in Sect. 4.2).

Can an agent influence the acceptance of an atom it does not believe? We see in Example 7 that the answer is yes: the strategic agent there is able to constructively Skept-manipulate w.r.t. a even though a is not among the skeptical beliefs of the agent itself. And, in fact, we are able to show that, when $\mu = \top$ and all bases are complete, Skept-manipulation is possible only under this assumption.

Proposition 3. *If the strategic agent constructively Skept-manipulates P with respect to an atom p, relative to the constraint $\mu = \top$ and operator $\Delta^{d_H, \Sigma}$, when all bases are complete, then $p \notin$ Skept(K^T).*

Proposition 3 can be seen as a positive result, one way of reading it being that if the strategic agent already accepts p (i.e., $p \in$ Skept(K^T)), then if it cannot impose p by submitting K^T itself, for the given parameters, then there is no other way of doing it. As such, this is the closest we can come to a strategyproofness result for constructive/destructive manipulation.

4.2 Manipulation with Respect to a Satisfaction Index

Constructive and destructive manipulation deals with the question of whether an agent can affect the acceptance of an atom in the aggregated outcome, regardless of the beliefs of the agent. In this section we look at the case when the agent improves the outcome with respect to its beliefs, where improvement is measured using the skeptical and credulous satisfaction indices i_{Acc}, for Acc $\in$ {Skept, Cred}.

The strategic agent *manipulates P with respect to i_{Acc} using K^F* if it holds that $i_{\text{Acc}}(K^T, \Delta_\mu(P + K^F)) < i_{\text{Acc}}(K^T, \Delta_\mu(P + K^T))$. In other words, an agent can improve its satisfaction index by submitting K^F instead of K^T. We say that an operator Δ is *strategy-proof with respect to a satisfaction index* i_{Acc} if there is no profile P, constraint μ and bases K^T and K^F such that the strategic agent, having K^T as its truthful position, manipulates P with respect to i_{Acc} using K^F.

Our definition of manipulability based on satisfaction indices is inspired by previous work on manipulation of propositional merging operators [11] but differs from it in an important respect: we measure the distance between the *accepted* atoms of the manipulating agent and the result, rather than between the sets of models themselves. A more minor (technical) difference is that, in our case, an agent is more satisfied when its index *decreases*.[2] This reflects the fact that the manipulated result gets closer to the agent's beliefs.

Example 8. In Example 2, we have $\text{Skept}(K_4^T) = a$ and $\text{Skept}(\Delta_\mu^{d_H,\Sigma}(P^T)) = b$. Thus, $i_{\text{Skept}}(K_4^T, \Delta_\mu^{d_H,\Sigma}(P^T)) = |a \triangle b| = 2$. However, by agent 4 submitting K_4^F instead of K_4^T, we get that $\text{Skept}(\Delta_\mu^{d_H,\Sigma}(P^F)) = ac$ and $i_{\text{Skept}}(K_4^T, \Delta_\mu^{d_H,\Sigma}(P^F)) = 1$. Thus, by submitting a position different from its truthful one, agent 4 is able to bring the (skeptically accepted atoms of) the merging result closer to its own position.

Example 8 shows that manipulation is possible in the general case for the merging operator $\Delta^{d_H,\Sigma}$ and the skeptical index. What is, now, the full picture with respect to manipulability? As for constructive and destructive manipulation, we first note that the identity $i_{\text{Skept}}(\varphi, \psi) = i_{\text{Cred}}(\overline{\varphi}, \overline{\psi})$ (see Sect. 3) allows us to turn a manipulation instance with respect to i_{Skept} into a manipulation instance with respect to i_{Cred} simply by replacing every formula involved with its dual.

For the operators $\Delta^{d,\text{gmax}}$ and $\Delta^{d,\text{max}}$ index manipulation turns out to be, like atom manipulation, unavoidable. This stays so even under heavy restrictions (i.e., complete bases and $\mu = \top$), and for any size $n \geq 2$ of the profile.

Theorem 3. *For* $d \in \{d_D, d_H\}$, $f \in \{\text{gmax}, \text{max}\}$ *and any* $n \geq 2$ *there exists a profile* $P = (K_1, \ldots, K_n)$ *and bases* K^T *and* K^F *such that the strategic agent manipulates* P *with respect to* i_{Acc}, *even if* $\mu = \top$ *and all bases* K_i, *for* $i \in \{1, \ldots, n\}$, *as well as* K^T *and* K^F, *are complete.*

The story is different for the operator $\Delta^{d_H,\Sigma}$: as seen in Proposition 3, constructive manipulation for skeptical acceptance, complete profiles, and $\mu = \top$ can only get an atom p into the result if the agent does not believe p. In other words, the result can be affected for p, but it is worth noting that the skeptical index does not increase by doing so. It turns out that this holds in general for the operator $\Delta_\top^{d_H,\Sigma}$, i.e., this operator is strategy-proof with respect to a satisfaction index i_{Acc}, for $\text{Acc} \in \{\text{Skept}, \text{Cred}\}$.

Theorem 4. *If all bases in the profile, as well as* K^T *and* K^F, *are complete and* $\mu = \top$, *then the operator* $\Delta_\top^{d_H,\Sigma}$ *is strategy-proof with respect to* i_{Skept} *and* i_{Cred}.

---

[2] As such, our indices can be interpreted as dissatisfaction indices; nevertheless we stick to the term satisfaction index.

Proof (sketch). For complete profiles, the operator $\Delta_\top^{d_H, \Sigma}$ returns models v that reflect majority opinion, i.e., if an atom p is true in a majority of bases, p is in v; if p is false in a majority of bases, then p is not in v; and if there is no majority (half of the bases have p in their model), then the result contains both a v with p and a v' without p in them. A strategic agent cannot increase its index: adding something to its model can make this skeptically accepted, but this is not in the agent's belief (similarly for other cases).

The restrictions on $\Delta^{d_H, \Sigma}$ in Theorem 4 are essential: weakening any of them results in the operator being manipulable.

Proposition 4. *If it is does not hold that $\mu = \top$ and all bases in P, as well as the truthful position of the strategic agent, are complete, then $\Delta^{d_H, \Sigma}$ is manipulable with respect to i_{Acc}.*

5   Influence of One Agent over the Outcome

Section 4 addresses the question of whether the strategic agent can modify the merging result to its advantage. But it is useful to take a step back and ask whether the strategic agent can modify the result in the first place, i.e., whether it matters if the strategic agent takes part in the merging process at all and, if yes, how exactly it can influence it. Given a profile P, an operator Δ, a constraint μ and a base K, we say that $\Delta_\mu(P)$ is *the intermediary result*, and $\Delta_\mu(P + K)$ is *the final result*.

There are, *a priori*, two ways in which the agent can change the intermediary result: one is by removing interpretations from $[\Delta_\mu(P)]$; i.e., by turning winning interpretations into non-winning interpretations; the other is by adding interpretations to $[\Delta_\mu(P)]$, i.e., by turning non-winning interpretations into winners. If w is an interpretation, we say that the strategic agent *demotes w from $\Delta_\mu(P)$ using K* if $w \in [\Delta_\mu(P)]$ and $w \notin [\Delta_\mu(P + K)]$, and that it *promotes w with respect to $\Delta_\mu(P)$ using K* if $w \notin [\Delta_\mu(P)]$ and $w \in [\Delta_\mu(P + K)]$.

It turns out that for a significant proportion of the operators we are working with the strategic agent can demote any number of interpretations from the intermediary result, using an easy strategy: focus on the wanted interpretations, and submit a base with those interpretations as models; the unwanted interpretations thus receive a penalty that renders them non-winning in the final result.

Proposition 5. *If P is a profile, μ is a constraint, $d \in \{d_H, d_D\}$, $f \in \{\Sigma, \text{gmax}\}$ and $W \subset [\Delta_\mu^{d, f}(P)]$ is a set of interpretations, then a strategic agent can demote all interpretations in $[\Delta_\mu^{d, f}(P)] \setminus W$ from $\Delta_\mu^{d, f}(P)$ by submitting K_W with $[K_W] = W$.*

On the other hand, promoting interpretations is more difficult: the strategic agent's ability to promote an interpretation w depends on the margin by which w loses out to the winning interpretations. We show this here for the operator $\Delta^{d_H, \Sigma}$.

Proposition 6. *If w is an interpretation such that $w \in [\mu]$ and $w \notin [\Delta_\mu^{d_H, \Sigma}(P)]$, then the strategic agent can promote w with respect to $\Delta_\mu^{d_H, \Sigma}(P)$ iff $d_H^\Sigma(w, P) - d_H^\Sigma(w_i, P) \leq d_H(w, w_i)$, for every $w_i \in [\Delta_\mu^{d_H, \Sigma}(P)]$.*

Intuitively, $d_H^\Sigma(w, P) - d_H^\Sigma(w_i, P)$ is the margin by which w loses out to a winning interpretation w_i in $\leq_P^{d, f}$. Proposition 6 then tells us that the strategic agent can reverse the order between w and w_i if and only if this margin is less than the Hamming distance between w and w_i. In general, the amount of support the strategic agent can give to w relative to w_i is at most $d_H(w, w_i)$ and thus, if w is trailing w_i by more than this amount, there is nothing the strategic agent can do for it. Using this result we note that, if possible for an agent to promote an interpretation w, then it can do so using a complete base.

Corollary 1. *If the strategic agent can promote an interpretation w with respect to $\Delta_\mu^{d, f}(P)$, then it can do so with a base K_w such that $[K_w] = \{w\}$.*

This result is similar in spirit to Theorem 2, and suggests something like a best strategy if the goal is to promote w: the strategic agent can always submit a base K_w with w as the sole model, since if w can be promoted to the final result then K_w is guaranteed to do it; otherwise, it does not matter what the agent submits.

Example 9. Suppose $[\mu] = \{w_1, w_2, w_3, w_4\}$, $[\Delta_\mu^{d, \Sigma}(P)] = \{w_1, w_2, w_3\}$, for $d \in \{d_H, d_D\}$. The strategic agent submits K with $[K] = \{w_1, w_2\}$. We write $d_H(w_1, P) = d_H(w_2, P) = d_H(w_3, P) = \beta$, $d_H(w_4, P) = \beta + \epsilon_4$ and $\delta_{3*} = \min\{\delta_{31}, \delta_{32}\}$, $\delta_{4*} = \min\{\delta_{41}, \delta_{42}\}$ for the distance from w_3 and w_4, respectively, to K (see Table 3). Notice now that $[\Delta_\mu^{d, \Sigma}(P + K)] = \{w_1, w_2\}$, i.e., the strategic agent demotes w_3 from $\Delta_\mu^{d, \Sigma}(P)$. To promote w_4 to the final result, the obvious strategy is for the strategic agent to submit K', with $[K'] = \{w_4\}$. In this case, promoting w_4 is successful only if $\epsilon_4 \leq \delta_{i4}$, where $\delta_{i4} = d_H(w_i, w_4)$, for $i \in \{1, 2, 3\}$ (again, see Table 3). The same argument applies to the drastic distance d_D, the only difference being that $\delta_{3*} = \delta_{4*} = \delta_{i4} = 1$, for $i \in \{1, 2, 3\}$.

With respect to atoms, an analogous question regarding the influence of an agent asks under what conditions a specific atom can be made part of the final result. The idea here turns out to be that no single agent can overturn majorities w.r.t. skeptical acceptances of the bases in the complete profile and $\mu \equiv \top$: if more than half of the agents skeptically accept a, then no strategic agent can alter this. This is the same fact that underwrites strategyproofness of $\Delta^{d_H, \Sigma}$. For non-complete profiles strategyproofness is lost, but a related result can be shown.

For a profile P, define agents' support for acceptances as $\texttt{Credsupp}_P(a) = |\{K \in P \mid a \in \texttt{Cred}(K)\}|$ and $\texttt{Skeptsupp}_P(a) = |\{K \in P \mid a \in \texttt{Skept}(K)\}|$. By generalizing a result from [7], we show that neither a majority of skeptical support nor a majority of credulous non-support can be altered, for aggregation under $\Delta_\top^{d_H, \Sigma}$.

Proposition 7. *Let $P = (K_1, \ldots, K_{n-1})$ be a profile, $X = \{x \mid \texttt{Skeptsupp}_P(x) > \frac{n}{2}\}$, and $Y = \{x \mid \texttt{Credsupp}_P(x) < \frac{n}{2}\}$. For any base K_n and $M = \Delta_\top^{d_H, \Sigma}(P + K_n)$, it holds that $X \subseteq \texttt{Skept}(M)$, and $Y \subseteq (\mathcal{P} \setminus \texttt{Cred}(M))$.*

A similar result does not hold for operator $\Delta_\top^{d_H,\max}$, i.e., when using `max` instead of Σ. Thus, for `max` majorities may be overturned, as illustrated in the next example.

Table 3. The agent penalizes w_3 by not including it in the models of its submitted base, and can only promote w_4 if the margin ϵ_4 by which it trails the other interpretations is sufficiently small.

	P	$\{w_1, w_2\}$	$\{w_4\}$	$d_H^\Sigma(\cdot, P+K)$	$d_H^\Sigma(\cdot, P+K')$
w_1	β	0	δ_{14}	β	$\beta + \delta_{14}$
w_2	β	0	δ_{24}	β	$\beta + \delta_{24}$
w_3	β	δ_{3*}	δ_{34}	$\beta + \delta_{3*}$	$\beta + \delta_{34}$
w_4	$\beta + \epsilon_4$	δ_{4*}	0	$\beta + \delta_{4*} + \epsilon_4$	$\beta + \epsilon_4$

Example 10. Take $[K_1] = \{b\}$, $[K_2] = \{c\}$, and $[K_3^T] = \{abc\}$. With $\Delta_\top^{d_H,\max}$ the result is $\{bc\}$. When agent 3 reports $[K_3^F] = \{ab\}$ instead, the result is $\{\emptyset, a, b, bc, abc\}$. Thus, agent 3 can get a to be true in a model of the output, even if less than half of the agents have a in some model of their base (in fact only agent 3 accepts a credulously).

6 Complexity of Constructive and Destructive Manipulation

By our results, if an agent can constructively or destructively **Skept**-manipulate the aggregation process, then it can do so by submitting a complete base (see Theorem 2). By Proposition 2, **Cred**-manipulation can always be achieved by the dual of a complete base (again a complete base), if manipulation is possible. By these results, for both constructive and destructive manipulation, deciding whether a profile is manipulable is in Σ_2^P. To see this, we first recall that computing the result of the merging process, i.e., whether $\Delta_\mu^{d,f}(P) \models \varphi$ holds, is a problem that can be solved via a deterministic polynomial time algorithm with access to an NP oracle, for all operators considered in this paper [19,20]. This implies that one can check whether an unmodified (non-altered) profile already returns the desired atom skeptically (credulously). If not, a non-deterministic construction ("guess") of a complete base with a subsequent new check of the result decides whether the constructed base results in a manipulation. For operator $\Delta_\mu^{d_H,\Sigma}$ and destructive **Skept**-manipulation, we also can show hardness for this class.

Theorem 5. *Deciding whether a profile can be destructively **Skept**-manipulated w.r.t. an atom and μ for operator $\Delta_\mu^{d_H,\Sigma}$ by submitting a complete base is Σ_2^P-complete.*

7 Related Work

Existing work on manipulation of belief merging operators [9,11] differs from ours in that satisfaction indices in [11] are not based on skeptical or credulous acceptance but on the models that the strategic agent and the result have in common. To highlight this difference, note that under the indices in [11] the strategic agent in Example 2 would be equally unsatisfied with both the truthful result $\Delta_\mu^{d_H,\Sigma}(P^T)$ and $\Delta_\mu^{d_H,\Sigma}(P^F)$, since K^T shares no model with either. Under our interpretation of the indices, $\Delta_\mu^{d_H,\Sigma}(P^F)$ ends up delivering a better result for the strategic agent than $\Delta_\mu^{d_H,\Sigma}(P^T)$, as under $\Delta_\mu^{d_H,\Sigma}(P^F)$ the atom a is guaranteed to be in the result, and there is a sense in which this is satisfactory for the strategic agent, as a is an atom that it skeptically accepts. Then, different to both [9,11], we also show results for acceptance manipulation (not based on indices), i.e., for constructive and destructive manipulation.

Belief merging invites comparison to multi-winner elections [1,2,14,23], combinatorial voting [22], and Judgment Aggregation [3,4,10]. We mention here that our use of acceptance notions and satisfaction indices, the compact encoding of sets of interpretations (agents' "top candidates") as propositional formulas, and the fact that we do not require the output to be of a specific size suggest that existing results in this area are not directly applicable to our setting. Our work intersects with social choice in the special case when the profile is complete and the number of bases is odd. In this case the aggregation problem corresponds to a Judgment Aggregation problem, with $\Delta_\top^{d_H,\Sigma}$ delivering the majority opinion on the atoms (considered as issues): this corresponds to the observation made in the Social Choice literature [5] that the majority opinion minimizes the sum of the Hamming distances to voters' approval ballots. Our strategy-proofness result for $\Delta_\top^{d_H,\Sigma}$ dovetails neatly with a similar result in Judgment Aggregation [4,10], though our treatment is slightly more general, as it accommodates both an even and an odd number of bases.

8 Conclusions

We have looked at the potential for manipulation in a belief merging framework [19,21], when results are obtained considering skeptical or credulous consequences. We have shown that manipulation is not only possible for well-known aggregation operators, but also that manipulation can be achieved by semantically simple (i.e., complete) bases, even if the complexity of doing so is in general high.

For future work, our aim is to extend these results to more merging operators, study best responses (strategies) by agents, manipulability in settings with incomplete information, and to consider extended settings of manipulation studied in Social Choice, e.g., bribery [3], where sets of agents can be "bribed" to form a joint manipulating coalition. We also want to look at properties from Social Choice used to understand strategyproofness at a more abstract level (e.g., monotonicity), and at how to adapt these properties to the merging framework.

This topic has received some attention [9,16], but more work is needed to establish connections to manipulation and strategyproofness.

Acknowledgements. We thank the anonymous reviewers for their helpful comments on an earlier version of the paper. This work was supported by the Austrian Science Fund (FWF): P30168-N31 and W1255-N23.

References

1. Amanatidis, G., Barrot, N., Lang, J., Markakis, E., Ries, B.: Multiple referenda and multiwinner elections using Hamming distances: complexity and manipulability. In: Weiss, G., Yolum, P., Bordini, R.H., Elkind, E. (eds.) Proceedings of the AAMAS 2015, pp. 715–723. ACM (2015)
2. Barrot, N., Lang, J., Yokoo, M.: Manipulation of Hamming-based approval voting for multiple referenda and committee elections. In: Larson, K., Winikoff, M., Das, S., Durfee, E.H. (eds.) Proceedings of the AAMAS 2017, pp. 597–605. ACM (2017)
3. Baumeister, D., Erdélyi, G., Erdélyi, O.J., Rothe, J.: Complexity of manipulation and bribery in judgment aggregation for uniform premise-based quota rules. Math. Soc. Sci. **76**, 19–30 (2015)
4. Baumeister, D., Rothe, J., Selker, A.K.: Strategic behavior in judgment aggregation. In: Endriss, U. (ed.) Trends in Computational Social Choice, pp. 145–168. AI Access (2017)
5. Brams, S.J., Kilgour, D.M., Sanver, M.R.: A minimax procedure for electing committees. Public Choice **132**(3), 401–420 (2007)
6. Conitzer, V., Walsh, T.: Barriers to manipulation in voting. In: Brandt, F., Conitzer, V., Endriss, U., Lang, J., Procaccia, A.D. (eds.) Handbook of Computational Social Choice, pp. 127–145. Cambridge University Press, Cambridge (2016)
7. Delobelle, J., Haret, A., Konieczny, S., Mailly, J., Rossit, J., Woltran, S.: Merging of abstract argumentation frameworks. In: Baral, C., Delgrande, J.P., Wolter, F. (eds.) Proceedings of the KR 2016, pp. 33–42. AAAI Press (2016)
8. Díaz, A.M., Pérez, R.P.: Impossibility in belief merging. Artif. Intell. **251**, 1–34 (2017)
9. Diaz, A.M., Perez, R.P.: Epistemic states, fusion and strategy-proofness. In: Ferme, E., Villata, S. (eds.) Proceedings of the NMR, pp. 176–185 (2018)
10. Endriss, U.: Judgment aggregation. In: Brandt, F., Conitzer, V., Endriss, U., Lang, J., Procaccia, A.D. (eds.) Handbook of Computational Social Choice, pp. 399–426. Cambridge University Press, Cambridge (2016)
11. Everaere, P., Konieczny, S., Marquis, P.: The strategy-proofness landscape of merging. J. Artif. Intell. Res. **28**, 49–105 (2007)
12. Everaere, P., Konieczny, S., Marquis, P.: Belief merging versus judgment aggregation. In: Weiss, G., Yolum, P., Bordini, R.H., Elkind, E. (eds.) Proceedings of the AAMAS 2015, pp. 999–1007. ACM (2015)
13. Faliszewski, P., Procaccia, A.D.: AI's war on manipulation: are we winning? AI Mag. **31**(4), 53–64 (2010)
14. Faliszewski, P., Skowron, P., Slinko, A., Talmon, N.: Multiwinner voting: a new challenge for social choice theory. In: Endriss, U. (ed.) Trends in Computational Social Choice, pp. 27–47. AI Access (2017)

15. Gabbay, D.M., Rodrigues, O., Pigozzi, G.: Connections between belief revision, belief merging and social choice. J. Log. Comput. **19**(3), 445–446 (2009)
16. Haret, A., Pfandler, A., Woltran, S.: Beyond IC postulates: classification criteria for merging operators. In: Kaminka, G.A., et al. (eds.) Proceedings of the ECAI 2016, pp. 372–380 (2016)
17. Haret, A., Wallner, J.P.: Manipulation of semantic aggregation procedures for propositional knowledge bases and argumentation frameworks. In: Ferme, E., Villata, S. (eds.) Proceedings of the NMR, pp. 146–155 (2018)
18. Haret, A., Wallner, J.P.: Manipulating skeptical and credulous consequences when merging beliefs. Technical report DBAI-TR-2019-114, TU Wien (2019). https://www.dbai.tuwien.ac.at/research/report/dbai-tr-2019-114.pdf
19. Konieczny, S., Lang, J., Marquis, P.: Distance based merging: a general framework and some complexity results. In: Fensel, D., Giunchiglia, F., McGuinness, D.L., Williams, M. (eds.) Proceedings of the KR 2002, pp. 97–108. Morgan Kaufmann (2002)
20. Konieczny, S., Lang, J., Marquis, P.: DA^2 merging operators. Artif. Intell. **157**(1–2), 49–79 (2004)
21. Konieczny, S., Pérez, R.P.: Logic based merging. J. Philosop. Log. **40**(2), 239–270 (2011)
22. Lang, J., Xia, L.: Voting in combinatorial domains. In: Brandt, F., Conitzer, V., Endriss, U., Lang, J., Procaccia, A.D. (eds.) Handbook of Computational Social Choice, pp. 197–222. Cambridge University Press, Cambridge (2016)
23. Meir, R., Procaccia, A.D., Rosenschein, J.S., Zohar, A.: Complexity of strategic behavior in multi-winner elections. J. Artif. Intell. Res. **33**, 149–178 (2008)
24. Strasser, C., Antonelli, G.A.: Non-monotonic logic. In: Zalta, E.N. (ed.) The Stanford Encyclopedia of Philosophy. Metaphysics Research Lab, Stanford University, summer 2018 edn. (2018)
25. Zwicker, W.S.: Introduction to the theory of voting. In: Brandt, F., Conitzer, V., Endriss, U., Lang, J., Procaccia, A.D. (eds.) Handbook of Computational Social Choice, pp. 23–56. Cambridge University Press, Cambridge (2016)

Repairing Non-monotonic Knowledge Bases

Markus Ulbricht[✉]

Department of Computer Science, Leipzig University, Leipzig, Germany
mulbricht@informatik.uni-leipzig.de

Abstract. Minimal inconsistent subsets of knowledge bases in monotonic logics play an important role when investigating the reasons for conflicts and trying to handle them. In the context of non-monotonic reasoning this notion is not as meaningful due to the possibility of resolving conflicts by adding information. In this paper we investigate inconsistency in non-monotonic logics while taking this issue into account. In particular, we show that the well-known classical duality between hitting sets of minimal inconsistent subsets and maximal consistent subsets generalizes to arbitrary logics even if we allow adding novel information to a given knowledge base. We illustrate the versatility of the main theorems by covering more sophisticated situations and demonstrate how to utilize our results to analyze inconsistency in abstract argumentation.

Keywords: Non-monotonic reasoning · Inconsistency · Abstract argumentation

1 Introduction

Inconsistency is an omnipresent phenomenon in logical accounts of knowledge representation and reasoning (KR) [7,12,13,18,19]. Classical logics usually suffer from the *principle of explosion* which renders reasoning meaningless, as everything can be derived from inconsistent theories. Therefore, reasoning under inconsistency [4,23,25] is an important research area in KR. In general, one can distinguish two paradigms in handling inconsistent information. The first paradigm advocates living with inconsistency but providing non-classical semantics that allow the derivation of non-trivial information, such as using paraconsistent reasoning [6], reasoning with possibilistic logic [13], or formal argumentation [2]. The second paradigm is about explicitly restoring consistency, thus changing the theory itself, as it is done in e.g. belief revision [19] or belief merging [24].

In a seminal paper belonging to the latter category Reiter [26] proves that consistency of $\mathcal{K}$ can be restored by computing a minimal hitting set of the

This work was funded by Deutsche Forschungsgemeinschaft DFG (Research Training Group 1763; project BR 1817/7-2).

© Springer Nature Switzerland AG 2019
F. Calimeri et al. (Eds.): JELIA 2019, LNAI 11468, pp. 151–167, 2019.
https://doi.org/10.1007/978-3-030-19570-0_10

minimal inconsistent subsets of $\mathcal{K}$ and eliminating the elements of the hitting set. Based on a strengthening of the notion of consistency this result generalizes to arbitrary, possibly non-monotonic logics [10]. Although appealing, this result neglects an important opportunity provided by non-monotonic logics: here consistencies cannot only be resolved by deleting formulas, but also by adding formulas. In fact, adding information to a knowledge base in order to represent additional assumptions might in some cases even be easier to justify than e.g. removing constraints. The main goal of this paper is thus to give duality characterizations for repairs while taking this into account.

The paper is organized as follows: we give necessary background in Sect. 2. Sections 3 and 4 investigate repairs based on addition as well as deletion of formulas and give characterizations in terms of hitting set dualities. Further aspects are investigated, in particular connections between the different notions. Section 5 discusses more sophisticated situations, namely forbidding removal of certain subsets of a knowledge base as well as modifying instead of deleting and adding formulas. Section 6 is a short case study demonstrating how our results and notions can be used to analyze inconsistency in abstract argumentation, that is, a given framework does not possess accepted arguments. Section 7 concludes.

2   Background

Hitting Sets and Tuples. In the present paper, minimality and maximality are to be understood with respect to the $\subseteq$-relation. So, if a set M is minimal with a certain property, this means there is no set $M' \subsetneq M$ satisfying it. Now let $\mathcal{M}$ be a set of sets. We call $\mathcal{S}$ a *hitting set* of $\mathcal{M}$ if $\mathcal{S} \cap M \neq \emptyset$ for each $M \in \mathcal{M}$. In this work, consideration of tuples of sets will be crucial. So given four sets X_1, Y_1, X_2, Y_2, we extend the basic set operations naturally by letting $(X_1, Y_1) \subseteq (X_2, Y_2)$ iff $\subseteq$ holds component wise. This definition also induces minimality and maximality for tuples. We let $(X_1, Y_1) \cap (X_2, Y_2) = (X_1 \cap X_2, Y_1 \cap Y_2)$. We write $(X_1, Y_1) \cap (X_2, Y_2) = \emptyset$ iff $X_1 \cap Y_1 = \emptyset$ and $X_2 \cap Y_2 = \emptyset$. Now the definition of a hitting set applies to a set $\mathcal{M}$ of sets of tuples in the natural way.

Answer Set Programming (ASP). Throughout the paper we use examples based on logic programs with disjunction in the head and two kinds of negation, classical negation $\neg$ and default negation *not*, under answer set semantics. Such programs consist of rules of the form

$$l_0 \leftarrow l_1, \ldots, l_m, \text{not } l_{m+1}, \ldots, \text{not } l_n. \tag{1}$$

where $0 \leq m \leq n$ and the l_i are ordinary literals. For programs without default negation $(m = n)$ the unique answer set is the smallest set of literals closed under all rules, where a set M is closed under a rule of form (1) without default negation iff $l_0 \in M$ whenever the body literals $l_1, \ldots, l_m$ are. If the answer set contains two complementary literals, then it is the set of all literals. For a program P with default negation, a set M of literals is an answer set iff M is the answer set of the reduced program P^M (without default negation) obtained from P by (i) deleting rules with "not l_j" in the body for some $l_j \in M$, and (ii) deleting default negated literals from the remaining rules. P is inconsistent iff all of its answer sets contain a complementary pair of literals. This includes the case where P has no answer sets at all. See [9] for more details.

Logics. Since we are going to consider arbitrary (non-monotonic) frameworks, we start by giving an abstract definition of a logic. We do so as in [11]. In a nutshell, a logic L consists of syntax and semantics of formulas. To model the syntax properly, we stipulate a set WF of so-called well-formed formulas. Any knowledge base $\mathcal{K}$ consists of a subset of WF. To model the semantics, we let BS be a set of so-called belief sets. Intuitively, given a knowledge base $\mathcal{K}$, the set of all that can be inferred from $\mathcal{K}$ is $B \subseteq$ BS. To formalize this, a mapping ACC assigns the set B of corresponding belief sets to each knowledge base $\mathcal{K}$. Finally, some belief sets are considered inconsistent. We call the set of all inconsistent belief sets INC. Hence, our definition of a logic is as follows.

Definition 1. *A logic L is a tuple $L = (WF, BS, INC, ACC)$ where WF is a set of well-formed formulas, BS is the set of belief sets, $INC \subseteq BS$ is an upward closed[1] set of inconsistent belief sets, and $ACC : 2^{WF} \to 2^{BS}$ is a mapping. A knowledge base $\mathcal{K}$ of L is a finite subset of WF.*

Observe that our definition of a logic is general enough to capture various monotonic and non-monotonic frameworks like propositional logic, ASP [17], abstract argumentation frameworks [14] etc.

Example 1. Let A be a set of propositional atoms. A propositional logic L_P can be defined as $L_P = (WF_P, BS_P, INC_P, ACC_P)$ where WF_P are the well-formed formulas over A, BS_P are the deductively closed sets of formulas and since any formula can be derived from a contradiction, $INC_P = \{WF\}$. The mapping ACC_P assigns to each $\mathcal{K} \subseteq WF_P$ the set containing its unique set of theorems.

Example 2. Let A be a set of propositional atoms. Extended logic programs under answer set semantics over A is $L_{ASP} = (WF_{ASP}, BS_{ASP}, INC_{ASP}, ACC_{ASP})$ where WF_{ASP} is the set of all rules of the form (1) over A, $BS_{ASP} = 2^A$, INC_{ASP} is the set containing all literals, and ACC_{ASP} assigns to a logic program $P \subseteq WF_{ASP}$ the set of all answer sets of P.

Definition 2. *Let L be a logic. A knowledge base $\mathcal{K}$ is called* inconsistent *iff $ACC(\mathcal{K}) \subseteq INC$. Let $I(\mathcal{K})$ and $I_{min}(\mathcal{K})$ denote the inconsistent and minimal inconsistent subsets of $\mathcal{K}$, respectively.*

All notions in this paper depend on the underlying logic L, so e.g. $I(\mathcal{K})$ should more precisely be called $I(\mathcal{K})^L$. We will omit these superscripts since there will be no risk of confusion. The only exception is Sect. 5.

Observe that Definition 2 captures cases where $\mathcal{K}$ has no belief sets at all.

---

[1] S is upward closed if $B \in S$, $B \subseteq B'$ implies $B' \in S$.

Example 3. Consider the logic program P given as follows.

$$P: \qquad a \leftarrow \text{not } a. \qquad\qquad a \leftarrow \text{not } b. \qquad\qquad b.$$

The reader may verify that the subprogram $H = \{a \leftarrow \text{not } a.\}$ is inconsistent since there is no answer set. Formally, $\text{ACC}(H) = \text{ACC}_{\text{ASP}}(H) = \emptyset \subseteq \text{INC}$. In contrast, $H' = H \cup \{a \leftarrow \text{not } b.\}$ is consistent as it possesses the answer set $\{a\}$. P itself is inconsistent.

Definition 3 [11]. *A logic* $L = (WF, BS, INC, ACC)$ *is sceptically monotonic whenever* $\mathcal{K}' \supseteq \mathcal{K}$ *implies: if* $B' \in ACC(\mathcal{K}')$ *then* $B' \supseteq B$ *for some* $B \in ACC(\mathcal{K})$. *We call such* L *monotonic for short.*

Note that in a monotonic logic conflicts cannot be resolved, i.e., if $\mathcal{K} \subseteq \mathcal{K}'$ holds for two knowledge bases $\mathcal{K}$ and $\mathcal{K}'$ where $\mathcal{K}$ is inconsistent, then so is $\mathcal{K}'$.

Example 4. Recall P and $H' \subseteq P$ from Example 3. We found $\text{ACC}(H) = \emptyset$ and $\text{ACC}(H') = \{\{a\}\}$. So, there is a set $B' \in \text{ACC}(H')$, namely $\{a\}$. However, there is no $B \in \text{ACC}(H)$ since the latter set is empty. In particular, there is no $B \in \text{ACC}(H)$ satisfying $B \subseteq B'$. Hence, ASP is non-monotonic.

Strong Inconsistency. Let us now discuss the notion of *strong inconsistency* and how it induces a hitting set duality for non-monotonic logics. As we do this quite briefly, we refer the reader to [11] for a more thorough discussion of strong inconsistency.

Definition 4. *For* $\mathcal{H}, \mathcal{K} \subseteq WF$ *with* $\mathcal{H} \subseteq \mathcal{K}$, $\mathcal{H}$ *is called* strongly $\mathcal{K}$-*inconsistent if* $\mathcal{H} \subseteq \mathcal{H}' \subseteq \mathcal{K}$ *implies* $\mathcal{H}'$ *is inconsistent. We call* $\mathcal{H}$ *simply* strongly inconsistent *when there is no risk of confusion. Let* $SI(\mathcal{K})$ *and* $SI_{min}(\mathcal{K})$ *denote the strongly inconsistent and minimal strongly inconsistent subsets of* $\mathcal{K}$, *respectively.*

Example 5. Consider again $H \subseteq H' \subseteq P$ from Example 3. We already found the inconsistent subset H which is however not *strongly* inconsistent due to the consistent superset H'. The reader may verify that $SI_{min}(P) = \{\{a \leftarrow \text{not } a., b.\}\}$.

We proceed with the well-known concept of (maximal) consistent subsets.

Definition 5. *We say* $\mathcal{H} \subseteq \mathcal{K}$ *is a* maximal consistent *subset of* $\mathcal{K}$ *if* $\mathcal{H}$ *is consistent and* $\mathcal{H} \subsetneq \mathcal{H}' \subseteq \mathcal{K}$ *implies* $\mathcal{H}'$ *is inconsistent. We denote the set of all maximal consistent subsets of* $\mathcal{K}$ *by* $C_{max}(\mathcal{K})$.

Now we are ready to phrase the duality result from [11].

Theorem 1. *Let* $\mathcal{K}$ *be a knowledge base. Then,* $\mathcal{S}$ *is a minimal hitting set of* $SI_{min}(\mathcal{K})$ *if and only if* $\mathcal{K} \backslash \mathcal{S} \in C_{max}(\mathcal{K})$.

Example 6. One can turn P from above into a consistent program by removing either $\{a \leftarrow \text{not } a.\}$ or $\{b.\}$. They are indeed the minimal hitting sets of $SI_{min}(P)$.

3 Addition-Based Repairs

Let us now consider repairs based on additional information. In general, it is not quite clear which information might be appropriate, especially when investigating a general logic as in the present paper. Moreover, it appears to be hard to give meaningful results when allowing an *arbitrary* superset of a knowledge base $\mathcal{K}$. We thus assume the set of potential additional information is given.

More precisely, we consider knowledge bases $\mathcal{K}$ (as usual) and $\mathcal{G}$ (of potential additional assumptions). The set $\mathcal{G}$ itself is not necessarily consistent. For technical convenience we assume $\mathcal{K}$ and $\mathcal{G}$ to be disjoint. This assumption also matches the intuitive meaning of $\mathcal{G}$ as a set of potential additional information. The following definition formally introduces repairs wrt. $\mathcal{G}$.

Definition 6. *Let $\mathcal{K}$ and $\mathcal{G}$ be disjoint knowledge bases. If for $\mathcal{A} \subseteq \mathcal{G}$, $\mathcal{K} \cup \mathcal{A}$ is consistent, then we call $\mathcal{A}$ a* repairing subset of $\mathcal{G}$ wrt. $\mathcal{K}$. *Let $\mathrm{REP}(\mathcal{K}, \mathcal{G}) = \{\mathcal{A} \subseteq \mathcal{G} \mid \mathcal{K} \cup \mathcal{A}$ is consistent$\}$. We denote the* minimal repairing subset *of $\mathcal{G}$ wrt. $\mathcal{K}$ by $\mathrm{REP}_{min}(\mathcal{K}, \mathcal{G})$.*

Example 7. Consider again the program P from Example 3. Assume we are given

$$G: \qquad\qquad a. \qquad\qquad\qquad c.$$
$$\qquad\qquad d. \qquad\qquad\qquad a \leftarrow d.$$

We see that $P \cup \{a.\}$ and $P \cup \{d., a \leftarrow d.\}$ are already consistent and thus

$$\mathrm{REP}_{min}(P, G) = \{\{a.\}, \{d., a \leftarrow d.\}\}$$

Our goal is to characterize the minimal repairing subsets for a given knowledge base $\mathcal{K}$ in terms of a hitting set duality, similar in spirit to Theorem 1. There the required notion was strong inconsistency, i.e., subsets $\mathcal{H}$ of a knowledge base $\mathcal{K}$ such that each set $\mathcal{H}'$ with $\mathcal{H} \subseteq \mathcal{H}' \subseteq \mathcal{K}$ is inconsistent. For addition-based repairs, our notion is a natural counterpart thereto, taking supersets of $\mathcal{K}$ into account rather than subsets.

Definition 7. *Let $\mathcal{K}$ and $\mathcal{G}$ be disjoint knowledge bases. If for $\mathcal{A} \subseteq \mathcal{G}$, $\mathcal{K}$ is* strongly $(\mathcal{K} \cup \mathcal{A})$-inconsistent, *i.e., $\mathcal{K} \in SI(\mathcal{K} \cup \mathcal{A})$, then we call $\mathcal{A}$ a* non-repairing subset *of $\mathcal{G}$ wrt. $\mathcal{K}$. Let $\mathrm{NREP}(\mathcal{K}, \mathcal{G}) = \{\mathcal{A} \subseteq \mathcal{G} \mid \mathcal{K} \in SI(\mathcal{K} \cup \mathcal{A})\}$. We denote the set of* maximal *non-repairing subsets of $\mathcal{G}$ wrt. $\mathcal{K}$ by $\mathrm{NREP}_{max}(\mathcal{K}, \mathcal{G})$.*

Example 8. Consider again P and G from Examples 3 and 7. The maximal non-repairing subsets of G are A_1 and a_2 where

$$A_1: \qquad c. \qquad\qquad a \leftarrow d. \qquad\qquad A_2: \qquad\qquad c. \qquad\qquad d.$$

Intuitively, in both cases we removed from G the sets of rules that could repair P. Neither A_i contains "a." or both "d." and "$a \leftarrow d$." to render P consistent.

Now, we are almost ready to phrase a duality result similar in spirit to Theorem 1. We need one more auxiliary definition.

Definition 8. *Let $\mathcal{K}$ and $\mathcal{G}$ be disjoint knowledge bases. A set $\overline{\mathcal{A}} \subseteq \mathcal{G}$ is in co-$\mathrm{NREP}_{max}(\mathcal{K}, \mathcal{G})$ if $\mathcal{G} \backslash \overline{\mathcal{A}}$ is in $\mathrm{NREP}_{max}(\mathcal{K}, \mathcal{G})$.*

As desired, the following theorem gives a characterization of $\mathrm{REP}_{min}(\mathcal{K}, \mathcal{G})$ in terms of a hitting set duality.

Theorem 2 (Superset Duality). *Let $\mathcal{K}$ and $\mathcal{G}$ be disjoint knowledge bases. Then, $\mathcal{S}$ is a minimal hitting set of co-$\mathrm{NREP}_{max}(\mathcal{K}, \mathcal{G})$ if and only if $\mathcal{S} \in \mathrm{REP}_{min}(\mathcal{K}, \mathcal{G})$.*

Example 9. For our programs P and G recall

$$\mathrm{REP}_{min}(P, G) = \{\{a.\}, \{d., a \leftarrow d.\}\},$$
$$\mathrm{NREP}_{max}(P, G) = \{\{c., a \leftarrow d.\}, \{c., d.\}\}.$$

In particular, co-$\mathrm{NREP}_{max}(P, G) = \{\{a., d.\}, \{a., a \leftarrow d.\}\}$. Indeed, REP_{min} (P, G) consists of the minimal hitting sets of co-$\mathrm{NREP}_{max}(P, G)$.

4 Arbitrary Repairs

Please observe that Theorem 2 is only meaningful whenever $\mathcal{K}$ is not strongly $(\mathcal{K} \cup \mathcal{G})$-inconsistent, i.e., whenever $\mathcal{G} \notin \mathrm{NREP}_{max}(\mathcal{K}, \mathcal{G})$. For example, this is naturally violated whenever the underlying logic is monotonic, but also when $\mathcal{G}$ is inappropriate when it comes to providing repair options for $\mathcal{K}$. This is an advantage of Theorem 1: Usually, a knowledge base contains consistent subsets and thus the theorem yields non-trivial results. Clearly, the finest solution would be combining the benefits of both Theorems 1 and 2. As it turns out, this can be achieved in a smooth and natural way.

Definition 9. *Let $\mathcal{K}$ and $\mathcal{G}$ be disjoint knowledge bases. We call $(\mathcal{D}, \mathcal{A})$ a bidirectional repair for $\mathcal{K}$ with respect to $\mathcal{G}$ if*

- *$\mathcal{D} \subseteq \mathcal{K}$ and $\mathcal{A} \subseteq \mathcal{G}$,*
- *$\mathcal{K} \backslash \mathcal{D} \cup \mathcal{A}$ is consistent.*

By $\mathrm{BI\text{-}REP}(\mathcal{K}, \mathcal{G})$ we denote the set of all bidirectional repairs for $\mathcal{K}$ with respect to $\mathcal{G}$. Let $\mathrm{BI\text{-}REP}_{min}(\mathcal{K}, \mathcal{G})$ be the set of all minimal ones, i.e., if $(\mathcal{D}, \mathcal{A}) \in \mathrm{BI\text{-}REP}_{min}(\mathcal{K}, \mathcal{G})$, then $(\mathcal{D}', \mathcal{A}') \in \mathrm{BI\text{-}REP}(\mathcal{K}, \mathcal{G})$ and $\mathcal{A}' \subseteq \mathcal{A}$ and $\mathcal{D}' \subseteq \mathcal{D}$ implies $(\mathcal{D}', \mathcal{A}') = (\mathcal{D}, \mathcal{A})$.

Example 10. For our programs P and G we already noticed that P can be repaired by removing either the rule "$a \leftarrow$ not $a.$" or "$b.$". Moreover, one might also add the repairing subsets of G. So,

$$\mathrm{BI\text{-}REP}_{min}(P, G) = \{(\{a \leftarrow \text{not } a.\}, \emptyset), (\{b.\}, \emptyset), (\emptyset, \{a.\}), (\emptyset, \{d., a \leftarrow d.\})\}.$$

Example 11. In the previous example, one of the sets in $(\mathcal{D}, \mathcal{A})$ was always empty for $(\mathcal{D}, \mathcal{A}) \in \text{BI-REP}_{min}(P, G)$. We want to illustrate that this is not necessarily the case in general. Consider P' given via

$$P' : \qquad\qquad a \leftarrow \text{not } a. \qquad\qquad b \leftarrow \text{not } b.$$

and G as before. Note that "$b \leftarrow \text{not } b$." will cause inconsistency no matter which rules from G are added. We thus find

$$\text{BI-REP}_{min}(P', G) = \{(P, \emptyset), (\{b \leftarrow \text{not } b.\}, \{a.\}), (\{b \leftarrow \text{not } b.\}, \{d., a \leftarrow d.\})\}.$$

Let us mention that bidirectional repairs generalize the notion of consistent subsets as well as repairing sets.

Proposition 1. *Let $\mathcal{K}$ and $\mathcal{G}$ be disjoint knowledge bases. Then,*

- *$(\mathcal{D}, \emptyset) \in \text{BI-REP}_{min}(\mathcal{K}, \mathcal{G})$ if and only if $\mathcal{H} = \mathcal{K} \backslash \mathcal{D} \in C_{max}(\mathcal{K})$,*
- *$(\emptyset, \mathcal{A}) \in \text{BI-REP}_{min}(\mathcal{K}, \mathcal{G})$ if and only if $\mathcal{A} \in \text{REP}_{min}(\mathcal{K}, \mathcal{G})$.*

Example 12. Consider once more our running example P, G. Recall $C_{max}(P) = \{P \backslash \{a \leftarrow \text{not } a.\}, P \backslash \{b.\}\}$. Indeed, corresponding tuples as claimed in Proposition 1 occur in $\text{BI-REP}_{min}(P, G)$ (see Example 10). Similarly, $\text{REP}_{min}(P, G) = \{\{a.\}, \{d., a \leftarrow d.\}\}$. Again, $\text{BI-REP}_{min}(P, G)$ contains the corresponding tuples.

Now let us reconsider the notions which led to the hitting set dualities in the previous theorems. In Theorem 1 the solution is the notion of strong inconsistency. Recall that $\mathcal{H}$ is minimal strongly $\mathcal{K}$-inconsistent if $\mathcal{H}$ is minimal such that $\mathcal{H} \subseteq \mathcal{H}' \subseteq \mathcal{K}$ implies inconsistency of $\mathcal{H}'$. To put it another way, $\mathcal{D}$ is maximal such that $\mathcal{K} \backslash \mathcal{D} \subseteq \mathcal{H}' \subseteq \mathcal{K}$ implies inconsistency of $\mathcal{H}'$ Analogously, Theorem 2 was based on the notion of maximal non-repairing subsets of $\mathcal{G}$. Here, a similar property is required considering $\mathcal{K} \cup \mathcal{A}$ rather than $\mathcal{K} \backslash \mathcal{D}$. So, roughly speaking, we always face a situation where $\mathcal{K}$ is surrounded by inconsistent sets. Hence, the following comes natural.

Definition 10. *Let $\mathcal{K}$ and $\mathcal{G}$ be disjoint knowledge bases. We call $(\mathcal{D}, \mathcal{A})$ a bidirectional non-repair for $\mathcal{K}$ with respect to $\mathcal{G}$ if*

- *$\mathcal{D} \subseteq \mathcal{K}$ and $\mathcal{A} \subseteq \mathcal{G}$,*
- *$\mathcal{K} \backslash \mathcal{D}$ is strongly $(\mathcal{K} \cup \mathcal{A})$-inconsistent, i.e., $\mathcal{K} \backslash \mathcal{D} \in SI(\mathcal{K} \cup \mathcal{A})$.*

Denote by $\text{BI-NREP}(\mathcal{K}, \mathcal{G})$ the set of all bidirectional non-repair for $\mathcal{K}$ with respect to $\mathcal{G}$ and by $\text{BI-NREP}_{max}(\mathcal{K}, \mathcal{G})$ the maximal ones.

Example 13. Recall our running example. Observe that removal of "$a \leftarrow \text{not } b$." from P is not beneficial in order to restore consistency. Moreover, the two maximal subsets of G which do *not* repair P are $A_1 = \{c., a \leftarrow d.\}$ and $A_2 = \{c., d.\}$ as found in Example 8. So, $P \backslash \{a \leftarrow \text{not } b.\} \in SI(P \cup A_i)$ for $i = 1, 2$. Hence

$$\text{BI-NREP}_{max}(P, G) = \{(\{a \leftarrow \text{not } b.\}, \{c, a \leftarrow d.\}), (\{a \leftarrow \text{not } b.\}, \{c., d.\})\}.$$

We make the following observations to emphasize how BI-NREP$_{max}(\mathcal{K},\mathcal{G})$ generalizes minimal (strong) inconsistency. First let us consider a monotonic logic. In this case, we do not expect $\mathcal{G}$ to play any role. Indeed, we find the following.

Proposition 2. *Let $\mathcal{K}$ and $\mathcal{G}$ be disjoint knowledge bases of a monotonic logic. Then, $(\mathcal{D},\mathcal{G}) \in$ BI-NREP$_{max}(\mathcal{K},\mathcal{G})$ if and only if $\mathcal{H} = \mathcal{K}\backslash\mathcal{D} \in SI_{min}(\mathcal{K})$.*

In the previous proposition $\mathcal{G}$ was irrelevant as the underlying logic was assumed to be monotonic. Clearly, a similar result holds whenever there is no set $\mathcal{G}$ at all.

Proposition 3. *Let $\mathcal{K}$ be a knowledge base and $\mathcal{G} = \emptyset$. Then, it holds that $(\mathcal{D},\emptyset) \in$ BI-NREP$_{max}(\mathcal{K},\mathcal{G})$ if and only if $\mathcal{H} = \mathcal{K}\backslash\mathcal{D} \in SI_{min}(\mathcal{K})$.*

A more advanced version of this result without restricting $\mathcal{G}$ is the following.

Proposition 4. *Let $\mathcal{K}$ and $\mathcal{G}$ be disjoint knowledge bases.*

- *If $(\mathcal{D},\mathcal{A}) \in$ BI-NREP$_{max}(\mathcal{K},\mathcal{G})$ then $\mathcal{H} = \mathcal{K}\backslash\mathcal{D} \in SI(\mathcal{K})$. In particular, there is a set $\mathcal{D}'$ with $\mathcal{D} \subseteq \mathcal{D}'$ such that $\mathcal{K}\backslash\mathcal{D}' \in SI_{min}(\mathcal{K})$.*
- *If $\mathcal{H} = \mathcal{K}\backslash\mathcal{D} \in SI_{min}(\mathcal{K})$, then there is a (not necessarily uniquely defined) $\mathcal{A} \subseteq \mathcal{G}$ such that $(\mathcal{D},\mathcal{A}) \in$ BI-NREP$_{max}(\mathcal{K},\mathcal{G})$.*

Example 14. Example 13 shows that BI-NREP$_{max}(P,G)$ contains two distinct tuples (D,A) with $D = \{a \leftarrow \text{not } b.\}$. We already have $H = P\backslash D = \{a \leftarrow \text{not } a., b.\} \in SI_{min}(P)$, so we can choose D' for the first item in Proposition 4. Since there are two tuples of this form in Example 13, it illustrates in particular that A in the second item in Proposition 4 is not uniquely defined in general.

Now let us compare BI-NREP$_{max}(\mathcal{K},\mathcal{G})$ to the non-repairing subsets of $\mathcal{G}$ from Definition 7. Considering cases where the underlying logic is monotonic or $\mathcal{G}$ is empty will clearly not yield insightful results when investigating NREP$(\mathcal{K},\mathcal{G})$. However, we find a counterpart to Proposition 4.

Proposition 5. *Let $\mathcal{K}$ and $\mathcal{G}$ be disjoint knowledge bases.*

- *If $(\mathcal{D},\mathcal{A}) \in$ BI-NREP$_{max}(\mathcal{K},\mathcal{G})$ then $\mathcal{A} \in$ NREP$(\mathcal{K},\mathcal{G})$. In particular, there is a set $\mathcal{A}'$ with $\mathcal{A} \subseteq \mathcal{A}'$ such that $\mathcal{A}' \in$ NREP$_{max}(\mathcal{K})$.*
- *If $\mathcal{A} \in$ NREP$_{max}(\mathcal{K},\mathcal{G})$, then there is a (not necessarily uniquely defined) $\mathcal{D} \subseteq \mathcal{K}$ such that $(\mathcal{D},\mathcal{A}) \in$ BI-NREP$_{max}(\mathcal{K},\mathcal{G})$.*

The duality result we aim at is similar to the previous ones. It is thus no surprise that we require a notion of *co*-BI-NREP$_{max}(\mathcal{K},\mathcal{G})$. The following is natural and well-behaving, extending the previous one component-wise.

Definition 11. *Let $\mathcal{K}$ and $\mathcal{G}$ be disjoint knowledge bases. A tuple $(\overline{\mathcal{A}},\overline{\mathcal{D}})$ is in co*-BI-NREP$_{max}(\mathcal{K},\mathcal{G})$ *if $(\mathcal{G}\backslash\overline{\mathcal{A}}, \mathcal{K}\backslash\overline{\mathcal{D}})$ is in* BI-NREP$_{max}(\mathcal{K},\mathcal{G})$.

Example 15. In order to summarize the relevant sets for our programs P and G, set $H = P\backslash\{a \leftarrow \text{not } b.\}$.

$$\text{BI-NREP}_{max}(P,G) = \{(\{a \leftarrow \text{not } b.\}, \{c, a \leftarrow d.\}), (\{a \leftarrow \text{not } b.\}, \{c., d.\})\}$$

$$co\text{-BI-NREP}_{max}(P,G) = \{(H, \{a, d\}), (H, \{a, a \leftarrow d.\})\}. \tag{2}$$

$$\text{BI-REP}_{min}(P,G) = \{(\{a \leftarrow \text{not } a.\}, \emptyset), (\{b.\}, \emptyset), (\emptyset, \{a.\}), (\emptyset, \{d., a \leftarrow d.\})\}$$

The following theorem states that the desired duality result is indeed obtained.

Theorem 3 (Subset-Superset Duality). *Let $\mathcal{K}$ and $\mathcal{G}$ be disjoint knowledge bases. Then, $\mathcal{S}$ is a minimal hitting set of co-BI-NREP$_{max}$($\mathcal{K}, \mathcal{G}$) if and only if $\mathcal{S} \in$ BI-REP$_{min}$($\mathcal{K}, \mathcal{G}$).*

Proof. We give the main idea for the proof, but some steps are just sketched. In principle, we prove a "dual" version of this theorem. Our first step is a lemma from [5]: Given a set $\mathcal{X} = \{X_1, \ldots, X_n\}$ of sets with $X_i \nsubseteq X_j$ for $i \neq j$. Then, $minHS(minHS(\mathcal{X})) = \mathcal{X}$, where $minHS$ assigns the set of minimal hitting sets to a set. Moreover, the following technical, but intuitively clear lemma will be convenient: Let $\mathcal{K}$ and $\mathcal{G}$ be disjoint knowledge bases. Let $\mathcal{A} \subseteq \mathcal{G}$ and $\mathcal{D} \subseteq \mathcal{K}$. Any set $\mathcal{H}$ with $\mathcal{K} \backslash \mathcal{D} \subseteq \mathcal{H} \subseteq \mathcal{K} \cup \mathcal{A}$ can be written as $\mathcal{H} = (\mathcal{K} \backslash \mathcal{D}') \cup \mathcal{A}'$ with $\mathcal{D}' \subseteq \mathcal{D}$ and $\mathcal{A}' \subseteq \mathcal{A}$. Due to the lemma about hitting sets, one may show that proving the following statement suffices: Let $\mathcal{K}$ and $\mathcal{G}$ be disjoint knowledge bases. Then, $\mathcal{S}$ is a minimal hitting set of BI-REP$_{min}$($\mathcal{K}, \mathcal{G}$) if and only if $\mathcal{S} \in$ co-BI-NREP$_{max}$($\mathcal{K}, \mathcal{G}$). This is done in a straight fashion, we demonstrate the direction "$\Rightarrow$":

Let $\mathcal{S} = (\mathcal{S}_{\mathcal{A}}, \mathcal{S}_{\mathcal{D}})$ be a minimal hitting set of BI-REP$_{min}$($\mathcal{K}, \mathcal{G}$). For the sake of contradiction assume that $(\mathcal{K} \backslash \mathcal{S}_{\mathcal{A}}, \mathcal{G} \backslash \mathcal{S}_{\mathcal{D}}) \notin$ BI-NREP$_{max}$($\mathcal{K}, \mathcal{G}$).

First assume $(\mathcal{G} \backslash \mathcal{S}_{\mathcal{A}}, \mathcal{K} \backslash \mathcal{S}_{\mathcal{D}}) \notin$ BI-NREP($\mathcal{K}, \mathcal{G}$). Then, by definition,

$$\mathcal{K} \backslash (\mathcal{K} \backslash \mathcal{S}_{\mathcal{D}}) \notin SI(\mathcal{K} \cup \mathcal{G} \backslash \mathcal{S}_{\mathcal{A}}),$$

and thus, $\mathcal{S}_{\mathcal{D}} \notin SI(\mathcal{K} \cup \mathcal{G} \backslash \mathcal{S}_{\mathcal{A}})$. So, there is a consistent set $\mathcal{H}$ with $\mathcal{S}_{\mathcal{D}} \subseteq \mathcal{H} \subseteq \mathcal{K} \cup (\mathcal{G} \backslash \mathcal{S}_{\mathcal{A}})$. Due to our lemma, we find $\mathcal{D} \subseteq \mathcal{K} \backslash \mathcal{S}_{\mathcal{D}}$ and $\mathcal{A} \subseteq \mathcal{G} \backslash \mathcal{S}_{\mathcal{A}}$ with $\mathcal{H} = \mathcal{K} \backslash \mathcal{D} \cup \mathcal{A}$. Due to finiteness of both knowledge bases we might assume $(\mathcal{D}, \mathcal{A}) \in$ BI-REP$_{min}$($\mathcal{K}, \mathcal{G}$). Now, $\mathcal{S}_{\mathcal{A}} \cap \mathcal{A} = \emptyset$ as well as $\mathcal{S}_{\mathcal{D}} \cap \mathcal{D} = \emptyset$ implies that $\mathcal{S} = (\mathcal{S}_{\mathcal{A}}, \mathcal{S}_{\mathcal{D}})$ is no hitting set of BI-REP$_{min}$($\mathcal{K}, \mathcal{G}$), a contradiction.

Now assume $(\mathcal{G} \backslash \mathcal{S}_{\mathcal{A}}, \mathcal{K} \backslash \mathcal{S}_{\mathcal{D}}) \subseteq$ NREP($\mathcal{K}, \mathcal{G}$), but the tuple is not maximal. We thus find a tuple $\mathcal{S}' = (\mathcal{S}_{\mathcal{A}'}, \mathcal{S}_{\mathcal{D}'}) \subseteq (\mathcal{S}_{\mathcal{A}}, \mathcal{S}_{\mathcal{D}}) = \mathcal{S}$ such that $(\mathcal{G} \backslash \mathcal{S}_{\mathcal{A}'}, \mathcal{K} \backslash \mathcal{S}_{\mathcal{D}'}) \in$ NREP$_{max}$($\mathcal{K}, \mathcal{G}$). We claim that $\mathcal{S}'$ is a hitting set of BI-REP$_{min}$($\mathcal{K}, \mathcal{G}$) as well. This can bee seen as follows: Assume this is not the case, i.e., there is a tuple $(\mathcal{D}, \mathcal{A}) \in$ BI-REP$_{min}$($\mathcal{K}, \mathcal{G}$) with $\mathcal{S}_{\mathcal{A}'} \cap \mathcal{A} = \emptyset$ as well as $\mathcal{S}_{\mathcal{D}'} \cap \mathcal{D} = \emptyset$. By assumption,

$$\mathcal{K} \backslash \mathcal{D} \cup \mathcal{A}$$

is consistent. Due to $\mathcal{S}_{\mathcal{A}'} \cap \mathcal{A} = \emptyset$ as well as $\mathcal{S}_{\mathcal{D}'} \cap \mathcal{D} = \emptyset$ we obtain $\mathcal{S}_{\mathcal{D}'} \subseteq \mathcal{K} \backslash \mathcal{D}$ and $\mathcal{A} \subseteq \mathcal{G} \backslash \mathcal{S}_{\mathcal{A}'}$. So,

$$\mathcal{S}_{\mathcal{D}'} \subseteq (\mathcal{K} \backslash \mathcal{D}) \subseteq (\mathcal{K} \cup \mathcal{A}) \backslash \mathcal{D} \subseteq (\mathcal{K} \cup (\mathcal{G} \backslash \mathcal{S}_{\mathcal{A}'})) \backslash \mathcal{D} \subseteq (\mathcal{K} \cup (\mathcal{G} \backslash \mathcal{S}_{\mathcal{A}'})).$$

In particular,

$$\mathcal{S}_{\mathcal{D}'} \subseteq (\mathcal{K} \cup \mathcal{A}) \backslash \mathcal{D} \subseteq (\mathcal{K} \cup (\mathcal{G} \backslash \mathcal{S}_{\mathcal{A}'})).$$

Due to consistency of $(\mathcal{K} \cup \mathcal{A}) \backslash \mathcal{D}$ we infer that $\mathcal{S}_{\mathcal{D}'} \notin SI(\mathcal{K} \cup (\mathcal{G} \backslash \mathcal{S}_{\mathcal{A}'}))$. So, by definition, $(\mathcal{G} \backslash \mathcal{S}_{\mathcal{A}'}, \mathcal{K} \backslash \mathcal{S}_{\mathcal{D}'}) \notin$ NREP($\mathcal{K}, \mathcal{G}$) which is a contradiction. So, $\mathcal{S}'$ must be a hitting set of BI-REP$_{min}$($\mathcal{K}, \mathcal{G}$) which contradicts minimality of $\mathcal{S}$. $\square$

Example 16. Recall (2) from Example 15. Again set $H = P \backslash \{a \leftarrow \text{not } b.\}$ and take $(\{a \leftarrow \text{not } a.\}, \emptyset) \in \text{BI-REP}_{min}(P, G)$. Indeed, this is a minimal hitting set of $co\text{-BI-NREP}_{max}(P, G)$ since

$$(\{a \leftarrow \text{not } a.\}, \emptyset) \cap (H, \{a, d\}) = (\{a \leftarrow \text{not } a.\}, \emptyset),$$
$$(\{a \leftarrow \text{not } a.\}, \emptyset) \cap (H, \{a, a \leftarrow d.\}) = (\{a \leftarrow \text{not } a.\}, \emptyset).$$

We want to make a few more observations in order to investigate the structural properties of hitting sets as well as the connections between the different cases we considered. Our first one is that hitting sets of $SI_{min}(\mathcal{K})$ can easily be turned into hitting sets of $co\text{-BI-NREP}_{max}(\mathcal{K}, \mathcal{G})$.

Proposition 6. *Let $\mathcal{K}$ and $\mathcal{G}$ be disjoint knowledge bases. If $C_{max}(\mathcal{K}) \neq \emptyset$, i.e., $\mathcal{K}$ possesses consistent subsets, then a set $\mathcal{S}_D$ is a minimal hitting set of $SI_{min}(\mathcal{K})$ if and only if $(\mathcal{S}_D, \emptyset)$ is a minimal hitting set of $co\text{-BI-NREP}_{max}(\mathcal{K}, \mathcal{G})$.*

Note in particular that $\mathcal{S}_D$ in Proposition 6 is independent of $\mathcal{G}$. So, once calculated for $\mathcal{K}$, it can be re-used for any $\mathcal{G}$. Similarly, we have:

Proposition 7. *Let $\mathcal{K}$ and $\mathcal{G}$ be disjoint knowledge bases. If $\text{REP}_{min}(\mathcal{K}, \mathcal{G}) \neq \emptyset$, i.e., there are repairing subsets of $\mathcal{G}$ wrt. $\mathcal{K}$, then a set $\mathcal{S}_A$ is a minimal hitting set of $co\text{-NREP}_{max}(\mathcal{K}, \mathcal{G})$ if and only if $(\emptyset, \mathcal{S}_A)$ is a minimal hitting set of $co\text{-BI-NREP}_{max}(\mathcal{K}, \mathcal{G})$.*

We want to emphasize that Proposition 6 in particular implies the following: If $(\overline{\mathcal{D}}, \overline{\mathcal{A}}) \in co\text{-BI-NREP}_{max}(\mathcal{K}, \mathcal{G})$, then $\overline{\mathcal{D}} \neq \emptyset$. Otherwise, $(\mathcal{S}_D, \emptyset)$ could not be a hitting set of $co\text{-BI-NREP}_{max}(\mathcal{K}, \mathcal{G})$. The same is true regarding Proposition 7.

Proposition 8. *Let $\mathcal{K}$ and $\mathcal{G}$ be disjoint knowledge bases.*

- *Let $C_{max}(\mathcal{K}) \neq \emptyset$. If $(\overline{\mathcal{D}}, \overline{\mathcal{A}}) \in co\text{-BI-NREP}_{max}(\mathcal{K}, \mathcal{G})$, then $\overline{\mathcal{D}} \neq \emptyset$.*
- *Let $\text{REP}_{min}(\mathcal{K}, \mathcal{G}) \neq \emptyset$. If $(\overline{\mathcal{D}}, \overline{\mathcal{A}}) \in co\text{-BI-NREP}_{max}(\mathcal{K}, \mathcal{G})$, then $\overline{\mathcal{A}} \neq \emptyset$.*

We believe that the results of this section are not only interesting regarding a generalized hitting set duality, but also point out quite encouraging structural properties of knowledge bases. The investigated notions which induce the duality results are symmetric in their spirit and generalize each other in a natural way. We are thus convinced that the properties we acquired in Propositions 1–8 are pleasant on their own, in addition to the main theorems.

5   Preferences and Refinements

The aim of this section is to investigate two further aspects that are of interest when dealing with inconsistent knowledge bases. First, we assume that certain information are undisputed due to their reliability, so we want repairs not to allow for removal of certain formulas in $\mathcal{B} \subseteq \mathcal{K}$. Then, we investigate refining instead of deleting and adding formulas, a more general approach. Our goal is again to characterize the minimal modifications in terms of a hitting set duality. Interestingly, we do not rely on novel proofs due to the versatility of Theorem 3. So let us start with a notion of repairs which insists on $\mathcal{B} \subseteq \mathcal{K}$.

Definition 12. *Let $\mathcal{K}$ and $\mathcal{G}$ be disjoint knowledge bases. Let $\mathcal{B} \subseteq \mathcal{K}$. Set*
$\text{BI-REP}_{min}(\mathcal{K}, \mathcal{G}, \mathcal{B}) = \{(\mathcal{D}, \mathcal{A}) \in \text{BI-REP}_{min}(\mathcal{K}, \mathcal{G}) \mid \mathcal{D} \cap \mathcal{B} = \emptyset\}.$

In order to apply Theorem 3, we redefine ACC to render subsets of $\mathcal{K}$ inconsistent whenever a formula in $\mathcal{B}$ is deleted. So let $L_{\mathcal{B}} = (\text{WF}, \text{BS}, \text{INC}, \text{ACC}_{\mathcal{B}})$ where $\text{ACC}_{\mathcal{B}}(\mathcal{K}) = \emptyset$ whenever $\mathcal{B} \not\subseteq \mathcal{K}$ and otherwise it coincides with $\text{ACC}(\mathcal{K})$. For this auxiliary logic $L_{\mathcal{B}}$ we obtain:

Lemma 1. *If L is a logic and $\mathcal{K}$ and $\mathcal{G}$ are disjoint knowledge bases, then*

- $\text{BI-REP}_{min}(\mathcal{K}, \mathcal{G})^{L_{\mathcal{B}}} = \text{BI-REP}_{min}(\mathcal{K}, \mathcal{G}, \mathcal{B})^{L}$,
- $\text{BI-NREP}_{max}(\mathcal{K}, \mathcal{G})^{L_{\mathcal{B}}} = \{(\mathcal{D} \cup \mathcal{B}, \mathcal{A}) \mid (\mathcal{D}, \mathcal{A}) \in \text{BI-NREP}_{max}(\mathcal{K}, \mathcal{G})^{L}\}$.

Hence, set $\text{BI-NREP}_{max}(\mathcal{K}, \mathcal{G}, \mathcal{B}) := \{(\mathcal{D} \cup \mathcal{B}, \mathcal{A}) \mid (\mathcal{D}, \mathcal{A}) \in \text{BI-NREP}_{max}(\mathcal{K}, \mathcal{G})\}$ and $\textit{co-}\text{BI-NREP}_{max}(\mathcal{K}, \mathcal{G}, \mathcal{B})$ as expected. Now apply Theorem 3 to the logic $L_{\mathcal{B}}$:

Corollary 1. *Let $\mathcal{K}$ and $\mathcal{G}$ be disjoint knowledge bases. Let $\mathcal{B} \subseteq \mathcal{K}$. Then, $\mathcal{S}$ is a minimal hitting set of $\textit{co-}\text{BI-NREP}_{max}(\mathcal{K}, \mathcal{G}, \mathcal{B})$ iff $\mathcal{S} \in \text{BI-REP}_{min}(\mathcal{K}, \mathcal{G}, \mathcal{B})$.*

Example 17. For our running example, assume that $B = \{a \leftarrow \text{not } a.\} \subseteq P$ is a rule in P that shall not be removed. Recalling (2) from Example 15, we find

$$\text{BI-REP}_{min}(P, G, B) = \{(\{b.\}, \emptyset), (\emptyset, \{a.\}), (\emptyset, \{d., a \leftarrow d.\})\}$$
$$\textit{co-}\text{BI-NREP}_{max}(P, G, B) = \{(\{b.\}, \{a, d\}), (\{b.\}, \{a, a \leftarrow d.\})\}.$$

Indeed, the duality claimed in Corollary 1 holds.

Let us continue with a more fine-grained modification to knowledge bases, namely weakening and strengthening instead of deleting and adding formulas. For that, we need a general notion for α_1 being a "stronger" formula than α_2:

Definition 13. *Let L be a logic. We say α_1 entails α_2, denoted by $\alpha_1 \models_L \alpha_2$, iff for all knowledge bases $\mathcal{K}$, $\alpha_1 \in \mathcal{K}$ implies $\text{ACC}(\mathcal{K}) = \text{ACC}(\mathcal{K} \cup \{\alpha_2\})$.*

To model modifications to formulas, let w, s (*weaker, stronger*) be mappings $w, s : \mathcal{K} \to \text{WF} \backslash \mathcal{K}$ with $s(\alpha) \models_L \alpha \models_L w(\alpha)$. For technical reasons we assume the sets $\mathcal{K}$, $w(\mathcal{K})$ and $s(\mathcal{K})$ to be pairwise disjoint. We consider the knowledge base $\mathcal{K}$ after applying w and s to two disjoint subsets $\mathcal{H}_w, \mathcal{H}_s \subseteq \mathcal{K}$, i.e., we let $\mathcal{K}[w(\mathcal{H}_w), s(\mathcal{H}_s)] = (\mathcal{K} \backslash (\mathcal{H}_w \cup \mathcal{H}_s)) \cup (w(\mathcal{H}_w) \cup s(\mathcal{H}_s))$.

Definition 14. *Let $\mathcal{K}$ be a knowledge base. If $\mathcal{H}_w, \mathcal{H}_s \subseteq \mathcal{K}$ are disjoint and $\mathcal{K}[w(\mathcal{H}_w), s(\mathcal{H}_s)]$ is consistent, then we call $(\mathcal{H}_w, s(\mathcal{H}_s))$ a consistency-restoring modification of $\mathcal{K}$ wrt. w, s. Let $\text{MOD}_{min}(\mathcal{K})$ denote the set of all minimal consistency-restoring modifications of $\mathcal{K}$ wrt. w, s.*

Note the intended asymmetry in the tuple $(\mathcal{H}_w, s(\mathcal{H}_s))$, which is chosen to conveniently phrase Lemmas 2 and 3 below. Again, we want to characterize $\text{MOD}_{min}(\mathcal{K})$ in terms of a hitting set duality. For this, consider $\tilde{\mathcal{K}}$ and $\tilde{\mathcal{G}}$ given as $\tilde{\mathcal{K}} = \mathcal{K} \cup w(\mathcal{K})$, i.e., $\tilde{\mathcal{K}}$ contains in addition the weakened formulas and $\tilde{\mathcal{G}} = s(\mathcal{K})$, i.e., $\tilde{\mathcal{G}}$ consists of the strengthened formulas. Please note that $\mathsf{ACC}(\tilde{\mathcal{K}}) = \mathsf{ACC}(\mathcal{K})$. In particular, if we remove $\alpha \in \mathcal{K}$ from $\tilde{\mathcal{K}}$, then the latter still contains $w(\alpha)$, i.e., $\mathsf{ACC}(\tilde{\mathcal{K}} \backslash \{\alpha\}) = \mathsf{ACC}(\mathcal{K}[w(\{\alpha\}), s(\emptyset)])$. Hence, this corresponds to weakening α. Similarly, adding a formula $s(\alpha) \in \tilde{G}$ to $\tilde{\mathcal{K}}$ corresponds to strengthening α. Now we can *almost* capture $\mathsf{MOD}_{min}(\mathcal{K})$.

Lemma 2. *Let $\mathcal{K}$ be a knowledge base. Then,* $\mathsf{BI\text{-}REP}_{min}(\tilde{\mathcal{K}}, \tilde{\mathcal{G}}) = \mathsf{MOD}_{min}(\mathcal{K}) \cup \{(\mathcal{D}, \mathcal{A}) \in \mathsf{BI\text{-}REP}_{min}(\tilde{\mathcal{K}}, \tilde{\mathcal{G}}) \mid w(\mathcal{K}) \cap \mathcal{D} \neq \emptyset\}$.

The difference is that one may in particular delete and not only weaken formulas. Depending on the desired outcome, one could either accept this or apply the technique from above in order to forbid removal of $\mathcal{B} := w(\mathcal{K}) \subseteq \tilde{\mathcal{K}}$. If we define $L_{\mathcal{B}}$ as above, Lemma 2 yields a characterization of $\mathsf{MOD}_{min}(\mathcal{K})$.

Lemma 3. *If $\mathcal{K}$ be a knowledge base, then* $\mathsf{BI\text{-}REP}_{min}(\tilde{\mathcal{K}}, \tilde{\mathcal{G}})^{L_{\mathcal{B}}} = \mathsf{MOD}_{min}(\mathcal{K})^{L}$.

By applying Theorem 3 we find a duality in terms of $\mathsf{BI\text{-}NREP}_{max}(\tilde{\mathcal{K}}, \tilde{\mathcal{G}})^{L_{\mathcal{B}}}$. So we are interested in the nature of this set.

Lemma 4. *Let $\mathcal{K}$ be a knowledge base. Then,* $\mathsf{BI\text{-}NREP}_{max}(\tilde{\mathcal{K}}, \tilde{\mathcal{G}})^{L_{\mathcal{B}}}$ *is the collection of all maximal tuples* $(\mathcal{D}, \mathcal{A}) = (\mathcal{H}_{w}, s(\mathcal{H}_{s}))$ *such that (i) the knowledge base* $\mathcal{K}[w(\mathcal{H}'_{w}), s(\mathcal{H}'_{s})]$ *is inconsistent for all* $(\mathcal{H}'_{w}, \mathcal{H}'_{s}) \subseteq (\mathcal{H}_{w}, \mathcal{H}_{s})$ *or (ii)* $\mathcal{D} \cap \mathcal{B} = \mathcal{D} \cap w(\mathcal{K}) \neq \emptyset$.

Finally, applying Theorem 3 yields the desired duality.

Corollary 2. *Let $\mathcal{K}$ be a knowledge base and $\tilde{\mathcal{K}}, \tilde{\mathcal{G}}$ and $\mathcal{B}$ as above. Then, $\mathcal{S}$ is a minimal hitting set of* $\text{co-}\mathsf{BI\text{-}NREP}_{max}(\tilde{\mathcal{K}}, \tilde{\mathcal{G}})^{L_{\mathcal{B}}}$ *iff $\mathcal{S} \in \mathsf{MOD}_{min}(\mathcal{K})^{L}$.*

We want to mention that more sophisticated situations can be covered via Theorem 3, for example consideration of more than one option to weaken and strengthen formulas. Of course, one can also enforce that certain subsets of $\mathcal{G}$ shall not be included. The two examples we have illustrated here are chosen since they can be elegantly presented in a concise way.

6   Excursus: Inconsistency in Abstract Argumentation

The aim of this section is to illustrate how the previous analysis can help to tackle situations where a given argumentation framework is inconsistent, i.e., it does not possess any accepted argument. In the original formulation [14], an *abstract argumentation framework* is a directed graph $F = (A, R)$ where nodes in A represent arguments and the relation R models *attack*, i.e., for $a, b \in A$, if $(a, b) \in R$ we say that a *attacks* b. For a set E we use E^{+} for $\{b \mid (a, b) \in R, a \in E\}$ and define $E^{\oplus} = E \cup E^{+}$. A further essential notion in argumentation is *defense*. Formally, an argument b is *defended by* a set A if each attacker of b is counter-attacked by some $a \in A$.

An *extension-based semantics* σ is a function which assigns to any AF $F = (A, R)$ a set of sets of arguments $\sigma(F) \subseteq 2^{A}$. Each one of them, so-called σ-*extension*, is considered to be acceptable with respect to F. Besides conflict-free and admissible sets (abbr. cf and ad) we consider stable, semi-stable, complete, preferred and grounded (abbr. stb, ss, co, pr and gr).

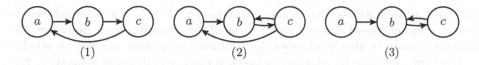

(1)   (2)   (3)

Fig. 1. The AFs from Example 18 (1), Example 19 (2) and Example 20 (3)

Definition 15. *Let $F = (A, R)$ be an AF and $E \subseteq A$.*

1. $E \in cf(F)$ iff for no $a, b \in E$, $(a, b) \in R$,
2. $E \in ad(F)$ iff $E \in cf(F)$ and E defends all its elements,
3. $E \in stb(F)$ iff $E \in cf(F)$ and $E^{\oplus} = A$,
4. $E \in ss(F)$ iff $E \in ad(F)$ and for no $\mathcal{I} \in ad(F)$, $E^{\oplus} \subset \mathcal{I}^{\oplus}$,
5. $E \in co(F)$ iff $E \in ad(F)$ and for any $a \in A$ defended by E, $a \in E$,
6. $E \in pr(F)$ iff $E \in co(F)$ and for no $\mathcal{I} \in co(F)$, $E \subset \mathcal{I}$,
7. $E \in gr(F)$ iff $E \in co(F)$ and for any $\mathcal{I} \in co(F)$, $E \subseteq \mathcal{I}$,

We demonstrate how to model argumentation frameworks under given semantics σ as a logic according to Definition 1. We assume a set A of arguments is fixed. We define a logic $L_{AF,\sigma}^{A} = (WF_{AF}^{A}, BS_{AF}^{A}, INC_{AF}^{A}, ACC_{AF,\sigma}^{A})$. For ease of presentation, we omit the superscript A whenever it is implicitly clear. The set WF_{AF} is the set of all possible attacks, i.e., $WF_{AF} = (A \times A)$. Belief sets are arbitrary sets of arguments, i.e., $BS_{AF} = 2^{A}$ and $INC_{AF} = \emptyset$ (there is no *inconsistent* extension). Now we define the acceptability function. Following [3], we consider one for both credulous as well as sceptical reasoning: Let $ACC_{AF,\sigma}^{cred}(F) = \bigcup \sigma(F)$ and $ACC_{AF,\sigma}^{scep}(F) = \bigcap \sigma(F)$ (where we stipulate $\bigcap \emptyset = \emptyset$). This yields different logics for each semantics and each reasoning mode (where we again omit the sub- and superscripts whenever the context is clear).

Example 18. The AF depicted in Fig. 1(1) can be represented as knowledge base $F = \{(a, b), (b, c), (c, a)\}$ over $A = \{a, b, c\}$. Note that F is inconsistent wrt. preferred semantics for both reasoning modes since $pr(F) = \emptyset$ and hence $ACC_{AF}^{scep}(F) = ACC_{AF}^{cred}(F) = \emptyset \subseteq INC_{AF}$ (recall Definition 2).

Please observe that the results from Sects. 3 and 4 hold for any semantics σ and both reasoning modes since we modeled AFs as a logic according to Definition 1.

Example 19. Consider $A = \{a, b, c\}$ and the AF F from above as well as $G = \{(c, b)\}$. The AF $F \cup G$ is depicted in Fig. 1(2). Consider preferred semantics and credulous reasoning. Observe $pr(F \cup G) = \{\{c\}\}$. So, $F \cup G$ is consistent and thus $(\mathcal{D}, \mathcal{A}) = (\emptyset, G) = (\emptyset, \{(c, b)\}) \in \text{BI-REP}_{min}(F, G)$. Moreover, removal of any attack turns F into a consistent AF. So,

$$\text{BI-REP}_{min}(F, G) = \{\{(\emptyset, \{(c, b)\})\}, \{(\{(a, b)\}, \emptyset)\}, \{(\{(b, c)\}, \emptyset)\}, \{(\{(c, a)\}, \emptyset)\}\}.$$

Now, by Theorem 3 we find that $co\text{-BI-NREP}_{max}(F, G)$ contains only the tuple (F, G). Consequently, $\text{BI-NREP}_{max}(F, G)$ consists of $\{(\emptyset, \emptyset)\}$. This is indeed true since any modification to F yields a consistent AF.

In [3] it has been noticed that deciding whether an AF $H \subseteq F$ is maximal consistent is computational demanding for most of the semantics from Definition 15. However, there is also good news: for grounded semantics, computing repairs is tractable and due to relations between repairs wrt. different semantics, the grounded case is a promising starting point when looking for consistent subsets of an AF. We are thus interested in extending the results from [3]. We find:

Proposition 9. *Let F and G be AFs with $F \cap G = \emptyset$. Let $\sigma \in \{ss, pr, co\}$. If $(\mathcal{D}, \mathcal{A}) \in$ BI-REP(F, G) wrt. gr semantics, then there is a tuple $(\mathcal{D}', \mathcal{A}') \subseteq (\mathcal{D}, \mathcal{A})$ with $(\mathcal{D}', \mathcal{A}') \in$ BI-REP$_{min}(F, G)$ wrt. σ. This holds for both reasoning modes.*

Example 20. Consider again F and G from Examples 18 and 19. A bidirectional repair for F wrt. grounded semantics is $(\mathcal{D}, \mathcal{A}) = (\{(c, a)\}, \{(c, b)\})$. The framework $F \setminus \{(c, a)\} \cup \{(c, b)\}$ is depicted in Fig. 1(3). Indeed, two of the minimal bidirectional repairs for F wrt. preferred semantics and credulous reasoning we found in Example 19 are $(\emptyset, \{(c, b)\}) \subseteq (\mathcal{D}, \mathcal{A})$ and $(\{(c, a)\}, \emptyset) \subseteq (\mathcal{D}, \mathcal{A})$.

Regarding stable semantics, we find a slightly weaker version of Proposition 9. Note that here, we have $(\mathcal{D}, \mathcal{A}) \subseteq (\mathcal{D}', \mathcal{A}')$ and no minimality for $(\mathcal{D}', \mathcal{A}')$.

Proposition 10. *Let F and G be AFs with $F \cap G = \emptyset$. If $(\mathcal{D}, \mathcal{A}) \in$ BI-REP(F, G) wrt. gr semantics, then there is a tuple $(\mathcal{D}, \mathcal{A}) \subseteq (\mathcal{D}', \mathcal{A}')$ with $(\mathcal{D}', \mathcal{A}') \in$ BI-REP(F, G) wrt. stb semantics. This holds for both reasoning modes.*

There is, however, a practical problem regarding Propositions 9 and 10. Note that there is a non-empty grounded extension if and only if there is an argument which is not attacked. This means there is never a reason to *add* attacks to obtain a framework which possesses a non-empty grounded extension.

Proposition 11. *Let F and G be AFs with $F \cap G = \emptyset$. If $(\mathcal{D}, \mathcal{A}) \in$ BI-REP(F, G) wrt. gr semantics, then the same is true for $(\mathcal{D}, \emptyset)$.*

Hence, even though one might start with a repair option $(\mathcal{D}, \mathcal{A})$ for grounded semantics, one can always ignore $\mathcal{D}$. For the semantics we investigate here, one could use stable semantics, as long as credulous reasoning is considered.

Proposition 12. *Let F and G be AFs with $F \cap G = \emptyset$. Let $\sigma \in \{ss, pr, co\}$. If $(\mathcal{D}, \mathcal{A}) \in$ BI-REP(F, G) wrt. stb semantics and credulous reasoning, then there is $(\mathcal{D}', \mathcal{A}') \subseteq (\mathcal{D}, \mathcal{A})$ s.t. $(\mathcal{D}', \mathcal{A}') \in$ BI-REP$_{min}(F, G)$ wrt. σ and credulous reasoning.*

Proposition 12 is not as appealing as Proposition 9 though, since checking whether an AF possesses a stable extension is known to be NP-complete in contrast to the tractability of the same problem for grounded semantics. Moreover, Proposition 12 does not work for sceptical reasoning. Finding relations that are similarly useful for the notions investigated here is left for future work.

7   Conclusions

In this paper we studied inconsistency in an abstract setting covering arbitrary logics, including non-monotonic ones. We extended the duality result from [11] to a setting which also allows for adding information to a given knowledge base and demonstrated relations between the different notions. We demonstrated the versatility of our results by applying them to more sophisticated situations. Moreover, we discussed our results in the context of abstract argumentation frameworks.

We are not aware of any work extending the well known hitting set duality to situations including adding new formulas to a knowledge base as we did in this paper. The closest to our work is probably [15]. The investigation in this paper is, however, restricted to multi-context systems [8]. They focus on the case where the source of inconsistency can be attributed to so-called bridge rules and consider modifying them rather than adding new rules. The paper [16] considers the problem of belief revision in ASP and analyzes, similar to the present paper, a setting where restoring consistency may be obtained due to additional rules.

We are convinced that an investigation of the computational complexity of the notions we considered in the present paper would be appealing. Indeed, they possess similar properties as the deletion-based ones discussed in [11]. A thorough discussion is, however, beyond the scope of this paper. In future work, one might also be interested in investigating specific frameworks similar in spirit to Sect. 6, including algorithms. Moreover, the present paper contributes to a thorough understanding of inconsistency in non-monotonic logics, which might help the research area of measuring inconsistency [1, 20–22, 27, 28].

References

1. Amgoud, L., Ben-Naim, J.: Measuring disagreement in argumentation graphs. In: Moral, S., Pivert, O., Sánchez, D., Marín, N. (eds.) SUM 2017. LNCS (LNAI), vol. 10564, pp. 208–222. Springer, Cham (2017). https://doi.org/10.1007/978-3-319-67582-4_15
2. Baroni, P., Caminada, M., Giacomin, M.: An introduction to argumentation semantics. Knowl. Eng. Rev. **26**(4), 365–410 (2011)
3. Baumann, R., Ulbricht, M.: If nothing is accepted - repairing argumentation frameworks. In: Principles of Knowledge Representation and Reasoning: Proceedings of the Sixteenth International Conference, KR 2018, Tempe, Arizona, 30 October–2 November 2018, pp. 108–117 (2018). https://aaai.org/ocs/index.php/KR/KR18/paper/view/17979
4. Benferhat, S., Dubois, D., Prade, H.: A local approach to reasoning under inconsistency in stratified knowledge bases. In: Froidevaux, C., Kohlas, J. (eds.) ECSQARU 1995. LNCS, vol. 946, pp. 36–43. Springer, Heidelberg (1995). https://doi.org/10.1007/3-540-60112-0_5
5. Berge, C.: Hypergraphs: Combinatorics of Finite Sets, vol. 45. North-Holland, Amsterdam (1989)
6. Béziau, J.Y., Carnielli, W., Gabbay, D. (eds.): Handbook of Paraconsistency. College Publications, London (2007)
7. Brachman, R.J., Levesque, H.J.: Knowledge Representation and Reasoning. The Morgan Kaufmann Series in Artificial Intelligence. Morgan Kaufmann Publishers, San Francisco (2004)

8. Brewka, G., Eiter, T.: Equilibria in heterogeneous nonmonotonic multi-context systems. In: Proceedings of the Twenty-Second AAAI Conference on Artificial Intelligence, Vancouver, British Columbia, Canada, 22–26 July 2007, pp. 385–390 (2007)

9. Brewka, G., Eiter, T., Truszczynski, M.: Answer set programming at a glance. Commun. ACM **54**(12), 92–103 (2011). https://doi.org/10.1145/2043174.2043195

10. Brewka, G., Thimm, M., Ulbricht, M.: Strong inconsistency in nonmonotonic reasoning. In: Proceedings of the Twenty-Sixth International Joint Conference on Artificial Intelligence, IJCAI 2017, pp. 901–907 (2017)

11. Brewka, G., Thimm, M., Ulbricht, M.: Strong inconsistency. Artif. Intell. **267**, 78–117 (2019)

12. Cholvy, L., Hunter, A.: Information fusion in logic: a brief overview. In: Gabbay, D.M., Kruse, R., Nonnengart, A., Ohlbach, H.J. (eds.) ECSQARU/FAPR -1997. LNCS, vol. 1244, pp. 86–95. Springer, Heidelberg (1997). https://doi.org/10.1007/BFb0035614

13. Dubois, D., Lang, J., Prade, H.: Inconsistency in possibilistic knowledge bases: to live with it or not live with it. In: Zadeh, L., Kacprzyk, J. (eds.) Fuzzy Logic for the Management of Uncertainty, pp. 335–351. Wiley, New York (1992)

14. Dung, P.M.: On the acceptability of arguments and its fundamental role in nonmonotonic reasoning, logic programming and n-person games. Artif. Intell. **77**(2), 321–358 (1995)

15. Eiter, T., Fink, M., Schüller, P., Weinzierl, A.: Finding explanations of inconsistency in multi-context systems. Artif. Intell. **216**, 233–274 (2014). https://doi.org/10.1016/j.artint.2014.07.008

16. Garcia, L., Lefèvre, C., Papini, O., Stéphan, I., Würbel, É.: A semantic characterization for ASP base revision. In: Moral, S., Pivert, O., Sánchez, D., Marín, N. (eds.) SUM 2017. LNCS (LNAI), vol. 10564, pp. 334–347. Springer, Cham (2017). https://doi.org/10.1007/978-3-319-67582-4_24

17. Gelfond, M., Lifschitz, V.: The stable model semantics for logic programming. In: ICLP/SLP, vol. 88, pp. 1070–1080 (1988)

18. Grant, J.: Classifications for inconsistent theories. Notre Dame J. Formal Log. **19**(3), 435–444 (1978)

19. Hansson, S.O.: A Textbook of Belief Dynamics. Kluwer Academic Publishers, Norwell (2001)

20. Hunter, A., Konieczny, S.: Approaches to measuring inconsistent information. In: Bertossi, L., Hunter, A., Schaub, T. (eds.) Inconsistency Tolerance. LNCS, vol. 3300, pp. 191–236. Springer, Heidelberg (2005). https://doi.org/10.1007/978-3-540-30597-2_7

21. Hunter, A.: Measuring inconsistency in argument graphs. Technical report. arXiv:1708.02851 (2017)

22. Hunter, A.: Measuring inconsistency in argument graphs. In: Grant, J., Martinez, M.V. (eds.) Measuring Inconsistency in Information. College Publications (2018)

23. Konieczny, S., Lang, J., Marquis, P.: Reasoning under inconsistency: the forgotten connective. In: Proceedings of IJCAI 2005, pp. 484–489 (2005)

24. Konieczny, S., Perez, R.P.: Logic based merging. J. Philos. Log. **40**, 239–270 (2011)

25. Lang, J., Marquis, P.: Reasoning under inconsistency: a forgetting-based approach. Artif. Intell. **174**(12–13), 799–823 (2010)

26. Reiter, R.: A theory of diagnosis from first principles. Artif. Intell. **32**(1), 57–95 (1987). https://doi.org/10.1016/0004-3702(87)90062-2

27. Ulbricht, M., Thimm, M., Brewka, G.: Inconsistency measures for disjunctive logic programs under answer set semantics. In: Grant, J., Martinez, M.V. (eds.) Measuring Inconsistency in Information, Studies in Logic, vol. 73. College Publications, February 2018
28. Ulbricht, M., Thimm, M., Brewka, G.: Measuring strong inconsistency. In: Proceedings of the 32nd AAAI Conference on Artificial Intelligence, AAAI 2018, February 2018

Causal, Defeasible and Inductive Reasoning

ACUOS²: A High-Performance System for Modular ACU Generalization with Subtyping and Inheritance

María Alpuente[1], Demis Ballis[2], Angel Cuenca-Ortega[1,3],
Santiago Escobar[1(✉)], and José Meseguer[4]

[1] DSIC -ELP, Universitat Politècnica de València,
Valencia, Spain
{alpuente,acuenca,sescobar}@dsic.upv.es
[2] DMIF, University of Udine,
Udine, Italy
demis.ballis@uniud.it
[3] Universidad de Guayaquil,
Guayaquil, Ecuador
angel.cuencao@ug.edu.ec
[4] University of Illinois at Urbana-Champaign,
Urbana, IL, USA
meseguer@illinois.edu

Abstract. Generalization in order-sorted theories with any combination of associativity (A), commutativity (C), and unity (U) algebraic axioms is finitary. However, existing tools for computing generalizers (also called "anti-unifiers") of two typed structures in such theories do not currently scale to real size problems. This paper describes the ACUOS² system that achieves high performance when computing a complete and minimal set of least general generalizations in these theories. We discuss how it can be used to address artificial intelligence (AI) problems that are representable as order-sorted ACU generalization, e.g., generalization in lists, trees, (multi-)sets, and typical hierarchical/structural relations. Experimental results demonstrate that ACUOS² greatly outperforms the predecessor tool ACUOS by running up to five orders of magnitude faster.

1 Introduction

Computing generalizations is relevant in a wide spectrum of automated reasoning areas where analogical reasoning and inductive inference are needed, such as analogy making, case-based reasoning, web and data mining, ontology learning, machine learning, theorem proving, program derivation, and inductive logic programming, among others [5,13,14].

This work has been partially supported by the EU (FEDER) and the Spanish MINECO under grant TIN 2015-69175-C4-1-R, by Generalitat Valenciana under grants PROMETEOII/2015/013 and PROMETEO/2019/098, and by NRL under contract number N00173-17-1-G002. Angel Cuenca-Ortega has been supported by the SENESCYT, Ecuador (scholarship program 2013).

© Springer Nature Switzerland AG 2019
F. Calimeri et al. (Eds.): JELIA 2019, LNAI 11468, pp. 171–181, 2019.
https://doi.org/10.1007/978-3-030-19570-0_11

This work presents ACUOS^2, a highly optimized implementation of the order-sorted ACU least general generalization algorithm formalized in [3]. ACUOS^2 is a new, high-performance version of a previous prototype called ACUOS [4]. ACUOS^2 runs up to five orders of magnitude faster than ACUOS and is able to solve complex generalization problems in which ACUOS fails to give a response. Both systems are written in Maude [10], a programming language and system that implements rewriting logic [12] and supports reasoning modulo algebraic properties, subtype polimorphism, and reflection. However, ACUOS was developed with a strong concern for simplicity and does not scale to real-life problem sizes, such as the biomedical domains often addressed in inductive logic programming and other AI applications, with a substantial number of variables, predicates and/or operators per problem instance. Scalability issues were not really unexpected since other equational problems (such as equational matching, equational unification, or equational embedding) are typically much more involved and costly than their corresponding "syntactic" counterparts, and achieving efficient implementations has required years of significant investigation effort.

Section 2 briefly summarizes the problem of generalizing two (typed) expressions in theories that satisfy any combination of associativity (A), commutativity (C) and unity axioms (U). In Sect. 3, we explain the main functionality of the ACUOS^2 system and describe the novel implementation ideas and optimizations that have boosted the tool performance. A nontrivial application of equational generalization to a biological domain is described in Sect. 4. An in-depth experimental evaluation of ACUOS^2 is given in Sect. 5. In Sect. 6 we briefly discuss some related work.

2   Least General Generalization Modulo A, C, and U

Computing a *least general generalization* (lgg) for two expressions t_1 and t_2 means finding the least general expression t such that both t_1 and t_2 are instances of t under appropriate substitutions. For instance, the expression `olympics(X,Y)` is a generalizer of both `olympics(1900,paris)` and `olympics(2024, paris)` but their least general generalizer, also known as *most specific generalizer* (msg) and *least common anti-instance* (lcai), is `olympics(X,paris)`.

Syntactic generalization has two important limitations. First, it cannot generalize common data structures such as records, lists, trees, or (multi-)sets, which satisfy specific premises such as, e.g., the order among the elements in a set being irrelevant. Second, it does not cope with types and subtypes, which can lead to more specific generalizers.

Consider the predicates `connected`, `flights`, `visited`, and `alliance` among cities, and let us introduce the constants `rome`, `paris`, `nyc`, `bonn`, `oslo`, `rio`, and `ulm`. Assume that the predicate `connected` is used to state that a pair of cities `C1;C2` are connected by transportation, with ";" being the *unordered pair constructor* operator so that the expressions `connected(nyc;paris)` and `connected(paris;nyc)` are considered to be equivalent modulo the commutativity of ";". The expressions `connected(nyc;paris)` and

connected(paris;bonn) can be generalized to connected(C;paris), whereas
the syntactic least general (or most specific) generalizer of these two expressions
is connected(C1;C2).

Similarly, assume that the predicate flights(C,L) is used to state that the
city C has direct flights to all of the cities in the list L. The *list concatenation*
operator "." records the cities[1] in the order given by the travel distance from
C. Due to the associativity of list concatenation, i.e., (X.Y).Z = X.(Y.Z), we
can use the flattened list rio.paris.oslo.nyc as a very compact and convenient representation of the congruence class (modulo associativity) whose
members are the different parenthesized list expressions ((rio.paris).oslo).
nyc, (rio.(paris.oslo)).nyc, rio.(paris.(oslo.nyc)), *etc.* Then, for
the expressions flights(rome,paris.oslo.nyc.rio) and flights(bonn,ulm.
oslo.rome), the least general generalizer is flights(C,L1.oslo.L2), which
reveals that oslo is the only common city that has a direct flight from rome and
bonn. Note that flights(C,L1.oslo.L2) is more general (modulo associativity) than flights(rome,paris.oslo.nyc.rio) by the substitution {C/rome,
L1/paris, L2/(nyc.rio)} and more general than flights(bonn,ulm.oslo.
rome) by the substitution {C/bonn, L1/ulm, L2/rome}.

Due to the equational axioms ACU, in general there can be more than one
least general generalizer of two expressions. As a simple example, let us record
the travel history of a person using a list that is ordered by the chronology in
which the visits were made; e.g., visited(paris.paris.bonn.nyc) denotes that
paris has been visited twice before visiting bonn and then nyc. The travel histories visited(paris.paris.bonn.nyc) and visited(bonn.bonn.rome) have
two incomparable least general generalizers: (a) visited(L1.bonn.L2) and (b)
visited(C.C.L), meaning that (a) the two travelers visited bonn, and (b) they
consecutively repeated a visit to their own first visited city. Note that the two
generalizers are least general and incomparable, since neither of them is an
instance (modulo associativity) of the other.

Furthermore, consider the predicate alliance(S) that checks whether the
cities in the set S have established an alliance. We introduce a new operator "&"
that satisfies associativity, commutativity, and unit element ∅; i.e., X & ∅ = X
and ∅ & X = X. We can use the flattened, multi-set notation alliance(nyc
& oslo & paris & rome) as a very compact and convenient representation
(with a total order on elements given by the lexicographic order) for the congruence class modulo ACU whose members are all of the different parenthesized permutations of the considered cities. Such permutations include as many
occurrences of ∅ as needed, due to unity [10]. In this scenario, the expressions (i) alliance(nyc & oslo & paris & rome) and (ii) alliance(bonn &
paris & rio & rome) have an infinite set of ACU generalizers of the form
alliance(paris & rome & S1 & ··· & Sn) yet they are all equivalent modulo

---

[1] A single city is automatically coerced into a singleton list.

ACU-renaming[2] so that we can choose one of them, typically the smallest one, as the class representative.

Regarding the handling of types and subtypes, let us assume that the constants rome, paris, oslo, ulm, and bonn belong to type European and that nyc and rio belong to type American. Furthermore, let us suppose that European and American are subtypes of a common type City that, in turn, is a subtype of the type Cities that can be used to model the typed version of the previous ACU (multi-)set structure. Subtyping implies automatic coercion: for instance, a European city also belongs to the type City and Cities. Note that the empty set, denoted by the unity ∅, only belongs to Cities.

In this typed environment, the above expressions (i) and (ii) have only one typed ACU least general generalizer alliance(paris & rome & C1:American & C2:European) that we choose as the representative of its infinite ACU congruence class. Note that alliance(paris & rome & S:Cities) is not a least general generalizer since it is strictly more general; it suffices to see that the typed ACU-lgg above is an instance of it modulo ACU with substitution {S:Cities/ (C1:American & C2:European)}.

For a discussion on how to achieve higher-order generalization in Maude we refer to [4].

3   ACUOS^2: A High Performance Generalization System

ACUOS^2 is a new, totally redesigned implementation of the ACUOS system presented in [4] that provides a remarkably faster and more optimized computation of least general generalizations. Generalizers are computed in an order-sorted, typed environment where inheritance and subtype relations are supported modulo any combination of associativity, commutativity, and unity axioms.

Both ACUOS and ACUOS^2 implement the generalization calculus of [3] but with remarkable differences concerning how they deal with the combinatorial explosion of different alternative possibilities; see [15] for some theoretical results on the complexity of generalization. Consider the generalization problem

$$\text{connected}(\text{paris};\text{bonn}) \overset{\triangle}{=} \text{connected}(\text{bonn};\text{paris})$$

that is written using the syntax of [3]. ACUOS already includes some optimizations but follows [3] straightforwardly and decomposes this problem (modulo commutativity of ";") into two simpler subproblems:

$$(P_1)\ \text{paris} \overset{\triangle}{=} \text{bonn} \wedge \text{bonn} \overset{\triangle}{=} \text{paris} \qquad (P_2)\ \text{paris} \overset{\triangle}{=} \text{paris} \wedge \text{bonn} \overset{\triangle}{=} \text{bonn}$$

According to [3], both are explored non-deterministically even if only the last subproblem would lead to the least general generalization. Much worse, due to axioms and types, a post-generation, time-expensive filtering phase is necessary

---

[2] i.e., the equivalence relation $\approx_{ACU}$ induced by the relative generality (subsumption) preorder $\leq_{ACU}$, i.e., $s \approx_{ACU} t$ iff $s \leq_{ACU} t$ and $t \leq_{ACU} s$.

to get rid of non-minimal generalizers. We have derived four groups of optimizations: (a) avoid non-deterministic exploration; (b) reduce the number of subproblems; (c) prune non-minimal paths to anticipate failure; and (d) filter out non-minimal solutions more efficiently.

(a) While ACUOS directly encoded the inference rules of [3] as rewrite rules that non-deterministically compute generalizers by exploring all branches of the search tree in a don't-know manner, i.e., each branch potentially leads to a different solution, ACUOS² smartly avoids non-deterministic exploration by using *synchronous rewriting* [7], also called *maximal parallel rewriting*, that allows ACUOS² to keep all current subproblems in a single data structure, e.g. $P_1 \mid P_2 \mid \cdots \mid P_n$, where all subproblems are simultaneously executed, avoiding any non-deterministic exploration at all. Synchronous rewriting is achieved in Maude by reformulating rewrite rules as oriented equations and, thanks to the different treatment of rules and equations in Maude [10], the deterministic encoding of the inference rules significantly reduces execution time and memory consumption. Also, built-in Maude memoization techniques are applied to speed up the evaluation of common subproblems, which can appear several times during the generalization process.

(b) Enumeration of all possible terms in a congruence class is extremely inefficient, and even nonterminating when the U axiom is considered. Therefore, it should not be used to effectively solve generalization problems when A, AC, or ACU axiom combinations are involved. For instance, if f is AC, the term $f(a_1, f(a_2, \ldots, f(a_{n-1}, a_n), \ldots))$ has $(2n-2)!/(n-1)!$ equivalent combinations; this number may grow exponentially for generalization problems that contain several symbols obeying distinct combinations of axioms.

ACUOS² avoids class element enumeration (specifically the expensive computation of argument permutations for AC operators). Instead, it relies on the extremely efficient Maude built-in support for equational matching to decompose generalization problems into simpler subproblems, thereby achieving a dramatic improvement in performance.

(c) It is extremely convenient to discard as early as possible any generalization subproblem that will not lead to a least general generalization. For example, trivial generalization problems such as paris $\overset{\triangle}{=}$ paris are immediately solved once and for all without any further synchronous rewrite. Similarly, dummy generalization problems with single variable generalizers such as nyc $\overset{\triangle}{=}$ paris are solved immediately. However, note that paris.oslo $\overset{\triangle}{=}$ nyc.oslo is not a dummy problem. ACUOS² also checks whether a subproblem is more general than another during the whole process, discarding the more general one. For instance, P_1 above contains two dummy subproblems and P_2 above contains two trivial subproblems, which *safely* allows ACUOS² to discard P_1 as being more general than P_2.

(d) Getting rid of non-minimal generalizers commonly implies too many pairwise comparisons, i.e., whether a generalizer l_1 is an instance *modulo* axioms of a generalizer l_2, or viceversa. Term size is a very convenient ally here since a term t' being bigger than another term t prevents t from being an instance of t'. Note that this property is no longer true when there is a unit element. For instance, `alliance(nyc & rome & S1:Cities & S2:Cities)` is bigger (modulo ACU) than `alliance(nyc & rome & S:Cities)`; but the latter is an instance of the former by the substitution {`S1/S, S2/∅`}. Term size can reduce the number of matching comparisons by half.

The ACUOS^2 backend has been implemented in Maude and consists of about 2300 lines of code. It can be directly invoked in the Maude environment by calling the generalization routine `lggs(M,t1,t2)`, which facilitates ACUOS^2 being integrated with third-party software. Furthermore, ACUOS^2 functionality can be accessed through an intuitive web interface that is publicly available at [1].

4   ACU Generalization in a Biological Domain

In this section, we show how ACUOS^2 can be used to analyze biological systems, e.g., to extract similarities and pinpoint discrepancies between two cell models that express distinct cellular states. We consider cell states that appear in the MAPK (Mitogen-Activated Protein Kinase) metabolic pathway that regulates growth, survival, proliferation, and differentiation of mammalian cells. Our cell formalization is inspired by and slightly modifies the data structures used in Pathway Logic (PL) [16]—a symbolic approach to the modeling and analysis of biological systems that is implemented in Maude. Specifically, a cell state can be specified as a typed term as follows.

We use sorts to classify cell entities. The main sorts are `Chemical`, `Protein`, and `Complex`, which are all subsorts of sort `Thing`, which specifies a generic entity. Cellular compartments are identified by sort `Location`, while `Modification` is a sort that is used to identify post-transactional protein modifications, which are defined by the operator "`[-]`" (e.g., the term `[EgfR - act]` represents the Egf (epidermal growth factor) receptor in an active state). A complex is a compound element that is specified by means of the associative ad commutative (AC) operator "`<=>`", which combines generic entities together.

A *cell state* is represented by a term of the form `[cellType | locs]`, where `cellType` specifies the cell type[3] and `locs` is a list (i.e., an associative data structure whose constructor symbol is "`,`") of cellular compartments (or locations). Each location is modeled by a term of the form `{ locName | comp }`, where `locName` is a name identifying the location (e.g., `CLm` represents the cell membrane location), and `comp` is a soup (i.e., an associative and commutative data structure with unity element `empty`) that specifies the entities included in that location. Note that cell states are built by means of a combination of A, AC, and ACU operators. The full formalization of the cell model is as follows.

```
fmod CELL-STRUCTURE is
  sorts Protein Thing Complex Chemical .
  subsorts Protein Complex Chemical < Thing .
```

---

[3] For simplicity, we only consider mammalian cells denoted by the constant `mcell`.

```
op _<=>_ : Thing Thing -> Complex [assoc comm] .
ops Egf EgfR Pi3k Gab1 Grb2 Hras Plcg Sos1 Src : -> Protein .
ops PIP2 PIP3 : -> Chemical .

sort Soup . subsort Thing < Soup .
op empty : -> Soup .
op __ : Soup Soup -> Soup [assoc comm id: empty] .

sort Modification .
ops act GTP GDP : -> Modification .
op [_-_] : Protein  Modification -> Protein .

sort Location LocName Locations .    subsort Location < Locations .
op {_|_} : LocName Soup -> Location .
ops CLc CLm CLi : -> LocName .
op _,_ : Locations Locations -> Locations [assoc] .

sorts Cell CellType .
op [_|_] : CellType Locations -> Cell .
op mcell : -> CellType .
endfm
```

Example 1. The term c_1

```
[ mcell | { Clc | Gab1 Grb2 Plcg Sos1 },
          { CLm | EgfR PIP2},
          { CLi | [Hras - GDP] Src } ]
```

models a cell state of the MAPK pathway with three locations: the cytoplasm (CLc) includes five proteins Gab1, Grb2, Pi3k, Plcg, and Sos1; the membrane (CLm) includes the protein EgfR and the chemical PIP2; the membrane interior (CLi) includes the proteins Hras (modified by GDP) and Src.

In this scenario, ACUOS² can be used to compare two cell states, c_1 and c_2. Indeed, any ACUOS² solution is a term whose non-variable part represents the common cell structure shared by c_1 and c_2, while its variables highlight discrepancy points where the two cell states differ.

Example 2. Consider the problem of generalizing the cell state of Example 1 plus the following MAPK cell state c_2

```
[ mcell | { CLc | Gab1 Plcg Sos1 },
          { CLm | PIP2 Egf <=> [EgfR - act] },
          { CLi | Grb2 Src [Hras - GDP] } ]
```

For instance, ACUOS² computes (in 4 ms) the following least general generalizer

```
[ mcell | { CLc | Gab1 Plcg Sos1 X1:Soup },
          { CLm | PIP2 X2:Thing },
          { CLi | Src X3:Soup [Hras - GDP] } ]
```

where X1:Soup, X2:Thing, and X3:Soup are typed variables. Each variable in the computed lgg detects a discrepancy between the two cell states. The variable X2:Thing represents a generic entity that abstracts two distinct elements in the membrane location CLm of the two cell states. In fact, c_1's membrane includes the (inactive) receptor EgfR, whereas c_2's membrane contains the complex Egf <=> [EgfR - act] that activates the receptor EgfR and binds it to the ligand Egf to start the metabolic process. Variables X1:Soup and X3:Soup indicate a protein relocation for Grb2, which appears in the location CLc in c_1 and in the membrane interior CLi in c_2. Note that the computed sort Soup is key in modeling the absence of Grb2 in a location, since it allows X1:Soup and X3:Soup to be bound to the empty soup.

5 Experimental Evaluation

To empirically evaluate the performance of ACUOS^2 we have considered the same generalization problems that were used to benchmark ACUOS in [4], together with some additional problems that deal with complex ACU structures such as graphs and biological models. All of the problems are available online at the tool web site [1] where the reader can also reproduce all of the experiments we conducted through the ACUOS^2 web interface. Specifically, the benchmarks used for the analysis are: (i) incompatible types, a problem without any generalizers; (ii) twins, ancestors, spouses, siblings, and children, some problems borrowed from the logic programming domain which are described in [4]; (iii) only-U, a generalization problem modulo (just) unity axioms, i.e., without A and C; (iv) synthetic, an involved example mixing A, C, and U axioms for different symbols; (v) multiple inheritance, which uses a classic example of multiple subtyping from [10] to illustrate the interaction of advanced type hierarchies with order-sorted generalization; (vi) rutherford, the classical analogy-making example that recognizes the duality between Rutherford's atom model and the solar system [11]; (vii) chemical, a variant of the case-based reasoning problem for chemical compounds discussed in [5]; (viii) alliance, the ACU example of Sect. 2; (ix) graph, the leading example of [9]; and (x) biological, the cell model discussed in Sect. 4.

We tested our implementations on a 3.30 GHz Intel(R) Xeon(R) E5-1660 with 64 Gb of RAM memory running Maude v2.7.1, and we considered the average of ten executions for each test. Table 1 shows our experimental results. For each problem, we show the size (i.e., number of operators) of the input terms, the computation time (ms.) until the first generalization is found[4], and the number #S of different subproblems that were generated so far, as a measure of how much the complexity of the problem has been simplified (before the optimizations, the number of produced subproblems was typically in the thousands for a term size of 100). In many cases, we cannot compare the time taken by each system to compute the set of all lggs, since the previous prototype ACUOS times

---

[4] The computation time for the incompatible types benchmark is the same for any input term since we provide two input terms of incompatible sorts.

Table 1. Experimental results

Benchmark	$\#S$	Size	ACUOS T1 (ms)	ACUOS² T2 (ms)	Speedup × (T1/T2)
incompatible types	0	20	30	1	30
	0	100	30	1	30
twins (C)	16	20	70	8	9
	42	100	23934	70	340
ancestors (A)	10	20	48	1	48
	31	100	TO	48	$>10^5$
spouses (A)	10	20	49	1	49
	31	100	TO	50	$>10^5$
spouses (AU)	10	20	531747	5	$\sim 10^5$
	61	100	TO	30	$>10^5$
siblings (AC)	16	20	TO	1	$>10^5$
	23	100	TO	150	$>10^5$
children (ACU)	12	20	TO	2	$>10^5$
	29	100	TO	3451	$>10^5$
only-U (U)	9	20	24	2	12
	9	100	TO	630	$>10^5$
synthetic (C+AU)	5	20	55	1	55
	5	100	31916	50	638
multiple inheritance (AC)	17	20	TO	10	$>10^5$
	31	100	TO	11067	$>10^5$
rutherford (AC+A+C)	5	20	48	1	48
	42	100	TO	320	$>10^5$
chemical (AU)	15	20	112	1	112
	31	100	TO	10	$>10^5$
graph (ACU+AU)	11	20	TO	1	$>10^5$
	31	100	TO	1002	$>10^5$
biological (ACU+AC+A)	22	20	TO	4	$>10^5$
	71	100	TO	50	$>10^5$
alliance (ACU)	11	20	TO	1	$>10^5$
	31	100	TO	9159	$>10^5$

out (for a generous timeout that we set to 60 min). Indeed, when we increase the size of the input terms from 20 to 100, the generalization process in ACUOS stops for most of the benchmarks due to timeout.

Considering the high combinatorial complexity of the ACU generalization problem, our implementation is highly efficient. All of the examples discussed in [4], except for `incompatible types`, `twins` (C), and `synthetic` (C + AU), fail to produce a generalization in ACUOS when the problem size is 100, whereas the time taken in $ACUOS^2$ is in the range from 1 to 11067 ms ($\sim$11 s). In all of the benchmarks, our figures demonstrate an impressive performance boost w.r.t. [4]: a speed up of five orders of magnitude for all of the ACU benchmarks.

6   Related Work

Related (but essentially different) problems of anti-unification for feature terms have been studied by [2,5,6]. The minimal and complete unranked anti-unification of [8] and the term graph anti-unification of [9] (together with the commutative extension) are also related to our work. The unranked anti-unification problems of [8,9] can be directly solved by using our techniques for associative anti-unification with the unit element by simply introducing sorts to distinguish between term variables and hedge variables (and their instantiations) [8]. Conversely, it is possible to simulate our calculus for associative least general generalization with the unit element in the minimal and complete unranked anti-unification algorithm of [8], but not the rules for associative-commutative least general generalization with the unit element.

As for the generalization of feature terms, this problem has two main similarities with computing (least general) generalizations modulo combinations of A, C, and U axioms: (1) feature terms are order-sorted (in contrast to the unsorted setting of unranked term anti-unification); and (2) there is no fixed order for arguments. However, the capability to deal with recursive, possibly cyclic data structures such as graphs in ACU anti-unification does not seem to have its counterpart in feature term anti-unification. Moreover, to generalize theories with a different number of clauses/equations (or a different number of atoms per clause), feature generalization algorithms resort to *ad hoc* mechanisms such as *background theories* and *projections* [11], whereas our approach naturally handles these kinds of generalizations by defining operators that obey the unity axiom.

References

1. The $ACUOS^2$ Website (2018). http://safe-tools.dsic.upv.es/acuos2
2. Aït-Kaci, H., Sasaki, Y.: An axiomatic approach to feature term generalization. In: De Raedt, L., Flach, P. (eds.) ECML 2001. LNCS (LNAI), vol. 2167, pp. 1–12. Springer, Heidelberg (2003). https://doi.org/10.1007/3-540-44795-4_1
3. Alpuente, M., Escobar, S., Espert, J., Meseguer, J.: A modular order-sorted equational generalization algorithm. Inf. Comput. **235**, 98–136 (2014)
4. Alpuente, M., Escobar, S., Espert, J., Meseguer, J.: ACUOS: a system for modular ACU generalization with subtyping and inheritance. In: Fermé, E., Leite, J. (eds.) JELIA 2014. LNCS (LNAI), vol. 8761, pp. 573–581. Springer, Cham (2014). https://doi.org/10.1007/978-3-319-11558-0_40
5. Armengol, E.: Usages of generalization in case-based reasoning. In: Weber, R.O., Richter, M.M. (eds.) ICCBR 2007. LNCS (LNAI), vol. 4626, pp. 31–45. Springer, Heidelberg (2007). https://doi.org/10.1007/978-3-540-74141-1_3

6. Armengol, E., Plaza, E.: Symbolic explanation of similarities in case-based reasoning. Comput. Artif. Intell. **25**(2–3), 153–171 (2006)
7. Baader, F., Nipkow, T.: Term Rewriting and All That. Cambridge University Press, Cambridge (1998)
8. Baumgartner, A., Kutsia, T., Levy, J., Villaret, M.: A variant of higher-order anti-unification. In: Proceedings of RTA 2013. LIPIcs, vol. 21, pp. 113–127 (2013)
9. Baumgartner, A., Kutsia, T., Levy, J., Villaret, M.: Term-graph anti-unification. In: Proceedings of FSCD 2018. LIPIcs, vol. 108, pp. 9:1–9:17 (2018)
10. Clavel, M., et al.: All About Maude - A High-Performance Logical Framework. LNCS, vol. 4350. Springer, Heidelberg (2007). https://doi.org/10.1007/978-3-540-71999-1
11. Gentner, D.: Structure-mapping: a theoretical framework for analogy*. Cogn. Sci. **7**(2), 155–170 (1983)
12. Meseguer, J.: Conditioned rewriting logic as a united model of concurrency. Theort. Comput. Sci. **96**(1), 73–155 (1992)
13. Muggleton, S.: Inductive logic programming: issues, results and the challenge of learning language in logic. Artif. Intell. **114**(1–2), 283–296 (1999)
14. Ontañón, S., Plaza, E.: Similarity measures over refinement graphs. Mach. Learn. **87**(1), 57–92 (2012)
15. Pottier, L.: Generalisation de termes en theorie equationelle: Cas associatif-commutatif. Technical report, Inria 1056, Norwegian Computing Center (1989)
16. Talcott, C.: Pathway logic. In: Bernardo, M., Degano, P., Zavattaro, G. (eds.) SFM 2008. LNCS, vol. 5016, pp. 21–53. Springer, Heidelberg (2008). https://doi.org/10.1007/978-3-540-68894-5_2

Taking Defeasible Entailment Beyond Rational Closure

Giovanni Casini[1]([⊠]) [iD], Thomas Meyer[2] [iD], and Ivan Varzinczak[3] [iD]

[1] CSC, Université du Luxembourg, Esch-sur-Alzette, Luxembourg
`giovanni.casini@uni.lu`
[2] CAIR, University of Cape Town, Cape Town, South Africa
`tmeyer@cs.uct.ac.za`
[3] CRIL, Univ. Artois & CNRS, Lens, France
`varzinczak@cril.fr`

Abstract. We present a systematic approach for extending the KLM framework for defeasible entailment. We first present a class of basic defeasible entailment relations, characterise it in three distinct ways and provide a high-level algorithm for computing it. This framework is then refined, with the refined version being characterised in a similar manner. We show that the two well-known forms of defeasible entailment, *rational closure* and *lexicographic closure*, fall within our refined framework, that rational closure is the most conservative of the defeasible entailment relations within the framework (with respect to subset inclusion), but that there are forms of defeasible entailment within our framework that are more "adventurous" than lexicographic closure.

1 Introduction

The approach by Kraus, Lehmann and Magidor [23] (a.k.a. KLM) is a well-known framework for defeasible reasoning. The KLM properties can be viewed as constraints on appropriate forms of defeasible entailment. We present what we believe to be the first systematic approach for extending the KLM framework. Our first proposal, *basic defeasible entailment*, strengthens the KLM framework by adding additional properties to it. We provide both a semantic characterisation in terms of a class of *ranked interpretations*, and a characterisation in terms of a class of functions that rank propositional (and defeasible) statements in a knowledge base according to their level of typicality. We also provide an algorithm for computing the framework. Next, we identify a crucial shortcoming in basic defeasible entailment, and propose a further strengthening, *rational defeasible entailment*, via an additional property. We prove that rational defeasible entailment can be characterised both semantically and in terms of ranks, and show that the algorithm is also applicable for computing rational defeasible entailment.

Currently there are two well-known forms of defeasible entailment satisfying those properties: rational closure (RC) [25] and lexicographic closure (LC) [24]. We show that both are rational (and basic) defeasible entailment relations, that

© Springer Nature Switzerland AG 2019
F. Calimeri et al. (Eds.): JELIA 2019, LNAI 11468, pp. 182–197, 2019.
https://doi.org/10.1007/978-3-030-19570-0_12

RC is the most conservative form of rational defeasible entailment, but there are forms of rational defeasible entailment that are "bolder" than LC. We argue that the framework for rational defeasible entailment is reminiscent of the AGM framework for belief change [1].

In the next section we provide the relevant background material, after which we present our work on basic defeasible entailment, rational defeasible entailment, and a discussion on the relation between lexicographic closure and rational defeasible entailment. We conclude with a discussion of related work, a summary, and suggestions for future work.

2   Background

For $\mathcal{P}$ being a finite set of propositional *atoms*, we use $p, q, \ldots$ as meta-variables for atoms. Propositional sentences are denoted by $\alpha, \beta, \ldots$, and are recursively defined in the usual way: $\alpha ::= \top \mid \bot \mid p \mid \neg\alpha \mid \alpha \wedge \alpha \mid \alpha \vee \alpha \mid \alpha \rightarrow \alpha \mid \alpha \leftrightarrow \alpha$. With $\mathcal{L}$ we denote the set of all propositional sentences. With $\mathcal{U} \equiv_{\text{def}} \{0,1\}^{\mathcal{P}}$ we denote the set of all propositional *valuations*, with 1 representing truth and 0 representing falsity. We use $u, v \ldots$ to denote valuations. Sometimes we represent valuations as sequences of atoms (e.g., p) and barred atoms (e.g., $\bar{p}$), with the understanding that the presence of a non-barred atom indicates that the atom is true in the valuation, while the presence of a barred atom indicates that the atom is false in the valuation. Satisfaction of a sentence $\alpha \in \mathcal{L}$ by $v \in \mathcal{U}$ is defined in the usual truth-functional way and is denoted by $v \Vdash \alpha$. The *models* of a set of sentences X is: $\llbracket X \rrbracket \equiv_{\text{def}} \{v \in \mathcal{U} \mid v \Vdash \alpha \text{ for every } \alpha \in X\}$.

2.1   KLM-Style Defeasible Implication

In the logic proposed by Kraus et al. [23], often referred to as the *KLM approach*, we are interested in defeasible implications (or DIs) of the form $\alpha \mathrel{\mid\!\sim} \beta$, read as "typically, if α, then β". The semantics of KLM-style rational defeasible implications is given by structures referred to as *ranked interpretations* [25]. In this work we adopt the following alternative representation thereof:

Definition 1. *A ranked interpretation $\mathscr{R}$ is a function from $\mathcal{U}$ to $\mathbb{N} \cup \{\infty\}$ s.t. $\mathscr{R}(u) = 0$ for some $u \in \mathcal{U}$, and satisfying the following* convexity *property: for every $i \in \mathbb{N}$, if $\mathscr{R}(v) = i$, then, for every j s.t. $0 \leq j < i$, there is a $u \in \mathcal{U}$ for which $\mathscr{R}(u) = j$.*

Given $\mathscr{R}$, we call $\mathscr{R}(v)$ the *rank* of v w.r.t. $\mathscr{R}$. Valuations with a lower rank are deemed more normal (or typical) than those with a higher rank, while those with an infinite rank are regarded as so atypical as to be impossible. With $\mathcal{U}^{\mathscr{R}} \equiv_{\text{def}} \{v \in \mathcal{U} \mid \mathscr{R}(v) < \infty\}$ we denote the *possible* valuations in $\mathscr{R}$. Given $\alpha \in \mathcal{L}$, we let $\llbracket\alpha\rrbracket^{\mathscr{R}} \equiv_{\text{def}} \{v \in \mathcal{U}^{\mathscr{R}} \mid v \Vdash \alpha\}$. $\mathscr{R}$ satisfies (is a ranked model of) α (denoted $\mathscr{R} \Vdash \alpha$) if $\mathcal{U}^{\mathscr{R}} \subseteq \llbracket\alpha\rrbracket^{\mathscr{R}}$.

Note that $\mathscr{R}$ generates a total preorder $\preceq_{\mathscr{R}}$ on $\mathcal{U}$ as follows: $v \preceq_{\mathscr{R}} u$ iff $\mathscr{R}(v) \leq \mathscr{R}(u)$. Given any total preorder $\preceq$ on $V \subseteq \mathcal{U}$, we can use its strict version $\prec$ to generate a ranked interpretation as follows. Let the *height* $h(v)$ of $v \in V$ be the length of the $\prec$-path between any one of the $\prec$-minimal elements of V and v (the length of the $\prec$-path between any of the $\prec$-minimal elements and a $\prec$-minimal element is 0). For $V \subseteq \mathcal{U}$ and a total preorder $\preceq$ on V, the ranked interpretation $\mathscr{R}^{\preceq}$ generated from $\preceq$ is defined as follows: for every $v \in \mathcal{U}$, $\mathscr{R}^{\preceq}(v) = h(v)$ if $v \in V$, and $\mathscr{R}^{\preceq}(v) = \infty$ otherwise.

Given a ranked interpretation $\mathscr{R}$ and $\alpha, \beta \in \mathcal{L}$, $\mathscr{R}$ satisfies (is a ranked model of) the conditional $\alpha \mathrel|\joinrel\sim \beta$ (denoted $\mathscr{R} \Vdash \alpha \mathrel|\joinrel\sim \beta$) if all the *possible* $\prec$-minimal α-valuations also satisfy β, i.e., if $\min_{\prec} [\![\alpha]\!]^{\mathscr{R}} \subseteq [\![\beta]\!]^{\mathscr{R}}$. $\mathscr{R}$ satisfies a set of conditionals $\mathcal{K}$ if $\mathscr{R} \Vdash \alpha \mathrel|\joinrel\sim \beta$ for every $\alpha \mathrel|\joinrel\sim \beta \in \mathcal{K}$.

Figure 1 depicts an example of a ranked interpretation for $\mathcal{P} = \{b, f, p\}$ satisfying $\mathcal{K} = \{p \rightarrow b, b \mathrel|\joinrel\sim f, p \mathrel|\joinrel\sim \neg f\}$. For brevity, we omit the valuations with rank ∞ in our graphical representations of ranked interpretations.

2	pbf		
1	$p\bar{b}f$	$pb\bar{f}$	
0	$\bar{p}bf$	$\bar{p}\bar{b}f$	$\bar{p}\bar{b}\bar{f}$

Fig. 1. A ranked interpretation for $\mathcal{P} = \{b, f, p\}$.

Observe that *all* classical propositional sentences can be expressed as DIs: $\mathscr{R} \Vdash \alpha$ iff $\mathscr{R} \Vdash \neg\alpha \mathrel|\joinrel\sim \bot$. The logic of defeasible implications can therefore be viewed as an extension of propositional logic.

2.2 Defeasible Entailment

Let a *knowledge base* $\mathcal{K}$ be a finite set of defeasible implications. The main question in this paper is to analyse *defeasible entailment* (denoted by $\approx$): what it means for a defeasible implication to be entailed by a *fixed* knowledge $\mathcal{K}$. It is well-accepted that defeasible entailment (unlike classical entailment) is not unique. For example, Lehmann and Magidor [25] put forward *rational closure* as an appropriate form of defeasible entailment, while Lehmann [24] proposed *lexicographic closure* as an alternative. We consider both of these in more detail below. In studying different forms of defeasible entailment, the position advocated by Lehmann and Magidor [25], and one we adopt here as well, is to consider a number of *rationality properties*, referred to as the KLM properties, for defeasible entailment.

$$
\begin{array}{lll}
\text{(Ref)} \ \mathcal{K} \approx \alpha \mathrel|\joinrel\sim \alpha & \text{(LLE)} \ \dfrac{\alpha \equiv \beta, \ \mathcal{K} \approx \alpha \mathrel|\joinrel\sim \gamma}{\mathcal{K} \approx \beta \mathrel|\joinrel\sim \gamma} & \text{(RW)} \ \dfrac{\mathcal{K} \approx \alpha \mathrel|\joinrel\sim \beta, \ \beta \models \gamma}{\mathcal{K} \approx \alpha \mathrel|\joinrel\sim \gamma} \\[3ex]
\text{(And)} \ \dfrac{\mathcal{K} \approx \alpha \mathrel|\joinrel\sim \beta, \ \mathcal{K} \approx \alpha \mathrel|\joinrel\sim \gamma}{\mathcal{K} \approx \alpha \mathrel|\joinrel\sim \beta \wedge \gamma} & \text{(Or)} \ \dfrac{\mathcal{K} \approx \alpha \mathrel|\joinrel\sim \gamma, \ \mathcal{K} \approx \beta \mathrel|\joinrel\sim \gamma}{\mathcal{K} \approx \alpha \vee \beta \mathrel|\joinrel\sim \gamma} & \text{(CM)} \ \dfrac{\mathcal{K} \approx \alpha \mathrel|\joinrel\sim \beta, \ \mathcal{K} \approx \alpha \mathrel|\joinrel\sim \gamma}{\mathcal{K} \approx \alpha \wedge \beta \mathrel|\joinrel\sim \gamma} \quad (1) \\[3ex]
\text{(RM)} \ \dfrac{\mathcal{K} \approx \alpha \mathrel|\joinrel\sim \gamma, \ \mathcal{K} \not\approx \alpha \mathrel|\joinrel\sim \neg\beta}{\mathcal{K} \approx \alpha \wedge \beta \mathrel|\joinrel\sim \gamma}
\end{array}
$$

Lehmann and Magidor argue that defeasible entailment ought to satisfy all the above KLM properties. We refer to this as *LM-rationality*.

Definition 2. *A ranked interpretation $\mathscr{R}$ is said to generate a defeasible $\mathcal{K}$-entailment relation $\approx_{\mathscr{R}}$ by setting $\mathcal{K} \approx_{\mathscr{R}} \alpha \mathrel{|\!\sim} \beta$ iff $\mathscr{R} \Vdash \alpha \mathrel{|\!\sim} \beta$. (If there isn't any ambiguity, we drop the subscript $\mathscr{R}$).*

Lehmann and Magidor proved the following useful result.

Observation 1 (Lehman and Magidor [25]). *A defeasible entailment relation is LM-rational iff it can be generated from a ranked interpretation.*

It is easy to see that rank entailment, defined next, is not LM-rational [25, Sect. 4.2].

Definition 3. *A defeasible implication $\alpha \mathrel{|\!\sim} \beta$ is rank entailed by a knowledge base $\mathcal{K}$ (denoted as $\mathcal{K} \approx_R \alpha \mathrel{|\!\sim} \beta$) if every ranked model of $\mathcal{K}$ satisfies $\alpha \mathrel{|\!\sim} \beta$.*

But rank entailment plays an important part in defining acceptable versions of defeasible entailment, since it can be viewed as the *monotonic core* of any appropriate form of defeasible entailment [16].

2.3 Rational Closure

The first version of defeasible entailment satisfying LM-rationality we consider is *rational closure* [25]. Consider the ordering $\preceq_{\mathcal{K}}$ on all ranked models of a knowledge base $\mathcal{K}$, which is defined as follows: $\mathscr{R}_1 \preceq_{\mathcal{K}} \mathscr{R}_2$ if for every $v \in \mathcal{U}$, $\mathscr{R}_1(v) \leq \mathscr{R}_2(v)$. Intuitively, ranked models lower down in the ordering are more typical. Giordano et al. [21] showed that there is a unique $\prec_{\mathcal{K}}$-minimal element.

Definition 4. *Let $\mathscr{R}_{\mathcal{K}}^{RC}$ be the minimum element of the ordering $\preceq_{\mathcal{K}}$ on ranked models of $\mathcal{K}$. A defeasible implication $\alpha \mathrel{|\!\sim} \beta$ is in the rational closure of $\mathcal{K}$ (denoted as $\mathcal{K} \approx_{RC} \alpha \mathrel{|\!\sim} \beta$) if $\mathscr{R}_{\mathcal{K}}^{RC} \Vdash \alpha \mathrel{|\!\sim} \beta$.*

Observe that there are two levels of typicality at work for rational closure, namely *within* ranked models of $\mathcal{K}$, where valuations lower down are viewed as more typical, and *between* ranked models of $\mathcal{K}$, where ranked models lower down in the ordering are viewed as more typical. The most typical ranked model $\mathscr{R}_{\mathcal{K}}^{RC}$ is the one in which valuations are as typical as $\mathcal{K}$ allows them to be.

Since rational closure can be defined in terms of a single ranked interpretation, it follows from Observation 1 that it is LM-rational (it satisfies all the KLM properties).

It will be useful to be able to refer to the possible valuations w.r.t. a knowledge base. We refer to $\mathcal{U}_R^{\mathcal{K}} \equiv_{\text{def}} \mathcal{U} \backslash \{u \in [\![\alpha]\!] \mid \mathcal{K} \approx_R \neg\alpha \mathrel{|\!\sim} \bot\}$ as the set of possible valuations w.r.t. $\mathcal{K}$. So $\mathcal{U}_R^{\mathcal{K}}$ refers to all the valuations not in conflict with rank entailment w.r.t. $\mathcal{K}$. From results by Lehmann and Magidor [25] (Lemmas 24 and 30) it follows that the possible valuations in the minimal model $\mathscr{R}_{\mathcal{K}}^{RC}$ are precisely the possible valuations w.r.t. $\mathcal{K}$: $\mathcal{U}_R^{\mathcal{K}} = \mathcal{U}^{\mathscr{R}_{\mathcal{K}}^{RC}}$.

Rational closure can also be defined in terms of the *base rank* of a statement. A propositional sentence α is said to be *exceptional* w.r.t. $\mathcal{K}$ if $\mathcal{K} \approx_R \top \vdash \neg\alpha$ (i.e., α is false in all the most typical valuations in every ranked model of $\mathcal{K}$). Let $\varepsilon(\mathcal{K}) = \{\alpha \vdash \beta \mid \mathcal{K} \approx_R \top \vdash \neg\alpha\}$. Define a sequence of knowledge bases $\mathcal{E}_0^{\mathcal{K}}, \ldots, \mathcal{E}_\infty^{\mathcal{K}}$ as follows: $\mathcal{E}_0^{\mathcal{K}} \equiv_{\text{def}} \mathcal{K}$, $\mathcal{E}_i^{\mathcal{K}} \equiv_{\text{def}} \varepsilon(\mathcal{E}_{i-1}^{\mathcal{K}})$, for $0 < i < n$, and $\mathcal{E}_\infty \equiv_{\text{def}} \mathcal{E}_n^{\mathcal{K}}$, where n is the smallest k for which $\mathcal{E}_k^{\mathcal{K}} = \mathcal{E}_{k+1}^{\mathcal{K}}$ (since $\mathcal{K}$ is finite, n must exist). The *base rank* $br_\mathcal{K}(\alpha)$ of a propositional statement α w.r.t. a knowledge base $\mathcal{K}$ is defined to be the smallest r for which α is *not* exceptional w.r.t. $\mathcal{E}_r^{\mathcal{K}}$. $br_\mathcal{K}(\alpha) \equiv_{\text{def}} \min\{r \mid \mathcal{E}_r^{\mathcal{K}} \not\approx_R \top \vdash \neg\alpha\}$.

Observation 2 (Giordano et al. [21]). $\mathcal{K} \approx_{RC} \alpha \vdash \beta$ *iff* $br_\mathcal{K}(\alpha) < br_\mathcal{K}(\alpha \wedge \neg\beta)$ *or* $br_\mathcal{K}(\alpha) = \infty$.

There is a fundamental connection between the base ranks of propositional statements w.r.t. $\mathcal{K}$ and the ranks of valuations in the minimal ranked model $\mathscr{R}_\mathcal{K}^{RC}$.

Observation 3 (Giordano et al. [21]). *For every knowledge base $\mathcal{K}$ and $\alpha \in \mathcal{L}$, $br_\mathcal{K}(\alpha) = \min\{i \mid$ there is a $v \in [\![\alpha]\!]$ s.t. $\mathscr{R}_\mathcal{K}^{RC}(v) = i\}$.*

From Observation 3 it follows that a classical statement α (or its defeasible representation $\neg\alpha \vdash \bot$) is in the rational closure of $\mathcal{K}$ iff the base rank of $\neg\alpha$ w.r.t. $\mathcal{K}$ is ∞. The definition of base rank can be extended to defeasible implications as follows: $br_\mathcal{K}(\alpha \vdash \beta) \equiv_{\text{def}} br_\mathcal{K}(\alpha)$. Assigning base ranks to defeasible implications in this way forms the basis of an algorithm for computing rational closure; an algorithm that can be reduced to a number of classical entailment checks. Define the *materialisation* of a knowledge base $\mathcal{K}$ as $\overrightarrow{\mathcal{K}} \equiv_{\text{def}} \{\alpha \to \beta \mid \alpha \vdash \beta \in \mathcal{K}\}$. It can be shown [25] that a sentence α is exceptional w.r.t. $\mathcal{K}$ iff $\overrightarrow{\mathcal{K}} \models \neg\alpha$. From this we can define a procedure BaseRank which partitions the materialisation of $\mathcal{K}$ into $n + 1$ classes according to base rank: $i = 0, \ldots n - 1, \infty$, $R_i \equiv_{\text{def}} \{\alpha \to \beta \mid \alpha \vdash \beta \in \mathcal{K}, br_\mathcal{K}(\alpha) = i\}$.

We use BaseRank to describe an algorithm originally proposed by Freund [18] for computing rational closure. It takes as input $\mathcal{K}$ and $\alpha \vdash \beta$, and returns **true** iff $\alpha \vdash \beta$ is in the rational closure of $\mathcal{K}$.

The algorithm keeps on removing (materialisations of) defeasible implications from (the materialisation of) $\mathcal{K}$, starting with the lowest base rank, and proceeding base rank by base rank, until it finds the first R which is classically consistent with α (and therefore α is not exceptional w.r.t. the defeasible version of R). $\alpha \vdash \beta$ is then taken to be in the rational closure of $\mathcal{K}$ iff R classically entails the materialisation of $\alpha \vdash \beta$.

Observation 4 (Freund [18]). *Given $\mathcal{K}$ and $\alpha \vdash \beta$, RationalClosure returns **true** iff $\mathcal{K} \approx_{RC} \alpha \vdash \beta$.*

Observe that RationalClosure involves a number of calls to a classical-entailment checker that is polynomial in the size of $\mathcal{K}$. Computing rational closure is therefore no harder than checking classical entailment.

Algorithm 1. `BaseRank`

Input: A knowledge base $\mathcal{K}$
Output: An ordered tuple $(R_0, \ldots, R_{n-1}, R_\infty, n)$

1 $i := 0;$
2 $E_0 := \overrightarrow{\mathcal{K}};$
3 **repeat**
4 | $\quad E_{i+1} := \{\alpha \to \beta \in E_i \mid E_i \models \neg\alpha\};$
5 | $\quad R_i := E_i \setminus E_{i+1};$
6 | $\quad i := i + 1;$
7 **until** $E_{i-1} = E_i;$
8 $R_\infty := E_{i-1};$
9 **if** $E_{i-1} = \emptyset$ **then**
10 | $\quad n := i \quad 1;$
11 **else**
12 | $\quad n := i;$
13 **return** $(R_0, \ldots, R_{n-1}, R_\infty, n)$

Algorithm 2. `RationalClosure`

Input: A knowledge base $\mathcal{K}$ and a DI $\alpha \mathrel{|\!\sim} \beta$
Output: **true**, if $\mathcal{K} \mathrel{\approx\!\!\!\!\mid} \alpha \mathrel{|\!\sim} \beta$, and **false**, otherwise

1 $(R_0, \ldots, R_{n-1}, R_\infty, n) := \texttt{BaseRank}(\mathcal{K});$
2 $i := 0;$
3 $R := \bigcup_{i=0}^{j<n} R_j;$
4 **while** $R_\infty \cup R \models \neg\alpha$ **and** $R \neq \emptyset$ **do**
5 | $\quad R := R \setminus R_i;$
6 | $\quad i := i + 1;$
7 **return** $R_\infty \cup R \models \alpha \to \beta;$

---

3   Basic Defeasible Entailment

Our departure point for defining defeasible entailment is that it ought to be LM-rational. The central question we address in this paper is whether LM-rationality is sufficient. The immediate answer is that it is not. For starters, we also require $\mathrel{\approx\!\!\!\!\mid}$ to satisfy Inclusion (all elements of $\mathcal{K}$ should be defeasibly entailed by $\mathcal{K}$):

(Inclusion) $\mathcal{K} \mathrel{\approx\!\!\!\!\mid} \alpha \mathrel{|\!\sim} \beta$ for every $\alpha \mathrel{|\!\sim} \beta \in \mathcal{K}$

and Classic Preservation—the classical defeasible implications (those corresponding to classical sentences) defeasibly entailed by $\mathcal{K}$ should correspond exactly to those in the monotonic core of $\mathcal{K}$ (i.e., those that are rank entailed by $\mathcal{K}$:

(Classic Preservation) $\mathcal{K} \approx \alpha \mathrel{\mid\!\sim} \bot$ iff $\mathcal{K} \approx_R \alpha \mathrel{\mid\!\sim} \bot$

An easy corollary of Classic Preservation is Classic Consistency, requiring that a knowledge base is consistent iff it is consistent w.r.t. rank entailment.

(Classic Consistency) $\mathcal{K} \approx \top \mathrel{\mid\!\sim} \bot$ iff $\mathcal{K} \approx_R \top \mathrel{\mid\!\sim} \bot$

We refer to a defeasible entailment relation satisfying LM-rationality, Inclusion, and Classic Preservation as a *basic defeasible entailment relation*.

We shall see below (using Theorem 1) that rational closure is a basic defeasible entailment relation. However, since ranked entailment does not satisfy RM, it is not LM-rational, and is therefore not a basic defeasible entailment relation.

Definition 5. *A ranked model $\mathscr{R}$ of $\mathcal{K}$ is said to be $\mathcal{K}$-faithful if the possible valuations in $\mathscr{R}$ are precisely the possible valuations w.r.t. $\mathcal{K}$: $\mathcal{U}^{\mathscr{R}} = \mathcal{U}_R^{\mathcal{K}}$.*

Note that the minimal model $\mathscr{R}_{\mathcal{K}}^{RC}$ is $\mathcal{K}$-faithful.

Our first fundamental result (using points 1 and 2b of Theorem 1 below) is a semantic characterisation of basic defeasible entailment in terms of the $\mathcal{K}$-faithful ranked models. From this it also follows immediately that basic defeasible entailment satisfies the following property.

(Rank Extension) If $\mathcal{K} \approx_R \alpha \mathrel{\mid\!\sim} \beta$, then $\mathcal{K} \approx \alpha \mathrel{\mid\!\sim} \beta$

Rank Extension requires $\approx$ to extend its monotonic core.

We can also characterise basic defeasible entailment by generalising the notion of base rank.

Definition 6. *Let $r : \mathcal{L} \longrightarrow \mathbb{N} \cup \{\infty\}$ be a rank function s.t. $r(\top) = 0$, satisfying the following* convexity *property: for every $i \in \mathbb{N}$, if $r(\alpha) = i$ then, for every j such that $0 \leq j < i$, there is a $\beta \in \mathcal{L}$ for which $r(\beta) = j$. r is entailment preserving if $\alpha \models \beta$ implies $r(\alpha) \geq r(\beta)$. r is $\mathcal{K}$-faithful if (i) it is entailment preserving; (ii) $r(\alpha) < r(\alpha \wedge \neg\beta)$ or $r(\alpha) = \infty$, for every $\alpha \mathrel{\mid\!\sim} \beta \in \mathcal{K}$, and (iii) $r(\alpha) = \infty$ iff $\mathcal{K} \approx_R \alpha \mathrel{\mid\!\sim} \bot$.*

Observe that the base rank $br_{\mathcal{K}}(\cdot)$ is $\mathcal{K}$-faithful.

Definition 7. *A rank function r generates a defeasible entailment relation $\approx$ whenever $\mathcal{K} \approx \alpha \mathrel{\mid\!\sim} \beta$ if $r(\alpha) < r(\alpha \wedge \neg\beta)$ or $r(\alpha) = \infty$.*

It follows (using points 1 and 2c of Theorem 1 below), that basic defeasible entailment can be characterised using the $\mathcal{K}$-faithful rank functions.

Next, we present an algorithm that computes the defeasible entailment relation generated by a $\mathcal{K}$-faithful rank function. It is a modified version of `RationalClosure`, differing from it in that the call to `BaseRank` is replaced with a call to the `Rank` algorithm described below. It receives as input a knowledge base $\mathcal{K}$ and a $\mathcal{K}$-faithful rank function r. It produces as output a sequence $(R_0, \ldots, R_{n-1}, R_\infty, n)$ where the R_is are *sentences*, unlike `BaseRank`, which produces sets of sentences. `DefeasibleEntailment` is then adjusted accordingly.

`DefeasibleEntailment` removes statements, starting with the lowest rank, and proceeding rank by rank, until it finds the first R which is classically consistent with α. $\alpha \mathrel{|\!\sim} \beta$ is then taken to be defeasibly entailed by $\mathcal{K}$ iff R classically entails the materialisation of $\alpha \mathrel{|\!\sim} \beta$. The R_is correspond to classical representations of defeasible information, with different R_is representing information with different levels of typicality, and with R_∞ corresponding to information that is classical. In fact, the set containing all the R_is is equivalent to the materialisation of $\mathcal{K}$.

Algorithm 3. `DefeasibleEntailment`

Input: A knowledge base $\mathcal{K}$, a $\mathcal{K}$-faithful rank function r, and a DI $\alpha \mathrel{|\!\sim} \beta$
Output: true, if $\mathcal{K} \mathrel{\approx} \alpha \mathrel{|\!\sim} \beta$, and **false**, otherwise

1 $(R_0, \ldots, R_{n-1}, R_\infty, n) := \text{Rank}(\mathcal{K}, r)$;
2 $i := 0$;
3 $R := \bigcup_{i=0}^{j<n} \{R_j\}$;
4 **while** $\{R_\infty\} \cup R \models \neg\alpha$ **and** $R \neq \emptyset$ **do**
5 $\quad\lfloor\; R := R \setminus \{R_i\}$;
6 $\quad\; i := i + 1$;
7 **return** $\{R_\infty\} \cup R \models \alpha \to \beta$;

Algorithm 4. `Rank`

Input: A knowledge base $\mathcal{K}$ and a $\mathcal{K}$-faithful rank function r
Output: An ordered tuple $(R_0, \ldots, R_{n-1}, R_\infty, n)$

1 $R_{\infty} := \neg \left(\bigvee_{r([\alpha]) = \infty} [\alpha] \right)$;
2 $n := \max\{i \in \mathbb{N} \mid \text{there is an } \alpha \in \mathcal{L} \text{ s.t. } r(\alpha) = i\}$;
3 **if** $n = 0$ **then**
4 $\quad\lfloor\; R_0 := \top; n := 1$;
5 **else**
6 $\quad$ **for** $i := 0$ **to** $n - 1$ **do**
7 $\quad\quad\lfloor\; R_i \equiv_{\text{def}} \neg \left(\bigvee_{r([\alpha]) = i+1} [\alpha] \right)$
8 **return** $(R_0, \ldots, R_{n-1}, R_\infty, n)$

For $\alpha \in \mathcal{L}$, let $[\alpha]$ be a canonical representative of the set $\{\beta \mid \beta \equiv \alpha\}$. Rank receives as input a knowledge base $\mathcal{K}$ and a $\mathcal{K}$-faithful rank function r and, as mentioned above, produces as output an ordered tuple of *sentences* $(R_0, \ldots, R_{n-1}, R_\infty, n)$.

If there is no α such that $r(\alpha) = \infty$, then R_∞ will be set to $\top$. This corresponds to the case where all information is defeasible. If $n = 0$, it corresponds to the case where there is no defeasible information. In this case we set n to 1 and set R_0 to $\top$.

Proposition 1. *Let* $(R_0, \ldots, R_{n-1}, R_\infty, n)$ *be the output obtained from the* Rank *algorithm, given a knowledge base* $\mathcal{K}$ *and a* $\mathcal{K}$*-faithful ranking function* r. *Then* $\{R_\infty\} \cup \bigcup_{i=0}^{j \leq n}\{R_j\} \equiv \overrightarrow{\mathcal{K}}$.

Example 1. Let $\mathcal{K} = \{\mathsf{p} \to \mathsf{b}, \mathsf{b} \mathrel{|\!\sim} \mathsf{f}, \mathsf{p} \mathrel{|\!\sim} \neg\mathsf{f}\}$. One can see there is only one ranking function r for which $r((\mathsf{b} \to \mathsf{f}) \to \mathsf{p}) = 1$, $r(\mathsf{p} \wedge (\mathsf{b} \to \mathsf{f})) = 2$, and $r(\neg(\mathsf{p} \to \mathsf{b})) = \infty$. Moreover, for every $\alpha \in \mathcal{L}$, $r(\alpha) = \infty$ or $r(\alpha) \leq 2$. Given $\mathcal{K}$ and r, Rank will output the ordered tuple $(R_0, R_1, R_\infty, 2)$, where $R_\infty \equiv \mathsf{p} \to \mathsf{b}$, $R_1 \equiv \neg(\mathsf{p} \wedge (\mathsf{b} \to \mathsf{f})) \equiv \mathsf{p} \to (\mathsf{b} \wedge \neg\mathsf{f})$, and $R_0 \equiv \neg((\mathsf{b} \to \mathsf{f}) \to \mathsf{p}) \equiv (\mathsf{b} \to \mathsf{f}) \wedge \neg\mathsf{p}$. Given $\mathcal{K}$, r, and $(\mathsf{p} \leftrightarrow \mathsf{b}) \wedge (\mathsf{b} \leftrightarrow \mathsf{f}) \mathrel{|\!\sim} \neg\mathsf{f}$, DefeasibleEntailment will return **true**. It will do so by first verifying that $\{R_0, R_1, R_\infty\} \not\models \neg((\mathsf{p} \leftrightarrow \mathsf{b}) \wedge (\mathsf{b} \leftrightarrow \mathsf{f}))$ and then checking whether $\{R_0, R_1, R_\infty\} \models ((\mathsf{p} \leftrightarrow \mathsf{b}) \wedge (\mathsf{b} \leftrightarrow \mathsf{f})) \to \neg\mathsf{f}$ (which it does). Note that, given this r, DefeasibleEntailment computes the rational closure of $\mathcal{K}$. □

Example 2. Let $\mathcal{K}$ be as in Example 1. It can be shown that there is only one ranking function r s.t. $r(\mathsf{f} \to \mathsf{p}) = 1$, $r((\mathsf{b} \vee \mathsf{f}) \to (\mathsf{p} \wedge \mathsf{f})) = 2$, and $r(\neg(\mathsf{p} \to \mathsf{b})) = \infty$, and that r is $\mathcal{K}$-faithful. Moreover, for r it will be the case that for every $\alpha \in \mathcal{L}$, $r(\alpha) = \infty$ or $r(\alpha) \leq 2$. Given $\mathcal{K}$ and r, the Rank algorithm will output the ordered tuple $(R_0, R_1, R_\infty, 2)$ where $R_\infty \equiv \mathsf{p} \to \mathsf{b}$, $R_1 \equiv \neg((\mathsf{b} \vee \mathsf{f}) \to (\mathsf{p} \wedge \mathsf{f})) \equiv (\neg\mathsf{b} \to \mathsf{f}) \wedge (\mathsf{p} \to \neg\mathsf{f})$, and $R_0 \equiv \neg(\mathsf{f} \to \mathsf{p}) \equiv \mathsf{f} \wedge \neg\mathsf{p}$. Given $\mathcal{K}$, r, and the DI $(\mathsf{p} \leftrightarrow \mathsf{b}) \wedge (\mathsf{b} \leftrightarrow \mathsf{f}) \mathrel{|\!\sim} \neg\mathsf{f}$, algorithm DefeasibleEntailment will return **false**. It will do so by first removing R_0 (since $\{R_0, R_1, R_\infty\} \models \neg((\mathsf{p} \leftrightarrow \mathsf{b}) \wedge (\mathsf{b} \leftrightarrow \mathsf{f}))$), then removing R_1 (since $\{R_1, R_\infty\} \models \neg((\mathsf{p} \leftrightarrow \mathsf{b}) \wedge (\mathsf{b} \leftrightarrow \mathsf{f}))$), and then, since $\{R_\infty\} \not\models \neg((\mathsf{p} \leftrightarrow \mathsf{b}) \wedge (\mathsf{b} \leftrightarrow \mathsf{f}))$, it will check whether $\{R_\infty\} \models ((\mathsf{p} \leftrightarrow \mathsf{b}) \wedge (\mathsf{b} \leftrightarrow \mathsf{f})) \to \neg\mathsf{f}$ (which it does not). □

Definition 8. DefeasibleEntailment *computes a defeasible entailment relation* $\mathrel{\approx\!\!\!|}$ *for a knowledge base* $\mathcal{K}$ *and a rank function* r *if* Defeasible-Entailment, *when presented with* $\mathcal{K}$, r, *and* $\alpha \mathrel{|\!\sim} \beta$, *returns* **true** *if and only if* $\mathcal{K} \mathrel{\approx\!\!\!|} \alpha \mathrel{|\!\sim} \beta$.

It follows (using points 1 and 2d of Theorem 1) that Defeasible-Entailment computes exactly basic defeasible entailment.

Theorem 1. *The following statements are equivalent: (1)* $\mathrel{\approx\!\!\!|}$ *is a basic defeasible* $\mathcal{K}$*-entailment relation, and (2) there is a* $\mathcal{K}$*-faithful ranked model* $\mathscr{R}$ *and a* $\mathcal{K}$*-faithful rank function* r *such that:*

a. $r(\alpha) = \min\{i \mid \text{there is a } v \in [\![\alpha]\!] \text{ s.t. } \mathscr{R}(v) = i\}$;
b. $\mathrel{\approx\!\!\!|}$ *can be generated from* $\mathscr{R}$;
c. $\mathrel{\approx\!\!\!|}$ *can be generated from* r;
d. $\mathrel{\approx\!\!\!|}$ *can be computed by* Defeasible Entailment, *given* $\mathcal{K}$ *and* r *as input.*

Note that points 1 and 2 in Theorem 1 establish a connection between $\mathscr{R}$ and r via a result that is a generalisation of Observation 3. And observe that DefeasibleEntailment involves a number of calls to a classic entailment checker that is linear in n times the size of $\mathcal{K}$ (where n is the number returned by the Rank algorithm). But note also that n may be exponential in the size of $\mathcal{K}$.

4   Rational Defeasible Entailment

We now proceed by suggesting that basic defeasible entailment is too permissive. We first show that it does not satisfy RC Extension:

(RC Extension) If $\mathcal{K} \mathrel{\vert\kern-0.3em\approx_{RC}} \alpha \mathrel{\vert\!\sim} \beta$, then $\mathcal{K} \mathrel{\vert\kern-0.3em\approx} \alpha \mathrel{\vert\!\sim} \beta$

To see that basic defeasible entailment does not satisfy RC Extension, consider the following example.

Example 3. Figure 2(a) depicts the ($\mathcal{K}$-faithful) minimal ranked model $\mathscr{R}_{\mathcal{K}}^{RC}$ of $\mathcal{K} = \{\mathsf{p} \rightarrow \mathsf{b}, \mathsf{b} \mathrel{\vert\!\sim} \mathsf{f}, \mathsf{p} \mathrel{\vert\!\sim} \neg\mathsf{f}\}$. Note that $\mathscr{R}_{\mathcal{K}}^{RC} \mathrel{\Vdash} \neg\mathsf{p} \wedge \neg\mathsf{f} \mathrel{\vert\!\sim} \neg\mathsf{b}$ and (from Definition 4) that $\mathcal{K} \mathrel{\vert\kern-0.3em\approx_{RC}} \neg\mathsf{p} \wedge \neg\mathsf{f} \mathrel{\vert\!\sim} \neg\mathsf{b}$. But for the $\mathcal{K}$-faithful ranked model $\mathscr{R}$ in Fig. 2(b) below it follows that $\mathscr{R} \mathrel{\nVdash} \neg\mathsf{p} \wedge \neg\mathsf{f} \mathrel{\vert\!\sim} \neg\mathsf{b}$. And from Theorem 1 it follows that for the basic defeasible $\mathcal{K}$-entailment relation $\mathrel{\vert\kern-0.3em\approx}$ generated from $\mathscr{R}$, $\mathcal{K} \mathrel{\vert\kern-0.3em\not\approx} \neg\mathsf{p} \wedge \neg\mathsf{f} \mathrel{\vert\!\sim} \neg\mathsf{b}$. So RC Extension does not hold.　　　□

2	pbf	
1	$\overline{\mathsf{p}}\mathsf{bf}$	$\mathsf{pb}\overline{\mathsf{f}}$
0	$\overline{\mathsf{p}}\mathsf{b}\overline{\mathsf{f}}$	$\overline{\mathsf{p}}\,\overline{\mathsf{b}}\mathsf{f}$	$\overline{\mathsf{p}}\,\overline{\mathsf{b}}\,\overline{\mathsf{f}}$

(a)

2	pbf		
1	$\overline{\mathsf{p}}\mathsf{bf}$	$\mathsf{pb}\overline{\mathsf{f}}$	$\overline{\mathsf{p}}\mathsf{b}\overline{\mathsf{f}}$
0	$\overline{\mathsf{p}}\,\overline{\mathsf{b}}\mathsf{f}$	$\overline{\mathsf{p}}\,\overline{\mathsf{b}}\,\overline{\mathsf{f}}$	

(b)

Fig. 2. Ranked models of the knowledge base in Example 3. (a) Shows the minimal $\mathcal{K}$-faithful ranked model $\mathscr{R}_{\mathcal{K}}^{RC}$, while (b) depicts the $\mathcal{K}$-faithful ranked model $\mathscr{R}$.

If a basic defeasible entailment relation also satisfies RC Extension, we refer to it as *rational* defeasible entailment. We propose the class of rational defeasible entailment relations as those worthy of the term *rational* and analyse them further in the remainder of this section. We start by showing (points 1 and 2b of Theorem 2) that rational defeasible entailment can be characterised in terms of a subset of the $\mathcal{K}$-faithful ranked models, referred to as *rank preserving*.

Definition 9. *A $\mathcal{K}$-faithful ranked model $\mathscr{R}$ is said to be rank preserving if the following condition holds: for all $v, u \in \mathcal{U}$, if $\mathscr{R}_{\mathcal{K}}^{RC}(v) < \mathscr{R}_{\mathcal{K}}^{RC}(u)$, then $\mathscr{R}(v) < \mathscr{R}(u)$.*

Informally, rank preservation requires the total preorder $\preceq_{\mathscr{R}}$ generated from $\mathscr{R}$ to respect the relative positions assigned to valuations in the minimal model $\mathscr{R}_{\mathcal{K}}^{RC}$ of $\mathcal{K}$.

We can also characterise rational defeasible entailment (points 1 and 2c of Theorem 2) using a subclass of $\mathcal{K}$-faithful rank functions referred to as *base rank preserving*.

Definition 10. *A $\mathcal{K}$-faithful rank function r is said to be base rank preserving if the following condition holds: for all $\alpha, \beta \in \mathcal{L}$, if $br_{\mathcal{K}}(\alpha) < br_{\mathcal{K}}(\beta)$, then $r(\alpha) < r(\beta)$.*

Base rank preserving rank functions (or, the relations $<$ derivable from base rank preserving rank functions) respect the base rank (or rather, the relation $<$ derivable from the base rank). We show (points 1 and 2d of Theorem 2) that DefeasibleEntailment described in the previous section can also be used to compute rational defeasible entailment, provided it receives base rank preserving rank functions as input.

Theorem 2. *The following statements are equivalent: (1) $\mathrel{\vcenter{\hbox{$\scriptstyle\approx$}}}$ is a rational defeasible $\mathcal{K}$-entailment relation, and (2) there is a rank preserving $\mathcal{K}$-faithful ranked model $\mathscr{R}$ and a $\mathcal{K}$-faithful base rank preserving rank function r s.t.:*

a. *$r(\alpha) = \min\{i \mid v \in [\![\alpha]\!]$ and $\mathscr{R}(v) = i\}$;*
b. *$\mathrel{\vcenter{\hbox{$\scriptstyle\approx$}}}$ can be generated from $\mathscr{R}$;*
c. *$\mathrel{\vcenter{\hbox{$\scriptstyle\approx$}}}$ can be generated from r;*
d. *$\mathrel{\vcenter{\hbox{$\scriptstyle\approx$}}}$ can be computed from DefeasibleEntailment, given $\mathcal{K}$ and r as input.*

Analogous to basic defeasible entailment, Points 1 and 2 of Theorem 2 establish a connection between $\mathscr{R}$ and r via a result that is a generalisation of Observation 3.

5   Lexicographic Closure

We now turn our attention to *lexicographic closure*, a second form of defeasible entailment that has been studied in the literature [24]. Our central result is that lexicographic closure is a rational defeasible entailment relation. We also show that lexicographic closure can be characterised in three different ways: semantically via a rank preserving $\mathcal{K}$-faithful ranked model, in terms of a base preserving $\mathcal{K}$-faithful rank function r, and via DefeasibleEntailment when it is presented with r (and a knowledge base $\mathcal{K}$) as input. While the semantic construction of lexicographic closure is known [24], the other two constructions are new. We also show that there are rational defeasible entailment relations that extend lexicographic closure, which means that lexicographic closure is not the "boldest" form of rational defeasible entailment, as has been the conjecture in the literature.

Let $\mathcal{C}^{\mathcal{K}}$ be a function from $\mathcal{U}$ to $\mathbb{N}$ s.t. $\mathcal{C}^{\mathcal{K}}(v) = \#\{\alpha \mathrel{\vcenter{\hbox{$\scriptstyle\sim$}}} \beta \in \mathcal{K} \mid v \Vdash \alpha \rightarrow \beta\}$ (where $\#X$ denotes the cardinality of the set X). The goal is to refine the ordering on $\mathcal{U}$ obtained from the minimal model $\mathscr{R}_{\mathcal{K}}^{RC}$ with $\mathcal{C}^{\mathcal{K}}$: in comparing two valuations with the same rank w.r.t. $\mathscr{R}_{\mathcal{K}}^{RC}$, the one with a higher number will be viewed as more typical.

We define an ordering $\preceq_{LC}^{\mathcal{K}}$ on $\mathcal{U}$: $v \preceq_{LC}^{\mathcal{K}} u$ if $\mathscr{R}_{\mathcal{K}}^{RC}(u) = \infty$, or $\mathscr{R}_{\mathcal{K}}^{RC}(v) < \mathscr{R}_{\mathcal{K}}^{RC}(u)$, or $\mathscr{R}_{\mathcal{K}}^{RC}(v) = \mathscr{R}_{\mathcal{K}}^{RC}(u)$ and $\mathcal{C}^{\mathcal{K}}(v) \geq \mathcal{C}^{\mathcal{K}}(u)$. Then let $\mathscr{R}_{\mathcal{K}}^{LC}$ be the ranked interpretation obtained from $\preceq_{LC}^{\mathcal{K}}$, which we call the *lexicographic ranked model* of $\mathcal{K}$.

Definition 11. *The lexicographic closure* $\approx_{LC}$ *of* $\mathcal{K}$ *is defined as follows:* $\mathcal{K} \approx_{LC} \alpha \mathrel{\vert\!\sim} \beta$ *if* $\mathscr{R}_{\mathcal{K}}^{LC} \Vdash \alpha \mathrel{\vert\!\sim} \beta$.

Proposition 2. $\mathscr{R}_{\mathcal{K}}^{LC}$ *is a* $\mathcal{K}$*-faithful and rank preserving ranked model.*

From this result it follows from Theorems 1 and 2 that lexicographic closure is a rational and basic defeasible entailment relation. Lehmann [24, Theorem 3] already showed that lexicographic closure satisfies RC Extension.

Example 4. Figure 3(a) depicts the minimal ranked model $\mathscr{R}_{\mathcal{K}}^{RC}$ of $\mathcal{K} = \{$p $\to$ b, b $\mathrel{\vert\!\sim}$ f, p $\mathrel{\vert\!\sim}$ ¬f, b $\mathrel{\vert\!\sim}$ w$\}$, while Fig. 3(b) depicts the lexicographic ranked model $\mathscr{R}_{\mathcal{K}}^{LC}$ of $\mathcal{K}$. From these two models we can see that p $\mathrel{\vert\!\sim}$ w (penguins usually have wings) is not in the rational closure of $\mathcal{K}$, but is in the lexicographic closure of $\mathcal{K}$. This is indicative of the difference between, what Lehmann refers to as Prototypical Reasoning and Presumptive Reasoning [24]. Presumptive Reasoning states that properties of a class are presumed to hold for all members of that class unless we have knowledge to the contrary. Because birds usually have wings we assume that penguins, being birds, usually have wings as well. Contrast this with Prototypical Reasoning which states that, while typical members of a class are presumed to inherit the properties of that class, the same does not hold for atypical members. According to Prototypical Reasoning, since penguins are atypical members of the class of birds, they do not inherit the property of having wings. Rational closure operates according to Prototypical Reasoning, while lexicographic closure adheres to Presumptive Reasoning. □

2	pbf̄w̄ pbfw
1	p̄bf̄w̄ p̄bf̄w pbf̄w̄ pbf̄w
0	p̄bf̄w̄ p̄bf̄w p̄bfw̄ p̄bfw pbfw̄ p̄bfw

(a)

5	pbfw̄
4	pbfw
3	pbf̄w̄ p̄bf̄w̄
2	pbf̄w p̄bf̄w
1	p̄bfw̄
0	p̄bfw̄ p̄bfw p̄bf̄w̄ p̄bf̄w pbfw

(b)

Fig. 3. Ranked models of the knowledge base in Example 4. (a) Shows the minimal model $\mathcal{K}$-faithful ranked model $\mathscr{R}_{\mathcal{K}}^{RC}$, while (b) depicts the lexicographic ranked model $\mathscr{R}_{\mathcal{K}}^{LC}$.

We have seen that lexicographic closure ($\approx_{LC}$) can be generated from a $\mathcal{K}$-faithful rank preserving model. From Theorem 2 it then follows that there is a $\mathcal{K}$-faithful base rank preserving rank function r from which $\approx_{LC}$ can be generated. Furthermore, it can be generated by DefeasibleEntailment, given $\mathcal{K}$ and r as input. We now show how to construct the $\mathcal{K}$-faithful base rank preserving rank function r mentioned above.

Definition 12. *The lexicographic rank w.r.t. a knowledge base $\mathcal{K}$ is defined as* $r_{\mathcal{K}}^{LC}(\alpha) \equiv_{def} \min\{\mathcal{R}_{\mathcal{K}}^{LC}(v) \mid v \in [\![\alpha]\!]\}$.

Proposition 3. *The lexicographic rank $r_{\mathcal{K}}^{LC}$ w.r.t. a knowledge base $\mathcal{K}$ is $\mathcal{K}$-faithful and base rank preserving.*

Now we show $r_{\mathcal{K}}^{LC}$ generates the same rational defeasible entailment relation as $\mathcal{R}_{\mathcal{K}}^{LC}$.

Proposition 4. $\mathcal{R}_{\mathcal{K}}^{LC} \Vdash \alpha \mathrel{|\!\sim} \beta$ *iff* $r_{\mathcal{K}}^{LC}(\alpha) < r_{\mathcal{K}}^{LC}(\alpha \wedge \neg\beta)$ *or* $r_{\mathcal{K}}^{LC}(\alpha) = \infty$.

Finally, `DefeasibleEntailment` computes the same (rational) defeasible entailment relation as $\mathcal{R}_{\mathcal{K}}^{LC}$ does when given the input $\mathcal{K}$ and $r_{\mathcal{K}}^{LC}$.

Proposition 5. `DefeasibleEntailment` *returns* **true** *when given the input* $\mathcal{K}$, $r_{\mathcal{K}}^{LC}$, *and* $\alpha \mathrel{|\!\sim} \beta$ *iff* $r_{\mathcal{K}}^{LC}(\alpha) < r_{\mathcal{K}}^{LC}(\alpha \wedge \neg\beta)$, *or* $r_{\mathcal{K}}^{LC}(\alpha) = \infty$.

We conclude this section with an example which shows that lexicographic closure is not (always) the "boldest" form of rational defeasible entailment.

Example 5. Consider the knowledge base $\mathcal{K}$ in Example 4 and let a $\mathcal{K}$-faithful ranked model $\mathcal{R}$ be as depicted in Fig. 4 below. $\mathcal{R}$ is a refinement of the lexicographic ranked model $\mathcal{R}_{\mathcal{K}}^{LC}$ in Fig. 3(b). It can be shown that $\mathcal{R}$ is rank base preserving, and therefore it generates a rational defeasible $\mathcal{K}$-entailment relation $\approx$, and that $\approx$ strictly extends lexicographic closure: If $\mathcal{K} \approx_{LC} \alpha \mathrel{|\!\sim} \beta$, then $\mathcal{K} \approx \alpha \mathrel{|\!\sim} \beta$, and there is at least one defeasible implication $\alpha \mathrel{|\!\sim} \beta$ such that $\mathcal{K} \approx \alpha \mathrel{|\!\sim} \beta$, but $\mathcal{K} \not\approx_{LC} \alpha \mathrel{|\!\sim} \beta$. For example, observe that $\mathcal{K} \approx b \wedge \neg f \wedge w \mathrel{|\!\sim} \neg p$, but $\mathcal{K} \not\approx_{LC} b \wedge \neg f \wedge w \mathrel{|\!\sim} \neg p$.   □

7	pbf$\bar{\text{w}}$
6	pbfw
5	pb$\bar{\text{f}}\bar{\text{w}}$
4	$\bar{\text{p}}$bf$\bar{\text{w}}$
3	pb$\bar{\text{f}}$w
2	$\bar{\text{p}}$bfw
1	$\bar{\text{p}}$b$\bar{\text{f}}\bar{\text{w}}$
0	$\bar{\text{p}}\bar{\text{b}}\bar{\text{f}}\bar{\text{w}}$ $\bar{\text{p}}\bar{\text{b}}\bar{\text{f}}$w $\bar{\text{p}}\bar{\text{b}}f\bar{\text{w}}$ $\bar{\text{p}}\bar{\text{b}}$fw $\bar{\text{p}}$b$\bar{\text{f}}$w

Fig. 4. The ranked model $\mathcal{R}$ of Example 5.

6 Related Work

The original work in the KLM style [23] was inspired by the work of Shoham [28], and investigated a class of non-monotonic consequence relations, where defeasible implication was viewed as a (non-monotonic) form of entailment. This approach was subsequently adapted by Lehmann and Magidor [25] to the case where $\vdash$ is viewed as an object-level connective for defeasible implication, and where the focus then shifts to defeasible entailment (i.e., $\approx$) for a logic language that extends propositional logic with the defeasible implication connective $\vdash$.

We are aware of four instances of defeasible entailment that have been studied: ranked entailment [25] which is not LM-rational, rational closure [4,7,21,25], and lexicographic closure [24] which are both regarded as appropriate forms of defeasible entailment, and relevant closure [17] which is also not LM-rational.

Our investigation here is reminiscent of the AGM framework for belief change [1,19], where classes of belief change operators are studied. Rational closure can be viewed as the defeasible entailment equivalent of *full-meet belief contraction or revision* since, by virtue of the property of RC Extension, it is the most conservative of those defeasible entailment relations regarded as appropriate. The boldest forms of rational defeasible entailment can be seen as analogous to *maxichoice* belief contraction and revision: maxichoice operators are obtained by imposing a linear ordering on the propositional valuations that are counter-models of a *belief set*, while the boldest forms of rational defeasible entailment are obtained by imposing a linear ordering on $\mathcal{U}_R^K$, the set of possible valuations w.r.t. a knowledge base $\mathcal{K}$ and then considering the defeasible entailment relations generated from the base rank preserving $\mathcal{K}$-faithful ranked models obtained from such linear orderings.

Studies of defeasible entailment beyond the propositional case include versions of defeasible implication in more expressive languages, most notably description logics [2,3,10,14,15,20,26,27] and modal logics [8,9,11]. A different type of extension is one in which defeasible implication is enriched by either introducing a notion of typicality in propositional logic [4–6] or a notion of defeasible modality [12,13].

7 Conclusion

The central focus of this paper is the question of determining what (defeasible) entailment means for propositional logic enriched with a defeasible implication connective. The short answer is that a defeasible entailment relation needs to be *rational* in a technical sense provided above. In arriving at this conclusion we have made a detour through the more permissive class of *basic* defeasible entailment relations.

There are at least three lines of research to which the work in this paper can lead. First is an analysis of concrete forms of rational defeasible entailment other than rational and lexicographic closure. Secondly, both basic and rational defeasible entailment is on the *knowledge level* [19] in the sense that the syntactic form of knowledge bases are, for the most part, irrelevant. But there is a strong case to be made for defining defeasible implication where syntax matters. This is analogous to the distinction between belief change on sets closed under classical consequence and base change [22], where the structure of the set of beliefs of an agent plays a role. And although lexicographic closure is an instance of rational defeasible entailment, it is an example of a form of entailment where the structure of the knowledge base matters. We conjecture that a syntax-based class of defeasible entailment will form a strict subclass of the class of rational defeasible entailment relations, and that lexicographic closure will be the strongest form of syntax-based rational defeasible entailment. Finally, we have presented an algorithm for computing any rational defeasible entailment relation, but the algorithm depends on the provision of a knowledge base $\mathcal{K}$, as well as a function that ranks all statements. With a syntax-based approach, it may be possible to use the structure of $\mathcal{K}$ to rank statements, in the way that the BaseRank algorithm does in the process of computing rational closure.

Acknowledgments. Giovanni Casini and Thomas Meyer have received funding from the EU Horizon 2020 research and innovation programme under the Marie Skłdowska-Curie grant agr. No. 690974 (MIREL). The work of Thomas Meyer has been supported in part by the National Research Foundation of South Africa (grant No. UID 98019).

References

1. Alchourrón, C., Gärdenfors, P., Makinson, D.: On the logic of theory change: partial meet contraction and revision functions. J. Symb. Log. **50**, 510–530 (1985)
2. Bonatti, P., Faella, M., Petrova, I., Sauro, L.: A new semantics for overriding in description logics. Artif. Intell. **222**, 1–48 (2015)
3. Bonatti, P., Sauro, L.: On the logical properties of the nonmonotonic description lógic DL^N. Artif. Intell. **248**, 85–111 (2017)
4. Booth, R., Casini, G., Meyer, T., Varzinczak, I.: On the entailment problem for a logic of typicality. In: IJCAI 2015, pp. 2805–2811 (2015)
5. Booth, R., Meyer, T., Varzinczak, I.: PTL: a propositional typicality logic. In: del Cerro, L.F., Herzig, A., Mengin, J. (eds.) JELIA 2012. LNCS (LNAI), vol. 7519, pp. 107–119. Springer, Heidelberg (2012). https://doi.org/10.1007/978-3-642-33353-8_9
6. Booth, R., Meyer, T., Varzinczak, I.: A propositional typicality logic for extending rational consequence. In: Fermé, E., Gabbay, D., Simari, G. (eds.) Trends in Belief Revision and Argumentation Dynamics, Studies in Logic - Logic and Cognitive Systems, vol. 48, pp. 123–154. King's College Publications (2013)
7. Booth, R., Paris, J.: A note on the rational closure of knowledge bases with both positive and negative knowledge. J. Log. Lang. Inf. **7**(2), 165–190 (1998)
8. Boutilier, C.: Conditional logics of normality: a modal approach. Artif. Intell. **68**(1), 87–154 (1994)
9. Britz, K., Meyer, T., Varzinczak, I.: Preferential reasoning for modal logics. Electron. Notes Theor. Comput. Sci. **278**, 55–69 (2011)
10. Britz, K., Meyer, T., Varzinczak, I.: Semantic foundation for preferential description logics. In: Wang, D., Reynolds, M. (eds.) AI 2011. LNCS (LNAI), vol. 7106, pp. 491–500. Springer, Heidelberg (2011). https://doi.org/10.1007/978-3-642-25832-9_50

11. Britz, K., Meyer, T., Varzinczak, I.: Normal modal preferential consequence. In: Thielscher, M., Zhang, D. (eds.) AI 2012. LNCS (LNAI), vol. 7691, pp. 505–516. Springer, Heidelberg (2012). https://doi.org/10.1007/978-3-642-35101-3_43
12. Britz, K., Varzinczak, I.: From KLM-style conditionals to defeasible modalities, and back. J. Appl. Non-Class. Log. (JANCL) **28**, 92–121 (2018)
13. Britz, K., Varzinczak, I.: Preferential accessibility and preferred worlds. J. Log. Lang. Inf. (JoLLI) **27**(2), 133–155 (2018)
14. Britz, K., Varzinczak, I.: Rationality and context in defeasible subsumption. In: Ferrarotti, F., Woltran, S. (eds.) FoIKS 2018. LNCS, vol. 10833, pp. 114–132. Springer, Cham (2018). https://doi.org/10.1007/978-3-319-90050-6_7
15. Casini, G., Straccia, U.: Defeasible inheritance-based description logics. JAIR **48**, 415–473 (2013)
16. Casini, G., Meyer, T.: Belief change in a preferential non-monotonic framework. In: IJCAI 2017, pp. 929–935 (2017)
17. Casini, G., Meyer, T., Moodley, K., Nortjé, R.: Relevant closure: a new form of defeasible reasoning for description logics. In: Fermé, E., Leite, J. (eds.) JELIA 2014. LNCS (LNAI), vol. 8761, pp. 92–106. Springer, Cham (2014). https://doi.org/10.1007/978-3-319-11558-0_7
18. Freund, M.: Preferential reasoning in the perspective of Poole default logic. Artif. Intell. **98**, 209–235 (1998). http://www.sciencedirect.com/science/article/pii/S0004370297000532
19. Gärdenfors, P.: Knowledge in Flux: Modeling the Dynamics of Epistemic States. MIT Press, Cambridge (1988)
20. Giordano, L., Gliozzi, V., Olivetti, N., Pozzato, G.: A non-monotonic description logic for reasoning about typicality. Artif. Intell. **195**, 165–202 (2013)
21. Giordano, L., Gliozzi, V., Olivetti, N., Pozzato, G.: Semantic characterization of rational closure: from propositional logic to description logics. Artif. Intell. **226**, 1–33 (2015)
22. Hansson, S.: A Textbook of Belief Dynamics: Theory Change and Database Updating. Kluwer, Boston (1999)
23. Kraus, S., Lehmann, D., Magidor, M.: Nonmonotonic reasoning, preferential models and cumulative logics. Artif. Intell. **44**, 167–207 (1990)
24. Lehmann, D.: Another perspective on default reasoning. Ann. Math. Artif. Intell. **15**(1), 61–82 (1995)
25. Lehmann, D., Magidor, M.: What does a conditional knowledge base entail? Artif. Intell. **55**, 1–60 (1992)
26. Pensel, M., Turhan, A.-Y.: Including quantification in defeasible reasoning for the description logic $\mathcal{EL}_\perp$. In: Balduccini, M., Janhunen, T. (eds.) LPNMR 2017. LNCS (LNAI), vol. 10377, pp. 78–84. Springer, Cham (2017). https://doi.org/10.1007/978-3-319-61660-5_9
27. Quantz, J., Royer, V.: A preference semantics for defaults in terminological logics. In: KR 1992, pp. 294–305 (1992)
28. Shoham, Y.: Reasoning About Change: Time and Causation from the Standpoint of Artificial Intelligence. MIT Press, Cambridge (1988)

Typed Meta-interpretive Learning of Logic Programs

Rolf Morel[✉], Andrew Cropper, and C.-H. Luke Ong

University of Oxford, Oxford, UK
{rolf.morel,andrew.cropper,luke.ong}@cs.ox.ac.uk

Abstract. Meta-interpretive learning (MIL) is a form of inductive logic programming that learns logic programs from background knowledge and examples. We claim that adding types to MIL can improve learning performance. We show that type checking can reduce the MIL hypothesis space by a cubic factor. We introduce two typed MIL systems: Metagol$_T$ and HEXMIL$_T$, implemented in Prolog and Answer Set Programming (ASP), respectively. Both systems support polymorphic types and can infer the types of invented predicates. Our experimental results show that types can substantially reduce learning times.

1 Introduction

Meta-interpretive learning (MIL) [8,22,23] is a form of inductive logic programming (ILP) [20]. MIL learns logic programs from examples and background knowledge (BK) by instantiating *metarules*, second-order Horn clauses with existentially quantified predicate variables. Metarules are a form of declarative bias [28] that define the structure of learnable programs. For instance, to learn the *grandparent/2* relation given the *parent/2* relation, the *chain* metarule would be suitable:

$$P(A, B) \leftarrow Q(A, C), R(C, B)$$

In this metarule[1] the letters P, Q, and R denote existentially quantified second-order variables (variables that can be bound to predicate symbols) and the letters A, B and C denote universally quantified first-order variables (variables that can be bound to constant symbols). Given the *chain* metarule, the background *parent/2* relation, and examples of the *grandparent/2* relation, a MIL learner will try to find the correct predicate substitutions, such as:

$$\{P/grandparent, Q/parent, R/parent\}$$

When applied to the *chain* metarule, these substitutions result in the theory:

$$grandparent(A, B) \leftarrow parent(A, C), parent(C, B)$$

---

[1] The fully quantified rule is $\exists P \exists Q \exists R \forall A \forall B \forall C \; P(A, B) \leftarrow Q(A, C), R(C, B)$.

R. Morel—Supported by Engineering and Physical Sciences Research Council [grant number EP/N509711/1].

© Springer Nature Switzerland AG 2019
F. Calimeri et al. (Eds.): JELIA 2019, LNAI 11468, pp. 198–213, 2019.
https://doi.org/10.1007/978-3-030-19570-0_13

The MIL hypothesis space grows quickly given more background relations [6, 11]. For instance, suppose that when learning the *grandparent/2* relation we have an additional k background relations, such as *head/2, tail/2, length/2*, etc. Then for the *chain* metarule, there are $k + 2$ substitutions for each predicate variable and thus $(k + 2)^3$ total substitutions. Existing MIL systems, such as Metagol [9] and HEXMIL [16], would potentially consider all these possible substitutions.

We claim that considering the types of predicates can significantly improve learning performance by reducing the number of predicate substitutions. For instance, suppose that when learning the *grandparent/2* relation we add types to the relations, such as *(person, person)* to *parent/2*, *(list(T), int)* to *length/2*, etc. Then given an example of the *grandparent/2* relation with the type *(person, person)*, only the *parent/2* relation (and *grandparent/2* itself) matches the example's type, and so the number of substitutions is reduced from $(k + 2)^3$ to 2^3.

Our main contributions are:

- We extend the MIL framework to support polymorphic types (Sect. 3.3).
- We show that type checking can reduce the MIL hypothesis space by a cubic factor (Sect. 3.4).
- We introduce Metagol$_T$ and HEXMIL$_T$ which extend Metagol and HEXMIL respectively. Both support polymorphic types and both can infer types for invented predicates (Sect. 4).
- We conduct experiments which show that types can substantially reduce learning times when there are irrelevant background relations (Sect. 5).

2   Related Work

Program Induction. Program synthesis is the automatic generation of a computer program from a specification. Deductive approaches [19] *deduce* a program from a full specification that precisely states the requirements and behaviour of the desired program. By contrast, program induction approaches *induce* (learn) a program from an incomplete specification, typically input/output examples. Many program induction approaches learn specific classes of programs, such as string transformations [33]. By contrast, MIL is general-purpose, and is, for instance, capable of grammar induction [22], learning robot strategies [7], and learning efficient algorithms [10].

Types in Program Induction. Functional program induction approaches often use types. For instance, bidirectional type checking is the foundation of the MYTH systems [26], where MYTH2 [14] supports polymorphic types. SYNQUID [27] forgoes input/output examples and only uses refinement types as its specification. The authors argue that refinement specifications are terser than examples. However, because of the need to supply correct and informative refinement types, SYNQUID is more similar to deductive synthesis approaches. In contrast to these inductive approaches, we focus on learning logic programs, including support for predicate invention, i.e. the introduction of new predicate symbols [36].

Inductive Logic Programming. ILP is a form of program induction which learns logic programs. ILP systems are typically untyped. The use of types in ILP is mostly restricted to *mode declarations* [21], which are used by many systems [17,21,29,31,35]. Mode declarations define what literals can appear in a program. In the mode language, *modeh* are declarations for head literals and *modeb* are declarations for body literals, where + and − are followed by the type of each argument and represent input and output arguments respectively, e.g. :-modeh(1,mult(+int,+int,-int)). Mode declarations are metalogical statements. By contrast, we introduce typed atoms (Definition 4) which are logical statements. As far as we are aware, our work is the first to declaratively represent types. In addition, in contrast to the existing approaches in ILP, our approach supports polymorphic types and we can also infer the types of invented predicates. Finally, to our best knowledge, we are the first to provide theoretical results that show that types can improve learning performance (Theorem 1).

MIL is a form of ILP that supports predicate invention and learning recursive programs. MIL is typically based on a Prolog meta-interpreter [9] but has also been encoded as SMT [1] and ASP problems [16]. We extend MIL to support learning with types. We demonstrate the approach in both Prolog and ASP settings. Farquhar et al. [13] considered adding types to MIL. However, their work is mainly concerned with applying MIL to learn strategies for interactive theorem proving and their work on types is minimal with only two simple types considered.

Types in Logic Programming. The main Prolog [5,38] and ASP [15] implementations do not explicitly support types. There are, however, typed Prolog-like languages, such as the functional-logic language Mercury [34] and the higher-order logic language λProlog [25]. Most work on adding types to logic programming [24,30] is motivated by reducing runtime errors by restricting the range of variables. By contrast, we are motivated by reducing learning times by restricting the range of variables.

3   Framework

3.1   Preliminaries

We assume familiarity with logic programming. We do, however, restate key terminology. We denote the predicate, constant, and function signatures as $\mathcal{P}$, $\mathcal{C}$, and $\mathcal{F}$ respectively. A variable is first-order if it can be bound to a constant symbol, a function symbol, or another first-order variable. A variable is second-order if it can be bound to a predicate symbol or another second-order variable. We denote the sets of first-order and second-order variables as $\mathcal{V}_1$ and $\mathcal{V}_2$ respectively. A term is a variable, a constant symbol, or a function symbol of arity n immediately followed by a bracketed n-tuple of terms. A term is ground if it contains no variables. An atom is a formula $p(t_1, \ldots, t_n)$, where p is a predicate symbol of arity n and each t_i is a term. An atom is ground if all of its terms are ground. We denote as p/n a predicate or function symbol p with arity n. A second-order term is a second-order variable or a predicate symbol. An atom is second-order if it has at least one second-order term. A literal is an atom A (a positive literal) or its negation $\neg A$ (a negative literal). A clause is a disjunction of literals. The variables in a clause are implicitly universally quantified. A Horn clause is a clause with at most one positive literal. A definite clause is a Horn clause with exactly one positive literal. A clause is second-order if it contains a second-order atom. A logic program is a set of Horn clauses. The constant symbols are distinct from the functional symbols, as the latter all have non-zero arity. We call a logic program without proper functional symbols a *datalog* program.

3.2   Meta-interpretive Learning

MIL was originally based on a Prolog meta-interpreter. The key difference between a MIL learner and a standard Prolog meta-interpreter is that whereas a standard Prolog meta-interpreter attempts to prove a goal by repeatedly fetching first-order clauses whose heads unify with a given goal, a MIL learner additionally attempts to prove a goal by fetching second-order metarules, supplied as BK, whose heads unify with the goal. The resulting predicate substitutions are saved and can be reused later in the proof. Following the proof of a set of goals, a logic program is induced by projecting the predicate substitutions onto their corresponding metarules.

We formally define the MIL setting, which we then extend with types. We first define metarules [6]:

Definition 1 *(Metarule).* *A metarule is a second-order formula of the form:*

$$\exists \pi \forall \mu \ A_0 \leftarrow A_1, \ldots, A_m$$

where $\pi \subseteq \mathcal{V}_1 \cup \mathcal{V}_2$, $\mu \subseteq \mathcal{V}_1 \cup \mathcal{V}_2$, π and μ are disjoint, and each A_i is an atom of the form $p(t_1, \ldots, t_n)$ such that $p/n \in \mathcal{P} \cup \pi \cup \mu$ and each $t_i \in \mathcal{C} \cup \mathcal{P} \cup \pi \cup \mu$.

When describing metarules, we typically omit the quantifiers and use the more terse notation shown in Fig. 1.

Name	Metarule
indent	$P(A,B) \leftarrow Q(A,B)$
dident	$P(A,B) \leftarrow Q(A,B), R(A,B)$
precon	$P(A,B) \leftarrow Q(A), R(A,B)$
curry	$P(A,B) \leftarrow Q(A,B,R)$
chain	$P(A,B) \leftarrow Q(A,C), R(C,B)$
tailrec	$P(A,B) \leftarrow Q(A,C), P(C,B)$

Fig. 1. Example metarules. The letters P, Q, and R denote existentially quantified second-order variables. The letters A, B, and C denote universally quantified first-order variables.

We define the standard MIL input:

Definition 2 (MIL input). *The MIL input is a triple* (B, E^+, E^-) *where:*

- $B = B_C \cup M$ *where* B_C *is a logic program representing BK and* M *is a set of metarules*
- E^+ *and* E^- *are disjoint sets of ground atoms representing positive and negative examples respectively*

We now define the hypotheses that MIL will consider. Given a set of metarules M, a logic program H is a hypothesis if each clause of H can be obtained by grounding the existentially quantified variables of a metarule in M. This hypothesis space definition enforces a strong inductive bias in MIL.

We define the standard MIL problem:

Definition 3 (MIL problem). *Given a MIL input* $(B_C \cup M, E^+, E^-)$, *the MIL problem is to find a logic program hypothesis* H *such that* $H \cup B_C \models E^+$ *and* $H \cup B_C \not\models E^-$. *We call* H *a solution to the MIL problem.*

3.3   Typed Meta-interpretive Learning

We extend MIL to support types. We assume a finite set $T_b \subseteq \mathcal{C}$ of base types (e.g. *int*, *bool*), a finite set $T_c \subseteq \mathcal{F}$ of polymorphic type constructors (e.g. *list*/1, *array*/1), and a set of type variables V_t. We inductively define a set $\mathcal{T}$ of types:

- if $\tau \in T_b \cup V_t$ then $\tau \in \mathcal{T}$
- if $c/n \in T_c$ and $\tau_1, \ldots, \tau_n \in \mathcal{T}$ then $c(\tau_1, \ldots, \tau_n) \in \mathcal{T}$
- if $\tau_1, \ldots, \tau_n \in \mathcal{T}$ then $(\tau_1, \ldots, \tau_n) \in \mathcal{T}$

The last case concerns types for predicates. For instance $(list(S), list(T), (S, T))$ is the type for the *map/3* predicate. We introduce *typed atoms*:

Definition 4 (Typed atom). *A typed atom is a formula* $p(\tau_1, \ldots, \tau_m, t_1, \ldots, t_m)$, *where* p *is a predicate symbol of arity* n, $m + m = n$, $\tau_1, \ldots, \tau_m \in \mathcal{T}$, *and each* t_i *is a first-order or second-order term.*

We can extend this notion to logic programs:

Definition 5 (Typed logic program). *A typed logic program is a logic program with typed atoms in place of atoms.*

To aid readability, in the rest of this paper we label each atom with its type. For instance we denote $succ(int, int, A, B)$ as $succ(A, B){:}(int, int)$, and $head(list(T), T, [H|\_], H)$ as $head([H|\_], H){:}(list(T), T)$. Note that the definition of typed logic programs also applies to metarules. For instance, the typed *chain* metarule is:

$$P(A, B){:}(Ta, Tb) \leftarrow Q(A, C){:}(Ta, Tc), R(C, B){:}(Tc, Tb)$$

We define the *typed MIL input*:

Definition 6 (Typed MIL input). *A typed MIL input is a triple* (B, E^+, E^-) *where:*

- $B = B_C \cup M$ *where* B_C *is a typed logic program and* M *is a set of typed metarules*
- E^+ *and* E^- *are disjoint sets of typed ground atoms representing positive and negative examples respectively*

The typed MIL problem easily follows:

Definition 7 (Typed MIL problem). *Given a typed MIL input* $(B_C \cup M, E^+, E^-)$, *the typed MIL problem is to find a typed logic program hypothesis* H *such that* $H \cup B_C \models E^+$ *and* $H \cup B_C \not\models E^-$.

3.4 Hypothesis Space Reduction

We now show that types can improve learning performance by reducing the size of the MIL hypothesis space which in turn reduces sample complexity and expected error. Note that in this section any reference to MIL typically also refers to typed MIL. In MIL, the size of the hypothesis space is a function of the number of metarules m, the number of predicate symbols p, and the maximum program size n. We typically restrict metarules by their body size and literal arity. For instance, the *chain* metarule is restricted to two body literals of arity two. We say that a metarule is in the fragment $\mathcal{M}_j^i$ if it has at most j literals in the body and each literal has arity at most i. By restricting the form of metarules, we can calculate the size of a MIL hypothesis space:

Proposition 1 (MIL hypothesis space [11]). *Given a MIL input with* p *predicate symbols and* m *metarules in* $\mathcal{M}_j^i$, *the number of programs expressible with at most* n *clauses is* $O((mp^{j+1})^n)$.

Proposition 1 shows the MIL hypothesis space grows exponentially both in the size of the target program and the number of body literals in a clause. For simplicity, let us only consider metarules in $\mathcal{M}_2^2$, such as the *chain* metarule. Then the corresponding MIL hypothesis space's size is $O((mp^3)^n)$.

We now consider the advantages of adding types, which we show can improve learning performance when they allow us to ignore irrelevant BK predicates. Informally, given a typed MIL input, a predicate symbol is *type relevant* when it can be used in a hypothesis that is type consistent with the BK and the examples. We define the *relevant ratio* to characterise the reduction of the hypothesis space:

Definition 8 (Relevant ratio). *Given a typed MIL input with* p *predicate symbols where only* p' *are type relevant, the relevant ratio is* $r = p'/p$.

The relevant ratio will always be between 0 and 1 with lower values indicating a greater reduction in the hypothesis space. We characterise this reduction:

Theorem 1 (Hypothesis space reduction). *Given a typed MIL input with* p *predicate symbols,* m *metarules in* $\mathcal{M}_2^2$, *a maximum program size* n, *and a relevant ratio* r, *typing reduces the size of the MIL hypothesis space by a factor of* r^{3n}.

Proof. Replacing p with rp in Proposition 1 and rearranging terms leads to $O(r^{3n}(mp^3)^n)$.

Theorem 1 shows that types can considerably reduce the size of hypothesis spaces[2]. The Blumer bound [2] says that given two hypothesis spaces of different sizes, searching the smaller space will result in less error and lower learning times compared to the larger space, assuming the target hypothesis is in both spaces. This result implies that types should improve learning performance, so long as they do not exclude the target hypothesis from the hypothesis space. In this next section we introduce Metagol$_T$ and HEXMIL$_T$ which implement this idea.

4   Metagol$_T$ and HEXMIL$_T$

We present two typed MIL systems: Metagol$_T$ and HEXMIL$_T$, which extend Metagol and HEXMIL respectively.

4.1   Metagol$_T$

Metagol$_T$ is based on an adapted Prolog meta-interpreter. Figure 2 shows the Metagol$_T$ algorithm described as Prolog code. Given a set of atoms representing positive examples, Metagol$_T$ tries to prove each atom in turn. Metagol$_T$ first tries to prove an atom using BK by delegating the proof to Prolog (line 9). Failing this, Metagol$_T$ tries to unify the atom with the head of a metarule (line 16) and to bind the existentially quantified variables in a metarule to symbols in the signature. Metagol$_T$ saves the resulting predicate substitution and tries to prove the body of the metarule. The predicate substitutions can be reused to prove atoms later on (line 11). After proving all atoms, Metagol$_T$ induces a logic program by projecting the predicate substitutions onto their corresponding metarules. Metagol$_T$ checks the consistency of the induced program with the negative examples. If the program is inconsistent, then Metagol$_T$ backtracks to explore different branches of the SLD-tree. Metagol uses iterative deepening to ensure that the first consistent hypothesis returned has the minimal number of clauses. At each depth d, Metagol$_T$ searches for a consistent hypothesis with at most d clauses. At each depth d, Metagol$_T$ introduces d-1 new predicate symbols, formed by taking the name of the task and adding underscores and numbers.

Metagol$_T$ extends Metagol to support types. We annotate each atom with its type using the syntax described in Sect. 3.3. For instance, the following Prolog code denotes an atom with ($list(char), int$) as its type:

---

[2] It is not hard too see that Theorem 1 generalizes to a reduction factor of $r^{(j+1)n}$ for any hypothesis space $\mathcal{M}_j^i$.

```
 1  learn(Pos,Neg,Prog):-
 2      prove(Pos,[],Prog),
 3      not(prove(Neg,Prog,Prog)).
 4  prove([],Prog,Prog).
 5  prove([Atom|Atoms],Prog1,Prog2):-
 6      prove_aux(Atom,Prog1,Prog3),
 7      prove(Atoms,Prog3,Prog2).
 8  prove_aux(Atom:DT:GT,Prog,Prog):-
 9      call(Atom:DT:GT).
10  prove_aux(Atom:DT:GT,Prog1,Prog2):-
11      member(sub(Name,GT,Subs),Prog1),
12      unifiable(DT,GT),
13      metarule(Name,Subs,(Atom:DT:GT:-Body)),
14      prove(Body,Prog1,Prog2).
15  prove_aux(Atom:DT:GT,Prog1,Prog2):-
16      metarule(Name,Subs,(Atom:DT:GT:-Body)),
17      prove(Body,[sub(Name,GT,Subs)|Prog1],Prog2).
```

Fig. 2. The Metagol$_T$ algorithm.

$$f([a,b,c],5):(list(char),int)$$

In Fig. 2, each atom and its type is denoted by the variables *Atom:DT*. The variable *DT* represents the *derivation type* of an atom. The derivation type is the type of the values of that atom. When trying to prove an atom, Metagol$_T$ ignores predicates whose derivation types do not match, which allows it to prune the hypothesis space (relative to untyped Metagol). This type check is done through unification. For instance, when trying to prove an atom using BK (line 9), unification ensures that Metagol$_T$ will only call a predicate in the BK if its derivation type matches the derivation type of the atom it is trying to prove. For invented predicate symbols, the derivation type is inferred from the type of the values used to induce that symbol. For instance, suppose we have induced the following theory to explain the above *f/2* atom:

$$f(A,B):(list(char),int) \leftarrow f_1(A,C):(list(char),int), succ(C,B):(int,int)$$
$$f_1(A,B):(list(char),int) \leftarrow length(A,C):(list(char),int), succ(C,B):(int,int)$$

In this theory the derivation type of the invented predicate symbol $f_1/2$ is $(list(char),int)$. Because $f_1/2$ is sufficiently general to be applied to lists of any type, we want to assign it a *general type* that will allow it to be polymorphically reused. For instance, we want the theory to also entail the atom $f([1,2,3,4],6):(list(int),int)$. To support polymorphic reuse, we annotate each atom with a second type that denotes the general type of its predicate symbol. The general type is the least general generalisation of the derivation types for an atom. For instance, given the atoms:

$$f([a, b, c], 5) : (list(char), int)$$
$$f([1, 2, 3, 4], 6) : (list(int), int)$$

We say that $(list(T), int)$ is the general type of $f/2$. When trying to prove an atom using an already invented predicate, line 12 in Fig. 2 checks that the derivation type of atom is an instance of the general type of the invented predicate.

4.2 HEXMIL$_T$

HEXMIL$_T$ extends the forward-chained state-based encoding of HEXMIL [16]. Forward-chained refers to a restricted class of metarules. For brevity we refer the reader to [16] for a full description of HEXMIL. Our main contribution is to extend HEXMIL with types. We do so by augmenting every atom in the ASP encoding with an additional argument that represents the type of that atom. For instance, the untyped successor relation

```
binary_bg(succ,A,B):-B=A+1,state(A).
```

becomes:

```
binary_bg(succ,(int,int),A,B):-B=A+1,state(A,int).
```

We likewise augment all the deduction rules with types.

Our second contribution is to extend the HEXMIL encoding to support learning second-order programs. However, as this extension is not crucial to the claims of this paper we leave a description to future work.

The full typed encoding is available as an online appendix[3].

5 Experiments

We now experimentally[4] examine the effect of adding types to MIL. We test the null hypothesis:

Null Hypothesis 1. *Adding types to MIL cannot reduce learning times.*

To test this null hypothesis we compare the learning times of the typed versus the untyped systems, i.e. Metagol$_T$ versus Metagol, and HEXMIL$_T$ versus HEXMIL.

5.1 Experiment 1: Ratio Influence

Theorem 1 shows that types can reduce the MIL hypothesis by a cubic factor depending on the relevant ratio (Definition 8), where a lower ratio indicates a greater reduction in the hypothesis space. In this experiment we vary the relevant ratio and measure the effect on learning times. In this experiment there is no solution to the MIL problem. The purpose of the experiment is to measure the time it takes to search the entire hypothesis space.

---

[3] HEXMIL$_T$ encoding file on https://github.com/rolfmorel/jelia19-typedmil.
[4] Experimental data available at https://github.com/rolfmorel/jelia19-typedmil.

Materials. We use a single positive example $p(1,0) : (int, int)$. We use 20 BK predicates, each a uniquely named copy of the $succ/2$ relation, e.g. $succ_1/2$, $succ_2/2, \ldots, succ_{20}/2$. The type of each predicate is either (int, int) or $(\bot, \bot)$, where $\bot$ is a dummy type. We use the *chain* metarule.

Methods. For each relevant ratio rp in $\{0, 0.05, 0.1, \ldots, 1.0\}$ we set the proportion of types (int, int) versus $(\bot, \bot)$ to rp. We consider program hypotheses with at most 3 clauses. We measure mean learning times and standard errors over 10 repetitions. For the HEXMIL experiments, we bound integers to the range 0 to 5000 to ensure the grounding is finite and tractable.

Results. Figure 3 shows that varying the relevant ratio (rp) does not affect the learning times of the untyped systems. By contrast, varying rp affects the learning times of the typed systems. Specifically, types reduce learning times for both typed systems when $rp \leq 0.95$. When rp is 0 the typed systems almost instantly determine that there is no solution. When rp is 0.5, types reduce learning time by approximately 500% with Metagol$_T$ and 300% with HEXMIL$_T$. When rp is 1 the typed systems take slightly longer than their untyped versions because of the small overhead in handling types. The flatter curve of HEXMIL$_T$ compared to Metagol$_T$ is because of implementation differences. The main cost of Metagol$_T$ is trying different predicate substitutions. By contrast, the main cost of HEXMIL$_T$ is grounding the $succ_i/2$ predicates. Overall these results suggest that we can reject the null hypothesis.

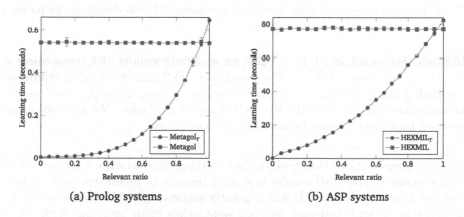

(a) Prolog systems   (b) ASP systems

Fig. 3. Relevant ratio experiment results.

5.2 Experiment 2: Droplasts

In this experiment we learn a *droplasts* program that takes lists of lists and drops the last element of each sublist. Figure 4 shows examples of this problem. We investigate how varying the amount of BK affects learning time.

droplasts([jelia,2019],[jeli,201]).
droplasts([artificial,intelligence],[artificia,intelligenc]).
droplasts([rende,cyprus,madeira,toulouse],[rend,cypru,madeir,toulous]).

Fig. 4. Example *droplasts/2* atoms.

Materials. We provide each system with two positive *droplasts*(x, y) examples where x is the input list and y is the output list. To generate an example, for the input list we select a random integer k between 2 and 5 that represents the number of sublists. We then randomly generate k sublists, where each sublist contains between three and five lowercase characters. The output list is the input list excluding the last element of each sublist. We use small list lengths because of grounding issues with the ASP systems. The Prolog systems can handle much larger values, as previously demonstrated [8]. Figure 5 shows the BK available in the experiments. We always use the *map/3*, *tail/2*, and *reverse/2* predicates, and sample others to include. We use the *chain* and *curry* metarules.

tail(A,B):(list(T),list(T)).	succ(A,B):(int,int).
map(A,B,F):(list(T),list(S),(S,T)).	last(A,B):(list(T),T).
reverse(A,B):(list(T),list(T)).	min_list(A,B):(list(int),int).
sumlist(A,B):(list(int),int).	pred(A,B):(int,int).
head(A,B):(list(T),T).	max_list(A,B):(list(int),int).

Fig. 5. BK predicates used in the *droplasts* experiment. We omit definitions for brevity.

Methods. For each k in $\{0, 1, \ldots, 25\}$, we uniformly sample with replacement k predicates from those shown in Fig. 5 and generate 2 positive training examples. For each learning system, we learn a *droplasts/2* program using the training examples and BK augmented with the k sampled predicates. We measure mean learning times and standard errors over 10 repetitions.

Results. Figure 6 shows that types reduce learning times in almost all cases. The high variance in the ASP results is mainly because of predicates that operate over integers (e.g. *length/2*), which greatly increase grounding complexity. In all cases both the typed and untyped approaches learn programs with 100% accuracy (plot omitted for brevity). Figure 7 shows an example program learned by Metagol$_T$. The Metagol systems show a clear distinction in the learning times that they require. For the HEXMIL systems intractability prohibits us from running the experiment with the full 25 predicates, though the greater variance and higher mean learning times for the untyped system are already apparent in Fig. 6. These results suggest that we can reject the null hypothesis.

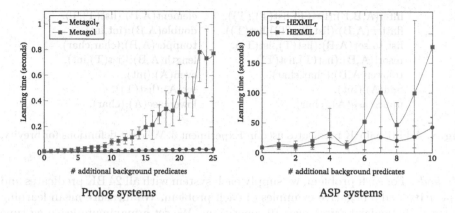

Fig. 6. Droplasts experiment results.

```
droplasts(A,B):(list(list(T)),list(list(T))):-
    map(A,C,droplasts_1):(list(list(T)),list(list(T)),(list(T),list(T))).
droplasts_1(A,B):(list(T),list(T)):-
    reverse(A,C):(list(T),list(T)),
    droplasts_2(C,B):(list(T),list(T)).
droplasts_2(A,B):(list(T),list(T)):-
    tail(A,C):(list(T),list(T)),
    reverse(C,B):(list(T),list(T)).
```

Fig. 7. An example *droplasts/2* program learned by Metagol$_T$. The predicate symbols *droplasts_1/2* and *droplasts_2/2* are invented by Metagol$_T$.

5.3 Experiment 3: More Problems

To further demonstrate that types can improve learning performance, we evaluate the untyped and typed systems on four additional problems:

- *filtercapslower/2* takes a list of characters, discards the lowercase characters, and makes the remaining letters lowercase
- *filterevendbl/2* takes a list of integers, discards the odd numbers, and doubles the even numbers
- *nestedincr/2* takes lists of lists of integers and increments each integer by two
- *finddups/2* takes a list of characters and returns the duplicate character

Materials. As with the previous experiment, we randomly generate examples of varying lengths. We omit full details for brevity. We use the BK from Experiment 2 (Fig. 5) augmented with 14 predicates (Fig. 8), i.e. a total of 24 background predicates. We use the *chain, curry, dident,* and *tailrec* metarules.

filter(A,B,F):(list(T),list(T),(T)).   element(A,B):(list(T),T).
flatten(A,B):(list(list(T)),list(T)).   double(A,B):(int,int).
list_to_set(A,B):(list(T),list(T)).   toupper(A,B):(char,char).
msort(A,B):(list(T),list(T)).   length(A,B):(list(T),int).
tolower(A,B):(char,char).   even(A):(int).
odd(A):(int).   set(A):(list(T)).
uppercase(A):(char).   lowercase(A):(char).

Fig. 8. Additional BK predicates used in Experiment 3. We omit definitions for brevity.

Methods. For each problem, we supply each system with all 24 BK predicates and 5 positive and 5 negative examples of each problem. We measure mean learning times and standard errors over 10 repetitions. We set a maximum learning time of 10 min.

Results. Figure 9 shows that types can significantly reduce learning times. The accuracy of the Prolog systems is identical in all cases, and is only less than 100% for the *finddups/2* program (4 out of 10 trials learned an erroneous hypothesis). The ASP timeouts are because the grounding is too large when using nested lists, integers, or recursive metarules. Again, the clear distinction in performance of the typed and untyped systems is evidence for rejecting the null hypothesis.

Problem	Metagol	Metagol$_T$	HEXMIL	HEXMIL$_T$
droplasts/2	0.93 ± 0.40	**0.07 ± 0.03**	timeout	timeout
filtercapslower/2	0.41 ± 0.21	**0.09 ± 0.11**	54 ± 27	10 ± 6
filterevendbl/2	0.34 ± 0.11	**0.06 ± 0.04**	timeout	timeout
nestedincr/2	0.67 ± 0.31	**0.05 ± 0.02**	timeout	timeout
finddups/2	4.50 ± 5.92	**2.09 ± 3.13**	timeout	timeout

Fig. 9. Experiment 3 results that show mean learning times and standard error.

6   Conclusions

We have extended MIL to support types. We have shown that types can reduce the MIL hypothesis space by a cubic factor (Theorem 1). We have introduced two typed MIL systems: Metagol$_T$, which extends Metagol, and HEXMIL$_T$ which extends HEXMIL. Both systems support polymorphic types and the inference of types for invented predicates. We have experimentally demonstrated that types can significantly reduce learning times for both systems.

Limitations and Future Work. Although we have focused on extending MIL with types, our results and techniques should be applicable to other areas of ILP and program induction. Because we declaratively represent types, our techniques should be directly transferable to other forms of ILP that use metarules [1,4,12, 32,37]. Future work should study the advantages of using types in these other approaches.

The MIL problem is decidable in the datalog setting [23]. However, because typed MIL supports polymorphic types, which are represented as function symbols, the decidability of the typed MIL problem is unclear. Future work should address this issue. A possible solution involves bounding the function application depth in the type terms while all relevant types for a hypothesis space remain expressible.

We have focused on polymorphic types. A natural extension, which has not been explored in ILP, is to support more complex types, such as refinement types [18].

MIL supports predicate invention so it is sensible to ask whether it can also support *type invention*. For instance, rather than treating strings as list of characters, it would be advantageous to ascribe more precise types, such as *postcode* or *email*. This idea is closely related to the idea of *learning declarative bias* [3].

References

1. Albarghouthi, A., Koutris, P., Naik, M., Smith, C.: Constraint-based synthesis of datalog programs. In: Beck, J.C. (ed.) CP 2017. LNCS, vol. 10416, pp. 689–706. Springer, Cham (2017). https://doi.org/10.1007/978-3-319-66158-2_44
2. Blumer, A., Ehrenfeucht, A., Haussler, D., Warmuth, M.: Learnability and the Vapnik-Chervonenkis dimension. J. ACM **36**(4), 929–965 (1989)
3. Bridewell, W., Todorovski, L.: Learning declarative bias. In: Blockeel, H., Ramon, J., Shavlik, J., Tadepalli, P. (eds.) ILP 2007. LNCS, vol. 4894, pp. 63–77. Springer, Heidelberg (2008). https://doi.org/10.1007/978-3-540-78469-2_10
4. Campero, A., Pareja, A., Klinger, T., Tenenbaum, J., Riedel, S.: Logical rule induction and theory learning using neural theorem proving. ArXiv e-prints, September 2018
5. Costa, V.S., Rocha, R., Damas, L.: The YAP Prolog system. TPLP **12**(1–2), 5–34 (2012)
6. Cropper, A.: Efficiently learning efficient programs. Ph.D. thesis. Imperial College London, UK (2017)
7. Cropper, A., Muggleton, S.H.: Learning efficient logical robot strategies involving composable objects. In: Yang, Q., Wooldridge, M. (eds.) Proceedings of the Twenty-Fourth International Joint Conference on Artificial Intelligence, IJCAI 2015, Buenos Aires, Argentina, 25–31 July 2015, pp. 3423–3429. AAAI Press (2015)
8. Cropper, A., Muggleton, S.H.: Learning higher-order logic programs through abstraction and invention. In: Kambhampati, S. (ed.) Proceedings of the Twenty-Fifth International Joint Conference on Artificial Intelligence, IJCAI 2016, New York, NY, USA, 9–15 July 2016, pp. 1418–1424. IJCAI/AAAI Press (2016)
9. Cropper, A., Muggleton, S.H.: Metagol system (2016). https://github.com/metagol/metagol

10. Cropper, A., Muggleton, S.H.: Learning efficient logic programs. Mach. Learn. 1–21 (2018)
11. Cropper, A., Tourret, S.: Derivation reduction of metarules in meta-interpretive learning. In: Riguzzi, F., Bellodi, E., Zese, R. (eds.) ILP 2018. LNCS, vol. 11105, pp. 1–21. Springer, Cham (2018). https://doi.org/10.1007/978-3-319-99960-9_1
12. Evans, R., Grefenstette, E.: Learning explanatory rules from noisy data. J. Artif. Intell. Res. **61**, 1–64 (2018)
13. Farquhar, C., Grov, G., Cropper, A., Muggleton, S., Bundy, A.: Typed meta-interpretive learning for proof strategies. In: CEUR Workshop Proceedings, vol. 1636, pp. 17–32 (2015)
14. Frankle, J., Osera, P., Walker, D., Zdancewic, S.: Example-directed synthesis: a type-theoretic interpretation. In: Bodík, R., Majumdar, R. (ed.) Proceedings of the 43rd Annual ACM SIGPLAN-SIGACT Symposium on Principles of Programming Languages, POPL 2016, St. Petersburg, FL, USA, 20–22 January 2016, pp. 802–815. ACM (2016)
15. Gebser, M., Kaufmann, B., Kaminski, R., Ostrowski, M., Schaub, T., Schneider, M.T.: Potassco: the Potsdam answer set solving collection. AI Commun. **24**(2), 107–124 (2011)
16. Kaminski, T., Eiter, T., Inoue, K.: Exploiting answer set programming with external sources for meta-interpretive learning. TPLP **18**(3–4), 571–588 (2018)
17. Law, M., Russo, A., Broda, K.: Inductive learning of answer set programs. In: Fermé, E., Leite, J. (eds.) JELIA 2014. LNCS, vol. 8761, pp. 311–325. Springer, Cham (2014). https://doi.org/10.1007/978-3-319-11558-0_22
18. Lovas, W., Pfenning, F.: Refinement types for logical frameworks and their interpretation as proof irrelevance. Log. Methods Comput. Sci. **6**(4) (2010)
19. Manna, Z., Waldinger, R.J.: A deductive approach to program synthesis. ACM Trans. Program. Lang. Syst. **2**(1), 90–121 (1980)
20. Muggleton, S.: Inductive logic programming. New Gener. Comput. **8**(4), 295–318 (1991)
21. Muggleton, S.: Inverse entailment and Progol. New Gener. Comput. **13**(3&4), 245–286 (1995)
22. Muggleton, S.H., Lin, D., Pahlavi, N., Tamaddoni-Nezhad, A.: Meta-interpretive learning: application to grammatical inference. Mach. Learn. **94**(1), 25–49 (2014)
23. Muggleton, S.H., Lin, D., Tamaddoni-Nezhad, A.: Meta-interpretive learning of higher-order dyadic datalog: predicate invention revisited. Mach. Learn. **100**(1), 49–73 (2015)
24. Mycroft, A., O'Keefe, R.A.: A polymorphic type system for Prolog. Artif. Intell. **23**(3), 295–307 (1984)
25. Nadathur, G., Miller, D.: An overview of lambda-PROLOG. In: Kowalski, R.A., Bowen, K.A. (eds.) Logic Programming, Proceedings of the Fifth International Conference and Symposium, Seattle, Washington, USA, 15–19 August 1988, vol. 2, pp. 810–827. MIT Press (1988)
26. Osera, P., Zdancewic, S.: Type-and-example-directed program synthesis. In: Grove, D., Blackburn, S. (eds.) Proceedings of the 36th ACM SIGPLAN Conference on Programming Language Design and Implementation, Portland, OR, USA, 15–17 June 2015, pp. 619–630. ACM (2015)
27. Polikarpova, N., Kuraj, I., Solar-Lezama, A.: Program synthesis from polymorphic refinement types. In: Proceedings of the 37th ACM SIGPLAN Conference on Programming Language Design and Implementation, PLDI 2016, New York, NY, USA, pp. 522–538. ACM (2016)

28. Raedt, L.: Declarative modeling for machine learning and data mining. In: Bshouty, N.H., Stoltz, G., Vayatis, N., Zeugmann, T. (eds.) ALT 2012. LNCS, vol. 7568, pp. 12–12. Springer, Heidelberg (2012). https://doi.org/10.1007/978-3-642-34106-9_2

29. Ray, O.: Nonmonotonic abductive inductive learning. J. Appl. Log. **7**(3), 329–340 (2009)

30. Schrijvers, T., Costa, V.S., Wielemaker, J., Demoen, B.: Towards typed Prolog. In: Garcia de la Banda, M., Pontelli, E. (eds.) ICLP 2008. LNCS, vol. 5366, pp. 693–697. Springer, Heidelberg (2008). https://doi.org/10.1007/978-3-540-89982-2_59

31. Schüller, P., Benz, M.: Best-effort inductive logic programming via fine-grained cost-based hypothesis generation - the inspire system at the inductive logic programming competition. Mach. Learn. **107**(7), 1141–1169 (2018)

32. Si, X., Lee, W., Zhang, R., Albarghouthi, A., Koutris, P., Naik, M.: Syntax-guided synthesis of datalog programs. In: Leavens, G.T., Garcia, A., Pasareanu, C.S. (eds.) Proceedings of the 2018 ACM Joint Meeting on European Software Engineering Conference and Symposium on the Foundations of Software Engineering, ESEC/SIGSOFT FSE 2018, Lake Buena Vista, FL, USA, 04–09 November 2018, pp. 515–527. ACM (2018)

33. Singh, R., Gulwani, S.: Synthesizing number transformations from input-output examples. In: Madhusudan, P., Seshia, S.A. (eds.) CAV 2012. LNCS, vol. 7358, pp. 634–651. Springer, Heidelberg (2012). https://doi.org/10.1007/978-3-642-31424-7_44

34. Somogyi, Z., Henderson, F.J., Conway, T.C.: Mercury, an efficient purely declarative logic programming language. Aust. Comput. Sci. Commun. **17**, 499–512 (1995)

35. Srinivasan, A.: The ALEPH manual. Machine Learning at the Computing Laboratory, Oxford University (2001)

36. Stahl, I.: The appropriateness of predicate invention as bias shift operation in ILP. Mach. Learn. **20**(1–2), 95–117 (1995)

37. Wang, W.Y., Mazaitis, K., Cohen, W.W.: Structure learning via parameter learning. In: Li, J., Wang, X.S., Garofalakis, M.N., Soboroff, I., Suel, T., Wang, M. (eds.) Proceedings of the 23rd ACM International Conference on Conference on Information and Knowledge Management, CIKM 2014, Shanghai, China, 3–7 November 2014, pp. 1199–1208. ACM (2014)

38. Wielemaker, J., Schrijvers, T., Triska, M., Lager, T.: SWI-Prolog. TPLP **12**(1–2), 67–96 (2012)

Explaining Actual Causation in Terms of Possible Causal Processes

Marc Denecker[1(✉)], Bart Bogaerts[1,2], and Joost Vennekens[1,3]

[1] Department of Computer Science, KU Leuven, Leuven, Belgium
{marc.denecker,bart.bogaerts,joost.vennekens}@cs.kuleuven.be
[2] Department of Computer Science, Vrije Universiteit Brussel (VUB),
Brussels, Belgium
[3] Department of Computer Science, KU Leuven, Campus De Nayer,
Sint-Katelijne-Waver, Belgium

Abstract. We point to several kinds of knowledge that play an important role in controversial examples of actual causation. One is knowledge about the causal mechanisms in the domain and the causal processes that result from them. Another is knowledge of what conditions trigger such mechanisms and what conditions can make them fail.

We argue that to solve questions of actual causation, such knowledge needs to be made explicit. To this end, we develop a new language in the family of CP-logic, in which causal mechanisms and causal processes are formal objects. We then build a framework for actual causation in which various "production" notions of actual causation are defined. Contrary to counterfactual definitions, these notions are defined directly in terms of the (formal) causal process that causes the possible world.

1 Introduction

Since the days of Hume [21], causal reasoning has been an active research domain in philosophy and (later) knowledge representation. With the groundbreaking work of Lewis [22] and Pearl [25], the structural equations and counterfactual reasoning approach became mainstream [9,10,14,15]. But the debate remains intense [11]. The counterfactual approach is contested by some [1,5,13]. In many scenarios, there is no agreement of what the actual causes are, and all definitions of actual causation have scenarios where they have been criticized. It shows that the informal notion of actual causation is vague and overloaded with many intuitions; it also show that many sorts of knowledge influence our judgment of actual causation. Science is not ready yet with unraveling all this.

Among the most striking examples are those where for the same formal causal model, different informal interpretations can be proposed that lead to different actual causes. Indeed, such examples are particularly interesting, because they demonstrate that some relevant knowledge is missing from the causal model. A powerful illustration is given by Halpern [16], who discusses 6 causal examples

Bart Bogaerts is a postdoctoral fellow of the Research Foundation – Flanders (FWO).

F. Calimeri et al. (Eds.): JELIA 2019, LNAI 11468, pp. 214–230, 2019.
https://doi.org/10.1007/978-3-030-19570-0_14

from the literature in which authors showed (often convincingly) that the actual causation definition of Halpern and Pearl [15], henceforth called HP, failed to predict the actual causes. He responds by proposing for each example an alternative informal interpretation leading to the *same* structural equation model but to intuitively *different* actual causes which, moreover, are those derived by HP! Halpern concludes that, as far as actual causation goes, the structural equation models are ambiguous. As for what knowledge is missing, he claims:

> "what turns out to arguably be the best way to do the disambiguation is to add [...] extra variables, which [...] capture the **mechanism of causality**" and "But all this talk of mechanisms [...] suggests that the mechanism should be part of the model."

That is, he argues that we should make knowledge of causal mechanisms explicit.

That such information is relevant for causal reasoning is not surprising. Many causal scenarios in the literature comes with an informal specification of causal mechanisms and, often, a sometimes partial *story* specifying which mechanisms are active and how they are rigged together in a causal process. As observed before [11, 27], most of this information is abstracted away in structural equation models. We illustrate to what problems this may lead with a simple example, an *ambiguity* of the same sort as tackled by Halpern [16]. Consider two scenarios involving two deadly poisons, arsenic and strychnine. In the first scenario, intake of any of these poisons triggers a deadly biochemical process. The corresponding structural equation is

$$Dead := Arsenic\_intake \lor Strychnine\_intake$$

If both poisons are taken, this is an instance of overdetermination; HP derives that both poisons are actual causes of death.

The second scenario is similar, except that arsenic, in addition to poisoning the victim, also *preempts* the chemical process by which strychnine poisons the victim. Now, the structural equation remains the same (i.e., the victim dies as soon as at least one poison is ingested) and so do the *possible worlds* (i.e., in both cases, there are 4 possible worlds: $\{D, A, S\}$, $\{D, A, \neg S\}$, $\{D, \neg A, S\}$ and $\{\neg D, \neg A, \neg S\}$)! However, the judgments of actual causation differ: when both poisons are ingested, only arsenic is a cause of death, since the effects of the strychnine are preempted. The conclusion is that the structural equation correctly predicts the possible worlds but does not contain enough information to explain the actual causes. What is missing is more detailed information about the *causal processes* that generate the possible worlds and about the individual causal mechanisms that constitute these processes.[1]

---

[1] A more intuitive structural equation for the second scenario is $Arsenic \lor (\neg Arsenic \land Strychnine)$. It is equivalent under standard semantics to the original equation. Nevertheless, it suggests an alternative way to resolve the ambiguity: developing a more refined semantics that distinguishes between the two equations. We suspect that structural equations under such a refined semantics might turn out to be quite similar to the logic we develop in this paper.

The following scenario, simplified from **Assassin** [20], illustrates another relevant sort of knowledge that is not expressed in structural equation models. *An assassin may kill a victim by administering deadly poison. A bodyguard may rescue the victim by administering an antidote.* The structural equation:

$$Dead := Poison\_intake \land No\_antidote\_intake$$

correctly characterizes the possible worlds. However, there is again a problem on the level of actual causes. When only poison is ingested, there is a strong intuition that it is the ingestion of poison that is the actual cause of death, not the absence of antidote. After all, it is the poison that activates the poisoning mechanism, not the absence of antidote. Yet, by the symmetry of the formal model, HP nor any other mathematical method can discover this from the above structural equation. The asymmetry here is that poison *triggers* the causal mechanism, while antidote *preempts* it, i.e., absence of antidote is only a condition to not *preempt* the mechanism. As we argue below, this distinction plays a role in many controversial causal examples and should be added to the causal model.

Halpern's solution to the first type of ambiguities is to *reify* the different causal mechanisms by auxiliary variables and structural equations representing when the mechanism *fires*. He applies this methodology to explicate the causal mechanisms in the different interpretations of each of the 6 cases. The causal models of the refined theories then not only encode the actual world, but also (part of) the causal process that creates it. For all 2×6 cases, HP was able to detect the intuitively expected actual causes using the refined theories.

These are great results, but they also raise some fundamental questions. First, Halpern's approach is to refine existing structural equation models to resolve *reported* ambiguities on them. What guarantee is there that all ambiguities are resolved now? To eradicate the problem of such ambiguities, we need a modelling language that supports expression of individual causal mechanisms. This is the first topic on which our paper contributes. Second, his analysis shows that knowledge of individual causal mechanisms and which of them fire influences our judgment of actual causation. But this does not explain how this works. Sure, HP was powerful enough to produce the expected answers, but HP is not based on causal mechanisms and processes, hence this method cannot explain why and how causal processes determine the actual causes. What is missing is a principled explanation of actual causation in terms of the causal process and the causal mechanisms. This is the second topic on which our paper contributes. Third, the second ambiguity, the one that appears in **Assassin**, is not a problem of discerning different causal mechanisms and Halpern's methodology is not applicable to this case. We argue that to resolve this type of ambiguities, it is necessary to express the distinction between conditions that *trigger* the causal process and conditions that, if false, *preempt* the causal mechanism. We propose a modelling language for this and we argue that making this distinction explains a number of controversies in causal reasoning, such as the difference between *early preemption* and *switch* scenarios.

2   The Causal Logic: Syntax and Informal Semantics

We propose a propositional causal modelling language to resolve the reported ambiguities. It can be lifted easily to the predicate level but this would merely increase the formal complexity without contributing to the essence of the paper.

To represent a causal domain, a *vocabulary* Σ of propositional symbols is chosen; each symbol expresses an atomic proposition in the domain. Literals are formulas of the form P or $\neg P$, with $P \in \Sigma$; slightly abusing notation, we use $\neg L$ to denote P if $L = \neg P$ and to denote $\neg P$ if $L = P$. As usual, we distinguish between *endogenous symbols*, for which the mechanisms that cause them are expressed in the theory, and *exogenous* symbols, for which no causal mechanisms are expressed.

A causal theory is a set of causal mechanisms. Each mechanism has *triggering conditions*, which set the mechanism in operation; *enabling conditions*, which if false, preempt the mechanism; and an *effect*. This leads to the following definition.

Definition 1. *A* causal mechanism *is a statement of the form*

$$L \leftarrow T \,\|\, C$$

where

- $\leftarrow$ *is the* causal operator *(not material implication),*
- L *is a literal of an endogenous symbol, called the* effect,
- T *is a sequence of literals called* triggering conditions,
- C *is a sequence of literals called* enabling conditions.

The causal mechanism $L \leftarrow \|$ *represents the unconditional causal mechanism causing* L. *Elements of* $T \cup C$ *are called* conditions *of the causal mechanism.*

A causal theory Δ *is a set of causal mechanisms that contains at least one mechanism for each endogenous symbol and such that:*

- Δ *is acyclic, i.e., there exists a strict well-founded order on symbols such that for each causal mechanism, the symbol in the effect is strictly larger than the symbols of the conditions.*
- Δ *does not contain mechanisms with contradictory effects* $P \leftarrow \dots$ *and* $\neg P \leftarrow \dots$.

The logic imposes two main constraints on causal theories: acyclicity and absence of contradictory effects. In many causal domains, cycles in causal mechanisms exist. Cycles are allowed in several causal rule formalisms [5–7,28]. Following [28], the logic proposed here can easily be extended with cycles. We do not implement it since the greater complexity would detract attention from the essence of this paper: the resolution of ambiguities. The absence of contradictory effects is an inherent aspect of the language and is explained below.

Example 1 **Arsenic and Strychnine.** The two causal scenarios mentioned in the introduction are represented as

$$\left\{ \begin{array}{l} Dead \leftarrow Arsenic\_intake \,|| \\ Dead \leftarrow Strychnine\_intake \,|| \end{array} \right\}, \text{ and}$$

$$\left\{ \begin{array}{l} Dead \leftarrow Arsenic\_intake \,|| \\ Dead \leftarrow Strychnine\_intake \,|| \,\neg Arsenic\_intake \end{array} \right\}$$

x respectively. Three of these rules have the empty sequence of enabling conditions. In the last rule, strychnine poisoning is triggered by strychnine but preempted by arsenic.

We now describe the informal semantics of the language. A causal theory does not impose constraints on the exogenous symbols and makes abstraction of causal mechanisms affecting them. For the endogenous symbols, the causal theory is assumed to contain *all* causal mechanisms affecting them. Each endogenous proposition has a *default* state L and a *deviant* state $\neg L$. The effect of a causal mechanism is always the deviant literal. A causal process starts in a state where endogenous properties are in their default state, and proceeds by firing *applicable but unsatisfied causal* mechanisms: mechanisms with true conditions but false effect. Firing a causal mechanism switches the effect on, moving the included proposition from its default to its deviant state. Once a deviant literal is true, it remains true. As such, with each endogenous proposition zero or one *event* is associated: zero if it stays in its default state, one if it switches. Such a switch event may be caused by multiple causal mechanisms causing L simultaneously. The process stops when all applicable causal mechanisms are satisfied. The resulting state is a possible causal world of the theory.

It can be seen that a form of the *law of inertia* is present in the logic: an endogenous symbol remains in the same state unless it is affected by some causal mechanism. Also, endogenous properties have a fixed default and deviant state and causal mechanisms cause deviant literals; hence, mechanisms have no contradictory effects.

The causal processes considered here are clearly of a limited kind. In many causal domains, endogenous properties evolve from true to false and back again, caused by mechanisms with contradictory effects. E.g., flipping a switch causes the light to be on if the light is not on and vice versa. Such domains, interesting as they are, fall outside the scope of this paper. First of all, the causal ambiguities studied here arise in causal domains modelled in non-temporal causal languages (structural equations, causal neuron diagrams, causal calculus, CP-logic, . . .). We argue that in the majority of such applications, the causal processes are of the simple kind considered here. Also, building a language for modelling causal worlds that are the result of complex dynamic causal processes is conceptually, mathematically, and computationally complex (e.g., causal processes may not terminate). This is outside the scope of this paper.

In worlds caused by causal processes of the sort we consider here, every deviant literal L has a causal explanation, namely the causal mechanism(s) that caused it. On the other hand, a default literal L that holds in the world is not caused by a specific causal mechanism; it is true by inertia. Nevertheless it has a causal explanation as well, namely, that every causal mechanism for $\neg L$ is blocked. Either way, the language implements Leibniz's principle of sufficient reason—that every true fact has a reason—(but only for endogenous facts).

Definition 2. *A world W is a complete and consistent set of literals, i.e., a set of literals such that for each $P \in \Sigma$, either $P \in W$ or $\neg P \in W$, but not both. The* exogenous state *of W is the set of its exogenous literals, denoted $Exo(W)$. As usual, an exogenous state is called a* context. *A symbol P is in its* deviant state *in W if its deviant literal holds in W, and in its* default state *otherwise.*

Definition 3. *A causal mechanism r of the form $L \leftarrow A \,\|\, B$ is blocked by a condition $K \in A \cup B$ in world W if $\neg K \in W$. The mechanism r is* active *in world W if $A \subseteq W$, that is, if all its triggering conditions hold in W; otherwise it is inactive. A causal mechanism is* applicable *in W if $A \cup B \subseteq W$. The mechanism r* fails *in W if it is active but is blocked by an enabling condition in W. A causal mechanism is* satisfied *in W if it is blocked, or if its effect holds in W.*

Triggering Conditions Versus Enabling Conditions. The distinction between triggering and enabling conditions of causal mechanisms is a new feature of our language. Often, a natural distinction can be made between the conditions that set the mechanism in operation and conditions that are necessary for the mechanism to succeed. E.g., to obtain a forest fire, at least two conditions are needed: a spark igniting a hotbed in the forest and absence of extinction operations. There is no difference between the two conditions on the level of counterfactual dependence. Nevertheless, it is the spark (in the form of a lightning or an unsafe camp fire) that triggers the causal mechanism; the condition of absence of extinction operations is there only because such operations would make the causal mechanism fail in achieving its effect. We argue that this explains the strong intuition shared by many that it is the spark that is the actual cause of the fire, and not the absence of fire extinction. Our goal here is to propose a formalization of this notion of actual causation. To define it, the nature of the conditions must be clear from the causal theory.

Example 2 (Hitchcock's **Assassin**, [20, p. 504]). Drinking coffee poisoned by Assassin causes Victim to die unless an antidote is administered by Bodyguard. We discuss three conditions here: presence of poison in the coffee (*Poison*), drinking the coffee (*Drink*), and absence of antidote ($\neg Antidote$). The poisoning process is physically triggered by the event of drinking the coffee. However, it is the intake of poison that triggers the poisoning process. Thus, the triggering conditions are *Drink* and *Poison*. Intake of an antidote causes the process to fail in achieving its effect. So, we argue for the following representation:

$$\neg Alive \leftarrow Drink, Poison \,\|\, \neg Antidote$$

Hitchcock pointed at the different "strengths" of the first conditions versus the third condition as causes for death. When the three conditions are true and Victim dies, drinking poisoned coffee seems to be a "stronger" cause of this than the absence of antidote. He argues that this is because absence of antidote is an *omission*, in particular, of the event of administering antidote. However, this cannot be the explanation. First, omissions are frequently perceived as strong causes [26]. Second (and illustrating the first point), if there is no poisoning or no drinking but antidote is administered, the omission of one or both of the first conditions seems to be the "stronger" actual cause for survival than the presence of antidote. The explanation we propose is in terms of triggering versus enabling conditions. When triggering and enabling conditions are true, we perceive the triggering conditions as "stronger" actual causes for the deviant effect than the enabling conditions. When triggering conditions and enabling conditions are both false, we see the omission of triggering conditions as the "stronger" actual causes for the absence of the effect; after all, if the causal mechanism is not even triggered, the falsity of its enabling conditions does not seem to matter. The only situation where an enabling condition plays a role as an actual cause is when the mechanism is active (its triggering conditions hold) but fails due to falsity of the enabling condition.

Even now, before having defined a formal semantics, it is intuitively clear how to transform causal theories to structural equations, namely by *predicate completion* [8]. E.g., the completion of the first causal theory of **Arsenic and Strychnine** is the propositional logic representation of the structural equation:

$$Dead := Arsenic\_intake \lor Strychnine\_intake$$

The completion of the second theory is syntactically different but logically equivalent.

$$Dead := Arsenic\_intake\lor$$
$$(Strychnine\_intake \land \neg Arsenic\_intake)$$

The transformation abstracts away the causal mechanisms and the distinction between triggering and enabling conditions.

3 Formal Semantics: Causal Processes and Possible Worlds

The formal semantics specifies for each causal theory Δ its causal processes and the world that each process leads to. Causal processes can be formalized in multiple ways. Vennekens et al. [28] formalize them as sequences of states in which at every state one causal mechanism is applied until all causal mechanisms are satisfied. This representation is precise and gives an account of, e.g., the "stories" in many causal examples. However, its high level of detail is not actually required for dealing with actual causation, e.g., it fixes the order of application of causal mechanisms which is largely irrelevant for determining actual causes. So, we opt to formalize a process as an acyclic dependency graph of the firing causal mechanisms. Let Δ be a causal theory throughout the rest of the paper.

Definition 4. *A possible causal process for Δ is a directed labeled graph $\mathcal{P}$ whose set of nodes is a world, denoted $World(\mathcal{P})$. Each arc from literal K to literal L is labeled with a mechanism r or $\neg r$. The graph satisfies the following conditions:*

- *For each deviant endogenous literal $L \in World(\mathcal{P})$, there exists a nonempty set F_L of applicable mechanisms with head L, called the firing set of L, such that for each condition K of each $r \in F_L$, there is an arc $L \xleftarrow{r} K$. There are no other arcs to L.*
- *For each default endogenous literal $L \in World(\mathcal{P})$, for each mechanism $r = \neg L \leftarrow \ldots$, the set B_r of conditions of r that are false in $World(\mathcal{P})$ is nonempty and there is an arc $L \xleftarrow{\neg r} \neg K \in \mathcal{P}$ for each $K \in B_r$. There are no other arcs to L.*

When the causal process in the real world leading up to the current world can be observed, the corresponding formal process can be extracted along the following lines. At each time the state changes during the process, one or more deviant literals L become true. For each, one detects the mechanisms that caused it and adds arcs from its conditions to L. When a default literal L remains true, one investigates why the mechanisms that could cause $\neg L$ did not fire, and adds arcs from the negation of all their false conditions to L.

Definition 5. *We call arcs $L \xleftarrow{r} K$ active arcs and distinguish between trigger arcs and enabling arcs depending on the type of the condition K is in r. We call arcs $L \xleftarrow{\neg r} \neg K \in \mathcal{P}$ blocking arcs and we distinguish between nontrigger arcs and failure arcs depending on the type of condition K is in r.*

The causal process semantics induces a possible world semantics.

Definition 6. *A causal process $\mathcal{P}$ realizes the world $World(\mathcal{P})$. We call W a possible world of causal theory Δ if it is realized by some causal process for Δ.*

The leafs of a causal process are the true exogenous literals of the world; the non-leafs are the true endogenous literals.

Definition 4 treats triggering and enabling conditions symmetrically, except for the names of arcs. As a consequence, the classification of the conditions in causal mechanisms has no impact on the possible causal worlds. However, it will play a key role in the definition(s) of actual causation.

Proposition 1. *A world W is a possible causal world of causal theory Δ iff W is a model of the completion of Δ.*

As such, the extra information[2] available in a causal theory Δ compared to its corresponding structural model (i.e., its completion) does not affect the possible worlds nor does it affect the answer to any inference problem that can be resolved by reasoning on possible worlds. However, it does affect the actual causation question. This was shown by the ambiguities.

---

[2] Information on different mechanisms, and triggering conditions versus enabling conditions.

Example 3 (**Drinking poisoned coffee, cont.**). Each of the eight exogenous states of this causal theory determines a unique process. E.g., the context $\{Drink, Poison, \neg Antidote\}$ is the only context in which the victim dies. The causal mechanism is active and fires and $\neg Alive$ has incoming trigger arcs from $Poison$ and $Drink$ and an enabling arc from $\neg Antidote$. In context $\{Drink, Poison, Antidote\}$, the mechanism is active but fails; $Alive$ has an incoming failure arc from $Antidote$. In $\{\neg Drink, \neg Poison, Antidote\}$, the mechanism is inactive and $Alive$ has nontrigger arcs from $\neg Drink, \neg Poison$ and a failure arc from $Antidote$. The latter context corresponds to **Bogus Prevention** [12,18].

The firing set F_L of a deviant literal L may contain more than one mechanism, in which case L is *overdetermined*.

In our framework, three sorts of preemption of causal mechanisms can be distinguished. The first one is that the causal mechanism is blocked by some triggering condition and is inactive. The second is that the mechanism is active but blocked by an enabling condition and thus *fails*. The third sort of preemption occurs when a causal mechanism r with effect L is applicable in world W (all its conditions hold) but L was caused by other mechanisms. This corresponds to *late preemption*.

Example 4 (**Window**, see [13]). Suzy and Billy throw rocks at a window. Each throw is a separate causal mechanism causing the same deviant state.

$$\left\{ \begin{array}{l} Broken \leftarrow SuzyT \parallel \\ Broken \leftarrow BillyT \parallel \end{array} \right\}$$

Assume that both throw. In the *overdetermination* scenario, they hit the window simultaneously. It corresponds to the causal process in which the fire set of $Broken$ contains both laws. In the *late preemption* scenario, Suzy's throw arrives first and smashes the window. It corresponds to the process in which only the first law belongs to the fire set of $Broken$. For the resulting world, this does not matter: the window is broken. Stated precisely, in the exogenous state $\{SuzyT, BillyT\}$, there are multiple possible causal processes. However, they are confluent: they lead to the same possible world.

4   Definitions of Actual Causation

The informal notion of actual causation is vague and overloaded with many different intuitions. It is the role of science to unravel these. Below, we propose several distinguished notions in the context of possible process semantics. A causal process $\mathcal{P}$ realizing world W provides a precise causal explanation of W. We define several notions of causation that can be "read off" from the actual causal process. They are *objective* notions in the sense that they are defined in terms of the *actual* causal process that shaped the actual world. In this respect, they are similar to the notion of *production* in [13] in the context of causal neuron diagrams, and they can be contrasted with counterfactual notions of causation such as HP which are defined in terms of a class of *hypothetical* worlds. Generally stated, we interpret a notion of actual causation as a "production" notion if it can be derived from the actual causal process only. The different notions of causation below are defined in terms of different sorts of causal paths in the causal process.

Definition 7. *Given a causal process P for a causal theory Δ, a literal K is an influence of literal L in P if there is a path from K to L in P.*

An influence of a literal L in a process P is any fact that has influenced the causal process causing L. We view the notion of influence as a "lower bound" for causation: in any reasonable notion of actual causation, an actual cause should be at least an influence. Stricter notions can be defined by limiting the paths that are considered: for instance, we call an influence *active* if the path contains only active arcs, i.e., if there is a chain of firing mechanisms between K and L. Active influences are similar to the notion of actual causation defined in [17] in the context of neuron diagrams.

The notion of influence is defined in terms of the causal process, whereas in most approaches actual causes are defined in the context of a possible world. As pointed out by Vennekens [27], even when we know the world, we may not know how it was caused and therefore, we may not be sure about the actual causes. This emerged in the different possible causal processes of **Window** when both Suzy and Billy throw. This uncertainty is reflected in the definition below.

Definition 8. *A literal K is a possible influence of L in a possible world W of Δ if there is a possible causal process P realizing W such that K is an influence of L in P. We call K a definite influence of L in W if it is an influence in every causal process realizing W.*

The notion of influence does not distinguish between triggers and enabling conditions. As we argued in the introduction and in Example 2, this sometimes leads to counterintuitive results. We now examine how the distinction between triggers and enabling conditions affects our judgment of causation. This will lead us to further refine the notion of influence. We consider three variants of the poisoned coffee example. **(1)** Victim drinks poisoned coffee without having received the antidote. In this case, $\neg Antidote$ is an influence of $\neg Alive$. Yet, the intuition, originally expressed by Hitchcock, is that it is the poison that caused his death, not the absence of antidote. In general, when L is caused by a mechanism r, the triggering conditions of r are actual causes for L, while its enabling conditions are not. **(2)** Victim is given an antidote, but the coffee is not poisoned. Here, both $\neg Poison$ and $Antidote$ are influences. However, only the absence of poison should be counted as an actual cause for his survival, not the antidote, since one cannot preempt an inactive mechanism. In general, if a mechanism r for $\neg L$ is inactive, the actual causes of L are the false triggering conditions of r, not its false enabling conditions. **(3)** Victim is poisoned and receives an antidote. Here, the antidote is an influence, and it *is* a cause for his survival. In general, if r fails, its false enabling conditions are causes.

These intuitions are implemented in the following definition.

Definition 9. *A literal L is an* actual P-cause *of literal K in process $\mathcal{P}$ if there is a path $K \rightarrow \ldots \rightarrow L$ in $\mathcal{P}$ without enabling arcs and without failure arcs of non-active causal mechanisms. Such a path consists of trigger and nontrigger arcs, and failure arcs of active causal mechanisms. We say that L is a* direct actual P-cause *of K if the length of the path is 1, and an* indirect actual P-cause *otherwise.*

The "P" stands for "production", the basic "material" sort of causation of this causal language, similar to production in [3,13]. This concept can be further constrained, e.g., to the notion of *active* actual P-cause.

The notion of actual P-cause is extended from processes to worlds in exactly the same way as was done for the notion of influence in Definition 8.

Proposition 2. *The notions of influence and actual P-cause in processes and worlds are transitive.*

All examples seen so far (**Arsenic and Strychnine, Drinking poisoning coffee** and **Window**) are modelled by simple causal theories which in every context has causal processes of length 1. As can be seen in the discussion preceding Definition 9, the actual P-causes of the endogenous literal match the intuitions expressed in the introduction.

Example 5. Assume in **Assassin**, that a crime syndicate ordered the murder. In this scenario, the following causal mechanism is in operation.

$$Poison \leftarrow CS\_Order$$

In the context $\{CS\_Order, Drink, \neg Antidote\}$, $Poison$ is a direct actual P-cause of $\neg Alive$ while CS_Order is an indirect actual P-cause of $\neg Alive$.

Example 6 **Double Preemption** [13]. Double preemption occurs when a potential preempter is preempted. It occurs in the following scenario. *Suzy fires a missile (SF) to bomb target (B); enemy fires a missile (EF) to hit Suzy's missile (SMH) and Billy fires a missile (BF) to hit Enemy's missile (EMH).* We see three causal mechanisms (annotated with names r_1, r_2, r_3).

$$\left\{ \begin{array}{ll} B \leftarrow SF \,\|\, \neg SMH & (r_1) \\ SMH \leftarrow EF \,\|\, \neg EMH & (r_2) \\ EMH \leftarrow BF \,\| & (r_3) \end{array} \right\}$$

In Fig. 1, three causal processes are graphically displayed. Red nodes are deviants, green nodes are defaults and grey nodes are exogenous. Full black arcs leave from trigger conditions; dotted purple arcs from enabling conditions. The arc is active if it ends in a red deviant node, it is blocking if it ends in a

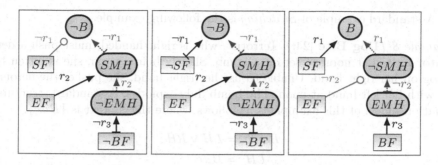

Fig. 1. Graphical representation of three causal processes. (Color figure online)

green default node. A third type of green arc leaves from a trigger condition in an active but failing mechanism that is preempted by an enabling condition.

The left process shows the causal process of context $\{SF, EF, \neg BF\}$ where Suzy's missile is destroyed by enemy fire and target is not bombed. The actual P-causes of $\neg B$ are SMH, EF. The middle shows the process in context $\{\neg SF, EF, \neg BF\}$ where the actual P-cause for $\neg B$ is false trigger $\neg SF$ but where SMH is another influence of $\neg B$. The right shows the causal process of context $\{SF, EF, BF\}$, where everyone fires, enemy's antimissile is destroyed by Billy's and the target is bombed. The actual P-cause of B is SF while $\neg SMH, EMH, BF$ are influences. The causal path $BF \rightarrow EMH \rightarrow \neg SMH \rightarrow B$ shows in the two last edges display a double preemption: the hit on enemy's missile preempts enemy's attempt at preempting Suzy's bombing. Some view that Billy's fire BF is an actual cause of B by double preemption. While this is not derived in our definition of actual P-cause, this kind of pattern can be read off from the causal process and is not difficult to formally define in the framework.

4.1 Early Preemption Versus Switch

A well-known issue in the actual causation literature concerns the relation between *Early Preemption* and *Switching* examples. Let us illustrate this by means of the following example of Early Preemption.

*Example 7 (***Backup** [20]*).* An assassin-in-training is on his first mission. Trainee is an excellent shot: if he shoots, the bullet will fell Victim. Supervisor is also present, in case Trainee has a last minute loss of nerve (a common affliction among student assassins) and fails to pull the trigger. If Trainee does not shoot, Supervisor will shoot Victim herself. In fact, Trainee performs admirably, firing his gun and killing Victim. The following is the standard structural equation model used in the literature for this story, where the context is such that *Trainee* is true.

$$Victim := Trainee \lor Supervisor$$
$$Supervisor := \neg Trainee$$

A standard example of *Switching* is the following example.

*Example 8 (***Dog Bite** [24]*)*. Terrorist, who is right-handed, must push a detonator button at noon to set off a bomb. Shortly before noon, she is bitten by a dog on her right hand. Unable to use her right hand, she pushes the detonator with her left hand at noon. The bomb duly explodes. A standard structural equation model of this example is as follows, where the context is $\{Bite\}$.

$$Bomb := LH \vee RH$$
$$LH := Bite$$
$$RH := \neg Bite$$

Let us now compare these two examples. The role of *Trainee* and *Bite* in the formal models of both examples are remarkably similar. Nevertheless, the common opinion is that in cases of Early Preemption, there *is* causation (i.e., Trainee caused Victim's death), whereas in cases of Switching, there is no causation (i.e., dog's bite did not cause the bomb to go off, even though it did cause Terrorist to push the detonator with her left hand).

The similarity between both causal models becomes even more striking when we extend the first example by an intermediate variable *Bullet*, that represents the fact that a bullet leaves Trainee's gun. In this case, we obtain:

$$Victim := Bullet \vee Supervisor$$
$$Bullet := Trainee$$
$$Supervisor := \neg Trainee$$

This model is now formally identical to the model for Dog Bite. However, the addition of the intermediate variable *Bullet* seems like it should not affect our causal judgments. Therefore, we now essentially have one formal model, from which we nevertheless would expect different actual causation answers depending on the informal interpretation. This is an ambiguity.

In the literature, several solutions have been proposed for this problem. According to Weslake [29], it is precisely the addition of the intermediate variable *Bullet* that turns this example from an instance of Early Preemption into an instance of Switching and he therefore does not agree with our intuition that adding this variable should preserve our causal judgments. Becker and Vennekens [4] and Hall [12] argue that an action such as shooting a victim can never be completely deterministic and that it is therefore necessary to change to a non-deterministic (or probabilistic) representation in order to correctly handle the examples. Hitchcock [19] and Halpern and Pearl [15] argue that the formal model we presented is not suitable for Switching examples, based on an analysis of the counterfactual interventions admitted by the model.

We offer a different explanation which we believe goes more to the heart of the difference between the two kinds of examples. Our opinion is that the ambiguity is of the same type as the second ambiguity in the introduction, the ambiguity in the context of **Assassin**: the difference between early preemption and switching is located in the subtle but important difference between triggering and enabling conditions.

If we now re-examine the two above examples, we see that, first of all, *Trainee* is obviously a triggering condition for *Bullet*, since it is Trainee's pulling of the literal trigger that sets in motion the causal mechanism that leads to the bullet's exiting the gun. The relevant causal mechanisms are therefore:

$$\left\{ \begin{array}{l} Victim \leftarrow Bullet \, \| \\ Victim \leftarrow Supervisor \, \| \\ Bullet \leftarrow Trainee \, \| \\ Supervisor \leftarrow \neg Trainee \, \| \end{array} \right\}$$

However, analyzing the Dog Bite example, we notice that neither the dog bite nor its absence is actually a trigger for the causal mechanism that leads to the detonator being pushed. Indeed, for all we know, the dog bite could have happened (or failed to happen) a long time before the detonator was actually pushed, giving Terrorist plenty of time to have a change of heart in between. The real trigger for the mechanism is Terrorist deciding to detonate the bomb. In our language, this example is therefore more appropriately modelled as:

$$\left\{ \begin{array}{l} Bomb \leftarrow LH \, \| \\ Bomb \leftarrow RH \, \| \\ LH \leftarrow DecideToDetonate \, \| \, Bite \\ RH \leftarrow DecideToDetonate \, \| \, \neg Bite \end{array} \right\}$$

(Here, we introduced the new variable *DecideToDenote* for clarity, but nothing changes in our analysis if we do not do this and leave the set of triggers empty).

By making the distinction between triggering conditions and enabling conditions, we believe to have a convincing answer to the question of what really distinguishes early preemption from switching. Indeed, our definitions now yield that *Trainee* is a actual P-cause of *Dead*, while *Bite* is not.

5   Related Work and Conclusions

We studied several sorts of knowledge that are important for actual causation: knowledge of causal mechanisms and which of them fire, and the distinction between triggering and enabling conditions. Causal mechanisms with enabling conditions can be considered as mechanisms with a failure option: a false enabling condition leads to failure of the mechanism. The relevance of these concepts was brought to light by ambiguities. We proposed a language to express them and defined a possible causal process semantics, which induces a possible world semantics. Using causal processes as an explanation of the world, we provided definitions for several notions of actual "production" causation. The notion of (active) influence is independent of the distinction between triggering and enabling conditions, while (active) actual P-cause takes them into account. We argued that the distinction explains the difference between early preemption and switching.

We evaluated these ideas in a range of examples. Our test set includes those of [11], where the definitions of Woodward [30] and HP [15] are put to the test. The notion of actual P-cause correctly derives the expected actual causes in most cases, including some where Woodwards and HP failed. In cases where actual P-cause fails, counterfactual reasoning is essential. Several examples can be tested at http://adams.cs.kuleuven.be/idp/server.html?chapter=intro/11-AC.

The aim to study actual causation in the context of causal processes is present in neuron diagrams approaches [23]. However, neuron diagrams do not represent individual mechanisms (similar to a structural equation) and do not distinguish between triggering and enabling conditions, and hence fall short for the sort of examples that motivated this paper. There exist other languages with a syntactic rule notation to express causal knowledge [5–7,28]. However, it is not clear to us whether our view of causal mechanisms matches with the view of causal rules in some of these formalisms. The only causal reasoning study that accounts for causal mechanisms, processes and worlds that we are aware of is the work on CP-logic [28]. CP-logic was used for various forms of reasoning such as probabilistic reasoning, interventions, and actual causation. The logic defined here is related in spirit to CP-logic but differs from it quite considerably. E.g., causal processes are formalized differently, and there is no distinction between triggering and enabling conditions in CP-logic. The actual causation method for CP-logic proposed by Vennekens [27] and refined by Beckers and Vennekens [2] is based on causal processes as well, but it is intuitively and mathematically completely different. It is a counterfactual method based on analysis of alternative causal processes, in a way related to the approaches of Hall [12,13]. The relation with our approach is not obvious and we leave a further analysis of this for future work.

Several other topics for future research exist. One is to determine the complexity of key computational problems, such as computing different notions of actual causation. Useful extensions of the language include non-deterministic, probabilistic and cyclic causation, first order features (e.g., quantification), and dynamic mechanisms that initiate some property at one time and terminate it at another. This we plan to do following CP-logic, which supports several of these extensions. Another challenge is to develop a proof-theoretical account of the logic.

Acknowledgements. We thank Alexander Bochman, Sander Beckers, Jorge Fandinno, Mathieu Beirlaen, and anonymous reviewers for many discussions and valuable feedback.

References

1. Baumgartner, M.: A regularity theoretic approach to actual causation. Erkenn **78**(Suppl), 1:85 (2013). https://doi.org/10.1007/s10670-013-9438-3
2. Beckers, S., Vennekens, J.: Counterfactual dependency and actual causation in CP-logic and structural models: a comparison. In: Proceedings of STAIRS, pp. 35–46 (2012)
3. Beckers, S., Vennekens, J.: A general framework for defining and extending actual causation using CP-logic. Int. J. Approx. Reason. **77**, 105–126 (2016)
4. Beckers, S., Vennekens, J.: A principled approach to defining actual causation. Synthese **195**(2), 835–862 (2018). https://doi.org/10.1007/s11229-016-1247-1
5. Bochman, A.: Actual causality in a logical setting. In: IJCAI (2018)
6. Bochman, A., Lifschitz, V.: Pearl's causality in a logical setting. In: Bonet, B., Koenig, S. (eds.) Proceedings of the Twenty-Ninth AAAI Conference on Artificial Intelligence, Austin, Texas, USA, 25–30 January 2015, pp. 1446–1452. AAAI Press (2015). http://www.aaai.org/ocs/index.php/AAAI/AAAI15/paper/view/9686
7. Cabalar, P., Fandinno, J.: Enablers and inhibitors in causal justifications of logic programs. TPLP **17**(1), 49–74 (2017). https://doi.org/10.1017/S1471068416000107
8. Clark, K.L.: Negation as failure. In: Logic and Data Bases, pp. 293–322. Plenum Press (1978)
9. Fenton-Glynn, L.: A proposed probabilistic extension of the Halpern and Pearl definition of 'actual cause'. Br. J. Philos. Sci. **68**(4), 1061–1124 (2015)
10. Gerstenberg, T., Goodman, N.D., Lagnado, D.A., Tenenbaum, J.B.: How, whether, why: causal judgments as counterfactual contrasts. In: Proceedings of the 37th Annual Conference of the Cognitive Science Society, pp. 782–787 (2015)
11. Glymour, C., et al.: Actual causation: a stone soup essay. Synthese **175**(2), 169–192 (2010)
12. Hall, N.: Structural equations and causation. Philos. Stud. **132**(1), 109–136 (2007)
13. Hall, N.: Two concepts of causation. In: Causation and Counterfactuals (2004)
14. Halpern, J.: Actual Causality. MIT Press, Cambridge (2016)
15. Halpern, J., Pearl, J.: Causes and explanations: a structural-model approach. Part I: causes. Br. J. Philos. Sci. **56**, 843–887 (2005)
16. Halpern, J.Y.: Appropriate causal models and the stability of causation. Rew. Symb. Log. **9**(1), 76–102 (2016)
17. Hiddleston, E.: Causal powers. Br. J. Philos. Sci. **56**(1), 27–59 (2005)
18. Hiddleston, E.: A causal theory of counterfactuals. Noûs **39**(4), 632–657 (2005)
19. Hitchcock, C.: The intransitivity of causation revealed in equations and graphs. J. Philos. **98**, 273–299 (2001)
20. Hitchcock, C.: Prevention, preemption, and the principle of sufficient reason. Philos. Rev. **116**(4), 495–532 (2007)
21. Hume, D.: A Treatise of Human Nature. John Noon, London (1739)
22. Lewis, D.: Causation. J. Philos. **70**, 113–126 (1973)
23. Lewis, D.: Postscripts to 'causation'. In: Lewis, D. (ed.) Philosophical Papers, vol. Ii. Oxford University Press (1986)
24. McDermott, M.: Redundant causation. Br. J. Philos. Sci. **XLVI**, 523–544 (1995)
25. Pearl, J.: Causality: Models, Reasoning, and Inference. Cambridge University Press, Cambridge (2000)
26. Schaffer, J.: Causes need not be physically connected to their effects: the case for negative causation. In: Hitchcock, C.R. (ed.) Contemporary Debates in Philosophy of Science, pp. 197–216. Blackwell (2004)

27. Vennekens, J.: Actual causation in CP-logic. Theory Pract. Log. Program. **11**, 647–662 (2011)
28. Vennekens, J., Denecker, M., Bruynooghe, M.: CP-logic: a language of causal probabilistic events and its relation to logic programming. TPLP **9**(3), 245–308 (2009)
29. Weslake, B.: A partial theory of actual causation. Br. J. Philos. Sci. (2015)
30. Woodward, J.: Making Things Happen: A Theory of Causal Explanation. Oxford University Press, Oxford (2003). Oxford scholarship online. https://books.google.be/books?id=LrAbrrj5te8C

Explaining Actual Causation
via Reasoning About Actions and Change

Emily LeBlanc[1]([✉]) [iD], Marcello Balduccini[2] [iD], and Joost Vennekens[3] [iD]

[1] Drexel University, Philadelphia, PA 19104, USA
leblanc@drexel.edu
[2] Saint Joseph's University, Philadelphia, PA 19131, USA
marcello.balduccini@sju.edu
[3] KU Leuven, 2860 Sint-Katelijne-Waver, Belgium
joost.vennekens@cs.kuleuven.be

Abstract. The study of actual causation concerns reasoning about events that have been instrumental in bringing about a particular outcome. Although the subject has long been studied in a number of fields including artificial intelligence, existing approaches have not yet reached the point where their results can be directly applied to explain causation in certain advanced scenarios, such as pin-pointing causes and responsibilities for the behavior of a complex cyber-physical system. We believe that this is due, at least in part, to a lack of distinction between the laws that govern individual states of the world and events whose occurrence cause state to evolve. In this paper, we present a novel approach to reasoning about actual causation that leverages techniques from Reasoning about Actions and Change to identify detailed causal explanations for how an outcome of interest came to be. We also present an implementation of the approach that leverages Answer Set Programming.

Keywords: Causal reasoning ·
Reasoning about Actions and Change ·
Knowledge representation and reasoning

1 Introduction

Actual causation concerns determining how a specified outcome came to be in a given scenario and has long been studied in numerous fields including law, philosophy, and, more recently, computer science and artificial intelligence (AI). Also referred to as *causation in fact*, actual causation is a broad term that encompasses all possible antecedents that have played a meaningful role in producing a consequence [8]. Sophisticated actual causal reasoning has long been prevalent in human society and continues to have an undeniable impact on the advancement of science, technology, medicine, and other important fields. From the development of ancient tools to modern root cause analysis in business and industry, reasoning about causeal influence over time in a sequence of events enables us

© Springer Nature Switzerland AG 2019
F. Calimeri et al. (Eds.): JELIA 2019, LNAI 11468, pp. 231–246, 2019.
https://doi.org/10.1007/978-3-030-19570-0_15

to diagnose the cause of an outcome of interest and gives us insight into how to bring about, or even prevent, similar outcomes in future scenarios.

The ability to automate this kind of reasoning will likely become even more important in the near future due to the ongoing advancement of *deep learning*. Indeed, entrusting important decisions to black-box machine learning algorithms brings with it significant societal risks. To counter these risks, there is a need for Artificial Intelligence systems that are able to explain their behavior in an intuitive way. This is recognized within the scientific community, as witnessed by the emergence of the *explainable AI* domain, and also by the measures enacted by policy makers. For instance, the General Data Protection Regulation (GDPR) has recently come into force in the European Union, a requirement of which is that companies must be able to provide their customers with explanations of algorithmic decisions that affect them.

Explaining the conclusions reached by a single neural network may perhaps not require sophisticated causal reasoning. However, if we consider the behavior of an advanced cyber-physical system, such as a self-driving car, reasoning about causation (e.g. blame or praise) becomes significantly more complex – the car typically contains a large number of software and hardware modules (possibly from different vendors), there may be other cars and pedestrians involved in the scenario of interest, and there may have been wireless communication with other vehicles or a central server, all of which may influence the actions taken by the car's control module over the course of its drive. To reach an intuitively satisfactory explanation of why some outcome of interest came to be in such a domain, the insights that have been produced by the decades-long study of actual causation seem indispensable.

Modern work on actual causation originated in philosophy with the seminal paper by Lewis [27]. His work, like that of other philosophers following him, was of course mainly theoretical and not intended to be put to practical use. The famous Halpern-Pearl (HP) paper [22] initiated interest in this concept within the field of AI and it constitutes a first milestone on the way towards applications of the concept of actual causation. However, neither the HP paper nor the many that have followed it (see also Sect. 6) have yet reached the point where their results could be directly applied, for example, in the context of a self-driving car as sketched above. We believe that this is due, at least in part, to a lack of distinction between the laws that govern individual states of the world and events whose occurrence cause state to evolve.

The goal of this work is to research and investigate the suitability of techniques from Reasoning about Actions and Change (RAC) for reasoning about and explaining actual causation in domains for which the evolution of the state of the world over time plays a critical role. We utilize the action language $\mathcal{AL}$ [2] to define the constructs of our theoretical framework. While our framework is not strongly tied to this choice of representation language, in this paper we adopt $\mathcal{AL}$ because the language enables us to represent the direct and indirect effects of events on the state of the world, as well as the evolution of state over time in response to their occurrence. $\mathcal{AL}$ also lends itself quite naturally to an automated translation to Answer Set Programming [15,17], using which, reasoning tasks of considerable complexity can be specified and automated.

The organization of the paper is as follows. In the following section, we provide background for the formalization of knowledge and events. Next, we present the technical details of the theoretical framework. Following that, we offer an approach to implementing the framework using Answer Set Programming. We then present an empirical study of the implementation's performance on a number of problem instances. Next, we present a summary of related work, and finally we draw conclusions and discuss directions for future research.

2   Preliminaries

For the representation of the domain and of its evolution over time we rely on action language $\mathcal{AL}$ [2]. $\mathcal{AL}$ is centered around a discrete-state-based representation of the evolution of a domain in response to events. The language $\mathcal{AL}$ builds upon an alphabet consisting of a set $\mathcal{F}$ of *fluents* and a set $\mathcal{E}$ of *elementary events*[1]. Fluents are boolean properties of the domain, whose truth value may change over time. A *(fluent) literal* is a fluent f or its negation $\neg f$. Additionally, we define $\overline{f} = \neg f$ and $\overline{\neg f} = f$. If $f \in \sigma$, we say that f *holds* in σ. A single elementary event is denoted by its element e in $\mathcal{E}$. A *compound event* is a set of elementary events $\epsilon = \{e_1, \ldots, e_n\}$. A statement of the form

$$e \text{ causes } l_0 \text{ if } l_1, \ldots, l_n \tag{1}$$

is a called a *dynamic (causal) law*. Intuitively, a law of form (1) says that if elementary event e[2] occurs in a state where literals $l_1, \ldots, l_n$ hold, then literal l_0 will hold in the next state. A statement

$$l_0 \text{ if } l_1, \ldots, l_n \tag{2}$$

is called a *state constraint* and says that in any state in which literals $l_1, \ldots, l_n$ hold, l_0 also holds. We say that l_0 is the *consequence* of the law. A statement of form (2) allows for an elegant and concise representation of *indirect effects* of events which enhances the expressive power of the language. Finally, a statement of the form

$$e \text{ impossible\_if } l_1, \ldots, l_n \tag{3}$$

is called an *executability condition* and states that an elementary event e cannot occur when $l_1, \ldots, l_n$ hold. A set of statements of $\mathcal{AL}$ is called an *action description*.

A set S of literals is *closed under a state constraint* (2) if $\{l_1, \ldots, l_n\} \not\subseteq S$ or $l_0 \in S$. Set S is *consistent* if, for every $f \in \mathcal{F}$, at most one of $\{f, \neg f\}$ is

---

[1] For convenience and compatibility with the terminology from RAC, in this paper we use *action* and *event* as synonyms.

[2] We focus on elementary actions for simplicity of presentation. It is straightforward to expand the statements to allow non-elementary actions.

in S. It is *complete* if at least one of $\{f, \neg f\}$ is in S. A *state* σ of an action description AD is a complete and consistent set of fluent literals closed under the state constraints of AD.

Given an elementary event e and a state σ, the set of *(direct) effects of e in σ*, denoted by $E(e, \sigma)$, is the set that contains a literal l_0 for every dynamic law (1) such that $\{l_1, \ldots, l_n\} \subseteq \sigma$. Given a compound event $\epsilon = \{e_1, \ldots, e_n\}$, the set of direct effects of ϵ in σ, therefore, is given by $E(\epsilon, \sigma) = E(e_1, \sigma) \cup \ldots \cup E(e_n, \sigma)$. Given a set S of literals and a set Z of state constraints, the *set $Cn_Z(S)$ of consequences of S under Z* is the smallest set of literals that contains S and is closed under every state constraint in Z. Finally, an event e is *non-executable* in a state σ if there exists an executability condition (3) such that $\{l_1, \ldots, l_n\} \subseteq \sigma$. Otherwise, the event is *executable*[3] in σ.

The semantics of an action description AD is defined by its *transition diagram* $\tau(AD)$, a directed graph $\langle N, A \rangle$ such that N is the collection of all states of AD; A is the set of all triples $\langle \sigma, \epsilon, \sigma' \rangle$ where σ, σ' are states, ϵ is an event executable in σ, and σ' satisfies the *successor state equation*:

$$\sigma' = Cn_Z(E(\epsilon, \sigma) \cup (\sigma \cap \sigma')) \tag{4}$$

where Z is the set of all state constraints of AD.

The argument of Cn_Z in (4) is the union of the set of direct effects $E(e, \sigma)$ for all $e \in \epsilon$ with the set $\sigma \cap \sigma'$ of the literals "preserved by inertia". The application of Cn_Z adds the "indirect effects" to this union. A triple $\langle \sigma, \epsilon, \sigma' \rangle \in E$ is called a *transition* of $\tau(AD)$ and σ' is a *successor state of* σ (under ϵ). A sequence $\langle \sigma_1, \epsilon_1, \sigma_2, \ldots, \epsilon_k, \sigma_{k+1} \rangle$ is a *path of* $\tau(AD)$ of length k if every $\langle \sigma_i, \epsilon_i, \sigma_{i+1} \rangle$ is a transition in $\tau(AD)$. We denote the *initial state* of a path ρ by σ_1.

3   Theoretical Framework

In this section we present the constructs of the causal reasoning framework and use them to characterize causal explanations. We then apply the framework to a variant of the well-known Yale Shooting Problem [23].

3.1   Definitions

A *problem* is a tuple $\psi = \langle \theta, \rho, AD \rangle$ where θ is a consistent set of literals we want to explain called an *outcome* and ρ is a path of $\tau(AD)$. We will leverage the framework to identify *causal explanations* for a problem ψ. The first step to explain how an outcome θ came to be in path ρ is to identify the *transition states* of θ in ρ. A transition state indicates the "appearance" of θ in the ρ.

Definition 1. *Given a problem $\psi = \langle \theta, \rho, AD \rangle$, a state σ_j in ρ is a transition state of θ if $\theta \not\subseteq \sigma_{j-1}$ and $\theta \subseteq \sigma_j$.*

---

[3] Note that an event may occur without having an effect on the state of the world, commonly referred to in the literature as a NOP action.

We denote by $T(\psi) = \{\sigma_{j_1}, \ldots, \sigma_{j_m}\}$ the set of transition states with respect to the problem ψ. Intuitively, state σ_j is a transition state of θ if the outcome is satisfied in σ_j but not in the immediately previous state σ_{j-1}. A *causing compound event* ϵ_i of literal l for a transition state σ_j of θ is the most recent compound event to σ_j to result in a transition state σ_{i+1} in ρ.

Definition 2. *Given a problem* $\psi = \langle \theta, \rho, AD \rangle$, *a state* σ_j *in* ρ, *and a literal* $l \in \sigma_j$, ϵ_i *is a causing compound event of* l *holding in* σ_j *if* σ_{i+1} *is a transition state of* $\{l\}$ *in* ρ, $i < j$, *and* $j - (i+1)$ *is minimal.*

Both direct and indirect causes of a literal l holding in a given state σ_j are members of the causing compound event ϵ_i of l holding in σ_j. A *direct cause* $e \in \epsilon_i$ of l is an elementary event in ϵ_i whose occurrence causes l to hold in the subsequent state.

Definition 3. *Given a problem* $\psi = \langle \theta, \rho, AD \rangle$, *a literal* $l \in \sigma_j$ *of* ρ, *and a causing compound event* ϵ_i *of* l, *the elementary event* $e' \in \epsilon_i$ *is a direct cause of* l *for* σ_j *if* l *is in the set* $E(e', \sigma_i)$.

We denote by $D(\sigma_j)$ the set containing a tuple $\langle \epsilon_i, e', l \rangle$ for every elementary event e' in each ϵ_i such that e' is a direct cause of a literal $l \in \theta$ for σ_j. Note that direct cause is defined so that multiple events in ϵ_i can be direct causes as long as l is in the corresponding sets of direct effects. An *indirect cause* of literal l is a subset[4] of a causing compound event of l.

Definition 4. *Given a problem* $\psi = \langle \theta, \rho, AD \rangle$, *state* σ_j *in* ρ, *a literal* $l \in \sigma_j$, *and a causing compound event* ϵ_i *of* l, *the compound event* $\epsilon' \subseteq \epsilon_i$ *is an indirect cause of* l *for* σ_j *if it is a smallest subset of* ϵ_i *such that the following conditions are satisfied:*

1. $l \notin E(\epsilon', \sigma_i)$
2. *There exists a transition* $t = \langle \sigma_i, \epsilon', \sigma'_{i+i} \rangle$ *in* $\tau(AD)$ *such that* σ'_{i+1} *is a transition state of* $\{l\}$ *in* t

We denote by $I(\sigma_j)$ a set containing a tuple $\langle \epsilon_i, \epsilon', l \rangle$ for every compound event ϵ' in every ϵ_i in ρ such that ϵ' is a indirect cause of l for σ_j in ρ.

Condition 1 ensures that l is not a direct effect of ϵ'. Condition 2 states that if ϵ' were to hypothetically occur by itself in state σ_i, then it would have caused l. In other words, we know that l does not hold in σ_i and that l is not a direct effect of ϵ'. Therefore, if ϵ' occurs by itself and l holds in the resulting state σ'_{i+1}, then it must be the case that l is an indirect effect of ϵ'. Finally, we require that ϵ' is a *smallest* subset of ϵ_i because we want to rule out any subsets including extraneous elementary events. For example, if ϵ' contains three events and only two are needed to indirectly cause l, then there would indeed

---

[4] In $\mathcal{AL}$, it is possible that a set of literals must hold simultaneously in order to cause a literal to hold. Consider $AD = \{a \textbf{ causes } b; c \textbf{ causes } d; e \textbf{ if } b, d\}$ of a causing compound event ϵ_i of l.

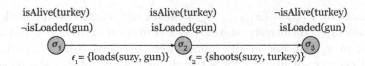

isAlive(turkey)   isAlive(turkey)   ¬isAlive(turkey)
¬isLoaded(gun)   isLoaded(gun)   isLoaded(gun)

σ_1 —— ϵ_1 = {loads(suzy, gun)} —— σ_2 —— ϵ_2 = {shoots(suzy, turkey)} —— σ_3

Fig. 1. Path ρ_Y is a representation of the Yale shooting scenario.

be transition $t = \langle \sigma_i, \epsilon', \sigma'_{i+1} \rangle$ in $\tau(AD)$ as required by condition 2. However, we want subsets containing *only* those events that have contributed to causing l.

By now we have defined direct and indirect causation of literals, however, these definitions alone do not provide a comprehensive explanation for an appearance of θ in ρ. Therefore, we define a *causal explanation*, which is a tuple containing the sets of direct and indirect causes of literals in θ in their respective transition state, given by $D(\sigma_j)$ and $I(\sigma_j)$.

Definition 5. *Given a problem $\psi = \langle \theta, \rho, AD \rangle$, a path $\rho \in \tau(AD)$, and a transition state σ_j of θ in ρ, a causal explanation of θ being satisfied in σ_j in path ρ is the tuple $\mathcal{C}(\psi, \sigma_j) = \langle D(\sigma_j), I(\sigma_j) \rangle$.*

Literals that were not caused by any event in ρ are omitted from the causal explanation. This choice is motivated by the idea that no cause can be identified for literals that were not caused.

3.2   Yale Shooting Problem

Here we use the framework defined above to solve a variant of the well-known Yale shooting problem (YSP) from [23]. The scenario is as follows:

Shooting a turkey with a loaded gun will kill it. Suzy shoots the turkey. What is the cause of the turkey's death?

The YSP problem is formalized by $\Psi_Y = \langle \theta_Y, v_Y, AD_Y \rangle$. The outcome of interest is $\theta_Y = \{\neg isAlive(turkey)\}$. The sequence of events is given by $v_Y = \{\epsilon_1, \epsilon_2\}$ where $\epsilon_1 = \{loads(suzy, gun)\}$ and $\epsilon_2 = \{shoots(suzy, turkey)\}$. The action description AD_Y characterizes the events of the YSP domain:

$$\left\{ \begin{array}{ll} shoots(X, turkey) \textbf{ causes } \neg isAlive(turkey) \textbf{ if } isAlive(turkey) & \text{(a)} \\ shoots(X, turkey) \textbf{ impossible\_if } \neg isLoaded(gun) & \text{(b)} \\ loads(X, gun) \textbf{ causes } isLoaded(gun) \textbf{ if } \neg isLoaded(gun) & \text{(c)} \end{array} \right. \quad (5)$$

Laws (5a) and (5c) are straightforward dynamic laws describing the effects of the events in the YSP domain. Law (5b) states that the turkey cannot be shot if the gun is not loaded. Consider the path ρ_Y, represented in Fig. 1. In the initial state of ρ_Y, the turkey is alive, and the turkey is dead in the final state of the path after the occurrence of $\epsilon_1 = \{loads(suzy, gun)\}$ and $\epsilon_2 = \{shoots(suzy, turkey)\}$.

It is straightforward to verify for the problem $\psi_Y = \langle \theta_Y, \rho_Y, AD_Y \rangle$ that σ_3 is the only transition state of θ_Y and that ϵ_2 is the causing compound event of $\neg isAlive(turkey)$. The elementary event $shoots(suzy, turkey)$ in ϵ_2 is a direct cause of $\neg isAlive(turkey)$ as per rule (5a). The causal explanation for Ψ_Y is therefore $C(\Psi_Y, \sigma_3) = \langle \{\langle \epsilon_2, shoots(suzy, turkey), \neg isAlive(turkey)\rangle\}, \{\} \rangle$. We have used the framework to identify only Suzy's shooting of the turkey as a direct cause of its death, which corresponds to the intuition about the problem. Moreover, we did not any identify indirect causes of the turkey's death, denoted in the explanation by the empty set for $I(\sigma_3)$. If we want to know why the gun was loaded so that Suzy could kill the turkey, we use rule (5b) to formulate the subproblem $\psi'_Y = \langle \{isLoaded(gun)\}, \rho_Y, AD_Y \rangle$ to determine that $loads(suzy, gun)$ directly caused the gun to be loaded. Appendix 2.1 of [26] of this paper presents a novel adaptation of YSP to demonstrate explaining the indirect causation of the turkey's death. Note that it is straightforward to represent and reason about other examples from the causality literature, such as the bottle-shattering example from [18].

4   ASP Implementation of the Framework

In this section, we present an approach to computing causal explanations via Answer Set Programming (ASP) [16, 18], a form of declarative programming that is useful in knowledge-intensive applications. In the ASP methodology, problem-solving tasks are reduced to computing answer sets of suitable logic programs. As demonstrated by a substantial body of literature (see, e.g., [1]), $\mathcal{AL}$ lends itself quite naturally to an automated translation to Answer Set Programming [15, 17], using which, reasoning tasks of considerable complexity can be specified and executed (see, e.g., [9, 11, 12]). As such, ASP is well suited to the task of computing causal explanations. We begin this section with a discussion of the syntax and semantics of Answer Set Programming.

4.1   Answer Set Programming

Let Σ be a signature containing constant, function and predicate symbols. Terms and atoms are formed as in first-order logic. A *literal* is an atom a or its strong negation $\neg a$. Literals are combined to form rules that represent both domain knowledge and events in our approach. A *rule* in ASP is a statement of the form:

$$h \leftarrow l_1, \ldots, l_m, \text{not } l_{m+1}, \ldots, \text{not } l_n$$

where h_i's (the head) and l_i's (the body) are literals and *not* is the so-called *default negation*. Intuitively, the meaning of default negation is the following: "if you believe $\{l_1, \ldots, l_m\}$ and have no reason to believe $\{l_{m+1}, \ldots, l_n\}$, then you must believe h". An ASP rule with an empty body is called a fact. In writing facts, the $\leftarrow$ connective is dropped. Rules of the form $\perp \leftarrow l_1, \ldots, \text{not } l_n$ are abbreviated $\leftarrow l_1, \ldots, \text{not } l_n$, and called *constraints*, intuitively meaning that $\{l_1, \ldots, \text{not } l_n\}$ must not be satisfied. A rule with variables (denoted by an uppercase initial) is interpreted as a shorthand for the set of rules obtained by replacing the variables with all possible variable-free terms. A *program* Π is a set of rules over Σ.

A consistent set S of domain literals is closed under a rule if $h \in S$ whenever $\{l_1, \ldots, l_m\} \subseteq S$ and $\{l_{m+1}, \ldots, l_n\} \cap S = \emptyset$. Set S is an answer set of a *not*-free program Π if S is the minimal set closed under its rules. The reduct, Π^S, of a program Π w.r.t. S is obtained from Π by removing every rule containing an expression "not l" s.t. $l \in S$ and by removing every other occurrence of not l. Finally, set S is an answer set of a program Π if S is the answer set of Π^S.

For a convenient representation of choices, in this paper we also use *constraint literals*, which are expressions of the form $m\{l_1, l_2, \ldots, l_k\}n$, where m, n are arithmetic expressions and l_i's are basic literals. A constraint literal is satisfied w.r.t. S whenever $m \leq |\{l_1, \ldots, l_k\} \cap S| \leq n$. Constraint literals are especially useful to reason about available choices. For example, a rule $1\{p, q, r\}1$. intuitively states that exactly one of $\{p, q, r\}$ should occur in every answer set.

4.2 Framework Implementation

We begin our approach to computing causal explanations by encoding the elements of a problem $\Psi = \langle \theta, \rho, AD \rangle$.

Problem Translation. For an outcome θ, set $\alpha(\theta)$ contains a fact $outcome(l, theta)$ as well as facts $inOutcome(l, theta)$, $olit(l)$, and $inOutcome$ $(l, olit(l))$ for every $l \in \theta$. We use the $olit(l)$ notation to denote the outcome coinciding with the singleton $\{l\}$.

The elements of a path ρ are given by the sets $\alpha(\rho_1)$, $\alpha(\rho_2)$, and $\alpha(\rho_3)$. The set $\alpha(\rho_1)$ contains a fact $occurs(e, i)$ for every $e \in \epsilon_i$ and a fact $holds(l, i)$ for each literal $l \in \sigma_i$ where $1 < i < k + 1$. The set also contains facts $event(e)$ and $fluent(f)$ for each $e \in \mathcal{E}$ and $f \in \mathcal{F}$, respectively. Next, the set $\alpha(\rho_2)$ contains the facts $subset(\lambda)$, where λ is a unique identifier for C, and $inSubset(e, \lambda)$ for every $e \in C$ for every subset C of $\mathcal{E}$. The subsets of $\mathcal{E}$ will be useful later to identify indirect causation, and are included as elements of ρ because they are specific to the path. The set $\alpha(\rho_3)$ characterizes the transitions of ρ as sequence of steps.

We refer to the steps of a path as *concrete steps*, or *c-steps*, to differentiate them from *hypothetical steps*, which will be discussed later in connection with indirect causes. For related reasons, we also represent the sequence of c-steps $cstep(1), cstep(2), \ldots, cstep(k + 1)$, where k is the length of the path, by means of the rule:

$$next(I1, I2) \leftarrow \quad cstep(I1), \ cstep(I2), \ I2 = I1 + 1. \tag{6}$$

Finally, $\alpha(\rho_3)$ includes the rule $step(I) \leftarrow cstep(I)$ which states that c-steps are types of steps. The set $\alpha(\rho) = \{\alpha(\rho_1) \cup \alpha(\rho_2) \cup \alpha(\rho_3)\}$ represents the path ρ.

We translate laws of $\mathcal{AL}$ to ASP as follows. For dynamic laws, the translation $\alpha(e \text{ causes } l_0 \text{ if } l_1, \ldots, l_n)$ is the collection of atoms $d\_law(d)$, $head(d, l_0)$, $event(d, e)$, $prec(d, 1, l_1), \ldots, prec(d, n, l_n)$, and $prec(d, n + 1, nil)$. For state constraints, $\alpha(l_0 \text{ if } l_1, \ldots, l_n)$ is the collection of atoms $s\_law(s)$, $head(s, l_0)$, $prec(s, 1, l_1), \ldots, prec(s, n, l_n)$, and $prec(s, n+1, nil)$. Finally, for executability conditions, $\alpha(e \text{ impossible\_if } l_1, \ldots, l_n)$ is the collection of atoms $i\_law(\iota)$, $event(\iota, e)$, $prec(\iota, 1, l_1), \ldots, prec(\iota, n, l_n)$, and $prec(\iota, n+1, nil)$.

The semantics of $\mathcal{AL}$ are captured by the rules of program Π, an approach is adapted from [1]. The program describes the effects of dynamic laws and state constraints and enforces executability conditions. It also defines when the preconditions of a translated law are satisfied (i.e. $prec(X, Y)$ atoms from the translation of $\mathcal{AL}$ laws to ASP), denoted by the predicate $prec_h(R, I)$ where R is the identifier of a translated $\mathcal{AL}$ law and I is a step in the ASP representation of ρ[5]. Finally, Π contains rules describing inertia [24] (i.e. things usually stay as they are) and consistency. See Appendix 1.2 of [26] for an expanded description of Π and a full listing of its rules.

Transition and Causing Steps. The rules in set Π_{σ_j} characterize a transition state σ_j of θ in path ρ. We use the term *transition step* in accordance with our representation of states in ρ as c-steps, a type of step.

$$
\Pi_{\sigma_j}
\begin{cases}
transitionStep(OC, J2) \leftarrow & step(J1), step(J2), next(J1, J2), \text{(a)} \\
 & next(J1, J2), outcome(OC), \\
 & ocSat(OC, J2), \neg ocSat(OC, J1). \\
\neg ocSat(OC, J) \leftarrow & step(J), inOutcome(OC, L), \text{(b)} \\
 & not\ holds(L, J). \\
ocSat(OC, J) \leftarrow & step(J), not\ \neg ocSat(OC, J). \text{(c)}
\end{cases}
\tag{7}
$$

Rule (7a) states that $J2$ is a transition step of outcome OC if it is satisfied in step $J2$ and not $J1$. (7b) and (7c) tell us when OC is or is not satisfied in a given step J, respectively. Note that transition steps leverage as *steps* rather than c-steps, allowing flexibility to reason about other types. The rules of Π_{ϵ_i} describe causing steps of a literal holding at step I.

$$
\Pi_{\epsilon_i}
\begin{cases}
possCausingStep(I, L, J) \leftarrow & cstep(I), cstep(J), I < J, \text{(a)} \\
 & transitionStep(olit(L), I+1), \\
 & transitionStep(theta, J). \\
\neg causingStep(I, L, J) \leftarrow & possCausingStep(I, L, J), \text{(b)} \\
 & possCausingStep(I', L, J), \\
 & I < I', I' < J. \\
causingStep(I, L, J) \leftarrow & possCausingStep(I, L, J), \text{(c)} \\
 & not\ \neg causingStep(I, L, J).
\end{cases}
\tag{8}
$$

Rule (8a) states that a c-step I is a *possible* causing step of L holding in J if it occurs prior to c-step J, $I+1$ is a transition step of $outcome(olit(L))$, and J is a transition step for the main outcome *theta*. It is easy to see that rule (8b) corresponds to the conditions of Definition 2 for compound causing events. Rule

---

[5] We will use the predicate $prec_h$ when computing both direct and indirect causes.

(8b) corresponds to condition 3 of Definition 2 by stating that c-step I cannot be a causing step of J if there is another possible causing step I' that closer to J. Again we can use inequalities to determine relative position, this time for two earlier c-steps. Finally, (8c) is a straightforward rule stating that a possible causing step I of L in c-step J is a causing step if we have no reason to believe that it is *not* a causing step.

Direct and Indirect Causes. Here we present ASP translations of the definitions of direct and indirect cause. The rules of Π_{D_θ} describe when an event that occurred at causing step I has directly caused L to hold in c-step I.

$$\Pi_{D_\theta} \begin{cases} directEffect(L,E,I) \leftarrow & cstep(I), d\_law(D), event(D,E), \quad \text{(a)} \\ & occurs(E,I), prec\_h(D,I), head(D,L). \\ directCause(E,I,L,J) \leftarrow & causingStep(I,L,J), \quad \text{(b)} \\ & directEffect(L,E,I). \end{cases} \quad (9)$$

Rule (9a) states that L is a direct effect of event E occurring at I when all of the preconditions of the dynamic law D are satisfied at I. Rule (9b) states that E occurring at I is a direct cause of L holding at c-step J if I is a causing step of L in J and L is a direct effect of E as per rule (9a).

Finally, the program Π_{I_θ} contains rules used to identify indirect causation. In the interest of space, we favor discussing the approach at a high level, presenting only the most significant rules of the program to facilitate the presentation. However, the full specification of Π_{I_θ} is given in Appendix 1.3 of [26]. Given a causing step I, we want to know if any subset of events that occurred at I caused the literal under consideration to hold indirectly. Program Π_{I_θ} states that an event subset C (i.e. $subset(C)$) occurring at step I is a possible indirect cause of L holding at step J if I is a causing step for L and we have no reason to believe that the event(s) in C (i.e. all $inSubset(E,C)$ atoms) caused L directly.

Recall that condition 2 of Definition 4 states that if $\epsilon' \in \epsilon_i$ is an indirect cause of l, then a transition t' must exist in $\tau(AD)$ such that if ϵ' occurring by itself in σ_i results in a transition step of $\{l\}$. Given a possible indirect causing subset C occurring at step I, we accomplish this reasoning in ASP by creating a sequence of two hypothetical steps, given by $hstep(\mu(C,I))$ and $hstep(\mu'(C,I))$, whose initial state is identical to I and testing to see if L holds after the occurrence of C's events. Once C has passed the hypothetical reasoning step, we are ready to determine indirect causation. With the use of a rule whose head $\neg smallest(C,L,I)$ becomes true when it is proven that C is a smallest possibly indirectly causing subset, the following rule describes when a subset C is an actual cause:

$$indirectCause(C,I,L,J) \leftarrow hypotheticalPass(C,I,L,J), \quad (10)$$
$$not \ \neg smallest(C,L,I).$$

In short, C occurring at c-step I is an indirect cause of L holding at c-step J if C passes the hypothetical step and there is no reason to believe that it is not a smallest possible causing subset of L at I. Note that this implementation returns information about direct and indirect causes of literals of translated θ, but no comprehensive causal explanation. A causal explanation can be easily extracted from an answer set through the literals formed by relations $directCause(E, I, L, J)$ and $indirectCause(C, I, L, J)$. See Appendices 2.2 and 2.3 [26] for ASP encodings of the direct and indirect Yale Shooting Problem adaptations from Sect. 3.

5 Empirical Study of the Implementation

Although an exhaustive experimental evaluation is beyond the scope of this paper, we present results from a preliminary evaluation aiming to assess the feasibility of the approach. To the best of our knowledge, there is no established set of benchmarks for the type of reasoning presented in this paper and so we have generated a set of novel problem instances that allow us to evaluate the framework's performance with respect to a number of problem features.

Problem instances are defined as follows. Given a number of literals L to explain and an allowed number of events per step EPS, the resulting problem instance's outcome contains L literals caused by E events distributed over $S = \lceil \frac{L}{E} \rceil$ steps of the instance's path. The transition step of the outcome is always $S + 1$. When $S = 1$, we say that the causes are *fully concurrent*. When $S = L$, on the other hand, we say that the causes occur in a *strict sequence*. We use the abbreviations FCDC and FCIC to denote full concurrency for direct causation and indirect causation, respectively. Similarly, we use SSDC and SSIC to denote strict sequences for direct and indirect causation.

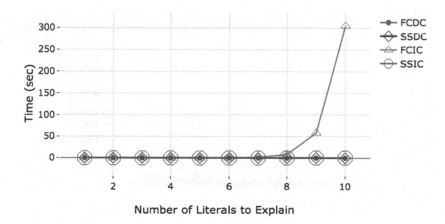

Fig. 2. Relating the explanation of literals and time (direct and indirect causation).

Explaining Cases of Full Concurrency and Strict Sequences. We first compared runtime needed to compute full concurrency and strict sequences for direct and indirect causes. In this experiment, we varied L from 1 to 10, allowed 10 events per step (EPS) for the fully concurrent cases, and allowed 1 event per step for the strict sequence cases.

The computation times are shown in Fig. 2. FCIC is the most challenging type of problem, taking approximately 300 s to compute 10 simultaneous indirect causes, overtaking computation of the other cases by a factor[6] of approximately 450. This can be explained by noticing that increasing the number of events occurring in a single step requires the program to perform exhaustive hypothetical reasoning for more and more subsets. Note that at 10 literals to explain there is little discernible difference in the time needed to compute explanations for SSDC, FCDC, and SSIC cases.

We also measured the framework's performance on greater values of L (i.e. larger outcomes). At 50 literals to explain, we found that SSIC overtakes both FCDC and SSDC by a factor of 240, with SSIC taking approximately 190 s and SSDC taking approximately 0.8 s (see Appendix 3 Fig. 2 of [26]). A possible explanation for this is that that the program must initially rule out the possibility that a subset is a direct cause and *then* perform the hypothetical step to confirm indirect causation.

Extending Fully Concurrent Causes Towards a Strict Sequence. Note that in the previous experiment, we were unable to see a significant difference in performance in direct cases for 50 literals. Here, we explore how L causes distributed over $\lceil \frac{L}{EPS} \rceil$ steps affects the performance of the framework for a subset of values for E between 1 and L for direct causes and indirect causes. In the direct causation case, we varied L between 1 and 50 and allowed EPS to take on the values between 1 and 50. The times for this experiment are shown in Fig. 3. SSDC, or $EPS = 1$, is the most challenging problem, overtaking $EPS = 2$

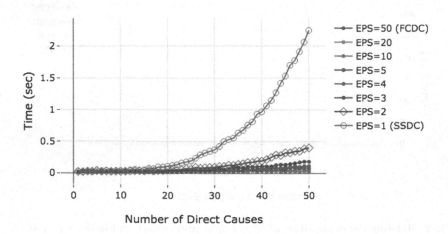

Fig. 3. Varying the number of events per step (EPS) for direct causes.

---

[6] The strict sequence indirect cause (SSIC) case takes the second to longest time to explain 10 literals at 0.67 s.

by a factor[7] of approximately 6.25. This can be explained by the fact that the program has to reason backward over the path to identify the causing event for all 50 literals in the outcome. In the FCIC case, the program only reasons back over one step for each literal. For the remaining values of $EPS > 2$, explaining 50 literals takes less than 0.25 s to compute.

In the case of indirect causation, we varied both L and EPS between 1 and 10. As we saw in Fig. 2, FCIC for 10 indirect causes takes approximately 300 s to compute (see Appendix 3 Fig. 3 of [26]). We observed that FCIC overtakes the second longest computation by a factor of approximately 2.6. While the computation time is large for $EPS = 8, 9, 10$, Fig. 3 shows little difference in performance for smaller values of EPS. In order to gain insight into the relationships among times to compute explanations for smaller values of EPS, Fig. 4 in Appendix 3 of [26] shows the performance for $EPS \leq 9$, showing that explaining 10 literals that were caused over $\lceil 10/9 \rceil = 2$ steps takes approximately 100 s, overtaking $EPS = 8$ by a factor of 5. For smaller values of EPS, the time is at most 5 s.

Overall Considerations. A comprehensive evaluation is needed before general claims can be made, but we believe these experiments show that the approach is promising. As we have already stated, the most challenging problem appears to be fully concurrent indirect causes due to an increasing number of event subsets to reason about for each literal that must be explained. However, when the value of EPS is closer to 1 for the indirect case, the literals can be explained in under 5 s. The best performance is seen for larger values of EPS nearing L for direct causation, requiring on average less than half a second to explain 50 directly caused literals.

6   Overview of Related Work

Attempts to mathematically characterize actual causation have largely pursued counterfactual analysis of structural equations [20,22,29,33], neuron diagrams [19], and other logical formalisms [5,25]. Counterfactual accounts of actual causation are typically inspired by the human intuition that if X caused Y, then not Y if not X [27]. It has been widely documented, however, that the counterfactual criteria alone is problematic and fails to recognize causation in a number of common cases such as overdetermination, preemption, and joint causation [10,17,28]. In cases of overdetermination, for example, removing one of the multiple sufficient causes from the scenario will not prevent the outcome from occurring. Therefore, if X and Y are both sufficient to cause Z, the counterfactual definition of cause may not identify X or Y as an actual cause because removing one or the other will not prevent Z. Similarly, it is straightforward to verify that the counterfactual approach may fail to identify causation in cases of preemption and joint causation.

---

[7] The SSDC case takes the second longest time to explain 50 literals at approximately 0.4 s.

More recent approaches such as [21,25,32] have addressed some of the short-comings associated with the counterfacual criterion by modifying the existing definitions of actual cause or by modeling change over time with some improved results. However, there is still no widely agreed upon counterfactual definition of actual cause in spite of a considerably large body of work aiming to find one. This suggests that alternate approaches should be explored to explain why an outcome of interest has come to be in a scenario.

In [4], the authors depart from the counterfactual approach, using a similar insight to our own that actual causation can be determined by inspecting a specific scenario rather than hypothesizing strictly about counterfactual worlds. Although the conceptual approach is similar, the technical approaches differ significantly. Leveraging the Situation Calculus (SC) to formalize knowledge, the approach identifies a sequence of event(s) that caused an SC formula ϕ to become true in a scenario. Our framework is capable of explaining a set of causal explanations for an outcome identifying not only causing events (or a sequence of events using multiple problems on the same path), but details about *how* each event influenced the outcome. There are also ramifications due to the choices for the formalization of the domain. Compared to $\mathcal{AL}$ formalizations, SC formalizations incur limitations when it comes to the representations of indirect effects of actions, which play an important role in our work, and the elaboration tolerance of the formalization. Additionally, SC relies on First-Order Logic, while $\mathcal{AL}$ features an independent and arguably simpler semantics.

A number of other interesting approaches exist linking causality and logic programming (LP) with varying goals (e.g. encoding the HP approach for LP [3,6], explaining answer sets of ASP programs [7,31], reasoning about causal information [13,14,30]). Research relating these topics is steadily advancing, prompting interdisciplinary discussion and exploration of the role and placement of causal reasoning and LP in the landscape of modern computer theory and the software industry.

7   Conclusions and Future Work

The aim of the work presented here is to lay the foundations of actual causal explanation from a representation and reasoning standpoint, leveraging techniques from Reasoning about Actions and Change to represent scenarios and identify actual causal explanations for an outcome of interest. We believe that we have demonstrated that our approach to representing and reasoning about actual causation is promising and practically feasible. In addition to further evaluating the implementation, an important next step will be to conduct a comparative analysis with related approaches to reasoning about actual causation. Another open problem is to investigate extensions of the framework to support the representation of time-delayed effects, probabilities, and triggered events.

References

1. Balduccini, M., Gelfond, M.: Diagnostic reasoning with A-Prolog. J. Theory Pract. Log. Program. (TPLP) **3**(4–5), 425–461 (2003)
2. Baral, C., Gelfond, M.: Reasoning agents in dynamic domains. In: Minker, J. (ed.) Logic-Based Artificial Intelligence. SECS, vol. 597, pp. 257–279. Springer, Boston (2000). https://doi.org/10.1007/978-1-4615-1567-8_12
3. Baral, C., Hunsaker, M.: Using the probabilistic logic programming language P-log for causal and counterfactual reasoning and non-naive conditioning. In: IJCAI, pp. 243–249 (2007)
4. Batusov, V., Soutchanski, M.: Situation calculus semantics for actual causality. In: 13th International Symposium on Commonsense Reasoning, vol. 6, University College London, UK, Monday, November 2017
5. Beckers, S., Vennekens, J.: A general framework for defining and extending actual causation using CP-logic. Int. J. Approximate Reasoning **77**, 105–126 (2016)
6. Bochman, A., Lifschitz, V.: Pearl's causality in a logical setting. In: AAAI, pp. 1446–1452 (2015)
7. Cabalar, P., Fandinno, J., Fink, M.: Causal graph justifications of logic programs. Theory Pract. Log. Program. **14**(4–5), 603–618 (2014)
8. Carpenter, C.E.: Concurrent causation. Univ. Pennsylvania Law Rev. Am. Law Reg. **83**(8), 941–952 (1935)
9. Dix, J., Kuter, U., Nau, D.: Planning in answer set programming using ordered task decomposition. In: Günter, A., Kruse, R., Neumann, B. (eds.) KI 2003. LNCS (LNAI), vol. 2821, pp. 490–504. Springer, Heidelberg (2003). https://doi.org/10.1007/978-3-540-39451-8_36
10. Dobbs, D.B.: Rethinking actual causation in tort law (2017)
11. Eiter, T., Faber, W., Leone, N., Pfeifer, G., Polleres, A.: Answer set planning under action costs. J. Artif. Intell. Res. **19**, 25–71 (2003)
12. Erdem, E., Gelfond, M., Leone, N.: Applications of answer set programming. AI Mag. **37**(3), 53–63 (2016)
13. Fandinno, J.: Deriving conclusions from non-monotonic cause-effect relations. Theory Pract. Log. Program. **16**(5–6), 670–687 (2016)
14. Fandinno, J.: Towards deriving conclusions from cause-effect relations. Fundamenta Informaticae **147**(1), 93–131 (2016)
15. Gelfond, M., Lifschitz, V.: The stable model semantics for logic programming. In: ICLP/SLP, vol. 88, pp. 1070–1080 (1988)
16. Gelfond, M., Lifschitz, V.: Classical negation in logic programs and disjunctive databases. New Gener. Comput. **9**, 365–385 (1991)
17. Glymour, C., Danks, D.: Actual causation: a stone soup essay. Synthese **175**(2), 169–192 (2010)
18. Hall, N.: Two concepts of causation. In: Causation and counterfactuals, pp. 225–276 (2004)
19. Hall, N.: Structural equations and causation. Philos. Stud. **132**(1), 109–136 (2007)
20. Halpern, J.Y.: Axiomatizing causal reasoning. J. Artif. Intell. Res. **12**, 317–337 (2000)
21. Halpern, J.Y.: Actual Causality. MIT Press, Cambridge (2016)
22. Halpern, J.Y., Pearl, J.: Causes and explanations: a structural-model approach. part I: causes. Br. J. Philos. Sci. **56**(4), 843–887 (2005)
23. Hanks, S., McDermott, D.: Nonmonotonic logic and temporal projection. Artif. intell. **33**(3), 379–412 (1987)

24. Hayes, P.J., McCarthy, J.: Some philosophical problems from the standpoint of artificial intelligence. In: Meltzer, B., Michie, D. (eds.) Machine Intelligence, vol. 4, pp. 463–502. Edinburgh University Press, Edinburgh (1969)
25. Hopkins, M., Pearl, J.: Causality and counterfactuals in the situation calculus. J. Log. Comput. **17**(5), 939–953 (2007)
26. LeBlanc, E., Balduccini, M., Vennekens, J.: Appendices of explaining actual causation via reasoning about actions and change, JELIA (2019). http://eleblanc.ai/files/lbv-jelia2019-appendices.pdf
27. Lewis, D.: Causation. J. Philos. **70**(17), 556–567 (1973)
28. Menzies, P.: Counterfactual theories of causation. The Stanford Encyclopedia of Philosophy (2001)
29. Pearl, J.: On the definition of actual cause. Technical report, University of California (1998)
30. Pereira, L.M., Saptawijaya, A.: Counterfactuals, logic programming and agent morality. In: Urbaniak, R., Payette, G. (eds.) Applications of Formal Philosophy: The Road Less Travelled. LARI, vol. 14. Springer, Cham (2017). https://doi.org/10.1007/978-3-319-58507-9_3
31. Pontelli, E., Son, T.C., Elkhatib, O.: Justifications for logic programs under answer set semantics. Theory Pract. Log. Program. **9**(1), 1–56 (2009)
32. Vennekens, J.: Actual causation in cp-logic. Theory Pract. Log. Program. **11**(4–5), 647–662 (2011)
33. Weslake, B.: A partial theory of actual causation. Br. J. Philos. Sci. (2015)

Advancements in Resource-Driven Substructural Defeasible Logic

Francesco Olivieri[1]([✉]) [iD], Guido Governatori[1] [iD], and Matteo Cristani[2] [iD]

[1] Data61, CSIRO, Brisbane, Australia
{francesco.olivieri,guido.governatori}@data61.csiro.au
[2] University of Verona, Strada Le Grazie 15, 37135 Verona, VR, Italy
matteo.cristani@univr.it

Abstract. Linear Logic and Defeasible Logic have been adopted to formalise different features of knowledge representation: consumption of resources and reasoning with exceptions. We propose a framework to combine sub-structural features, corresponding to the consumption of resources, with defeasibility aspects to handle potentially conflicting information, and we discuss the design choices.

1 Introduction

Logic is often described as the "art" of reasoning or, in other terms, its subject matter is how to derive conclusions from given premises. Under this perspective we can distinguish *rules* (or *sequents*) and *inference* (or *derivation*) *rules*. A *rule* specifies that some consequences follow from some premises, while a *derivation rule* provides a recipe to determine the valid steps in a proof, or derivation. A classical example of a derivation rule is Modus Ponens (i.e., from '$\alpha \to \beta$' and α to derive β). A rule can be understood as a pair "$\Gamma \vdash \Theta$", where Γ and Θ are collections of formulas in an underlying language.

In Classical Logic, Γ and Θ are sets of formulas, and in Intuitionistic Logic Θ is a singleton. Thus, the Classical Logic rules '$\alpha, \beta \vdash \gamma, \delta$' and '$\beta, \alpha \vdash \delta, \gamma$' are the same rule. Here ',' is understood as conjunction in the antecedent Γ, and disjunction in the consequent Θ. In substructural logics (e.g., Lambek Calculus, and the family of Linear Logics), Γ and Θ are assumed to have an internal structure, and they are considered as multi-sets or sequences. An interpretation of a rule is how to transform the premises into the conclusion. Therefore, the rule '$\alpha, \beta, \alpha \vdash \gamma$' can be taken to mean that we need two instances of α with one instance of β in between to produce an instance of γ. Derivation rules, on the other hand, tell us how to combine rules to obtain new rules. For example, the derivation rule

$$\frac{\Gamma \vdash \alpha \qquad \Theta \vdash \alpha \to \beta}{\Gamma, \Theta \vdash \alpha, \alpha \to \beta, \beta}$$

establishes that if we have a derivation of α from Γ and a derivation of $\alpha \to \beta$ from Θ, then we can combine the Γ and Θ to obtain a new derivation, where we have α followed by $\alpha \to \beta$ and then β. If the formulae denote activities

© Springer Nature Switzerland AG 2019
F. Calimeri et al. (Eds.): JELIA 2019, LNAI 11468, pp. 247–258, 2019.
https://doi.org/10.1007/978-3-030-19570-0_16

(or tasks) and resources, then the consequent is a sequence of tasks describing the activities to be done (and the order in which they have to be executed) to produce an outcome (and also, what resources are needed). Hence, we can use the rules to model transformation in a business process, and derivations as the process traces (or the ways in which the process can be executed).

A formalism that properly models processes should feature some key characteristics, and one of the most important ones is to identify which resources are *consumed* after a task has finished its execution. Consider a vending machine scenario, where the dollar resource is spent to *produce* the can of cola. Trivially, once we get the cola, the dollar resource is no longer spendable (unless it can be, somehow, *replenished*). However, the specifications of a process may include thousands of rules to represent, at their best, all the various situations that may occur during the execution of the process itself: situations where the information at hand may be incomplete and, sometimes, even contradictory, and rules encoding possible exceptions. This means that we have to adopt a formalism that is able to represent and reason with *exceptions*, and *partial information*.

Defeasible Logic (DL) [11] is a non-monotonic rule based formalism, that has been used to model exceptions and processes. We chose DL as base for its ability in managing non-monotonic aspects of logical conclusion/derivation mechanisms; most importantly, very efficient implementations have been developed capable to handle very large knowledge bases [10]. The starting point here is that, while rules define a relation between premises and conclusion, DL takes the stance that multiple relations are possible, and it focuses on the "strength" of the relationships (i.e., rules can be prevented to draw conclusions). An example of rules with a baseline condition and exception is the scenario of the vending machine: the outcome is that we get a cola, unless the machine is out of order or switched off. We can thus represent this scenario with the rules (see Sect. 2):

$$r_1 : 1\$ \Rightarrow cola \qquad r_2 : OutOfOrder \Rightarrow \neg cola \qquad r_3 : Off \Rightarrow \neg cola.$$

The motivation of the paper is to combine, from a logic perspective, mechanisms of defeasibility with mechanisms from substructural logic in order to capture:

1. **Ordered list of antecedents:** sometimes it is meaningful to consider an *ordered sequence* of atoms in the head of a rule, instead of an *unordered set* of antecedents (hence rules '$r : a, b \Rightarrow c$' and '$r : b, a \Rightarrow c$' are semantically different).
2. **Multi-occurrence/repetitions of literals:** literals may appear in multiple instances (again, rules '$r : a; a; b \Rightarrow c$' and '$s : a; b; a \Rightarrow c$' are semantically different).
3. **Resources consumption:** some literals represent resources that are *consumed* during the derivation process, if they appear in the antecedent of a rule and such a rule produces its conclusion, then the other rules with the same literals in their antecedent can no longer fire (unless there are multiple occurrences).
4. **Concurrent production:** symmetrically, consider two rules with the same conclusion: '$r : a \Rightarrow c$' and '$s : b \Rightarrow c$'. It now seems reasonable that, if both a and b are derived, then we conclude two instances of c.

5. **Team defeater and resource consumption:** when two rules for opposite conclusions may fire, in sceptical formalisms typically only one produces its conclusion. Thus the question is whether defeated rules consume resources, or not.

6. **Multiple conclusions:** rules can produce more than one conclusion at a time (like '$r : a, b \Rightarrow c, d$'). This cannot be obtained by the two rules '$t : a, b \Rightarrow c$' and '$s : a, b \Rightarrow d$' since, due to resource consumption, only one of them would fire.

7. **Loops:** play a fundamental role in many real life applications, like business processes.

For a more comprehensive discussion, the reader is referred to [13], where they can find real-life examples for each item. It is clear that the resulting combination of logical machinery could provide a much better formalism for the representation of processes.

2   Language and Logical Formalisation of RSDL

The logics presented here considers consumable literals only: the formalisation of non-consumable literals is the same of that in Standard DL (SDL) [1], and thus the process would not add any value to this contribution. Also we will have either multi-sets or sequences of literals, but *not* combinations of those: again this is trivial and left out due to space limits.

Our logics deals with two types of derivations: *strict* and *defeasible*. *Strict rules* derive indisputable conclusions, i.e., conclusions that which are always true. Thus, if two strict rules have opposite conclusions, then the resulting logic is inconsistent. On the contrary, defeasible rules are to derive pieces of information that can be defeated by contrary evidence. Finally, defeaters are special type of rules whose purpose is to block/prevent contrary evidence: they cannot be used to directly derive conclusions.

We now introduce the language of Resource-driven Substructural Defeasible Logic (RSDL). PROP is the set of propositional atoms, the set Lit = PROP $\cup$ $\{\neg p | p \in$ PROP$\}$ is the set of literals. The *complement* of a literal p is denoted by $\sim q$; if q is a positive literal p, then $\neg q$ is $\neg p$, and if q is a negative literal $\neg p$, then $\sim q$ is p.

Definition 1. *Let* Lab *be a set of arbitrary labels. Rules have form "$r : A(r) \hookrightarrow C(r)$": (1) $r \in$ Lab is a unique name; (2) $A(r)$ is the* antecedent, *or* body, *of the rule. $A(r)$ can either have the form $A(r) = a_1, \ldots, a_n$ to denote a multi-set, or $A(r) = a_1; \ldots; a_n$ to denote a sequence; (3) $\hookrightarrow \in \{\rightarrow, \Rightarrow, \rightsquigarrow\}$ denotes a strict rule, a defeasible rule, and a defeater, respectively; (4) $C(r)$ is the* consequent, *or* head, *of the rule. For the head, we consider three options: (i) The head is a single literal 'p', (ii) The head is a multi-set '$p_1, \ldots, p_m$', or (iii) the head is a sequence '$p_1; \ldots; p_m$'.*

With abuse of notation, we will often refer to $p_1, \ldots, p_m$ as a set, and overload standard set theoretic notation. Given a set of rules R and a rule $r : A(r) \hookrightarrow C(r)$, we use the following abbreviations: (i) R_s is the subset of strict rules, (ii) R_{sd} is the set of strict and defeasible rules, (iii) $R[p; i]$ is the set of rules where p appears at index i in the consequent where the consequent is a sequence, (iv) $R[p, i]$ when the consequent is a multi-set containing p.

Definition 2. *A resource-driven substructural defeasible theory is a tuple $(F, R, \succ)$ where: (i) $F \subseteq$ Lit are pieces of information denoting the resources available at the beginning of the computation. This differs strikingly from SDL, where facts denote always-true statements; (ii) R is the set of rules; (iii) $\succ: R \times R$ is the superiority relation.*

A theory is *finite* if the sets of facts and rules are finite. In SDL, a *proof* P of length n is a finite sequence $P(1), \ldots, P(n)$ of *tagged literals* of the type $\pm\Delta p$, $\pm\partial p$. The idea is that, at every step of the derivation, a literal is either proven or disproven.

In our logic, we must be able to derive multiple conclusions in a single derivation step, and hence we require a mechanism to determine when premises have been used to derive a conclusion. Accordingly, we modify the definition of proof to be a matrix.

Definition 3. *A proof P in RSDL is a finite matrix $P(1, 1), \ldots, P(l, c)$ of tagged literals of the type $\pm\Delta p$, $\pm\partial p$, $+\sigma p$, $+\Delta p^{\checkmark}$, and $+\partial p^{\checkmark}$.*

We assume that facts are simultaneously true at the beginning of the computation. Notation $+\#p^{\checkmark}$, $\# \in \{\Delta, \partial\}$ denotes that p has been consumed. The distinctive notation for when a literal is proven and when it is consumed will play a key role to determine which rules are applicable. The tagged literal $\pm\Delta p$ means that p is *strictly proved/refuted* in D, and, symmetrically, $\pm\partial p$ means that p is *defeasibly proven/refuted*, $+\sigma p$ indicates that there are applicable rules for p, but some of their resources have already been used.

The set of positive and negative conclusions is called *extension*. In SDL, given a set of facts, a set of rules, and a superiority relation, the extension is unique. It is clear that this is not the case when resource consumption and ordered sequences are to be taken into account: depending on the order in which the rules are applied, different extensions can be obtained. In RSDL every distinct derivation corresponds to an extension.

In SDL, derivations are based on the notions of a rule being *applicable* or *discarded*. Intuitively, a rule is applicable when every literal in the antecedent has been proven at a previous step. We report hereafter the defeasible proof tag in SDL to give the reader a better understanding of how defeasible conclusions can be drawn.

If $P(n + 1) = +\partial p$ then
(1) $\exists r \in R_{sd}[p]$: r is applicable and
(2) $\forall s \in R[\sim p]$ either (1) s is discarded or (2) $\exists t \in R[p]$: t is applicable and $t \succ s$.

A literal is defeasibly proven when there exists an applicable rule for such a conclusion and all the rules of the opposite are either discarded, or defeated by stronger rules. (Strict derivations only differ in that, when a rule is applicable, we do not care about contrary evidence, and the rule will always produce its conclusion nonetheless).

As for SDL, we obtain variants of the logic by providing different definitions of being *applicable* and *discarded*. More specifically, for RSDL, definitions of applicability and discardability need to take into account (i) the number of times a literal appears in the body of a rule, (ii) how many times they have been derived[1], (iii) the order in which the literals occur in the body of a rule and in a derivation. In addition, we have to extend the structure of the proof conditions to include mechanisms or conditions to determine when literals/resources have been used to derive new literals/resources.

We shall proceed incrementally. First, we provide definitions for multi-sets. We then provide definitions for sequences. In both cases, we consider rules with a *single* literal for conclusion. Only after those concepts will be clear, we move forward and propose definitions to describe rules with multiple conclusions.

Definition 4. *A rule r is #-applicable, $\# \in \{\Delta, \partial, \sigma\}$, at $P(l + 1, c + 1)$ iff $\forall$ $a_i \in A(r)$ then $+\#a_i \in P[(1,1)..(l,c)]$. Moreover, we say that r is #-consumable iff r is #-applicable and $\exists \, l' \leq l$ such that $P(l', c) = +\#a_i$.*

A rule is consumable if it is applicable and, for every literal in its antecedent, there is an *unused* occurrence. Discardability is the strong negation of applicability.

Definition 5. *A rule r is #-discarded, $\# \in \{\Delta, \partial\}$, at $P(l + 1, c + 1)$ iff $\exists$ $a_i \in A(r)$ such that $-\#a_i \in P[(1,1)..(l,c)]$. Moreover, we say that r is #-non-consumable iff either r is discarded, or $\forall \, l' \leq l$, $P(l', c) \neq +\partial a_i$.*

Lastly, we define the conditions describing when a literal is consumed.

Definition 6. *Given rule r, a literal $a \in A(r)$ is #-consumed, $\# \in \{\Delta, \partial\}$, at $P(l+1, c+1)$, iff 1. $\exists \, l' \leq l$ such that $P(l', c) = +\#a$, and 2. $P(l', c+1) = +\#a^{\checkmark}$.*

Example 1 illustrates how we use $+\partial p^{\checkmark}$ within the resource consumption mechanism.

Example 1. Consider $D = (\{a\}, R, \emptyset)$, where $R = \{r_0 : a \Rightarrow b, r_1 : b \Rightarrow c, r_2 : b \to d\}$ and (one of) the corresponding proof table(s):

P	1	2	3	4
1	$+\Delta a$	$+\Delta a^{\checkmark}$	$+\Delta a^{\checkmark}$	$+\Delta a^{\checkmark}$
2		$+\partial b$	$+\partial b^{\checkmark}$	$+\partial b^{\checkmark}$
3			$+\partial c$	$+\partial c$
4				$-\partial d$

---

[1] Trivially, e.g., if literal a has been derived twice, but it appears in the antecedent of three rules, only two of such rules can produce their conclusions.

Naturally, two mutually exclusive extensions are possible, based on whether $+\partial b$ is used by r_1 to derive $+\partial c$, or by r_2 to derive $+\partial d$. Table 1 shows the former case. At $P(1,1)$ we obtain $+\Delta a$, instance that is consumed in deriving $+\partial b$ at $P(2,2)$. Thus, $P(1,2) = +\Delta a^{\checkmark}$. Symmetric situation for activating r_1 at the third derivation step, which results in $P(2,3) = +\partial b^{\checkmark}$ and $P(3,3) = +\partial c$. Now, at $P(4,4)$, r_2 is applicable but non-consumable, and hence $P(4,4) = -\partial d$. Note that if r_2 instead of r_1 is activated, we would have had $P(3,3) = +\partial d$.

Proof Tags for Multi-sets in the Antecedent and Single Conclusion

We begin with: (1) the antecedent is a multi-set, (2) single literal in the conclusion.

$+\Delta$: If $P(l+1, c+1) = +\Delta p$ then
    (1) $p \in F$, or (2) $\exists r \in R_s[p]$ s.t. r is Δ-consumable and $\forall a_j \in A(r)$, a_j is Δ-consumed.

Literal q is definitely provable if either is a fact, or there is a strict consumable rule for p. Condition (2) actually consumes the literals by replacing $+\Delta a_j$ with $+\Delta a_j^{\checkmark}$.

$-\Delta$: If $P(l+1, c+1) = -\Delta p$ then
    (1) $p \notin F$ and (2) $\forall r \in R_s[p]$, r is Δ-non-consumable.

Literal q is definitely refuted if p is not a fact, and every rule for p is non-consumable.

$+\partial$: If $P(l+1, c+1) = +\partial p$, then
    (1) $+\Delta p \in P(l,c)$ or
    (2) (1) $-\Delta{\sim}p \in P(l,c)$ and
        (2) $\exists r \in R_{sd}[p]$ ∂-consumable and
        (3) $\forall s \in R[{\sim}p]$ either (1) s is ∂-discarded, or
            (2) $\exists t \in R[p]$ ∂-consumable, $t \succ s$, and
                if $\exists w \in R[{\sim}p]$ ∂-applicable, $t \succ w$, then
                    $\forall a_j \in A(t)$, a_j is ∂-consumed, otherwise $\forall a_k \in A(r)$, a_k is ∂-consumed.

Condition (1) is to inherit a defeasible derivation from a definite one. Condition (2.1) ensures that the logic is sound. Condition (2.2) requires that there is a rule r that is triggered by literals that have been previously proven but not consumed. Clause (2.3) is that, to rebut an attacking argument, either we show that some of its premises have been refuted, or is defeated by stronger, consumable rules. The final part is to determine which resources are consumed during the derivation of p. This variant assumes that only the rules in the winning team defeater consume resources, whilst the 'defeated rules' do not.

For $-\partial$, we use the strategy similar to that used in [1] to provide proof conditions for the ambiguity propagating variant of SDL, that is, we make it easier to attack a rule (2.2.2). In line with above, literals tagged with $-\partial$ do not consume of resources.

$-\partial$: If $P(l+1, c+1) = -\partial p$, then

(1) $-\Delta p \in P[l, c]$ and

(2) (1) $+\Delta\sim p \in P[l, c]$ or

    (2) $\forall r \in R_{sd}[p]$ either r is ∂-discarded or

       (1) $\exists s \in R[\sim p]$ s.t. s is σ-applicable and

       (2) $\forall t \in R[p]$ either t is ∂-discarded or $t \not\succ s$.

The idea behind $+\sigma$ is that there are applicable, non-defeated rules for the consequent, irrespective whether the premises have been used or not.

$+\sigma$: If $P(l+1, c+1) = +\sigma p$ then

(1) $\Delta p \in P[l, c]$ or

(2) $\exists r \in R_{sd}[p]$ s.t. (1) r is σ-applicable and (2) $\forall s \in R[\sim p]$ either s is ∂-discarded or $s \not\succ r$.

Example 2. Consider $D = (\{a, b, c\}, R = \{r_0 : a \Rightarrow d, r_1 : a \to e, r_2 : b \Rightarrow d, r_3 : c \Rightarrow \sim d\}, \succ = \{(r_2, r_3)\})$ and the corresponding proof table:

P	1	2	3	4	5
1	$+\Delta a$	$+\Delta a$	$+\Delta a$	$+\Delta a$	$+\Delta a^{\checkmark}$
2		$+\Delta b$	$+\Delta b$	$+\Delta b^{\checkmark}$	$+\Delta b^{\checkmark}$
3			$+\Delta c$	$+\Delta c$	$+\Delta c$
4				$+\partial d$	$+\partial d$
5					$+\partial e$

Assume that, at $P(4, 4)$, r_0 is taken into consideration; r_0 is consumable, but so is r_3, and no superiority is given between r_0 and r_3. Actually, r_2 is consumable and stronger than r_3. Accordingly, the team defeater allows us to prove $+\partial d$, and only b is consumed in this process. Thus a is still available, and can be used at $P(5, 5)$ to get $+\partial e$, via r_1. Note that we do not consume resource $+\Delta c$, since $r_2 \succ r_3$.

Proof Tags for Sequences in the Antecedent and Single Conclusion

When considering sequences in the antecedent, definitions of applicable, discarded, and consumable must be revised. A rule is *sequence applicable* when the derivation order reflects the order in which the literals appear in the antecedent.

Definition 7. *A rule $r \in R[p]$ is #-sequence applicable, $\# \in \{\Delta, \partial\}$, at $P(l+1, c+1)$ iff for all $a_i \in A(r)$ there exists $c_i \leq c$ such that $P(l_i, c_i) = +\#a_i$, $l_i \leq l$, and for all $a_j \in A(r)$ such that $i < j$, then for all $c_j \leq c$ such that $P(l_j, c_j) = +\#a_j$, $l_j \leq l$ then $l_i < l_j$ and $c_i < c_j$. We say that r is #-sequence consumable iff is #-applicable and 4. $P(l_i, c) = +\#a_i$.*

A rule is sequence discarded if there exists a literal in the antecedent which has been disproven, or there are two proven literals in the antecedent, say a and b, with a before b, and one proof for b is before every proof for a.

Definition 8. *A rule $r \in R[p]$ is #-sequence discarded, $\# \in \{\Delta, \partial\}$, at $P(l+1, c+1)$ iff for there exists $a_i \in A(r)$ such that either $-\#a_i \in P(l-1, c-1)$, or for all $c_i \leq c$ such that $P(l_j, c_i) = +\#a_i$, $l_i \leq l$, then there exists $a_j \in A(r)$, with $i < j$, such that there exists $c_j \leq c$ such that $P(l_j, c_j) = +\#a_j$, $l_j \leq l$, and $c_i > c_j$, $l_i > l_j$.*

The definition of being #-consumed remains the same. The proof tags for strict and defeasible conclusions with sequences in the antecedent and a single conclusion can be obtained by simply replacing: (a) #-applicable with #-sequence applicable, (b) #-consumable with #-sequence consumable, and (c) #-discarded with #-sequence discarded.

Example 3. Consider $D = (\{c, d, e\}, R, \succ = \emptyset)$, where $R = \{r_0 : a, b, a \Rightarrow f, r_1 : c \Rightarrow a, r_2 : d \Rightarrow a, r_3 : e \Rightarrow b\}$.

Assume the rules are activated in this order: first r_1, then r_2, last r_3. Thus, $P(4, 4) = +\partial a$, $P(5, 5) = +\partial a$, and $P(6, 6) = +\partial b$. The derivation order between b and the second occurrence of a has not been complied with, and r_0 is sequence discarded. Same if the order is 'r_3, r_1, r_2', whilst 'r_2, r_3, r_1' is a legit order to let r_0 be sequence applicable.

Proof Tags for Sequences in Both the Antecedent and Conclusion

Even when we consider sequences in the consequent, a literal's strict provability or refutability depends only upon whether the strict rule (where the literal occurs) is sequence consumable or not. As such, given a strict rule $r \in R_s[p; j]$, still p's strict provability/refutability depends only upon whether r is strictly sequence consumable or not. However, now we also have to verify that, if $r \in R_s[q; j - 1]$, we prove p immediately after q. The resulting new formalisations of $+\Delta$ and $+\partial$ are as follows (negative proof tags are trivial and thus omitted):

$+\Delta$: If $P(l + 1, c + 1) = +\Delta p$ then
    (1) $p \in F$, or
    (2) (1) $\exists r \in R_s[p; j]$ r is Δ-sequence-consumable, $r \in R_s[q; j - 1]$, $P(l + i - 1, c + 1) = +\Delta q$,
        (2) $\forall a_j \in A(r)$, a_j is Δ-consumed.

$+\partial$: If $P(l + i, c + 1) = +\partial p$, then
    (1) $+\Delta p \in P(l, c)$ or
    (2) (1) $-\Delta \sim p \in P(l, c)$ and
        (2) (1) $\exists r \in R_{sd}[p; j]$ ∂-sequence-consumable and
            (2) $\exists r \in R[q; j - 1]$ and $P(l + i - 1, c + 1) = +\partial q$, and
        (3) $\forall s \in R[\sim p]$ either s is ∂-sequence-discarded, or
            (1) $\exists t \in R[p]$ ∂-sequence-consumable, $t \succ s$, and
            (2) if $\exists w \in R[\sim p]$ ∂-sequence-applicable, $t \succ w$, then
                (1) $\forall a_j \in A(t)$, a_j is ∂-consumed, otherwise (2) $\forall a_k \in A(r)$, a_k is ∂-consumed.

Example 4. Consider $D = (\{a, b\}, R = \{r_0 : a \Rightarrow c; d; e$ and $r_1 : b \Rightarrow \sim d\}, \succ = \emptyset)$. We obtain $+\partial c$ and $-\partial d$ since r_1 is sequence-applicable and $r_0 \not\succ r_1$. Thus, we prove $-\partial e$.

Proof Tags for Sequences in the Antecedent and Multi-sets in the Conclusion

We now consider multi-sets in the conclusion. Strict provability does not change with respect to the one described in the previous section, and is therefore omitted. When considering a 'team defeater fight', two variants are possible. In this first variant, we draw a conclusion only if there is a winning team defeater for each literal in the conclusion.

$+\partial$: If $P(l+i, c+1) = +\partial p$, then
    (1) $+\Delta p \in P(l, c)$ or
    (2) (1) $-\Delta\sim p \in P(l, c)$ and
        (2) $\exists r \in R_{sd}[p, j]$ ∂-sequence-consumable and
        (3) $\forall s \in R[\sim q]$ such that $q \in C(r)$ either s is ∂-sequence-discarded, or
            (1) $\exists t \in R[q]$ ∂-sequence-consumable, $t \succ s$, and
            (2) if $\exists w \in R[\sim p]$ ∂-sequence-applicable, $t \succ w$, then
                (1) $\forall a_j \in A(t)$, a_j is ∂-consumed, otherwise (2) $\forall a_k \in A(r)$, a_k is ∂-consumed.

Consider D of Example 4, with $C(r_0) = \{c, d, e\}$ (now multi-set). Here, even if $C(r_1) = \sim d$, since there is no stronger rule, r_1 prevents r_0 to derive $+\partial c$, as well as $+\partial d$ and $+\partial e$.

In this latter variant, we limit the comparison on the individual literal.

$+\partial$: If $P(l+i, c+1) = +\partial p$, then
    (1) $+\Delta p \in P(l, c)$ or
    (2) (1) $-\Delta\sim p \in P(l, c)$ and
        (2) $\exists r \in R_{sd}[p, j]$ ∂-sequence-consumable and
        (3) $\forall s \in R[\sim p]$ either s is ∂-sequence-discarded, or
            (1) $\exists t \in R[p]$ ∂-sequence-consumable, $t \succ s$, and
            (2) if $\exists w \in R[\sim p]$ ∂-sequence-applicable, $t \succ w$, then
                (1) $\forall a_j \in A(t)$, a_j is ∂-consumed, otherwise (2) $\forall a_k \in A(r)$, a_k is ∂-consumed.

Consider D of Example 4, again with $C(r_0) = \{c, d, e\}$. Now r_1 can prevent r_0 only to prove $+\partial d$. Since there are no stronger rules for $\sim c$ nor $\sim e$, we now prove $+\partial c$ and $+\partial e$.

3   Results

A logical system enjoys the *Finite Model Property* (FMP) when for every set of formulae, the associated meaning to each formula requires a finite set of elements in the semantics for every model of that set. In the case of RSDL, the semantics is determined by the derivations that are possible given a theory. As a consequence of the aforementioned notions we shall prove one property that regards acyclic RSDL. The Atom Dependency Graph (ADG)[2] of a defeasible theory has been defined in many different contexts, specifically in the analysis of preferences, as in [6]. Acyclic RSDLs are theories in which no cycle appears in the ADG. This means that when a rule is used to produce a conclusion, the resources in the antecedent of the rules cannot be replenished, and we reach nodes, literals, that can be produced by the theory only if they are given (node, with no incoming edges in the ADG).

Theorem 1. *Acyclic finite RSDL theories enjoy the FMP.*

---

[2] The atomic propositions are the nodes, and there is a directed edge between nodes if there is a rule containing the source or its negation in the body, and the target or its negation in the head.

Proof. With no cycles in the ADG, every time a rule is used to derive a positive conclusion, the number of available resources decreases. Thus, the maximum number of literals that can appear in a proof is bound and proportional to the number of literals occurring in the rule heads. Hence, every derivation is finite, and the theory has the FMP.

Note that the theory with a as a fact and the rule $a \Rightarrow a$ can generate a derivation with infinitely many occurrences of a. The acyclicity condition allows us to compute in finite time the extension of a theory. However, this is not the case for cyclic theory, where the computation is not guaranteed to terminate. Accordingly:

Theorem 2. *Computing extensions of cyclic RSDL theories is semi-decidable.*

For acyclic theories, we have the FMP. Thus, since acyclic theories can be checked for model existence in finite time, when the model does not exist, and by brute force methods, we can trivially claim the following result.

Theorem 3. *The problem of computing extensions of acyclic RSDL theories is decidable.*

SDL is efficient in terms of time and space, since the extension can be computed in linear time in the number of literals. This property, however, cannot be claimed for RSDL. In particular, we can show that RSDL can be used to represent a classical 3-SAT problem, and thus prove that the complexity cannot be polynomial on deterministic machines.

The basic idea of reducing to 3-SAT is as follows. A 3-SAT problem P is a clause representing a finite conjunction of triplets (t_i), each formed by three literals (t_i^1, t_i^2, t_i^3), that we assume to be conjuncted in the sub-clause, where we ask whether the clause is satisfiable, or not. We map each literal appearing in the clause in a positive literal $\widehat{t_i^x}$ (with $x = 1, 2, 3$), not appearing in the clause, and add one positive literal $\widehat{t_i}$ for every triplet, again not appearing in the triplets. Subsequently, we add one rule $\widehat{t_i} \Rightarrow \widehat{t_i^x}$ for each of the three values $x = 1, 2, 3$ and three rules $\widehat{t_i^x} \Rightarrow t_i^x$ for each of the values $x = 1, 2, 3$. Finally, we add one fact for every literal $\widehat{t_i}$. Conclusively, we have mapped every triplet in six RSDL rules. The resulting RSDL theory has a derivation containing at least one literal for each clause if and only if the original problem P is a satisfiable clause. For example, consider the clause $(\alpha \lor \beta \lor \gamma) \land (\neg\alpha \lor \neg\beta \lor \delta)$. Using c_1 and c_2 for the triplets, and $c_1^1, c_1^2, c_1^3, c_2^1, c_2^2, c_2^3$ for the elements in the triplets, the theory encoding the clause is:

$$c_1 \qquad c_1 \Rightarrow c_1^2 \qquad c_2 \Rightarrow c_2^2 \qquad c_1^2 \Rightarrow \beta \qquad c_2^2 \Rightarrow \sim\beta$$

$$c_2 \qquad c_1 \Rightarrow c_1^3 \qquad c_2 \Rightarrow c_2^3 \qquad c_1^3 \Rightarrow \gamma \qquad c_2^3 \Rightarrow \delta$$

$$c_1 \Rightarrow c_1^1 \qquad c_2 \Rightarrow c_2^1 \qquad c_1^1 \Rightarrow \alpha \qquad c_2^1 \Rightarrow \sim\alpha.$$

4   Conclusions and Related Work

We proposed a fresh logical apparatus that deals with the problem of manipulating resource consumption in non-monotonic reasoning. The combination of linear with defeasible features is a complete novelty and we believe that it can be useful in several areas of AI and knowledge representation, like agent modelling and business processes.

Studies on light linear logic versions, with specific aspects of linearity related to resource consumption have been devised such as *light* and *soft linear logic* [3,5]. Both SDL and Linear Logic (for different reasons and techniques) have been used for modelling business processes [2,4,8,12,14,17,18]. Applications of linear logic to problems indirectly related to business processes such as Petri Nets can be found in [2,8,18]. However, such approaches are not able to handle in a natural fashion the aspect of exceptions. In [9,15,16], the authors propose the use of Linear Logic to generate which plans the agent adopts to achieve its goals. In the same spirit, [7] addresses the problem of agents that have to take decisions from partial, and possibly inconsistent, information.

References

1. Antoniou, G., Billington, D., Governatori, G., Maher, M.J.: Representation results for defeasible logic. ACM Trans. Comput. Logic 2(2), 255–287 (2001)
2. Engberg, U., Winskel, G.: Completeness results for linear logic on Petri nets. Ann. Pure Appl. Logic 86(2), 101–135 (1997)
3. Gaboardi, M., Marion, J.Y., Ronchi Della Rocca, S.: Soft linear logic and polynomial complexity classes. Electron. Notes Theoret. Comput. Sci. 205(C), 67–87 (2008)
4. Ghooshchi, N.G., van Beest, N., Governatori, G., Olivieri, F., Sattar, A.: Visualisation of compliant declarative business processes. In: EDOC 2017, pp. 89–94. IEEE (2017)
5. Girard, J.Y.: Light linear logic. Inf. Comput. 143(2), 175–204 (1998)
6. Governatori, G., Olivieri, F., Cristani, M., Scannapieco, S.: Revision of defeasible preferences. Int. J. Approx. Reasoning 104, 205–230 (2019)
7. Governatori, G., Olivieri, F., Scannapieco, S., Rotolo, A., Cristani, M.: The rationale behind the concept of goal. Theory Pract. Log. Program. 16(3), 296–324 (2016)
8. Kanovich, M., Ito, T.: Temporal linear logic specifications for concurrent processes. In: LICS 1997, pp. 48–57. IEEE Computer Society (1997)
9. Küngas, P., Matskin, M.: Linear logic, partial deduction and cooperative problem solving. In: Leite, J., Omicini, A., Sterling, L., Torroni, P. (eds.) DALT 2003. LNCS (LNAI), vol. 2990, pp. 263–279. Springer, Heidelberg (2004). https://doi.org/10.1007/978-3-540-25932-9_14

10. Lam, H.-P., Governatori, G.: The making of SPINdle. In: Governatori, G., Hall, J., Paschke, A. (eds.) RuleML 2009. LNCS, vol. 5858, pp. 315–322. Springer, Heidelberg (2009). https://doi.org/10.1007/978-3-642-04985-9_29

11. Nute, D.: Defeasible logic. In: Handbook of Logic in Artificial Intelligence and Logic Programming, vol. 3. Oxford University Press (1987)

12. Olivieri, F., Cristani, M., Governatori, G.: Compliant business processes with exclusive choices from agent specification. In: Chen, Q., Torroni, P., Villata, S., Hsu, J., Omicini, A. (eds.) PRIMA 2015. LNCS (LNAI), vol. 9387, pp. 603–612. Springer, Cham (2015). https://doi.org/10.1007/978-3-319-25524-8_43

13. Olivieri, F., Governatori, G., Cristani, M., van Beest, N., Colombo-Tosatto, S.: Resource-driven substructural defeasible logic. In: Miller, T., Oren, N., Sakurai, Y., Noda, I., Savarimuthu, B.T.R., Cao Son, T. (eds.) PRIMA 2018. LNCS (LNAI), vol. 11224, pp. 594–602. Springer, Cham (2018). https://doi.org/10.1007/978-3-030-03098-8_46

14. Olivieri, F., Governatori, G., Scannapieco, S., Cristani, M.: Compliant business process design by declarative specifications. In: Boella, G., Elkind, E., Savarimuthu, B.T.R., Dignum, F., Purvis, M.K. (eds.) PRIMA 2013. LNCS (LNAI), vol. 8291, pp. 213–228. Springer, Heidelberg (2013). https://doi.org/10.1007/978-3-642-44927-7_15

15. Pham, D.Q., Harland, J.: Temporal linear logic as a basis for flexible agent interactions. In: AAMAS 2007, pp. 28:1–28:8. ACM (2007)

16. Pham, D.Q., Harland, J., Winikoff, M.: Modeling agents' choices in temporal linear logic. In: Baldoni, M., Son, T.C., van Riemsdijk, M.B., Winikoff, M. (eds.) DALT 2007. LNCS (LNAI), vol. 4897, pp. 140–157. Springer, Heidelberg (2008). https://doi.org/10.1007/978-3-540-77564-5_9

17. Rao, J., Küngas, P., Matskin, M.: Composition of semantic web services using linear logic theorem proving. Inf. Syst. **31**(4–5), 340–360 (2006)

18. Tanabe, M.: Timed Petri nets and temporal linear logic. In: Azéma, P., Balbo, G. (eds.) ICATPN 1997. LNCS, vol. 1248, pp. 156–174. Springer, Heidelberg (1997). https://doi.org/10.1007/3-540-63139-9_35

SLD-Resolution Reduction
of Second-Order Horn Fragments

Sophie Tourret[1]([⊠])[iD] and Andrew Cropper[2][iD]

[1] Max Planck Institute for Informatics, Saarland Informatics Campus,
Saarbrücken, Germany
sophie.tourret@mpi-inf.mpg.de
[2] University of Oxford, Oxford, UK
andrew.cropper@cs.ox.ac.uk

Abstract. We present the *derivation reduction* problem for SLD-resolution, the undecidable problem of finding a finite subset of a set of clauses from which the whole set can be derived using SLD-resolution. We study the reducibility of various fragments of second-order Horn logic with particular applications in Inductive Logic Programming. We also discuss how these results extend to standard resolution.

1 Introduction

Detecting and eliminating redundancy in a clausal theory (a set of clauses) is useful in many areas of computer science [3,19]. Eliminating redundancy can make a theory easier to understand and may also have computational efficiency advantages [9]. The two standard criteria for redundancy are entailment [28,29,34] and subsumption [5,16,38]. In the case of entailment, a clause C is redundant in a clausal theory $T \cup \{C\}$ when $T \models C$. In the case of subsumption, a clause C is redundant in a clausal theory $T \cup \{C\}$ when there exists a clause $D \in T$ such that D subsumes C. For instance, consider the clausal theory T_1:

$$C_1 = p(x) \leftarrow q(x)$$
$$C_2 = p(x) \leftarrow q(x), r(x)$$

The clause C_2 is entailment and subsumption redundant because it is a logical consequence of C_1 (and is also subsumed by C_1). However, as we will soon show, entailment and subsumption redundancy can be too strong for some applications. To overcome this issue, we introduce a new form of redundancy based on whether a clause is *derivable* from a clausal theory using SLD-resolution [26]. Let $\vdash^*$ represent derivability in SLD-resolution. Then a Horn clause C is *derivationally redundant* in a Horn theory $T \cup \{C\}$ when $T \vdash^* C$. For instance, in T_1, although C_1 entails C_2, we cannot derive C_2 from C_1 using SLD-resolution because it is impossible to derive a clause with three literals from a clause with two literals.

We focus on whether theories formed of second-order function-free Horn clauses can be derivationally reduced to minimal (i.e. irreducible) finite theories

© Springer Nature Switzerland AG 2019
F. Calimeri et al. (Eds.): JELIA 2019, LNAI 11468, pp. 259–276, 2019.
https://doi.org/10.1007/978-3-030-19570-0_17

from which the original theory can be derived using SLD-resolution. For instance, consider the following theory T_2, where the symbols P_i represent second-order variables (i.e. variables that can be substituted by predicate symbols):

$$C_1 = P_0(x) \leftarrow P_1(x)$$
$$C_2 = P_0(x) \leftarrow P_1(x), P_2(x)$$
$$C_3 = P_0(x) \leftarrow P_1(x), P_2(x), P_3(x)$$

Although C_1 subsumes C_2 and C_3, the two clauses cannot be derived from C_1 for the same reason as in the previous example. However, C_3 is derivationally redundant because it can be derived by self-resolving C_2. A minimal *derivation reduction* of T_2 is the theory $\{C_1, C_2\}$ because C_2 cannot be derived from C_1 and vice versa.

1.1 Motivation

Our interest in this form of redundancy comes from Inductive Logic Programming (ILP) [33], a form of machine learning which induces hypotheses from examples and background knowledge, where the hypotheses, examples, and background knowledge are represented as logic programs. Many forms of ILP [1,10,25,35,40,44] and ILP variants [6,15,42,47] use second-order Horn clauses as templates to denote the form of programs that may be induced. For instance, consider the father kinship relation:

$$father(A, B) \leftarrow parent(A, B), male(A).$$

A suitable clause template to induce this relation is:

$$P_0(A, B) \leftarrow P_1(A, B), P_2(A).$$

Determining which clauses to use for a given learning task is a major open problem in ILP [8,9,35], and most approaches uses clauses provided by the designers of the systems without any theoretical justifications [1,6,10,25,42,44, 47]. The problem is challenging because on the one hand, you want to provide clauses sufficiently expressive to solve the given learning problem. For instance, it is impossible to learn the father relation using only monadic clauses. On the other hand, you want to remove redundant clauses to improve learning efficiency [9].

To illustrate this point, suppose you have the theory T_3:

$$C_1 = P_0(A, B) \leftarrow P_1(A, B)$$
$$C_2 = P_0(A, B) \leftarrow P_1(A, B), P_2(A)$$
$$C_3 = P_0(A, B) \leftarrow P_1(A, B), P_2(A, B)$$
$$C_4 = P_0(A, B) \leftarrow P_1(A, B), P_2(A, B), P_3(A, B)$$

Running entailment reduction on T_3 would remove C_2, C_3, and C_4 because they are logical consequence of C_1. But it is impossible to learn the intended father relation given only C_1. By contrast, running derivation reduction on T_3

would only remove C_4 because it can be *derived* by self-resolving C_3. As this example illustrates, any clause removed by derivation reduction can be recovered by derivation if necessary, while entailment reduction can be too strong and remove important clauses with no way to get them back using SLD-resolution. In this paper, we address this issue by studying the derivation reducibility of fragments of second-order Horn logic relevant to ILP. Although our notion of derivation reduction can be defined for any proof system, we initially focus on SLD-resolution because (1) most forms of ILP learn definite logic programs (typically Prolog programs), and (2) we want to reduce sets of metarules, which are themselves definite clauses (although second-order rather than first-order). The logic fragments we consider here also correspond to the search spaces typically targeted by ILP systems.

1.2 Contributions

Our main contributions are:

- We state the derivation reduction problem for SLD-resolution (Sect. 3) that we originally introduced in [12].
- We describe fragments of second-order Horn logic particularly relevant for ILP (Sect. 4).
- We show that, by constraining the arity of the predicates, an infinite fragment of connected Horn clauses can be derivationally reduced to a finite fragment made of clauses that contain at most two literals in the body (Sect. 5).
- We show that an infinite fragment of 2-connected (i.e. connected and without singleton occurrences of variables) Horn clauses *cannot* be derivationally reduced to any finite fragments (Sect. 6).
- We show similar but incomplete negative results for a more expressive 2-connected fragment (Sect. 7).
- We extend the reducibility results to standard resolution (Sect. 8).

A technical report including detailed proofs of all the results (including the ones only sketched in this paper) has been created as a separate document [46].

2   Related Work

In clausal logic there are two main forms of redundancy: (1) a literal may be redundant in a clause, and (2) a clause may be redundant in a clausal theory.

Literal Redundancy. Plotkin [38] used subsumption to decide whether a literal is redundant in a first-order clause. Joyner [24] independently studied the same problem, which he called *clause condensation*, where a condensation of a clause C is a minimum cardinality subset C' of C such that $C' \models C$. Gottlob and Fermüller [16] showed that determining whether a clause is condensed is coNP-complete. In contrast to eliminating literals from clauses, we focus on removing *clauses* from theories.

Clause Redundancy. Plotkin [38] also introduced methods to decide whether a clause is subsumption redundant in a first-order clausal theory. The same problem, and slight variants, has been extensively studied in the propositional logic [28,29] and has numerous applications, such as to improve the efficiency of SAT solving [19]. This problem has also been extensively studied in the context of first-order logic with equality due to its application in superposition-based theorem proving [20,48]. Langlois et al. [27] studied combinatorial problems for propositional Horn clauses. Their results include bounds on entailment reduced sets of propositional Horn fragments. In contrast to these works, we focus on removing *second-order* Horn clauses (without equality) that are *derivationally* redundant.

Much closer to this paper is the work of Cropper and Muggleton [9]. They used entailment reduction [34] on sets of second-order Horn clauses to identify theories that are (1) entailment complete for certain fragments of second-order Horn logic, and (2) minimal or irreducible, in that no further reductions are possible. They demonstrate that in some cases as few as two clauses are sufficient to entail an infinite language.

In contrast to all these works, we go beyond entailment reduction and introduce *derivation reduction* because, as stated in the previous section, the former can be too strong to be of use in ILP. Thus our focus is on *derivationally* reducing sets of *second-order Horn* clauses.

Theory Minimisation and Program Transformation. In theory minimisation [18] the goal is to find a minimum equivalent formula to a given input formula. The fold/unfold transformations of first-order rules are used, e.g. to improve the efficiency of logic programs or to synthesise definite programs from arbitrary specifications [43]. Both allow for the introduction of new formulæ. By contrast, the derivation reduction problem only allows for the *removal* of redundant clauses.

Prime Implicates. Implicates of a theory T are the clauses entailed by T. They are called prime when they do not themselves entail other implicates of T. This notion differs from the redundancy elimination in this paper because (1) the notion of a prime implicate has been studied only in propositional, first-order, and some modal logics [4,14,31], and (2) implicates are defined using entailment, which as already stated is too strong for our purpose.

Descriptive Complexity. Second-order Horn logic is often the focus in descriptive complexity [23], which studies how expressive a logic must be to describe a given formal language. For instance, Grädel showed that existential second-order Horn logic can describe all polynomial-time algorithms [17]. In this paper, we do not study the expressiveness of the logic but whether the logic can be logically reduced.

Higher-Order Calculi. SLD-resolution on second-order clauses, as used in this paper, supports the unification of predicate variables. By contrast, there are extensions of SLD-resolution and standard resolution that handle the full expressivity of higher-order logic [7,22]. These richer extensions handle more complex clauses, e.g. clauses including function symbols and λ-terms. We do not consider such complex clauses because most ILP approaches use second-order Horn clauses to learn function-free first-order Horn programs [1,10,15,25,35]. Extending our results to full higher-order logic is left for future work.

Second-Order Logic Templates. McCarthy [32] and Lloyd [30] advocated using second-order logic to represent knowledge. Similarly, in [36], the authors argued for using second-order representations in ILP to represent knowledge. As mentioned in the introduction, many forms of ILP use second-order Horn clauses as a form of declarative bias [39] to denote the structure of rules that may be induced. However, most approaches either (1) assume correct templates as input, or (2) use clauses without any theoretical justifications. Recent work [9] has attempted to address this issue by reasoning about the completeness of these templates, where the goal is to identify finite sets of templates sufficiently expressive to induce all logic programs in a given fragment. Our work contributes to this goal by exploring the derivation redundancy of sets of templates.

Derivation Reduction. In earlier work [12] we introduced the derivation reduction problem and a simple algorithm to compute reduction cores. We also experimentally studied the effect of using derivationally reduced templates on ILP benchmarks. Whereas our earlier paper mainly focuses on the application of derivation reduction to ILP, the current paper investigates derivation reduction itself in a broader perspective, with more emphasis on whether infinite fragments can be reduced to finite subsets. Another main distinction between the two papers is that here we focus on derivation reduction modulo first-order variable unification. The overlap includes the definition of derivation reduction and Sect. 4.2 in [12] which covers in less detail the same topic as our Sect. 6.

3   Problem Statement and Decidability

We now define the derivation reduction problem, i.e. the problem of removing derivationally redundant clauses from a clausal theory.

3.1   Preliminaries

We focus on function-free second-order Horn logic. We assume infinite enumerable sets of *term variables* $\{x_1, x_2, \ldots\}$ and *predicate variables* $\{P, P_0, P_1, \ldots\}$. An *atom* $P(x_{k_1}, \ldots, x_{k_a})$ consists of a predicate variable P of arity a followed by a term variables. A *literal* is an atom (*positive* literal) or the negation of an atom (*negative* literal). A *clause* is a finite disjunction of literals. A *Horn clause* is a clause with at most one positive literal. From this point on, we omit the term *Horn* because all clauses in the rest of the paper are Horn clauses (λ-free function-free second-order Horn clauses to be precise). The positive literal of a clause C, when it exists, is its *head* and is denoted as $h(C)$. The set of negative literals of C is called its *body* and is denoted as $b(C)$. The clause C is written as $h(C) \leftarrow b(C)$. We denote the empty clause as $\square$. We denote the number of literals occurring in $b(C)$ as $|b(C)|$, i.e. the body size of C. A *theory* T is a set of clauses.

A *substitution* σ is a function mapping term variables to term variables, and predicate variables to predicate variables with the same arity. The application of a substitution σ to a clause C is written $C\sigma$. A substitution σ is a *unifier* of two literals when they are equal after substitution. A substitution σ is a *most general unifier* of two literals, denoted as m.g.u., when no smaller substitution is also a unifier of the two literals, i.e. there exist no σ' and γ such that σ' unifies the two literals and $\sigma = \sigma' \circ \gamma$. The variables in a clause are implicitly universally quantified. In practice, ILP approaches typically use existentially quantified predicate variables [1,9,15,35]. However, we ignore the quantification of the predicate variables because we are not concerned with the semantics of the clauses, only their syntactic form.

3.2 Derivation Reduction

The derivation reduction problem can be defined for any proof system but we focus on SLD-resolution [26] because of the direct application to ILP. SLD-resolution is a restricted form of resolution [41] based on linear resolution with two main additional constraints (1) it is restricted to Horn clauses, and (2) it does not use factors, where factoring unifies two literals in the same clause during the application of the resolution inference rule (this implies that all resolvents are binary resolvents). SLD-resolution is usually defined for first-order logic. To apply it to the second-order clauses in this paper, we replace the standard notion of a m.g.u. with the one defined in the previous paragraph that also handles predicate variables. An SLD-resolution inference is denoted as $C_1, C_2 \vdash C$ where the necessary m.g.u. is implicitly applied on C. The clauses C_1 and C_2 are the *premises* and C is the *resolvent* of the inference. The literal being resolved upon in C_1 and C_2 is called the *pivot* of the resolution. We define a function $S^n(T)$ of a theory T as:

$$S^0(T) = T$$
$$S^n(T) = \{C \mid C_1 \in S^{n-1}(T), C_2 \in T, s.t.\ C_1, C_2 \vdash C\}$$

The *SLD-closure* of a theory T is defined as:

$$S^*(T) = \bigcup_{n \in \mathbb{N}} S^n(T)$$

A clause C is *derivable* from the theory T, written $T \vdash^* C$, if and only if $C \in S^*(T)$. Given a theory T, a clause $C \in T$ is *reducible* if it is the resolvent of an inference whose premises all belong to T and have a body size smaller than $|b(C)|$. A clause C is *redundant* in the theory $T \cup \{C\}$ if and only if $T \vdash^* C$. By extension, a theory T is *redundant* to another theory $T' \subseteq T$ if for all $C \in T$, $T' \vdash^* C$. A theory is *reduced* if and only if it does not contain any redundant clauses. We state the *reduction problem*:

Definition 1 (Reduction Problem). *Given a possibly infinite theory T, the reduction problem is to find a finite theory $T' \subseteq T$ such that (1) T is redundant to T', and (2) T' is reduced. In this case, we say that T' is a reduction core of T.*

Note that in the case of a finite theory T, the existence of a reduction core is obvious since at worst it is T itself. However, for arbitrary theories it is impossible to compute or a reduction core because the derivation reduction problem is undecidable [12].

4 Fragments of Interest in $\mathcal{H}$

From Sect. 5 onwards we study whether derivationally reduced theories exist for various fragments of Horn logic. Horn logic with function symbols has the expressive power of Turing machines and is consequently undecidable [45], hence ILP approaches typically learn programs without function symbols [37], which are decidable [13]. We therefore focus on function-free Horn clauses. We denote the set of all second-order function-free Horn clauses as $\mathcal{H}$.

We further impose syntactic restrictions on clauses in $\mathcal{H}$ principally on the arity of the literals and on the number of literals in the clauses. Let us consider a fragment $\mathcal{F}$ of $\mathcal{H}$. We write $\mathcal{F}_{a,b}$ to denote clauses in $\mathcal{F}$ that contain literals of arity at most a and clauses of body size at most b. For example, the clause $P_0(x_1) \leftarrow P_1(x_2, x_3, x_4)$ is in $\mathcal{H}_{3,1}$. When one of these restrictions is not imposed, the symbol ∞ replaces the corresponding number. When restrictions are imposed on a fragment that is already restricted, the stricter restrictions are kept. For example, $(\mathcal{H}_{4,1})_{3,\infty} = \mathcal{H}_{3,1} = \mathcal{H}_{4,1} \cap \mathcal{H}_{3,\infty}$. We rely on the body size restriction to bound the reduction cores of the studied fragments.

We also constrain the fragments so that they are defined modulo variable renaming and so that only the most general clauses up to variable unification are considered. Let C be a clause verifying the syntactic restrictions of a given fragment $\mathcal{F}$. Then there exists a clause $C_{\mathcal{F}} \in \mathcal{F}$ such that $C_{\mathcal{F}}\sigma = C$ for some substitution σ. The motivation behind this restriction is that SLD-resolution only applies m.g.u.s and not any unifiers but some clauses like C' may need more specific unifiers to be generated and can thus be unreachable by SLD-resolution. This is not restrictive because up to variable renaming any such C' can be obtained from C by renaming and unifying variables.

Definition 2 (Reducible fragment). *A fragment $\mathcal{F}$ of $\mathcal{H}$ is reducible to $\mathcal{F}_{\infty,b}$ when, for all $C \in \mathcal{F}$ such that $b < |\mathsf{b}(C)|$, there exists $b' < |\mathsf{b}(C)|$ such that $\mathcal{F}_{\infty,b'} \vdash C$, i.e. C is the resolvent of an inference with premises in $\mathcal{F}_{\infty,b'}$.*

The following results are consequences of this definition and of the reduction problem statement.

Proposition 3 (Reduciblility). *If a fragment $\mathcal{F}$ is reducible to $\mathcal{F}_{\infty,b}$ then $\mathcal{F}$ is redundant to $\mathcal{F}_{\infty,b}$.*

Theorem 4 (Cores of Reducible Fragments). *If a fragment $\mathcal{F}$ is reducible to $\mathcal{F}_{\infty,b}$ then the solutions of the reduction problem for $\mathcal{F}$ and $\mathcal{F}_{\infty,b}$ are the same, i.e. the reduction cores of $\mathcal{F}$ and $\mathcal{F}_{\infty,b}$ are the same.*

Because we are motivated by applications in ILP, we focus on connected clauses [1,9,15,25,37]:

Definition 5 (Connected Fragment). *A clause is connected if the literals in the clause cannot be partitioned into two non-empty sets such that the variables appearing in the literals of one set are disjoint from the variables appearing in the literals of the other set. The* connected *fragment, denoted as $\mathcal{H}^c$, is the subset of $\mathcal{H}$ where all clauses are connected.*

Example 6. The clause $C_1 = P_0(x_1,x_2) \leftarrow P_1(x_3,x_1), P_2(x_2), P_3(x_3)$ is in $\mathcal{H}^c$, but the clause $C_2 = P_0(x_1,x_2) \leftarrow P_1(x_3,x_4), P_2(x_2), P_3(x_3)$ is not because none of the variables in P_0 and P_2 (x_1 and x_2) appear in P_1 and P_3 and vice versa.

A stricter version of connectedness, denoted here as 2-connectedness, describes the fragment that is used the most in ILP [9]. It essentially eliminates singleton variables.

Definition 7 (2-Connected Fragment). *The* 2-connected *fragment, denoted as $\mathcal{H}^{2c}$, is the subset of $\mathcal{H}^c$ such that all the term variables occur at least twice in distinct literals. In this context, a term variable that does not follow this restriction is denoted as* pending.

Example 8. The clause C_1 from Example 6 is in $\mathcal{H}^{2c}$ because x_1 is in P_0 and P_1, x_2 is in P_0 and P_2, and x_3 is in P_1 and P_3. By contrast, the clause $C_3 = P_0(x_1,x_2) \leftarrow P_1(x_3,x_1), P_2(x_1), P_3(x_3)$ is in $\mathcal{H}^c$ but not in $\mathcal{H}^{2c}$ because x_2 only occurs once and is thus pending.

Note that the simple syntactic restrictions can be combined with both connectedness and 2-connectedness. In the following sections we consider the reduction problem for $\mathcal{H}^c$ (Sect. 5), $\mathcal{H}^{2c}_{2,\infty}$ (Sect. 6), and $\mathcal{H}^{2c}_{3,\infty}$ (Sect. 7).

5   The Fragment $\mathcal{H}^c$ Is Reducible to $\mathcal{H}^c_{\infty,2}$

We now study whether certain fragments can be reduced. Our first focus is on the fragment $\mathcal{H}^c$which contains all connected clauses. We are primarily interested in whether this fragment can be reduced using SLD-resolution to a minimal fragment, preferably with only two literals in the body ($\mathcal{H}^c_{\infty,2}$).

5.1   Graph Encoding

To prove the reducibility of $\mathcal{H}^c$ we consider $\mathcal{H}^c_{a,\infty}$ for any $a \in \mathbb{N}^*$ and show that it can be reduced to $\mathcal{H}^c_{a,2}$. To reduce all clauses in $\mathcal{H}^c_{a,\infty}$ of body size greater than two, we rely on the following graph encoding to create connected premises to infer C. We assume reader familiarity with basic notions of graph theory, in particular, notions of *spanning trees*, *connected graphs*, *degree* of vertices and *outgoing* edges (from a set of vertices).

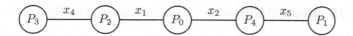

Fig. 1. Encoding of $C = P_0(x_1, x_2) \leftarrow P_2(x_1, x_3, x_4), P_3(x_4), P_4(x_2, x_5), P_1(x_5, x_6)$ where vertices correspond to literals and edges represent variables shared by two literals

Definition 9 (Graph Encoding). *Let C be a clause in $\mathcal{H}^c_{m,\infty}$. The undirected graph $\mathcal{G}_C$ is such that:*

- *There is a bijection between the vertices of $\mathcal{G}_C$ and the predicate variable occurrences in C (head and body).*
- *There is an edge in $\mathcal{G}_C$ between each pair of vertices for each corresponding pair of literals that share a common term variable. The edge is labeled with the corresponding variable.*

Example 10. $C = P_0(x_1, x_2) \leftarrow P_2(x_1, x_3, x_4), P_3(x_4), P_4(x_2, x_5), P_1(x_5, x_6)$ is mapped to $\mathcal{G}_C$ as illustrated in Fig. 1. Note that since the variables x_3 and x_6 occur only in P_2 and P_1 respectively, they are not present in $\mathcal{G}_C$. In fact $\mathcal{G}_C$ also represents many other clauses, e.g. $P_1(x_5, x_5) \leftarrow P_0(x_2, x_1)$, $P_2(x_4, x_3, x_1), P_3(x_4), P_4(x_2, x_5)$.

This graph encoding allows us to focus on connectivity, as stated in the following proposition.

Proposition 11. *Let $C \in \mathcal{H}$. The graph $\mathcal{G}_C$ is connected if and only if $C \in \mathcal{H}^c$.*

In other words, the notion of connectedness that we introduced for clauses in Definition 5 is equivalent to graph connectedness when encoding the clauses in graph form using Definition 9. Because we are only interested in connected clauses, we only handle connected graphs.

5.2 Reducibility of $\mathcal{H}^c$

Proposition 12 is the main intermediary step in the proof of reducibility of the connected fragment (Theorem 13). A detailed proof of this result is available in the technical report version of this paper [46].

Proposition 12 (Spanning Tree). *For any clause $C \in \mathcal{H}^c_{a,\infty}$, $a \in \mathbb{N}^*$, there exists a spanning tree of $\mathcal{G}_C$ in which there exist two adjacent vertices such that the number of edges outgoing from this pair of vertices is at most a.*

Proof sketch. Assuming no such pair of vertices exists in any spanning tree of $\mathcal{G}_C$, we show in a case analysis that it is always possible to transform a spanning tree into another one where such a pair exists, a contradiction.

The main result of this section is the next theorem stating that any connected fragment of constrained arity has a reduction core containing clauses of body size at most two.

Theorem 13 (Reducibility of $\mathcal{H}^c_{a,\infty}$). *For any $a \in \mathbb{N}^*$, $\mathcal{H}^c_{a,\infty}$ is reducible to $\mathcal{H}^c_{a,2}$.*

Proof. Let $a \in \mathbb{N}^*$ be fixed and $C = P_0(..) \leftarrow P_1(..), .., P_k(..) \in \mathcal{H}^c_{a,\infty}$ ($k \geq 3$). By applying Proposition 12, it is possible to identify two adjacent vertices v and v' in $\mathcal{G}_C$ such that there exists a spanning tree $\mathcal{S}$ of $\mathcal{G}_C$ where the number of edges outgoing from the pair v, v' is less than or equal to a. Let P_v and $P_{v'}$ be the predicate variables respectively corresponding to v and v' in C. Let $x_1, .., x_{a'}$ ($a' \leq a$) be the variables corresponding to the edges outgoing from the pair of vertices v, v'. Let P'_0 be an unused predicate variable of arity a'. We define: $C_1 = P_0(..) \leftarrow P'_0(x_1, .., x_{a'}), P_1(..), .., P_k(..) \backslash \{P_v(..), P_{v'}(..)\}$ and $C_2 = P'_0(x_1, .., x_{a'}) \leftarrow P_v(..), P_{v'}(..)$. These clauses are such that $C_1, C_2 \in \mathcal{H}^c_{a',\infty}$ and $C_1, C_2 \vdash C$ modulo variable unification.[1] Thus, C is reducible.

We extend this result to the whole connected fragment.

Theorem 14 (Reducibility of $\mathcal{H}^c$). *The fragment $\mathcal{H}^c$ is reducible to $\mathcal{H}^c_{\infty,2}$.*

Note that Theorem 14 does not imply that $\mathcal{H}^c$ has a reduction core because $\mathcal{H}^c_{\infty,2}$ is also infinite. In fact, since it is not possible to increase the arity of literals through SLD-resolution, any fragment where this arity is not constrained is guaranteed to have no reduction core since at least one literal of each arity must occur in it and the number of literals that occur in a clause is finite.

6   Reducibility of $\mathcal{H}^{2c}_{2,\infty}$

We now consider the reducibility of $\mathcal{H}^{2c}_{2,\infty}$. The restriction to monadic and dyadic literals is common not only in ILP [1,6,15,35] but also in description logics [2] and in ontology reasoning [21]. Although this fragment is only slightly more constrained than $\mathcal{H}^c_{2,\infty}$, itself reducible to $\mathcal{H}^c_{2,2}$, we show that it is impossible to reduce $\mathcal{H}^{2c}_{2,\infty}$ to any size-constrained sub-fragment. To do so we exhibit a subset $\mathcal{H}^{nr}$ in $\mathcal{H}^{2c}_{2,\infty}$ that cannot be reduced. This set contains clauses of arbitrary size. In practice, this means that in $\mathcal{H}^{2c}_{2,\infty}$ given any integer k it is possible to exhibit a clause of body size superior or equal to k that cannot be reduced, thus preventing $\mathcal{H}^{2c}_{2,\infty}$ itself to be reducible to $\mathcal{H}^{2c}_{2,k}$ no matter how big k is. We start by defining the clause $C_{base} \in \mathcal{H}^{nr}$.

Definition 15 (C_{base}).

$$C_{base} = P_0(x_1, x_2) \leftarrow P_1(x_1, x_3), P_2(x_1, x_4), P_3(x_2, x_3), P_4(x_2, x_4), P_5(x_3, x_4).$$

In C_{base} all the literals are symmetrical to each other. Each literal (vertex) has (1) two neighbours connected by their first variable, (2) two other neighbours connected by their second variable, and (3) another literal that it is not connected to but which all the other literals are. This symmetry is better seen on

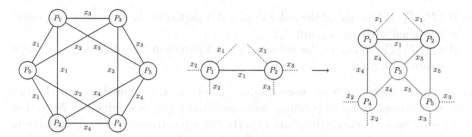

(a) Graph encoding of C_{base}, $\mathcal{G}_{C_{base}}$

(b) Partial graph encoding of a clause before and after a non-red preserving transformation

Fig. 2. Graph encoding of $\mathcal{H}^{nr}$ base and construction rule (Color figure online)

the graphical representation of C_{base} in Fig. 2a. For example P_0 does not share literals with P_5 but does with all other predicates.

Proposition 16 (Non-reducibility of C_{base}). C_{base} *is irreducible.*

Proof. To derive C_{base} from two smaller clauses, these two smaller clauses C_1 and C_2 must form a partition of the literals in C_{base} if one excludes the pivot. To solve this problem, we partition the vertices of $\mathcal{G}_{C_{base}}$ in two sets and count the number of edges with distinct labels that link vertices from the two sets. These edges correspond to pending variables in one of the sets, i.e. to the variables that must occur in the pivot that will be added in both sets to form C_1 and C_2. If there are more than two of these variables, the pivot cannot contain all of them, thus at least one of C_1 and C_2 is not in $\mathcal{H}^{2c}_{2,\infty}$ for lack of 2-connectivity. Each of the two sets in the partition must contain at least two elements, otherwise one of C_1, C_2 is as big as C_{base} which does not make C_{base} reducible even though it is derivable from C_1, C_2. The symmetries in $\mathcal{G}_{C_{base}}$ are exploited to reduce the number of cases to consider to only four that vary along two dimensions: the cardinalities of the two subsets, either 2-4 or 3-3 respectively; and the connectedness of the subsets. In the 2-4 partition, only the following cases or symmetric ones are possible:

- if $\{P_0, P_5\}$ is the subset of cardinality 2 in a 2-4 partition, then the edges outgoing from this subset, connecting the two subsets and that correspond to pending variables, are labeled with x_1, x_2, x_3 and x_4;
- if $\{P_0, P_1\}$ is the subset of cardinality 2 in a 2-4 partition, then the outgoing edges are labeled with x_1, x_2 and x_3.

All the remaining 2-4 cases where P_0 is in the subset of cardinality 2 are symmetric to this case. The other 2-4 cases are symmetric to either one of these two cases. Similarly, all the 3-3 partition are symmetric to one of the following cases:

---

[1] Some connections may be lost between variables in C_1 and C_2 since only the ones occurring in the spanning tree $\mathcal{S}$ are preserved. However, they can be recovered by unifying the disconnected variables together in the resolvent.

- if $\{P_0, P_1, P_2\}$ is one of the subsets in a 3-3 partition then the outgoing edges are labeled with x_2, x_3 and x_4;
- if $\{P_0, P_1, P_4\}$ is one of the subsets in a 3-3 partition then the outgoing edges are labeled with x_1, x_2, x_3 and x_4.

In all cases, there are 3 or more distinct labels on the edges between the two subsets, corresponding to pending variables, thus C_{base} is irreducible. Note that this proof works because there are exactly three occurrences of each variable in C_{base}. Otherwise it would not be possible to match the labels with the pending variables.

We define a transformation that turns a clause into a bigger clause (Definition 17) such that when applied to an irreducible clause verifying some syntactic property, the resulting clause is also irreducible (Proposition 18).

Definition 17 (Non-red Preserving Extension). *Let the body of a clause $C \in \mathcal{H}_{2,\infty}^{2c}$ contain two dyadic literals sharing a common variable, e.g. $P_1(x_1, x_2)$ and $P_2(x_1, x_3)$, without loss of generality. A non-red preserving extension of C is any transformation which replaces two such literals in C by the following set of literals: $P_1(x_1, x_4)$, $P_2(x_1, x_5)$, $P_3(x_4, x_5)$, $P_4(x_4, x_2)$, $P_5(x_5, x_3)$ where P_3, P_4, P_5, x_4 and x_5 are new predicate and term variables.*

Proposition 18 (Non-red Preserving Extension). *If a clause C is irreducible and all the term variables it contains occur three times then any non-red preserving extension of C is also irreducible.*

Proof sketch. We assume that a non-red preserving extension of C is reducible and we use a case analysis to show that this implies that C is also reducible, a contradiction. This proof heavily exploits the symmetry that can be seen on Fig. 2b to reduce the number of cases to consider.

Starting from C_{base} and using this extension, we define $\mathcal{H}^{nr}$ formally (Definition 19) and, as a consequence of Proposition 18, $\mathcal{H}^{nr}$ contains only irreducible clauses (Proposition 20).

Definition 19 (Non-reducible Fragment). *The subset $\mathcal{H}^{nr}$ of $\mathcal{H}_{2,\infty}^{2c}$ contains C_{base} and all the clauses that can be obtained by applying a non-red extension to another clause in $\mathcal{H}^{nr}$.*

Proposition 20 (Non-reducibility of $\mathcal{H}^{nr}$). *For all $C \in \mathcal{H}^{nr}$, C is irreducible.*

The non-reducibility of $\mathcal{H}^{nr}$ ensures that the body size of the clauses in a hypothetical reduction core of $\mathcal{H}_{2,\infty}^{2c}$ cannot be bounded, which in turn prevents the existence of this reduction core. This result has negative consequences on ILP approaches that use second-order templates. We discuss these consequences in the conclusion.

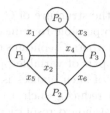

Fig. 3. $\mathcal{G}_C$ for $C = P_0(x_1, x_2, x_3) \leftarrow P_1(x_1, x_4, x_5), P_2(x_2, x_5, x_6), P_3(x_3, x_4, x_6)$

7   Reducibility of $\mathcal{H}^{2c}_{3,\infty}$

The reducibility of $\mathcal{H}^{2c}_{3,\infty}$ is still an open problem. However, we know that it cannot be reduced to $\mathcal{H}^{2c}_{3,2}$.

Theorem 21 (Non-reducibility of $\mathcal{H}^{2c}_{3,2}$). $\mathcal{H}^{2c}_{3,\infty}$ *cannot be reduced to* $\mathcal{H}^{2c}_{3,2}$

Proof. The clause $C = P_0(x_1, x_2, x_3) \leftarrow P_1(x_1, x_4, x_5), P_2(x_2, x_5, x_6), P_3(x_3, x_4, x_6)$, shown in graph form in Fig. 3, is a counter-example because any pair of literals in it contain exactly four pending variables. For example, consider the following pair of literals: $(P_1(x_1, x_4, x_5), P_0(x_1, x_2, x_3))$ leaves x_2, x_3, x_4, x_5 pending. By symmetry the same holds for all the other pairs of literals. Thus none of these pairs can be completed by a triadic (or less) pivot. In addition, the removal of any single literal from C does not lead to a reduction of the clause since all the variables occurring in the literal then occur only once in each subset of the clause. For example, to replace $P_1(x_1, x_4, x_5)$, a triadic literal containing x_1, x_4 and x_5 needs to be added, creating a clause identical to C up to the name of one predicate variable and the order of the term variables in it. Therefore C is irreducible in $\mathcal{H}^{2c}_{3,\infty}$, thus $\mathcal{H}^{2c}_{3,\infty}$ cannot be reduced to $\mathcal{H}^{2c}_{3,2}$.

In addition to this result, for lack of finding a reduction to $P_0(x_1, x_2, x_3) \leftarrow P_1(x_1, x_5, x_6), P_2(x_2, x_4, x_8), P_3(x_6, x_7, x_8), P_4(x_4, x_5, x_7), P_5(x_3, x_4, x_7)$ (not formally proved) we conjecture that $\mathcal{H}^{2c}_{3,\infty}$ cannot be reduced to $\mathcal{H}^{2c}_{3,4}$. Clarifying this situation and that of any $\mathcal{H}^{2c}_{a,\infty}$ with $a \geq 3$ is left as future work.

8   Extension to Standard Resolution

Although we introduced the derivation reduction problem for SLD-resolution, the principle applies to any standard deductive proof system, and in particular, it can be applied to standard resolution, extended from first to second-order logic in the same way that was used for SLD-resolution. Given that SLD-resolution is but a restriction of resolution, the positive reducibility result for $\mathcal{H}^c_{2,\infty}$ is directly transferable to standard resolution. On the contrary, the fragment $\mathcal{H}^{2c}_{2,\infty}$, that we proved irreducible with SLD-resolution, can be reduced to $\mathcal{H}^{2c}_{2,2}$ with standard resolution.

Theorem 22 (Reducibility$_R$ of $\mathcal{H}^{2c}_{2,\infty}$). $\mathcal{H}^{2c}_{2,\infty}$ *is reducible$_R$ to* $\mathcal{H}^{2c}_{2,2}$

Proof sketch. We first analyse the structure of C and show how to reduce C in the simple cases where it is also possible to reduce C using SLD-resolution. We are then left to consider clauses where C contains only dyadic predicates, no two predicates in C have the same pair of variables and all variables occur exactly three times in C. An example of such clauses is the $\mathcal{H}^{nr}$ family from Sect. 6. Then we present a method to reduce$_R$ such a clause C. The key point that justifies Theorem 22 is that in standard resolution, factorisation is allowed and thus allows inferences that remove duplicate literals. The removal of duplicate literals would be also possible with SLD-resolution but only when the fragment contains bodyless clauses which is prevented by 2-connectedness.

Let us consider an example of additional inferences allowed with resolution but not with SLD-resolution in the $\mathcal{H}^{2c}_{2,\infty}$ fragment, that make the C_{base} clause redundant:

$$P_0(x_1, x_2) \leftarrow P_1(x_1, x_3), P_2(x_1, x_4), P_3(x_2, x_3), H(x_2, x_4)$$
$$H'(x_2', x_4') \leftarrow P_3'(x_2', x_3'), P_4'(x_2', x_4'), P_5'(x_3', x_4')$$
$$\overline{P_0(x_1, x_2) \leftarrow P_1(x_1, x_3), P_2(x_1, x_4), P_3(x_2, x_3), P_3'(x_2, x_3'), P_4'(x_2, x_4), P_5'(x_3', x_4)}$$
$$P_0(x_1, x_2) \leftarrow P_1(x_1, x_3), P_2(x_1, x_4), P_3(x_2, x_3), P_4'(x_2, x_4), P_5'(x_3, x_4)$$

The first step is a resolution that unifies H' with H, x_2' with x_2 and x_4' with x_4 and uses $H(x_2, x_4)$ as pivot. The second step is a factorisation that unifies P_3' with P_3, and x_3' with x_3. The result is C_{base} up to variable renaming.

Finally, the result that we presented for $\mathcal{H}^{2c}_{3,\infty}$ is also transferable from SLD- to standard resolution since the proof of Theorem 21 remains the same. This is because the size of the considered clauses does not allow for the kind of resolution inferences that make Theorem 22 possible. Table 1 summarises our findings and their extension to standard resolution.

9   Conclusion

We have introduced the derivation reduction problem for second-order Horn clauses ($\mathcal{H}$), i.e. the undecidable problem of finding a finite subset of a set of clauses from which the whole set can be derived using SLD-resolution. We have considered the derivation reducibility of several fragments of $\mathcal{H}$, for which the results are summarised in Table 1. We have also extended the results from SLD-resolution to standard resolution. Further work is necessary to clarify the situation for $\mathcal{H}^{2c}_{3,\infty}$ and for fragments with higher arity constraints.

Although we have positive results regarding the reducibility of certain fragments, we have not identified the reductions of those fragments, nor have we provided any results regarding the cardinality of the reductions. Future work should address this limitation by introducing algorithms to compute the reductions.

Our results have direct implications in ILP. As described in the introduction, many ILP systems use second-order Horn clauses as templates to define the hypothesis space. An open question [8,9,35] is whether there exists finite sets of

Table 1. Summary of the results. When a fragment is preceded with > the entry must be read as "no reduction up to this fragment". The word *possibly* precedes results that have not been proved and are only conjectured.

Fragment	Reducibility	
	SLD-resolution	Standard resolution
$\mathcal{H}^c$	$\mathcal{H}^c_{\infty,2}$	$\mathcal{H}^c_{\infty,2}$
$\mathcal{H}^{2c}_{2,\infty}$	no	$\mathcal{H}^{2c}_{2,2}$
$\mathcal{H}^{2c}_{3,\infty}$	$> \mathcal{H}^{2c}_{3,2}$	$> \mathcal{H}^{2c}_{3,2}$
	possibly $> \mathcal{H}^{2c}_{3,4}$	possibly $> \mathcal{H}^{2c}_{3,4}$

such clauses from which these systems could induce any logic program in a specific fragment of logic. Proposition 20 shows that for the $\mathcal{H}^{2c}_{2,\infty}$ fragment, which is often the focus of ILP, the answer is no. This result implies that ILP systems, such as Metagol [11] and HEXMIL [25], are incomplete in that they cannot learn all programs in this fragment without being given an infinite set of clauses (these approaches require a finite set of such clauses hence the incompleteness).

Our work now opens up a new challenge of overcoming this negative result for $\mathcal{H}^{2c}_{2,\infty}$ (and negative conjectures for $\mathcal{H}^{2c}_{3,\infty}$). One possible solution would be to allow the use of triadic literals as pivot in inferences in specific cases where SLD-resolution fails to derive the desired clause, but this idea requires further investigation.

Acknowledgements. The authors thank Katsumi Inoue and Stephen Muggleton for discussions on this work.

References

1. Albarghouthi, A., Koutris, P., Naik, M., Smith, C.: Constraint-based synthesis of datalog programs. In: Beck, J.C. (ed.) CP 2017. LNCS, vol. 10416, pp. 689–706. Springer, Cham (2017). https://doi.org/10.1007/978-3-319-66158-2_44
2. Baader, F., Horrocks, I., Lutz, C., Sattler, U.: An Introduction to Description Logic. Cambridge University Press, Cambridge (2017)
3. Balcázar, J.L.: Redundancy, deduction schemes, and minimum-size bases for association rules. Log. Methods Comput. Sci. **6**(2), 1–33 (2010)
4. Bienvenu, M.: Prime implicates and prime implicants in modal logic. In: Proceedings of the National Conference on Artificial Intelligence, vol. 22, p. 379. AAAI Press/MIT Press, Menlo Park/Cambridge (2007)
5. Buntine, W.: Generalized subsumption and its applications to induction and redundancy. Artif. Intell. **36**(2), 149–176 (1988). https://doi.org/10.1016/0004-3702(88)90001-X
6. Campero, A., Pareja, A., Klinger, T., Tenenbaum, J., Riedel, S.: Logical rule induction and theory learning using neural theorem proving. ArXiv e-prints, September 2018

7. Charalambidis, A., Handjopoulos, K., Rondogiannis, P., Wadge, W.W.: Extensional higher-order logic programming. ACM Trans. Comput. Log. **14**(3), 21:1–21:40 (2013). https://doi.org/10.1145/2499937.2499942
8. Cropper, A.: Efficiently learning efficient programs. Ph.D. thesis, Imperial College London, UK (2017)
9. Cropper, A., Muggleton, S.H.: Logical minimisation of meta-rules within meta-interpretive learning. In: Davis, J., Ramon, J. (eds.) ILP 2014. LNCS (LNAI), vol. 9046, pp. 62–75. Springer, Cham (2015). https://doi.org/10.1007/978-3-319-23708-4_5
10. Cropper, A., Muggleton, S.H.: Learning higher-order logic programs through abstraction and invention. In: Kambhampati, S. (ed.) Proceedings of the Twenty-Fifth International Joint Conference on Artificial Intelligence, IJCAI 2016, 9–15 July 2016, New York, pp. 1418–1424. IJCAI/AAAI Press (2016)
11. Cropper, A., Muggleton, S.H.: Metagol system (2016). https://github.com/metagol/metagol
12. Cropper, A., Tourret, S.: Derivation reduction of metarules in meta-interpretive learning. In: Proceedings of Inductive Logic Programming - 28th International Conference, ILP 2018, 2–4 September 2018, Ferrara, Italy, pp. 1–21 (2018). https://doi.org/10.1007/978-3-319-99960-9_1
13. Dantsin, E., Eiter, T., Gottlob, G., Voronkov, A.: Complexity and expressive power of logic programming. ACM Comput. Surv. **33**(3), 374–425 (2001). https://doi.org/10.1145/502807.502810
14. Echenim, M., Peltier, N., Tourret, S.: Quantifier-free equational logic and prime implicate generation. In: Felty, A.P., Middeldorp, A. (eds.) CADE 2015. LNCS (LNAI), vol. 9195, pp. 311–325. Springer, Cham (2015). https://doi.org/10.1007/978-3-319-21401-6_21
15. Evans, R., Grefenstette, E.: Learning explanatory rules from noisy data. J. Artif. Intell. Res. **61**, 1–64 (2018). https://doi.org/10.1613/jair.5714
16. Gottlob, G., Fermüller, C.G.: Removing redundancy from a clause. Artif. Intell. **61**(2), 263–289 (1993)
17. Grädel, E.: The expressive power of second order Horn logic. In: Choffrut, C., Jantzen, M. (eds.) STACS 1991. LNCS, vol. 480, pp. 466–477. Springer, Heidelberg (1991). https://doi.org/10.1007/BFb0020821
18. Hemaspaandra, E., Schnoor, H.: Minimization for generalized Boolean formulas. In: IJCAI Proceedings-International Joint Conference on Artificial Intelligence, vol. 22, p. 566 (2011)
19. Heule, M., Järvisalo, M., Lonsing, F., Seidl, M., Biere, A.: Clause elimination for SAT and QSAT. J. Artif. Intell. Res. **53**, 127–168 (2015)
20. Hillenbrand, T., Piskac, R., Waldmann, U., Weidenbach, C.: From search to computation: redundancy criteria and simplification at work. In: Voronkov, A., Weidenbach, C. (eds.) Programming Logics. LNCS, vol. 7797, pp. 169–193. Springer, Heidelberg (2013). https://doi.org/10.1007/978-3-642-37651-1_7
21. Hohenecker, P., Lukasiewicz, T.: Deep learning for ontology reasoning. CoRR abs/1705.10342 (2017)
22. Huet, G.P.: A mechanization of type theory. In: Proceedings of the 3rd International Joint Conference on Artificial Intelligence, pp. 139–146 (1973)
23. Immerman, N.: Descriptive Complexity. Springer, New York (2012). https://doi.org/10.1007/978-1-4612-0539-5
24. Joyner Jr., W.H.: Resolution strategies as decision procedures. J. ACM **23**(3), 398–417 (1976). https://doi.org/10.1145/321958.321960

25. Kaminski, T., Eiter, T., Inoue, K.: Exploiting answer set programming with external sources for meta-interpretive learning. In: 34th International Conference on Logic Programming (2018)
26. Kowalski, R.A.: Predicate logic as programming language. In: IFIP Congress, pp. 569–574 (1974)
27. Langlois, M., Mubayi, D., Sloan, R.H., Turán, G.: Combinatorial problems for Horn clauses. In: Lipshteyn, M., Levit, V.E., McConnell, R.M. (eds.) Graph Theory, Computational Intelligence and Thought. LNCS, vol. 5420, pp. 54–65. Springer, Heidelberg (2009). https://doi.org/10.1007/978-3-642-02029-2_6
28. Liberatore, P.: Redundancy in logic I: CNF propositional formulae. Artif. Intell. **163**(2), 203–232 (2005). https://doi.org/10.1016/j.artint.2004.11.002
29. Liberatore, P.: Redundancy in logic II: 2CNF and Horn propositional formulae. Artif. Intell. **172**(2–3), 265–299 (2008). https://doi.org/10.1016/j.artint.2007.06.003
30. Lloyd, J.: Logic for Learning. COGTECH. Springer, Heidelberg (2003). https://doi.org/10.1007/978-3-662-08406-9
31. Marquis, P.: Consequence finding algorithms. In: Kohlas, J., Moral, S. (eds.) Handbook of Defeasible Reasoning and Uncertainty Management Systems, pp. 41–145. Springer, Dordrecht (2000). https://doi.org/10.1007/978-94-017-1737-3
32. McCarthy, J.: Making robots conscious of their mental states. In: Machine Intelligence 15, Intelligent Agents, July 1995, pp. 3–17. St. Catherine's College, Oxford (1995)
33. Muggleton, S.: Inductive logic programming. New Gener. Comput. **8**(4), 295–318 (1991)
34. Muggleton, S.: Inverse entailment and Progol. New Gener. Comput. **13**, 245–286 (1995)
35. Muggleton, S., Lin, D., Tamaddoni-Nezhad, A.: Meta-interpretive learning of higher-order dyadic datalog: predicate invention revisited. Mach. Learn. **100**(1), 49–73 (2015)
36. Muggleton, S., et al.: ILP turns 20 - biography and future challenges. Mach. Learn. **86**(1), 3–23 (2012). https://doi.org/10.1007/s10994-011-5259-2
37. Nienhuys-Cheng, S.H., De Wolf, R.: Foundations of Inductive Logic Programming. Springer, New York (1997). https://doi.org/10.1007/3-540-62927-0
38. Plotkin, G.: Automatic methods of inductive inference. Ph.D. thesis, Edinburgh University, August 1971
39. Raedt, L.D.: Declarative modeling for machine learning and data mining. In: Proceedings of Algorithmic Learning Theory - 23rd International Conference, ALT, p. 12 (2012). https://doi.org/10.1007/978-3-642-34106-9_2
40. Raedt, L.D., Bruynooghe, M.: Interactive concept-learning and constructive induction by analogy. Mach. Learn. **8**, 107–150 (1992). https://doi.org/10.1007/BF00992861
41. Robinson, J.A.: A machine-oriented logic based on the resolution principle. J. ACM **12**(1), 23–41 (1965). https://doi.org/10.1145/321250.321253
42. Rocktäschel, T., Riedel, S.: End-to-end differentiable proving. In: Guyon, I., et al. (eds.) Advances in Neural Information Processing Systems 30: Annual Conference on Neural Information Processing Systems 2017, pp. 3791–3803 (2017)
43. Sato, T.: Equivalence-preserving first-order unfold/fold transformation systems. Theor. Comput. Sci. **105**(1), 57–84 (1992). https://doi.org/10.1016/0304-3975(92)90287-P

44. Si, X., Lee, W., Zhang, R., Albarghouthi, A., Koutris, P., Naik, M.: Syntax-guided synthesis of datalog programs. In: Leavens, G.T., Garcia, A., Pasareanu, C.S. (eds.) Proceedings of the 2018 ACM Joint Meeting on European Software Engineering Conference and Symposium on the Foundations of Software Engineering, ESEC/SIGSOFT FSE 2018, pp. 515–527. ACM (2018). https://doi.org/10.1145/3236024.3236034
45. Tärnlund, S.: Horn clause computability. BIT **17**(2), 215–226 (1977)
46. Tourret, S., Cropper, A.: SLD-resolution reduction of second-order Horn fragments. Technical report (2018). https://arxiv.org/abs/1902.09900
47. Wang, W.Y., Mazaitis, K., Cohen, W.W.: Structure learning via parameter learning. In: Proceedings of the 23rd ACM International Conference on Conference on Information and Knowledge Management, pp. 1199–1208. ACM (2014)
48. Weidenbach, C., Wischnewski, P.: Subterm contextual rewriting. AI Commun. **23**(2–3), 97–109 (2010). https://doi.org/10.3233/AIC-2010-0459

Conditional, Probabilistic and Propositional Logic

Systematic Generation of Conditional Knowledge Bases up to Renaming and Equivalence

Christoph Beierle[✉] and Steven Kutsch

Faculty of Mathematics and Computer Science, FernUniversität in Hagen,
58084 Hagen, Germany
beierle@fernuni-hagen.de

Abstract. A conditional of the form "If A then usually B" establishes a plausible connection between A and B, while still allowing for exceptions. A conditional knowledge base consists of a finite set of conditionals, inducing various nonmonotonic inference relations. Sets of knowledge bases are of interest for, e.g., experimenting with systems implementing conditional reasoning and for empirically evaluating them. In this paper, we present an approach for systematically generating knowledge bases over a given signature. The approach is minimal in the sense that no two knowledge bases are generated that can be transformed into each other by a syntactic renaming or that are elementwise equivalent. Furthermore, the approach is complete in the sense that, taking renamings and equivalences into account, every consistent knowledge base is generated.

Keywords: Conditional · Normal form conditional ·
Canonical normal form conditional · Conditional knowledge base ·
Equivalence · Elementwise equivalence · Renaming · Isomorphism ·
Generation of knowledge bases

1 Introduction

A conditional *"if A then usually B"*, denoted by $(B|A)$, establishes a plausible connection between the *antecedent* A and the *consequence* B partitions the set of possible worlds in three parts: those worlds satisfying AB, thus *verifying* the conditional, those worlds satisfying $A\overline{B}$, thus *falsifying* the conditional, and those worlds not fulfilling the premise A and so which the conditional may not be applied to at all [7]. To give appropriate semantics to conditionals, they are usually considered within structures providing some kind of ordering on possible worlds. Examples are Lewis' system of spheres [13], conditional objects evaluated using boolean intervals [8], possibility distributions [6], ranking functions [15,16], or special classes of ranking functions like c-representations [10]. A common feature of these semantics is that $(B|A)$ is accepted if its verification is considered more plausible, more possible, less surprising, etc. than its

© Springer Nature Switzerland AG 2019
F. Calimeri et al. (Eds.): JELIA 2019, LNAI 11468, pp. 279–286, 2019.
https://doi.org/10.1007/978-3-030-19570-0_18

falsification. For a knowledge base $\mathcal{R}$ consisting of a set of conditionals, various nonmonotonic inference relations induced by $\mathcal{R}$ have been proposed, e.g., [3,11,12,14]. For their empirical comparison and evaluation, for instance with the help of implemented reasoning systems like [4], sets of different knowledge bases are needed. In this paper, we develop an approach for the systematic generation of conditional knowledge bases. The algorithm we present will generate precisely all consistent knowledge bases while taking both syntactic renamings and semantic elementwise equivalence into account.

2   Background: Conditional Logic

Let $\mathcal{L}$ be a propositional language over a finite set Σ of atoms $a, b, c, \ldots$. The formulas of $\mathcal{L}$ will be denoted by letters $A, B, C, \ldots$. We write AB for $A \wedge B$ and $\overline{A}$ for $\neg A$. We identify the set of all complete conjunctions over Σ with the set Ω of possible worlds over $\mathcal{L}$. For $\omega \in \Omega$, $\omega \models A$ means that $A \in \mathcal{L}$ holds in ω. By introducing a new binary operator $|$, we obtain the set $(\mathcal{L} \mid \mathcal{L}) = \{(B|A) \mid A, B \in \mathcal{L}\}$ of conditionals over $\mathcal{L}$. The counter conditional of a conditional $r = (B|A)$ is $\overline{r} = (\overline{B}|A)$. As an example of semantics for conditionals, consider ordinal conditional functions, OCFs [16]. An OCF is a function $\kappa : \Omega \to \mathbb{N}$ expressing degrees of plausibility of possible worlds where a lower degree denotes "less surprising". At least one world must be regarded as being normal; therefore, $\kappa(\omega) = 0$ for at least one $\omega \in \Omega$. Each κ uniquely extends to a function mapping sentences to $\mathbb{N} \cup \{\infty\}$ given by $\kappa(A) = \min\{\kappa(\omega) \mid \omega \models A\}$ where $\min \emptyset = \infty$. An OCF κ accepts a conditional $(B|A)$ if the verification of the conditional is less surprising than its falsification, i.e., if $\kappa(AB) < \kappa(A\overline{B})$. A finite set $\mathcal{R} \subseteq (\mathcal{L}|\mathcal{L})$ of conditionals is called a knowledge base. An OCF κ accepts $\mathcal{R}$ if κ accepts all conditionals in $\mathcal{R}$, and $\mathcal{R}$ is consistent if an OCF accepting $\mathcal{R}$ exists [9].

3   Orderings and Normal Forms for Conditionals

Under all semantics for conditionals mentioned above, two conditionals are equivalent if they partition the set of worlds in the same way; thus, $(B|A) \equiv (B'|A')$ if $A \equiv A'$ and $AB \equiv A'B'$. Furthermore, conditionals that are self-fulfilling $(A \models B)$ or contradictory $(A \models \overline{B})$, called trivial conditionals in the following, are of little interest because they can not be falsified or verified, respectively.

Definition 1 ($\leqslant_{lex}$, $\leqslant_{set}$ induced ordering on strings and sets). For an ordering relation $\leqslant$ on a set M, its lexicographic extension to strings over M is denoted by $\leqslant_{lex}$. For ordered sets $S, S' \subseteq M$ with $S = \{e_1, \ldots, e_n\}$ and $S' = \{e'_1, \ldots, e'_{n'}\}$ where $e_i \leqslant e_{i+1}$ and $e'_j \leqslant e'_{j+1}$ its extension $\leqslant_{set}$ to sets is:

$$S \leqslant_{set} S' \text{ iff } n < n', \text{ or } n = n' \text{ and } e_1 \ldots e_n \leqslant_{lex} e'_1 \ldots e'_{n'} \tag{1}$$

As a running example, we will use the signature $\Sigma_{ab} = \{a, b\}$ with the linear ordering $\lessdot$ given by $a \lessdot b$. For Σ_{ab} we have $\{a\} \leqslant_{set} \{b\}$ and $\{b\} \leqslant_{set} \{a, b\}$. For any set M with an ordering relation $\leqslant$, as usual, the induced ordering relation $<$ is defined by $m < m'$ iff both $m \leqslant m'$ and $m' \not\leqslant m$.

For defining a normal form for conditionals, we will use the representation of a propositional formula F by its set of possible worlds

$$\Omega_F = \{\omega \mid \omega \models F\}.$$

For instance, given Σ_{ab}, we have $\Omega_{a \vee \bar{b}} = \{ab, a\bar{b}, \bar{a}\bar{b}\}$. Furthermore, for each possible world ω over Σ with ordering relation $<$, $[\![\omega]\!]_<$ denotes the usual interpretation of ω as a binary number; e.g., $[\![ab]\!]_< = 3$, $[\![a\bar{b}]\!]_< = 2$, $[\![\bar{a}b]\!]_< = 1$, and $[\![\bar{a}\bar{b}]\!]_< = 0$.

Definition 2 (induced ordering on formulas and conditionals). *Let Σ be a signature with linear ordering $<$. The orderings induced by $<$ on worlds ω, ω' and conditionals $(B|A), (B'|A')$ over Σ are given by:*

$$\omega \overset{w}{\leqslant} \omega' \text{ iff } [\![\omega]\!]_< \geqslant [\![\omega']\!]_< \tag{2}$$

$$(B|A) \overset{c}{\leqslant} (B'|A') \text{ iff } \Omega_A \overset{w}{<}_{set} \Omega_{A'}, \text{ or } \Omega_A = \Omega_{A'} \text{ and } \Omega_B \overset{w}{\leqslant}_{set} \Omega_{B'} \tag{3}$$

In order to ease our notation, we will omit the upper symbol in $\overset{w}{<}$ and $\overset{c}{<}$, and write just $<$ instead, and analogously $\leqslant$ for the non-strict variants. For instance, for Σ_{ab} we have $ab < a\bar{b} < \bar{a}b < \bar{a}\bar{b}$ for worlds, and $(ab|ab \vee a\bar{b}) < (ab|ab \vee \bar{a}b)$ and $(ab \vee \bar{a}\bar{b}|ab \vee a\bar{b} \vee \bar{a}\bar{b}) < (\bar{a}\bar{b}|ab \vee a\bar{b} \vee \bar{a}b \vee \bar{a}\bar{b})$ for conditionals.

We may also use the set Ω_F instead of F within a conditional. Using this notation, in [5] conditionals of the form $(B|A)$ are generated where the conditions $B \subsetneq A$ and $B \neq \emptyset$ ensure the falsifiability and the verifiability of $(B|A)$. This leads to the following proposition providing an effective characterization of a complete and minimal set of all nontrivial conditionals over a given signature.

Proposition 1 (NFC(Σ)). *For the set of conditionals*

$$NFC(\Sigma) = \{(B|A) \mid A \subseteq \Omega_A, \ B \subsetneq A, \ B \neq \emptyset\},$$

called the set of normal form conditionals *over a signature Σ, the following holds:*

(nontrivial) *$NFC(\Sigma)$ does not contain any trivial conditional.*
(complete) *For every nontrivial conditional over Σ there is an equivalent conditional in $NFC(\Sigma)$.*
(minimal) *All conditional in $NFC(\Sigma)$ are pairwise non-equivalent.*

For instance, we have $(\{ab, a\bar{b}\}|\{ab, \bar{a}\bar{b}\}) \equiv (\{ab\}|\{ab, \bar{a}\bar{b}\}) \in NFC(\Sigma_{ab})$. Note that the normal form of the counter conditional of $(\{ab\}|\{ab, \bar{a}\bar{b}\})$ is $(\{\bar{a}\bar{b}\}|\{ab, \bar{a}\bar{b}\})$ and not $(\{a\bar{b}, \bar{a}b, \bar{a}\bar{b}\}|\{ab, \bar{a}\bar{b}\})$ since the latter is not in $NFC(\Sigma_{ab})$. Using sets of worlds as formulas yields $2^{2^{|\Sigma|}}$ different formulas and thus $2^{2^{|\Sigma|} \times 2}$ different conditionals over Σ. Out of the 256 conditionals over Σ_{ab} only 50 are in $NFC(\Sigma_{ab})$; a complete listing of these 50 conditionals is given in Table 1. The following observation will be exploited for equivalences respecting isomorphisms.

Proposition 2 (*NFC*(Σ)). *For every linear ordering $<$ on a signature Σ, the induced ordering $\prec$ on conditionals according to Definition 2 is a linear ordering on NFC(Σ).*

4   Knowledge Base Equivalences and Isomorphisms

When systematically generating knowledge bases, we are not interested in merely syntactic variants. The following notion of equivalence, presented in [2] and generalized in [1], employs the idea that each piece of knowledge in one knowledge base directly corresponds to a piece of knowledge in the other knowledge base.

Definition 3 ([2] **equivalence** $\equiv_{ee}$). *Let $\mathcal{R}, \mathcal{R}'$ be knowledge bases.*

– *$\mathcal{R}$ is an elementwise equivalent sub-knowledge base of $\mathcal{R}'$, denoted by $\mathcal{R} \ll_{ee} \mathcal{R}'$, if for every conditional $(B'|A') \in \mathcal{R}'$ that is not self-fulfilling there is a conditional $(B|A) \in \mathcal{R}$ such that $(B|A) \equiv (B'|A')$.*
– *$\mathcal{R}$ and $\mathcal{R}'$ are strictly elementwise equivalent if $\mathcal{R} \ll_{ee} \mathcal{R}'$ and $\mathcal{R}' \ll_{ee} \mathcal{R}$.*
– *$\mathcal{R}$ and $\mathcal{R}'$ are elementwise equivalent, denoted by $\mathcal{R} \equiv_{ee} \mathcal{R}'$, if either both are inconsistent, or both are consistent and strictly elementwise equivalent.*

Apart from avoiding to generate elementwise equivalent knowledge bases, we also want to take isomorphisms into account. For a signature Σ, a function $\rho : \Sigma \to \Sigma'$ is a *renaming* if ρ is a bijection. For instance, the function ρ_{ab} with $\rho_{ab}(a) = b$ and $\rho_{ab}(b) = a$ is a renaming for Σ_{ab}. As usual, ρ is extended canonically to worlds, formulas, conditionals, knowledge bases, and to sets thereof. For a set M, $m \in M$, and an equivalence relation $\equiv$ on M, the set of equivalence classes induced by $\equiv$ is denoted by $[M]_{/\equiv}$, and the unique equivalence class containing m is denoted by $[m]_{\equiv}$.

Definition 4 ($\simeq$). *Let X, X' be two signatures, worlds, formulas, knowledge bases, or sets over one of these items. We say that X and X' are isomorphic, denoted by $X \simeq X'$, if there exists a renaming ρ such that $\rho(X) = X'$.*

For instance, $[\Omega_{\Sigma_{ab}}]_{/\simeq} = \{[ab], [a\overline{b}, \overline{a}b], [\overline{a}\overline{b}]\}$ are the three equivalence classes of worlds over Σ_{ab}, and we have $[(ab|ab \vee a\overline{b})]_{\simeq} = [(ab|ab \vee \overline{a}b)]_{\simeq}$.

Given the ordering $<$ on *NFC*(Σ) from Proposition 2, we will now define a new ordering $\prec$ on these conditionals that takes isomorphisms into account and prioritizes the $<$-minimal elements in each equivalence class in $[NFC(\Sigma)]_{/\simeq}$.

Definition 5 (*cNFC*(Σ), $\prec$). *Given a signature Σ with linear ordering $<$, let $[NFC(\Sigma)]_{/\simeq} = \{[r_1]_{\simeq}, \ldots, [r_m]_{\simeq}\}$ be the equivalence classes of NFC(Σ) induced by isomorphisms such that for each $i \in \{1, \ldots, m\}$, the conditional r_i is the minimal element in $[r_i]_{\simeq}$ with respect to $<$, and $r_1 < \ldots < r_m$.*

1. *The* canonical normal form conditionals *over Σ are*

$$cNFC(\Sigma) = \{r_1, \ldots, r_m\}.$$

2. *The* canonical ordering *on* $NFC(\Sigma)$, *denoted by* $\prec$, *is given by the schema*

$$r_1 \prec \ldots \prec r_m \prec [r_1]_{\simeq} \setminus \{r_1\} \prec \ldots \prec [r_m]_{\simeq} \setminus \{r_m\}$$

where $r \prec r'$ *iff* $r \ll r'$ *for all* $i \in \{1, \ldots, m\}$ *and all* $r, r' \in [r_i]_{\simeq} \setminus \{r_i\}$.

Table 1. Conditionals $r_{01} \prec \ldots \prec r_{50}$ in $NFC(\Sigma_{ab})$ with $cNFC(\Sigma) = \{r_{01}, \ldots, r_{31}\}$ for $\Sigma_{ab} = \{a, b\}$, their counter conditionals $\overline{r_i}$, and their isomorphisms induced equivalence classes $[01], \ldots, [31]$. Formulas in conditionals are given by sets of worlds, and worlds are represented by their binary number interpretation; e.g., $r_{03}: (\{3\}|\{3,0\})$ stands for $(\{ab\}|\{ab, \overline{a}\overline{b}\})$.

Class	First conditional	Second conditional	Counter conditionals
[01]	$r_{01}: (\{3\}|\{3,2\})$	$r_{32}: (\{3\}|\{3,1\})$	$\overline{r_{01}}: r_{02}, \overline{r_{32}}: r_{33}$
[02]	$r_{02}: (\{2\}|\{3,2\})$	$r_{33}: (\{1\}|\{3,1\})$	$\overline{r_{02}}: r_{01}, \overline{r_{33}}: r_{32}$
[03]	$r_{03}: (\{3\}|\{3,0\})$		$\overline{r_{03}}: r_{04}$
[04]	$r_{04}: (\{0\}|\{3,0\})$		$\overline{r_{04}}: r_{03}$
[05]	$r_{05}: (\{2\}|\{2,1\})$	$r_{34}: (\{1\}|\{2,1\})$	$\overline{r_{05}}: r_{34}, \overline{r_{34}}: r_{05}$
[06]	$r_{06}: (\{2\}|\{2,0\})$	$r_{35}: (\{1\}|\{1,0\})$	$\overline{r_{06}}: r_{07}, \overline{r_{35}}: r_{36}$
[07]	$r_{07}: (\{0\}|\{2,0\})$	$r_{36}: (\{0\}|\{1,0\})$	$\overline{r_{07}}: r_{06}, \overline{r_{36}}: r_{35}$
[08]	$r_{08}: (\{3\}|\{3,2,1\})$		$\overline{r_{08}}: r_{16}$
[09]	$r_{09}: (\{2\}|\{3,2,1\})$	$r_{37}: (\{1\}|\{3,2,1\})$	$\overline{r_{09}}: r_{42}, \overline{r_{37}}: r_{15}$
[10]	$r_{10}: (\{3\}|\{3,2,0\})$	$r_{38}: (\{3\}|\{3,1,0\})$	$\overline{r_{10}}: r_{19}, \overline{r_{38}}: r_{45}$
[11]	$r_{11}: (\{2\}|\{3,2,0\})$	$r_{39}: (\{1\}|\{3,1,0\})$	$\overline{r_{11}}: r_{18}, r_{39}: r_{44}$
[12]	$r_{12}: (\{0\}|\{3,2,0\})$	$r_{40}: (\{0\}|\{3,1,0\})$	$\overline{r_{12}}: r_{17}, \overline{r_{40}}: r_{43}$
[13]	$r_{13}: (\{2\}|\{2,1,0\})$	$r_{41}: (\{1\}|\{2,1,0\})$	$\overline{r_{13}}: r_{46}, \overline{r_{41}}: r_{21}$
[14]	$r_{14}: (\{0\}|\{2,1,0\})$		$\overline{r_{14}}: r_{20}$
[15]	$r_{15}: (\{3,2\}|\{3,2,1\})$	$r_{42}: (\{3,1\}|\{3,2,1\})$	$\overline{r_{15}}: r_{37}, \overline{r_{42}}: r_{09}$
[16]	$r_{16}: (\{2,1\}|\{3,2,1\})$		$\overline{r_{16}}: r_{08}$
[17]	$r_{17}: (\{3,2\}|\{3,2,0\})$	$r_{43}: (\{3,1\}|\{3,1,0\})$	$\overline{r_{17}}: r_{12}, \overline{r_{43}}: r_{40}$
[18]	$r_{18}: (\{3,0\}|\{3,2,0\})$	$r_{44}: (\{3,0\}|\{3,1,0\})$	$\overline{r_{18}}: r_{11}, \overline{r_{44}}: r_{39}$
[19]	$r_{19}: (\{2,0\}|\{3,2,0\})$	$r_{45}: (\{1,0\}|\{3,1,0\})$	$\overline{r_{19}}: r_{10}, \overline{r_{45}}: r_{38}$
[20]	$r_{20}: (\{2,1\}|\{2,1,0\})$		$\overline{r_{20}}: r_{14}$
[21]	$r_{21}: (\{2,0\}|\{2,1,0\})$	$r_{46}: (\{1,0\}|\{2,1,0\})$	$\overline{r_{21}}: r_{41}, \overline{r_{46}}: r_{13}$
[22]	$r_{22}: (\{3\}|\{3,2,1,0\})$		$\overline{r_{22}}: r_{31}$
[23]	$r_{23}: (\{2\}|\{3,2,1,0\})$	$r_{47}: (\{1\}|\{3,2,1,0\})$	$\overline{r_{23}}: r_{50}, \overline{r_{47}}: r_{30}$
[24]	$r_{24}: (\{0\}|\{3,2,1,0\})$		$\overline{r_{24}}: r_{29}$
[25]	$r_{25}: (\{3,2\}|\{3,2,1,0\})$	$r_{48}: (\{3,1\}|\{3,2,1,0\})$	$\overline{r_{25}}: r_{49}, \overline{r_{48}}: r_{28}$
[26]	$r_{26}: (\{3,0\}|\{3,2,1,0\})$		$\overline{r_{26}}: r_{27}$
[27]	$r_{27}: (\{2,1\}|\{3,2,1,0\})$		$\overline{r_{27}}: r_{26}$
[28]	$r_{28}: (\{2,0\}|\{3,2,1,0\})$	$r_{49}: (\{1,0\}|\{3,2,1,0\})$	$\overline{r_{28}}: r_{48}, \overline{r_{49}}: r_{25}$
[29]	$r_{29}: (\{3,2,1\}|\{3,2,1,0\})$		$\overline{r_{29}}: r_{24}$
[30]	$r_{30}: (\{3,2,0\}|\{3,2,1,0\})$	$r_{50}: (\{3,1,0\}|\{3,2,1,0\})$	$\overline{r_{30}}: r_{47}, \overline{r_{50}}: r_{23}$
[31]	$r_{31}: (\{2,1,0\}|\{3,2,1,0\})$		$\overline{r_{31}}: r_{22}$

Whereas $NFC(\Sigma_{ab})$ contains 50 conditionals, $cNFC(\Sigma_{ab})$ has only 31 elements, labelled $r_{01}, \ldots, r_{31}$ in Table 1. The ordering $\prec$ on $NFC(\Sigma_{ab})$ is given by $r_{01} \prec \ldots \prec r_{50}$ (cf. Table 1), and in general we have:

Algorithm 1. *GenKB* – Generate all knowledge bases over Σ

Input: signature Σ with linear ordering $<$
Output: set of all consistent, pairwise elementwise non-equivalent and non-isomorphic knowledge bases $\mathcal{KB}$ over Σ

1: $L_1 \leftarrow \emptyset$
2: $k \leftarrow 1$
3: **for** $r \in cNFC(\Sigma)$ **do**   ▷ only canonical conditionals for initialization
4:    $D \leftarrow \{d \mid d \in NFC(\Sigma), d \preccurlyeq r\}$ ▷ conditionals D can not extend $\{r\}$
5:    $L_1 \leftarrow L_1 \cup \{\langle \{r\}, NFC(\Sigma) \setminus (\{\overline{r}\} \cup D) \rangle\}$ ▷ $\overline{r}$ can not extend $\{r\}$
6: **while** $L_k \neq \emptyset$ **do**
7:    $L_{k+1} \leftarrow \emptyset$
8:    **for** $\langle \mathcal{R}, C \rangle \in L_k$ **do**   ▷ $\mathcal{R}$ knowledge base, C candidates for extending $\mathcal{R}$
9:       **for** $r \in C$ **do**
10:         **if** $\mathcal{R} \cup \{r\}$ is consistent **then**   ▷ extend $\mathcal{R}$ with conditional r
11:            $D \leftarrow \{d \mid d \in C, d \preccurlyeq r\}$ ▷ conditionals D can not extend $\mathcal{R} \cup \{r\}$
12:            $L_{k+1} \leftarrow L_{k+1} \cup \{\langle \mathcal{R} \cup \{r\}, C \setminus (\{\overline{r}\} \cup D) \rangle\}$ ▷ $\overline{r}$ can not extend $\mathcal{R} \cup \{r\}$
13:    $k \leftarrow k + 1$
14: **return** $\mathcal{KB} = \{\mathcal{R} \mid \langle \mathcal{R}, C \rangle \in L_i, i \in \{1, \ldots, k\}\}$

Proposition 3 (*cNFC*(Σ), $\prec$). *For every linear ordering $<$ on a signature Σ, the induced ordering $\prec$ on conditionals according to Definition 2 is a linear ordering on $cNFC(\Sigma)$.*

5   Systematic Generation of Knowledge Bases

The algorithm *GenKB* (Algorithm 1) generates all consistent knowledge bases up to elementwise equivalence and up to isomorphisms. It uses pairs $\langle \mathcal{R}, C \rangle$ where $\mathcal{R}$ is a knowledge base and C is a set of conditionals that are candidates to be used to extend $\mathcal{R}$ to obtain a new knowledge base. For systematically extending a knowledge base, the ordering $\prec$ is taking into account. Note that in Lines 3–5, only the canonical conditionals (which are minimal with respect to $\prec$) are used for initializing the set of one-element knowledge bases. In Lines 4 and 11, the set D collects those conditionals that are smaller (with respect to $\preccurlyeq$) than the conditional r selected for extending the current knowledge base since these do not have to be taken into account for extending $\mathcal{R}$. Similarly, the counter conditional $\overline{r}$ can be removed form the set of remaining candidates since any knowledge base containing both r and $\overline{r}$ is inconsistent. The consistency test used in Line 10 can easily be implemented by the well-known tolerance test for conditional knowledge bases [9].

Proposition 4 (GenKB). *Let Σ be a signature with linear ordering $<$. Then applying GenKB to it terminates and returns $\mathcal{KB}$ for which the following holds:*

(correctness) *$\mathcal{KB}$ is a set of knowledge bases over Σ.*
($\equiv_{ee}$ minimality) *All knowledge bases in $\mathcal{KB}$ are pairwise not elementwise equivalent.*
($\simeq$ minimality) *All knowledge bases in $\mathcal{KB}$ are pairwise not isomorphic.*
(consistency) *$\mathcal{KB}$ does not contain any inconsistent knowledge base.*
(completeness) *For every consistent $\mathcal{R}$ over Σ there is a knowledge base $\mathcal{R}'$ in $\mathcal{KB}$ and an isomorphism ρ such that $\mathcal{R}$ and $\rho(\mathcal{R}')$ are elementwise equivalent.*

Proof (Sketch). The proof is obtained by formalizing the description of *GenKB* given above and the following observations. Note that *GenKB* exploits the fact that every subset of a consistent knowledge base is again a consistent knowledge base. Thus building up knowledge bases by systematically adding remaining conditionals according to their linear ordering ensures completeness. Checking consistency when adding a new conditional ensures consistency of the resulting knowledge bases. $\equiv_{ee}$-Minimality is guaranteed because all conditionals in $NFC(\Sigma)$ are pairwise non-equivalent (Proposition 1), and $\simeq$-minimality can be shown by induction on the number of conditionals in a knowledge base. $\square$

For instance, $GenKB(\Sigma_{ab})$ will generate

$$\{r_{01}\colon (\{ab\}|\{ab, a\overline{b}\}),\ r_{03}\colon (\{ab\}|\{ab, \overline{a}\overline{b}\})\}$$

but not the isomorphic knowledge base

$$\{r_{03}\colon (\{ab\}|\{ab, \overline{a}\overline{b}\}),\ r_{32}\colon (\{ab\}|\{ab, \overline{a}\overline{b}\})\}.$$

6 Conclusions and Further Work

Based on a notion of normal forms for conditionals, we presented an algorithm *GenKB* for systematically generating all consistent knowledge bases over a given signature while taking both syntactic renamings and semantic elementwise equivalence into account. In our current work, we are working with *GenKB* and the reasoning system InfOCF [4] for empirically investigating various nonmonotonic inference relations induced by a conditional knowledge base.

References

1. Beierle, C.: Inferential equivalence, normal forms, and isomorphisms of knowledge bases in institutions of conditional logics. In: The 34th ACM/SIGAPP Symposium on Applied Computing (SAC 2019) 8–12 April 2019, Limassol, Cyprus. ACM, New York (2019, to appear). https://doi.org/10.1145/3297280.3297391
2. Beierle, C., Eichhorn, C., Kern-Isberner, G.: A transformation system for unique minimal normal forms of conditional knowledge bases. In: Antonucci, A., Cholvy, L., Papini, O. (eds.) ECSQARU 2017. LNCS (LNAI), vol. 10369, pp. 236–245. Springer, Cham (2017). https://doi.org/10.1007/978-3-319-61581-3_22

3. Beierle, C., Eichhorn, C., Kern-Isberner, G., Kutsch, S.: Skeptical, weakly skeptical, and credulous inference based on preferred ranking functions. In: Kaminka, G.A., et al. (eds.) Proceedings 22nd European Conference on Artificial Intelligence, ECAI-2016, vol. 285, pp. 1149–1157. IOS Press, Amsterdam (2016)
4. Beierle, C., Eichhorn, C., Kutsch, S.: A practical comparison of qualitative inferences with preferred ranking models. KI - Künstliche Intell. **31**(1), 41–52 (2017)
5. Beierle, C., Kutsch, S.: Computation and comparison of nonmonotonic skeptical inference relations induced by sets of ranking models for the realization of intelligent agents. Appl. Intell. **49**(1), 28–43 (2019)
6. Benferhat, S., Dubois, D., Prade, H.: Possibilistic and standard probabilistic semantics of conditional knowledge bases. J. Log. Comput. **9**(6), 873–895 (1999)
7. de Finetti, B.: La prévision, ses lois logiques et ses sources subjectives. Ann. Inst. H. Poincaré **7**(1), 1–68 (1937). Engl. transl. Theory of Probability, J. Wiley & Sons (1974)
8. Dubois, D., Prade, H.: Conditional objects as nonmonotonic consequence relations: main results. In: Proceedings of the KR 1994, pp. 170–177. Morgan Kaufmann Publishers (1994)
9. Goldszmidt, M., Pearl, J.: Qualitative probabilities for default reasoning, belief revision, and causal modeling. Artif. Intell. **84**, 57–112 (1996)
10. Kern-Isberner, G.: Conditionals in Nonmonotonic Reasoning and Belief Revision. LNCS (LNAI), vol. 2087. Springer, Heidelberg (2001). https://doi.org/10.1007/3-540-44600-1
11. Kraus, S., Lehmann, D., Magidor, M.: Nonmonotonic reasoning, preferential models and cumulative logics. Artif. Intell. **44**, 167–207 (1990)
12. Lehmann, D.J., Magidor, M.: What does a conditional knowledge base entail? Artif. Intell. **55**(1), 1–60 (1992)
13. Lewis, D.: Counterfactuals. Harvard University Press, Cambridge (1973)
14. Paris, J.: The Uncertain Reasoner's Companion - A Mathematical Perspective. Cambridge University Press, Cambridge (1994)
15. Spohn, W.: Ordinal conditional functions: a dynamic theory of epistemic states. In: Harper, W., Skyrms, B. (eds.) Causation in Decision, Belief Change, and Statistics, vol. 2, pp. 105–134. Kluwer Academic Publishers, Dordrecht (1988)
16. Spohn, W.: The Laws of Belief: Ranking Theory and Its Philosophical Applications. Oxford University Press, Oxford (2012)

Unifying Reasoning and Core-Guided Search for Maximum Satisfiability

Jeremias Berg⬤ and Matti Järvisalo(✉)⬤

HIIT, Department of Computer Science, University of Helsinki, Helsinki, Finland
{jeremias.berg,matti.jarvisalo}@helsinki.fi

Abstract. A central algorithmic paradigm in maximum satisfiability solving geared towards real world optimization problems is the core-guided approach. Furthermore, recent progress on preprocessing techniques is bringing in additional reasoning techniques to MaxSAT solving. Towards realizing their combined potential, understanding formal underpinnings of interleavings of preprocessing-style reasoning and core-guided algorithms is important. It turns out that earlier proposed notions for establishing correctness of core-guided algorithms and preprocessing, respectively, are not enough for capturing correctness of interleavings of the techniques. We provide an in-depth analysis of these and related MaxSAT instance transformations, and propose correction set reducibility as a notion that captures inprocessing MaxSAT solving within a state-transition style abstract MaxSAT solving framework. Furthermore, we establish a general theorem of correctness for applications of SAT-based preprocessing techniques in MaxSAT. The results pave way for generic techniques for arguing about the formal correctness of MaxSAT algorithms.

Keywords: Maximum satisfiability · Core-guided reasoning ·
Preprocessing · Instance transformations · Inprocessing

1 Introduction

Maximum satisfiability (MaxSAT), the optimization variant of Boolean satisfiability (SAT), provides a competitive approach to various real-world optimization problems arising from AI and industrial applications, see e.g. [6,7,14,18, 25,33,34]. Most of the modern MaxSAT solvers are based on iteratively transforming an input problem instance in specific ways towards a representation from which an optimal solution is in some sense "easy" to compute. In particular, a central algorithmic paradigm in modern MaxSAT solving geared towards real-world optimization problems is the so-called core-guided approach [2,27]. Core-guided MaxSAT solvers reduce the search for an optimal solution to a sequence of SAT instances, forming the next instance in the sequence by transforming the current one based on an unsatisfiable core reported by a SAT solver until a solution is found. In addition to the core-guided approach, MaxSAT preprocessing [4,5,8,19] also iteratively applies instance transformations through

© Springer Nature Switzerland AG 2019
F. Calimeri et al. (Eds.): JELIA 2019, LNAI 11468, pp. 287–303, 2019.
https://doi.org/10.1007/978-3-030-19570-0_19

simplification (or reasoning) techniques which, however, significantly differ from core-guided transformations.

The formal underpinning of inprocessing SAT solving [17], a popular approach to modern SAT solving based on interleaving preprocessing techniques with conflict-driven clause learning search, is today well-understood. In contrast, preprocessing for MaxSAT, including the realization of liftings of SAT preprocessing to MaxSAT [5], is a more recent line of development. In fact, so far only a few specific liftings of SAT preprocessing techniques have been shown to be correct for MaxSAT [5]. Furthermore, towards lifting the inprocessing SAT solving paradigm to the realm of MaxSAT, understanding how to interleave core-guided MaxSAT inferences and inference steps made by MaxSAT preprocessing techniques is important. While formal notions of instance transformations have been proposed for establishing correctness of core-guided algorithms and preprocessing, respectively, these notions in themselves are not expressive enough for capturing correctness of interleavings of the two types of transformations.

To address these shortcomings, we focus in this paper on providing further understanding of correct instance transformations for generic MaxSAT solving. To this end, we analyze both earlier proposed formal notions of instance transformations [2,5], and explain why they are fundamentally different and therefore individually not enough to capture interleaving of core-guided and preprocessing-style instance transformations; both types of transformations are required in order to obtain a framework capable of modelling MaxSAT solving without relying on the correctness of SAT solvers. We propose correction set reducibility as a general notion of instance transformations that captures to a far extent transformations applied in both core-guided solvers and MaxSAT preprocessing. We base our analysis on a formal framework as an abstract state transition system based on different sets of sequences of MaxSAT instances. This allows for reasoning about correctness of core-guided solving and MaxSAT preprocessing in a unified manner which can ease the development of new MaxSAT solving methods, including inprocessing. Furthermore, as a further form of instance transformation, we lift the notion of resolution asymmetric tautologies (RAT clauses), a simple yet powerful notion capturing SAT preprocessing techniques at large in a unified way [17], to MaxSAT. By doing so, we establish a general proof of correctness for natural liftings of SAT preprocessing techniques to MaxSAT, thereby significantly generalizing the correctness proofs earlier presented for MaxSAT liftings of specific SAT preprocessing techniques [5]. The results pave way for generic techniques for arguing about the formal correctness of MaxSAT algorithms.

2   Maximum Satisfiability, MaxSAT Solving and Preprocessing

A literal l is a Boolean variable x or its negation $\neg x$. For a set L of literals, the set $\neg L$ contains the negations of the literals in L; L is consistent if L and $\neg L$ are disjoint. A clause is a disjunction (logical OR) of literals (represented as a set of its literals) and a CNF formula F is a conjunction (logical AND) of clauses (represented as a set of its clauses). A clause C is a tautology if $\{x, \neg x\} \subset C$ for some variable x. The set $\text{VAR}(C)$ contains all variables x for which $x \in C$ or $\neg x \in C$. The set $\text{VAR}(F)$ of the variables of F is $\cup_{C \in F} \text{VAR}(C)$ and the set $\text{LIT}(F)$ is $\cup_{C \in F} C$ (each C seen as a set of literals). For a literal $l \in \text{LIT}(F)$ we use $\text{CL}_F(l)$ to denote the set of clauses in F which contain l, dropping the subscript when clear from context.

A (truth) assignment τ is a consistent set of literals. A literal l is true under τ ($\tau(l) = 1$) if $l \in \tau$ and false ($\tau(l) = 0$) if $\neg l \in \tau$. A literal l true or false under τ is *assigned* in (or assigned by) τ, and unassigned otherwise. An assignment τ satisfies a clause C ($\tau(C) = 1$) if $\tau(l) = 1$ for some literal l in C, i.e., if $\tau \cap C \neq \emptyset$. τ satisfies a formula F ($\tau(F) = 1$) if it satisfies all clauses in it. A formula is satisfiable if there is an assignment that satisfies it, and else unsatisfiable. An assignment τ is a complete assignment to a CNF formula F if every literal $l \in \text{LIT}(F)$ is assigned in τ, else it is partial. The restriction $F|_\tau$ of a formula F under an assignment τ is the CNF formula $F \wedge \bigwedge_{l \in \tau}(l)$.

A (weighted partial) MaxSAT instance is a triplet $\mathcal{F} = (F_h, F_s, w)$ consisting of a set F_h of hard clauses, a set F_s of soft clauses and a weight function $w : F_s \rightarrow \mathbb{N}$. The instance is partial if $F_h \neq \emptyset$ and unweighted if $w(C) = k$ for some constant $k \in \mathbb{N}$ and all $C \in F_s$. The core-guided MaxSAT algorithms we focus on in this work solve the most general case of weighted partial MaxSAT and do not treat any variant of it any differently (cf. Sect. 2.2). Hence we will refer to weighted partial MaxSAT simply by MaxSAT. The cost $\text{COST}(\mathcal{F}, \tau)$ of a complete assignment to $F_h \wedge F_s$ is ∞ if $\tau(F_h) = 0$ and $\sum_{C \in F_s}(1 - \tau(C)) \cdot w(C)$ otherwise. We say that τ is a solution to $\mathcal{F}$ if $\tau(F_h) = 1$ and optimal if $\text{COST}(\mathcal{F}, \tau) \leq \text{COST}(\mathcal{F}, \tau^\star)$ for all compete truth assignments $\tau^\star$ to $F_h \wedge F_s$. We denote the cost of the optimal solutions to $\mathcal{F}$ by $\text{COST}(\mathcal{F})$. The cost of a partial assignment τ^p to $F_h \wedge F_s$ is the cost of an "optimal extension" of τ^p into a complete assignment, i.e., $\text{COST}(\mathcal{F}, \tau^p) = \text{COST}(\mathcal{F}^{\tau^p})$, where $\mathcal{F}^{\tau^p} = (F_h|_{\tau^p}, F_s, w)$.

A subset $\kappa \subset F_s$ is an unsatisfiable subset (or core) of $\mathcal{F}$ if $F_h \wedge \kappa$ is unsatisfiable and a minimal unsatisfiable subset (MUS) if $F_h \wedge \kappa_s$ is satisfiable for all $\kappa_s \subsetneq \kappa$. A set H is a correction set (CS) if $F_h \wedge (F_s \setminus H)$ is satisfiable and a minimal correction set (an MCS) if $F_h \wedge (F_s \setminus H_s)$ is unsatisfiable for all $H_s \subsetneq H$. The sets of MUSes and MCSes of $\mathcal{F}$ are denoted by $\text{MUS}(\mathcal{F})$ and $\text{MCS}(\mathcal{F})$, respectively. For a solution τ to $\mathcal{F}$ the set $U(\mathcal{F}, \tau) = \{C \mid \tau(C) = 0\}$ contains the soft clauses falsified by τ. We say that the solution τ corresponds to the correction set $U(\mathcal{F}, \tau)$. Similarly, a correction set H corresponds to a solution τ if $H = U(\mathcal{F}, \tau)$. A correction set H is optimal if it corresponds to an optimal solution τ to $\mathcal{F}$. It is easy to show that every solution corresponds to a correction set and every correction set corresponds to some solution.

2.1   Core-Guided MaxSAT Solving and MaxSAT-Reducibility

When solving a MaxSAT instance $\mathcal{F}$, a core-guided MaxSAT algorithm maintains a working instance $\mathcal{F}^i = (F_h^i, F_s^i, w^i)$, initialized to $\mathcal{F}$. During each iteration of the search, a SAT solver is queried for the satisfiability of $F_h^i \wedge F_s^i$. If the formula is satisfiable, i.e., if $\mathrm{COST}(\mathcal{F}^i) = 0$, any assignment τ^o satisfying $F_h^i \wedge F_s^i$ is an optimal solution to $\mathcal{F}$. Otherwise, the SAT solver returns a core κ^i of $\mathcal{F}^i$. The next working instance $\mathcal{F}^{i+1}$ is then formed by transforming $\mathcal{F}^i$ in a way that rules out κ^i as a source of unsatisfiability and lowers the optimal cost of $\mathcal{F}^i$ by $\min\{w^i(C) \mid C \in \kappa^i\}$. Many existing core-guided algorithms fit this high-level description and differ mainly in the the specific transformation used to form the next working instance [1,3,15,26,29]. The correctness of such solvers, i.e., that the final assignment returned will indeed be an optimal solution to the input instance, is often established by proving that $\mathcal{F}^i$ is MaxSAT-reducible [2] to $\mathcal{F}^{i+1}$.

Definition 1. *An instance $\mathcal{F}$ is MaxSAT-reducible (or k-reducible) to the instance $\mathcal{F}^R$ if $\mathrm{COST}(\mathcal{F}, \tau) = \mathrm{COST}(\mathcal{F}^R, \tau) + k$ for some integer k and for all complete assignments τ to $\mathcal{F}$. The constant k can depend on $\mathcal{F}$ but not on the assignment τ.*

An important motivation for the abstract model of MaxSAT solving we detail in Sect. 3 relates to the specifics of how cores are extracted with SAT solvers. In practice, a core κ of an instance $\mathcal{F} = (F_h, F_s, w)$ is extracted by extending each soft clause $C_i \in F_s$ with an unique *assumption variable* a_i to form the clause $C_i \vee a_i$. Afterwards the so-called assumption interface of the SAT solver [28] is used to query the satisfiability of $(F_h \wedge F_s^A)|_{\neg \mathcal{A}}$, where F_s^A is the set of extended soft clauses and $\mathcal{A}$ the set of all assumption variables. If the result is satisfiable, the obtained assignment satisfies $(F_h \wedge F_s^A) \wedge \bigwedge_{a \in \mathcal{A}}(\neg a)$ and hence also $(F_h \wedge F_s)$. If the formula is unsatisfiable, the SAT solver instead returns a subset $A_s \subset \mathcal{A}$ for which $F_h \wedge F_s|_{\neg A_s}$ is unsatisfiable as well. Indeed, as we illustrate in Example 1, modern core-guided solvers represent cores in terms of the variables in A_s [1,26,29].

2.2 MaxSAT Preprocessing and MCS-Equivalence

MaxSAT preprocessing refers to the application of different simplification and deduction rules to an instance $\mathcal{F} = (F_h, F_s, w)$, resulting in another instance $\mathcal{F}^p$. A simple example is the so-called subsumption rule which allows removing a clause $D \in (F_h \wedge F_s)$ if there is a clause $C \in F_h$ for which $C \subset D$. The goal of correct and effective preprocessing for MaxSAT is to make the time required to transform $\mathcal{F}$, solve $\mathcal{F}^p$ and reconstruct an optimal solution to $\mathcal{F}$ lower than the time required to solve $\mathcal{F}$ directly. The previously proposed notion for proving correctness of MaxSAT preprocessing requires the use of the following literal-based definition of MaxSAT [5]. In particular, for the remainder of this paper, we will apply the following literal-based definitions of MaxSAT.

A MaxSAT instance $\mathcal{F}$ consists of a CNF formula $\mathrm{CLAUSES}(\mathcal{F})$ and a weight function $w^{\mathcal{F}} : \mathrm{VAR}(\mathrm{CLAUSES}(\mathcal{F})) \to \mathbb{N}$, assigning a weight to each variable of $\mathcal{F}$. Whenever clear from context, we use $\mathcal{F}$ and $\mathrm{CLAUSES}(\mathcal{F})$ interchangeably. A variable $x \in \mathrm{VAR}(\mathcal{F})$ is soft in $\mathcal{F}$ if $w^{\mathcal{F}}(x) > 0$. The set $\mathcal{S}(\mathcal{F})$ contains all soft variables of $\mathcal{F}$. The complement S^c of a $S \subset \mathcal{S}(\mathcal{F})$ is $\mathcal{S}(\mathcal{F}) \setminus S$.

The other concepts related to MaxSAT discussed earlier are lifted from soft clauses to soft variables in a natural way. An assignment τ is a solution to $\mathcal{F}$ if $\tau(\mathcal{F}) = 1$ and has cost $\text{COST}(\mathcal{F}, \tau) = \sum_{x \in \text{VAR}(\mathcal{F})} \tau(x) \cdot w(x)$. A set $\kappa \subset \mathcal{S}(\mathcal{F})$ is a a core of $\mathcal{F}$ if $\mathcal{F}|_{\neg\kappa}$ is unsatisfiable. Similarly $H \subset \mathcal{S}(\mathcal{F})$ is a CS of $\mathcal{F}$ if $\mathcal{F}|_{\neg(H^c)}$ is satisfiable and an MCS if no $H_s \subsetneq H$ is a CS of $\mathcal{F}$. Notice that under the literal-based definitions, the set $U(\mathcal{F}, \tau)$ is simply $\tau \cap \mathcal{S}(\mathcal{F})$. Using these definitions, the notion of MCS-$equivalence$ has been used as a basis for showing correctness of the liftings of four specific preprocessing rules proposed for SAT solving to MaxSAT [5].

Definition 2. *The instance $\mathcal{F}$ is MCS-equivalent with the instance $\mathcal{F}^R$ (and vice-versa) if* $\text{MCS}(\mathcal{F}) = \text{MCS}(\mathcal{F}^R)$ *and* $w^{\mathcal{F}}(x) = w^{\mathcal{F}^R}(x)$ *for all* $x \in \text{VAR}(\mathcal{F}) \cap \text{VAR}(\mathcal{F}^R)$.

As we will demonstrate, defining MaxSAT based on soft variables instead of soft clauses allows reasoning about core-guided solving and MaxSAT preprocessing in a unified manner. We emphasize that the literal-based definition is equivalent to the clause-based one. Furthermore, the literal-based definitions correspond more closely with the representation of MaxSAT instances that core-guided solvers and MaxSAT preprocessors actually operate on. Given any MaxSAT instance (partial or not), a core-guided solver and similarly a MaxSAT preprocessor will add an explicit variable a_i to each soft clause. During solving and preprocessing, the extended soft clauses and hard clauses are treated equally. Instead, special treatment is given to the added variables; for correctness, a preprocessor is restricted from resolving on them, and a core-guided solver extracts cores and applies transformations in terms of the a_i's, instead of in terms of the soft clauses directly. The concept of a soft variable makes the role of these "special" variables explicit, highlighting the similarities of core-guided solving and preprocessing. Furthermore, applications of specific preprocessing techniques such as bounded variable elimination will result in clauses with several soft variables; the literal-based view also uniformly covers this. The literal-based definitions also allow describing the transformations used by modern core-guided solvers in a succinct manner.

Example 1. Let $\mathcal{F}$ be a MaxSAT instance, $\kappa = \{l_1, \ldots, l_n\}$ a core of $\mathcal{F}$, and $w_\kappa = \min_{l \in \kappa}\{w^{\mathcal{F}}(l)\}$. The instance transformation used by the PMRES core-guided algorithm [29] forms the instance $\mathcal{F}^R = \mathcal{F} \wedge \bigwedge_{i=1}^{n-1}(c_i \leftrightarrow (c_{i+1} \vee l_{i+1})) \wedge \bigwedge_{i=1}^{n-1}((\neg c_i \vee \neg l_i \vee r_i)) \wedge (\neg c_n)$ with the equivalence expressed as clauses in the standard way. Each c_i and r_i are new variables that do not appear in $\text{VAR}(\mathcal{F})$. The weights of the variables $\mathcal{F}^R$ are modified by (i) decreasing the weight of each $l \in \kappa$ by w_κ, (ii) setting the weight of each c_i to 0, (iii) setting the weight of each r_i to w_κ and (iv) keeping the weights of all other variables the same as in $\mathcal{F}$. The fact that $\mathcal{F}$ is MaxSAT-reducible to $\mathcal{F}^R$ was first shown in [29].

3 An Abstract MaxSAT Solving Framework

In the rest of this work we study MaxSAT-reducibility, MCS-equivalence and other notions of transformation properties in an abstract framework based on sequences of MaxSAT instances (or sequences for short). For example, solving an instance $\mathcal{F}$ with a core-guided MaxSAT solver is identified with a sequence $\langle \mathcal{F} = \mathcal{F}_1, \ldots, \mathcal{F}_n \rangle$, where each instance $\mathcal{F}_i$ is MaxSAT-reducible to $\mathcal{F}_{i+1}$ and $\mathrm{COST}(\mathcal{F}_n) = 0$. Similarly, preprocessing $\mathcal{F}$ is identified with a sequence $\langle \mathcal{F} = \mathcal{F}_1, \ldots, \mathcal{F}_n \rangle$, where each $\mathcal{F}_i$ is MCS-equivalent with $\mathcal{F}_{i+1}$. The notion of MaxSAT-reducibility (MCS-equivalence) is lifted to sequences of instances by the set MSRED (MCSEQ) containing all sequences $\langle \mathcal{F}_1, \ldots, \mathcal{F}_n \rangle$ for which $\mathcal{F}_i$ is MaxSAT-reducible to (MCS-equivalent with) $\mathcal{F}_{i+1}$ for all $i = 1, \ldots, n-1$.

More generally, the framework captures MaxSAT solving techniques that iteratively transform an input MaxSAT instance toward a specific final instance, from which an optimal solution to the input instance can then be obtained based on an optimal solution to the final instance. As the final instance we use the (unique) MaxSAT instance $\mathcal{F}_F = \emptyset$ that contains no clauses and to which any assignment τ is an optimal solution to. The following notion of a terminating sequence represents MaxSAT solving within the general framework.

Definition 3. *A sequence $\langle \mathcal{F}, \ldots, \mathcal{F}_n \rangle$ is terminating if $\mathcal{F}_n = \mathcal{F}_F$.*

An important observation to make regarding the sets of sequences that we work with is that the membership of a sequence $\langle \mathcal{F}_1, \ldots, \mathcal{F}_n \rangle$ in each set can be determined "locally" by checking if some property holds between $\mathcal{F}_i$ and $\mathcal{F}_{i+1}$ for all $i = 1, \ldots, n-1$. For example, $\langle \mathcal{F}_1, \ldots, \mathcal{F}_n \rangle \in$ MSRED can be checked by verifying that $\mathcal{F}_i$ is MaxSAT-reducible to $\mathcal{F}_{i+1}$ for all i. More formally, we say that a set S of sequences is decomposable if $\langle \mathcal{F}_1, \ldots, \mathcal{F}_n \rangle \in$ S if and only if $\langle \mathcal{F}_i, \mathcal{F}_{i+1} \rangle \in$ S for all $i = 1, \ldots, n-1$. All sets of sequences that we consider in this work with are decomposable, including the already defined MSRED and MCSEQ.

The following notion of allows for combining sets of sequences for modelling interleavings of different types of instance transformations.

Definition 4. *The combination $S_1 \circ S_2$ of two sets S_1 and S_2 of sequences contains all sequences $\langle \mathcal{F}_1, \ldots, \mathcal{F}_n \rangle$ for which $\langle \mathcal{F}_i, \mathcal{F}_{i+1} \rangle \in S_1 \cup S_2$.*

For example, the set MCSEQ $\circ$ MSRED contains all sequences $\langle \mathcal{F}_1, \ldots, \mathcal{F}_n \rangle$ where $\mathcal{F}_i$ is either MaxSAT-reducible to, or MCS equivalent with, $\mathcal{F}_{i+1}$ for all i. Informally speaking, MCSEQ $\circ$ MSRED models inprocessing MaxSAT solving, interleaving preprocessing and core-guided search.

When analyzing a set S of sequences, we focus on three central properties that are interesting in the context of MaxSAT solving. The first property is *sufficiency*: that for any instance $\mathcal{F}$ there is a terminating sequence in S that starts from $\mathcal{F}$.

Definition 5. *Let $\mathcal{F}$ be a MaxSAT instance. A set S of sequences is sufficient (for reaching the final state) if there is a terminating sequence $\langle \mathcal{F}, \ldots, \mathcal{F}_F \rangle \in$ S.*

The second property, *effectiveness*, captures the idea that for practical applicability, an optimal solution τ_n to the last instance $\mathcal{F}_n$ in a sequence $\langle \mathcal{F}, \ldots, \mathcal{F}_n \rangle$ should be applicable or "useful" for obtaining an optimal solution τ to $\mathcal{F}$. In the following, we say that a function that on input $\langle \mathcal{F}, \ldots, \mathcal{F}_n \rangle$ and τ_n computes τ is a reconstruction function for $\langle \mathcal{F}, \ldots, \mathcal{F}_n \rangle$.

Definition 6. *Let* S *be a set of sequences and* $\langle \mathcal{F}, \mathcal{F}^T \rangle \in$ S *any sequence of length two in* S. *The set* S *is* effective *(for MaxSAT solving) if there is a reconstruction function for* $\langle \mathcal{F}, \mathcal{F}^T \rangle$ *computable in polynomial time with respect to* $|\mathcal{F}|$.

If the set S is decomposable, as all of the sets we work with are, the ability to reconstruct optimal solutions is extended to sequences of arbitrary lengths.

Observation 1. *Let* S *be an effective decomposable set of sequences and consider a sequence* $\langle \mathcal{F}_1, \ldots, \mathcal{F}_n \rangle \in$ S. *Assume that* $|\mathcal{F}_i|$ *is polynomial in* $|\mathcal{F}_1|$ *for all* i. *Then there is a reconstruction function for* $\langle \mathcal{F}_1, \ldots, \mathcal{F}_n \rangle$ *computable in time* $\mathcal{O}(n \times g(|\mathcal{F}_1|))$ *for some polynomial* g.

An alternative view of effectiveness is hence that a sequence $\langle \mathcal{F}_1, \ldots, \mathcal{F}_n \rangle \in$ S of an effective decomposable set S is one where each $\mathcal{F}_{i+1}$ is formed from $\mathcal{F}_i$ by a transformation that preserves enough information to allow effective reconstruction of an optimal solution. For example, a set containing $\langle \mathcal{F}, \mathcal{F}_F \rangle$ for all instances $\mathcal{F}$ is clearly sufficient. However, it is not effective as no "useful" information is preserved when transforming $\mathcal{F}$ to $\mathcal{F}_F$ (in most cases).

Finally, *generality* allows for comparing sets of sequences in a natural way.

Definition 7. *Let* S_1 *and* S_2 *be two sets of sequences of instances. We say that*

(i) S_1 *is at least as general as* S_2 *if* $S_2 \subset S_1$;
(ii) S_2 *is not as general as* S_1 *if* $S_1 \setminus S_2 \neq \emptyset$; *and*
(iii) S_1 *is more general than* S_2 *if* S_1 *is at least as general and* S_2 *is not as general.*

4   Overview of Results

Figure 1 gives an overview of our main results. Considering previously proposed types of instance transformations, we establish that the sets MSRED and MCSEQ are individually not expressive enough to be sufficient within our generic framework, while their combination MSRED ∘ MCSEQ is. Indeed, MSRED and MCSEQ are orthogonal in the sense that neither one is as general as the other; we will give concrete examples of sequences $\langle \mathcal{F}, \mathcal{F}^R \rangle \in$ MSRED \ MCSEQ and $\langle \mathcal{F}, \mathcal{F}^R \rangle \in$ MCSEQ \ MSRED. Thus, neither one of these previously proposed formalisms for MaxSAT solving techniques is expressive enough to capture hybrid forms of MaxSAT solving that combine the core-guided approach with preprocessing-style reasoning.

In addition to MSRED and MCSEQ, we will also consider several other sets of sequences. The set MSEQUIV in Fig. 1 contains sequences where subsequent instances are MaxSAT-equivalent with each other. MaxSAT-equivalence has previously been shown to be a special case of MaxSAT resolution [2,10] and included in this work mainly for completeness. We also propose two new sets of sequences, MAX-RAT and CSRED, with different motivations. As detailed in Sect. 6, we propose MAX-RAT as a natural lifting of the notion of resolution asymmetric tautology, which has been shown to give a basis for formalizing inprocessing SAT solving [17], to the context of MaxSAT. As a main result, we show that MAX-RAT yields a general proof of correctness of liftings of SAT preprocessing techniques to MaxSAT, noticeably generalizing earlier correctness proofs of liftings of specific SAT preprocessing techniques [5]. Towards more general instance transformations, we also propose the notion of correction-set reducibility, CSRED containing sequences in which each instance is correction-set reducible to the next one. We show that CSRED surpasses the combination of MSRED and MCSEQ; even its effective subset CSRED-E captures essentially all current core-guided and preprocessing-style transformations we are aware of.

5   Analysis of Known Transformations

We begin the detailed analysis with MaxSAT-reducibility and MCS-equivalence, their combination, and MaxSAT-equivalence.

5.1   MaxSAT-Reducibility

First, we show that MSRED is not sufficient for reaching the final state. Informally, the result follows from the fact that MaxSAT-reducibility requires preserving all of the solutions to an instance while not being expressive enough to affect the cost of different solutions in different ways. Hence any instance $\mathcal{F}$ which has two solutions τ^1 and τ^2 such that $\text{COST}(\mathcal{F}, \tau^1) \neq \text{COST}(\mathcal{F}, \tau^2)$ is not MaxSAT-reducible to the final instance $\mathcal{F}_F$ to which all solutions have the same cost. We generalize this argument to sequences to establish the following.

Proposition 1. MSRED *is not sufficient for reaching the final state.*

Note that in practice core-guided solvers that use MaxSAT-reducible transformations terminate once the cost of the working instance becomes 0, which is not the same as the working instance being $\mathcal{F}_F$. This "contrast" arises from the fact that core-guided solvers rely on a SAT solver for termination.

The effectiveness of MSRED follows by showing that τ_2, an optimal solution to $\mathcal{F}_2$ in $\langle \mathcal{F}_1, \mathcal{F}_2 \rangle \in$ MSRED satisfies $\mathcal{F}_1$ and assigns all variables in $\mathcal{S}(\mathcal{F}_1)$. Thus an optimal solution to $\mathcal{F}_1$ can be obtained by (i) restricting τ_2 to $\text{LIT}(\mathcal{F}_1)$ and (ii) assigning any unassigned variables of $\text{VAR}(\mathcal{F}_1)$ arbitrarily.

Proposition 2. MSRED *is effective.*

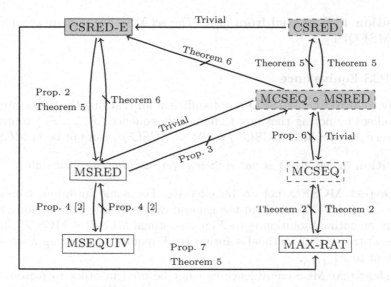

Fig. 1. Relationships between sets of sequences. Here $S_1 \rightarrow S_2$ denotes that S_1 is at least as general as S_2, $S_1 \nrightarrow S_2$ that S_1 is not as general as S_2. Transitive edges are not shown. The types of transformations that are sufficient for reaching the final state are coloured green, and effective transformations are drawn with continuous lines. (Color figure online)

The next proposition implies that MaxSAT-reducibility can not be used as basis for reasoning about the correctness of MaxSAT preprocessing.

Proposition 3. MSRED *is not as general as* MCSEQ.

Proof. Consider the sequence $\langle \mathcal{F}, \mathcal{F}_F \rangle$, where $\mathcal{F} = \{(l \vee x)\}$ with $w^{\mathcal{F}}(l) = 1$ and $w^{\mathcal{F}}(x) = 0$. Since $\mathrm{COST}(\mathcal{F}) = 0$ it follows that $\mathrm{MCS}(\mathcal{F}) = \{\emptyset\} = \mathrm{MCS}(\mathcal{F}_F)$. This implies that $\langle \mathcal{F}, \mathcal{F}_F \rangle \in \mathrm{MCSEQ}$. To see that $\langle \mathcal{F}, \mathcal{F}_F \rangle \notin \mathrm{MSRED}$, consider the solutions $\tau^1 = \{l, \neg x\}$ and $\tau^2 = \{\neg l, x\}$ to $\mathcal{F}$. Since $\mathrm{COST}(\mathcal{F}, \tau^1) = 1 = 0 + 1 = \mathrm{COST}(\mathcal{F}_F, \tau^1) + 1$ while $\mathrm{COST}(\mathcal{F}, \tau^2) = 0 = 0 + 0 = \mathrm{COST}(\mathcal{F}_F, \tau^2) + 0$, it follows that $\mathcal{F}$ is not MaxSAT-reducible (for any k) to $\mathcal{F}_F$. □

Finally, *MaxSAT-equivalence* is a special case of MaxSAT-reducibility [2,10].

Definition 8. *The instance* $\mathcal{F}$ *is MaxSAT equivalent to the instance* $\mathcal{F}^R$ *if* $\mathrm{COST}(\mathcal{F}, \tau) = \mathrm{COST}(\mathcal{F}^R, \tau) + k$ *for some positive integer* k *and all complete truth assignments* τ *for both* $\mathcal{F}$ *and* $\mathcal{F}^R$.

Again, the constant k may depend on $\mathcal{F}$ but not on the particular assignment τ. The set MSEQUIV contains all sequences of MaxSAT instances where subsequent instances are MaxSAT equivalent. MaxSAT-reducibility subsumes MaxSAT-equivalence in terms of the generality of MSRED and MSEQUIV, which follows from comparing the definitions. The following result was first shown in [2] and included here for completeness.

Proposition 4 (Restated from [2]). *The set* MSRED *is more general than the set* MSEQUIV.

5.2   MCS-Equivalence

Similarly to MSRED, MCSEQ is not sufficient for reaching the final state. The result follows by noting that any terminating sequence $\langle \mathcal{F}, \ldots, \mathcal{F}_F \rangle$ containing an instance $\mathcal{F}_i$ for which $\mathrm{MCS}(\mathcal{F}_i) \neq \{\emptyset\} = \mathrm{MCS}(\mathcal{F}_F)$ can not be in MCSEQ.

Proposition 5. MCSEQ *is not sufficient for reaching the final state.*

We expect MCSEQ not to be effective. For some intuition, consider a sequence $\langle \mathcal{F}, \mathcal{F}_2 \rangle \in$ MCSEQ. In the general case, the only information obtainable from an optimal solution τ_2 to $\mathcal{F}_2$ is an optimal MCS $H \in \mathrm{MCS}(\mathcal{F})$. In this case, reconstructing an optimal solution to $\mathcal{F}$ requires computing a satisfying assignment to $\mathcal{F}|_{\neg(H^c)}$.

We show that MCS-equivalence can not be used in order to reason about the correctness of core-guided solving, i.e., that MCSEQ is not as general as MSRED. Informally, the result follows by noting that $\mathrm{COST}(\mathcal{F}) = \mathrm{COST}(\mathcal{F}_2)$ for any MCS-equivalent instances $\mathcal{F}_1$ and $\mathcal{F}_2$. In contrast, there are sequences $\langle \mathcal{F}_1, \ldots, \mathcal{F}_n \rangle \in$ MSRED for which $\mathrm{COST}(\mathcal{F}_1) > \mathrm{COST}(\mathcal{F}_n)$.

Proposition 6. MCSEQ *is not as general as* MSRED.

5.3   Combining MSRED and MCSEQ

So far, we have established that neither MSRED nor MCSEQ is individually sufficient for reaching the final state, and that neither one is as general as the other. The reasons for insufficiency, however, are in a sense orthogonal. While there are sequences $\langle \mathcal{F}_1, \ldots, \mathcal{F}_n \rangle \in$ MSRED for which $\mathrm{COST}(\mathcal{F}_1) > \mathrm{COST}(\mathcal{F}_n)$, any solution to $\mathcal{F}_1$ is also a solution to $\mathcal{F}_n$. In other words, MaxSAT-reducibility can lower the optimal cost of instances but not rule out non-optimal solutions. In contrast, while $\mathrm{COST}(\mathcal{F}_i) = \mathrm{COST}(\mathcal{F}_j)$ for any two instances in a sequence $\langle \mathcal{F}_1, \ldots, \mathcal{F}_n \rangle \in$ MCSEQ, there can be solutions to $\mathcal{F}_1$ that are not solutions to $\mathcal{F}_n$. More informally, MCS-equivalence can be used to rule out non-optimal solutions, but not to lower the optimal cost of instances. Since a terminating sequence starting from an arbitrary instance $\mathcal{F}$ requires both lowering the optimal cost of $\mathcal{F}$ to 0 and ruling out non-optimal solutions, using both MSRED and MCSEQ obtains a sufficient set of sequences.

Theorem 1. MSRED $\circ$ MCSEQ *is sufficient for reaching the final state.*

Proof. (Sketch) Let $\mathcal{F}$ be a MaxSAT instance. By correctness of the PMRES algorithm discussed in Example 1 [29], there is a sequence $\langle \mathcal{F}, \ldots, \mathcal{F}_S \rangle \in$ MSRED for which $\mathrm{COST}(\mathcal{F}_S) = 0$ and hence $\mathrm{MCS}(\mathcal{F}_S) = \{\emptyset\}$. The terminating sequence $\langle \mathcal{F}, \ldots, \mathcal{F}_S, \mathcal{F}_F \rangle \in$ MSRED $\circ$ MCSEQ witnesses the claim. $\square$

6   RAT Clauses in MaxSAT

We propose and analyze two novel notions for transforming MaxSAT instances and their corresponding sets of sequences, MAX-RAT and CSRED. First we adapt the idea of resolution asymmetric tautologies (RAT) to MaxSAT to obtain MAX-RAT, an effective subset of MCSEQ. RAT is a simple yet powerful notion for characterizing preprocessing and inprocessing in SAT solving [17] which provides a basis for a general proof of correctness for natural liftings of SAT preprocessing techniques that can be expressed as sequences adding and removing RAT clauses.

Given two clauses $C = l \vee C'$ and $D = \neg l \vee D'$, the resolvent $C \bowtie_l D = C' \vee D'$ of C and D is obtained by *resolving* them on l. Resolution is extended to sets of clauses by $\mathrm{CL}(l) \bowtie_l \mathrm{CL}(\neg l) = \{C \bowtie_l D \mid C \in \mathrm{CL}(l), D \in \mathrm{CL}(\neg l)\}$. Let $\mathcal{F}$ be a MaxSAT instance and C a clause. Denote by $\mathrm{ALA}(\mathcal{F}, C)$ (asymmetric literal addition) the unique clause resulting from repeating the following until fixpoint: if $l_1, \ldots, l_k \subset C$ and there is a clause $(l_1 \vee \cdots \vee l_k \vee l) \in \mathcal{F} \setminus \{C\}$, set $C := C \cup \{\neg l\}$. We say that C has solution resolution asymmetric tautology (SRAT) with respect to $\mathcal{F}$ if either $C = (x \vee \neg x)$ for some variable x or there is a literal $l \in C \setminus \mathcal{S}(\mathcal{F})$ such that $\mathrm{ALA}(\mathcal{F}, C \bowtie_l D)$ is a tautology for all clauses $D \in \mathrm{CL}(\neg l)$. In the second case, we say that C has SRAT on l. When $\mathcal{F}$ is clear from context, we say that C is an SRAT clause. We emphasize that the only restriction put on l is that it is not a soft variable. Specifically, l can still be the negation of a soft variable. Notice also that any clause C that has SRAT with respect to to an instance F also has RAT as defined in [17] with respect to to the CNF formula $\mathrm{CLAUSES}(\mathcal{F})$ but the converse is not true. We use the terms SRAT clause to refer to the concept for MaxSAT as defined here, and RAT clause to refer to the SAT-specific concept from [17].

Given a MaxSAT instance $\mathcal{F}$ and an SRAT clause C, the instance $\mathrm{ADD}(\mathcal{F}, C)$ is obtained by (i) adding C to $\mathcal{F}$ and (ii) extending $w^{\mathcal{F}}$ by setting the weight of each variable (if any) in $\mathrm{VAR}(C) \setminus \mathrm{VAR}(\mathcal{F})$ arbitrarily. Similarly, the instance $\mathrm{REMOVE}(\mathcal{F}, C)$ is obtained by (i) removing C from $\mathcal{F}$ and (ii) restricting $w^{\mathcal{F}}$ onto $\mathrm{VAR}(\mathcal{F} \setminus \{C\})$. These transformations are lifted to sequences of instances by the set MAX-RAT.

Definition 9. *The set* MAX-RAT *contains all sequences* $\langle \mathcal{F}_1, \ldots, \mathcal{F}_n \rangle$*, where* $\mathcal{F}_{i+1} = \mathrm{ADD}(\mathcal{F}_i, C)$ *or* $\mathcal{F}_{i+1} = \mathrm{REMOVE}(\mathcal{F}_i, C)$ *for all* $i = 1, \ldots, n-1$.

While simple, the sequences in MAX-RAT are fairly expressive. As discussed in [17], SAT solving techniques, including forms of preprocessing, can very generally be viewed as sequences of adding and removing RAT clauses and can thus be easily lifted to MaxSAT with SRAT.

Example 2. Let $\mathcal{F}$ be an instance, $x \in \mathrm{VAR}(\mathcal{F}) \setminus \mathcal{S}(\mathcal{F})$, $\mathrm{CL}(x) \cup \mathrm{CL}(\neg x) = \{C_1, \ldots, C_n\}$ and $\mathrm{CL}(x) \bowtie_x \mathrm{CL}(\neg x) = \{D_1, \ldots, D_t\}$. The well-known variable elimination rule allows eliminating x from $\mathcal{F}$ by transforming it to $\mathcal{F}^R = \mathcal{F} \setminus (\mathrm{CL}(x) \cup \mathrm{CL}(\neg x)) \cup (\mathrm{CL}(x) \bowtie_x \mathrm{CL}(\neg x))$. This corresponds to the sequence $\langle \mathcal{F} = \mathcal{F}_0, \mathcal{F}_1, \ldots, \mathcal{F}_t, \ldots, \mathcal{F}_{t+n} \rangle$ with $\mathcal{F}_i = \mathrm{ADD}(\mathcal{F}_{i-1}, D_i)$ for $i = 1, \ldots, t$ and $\mathcal{F}_i = \mathrm{REMOVE}(\mathcal{F}_{i-1}, C_{i-t})$ for $i = t+1, \ldots, t+n$. This sequence is in MAX-RAT.

Both $\text{ADD}(\mathcal{F}, C)$ and $\text{REMOVE}(\mathcal{F}, C)$ are MCS-equivalent with $\mathcal{F}$; this is because soft variables of $\mathcal{F}$ contained only in C are not members of any MCSes of $\mathcal{F}$.

Theorem 2. MCSEQ *is more general than* MAX-RAT.

In addition, generalizing results from [17], we show that MAX-RAT is effective. Given an instance $\mathcal{F}$ and a clause C that has SRAT with respect to a literal l, we show that if τ is a solution to $\mathcal{F}$ but not $\text{ADD}(\mathcal{F}, C)$, then $\tau^R = \tau \setminus \{\neg l\} \cup \{l\}$ is a solution to both $\mathcal{F}$ and $\text{ADD}(\mathcal{F}, C)$. While this also holds for RAT clauses [17], the added assumption $l \notin \mathcal{S}(\mathcal{F})$ of SRAT is needed to show $\text{COST}(\mathcal{F}, \tau) \geq \text{COST}(\mathcal{F}, \tau^R) = \text{COST}(\text{ADD}(\mathcal{F}, C), \tau^R)$, which in turn implies the existence of effective reconstruction functions for sequences in MAX-RAT.

Proposition 7. MAX-RAT *is effective*.

More generally, MAX-RAT provides a natural way of correctly lifting all of the preprocessing rules proposed for SAT solving that can be modelled with RAT based transformations to MaxSAT; this noticeably generalizes correctness proofs of the four particular liftings considered in [5].

Theorem 3. *Let $\mathcal{F}$ be a MaxSAT instance and $\mathcal{F}^R$ the instance obtained by applying a SAT preprocessing technique that can be viewed as a sequence $\langle \mathcal{F}, \ldots, \mathcal{F}^R \rangle$ of RAT clause additions and deletions. Assume that all of the added and removed clauses also have SRAT. Then an optimal solution to $\mathcal{F}$ can be effectively computed based on an optimal solution to $\mathcal{F}^R$.*

RAT and, by extension, SRAT are very powerful concepts, allowing for simulating essentially all SAT preprocessing techniques, including both resolution-based and clause elimination techniques [17]. Hence Theorem 3 gives a very general proof of correctness for natural liftings of SAT-based preprocessing techniques to MaxSAT.

The MAX-RAT sequences also detail the relationship between core-guided MaxSAT solvers and the abstract model of MaxSAT solving that we work with. Since the transformations in MAX-RAT can model SAT solving [17], the abstract state transition system models both the transformations employed by the outer core-guided MaxSAT algorithm, and the internal SAT solver used by it to extract cores and compute satisfying assignments. For example, the soundness of keeping learned clauses of the internal SAT solver between iterations follows easily from the fact that a SAT solver only learns clauses that have SRAT with respect to the current instance. Therefore the combination of MAX-RAT and MSRED captures the correctness of core-guided algorithms and their interleavings with liftings of SAT-based preprocessing techniques.

Theorem 4. MSRED ∘ MAX-RAT *is effective and sufficient for reaching the final state.*

However, as we will discuss next, there are instance transformations, some of which arise from MaxSAT-specific preprocessing techniques without counterparts in SAT preprocessing, that are not captured by MSRED ∘ MAX-RAT. This motivates the study of more expressive instance transformations.

7 Correction Set Reducible Transformations

The second novel notion for transforming MaxSAT instances that we propose is correction set reducibility (CS-reducibility). CS-reducibility is a more general form of instance transformations, surpassing the combination of MaxSAT-reducibility and MCS-equivalence, and thereby providing a wide basis for reasoning about the correctness of MaxSAT solving.

Definition 10. *The instance $\mathcal{F}$ is correction set reducible (CS-reducible) to the instance $\mathcal{F}^R$ if $U(\mathcal{F}, \tau^R) = \tau^R \cap \mathcal{S}(\mathcal{F})$ is an optimal MCS of $\mathcal{F}$ whenever τ^R is an optimal solution to $\mathcal{F}^R$.*

Example 3. Let $\mathcal{F} = \{(l_1 \vee l_2)\}$ and $\mathcal{F}^R = \{(l_1 \vee l_2), (\neg l_2)\}$ be two instances with $w^{\mathcal{F}}(l_1) = w^{\mathcal{F}^R}(l_1) = 1$ and $w^{\mathcal{F}}(l_2) = w^{\mathcal{F}^R}(l_2) = 2$. Then $\mathcal{F}$ is CS reducible to $\mathcal{F}^R$ which follows from $\tau^R = \{l_1, \neg l_2\}$ being the only optimal solution of $\mathcal{F}^R$ and $\tau^R \cap \mathcal{S}(\mathcal{F}) = \{l_1\}$ being an optimal MCS of $\mathcal{F}$.

Similarly to other transformations, let CSRED be the set of sequences that contains all sequences $\langle \mathcal{F}_1, \ldots, \mathcal{F}_n \rangle$ for which $\mathcal{F}_i$ is CS-reducible to $\mathcal{F}_{i+1}$ for $i = 1, \ldots, n-1$. In contrast to MaxSAT-reducibility, CS-reducibility does not require uniformly changing costs of all assignments. This allows transformations that rule out non-optimal solutions. In contrast to MCS-equivalence, CS-reducibility only requires that an optimal solution to the transformed instance corresponds to an optimal MCS of the original instance; an optimal MCS of the original instance does not have to be an MCS of the transformed instance nor do all MCSes of the instance need to be preserved. This allows transformations that lower the optimal cost of instances.

Theorem 5. CSRED *is more general than* MSRED ∘ MCSEQ.

Notice that Theorem 5 also implies that CSRED is sufficient for reaching the final state.

As CSRED is at least as general as MCSEQ we do not expect it to be effective. However, CSRED-E, the effective subset of CSRED, is in itself relatively expressive.

Theorem 6. CSRED-E *is sufficient for reaching the final state. Furthermore,* MSRED ∘ MCSEQ, *is not as general as* CSRED-E.

Proof. The first claim follows directly from Theorems 4 and 5. For the second claim, consider the sequence $\langle \mathcal{F}, \mathcal{F}^R \rangle$ formed by the instances defined in Example 3. The claim $\langle \mathcal{F}, \mathcal{F}^R \rangle \in$ CSRED-E follows from the fact that the sets of optimal solutions of $\mathcal{F}$ and $\mathcal{F}^R$ are equal. To show that $\langle \mathcal{F}, \mathcal{F}^R \rangle \notin$ MSRED $\circ$ MCSEQ we demonstrate that $\mathcal{F}$ is neither MaxSAT-reducible to, or MCS-equivalent with, $\mathcal{F}^R$. The former follows by considering the solution $\tau = \{l_2, \neg l_1\}$ to $\mathcal{F}$ and the latter from $\mathrm{MCS}(\mathcal{F}) = \{\{l_1\}, \{l_2\}\} \neq \{\{l_1\}\} = \mathrm{MCS}(\mathcal{F}^R)$.   □

Note that Theorem 6 implies that MSRED $\circ$ MAX-RAT is not as general as CSRED-E and that the sequence $\langle \mathcal{F}, \mathcal{F}^R \rangle$ corresponds to applying the MaxSAT-specific preprocessing of subsumed label elimination [8] on $\mathcal{F}$. Thus effective CS-reducibility captures existing MaxSAT preprocessing techniques not captured by MSRED $\circ$ MAX-RAT.

8   Related Work

In terms of previously proposed formal systems for MaxSAT, MaxSAT resolution [10,20] was proposed as a generalization of the resolution proof system. It is a complete rule for MaxSAT in that iteratively applying MaxSAT resolution to the clauses of a MaxSAT instance $\mathcal{F}$ gives another instance $\mathcal{F}^{\mathrm{RES}}$ such that $\mathrm{COST}(\mathcal{F}^{\mathrm{RES}}) = 0$ and any satisfying assignment to $\mathcal{F}^S|_{\neg \mathcal{S}(\mathcal{F}^S)}$ is an optimal solution to $\mathcal{F}$. The correctness of MaxSAT resolution was shown by establishing that $\mathcal{F}$ is MaxSAT-equivalent to $\mathcal{F}^{\mathrm{RES}}$. As implied by our analysis, this means that MaxSAT resolution can be used to determine the optimal cost of an instance, but finding an optimal solution requires computing a satisfying assignment to a satisfiable CNF formula. While MaxSAT resolution and its restrictions give rise to simplification rules used in conjunction with branch-and-bound MaxSAT solvers [4,16,21,22] (and also yields a proof system for SAT [9]), we focus on the current state-of-the-art core-guided approaches and central SAT-based preprocessing techniques. (The recent clause tableaux proof system for MaxSAT [23] does not capture core-guided transformations or MaxSAT preprocessing, either.) The recent formalization of implicit hitting set (IHS) algorithms for optimization modulo theories of [13] captures solely extensions of the IHS approach [12,32], extending the DPLL(T) framework [31] which has also earlier been extended to optimization modulo theories [30] and adapted for formalizing answer set solvers [11,24] (without optimization statements).

9   Conclusions

We studied the formal underpinnings of unifying preprocessing-style reasoning and core-guided transformations for MaxSAT. To this end, we formalized a generic framework for MaxSAT solving based on sequences of MaxSAT instances, and analyzed previously proposed notions of instance transformations underlying core-guided search and SAT-based preprocessing for MaxSAT within the framework. We showed that these notions individually do not capture each other (i.e., inprocessing core-guided MaxSAT solving), and therefore neither can be used for arguing about the correctness of the other. We proposed correction set reducibility as a new type of MaxSAT instance transformation which unifies core-guided

MaxSAT solving and MaxSAT preprocessing, including SAT-based preprocessing lifted to MaxSAT. Furthermore, we generalized the concept of resolution asymmetric tautologies from SAT solving to MaxSAT solving, thereby obtaining a very general proof of correctness for lifting SAT preprocessing techniques to MaxSAT. All in all, the results build ground for generic techniques for arguing about the formal correctness of MaxSAT algorithms.

Acknowledgments. The work has been financially supported by Academy of Finland (grants 276412 and 312662) and University of Helsinki Doctoral Programme in Computer Science.

References

1. Alviano, M., Dodaro, C., Ricca, F.: A MaxSAT algorithm using cardinality constraints of bounded size. In: Proceedings of IJCAI, pp. 2677–2683. AAAI Press (2015)
2. Ansótegui, C., Bonet, M., Levy, J.: SAT-based MaxSAT algorithms. Artif. Intell. **196**, 77–105 (2013)
3. Ansótegui, C., Didier, F., Gabàs, J.: Exploiting the structure of unsatisfiable cores in MaxSAT. In: Proceedings of IJCAI, pp. 283–289. AAAI Press (2015)
4. Argelich, J., Li, C.M., Manyà, F.: A preprocessor for Max-SAT solvers. In: Kleine Büning, H., Zhao, X. (eds.) SAT 2008. LNCS, vol. 4996, pp. 15–20. Springer, Heidelberg (2008). https://doi.org/10.1007/978-3-540-79719-7_2
5. Belov, A., Morgado, A., Marques-Silva, J.: SAT-based preprocessing for MaxSAT. In: McMillan, K., Middeldorp, A., Voronkov, A. (eds.) LPAR 2013. LNCS, vol. 8312, pp. 96–111. Springer, Heidelberg (2013). https://doi.org/10.1007/978-3-642-45221-5_7
6. Benedetti, M., Mori, M.: Parametric RBAC maintenance via Max-SAT. In: Proceedings of SACMAT, pp. 15–25. ACM (2018)
7. Berg, J., Järvisalo, M.: Cost-optimal constrained correlation clustering via weighted partial maximum satisfiability. Artif. Intell. **244**, 110–143 (2017)
8. Berg, J., Saikko, P., Järvisalo, M.: Subsumed label elimination for maximum satisfiability. In: Proceedings of ECAI, Frontiers in Artificial Intelligence and Applications, vol. 285, pp. 630–638. IOS Press (2016)
9. Bonet, M.L., Buss, S., Ignatiev, A., Marques-Silva, J., Morgado, A.: MaxSAT resolution with the dual rail encoding. In: Proceedings of AAAI. AAAI Press (2018)
10. Bonet, M.L., Levy, J., Manyà, F.: Resolution for Max-SAT. Artif. Intell. **171**(8–9), 606–618 (2007)
11. Brochenin, R., Maratea, M., Lierler, Y.: Disjunctive answer set solvers via templates. Theory Pract. Logic Program. **16**(4), 465–497 (2016)
12. Davies, J., Bacchus, F.: Exploiting the power of MIP solvers in MAXSAT. In: Järvisalo, M., Van Gelder, A. (eds.) SAT 2013. LNCS, vol. 7962, pp. 166–181. Springer, Heidelberg (2013). https://doi.org/10.1007/978-3-642-39071-5_13
13. Fazekas, K., Bacchus, F., Biere, A.: Implicit hitting set algorithms for maximum satisfiability modulo theories. In: Galmiche, D., Schulz, S., Sebastiani, R. (eds.) IJCAR 2018. LNCS (LNAI), vol. 10900, pp. 134–151. Springer, Cham (2018). https://doi.org/10.1007/978-3-319-94205-6_10

302   J. Berg and M. Järvisalo

14. Feng, Y., Bastani, O., Martins, R., Dillig, I., Anand, S.: Automated synthesis of semantic malware signatures using maximum satisfiability. In: Proceedings of NDSS. The Internet Society (2017)

15. Heras, F., Morgado, A., Marques-Silva, J.: Core-guided binary search algorithms for maximum satisfiability. In: Proceedings of AAAI. AAAI Press (2011)

16. Heras, F., Larrosa, J., Oliveras, A.: MiniMaxSAT: an efficient weighted Max-SAT solver. J. Artif. Intell. Res. **31**, 1–32 (2008)

17. Järvisalo, M., Heule, M.J.H., Biere, A.: Inprocessing rules. In: Gramlich, B., Miller, D., Sattler, U. (eds.) IJCAR 2012. LNCS (LNAI), vol. 7364, pp. 355–370. Springer, Heidelberg (2012). https://doi.org/10.1007/978-3-642-31365-3_28

18. Jose, M., Majumdar, R.: Cause clue clauses: error localization using maximum satisfiability. In: Proceedings of PLDI, pp. 437–446. ACM (2011)

19. Korhonen, T., Berg, J., Saikko, P., Järvisalo, M.: MaxPre: an extended MaxSAT preprocessor. In: Gaspers, S., Walsh, T. (eds.) SAT 2017. LNCS, vol. 10491, pp. 449–456. Springer, Cham (2017). https://doi.org/10.1007/978-3-319-66263-3_28

20. Larrosa, J., Heras, F.: Resolution in Max-SAT and its relation to local consistency in weighted CSPs. In: Proceedings of IJCAI, pp. 193–198. Professional Book Center (2005)

21. Larrosa, J., Heras, F., de Givry, S.: A logical approach to efficient Max-SAT solving. Artif. Intell. **172**(2–3), 204–233 (2008)

22. Li, C.M., Manyà, F., Mohamedou, N.O., Planes, J.: Resolution-based lower bounds in MaxSAT. Constraints **15**(4), 456–484 (2010)

23. Li, C.M., Manyà, F., Soler, J.R.: A clause tableau calculus for MinSAT. In: Proceedings of CCIA, Frontiers in Artificial Intelligence and Applications, vol. 288, pp. 88–97. IOS Press (2016)

24. Lierler, Y., Truszczynski, M.: On abstract modular inference systems and solvers. Artif. Intell. **236**, 65–89 (2016)

25. Marques-Silva, J., Janota, M., Ignatiev, A., Morgado, A.: Efficient model based diagnosis with maximum satisfiability. In: Proceedings of IJCAI, pp. 1966–1972. AAAI Press (2015)

26. Morgado, A., Dodaro, C., Marques-Silva, J.: Core-guided MaxSAT with soft cardinality constraints. In: O'Sullivan, B. (ed.) CP 2014. LNCS, vol. 8656, pp. 564–573. Springer, Cham (2014). https://doi.org/10.1007/978-3-319-10428-7_41

27. Morgado, A., Heras, F., Liffiton, M., Planes, J., Marques-Silva, J.: Iterative and core-guided MaxSAT solving: a survey and assessment. Constraints **18**(4), 478–534 (2013)

28. Nadel, A., Ryvchin, V.: Efficient SAT solving under assumptions. In: Cimatti, A., Sebastiani, R. (eds.) SAT 2012. LNCS, vol. 7317, pp. 242–255. Springer, Heidelberg (2012). https://doi.org/10.1007/978-3-642-31612-8_19

29. Narodytska, N., Bacchus, F.: Maximum satisfiability using core-guided MaxSAT resolution. In: Proceedings of AAAI, pp. 2717–2723. AAAI Press (2014)

30. Nieuwenhuis, R., Oliveras, A.: On SAT modulo theories and optimization problems. In: Biere, A., Gomes, C.P. (eds.) SAT 2006. LNCS, vol. 4121, pp. 156–169. Springer, Heidelberg (2006). https://doi.org/10.1007/11814948_18

31. Nieuwenhuis, R., Oliveras, A., Tinelli, C.: Solving SAT and SAT modulo theories: from an abstract Davis-Putnam-Logemann-Loveland procedure to DPLL(T). J. ACM **53**, 2006 (2006)

32. Saikko, P., Berg, J., Järvisalo, M.: LMHS: a SAT-IP hybrid MaxSAT solver. In: Creignou, N., Le Berre, D. (eds.) SAT 2016. LNCS, vol. 9710, pp. 539–546. Springer, Cham (2016). https://doi.org/10.1007/978-3-319-40970-2_34

33. Wallner, J.P., Niskanen, A., Järvisalo, M.: Complexity results and algorithms for extension enforcement in abstract argumentation. J. Artif. Intel. Res. **60**, 1–40 (2017)
34. Zhu, C., Weissenbacher, G., Malik, S.: Post-silicon fault localisation using maximum satisfiability and backbones. In: Proceedings of FMCAD, pp. 63–66. FMCAD Inc. (2011)

Facets of Distribution Identities in Probabilistic Team Semantics

Miika Hannula[1] , Åsa Hirvonen[1] , Juha Kontinen[1] , Vadim Kulikov[1,2],
and Jonni Virtema[3(✉)]

[1] University of Helsinki, Helsinki, Finland
{miika.hannula,asa.hirvonen,juha.kontinen}@helsinki.fi
[2] Aalto University, Espoo, Finland
vadim.kulikov@iki.fi
[3] Hasselt University, Hasselt, Belgium
jonni.virtema@uhasselt.be

Abstract. We study probabilistic team semantics which is a semantical framework allowing the study of logical and probabilistic dependencies simultaneously. We examine and classify the expressive power of logical formalisms arising by different probabilistic atoms such as conditional independence and different variants of marginal distribution equivalences. We also relate the framework to the first-order theory of the reals and apply our methods to the open question on the complexity of the implication problem of conditional independence.

Keywords: Team semantics · Probabilistic logic ·
Conditional independence

1 Introduction

Team semantics, introduced by Hodges [21] and popularised by Väänänen [26], shifts the focus of logics away from assignments as the primitive notion connected to satisfaction. In team semantics formulae are evaluated with respect to sets of assignments (i.e., teams) as opposed to single assignments of Tarskian semantics. During the last decade the research on team semantics has flourished, many logical formalisms have been defined, and surprising connections to other fields identified. In particular, several promising application areas of team semantics have been identified recently. Krebs et al. [23] developed a team based approach to linear temporal logic for the verification of information flow properties. In applications to database theory, a team corresponds exactly to a database table (see, e.g., [17]). Hannula et al. [19] introduced a framework that extends the connection of team semantics and database theory to polyrelational databases and data exchange.

The first and the third author were supported by grant 308712, the fourth by grant 285203 of the Academy of Finland.

F. Calimeri et al. (Eds.): JELIA 2019, LNAI 11468, pp. 304–320, 2019.
https://doi.org/10.1007/978-3-030-19570-0_20

The focus of this article is probabilistic team semantics which connects team based logics to probabilistic dependency notions. Probabilistic team semantics is built compositionally upon the notion of a probabilistic team, that is, a probability distribution over variable assignments. While the first ideas of probabilistic teams trace back to the works of Galliani [11] and Hyttinen et al. [22], the systematic study of the topic was initiated and further continued by Durand et al. in [8,9]. It is worth noting that in [2] so-called causal teams have been introduced to logically model causality and interventions. Probabilistic team semantics has also a close connection to the area of metafinite model theory [14]. In metafinite model theory, finite structures are extended with an another (infinite) domain sort such as the real numbers (often with arithmetic) and with weight functions that work as a bridge between the two sorts. This approach provides an elegant way to model weighted graphs and other structures that refer to infinite structures. The exact relationship between probabilistic team semantics and logics over metafinite models as well as with probabilistic databases of [6] will be a topic of future research.

The starting point of this work comes from [9] in which probabilistic team semantics was defined following the lines of [11]. The main theme in [9] was to characterize logical formalisms in this framework in terms of existential second-order logic. Two main probabilistic dependency atoms were examined. The probabilistic conditional independence atom $y \perp\!\!\!\perp_x z$ states that the two variable tuples y and z are independent given the third tuple x. The marginal identity atom $x \approx y$ states that the marginal distributions induced from the two tuples x and y (of the same length) are identical. The extension of first-order logic with these atoms $(\mathrm{FO}(\perp\!\!\!\perp_c, \approx))$ was then shown to correspond to a two-sorted variant of existential second-order logic that allows a restricted access to arithmetical operations for numerical function terms. What was left unexamined were the relationships between different logical formalisms in probabilistic team semantics. In fact, it was unknown whether there are any meaningful probabilistic dependency notions such that the properties definable with one notion are comparable to those definable with another.

In this article we study the relative expressivity of first-order logic with probabilistic conditional independence atoms $(\mathrm{FO}(\perp\!\!\!\perp_c))$ and with marginal identity atoms $(\mathrm{FO}(\approx))$. The logic $\mathrm{FO}(\approx)$ is a probabilistic variant of *inclusion logic* that is strictly less expressive than *independence logic*, after which $\mathrm{FO}(\perp\!\!\!\perp_c)$ is modelled [12,15]. In addition, we examine $\mathrm{FO}(\approx^*)$ which is another extension defined in terms of so-called marginal distribution equivalence. The *marginal distribution equivalence atom* $x \approx^* y$ for two variable tuples x and y (not necessarily of the same length) relaxes the truth condition of the marginal identity atom in that the two distributions induced from x and y are required to determine the same multisets of probabilities. The aforementioned open question is now answered in the positive. The logics mentioned above are not only comparable, but they form a linear expressivity hierarchy: $\mathrm{FO}(\approx) < \mathrm{FO}(\approx^*) \leq \mathrm{FO}(\perp\!\!\!\perp_c)$. We also show that $\mathrm{FO}(\approx)$ enjoys a union closure property that is a generalization of the union closure property of inclusion logic, and that conditional independence atoms $y \perp\!\!\!\perp_x z$ can be defined with an access to only marginal independence atoms $x \perp\!\!\!\perp y$ between two variable tuples. Furthermore, we show that, surprisingly, $FO(\approx^*)$ corresponds to $FO(\approx, =(\cdot))$, where $=(\cdot)$ refers to the dependence atom defined as a declaration of functional dependence over the support of the probabilistic team. The question whether $FO(\approx, =(\cdot))$ is strictly less expressive than $FO(\perp\!\!\!\perp_c)$ is left as an open question; in team semantics the corresponding logics are known to be equivalent. The above findings look outwardly very similar to many results in team semantics. However, it is important to note that, apart perhaps from the union closure property, the results of this paper base on entirely new ideas and do not recycle old arguments from the team semantics context.

We also investigate (quantified) propositional logics with probabilistic team semantics. By connecting these logics to the arithmetic of the reals we show upper bounds for their associated computational problems. Our results suggest that the addition of probabilities to team semantics entails an increase in the complexity. Satisfiability of propositional team logic $(PL(\sim))$, i.e., propositional logic with classical negation is in team semantics known to be complete for alternating exponential time with polynomially many alternations [20]. Shifting to probabilistic team semantics analogous problems are here shown to enjoy double exponential space upper bound. This is still lower than the complexity of satisfiability for modal team logic $(ML(\sim))$ in team semantics, known to be complete for the non-elementary complexity class $TOWER(poly)$ which consists of problems solvable in time restricted by some tower of exponentials of polynomial height [24]. One intriguing consequence of our translation to real arithmetic is that the implication problem of conditional independence statements over binary distributions is decidable in exponential space. The decidability of this problem is open relative to all discrete probability distributions [25].

2   Preliminaries

First-order variables are denoted by x, y, z and tuples of first-order variables by $\boldsymbol{x}, \boldsymbol{y}, \boldsymbol{z}$. By $Var(\boldsymbol{x})$ we denote the set of variables that appear in the variable sequence $\boldsymbol{x}$. The length of the tuple $\boldsymbol{x}$ is denoted by $|\boldsymbol{x}|$. A *vocabulary* τ is a set of relation symbols and function symbols with prescribed arities. We mostly denote relation symbols by R and function symbols by f, and the related arities by $ar(R)$ and $ar(f)$, respectively. The closed interval of real numbers between 0 and 1 is denoted by $[0, 1]$. Given a finite set A, a function $f \colon A \to [0, 1]$ is called a *(probability) distribution* if $\sum_{s \in A} f(s) = 1$. In addition, the empty function is a *distribution*.

The probabilistic logics investigated in this paper are extensions of first-order logic FO over a vocabulary τ given by the grammar rules:

$$\phi ::= x = y \mid x \neq y \mid R(\boldsymbol{x}) \mid \neg R(\boldsymbol{x}) \mid (\phi \wedge \phi) \mid (\phi \vee \phi) \mid \exists x \phi \mid \forall x \phi,$$

where $\boldsymbol{x}$ is a tuple of first-order variables and R a relation symbol from τ.

Let D be a finite set of first-order variables and A be a nonempty set. A function $s\colon D \to A$ is called an *assignment*. For a variable x and $a \in A$, the assignment $s(a/x)\colon D \cup \{x\} \to A$ is equal to s with the exception that $s(a/x)(x) = a$. A *team* X is a finite set of assignments from D to A. The set D is called the *domain* of X (written $\mathrm{Dom}(X)$) and the set A the *range* of X (written $\mathrm{Ran}(X)$). Let X be a team with range A, and let $F\colon X \to \mathcal{P}(A) \setminus \{\emptyset\}$ be a function. We denote by $X[A/x]$ the modified team $\{s(a/x) \mid s \in X, a \in A\}$, and by $X[F/x]$ the team $\{s(a/x) \mid s \in X, a \in F(s)\}$. A *probabilistic team* $\mathbb{X}$ is a distribution $\mathbb{X}\colon X \to [0,1]$. Let $\mathfrak{A}$ be a τ-structure and $\mathbb{X}\colon X \to [0,1]$ a probabilistic team such that the domain of $\mathfrak{A}$ is the range of X. Then we say that $\mathbb{X}$ is a probabilistic team of $\mathfrak{A}$. In the following, we will define two notations $\mathbb{X}[A/x]$ and $\mathbb{X}[F/x]$. Let $\mathbb{X}\colon X \to [0,1]$ be a probabilistic team, A a finite non-empty set, p_A the set of all probability distributions $d\colon A \to [0,1]$, and $F\colon X \to p_A$ a function. We denote by $\mathbb{X}[A/x]$ the probabilistic team $X[A/x] \to [0,1]$ such that

$$\mathbb{X}[A/x](s(a/x)) = \sum_{\substack{t \in X \\ t(a/x)=s(a/x)}} \mathbb{X}(t) \cdot \frac{1}{|A|},$$

for each $a \in A$ and $s \in X$. Note that if x does not belong to the domain of X then the righthand side of the above equation is simply $\mathbb{X}(s) \cdot \frac{1}{|A|}$. By $\mathbb{X}[F/x]$ we denote the probabilistic team $X[A/x] \to [0,1]$ defined such that

$$\mathbb{X}[F/x](s(a/x)) = \sum_{\substack{t \in X \\ t(a/x)=s(a/x)}} \mathbb{X}(t) \cdot F(t)(a),$$

for each $a \in A$ and $s \in X$. Again if x does not belong to the domain of X, $\sum$ can be dropped from the above equation.

If $\mathbb{Y}\colon X \to [0,1]$ and $\mathbb{Z}\colon X \to [0,1]$ are probabilistic teams and $k \in [0,1]$, then we write $\mathbb{Y} \sqcup_k \mathbb{Z}$ for the k-scaled union of $\mathbb{Y}$ and $\mathbb{Z}$, that is, the probabilistic team $\mathbb{Y} \sqcup_k \mathbb{Z}\colon X \to [0,1]$ defined such that $(\mathbb{Y} \sqcup_k \mathbb{Z})(s) = k \cdot \mathbb{Y}(s) + (1-k) \cdot \mathbb{Z}(s)$ for each $s \in X$.

We may now define probabilistic team semantics for first-order formulae. The definition is the same as in [9]. The only exception is that it is here applied to probabilistic teams that have real probabilities, whereas in [9] rational probabilities were used.

Definition 1. *Let $\mathfrak{A}$ be a probabilistic τ-structure over a finite domain A, and $\mathbb{X}\colon X \to [0,1]$ a probabilistic team of $\mathfrak{A}$. The satisfaction relation $\models_{\mathbb{X}}$ for first-order logic is defined as follows:*

$\mathfrak{A} \models_{\mathbb{X}} x = y \;\Leftrightarrow\;$ *for all $s \in X$: if $\mathbb{X}(s) > 0$, then $s(x) = s(y)$*

$\mathfrak{A} \models_{\mathbb{X}} x \neq y \;\Leftrightarrow\;$ *for all $s \in X$: if $\mathbb{X}(s) > 0$, then $s(x) \neq s(y)$*

$\mathfrak{A} \models_{\mathbb{X}} R(\boldsymbol{x}) \;\Leftrightarrow\;$ *for all $s \in X$: if $\mathbb{X}(s) > 0$, then $s(\boldsymbol{x}) \in R^{\mathfrak{A}}$*

$\mathfrak{A} \models_{\mathbb{X}} \neg R(\boldsymbol{x}) \;\Leftrightarrow\;$ *for all $s \in X$: if $\mathbb{X}(s) > 0$, then $s(\boldsymbol{x}) \notin R^{\mathfrak{A}}$*

$\mathfrak{A} \models_{\mathbb{X}} (\psi \wedge \theta) \;\Leftrightarrow\; \mathfrak{A} \models_{\mathbb{X}} \psi$ *and* $\mathfrak{A} \models_{\mathbb{X}} \theta$

$\mathfrak{A} \models_{\mathbb{X}} (\psi \vee \theta) \;\Leftrightarrow\; \mathfrak{A} \models_{\mathbb{Y}} \psi$ *and* $\mathfrak{A} \models_{\mathbb{Z}} \theta$ *for some* $\mathbb{Y}, \mathbb{Z}, k$ *s.t.* $\mathbb{Y} \sqcup_k \mathbb{Z} = \mathbb{X}$

$$\mathfrak{A} \models_\mathbb{X} \forall x \psi \quad \Leftrightarrow \mathfrak{A} \models_{\mathbb{X}[A/x]} \psi$$
$$\mathfrak{A} \models_\mathbb{X} \exists x \psi \quad \Leftrightarrow \mathfrak{A} \models_{\mathbb{X}[F/x]} \psi \text{ holds for some } F \colon X \to p_A.$$

Probabilistic team semantics is in line with Tarski-semantics of first-order formulae ($\models_s$):

$$\mathfrak{A} \models_\mathbb{X} \psi \Leftrightarrow \forall s \in X \text{ such that } \mathbb{X}(s) > 0 : \mathfrak{A} \models_s \psi.$$

In particular the non-classical semantics for negation is required for the above equivalence to hold.

In this paper we consider three probabilistic atoms: marginal identity, probabilistic independence, and marginal distribution equivalence atom. The first two were first introduced in the context of multiteam semantics in [8], and they extend the notions of inclusion and independence atoms from team semantics [12].

We define $|\mathbb{X}_{x=a}|$ where x is a tuple of variables and a a tuple of values, as

$$|\mathbb{X}_{x=a}| := \sum_{\substack{s(x)=a \\ s \in X}} \mathbb{X}(s).$$

If ϕ is some first-order formula, then $|\mathbb{X}_\phi|$ is defined analogously as the total sum of weights of those assignments in X that satisfy ϕ.

If x, y are variable sequences of length k, then $x \approx y$ is a *marginal identity atom* with the following semantics:

$$\mathfrak{A} \models_\mathbb{X} x \approx y \Leftrightarrow |\mathbb{X}_{x=a}| = |\mathbb{X}_{y=a}| \text{ for each } a \in A^k. \tag{1}$$

Note that the equality $|\mathbb{X}_{x=a}| = |\mathbb{X}_{y=a}|$ in (1) can be equivalently replaced with $|\mathbb{X}_{x=a}| \leq |\mathbb{X}_{y=a}|$ since the tuples a range over A^k for a finite A (see [8, Definition 7] for details). Due to this alternative formulation, marginal identity atoms were in [8] called probabilistic inclusion atoms. Intuitively, the atom $x \approx y$ states that the distributions induced from x and y are identical.

The marginal distribution equivalence atom is defined in terms of multisets of assignment weights. We distinguish multisets from sets by using double wave brackets, e.g., $\{\{a, a, b\}\}$ denotes the multiset $(\{a, b\}, m)$ where a and b are given multiplicities $m(a) = 2$ and $m(b) = 1$. If x, y are variable sequences, then $x \approx^* y$ is a *marginal distribution equivalence atom* with the following semantics:

$$\mathfrak{A} \models_\mathbb{X} x \approx^* y \Leftrightarrow \{\{|\mathbb{X}_{x=a}| > 0 \mid a \in A^{|x|}\}\} = \{\{|\mathbb{X}_{y=b}| > 0 \mid b \in A^{|y|}\}\}.$$

The next example illustrates the relationships between marginal distribution equivalence and marginal identity atoms; the latter implies the former, but not vice versa.

Example 2. Let $\mathbb{X}$ be the probabilistic team depicted in Fig. 1. The team $\mathbb{X}$ satisfies the atoms $xy \approx^* y$, $x \approx^* y$, $y \approx^* z$, and $y \approx z$. The team $\mathbb{X}$ falsies the atom $x \approx y$, whereas $xy \approx y$ is not a well formed formula.

X			
x	y	z	P
a	b	c	1/2
b	c	b	1/2

Fig. 1. A representation of a probabilistic team X, for Example 2, with domain $\{x, y, z\}$ that consists of two assignments whose probabilities are 1/2.

If x, y, z are variable sequences, then $y \perp\!\!\!\perp_x z$ is a *probabilistic conditional independence atom* with the satisfaction relation defined as

$$\mathfrak{A} \models_{\mathbb{X}} y \perp\!\!\!\perp_x z$$

if for all $s: \text{Var}(xyz) \to A$ it holds that

$$|\mathbb{X}_{xy=s(xy)}| \cdot |\mathbb{X}_{xz=s(xz)}| = |\mathbb{X}_{xyz=s(xyz)}| \cdot |\mathbb{X}_{x=s(x)}|.$$

Furthermore, we define *probabilistic marginal independence atom* $x \perp\!\!\!\perp y$ as $x \perp\!\!\!\perp_\emptyset y$, i.e., probabilistic independence conditioned by the empty tuple.

In addition to atoms based on counting or arithmetic operations, we may also include all dependency atoms from the team semantics literature. Let α be an atom that is interpreted in team semantics, let $\mathfrak{A}$ be a finite structure, and $\mathbb{X} : X \to [0,1]$ a probabilistic team. We define $\mathfrak{A} \models_{\mathbb{X}} \alpha$ if $\mathfrak{A} \models_{X^+} \alpha$, where X^+ consists of those assignments of X that are given positive weight by $\mathbb{X}$. In this paper we will discuss dependence atoms also in the context of probabilistic team semantics. If x, y are two variable sequences, then $=(x, y)$ is a *dependence atom* with team semantics:

$$\mathfrak{A} \models_X =(x, y) \Leftrightarrow s(x) = s'(x) \text{ implies } s(y) = s'(y) \text{ for all } s, s' \in X.$$

A dependence atom of the form $=(\emptyset, x)$ is called a *constancy atom*, written $=(x)$ in shorthand notation. Dependence atoms can be expressed by using probabilistic independence atoms. This has been shown for multiteams in [8], and the proof applies to probabilistic teams.

Proposition 3 ([8])**.** *Let $\mathfrak{A}$ be a structure, $\mathbb{X} : X \to [0, 1]$ a probabilistic team of $\mathfrak{A}$, and x and y two sequences of variables. Then $\mathfrak{A} \models_{\mathbb{X}} =(x, y) \Leftrightarrow \mathfrak{A} \models_{\mathbb{X}} y \perp\!\!\!\perp_x y$.*

Given a collection C of atoms from $\{\perp\!\!\!\perp_c, \perp\!\!\!\perp, \approx, \approx^*, =(\cdot)\}$, we write FO($C$) for the logic that extends FO with the atoms in C.

Example 4. Let $f_1, \ldots, f_n, g$ be univariate distributions. Then g is a *finite mixture* of $f_1, \ldots, f_n$ if it can be expressed as a convex combination of $f_1, \ldots, f_n$, i.e., if there are non-negative real numbers $r_1, \ldots, r_n$ such that $r_1 + \ldots + r_n = 1$ and $g(a) = \sum_{i=1}^{n} r_i f_i(a)$. A probabilistic team $\mathbb{X} : X \to [0, 1]$ gives rise to a univariate distribution $f_x(a) := |\mathbb{X}_{x=a}|$ for each variable x from the domain of X. The next formula expresses that the distribution f_y is a finite mixture of the distributions $f_{x_1}, \ldots, f_{x_n}$:

$$\exists qr\left[x_1 \ldots x_n \perp\!\!\!\perp r \wedge \bigvee_{i=1}^{n} r = i \wedge \bigwedge_{i=1}^{n} \exists x'r'\left(x_i r \approx x'r' \wedge [(q = i \vee r' = i) \rightarrow yq = x'r']\right)\right],$$

where the indices $1, \ldots, n$ are also thought of as distinct constants, and $(q = i \vee r' = i) \rightarrow yq = x'r'$ stands for $\neg(q \neq i \wedge r' \neq i) \vee yq = x'r'$. The non-negative real numbers r_i are represented by the weights of $r = i$ where r is distributed independently of each x_i. The summand $r_i f_{x_i}(a)$ is then represented by the weight of $x_i r = ai$ and $f_y(a)$ by the weight of $y = a$. The quantified subformula expresses that the former weight matches the weight of $yq = ai$, which implies that $f_y(a)$ is $r_1 f_{x_1}(a) + \ldots + r_n f_{x_n}(a)$.

Example 5. Probabilistic team semantics can be also used to model properties of data obtained from a quantum experiment (adapting the approach of [1]). Consider a probabilistic team $\mathbb{X}$ over variables $m_1, \ldots, m_n, o_1, \ldots, o_n$. The intended interpretation of $\mathbb{X}(s) = r$ is that the joint probability that $s(m_i)$ was measured with outcome $s(o_i)$, for $1 \leq i \leq m$, is r. In this setting many important properties of the experiment can be expressed using our formalism. For example the formula

$$o_i \perp\!\!\!\perp_m (o_1, \ldots, o_{i-1}, o_{i+1}, \ldots, o_m)$$

expresses a property called *Outcome-Independence*; given the measurements m, the outcome at i is independent of the outcomes at other positions. The dependence atom $=(m, o)$ on the other hand corresponds to a property called *Weak-Determinism*. Moreover, if ϕ describes some property of hidden-variable models (Outcome-Independence, etc.), then the formula $\exists \lambda \phi$ expresses that the experiment can be explained by a hidden-variable model satisfying that property.

The next example relates probabilistic team semantics to Bayesian networks. The example is an adaptation of an example discussed also in [8].

Example 6. Consider the Bayesian network $\mathbb{G}$ in Fig. 2 that models beliefs about house safety using four Boolean random variables thief, cat, guard and alarm. We refer to these variables by t, c, g, a. The dependence structure of a Bayesian network is characterized by the so-called local directed Markov property stating that each variable is conditionally independent of its non-descendants given its parents. For our network $\mathbb{G}$ the only non-trivial independence given by this property is $g \perp\!\!\!\perp_{tc} a$. Hence a joint distribution P over t, c, g, a factorizes according to $\mathbb{G}$ if $\mathbb{X}$ satisfies $g \perp\!\!\!\perp_{tc} a$. In this case P can be factorized by

$$P(t, c, g, a) = P(t) \cdot P(c \mid t) \cdot P(g \mid t, c) \cdot P(a \mid t, c)$$

where, for instance, t abbreviates either thief $= T$ or thief $= F$, and $P(c \mid t)$ is the probability of c given t. The joint probability distribution (i.e., the team $\mathbb{X}$) can hence be stored as in Fig. 2. Note that while $\mathbb{G}$ expresses the independence statement $g \perp\!\!\!\perp_{tc} a$, $FO(\perp\!\!\!\perp_c, \approx)$-formulas can be used to further refine the joint probability distribution as follows. Assume we have information suggesting that we may safely assume an $FO(\perp\!\!\!\perp_c, \approx)$ formula ϕ on $\mathbb{X}$:

- $\phi := t = F \rightarrow g = F$ indicates that guard never raises alarm in absence of thief. In this case the two bottom rows of the conditional probability distribution for guard become superfluous.
- the assumption that ϕ is satisfied also exemplifies an interesting form of *context-specific* independence (CSI) that cannot be formalized by the usual Bayesian networks (see, e.g., [7]). Namely, ϕ implies that guard is independent of cat in the context thief $= F$. Interestingly such CSI statements can be formalized utilizing the disjunction of $FO(\perp\!\!\!\perp_c, \approx)$:

$$t = T \vee (t = F \wedge g \perp\!\!\!\perp c).$$

- satisfaction of $\phi := tca \approx tcg$ would imply that alarm and guard have the same reliability for any given value of thief and cat. Consequently, the conditional distributions for alarm and guard are equal and one of the them could be removed.

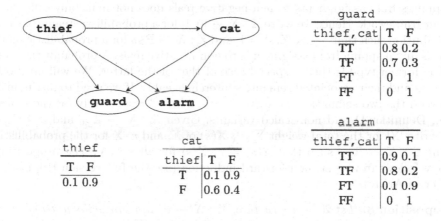

guard		
thief,cat	T	F
TT	0.8	0.2
TF	0.7	0.3
FT	0	1
FF	0	1

alarm		
thief,cat	T	F
TT	0.9	0.1
TF	0.8	0.2
FT	0.1	0.9
FF	0	1

thief	
T	F
0.1	0.9

cat		
thief	T	F
T	0.1	0.9
F	0.6	0.4

Fig. 2. Bayesian network $\mathbb{G}$ and its related conditional distributions.

The following locality property dictates that satisfaction of a formula ϕ in probabilistic team semantics depends only on the free variables of ϕ. For this, we define the *restriction* of a team X to V as $X \restriction V = \{s \restriction V \mid s \in X\}$ where $s \restriction V$ denotes the restriction of the assignment s to V. The restriction of a probabilistic team $\mathbb{X} : X \rightarrow [0,1]$ to V is then defined as the probabilistic team $\mathbb{Y} : X \restriction V \rightarrow [0,1]$ where $\mathbb{Y}(s) = \sum_{s' \restriction V = s} \mathbb{X}(s')$. The set of *free variables* $\mathrm{Fr}(\phi)$ of a formula over probabilistic team semantics is defined recursively as in first-order logic; note that for any atom ϕ, $\mathrm{Fr}(\phi)$ consists of all variables that appear in ϕ.

Proposition 7 (Locality, [9]). *Let $\phi(\boldsymbol{x}) \in \text{FO}(\perp\!\!\!\perp_c, \approx, \approx^*, = (\cdot))$ be a formula with free variables from $\boldsymbol{x} = (x_1, \ldots, x_n)$. Then for all structures $\mathfrak{A}$ and probabilistic teams $\mathbb{X} : X \to [0, 1]$ where $\{x_1, \ldots, x_n\} \subseteq V \subseteq \text{Dom}(X)$, $\mathfrak{A} \models_\mathbb{X} \phi \iff \mathfrak{A} \models_{\mathbb{X} \upharpoonright V} \phi$.*

Given two logics $\mathcal{L}$ and $\mathcal{L}'$ over probabilistic team semantics, we write $\mathcal{L} \leq \mathcal{L}'$ if for all open formulae $\phi(\boldsymbol{x}) \in \mathcal{L}$ there is a formula $\psi(\boldsymbol{x}) \in \mathcal{L}'$ such that $\mathfrak{A} \models_\mathbb{X} \phi \Leftrightarrow \mathfrak{A} \models_\mathbb{X} \psi$, for all structures $\mathfrak{A}$ and probabilistic teams $\mathbb{X}$. The equality "$\equiv$" and strict inequality "$<$" relations between $\mathcal{L}$ and $\mathcal{L}'$ are defined from "$\leq$" in the standard way.

Alternative Definition. Probabilistic teams can also be defined as mappings $\mathbb{X} : X \to \mathbb{R}_{\geq 0}$ that have no restriction for the total sum of assignment weights, $\mathbb{R}_{\geq 0}$ being the set of all non-negative reals. Probabilistic team semantics with respect to such real weighted teams is then given exactly as in Definition 1, except that we define disjunction without scaling:

$$\mathfrak{A} \models_\mathbb{X} (\psi \vee \theta) \Leftrightarrow \mathfrak{A} \models_\mathbb{Y} \psi \text{ and } \mathfrak{A} \models_\mathbb{Z} \theta \text{ for some } \mathbb{Y}, \mathbb{Z} \text{ s.t. } \mathbb{Y} \sqcup \mathbb{Z} = \mathbb{X},$$

where the union $\mathbb{Y} \sqcup \mathbb{Z}$ is defined such that $(\mathbb{Y} \sqcup \mathbb{Z})(s) = \mathbb{Y}(s) + \mathbb{Z}(s)$ for each s. Whether interpreting probabilistic teams as probability distributions or just mappings from assignments to non-negative reals does not make any difference in our framework. Hence we write $\mathbb{X} : X \to [0, 1]$ for a probabilistic team that is a distribution such that $\sum_{s \in X} \mathbb{X}(s) = 1$, and $\mathbb{X} : X \to \mathbb{R}_{\geq 0}$ for a probabilistic team that is any mapping from assignments to non-negative reals. A probabilistic team of the former type is then a special case of that of the latter. We will use both notions and their associated semantics interchangeably. If we need to distinguish between the two semantics, we write $\models^{[0,1]}$ and $\models^{\geq 0}$ respectively for the scaled (i.e., Definition 1) and non-scaled variants. Given $\mathbb{X} : X \to \mathbb{R}_{\geq 0}$ and $r \in \mathbb{R}_{\geq 0}$, we write $|\mathbb{X}|$ for the total weight $\sum_{s \in X} \mathbb{X}(s)$ of $\mathbb{X}$, and $r \cdot \mathbb{X}$ for the probabilistic team $\mathbb{Y} : X \to \mathbb{R}_{\geq 0}$ such that $\mathbb{Y}(s) = r \cdot \mathbb{X}(s)$ for all $s \in X$. The proposition below follows from a straightforward induction (see the full version [16] of this paper in ArXiv).

Proposition 8. *Let $\mathfrak{A}$ be a structure, $\mathbb{X} : X \to \mathbb{R}_{\geq 0}$ a probabilistic team of $\mathfrak{A}$, and $\phi \in \text{FO}(\perp\!\!\!\perp_c, \approx, \approx^*, = (\cdot))$. Then $\mathfrak{A} \models^{\geq 0}_\mathbb{X} \phi \Leftrightarrow \mathfrak{A} \models^{[0,1]}_{\frac{1}{|\mathbb{X}|} \cdot \mathbb{X}} \phi$.*

3   Expressiveness of FO($\perp\!\!\!\perp$)

Let $\mathbb{X} : X \to [0, 1]$ be a probabilistic team where X is a finite set of assignments from a finite set D of variables. A variable $x \in D$ is *uniformly distributed* in $\mathbb{X}$ over a set of values S, if

$$\mathbb{X}_{x=a} = \frac{1}{|S|} \text{ for all } a \in S \text{ and } \mathbb{X}_{x=a} = 0 \text{ otherwise.}$$

The following lemma says essentially that if we can express constancy and independence for a uniform distribution, then we can express $\approx$. Note that it may happen that we can express "x uniformly distributed and independent of y" even when we cannot express "x is independent of y" in general. For a proof of the lemma, see the full ArXiv version [16] of this paper.

Lemma 9. *Let $\mathfrak{A}$ be a structure with at least two elements and z an n-tuple of variables. Let $\phi(z, d, c_1, c_2)$ be a formula s.t. for all probabilistic teams $\mathbb{X}$, whose variable domain includes z, d, c_1, c_2 and for which $\mathfrak{A} \models_{\mathbb{X}} c_1 \neq c_2$ and $\mathfrak{A} \models_{\mathbb{X}} =(c_1) \land =(c_2)$, it holds that*

$$M \models_{\mathbb{X}} \phi \quad \Leftrightarrow \quad d \text{ is uniformly distributed over the two values of } c_1, c_2 \tag{2}$$

$$\text{and } d \text{ is independent of } z.$$

Then $x \approx y$ can be expressed for n-tuples x and y using ϕ and the constancy atom.

Theorem 10. $\mathrm{FO}(\approx) \leq \mathrm{FO}(\perp\!\!\!\perp)$.

Proof. Proposition 3 established that the constancy atom $=(x)$ can be equivalently expressed by the independence atom $x \perp\!\!\!\perp x$. Hence it is enough to show that we can define the formula ϕ of Lemma 9 by using $\perp\!\!\!\perp$.

Let $\mathfrak{A}$ and $\mathbb{X}$ be as assumed in Lemma 9. We use below $\exists b \in \{c_1, c_2\} \theta$ as an abbreviation for $\exists b (b = c_1 \lor b = c_2) \land \theta$, and $\forall b \in \{c_1, c_2\} \theta$ for $\forall b (b \neq c_1 \land b \neq c_2) \lor ((b = c_1 \lor b = c_2) \land \theta)$. Define $\phi(z, d, c_1, c_2)$ as

$$(z \perp\!\!\!\perp d) \land \forall a \in \{c_1, c_2\} \exists b \in \{c_1, c_2\} [(a \perp\!\!\!\perp b) \land ((a = b \land d = c_1) \lor (a \neq b \land d = c_2))].$$

It suffices to prove (2). The formula ϕ clearly states that z and d are independent. The formula also states that the values of d range over the values of c_1 and c_2. It remains to be shown, conditioned on that z and d are independent, that

$\mathfrak{A} \models_{\mathbb{X}} \phi$ if and only if d is uniformly distributed over c_1 and c_2.

Note that, by assumption of Lemma 9, c_1 and c_2 are distinct constants. Let $\mathbb{X}_1$ be a team obtained from $\mathbb{X}$ by the quantification of a and b. By the definition of universal quantification, in $\mathbb{X}_1$ a is uniformly distributed and independent of everything else except maybe b. Note that d is uniformly distributed over the values of c_1 and c_2 in $\mathbb{X}$ if and only if it is in $\mathbb{X}_1$.

If d is uniformly distributed over the values of c_1 and c_2, then picking values of b with a uniform probability such that the right conjunct in

$$[(a \perp\!\!\!\perp b) \land ((a = b \land d = c_1) \lor (a \neq b \land d = c_2))] \tag{3}$$

holds clearly yields a team in which the left conjunct also holds. However, if d is not uniformly distributed over c_1 and c_2, then picking values for b such that the right conjunct of (3) holds will yield b that is not independent on a.   □

We also note that conditional independence is definable using marginal independence. The proof applies ideas from [9] and can be found in the full ArXiv version [16].

Theorem 11. $\mathrm{FO}(\perp\!\!\!\perp) \equiv \mathrm{FO}(\perp\!\!\!\perp_c)$.

4 Expressiveness of FO($\approx^*$) and FO($\approx$)

Initially it may seem that first-order logic with marginal distribution equivalence atoms is less expressive than that with marginal identity atoms, as the former atoms are given a strictly weaker truth condition. Contrary to this intuition, however, we will in this section show that FO($\approx^*$) is actually strictly more expressive than FO($\approx$). The result is proven in two phases. First, in Sect. 4.1 we show that dependence and marginal identity can be defined in FO($\approx^*$), the former by a single marginal distribution equivalence atom and the latter by a more complex formula. Second, in Sect. 4.2 we show that the expressiveness of FO($\approx$) is restricted by a union closure property which is similar to that of inclusion logic in team semantics. Since dependence atoms lack this property, the strict inequality between FO($\approx$) and FO($\approx^*$) follows.

4.1 Translations of Dependence and Marginal Identity to FO($\approx^*$)

We observe first that dependence atoms can be expressed in terms of marginal distribution equivalence atoms, which in turn are definable using marginal identity and dependence atoms.

Proposition 12. *The following equivalences hold:*

1. $=(\boldsymbol{x}, y) \equiv \boldsymbol{x}y \approx^* \boldsymbol{x}$,
2. $\boldsymbol{x} \approx^* \boldsymbol{y} \equiv \exists \boldsymbol{z}(=(\boldsymbol{y}, \boldsymbol{z}) \wedge\ =(\boldsymbol{z}, \boldsymbol{y}) \wedge \boldsymbol{x} \approx \boldsymbol{z})$.

Defining marginal identity atoms in FO($\approx^*$) is more cumbersome. Let $\mathbb{X} : X \to \mathbb{R}_{\geq 0}$ be a probabilistic team, and ϕ a quantifier-free first-order formula over the empty vocabulary (i.e., such that its satisfaction depends only on the variable assignment). We define $\mathbb{X}_\phi : X \to \mathbb{R}_{\geq 0}$ as the probabilistic team such that $\mathbb{X}_\phi(s) = \mathbb{X}(s)$ if s satisfies ϕ, and $\mathbb{X}_\phi(s) = 0$ otherwise. Given two sequences of variables $\boldsymbol{x} = (x_1, \dots, x_n)$ and $\boldsymbol{y} = (y_1, \dots, y_n)$, we write $\boldsymbol{x} \neq \boldsymbol{y}$ as a shorthand for $\bigvee_{i=1}^{n} \neg x_i = y_i$.

Theorem 13. $\boldsymbol{x} \approx \boldsymbol{y}$ *is equivalent to* $\phi \in$ FO($\approx^*$) *where*

$$\phi := \forall \boldsymbol{z}\big((\boldsymbol{z} \neq \boldsymbol{x} \wedge \boldsymbol{z} \neq \boldsymbol{y}) \vee ((\boldsymbol{z} = \boldsymbol{x} \vee \boldsymbol{z} = \boldsymbol{y}) \wedge \boldsymbol{z} \approx^* \boldsymbol{x} \wedge \boldsymbol{z} \approx^* \boldsymbol{y})\big).$$

Proof. Assume that $\boldsymbol{x}, \boldsymbol{y}, \boldsymbol{z}$ are all m-ary. Let $\mathfrak{A}$ be a structure with domain $A = \{1, \dots, n\}$, and let $\mathbb{X} : X \to \mathbb{R}_{\geq 0}$ a probabilistic team. Assume first that $\mathfrak{A} \models_\mathbb{X} \boldsymbol{x} \approx \boldsymbol{y}$, that is, for all $i \in A^m$, the weights $|\mathbb{X}_{\boldsymbol{x}=i}|$ and $|\mathbb{X}_{\boldsymbol{y}=i}|$ coincide. It suffices to show that $\mathfrak{A} \models_\mathbb{Y} \boldsymbol{z} \approx^* \boldsymbol{x} \wedge \boldsymbol{z} \approx^* \boldsymbol{y}$ for $\mathbb{Y} := \mathbb{X}'_\theta$ where θ is $\boldsymbol{z} = \boldsymbol{x} \vee \boldsymbol{z} = \boldsymbol{y}$ and $\mathbb{X}' = \mathbb{X}[A^m/\boldsymbol{z}]$ is the probabilistic team obtained from $\mathbb{X}$ by distributing A^m to $\boldsymbol{z}$ uniformly. For each $i \in A^m$ we consider three weight measures, obtained by dividing assignments associated with i into three parts, $l_i := |\mathbb{X}_{\boldsymbol{x}=i \wedge \boldsymbol{x} \neq \boldsymbol{y}}|$, $r_i := |\mathbb{X}_{\boldsymbol{y}=i \wedge \boldsymbol{x} \neq \boldsymbol{y}}|$, and $c_i := |\mathbb{X}_{\boldsymbol{x}=i \wedge \boldsymbol{y}=i}|$. Then

$$|\mathbb{Y}_{\boldsymbol{x}=i}| = |\mathbb{X}'_{\theta \wedge \boldsymbol{x}=i}| = |\mathbb{X}'_{\theta \wedge \boldsymbol{x}=i \wedge \boldsymbol{x} \neq \boldsymbol{y}}| + |\mathbb{X}'_{\theta \wedge \boldsymbol{x}=i \wedge \boldsymbol{y}=i}| = \frac{2l_i + c_i}{n^m}.$$

Observe that for $\mathbb{X}'_{\theta \wedge x = i \wedge x \neq y}$ we first partition each assignment in $\mathbb{X}_{x = i \wedge x \neq y}$ uniformly to n^m parts in terms of the value of z and then keep only those parts where θ holds. Since x and y disagree for every assignment in $\mathbb{X}'_{x = i \wedge x \neq y}$, the total weight of $\mathbb{X}'_{\theta \wedge x = i \wedge x \neq y}$ is obtained by multiplying l_i with $\frac{2}{n^m}$. For $\mathbb{X}'_{\theta \wedge x = i \wedge y = i}$ we have identical x and y, and hence its weight is obtained by multiplying c_i with $\frac{1}{n^m}$. By analogous reasoning we obtain that

$$|\mathbb{Y}_{y=i}| = \frac{2r_i + c_i}{n^m} \text{ and } |\mathbb{Y}_{z=i}| = \frac{r_i + l_i + c_i}{n^m}.$$

Since our assumption implies $l_i = r_i$ for all i, the claim now follows from the observation that $\{\{|\mathbb{Y}_{u=i}| \mid i \in A^m\}\}$ are identical multisets for $u \in \{x, y, z\}$.

Vice versa, assuming $\mathfrak{A} \models_{\mathbb{X}} \phi$ we show $\mathfrak{A} \models_{\mathbb{X}} x \approx y$. Let the weights l_i, r_i, c_i and the probabilistic team $\mathbb{Y}$ be as above. By assumption we have $\mathfrak{A} \models_{\mathbb{Y}} z \approx^* x \wedge z \approx^* y$, and thus the following multisets are identical:

$$W_x := \{\{2l_1 + c_1, \ldots, 2l_n + c_n\}\},$$
$$W_y := \{\{2r_1 + c_1, \ldots, 2r_n + c_n\}\},$$
$$W_z := \{\{l_1 + r_1 + c_1, \ldots, l_n + r_n + c_n\}\},$$

where $\mathbf{1} = (1, \ldots, 1)$ and $\mathbf{n} = (n, \ldots, n)$. Assume to the contrary that $\mathfrak{A} \not\models_{\mathbb{X}} x \approx y$, that is, $l_i \neq r_i$ for some i. Observe that whenever $l_j = r_j$ agree, then j contributes the same weight to all W_x, W_y, and W_z. Therefore, we may assume without loss of generality that $l_i \neq r_i$ for all i. Assume that $2l_j + c_j$ is the smallest element from W_x. Since $W_x = W_z$, it follows that $2l_j + c_j = l_k + r_k + c_k$ for some k. If $l_k < r_k$, then $2l_k + c_k < l_k + r_k + c_k$ which contradicts the assumption that $2l_j + c_j$ is smallest. Since $W_x = W_y$, similar contradiction follows from $r_k < l_k$, too. Hence, $\mathfrak{A} \models_{\mathbb{X}} x \approx y$ which concludes the proof. $\square$

The following theorem now combines the results of this section. Note that the translations to both directions are of linear size.

Theorem 14. $\mathrm{FO}(\approx^*) \equiv \mathrm{FO}(\approx, =(\cdot))$.

4.2 Scaled Union Closure of FO($\approx$)

Inclusion logic is known to be union closed over teams. This means that for all structures $\mathfrak{A}$, teams X, and inclusion logic formulae ϕ: if $\mathfrak{A} \models_X \phi$ and $\mathfrak{A} \models_Y \phi$, then $\mathfrak{A} \models_{X \cup Y} \phi$. The following proposition, proven in the full ArXiv version [16] of this paper, demonstrates that $\mathrm{FO}(\approx)$ is endowed with an analogous closure property, namely, that all formulae of $\mathrm{FO}(\approx)$ are closed under all k-scaled unions of probabilistic teams.

Proposition 15. *Let $\mathfrak{A}$ be a model, $\phi \in \mathrm{FO}(\approx)$ a formula, and $\mathbb{X} : X \to [0, 1]$ and $\mathbb{Y} : X \to [0, 1]$ two probabilistic teams. Then for all $k \in [0, 1]$:*

if $\mathfrak{A} \models_{\mathbb{X}} \phi$ and $\mathfrak{A} \models_{\mathbb{Y}} \phi$, then $\mathfrak{A} \models_{\mathbb{X} \sqcup_k \mathbb{Y}} \phi$.

As a corollary we observe that FO($\approx$) is strictly weaker than FO($\approx^*$). Recall from Proposition 12 that the constancy atom $=(x)$ is definable in FO($\approx^*$). However, constancy is clearly not preserved under k-scaled unions, therefore falling outside the scope of FO($\approx$). Furthermore, by Theorem 13 FO($\approx^*$) is at least as expressive as FO($\approx$).

Corollary 16. FO($\approx$) < FO($\approx^*$).

5 Binary Probabilistic Teams

In this section we restrict attention to binary probabilistic teams and propositional logic extended with quantifiers (see [18] for related work). We define the syntax of *quantified propositional logic* QPL by the following grammar

$$\phi ::= p \mid \neg p \mid \phi \vee \phi \mid \phi \wedge \phi \mid \exists p \phi \mid \forall p \phi, \tag{4}$$

where p is a proposition variable. The probabilistic team semantics of QPL is defined analogously to that of first-order formulae. We say that a probabilistic team $\mathbb{X} : X \to [0,1]$ is *binary* if X assigns variables into $\{0,1\}$. For a QPL formula ϕ and a binary probabilistic team $\mathbb{X} : X \to [0,1]$, we write $\mathbb{X} \models \phi$ iff $\mathfrak{A} \models_{\mathbb{X}} \phi^*$, where ϕ^* is the first-order formula obtained from ϕ by substituting $P(p)$ for p and $\neg P(p)$ for $\neg p$, and letting $\mathfrak{A} := (\{0,1\}, P^{\mathfrak{A}} := \{1\})$. Furthermore, we denote classical negation by "$\sim$". That is, we write $\mathbb{X} \models \sim \phi$ if $\mathbb{X} \not\models \phi$. We let QPL($\sim$) denote the logic obtained by the grammar (4) extended with $\sim\phi$, and denote by QPL($\sim$, C) the extension of QPL($\sim$) by any collection of dependencies C.

We observe that QPL($\sim, \perp_c, \approx$) can be interpreted as statements of real arithmetic. As truth in real arithmetic is decidable, this gives us some fairly conservative upper bounds with respect to the complexity of satisfiability and validity of QPL($\sim, \perp_c, \approx$). We say that $\phi \in$ QPL($\sim, \perp_c, \approx$) is *satisfiable* if ϕ is satisfied by some non-empty binary probabilistic team.[1] Also, ϕ is *valid* is ϕ is satisfied by all binary probabilistic teams. Note that the *free variables* of a QPL($\sim, C$) formula are defined analogously to the first-order case.

Theorem 17. *For each $\phi \in$ QPL($\sim, \perp_c$) ($\phi \in$ QPL($\sim, \approx$), resp.) there exists a first-order sentence ψ over vocabulary $\{+, \times, \leq, 0, 1\}$ ($\{+, \leq, 0\}$, resp.) such that ϕ is satisfiable iff $(\mathbb{R}, +, \times, \leq, 0, 1) \models \psi$ (($\mathbb{R}, +, \leq, 0) \models \psi$, resp.).*

Proof. We show that satisfiability of a formula $\phi \in$ QPL($\sim, \perp_c$) is definable in real arithmetic in terms of the non-scaled variant of probabilistic team semantics. For a given tuple $\boldsymbol{p} = (p_1, \ldots, p_n)$ of proposition variables, we introduce fresh first-order variables $s_{\boldsymbol{p}=i}$ for each propositional assignment $s(\boldsymbol{p}) = \boldsymbol{i}$, where $\boldsymbol{i}$ is a binary string of length n. We write $\boldsymbol{s}$ to denote the complete tuple of these variables. For a $\boldsymbol{p}$ listing the free variables of ϕ, we define

---

[1] Empty team satisfies every formula without $\sim$; with $\sim$ it is a non-interesting special case [20].

$$\psi := \exists s_{p=0} \ldots s_{p=1} \big(\bigwedge_i 0 \le s_{p=i} \; \wedge \; \neg 0 = \sum_i s_{p=i} \wedge \phi^*(s)\big)$$

where the mapping $\phi(p) \mapsto \phi^*(s)$ is defined recursively as follows:

- If $\phi(p)$ is a propositional literal, then $\phi^*(s) := \bigwedge_{s \not\models \phi} s = 0$.
- If $\phi(p)$ is $b \perp\!\!\!\perp_a c$, where $p = abcd$ for some d, then $\phi^*(s)$ is defined as

$$\bigwedge_{ijk} \big(\sum_{l'} s_{abcd=ijkl'} \times \sum_{j'k'l'} s_{abcd=ij'k'l'} = \sum_{k'l'} s_{abcd=ijk'l'} \times \sum_{j'l'} s_{abcd=ij'kl'}\big).$$

- If $\phi(p)$ is $a \approx b$, where $p = abc$ for some c, then

$$\phi^*(s) := \bigwedge_i \sum_{j'k'} s_{abc=ij'k'} = \sum_{j'k'} s_{abc=j'ik'}.$$

- If $\phi(p)$ is $\sim\eta(p)$, then $\phi^*(s) := \neg\eta^*(s)$.
- If $\phi(p)$ is $\eta(p) \wedge \chi(p)$, then $\phi^*(s) := \eta^*(s) \wedge \chi^*(s)$.
- If $\phi(p)$ is $\eta(p) \vee \chi(p)$, then

$$\phi^*(s) := \exists t_{p=0} r_{p=0} \ldots t_{p=1} r_{p=1} \big(\bigwedge_i (0 \le t_{p=i} \wedge 0 \le r_{p=i} \wedge$$

$$s_{p=i} = t_{p=i} + r_{p=i}) \wedge \eta^*(t) \wedge \chi^*(r)\big).$$

- If $\phi(p)$ is $\exists q \eta(p, q)$, then

$$\phi^*(s) := \exists t_{pq=00} \ldots t_{pq=11} \big(\bigwedge_{ij} (0 \le t_{pq=ij} \wedge s_{p=i} = t_{p=i0} + t_{p=i1}) \wedge \eta(t)\big).$$

- If $\phi(p)$ is $\forall y \eta(p, q)$, then

$$\phi^*(s) := \exists t_{pq=00} \ldots t_{pq=11} \big(\bigwedge_{ij} (0 \le t_{pq=ij} \wedge s_{p=i} = t_{p=i0} + t_{p=i1} \wedge$$

$$t_{p=i0} = t_{p=i1}) \wedge \eta(t)\big).$$

It is straightforward to check that the claim follows.   □

From the translation above we immediately obtain some complexity bounds for the satisfiability and validity problems of quantified propositional logics over probabilistic team semantics. We write 2-EXPSPACE for the class of problems solvable in space $O(2^{2^{p(n)}})$, and AEXPTIME($f(n)$) (2-AEXPTIME($f(n)$), resp.) for the class of problems solvable by alternating Turing machine in time $O(2^{p(n)})$ $(O(2^{2^{p(n)}})$, resp.) with $f(n)$ many alternations, where p is a polynomial.

Theorem 18. *The satisfiability/validity problems for* QPL($\perp\!\!\!\perp_c, \sim$) *and* QPL $(\approx, \sim)$ *are in* 2-EXPSPACE *and* 2-AEXPTIME($2^{O(n)}$), *respectively.*

Proof. By the proof of Theorem 17, satisfiability and validity of quantified propositional formulae can be reduced to truth of a real arithmetic sentence of size $2^{O(n)}$. The stated upper bounds for $\text{QPL}(\sim, \perp\!\!\!\perp_c)$ and $\text{QPL}(\sim, \approx)$ then follow because the theory of real-closed fields, $\text{Th}(\mathbb{R}, +, \times, \leq, 0, 1)$, is in EXPSPACE [3], and the theory of real addition, $\text{Th}(\mathbb{R}, +, \leq, 0)$, is in AEXPTIME($n$) [4,10].   □

We also obtain an upper bound for the implication problem of conditional independence over binary probability distributions. The *implication problem* for conditional independence is given as a finite set $\Sigma \cup \{\sigma\}$ of conditional independence statements, and the problem is to decide whether all probability distributions that satisfy Σ satisfy also σ. It is a famous open problem to determine whether implication of conditional independence is decidable over discrete distributions. Since binary probabilistic teams can be interpreted as discrete distributions of binary random variables, we obtain that the implication problem for conditional independence statements is decidable in exponential space over binary distributions. The result follows since any instance of such an implication problem can be expressed as an existential formula of exponential size (Theorem 17), and since the existential theory of real-closed fields is in PSPACE [5].

Corollary 19. *The implication problem for conditional independence over binary probability distributions is in* EXPSPACE.

It may be conjectured that the obtained complexity bounds are not optimal. The first-order translations provide only access to a very restricted type of arithmetic expressions. For instance, real multiplication is only available between sums of reals from the unit interval. We leave it as an open problem to determine whether the results of this section can be optimized using more refined arguments.

Table 1. Relative expressivity in probabilistic team semantics (PTS) and team semantics (TS)

PTS:	$\text{FO}(\approx) < \text{FO}(\approx, =(\cdot)) \equiv \text{FO}(\approx^*) \leq \text{FO}(\perp\!\!\!\perp) \equiv \text{FO}(\perp\!\!\!\perp_c)$
TS:	$\text{FO}(\subseteq) < \text{FO}(\subseteq, =(\cdot)) \equiv \text{FO}(\perp) \equiv \text{FO}(\perp_c)$ [12,13]

6   Conclusions and Further Directions

We have studied probabilistic team semantics in association with three notions of dependency atoms: probabilistic independence, marginal identity, and marginal distribution equivalence atoms. Our investigations give rise to an overall classification that is already familiar from the team semantics context (see Table 1). Similar to inclusion logic ($\text{FO}(\subseteq)$) in team semantics, we observed that $\text{FO}(\approx)$

enjoys a union closure property which renders it strictly less expressive than $FO(\approx, =(\cdot))$. A further analogous fact is that both dependence and marginal identity are definable with conditional independence, which in turn is definable using only marginal independence. An interesting open question is to determine the relationship between $FO(\approx, =(\cdot))$ (or equivalently $FO(\approx^*)$) and $FO(\perp\!\!\!\perp_c)$. Contrary to the picture arising from team semantics, we conjecture that the latter is strictly more expressive.

One motivation behind our marginal distribution equivalence atom was that it seemed to be weaker than marginal identity but still enough to guarantee the same entropy of two distributions. A natural next step would be to consider some form of entropy atom/atoms and study the expressive power of the resulting logics. The exact formulation of such atoms will make all the difference, as one can detect both functional dependencies and marginal independence if one has full access to the conditional entropy as a function.

We also studied (quantified) propositional logics with probabilistic team semantics. By connecting real-valued probabilistic teams to real arithmetic we showed upper bounds for computational problems associated with these logics. As a consequence of our translation to real arithmetic we also obtained an EXPSPACE upper bound for the implication problem of conditional independence statements over binary distributions.

References

1. Abramsky, S.: Relational hidden variables and non-locality. Studia Logica **101**(2), 411–452 (2013)
2. Barbero, F., Sandu, G.: Interventionist counterfactuals on causal teams. In: Finkbeiner, B., Kleinberg, S. (eds.) Proceedings 3rd Workshop on Formal Reasoning About Causation, Responsibility, and Explanations in Science and Technology, Thessaloniki, Greece, 21st April 2018. Electronic Proceedings in Theoretical Computer Science, vol. 286, pp. 16–30. Open Publishing Association (2019). https://doi.org/10.4204/EPTCS.286.2
3. Ben-Or, M., Kozen, D., Reif, J.: The complexity of elementary algebra and geometry. J. Comput. Syst. Sci. **32**(2), 251–264 (1986)
4. Berman, L.: The complexity of logical theories. Theoret. Comput. Sci. **11**(1), 71–77 (1980)
5. Canny, J.: Some algebraic and geometric computations in PSPACE. In: Proceedings of the Twentieth Annual ACM Symposium on Theory of Computing, STOC 1988, pp. 460–467. ACM, New York (1988)
6. Cavallo, R., Pittarelli, M.: The theory of probabilistic databases. In: Proceedings of the 13th International Conference on Very Large Data Bases, VLDB 1987, pp. 71–81. Morgan Kaufmann Publishers Inc., San Francisco (1987)
7. Corander, J., Hyttinen, A., Kontinen, J., Pensar, J., Väänänen, J.: A logical approach to context-specific independence. In: Väänänen, J., Hirvonen, Å., de Queiroz, R. (eds.) WoLLIC 2016. LNCS, vol. 9803, pp. 165–182. Springer, Heidelberg (2016). https://doi.org/10.1007/978-3-662-52921-8_11
8. Durand, A., Hannula, M., Kontinen, J., Meier, A., Virtema, J.: Approximation and dependence via multiteam semantics. Ann. Math. Artif. Intell. **83**(3–4), 297–320 (2018). https://doi.org/10.1007/s10472-017-9568-4

9. Durand, A., Hannula, M., Kontinen, J., Meier, A., Virtema, J.: Probabilistic team semantics. In: Ferrarotti, F., Woltran, S. (eds.) FoIKS 2018. LNCS, vol. 10833, pp. 186–206. Springer, Cham (2018). https://doi.org/10.1007/978-3-319-90050-6_11
10. Ferrante, J., Rackoff, C.: A decision procedure for the first order theory of real addition with order. SIAM J. Comput. **4**(1), 69–76 (1975). https://doi.org/10.1137/0204006
11. Galliani, P.: Game values and equilibria for undetermined sentences of dependence logic. MSc thesis. ILLC Publications, MoL-2008-08 (2008)
12. Galliani, P.: Inclusion and exclusion dependencies in team semantics: on some logics of imperfect information. Ann. Pure Appl. Logic **163**(1), 68–84 (2012)
13. Galliani, P., Väänänen, J.: On dependence logic. In: Baltag, A., Smets, S. (eds.) Johan van Benthem on Logic and Information Dynamics. OCL, vol. 5, pp. 101–119. Springer, Cham (2014). https://doi.org/10.1007/978-3-319-06025-5_4
14. Grädel, E., Gurevich, Y.: Metafinite model theory. Inf. Comput. **140**(1), 26–81 (1998). https://doi.org/10.1006/inco.1997.2675
15. Grädel, E., Väänänen, J.: Dependence and independence. Studia Logica **101**(2), 399–410 (2013). https://doi.org/10.1007/s11225-013-9479-2
16. Hannula, M., Hirvonen, Å., Kontinen, J., Kulikov, V., Virtema, J.: Facets of distribution identities in probabilistic team semantics. CoRR abs/1812.05873 (2018). http://arxiv.org/abs/1812.05873
17. Hannula, M., Kontinen, J.: A finite axiomatization of conditional independence and inclusion dependencies. Inf. Comput. **249**, 121–137 (2016). https://doi.org/10.1016/j.ic.2016.04.001
18. Hannula, M., Kontinen, J., Lück, M., Virtema, J.: On quantified propositional logics and the exponential time hierarchy. In: GandALF. EPTCS, vol. 226, pp. 198–212 (2016)
19. Hannula, M., Kontinen, J., Virtema, J.: Polyteam semantics. In: Artemov, S., Nerode, A. (eds.) LFCS 2018. LNCS, vol. 10703, pp. 190–210. Springer, Cham (2018). https://doi.org/10.1007/978-3-319-72056-2_12
20. Hannula, M., Kontinen, J., Virtema, J., Vollmer, H.: Complexity of propositional logics in team semantic. ACM Trans. Comput. Log. **19**(1), 2:1–2:14 (2018). https://doi.org/10.1145/3157054
21. Hodges, W.: Compositional semantics for a language of imperfect information. J. Interest Group Pure Appl. Logics **5**(4), 539–563 (1997)
22. Hyttinen, T., Paolini, G., Väänänen, J.: A logic for arguing about probabilities in measure teams. Arch. Math. Logic **56**(5-6), 475–489 (2017). https://doi.org/10.1007/s00153-017-0535-x
23. Krebs, A., Meier, A., Virtema, J., Zimmermann, M.: Team semantics for the specification and verification of hyperproperties. In: Potapov, I., Spirakis, P., Worrell, J. (eds.) 43rd International Symposium on Mathematical Foundations of Computer Science (MFCS 2018). Leibniz International Proceedings in Informatics (LIPIcs), vol. 117, pp. 10:1–10:16. Schloss Dagstuhl-Leibniz-Zentrum fuer Informatik, Dagstuhl (2018). https://doi.org/10.4230/LIPIcs.MFCS.2018.10
24. Lück, M.: Canonical models and the complexity of modal team logic. In: 27th EACSL Annual Conference on Computer Science Logic, CSL 2018, 4–7 September 2018, Birmingham, UK, pp. 30:1–30:23 (2018). https://doi.org/10.4230/LIPIcs.CSL.2018.30
25. Niepert, M., Gyssens, M., Sayrafi, B., Gucht, D.V.: On the conditional independence implication problem: a lattice-theoretic approach. Artif. Intell. **202**, 29–51 (2013). https://doi.org/10.1016/j.artint.2013.06.005
26. Väänänen, J.: Dependence Logic. Cambridge University Press, Cambridge (2007)

Description Logics

Privacy-Preserving Ontology Publishing for $\mathcal{EL}$ Instance Stores

Franz Baader[ID], Francesco Kriegel[ID], and Adrian Nuradiansyah[✉][ID]

Theoretical Computer Science, TU Dresden, Dresden, Germany
{franz.baader,francesco.kriegel,adrian.nuradiansyah}@tu-dresden.de

Abstract. We make a first step towards adapting an existing approach for privacy-preserving publishing of linked data to Description Logic (DL) ontologies. We consider the case where both the knowledge about individuals and the privacy policies are expressed using concepts of the DL $\mathcal{EL}$, which corresponds to the setting where the ontology is an $\mathcal{EL}$ instance store. We introduce the notions of compliance of a concept with a policy and of safety of a concept for a policy, and show how optimal compliant (safe) generalizations of a given $\mathcal{EL}$ concept can be computed. In addition, we investigate the complexity of the optimality problem.

1 Introduction

When publishing information about individuals, one needs to ensure that certain privacy constraints are fulfilled. These constraints are encoded as *privacy policies*, and before publishing the information one needs to check whether the information is *compliant* with these policies [10]. We illustrate this setting using an example from [10]: when publishing information about hospitals, doctors, and patients, the policy may require that one should not be able to find out who are the cancer patients. In case the information to be published is not policy compliant, it first needs to be modified in a minimal way to make it compliant. However, compliance per se is not enough if a possible attacker can also obtain relevant information from other sources, which together with the published information might violate the privacy policy. *Safety* requires that the combination of the published information with any other compliant information is again compliant [10]. More information on privacy-preserving data publishing can be found in the survey [13].

In [10], privacy-preserving data publishing was investigated in a setting where the information to be published is given as a relational dataset with (labeled) null values, and the policy is given by a conjunctive query. In order to make a given dataset compliant or safe, one is basically allowed to replace constants (or null values) by new null values. The paper investigates the complexity of deciding compliance (Is a given modification of a dataset policy compliant?),

---

F. Baader—Partially funded by the Deutsche Forschungsgemeinschaft (DFG, German Research Foundation) – Projektnummer 389792660 – TRR 248.

A. Nuradiansyah—Funded by DFG within the Research Training Group 1907 "RoSI".

F. Calimeri et al. (Eds.): JELIA 2019, LNAI 11468, pp. 323–338, 2019.
https://doi.org/10.1007/978-3-030-19570-0_21

safety (Is a given modification of a dataset safe w.r.t. a policy?), and optimality (Is a given modification of a dataset safe w.r.t. a policy and does it change the dataset in a minimal way?). The obtained complexity results depend on whether combined or data complexity is considered, and whether closed- or open-world semantics are used. For combined complexity, they lie on the second and third level of the polynomial hierarchy. The paper does not consider the case where the information in the dataset is augmented by ontological knowledge. In [8], ontologies are used to formulate privacy policies, but the policies considered there concerned with meta-information like location and duration of data storage, intended use of data, etc. In contrast, the policies considered in [10] and in the present paper specify what information needs to be hidden.

In the present paper, we make a first step towards handling ontologies in the context of privacy-preserving data publishing, but consider a quite restricted setting, where information about an individual is given by a concept of the inexpressive Description Logic (DL) $\mathcal{EL}$. Basically, this is the setting where the ontology consists of an ABox containing only concept assertions of the form $C(a)$ for possibly complex concepts C, but no role assertion. In [15], such an ABox was called an *instance store*. In addition, we assume that there is no TBox, i.e., all the information about the individual a is given by the concept C.[1] A policy is then given by an instance query, i.e., by an $\mathcal{EL}$ concept D. A concept C (giving information about some individual a) is *compliant* with this policy, if it is not subsumed by D, i.e., if $C(a)$ does not imply $D(a)$. In our example, the policy could be formalized as the $\mathcal{EL}$ concept

$$D = Patient \sqcap \exists seen\_by.(Doctor \sqcap \exists works\_in.Oncology),$$

which says that one should not be able to find out who are the patients that are seen by a doctor that works for the oncology department. The concept

$$C = Patient \sqcap Male \sqcap \exists seen\_by.(Doctor \sqcap Female \sqcap \exists works\_in.Oncology)$$

is not compliant with the policy D since $C \sqsubseteq D$. The concept

$$C' = Male \sqcap \exists seen\_by.(Doctor \sqcap Female \sqcap \exists works\_in.Oncology)$$

is a compliant generalization of C, i.e., $C \sqsubseteq C'$ and $C' \not\sqsubseteq D$. However, it is not safe since $C' \sqcap Patient \sqsubseteq D$, i.e., if the attacker already knows that a is a patient then together with $C'(a)$ the hidden information D is revealed. In contrast,

$$C'' = Male \sqcap \exists seen\_by.(Doctor \sqcap Female \sqcap \exists works\_in.\top),$$

is a safe generalization of C, though it is less obvious to see this. This concept is, however, not optimal since more information than necessary is removed. In fact, the concept

$$C''' = Male \sqcap \exists seen\_by.(Doctor \sqcap Female \sqcap \exists works\_in.\top) \sqcap$$
$$\exists seen\_by.(Female \sqcap \exists works\_in.Oncology)$$

---

[1] Since $\mathcal{EL}$ concepts are closed under conjunction, we can assume that the ABox contains only one assertion for each individual a.

is a safe generalization of C that is more specific than C'', i.e., $C \sqsubseteq C''' \sqsubset C''$.

We will show how to compute optimal compliant and optimal safe generalizations of $\mathcal{EL}$ concepts C with $\mathcal{EL}$ policies, but instead of only one policy concept we allow for a finite set of $\mathcal{EL}$ concepts as policy, where a concept C' is compliant with the policy $\{D_1, \ldots, D_p\}$ iff it is compliant with each element of this set, i.e., $C \not\sqsubseteq D_i$ holds for all $i = 1, \ldots, p$. In addition, following [10], we will also view optimality as a decision problem, and investigate its complexity. A short version of this paper, without the results of Sect. 5, was presented at DL 2018 [7]. Due to space restrictions, we cannot give detailed proofs of all our results. They can be found in [3].

2 Preliminaries

A wide range of DLs of different expressive power has been investigated in the literature [2]. Here, we only introduce the DL $\mathcal{EL}$, for which reasoning is tractable [1,5,9]. Let N_C and N_R be mutually disjoint sets of *concept* and *role names*, respectively. Then $\mathcal{EL}$ *concepts* over these names are constructed from concept names using the constructors top concept ($\top$), conjunction ($C \sqcap D$), and existential restriction ($\exists r.C$). The *size* of an $\mathcal{EL}$ concept C is the number of occurrences of $\top$ as well as concept and role names in C, its *role depth* is the maximal nesting of existential restrictions, and its *signature* $sig(C)$ is the set of all concept and role names occurring in C.

The semantics of $\mathcal{EL}$ is defined through *interpretations* $\mathcal{I} = (\Delta^{\mathcal{I}}, \cdot^{\mathcal{I}})$, where $\Delta^{\mathcal{I}}$ is a non-empty set, called the *domain*, and $\cdot^{\mathcal{I}}$ is the *interpretation function*, which maps every $A \in N_C$ to a set $A^{\mathcal{I}} \subseteq \Delta^{\mathcal{I}}$ and every $r \in N_R$ to a binary relation $r^{\mathcal{I}} \subseteq \Delta^{\mathcal{I}} \times \Delta^{\mathcal{I}}$. This function $\cdot^{\mathcal{I}}$ is extended to arbitrary $\mathcal{EL}$ concepts by setting $\top^{\mathcal{I}} := \Delta^{\mathcal{I}}$, $(C \sqcap D)^{\mathcal{I}} := C^{\mathcal{I}} \sqcap D^{\mathcal{I}}$, and $(\exists r.C)^{\mathcal{I}} := \{\delta \in \Delta^{\mathcal{I}} \mid \exists \eta \in C^{\mathcal{I}}.(\delta, \eta) \in r^{\mathcal{I}}\}$.

The $\mathcal{EL}$ concept C is *subsumed by* the $\mathcal{EL}$ concept D (written $C \sqsubseteq D$) if $C^{\mathcal{I}} \subseteq D^{\mathcal{I}}$ holds for all interpretations $\mathcal{I}$. Strict subsumption (written $C \sqsubset D$) holds if $C \sqsubseteq D$ and $D \not\sqsubseteq C$, and we say that C is *equivalent* to D (written $C \equiv D$) if $C \sqsubseteq D$ and $D \sqsubseteq C$.

Subsumption between $\mathcal{EL}$ concepts can be decided in polynomial time. In [5], this was shown using a homomorphism characterization of subsumption, but it is also an easy consequence of the following result of Küsters. Given an $\mathcal{EL}$ concept C, we *reduce* it by exhaustively replacing subconcepts of the form $E \sqcap F$ with $E \sqsubseteq F$ by E (modulo associativity and commutativity of $\sqcap$). As shown in [17], this can be done in polynomial time, and two concepts C, D are equivalent iff their reduced forms are equal up to associativity and commutativity of $\sqcap$.

We are now ready to define the important notions regarding privacy-preserving publishing of ontological information that will be investigated in this paper. As mentioned in the introduction, policies are finite sets of $\mathcal{EL}$ concepts. We assume in the following, that the concepts occurring in the policy are not equivalent to top since otherwise there would not be compliant concepts.

Definition 1. *A* policy *is a finite set* $\mathcal{P} = \{D_1, \ldots, D_p\}$ *of* $\mathcal{EL}$ *concepts such that* $\top \not\equiv D_i$ *for* $i = 1, \ldots, p$. *Given an* $\mathcal{EL}$ *concept* C *and a policy* $\mathcal{P} = \{D_1, \ldots, D_p\}$, *the* $\mathcal{EL}$ *concept* C' *is*

- compliant *with* $\mathcal{P}$ *if* $C' \not\sqsubseteq D_i$ *holds for all* $i = 1, \ldots, p$;
- safe *for* $\mathcal{P}$ *if* $C' \sqcap C''$ *is compliant with* $\mathcal{P}$ *for all* $\mathcal{EL}$ *concepts* C'' *that are compliant with* $\mathcal{P}$;
- *a* $\mathcal{P}$-compliant generalization *of* C *if* $C \sqsubseteq C'$ *and* C' *is compliant with* $\mathcal{P}$;
- *an* optimal $\mathcal{P}$-compliant generalization *of* C *if it is a* $\mathcal{P}$-*compliant generalization of* C *and there is no* $\mathcal{P}$-*compliant generalization* C'' *of* C *such that* $C'' \sqsubset C'$;
- *a* $\mathcal{P}$-safe generalization *of* C *if* $C \sqsubseteq C'$ *and* C' *is safe for* $\mathcal{P}$;
- *an* optimal $\mathcal{P}$ -safe generalization *of* C *if it is a* $\mathcal{P}$-*safe generalization of* C *and there is no* $\mathcal{P}$-*safe generalization* C'' *of* C *such that* $C'' \sqsubset C'$.

It is easy to see that safety implies compliance since the top concept is always compliant: if C' is safe for $\mathcal{P}$, then $\top \sqcap C' \equiv C'$ is compliant.

3   Computing Optimal Compliant Generalizations

In this section, we characterize the concepts that are compliant with a given policy $\mathcal{P}$, and use this to develop an algorithm that computes all optimal $\mathcal{P}$-compliant generalizations of a given $\mathcal{EL}$ concept C.

But first, we recall the recursive characterization of subsumption in $\mathcal{EL}$ given in [6]. We call an $\mathcal{EL}$ concept an *atom* if it is a concept name or an existential restriction. Given an $\mathcal{EL}$ concept C, we denote the set of atoms occurring in its top-level conjunction with $\mathbf{con}(C)$. For example, if $C = A \sqcap \exists r.(B \sqcap \exists s.A)$, then $\mathbf{con}(C) = \{A, \exists r.(B \sqcap \exists s.A)\}$. Subsumption between atoms E, F can be characterized as follows: $E \sqsubseteq F$ iff

- $E = F \in N_C$ or
- there is $r \in N_R$ such that $E = \exists r.E', F = \exists r.F'$ and $E' \sqsubseteq F'$.

Definition 2. *Let* S, T *be sets of atoms. Then we say that* S covers T *if for every* $F \in T$ *there is* $E \in S$ *such that* $E \sqsubseteq F$.

With this notation, subsumption in $\mathcal{EL}$ can be characterized as follows.

Proposition 1. *Let* C, D *be* $\mathcal{EL}$ *concepts. Then* $C \sqsubseteq D$ *iff* $\mathbf{con}(C)$ *covers* $\mathbf{con}(D)$.

The following (polynomial-time decidable) characterization of compliance is an immediate consequence of this proposition.

Proposition 2. *The* $\mathcal{EL}$ *concept* C' *is compliant with the policy* $\mathcal{P} = \{D_1, \ldots, D_p\}$ *iff* $\mathbf{con}(C')$ *does not cover* $\mathbf{con}(D_i)$ *for any* $i = 1, \ldots, p$, *i.e., for every* $i = 1, \ldots, p$, *at least one of the following two properties holds:*

- there is a concept name $A \in con(D_i)$ such that $A \notin con(C')$; or
- there is an existential restriction $\exists r.D \in con(D_i)$ such that $C \not\sqsubseteq D$ for all existential restrictions of the form $\exists r.C \in con(C')$.

Now assume that we are given an $\mathcal{EL}$ concept C and a policy $\mathcal{P} = \{D_1, \ldots, D_p\}$, and we want to construct a $\mathcal{P}$-compliant generalization C' of C. For C' to satisfy the condition of Proposition 2, there needs to exist for every $i = 1, \ldots, p$ an element of $con(D_i)$ that is not covered by any element of $con(C')$. In case $con(C)$ contains elements covering such an atom, we need to remove or generalize them appropriately.

Definition 3. *We say that $H \subseteq con(D_1) \cup \ldots \cup con(D_p)$ is a hitting set of $con(D_1), \ldots, con(D_p)$ if $H \cap con(D_i) \neq \emptyset$ for every $i = 1, \ldots, p$. This hitting set is* minimal *if there is no other hitting set strictly contained in it.*

Basically, the idea is now to choose a hitting set H of $con(D_1), \ldots, con(D_p)$ and use H to guide the construction of a compliant generalization of C. In order to make this generalization as specific as possible, we use minimal hitting sets. In case the policy contains concepts D_i with which C is already compliant (i.e., $C \not\sqsubseteq D_i$ holds), nothing needs to be done w.r.t. these concepts. This is why, in the following definition, $con(D_i)$ does not take part in the construction of the hitting set if $C \not\sqsubseteq D_i$.

Definition 4. *Let C be an $\mathcal{EL}$-concept and $\mathcal{P} = \{D_1, \ldots, D_p\}$ a policy. The set $SCG(C, \mathcal{P})$ of specific compliant generalizations of C w.r.t. $\mathcal{P}$ consists of the concepts that can be constructed from C as follows:*

- *If C is compliant with $\mathcal{P}$, then $SCG(C, \mathcal{P}) = \{C\}$.*
- *Otherwise, choose a minimal hitting set H of $con(D_{i_1}), \ldots, con(D_{i_q})$ where $i_1, \ldots, i_q$ are exactly the indices i for which $C \sqsubseteq D_i$. Note that $q \geq 1$ since we are in the case where C is not compliant with $\mathcal{P}$. In addition, according to our definition of a policy, none of the concepts D_i is equivalent to $\top$, and thus the sets $con(D_{i_j})$ are non-empty. Consequently, at least one minimal hitting set exists. Each minimal hitting set H yields a concept in $SCG(C, \mathcal{P})$ by removing or modifying atoms in the top-level conjunction of C in the following way:*
  - *For every concept name $A \in con(C)$, remove A from the top-level conjunction of C if $A \in H$;*
  - *For every existential restriction $\exists r_i.C_i \in con(C)$, consider the set*

$$\mathcal{P}_i := \{G \mid \text{there is } \exists r_i.G \in H \text{ such that } C_i \sqsubseteq G\}.$$

  - *If $\mathcal{P}_i = \emptyset$, then leave $\exists r_i.C_i$ as it is.*
  - *If $\top \in \mathcal{P}_i$, then remove $\exists r_i.C_i$.*
  - *Otherwise, replace $\exists r_i.C_i$ with $\bigsqcap_{F \in SCG(C_i, \mathcal{P}_i)} \exists r_i.F$.*

First, we show that every element of $SCG(C, \mathcal{P})$ is indeed a compliant generalization of C.

Proposition 3. *Let C be an $\mathcal{EL}$-concept and $\mathcal{P} = \{D_1, \ldots, D_p\}$ a policy. If $C' \in SCG(C, \mathcal{P})$, then C' is a $\mathcal{P}$-compliant generalization of C.*

Proof. In case C is already compliant with $\mathcal{P}$, then $C = C'$ and we are done. Thus, assume that C is not compliant with $\mathcal{P}$. We show that C' is a compliant generalization of C by induction on the role depth of C.

First, we show that C' is a generalization of C, i.e., $C \sqsubseteq C'$. This is an easy consequence of the fact that, when constructing C' from C, atoms from the top-level conjunction of C are left unchanged, are removed, or are replaced by a conjunction of more general atoms. The only non-trivial case is where we replace an existential restriction $\exists r_i.C_i$ with the conjunction $\bigsqcap_{F \in SCG(C_i, \mathcal{P}_i)} \exists r_i.F$. By induction, we know that $C_i \sqsubseteq F$ for all $F \in SCG(C_i, \mathcal{P}_i)$, and thus $\exists r_i.C_i \sqsubseteq \bigsqcap_{F \in SCG(C_i, \mathcal{P}_i)} \exists r_i.F$.

Second, we show that C' is compliant with $\mathcal{P}$, i.e., $C' \not\sqsubseteq D_i$ holds for $i = 1, \ldots, p$. For the indices i with $C \not\sqsubseteq D_i$, we clearly also have $C' \not\sqsubseteq D_i$ since $C \sqsubseteq C'$. Now, consider one of the remaining indices $i_j \in \{i_1, \ldots, i_q\}$, where $i_1, \ldots, i_q$ are exactly the indices for which $C \sqsubseteq D_i$. The concept C' was constructed by taking some minimal hitting set H of $con(D_{i_1}), \ldots, con(D_{i_q})$. If the element in H hitting $con(D_{i_j})$ is a concept name, then this concept name does not occur in $con(C')$, and thus $C' \not\sqsubseteq D_{i_j}$. Thus, assume that it is an existential restriction $\exists r_i.G$. But then each existential restriction $\exists r_i.C_i$ in $con(C)$ with $C_i \sqsubseteq G$ is either removed or replaced by a conjunction of existential restrictions $\exists r_i.F$ such that (by induction) $F \not\sqsubseteq G$. In addition, other existential restrictions are either removed or generalized. This clearly implies $C' \not\sqsubseteq D_{i_j}$ since $\exists r_i.G$ in $con(D_{i_j})$ is not covered by any element of $con(C')$.   □

However, $SCG(C, \mathcal{P})$ may also contain compliant generalizations of C that are not optimal, as illustrated by the following example.

Example 1. Let $C = \exists r.(A_1 \sqcap A_2 \sqcap A_3 \sqcap A_4)$ and $\mathcal{P} = \{D_1, D_2\}$, where

$$D_1 = \exists r.A_1 \sqcap \exists r.(A_2 \sqcap A_3) \quad \text{and} \quad D_2 = \exists r.A_2 \sqcap \exists r.A_4.$$

We have $C \sqsubseteq D_1$ and $C \sqsubseteq D_2$, and thus C is not compliant with $\mathcal{P}$. Consequently, the elements of $SCG(C, \mathcal{P})$ are obtained by considering the minimal hitting sets of $\{\exists r.A_1, \exists r.(A_2 \sqcap A_3)\}$ and $\{\exists r.A_2, \exists r.A_4\}$.

If we take the minimal hitting set $H = \{\exists r.(A_2 \sqcap A_3), \exists r.A_2\}$ and consider the only existential restriction in $con(C)$, the corresponding set $\mathcal{P}_i$ consists of $A_2 \sqcap A_3$ and A_2. It is easy to see that $SCG(A_1 \sqcap A_2 \sqcap A_3 \sqcap A_4, \mathcal{P}_i) = \{A_1 \sqcap A_3 \sqcap A_4\}$ since the only minimal hitting set of $\{A_1, A_2\}$ and $\{A_2\}$ is $\{A_2\}$. Thus, we obtain $C' := \exists r.(A_1 \sqcap A_3 \sqcap A_4)$ as an element of $SCG(C, \mathcal{P})$.

However, if we take the minimal hitting set $H' = \{\exists r.A_1, \exists r.A_2\}$ instead, then the set $\mathcal{P}_i'$ corresponding to the only existential restriction in $con(C)$ is $\{A_1, A_2\}$. Consequently, in this case $SCG(A_1 \sqcap A_2 \sqcap A_3 \sqcap A_4, \mathcal{P}_i') = \{A_3 \sqcap A_4\}$ since the only minimal hitting set of $\{A_1\}$ and $\{A_2\}$ is $\{A_1, A_2\}$. This yields $C'' := \exists r.(A_3 \sqcap A_4)$ as another element of $SCG(C, \mathcal{P})$. Since $C' \sqsubset C''$, the element C'' cannot be optimal.

The next lemma states that every compliant generalization of C subsumes some element of $SCG(C, \mathcal{P})$.

Lemma 1. *Let C be an $\mathcal{EL}$-concept and $\mathcal{P} = \{D_1, \ldots, D_p\}$ a policy. If C'' is a $\mathcal{P}$-compliant generalization of C, then there is $C' \in SCG(C, \mathcal{P})$ such that $C' \sqsubseteq C''$.*

Proof. If C is compliant with $\mathcal{P}$, then we have $C \in SCG(C, \mathcal{P})$ and $C \sqsubseteq C''$ since C'' is a generalization of C. Thus, assume that C is not compliant with $\mathcal{P}$, and let $i_1, \ldots, i_q$ be exactly the indices for which $C \sqsubseteq D_i$.

Now, let i_j be such an index. We have $C \sqsubseteq C'' \not\sqsubseteq D_{i_j}$ and $C \sqsubseteq D_{i_j}$. Since $C'' \not\sqsubseteq D_{i_j}$, there is an element $E_j \in \mathrm{con}(D_{i_j})$ that is not covered by any element of $\mathrm{con}(C'')$. Obviously, $H'' := \{E_1, \ldots, E_q\}$ is a hitting set of $\mathrm{con}(D_{i_1}), \ldots, \mathrm{con}(D_{i_q})$. Thus, there is a minimal hitting set H of $\mathrm{con}(D_{i_1}), \ldots, \mathrm{con}(D_{i_q})$ such that $H \subseteq H''$. Let C' be the element of $SCG(C, \mathcal{P})$ that was constructed using this hitting set H. We claim that $C' \sqsubseteq C''$. For this, it is sufficient to show that $\mathrm{con}(C')$ covers $\mathrm{con}(C'')$.

First, consider a concept name $A \in \mathrm{con}(C'')$. Since $C \sqsubseteq C''$, we also have $A \in \mathrm{con}(C)$. If $A \notin H''$, then $A \notin H$, and thus A is not removed in the construction of C'. Consequently, $A \in \mathrm{con}(C')$ covers $A \in \mathrm{con}(C'')$. If $A \in H''$, then A is not covered by any element of $\mathrm{con}(C'')$ according to our definition of H'', which contradicts our assumption that $A \in \mathrm{con}(C'')$.

Second, consider an existential restriction $\exists r_i.E \in \mathrm{con}(C'')$. Since $C \sqsubseteq C''$, there is an existential restriction $\exists r_i.C_i$ in $\mathrm{con}(C)$ such that $C_i \sqsubseteq E$. If this restriction is not removed or generalized when constructing C', then we are done since this restriction then belongs to $\mathrm{con}(C')$ and covers $\exists r_i.E$. Otherwise, $\mathcal{P}_i = \{G \mid \text{there is } \exists r_i.G \in H \text{ such that } C_i \sqsubseteq G\}$ is non-empty.

If $\top \in \mathcal{P}_i$, then $\exists r_i.\top \in H \subseteq H''$. However, then $\exists r_i.E \in \mathrm{con}(C'')$ covers an element of H'', which is a contradiction.

Consequently, $\top \notin \mathcal{P}_i$, and thus $\exists r_i.C_i$ is replaced with $\bigsqcap_{F \in SCG(C_i, \mathcal{P}_i)} \exists r_i.F$ when constructing C' from C. According to our definition of H'' and the fact that $H \subseteq H''$, none of the existential restrictions $\exists r_i.G$ considered in the definition of $\mathcal{P}_i$ is covered by $\exists r_i.E \in \mathrm{con}(C'')$. This implies that E is a $\mathcal{P}_i$-compliant generalization of C_i. By induction (on the role depth) we can thus assume that there is an $F \in SCG(C_i, \mathcal{P}_i)$ such that $F \sqsubseteq E$. This shows that $\exists r_i.E \in \mathrm{con}(C'')$ is covered by $\exists r_i.F \in \mathrm{con}(C')$. $\qquad\square$

As an easy consequence of this lemma, we obtain that all optimal compliant generalizations of C must belong to $SCG(C, \mathcal{P})$.

Proposition 4. *Let C be an $\mathcal{EL}$-concept and $\mathcal{P} = \{D_1, \ldots, D_p\}$ a policy. If C'' is an optimal $\mathcal{P}$-compliant generalization of C, then $C'' \in SCG(C, \mathcal{P})$ (up to equivalence of concepts).*

Proof. Let C'' be an optimal $\mathcal{P}$-compliant generalization of C. By Lemma 1, there is an element $C' \in SCG(C, \mathcal{P})$ such that $C' \sqsubseteq C''$. In addition, by Proposition 3, C' is a $\mathcal{P}$-compliant generalization of C. Thus, optimality of C'' implies $C'' \equiv C'$. $\qquad\square$

We are now ready to formulate and prove the main result of this section.

Theorem 1. *Let C be an $\mathcal{EL}$-concept and $\mathcal{P} = \{D_1, \ldots, D_p\}$ a policy. Then the set of all optimal $\mathcal{P}$-compliant generalizations of C can be computed in time exponential in the size of C and $D_1, \ldots, D_p$.*

Proof. It is sufficient to show that the set $SCG(C, \mathcal{P})$ can be computed in exponential time. In fact, given $SCG(C, \mathcal{P})$, we can compute the set of all optimal $\mathcal{P}$-compliant generalizations of C by removing elements that are not minimal w.r.t. subsumption, which requires at most exponentially many subsumption tests. Each subsumption test takes at most exponential time since subsumption in $\mathcal{EL}$ is in P, and the elements of $SCG(C, \mathcal{P})$ have at most exponential size, as shown below.

We show by induction on the role depth that $SCG(C, \mathcal{P})$ consists of at most exponentially many elements of at most exponential size. The at most exponential cardinality of $SCG(C, \mathcal{P})$ is an immediate consequence of the fact that there are at most exponentially many hitting sets of $\mathrm{con}(D_{i_1}), \ldots, \mathrm{con}(D_{i_q})$, and each yields exactly one element of $SCG(C, \mathcal{P})$ (see Definition 4). Regarding the size of these elements, note that we may assume by induction that an existential restriction may be replaced by a conjunction of at most exponentially many existential restrictions, where each is of at most exponential size. The overall size of the concept description obtained this way is thus also of at most exponential size. Given this, it is easy to see that the computation of these elements also takes at most exponential time. □

The following example shows that the exponential upper bounds can indeed by reached.

Example 2. Let $C = P_1 \sqcap Q_1 \sqcap \ldots \sqcap P_n \sqcap Q_n$ and $\mathcal{P} = \{P_i \sqcap Q_i \mid 1 \leq i \leq n\}$. Then $SCG(C, \mathcal{P})$ contains 2^n elements since the sets $\{P_1, Q_1\}, \ldots, \{P_n, Q_n\}$ obviously have exponentially many hitting sets. To be more precise,

$$SCG(C, \mathcal{P}) = \{X_1 \sqcap \ldots \sqcap X_n \mid X_i \in \{P_i, Q_i\} \text{ for } i = 1, \ldots, n\}.$$

This example can easily be modified to enforce an element of exponential size. Consider $\widehat{C} = \exists r.C$ and $\widehat{\mathcal{P}} = \{\exists r.(P_i \sqcap Q_i) \mid 1 \leq i \leq n\}$. Then $SCG(\widehat{C}, \widehat{\mathcal{P}}) = \{\sqcap_{F \in SCG(C, \mathcal{P})} \exists r.F\}$. We leave it to the reader to further modify the example in order to obtain exponentially many elements of exponential size.

4   Computing Optimal Safe Generalizations

Before we can characterize safety, we need to remove redundant elements from $\mathcal{P}$. We say that $D_i \in \mathcal{P}$ is *redundant* if there is a different element $D_j \in \mathcal{P}$ such that $D_i \sqsubseteq D_j$. The following lemma is easy to prove.

Lemma 2. *Let $\mathcal{P}$ be a policy and assume that $D_i \in \mathcal{P}$ is redundant. Then the following holds for all $\mathcal{EL}$ concepts C, C':*

- C' is compliant with $\mathcal{P}$ iff C' is compliant with $\mathcal{P} \setminus \{D_i\}$;
- C is safe for $\mathcal{P}$ iff C is safe for $\mathcal{P} \setminus \{D_i\}$.

This lemma shows that we can assume without loss of generality that our policies do not contain redundant concepts. However, elements of D_i of $\mathcal{P}$ may also contain redundant atoms. This can be avoided by reducing the policy concepts. We call a policy *redundancy-free* if it does not contain redundant elements and every element is reduced.

The following proposition characterizes safety for redundancy-free policies.

Proposition 5. *Let $\mathcal{P} = \{D_1, \ldots, D_p\}$ be a redundancy-free policy. The $\mathcal{EL}$ concept C' is safe for $\mathcal{P}$ iff there is no pair of atoms (E, F) such that $E \in con(C')$, $F \in con(D_1) \cup \ldots \cup con(D_p)$, and $E \sqsubseteq F$.*

Proof. First, assume that C' is not safe for $\mathcal{P}$, i.e., there is an $\mathcal{EL}$ concept C'' that is compliant with $\mathcal{P}$, but for which $C' \sqcap C''$ is not compliant with $\mathcal{P}$. The latter implies that there is $D_i \in \mathcal{P}$ such that $C' \sqcap C'' \sqsubseteq D_i$, which is equivalent to saying that $con(C') \cup con(C'')$ covers $con(D_i)$. On the other hand, we know that $con(C'')$ does not cover $con(D_i)$ since C'' is compliant with $\mathcal{P}$. Thus, there is an element $F \in con(D_i)$ that is covered by an element E of $con(C')$. This yields (E, F) such that $E \in con(C')$, $F \in con(D_1) \cup \ldots \cup con(D_p)$, and $E \sqsubseteq F$.

Conversely, assume that there is a pair of atoms (E, F) such that $E \in con(C')$, $F \in con(D_i)$, and $E \sqsubseteq F$. Let C'' be the concept obtained from D_i by removing F from the top-level conjunction of D_i. Then we clearly have $D_i \sqsubseteq C''$. In addition, since D_i is reduced, we also have $C'' \not\sqsubseteq D_i$. Consider $D_j \in \mathcal{P}$ different from D_i, and assume that $C'' \sqsubseteq D_j$. But then $D_i \sqsubseteq C'' \sqsubseteq D_j$ contradicts our assumption that $\mathcal{P}$ does not contain redundant elements. Thus, we have shown that C'' is compliant with $\mathcal{P}$. In addition, $con(C') \cup con(C'')$ covers $con(D_i)$. In fact, the elements of $con(D_i) \setminus \{F\}$ belong to $con(C'')$, and thus cover themselves. In addition, F is covered by $E \in con(C')$. Thus $C' \sqcap C'' \sqsubseteq D_i$, which shows that C' is not safe for $\mathcal{P}$. $\square$

Clearly, the necessary and sufficient condition for safety stated in this proposition can be decided in polynomial time. If needed, the policy can first be made redundancy-free, which can also be done in polynomial time.

Corollary 1. *Safety of an $\mathcal{EL}$ concept for an $\mathcal{EL}$ policy is in P.*

We now consider the problem of computing optimal $\mathcal{P}$-safe generalizations of a given $\mathcal{EL}$ concept C. First note that, up to equivalence, there can be only one optimal $\mathcal{P}$-safe generalization of C. This is an immediate consequence of the fact that the conjunction of safe concepts is again safe.

Lemma 3. *Let C'_1, C'_2 be two $\mathcal{EL}$ concepts that are $\mathcal{P}$-safe generalizations of C, where $\mathcal{P}$ is redundancy-free. Then $C'_1 \sqcap C'_2$ is also a $\mathcal{P}$-safe generalization of C.*

Thus there cannot be non-equivalent optimal $\mathcal{P}$-safe generalizations of a given $\mathcal{EL}$ concept C since their conjunction would then be more specific, contradicting their optimality. This property is independent of whether the policy is redundancy-free or not since turning a policy into one that is redundancy-free preserves the set of concepts that are compliant with (safe for) the policy.

Proposition 6. *If C'_1, C'_2 are optimal $\mathcal{P}$-safe generalizations of the $\mathcal{EL}$ concept C, then $C'_1 \equiv C'_2$.*

The following theorem, whose proof can be found in [3], shows how an optimal safe generalization of C can be constructed.

Theorem 2. *Let C be an $\mathcal{EL}$ concept and $\mathcal{P} = \{D_1, \ldots, D_p\}$ a redundancy-free policy. We construct the concept C' from C by removing or modifying atoms in the top-level conjunction of C in the following way:*

- *For every concept name $A \in \mathbf{con}(C)$, remove A from the top-level conjunction of C if $A \in \mathbf{con}(D_1) \cup \ldots \cup \mathbf{con}(D_p)$;*
- *For every existential restriction $\exists r_i.C_i \in \mathbf{con}(C)$, consider the set of concepts*

$$\mathcal{P}_i := \{G \mid \text{ there is } \exists r_i.G \in \mathbf{con}(D_1) \cup \ldots \cup \mathbf{con}(D_p) \text{ such that } C_i \sqsubseteq G\}.$$

  - *If $\mathcal{P}_i = \emptyset$, then leave $\exists r_i.C_i$ as it is.*
  - *If $\top \in \mathcal{P}_i$, then remove $\exists r_i.C_i$.*
  - *Otherwise, replace $\exists r_i.C_i$ with $\bigsqcap_{F \in OCG(C_i, \mathcal{P}_i)} \exists r_i.F$, where $OCG(C_i, \mathcal{P}_i)$ is the set of all optimal $\mathcal{P}_i$-compliant generalizations of C_i.*

Then C' is an optimal $\mathcal{P}$-safe generalization of C.

Since, by Theorem 1, $OCG(C_i, \mathcal{P}_i)$ can be computed in exponential time, the construction described in Theorem 2 can also be performed in exponential time.

Corollary 2. *Let C be an $\mathcal{EL}$ concept and $\mathcal{P} = \{D_1, \ldots, D_p\}$ a redundancy-free policy. Then an optimal $\mathcal{P}$-safe generalization of C can be computed in exponential time.*

Example 2 can easily be modified to provide an example that shows that this exponential bound can actually not be improved since there are cases where the safe generalization is of exponential size.

5   The Complexity of Deciding Optimality

In this section, we consider *optimality as a decision problem*, i.e., given $\mathcal{EL}$ concepts C, C' such that $C \sqsubseteq C'$ and a policy $\mathcal{P}$, decide whether C' is an optimal $\mathcal{P}$-compliant ($\mathcal{P}$-safe) generalization of C.

Theorem 1 and Corollary 2 show that the optimality problem is *in ExpTime* both for compliance and for safety. In fact, according to Theorem 1, given C and $\mathcal{P}$, we can compute the set of all optimal $\mathcal{P}$-compliant generalizations of C (up to equivalence) in exponential time. Consequently, this set contains at most exponentially many elements and each element has at most exponential size. This implies that we can test, in exponential time, whether a given concept C'

is equivalent to one of the elements of this set. If this is the case, then C' is an optimal $\mathcal{P}$-compliant generalization of C, and otherwise not. The case of safety can be treated similarly, using Corollary 2 instead of Theorem 1.

In the following, we show that this complexity upper bound can be improved to coNP. Actually, we will prove this upper bound not just for compliance and safety, but for a whole class of properties.

Definition 5. *Let F be a function that assigns a set of $\mathcal{EL}$ concepts to every input consisting of an $\mathcal{EL}$ concept C and a policy $\mathcal{P}$. We say that the function F defines a* polynomial, upward-closed property *if the following holds for every input $C, \mathcal{P}$:*

- *for every $\mathcal{EL}$ concept C', we can decide $C' \in F(C, \mathcal{P})$ in time polynomial in $C, C', \mathcal{P}$ (polynomiality);*
- *if $C' \in F(C, \mathcal{P})$ and $C' \sqsubseteq C''$, then $C'' \in F(C, \mathcal{P})$ (upward-closedness).*

We say that C' is an optimal F-generalization *of C w.r.t. $\mathcal{P}$ if $C \sqsubseteq C'$, $C' \in F(C, \mathcal{P})$, and there is no $C \sqsubseteq C'' \sqsubset C'$ such that $C'' \in F(C, \mathcal{P})$.*

It is easy to see that compliance and safety are polynomial, upward-closed properties. In fact, upward-closedness is an obvious consequence of the definition of compliance (safety). For compliance, polynomiality follows from the fact that subsumption in $\mathcal{EL}$ can be decided in polynomial time. For safety, it is stated in Corollary 1. In addition, the notion of optimality introduced in the above definition coincides with the notion of optimality introduced in Definition 1 for compliance and safety.

We will show that, for polynomial, upward-closed properties, the optimality problem is in coNP, i.e., there is an *NP-algorithm* that, on input $C \sqsubset C'$ and $\mathcal{P}$, succeeds iff C' is *not* an optimal F-generalization of C w.r.t. $\mathcal{P}$. Basically, this algorithm proceeds as follows. It guesses a lower neighbor C'' of C' subsuming C, i.e., a concept C'' such that (i) $C \sqsubseteq C'' \sqsubset C'$ and (ii) there is no concept C''' with $C'' \sqsubset C''' \sqsubset C'$. If $C'' \in F(C, \mathcal{P})$, then the algorithm succeeds, and otherwise it fails.

To make this algorithm more concrete, we need to investigate the strict subsumption relation $\sqsubset$ on $\mathcal{EL}$ concepts in more detail. Following [4], we define the *one-step relation* $\sqsubset_1$ induced by $\sqsubset$ as

$$\sqsubset_1 := \{(C'', C') \in \sqsubset \mid \text{there is no } C''' \text{ such that } C'' \sqsubset C''' \sqsubset C'\}.$$

If $C'' \sqsubset_1 C'$ then we call C' an *upper neighbor* of C'' and C'' a *lower neighbor* of C'. In [4] it was shown that the relation $\sqsubset$ on $\mathcal{EL}$ concepts is *one-step generated*, i.e., the transitive closure of $\sqsubset_1$ is again $\sqsubset$. In the context of the optimality problem for polynomial, upward-closed properties, this implies the following: whenever there is a counterexample to the optimality of C' (i.e., a concept C'' such that $C \sqsubseteq C'' \sqsubset C'$ and $C'' \in F(C, \mathcal{P})$), then there is a lower neighbor of C' that provides such a counterexample. To see this, just note that $C'' \sqsubset C'$ implies that C' can be reached by a $\sqsubset_1$-chain from C''. The last element in this chain before C' is a lower neighbor of C', and it belongs to $F(C, \mathcal{P})$ since F is upward-closed.

Another interesting result in [4] is the following characterization of upper neighbors: for a given *reduced* $\mathcal{EL}$ concept C, the set of upper neighbors of C consists (up to equivalence) of the concepts D obtained from C as follows:

- Remove a concept name A from the top-level conjunction of C.
- Remove an existential restriction $\exists r.E$ from the top-level conjunction of C, and replace it by the conjunction of all existential restrictions $\exists r.F$ where F ranges over all upper neighbors of E.

Note that a special case of the second item is the removal of an existential restriction of the form $\exists r.\top$ since $\top$ does not have any upper neighbors. As shown in [16], this characterization implies that a given concept has only polynomially many upper neighbors, each of which is of polynomial size. As an easy consequence, we obtain the following lemma:

Lemma 4. *The one-step relation* $\sqsubseteq_1$ *induced by* $\sqsubseteq$ *on* $\mathcal{EL}$ *concepts is decidable in polynomial time.*

Regarding lower neighbors, it is sufficient for our purposes to show that they can be guessed in non-deterministic polynomial time. Thus, we are looking for an NP-algorithm that, given input concepts $C \sqsubseteq C'$, generates exactly the lower neighbors of C' that subsume C. Below, we sketch how an appropriate NP-algorithm can be obtained. A more detailed description as well as *proofs can be found in* [16]. First, note that the lower neighbors C'' of C' can be obtained by conjoining an atom not implied by C' to C'. In addition, $C \sqsubseteq C''$ implies that $sig(C'') \subseteq sig(C)$. Given an $\mathcal{EL}$ concept C' and a finite set Σ as names, the set of *lowering atoms* for C' w.r.t. Σ is defined as

$$LA_\Sigma(C') := \{A \in \Sigma \cap N_C \mid A \notin \text{con}(C')\} \cup \{\exists r.D \mid r \in \Sigma \cap N_R, sig(D) \subseteq \Sigma,$$
$$C' \not\sqsubseteq \exists r.D, \text{ and } C' \sqsubseteq \exists r.E \text{ for all } E \text{ with } D \sqsubseteq_1 E\}.$$

Lemma 5. *Let C' be an $\mathcal{EL}$ concept and Σ a finite set of concept and role names with $sig(C') \subseteq \Sigma$. Then C'' is a lower neighbor of C' with $sig(C'') \subseteq \Sigma$ iff there is an atom $At \in LA_\Sigma(C')$ such that $C'' \equiv C' \sqcap At$.*

Intuitively, adding a single atom to the top-level conjunction of C' is sufficient to obtain a lower neighbor since adding two (non-redundant) atoms would step too far down in the subsumption hierarchy. The same is true for adding an existential restriction $\exists r.D$ for which $\exists r.E$ with $D \sqsubseteq_1 E$ does not subsume C' since then $C' \sqcap \exists r.D \sqsubseteq C' \sqcap \exists r.E \sqsubseteq C'$ would hold.

Example 3. Let $\Sigma := \{r, A_1, A_2, B_1, B_2, C_1, C_2\}$ and

$$C' := \exists r.(A_1 \sqcap A_2 \sqcap B_1 \sqcap B_2) \sqcap \exists r.(A_1 \sqcap A_2 \sqcap C_1 \sqcap C_2) \sqcap \exists r.(B_1 \sqcap B_2 \sqcap C_1 \sqcap C_2).$$

Then, for all $i, j, k \in \{1, 2\}$, the existential restriction $\exists r.D$ with $D := A_i \sqcap B_j \sqcap C_k$ belongs to $LA_\Sigma(C')$. In fact, $C' \not\sqsubseteq \exists r.D$ is obviously true, and since the upper neighbors of D are $A_i \sqcap B_j$, $B_j \sqcap C_k$, and $A_i \sqcap C_k$, we also have $C' \sqsubseteq \exists r.E$ for all E with $D \sqsubset_1 E$. Obviously, by using n instead of three pairs of concept names, we can produce a generalized version of this example that shows that the cardinality of $LA_\Sigma(C')$ can be exponential in the size of C' and Σ.

In order to obtain an NP-algorithm that generates exactly the lower neighbors of C' that subsume C, it is sufficient to generate all lowering atoms for C' w.r.t. $\Sigma := sig(C)$, and then remove the ones that do not subsume C. Unfortunately, the definition of lowering atoms given above Lemma 5 does not tell us directly how appropriate existential restrictions $\exists r.D$ can be found. The following necessary conditions follows from the characterization of lower neighbors given in [16].

Lemma 6. *Let C' be reduced. If $\exists r.D \in LA_\Sigma(C')$, then there is a set of existential restrictions $\{\exists r.F_1', \ldots, \exists r.F_k'\} \subseteq con(C')$ and $F_1 \in LA_\Sigma(F_1'), \ldots, F_k \in LA_\Sigma(F_k')$ such that $D \equiv F_1 \sqcap \ldots \sqcap F_k$.*

We illustrate this lemma using the lowering atom $D = A_i \sqcap B_j \sqcap C_k$ in Example 3. Here we take the set of all existential restrictions in $con(C')$ and choose $C_k \in LA_\Sigma(A_1 \sqcap A_2 \sqcap B_1 \sqcap B_2)$, $B_j \in LA_\Sigma(A_1 \sqcap A_2 \sqcap C_1 \sqcap C_2)$, and $A_i \in LA_\Sigma(B_1 \sqcap B_2 \sqcap C_1 \sqcap C_2)$. Obviously, D is indeed equivalent to the conjunction of these three atoms.

In general, not all choices of subsets and lower neighbors yields an appropriate existential restriction. For instance, if we take a smaller set of existential restrictions in our example (e.g., $\{\exists r.(A_1 \sqcap A_2 \sqcap C_1 \sqcap C_2), \exists r.(B_1 \sqcap B_2 \sqcap C_1 \sqcap C_2)\}$), then the obtained conjunction of lowering atoms (e.g., $B_1 \sqcap A_2$) is not appropriate since the corresponding existential restriction (e.g., $\exists r.(B_1 \sqcap A_2)$) is subsumed by C'.

The *NP-algorithm* generating exactly the elements of $LA_\Sigma(C')$ works as follows: given a reduced concept C' and a finite set Σ of concept and role names such that $sig(C') \subseteq \Sigma$, it non-deterministically chooses one of the following two alternatives:

1. Choose a concept name $A \in \Sigma \setminus con(C')$, and output A. If there is no such concept name, fail.
2. Choose $r \in \Sigma \cap N_R$, a set of existential restrictions $\{\exists r.F_1', \ldots, \exists r.F_k'\} \subseteq con(C')$, and recursively guess elements $F_1 \in LA_\Sigma(F_1'), \ldots, F_k \in LA_\Sigma(F_k')$. If for some $i, 1 \le i \le k$, the attempt to produce the atom $F_i \in LA_\Sigma(F_i')$ fails, or if $C' \sqsubseteq \exists r.(F_1 \sqcap \ldots \sqcap F_k)$, or if $F_1 \sqcap \ldots \sqcap F_k$ has an upper neighbor E such that $C' \not\sqsubseteq \exists r.E$, then fail. Otherwise, output $\exists r.(F_1 \sqcap \ldots \sqcap F_k)$.

Lemma 7. *The algorithm described above runs in non-deterministic polynomial time, and its non-failing runs produce exactly the elements of $LA_\Sigma(C')$.*

Proof. Soundness of the algorithm is an immediate consequence of the fact that, in the second case, we explicitly test whether the conditions in the definition of lowering atoms are satisfied. Completeness is an easy consequence of Lemma 6. Finally, the choice of a concept name, a role name, and a subset of the existential restrictions in $con(C')$, can clearly be achieved by making polynomially many binary choices. By induction on the role depth, we can assume that the algorithm can produce the elements $F_i \in LA_\Sigma(F_i')$ in non-deterministic polynomial time, which shows that the overall algorithm runs in non-deterministic polynomial time. □

With this lemma in place, we can now show that the optimality problem for polynomial, upward-closed properties is in coNP.

Theorem 3. *Let F be a polynomial, upward-closed property. The problem of deciding, for a given input $C, C', \mathcal{P}$, whether C' is an optimal F-generalization of C w.r.t. $\mathcal{P}$ is in coNP.*

Proof. We show that non-optimality can be decided by an NP-algorithm, i.e., we describe an NP-algorithm that, given $C, C', \mathcal{P}$, succeeds iff C' is *not* an optimal F-generalization of C w.r.t. $\mathcal{P}$.

1. Check whether $C \sqsubseteq C'$ and $C' \in F(C, \mathcal{P})$. If this is not the case, then succeed. Otherwise, continue with the next step. Polynomiality of F and of subsumption in $\mathcal{EL}$ implies that this test can be done in polynomial time.
2. Set $\Sigma := sig(C)$ and guess a lowering atom $At \in LA_\Sigma(C')$. If $C \not\sqsubseteq At$, then fail. Otherwise, we know that $C'' := C' \sqcap At$ is a lower neighbor of C' that subsumes C, and we continue with the next step. As shown above, the elements of $LA_\Sigma(C')$ can be generated by an NP-algorithm.
3. Check whether $C'' \in F(C, \mathcal{P})$. If this is the case, then succeed, and otherwise fail.

It is easy to see that this algorithm is correct and runs in non-deterministic polynomial time. □

Since compliance and safety are polynomial, upward-closed properties, the following corollary is an immediate consequence of this theorem.

Corollary 3. *The optimality problem is in coNP for compliance and for safety.*

At the moment, we do not know whether these problems are also coNP-hard. We can show, however, that the Hypergraph Duality Problem [11] can be reduced to them. Note that this problem is in coNP, but conjectured to be neither in P nor coNP-hard [12,14]. Given two finite families of inclusion-incomparable sets $\mathcal{G}$ and $\mathcal{H}$, the *Hypergraph Duality Problem* (DUAL) asks whether $\mathcal{H}$ consists exactly of the minimal hitting sets of $\mathcal{G}$.

Proposition 7. *There is a polynomial reduction of DUAL to the optimality problem that works both for compliance and for safety.*

Proof. Let $\mathcal{G} = \{G_1, \ldots, G_g\}, \mathcal{H} = \{H_1, \ldots, H_h\}$ be finite families of inclusion-incomparable sets and $G := G_1 \cup \ldots \cup G_g$. Since it can be checked in polynomial time whether a given set H is a minimal hitting set of $\mathcal{G}$, we can assume without loss of generality that all sets H_i are indeed minimal hitting sets of $\mathcal{G}$. The problem to be decided by our reduction is thus whether $\mathcal{H}$ really contains *all* minimal hitting sets of $\mathcal{G}$. We view the elements of G as concept names, for $S \subseteq G$ write $\bigsqcap S$ for the conjunction of the concept names in S, and define

- $C := \exists r_1.\bigsqcap G$ and $\mathcal{P} := \{D_1 := \exists r_1.\bigsqcap G_1, \ldots, D_g := \exists r_1.\bigsqcap G_g\}$;
- $C' := \exists r_1.\bigsqcap(G \setminus H_1) \sqcap \ldots \sqcap \exists r_1.\bigsqcap(G \setminus H_h)$.

It is easy to see that C' is a $\mathcal{P}$-compliant and $\mathcal{P}$-safe generalization of C.

According to Definition 4 and the proof of Theorem 1, C has exactly one optimal $\mathcal{P}$-compliant generalization, which is obtained as follows. First, note that the top-level conjunctions of C and $D_1, \ldots, D_g$ respectively consist of a single existential restriction for the same role r_1, and that the concepts D_i are pairwise incomparable. This implies that on this level only one hitting set is considered, which is $\mathcal{P}$. On the next role level, we have $\mathcal{P}_1 = \{\bigsqcap G_1, \ldots, \bigsqcap G_g\}$. The optimal $\mathcal{P}_1$-compliant generalizations of $C_1 := \bigsqcap G$ are obtained by considering all minimal hitting sets of $G_1, \ldots, G_g$, and removing their elements from the top-level conjunction of C_1. Consequently, the optimal $\mathcal{P}$-compliant generalization of C is given as

$$C'' := \bigsqcap_{H \text{ minimal hitting set of } \mathcal{G}} \exists r_1.\bigsqcap(G \setminus H).$$

A close look at Theorem 2 reveals that C'' is also the optimal $\mathcal{P}$-safe generalization of C. This shows that C' is optimal for compliance (safety) iff $\mathcal{H}$ contains all minimal hitting sets of $\mathcal{G}$. □

6 Conclusion

We have introduced the notions of compliance with and safety for a policy in the simple setting where both the knowledge about individuals and the policy are given by $\mathcal{EL}$ concepts. In this setting, we were able to characterize compliant (safe) generalization of a given concept w.r.t. a policy, and have used these characterizations to obtain algorithms for computing optimal generalizations. These algorithms need exponential time, which is optimal since the generalizations may be of exponential size. For the optimality problems, we have provided a coNP upper bound, and have shown by a reduction from DUAL that they are unlikely to be in P since this would show DUAL $\in$ P, a problem that has been open for a long time.

In the future, we intend to extend this work in two directions. On the one hand, we will consider $\mathcal{EL}$ concepts w.r.t. a background ontology. On the other hand, we will consider a setting where the ABox contains not just concept assertions, but also role assertions. In the latter case, one can use not just generalization of concepts, but also renaming of individuals as operations for achieving compliance (safety). Finally, of course, these two extensions should be combined.

References

1. Baader, F., Brandt, S., Lutz, C.: Pushing the $\mathcal{EL}$ envelope. In: Proceedings of the Nineteenth International Joint Conference on Artificial Intelligence, IJCAI 2005, Edinburgh, UK. Morgan-Kaufmann Publishers (2005)

2. Baader, F., Calvanese, D., McGuinness, D.L., Nardi, D., Patel-Schneider, P.F. (eds.): The Description Logic Handbook: Theory, Implementation, and Applications. Cambridge University Press, New York (2003)
3. Baader, F., Kriegel, F., Nuradiansyah, A.: Privacy-preserving ontology publishing for $\mathcal{EL}$ instance stores (extended version). LTCS-Report 19–01, Chair of Automata Theory, Institute of Theoretical Computer Science, TU Dresden, Dresden, Germany (2019). https://tu-dresden.de/inf/lat/reports#BaKrNu-LTCS-19-01
4. Baader, F., Kriegel, F., Nuradiansyah, A., Peñaloza, R.: Making repairs in description logics more gentle. In: Principles of Knowledge Representation and Reasoning: Proceedings of the Sixteenth International Conference, KR 2018, Tempe, Arizona, 30 October–2 November 2018, pp. 319–328 (2018)
5. Baader, F., Küsters, R., Molitor, R.: Computing least common subsumers in description logics with existential restrictions. In: Proceedings of the 16th International Joint Conference on Artificial Intelligence (IJCAI 1999), pp. 96–101 (1999)
6. Baader, F., Morawska, B.: Unification in the description logic $\mathcal{EL}$. Logical Methods Comput. Sci. **6**(3), 31 p. (2010)
7. Baader, F., Nuradiansyah, A.: Towards privacy-preserving ontology publishing. In: Ortiz, M., Schneider, T. (eds.) Proceedings of the 31st International Workshop on Description Logics (DL 2018). CEUR Workshop Proceedings (2018)
8. Bonatti, P.A.: Fast compliance checking in an OWL2 fragment. In: Lang, J. (ed.) Proceedings of the Twenty-Seventh International Joint Conference on Artificial Intelligence (IJCAI 2018), pp. 1746–1752. ijcai.org (2018)
9. Brandt, S.: Polynomial time reasoning in a description logic with existential restrictions, GCI axioms, and—what else? In: de Mántaras, R.L., Saitta, L. (eds.) Proceedings of the 16th European Conference on Artificial Intelligence (ECAI 2004), pp. 298–302 (2004)
10. Cuenca Grau, B., Kostylev, E.V.: Logical foundations of privacy-preserving publishing of linked data. In: Proceedings of the Thirtieth AAAI Conference on Artificial Intelligence, Phoenix, Arizona, USA, 12–17 February 2016, pp. 943–949 (2016)
11. Eiter, T., Gottlob, G.: Hypergraph transversal computation and related problems in logic and AI. In: Flesca, S., Greco, S., Ianni, G., Leone, N. (eds.) JELIA 2002. LNCS (LNAI), vol. 2424, pp. 549–564. Springer, Heidelberg (2002). https://doi.org/10.1007/3-540-45757-7_53
12. Fredman, M.L., Khachiyan, L.: On the complexity of dualization of monotone disjunctive normal forms. J. Algorithms **21**(3), 618–628 (1996)
13. Fung, B.C.M., Wang, K., Chen, R., Yu, P.S.: Privacy-preserving data publishing: a survey of recent developments. ACM Comput. Surv. **42**(4), 14:1–14:53 (2010)
14. Gottlob, G., Malizia, E.: Achieving new upper bounds for the hypergraph duality problem through logic. SIAM J. Comput. **47**(2), 456–492 (2018)
15. Horrocks, I., Li, L., Turi, D., Bechhofer, S.: The instance store: DL reasoning with large numbers of individuals. In: Proceedings of the 2004 International Workshop on Description Logics (DL 2004), Whistler, British Columbia, Canada, 6–8 June 2004 (2004)
16. Kriegel, F.: The distributive, graded lattice of $\mathcal{EL}$ concept descriptions and its neighborhood relation (extended version). LTCS-Report 18–10, Chair of Automata Theory, Institute of Theoretical Computer Science, TU Dresden, Dresden, Germany (2018). https://tu-dresden.de/inf/lat/reports#Kr-LTCS-18-10
17. Küsters, R.: Non-standard Inferences in Description Logics. Lecture Notes in Artificial Intelligence, vol. 2100. Springer, Heidelberg (2001). https://doi.org/10.1007/3-540-44613-3

A Bayesian Extension of the Description Logic $\mathcal{ALC}$

Leonard Botha[1], Thomas Meyer[1], and Rafael Peñaloza[2]([✉])

^{1} University of Cape Town and CAIR, Cape Town, South Africa
leonardzbotha@gmail.com, tmeyer@cs.uct.ac.za
^{2} University of Milano-Bicocca, Milano, Italy
rafael.penaloza@unibz.it

Abstract. Description logics (DLs) are well-known knowledge representation formalisms focused on the representation of terminological knowledge. A probabilistic extension of a light-weight DL was recently proposed for dealing with certain knowledge occurring in uncertain contexts. In this paper, we continue that line of research by introducing the Bayesian extension $\mathcal{BALC}$ of the DL $\mathcal{ALC}$. We present a tableau-based procedure for deciding consistency, and adapt it to solve other probabilistic, contextual, and general inferences in this logic. We also show that all these problems remain ExpTime-complete, the same as reasoning in the underlying classical $\mathcal{ALC}$.

1 Introduction

Description logics (DLs) [1] are a family of logic-based knowledge representation formalisms designed to describe the terminological knowledge of an application domain. Due to their clear syntax, formal semantics, and the existence of efficient reasoners alongside their expressivity, they have been successfully applied to model several domains, especially from the biomedical sciences. However, in their classical form, these logics are not capable of dealing with uncertainty, which is an unavoidable staple in real-world knowledge. To overcome this limitation, several probabilistic extensions of DLs have been suggested in the literature. The landscape of probabilistic extensions of DLs is too large to be covered in detail in this work. These logics differentiate themselves according to their underlying logical formalism, their interpretation of probabilities, and the kind of uncertainty that they are able to express. For a relevant, although slightly outdated survey, where all these differences are showcased, see [16].

A recently proposed probabilistic DL is the Bayesian extension $\mathcal{BEL}$ of the light-weight $\mathcal{EL}$. This logic focuses on modelling certain knowledge that holds only in some contexts, together with uncertainty about the current context. One advantage of the formalism underlying $\mathcal{BEL}$ is that it separates the contextual

---

R. Peñaloza—This work was carried out while the third author was at the Free University of Bozen-Bolzano, Italy.

F. Calimeri et al. (Eds.): JELIA 2019, LNAI 11468, pp. 339–354, 2019.
https://doi.org/10.1007/978-3-030-19570-0_22

knowledge, which is *de facto* a classical ontology, from the likelihood of observing this context. As a simple example of the importance of contextual knowledge, consider the knowledge of construction techniques and materials that vary through time. In the context of a modern house, asbestos and modern pipes are not observable, while some classes of houses built during the 1970s do contain both. However, in all contexts we know that asbestos and lead in drinking water have grave health effects. Still, when confronted with a random house, one might not know to which of these contexts it belongs, and by extension whether it is safe to live in. But construction data may be used to derive the probabilities of these contexts.

To allow for complex probabilistic relationships between the contexts, their joint probability distribution is encoded via a Bayesian network (BN) [18]. This logic is closely related to the probabilistic extension of DL-Lite proposed in [12], but uses a less restrictive semantics (for a discussion on the differences between these logics, see [11]). Another similar proposal is Probabilistic Datalog$^{\pm}$ [13], with the difference that uncertainty is represented via a Markov Logic Network, instead of a BN. Since the introduction of $\mathcal{BEL}$, the main notions behind it have been generalised to arbitrary ontology languages [8]. However, it has also been shown that efficient and complexity-optimal reasoning methods can only be achieved by studying the properties of each underlying ontology language [11].

In this paper, we continue with that line of research and study the Bayesian extension of the propositionally closed DL $\mathcal{ALC}$. As our main result, we present an algorithm, based on a glass-box modification of the classical tableaux method for reasoning in $\mathcal{ALC}$, that outputs a description of all the contexts encoding inconsistent knowledge. Using this algorithm, we describe an effective method for deciding consistency of a $\mathcal{BALC}$ knowledge base. We also provide a tight ExpTime complexity bound for this problem.

This is followed by a study of several crisp and probabilistic variants of the standard DL decision problems; namely, concept satisfiability, subsumption, and instance checking. Interestingly, our work shows that all our problems can be reduced to some basic computations over a context describing inconsistency, and hence are ExpTime-complete as well. These complexity bounds are not completely surprising, given the high complexity of the classical $\mathcal{ALC}$. However, our tableaux-based algorithm has the potential to behave better in practical scenarios. This work details and deepens results that have previously been presented in [5, 6].

2   Preliminaries

We start by briefly introducing Bayesian networks and the description logic (DL) $\mathcal{ALC}$, which form the basis for $\mathcal{BALC}$.

Bayesian networks (BNs) are graphical models capable of representing the joint probability distribution (JPD) of several discrete random variables in a compact manner [18]. Given a random variable X, $\mathsf{val}(X)$ denotes the set of values that

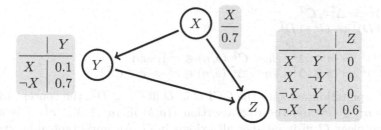

	Y
X	0.1
$\neg X$	0.7

	X
	0.7

		Z
X	Y	0
X	$\neg Y$	0
$\neg X$	Y	0
$\neg X$	$\neg Y$	0.6

Fig. 1. A Bayesian network with three Boolean variables.

X can take. For $x \in val(X)$, $X = x$ is the *valuation* of X taking the value x. This notation is extended to sets of variables in the obvious way. Given a set of random variables V, a *world* ω is a set of valuations containing exactly one valuation for every random variable $X \in V$. A V-*literal* is an ordered pair of the form (X_i, x), where $X_i \in V$ and $x \in val(X_i)$. V-literals generalise Boolean literals denoted as x or $\neg x$ for the random variable X. For simplicity, in this paper we will often use the notation X for (X, T) and $\neg X$ for (X, F). A V-*context* is any set of V-literals. It is *consistent* if it contains at most one literal for each random variable. We will often call V-contexts *primitive contexts*.

A *Bayesian network* is a pair $\mathcal{B} = (G, \Theta)$ where $G = (V, E)$ is a directed acyclic graph (DAG) and Θ is a set of conditional probability distributions for every variable $X \in V$ given its parents $\pi(X)$ on the DAG G; more precisely, $\Theta = \{P(X = x | \pi(X) = \boldsymbol{x}') \mid X \in V\}$. $\mathcal{B}$ encodes the JPD of V through the chain rule $P(\boldsymbol{X} = \boldsymbol{x}) = \prod_{X_i \in V} P(X_i = x_i \mid \pi(X_i) = \boldsymbol{x}_j)$.

Figure 1 depicts a BN with three random variables denoting the likelihood of different characteristics of a construction: X stands for a post-1986 building, Y for a renovated building, and Z for the presence of lead pipes. In this case, $P(X, Y, Z) = 0.7 \cdot 0.1 \cdot 0 = 0$; i.e., a renovated post-1986 house has no lead pipes. The description logic $\mathcal{ALC}$ is the smallest propositionally closed DL [1,20]. It is based on *concepts* which correspond to unary predicates of first-order logic, and *roles* corresponding to binary predicates. Formally, given the mutually disjoint sets N_I, N_C, and N_R of *individual, concept,* and *role names*, respectively, $\mathcal{ALC}$ *concepts* are built by the grammar rule $C ::= A \mid \neg C \mid C \sqcap C \mid C \sqcup C \mid \exists r.C \mid \forall r.C$, where $A \in N_C$ and $r \in N_R$. $\mathcal{ALC}$ *axioms* are either *general concept inclusions* (GCIs) of the form $C \sqsubseteq D$, *concept assertions* $C(a)$, or *role assertions* $r(a, b)$ where $a, b \in N_I, r \in N_R$, and C, D are concepts. An *ontology* is a finite set of axioms. We sometimes partition an ontology into the *TBox* $\mathcal{T}$ composed exclusively of GCIs, and the *ABox* $\mathcal{A}$ containing all concept and role assertions.

The semantics of $\mathcal{ALC}$ is defined by *interpretations*, which are pairs of the form $\mathcal{I} = (\Delta^{\mathcal{I}}, \cdot^{\mathcal{I}})$ where $\Delta^{\mathcal{I}}$ is a non-empty set called the *domain* and $\cdot^{\mathcal{I}}$ is the *interpretation function* that maps every $a \in N_I$ to an element $a^{\mathcal{I}} \in \Delta^{\mathcal{I}}$, every $A \in N_C$ to a set $A^{\mathcal{I}} \subseteq \Delta^{\mathcal{I}}$ and every $r \in N_R$ to a binary relation $r^{\mathcal{I}} \subseteq \Delta^{\mathcal{I}} \times \Delta^{\mathcal{I}}$. The interpretation function is extended to arbitrary concepts by defining for any two concepts C, D:

- $(\neg C)^{\mathcal{I}} := \Delta^{\mathcal{I}} \setminus C^{\mathcal{I}}$,
- $(C \sqcap D)^{\mathcal{I}} := C^{\mathcal{I}} \cap D^{\mathcal{I}}$,
- $(C \sqcup D)^{\mathcal{I}} := C^{\mathcal{I}} \cup D^{\mathcal{I}}$,
- $(\exists r.C)^{\mathcal{I}} := \{\delta \in \Delta^{\mathcal{I}} \mid \exists \eta \in C^{\mathcal{I}}.(\delta, \eta) \in r^{\mathcal{I}}\}$, and
- $(\forall r.C)^{\mathcal{I}} := \{\delta \in \Delta^{\mathcal{I}} \mid \forall \eta \in \Delta^{\mathcal{I}}.(\delta, \eta) \in r^{\mathcal{I}} \Rightarrow \eta \in C^{\mathcal{I}}\}$.

This interpretation *satisfies* the GCI $C \sqsubseteq D$ iff $C^{\mathcal{I}} \subseteq D^{\mathcal{I}}$, the concept assertion $C(a)$ iff $a^{\mathcal{I}} \in C^{\mathcal{I}}$ and the role assertion $r(a, b)$ iff $(a^{\mathcal{I}}, b^{\mathcal{I}}) \in r^{\mathcal{I}}$. $\mathcal{I}$ is a *model* of the ontology $\mathcal{O}$ iff it satisfies all axioms in $\mathcal{O}$. An important abbreviation in $\mathcal{ALC}$ is the bottom concept $\bot := A \sqcap \neg A$, where A is any concept name. For any interpretation $\mathcal{I}$, $\bot^{\mathcal{I}} = \emptyset$.

As a simple example, one can express the notion that water pipes do not contain lead through the GCI Pipe $\sqsubseteq \forall$contains.$\neg$Lead.

3 $\mathcal{BALC}$

$\mathcal{BALC}$ is a probabilistic extension of $\mathcal{ALC}$, in which axioms are considered to hold only in a given (possibly uncertain) context expressed through annotations.

Definition 1 (KB). *Let V be a finite set of discrete random variables. A V-restricted axiom (V-axiom) is an expression of the form α^κ, where α is an $\mathcal{ALC}$ axiom and κ is a V-context. A V-ontology is a finite set of V-axioms. A $\mathcal{BALC}$ knowledge base (KB) over V is a pair $\mathcal{K} = (\mathcal{O}, \mathcal{B})$ where $\mathcal{B}$ is a BN over V, and $\mathcal{O}$ is a V-ontology.*

To define the semantics of $\mathcal{BALC}$, we extend the notion of an interpretation to also take contexts into account, and interpret the probabilities based on a multiple-world approach. Formally, a *V-interpretation* is a tuple $\mathcal{V} = (\Delta^{\mathcal{V}}, \cdot^{\mathcal{V}}, v^{\mathcal{V}})$ where $(\Delta^{\mathcal{V}}, \cdot^{\mathcal{V}})$ is an $\mathcal{ALC}$ interpretation and $v^{\mathcal{V}} : V \to \cup_{X \in V} val(X)$ is a *valuation function* such that $v^{\mathcal{V}}(X) \in val(X)$.

Given a valuation function $v^{\mathcal{V}}$, a Bayesian world ω, and a context κ we denote $v^{\mathcal{V}} = \omega$ when $v^{\mathcal{V}}$ assigns to each random variable the same value as it has in ω; $v^{\mathcal{V}} \models \kappa$ when $v^{\mathcal{V}}(X) = x$ for all $(X, x) \in \kappa$; and $\omega \models \kappa$ when there is $\omega = v^{\mathcal{V}}$ such that $v^{\mathcal{V}} \models \kappa$.

Definition 2 (Model). *The V-interpretation $\mathcal{V}$ is a model of the V-axiom α^κ, ($\mathcal{V} \models \alpha^\kappa$), iff (i) $v^{\mathcal{V}} \not\models \kappa$, or (ii) $(\Delta^{\mathcal{V}}, \cdot^{\mathcal{V}})$ satisfies α. It is a model of the ontology $\mathcal{O}$ iff it is a model of all axioms in $\mathcal{O}$.*

Notice that $\mathcal{BALC}$ is a generalisation of $\mathcal{ALC}$. The axiom $\alpha^\emptyset$ holds in all contexts, and hence every $\mathcal{ALC}$ ontology is also a V-ontology from $\mathcal{BALC}$. In particular, this means that reasoning in $\mathcal{BALC}$ should be at least as hard as doing so in $\mathcal{ALC}$. For brevity, for the rest of this paper we will abbreviate axioms of the form $\alpha^\emptyset$ simply as α. When it is clear from the context, we will omit the V prefix and refer only to e.g., contexts, GCIs, or ontologies.

V-interpretations focus on only a single world, but KBs have information about the uncertainty of being in one world or another. Probabilistic interpretations combine multiple V-interpretations and the probability distribution from the BN to give information about the uncertainty of some consequences.

Definition 3 (Probabilistic model). *A probabilistic interpretation is a pair of the form* $\mathcal{P} = (\mathcal{J}, \mathcal{P}_{\mathcal{J}})$, *where* $\mathcal{J}$ *is a finite set of V-interpretations and* $\mathcal{P}_{\mathcal{J}}$ *is a probability distribution over* $\mathcal{J}$ *such that* $\mathcal{P}_{\mathcal{J}}(\mathcal{V}) > 0$ *for all* $\mathcal{V} \in \mathcal{J}$. *The probabilistic interpretation* $\mathcal{P}$ *is a* model *of the axiom* α^{κ} ($\mathcal{P} \models \alpha^{\kappa}$) *iff every* $\mathcal{V} \in \mathcal{J}$ *is a model of* α^{κ}. $\mathcal{P}$ *is a model of the ontology* $\mathcal{O}$ *iff every* $\mathcal{V} \in \mathcal{J}$ *is a model of* $\mathcal{O}$.

The distribution $\mathcal{P}_{\mathcal{J}}$ is consistent with the BN $\mathcal{B}$ if for every possible world ω of the variables in V it holds that

$$\sum_{\mathcal{V} \in \mathcal{J}, v^{\mathcal{V}} = \omega} \mathcal{P}_{\mathcal{J}}(\mathcal{V}) = P_{\mathcal{B}}(\omega),$$

where $P_{\mathcal{B}}$ is the joint probability distribution defined by the BN $\mathcal{B}$. The probabilistic interpretation $\mathcal{P}$ is a model of the KB $\mathcal{K} = (\mathcal{O}, \mathcal{B})$ iff it is a (probabilistic) model of $\mathcal{O}$, and is consistent with $\mathcal{B}$.

Consider for example the KB $\mathcal{K} = (\mathcal{O}, \mathcal{B})$ where $\mathcal{B}$ is the BN from Fig. 1, and $\mathcal{O}$ contains the axioms

Pipe $\sqsubseteq \forall$contains.$\neg$Lead^X Pipe $\sqsubseteq \forall$contains.$\neg$Lead^Y

Pipe $\sqsubseteq \exists$contains.Lead^Z Water $\sqcap \exists$hasAlkalinity.Low $\sqsubseteq \neg$Drinkable^Z.

The axioms in the first row express that pipes in post-1986 (context X) and in renovated buildings (context Y) do not contain lead. The axioms in the second row refer exclusively to the context of lead pipes (Z). In this case, our knowledge is that pipes do contain lead, and that water with low alkalinity is not drinkable, as it absorbs the lead from the pipes it travels on. Notice that the first two axioms contradict the third one. This is not a problem because they are required to hold in different contexts. Indeed, notice that any context that makes Z, and either X or Y true has probability 0, and hence can be ignored in the construction of a model.

A *complex context* ϕ is a finite non-empty set of primitive contexts. Note that primitive contexts can be seen as complex ones; e.g., the primitive context κ corresponds to the complex context $\{\kappa\}$. Given a valuation function $v^{\mathcal{V}}$ and a complex context $\phi = \{\alpha_1, \ldots, \alpha_n\}$ we say that $v^{\mathcal{V}}$ satisfies ϕ (written as $v^{\mathcal{V}} \models \phi$) iff $v^{\mathcal{V}}$ satisfies at least one $\alpha_i \in \phi$; in particular, if $v^{\mathcal{V}} \models \kappa$ then $v^{\mathcal{V}} \models \{\kappa\}$. Thus, in the following we assume that all contexts are in complex form unless explicitly stated otherwise. Finally we say that ϕ entails ψ ($\phi \models \psi$) iff for all $v^{\mathcal{V}}$ such that $v^{\mathcal{V}} \models \phi$ it follows that $v^{\mathcal{V}} \models \psi$. Or alternatively $\phi \models \psi$ iff for all Bayesian worlds ω such that $\omega \models \phi$ it follows that $\omega \models \psi$.

Given complex contexts $\phi = \{\alpha_1, \ldots, \alpha_n\}$ and $\psi = \{\beta_1, \ldots, \beta_m\}$ we define the operations

$$\phi \vee \psi := \phi \cup \psi, \hspace{4cm} \text{and}$$

$$\phi \wedge \psi := \bigcup_{\alpha \in \phi, \beta \in \psi} \{\alpha \cup \beta\} = \{\alpha \cup \beta \mid \alpha \in \phi, \beta \in \psi\}.$$

These operations generalise propositional disjunction ($\vee$) and propositional conjunction ($\wedge$), where disjunction has the property that either one of the two contexts holds and conjunction requires that both hold. It is easy to see that for all worlds ω and complex contexts ϕ, ψ it holds that (i) $\omega \models \phi \vee \psi$ iff $\omega \models \phi$ or $\omega \models \psi$, and (ii) $\omega \models \phi \wedge \psi$ iff $\omega \models \phi$ and $\omega \models \psi$. Two important special complex contexts are top ($\top$) and bottom ($\bot$), which are satisfied by all or no world, respectively. If there are n consistent primitive contexts and κ is an inconsistent context, these are defined as $\top := \{\alpha_1, \ldots, \alpha_n\}$ and $\bot := \kappa$.

In the next section, we study the problem of consistency of a $\mathcal{BALC}$ KB, and its relation to other reasoning problems.

4   Consistency

The most basic decision problem one can consider is *consistency*. That is, deciding whether a given $\mathcal{BALC}$ KB $\mathcal{K}$ has a probabilistic model or not. To deal with this problem, it is convenient to consider the classical $\mathcal{ALC}$ ontologies that should hold at each specific world. Formally, given the $\mathcal{BALC}$ KB $\mathcal{K} = (\mathcal{O}, \mathcal{B})$ and the world ω, the *restriction* of $\mathcal{O}$ to ω is

$$\mathcal{O}_\omega := \{\alpha \mid \alpha^\kappa \in \mathcal{O}, \omega \models \kappa\}.$$

Recall that a probabilistic model $\mathcal{P} = (\mathcal{J}, \mathcal{P}_\mathcal{J})$ of $\mathcal{K}$ is a class of classical interpretations associated to worlds $(\Delta^\mathcal{V}, \cdot^\mathcal{V}, \omega)$, such that $(\Delta^\mathcal{V}, \cdot^\mathcal{V})$ is a classical model of $\mathcal{O}_\omega$. Moreover, all the interpretations associated with the world ω must add to the probability $P_\mathcal{B}(\omega)$ specified by $\mathcal{B}$. Using this insight, we obtain the following result.

Theorem 4. *The $\mathcal{BALC}$ KB $\mathcal{K} = (\mathcal{O}, \mathcal{B})$ is consistent iff for every world ω with $P_\mathcal{B}(\omega) > 0$ $\mathcal{O}_\omega$ is consistent.*

Based on this result, we can derive a process for deciding consistency that provides a tight complexity bound for this problem.

Corollary 5. *$\mathcal{BALC}$ KB consistency is* ExpTime-*complete.*

Proof. There are exponentially many worlds ω. For each of them, we have to check (classical) consistency of $\mathcal{O}_\omega$ (in exponential time) and that $P_\mathcal{B}(\omega) > 0$, which is linear in the size of $\mathcal{B}$. □

The algorithm described in the proof of this corollary is optimal in terms of *worst-case* complexity, but it also runs in exponential time in the *best case*. Indeed, it enumerates all the (exponentially many) Bayesian worlds. In practice, it is infeasible to use an algorithm that requires exponential time on every instance. For that reason, we present a new algorithm based on the tableau method originally developed for $\mathcal{ALC}$. To describe this algorithm, we need to introduce some additional notation.

⊓-rule	if $(C_1 \sqcap C_2)(x)^\phi \in \mathcal{A}$, and either $C_1(x)^\phi$ or $C_2(x)^\phi$ is $\mathcal{A}$-insertable
	then $\mathcal{A}' := (\mathcal{A} \oplus C_1(x)^\phi) \oplus C_2(x)^\phi$
⊔-rule	if $(C_1 \sqcup C_2)(x)^\phi \in \mathcal{A}$, and both $C_1(x)^\phi$ and $C_2(x)^\phi$ are $\mathcal{A}$-insertable
	then $\mathcal{A}' := \mathcal{A} \oplus C_1(x)^\phi$, $\mathcal{A}'' := \mathcal{A} \oplus C_2(x)^\phi$
∃-rule	if $(\exists R.C)(x)^\phi \in \mathcal{A}$, there is no z such that neither $R(x,z)^\phi$ nor $C(z)^\phi$ is $\mathcal{A}$-insertable, and x is not blocked
	then $\mathcal{A}' := (\mathcal{A} \oplus R(x,y)^\phi) \oplus C(y)^\phi$, where y is a new individual name
∀-rule	if $\{(\forall R.C)(x)^\phi, R(x,y)^\psi\} \subseteq \mathcal{A}$, and $C(y)^{\phi \wedge \psi}$ is $\mathcal{A}$-insertable
	then $\mathcal{A}' := \mathcal{A} \oplus C(y)^{\phi \wedge \psi}$
⊑-rule	if $(C \sqsubseteq D)^\phi \in \mathcal{O}$, x appears in $\mathcal{A}$, and $(\neg C \sqcup D)(x)^\phi$ is $\mathcal{A}$-insertable
	then $\mathcal{A}' := \mathcal{A} \oplus (\neg C \sqcup D)(x)^\phi$

Fig. 2. Expansion rules for constructing $\phi_{\mathcal{K}}^\perp$

We denote the context that describes all worlds ω such that $\mathcal{O}_\omega$ is inconsistent as $\phi_{\mathcal{K}}^\perp$. That is $\omega \models \phi_{\mathcal{K}}^\perp$ iff $\mathcal{O}_\omega$ is inconsistent. Moreover, $\phi_{\mathcal{B}}$ is a context such that $\omega \models \phi_{\mathcal{B}}$ iff $P(\omega) = 0$. Theorem 4 states that $\mathcal{K}$ is inconsistent whenever there is a world that models both $\phi_{\mathcal{K}}^\perp$ and $\phi_{\mathcal{B}}$. This is formalized in the following result.

Theorem 6. *The KB $\mathcal{K}$ is inconsistent iff $\phi_{\mathcal{K}}^\perp \wedge \neg \phi_{\mathcal{B}}$ is satisfiable.*

To decide consistency, it then suffices to find a method for deriving the contexts $\phi_{\mathcal{K}}^\perp$ and $\phi_{\mathcal{B}}$. For the former, we present a variant of the glass-box approach for so-called axiom pinpointing [4,15,17], originally based on the ideas from [2]. This approach modifies the standard tableaux algorithm for $\mathcal{ALC}$ to keep track of the contexts in which the derived elements in the tableau hold. In a nutshell, whenever a rule application requires the use of an axiom from the ontology, this fact is registered as part of a propositional formula. In our case, we need a context, rather than a propositional formula, to take care of the multiple values that the random variables take.

The algorithm starts with the ABox $\mathcal{A}$ from $\mathcal{O}$. Recall that all the axioms in $\mathcal{A}$ are labeled with a context. The algorithm then creates a set of ABoxes $\mathfrak{A}$ following the rules from Fig. 2. As a pre-requisite for the execution of the algorithm, we assume that all concepts appearing in the ontology are in *negation normal form* (NNF); that is, only concept names can appear in the scope of a negation operator. This assumption is w.l.o.g. because every concept can be transformed into NNF in linear time by applying the De Morgan laws, the duality of the quantifiers, and eliminating double negations. Each rule application chooses an ABox $\mathcal{A} \in \mathfrak{A}$ and replaces it by one or two new ABoxes that expand $\mathcal{A}$. We explain the details of these rule applications next.

An assertion α^ϕ is $\mathcal{A}$-*insertable* to $\mathcal{A}$ iff for all ψ such that $\alpha^\psi \in \mathcal{A}$, $\phi \not\models \psi$. In the expansion rules $\oplus$ is used as shorthand for $\mathcal{A} \oplus \alpha^\phi := (\mathcal{A} \setminus \{\alpha^\psi\}) \cup \{\alpha^{\phi \vee \psi}\}$ if $\alpha^\psi \in \mathcal{A}$ and $\mathcal{A} \cup \{\alpha^\phi\}$ otherwise. The individual x is an *ancestor* of y if there is a chain of role assertions connecting x to y; x *blocks* y iff x is an ancestor of y and for every $C(y)^\psi \in \mathcal{A}$, there is a ϕ such that $C(x)^\phi \in \mathcal{A}$ and $\psi \models \phi$; y is *blocked* if there is a node that block it.

The algorithm applies the expansion rules until $\mathfrak{A}$ is *saturated*; i.e., until no rule is applicable to any $\mathcal{A} \in \mathfrak{A}$. $\mathcal{A}$ contains a *clash* if $\{A(x)^\phi, \neg A(x)^\psi\} \subseteq \mathcal{A}$ for some individual x and concept name A. We define the context

$$\phi_{\mathcal{A}} := \bigvee_{A(x)^\phi, \neg A(x)^\psi \in \mathcal{A}} \phi \wedge \psi,$$

which intuitively describes all the clashes that appear in $\mathcal{A}$. When $\mathfrak{A}$ is saturated, we return the context $\phi_{\mathcal{K}}^{\perp} = \bigwedge_{\mathcal{A} \in \mathfrak{A}} \phi_{\mathcal{A}}$ expressing the need of having clashes in every ABox $\mathcal{A}$ for inconsistency to follow. It is important to notice that the definition of a clash does not impose any constraints on the contexts ϕ and ψ labelling the assertions $A(x)$ and $\neg A(x)$, respectively. Indeed, $A(x)$ and $\neg A(x)$ could hold in contradictory contexts. In that case, the conjunction appearing in $\phi_{\mathcal{A}}$ would not be affected; i.e., this clash will not provide any new information about inconsistency.

Informally, the formula $\phi_{\mathcal{K}}^{\perp}$ corresponds to the clash formula (or pinpointing formula) for explaining inconsistency of an $\mathcal{ALC}$ ontology [4,15]. The main differences are that the variables appearing in a context are not necessarily Boolean, but multi-valued, and that the axioms in $\mathcal{O}$ are not labelled with unique variables, but rather with contexts already. Notice that the expansion rules in Fig. 2 generalise the expansion rules for $\mathcal{ALC}$, but may require new rule applications to guarantee that all possible derivations of a clash are detected. As observed in [3,4], one has to be careful with termination of the modified method. However, since all the assertions used are unary and binary, the sufficient termination conditions from [4,19] are satisfied. Hence we obtain the following result.

Theorem 7. *The modified tableau algorithm terminates, and the context $\phi_{\mathcal{K}}^{\perp}$ is such that for every world ω, $\omega \models \phi_{\mathcal{K}}^{\perp}$ iff $\mathcal{K}_\omega$ is inconsistent.*

We now turn our attention to the computation of the formula $\phi_{\mathcal{B}}$. Recall that in a BN, the joint probability distribution is the product of the conditional probabilities of each variable given its parents. Hence a world ω can only have probability 0 if it evaluates some variable in $X \in V$ and its parents $\pi(X)$ to values x and $\boldsymbol{x}$, respectively, such that $P(X = x \mid \pi(X) = \boldsymbol{x}) = 0$. Thus, to compute $\phi_{\mathcal{B}}$ it suffices to find out the cells in the conditional probability tables in Θ with value 0.

Theorem 8. *Let $\mathcal{B} = (V, \Theta)$ be a BN, and define*

$$\phi_{\mathcal{B}} := \bigvee_{P(X=x|\pi(X)=\boldsymbol{x})=0} \left((X, x) \wedge \bigwedge_{Y \in \pi(X)} (Y, y) \right).$$

Then for every world ω, $\omega \models \phi_{\mathcal{B}}$ iff $P_{\mathcal{B}}(\omega) = 0$.

Notice that, in general, the context $\phi_{\mathcal{B}}$ can be computed faster than simply enumerating all possible worlds. In particular, if the conditional probability tables in Θ contain no 0-valued cell, then $\phi_{\mathcal{B}} = \perp$; i.e., it is satisfied by no world.

Although consistency is a very important problem to be studied, we are interested also in other reasoning tasks. In particular, we should also take into account the contexts and the probabilities provided by the BN beyond the question of whether they are positive or not. In the next section we study variants of satisfiability and subsumption problems, before turning our attention to instance checking.

5 Satisfiability and Subsumption

In this section, we focus on two problems that depend only on the TBox part of an ontology, and hence assume for the sake of simplicity that the ABox is empty. Thus, we will write a $\mathcal{BALC}$ KB as a pair $(\mathcal{T}, \mathcal{B})$ where $\mathcal{T}$ is a TBox and $\mathcal{B}$ is a BN. We are in general interested in understanding the properties and relationships of concepts.

Given two concepts C, D and a $\mathcal{BALC}$ KB $\mathcal{K}$, we say that C is *satisfiable* w.r.t. $\mathcal{K}$ iff there exists a probabilistic model $\mathcal{P} = (\mathcal{J}, P_{\mathcal{J}})$ of $\mathcal{K}$ s.t. $C^{\mathcal{V}} \neq \emptyset$ for all $\mathcal{V} \in \mathcal{J}$. C is *subsumed* by D w.r.t. $\mathcal{K}$ iff for all models $\mathcal{P} = (\mathcal{J}, P_{\mathcal{J}})$ of $\mathcal{K}$ and all $\mathcal{V} \in \mathcal{J}$ $C^{\mathcal{V}} \subseteq D^{\mathcal{V}}$. It is possible to adapt the well known reductions from the classical case to show that these two problems are ExpTime-complete.

Theorem 9. *Satisfiability and subsumption w.r.t. $\mathcal{BALC}$ KBs are* ExpTime-*complete.*

Proof. Let $\mathcal{K} = (\mathcal{T}, \mathcal{B})$ and C, D be concepts. It is easy to see that C is subsumed by D w.r.t. $\mathcal{K}$ iff $\mathcal{K}' = (\mathcal{T} \cup \{(C \sqcap \neg D)(a)^{\emptyset}\}, \mathcal{B})$ is inconsistent, where a is an arbitrary individual name. Similarly, C is satisfiable iff $\mathcal{K}'' = (\mathcal{T} \cup \{C(a)^{\emptyset}\}, \mathcal{B})$ is consistent. □

In the following, we study variants of these problems. For a more concise presentation, we will present only the cases for subsumption. Analogous results hold for satisfiability based on the fact that for every $\mathcal{ALC}$ interpretation $\mathcal{I}$, it holds that $C^{\mathcal{I}} = \emptyset$ iff $C^{\mathcal{I}} \subseteq \perp^{\mathcal{I}}$. First we consider additional information about contexts; afterwards we compute the probability of an entailment, and then the combination of both.

Definition 10 (contextual subsumption). *Let $\mathcal{K} = (\mathcal{T}, \mathcal{B})$ be a $\mathcal{BALC}$ KB, C, D concepts, and κ a context. C is subsumed in context κ w.r.t. $\mathcal{K}$, denoted as $\mathcal{K} \models (C \sqsubseteq D)^{\kappa}$ if every probabilistic model of $\mathcal{K}$ is also a model of $(C \sqsubseteq D)^{\kappa}$.*

This is the natural extension of entailment to consider also the contexts. In our setting, however, contexts provide a means to express and reason with probabilities.

Definition 11 (subsumption probability). *Let $\mathcal{P} = (\mathcal{J}, P_{\mathcal{J}})$ be a probabilistic model of the KB $\mathcal{K}$, κ a context, and C, D two concepts. The probability of $(C \sqsubseteq D)^{\kappa}$ w.r.t. $\mathcal{P}$ is*

$$P_{\mathcal{P}}((C \sqsubseteq D)^{\kappa}) = \sum_{\mathcal{V} \in \mathcal{J}, \mathcal{V} \models (C \sqsubseteq D)^{\kappa}} P_{\mathcal{J}}(\mathcal{V}).$$

The probability of $(C \sqsubseteq D)^\kappa$ *w.r.t.* $\mathcal{K}$ *is*

$$P_\mathcal{K}((C \sqsubseteq D)^\kappa) = \inf_{\mathcal{P} \models \mathcal{K}} P_\mathcal{P}((C \sqsubseteq D)^\kappa).$$

C *is* positively subsumed *by* D *in* κ *iff* $P_\mathcal{K}((C \sqsubseteq D)^\kappa) > 0$; *it is* p-subsumed *iff* $P_\mathcal{K}((C \sqsubseteq D)^\kappa) \geq p$; *it is* exactly p-subsumed *iff* $P_\mathcal{K}((C \sqsubseteq D)^\kappa) = p$, *and it is* almost certainly subsumed *iff* $P_\mathcal{K}((C \sqsubseteq D)^\kappa) = 1$.

That is, the probability of a subsumption in a specific model is the sum of the probabilities of the worlds in which C is subsumed by D in context κ; notice that this trivially includes all worlds where κ does not hold. In the case where $\mathcal{K}$ is inconsistent we define the probability of all subsumptions as 1 to ensure our definition is consistent with general probability theory (recall that $\inf(\emptyset) = \infty$ in general).

Contextual subsumption is related to subsumption probability in the obvious way. Namely, a KB $\mathcal{K}$ entails a contextual subsumption iff the probability of the subsumption in $\mathcal{K}$ is 1.

Theorem 12. *Given a KB* $\mathcal{K}$, *concepts* C *and* D, *and a context* κ, *it holds that:*

$$\mathcal{K} \models (C \sqsubseteq D)^\kappa \quad \textit{iff} \quad P_\mathcal{K}((C \sqsubseteq D)^\kappa) = 1.$$

This is convenient as it provides a method of reusing our results from Sect. 4 to compute subsumption probabilities.

Theorem 13. *Let* $\mathcal{K} = (\mathcal{T}, \mathcal{B})$ *be a consistent KB,* C, D *two concepts, and* κ *a context. For the KB* $\mathcal{K}' = (\mathcal{T} \cup \{C(a)^\kappa, \neg D(a)^\kappa\}, \mathcal{B})$ *it holds that*

$$P_\mathcal{K}((C \sqsubseteq D)^\kappa) = \sum_{\omega \models \phi_{\mathcal{K}'}^\perp} P_\mathcal{B}(\omega) + 1 - P_\mathcal{B}(\kappa).$$

Notice that the formula $\phi_{\mathcal{K}'}^\perp$ requires at most exponential space on the size of $\mathcal{T}$ to be encoded. For each of the exponentially many worlds, computing $P_\mathcal{B}(\omega)$ requires polynomial time due to the chain rule. Hence, overall, the computation of the subsumption probabilities requires exponential time. Importantly, this bound does not depend on how $\phi_{\mathcal{K}'}^\perp$ was computed. This provides an exponential upper bound for computing the probability of a subsumption.

Corollary 14. *The probability of a subsumption w.r.t. a KB can be computed in exponential time on the size of the KB.*

Obviously, an exponential-time upper bound for computing the exact probability of a subsumption relation immediately yields an ExpTime upper bound for deciding the other problems introduced in Definition 11. All these problems are also generalisations of the subsumption problem in $\mathcal{ALC}$. More precisely, given an $\mathcal{ALC}$ TBox $\mathcal{T}$, we can create the $\mathcal{BALC}$ KB $\mathcal{K} = (\mathcal{T}', \mathcal{B})$ where $\mathcal{T}'$ contains all the axioms in $\mathcal{T}$ labelled with the context x and $\mathcal{B}$ contains only one Boolean node x that holds with probability 1. Given two concepts C, D $\mathcal{T} \models C \sqsubseteq D$ iff

C is almost certainly subsumed by D in context x. Since subsumption in $\mathcal{ALC}$ is already ExpTime-hard, we get that all these problems are ExpTime-complete.

In practice, however, it may be too expensive to compute the exact probability when we are only interested in determining lower bounds, or the possibility of observing an entailment; for instance, when considering positive subsumption. Notice that, according to our semantics, a contextual GCI $(C \sqsubseteq D)^\kappa$ will hold in any world ω such that $\omega \not\models \kappa$. Thus, if the probability of this world is positive $(P_\mathcal{B}(\omega) > 0)$, we can immediately guarantee that $P_\mathcal{K}((C \sqsubseteq D)^\kappa) > 0$. Thus, positive subsumption can be decided without any ontological reasoning for any context that is not almost certain. In all other cases, the problem can still be reduced to inconsistency.

Theorem 15. *The concept C is positively subsumed by D in context κ w.r.t. $\mathcal{K} = (\mathcal{T}, \mathcal{B})$ iff $\mathcal{K}' = (\mathcal{T} \cup \{C(a)^\kappa, \neg D(a)^\kappa\}, \mathcal{B})$ is inconsistent or $P_\mathcal{B}(\kappa) < 1$.*

Assuming that the KB $\mathcal{K}$ is consistent, the inconsistency in the KB $\mathcal{K}'$ from this theorem can only arise from the inclusion of the two assertions which are required to hold in context κ. If the context κ is not known before hand, it is also possible to leverage the inconsistency decision process, which is the most expensive part of this method. Let $\mathcal{K}_\emptyset := (\mathcal{T} \cup \{C(a)^\emptyset, \neg D(a)^\emptyset\}, \mathcal{B})$. That is, we extend $\mathcal{K}$ with assertions negating the subsumption relation, which should hold in all contexts. From Theorem 7 we conclude that $\phi^\perp_{\mathcal{K}_\emptyset}$ encodes all the contexts in which $C \sqsubseteq D$ must hold. Notice that the computation of $\phi^\perp_{\mathcal{K}_\emptyset}$ does not depend on the context κ but can be used to decide positive subsumption for any context.

Corollary 16. *The concept C is positively subsumed by D in context κ w.r.t. $\mathcal{K} = (\mathcal{T}, \mathcal{B})$ iff κ entails $\phi^\perp_{\mathcal{K}_\emptyset}$ or $P_\mathcal{B}(\kappa) < 1$.*

Considering the probabilities of contextual subsumption relations may lead to unexpected results arising from the contextual semantics. Indeed, it always holds (see Theorem 15) that $P_\mathcal{K}((C \sqsubseteq D)^\kappa) \geq 1 - P_\mathcal{B}(\kappa)$. In other words, the probability of a subsumption in a very unlikely context will always be very high, regardless of the KB and concepts used. In some cases, it may be more meaningful to consider a *conditional* probability under the assumption that the context κ holds.

Definition 17 (conditional subsumption). *Let $\mathcal{P} = (\mathcal{J}, P_\mathcal{J})$ be a probabilistic model of the KB $\mathcal{K}$, κ, λ two contexts with $P_\mathcal{B}(\lambda) > 0$, and C, D two concepts. The* conditional probability *of $(C \sqsubseteq D)^\kappa$ given λ w.r.t. $\mathcal{P}$ is*

$$P_\mathcal{P}((C \sqsubseteq D)^\kappa \mid \lambda) = \frac{\sum_{\mathcal{V} \in \mathcal{J}, v^\mathcal{V} \models \lambda, \mathcal{V} \models (C \sqsubseteq D)^\kappa} P_\mathcal{J}(\mathcal{V})}{P_\mathcal{B}(\lambda)}.$$

The conditional probability *of $(C \sqsubseteq D)^\kappa$ given λ w.r.t. $\mathcal{K}$ is*

$$P_\mathcal{K}((C \sqsubseteq D)^\kappa \mid \lambda) = \inf_{\mathcal{P} \models \mathcal{K}} P_\mathcal{P}((C \sqsubseteq D)^\kappa \mid \lambda).$$

This definition follows the same principles of conditioning in probability theory, but extended to the open world interpretation provided by our model-based semantics. Notice that, in addition to the scaling factor $P_B(\lambda)$ in the denominator, the nominator is also differentiated from Definition 11 by considering only the worlds that satisfy the context λ already.

Consider the numerator in the definition of conditional probabilities. Notice that it is pretty similar to Definition 11, except that the sum restricts to only the worlds that satisfy the context λ. Thus, the numerator can be obtained from the contextual probability in the context $\kappa \wedge \lambda$ excluding the worlds that violate λ. More formally, we have that

$$\sum_{\mathcal{V} \in \mathcal{J}, v^{\mathcal{V}} \models \lambda, \mathcal{V} \models (C \sqsubseteq D)^\kappa} P_{\mathcal{J}}(\mathcal{V}) = \sum_{v^{\mathcal{V}} \models \lambda, v^{\mathcal{V}} \not\models \kappa} P_{\mathcal{J}}(\mathcal{V}) + \sum_{v^{\mathcal{V}} \models \lambda \wedge \kappa, \mathcal{V} \models C \sqsubseteq D} P_{\mathcal{J}}(\mathcal{V})$$

$$= P_B(\lambda) - P_B(\lambda \wedge \kappa) + P_P((C \sqsubseteq D)^{\lambda \wedge \kappa}) - 1 + P_B(\lambda \wedge \kappa)$$

$$= P_P((C \sqsubseteq D)^{\lambda \wedge \kappa}) + P_B(\lambda) - 1.$$

Thus we get the following result.

Theorem 18. $P_K((C \sqsubseteq D)^\kappa \mid \lambda) = \frac{P_P((C \sqsubseteq D)^{\lambda \wedge \kappa}) + P_B(\lambda) - 1}{P_B(\lambda)}$.

In particular, this means that also conditional probabilities can be computed through contextual probabilities, with a small overhead of computing the probability (on the BN B) of the conditioning context λ.

As in the contextual case, if one is only interested in knowing that the subsumption is possible (that is, that it has a positive probability), then one can exploit the complex context describing the inconsistent contexts which, as mentioned before, can be precompiled to obtain the contexts in which a subsumption relation must be satisfied. However, in this case, entailment between contexts is not sufficient; one must still compute the probability of the contextual subsumption.

Corollary 19. Let $K = (\mathcal{T}, B)$ be a consistent KB, C, D concepts, and κ, λ contexts s.t. $P_B(\lambda) > 0$. $P_K((C \sqsubseteq D)^\kappa \mid \lambda) > 0$ iff $P_P((C \sqsubseteq D)^{\lambda \wedge \kappa}) > 1 - P_B(\lambda)$.

In other words, $P((C \sqsubseteq D)^\kappa \mid \lambda) > 0$ iff C is p-subsumed by D in $\kappa \wedge \lambda$ with $p = 1 - P_B(\lambda)$.

Analogously to Definitions 10, 11, and 17, it is possible to define the notions of consistency of a concept C to hold in only some contexts, and based on it, the (potentially conditional) probability of such a contextual consistency problem. As mentioned already, it is well known that for every $\mathcal{ALC}$ interpretation $\mathcal{I}$ it holds that $C^{\mathcal{I}} = \emptyset$ iff $C^{\mathcal{I}} \sqsubseteq \bot^{\mathcal{I}}$. Hence, all these problems can be solved through a direct reduction to their related subsumption problem.

We now turn our attention to the problem of instance checking. In this problem, the ABox also plays a role. Hence, we consider once again ontologies $\mathcal{O}$ that can have in addition to GCIs, concept and role assertions.

6   Instance Checking

We consider a probabilistic extension to the classical instance checking problem. In $\mathcal{BALC}$ we call this problem probabilistic instance checking and we define both a decision problem and probability calculation for it next.

Given a KB $\mathcal{K}$ and a context κ, the individual name a is an *instance* of the concept C in κ w.r.t. $\mathcal{K}$, written $\mathcal{K} \models C(a)^\kappa$, iff for all probabilistic models $\mathcal{P} = (\mathcal{J}, P_{\mathcal{J}})$ of $\mathcal{K}$ and for all $\mathcal{V} \in \mathcal{J}$ it holds that $\mathcal{V} \models C(a)^\kappa$. That is, if every interpretation in $\mathcal{P}$ satisfies the assertion $C(a)^\kappa$. Note that as before, instance checking in $\mathcal{ALC}$ is a special case of this definition, that can be obtained by considering a BN with only one variable that is true with probability 1. Notice that, contrary to the case of satisfiability studied at the end of the last section, it is not possible to reduce instance checking to subsumption since an instance may be caused by ABox assertions. However, it may be reduced to consistency.

Theorem 20. *Given $a \in N_I$, a concept C, a context κ, and a KB $\mathcal{K} = (\mathcal{O}, \mathcal{B})$, $\mathcal{K} \models C(a)^\kappa$ iff the KB $\mathcal{K}' = (\mathcal{O} \cup \{(\neg C(a))^\kappa\}, \mathcal{B})$ is inconsistent.*

In particular, this means that instance checking is at most as hard as deciding consistency. As mentioned already, it is also at least as hard as instance checking in the classical $\mathcal{ALC}$. Hence we get the following result.

Lemma 21. *Instance checking in a $\mathcal{BALC}$ KB is* ExpTime-*complete.*

Let us now consider the probabilistic entailments related to instance checking.

Definition 22 (instance probability). *The* probability of an instance *in a probabilistic model $\mathcal{P} = (\mathcal{J}, P_{\mathcal{J}})$ of the KB $\mathcal{K}$ is*

$$P_{\mathcal{P}}(C(x)^\kappa) = \sum_{\mathcal{V} \in \mathcal{J}, \mathcal{V} \models C(x)^\kappa} P_{\mathcal{J}}(\mathcal{V}).$$

The instance probability *w.r.t. a KB $\mathcal{K}$ is*

$$P_{\mathcal{K}}(C(x)^\kappa) = \inf_{\mathcal{P} \models \mathcal{K}} P_{\mathcal{P}}(C(x)^\kappa).$$

The conditional probability *of an instance in a particular probabilistic model $\mathcal{P} = (\mathcal{J}, P_{\mathcal{J}})$ is*

$$P_{\mathcal{P}}(C(x)^\kappa \mid \lambda) = \frac{\sum_{\mathcal{V} \in \mathcal{J}, v^{\mathcal{V}} \models \lambda, \mathcal{V} \models C(x)^\kappa} P_{\mathcal{J}}(\mathcal{V})}{P_{\mathcal{B}}(\lambda)},$$

The probability of the conditional instance *in $\mathcal{K}$ is:*

$$P_{\mathcal{K}}(C(x)^\kappa \mid \lambda) = \inf_{\mathcal{P} \models \mathcal{K}} P_{\mathcal{P}}(C(x)^\kappa \mid \lambda)$$

The probability of all instance checks for an inconsistent KB is always 1 to keep our definitions consistent with probability theory.

As we did for subsumption, we can exploit the reasoning techniques for deciding inconsistency of a $\mathcal{BALC}$ KB to find out the contextual and conditional probabilities of an instance. Moreover, the method can be further optimised in the cases where we are only interested in probabilistic bounds. In particular, we can adapt Theorem 18 to this case.

Theorem 23. $P_{\mathcal{K}}(C(x)^{\kappa} \mid \lambda) = \frac{P_{\mathcal{K}}(C(x)^{\kappa \wedge \lambda}) + P_{\mathcal{B}}(\lambda) - 1}{P(\lambda)}.$

7   Conclusions

We have presented a new probabilistic extension of the DL $\mathcal{ALC}$ based on the ideas of Bayesian ontology languages, in which certain knowledge is dependent on the uncertain context where it holds. Our work extends the results on $\mathcal{BEL}$ [9,10] to a propositionally closed ontology language. The main notions follow the basic ideas of Bayesian ontology languages [11]; however, by focusing on a specific logic, we are able to produce a tableaux-based decision algorithm for KB consistency, in contrast to the generic black-box algorithms proposed in the literature. Our algorithm extends the classical tableau algorithm for $\mathcal{ALC}$ with techniques originally developed for axiom pinpointing. The main differences are the use of multi-valued variables in the definition of the contexts, and the possibility of having complex contexts (not only unique variables) labeling individual axioms. In general, we have shown that adding context-based uncertainty to an ontology does not increase the complexity of reasoning in this logic: all (probabilistic) reasoning problems can still be solved in exponential time.

Theorems 6, 7 and 8 yield an effective decision method $\mathcal{BALC}$ KB consistency, through the computation and handling of two complex contexts. Notice that $\phi_{\mathcal{B}}$ can be computed in linear time on the size of $\mathcal{B}$, and satisfiability of the context $\phi_{\mathcal{K}}^{\perp} \wedge \phi_{\mathcal{B}}$ can be checked in non-deterministic polynomial time in the size of this context. However, the tableau algorithm for computing $\phi_{\mathcal{K}}^{\perp}$ is not optimal w.r.t. worst-case complexity. In fact, in the worst case it requires double exponential time, although the formula itself is only of exponential size. The benefit of this method, as in the classical case, is that it provides a better behaviour in the average case. To further improve the efficiency of our approach, one can think of adapting the methods from [21] to construct a compact representation of the context—akin to a binary decision diagram (BDD) [7,14] for multi-valued variables—allowing for efficient weighted model counting. A task for future work is to exploit these data structures for practical development of our methods.

Recall that the most expensive part of our approach is the computation of the context $\phi_{\mathcal{K}}^{\perp}$. By slightly modifying the KB, we have shown that one computation of this context suffices to solve different problems of interest; in particular, contextual and conditional entailments—being subsumption, satisfiability, or instance checking—can be solved using $\phi_{\mathcal{K}'}^{\perp}$, for an adequately constructed $\mathcal{K}'$, regardless of the contexts under consideration.

An important next step will be to implement the methods described here, and compare the efficiency of our system to other probabilistic DL reasoners based on similar semantics. In particular, we would like to compare against the tools from [21]. Even though this latter system is also based on an extension of the tableaux algorithm for DLs, and use multiple-world semantics closely related to ours, a direct comparison would be unfair. Indeed, [21] makes use of stronger independence assumptions than ours. However, a well-designed experiment can shed light on the advantages and disadvantages of each method.

Another interesting problem for future work is to extend the query language beyond instance queries. To maintain some efficiency, this may require some additional restrictions on the language or the probabilistic structure. A more detailed study of this issue is needed.

References

1. Baader, F., Calvanese, D., McGuinness, D., Nardi, D., Patel-Schneider, P. (eds.): The Description Logic Handbook: Theory, Implementation, and Applications, 2nd edn. Cambridge University Press, Cambridge (2007)
2. Baader, F., Hollunder, B.: Embedding defaults into terminological knowledge representation formalisms. J. Autom. Reasoning **14**(1), 149–180 (1995). https://doi.org/10.1007/BF00883932
3. Baader, F., Peñaloza, R.: Axiom pinpointing in general tableaux. In: Olivetti, N. (ed.) TABLEAUX 2007. LNCS (LNAI), vol. 4548, pp. 11–27. Springer, Heidelberg (2007). https://doi.org/10.1007/978-3-540-73099-6_4
4. Baader, F., Peñaloza, R.: Axiom pinpointing in general tableaux. J. Logic Comput. **20**(1), 5–34 (2010). https://doi.org/10.1093/logcom/exn058. Special issue: Tableaux and analytic proof methods
5. Botha, L.: The Bayesian description logic ALC. Master's thesis, University of Cape Town, South Africa (2018)
6. Botha, L., Meyer, T., Peñaloza, R.: The Bayesian description logic BALC. In: Ortiz, M., Schneider, T. (eds.) Proceedings of the 31st International Workshop on Description Logics (DL 2018), CEUR Workshop Proceedings, vol. 2211. CEUR-WS.org (2018). http://ceur-ws.org/Vol-2211/paper-09.pdf
7. Brace, K.S., Rudell, R.L., Bryant, R.E.: Efficient implementation of a BDD package. In: Proceedings of the 27th ACM/IEEE Design Automation Conference, DAC 1990, pp. 40–45. ACM, New York (1990). https://doi.org/10.1145/123186.123222
8. Ceylan, İ.İ.: Query answering in probabilistic data and knowledge bases. Ph.D. thesis, Dresden University of Technology, Germany (2018)
9. Ceylan, İ.İ., Peñaloza, R.: The Bayesian description logic $\mathcal{BEL}$. In: Demri, S., Kapur, D., Weidenbach, C. (eds.) IJCAR 2014. LNCS (LNAI), vol. 8562, pp. 480–494. Springer, Cham (2014). https://doi.org/10.1007/978-3-319-08587-6_37
10. Ceylan, İ.İ., Peñaloza, R.: Tight complexity bounds for reasoning in the description logic $\mathcal{BEL}$. In: Fermé, E., Leite, J. (eds.) JELIA 2014. LNCS (LNAI), vol. 8761, pp. 77–91. Springer, Cham (2014). https://doi.org/10.1007/978-3-319-11558-0_6
11. Ceylan, İ.İ., Peñaloza, R.: The Bayesian ontology language BEL. J. Autom. Reasoning **58**(1), 67–95 (2017). https://doi.org/10.1007/s10817-016-9386-0

12. d'Amato, C., Fanizzi, N., Lukasiewicz, T.: Tractable reasoning with bayesian description logics. In: Greco, S., Lukasiewicz, T. (eds.) SUM 2008. LNCS (LNAI), vol. 5291, pp. 146–159. Springer, Heidelberg (2008). https://doi.org/10.1007/978-3-540-87993-0_13

13. Gottlob, G., Lukasiewicz, T., Simari, G.I.: Answering threshold queries in probabilistic datalog+/– ontologies. In: Benferhat, S., Grant, J. (eds.) SUM 2011. LNCS (LNAI), vol. 6929, pp. 401–414. Springer, Heidelberg (2011). https://doi.org/10.1007/978-3-642-23963-2_31

14. Lee, C.Y.: Representation of switching circuits by binary-decision programs. Bell Syst. Tech. J. **38**, 985–999 (1959)

15. Lee, K., Meyer, T.A., Pan, J.Z., Booth, R.: Computing maximally satisfiable terminologies for the description logic ALC with cyclic definitions. In: Parsia, B., Sattler, U., Toman, D. (eds.) Proceedings of the 2006 International Workshop on Description Logics (DL 2006), CEUR Workshop Proceedings, vol. 189. CEUR-WS.org (2006). http://ceur-ws.org/Vol-189/submission_29.pdf

16. Lukasiewicz, T., Straccia, U.: Managing uncertainty and vagueness in description logics for the semantic web. J. Web Semant. **6**(4), 291–308 (2008). https://doi.org/10.1016/j.websem.2008.04.001

17. Meyer, T.A., Lee, K., Booth, R., Pan, J.Z.: Finding maximally satisfiable terminologies for the description logic ALC. In: Proceedings of the Twenty-First National Conference on Artificial Intelligence and the Eighteenth Innovative Applications of Artificial Intelligence Conference, pp. 269–274. AAAI Press (2006). http://www.aaai.org/Library/AAAI/2006/aaai06-043.php

18. Pearl, J.: Bayesian networks: a model of self-activated memory for evidential reasoning. In: Proceedings of Cognitive Science Society (CSS-7), pp. 329–334 (1985)

19. Peñaloza, R.: Axiom-pinpointing in description logics and beyond. Ph.D. thesis, Dresden University of Technology, Germany (2009)

20. Schmidt-Schauß, M., Smolka, G.: Attributive concept descriptions with complements. Artif. Intell. **48**(1), 1–26 (1991). https://doi.org/10.1016/0004-3702(91)90078-X

21. Zese, R., Bellodi, E., Riguzzi, F., Cota, G., Lamma, E.: Tableau reasoning for description logics and its extension to probabilities. Ann. Math. Artif. Intell. **82**(1–3), 101–130 (2018). https://doi.org/10.1007/s10472-016-9529-3

Computing Minimal Projection Modules for $\mathcal{ELH}^r$-Terminologies

Jieying Chen[1(✉)] , Michel Ludwig[2] , Yue Ma[1] , and Dirk Walther[3]

[1] Laboratoire de Recherche en Informatique, Université Paris-Saclay, Paris, France
{jieying.chen,yue.ma}@lri.fr
[2] Beaufort, Luxembourg
michel.ludwig@gmail.com
[3] Fraunhofer IVI, Dresden, Germany
dirk.walther@ivi.fraunhofer.de

Abstract. For the development of large-scale representations of knowledge, the application of methodologies and design principles becomes relevant. The knowledge may be organized in ontologies in a modular and hierarchical fashion. An upper-level (reference) ontology typically provides specifications of requirements, functions, design or standards that are to be complied with by domain ontologies for a specific task on a lower level (task ontology) in the hierarchy. Verifying whether and how specifications have been implemented by a task ontology becomes a challenge when relevant axioms of the domain ontology need to be inspected. We consider specifications to be defined using entailments of certain queries over a given vocabulary. For selecting the relevant axioms from task ontologies, we propose a novel module notion called *projection module* that entails the queries that follow from a reference ontology. We develop algorithms for computing minimal projection modules of Description Logic terminologies for subsumption, instance and conjunctive queries.

1 Introduction

A common practice in the area of the Semantic Web is to reuse and extend existing ontologies for a specific task. Therefore, an approach to comparing multiple ontologies is often desired. In this paper, we propose the notion of *projection module* which characterizes the relative knowledge of an ontology, say, an ontology developed for a specific task (called *task ontology*), by taking another ontology as a reference (called *reference ontology*), e.g. an upper-level ontology. This can thus lead to (1) a method for comparing the entailment capacities of any two ontologies about a given vocabulary of interest, and (2) a fine-grained ontology comparison measurement between two ontologies.

As illustrated in Fig. 1, for a user interest expressed as a set Σ of concept and role names, the reference ontology $\mathcal{T}_1$ (resp. task ontology $\mathcal{T}_2$) contains

---

This work is partially funded by the ANR project GoAsQ (ANR-15-CE23-0022).

F. Calimeri et al. (Eds.): JELIA 2019, LNAI 11468, pp. 355–370, 2019.
https://doi.org/10.1007/978-3-030-19570-0_23

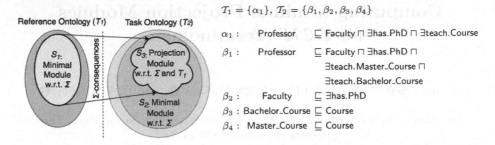

$T_1 = \{\alpha_1\}$, $T_2 = \{\beta_1, \beta_2, \beta_3, \beta_4\}$

α_1 :   Professor   ⊑ Faculty ⊓ ∃has.PhD ⊓ ∃teach.Course

β_1 :   Professor   ⊑ Faculty ⊓ ∃has.PhD ⊓
                                    ∃teach.Master_Course ⊓
                                    ∃teach.Bachelor_Course

β_2 :   Faculty   ⊑ ∃has.PhD

β_3 : Bachelor_Course ⊑ Course

β_4 : Master_Course ⊑ Course

Fig. 1. Projection module   **Fig. 2.** Example: minimal projection modules

S_1 (resp. S_2) as a sub-ontology, e.g., a minimal module [9,10], that provides a minimal number of axioms entailing all Σ-consequences. A projection module, on the other hand, additionally takes a reference ontology into account as to preserve the relevant Σ-knowledge only, which can yield an even smaller module S_3 of T_2. Figure 2 shows a concrete example with T_1 being the upper-level (reference) ontology modelling aspects of a university domain, and a task ontology T_2 as an extended and modified version of T_1. Consider the signature Σ = {Professor, Faculty, has, PhD, teach, Course} (consisting of the symbols marked in blue in Fig. 2). Then T_1 has merely one module $S_1 = \{\alpha_1\}$ that preserves T_1's knowledge about Σ. When extracting modules of T_2 for Σ, we obtain T_2 itself using existent module notions such as modules based on locality [14] or the module extracted by MEX [20]. Here we have two candidates for a minimal module S_2 of T_2 that each preserve all inclusions over Σ: $\{\beta_1, \beta_2, \beta_3\}$ and $\{\beta_1, \beta_2, \beta_4\}$ [9]. The projection modules of T_2, however, preserving the Σ-inclusions entailed by T_1 are even smaller with $S_3 = \{\beta_1, \beta_3\}$ or $S_3 = \{\beta_1, \beta_4\}$. Every projection module S_3 is a strict subset of a minimal module of T_2, which is in line with the fact that the task ontology T_2 has extended the reference ontology T_1 with new Σ-consequences, e.g., Faculty ⊑ ∃has.PhD.

Various approaches to comparing ontologies have been suggested, including ontology matching [13] and logical difference [22–24,26]. Ontology matching is the process of determining correspondences, e.g., the subsumption relations between two concept or role names from different ontologies, for which a good concept similarity [1,25] is often helpful. In contrast, logical difference focuses on the comparison of entailed logical consequences from each ontology and returns difference witnesses if differences are present. When an ontology has no logical difference compared to another one, our approach further extracts sub-ontologies of the first that contain the knowledge as represented by the second ontology.

Ontology modularity [9,18,22,24,27,28] is about the extraction of sub-ontologies that preserve all logical consequences over a signature. The proposed projection module is different from modules of a single ontology, as illustrated by the example in Fig. 2. To compute projection modules, in this paper, we generalize the notion of justification to the notion of *subsumption justification* as a minimal set of axioms that maintains the entailment of a consequence. Our algorithm employs the classical notion of justification to compute subsumption justifications. Currently, the approaches for computing all justifications of an ontology for a consequence can be classified into two categories: "glass-box" [2,5,16,17] and "black-box" [11,16,29].

We proceed as follows. After reviewing some preliminaries in Sect. 2, the notion of a minimal project module for subsumption, instance and conjunctive queries is introduced in Sect. 3. In Sect. 4, we introduce the algorithm for computing minimal projection modules. In Sect. 5, two applications of minimal projection modules are presented. Finally, we close the paper with a conclusion in Sect. 6.

2 Preliminaries

We start by reviewing the description logic $\mathcal{EL}$ and several of its extensions.

Let N_C, N_R and N_I be mutually disjoint and countably infinite sets of concept names, role names and instance names. The signature $\mathrm{sig}(\xi)$ is the set of concept and role names occurring in ξ, where ξ ranges over any syntactic object. The sets of $\mathcal{EL}$ -concepts C, $\mathcal{EL}^{\mathsf{ran}}$ -concepts D, $\mathcal{EL}^{\sqcap}$ -concepts E, and $\mathcal{EL}^{\sqcap,u}$ -concepts F, and the sets of $\mathcal{ELH}^r$ -inclusions α, $\mathcal{EL}^{\mathsf{ran}}$ -inclusions β and $\mathcal{EL}^{\mathsf{ran},\sqcap,u}$ -inclusions γ are built according to the grammar rules:

$$
\begin{aligned}
C &::= A \mid C \sqcap C \mid \exists r.C \mid \mathsf{dom}(r) \\
D &::= A \mid D \sqcap D \mid \exists r.D \mid \mathsf{dom}(r) \mid \mathsf{ran}(r) \\
E &::= A \mid E \sqcap F \mid \exists R.E \\
F &::= A \mid F \sqcap F \mid \exists R.F \mid \exists u.F \\
\alpha &::= C \sqsubseteq C \mid \mathsf{ran}(r) \sqsubseteq C \mid \mathsf{ran}(r) \sqcap C \sqsubseteq C \mid C \equiv C \mid r \sqsubseteq s \\
\beta &::= D \sqsubseteq C \mid r \sqsubseteq s \\
\gamma &::= D \sqsubseteq F \mid r \sqsubseteq s
\end{aligned}
$$

where $A \in N_C$, $r, s \in N_R$, u is a fresh logical symbol (the *universal role*) and $R = r_1 \sqcap \ldots \sqcap r_n$ with $r_1, ..., r_n \in N_R$, for $n \geq 1$. We refer to inclusions also as *axioms*. A Γ-*TBox* is a finite set of Γ-inclusions, where Γ ranges over the sets of $\mathcal{ELH}^r$- and $\mathcal{EL}^{\mathsf{ran},\sqcap,u}$-inclusions. We use $\mathrm{lhs}(\alpha)$ (resp. $\mathrm{rhs}(\alpha)$) to represent the left-hand side (resp. right-hand side) of an inclusion α.

The semantics is defined as usual in terms of interpretations interpreting concept/role names as unary/binary relations and are then inductively extended to complex concepts. The notions of satisfaction of a concept, axiom and TBox as well as the notions of a model and the logical consequence relation are defined as usual [4].

An $\mathcal{ELH}^r$ -*terminology* $\mathcal{T}$ is an $\mathcal{ELH}^r$-TBox consisting of axioms α of the form $A \sqsubseteq C$, $A \equiv C$, $r \sqsubseteq s$, $\mathsf{ran}(r) \sqsubseteq C$ or $\mathsf{dom}(r) \sqsubseteq C$, where A is a concept name, C an $\mathcal{EL}$-concept and no concept name occurs more than once on the left-hand side of an axiom. To simplify the presentation we assume that terminologies do not contain axioms of the form $A \equiv B$ or $A \equiv \top$ (after having removed multiple $\top$-conjuncts) for concept names A and B. For a terminology $\mathcal{T}$, let $\prec_{\mathcal{T}}$ be a binary relation over N_C satisfying that $A \prec_{\mathcal{T}} B$ iff there is an axiom of the form

$A \sqsubseteq C$ or $A \equiv C$ in $\mathcal{T}$ such that $B \in \text{sig}(C)$. A terminology $\mathcal{T}$ is *acyclic* if the transitive closure $\prec_{\mathcal{T}}^+$ of $\prec_{\mathcal{T}}$ is irreflexive; otherwise $\mathcal{T}$ is *cyclic*. We say that a concept name A is *conjunctive in* $\mathcal{T}$ iff there exist concept names $B_1, \ldots, B_n$, $n > 0$, such that $A \equiv B_1 \sqcap \ldots \sqcap B_n \in \mathcal{T}$; otherwise A is said to be *non-conjunctive in* $\mathcal{T}$. An $\mathcal{ELH}^r$-terminology $\mathcal{T}$ is *normalised* iff it only contains axioms of the forms

- $r \sqsubseteq s$, $\varphi \sqsubseteq B_1 \sqcap \ldots \sqcap B_n$, $A \sqsubseteq \exists r.B$, $A \sqsubseteq \text{dom}(r)$, and
- $A \equiv B_1 \sqcap \ldots \sqcap B_m$, $A \equiv \exists r.B$,

where $\varphi \in \{A, \text{dom}(s), \text{ran}(s)\}$, $n \geq 1$, $m \geq 2$, $A, B, B_i \in \mathsf{N_C}$, $r, s \in \mathsf{N_R}$, and each conjunct B_i is non-conjunctive in $\mathcal{T}$. Every $\mathcal{ELH}^r$-terminology $\mathcal{T}$ can be normalised in polynomial time such that the resulting terminology is a conservative extension of $\mathcal{T}$ [19]. A subset $M \subseteq \mathcal{T}$ is called a *justification for an $\mathcal{ELH}$ -concept inclusion* α *from* $\mathcal{T}$ iff $M \models \alpha$ and $M' \not\models \alpha$ for every $M' \subsetneq M$.

We denote the set of all justifications for an $\mathcal{ELH}$-concept inclusion α from an $\mathcal{ELH}$-terminology $\mathcal{T}$ with $\text{Just}_{\mathcal{T}}(\alpha)$. The latter may contain exponentially many justifications in the number of axioms in $\mathcal{T}$. An ABox contains *assertions* of the form $\top(a)$, $A(a)$ and $r(a,b)$, where $a, b \in \mathsf{N_I}$ and $r \in \mathsf{N_R}$. An *ABox* consists of finitely many ABox assertions.

Let $\mathsf{N_I}$ and $\mathsf{N_V}$ be disjoint sets of individual and variable names. A conjunctive query is a first-order formula built according to the following format: $\exists y_1 \ldots \exists y_n. \bigwedge_{i \in I_1} A_i(s_i) \wedge \bigwedge_{j \in I_2} r_j(t_j, t_j')$, where $y_1, \ldots, y_n \in \mathsf{N_V}$ for $n \geq 1$ are variable names, I_1, I_2 are finite sets of indices, and for $i \in I_1$ and $j \in I_2$, A_i ranges over concept names in $\mathsf{N_C}$, r_j ranges over role names in $\mathsf{N_R}$, and s_i, t_j, t_j' range over individual and variable names in $\mathsf{N_I} \cup \mathsf{N_V}$.

A signature Σ is a finite set of symbols from $\mathsf{N_C}$ and $\mathsf{N_R}$. The symbol Σ is used as a subscript to sets of concepts or inclusions to denote that the elements only use symbols from Σ, e.g., $\mathcal{ELH}^r_{\Sigma}$ and $\mathcal{EL}^{\text{ran},\sqcap,u}_{\Sigma}$. For a signature Σ, let $\Sigma^{\text{dom}} = \{\text{dom}(r) \mid r \in \mathsf{N_R} \cap \Sigma\}$ and $\Sigma^{\text{ran}} = \{\text{ran}(r) \mid r \in \mathsf{N_R} \cap \Sigma\}$ be the sets consisting of concepts of the form $\text{dom}(r)$ and $\text{ran}(r)$ for every role name r in Σ, respectively. We recall the notion of logical difference for concept subsumption queries, instance queries and conjunctive queries from [19,23]. For a more detailed introduction to description logics, we refer to [3,4]. For latest results on logical inseparability see [7,8,15], and for a survey on query inseparability, see [6].

Definition 1 (Logical Difference). *The $\mathcal{L}$-subsumption query difference, for some logic $\mathcal{L}$, the instance and conjunctive query difference between $\mathcal{T}_1$ and $\mathcal{T}_2$ w.r.t. Σ are the sets $\text{cDiff}^{\mathcal{L}}_{\Sigma}(\mathcal{T}_1, \mathcal{T}_2)$, $\text{iDiff}_{\Sigma}(\mathcal{T}_1, \mathcal{T}_2)$, and $\text{qDiff}_{\Sigma}(\mathcal{T}_1, \mathcal{T}_2)$, respectively, where*

- $\varphi \in \text{cDiff}^{\mathcal{L}}_{\Sigma}(\mathcal{T}_1, \mathcal{T}_2)$ *iff φ is an $\mathcal{L}$-inclusion, $\mathcal{T}_1 \models \varphi$ and $\mathcal{T}_2 \not\models \varphi$;*
- $(\mathcal{A}, \lambda) \in \text{iDiff}_{\Sigma}(\mathcal{T}_1, \mathcal{T}_2)$ *iff $\mathcal{A}$ is a Σ-ABox and λ a Σ-instance assertion such that $(\mathcal{T}_1, \mathcal{A}) \models \lambda$ and $(\mathcal{T}_2, \mathcal{A}) \not\models \lambda$;*
- $(\mathcal{A}, q(\boldsymbol{a})) \in \text{qDiff}_{\Sigma}(\mathcal{T}_1, \mathcal{T}_2)$ *iff $\mathcal{A}$ is a Σ-ABox and $q(\boldsymbol{a})$ a Σ-conjunctive query such that $(\mathcal{T}_1, \mathcal{A}) \models q(\boldsymbol{a})$ and $(\mathcal{T}_2, \mathcal{A}) \not\models q(\boldsymbol{a})$.*

According to [19], $\mathcal{L}$-subsumption queries for $\mathcal{L} = \mathcal{EL}^{\mathrm{ran}}$ and $\mathcal{L} = \mathcal{EL}^{\mathrm{ran},\sqcap,u}$ are sufficient to detect the absence of any instance query and conjunctive query differences, respectively. Therefore, we only consider how to detect $\mathcal{L}$-subsumption queries for $\mathcal{L} = \{\mathcal{ELH}^r, \mathcal{EL}^{\mathrm{ran}}, \mathcal{EL}^{\mathrm{ran},\sqcap,u}\}$. Let $\alpha_\Sigma^\mathcal{L}$ be an $\mathcal{L}$-inclusion that only uses symbols in Σ. We organise the Σ-symbols (and the domain and range concepts over role names from Σ) that occur as "witnesses" of a $\mathcal{L}$-subsumption query difference between $\mathcal{T}_1$ and $\mathcal{T}_2$ as follows:

$$\mathsf{Wtn}_\Sigma^\mathcal{L}(\mathcal{T}_1, \mathcal{T}_2) := (\mathsf{roleWtn}_\Sigma^\mathcal{L}(\mathcal{T}_1, \mathcal{T}_2), \mathsf{lhsWtn}_\Sigma^\mathcal{L}(\mathcal{T}_1, \mathcal{T}_2), \mathsf{rhsWtn}_\Sigma^\mathcal{L}(\mathcal{T}_1, \mathcal{T}_2)),$$

where $\mathsf{roleWtn}_\Sigma^\mathcal{L}(\mathcal{T}_1, \mathcal{T}_2) = \{\, r \in \Sigma \cap \mathsf{N_R} \mid r \sqsubseteq s \text{ or } s \sqsubseteq r \in \mathsf{cDiff}_\Sigma^\mathcal{L}(\mathcal{T}_1, \mathcal{T}_2)\,\}$, $\mathsf{lhsWtn}_\Sigma^\mathcal{L}(\mathcal{T}_1, \mathcal{T}_2) = \{\, \varphi \in (\Sigma \cap \mathsf{N_C}) \cup \Sigma^{\mathrm{dom}} \cup \Sigma^{\mathrm{ran}} \mid \varphi \sqsubseteq \mathrm{rhs}(\alpha_\Sigma^\mathcal{L}) \text{ and } \alpha \text{ is a } \mathcal{L}_\Sigma - \text{inclusion}\}$ and $\mathsf{rhsWtn}_\Sigma^\mathcal{L}(\mathcal{T}_1, \mathcal{T}_2) = \{\, A \in \Sigma \cap \mathsf{N_C} \mid \mathrm{lhs}(\alpha_\Sigma^\mathcal{L}) \sqsubseteq A \in \mathsf{cDiff}_\Sigma^Q(\mathcal{T}_1, \mathcal{T}_2)\,\}$. The set $\mathsf{Wtn}_\Sigma^\mathcal{L}(\mathcal{T}_1, \mathcal{T}_2)$ can be seen as a finite representation of the set $\mathsf{cDiff}_\Sigma^\mathcal{L}(\mathcal{T}_1, \mathcal{T}_2)$, which is typically infinite when it is not empty. It follows from the "primitive witnesses" theorems in [19] that $\mathsf{cDiff}_\Sigma^\mathcal{L}(\mathcal{T}_1, \mathcal{T}_2) = \emptyset$ iff $\mathsf{Wtn}_\Sigma^\mathcal{L}(\mathcal{T}_1, \mathcal{T}_2) = (\emptyset, \emptyset, \emptyset)$. Thus, deciding the existence of logical differences is equivalent to decide non-emptiness of the three witness sets.

3   Projection Modules

To understand the relations among different ontologies, we introduce the notion of projection module, as a way to explain how the knowledge that is encoded in a reference ontology is implemented in a task ontology. We are interested in computing *all* projection modules, since it provides a complete list of all implementations of an ontology regarding a reference, each of which may be necessary to be checked. To enable a manual validation by domain experts, we need to present only necessary information, so we focus on computing *minimal* projection modules.

A terminology $\mathcal{T}_1$ together with a signature Σ and a type of query Q determine a set Φ of queries from Q formulated using only symbols from Σ that follow from $\mathcal{T}_1$. A projection module of another terminology $\mathcal{T}_2$ is a subset of $\mathcal{T}_2$ that entails the queries in Φ. For convenience, we bundle the parameters together in a tuple $\rho = \langle \mathcal{T}_1, \Sigma, \mathcal{T}_2 \rangle$, which we call a *projection setting*.

Definition 2 (Projection Module). *Let $\rho = \langle \mathcal{T}_1, \Sigma, \mathcal{T}_2 \rangle$ be a projection setting, $\mathcal{A}$ be a Σ-ABox. A subset $\mathcal{M} \subseteq \mathcal{T}_2$ is a subsumption (resp. instance, conjunctive) query projection module under projection setting ρ, denoted as $\mathcal{M}_\rho^c$ (resp. $\mathcal{M}_\rho^i$, $\mathcal{M}_\rho^q$) iff:*

- *$\mathcal{M}_\rho^c$: for each $\mathcal{ELH}_\Sigma^r$-inclusion α, if $\mathcal{T}_1 \models \alpha$, then $\mathcal{M} \models \alpha$;*
- *$\mathcal{M}_\rho^i$: for each Σ-instance assertion λ, if $(\mathcal{T}_1, \mathcal{A}) \models \lambda$, then $(\mathcal{M}, \mathcal{A}) \models \lambda$;*
- *$\mathcal{M}_\rho^q$: for each $q(\boldsymbol{a})$, if $(\mathcal{T}_1, \mathcal{A}) \models q(\boldsymbol{a})$, then $(\mathcal{M}, \mathcal{A}) \models q(\boldsymbol{a})$, where $\boldsymbol{a}$ is a tuple of individual names from $\mathcal{A}$ and $q(\boldsymbol{a})$ is a Σ-conjunctive query.*

A *minimal subsumption (resp. instance, conjunctive) query projection module is a projection module* $\mathcal{M}_\rho^c$ *(resp.* $\mathcal{M}_\rho^i, \mathcal{M}_\rho^q$*) minimal w.r.t.* $\subsetneq$.

Note that there may exist several, even exponentially many minimal projection modules. It can readily be checked that $\mathsf{cDiff}_\Sigma^{\mathcal{L}}(\mathcal{T}_1, \mathcal{M}_\rho^c) = \emptyset$, for $\mathcal{L} = \mathcal{ELH}^r$, $\mathsf{iDiff}_\Sigma(\mathcal{T}_1, \mathcal{M}_\rho^i) = \emptyset$ and $\mathsf{qDiff}_\Sigma(\mathcal{T}_1, \mathcal{M}_\rho^q) = \emptyset$ (cf. Definition 1).

Example 1. Suppose $\mathcal{T}_1 = \{A_1 \sqsubseteq A_2, A_2 \sqsubseteq A_3\}$, $\mathcal{T}_2 = \{A_1 \sqsubseteq A_3 \sqcap B_1, B_1 \sqsubseteq \exists r.A_3\}$, and the interested vocabulary $\Sigma = \{A_1, A_3, r\}$. $\mathcal{T}_2$ has no logical difference from $\mathcal{T}_1$. However, the concept project module of $\mathcal{T}_2$ with respect to $\mathcal{T}_1$ and Σ is $\{A_1 \sqsubseteq A_3 \sqcap B_1\} \subsetneq \mathcal{T}_2$. This means that a strict sub-ontology of $\mathcal{T}_2$ is sufficient to capture all the information of $\mathcal{T}_1$ about Σ. Moreover, $\mathcal{T}_2$ also entails a consequence $A_1 \sqsubseteq \exists r.A_3$, which is not the case for $\mathcal{T}_1$.

The following example shows that the three notions of projection modules based on different query languages are distinct.

Example 2. Let $\mathcal{T} = \{X \sqsubseteq Y, Y \sqsubseteq \exists t.Z, \mathsf{ran}(r) \sqsubseteq A_1, \mathsf{ran}(s) \sqsubseteq A_2, B \equiv A_1 \sqcap A_2\}$, $\Sigma = \{X, Y, Z, B, r, s\}$, and $\rho = \langle \mathcal{T}, \sigma, \mathcal{T} \rangle$. We have that $\mathcal{M}_\rho^c = \{X \sqsubseteq Y\}$, $\mathcal{M}_\rho^i = \mathcal{M}_\rho^c \cup \{\mathsf{ran}(r) \sqsubseteq A_1, \mathsf{ran}(s) \sqsubseteq A_2, B \equiv A_1 \sqcap A_2\}$ and $\mathcal{M}_\rho^q = \mathcal{T}$.

Definition 3. *Let* $Q \in \{c, i, q\}$. *The relationship between* $\mathcal{T}_1$ *and* $\mathcal{T}_2$ *is a* $\langle \Sigma, Q \rangle$-*implementation, denoted* $\mathcal{T}_1 \leadsto_\Sigma^Q \mathcal{T}_2$, *iff there exists a projection module* $\mathcal{M}_\rho^Q$ *under the setting* $\rho = \langle \mathcal{T}_1, \Sigma, \mathcal{T}_2 \rangle$.

If $\mathcal{T}_1 \leadsto_\Sigma^Q \mathcal{T}_2$, we also say that $\mathcal{T}_2 \langle \Sigma, Q \rangle$-implements $\mathcal{T}_1$. In case $\mathcal{T}_1$ and $\mathcal{T}_2 \langle \Sigma, Q \rangle$-implement each other, they cannot be separated using the query language Q.

Proposition 1. *Let* $\mathcal{T}_1 \leadsto_\Sigma^Q \mathcal{T}_2$ *and* $\mathcal{T}_2 \leadsto_\Sigma^Q \mathcal{T}_1$. *Then:*

- $Q = c$: $\mathsf{cDiff}_\Sigma^{\mathcal{L}}(\mathcal{T}_1, \mathcal{T}_2) = \mathsf{cDiff}_\Sigma^{\mathcal{L}}(\mathcal{T}_2, \mathcal{T}_1) = \emptyset$, *for* $\mathcal{L} = \mathcal{ELH}^r$;
- $Q = i$: $\mathsf{iDiff}_\Sigma(\mathcal{T}_1, \mathcal{T}_2) = \mathsf{iDiff}_\Sigma(\mathcal{T}_2, \mathcal{T}_1) = \emptyset$; *and*
- $Q = q$: $\mathsf{qDiff}_\Sigma(\mathcal{T}_1, \mathcal{T}_2) = \mathsf{qDiff}_\Sigma(\mathcal{T}_2, \mathcal{T}_1) = \emptyset$.

We obtain the following monotonicity properties of the $\langle \Sigma, Q \rangle$-implementation relation.

Proposition 2 (Implementation Monotonicity).

(i) If $\mathcal{T}_2 \subseteq \mathcal{T}_3$ and $\mathcal{T}_1 \leadsto_\Sigma^Q \mathcal{T}_2$, then $\mathcal{T}_1 \leadsto_\Sigma^Q \mathcal{T}_3$;
(ii) If $\mathcal{T}_1 \subseteq \mathcal{T}_2$ and $\mathcal{T}_2 \leadsto_\Sigma^Q \mathcal{T}_3$, then $\mathcal{T}_1 \leadsto_\Sigma^Q \mathcal{T}_3$.

Property (i) states that if a terminology $\mathcal{T}_3$ is obtained from $\mathcal{T}_2$ by adding further axioms to it, then it $\langle \Sigma, Q \rangle$-implements all the terminologies $\mathcal{T}_1$ that $\mathcal{T}_2 \langle \Sigma, Q \rangle$-implements. Property (ii) states $\mathcal{T}_3 \langle \Sigma, Q \rangle$-implements all subsets $\mathcal{T}_1$ of $\mathcal{T}_2$ provided that $\mathcal{T}_3 \langle \Sigma, Q \rangle$-implements $\mathcal{T}_2$. We leave investigating certain robustness properties of $\leadsto_\Sigma^Q$ regarding signature extensions and varying query languages for future work; see, e.g., [21].

4 Computing Minimal Projection Modules

It is shown in [19] that detecting concept inclusion differences formulated in $\mathcal{EL}^{\mathrm{ran}}$ and $\mathcal{EL}^{\mathrm{ran},\sqcap,u}$ is equivalent to detecting a difference with instance and conjunctive queries, respectively. We therefore consider subsumption queries from $\mathcal{EL}^{\mathrm{ran}}$ and $\mathcal{EL}^{\mathrm{ran},\sqcap,u}$ to compute minimal projection justifications for instance and conjunctive queries, respectively.

4.1 Definition of Subsumption Projection Justifications

For computing minimal subsumption projection modules for subsumption queries, we introduce the notion of a subsumption projection justification between two terminologies. As the notion depends on several parameters, we organise them for better readability in a tuple χ of the form $\langle \mathcal{T}_1, X_1, \Sigma, \mathcal{T}_2, X_2, \mathcal{L} \rangle$, where $\mathcal{T}_1$ and $\mathcal{T}_2$ are normalised $\mathcal{ELH}^r$-terminologies, Σ is a signature, $X_1, X_2 \in \mathsf{N_C} \cup \{\,\mathsf{dom}(r), \mathsf{ran}(r) \mid r \in \mathsf{N_R}\,\}$, and $\mathcal{L} \in \{\mathcal{ELH}^r, \mathcal{EL}^{\mathrm{ran}}, \mathcal{EL}^{\mathrm{ran},\sqcap,u}\}$.

To obtain subsumption modules, we use an operator '$\otimes$' to combine sets of role, subsumee and subsumer projection justifications. Given a set S and sets of sets $\mathbb{S}_1, \mathbb{S}_2 \subseteq 2^S$, we define $\mathbb{S}_1 \otimes \mathbb{S}_2 := \{\, S_1 \cup S_2 \mid S_1 \in \mathbb{S}_1, S_2 \in \mathbb{S}_2 \,\}$. For instance, if $\mathbb{S}_1 = \{\{\alpha_1, \alpha_2\}, \{\alpha_3\}\}$ and $\mathbb{S}_2 = \{\{\alpha_1, \alpha_3\}, \{\alpha_4, \alpha_5\}\}$, then $\mathbb{S}_1 \otimes \mathbb{S}_2 = \{\{\alpha_1, \alpha_2, \alpha_3\}, \{\alpha_1, \alpha_2, \alpha_4, \alpha_5\}, \{\alpha_3, \alpha_4, \alpha_5\}, \{\alpha_1, \alpha_3\}\}$. For a set $\mathbb{M}$ of sets, we define a function $\mathrm{Minimise}_{\subseteq}(\mathbb{M})$ as follows: $\mathcal{M} \in \mathrm{Minimise}_{\subseteq}(\mathbb{M})$ iff $\mathcal{M} \in \mathbb{M}$ and there does not exist a set $\mathcal{M}' \in \mathbb{M}$ such that $\mathcal{M}' \subsetneq \mathcal{M}$. Continuing with the example, $\mathrm{Minimise}_{\subseteq}(\mathbb{S}_1 \otimes \mathbb{S}_2) = \{\{\alpha_1, \alpha_3\}, \{\alpha_1, \alpha_2, \alpha_4, \alpha_5\}, \{\alpha_3, \alpha_4, \alpha_5\}\}$.

Definition 4 (Subsumption Projection Justification). *Let $\chi = \langle \mathcal{T}_1, X_1, \Sigma, \mathcal{T}_2, X_2, \mathcal{L} \rangle$. A set $\mathcal{M}$ is a* subsumee module *under χ iff $\mathcal{M} \subseteq \mathcal{T}_2$ and for every $\mathcal{L}_\Sigma$-inclusion α: $\mathcal{T}_1 \models \mathit{lhs}(\alpha) \sqsubseteq X_1$ implies $\mathcal{M} \models \mathit{lhs}(\alpha) \sqsubseteq X_2$; and $\mathcal{M}$ is a* subsumer module *under χ iff $\mathcal{M} \subseteq \mathcal{T}_2$ and for every $\mathcal{L}_\Sigma$-inclusion α: $\mathcal{T}_1 \models X_1 \sqsubseteq \mathit{rhs}(\alpha)$ implies $\mathcal{M} \models X_2 \sqsubseteq \mathit{rhs}(\alpha)$.*

$\mathcal{M}$ is called a subsumption projection module *under χ iff $\mathcal{M}$ is a subsumee and a subsumer projection module under χ. A* subsumee (subsumer, subsumption) projection justification *under χ is a subsumee (resp. subsumer, subsumption) projection module under χ that is minimal w.r.t. $\subsetneq$.*

We denote the set of all subsumee (resp. subsumer, subsumption) justifications under χ as $\mathbb{J}_{\chi}^{\leftarrow}$ (resp. $\mathbb{J}_{\chi}^{\rightarrow}$, $\mathbb{J}_{\chi}$), where $\chi = \langle \mathcal{T}_1, \varphi_1, \Sigma, \mathcal{T}_2, \varphi_2, \mathcal{L} \rangle$, and $\varphi_1, \varphi_2 \in (\mathsf{N_C} \cap \Sigma) \cup \Sigma^{\mathrm{dom}} \cup \Sigma^{\mathrm{ran}}$.

Definition 5 (Role Subsumption Projection Justification). *Let $\rho = \langle \mathcal{T}_1, \Sigma, \mathcal{T}_2 \rangle$ be a projection setting. A set $\mathcal{M}$ is called a* role subsumption module *under ρ iff $\mathcal{M} \subseteq \mathcal{T}_2$ and for every $r, s \in \mathsf{N_R} \cap \Sigma$, $\mathcal{T}_1 \models r \sqsubseteq s$ implies $\mathcal{M} \models r \sqsubseteq s$. A* minimal role subsumption projection justification *under ρ is the role subsumption module under ρ that is minimal w.r.t. $\subsetneq$.*

We denote the set of all role subsumption projection justifications under ρ as $\mathbb{J}_\rho^R$. The following lemma states how role subsumption projection justifications can be computed. The lemma can be shown using Definition 5 and the notion of justification.

Lemma 1. *Let* $\rho = \langle \mathcal{T}_1, \Sigma, \mathcal{T}_2 \rangle$ *be a projection setting.*

$$\mathbb{J}_\rho^R = Minimize_\subseteq \Big(\bigotimes_{r,s \in \Sigma \cap \mathsf{N_R}, \mathcal{T}_1 \models r \sqsubseteq s} Just_{\mathcal{T}_2}(r \sqsubseteq s) \Big)$$

Using Definitions 1 and 4, we obtain the following lemma stating the absence of certain concept names, and domain and range concepts over role names as left-hand and right-hand difference witnesses between two terminologies $\mathcal{T}_1$ and $\mathcal{T}_2$.

Lemma 2. *Let* $\varphi \in (\mathsf{N_C} \cap \Sigma) \cup \Sigma^{\mathsf{dom}} \cup \Sigma^{\mathsf{ran}}$ *and let* $A \in \Sigma \cap \mathsf{N_C}$. *Additionally, let* $\chi = \langle \mathcal{T}_1, \varphi, \Sigma, \mathcal{T}_2, \varphi, \mathcal{L} \rangle$, $\chi' = \langle \mathcal{T}_1, A, \Sigma, \mathcal{T}_2, A, \mathcal{L} \rangle$ *and* $\mathcal{L} \in \{\mathcal{ELH}^r, \mathcal{EL}^{\mathsf{ran}}, \mathcal{EL}^{\mathsf{ran},\sqcap,u}\}$. *Then:*

- $\varphi \notin \mathsf{lhsWtn}_\Sigma^{\mathcal{L}}(\mathcal{T}_1, J_\varphi)$ *for every* $J_\varphi \in \mathbb{J}_\chi^\rightarrow$;
- $A \notin \mathsf{rhsWtn}_\Sigma^{\mathcal{L}}(\mathcal{T}_1, J_A)$ *for every* $J_A \in \mathbb{J}_{\chi'}^\leftarrow$;
- $\mathsf{roleWtn}_\Sigma^{\mathcal{L}}(\mathcal{T}_1, J) = \emptyset$ *for every* $J \in \mathbb{J}_\rho^R$.

We need at least one subsumption justification, for every potential difference witness, to be contained in a projection module in order to prevent the witness; cf. Lemma 2. This is made precise in the following theorem.

Theorem 1. *Let* $\rho = \langle \mathcal{T}_1, \Sigma, \mathcal{T}_2 \rangle$ *be a projection setting and let* $Q \in \{c, i, q\}$. *Additionally, let* $\mathbb{M}_\rho^Q$ *be the set of all minimal projection modules under* ρ *for query type* Q. *Finally, let*

$$\mathbb{S}_\rho^{\mathcal{L}} = Minimize_\subseteq \big(\mathbb{J}_\rho^R \otimes \bigotimes_{\varphi \in (\Sigma \cap \mathsf{N_C}) \cup \Sigma^{\mathsf{dom}} \cup \Sigma^{\mathsf{ran}}} \mathbb{J}_{\chi(\varphi,\mathcal{L})}^\rightarrow \otimes \bigotimes_{A \in \Sigma \cap \mathsf{N_C}} \mathbb{J}_{\chi(A,\mathcal{L})}^\leftarrow \big)$$

where $\chi(\psi, \mathcal{L}) = \langle \mathcal{T}_1, \psi, \Sigma, \mathcal{T}_2, \psi, \mathcal{L} \rangle$, *and* $\mathcal{L} = \mathcal{ELH}^r$ *if* $Q = c$, $\mathcal{L} = \mathcal{EL}^{\mathsf{ran}}$ *if* $Q = i$, *and* $\mathcal{L} = \mathcal{EL}^{\mathsf{ran},\sqcap,u}$ *if* $Q = q$. *Then it holds that* $\mathbb{M}_\rho^Q = \mathbb{S}_\rho^{\mathcal{L}}$.

In this paper, we present an algorithm for computing subsumee projection justifications for subsumption queries of $\mathcal{EL}^{\mathsf{ran},\sqcap,u}$. Recall that $\mathcal{EL}^{\mathsf{ran},\sqcap,u}$-inclusions are sufficient to detect any difference that is detectable with conjunctive queries. The algorithm for computing subsumer projection justifications, and the algorithms for the other query languages are similar.

4.2   Computing Subsumee Projection Justifications

We now present the algorithm for computing subsumee projection justifications (Fig. 3). The basic idea of the algorithm is to collect as few axioms from a terminology $\mathcal{T}_2$ as possible while ensuring the existence of a so-called subsumee simulation between another terminology $\mathcal{T}_1$ and $\mathcal{T}_2$ [12,26].

Algorithm 1: Computing all Subsumee Projection Justifications

1 **function** COVER$_\leftarrow$ $(\mathcal{T}_1, X_1, \Sigma, \mathcal{T}_2, X_2, \zeta)$
2   **if** X_1 *is not* Σ*-entailed w.r.t.* $\mathcal{T}_1$ **then**
3   **return** $\{\emptyset\}$
4    $M^\leftarrow_{(X_1,X_2)} := \text{COVER}^{N_C}_\leftarrow(\mathcal{T}_1, X_1, \Sigma, \mathcal{T}_2, X_2, \zeta)$
5   **if** X_1 *is not complex* Σ*-entailed in* $\mathcal{T}_1$ **then**
6   **return** $M^\leftarrow_{(X_1,X_2)}$
7   **if** $X_1 \equiv \exists r.Y \in \mathcal{T}_1$, *and* r, Y *are* Σ*-entailed w.r.t.* $\mathcal{T}_1$ **then**
8      $M^\leftarrow_{(X_1,X_2)} :=$
       $M^\leftarrow_{(X_1,X_2)} \otimes \text{COVER}^\exists_\leftarrow(\mathcal{T}_1, X_1, \Sigma, \mathcal{T}_2, X_2, \zeta)$
9   **else if** $X_1 \equiv Y_1 \sqcap \ldots \sqcap Y_m \in \mathcal{T}_1$ **then**
10      $M^\leftarrow_{(X_1,X_2)} :=$
       $M^\leftarrow_{(X_1,X_2)} \otimes \text{COVER}^\sqcap_\leftarrow(\mathcal{T}_1, X_1, \Sigma, \mathcal{T}_2, X_2, \zeta)$
11   **return** Minimise$_\subseteq(M^\leftarrow_{(X_1,X_2)})$

Algorithm 2: Computing all Subsumee Projection Justifications $(S^\leftarrow_\exists)$

1 **function** COVER$^\exists_\leftarrow$ $(\mathcal{T}_1, X_1, \Sigma, \mathcal{T}_2, X_2, \zeta)$
2   **let** $\alpha_{X_1} := X_1 \equiv \exists r.Y_1 \in \mathcal{T}_1$
3    $M^\leftarrow_{(X_1,X_2)} := \{\text{max-tree}^\sqcap_{\mathcal{T}_2}(X_2)\}$
4   **for every** $s \in N_R \cap \Sigma$ *such that* $\mathcal{T}_1 \models s \sqsubseteq r$ **do**
5   **for every** $X'_2 \in$ *non-conj*$_{\mathcal{T}_2}(X_2)$ *such that* $\zeta \neq \varepsilon$ *implies* $\mathcal{T}_2 \not\models \text{ran}(\zeta) \sqsubseteq X'_2$ *and* $\mathcal{T}_2 \not\models \text{dom}(s) \sqsubseteq X'_2$ **do**
6   **let** $\alpha_{X'_2} := X'_2 \equiv \exists r'.Y'_2 \in \mathcal{T}_2$
       $M^\leftarrow_{Y'_2} := \text{COVER}_\leftarrow(\mathcal{T}_1, Y_1, \Sigma, \mathcal{T}_2, Y'_2, s)$
       $M^\leftarrow_{(X_1,X_2)} := M^\leftarrow_{(X_1,X_2)}$
       $\otimes (\{\{\alpha_{X'_2}\}\} \otimes \text{Just}_{\mathcal{T}_2}(s \sqsubseteq r) \otimes M^\leftarrow_{Y'_2})$
7   **return** $M^\leftarrow_{(X_1,X_2)}$

Algorithm 3: Computing all Subsumee Projection Justifications $(S^\leftarrow_{N_C})$

1 **function** COVER$^{N_C}_\leftarrow$ $(\mathcal{T}_1, X_1, \Sigma, \mathcal{T}_2, X_2, \zeta)$
2    $M^\leftarrow_{(X_1,X_2)} := \{\emptyset\}$
3   **for every** $B \in \Sigma^\zeta$ *such that* $\mathcal{T}_1 \models B \sqsubseteq X_1$ **do**
4   **for every** $X_2 \in$ *non-conj*$_{\mathcal{T}_2}(X_1)$ *such that* $\zeta = \varepsilon$ *or* $\mathcal{T}_2 \models \text{ran}(\zeta) \sqsubseteq X_2$ **do**
5        $M^\leftarrow_{(X_1,X_2)} := M^\leftarrow_{(X_1,X_2)} \otimes \text{Just}_{\mathcal{T}_2}(B \sqsubseteq X_2)$
6   **return** $M^\leftarrow_{(X_1,X_2)}$

Algorithm 4: Computing all Subsumee Projection Justifications $(S^\leftarrow_\sqcap)$

1 **function** COVER$^\sqcap_\leftarrow$ $(\mathcal{T}_1, X_1, \Sigma, \mathcal{T}_2, X_2, \zeta)$
2   **let** $\alpha_{X_1} := X_1 \equiv Y_1 \sqcap \ldots \sqcap Y_m \in \mathcal{T}_1$
3    $M^\leftarrow_{(X_1,X_2)} := \emptyset$
4   **for every** $\Gamma \in \text{DefForest}^\sqcap_{\mathcal{T}_2}(X_2)$ **do**
5   **let** $\delta_\Gamma := \{\text{def}^\sqcap_{\mathcal{T}_2}(X') \mid X' \in \text{leaves}(\Gamma) \cap \text{def}^\sqcap_{\mathcal{T}_2}\}$
6      $M^\leftarrow_\Gamma := \{\Gamma\}$
7   **for every** $X'_2 \in \text{leaves}(\Gamma)$ *such that* $\zeta = \varepsilon$ *or* $\mathcal{T}_2 \not\models \text{ran}(\zeta) \sqsubseteq X'_2$ **do**
8        $M^\leftarrow_{X'_2} := \emptyset$
9   **for every** $X'_1 \in$ *non-conj*$_{\mathcal{T}_1}(X_1)$ *such that* $\zeta = \varepsilon$ *or* $\mathcal{T}_2 \not\models \text{ran}(\zeta) \sqsubseteq X'_1$ **do**
10   **if** $\langle \mathcal{T}_1, X'_1 \rangle \sim_{\Sigma,\zeta} \langle \mathcal{T}_2 \setminus \delta_\Gamma, X'_2 \rangle$ **then**
11            $M^\leftarrow_{X'_2} := M^\leftarrow_{X'_2} \cup$
           $\text{COVER}_\leftarrow(\mathcal{T}_1, X'_1, \Sigma, \mathcal{T}_2 \setminus \delta_\Gamma, X'_2, \varepsilon)$
12        $M^\leftarrow_\Gamma := M^\leftarrow_\Gamma \otimes M^\leftarrow_{X'_2}$
13      $M^\leftarrow_{(X_1,X_2)} := M^\leftarrow_{(X_1,X_2)} \cup M^\leftarrow_\Gamma$
14   **return** $M^\leftarrow_{(X_1,X_2)}$

Fig. 3. Algorithms for computing all subsumee justifications

Inclusions of the form $\text{ran}(r) \sqsubseteq X$ might cause non-trivial entailments. For example, let $\mathcal{T}_1 = \{X \equiv \exists r.Y, Y \equiv A_1 \sqcap A_2\}$ and $\Sigma = \{X, A_1, A_2, r\}$. Then $\mathcal{T}_1$ entails that X is subsumed by the Σ-concepts $\exists r.\top$ and $\exists r.(A_1 \sqcap A_2)$ (modulo equivalence). For $\mathcal{T}_2 = \mathcal{T}_1 \cup \{\text{ran}(r) \sqsubseteq A_1\}$, however, we additionally obtain $\mathcal{T}_2 \models \exists r.A_2 \sqsubseteq X$. Hence, when formulating the algorithms for computing subsumee simulations, an additional parameter $\zeta \in \{\epsilon\} \cup (N_R \cap \Sigma)$ is needed which is used in range concepts of the form $\text{ran}(\zeta)$. We call this parameter *context of a role*. We treat ϵ as a special role name and set $\text{ran}(\epsilon) = \top$. The set of all role contexts, in symbols $\mathcal{C}^\Sigma$, is defined as $\mathcal{C}^\Sigma = \{\epsilon\} \cup (N_R \cap \Sigma)$.

To identify concept and role names that are relevant for a subsumee simulation that we propose later, we first use the following notion of Σ-entailment:

- $A \in N_C$ is Σ-*entailed in* $\mathcal{T}$ iff there is an $\mathcal{EL}^{\text{ran}}_\Sigma$-concept C such that $\mathcal{T} \models C \sqsubseteq A$;
- $s \in N_R$ is Σ-*entailed in* $\mathcal{T}$ iff there exists $s' \in N_R \cap \Sigma$ such that $\mathcal{T} \models s' \sqsubseteq s$;
- $A \in N_C$ is (Σ, s)-*entailed in* $\mathcal{T}$ iff there is an $\mathcal{EL}^{\text{ran}}_\Sigma$-concept C such that $\mathcal{T} \models C \sqcap \text{ran}(s) \sqsubseteq A$.

Moreover, we say that $X \in \mathsf{N_C}$ is *complex Σ-entailed* w.r.t. $\mathcal{T}$ iff for every $Y \in \text{non-conj}_{\mathcal{T}}(X)$ one of the following conditions holds:

- there exists $B \in \Sigma$ such that $\mathcal{T} \models B \sqsubseteq Y$ and $\mathcal{T} \not\models B \sqsubseteq X$;
- there exists $Y \equiv \exists r.Z \in \mathcal{T}$ and r, Z are Σ-entailed in $\mathcal{T}$.

X is said to be *simply Σ-entailed* if X is Σ-entailed but not complex Σ-entailed. For example, let $\mathcal{T} = \{X \equiv X_1 \sqcap X_2, B_1 \sqsubseteq X_1, X_2 \equiv \exists r.Z, B_2 \sqsubseteq Z, s \sqsubseteq r\}$. We have that $\text{non-conj}_{\mathcal{T}}(X) = \{X_1, X_2\}$, then r is Σ-entailed w.r.t. $\mathcal{T}$; X is complex Σ-entailed w.r.t. $\mathcal{T}$ for $\Sigma = \{B_1, B_2, s\}$; but X is not complex Σ'-entailed w.r.t. $\mathcal{T}$, where Σ' ranges over $\{B_1, B_2\}$, $\{B_1, s\}$, $\{B_2, s\}$. Additionally, X is not complex Σ-entailed w.r.t. $\mathcal{T} \cup \{B_1 \sqsubseteq X\}$.

We now define the notion of a *subsumee simulation* from $\mathcal{T}_1$ to $\mathcal{T}_2$ as a subset of $(\mathsf{N_C} \cap \text{sig}(\mathcal{T}_1)) \times (\mathsf{N_C} \cap \text{sig}(\mathcal{T}_2)) \times \mathcal{C}_{\mathcal{T}_1}^{\Sigma}$, where $\mathcal{C}_{\mathcal{T}_1}^{\Sigma} := \{\epsilon\} \cup (\mathsf{N_R} \cap (\Sigma \cup \text{sig}(\mathcal{T}_1)))$ is the range of role contexts.

Definition 6 (Subsumee Simulation). *A relation* $S \subseteq \text{sig}^{\mathsf{N_C}}(\mathcal{T}_1) \times \text{sig}^{\mathsf{N_C}}(\mathcal{T}_2) \times \mathcal{C}_{\mathcal{T}_1}^{\Sigma}$ *is a Σ-subsumee simulation from $\mathcal{T}_1$ to $\mathcal{T}_2$ iff the following conditions hold:*

$(S_{\mathsf{N_C}}^{\leftarrow})$ *if* $(X_1, X_2, \zeta) \in S$, *then for every* $\varphi \in \Sigma^{\zeta}$ *and for every* $X_2' \in \text{non-conj}_{\mathcal{T}_2}(X_2)$ *with* $\mathcal{T}_2 \not\models \text{ran}(\zeta) \sqsubseteq X_2'$, $\mathcal{T}_1 \models \varphi \sqsubseteq X_1$ *implies* $\mathcal{T}_2 \models \varphi \sqsubseteq X_2'$;

$(S_{\exists}^{\leftarrow})$ *if* $(X_1, X_2, \zeta) \in S$ *and* $X_1 \equiv \exists r.Y_1 \in \mathcal{T}_1$ *such that* $\mathcal{T}_1 \models s \sqsubseteq r$ *for* $s \in \Sigma$ *and* Y_1 *is* (Σ, s)*-entailed in* $\mathcal{T}_1$, *then for every* $X_2' \in \text{non-conj}_{\mathcal{T}_2}(X_2)$ *not entailed by* $\text{dom}(s)$ *or* $\text{ran}(\zeta)$ *w.r.t.* $\mathcal{T}_2$, *there exists* $X_2' \equiv \exists r'.Y_2 \in \mathcal{T}_2$ *such that* $\mathcal{T}_2 \models s \sqsubseteq r'$ *and* $(Y_1, Y_2, s) \in S$;

$(S_{\sqcap}^{\leftarrow})$ *if* $(X_1, X_2, \zeta) \in S$ *and* $X_1 \equiv Y_1 \sqcap Y_2 \sqcap \ldots \sqcap Y_n \in \mathcal{T}_1$, *then for every* $Y_2 \in \text{non-conj}_{\mathcal{T}_2}(X_2)$ *not entailed by* $\text{ran}(\zeta)$ *w.r.t.* $\mathcal{T}_2$, *there exists* $Y_1 \in \text{non-conj}_{\mathcal{T}_1}(X_1)$ *not entailed by* $\text{ran}(\zeta)$ *w.r.t.* $\mathcal{T}_2$ *with* $(Y_1, Y_2, \epsilon) \in S$.

We write $\mathcal{T}_1 \sim_{\Sigma}^{\leftarrow} \mathcal{T}_2$ *iff there is a Σ-subsumee simulation S from $\mathcal{T}_1$ to $\mathcal{T}_2$ such that for every* $A \in \mathsf{N_C} \cap \Sigma$: $(A, A, \epsilon) \in S$.

For $\zeta \in \Sigma \cap \mathsf{N_R}$, *we write* $\langle \mathcal{T}_1, X_1 \rangle \sim_{\Sigma, \zeta}^{\leftarrow} \langle \mathcal{T}_2, X_2 \rangle$ *iff there is a Σ-subsumee simulation S from $\mathcal{T}_1$ to $\mathcal{T}_2$ with* $(X_1, X_2, \zeta) \in S$ *for which* $\mathcal{T}_1 \sim_{\Sigma}^{\leftarrow} \mathcal{T}_2$.

A subsumee simulation captures the set of subsumees in the sense that $\mathcal{T}_1 \sim_{\Sigma}^{\leftarrow} \mathcal{T}_2$ iff $\text{rhsWtn}_{\Sigma}(\mathcal{T}_1, \mathcal{T}_2) = \emptyset$. Moreover, if a concept name X_2 in $\mathcal{T}_2$ Σ-subsumee simulates a concept name X_1 in $\mathcal{T}_1$, then X_2 subsumes all Σ-concepts w.r.t. $\mathcal{T}_2$ that are subsumed by X_1 w.r.t. $\mathcal{T}_1$. Formally: $\langle \mathcal{T}_1, X_1 \rangle \sim_{\Sigma, \zeta}^{\leftarrow} \langle \mathcal{T}_2, X_2 \rangle$ iff for every $C \in \mathcal{EL}_{\Sigma}^{\text{ran}}: \mathcal{T}_1 \models C \sqsubseteq X_1$ implies $\mathcal{T}_2 \models C \sqsubseteq X_2$ [26].

Algorithm 1 provides the function COVER$_{\leftarrow}$ for computing the set of all subsumee justifications. The algorithm recursively computes sets of axioms sufficient to construct a subsumee simulation. For better readability, the algorithm is structured into several parts, one for each condition of a subsumee simulation, cf. Definition 6. Algorithm 3 handles Case $(S_{\mathsf{N_C}}^{\leftarrow})$, Algorithm 2 takes care of Case $(S_{\exists}^{\leftarrow})$ and Algorithm 4 is responsible for Case $(S_{\sqcap}^{\leftarrow})$. Note that each of these algorithms requires a role context ζ as an input parameter. The notion of complex Σ-entailment is employed in Algorithm 1. If X is not complex Σ-entailment, then neither the existential nor the conjunctive case need to be considered, and Algorithm 1 terminates in Line 6.

Compared with computing subsumer projection justifications, the challenge of computing subsumee projection justifications is to handle conjunctions on the left-hand side of subsumptions. Concept names defined as conjunctions in $\mathcal{T}_2$ use conjuncts which in turn may also be defined as conjunctions. Such axioms form tree structures. When selecting axioms, all minimal subsets of $\mathcal{T}_2$, i.e., all sub-trees, that maintain a subsumee simulation need to be considered. To this end, we define for each concept name X a so-called *definitorial forest* consisting of sets of axioms of the form $Y \equiv Y_1 \sqcap \ldots \sqcap Y_n$ which can be thought of as forming *trees*. Any $\langle X, \Sigma \rangle$-subsumee projection justification contains the axioms of a selection of these trees, i.e., one tree for every conjunction formulated over Σ that entails X w.r.t. $\mathcal{T}$. Formally, we define a set of a DefForest$_\mathcal{T}^\sqcap(X) \subseteq 2^\mathcal{T}$ to be the smallest set closed under the following conditions:

- $\emptyset \in$ DefForest$_\mathcal{T}^\sqcap(X)$;
- $\{\alpha\} \in$ DefForest$_\mathcal{T}^\sqcap(X)$ for $\alpha := X \equiv X_1 \sqcap \ldots \sqcap X_n \in \mathcal{T}$; and
- $\Gamma \cup \{\alpha\} \in$ DefForest$_\mathcal{T}^\sqcap(X)$ for $\Gamma \in$ DefForest$_\mathcal{T}^\sqcap(X)$ with $Z \equiv Z_1 \sqcap \ldots \sqcap Z_k \in \Gamma$ and $\alpha := Z_i \equiv Z_i^1 \sqcap \ldots \sqcap Z_i^n \in \mathcal{T}$.

Given a tree $\Gamma \in$ DefForest$_\mathcal{T}^\sqcap(X)$ rooted at X, we use leaves(Γ) to denote the set $\mathrm{sig}(\Gamma) \setminus \{ X \in \mathrm{sig}(C) \mid X \equiv C \in \Gamma \}$ of leaves if $\Gamma \neq \emptyset$; and $\{X\}$ otherwise. We denote with max-tree$_\mathcal{T}^\sqcap(X)$ the set in DefForest$_\mathcal{T}^\sqcap(X)$ that is maximal w.r.t. $\subseteq$. Finally, we set non-conj$_\mathcal{T}(X) :=$ leaves(max-tree$_\mathcal{T}^\sqcap(X)$) to be the set of leaves of the maximal tree. For example, for $\mathcal{T} = \{\alpha_1, \alpha_2, \alpha_3\}$ with $\alpha_1 := X \equiv Y \sqcap Z$, $\alpha_2 := Y \equiv Y_1 \sqcap Y_2$, and $\alpha_3 := Z \equiv Z_1 \sqcap Z_2$, we obtain DefForest$_\mathcal{T}^\sqcap(X) = \{\emptyset, \{\alpha_1\}, \{\alpha_1, \alpha_2\}, \{\alpha_1, \alpha_3\}, \{\alpha_1, \alpha_2, \alpha_3\}\}$. Moreover, we have that leaves$(\{\alpha_1, \alpha_3\}) = \{Y, Z_1, Z_2\}$, max-tree$_\mathcal{T}^\sqcap(X) = \{\alpha_1, \alpha_2, \alpha_3\}$, and non-conj$_\mathcal{T}(X) = \{Y_1, Y_2, Z_1, Z_2\}$.

The definitorial forest is used to enumerate and find all trees for which Case $(S_\sqcap^\leftarrow)$ holds, which is done in Algorithm 4. The set non-conj$_\mathcal{T}(X)$, however, is also used in Algorithm 2, which we discuss next. The existence of axiom $\alpha_{X_1} := X_1 \equiv \exists r.Y_1 \in \mathcal{T}_1$ in Line 2 of Algorithm 2 is guaranteed by Line 7 of Algorithm 1. The axiom $\alpha_{X_2'} := X_2' \equiv \exists r'.Y_2' \in \mathcal{T}_2$ in Line 6 of Algorithm 2 exists as we assume that $\mathcal{T}_2, X_2$ subsumee-simulates $\mathcal{T}_1, X_1$ w.r.t. Σ. Moreover, there is at most one axiom $\alpha_{X_1} \in \mathcal{T}_1$ and at most one $\alpha_{X_2'} \in \mathcal{T}_2$ as $\mathcal{T}_1$ and $\mathcal{T}_2$ are terminologies. The concept name X_2 may be defined as a conjunction in $\mathcal{T}_2$ whose conjuncts in turn may also be defined as a conjunction in $\mathcal{T}_2$ and so forth. In Line 3 all axioms forming the maximal resulting definitorial conjunctive tree are collected.

For the next algorithm, we define def$_\mathcal{T}^\sqcap := \{ X \in \mathrm{sig}^{\mathsf{Nc}}(\mathcal{T}) \mid X \equiv Y_1 \sqcap \ldots \sqcap Y_n \in \mathcal{T} \}$ to be the set of concept names that are conjunctively defined in $\mathcal{T}$. For every $X \in$ def$_\mathcal{T}^\sqcap$, we set def$_\mathcal{T}^\sqcap(X) := \alpha$, where $\alpha = X \equiv Y_1 \sqcap \ldots \sqcap Y_n \in \mathcal{T}$.

The axiom $\alpha_{X_1} := X_1 \equiv Y_1 \sqcap \ldots \sqcap Y_m \in \mathcal{T}_1$ in Line 2 of Algorithm 4 is guaranteed to exist by Line 9 of Algorithm 4. In case X_2 is defined as a conjunction in $\mathcal{T}_2$, the pair consisting of $\mathcal{T}_2$ containing only a partial conjunctive tree rooted at X_2 and X_2 needs to be considered to be sufficient to subsumee simulate T_1, X_1. Therefore Algorithm 4 considers every partial conjunctive tree Γ from $\mathrm{DefForest}_{T_2}^{\sqcap}(X_2)$ in Line 4 and removes the axioms in δ_Γ connecting the leaves of Γ with the remaining conjunctive tree from T_2 in lines 10 and 11.

The following theorem states that Algorithm 1 indeed computes the set of subsumee projection justifications. The proof establishes that Algorithm 1 computes all possible subsets of T_2 that are minimal w.r.t. $\subsetneq$ while preserving one of the considered Σ-subsumee simulations from T_1 to T_2.

Theorem 2. *Let* $\chi = \langle T_1, \varphi_1, \Sigma, T_2, \varphi_2, \mathcal{EL}^{\mathrm{ran},\sqcap,u}\rangle$, *and* $\varphi_1, \varphi_2 \in (\mathsf{N_C} \cap \Sigma) \cup \{\mathrm{dom}(r), \mathrm{ran}(r) \mid r \in \mathsf{N_R} \cap \Sigma\}$. *Additionally, let* $\mathbb{M} := \mathrm{COVER}_\leftarrow(T_1, \varphi_1, \Sigma, T_2, \varphi_2, \epsilon)$ *using Algorithm 1. Then* $\mathbb{M}$ *is the set of all subsumee justifications under* χ.

Algorithm 1 runs in exponential time in the number of axioms contained in the input terminologies, in the worst case. On the one hand, the algorithm uses justifications (see Line 6 of Alg. 2 and Line 5 of Alg. 3) whose number grows exponentially for role inclusions as well as concept name inclusions. The different justifications are each incorporated using the operator $\otimes$ resulting in possibly different subsumption justifications. The majority of the running time will be spent on computing justifications. Another source of exponential blowup is contained in Line 4 of Algorithm 4. The number of elements in the set $\mathrm{DefForest}_T^{\sqcap}(X)$ grows exponentially in $|T|$. According to our experience so far, however, it seems plausible to assume that definitorial forests in practical ontologies remain rather small and, thus, they do not cause a serious slowdown of the algorithm.

5 Application of Minimal Projection Modules

In this section, we discuss two applications of minimal projection modules.

5.1 Computing Minimal Query Modules

We first define the minimal query modules for different queries.

Definition 7 (Query Module). *A set* $M \subseteq T$ *is a subsumption (resp. instance, conjunctive) query module of* T, *denoted as* M_Σ^c *(resp.* M_Σ^i, M_Σ^q*).*

- M_Σ^c: *for each* $\mathcal{ELH}_\Sigma^r$-*inclusion* α, *if* $T \models \alpha$, *then* $M \models \alpha$;
- M_Σ^i: *for each* Σ-*instance assertion* λ, *if* $(T, \mathcal{A}) \models \lambda$, *then* $(M, \mathcal{A}) \models \lambda$;
- M_Σ^q: *for each* $q(\boldsymbol{a})$, *if* $(T, \mathcal{A}) \models q(\boldsymbol{a})$, *then* $(M, \mathcal{A}) \models q(\boldsymbol{a})$, *where* $\boldsymbol{a}$ *is a tuple of individual names from* $\mathcal{A}$ *and* $q(\boldsymbol{a})$ *is a* Σ-*conjunctive query.*

A subsumption (resp. instance, conjunctive) query module is called a *minimal* subsumption (resp. instance, conjunctive) query module iff it is minimal w.r.t. $\subsetneq$.

In general, the reference and the implementing/task ontologies do not coincide. Intuitively, the task ontology T_2 might contain more knowledge about Σ than the reference ontology T_1. The following lemma illustrates the relationship between minimal projection modules and minimal query modules.

Lemma 3. *Let $Q \in \{c, i, q\}$ and $\rho = \{\mathcal{T}_1, \Sigma, \mathcal{T}_2\}$. Then: for every minimal projection module $\mathcal{M}_\rho^Q$ for a query type Q and under a projection setting ρ, there exists a minimal Q-query module M_Σ^Q of $\mathcal{T}_2$ such that $\mathcal{M}_\rho^Q \subseteq M_\Sigma^Q$.*

Example 3 (Fig. 2 contd.). The minimal projection module of $\mathcal{T}_2$ under $\rho = \{\mathcal{T}_1, \Sigma, \mathcal{T}_2\}$ is $\{\{\beta_1, \beta_3\}, \{\beta_1, \beta_4\}\}$, for any query type $Q \in \{c, i, q\}$. The minimal Q-query module of $\mathcal{T}_2$ w.r.t. Σ is $\{\{\beta_1, \beta_2, \beta_3\}, \{\beta_1, \beta_2, \beta_4\}\}$. The minimal Q-query module of $\mathcal{T}_1$ is $\{\alpha_1\}$.

One solution for importing Σ-knowledge of a reference ontology to a task ontology is to import a minimal Q-query module of the reference ontology. However, one can see that if we include α_1 to $\mathcal{T}_2$, then α_1 repeats the Σ-knowledge that is already represented by β_1. Besides, the resulting ontology would not be a terminology anymore.

Consider a special projection setting of the form $\langle \mathcal{T}, \Sigma, \mathcal{T} \rangle$, where the reference ontology $\mathcal{T}$ is also the implementing ontology. We denote such reflexive projection settings with $\rho^\circlearrowleft$. A projection module $\mathcal{M}$ of $\mathcal{T}$ under $\rho^\circlearrowleft$ for subsumption (resp. instance, conjunctive) queries is a subset of $\mathcal{T}$ that preserves the answers to Σ-concept subsumption (resp. instance, conjunctive) queries as given by $\mathcal{T}$. It can readily be verified that a minimal projection module under a reflexive projection setting coincides with a *minimal module* for the type of queries considered.

5.2   Ontology Comparison Measure

In existent methods for measuring the entailment capacity of a terminology about a signature Σ for a query language, one can use logical difference. However, the following example shows that using logical difference can be not sufficient in some case.

Example 4. Let $\alpha_1 := A \sqsubseteq B_1 \sqcap B_2 \sqcap B_3 \sqcap B_4$, $\alpha_2 := B_1 \sqsubseteq B_2 \sqcap B_3$, $\alpha_3 := B_2 \sqsubseteq B_4$, $\alpha_4 := B_3 \sqsubseteq B_4$. Let $\mathcal{T}_1 = \{\alpha_1\}$, $\mathcal{T}_2 = \{\alpha_1, \alpha_2\}$, $\mathcal{T}_3 = \{\alpha_1, \alpha_2, \alpha_3, \alpha_4\}$ and $\Sigma = \{A, B_1, B_2, B_3, B_4\}$. We have that $\mathrm{Wtn}_\Sigma^{\mathcal{L}}(\mathcal{T}_1, \mathcal{T}_2) = \mathrm{Wtn}_\Sigma^{\mathcal{L}}(\mathcal{T}_1, \mathcal{T}_3) = (\emptyset, \emptyset, \emptyset)$, for $\mathcal{L} \in \{\mathcal{ELH}^r, \mathcal{EL}^{\mathrm{ran}}, \mathcal{EL}^{\mathrm{ran}, \sqcap, u}\}$.

In Example 4, the notion of logical difference cannot be used to distinguish between $\mathcal{T}_2$ and $\mathcal{T}_3$ w.r.t. Σ as $\mathcal{T}_2$ and $\mathcal{T}_3$ preserve the Σ-knowledge w.r.t. $\mathcal{T}_1$. However, intuitively, $\mathcal{T}_2$ and $\mathcal{T}_3$ each contain more information about the Σ-concept names B_1, B_2 and B_4 than $\mathcal{T}_1$. We therefore propose a new measure based on the notions of minimal projection module and query module for different query languages.

Definition 8 (Projection Rate). *Let $Q \in \{c, i, q\}$ and let $\mathcal{M}_\rho^Q$ range over minimal projection modules under $\rho = \langle \mathcal{T}_1, \Sigma, \mathcal{T}_2 \rangle$ and the query type Q. Additionally, let M_Σ^Q range over minimal modules of $\mathcal{T}_2$ for the query type Q. The projection rate P^Q of $\mathcal{T}_1$ over $\mathcal{T}_2$ is defined as:*

$$P^Q = \frac{|\bigcup \mathcal{M}_\rho^Q|}{|\bigcup M_\Sigma^Q|}$$

Note that $p \leq 1$ always holds by Lemma 3. Intuitively, the lower the projection rate, the more Σ-knowledge is contained in $\mathcal{T}_2$ compared with $\mathcal{T}_1$.

Example 5 (Example 4 contd.). Considering when $Q = c$, we have that $\mathcal{M}_\rho^c = \mathcal{M}_{\rho'}^c = \{\alpha_1\}$ under $\rho = \langle \mathcal{T}_1, \Sigma, \mathcal{T}_2 \rangle$ and $\rho' = \langle \mathcal{T}_1, \Sigma, \mathcal{T}_3 \rangle$. The minimal subsumption query module of $\mathcal{T}_2$ w.r.t. Σ is $\{\alpha_1, \alpha_2\}$. But there exists two minimal subsumption query module of $\mathcal{T}_3$ w.r.t. Σ, which are $\{\alpha_1, \alpha_2, \alpha_3\}$ and $\{\alpha_1, \alpha_2, \alpha_4\}$. So the union of minimal subsumption query module of $\mathcal{T}_3$ w.r.t. Σ is $\mathcal{T}_3$ that contains four axioms. Therefore, the projection rate P^c of $\mathcal{T}_1$ over $\mathcal{T}_2$ is $P^c = 1/2$ and the projection rate P^c of $\mathcal{T}_1$ over $\mathcal{T}_3$ is $P^c = 1/4$. So $\mathcal{T}_3$ contains more Σ-knowledge compared with $\mathcal{T}_2$ as $1/4 < 1/2$.

6   Conclusion

We proposed a novel module notion called projection module that entails the queries that follow from a reference ontology. We presented an algorithm for computing all minimal projection modules of acyclic $\mathcal{ELH}^r$-terminologies and two applications of minimal projection modules. We expect that the algorithms can be extended to deal with cyclic terminologies and possibly general $\mathcal{ELH}^r$-TBoxes, and to yield a ranking between different projection modules, e.g., via weighted signatures.

References

1. Alsubait, T., Parsia, B., Sattler, U.: Measuring similarity in ontologies: a new family of measures. In: Janowicz, K., Schlobach, S., Lambrix, P., Hyvönen, E. (eds.) EKAW 2014. LNCS (LNAI), vol. 8876, pp. 13–25. Springer, Cham (2014). https://doi.org/10.1007/978-3-319-13704-9_2
2. Arif, M.F., Mencía, C., Ignatiev, A., Manthey, N., Peñaloza, R., Marques-Silva, J.: BEACON: an efficient SAT-based tool for debugging $\mathcal{EL}^+$ ontologies. In: Creignou, N., Le Berre, D. (eds.) SAT 2016. LNCS, vol. 9710, pp. 521–530. Springer, Cham (2016). https://doi.org/10.1007/978-3-319-40970-2_32
3. Baader, F., Calvanese, D., McGuinness, D.L., Nardi, D., Patel-Schneider, P.F. (eds.): The Description Logic Handbook: Theory, Implementation, and Applications, 2 edn. Cambridge University Press, June 2010
4. Baader, F., Horrocks, I., Lutz, C., Sattler, U.: An Introduction to Description Logic. Cambridge University Press, Cambridge (2017)
5. Baader, F., Peñaloza, R., Suntisrivaraporn, B.: Pinpointing in the description logic $\mathcal{EL}$. In: Proceedings of DL 2007: The 20th International Workshop on Description Logics (2007)
6. Botoeva, E., Konev, B., Lutz, C., Ryzhikov, V., Wolter, F., Zakharyaschev, M.: Inseparability and conservative extensions of description logic ontologies: a survey. In: Pan, J.Z., et al. (eds.) Reasoning Web 2016. LNCS, vol. 9885, pp. 27–89. Springer, Cham (2017). https://doi.org/10.1007/978-3-319-49493-7_2
7. Botoeva, E., Kontchakov, R., Ryzhikov, V., Wolter, F., Zakharyaschev, M.: Games for query inseparability of description logic knowledge bases. Artif. Intell. **234**, 78–119 (2016)

8. Botoeva, E., Lutz, C., Ryzhikov, V., Wolter, F., Zakharyaschev, M.: Query-based entailment and inseparability for ALC ontologies. In: Proceedings of IJCAI 2016: The 25th International Joint Conference on Artificial Intelligence, pp. 1001–1007. AAAI Press (2016)

9. Chen, J., Ludwig, M., Ma, Y., Walther, D.: Zooming in on ontologies: minimal modules and best excerpts. In: d'Amato, C., et al. (eds.) ISWC 2017. LNCS, vol. 10587, pp. 173–189. Springer, Cham (2017). https://doi.org/10.1007/978-3-319-68288-4_11

10. Chen, J., Ludwig, M., Walther, D.: Computing minimal subsumption modules of ontologies. In: Proceedings of GCAI 2018: The 4th Global Conference on Artificial Intelligence, pp. 41–53 (2018)

11. Domingue, J., Anutariya, C. (eds.): ASWC 2008. LNCS, vol. 5367. Springer, Heidelberg (2008). https://doi.org/10.1007/978-3-540-89704-0

12. Ecke, A., Ludwig, M., Walther, D.: The concept difference for $\mathcal{EL}$-terminologies using hypergraphs. In: Proceedings of DChanges 2013: The International workshop on (Document) Changes: Modeling, Detection, Storage and Visualization (2013)

13. Euzenat, J., Shvaiko, P.: Ontology Matching, 2nd edn. Springer, Heidelberg (2013). https://doi.org/10.1007/978-3-642-38721-0

14. Grau, B.C., Horrocks, I., Kazakov, Y., Sattler, U.: Modular reuse of ontologies: theory and practice. J. Artif. Intell. Res. **31**(1), 273–318 (2008)

15. Jung, J.C., Lutz, C., Martel, M., Schneider, T.: Query conservative extensions in horn description logics with inverse roles. In: Proceedings of IJCAI 2017: The 26th International Joint Conference on Artificial Intelligence, pp. 1116–1122. AAAI Press (2017)

16. Kalyanpur, A., Parsia, B., Sirin, E., Hendler, J.A.: Debugging unsatisfiable classes in OWL ontologies. J. Web Semant. **3**(4), 268–293 (2005)

17. Kazakov, Y., Skocovsky, P.: Enumerating justifications using resolution. In: Proceedings of DL 2017: The 30th International Workshop on Description Logics (2017)

18. Konev, B., Kontchakov, R., Ludwig, M., Schneider, T., Wolter, F., Zakharyaschev, M.: Conjunctive query inseparability of OWL 2 QL TBoxes. In: Proceedings of AAAI 2011: The 25th Conference on Artificial Intelligence. AAAI Press (2011)

19. Konev, B., Ludwig, M., Walther, D., Wolter, F.: The logical difference for the lightweight description logic EL. J. Artif. Intell. Res. **44**, 633–708 (2012)

20. Konev, B., Lutz, C., Walther, D., Wolter, F.: Semantic modularity and module extraction in description logics. In: Proceedings of ECAI 2008: The 18th European Conference on Artificial Intelligence, pp. 55–59. IOS Press (2008)

21. Konev, B., Lutz, C., Walther, D., Wolter, F.: Formal properties of modularisation. In: Stuckenschmidt, H., Parent, C., Spaccapietra, S. (eds.) Modular Ontologies. LNCS, vol. 5445, pp. 25–66. Springer, Heidelberg (2009). https://doi.org/10.1007/978-3-642-01907-4_3

22. Konev, B., Lutz, C., Walther, D., Wolter, F.: Model-theoretic inseparability and modularity of description logic ontologies. Artif. Intell. **203**, 66–103 (2013)

23. Konev, B., Walther, D., Wolter, F.: The logical difference problem for description logic terminologies. In: Armando, A., Baumgartner, P., Dowek, G. (eds.) IJCAR 2008. LNCS (LNAI), vol. 5195, pp. 259–274. Springer, Heidelberg (2008). https://doi.org/10.1007/978-3-540-71070-7_21

24. Kontchakov, R., Wolter, F., Zakharyaschev, M.: Logic-based ontology comparison and module extraction, with an application to DL-Lite. Artif. Intell. **174**(15), 1093–1141 (2010)

25. Lehmann, K., Turhan, A.-Y.: A framework for semantic-based similarity measures for $\mathcal{ELH}$-concepts. In: del Cerro, L.F., Herzig, A., Mengin, J. (eds.) JELIA 2012. LNCS (LNAI), vol. 7519, pp. 307–319. Springer, Heidelberg (2012). https://doi.org/10.1007/978-3-642-33353-8_24

26. Ludwig, M., Walther, D.: The logical difference for $\mathcal{ELH}^r$-terminologies using hypergraphs. In: Proceedings of ECAI 2014: The 21st European Conference on Artificial Intelligence, pp. 555–560 (2014)

27. Romero, A.A., Kaminski, M., Grau, B.C., Horrocks, I.: Module extraction in expressive ontology languages via datalog reasoning. J. Artif. Intell. Res. **55**, 499–564 (2016)

28. Sattler, U., Schneider, T., Zakharyaschev, M.: Which kind of module should I extract? In: Proceedings of DL 2009. CEUR Workshop Proceedings, vol. 477. CEUR-WS.org (2009)

29. Zhou, Z., Qi, G., Suntisrivaraporn, B.: A new method of finding all justifications in OWL 2 EL. In: Proceedings of WI 2013: IEEE/WIC/ACM International Conferences on Web Intelligence, pp. 213–220 (2013)

Closed-World Semantics for Conjunctive Queries with Negation over $\mathcal{ELH}_\perp$ Ontologies

Stefan Borgwardt$^{(\boxtimes)}$ and Walter Forkel

Chair for Automata Theory, Technische Universität Dresden, Dresden, Germany
{stefan.borgwardt,walter.forkel}@tu-dresden.de

Abstract. Ontology-mediated query answering is a popular paradigm for enriching answers to user queries with background knowledge. For querying the *absence* of information, however, there exist only few ontology-based approaches. Moreover, these proposals conflate the closed-domain and closed-world assumption, and therefore are not suited to deal with the anonymous objects that are common in ontological reasoning. We propose a new closed-world semantics for answering conjunctive queries with negation over ontologies formulated in the description logic $\mathcal{ELH}_\perp$, which is based on the *minimal* canonical model. We propose a rewriting strategy for dealing with negated query atoms, which shows that query answering is possible in polynomial time in data complexity.

1 Introduction

Ontology-mediated query answering (OMQA) allows using background knowledge for answering user queries, supporting data-focused applications offering search, analytics, or data integration functionality. An *ontology* is a logical theory formulated in a decidable fragment of first-order logic, with a trade-off between the expressivity of the ontology and the efficiency of query answering. *Rewritability* is a popular topic of research, the idea being to reformulate ontological queries into database queries that can be answered by traditional database management systems [8,10,15,21,27].

Ontology-based systems do not use the *closed-domain* and *closed-world* semantics of databases. Instead, they acknowledge that unknown (*anonymous*) objects may exist (*open domain*) and that facts that are not explicitly stated may still be true (*open world*). Anonymous objects are related to *null* values in databases, but are not used explicitly; for example, if we know that every person has a mother, then first-order models include all mothers, even though they may not be mentioned in the input dataset. The open-world assumption ensures that, if the dataset does not contain an entry on, e.g. whether a person is

---

This work was supported by the DFG grant BA 1122/19-1 (GOASQ) and grant 389792660 (TRR 248) (see https://perspicuous-computing.science).

© Springer Nature Switzerland AG 2019
F. Calimeri et al. (Eds.): JELIA 2019, LNAI 11468, pp. 371–386, 2019.
https://doi.org/10.1007/978-3-030-19570-0_24

male or female, then we do not infer that this person is neither male nor female, but rather consider all possibilities.

The biomedical domain is a fruitful area for OMQA methods, due to the availability of large ontologies covering a multitude of topics[1] and the demand for managing large amounts of patient data, in the form of *electronic health records (EHRs)* [12]. For example, for the preparation of clinical trials[2] a large number of patients need to be screened for eligibility, and an important area of current research is how to automate this process [7,23,28,29,31].[3]

However, ontologies and EHRs mostly contain *positive* information, while clinical trials also require certain *exclusion criteria* to be absent in the patients. For example, we may want to select only patients that have *not* been diagnosed with cancer,[4] but such information cannot be entailed from the given knowledge. The culprit for this problem is the open-world semantics, which considers a cancer diagnosis possible unless it has been explicitly ruled out.

One possibility is to introduce (partial) closed-world semantics to ontology languages [1,24]. For example, one can declare the predicate *human* to be "closed", i.e. if an object is not explicitly listed as *human* in the dataset, then it is considered to be not human. However, such approaches fail to deal with anonymous objects; indeed, they conflate the open-world and open-domain assumptions by requiring that all closed information is restricted to the known objects. For example, even if we don't know the mother of a person, we still know that she is human, even though this may not be explicitly stated in the ontology (but entailed by it). Using the semantics of [1,24] would hence enforce a partial *closed-domain* assumption as well, in that A's mother would have to be a known object from the dataset.

Epistemic logics are another way to give a closed-world-like semantics to negated formulas; e.g. one can formulate queries like "no cancer diagnosis is *known*" using the epistemic knowledge modality **K**. Such formalisms are also unable to deal with closed-world knowledge over anonymous objects [11,32]. Most closely related to our proposal are Datalog-based semantics for negation, based on the (Skolem) chase construction [2,18]. We compare all these existing semantics in detail in Sect. 3.

The contribution of this paper is a new closed-world semantics to answer *conjunctive queries with (guarded) negation* [6] over ontologies formulated in $\mathcal{ELH}_\perp$, an ontology language that covers many biomedical ontologies. Our semantics is based on the *minimal canonical model*, which encodes all inferences of the ontology in the most concise way possible. As a side effect, this means that standard CQs without negation are interpreted under the standard open-world semantics. In order to properly handle negative knowledge about anonymous objects, however, we have to be careful in the construction of the canonical model, in particular about the number and type of anonymous objects that are introduced.

---

[1] https://bioportal.bioontology.org.

[2] https://clinicaltrials.gov.

[3] https://n2c2.dbmi.hms.harvard.edu.

[4] An exclusion criterion in https://clinicaltrials.gov/ct2/show/NCT01463215.

Since in general the minimal canonical model is infinite, we develop a rewriting technique, in the spirit of the combined approach of [22, 25], and most closely inspired by [8, 15], which allows us to evaluate conjunctive queries with negation over a finite part of the canonical model, using traditional database techniques.

An extended version of this paper, including an appendix with full proofs, can be found at https://tu-dresden.de/inf/lat/papers.

2 Preliminaries

We recall the definitions of $\mathcal{ELH}_\perp$ and first-order queries, which are needed for our rewriting of conjunctive queries with negation.

The Description Logic $\mathcal{ELH}_\perp$. Let N_C, N_R, N_I be countably infinite sets of *concept, role,* and *individual names,* respectively. A *concept* is built according to the syntax rule $C ::= A \mid \top \mid \perp \mid C \sqcap C \mid \exists r.C$, where $A \in N_C$ and $r \in N_R$. An *ABox* is a finite set of *concept assertions* $A(a)$ and *role assertions* $r(a, b)$, where $a, b \in N_I$. A *TBox* is a finite set of *concept inclusions* $C \sqsubseteq D$ and *role inclusions* $r \sqsubseteq s$, where C, D are concepts and r, s are roles. In the following we assume the TBox to be in normal form, i.e. that it contains only inclusions of the form

$$A_1 \sqcap \cdots \sqcap A_n \sqsubseteq B, \qquad A \sqsubseteq \exists r.B, \qquad \exists r.A \sqsubseteq B, \qquad r \sqsubseteq s$$

where $A_{(i)} \in N_C \cup \{\top\}$, $B \in N_C \cup \{\perp\}$, $r, s \in N_R$, and $n \geq 1$. A *knowledge base (KB)* (or *ontology*) $\mathcal{K} = (\mathcal{T}, \mathcal{A})$ is a pair of a TBox $\mathcal{T}$ and an ABox $\mathcal{A}$. We refer to the set of individual names occurring in $\mathcal{K}$ by $\mathrm{Ind}(\mathcal{K})$. We write $C \equiv D$ to abbreviate the two inclusions $C \sqsubseteq D$, $D \sqsubseteq C$, and similarly for role inclusions.

The semantics of $\mathcal{ELH}_\perp$ is defined in terms of interpretations $I = (\Delta^I, \cdot^I)$ as usual [5]. In the following, we assume all KBs to be consistent and make the standard name assumption, i.e. that for every individual name a in any interpretation I we have $a^I = a$. An axiom α is *entailed* by $\mathcal{K}$ (written $\mathcal{K} \models \alpha$) if α is satisfied in all models of $\mathcal{K}$. We abbreviate $\mathcal{K} \models C \sqsubseteq D$ to $C \sqsubseteq_{\mathcal{T}} D$, and similarly for role inclusions; note that the ABox does not influence the entailment of inclusions. Entailment in $\mathcal{ELH}_\perp$ can be decided in polynomial time [4].

Query Answering. Let N_V be a countably infinite set of *variables.* The set of *terms* is $N_T := N_V \cup N_I$. A *first-order query* $\phi(\mathbf{x})$ is a first-order formula built from *concept atoms* $A(t)$ and *role atoms* $r(t, t')$ with $A \in N_C, r \in N_R$, and $t_i \in N_T$, using the boolean connectives $(\wedge, \vee, \neg, \rightarrow)$ and universal and existential quantifiers $(\forall x, \exists x)$. The free variables $\mathbf{x}$ of $\phi(\mathbf{x})$ are called *answer variables* and we say that ϕ is k-ary if there are k answer variables. The remaining variables are the *quantified variables.* We use $\mathrm{Var}(\phi)$ to denote the set of all variables in ϕ. A query without any answer variables is called a *Boolean query.*

Let $I = (\Delta, \cdot^I)$ be an interpretation. An *assignment* $\pi \colon \mathrm{Var}(\phi) \rightarrow \Delta$ *satisfies* ϕ in I, if $I, \pi \models \phi$ under the standard semantics of first-order logic. We write $I \models \phi$ if there is a satisfying assignment for ϕ in I. Let $\mathcal{K}$ be a KB. A k-tuple $\mathbf{a}$ of individual names from $\mathrm{Ind}(\mathcal{K})$ is an *answer* to ϕ in I if ϕ has a satisfying assignment π in I with $\pi(\mathbf{x}) = \mathbf{a}$; it is a *certain answer* to q over $\mathcal{K}$ if it is an answer to q in all models of $\mathcal{K}$. We denote the set of all answers to ϕ in I by ans(ϕ, I), and the set of all certain answers to ϕ over $\mathcal{K}$ by cert$(\phi, \mathcal{K})$.

A *conjunctive query* (CQ) $q(\mathbf{x})$ is a first-order query of the form $\exists \mathbf{y}. \varphi(\mathbf{x}, \mathbf{y})$, where φ is a conjunction of atoms. Abusing notation, we write $\alpha \in q$ if the atom α occurs in q, and conversely may treat a set of atoms as a conjunction. The *leaf variables* x in q are those that do not occur in any atoms of the form $r(x, y)$. Clearly, q is satisfied in an interpretation if there is a satisfying assignment for $\varphi(\mathbf{x}, \mathbf{y})$, which is often called a *match* for q. A CQ is *rooted* if all variables are connected to an answer variable through role atoms.

CQ answering over $\mathcal{ELH}_\perp$ KBs is *combined first-order rewritable* [25]: For any CQ q and consistent KB $\mathcal{K} = (\mathcal{T}, \mathcal{A})$ we can find a first-order query $q_\mathcal{T}$ and a finite interpretation $I_\mathcal{K}$ such that cert$(q, \mathcal{K}) = $ ans$(q_\mathcal{T}, I_\mathcal{K})$. Importantly, $I_\mathcal{K}$ is independent of q, i.e. can be reused to answer many different queries, while $q_\mathcal{T}$ is independent of $\mathcal{A}$, i.e. each query can be rewritten without using the (possibly large) dataset. The rewritability results are based crucially on the *canonical model* property of $\mathcal{ELH}_\perp$: For any consistent KB $\mathcal{K}$ one can construct a model $I_\mathcal{K}$ that is homomorphically contained in any other model. This is a very useful property since any match in the canonical model corresponds to matches in all other models of $\mathcal{K}$, and therefore cert$(q, \mathcal{K}) = $ ans$(q, I_\mathcal{K})$ holds for all CQs q.

3   Conjunctive Queries with Negation

We are interested in answering queries of the following form.

Definition 1. *Conjunctive queries with (guarded) negation (NCQs) are constructed by extending CQs with negated concept atoms $\neg A(t)$ and negated role atoms $\neg r(t, t')$, such that, for any negated atom over terms t (and t') the query contains at least one positive atom over t (and t').*

We first discuss different ways of handling the negated atoms, and then propose a new semantics that is based on a particular kind of *minimal* canonical model. For this, we consider an example based on real EHRs (ABoxes) from the MIMIC-III database [20], criteria (NCQs) from clinicaltrials.gov, and the large medical ontology SNOMED CT[5] (the TBox). We omit here the "role groups" used in SNOMED CT, which do not affect the example. We also simplify the concept names and their definitions for ease of presentation. We assume that the ABoxes have been extracted from EHRs by a natural language processing tool based, e.g. on existing concept taggers like [3, 30]; of course, this extraction is an entire research field in itself, which we do not attempt to tackle in this paper.

Example 2. We consider three patients. Patient p_1 (patient 2693 in the MIMIC-III dataset) is diagnosed with breast cancer and an unspecified form of cancer (this often occurs when there are multiple mentions of cancer in a patient's EHR,

---

[5] https://www.snomed.org/snomed-ct.

which cannot be resolved to be the same entity). Patient p_2 (patient 32304 in the MIMIC-III dataset) suffers from breast cancer and skin cancer ("[S]tage IV breast cancer with mets to skin, bone, and liver".) For p_3 (patient 88432 in the MIMIC-III dataset), we know that p_3 has breast cancer that involves the skin ("Skin, left breast, punch biopsy: Poorly differentiated carcinoma").

Since SNOMED CT does not model patients, we add a special role name *diagnosedWith* that connects patients with their diagnoses. One can use this to express diagnoses in two ways. First, one can explicitly introduce individual names for diagnoses in assertions like diagnosedWith(p_1, d_1), BreastCancer(d_1), diagnosedWith(p_1, d_2), Cancer(d_2), implying that these diagnoses are treated as distinct entities under the standard name assumption. Alternatively, one can use complex assertions like $\exists$diagnosedWith.Cancer(p_1), which allows the logical semantics to resolve whether two diagnoses actually refer to the same object. Since ABoxes only contain concept names, in this case one has to introduce auxiliary definitions like CancerPatient $\equiv$ $\exists$diagnosedWith.Cancer into the TBox. We use both variants in our example, to illustrate their different behaviours.

We obtain the KB $\mathcal{K}_C$, containing knowledge about different kinds of cancers and cancer patients, together with information about the three patients. The information about cancers is taken from SNOMED CT (in simplified form):

$$\text{SkinCancer} \equiv \text{Cancer} \sqcap \exists\text{findingSite.SkinStructure}$$
$$\text{BreastCancer} \equiv \text{Cancer} \sqcap \exists\text{findingSite.BreastStructure}$$
$$\text{SkinOfBreastCancer} \equiv \text{Cancer} \sqcap \exists\text{findingSite.SkinOfBreastStructure}$$
$$\text{SkinOfBreastStructure} \sqsubseteq \text{BreastStructure} \sqcap \text{SkinStructure}$$

The EHRs are compiled into several assertions per patient:

$$\text{Patient } p_1 : \text{BreastCancerPatient}(p_1),\ \text{CancerPatient}(p_1)$$
$$\text{Patient } p_2 : \text{SkinCancerPatient}(p_2),\ \text{BreastCancerPatient}(p_2)$$
$$\text{Patient } p_3 : \text{diagnosedWith}(p_3, c_3),\ \text{SkinOfBreastCancer}(c_3)$$

Additionally, we add the following auxiliary definitions to the TBox:

$$\text{CancerPatient} \equiv \exists\text{diagnosedWith.Cancer}$$
$$\text{SkinCancerPatient} \equiv \exists\text{diagnosedWith.SkinCancer}$$
$$\text{BreastCancerPatient} \equiv \exists\text{diagnosedWith.BreastCancer}$$

For example, skin cancers and breast cancers are cancers occurring at specific parts of the body ("body structure" in SNOMED CT), and a breast cancer patient is someone who is diagnosed with breast cancer. This means that, in every model of $\mathcal{K}_C$, every object that satisfies BreastCancerPatient (in particular p_2) must have a diagnosedWith-connected object that satisfies BreastCancer, and so on.

For a clinical trial,[6] we want to find patients that have "breast cancer", but not "breast cancer that involves the skin." This can be translated into an NCQ:

$$q_B(x) := \exists y, z.\, \text{diagnosedWith}(x, y) \wedge \text{Cancer}(y) \wedge \text{findingSite}(y, z) \wedge$$
$$\text{BreastStructure}(z) \wedge \neg \text{SkinStructure}(z)$$

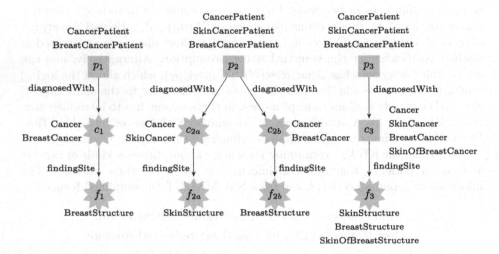

Fig. 1. The minimal canonical model $I_{\mathcal{K}_C}$. Named individuals are depicted by squares, anonymous objects by stars.

We know that p_1 is diagnosed with BreastCancer as well as Cancer. Since the former is more specific, we assume that the latter refers to the same Breast-Cancer. However, since we have no information about an involvement of the skin, p_1 should be returned as an answer to q_B.

We know that p_2 suffers from cancer in the skin and the breast, but not if the skin of the breast is also affected. Since neither location is implied by the other, we assume that they refer to distinct areas. p_2 should thus be an answer to q_B.

In the case of p_3, it is explicitly stated that it is the same cancer that is occurring (not necessarily exclusively) at the skin of the breast. In this case, the ABox assertions override the distinctness assumption we made for p_2. Thus, p_3 should not be an answer to q_B.   ∎

In practice, more complicated cases than in our example can occur: The nesting of anonymous objects will be deeper and more branched when using large biomedical ontologies. For example, in SNOMED CT it is possible to describe many details of a cancer, such as the kind of cancer, whether it is a primary or secondary cancer, and in which part of the body it is found. This means

---

[6] https://clinicaltrials.gov/ct2/show/NCT01960803.

that even a single assertion can lead to the introduction of multiple levels of anonymous objects in the canonical model. In some ontologies there are even cyclic concept inclusions, which lead to infinitely many anonymous individuals, e.g. in the GALEN ontology[7]. We focus on Example 2 in this paper, to illustrate the relevant issues in a clear and easy to follow manner.

We now evaluate existing semantics on this example.

Standard Certain Answer Semantics as defined in Sect. 2 is clearly not suited here, because one can easily construct a model of $\mathcal{K}_C$ in which c_1 is also a skin cancer, and hence p_1 is not an element of $\text{cert}(q_B, \mathcal{K}_C)$. Moreover, under certain answer semantics answering CQs with guarded negation is already coNP-complete [17], and hence not (combined) rewritable.

Epistemic Logic allows us to selectively apply closed-world reasoning using the modal knowledge operator **K**. For a formula **K**φ to be true, it has to hold in all "connected worlds", which is often considered to mean all possible models of the KB, adopting an $S5$-like view [11]. For q_B, we could read $\neg\text{SkinStructure}(z)$ as "not known to be a skin structure", i.e. $\neg\textbf{K}\text{SkinStructure}(z)$. Consider the model $I_{\mathcal{K}_C}$ in Fig. 1 and the assignment $\pi = \{x \mapsto p_3, y \mapsto c_3, z \mapsto f_3\}$, for which we want to check whether it is a match for q_B. Under epistemic semantics, $\neg\textbf{K}\text{SkinStructure}(z)$ is considered true if $\mathcal{K}$ has a (different) model in which f_3 does not belong to SkinStructure. However, f_3 is an anonymous object, and hence its name is not fixed. For example, we can easily obtain another model by renaming f_3 to f_1 and vice versa. Then f_3 would not be a skin structure, which means that $\neg\textbf{K}\text{SkinStructure}(z)$ is true in the original model $I_{\mathcal{K}_C}$, which is not what we expected. This is a known problem with epistemic first-order logics [32].

Skolemization can enforce a stricter comparison of anonymous objects between models. The inclusion SkinOfBreastCancer $\sqsubseteq$ ∃findingSite.SkinOfBreast could be rewritten as the first-order sentence

$$\forall x. \Big(\text{SkinOfBreastCancer}(x) \rightarrow \text{findingSite}\big(x, f(x)\big) \wedge \text{SkinOfBreast}\big(f(x)\big) \Big),$$

where f is a fresh function symbol. This means that c_3 would be connected to a finding site that has the unique name $f(c_3)$ in every model. Queries would be evaluated over Herbrand models only. Hence, for evaluating $\neg\textbf{K}\text{SkinStructure}(z)$ when z is mapped to $f(c_3)$, we would only be allowed to compare the behavior of $f(c_3)$ in other Herbrand models. The general behavior of this anonymous individual is fixed, however, since in all Herbrand models it is *the* finding site of c_3. While this improves the comparison by introducing pseudo-names for all anonymous individuals, it limits us in different ways: Since p_3 is inferred to be a BreastCancerPatient, the Skolemized version of BreastCancerPatient $\sqsubseteq$ ∃diagnosedWith.BreastCancer introduces a new successor $g(p_3)$ of p_3 satisfying BreastCancer, which, together with the definition of BreastCancer, means that p_3 is an answer to q_B since there is an additional breast cancer diagnosis that does not involve the skin.

---

[7] http://www.opengalen.org/.

Datalog-Based Ontology Languages with negation [2,18] are closely related to Skolemized ontologies, since their semantics is often based on the so-called *Skolem chase* [26]. This is closer to the semantics we propose in Sect. 3.1, in that a single canonical model is used for all inferences. However, it suffers from the same drawback of Skolemization described above, due to superfluous successors. To avoid this, our semantics uses a special minimal canonical model (see Definition 4), which is similar to the *restricted chase* [16] or the *core chase* [14], but always produces a unique model without having to merge domain elements. To the best of our knowledge, there exist no complexity results for Datalog-based languages with negation over the these other chase variants.

Closed Predicates are a way to declare, for example, the concept name Skin-Structure as "closed", which means that all skin structures must be declared explicitly, and no other SkinStructure object can exist [1,24]. This provides a way to give answers to negated atoms as in q_B. However, as explained in the introduction, this mechanism is not suitable for anonymous objects since it means that only named individuals can satisfy SkinStructure. When applied to $\mathcal{K}_C$, the result is even worse: Since there is no (named) SkinStructure object, no skin structures can exist at all and $\mathcal{K}_C$ becomes inconsistent. Closed predicates are appropriate in cases where the KB contains a full list of all instances of a certain concept name, and no other objects should satisfy it; but they are not suitable to infer negative information about anonymous objects. Moreover, CQ answering with closed predicates in $\mathcal{ELH}_\bot$ is already coNP-hard [24].

3.1   Semantics for NCQs

We propose to answer NCQs over a special canonical model of the knowledge base. On the one hand, this eliminates the problem of tracking anonymous objects across different models, and on the other hand enables us to encode our assumptions directly into the construction of the model. In particular, we should only introduce the minimum necessary number of anonymous objects since, unlike in standard CQ answering, the precise shape and number of anonymous objects has an impact on the semantics of negated atoms.

Given $\mathcal{K}_C$, in contrast to the Skolemized semantics, we will not create both a generic "Cancer" and another "BreastCancer" successor for p_1, because the BreastCancer is also a Cancer, and hence the first object is redundant. Therefore, in the minimal canonical model of $\mathcal{K}_C$ depicted in Fig. 1, for patient p_1 only one successor is introduced to satisfy the definitions of both BreastCancerPatient and CancerPatient at the same time. In contrast, p_2 has two successors, because BreastCancer and SkinCancer do not imply each other. Finally, for p_3 the ABox contains a single successor that is a SkinOfBreastCancer, which implies a single findingSite-successor that satisfies both SkinStructure and BreastStructure.

To detect whether an object required by an existential restriction $\exists r.A$ is redundant, we use the following notion of minimality.

Definition 3 (Structural Subsumption). *Let $\exists r.A$, $\exists t.B$ be concepts with $A, B \in N_C$ and $r, t \in N_R$. We say that $\exists r.A$ is structurally subsumed by $\exists t.B$ (written $\exists r.A \sqsubseteq^s_\mathcal{T} \exists t.B$) if $r \sqsubseteq_\mathcal{T} t$ and $A \sqsubseteq_\mathcal{T} B$.*

Given a set V of existential restrictions, we say that $\exists r.A \in V$ is minimal w.r.t. $\sqsubseteq^s_\mathcal{T}$ (in V) if there is no $\exists t.B \in V$ such that $\exists t.B \sqsubseteq^s_\mathcal{T} \exists r.A$.

A CQ $q_1(\mathbf{x})$ is structurally subsumed by a CQ $q_2(\mathbf{x})$ with the same answer variables (written $q_1 \sqsubseteq^s_\mathcal{T} q_2$) if, for all $x, y \in \mathbf{x}$, it holds that

$$\bigsqcap_{\alpha(x) \in q_1} \alpha \sqsubseteq_\mathcal{T} \bigsqcap_{\alpha(x) \in q_2} \alpha, \quad \text{and} \quad \bigsqcap_{\alpha(x,y) \in q_1} \alpha \sqsubseteq_\mathcal{T} \bigsqcap_{\alpha(x,y) \in q_2} \alpha,$$

where role conjunction is interpreted in the standard way [5].

In contrast to standard subsumption, $\exists r.A$ is not structurally subsumed by $\exists t.B$ w.r.t. the TBox $\mathcal{T} = \{\exists r.A \sqsubseteq \exists t.B\}$, as neither $r \sqsubseteq_\mathcal{T} t$ nor $A \sqsubseteq_\mathcal{T} B$ hold. Similarly, structural subsumption for CQs considers all (pairs of) variables separately.

We use this notion to define the minimal canonical model.

Definition 4 (Minimal Canonical Model). *Let $\mathcal{K} = (\mathcal{T}, \mathcal{A})$ be an $\mathcal{ELH}_\perp$ KB. We construct the minimal canonical model $I_\mathcal{K}$ of $\mathcal{K}$ as follows:*

1. *Set $\Delta^{I_\mathcal{K}} := N_I$ and $a^{I_\mathcal{K}} := a$ for all $a \in N_I$.*
2. *Define $A^{I_\mathcal{K}} := \{a \mid \mathcal{K} \models A(a)\}$ for all $A \in N_C$ and $r^{I_\mathcal{K}} := \{(a, b) \mid \mathcal{K} \models r(a, b)\}$ for all $r \in N_R$.*
3. *Repeat:*
   (a) *Select an element $d \in \Delta^{I_\mathcal{K}}$ that has not been selected before and let $V := \{\exists r.B \mid d \in A^{I_\mathcal{K}} \text{ and } d \notin (\exists r.B)^{I_\mathcal{K}} \text{ with } A \sqsubseteq_\mathcal{T} \exists r.B, A, B \in N_C\}$.*
   (b) *For each $\exists r.B \in V$ that is minimal w.r.t. $\sqsubseteq^s_\mathcal{T}$, add a fresh element e to $\Delta^{I_\mathcal{K}}$, for each $B \sqsubseteq_\mathcal{T} A$ add e to $A^{I_\mathcal{K}}$, and for each $r \sqsubseteq_\mathcal{T} s$ add (d, e) to $s^{I_\mathcal{K}}$.*

By $I_\mathcal{A}$ we denote the restriction of $I_\mathcal{K}$ to named individuals, i.e. the result of applying only Steps 1 and 2, but not Step 3.

If Step 3 is applied fairly, i.e. such that each new domain element that is created in (b) is eventually also selected in (a), then $I_\mathcal{K}$ is indeed a model of $\mathcal{K}$ (if $\mathcal{K}$ is consistent at all). In particular, all required existential restrictions are satisfied at each domain element, because the existential restrictions that are minimal w.r.t. $\sqsubseteq^s_\mathcal{T}$ entail all others.

Moreover, $I_\mathcal{K}$ satisfies the properties expected of a canonical model [15,25]: it can be homomorphically embedded into any other model of $\mathcal{K}$, and therefore $\text{cert}(q, \mathcal{K}) = \text{ans}(q, I_\mathcal{K})$ holds for all CQs q. We now define the semantics of NCQs as described before, i.e. by evaluating them as first-order formulas over the minimal canonical model $I_\mathcal{K}$, which ensures that our semantics is compatible with the usual certain-answer semantics for CQs.

Definition 5 (Minimal-World Semantics). *The (minimal-world) answers to an NCQ q over a consistent $\mathcal{ELH}_\perp$ KB $\mathcal{K}$ are $\text{mwa}(q, \mathcal{K}) := \text{ans}(q, I_\mathcal{K})$.*

For Example 2, we get $\mathrm{mwa}(q_B, \mathcal{K}_C) = \{p_1, p_2\}$ (see Fig. 1), which is exactly as intended. Unfortunately, in general the minimal canonical model is infinite, and we cannot evaluate the answers directly. Hence, we employ a rewriting app-roach to reduce NCQ answering over the minimal canonical model to (first-order) query answering over $I_{\mathcal{A}}$ only.

4   A Combined Rewriting for NCQs

We show that NCQ answering is combined first-order rewritable. As target rep-resentation, we obtain first-order queries of a special form.

Definition 6 (Filtered query). *Let* $\mathcal{K} = (\mathcal{T}, \mathcal{A})$ *be an* $\mathcal{ELH}_{\perp}$ *KB. A filter on a variable* z *is a first-order expression* $\psi(z)$ *of the form*

$$\big(\exists z'.\psi^+(z, z')\big) \rightarrow \big(\exists z'.\psi^+(z, z') \wedge \psi^-(z, z') \wedge \Psi\big) \tag{1}$$

where $\psi^+(z, z')$ *is a conjunction of atoms of the form* $A(z')$ *or* $r(z, z')$, *that contains at least one role atom,* $\psi^-(z, z')$ *is a conjunction of negated atoms* $\neg A(z')$ *or* $\neg r(z, z')$, *and* Ψ *is a (possibly empty) set of filters on* z'.

A filtered query ϕ *is of the form* $\exists \mathbf{y}.\big(\varphi(\mathbf{x}, \mathbf{y}) \wedge \Psi\big)$ *where* $\exists \mathbf{y}.\varphi(\mathbf{x}, \mathbf{y})$ *is an NCQ and* Ψ *is a set of filters on leaf variables in* φ. *It is rooted if* $\exists \mathbf{y}.\varphi(\mathbf{x}, \mathbf{y})$ *is rooted.*

Note that every NCQ is a filtered query where the set of filters Ψ is empty.

We will use filters to check for the existence of "typical" successors, i.e. role successors that behave like the ones that are introduced by the canonical model construction to satisfy an existential restriction. In particular, a typical successor does not satisfy any superfluous concept or role atoms. For exam-ple, in Fig. 1 the element c_1 introduced to satisfy $\exists$diagnosedWith.BreastCancer for p_1 is a typical successor, because it satisfies only BreastCancer and Can-cer and not, e.g. SkinCancer. In contrast, the diagnosedWith-successor c_3 of p_3 is atypical, since the ontology does not contain an existential restriction $\exists$diagnosedWith.SkinOfBreastCancer that could have introduced such a succes-sor in the canonical model.

The idea of the rewriting procedure is to not only rewrite the positive part of the query, as in [8,15], but to also ensure that no critical information is lost. This is accomplished by rewriting the negative parts and by saving the structure of the eliminated part of the query in the filter. A filter on z ensures that the rewritten query can only be satisfied by mapping z to an anonymous individual in the canonical model, or to a named individual that behaves in a similar way.

Definition 7 (Rewriting). *Let* $\mathcal{K} = (\mathcal{T}, \mathcal{A})$ *be a KB and* $\phi = \exists \mathbf{y}.\varphi(\mathbf{x}, \mathbf{y}) \wedge \Psi$ *be a rooted filtered query. We write* $\phi \rightarrow_{\mathcal{T}} \phi'$ *if* ϕ' *can be obtained from* ϕ *by applying the following steps:*

(S1) Select a quantified leaf variable $\hat{x}$ *in* φ. *Let* $\hat{y}$ *be a fresh variable and select*

$$\mathsf{Pred} := \{y \mid r(y, \hat{x}) \in \varphi\} \cup \{y \mid \neg r(y, \hat{x}) \in \varphi\} \qquad (\text{predecessors of } \hat{x}),$$

$$\mathsf{Pos} := \{A(\hat{x}) \in \varphi\} \cup \{r(\hat{y}, \hat{x}) \mid r(y, \hat{x}) \in \varphi\} \qquad (\text{positive atoms for } \hat{x}),$$

$$\mathsf{Neg} := \{\neg A(\hat{x}) \in \varphi\} \cup \{\neg r(\hat{y}, \hat{x}) \mid \neg r(y, \hat{x}) \in \varphi\} \quad (\text{negative atoms for } \hat{x}).$$

(S2) Select some $M \sqsubseteq_\mathcal{T} \exists s.N$ with $M, N \in N_C$ that satisfies all of the following:
  (a) $s(\hat{y}, \hat{x}) \wedge N(\hat{x}) \sqsubseteq_\mathcal{T}^s$ Pos, and
  (b) $s(\hat{y}, \hat{x}) \wedge N(\hat{x}) \not\sqsubseteq_\mathcal{T}^s \alpha$ for all $\neg\alpha \in$ Neg.
(S3) Let $\mathcal{M}'$ be the set of all $M' \in N_C$ such that $M' \sqsubseteq_\mathcal{T} \exists s'.N'$ with $N' \in N_C$,
  (a) $\exists s'.N' \sqsubseteq_\mathcal{T}^s \exists s.N$ (where $\exists s.N$ was chosen in *(S2)*), and
  (b) $s'(\hat{y}, \hat{x}) \wedge N'(\hat{x}) \sqsubseteq_\mathcal{T}^s \alpha$ for some $\neg\alpha \in$ Neg.
(S4) Drop from φ every atom that contains $\hat{x}$.
(S5) Replace all variables $y \in$ Pred in φ with $\hat{y}$.
(S6) Add the atoms $M(\hat{y})$ and $\{\neg M'(\hat{y}) \mid M' \in \mathcal{M}'\}$ to φ.
(S7) Set the new filters to $\Psi' := \Psi \cup \{\psi^*(\hat{y})\} \setminus \Psi_{\hat{x}}$, where $\Psi_{\hat{x}} := \{\psi(\hat{x}) \in \Psi\}$ and

$$\psi^*(\hat{y}) := \big(\exists \hat{x}.\, s(\hat{y}, \hat{x}) \wedge N(\hat{x})\big) \rightarrow \big(\exists \hat{x}.\, s(\hat{y}, \hat{x}) \wedge N(\hat{x}) \wedge \mathsf{Neg} \wedge \Psi_{\hat{x}}\big).$$

We write $\phi \rightarrow_\mathcal{T}^* \phi'$ if there exists a finite sequence $\phi \rightarrow_\mathcal{T} \cdots \rightarrow_\mathcal{T} \phi'$. Furthermore, let $\mathrm{rew}_\mathcal{T}(\phi) := \{\phi' \mid \phi \rightarrow_\mathcal{T}^* \phi'\}$ denote the finite set of all rewritings of ϕ.

There can only be a finite number of rewritings for a given query since there is only a finite number of possible subsumptions $M \sqsubseteq_\mathcal{T} \exists s.N$ that can be used for rewriting steps. Additionally, in every step one variable $(\hat{x})$ is eliminated from the NCQ part of the filtered query. Since the query is rooted, there always exists at least one predecessor that is renamed to $\hat{y}$, hence the introduction of $\hat{y}$ never increases the number of variables. Finally, it is easy to see that rewriting a rooted query always yields a rooted query.

The rewriting of Neg to the new negated atoms (via $\mathcal{M}'$ in (S6)) ensures that we do not lose important exclusion criteria, which may result in too many answers. Similarly, the filters exclude atypical successors in the ABox that may result in spurious answers. Both of these constructions are necessary.

Example 8. Consider the query q_B from Example 2. Using Definition 7, we obtain the first-order queries $\psi_B = q_B$, ϕ_B', and ϕ_B'', where

$$\phi_B' = \exists y.\, \mathrm{diagnosedWith}(x, y) \wedge \mathrm{BreastCancer}(y) \wedge \neg\mathrm{SkinOfBreastCancer}(y) \wedge$$

$$\big((\exists z.\, \mathrm{findingSite}(y, z) \wedge \mathrm{BreastStructure}(z)) \rightarrow$$

$$(\exists z.\, \mathrm{findingSite}(y, z) \wedge \mathrm{BreastStructure}(z) \wedge \neg\mathrm{SkinStructure}(z))\big)$$

results from choosing z in (S1), $\mathrm{BreastCancer} \sqsubseteq_{\mathcal{K}_C} \exists\mathrm{findingSite}.\mathrm{BreastStructure}$ in (S2), and computing $\mathcal{M}' = \{\mathrm{SkinOfBreastCancer}\}$ in (S3), and

$$\phi_B'' = \mathrm{BreastCancerPatient}(x) \wedge$$

$$\big((\exists y.\, \mathrm{diagnosedWith}(x, y) \wedge \mathrm{BreastCancer}(y)) \rightarrow$$

$$(\exists y.\, \mathrm{diagnosedWith}(x, y) \wedge \mathrm{BreastCancer}(y) \wedge \neg\mathrm{SkinOfBreastCancer}(y)) \wedge$$

$$((\exists z.\, \mathrm{findingSite}(y, z) \wedge \mathrm{BreastStructure}(z)) \rightarrow$$

$$(\exists z.\, \mathrm{findingSite}(y, z) \wedge \mathrm{BreastStructure}(z) \wedge \neg\mathrm{SkinStructure}(z)))\big)$$

is obtained due to BreastCancerPatient $\sqsubseteq_{\mathcal{K}_C}$ ∃diagnosedWith.BreastCancer. We omitted the redundant atoms Cancer(y) for clarity.

The finite interpretation $I_{\mathcal{A}_C}$ can be seen in Fig. 1 by ignoring all star-shaped nodes. When computing the answers over $I_{\mathcal{A}_C}$, we obtain

$$\text{ans}(\phi_B, I_{\mathcal{A}_C}) = \emptyset, \;\; \text{ans}(\phi'_B, I_{\mathcal{A}_C}) = \emptyset, \;\; \text{and} \;\; \text{ans}(\phi''_B, I_{\mathcal{A}_C}) = \{p_1, p_2\}.$$

For ϕ'_B, the conjunct ¬SkinOfBreastCancer(y) is necessary to exclude p_3 as an answer. In ϕ''_B, p_3 is excluded due to the filter that detects c_3 as an atypical successor, because it satisfies not only BreastCancer, but also SkinOfBreast-Cancer. Hence, both (S6) and (S7) are necessary steps in our rewriting. ∎

4.1 Correctness

In Definition 7, the new filter $\psi^*(\hat{y})$ may end up inside another filter expression after applying subsequent rewriting steps, i.e. by rewriting w.r.t. $\hat{y}$. In this case, however, the original structure of the rewriting is preserved, including all internal filters as well as the atoms $M(\hat{y})$, which are included implicitly by $\exists s.N \sqsubseteq M$, and $\{\neg M'(\hat{y}) \mid M' \in \mathcal{M}'\}$, which are included in Neg. We exploit this behavior to show that, whenever a rewritten query is satisfied in the finite interpretation $I_{\mathcal{A}}$, then it is also satisfied in $I_{\mathcal{K}}$. This is the most interesting part of the correctness proof, because it differs from the known constructions for ordinary CQs, for which this step is trivial.

Lemma 9. Let $\mathcal{K} = (\mathcal{T}, \mathcal{A})$ be a consistent $\mathcal{ELH}_\perp$ KB and ϕ be a rooted NCQ. Then, for all $\phi' \in \text{rew}_{\mathcal{T}}(\phi)$,

$$\text{ans}(\phi', I_{\mathcal{A}}) \subseteq \text{mwa}(\phi', \mathcal{K}).$$

Proof. Let $\phi' = \exists \mathbf{y}.(\varphi(\mathbf{x}, \mathbf{y}) \wedge \Psi)$ and π be an assignment of $\mathbf{x}, \mathbf{y}$ to N_I such that $I_{\mathcal{A}}, \pi \models \varphi(\mathbf{x}, \mathbf{y})$. Since $I_{\mathcal{A}}$ and $I_{\mathcal{K}}$ coincide on the domain N_I, we also have $I_{\mathcal{K}}, \pi \models \varphi(\mathbf{x}, \mathbf{y})$. Consider any filter $\psi(z) = \exists z'.\psi^+(z, z') \to \exists z'.(\beta(z, z') \wedge \Psi^*)$ in Ψ, where $\beta(z, z') := \psi^+(z, z') \wedge \psi^-(z, z')$. Then $\psi(z)$ was introduced at some point during the rewriting, suppose by selecting $M \sqsubseteq_{\mathcal{T}} \exists s.N$ in (S2). This means that φ contains the atom $M(z)$, and hence $d := \pi(z)$ is a named individual that is contained in $M^{I_{\mathcal{A}}} \subseteq M^{I_{\mathcal{K}}}$. By (S2), this means that $I_{\mathcal{K}}, \pi \models \exists z'.\psi^+(z, z')$, and we have to show that $I_{\mathcal{K}}, \pi \models \exists z'.(\beta(z, z') \wedge \Psi^*)$:

1. If $I_{\mathcal{A}}, \pi \models \exists z'.\beta(z, z')$, then $I_{\mathcal{K}}, \pi \models \exists z'.\beta(z, z')$ by the same argument as for $\varphi(\mathbf{x}, \mathbf{y})$ above, and we can proceed by induction on the structure of the filters to show that the inner filters Ψ^* are satisfied by the assignment π (extended appropriately for z').
2. If $I_{\mathcal{A}}, \pi \not\models \exists z'.\beta(z, z')$, then we cannot use a named individual to satisfy the filter $\psi(z)$ in $I_{\mathcal{K}}$. Moreover, since $I_{\mathcal{A}}$ satisfies $\psi(z)$, we also know that $I_{\mathcal{A}}, \pi \not\models \exists z'.\psi^+(z, z')$. Since $\psi^+(z, z') = s(z, z') \wedge N(z')$, this implies that $d \notin (\exists s.N)^{I_{\mathcal{A}}}$. Hence, $\exists s.N$ is included in the set V constructed in Step 3(a) of the canonical model construction for the element $d = \pi(z)$. Thus, there exists

$M' \sqsubseteq_\mathcal{T} \exists s'.N'$ such that $d \in (M')^{I_\mathcal{A}}$, $d \notin (\exists s'.N')^{I_\mathcal{A}}$, and $\exists s'.N' \sqsubseteq_\mathcal{T}^s \exists s.N$. By Step 3(b), $I_\mathcal{K}$ must contain an element d' such that $d' \in A^{I_\mathcal{K}}$ iff $N' \sqsubseteq_\mathcal{T} A$ and $(d, d') \in r^{I_\mathcal{K}}$ iff $s' \sqsubseteq_\mathcal{T} r$. Since $N' \sqsubseteq_\mathcal{T} N$ and $s' \sqsubseteq_\mathcal{T} s$, we obtain that $I_\mathcal{K}, \pi \cup \{z' \mapsto d'\} \models \psi^+(z, z')$.

We show that the assignment $\pi \cup \{z' \mapsto d'\}$ also satisfies $\psi^-(z, z') = \mathsf{Neg}$. Assume to the contrary that there is $\neg A(z') \in \mathsf{Neg}$ such that $d' \in A^{I_\mathcal{K}}$ (the case of negated role atoms is again analogous). Then we have $N' \sqsubseteq_\mathcal{T} A$, which shows that all conditions of (S3) are satisfied, and hence M' must be included in $\mathcal{M}'$. Since the atoms $\{\neg M'(\hat{y}) \mid M' \in \mathcal{M}'\}$ are contained in φ, we know that they are satisfied by π in $I_\mathcal{K}$, i.e. $d \notin (M')^{I_\mathcal{K}}$ and hence also $d \notin (M')^{I_\mathcal{A}}$, which is a contradiction.

It remains to show that the inner filters Ψ^* are satisfied by the assignment $\pi \cup \{z' \mapsto d'\}$ in $I_\mathcal{K}$. Since we are now dealing with an anonymous domain element d', we can use similar, but simpler, arguments as above to prove this by induction on the structure of the filters. This is possible because the atoms $s(\hat{y}, \hat{x})$, $N(\hat{x})$ implied by $M(\hat{y})$ and the negated atoms induced by $\mathcal{M}'$ are present in the query even if the filter is integrated into another filter during a subsequent rewriting step. □

We can use this lemma to show correctness of our approach, i.e. the answers returned for the *union* of queries given by $\mathrm{rew}_\mathcal{T}(\phi)$ over $I_\mathcal{A}$ are exactly the answers of the original NCQ ϕ over $I_\mathcal{K}$. The proof, which can be found in the extended version, is based on existing proofs for ordinary CQs [8,15], extended appropriately to deal with the filters.

Lemma 10. *Let* $\mathcal{K} = (\mathcal{T}, \mathcal{A})$ *be a consistent* $\mathcal{ELH}_\perp$ *KB and let* $\phi(\mathbf{x})$ *be a rooted NCQ. Then, for all* $\phi' \in \mathrm{rew}_\mathcal{T}(\phi)$,

$$\mathrm{mwa}(\phi, \mathcal{K}) = \bigcup_{\phi' \in \mathrm{rew}_\mathcal{T}(\phi)} \mathrm{ans}(\phi', I_\mathcal{A}).$$

We obtain the claimed complexity result.

Theorem 11. *Checking whether a given tuple* $\mathbf{a}$ *is a closed-world answer to an NCQ* ϕ *over a consistent* $\mathcal{ELH}_\perp$ *KB* $\mathcal{K}$ *can be done in polynomial time in data complexity.*

Under data complexity assumptions, ϕ and $\mathcal{T}$, and hence $\mathrm{rew}_\mathcal{T}(\phi)$, are fixed, and $I_\mathcal{A}$ is of polynomial size in the size of $\mathcal{A}$. However, if we want to use complex assertions in $\mathcal{A}$, as in Example 2, this leads to the introduction of additional acyclic definitions $\mathcal{T}'$, which are not fixed. The complexity nevertheless remains the same: Since $\mathcal{T}$ does not use the new concept names in $\mathcal{T}'$, we can apply the rewriting only w.r.t. $\mathcal{T}$, and extend $I_\mathcal{A}$ by a polynomial number of new elements that result from applying Definition 4 only w.r.t. $\mathcal{T}'$.

What is more important than the complexity result is that this approach can be used to evaluate NCQs using standard database methods, e.g. using views to define the finite interpretation $I_\mathcal{A}$ based on the input data given in $\mathcal{A}$, and SQL queries to evaluate the elements of $\mathrm{rew}_\mathcal{T}(\phi)$ over these views [22].

5   Conclusion

Dealing with the absence of information is an important and at the same time challenging task. In many real-world scenarios, it is not clear whether a piece of information is missing because it is unknown or because it is false. EHRs mostly talk about positive diagnoses and it would be impossible to list all the negative diagnoses, i.e. the diseases a patient does not suffer from. We showed that such a setting cannot be handled adequately by existing logic-based approaches, mostly because they do not deal with closed-world negation over anonymous objects. We introduced a novel semantics for answering conjunctive queries with negation and showed that it is well-behaved also for anonymous objects. Moreover, we demonstrated combined first-order rewritability, which allows us to answer NCQs by using conventional relational database technologies.

We are working on an optimized implementation of this method with the aim to deal with queries over large ontologies such as SNOMED CT. On the theoretical side, we will further develop our approach to also represent temporal and numeric information, such as the precise order and duration of a patient's illnesses and treatments, and the dosage of medications. Such information is important for evaluating the eligibility criteria of clinical trials [9,13,19].

References

1. Ahmetaj, S., Ortiz, M., Simkus, M.: Polynomial datalog rewritings for expressive description logics with closed predicates. In: Kambhampati, S. (ed.) Proceedings of the 25th International Joint Conference on Artificial Intelligence (IJCAI 2016), pp. 878–885. AAAI Press (2016). https://www.ijcai.org/Abstract/16/129
2. Arenas, M., Gottlob, G., Pieris, A.: Expressive languages for querying the semantic web. In: Hull, R., Grohe, M. (eds.) Proceedings of the 33rd Symposium on Principles of Database Systems (PODS 2014), pp. 14–26. ACM (2014). https://doi.org/10.1145/2594538.2594555
3. Aronson, A.R.: Effective mapping of biomedical text to the UMLS Metathesaurus: the MetaMap program. In: Proceedings of the AMIA Symposium, pp. 17–21. American Medical Informatics Association (2001)
4. Baader, F., Brandt, S., Lutz, C.: Pushing the $\mathcal{EL}$ envelope. In: Kaelbling, L.P., Saffiotti, A. (eds.) Proceedings of the 19th International Joint Conference on Artificial Intelligence (IJCAI 2005), pp. 364–369. Professional Book Center (2005). http://ijcai.org/Proceedings/09/Papers/053.pdf
5. Baader, F., Calvanese, D., McGuinness, D.L., Nardi, D., Patel-Schneider, P.F. (eds.): The Description Logic Handbook: Theory, Implementation, and Applications, 2nd edn. Cambridge University Press, Cambridge (2007)
6. Bárány, V., ten Cate, B., Otto, M.: Queries with guarded negation. Proc. VLDB Endow. 5(11), 1328–1339 (2012). https://doi.org/10.14778/2350229.2350250
7. Besana, P., Cuggia, M., Zekri, O., Bourde, A., Burgun, A.: Using semantic web technologies for clinical trial recruitment. In: Patel-Schneider, P.F., et al. (eds.) ISWC 2010. LNCS, vol. 6497, pp. 34–49. Springer, Heidelberg (2010). https://doi.org/10.1007/978-3-642-17749-1_3

8. Bienvenu, M., Ortiz, M.: Ontology-mediated query answering with data-tractable description logics. In: Faber, W., Paschke, A. (eds.) Reasoning Web 2015. LNCS, vol. 9203, pp. 218–307. Springer, Cham (2015). https://doi.org/10.1007/978-3-319-21768-0_9

9. Bonomi, L., Jiang, X.: Patient ranking with temporally annotated data. J. Biomed. Inform. **78**, 43–53 (2018). https://doi.org/10.1016/j.jbi.2017.12.007

10. Calvanese, D., et al.: Ontop: answering SPARQL queries over relational databases. Semant. Web **8**, 471–487 (2017)

11. Calvanese, D., De Giacomo, G., Lembo, D., Lenzerini, M., Rosati, R.: Epistemic first-order queries over description logic knowledge bases. In: Parsia, B., Sattler, U., Toman, D. (eds.) Proceedings of the 19th International Workshop on Description Logics (DL 2006). CEUR Workshop Proceedings, vol. 189, pp. 51–61 (2006)

12. Cresswell, K.M., Sheikh, A.: Inpatient clinical information systems. In: Sheikh, A., Cresswell, K.M., Wright, A., Bates, D.W. (eds.) Key Advances in Clinical Informatics, Chap. 2, pp. 13–29. Academic Press (2017). https://doi.org/10.1016/B978-0-12-809523-2.00002-9

13. Crowe, C.L., Tao, C.: Designing ontology-based patterns for the representation of the time-relevant eligibility criteria of clinical protocols. AMIA Joint Summits Transl. Sci. Proc. **2015**, 173–177 (2015). https://www.ncbi.nlm.nih.gov/pmc/articles/PMC4525239/

14. Deutsch, A., Nash, A., Remmel, J.B.: The chase revisited. In: Lenzerini, M., Lembo, D. (eds.) Proceedings of the 27th ACM SIGMOD-SIGACT-SIGART Symposium on Principles of Database Systems (PODS 2008), pp. 149–158. ACM (2008). https://doi.org/10.1145/1376916.1376938

15. Eiter, T., Ortiz, M., Šimkus, M., Tran, T.K., Xiao, G.: Query rewriting for horn-$\mathcal{SHIQ}$ plus rules. In: Hoffmann, J., Selman, B. (eds.) Proceedings of the 26th AAAI Conference on Artificial Intelligence (AAAI 2012), pp. 726–733. AAAI Press (2012). http://www.aaai.org/ocs/index.php/AAAI/AAAI12/paper/view/4931

16. Fagin, R., Kolaitis, P.G., Miller, R.J., Popa, L.: Data exchange: semantics and query answering. Theor. Comput. Sci. **336**(1), 89–124 (2005). https://doi.org/10.1016/j.tcs.2004.10.033

17. Gutiérrez-Basulto, V., Ibáñez-García, Y., Kontchakov, R., Kostylev, E.V.: Queries with negation and inequalities over lightweight ontologies. J. Web Semant. **35**, 184–202 (2015). https://doi.org/10.1016/j.websem.2015.06.002

18. Hernich, A., Kupke, C., Lukasiewicz, T., Gottlob, G.: Well-founded semantics for extended datalog and ontological reasoning. In: Hull, R., Fan, W. (eds.) Proceedings of the 32nd Symposium on Principles of Database Systems (PODS 2013), pp. 225–236. ACM (2013). https://doi.org/10.1145/2463664.2465229

19. Hripcsak, G., Zhou, L., Parsons, S., Das, A.K., Johnson, S.B.: Modeling electronic discharge summaries as a simple temporal constraint satisfaction problem. J. Am. Med. Inform. Assoc. **12**(1), 55–63 (2005). https://doi.org/10.1197/jamia.m1623

20. Johnson, A.E.W., et al.: MIMIC-III, a freely accessible critical care database. Sci. Data **3**(160035), 1–9 (2016). https://doi.org/10.1038/sdata.2016.35

21. Kharlamov, E., et al.: Ontology based data access in Statoil. Web Semant. **44**, 3–36 (2017). https://doi.org/10.1016/j.websem.2017.05.005

22. Kontchakov, R., Lutz, C., Toman, D., Wolter, F., Zakharyaschev, M.: The combined approach to ontology-based data access. In: Walsh, T. (ed.) Proceedings of the 22nd International Joint Conference on Artificial Intelligence (IJCAI 2011), pp. 2656–2661. AAAI Press (2011). https://doi.org/10.5591/978-1-57735-516-8/IJCAI11-442

23. Köpcke, F., Prokosch, H.U.: Employing computers for the recruitment into clinical trials: a comprehensive systematic review. J. Med. Internet Res. 16(7), e161 (2014). https://doi.org/10.2196/jmir.3446
24. Lutz, C., Seylan, I., Wolter, F.: Ontology-based data access with closed predicates is inherently intractable (sometimes). In: Rossi, F. (ed.) Proceedings of the 23rd International Joint Conference on Artificial Intelligence (IJCAI 2013), pp. 1024–1030. AAAI Press (2013). https://www.ijcai.org/Abstract/13/156
25. Lutz, C., Toman, D., Wolter, F.: Conjunctive query answering in the description logic $\mathcal{EL}$ using a relational database system. In: Boutilier, C. (ed.) Proceedings of the 21st International Joint Conference on Artificial Intelligence (IJCAI 2009), pp. 2070–2075. AAAI Press (2009)
26. Marnette, B.: Generalized schema mappings: from termination to tractability. In: Paredaens, J., Su, J. (eds.) Proceedings of the 28th Symposium on Principles of Database Systems (PODS 2009), pp. 13–22. ACM (2009). https://doi.org/10.1145/1559795.1559799
27. Mugnier, M.-L., Thomazo, M.: An introduction to ontology-based query answering with existential rules. In: Koubarakis, M., et al. (eds.) Reasoning Web 2014. LNCS, vol. 8714, pp. 245–278. Springer, Cham (2014). https://doi.org/10.1007/978-3-319-10587-1_6
28. Ni, Y., et al.: Increasing the efficiency of trial-patient matching: Automated clinical trial eligibility pre-screening for pediatric oncology patients. BMC Med. Inform. Decis. Making 15, 1–10 (2015). https://doi.org/10.1186/s12911-015-0149-3
29. Patel, C., et al.: Matching patient records to clinical trials using ontologies. In: Aberer, K., et al. (eds.) ASWC/ISWC 2007. LNCS, vol. 4825, pp. 816–829. Springer, Heidelberg (2007). https://doi.org/10.1007/978-3-540-76298-0_59
30. Savova, G.K., et al.: Mayo clinical text analysis and knowledge extraction system (cTAKES): architecture, component evaluation and applications. J. Am. Med. Inform. Assoc. 17(5), 507–513 (2010)
31. Tagaris, A., et al.: Exploiting ontology based search and EHR interoperability to facilitate clinical trial design. In: Koutsouris, D.-D., Lazakidou, A.A. (eds.) Concepts and Trends in Healthcare Information Systems. AIS, vol. 16, pp. 21–42. Springer, Cham (2014). https://doi.org/10.1007/978-3-319-06844-2_3
32. Wolter, F.: First order common knowledge logics. Studia Logica 65(2), 249–271 (2000). https://doi.org/10.1023/A:1005271815356

Extending $\mathcal{ALC}$ with the Power-Set Construct

Laura Giordano[1](✉) and Alberto Policriti[2]

[1] DISIT - Università del Piemonte Orientale, Alessandria, Italy
laura.giordano@uniupo.it
[2] Dipartimento di Scienze Matematiche, Informatiche e Fisiche,
Università di Udine, Udine, Italy
alberto.policriti@uniud.it

Abstract. We continue our exploration of the relationships between Description Logics and Set Theory, which started with the definition of the description logic $\mathcal{ALC}^\Omega$. We develop a set-theoretic translation of the description logic $\mathcal{ALC}^\Omega$ in the set theory Ω, exploiting a technique originally proposed for translating normal modal and polymodal logics into Ω.

We first define a set-theoretic translation of $\mathcal{ALC}$ based on Schild's correspondence with polymodal logics. Then we propose a translation of the fragment $\mathcal{LC}^\Omega$ of $\mathcal{ALC}^\Omega$ without roles and individual names. In this—simple—case the power-set concept is mapped, as expected, to the set-theoretic power-set, making clearer the real nature of the power-set concept in $\mathcal{ALC}^\Omega$. Finally, we encode the whole language of $\mathcal{ALC}^\Omega$ into its fragment without roles, showing that such a fragment is as expressive as $\mathcal{ALC}^\Omega$. The encoding provides, as a by-product, a set-theoretic translation of $\mathcal{ALC}^\Omega$ into the theory Ω, which can be used as basis for extending other, more expressive, DLs with the power-set construct.

1 Introduction

In this paper we continue our investigation of the relationships between Description Logics and Set Theory, starting from the description logic $\mathcal{ALC}^\Omega$, introduced in [5], which extends the language of $\mathcal{ALC}$ with the power set concept and with membership axioms. In $\mathcal{ALC}^\Omega$ concepts are interpreted as *sets* living in a model of a simple theory Ω, a very rudimentary axiomatic set theory (introduced in Sect. 2.2), consisting of only four axioms characterizing binary union, set difference, inclusion, and the power-set. Hence, concepts are interpreted as sets of sets (which are not necessarily well-founded), and membership among concepts has the obvious semantic interpretation as a natural generalization of DL assertions $C(a)$.

The idea of enhancing the language of description logics with statements of the form $C \in D$, with C and D concepts is not new, as assertions of the form $D(A)$, with A a concept name, are allowed in OWL-Full [15], and, starting from [11], where two alternative semantics (the Contextual π-semantics and the Hilog

© Springer Nature Switzerland AG 2019
F. Calimeri et al. (Eds.): JELIA 2019, LNAI 11468, pp. 387–398, 2019.
https://doi.org/10.1007/978-3-030-19570-0_25

ν-semantics) are proposed for metamodeling, many approaches to metamodeling have been proposed in the literature including membership among concepts. Most of them [4,8–10] are based on a Hilog semantics, while [12,14] define extensions of OWL DL and of $\mathcal{SHIQ}$ (respectively), based on semantics interpreting concepts as well-founded sets. None of these proposals includes the power-set concept in the language.

Considering an example taken from [11,17], using membership axioms, we can represent the fact that eagles are in the red list of endangered species, by the axiom $Eagle \in RedListSpecies$ and that Harry is an eagle, by the assertion $Eagle(harry)$. We could further consider a concept $NotModifiableList$, consisting of those lists that cannot be modified (if not by, say, a specifically enforced law) and, for example, it would be reasonable to ask $RedListSpecies \in NotModifiableList$. However, much more interestingly, we would also clearly want $NotModifiableList \in NotModifiableList$.

The power-set concept, $\mathrm{Pow}(C)$, allows to capture in a natural way the interactions between concepts and metaconcepts. Considering again the example above, the statement "all the instances of species in the Red List are not allowed to be hunted", observe that it can be naturally represented by the concept inclusion axiom: $RedListSpecies \sqsubseteq \mathrm{Pow}(CannotHunt)$, meaning that all the instances in the $RedListSpecies$ (as the class $Eagle$) are collections of individuals of the class $CannotHunt$. Notice, however, that $\mathrm{Pow}(CannotHunt)$ is not limited to include $RedListSpecies$ but can include a much larger universe of sets (e.g. anything belonging to $\mathrm{Pow}(Humans)$).

In [5] we proved that $\mathcal{ALC}^{\Omega}$ is decidable by defining, for any $\mathcal{ALC}^{\Omega}$ knowledge base K, a polynomial translation K^T into $\mathcal{ALCOI}$, exploiting a technique—originally proposed and studied in [3]—consisting in identifying the membership relation $\in$ with the accessibility relation of a normal modality. Such an identification naturally leads to a correspondence between the power-set operator and the modal necessity operator $\Box$. We showed that the translation has the finite model property and concept satisfiability in $\mathcal{ALC}^{\Omega}$ is in ExpTime.

In this paper we exploit the correspondence between $\in$ and the accessibility relation of a normal modality in another direction, to provide a polynomial set-theoretic translation of $\mathcal{ALC}^{\Omega}$ in the set theory Ω. Our aim is to understand the real nature of the power-set concept in $\mathcal{ALC}^{\Omega}$, as well as showing that a description logic with just the power-set concept, but no roles and no individual names, is as expressive as $\mathcal{ALC}^{\Omega}$.

We proceed step by step by first defining a set-theoretic translation of $\mathcal{ALC}$ based on Schild's correspondence result [16] and on the set-theoretic translation for normal polymodal logics in [3]. Then, we consider the fragment of $\mathcal{ALC}^{\Omega}$ containing union, intersection, (set-)difference, complement, and power-set (but neither roles nor named individuals) and we show that this fragment, that we call $\mathcal{LC}^{\Omega}$, has an immediate set-theoretic translation into Ω, where the power-set concept is translated as the power-set in Ω. Finally, we provide an encoding of the whole $\mathcal{ALC}^{\Omega}$ into $\mathcal{LC}^{\Omega}$. This encoding shows that $\mathcal{LC}^{\Omega}$ is as expressive as $\mathcal{ALC}^{\Omega}$. The full path leads to a set-theoretic translation of both the universal restriction and power-set concept of $\mathcal{ALC}^{\Omega}$ in the theory Ω using the single relational symbol $\in$. We refer to [6] for the proofs of the results.

2 Preliminaries

2.1 The Description Logic $\mathcal{ALC}$

Let N_C be a set of concept names, N_R a set of role names and N_I a set of individual names. The set $\mathcal{C}$ of $\mathcal{ALC}$ *concepts* can be inductively defined as follows:

- $A \in N_C$, $\top$ and $\perp$ are concepts in $\mathcal{C}$;
- if $C, D \in \mathcal{C}$ and $R \in N_R$, then $C \sqcap D, C \sqcup D, \neg C, \forall R.C, \exists R.C$ are concepts in $\mathcal{C}$.

A knowledge base (KB) K is a pair $(\mathcal{T}, \mathcal{A})$, where $\mathcal{T}$ is a TBox and $\mathcal{A}$ is an ABox. The TBox $\mathcal{T}$ is a set of concept inclusions (or subsumptions) $C \sqsubseteq D$, where C, D are concepts in $\mathcal{C}$. The ABox $\mathcal{A}$ is a set of assertions of the form $C(a)$ and $R(a, b)$ where C is a concept, $R \in N_R$, and $a, b \in N_I$.
An interpretation for $\mathcal{ALC}$ (see [2]) is a pair $I = \langle \Delta, \cdot^I \rangle$ where:

- Δ is a domain—a set whose elements are denoted by $x, y, z, \ldots$ —and
- $\cdot^I$ is an extension function that maps each concept name $C \in N_C$ to a set $C^I \subseteq \Delta$, each role name $R \in N_R$ to a binary relation $R^I \subseteq \Delta \times \Delta$, and each individual name $a \in N_I$ to an element $a^I \in \Delta$.

The function $\cdot^I$ is extended to complex concepts as follows: $\top^I = \Delta$, $\perp^I = \emptyset$, $(\neg C)^I = \Delta \backslash C^I$, $(C \sqcap D)^I = C^I \cap D^I$, $(C \sqcup D)^I = C^I \cup D^I$, and

$$(\forall R.C)^I = \{x \in \Delta \mid \forall y.(x, y) \in R^I \mapsto y \in C^I\},$$
$$(\exists R.C)^I = \{x \in \Delta \mid \exists y.(x, y) \in R^I \ \& \ y \in C^I\}.$$

The notion of satisfiability of a KB in an interpretation is defined as follows:

Definition 1 (Satisfiability and entailment). *Given an $\mathcal{ALC}$ interpretation* $I = \langle \Delta, \cdot^I \rangle$:

- *I satisfies an inclusion $C \sqsubseteq D$ if $C^I \subseteq D^I$;*
- *I satisfies an assertion $C(a)$ if $a^I \in C^I$ and an assertion $R(a, b)$ if $(a^I, b^I) \in R^I$.*

Given a KB $K = (\mathcal{T}, \mathcal{A})$, an interpretation I satisfies $\mathcal{T}$ (resp. $\mathcal{A}$) if I satisfies all inclusions in $\mathcal{T}$ (resp. all assertions in $\mathcal{A}$); I is a model of K if I satisfies $\mathcal{T}$ and $\mathcal{A}$.

Letting a query F be either an inclusion $C \sqsubseteq D$ (where C and D are concepts) or an assertion $C(a)$, F is entailed by K, written $K \models F$, if for all models $I = \langle \Delta, \cdot^I \rangle$ of K, I satisfies F.

Given a KB K, the *subsumption* problem is the problem of deciding whether an inclusion $C \sqsubseteq D$ is entailed by K. The *instance checking* problem is the problem of deciding whether an assertion $C(a)$ is entailed by K. The *concept satisfiability* problem is the problem of deciding, for a concept C, whether C is consistent with K, that is, whether there exists a model I of K, such that $C^I \neq \emptyset$.

2.2   The Theory Ω

The first-order theory Ω consists of the following four axioms in the language with relational symbols $\in$ and $\subseteq$, and functional symbols $\cup$, $\setminus$, Pow:

$$x \in y \cup z \leftrightarrow x \in y \vee x \in z;$$
$$x \in y \setminus z \leftrightarrow x \in y \wedge x \notin z;$$
$$x \subseteq y \leftrightarrow \forall z (z \in x \rightarrow z \in y);$$
$$x \in Pow(y) \leftrightarrow x \subseteq y.$$

In an Ω-model *everything* is supposed to be a set. Hence, a set will have (only) sets as its elements and circular definition of sets are allowed (such as a set admitting itself as one of its elements). Moreover, not postulating in Ω any *link* between membership $\in$ and equality—in axiomatic terms, having no *extensionality* (axiom)—Ω-models in which there are different sets with equal collection of elements, are admissible.

The most natural Ω-model—in which different sets are, in fact, always extensionally different—is the collection of well-founded sets $\mathsf{HF} = \mathsf{HF}^0 = \bigcup_{n \in \mathbb{N}} \mathsf{HF}_n$, where: $\mathsf{HF}_0 = \emptyset$ and $\mathsf{HF}_{n+1} = Pow(\mathsf{HF}_n)$. A close relative of HF^0, in which sets are not required to be well-founded, goes under the name of $\mathsf{HF}^{1/2}$ (see [1,13]). HF^0 or $\mathsf{HF}^{1/2}$ can be seen as the collection of finite (either acyclic or cyclic) graphs where sets are represented by nodes and arcs depict the membership relation among sets (see [13]).

A further enrichment of both HF^0 and $\mathsf{HF}^{1/2}$ is obtained by adding *atoms*, that is copies of the empty-set, to be denoted by $\mathsf{a}_1, \mathsf{a}_2, \ldots$ and collectively represented by $\mathbb{A} = \{\mathsf{a}_1, \mathsf{a}_2, \ldots\}$. The resulting universes will be denoted by $\mathsf{HF}^0(\mathbb{A})$ and $\mathsf{HF}^{1/2}(\mathbb{A})$.

We will regard the domain Δ of an $\mathcal{ALC}^\Omega$ interpretation as a fragment of the universe of an Ω-model, i.e. as a set of sets of the theory Ω rather than as a set of individuals, as customary in description logics.

2.3   The Description Logic $\mathcal{ALC}^\Omega$

In [5] $\mathcal{ALC}$ has been extended by allowing concepts to be interpreted as sets in a universe of the set theory Ω, introducing the power-set as a new concept constructor, and admitting membership relations among concepts to occur in the knowledge base. The resulting extension of $\mathcal{ALC}$ has been called $\mathcal{ALC}^\Omega$. We recap its definition.

Let N_I, N_C, and N_R be as in Sect. 2.1. We extend the language of $\mathcal{ALC}$ by allowing, for all $\mathcal{ALC}^\Omega$ concepts C, D:

- the *difference concept* $C \setminus D$ and
- the *power-set concept* $\mathrm{Pow}(C)$.

While the concept $C \setminus D$ can be easily defined in $\mathcal{ALC}$ as $C \sqcap \neg D$, this is not the case for the concept $\mathrm{Pow}(C)$. Informally, the instances of concept $\mathrm{Pow}(C)$ are all the subsets of the instances of concept C, which are "visible" in (i.e. which belong to) Δ.

Besides usual assertions of the forms $C(a)$ and $R(a, b)$ with $a, b \in N_I$, $\mathcal{ALC}^\Omega$ allows in the ABox *concept membership axioms* and *role membership axioms* of the forms $C \in D$ and $(C, D) \in R$, respectively, where C and D are $\mathcal{ALC}^\Omega$ concepts and R is a role name.

Considering again the example from the Introduction, the additional expressivity of the language allows for instance to represent the fact that polar bears are in the red list of endangered species, by the axiom *Polar $\sqcap$ Bear $\in$ RedListSpecies*. We can further represent the fact the polar bears are more endangered than eagles by the role membership axiom *(Polar $\sqcap$ Bear, Eagle) $\in$ moreEndangered*.

We define a semantics for $\mathcal{ALC}^\Omega$ extending the $\mathcal{ALC}$ semantics in Sect. 2.1 to capture the meaning of concepts (including concept $\text{Pow}(C)$) as elements (sets) of the domain Δ, chosen as a *transitive* set (i.e. a set x satisfying $(\forall y \in x)(y \subseteq x)$) in a model of Ω. Individual names are (essentially) interpreted as elements of a set of *atoms* $\mathbb{A}$, i.e. pairwise distinct copies of the empty-set from which the remaining sets in Δ are built.

Definition 2. *An interpretation for $\mathcal{ALC}^\Omega$ is a pair $I = \langle \Delta, \cdot^I \rangle$ over a set of atoms $\mathbb{A}$ where: (i) the non-empty domain Δ is a transitive set chosen in the universe $\mathcal{U}$ of a model $\mathcal{M}$ of Ω over the atoms in $\mathbb{A}$;[1] (ii) the extension function $\cdot^I$ maps each concept name $A \in N_C$ to an element $A^I \in \Delta$; each role name $R \in N_R$ to a binary relation $R^I \subseteq \Delta \times \Delta$; and each individual name $a \in N_I$ to an element $a^I \in \mathbb{A} \subseteq \Delta$. The function $\cdot^I$ is extended to complex concepts of $\mathcal{ALC}^\Omega$, as in Sect. 2.1 for $\mathcal{ALC}$, but for the two additional cases: $(\text{Pow}(C))^I = \text{Pow}(C^I) \cap \Delta$ and $(C \backslash D)^I = (C^I \backslash D^I)$.*

Observe that $\mathbb{A} \subseteq \Delta \in \mathcal{U}$. As Δ is not guaranteed to be closed under union, intersection, etc., the interpretation C^I of a concept C is a set in $\mathcal{U}$ but not necessarily an element of Δ. However, given the interpretation of the power-set concept as the portion of the (set-theoretic) power-set *visible in* Δ, it easy to see by induction that, for each C, the extension of C^I is a subset of Δ.

Given an interpretation I, the satisfiability of inclusions and assertions is defined as in $\mathcal{ALC}$ interpretations (Definition 1). Satisfiability of (concept and role) membership axioms in an interpretation I is defined as follows: I *satisfies* $C \in D$ if $C^I \in D^I$; I *satisfies* $(C, D) \in R$ if $(C^I, D^I) \in R^I$. With this addition, the notions of satisfiability of a KB and of entailment in $\mathcal{ALC}^\Omega$ (denoted $\models_{\mathcal{ALC}^\Omega}$) can be defined as in Sect. 2.1.

The problem of instance checking in $\mathcal{ALC}^\Omega$ includes both the problem of verifying whether an assertion $C(a)$ is a logical consequence of the KB and the problem of verifying whether a membership $C \in D$ is a logical consequence of the KB (i.e., whether C is an instance of D).

---

[1] In the following, for readability, we will denote by $\in$, Pow, $\cup$, $\backslash$ (rather than $Pow^\mathcal{M}$, $\cup^\mathcal{M}$, $\backslash^\mathcal{M}$) the interpretation in a model $\mathcal{M}$ of the predicate and function symbols $\in$, Pow, $\cup$, $\backslash$.

A translation of the logic $\mathcal{ALC}^{\Omega}$ into the description logic $\mathcal{ALCOI}$, including inverse roles and nominals, has been defined in [5], based on the correspondence between $\in$ and the accessibility relation of a modality explored in [3]. There, the membership relation $\in$ is used to represent a normal modality R. In [5], vice-versa, a new (reserved) role e in N_R is introduced to represent the inverse of the membership relation, restricted to the sets in Δ: in any interpretation I, $(x, y) \in e^I$ will stand for $y \in x$. The idea underlying the translation is that each element u of the domain Δ in an $\mathcal{ALCOI}$ interpretation $I = \langle \Delta, \cdot^I \rangle$ can be regarded as the set of all the elements v such that $(u, v) \in e^I$.

Soundness and completeness of this polynomial translation (see [5,6]) provide, besides decidability, an EXPTIME upper bound for satisfiability in $\mathcal{ALC}^{\Omega}$. In [5] it was also proved that if the translation K^T has a model in $\mathcal{ALCOI}$, then it has a finite model. From the soundness and completeness of the translation, it follows that $\mathcal{ALC}^{\Omega}$ has the *finite model property*.

3 A Set Theoretic Translation of $\mathcal{ALC}^{\Omega}$

We define a set-theoretic translation of $\mathcal{ALC}^{\Omega}$ in the set theory Ω, exploiting the correspondence between $\in$ and the accessibility relation of a normal modality studied in [3]. In Sect. 3.1, we define a set-theoretic translation of $\mathcal{ALC}$, based on the translation introduced by D'Agostino et al. for normal, complete finitely axiomatizable polymodal logics [3]. Here, according to the well known correspondence between description logics and modal logics studied by Schild [16], concepts (sets of elements) play the role of propositions (sets of worlds) in the polymodal logic, while universal and existential restrictions $\forall R$ and $\exists R$ play the role of universal and existential modalities $\Box_i$ and $\Diamond_i$.

In Sect. 3.2 we focus on the fragment of $\mathcal{ALC}^{\Omega}$ admitting no roles, no individual names and no existential and universal restrictions, that we call $\mathcal{LC}^{\Omega}$. We show that $\mathcal{LC}^{\Omega}$ can be given a simple set-theoretic translation in Ω. Finally, in Sect. 3.3, we see that this set-theoretic translation can be naturally extended to the full $\mathcal{ALC}^{\Omega}$. In particular, we encode $\mathcal{ALC}^{\Omega}$ into its fragment $\mathcal{LC}^{\Omega}$, showing that $\mathcal{LC}^{\Omega}$ is as expressive as $\mathcal{ALC}^{\Omega}$ and providing a set-theoretic translation of $\mathcal{ALC}^{\Omega}$ in which $\forall R_i.C$ and the power-set concept $\text{Pow}(C)$ are encoded in a uniform way.

3.1 A Set Theoretic Translation of $\mathcal{ALC}$ with Empty ABox

Let $R_1, \ldots, R_k$ be the roles occurring in the knowledge base $K = (\mathcal{T}, \mathcal{A})$ and let $A_1, \ldots, A_n$ be the concept names occurring in K. Given a concept C of $\mathcal{ALC}$, built from the concept names and role names in K, its set-theoretic translation is a set-theoretic term $C^S(x, y_1, \ldots, y_k, x_1, \ldots, x_n)$, where $x, y_1, \ldots, y_k, x_1, \ldots, x_n$ are set-theoretic variables, inductively defined as follows:

$$\top^S = x; \qquad\qquad\qquad \bot^S = \emptyset;$$
$$A_i^S = x_i, \text{ for } A_i \text{ in } K; \qquad (\neg C)^S = x \backslash C^S;$$
$$(C \sqcap D)^S = C^S \cap D^S; \qquad (C \sqcup D)^S = C^S \cup D^S;$$
$$(\forall R_i.C)^S = Pow(((x \cup y_1 \cup \ldots \cup y_k)\backslash y_i) \cup Pow(C^S)), \qquad \text{for } R_i \text{ in } K;$$

$(\exists R_i.C)^S$ is translated to the set-theoretic term $(\neg \forall R_i.\neg C)^S$. Each $\mathcal{ALC}$ concept C is represented by a set-theoretic term C^S and interpreted as a set in each model of Ω. Membership is used to give an interpretation of roles, as for modalities in the polymodal logics in [3].

For a single role R, by *imitating* the relation R^I with $\in$ (where $v \in u$ corresponds to $(u, v) \in R^I$), we naturally obtain that $Pow(C)$ corresponds to the universal restriction $\forall R.C$. For multiple roles, in order to encode the different relations $R_1, \ldots, R_k$, k sets U_i are considered. Informally, each set U_i (represented by the variable y_i) is such that $(v, v') \in R_i^I$ iff there is some $u_i \in U_i$ such that $u_i \in v$ and $v' \in u_i$.

Given an $\mathcal{ALC}$ knowledge base $K = (\mathcal{T}, \mathcal{A})$ with $\mathcal{A} = \emptyset$, we define the translation of the TBox axioms as follows:

$$TBox_{\mathcal{T}}(x, y_1, \ldots, y_k, x_1, \ldots, x_k) = \{C_1^S \cap x \subseteq C_2^S \mid C_1 \sqsubseteq C_2 \in \mathcal{T}\}$$

We can then establish a correspondence between subsumption in $\mathcal{ALC}^\Omega$ and derivability in the set theory Ω, instantiating the result of Theorem 5 in [3] as follows:

Proposition 1. *For all concepts C and D on the language of the theory K:*

$$K \models_{\mathcal{ALC}} C \sqsubseteq D \text{ if and only if}$$
$$\Omega \vdash \forall x \forall y_1 \ldots \forall y_k (Trans^2(x) \wedge Axiom_H(x, y_1, \ldots, y_k)$$
$$\rightarrow \forall x_1, \ldots, \forall x_n (\bigwedge TBox_{\mathcal{T}} \rightarrow C^S \cap x \subseteq D^S))$$

where $Trans^2(x)$ stands for $\forall y \forall z(y \in z \wedge z \in x \rightarrow y \subseteq x)$, that is, $x \subseteq Pow(Pow(x))$.

The property $Trans^2(x)$ on the set x, which here represents the domain Δ of an $\mathcal{ALC}^\Omega$ interpretation (a transitive set), is needed, as in the polymodal case in [3], to guarantee that elements accessible through R_i turn out to be in x. The set $Axiom_H(x, y_1, \ldots, y_k)$, which in [3] contains the translation of the specific axioms of a polymodal logic, here is empty, as in $\mathcal{ALC}^\Omega$ roles do not have any specific additional properties, and they correspond to the modalities of the normal polymodal logic K_m.

Roughly speaking, the meaning of Proposition 1 is that, for all the instances of x representing the domain Δ, for all the instances $U_1, \ldots, U_k$ of the set variables $y_1, \ldots, y_k$, any choice for the interpretation $x_1, \ldots, x_n$ of the atomic concepts $A_1, \ldots, A_n$ in K which satisfies the TBox axioms over the elements in x (i.e., over the domain Δ), also satisfies the inclusion $C^S \subseteq D^S$ over Δ.

From the correspondence of the logic $\mathcal{ALC}$ with the normal polymodal logic K_m in [16] and from the soundness and completeness of the set-theoretic translation for normal polymodal logics (Theorems 17 and 18 in [3]), we can conclude that, for $\mathcal{ALC}$, the set-theoretic translation above is sound and complete.

This set-theoretic translation can be naturally extended to more expressive description logics adding in $Axiom_H(x, \overline{y})$ the set-theoretic encoding of the semantic properties of the DL constructs. For instance, role hierarchy axioms, $R_j \sqsubseteq R_i$, with semantic condition $R_j^I \subseteq R_i^I$, can be simply captured by adding in $Axiom_H(x, y_1, \ldots, y_k)$ the condition $y_j \subseteq y_i$. The inverse role R_j of a role R_i (i.e., $R_j = R_i^-$) can be captured by encoding the semantic condition $(v, y) \in R_j$ if and only if $(y, v) \in R_i$ by the axiom: $\forall y, v(y \in x \wedge v \in x \rightarrow (\exists u(u \in y \wedge u \in y_j \wedge v \in u) \leftrightarrow \exists u'(u' \in v \wedge u' \in y_i \wedge y \in u')))$.

3.2   Translating the Fragment $\mathcal{LC}^\Omega$

In this section we focus on the fragment $\mathcal{LC}^\Omega$ of $\mathcal{ALC}^\Omega$ without roles, individual names, universal and existential restrictions and role assertions, and we show that it can be given a simple set-theoretic translation in the set theory Ω. This translation provides some insight in the nature of the power-set construct in $\mathcal{ALC}^\Omega$.

Let us consider a fragment of $\mathcal{ALC}^\Omega$ which does neither allow existential and universal restrictions nor role assertions. We call $\mathcal{LC}^\Omega$ such a fragment, whose concepts are defined inductively as follows:

– $A \in N_C$, $\top$ and $\bot$ are $\mathcal{LC}^\Omega$ concepts;
– if C, D are $\mathcal{LC}^\Omega$ concepts, then the following are $\mathcal{LC}^\Omega$ concepts:

$$C \sqcap D, C \sqcup D, \neg C, C \backslash D, \text{Pow}(C)$$

An $\mathcal{LC}^\Omega$ knowledge base K is a pair $(\mathcal{T}, \mathcal{A})$, where the TBox $\mathcal{T}$ is a set of concept inclusions $C \sqsubseteq D$, and the ABox $\mathcal{A}$ is a set of membership axioms $C \in D$.

Given an $\mathcal{LC}^\Omega$ knowledge base $K = (\mathcal{T}, \mathcal{A})$, let $A_1, \ldots, A_n$ be the concept names occurring in K. We define a translation of an $\mathcal{LC}^\Omega$ concept C over the language of K to a set-theoretic term $C^S(x, x_1, \ldots, x_n)$, where $x, x_1, \ldots, x_n$ are set-theoretic variables, by induction on the structure of concepts, as follows:

$$\top^S = x; \quad \bot^S = \emptyset; \quad A_i^S = x_i, \text{ for } i = 1, \ldots, n; \quad (\neg C)^S = x \backslash C^S;$$
$$(\neg C)^S = x \backslash C^S; \quad (C \sqcap D)^S = C^S \cap D^S; \quad (C \sqcup D)^S = C^S \cup D^S;$$
$$(C \backslash D)^S = C^S \backslash D^S; \quad (\text{Pow}(C))^S = Pow(C^S).$$

Given a knowledge base $K = (\mathcal{T}, \mathcal{A})$, the translation for the TBox $\mathcal{T}$ and ABox $\mathcal{A}$ is defined as follows:

$$TBox_{\mathcal{T}}(x, x_1, \ldots, x_n) = \{C_1^S \cap x \subseteq C_2^S \mid C_1 \sqsubseteq C_2 \in \mathcal{T}\} \cup \{A_i^S \in x \mid i = 1, \ldots, n\}$$
$$ABox_{\mathcal{A}}(x, x_1, \ldots, x_n) = \{C_1^S \in C_2^S \cap x \mid (C_1 \in C_2) \in \mathcal{A}\}$$

We can now establish a correspondence between subsumption in $\mathcal{LC}^\Omega$ and derivability in the set theory Ω.

Proposition 2 (Soundness and Completeness of the Translation of $\mathcal{LC}^\Omega$). *For all concepts C and D on the language of the knowledge base K:*

$$K \models_{\mathcal{LC}^\Omega} C \sqsubseteq D \text{ if and only if}$$

$$\Omega \models \forall x(Trans(x) \to \forall x_1, \ldots, \forall x_n(\bigwedge ABox_\mathcal{A} \wedge \bigwedge TBox_\mathcal{T} \to C^S \cap x \subseteq D^S))$$

where $Trans(x)$ stands for $\forall y(y \in x \to y \subseteq x)$, that is, $x \subseteq Pow(x)$, and $Axiom_H(x, y_1, \ldots, y_k)$ has been omitted as it is empty.

We refer to [6] for the proof. A similar correspondence result can be proved for *instance checking*, by replacing the inclusion $C^S \cap x \in D^S$ in Proposition 2 with $C^S \in D^S \cap x$.

As we can see from the translation above, the power-set construct in $\mathcal{LC}^\Omega$ is defined precisely as the set-theoretic power-set. From the translation it is clear that only the part of the power-set which is in x (the domain Δ) is relevant when evaluating the axioms in K or a query, as all the axioms in the knowledge base are only required to be satisfied over the elements of the transitive set x. Notice that it is the same as in the set-theoretic translation of $\mathcal{ALC}$. Observe also that, in both $\mathcal{ALC}$ and $\mathcal{LC}^\Omega$, $\top$ is interpreted as the transitive set x. It would not be correct to interpret $\top$ as the universe $\mathcal{U}$ of a model of Ω, as $\mathcal{U}$ might not be a set. Furthermore, $Pow(\top)$ is in the language of concepts and the interpretation of $Pow(\top)$ must be larger than the interpretation of $\top$.

3.3 Translating $\mathcal{ALC}^\Omega$ by Encoding into $\mathcal{LC}^\Omega$

It can be shown that $\mathcal{LC}^\Omega$ has the same expressive power as $\mathcal{ALC}^\Omega$, as universal and existential restrictions of the language $\mathcal{ALC}^\Omega$ (as well as role assertions) can be encoded into $\mathcal{LC}^\Omega$. The encoding, together with the set-theoretic translation of $\mathcal{LC}^\Omega$ given in the previous section, determines a set-theoretic translation for $\mathcal{ALC}^\Omega$, in which both the roles and the power-set construct are translated in a similar fashion, according to the polymodal translation in [3]. For space limitations, here we omit the treatment of role assertions and role membership axioms in the translation, and refer to [6].

Given an $\mathcal{ALC}^\Omega$ knowledge base $K = (\mathcal{T}, \mathcal{A})$, let $R_1, \ldots, R_k$ be the role names occurring in K, $A_1, \ldots, A_n$ the concept names occurring in K, and $a_1, \ldots, a_r$ the individual names occurring in K. We introduce k new concept names $U_1, \ldots, U_k$ in the language, one for each role R_i. These concepts (that are not in N_C) will be used to encode universal restrictions $\forall R_i.C$ as well as the power-set concept $Pow(C)$ of $\mathcal{ALC}^\Omega$ into $\mathcal{LC}^\Omega$. We further introduce a new concept name B_i for each individual name a_i occurring in K^2.

For an $\mathcal{ALC}^\Omega$ concept C, the encoding C^E in $\mathcal{LC}^\Omega$ can be defined by recursively replacing: every named individual a_i with the new concept name B_i, every

---

[2] Further concept names would be needed to translate role assertions.

subconcept $\forall R_i.C$ with $(\forall R_i.C)^E$ and every subconcept $\mathrm{Pow}(C)$ with $(\mathrm{Pow}(C))^E$, as defined below, while the encoding E commutes with concept constructors in all other cases:

$$a_i^E = B_i$$
$$(\forall R_i.C)^E = \mathrm{Pow}(\neg U_i \sqcup \mathrm{Pow}(C^E))$$
$$(\mathrm{Pow}(C))^E = \mathrm{Pow}(U_1 \sqcup \ldots \sqcup U_k \sqcup C^E)$$

For the encoding of the power-set, the idea is the same underlying the encoding of $\forall R_i.C$, as described in Sect. 3.1. For each $(\mathrm{Pow}(C))^E$-element y, we require that all its elements $y' \in y$, which are not $U_1 \sqcup \ldots \sqcup U_k$-elements, are C^E-elements. This is needed to keep the encoding of $\forall R_i.C$ and $\mathrm{Pow}(C)$ (both based on the set-theoretic power-set) independent of each other.

Given an $\mathcal{ALC}^\Omega$ knowledge base K, and a query F (over the language of K), the encoding K^E of K, and the encoding F^E of the query F in $\mathcal{LC}^\Omega$ are defined as follows. K^E contains: an inclusion axiom $C^E \sqcap \neg(U_1 \sqcup \ldots \sqcup U_k) \sqsubseteq D^E$ for each $C \sqsubseteq D \in K$; a membership axiom $C^E \in D^E \sqcap \neg(U_1 \sqcup \ldots \sqcup U_k)$ for each $C \in D$ in K; an axiom $a_i^E \in C^E \sqcap \neg(U_1 \sqcup \ldots \sqcup U_k)$ for each $C(a_i)$ in K; an axioms $A_i \in \neg(U_1 \sqcup \ldots \sqcup U_k)$, for all A_i in K. Finally, axiom $\neg(U_1 \sqcup \ldots \sqcup U_k) \sqsubseteq \mathrm{Pow}(\mathrm{Pow}(\neg(U_1 \sqcup \ldots \sqcup U_k)))$. The last one enforces the property $Trans^2(\Delta \backslash (U_1 \sqcup \ldots \sqcup U_k)^I$.

For a query F, if F is an inclusion $C \sqsubseteq D$, its translation is $C^E \sqsubseteq D^E$; if F is an assertion $C(a_i)$, its translation is $a_i^E \in C^E$; if F is a membership axioms $C \in D$, its translation is $C^E \in D^E$. It can be proved that the encoding above is sound and complete, that is: $K \models_{\mathcal{ALC}^\Omega} F$ if and only if $K^E \models_{\mathcal{LC}^\Omega} F^E$.

Combining this encoding with the set-theoretic translation for $\mathcal{LC}^\Omega$ of Sect. 3.2, a set-theoretic translation for $\mathcal{ALC}^\Omega$ can be obtained which extends the translation of $\mathcal{ALC}$ in Sect. 3.1 to the power-set concept. Given a concept C of $\mathcal{ALC}^\Omega$ on the language of K, its set-theoretic translation $(C^E)^S$ is a set-theoretic term C^*:

$$\top^* = x; \qquad\qquad \bot^* = \emptyset;$$
$$A_i^* = x_i, \text{ for } A_i \text{ in } K; \qquad (\neg C)^* = x \backslash C^*;$$
$$(C \sqcap D)^* = C^* \cap D^*; \qquad (C \sqcup D)^* = C^* \cup D^*;$$
$$(\forall R_i.C)^* = Pow(((x \cup y_1 \cup \ldots \cup y_k) \backslash y_i) \cup Pow(C^*)), \text{ for } R_i \text{ in } K;$$
$$\mathrm{Pow}(C)^* = Pow((y_1 \cup \ldots \cup y_k \cup C^*).$$

The translation of an $\mathcal{ALC}^\Omega$ knowledge base K can be defined accordingly, and a correspondence result follows from Propositions 2.

4   Conclusions and Related Work

The similarities between Description Logics and Set Theory have led to the definition of an extension of $\mathcal{ALC}$, called $\mathcal{ALC}^\Omega$, with a power-set construct and membership relationships among arbitrary concepts [5]. It was shown that an

$\mathcal{ALC}^{\Omega}$ knowledge base can be polynomially translated into an $\mathcal{ALCOI}$ knowledge base, providing an ExpTime upper bound for satisfiability in $\mathcal{ALC}^{\Omega}$. In this paper, we have developed a set-theoretic translation for the description logic $\mathcal{ALC}^{\Omega}$ into the set theory Ω exploiting a technique, originally proposed in [3], for translating normal modal and polymodal logics into Ω. The translation has been defined step by step, first translating $\mathcal{ALC}$ with empty ABox, then translating the fragment of $\mathcal{ALC}^{\Omega}$ without roles and individual names and, finally, providing an encoding of $\mathcal{ALC}^{\Omega}$ into this fragment. The translation of role assertions and role membership is omitted for space limitations and can be found in [6].

The set-theoretic translation allows, on the one hand, to shed some light on the nature of the power-set concept (which indeed corresponds to the set theoretic power-set) and, on the other hand, to show that the fragment of $\mathcal{ALC}^{\Omega}$ without roles and individual names is as expressive as whole $\mathcal{ALC}^{\Omega}$. The correspondence among fragments of set-theory and description logics opens to the possibility of transferring proof methods and decidability results across the two formalisms.

Up to our knowledge, the power-set construct has not been considered for DLs before. However, the issue of metamodelling, and the extension of DLs with membership among concept, have been widely studied in DLs [4, 7–10, 12], starting with the work by Motik [11], and we refer to [5] for comparisons.

Acknowledgement. This research is partially supported by INDAM-GNCS Project 2019: Metodi di prova orientati al ragionamento automatico per logiche non-classiche.

References

1. Aczel, P.: Non-Well-Founded Sets, vol. 14. CSLI Lecture Notes, Stanford (1988)
2. Baader, F., Calvanese, D., McGuinness, D.L., Nardi, D., Patel-Schneider, P.F.: The Description Logic Handbook - Theory, Implementation, and Applications. Cambridge University Press, Cambridge (2007)
3. D'Agostino, G., Montanari, A., Policriti, A.: A set-theoretic translation method for polymodal logics. J. Autom. Reasoning **15**(3), 317–337 (1995)
4. De Giacomo, G., Lenzerini, M., Rosati, R.: Higher-order description logics for domain metamodeling. In: Proceedings of AAAI 2011, San Francisco, California, USA, 7–11 August 2011
5. Giordano, L., Policriti, A.: Power(Set) ALC. In ICTCS, 19th Italian Conference on Theoretical Computer Science, Urbino, Italy, 18–20 September 2018
6. Giordano, L., Policriti, A.: Adding the Power-Set to Description Logics. CoRR abs/1902.09844, February 2019
7. Glimm, B., Rudolph, S., Völker, J.: Integrated metamodeling and diagnosis in OWL 2. In: Patel-Schneider, P.F., Pan, Y., Hitzler, P., Mika, P., Zhang, L., Pan, J.Z., Horrocks, I., Glimm, B. (eds.) ISWC 2010. LNCS, vol. 6496, pp. 257–272. Springer, Heidelberg (2010). https://doi.org/10.1007/978-3-642-17746-0_17
8. Gu, Z.: Meta-modeling extension of Horn-SROIQ and query answering. In: Proceedings of the 29th International Workshop on Description Logics, Cape Town, South Africa, 22–25 April 2016

9. Homola, M., Kluka, J., Svátek, V., Vacura, M.: Typed higher-order variant of SROIQ - why not? In: Proceedings 27th International Workshop on Description Logics, Vienna, Austria, 17–20 July, pp. 567–578 (2014)
10. Kubincová, P., Kluka, J., Homola, M.: Towards expressive metamodelling with instantiation. In: Proceedings of the 28th International Workshop on Description Logics, Athens, 7–10 June 2015
11. Motik, B.: On the Properties of Metamodeling in OWL. In: Gil, Y., Motta, E., Benjamins, V.R., Musen, M.A. (eds.) ISWC 2005. LNCS, vol. 3729, pp. 548–562. Springer, Heidelberg (2005). https://doi.org/10.1007/11574620_40
12. Motz, R., Rohrer, E., Severi, P.: The description logic SHIQ with a flexible meta-modelling hierarchy. J. Web Sem. **35**, 214–234 (2015)
13. Omodeo, E.G., Policriti, A., Tomescu, A.I.: Perspectives Logic Combinatorics. On Sets and Graphs. Springer, Cham (2017). https://doi.org/10.1007/978-3-319-54981-1
14. Pan, J.Z., Horrocks, I., Schreiber, G.: OWL FA: A metamodeling extension of OWL DL. In Proceedings of OWLED 2005 Workshop, Galway, Ireland, 11–12 November 2005
15. Patel-Schneider, P.F., Hayes, P.H., Horrocks. I.: OWL Web Ontology Language; Semantics and Abstract Syntax (2002). http://www.w3.org/TR/owl-semantics/
16. Schild, K.: A correspondence theory for terminological logics: preliminary report. In: Proceedings IJCAI 1991, Sydney, Australia, 24–30 August 1991, pp. 466–471 (1991)
17. Welty, C., Ferrucci, D.: What's in an instance? Technical report, pp. 94–18, Max-Plank-Institut, RPI computer Science (1994)

Learning Description Logic Axioms from Discrete Probability Distributions over Description Graphs

Francesco Kriegel$^{(\boxtimes)}$ (iD)

Institute of Theoretical Computer Science, Technische Universität Dresden,
Dresden, Germany
francesco.kriegel@tu-dresden.de

Abstract. Description logics in their standard setting only allow for representing and reasoning with crisp knowledge without any degree of uncertainty. Of course, this is a serious shortcoming for use cases where it is impossible to perfectly determine the truth of a statement. For resolving this expressivity restriction, probabilistic variants of description logics have been introduced. Their model-theoretic semantics is built upon so-called probabilistic interpretations, that is, families of directed graphs the vertices and edges of which are labeled and for which there exists a probability measure on this graph family. Results of scientific experiments, e.g., in medicine, psychology, or biology, that are repeated several times can induce probabilistic interpretations in a natural way. In this document, we shall develop a suitable axiomatization technique for deducing terminological knowledge from the assertional data given in such probabilistic interpretations. More specifically, we consider a probabilistic variant of the description logic $\mathcal{EL}^\perp$, and provide a method for constructing a set of rules, so-called concept inclusions, from probabilistic interpretations in a sound and complete manner.

Keywords: Data mining · Knowledge acquisition ·
Probabilistic description logic · Knowledge base ·
Probabilistic interpretation · Concept inclusion

1 Introduction

Description Logics (abbrv. DLs) [2] are frequently used knowledge representation and reasoning formalisms with a strong logical foundation. In particular, these provide their users with automated inference services that can derive implicit knowledge from the explicitly represented knowledge. Decidability and computational complexity of common reasoning tasks have been widely explored for most DLs. Besides being used in various application domains, their most notable success is the fact that DLs constitute the logical underpinning of the *Web Ontology Language* (abbrv. OWL) and its profiles.

© Springer Nature Switzerland AG 2019
F. Calimeri et al. (Eds.): JELIA 2019, LNAI 11468, pp. 399–417, 2019.
https://doi.org/10.1007/978-3-030-19570-0_26

Logics in their standard form only allow for representing and reasoning with *crisp* knowledge without any degree of *uncertainty*. Of course, this is a serious shortcoming for use cases where it is impossible to perfectly determine the truth of a statement or where there exist degrees of truth. For resolving this expressivity restriction, probabilistic variants of logics have been introduced. A thorough article on extending first-order logics with means for representing and reasoning with probabilistic knowledge was published by Halpern [12]. In particular, Halpern explains why it is important to distinguish between two contrary types of probabilities: *statistical information* (type 1) and *degrees of belief* (type 2). The crucial difference between both types is that type-1 probabilities represent information about one particular world, the *real* world, and assume that there is a probability distribution on the objects, while type-2 probabilities represent information about a multi-world view such that there is a probability distribution on the set of possible worlds. Following his arguments and citing two of his examples, the first following statement can only be expressed in type-1 probabilistic logics and the second one is only expressible in type-2 probabilistic logics.

1. *"The probability that a randomly chosen bird will fly is greater than 0.9."*
2. *"The probability that Tweety (a particular bird) flies is greater than 0.9."*

Bacchus has published a further early work on probabilistic logics [3]. In particular, he defined the probabilistic first-order logic **Lp**, which allows to express various kinds of probabilistic/statistical knowledge: relative, interval, functional, conditional, independence. It is of type 1, since its semantics is based on probability measures over the domain of discourse (the objects). However, it also supports the deduction of degrees of belief (type 2) from given knowledge by means of an inference mechanism that is called *belief formation* and is based on an *inductive assumption of randomization*.

In [13], Heinsohn introduced the probabilistic description logic $\mathcal{ALCP}$ as an extension of $\mathcal{ALC}$. An $\mathcal{ALCP}$ ontology is a union of some acyclic $\mathcal{ALC}$ TBox and a finite set of so-called *p-conditionings*, which are expressions of the form $C \xrightarrow{[p,q]} D$ where C and D are Boolean combinations of concept names and where p and q are real numbers from the unit interval $[0, 1]$. $\mathcal{ALCP}$ allows for expressing type-1 probabilities only, since a p-conditioning $C \xrightarrow{[p,q]} D$ is defined to be valid in an interpretation $\mathcal{I}$ if it holds true that $p \leq |C^{\mathcal{I}} \cap D^{\mathcal{I}}|/|C^{\mathcal{I}}| \leq q$, that is, a uniform distribution on the domain of $\mathcal{I}$ is assumed and it is measured which percentage of the objects satisfying the premise C also satisfies the conclusion D. In particular, this means that only finite models are considered, which is a major restriction. Heinsohn shows how important reasoning problems (consistency and determining minimal p-conditionings) can be translated into problems of linear algebra. Please note that there is a strong correspondence with the notion of *confidence* of a concept inclusion as utilized by Borchmann in [4], cf. Sect. 2.

Another probabilistic extension of $\mathcal{ALC}$ was devised by Jaeger [14]: the description logic $\mathcal{PALC}$. Probabilities can be assigned to both terminological information and assertional information, rendering it a mixture of means for expressing type-1 and type-2 probabilities. A $\mathcal{PALC}$ ontology is a union of an acyclic $\mathcal{ALC}$ TBox, a finite set of *probabilistic terminological axioms* of the form $P(C \mid D) = p$, and a finite set of *probabilistic assertions* of the form $P(a \in C) = p$. The model-theoretic semantics are defined by extending the usual notion of a model with a probability measures: one measure μ dedicated to the probabilistic terminological axioms, and one measure ν_a dedicated to the probabilistic assertions for each individual a. Furthermore, these probability measures are defined on some finite subalgebra of the Lindenbaum-Tarski algebra of $\mathcal{ALC}$ concept descriptions that is generated by the concept descriptions occurring in the ontology, and it is further required that each ABox measure ν_a has minimal *cross entropy* to the TBox measure μ.

Lukasiewicz introduced in [23] the description logics P-*DL-Lite*, P-$\mathcal{SHIF}(\mathbf{D})$, and P-$\mathcal{SHOIN}(\mathbf{D})$ that are probabilistic extensions of *DL-Lite* and of the DLs underlying OWL Lite and OWL DL, respectively. We shall now briefly explain P-$\mathcal{SHOIN}(\mathbf{D})$, the others are analogous. It allows for expressing *conditional constraints* of the form $(\phi|\psi)[l, u]$ where ϕ and ψ are elements from some fixed, finite set $\mathcal{C}$ of $\mathcal{SHOIN}(\mathbf{D})$ concept descriptions, so-called *basic classification concepts*, and where l and u are real numbers from the unit interval $[0, 1]$. Similar to $\mathcal{PALC}$, P-$\mathcal{SHOIN}(\mathbf{D})$ ontologies are unions of some $\mathcal{SHOIN}(\mathbf{D})$ ontology, a finite set of conditional constraints ($PTBox$) as probabilistic terminological knowledge, and a finite set of conditional constraints ($PABox$) as probabilistic assertional knowledge for each probabilistic individual. The semantics are then defined using interpretations that are additionally equipped with a discrete probability measure on the Lindenbaum-Tarski algebra generated by $\mathcal{C}$. Note that, in contrast to $\mathcal{PALC}$, there is only one probability measure available in each interpretation. While the terminological knowledge is, just like for $\mathcal{PALC}$, the default knowledge from which we only differ for a particular individual if the corresponding knowledge requires us to do so, the inference process is different, i.e., cross entropy is not utilized in any way. In order to allow for drawing inferences from a P-$\mathcal{SHOIN}(\mathbf{D})$ ontology, *lexicographic entailment* is defined for deciding whether a conditional constraint follows from the terminological part or for a certain individual. A thorough complexity analysis shows that the decision problems in these three logics are **NP**-complete, **EXP**-complete, and **NEXP**-complete, respectively.

Gutiérrez-Basulto, Jung, Lutz, and Schröder consider in [11] the probabilistic description logics Prob-$\mathcal{ALC}$ and Prob-$\mathcal{EL}$ where probabilities are always interpreted as degrees of belief (type 2). Among other language constructs, a new concept constructor is introduced that allows to probabilistically quantify a concept description. The semantics are based on multi-world interpretations where a discrete probability measure on the set of worlds is defined. Consistency and entailment is then defined just as usual, but using such probabilistic interpretations. A thorough investigation of computational complexity for various probabilistic extensions of DLs is provided: for instance, the common reasoning problems in Prob-$\mathcal{EL}$ and in Prob-$\mathcal{ALC}$ are **EXP**-complete, that is, not more expensive than the same problems in $\mathcal{ALC}$.

One should never mix up probabilistic and fuzzy variants of (description) logics. Although at first sight one could get the impression that both are suitable for any use cases where imprecise knowledge is to be represented and reasoned with, this is definitely not the case. A very simple argument against this is that in fuzzy logics we can easily evaluate conjunctions by means of the underlying fixed triangular norm (abbrv. t-norm), while it is not (always) possible to deduce the probability of a conjunction given the probabilities of the conjuncts. For instance, consider statements α and β. If both have fuzzy truth degree $1/2$ and the t-norm is Gödel's minimum, then $\alpha \wedge \beta$ has the fuzzy truth degree $1/2$ as well. In contrast, if both have probabilistic truth degree $1/2$, then the probability of $\alpha \wedge \beta$ might be any value in the interval $[0, 1/2]$, but without additional information we cannot bound it further or even determine it exactly.

Within this document, we make use of the syntax and semantics of [11]. It is easy to see that the probabilistic multi-world interpretations can be represented as families of directed graphs the vertices and edges of which are labeled and for which there exists a probability measure on this graph family. More specifically, we shall develop a suitable axiomatization technique for deducing terminological knowledge from the assertional data given in such probabilistic interpretations. In order to prevent the generated ontology from *overfitting*, a description logic that is not closed under Boolean operations is chosen. Since conjunction is essential, this implies that we leave out disjunction and negation. We consider a probabilistic variant $\mathsf{Prob}^{>}\mathcal{EL}^{\perp}$ of the description logic $\mathcal{EL}^{\perp}$, show that reasoning in $\mathsf{Prob}^{>}\mathcal{EL}^{\perp}$ is **EXP**-complete, and provide a method for constructing a set of rules, so-called concept inclusions, from probabilistic interpretations in a sound and complete manner. Within this document, the usage of probability restrictions is only allowed for lower probability bounds. This choice shall ease readability; it is not hard to verify that similar results can be obtained when additionally allowing for upper probability bounds.

Results of scientific experiments, e.g., in medicine, psychology, biology, finance, or economy, that are repeated several times can induce probabilistic interpretations in a natural way. Each repetition corresponds to a world, and the results of a particular repetition are encoded in the graph structure of that world. For instance, a researcher could collect data on consumption of the drugs ethanol and nicotine as well as on occurrence of serious health effects, e.g., cancer, psychological disorders, pneumonia, etc., such that a world corresponds to a single person and all worlds are equally likely. Then, the resulting probabilistic interpretation could be analyzed with the procedure described in the sequel of this document, which produces a *sound and complete axiomatization* of it. In particular, the outcome would then be a *logical-statistical evaluation* of the input data, and could include concept inclusions like the following.[1]

---

[1] Please note that, although similar statements with adjusted probability bounds do hold true in real world, the mentioned statements are not taken from any publications in the medical or psychological domain. The author has simply read according Wikipedia articles and then wrote down the statements.

∃ drinks. (Alcohol ⊓ ∃ frequency. TwiceAWeek)
⊑ d ≥ ¹/₁₀. ∃ suffersFrom. Cancer ⊓ d ≥ ¹/₅. ∃ develops. PsychologicalDisorder

∃ smokes. Tobacco
⊑ d ≥ ¹/₄. ∃ suffersFrom. Cancer ⊓ d ≥ ¹/₃. ∃ suffersFrom. Pneumonia

The first one states that any person who drinks alcohol twice a week suffers from cancer with a probability of at least 10% and develops some psychological disorder with a probability of at least 20%; the second one expresses that each person smoking tobacco suffers from cancer with a probability of at least 25% and suffers from pneumonia with a probability of at least 33¹/₃%.

However, one should be cautious when interpreting the results, since the procedure, like any other existing statistical evaluation techniques, cannot distinguish between *causality* and *correlation*. It might as well be the case that an application of our procedure yields concept inclusions of the following type.

d ≥ ¹/₂. ∃ develops. PsychologicalDisorder
⊑ d ≥ ¹/₃. ∃ drinks. (Alcohol ⊓ ∃ frequency. Daily)

The above concept inclusion reads as follows: any person who develops a psychological disorder with a probability of at least 50% drinks alcohol on a daily basis with a probability of at least 33¹/₃%.

It should further be mentioned that for evaluating observations by means of the proposed technique no hypotheses are necessary. Instead, the procedure simply provides a sound and complete axiomatization of the observations, and the output is, on the one hand, not too hard to be understood by humans (at least if the probability depth is not set too high) and, on the other hand, well-suited to be further processed by a computer.

This document also resolves an issue found by Franz Baader with the techniques described by the author in [15, Sections 5 and 6]. In particular, the concept inclusion base proposed therein in Proposition 2 is only complete with respect to those probabilistic interpretations that are also quasi-uniform with a probability ε of each world. Herein, we describe a more sophisticated axiomatization technique of not necessarily quasi-uniform probabilistic interpretations that ensures completeness of the constructed concept inclusion base with respect to *all* probabilistic interpretations, but which, however, only allows for bounded nesting of probability restrictions. It is not hard to generalize the following results to a more expressive probabilistic description logic, for example to a probabilistic variant Prob$^>\mathcal{M}$ of the description logic $\mathcal{M}$, for which an axiomatization technique is available [17]. That way, we can regain the same, or even a greater, expressivity as the author has tried to tackle in [15], but without the possibility to nest probability restrictions arbitrarily deep. A first step for resolving this issue has already been made in [20] where a nesting of probability restrictions is not supported. As a follow-up, we now expand on these results in [20] with the goal to allow for nesting of probabilistically quantified concept descriptions.

Due to space constraints, no proofs could be included here, but have rather been moved to a corresponding technical report [21].

2   Related Work

So far, several approaches for axiomatizing concept inclusions (abbrv.CIs) in different description logics have been developed, and many of these utilize sophisticated techniques from Formal Concept Analysis [8,9]: on the one hand, there is the so-called *canonical base*, cf. Guigues and Duquenne in [10], that provides a concise representation of the implicative theory of a formal context in a sound and complete manner and, on the other hand, the interactive algorithm *attribute exploration* exists, which guides an expert through the process of axiomatizing the theory of implications that are valid in a domain of interest, cf. Ganter in [7]. In particular, attribute exploration is an interactive variant of an algorithm for computing canonical bases [7], and it works as follows: the input is a formal context that only partially describes the domain of interest (that is, there may be implications that are not valid, but for which this partial description does not provide a counterexample), and during the run of the exploration process a minimal number of questions is enumerated and posed to the expert (such a question is an implication for which no counterexample has been explored, and the expert can either confirm its validity or provide a suitable counterexample). On termination, a minimal sound and complete representation of the theory of implications that are valid in the considered domain has been generated.

A first pioneering work on axiomatizing CIs in the description logic $\mathcal{FLE}$ has been developed by Rudolph [24], which allows for the exploration of a CI base for a given interpretation in a multi-step approach such that each step increases the role depth of concept descriptions occurring in the CIs. Later, a refined approach has been developed by Baader and Distel [1,6] for axiomatizing CI bases in the description logic $\mathcal{EL}^{\perp}$. They found techniques for computing and for exploring such bases that contain a *minimal* number of CIs and that are both sound and complete not only for those valid CIs up to certain role depth but instead for *all* valid ones. However, due to possible presence of cycles in the input interpretation they need to apply greatest fixed-point semantics; luckily, there is a finite *closure ordinal* for any finitely representable interpretation, that is, there is a certain role depth up to which the concept descriptions in the base can be unraveled to obtain a base for *all* valid CIs with respect to the standard semantics. Borchmann, Distel, and the author devised a variant of these techniques in [5] that circumvents the use of greatest fixed-point semantics, but which can only compute *minimal* CI bases that are sound and complete for all concept inclusions up to a set role depth—of course, if one chooses the closure ordinal as role-depth bound, then also these bases are sound and complete for *all* valid CIs w.r.t. standard semantics. Further variants that allow for the incorporation of background knowledge or allow for a more expressive description logic can be found in [16,17,22].

However, all of the mentioned approaches have in common that they heavily rely on the assumption that the given input interpretation to be axiomatized does not contain errors—otherwise these errors would be reflected in the constructed CI base. A reasonable solution avoiding this assumption has been proposed by Borchmann in [4]. He defined the notion of *confidence* as a statistical measure of validity of a CI in a given interpretation, and developed means for the computation and exploration of CI bases in $\mathcal{EL}^\perp$ that are sound and complete for those CIs the confidence of which exceeds a pre-defined threshold. Furthermore, in [19] the author defined the notion of *probability* of a CI in a probabilistic interpretation, and showed how corresponding bases of CIs exceeding a probability threshold can be constructed in a sound and complete manner. Both works have in common that they only allow for a statistical or probabilistic quantification of CIs, that is, it is only possible to assign a degree of truth to whole CIs, and not to concept descriptions occurring in these. For instance, one can express that $A \sqsubseteq \exists r.B$ has a confidence or probability of $2/3$, but one cannot write that every object which satisfies A with a probability of $5/6$ also satisfies $\exists r.B$ with a probability of $1/3$. As a solution to this, the author first considered in [18] implications over so-called probabilistic attributes in Formal Concept Analysis and showed how these can be axiomatized from a probabilistic formal context. Then in [20], his results have been extended to the probabilistic description logic $\mathsf{Prob}_1^{\ge}\mathcal{EL}^\perp$, a sublogic of $\mathsf{Prob}^{\ge}\mathcal{EL}^\perp$ that does not allow for nesting of probabilistically quantified concept descriptions. In Sect. 5 we shall expand on the results from [20] with the goal to constitute an effective procedure for axiomatizing CI bases in $\mathsf{Prob}^{\ge}\mathcal{EL}^\perp$, that is, we extend the procedure in [20] to allow for nesting of probabilistically quantified concept descriptions.

3   The Probabilistic Description Logic $\mathsf{Prob}^{\ge}\mathcal{EL}^\perp$

The probabilistic description logic $\mathsf{Prob}^{\ge}\mathcal{EL}^\perp$ constitutes an extension of the tractable description logic $\mathcal{EL}^\perp$ [2] that allows for expressing and reasoning with probabilities. More specifically, it is a sublogic of $\mathsf{Prob}\text{-}\mathcal{EL}$ introduced by Gutiérrez-Basulto, Jung, Lutz, and Schröder in [11] in which only the relation symbols $>$ and $\ge$ are available for the probability restrictions, and in which the bottom concept description $\perp$ is present.[2] In the sequel of this section, we shall introduce the syntax and semantics of $\mathsf{Prob}^{\ge}\mathcal{EL}^\perp$. Furthermore, we will show that a common inference problem in $\mathsf{Prob}^{\ge}\mathcal{EL}^\perp$ is **EXP**-complete and, thus, more expensive than in $\mathcal{EL}^\perp$ where the same problem is **P**-complete.

Throughout the whole document, assume that Σ is an arbitrary but fixed *signature*, that is, Σ is a disjoint union of a set Σ_{C} of *concept names* and a set Σ_{R} of *role names*. Then, $\mathsf{Prob}^{\ge}\mathcal{EL}^\perp$ *concept descriptions* C over Σ may be inductively constructed by means of the following grammar rule (where $A \in \Sigma_{\mathsf{C}}$, $r \in \Sigma_{\mathsf{R}}$, $\ge \in \{\ge, >\}$ and $p \in [0,1] \cap \mathbb{Q}$).

$$
\begin{aligned}
C ::= \ &\perp && \textit{(bottom concept description/contradiction)} \\
\mid\ &\top && \textit{(top concept description/tautology)} \\
\mid\ &A && \textit{(concept name)} \\
\mid\ &C \sqcap C && \textit{(conjunction)}
\end{aligned}
$$

---

[2] We merely introduce $\perp$ as syntactic sugar; of course, it is semantically equivalent to the unsatisfiable probabilistic restriction $\mathsf{d} > 1. \top$.

$$| \, \exists \, r. \, C \qquad\qquad\qquad\qquad \textit{(existential restriction)}$$

$$| \, \mathsf{d} > p. \, C \qquad\qquad\qquad\qquad \textit{(probability restriction)}$$

Within this document, we stick to the default conventions and denote concept names by letters A or B, denote concept descriptions by letters C, D, E, etc., and denote role names by letters r, s, t, etc., each possibly with sub- or superscripts. Furthermore, we write $\mathsf{Prob}^{>}\mathcal{EL}^{\perp}(\Sigma)$ for the set of all $\mathsf{Prob}^{>}\mathcal{EL}^{\perp}$ concept descriptions over Σ. An $\mathcal{EL}^{\perp}$ *concept description* is a $\mathsf{Prob}^{>}\mathcal{EL}^{\perp}$ concept description not containing any subconcept of the form $\mathsf{d} > p. \, C$,[3] and we shall write $\mathcal{EL}^{\perp}(\Sigma)$ for the set of all $\mathcal{EL}^{\perp}$ concept descriptions over Σ. If both C and D are concept descriptions, then the expression $C \sqsubseteq D$ is a *concept inclusion* (abbrv.CI), and the expression $C \equiv D$ is a *concept equivalence* (abbrv.CE). A *terminological box* (abbrv.TBox) is a finite set of CIs and CEs.

An example of a $\mathsf{Prob}^{>}\mathcal{EL}^{\perp}$ concept description is the following; it describes cats that are both alive and dead with a respective probability of at least 50%. In particular, we could consider the below concept description as a formalization of the famous thought experiment *Schrödinger's Cat*.

$$\mathsf{Cat} \sqcap \mathsf{d} \geq {}^{1}\!/_{2}. \, \exists \, \mathsf{hasPhysicalCondition}. \, \mathsf{Alive}$$

$$\sqcap \, \mathsf{d} \geq {}^{1}\!/_{2}. \, \exists \, \mathsf{hasPhysicalCondition}. \, \mathsf{Dead} \qquad\qquad (1)$$

The *probability depth* $\mathsf{pd}(C)$ of a $\mathsf{Prob}^{>}\mathcal{EL}^{\perp}$ concept description C is defined as the maximal nesting depth of probability restrictions within C, and we formally define it as follows: $\mathsf{pd}(A) := 0$ for each $A \in \Sigma_{\mathsf{C}} \cup \{\perp, \top\}$, $\mathsf{pd}(C \sqcap D) := \mathsf{pd}(C) \vee \mathsf{pd}(D)$,[4] $\mathsf{pd}(\exists \, r. \, C) := \mathsf{pd}(C)$, and $\mathsf{pd}(\mathsf{d} > p. \, C) := 1 + \mathsf{pd}(C)$. Then, $\mathsf{Prob}^{>}_{n}\mathcal{EL}^{\perp}(\Sigma)$ denotes the set of all $\mathsf{Prob}^{>}\mathcal{EL}^{\perp}$ concept descriptions over Σ the probability depth of which does not exceed n.

Our considered logic $\mathsf{Prob}^{>}\mathcal{EL}^{\perp}$ possesses a model-theoretic semantics; so-called probabilistic interpretations function as models. Such a *probabilistic interpretation* over Σ is a tuple $\mathcal{I} := (\Delta^{\mathcal{I}}, \Omega^{\mathcal{I}}, \cdot^{\mathcal{I}}, \mathbb{P}^{\mathcal{I}})$ that consists of a non-empty set $\Delta^{\mathcal{I}}$ of *objects*, called the *domain*, a non-empty, countable set $\Omega^{\mathcal{I}}$ of *worlds*, a discrete probability measure $\mathbb{P}^{\mathcal{I}}$ on $\Omega^{\mathcal{I}}$, and an *extension function* $\cdot^{\mathcal{I}}$ such that, for each world $\omega \in \Omega^{\mathcal{I}}$, any concept name $A \in \Sigma_{\mathsf{C}}$ is mapped to a subset $A^{\mathcal{I}(\omega)} \subseteq \Delta^{\mathcal{I}}$ and each role name $r \in \Sigma_{\mathsf{R}}$ is mapped to a binary relation $r^{\mathcal{I}(\omega)} \subseteq \Delta^{\mathcal{I}} \times \Delta^{\mathcal{I}}$. We remark that the discrete probability measure is a mapping $\mathbb{P}^{\mathcal{I}} \colon \wp(\Omega^{\mathcal{I}}) \to [0, 1]$ which satisfies $\mathbb{P}^{\mathcal{I}}(\emptyset) = 0$ and $\mathbb{P}^{\mathcal{I}}(\Omega^{\mathcal{I}}) = 1$, and which is σ-*additive*, that is, for all countable families $(U_n \mid n \in \mathbb{N})$ of pairwise disjoint sets $U_n \subseteq \Omega^{\mathcal{I}}$ it holds true that $\mathbb{P}^{\mathcal{I}}(\bigcup\{U_n \mid n \in \mathbb{N}\}) = \sum(\mathbb{P}^{\mathcal{I}}(U_n) \mid n \in \mathbb{N})$.

We shall follow the assumption in [11, Section 2.6] and consider only probabilistic interpretations without any infinitely improbable worlds, i.e., which do

---

[3] The author does not use the denotation $P_{>p}C$ for probability restrictions as in [11], since quantifiers are usually single letters rotated by 180°.

[4] Note that $\vee$ denotes the binary supremum operator for numbers, which here coincides with the maximum operator, since there are only finitely many arguments.

not contain any world $\omega \in \Omega^{\mathcal{I}}$ with $\mathbb{P}^{\mathcal{I}}\{\omega\} = 0$. Furthermore, a probabilistic interpretation $\mathcal{I}$ is *finitely representable* if $\Delta^{\mathcal{I}}$ is finite, $\Omega^{\mathcal{I}}$ is finite, the *active signature*

$$\Sigma^{\mathcal{I}} := \{\, \sigma \mid \sigma \in \Sigma \text{ and } \sigma^{\mathcal{I}(\omega)} \neq \emptyset \text{ for some } \omega \in \Omega^{\mathcal{I}} \,\}$$

is finite, and if $\mathbb{P}^{\mathcal{I}}$ has only rational values.

It is easy to see that, for any probabilistic interpretation $\mathcal{I}$, each world $\omega \in \Omega^{\mathcal{I}}$ can be represented as a labeled, directed graph: the node set is the domain $\Delta^{\mathcal{I}}$, the edge set is $\bigcup \{\, r^{\mathcal{I}(\omega)} \mid r \in \Sigma_{\mathsf{R}} \,\}$, any node δ is labeled with all those concept names A that satisfy $\delta \in A^{\mathcal{I}(\omega)}$, and any edge (δ, ϵ) has a role name r as a label if $(\delta, \epsilon) \in r^{\mathcal{I}(\omega)}$ holds true. That way, we can regard probabilistic interpretations also as discrete probability distributions over description graphs.

Later, we will also use the notion of *interpretations*, which are the models upon which the semantics of $\mathcal{EL}^{\perp}$ is built. Put simply, these are probabilistic interpretations with only one world, that is, these are tuples $\mathcal{I} := (\Delta^{\mathcal{I}}, \cdot^{\mathcal{I}})$ where $\Delta^{\mathcal{I}}$ is a non-empty set of *objects*, called *domain*, and where $\cdot^{\mathcal{I}}$ is an *extension function* that maps concept names $A \in \Sigma_{\mathsf{C}}$ to subsets $A^{\mathcal{I}} \subseteq \Delta^{\mathcal{I}}$ and maps role names $r \in \Sigma_{\mathsf{R}}$ to binary relations $r^{\mathcal{I}} \subseteq \Delta^{\mathcal{I}} \times \Delta^{\mathcal{I}}$.

Let $\mathcal{I}$ be a probabilistic interpretation. Then, the *extension* $C^{\mathcal{I}(\omega)}$ of a $\mathrm{Prob}^{>} \mathcal{EL}^{\perp}$ concept description C in a world ω of $\mathcal{I}$ is recursively defined as follows.

$$\perp^{\mathcal{I}(\omega)} := \emptyset \qquad \top^{\mathcal{I}(\omega)} := \Delta^{\mathcal{I}} \qquad (C \sqcap D)^{\mathcal{I}(\omega)} := C^{\mathcal{I}(\omega)} \cap D^{\mathcal{I}(\omega)}$$

$$(\exists\, r.\, C)^{\mathcal{I}(\omega)} := \{\, \delta \mid \delta \in \Delta^{\mathcal{I}}, \ (\delta, \epsilon) \in r^{\mathcal{I}(\omega)}, \text{ and } \epsilon \in C^{\mathcal{I}(\omega)} \text{ for some } \epsilon \in \Delta^{\mathcal{I}} \,\}$$

$$(\mathsf{d} > p.\, C)^{\mathcal{I}(\omega)} := \{\, \delta \mid \delta \in \Delta^{\mathcal{I}} \text{ and } \mathbb{P}^{\mathcal{I}}\{\delta \in C^{\mathcal{I}}\} > p \,\}$$

In the last of the above definitions we use the abbreviation

$$\{\delta \in C^{\mathcal{I}}\} := \{\, \omega \mid \omega \in \Omega^{\mathcal{I}} \text{ and } \delta \in C^{\mathcal{I}(\omega)} \,\}.$$

All but the last formula can be used in a similar manner to define the *extension* $C^{\mathcal{I}}$ of an $\mathcal{EL}^{\perp}$ concept description C in an interpretation $\mathcal{I}$. Please note that, in accordance with [11], there is nothing wrong with the above definition of extensions; in particular, it is true that the extension $(\mathsf{d} > p.\, C)^{\mathcal{I}(\omega)}$ of a probabilistic restriction $\mathsf{d} > p.\, C$ is indeed independent of the concrete world ω, i.e., it holds true that $(\mathsf{d} > p.\, C)^{\mathcal{I}(\omega)} = (\mathsf{d} > p.\, C)^{\mathcal{I}(\psi)}$ whenever ω and ψ are arbitrary worlds in $\Omega^{\mathcal{I}}$. This is due to the intended meaning of $\mathsf{d} > p.\, C$: it describes the class of objects for which the probability of being a C is $> p$. As a probabilistic interpretation $\mathcal{I}$ provides a multi-world view where probabilities can be assigned to sets of worlds, the probability of an object $\delta \in \Delta^{\mathcal{I}}$ being a C is defined as the probability of the set of all those worlds in which δ is some C, just like we have defined it above. We shall elaborate on this again as soon as we have defined validity of concept inclusions in probabilistic interpretations, and mind that extensions of a fixed probabilistic quantification are equal in all worlds.

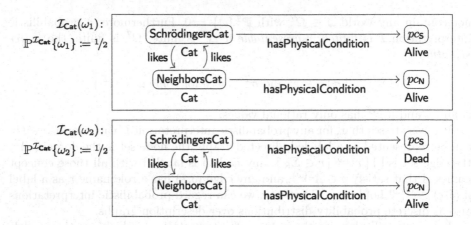

Fig. 1. An exemplary probabilistic interpretation

A toy example of a probabilistic interpretation is $\mathcal{I}_{\mathsf{Cat}}$ shown in Fig. 1. As one quickly verifies, only the object SchrödingersCat belongs to the extension of the concept description from Eq. (1).

A concept inclusion $C \sqsubseteq D$ or a concept equivalence $C \equiv D$ is *valid* in $\mathcal{I}$ if, for each world $\omega \in \Omega^{\mathcal{I}}$, it holds true that $C^{\mathcal{I}(\omega)} \subseteq D^{\mathcal{I}(\omega)}$ or $C^{\mathcal{I}(\omega)} = D^{\mathcal{I}(\omega)}$, respectively, and we shall then write $\mathcal{I} \models C \sqsubseteq D$ or $\mathcal{I} \models C \equiv D$, respectively. Furthermore, $\mathcal{I}$ is a *model* of a TBox $\mathcal{T}$, denoted as $\mathcal{I} \models \mathcal{T}$, if every concept inclusion or concept equivalence in $\mathcal{T}$ is valid in $\mathcal{I}$. A TBox $\mathcal{T}$ *entails* a concept inclusion or concept equivalence α, symbolized by $\mathcal{T} \models \alpha$, if α is valid in every model of $\mathcal{T}$. In case $\mathcal{T} \models C \sqsubseteq D$ we say that C is *subsumed* by D with respect to $\mathcal{T}$, and if $\mathcal{T} \models C \equiv D$, then we call C and D *equivalent* to each other with respect to $\mathcal{T}$.

If $\mathcal{Y}$ is either an interpretation or a terminological box and $\leq$ is a suitable relation symbol, e.g., one of $\sqsubseteq, \equiv, \sqsupseteq$, then we may also use the denotation $C \leq_{\mathcal{Y}} D$ instead of $\mathcal{Y} \models C \leq D$ and, analogously, we may write $C \not\leq_{\mathcal{Y}} D$ for $\mathcal{Y} \not\models C \leq D$.

Considering again the above definition of extensions of concept descriptions together with the just defined validity of concept inclusions, we can also justify the independence of $(\mathsf{d} > p.\, C)^{\mathcal{I}(\omega)}$ from world ω in the following way. Fix some probabilistic interpretation as well as some concept inclusion $C \sqsubseteq D$. Since concept inclusions are terminological axioms, and as such represent knowledge that globally holds true, it is only natural to say that $C \sqsubseteq D$ is valid in $\mathcal{I}$ if, and only if, $C \sqsubseteq D$ is valid in each *slice* $\mathcal{I}(\omega)$ for any world $\omega \in \Omega^{\mathcal{I}}$— apparently, this is what we have defined above. If $C = \mathsf{d} \geq p.\, C'$ and $D = \mathsf{d} \geq q.\, D'$ are probabilistic restrictions, then the intended meaning of the concept inclusion $\mathsf{d} \geq p.\, C' \sqsubseteq \mathsf{d} \geq q.\, D'$ is that any object being a C' with probability at least p is also a D' with probability q or greater. Of course, this is equivalent to $(\mathsf{d} \geq p.\, C')^{\mathcal{I}(\omega)} \subseteq (\mathsf{d} \geq q.\, D')^{\mathcal{I}(\omega)}$ for each world $\omega \in \Omega^{\mathcal{I}}$, that is, to $\mathcal{I} \models$

$d \geq p.\,C' \sqsubseteq d \geq q.\,D'$. This argumentation can now be extended to the general case where C and D are arbitrary $\mathsf{Prob}^{>}\mathcal{EL}^{\perp}$ concept descriptions.

For a complexity analysis, we consider the following *subsumption problem*.

Instance: Let $\mathcal{T}$ be a TBox and let $C \sqsubseteq D$ be a concept inclusion.
Question: Is C subsumed by D w.r.t. $\mathcal{T}$, i.e., does $C \sqsubseteq_{\mathcal{T}} D$ hold true?

The next proposition shows that this problem is **EXP**-complete and, consequently, more expensive than deciding subsumption w.r.t. a TBox in its non-probabilistic sibling $\mathcal{EL}^{\perp}$—a problem which is well-known to be **P**-complete. We conclude that reasoning in $\mathsf{Prob}^{>}\mathcal{EL}^{\perp}$ is worst-case intractable, while reasoning in $\mathcal{EL}^{\perp}$ is always tractable.

Proposition 1. *In* $\mathsf{Prob}^{>}\mathcal{EL}^{\perp}$, *the subsumption problem is* **EXP**-*complete.*

4   Concept Inclusion Bases in $\mathcal{EL}^{\perp}$

When developing a method for axiomatizing $\mathsf{Prob}^{>}\mathcal{EL}^{\perp}$ concept inclusions valid in a given probabilistic interpretation in the next section, we will use techniques for axiomatizing $\mathcal{EL}^{\perp}$ CIs valid in an interpretation as developed by Baader and Distel in [1,6] for greatest fixed-point semantics, and as adjusted by Borchmann, Distel, and the author in [5] for the role-depth-bounded case. A brief introduction is as follows. A *concept inclusion base* for an interpretation $\mathcal{I}$ is a TBox $\mathcal{T}$ such that, for each CI $C \sqsubseteq D$, it holds true that $C \sqsubseteq_{\mathcal{I}} D$ if, and only if, $C \sqsubseteq_{\mathcal{T}} D$. For each finite interpretation $\mathcal{I}$ with finite active signature, there is a *canonical base* $\mathsf{Can}(\mathcal{I})$ with respect to greatest fixed-point semantics, which contains a minimal number of CIs among all concept inclusion bases for $\mathcal{I}$, cf. [6, Corollary 5.13 and Theorem 5.18], and similarly there is a minimal *canonical base* $\mathsf{Can}(\mathcal{I}, d)$ with respect to an upper bound $d \in \mathbb{N}$ on the role depths, cf. [5, Theorem 4.32]. The construction of both canonical bases is built upon the notion of a *model-based most specific concept description* (abbrv.MMSC), which, for an interpretation $\mathcal{I}$ and some subset $\varXi \subseteq \Delta^{\mathcal{I}}$, is a concept description C such that $\varXi \subseteq C^{\mathcal{I}}$ and, for each concept description D, it holds true that $\varXi \subseteq D^{\mathcal{I}}$ implies $C \sqsubseteq_{\emptyset} D$. These exist either if greatest fixed-point semantics is applied (in order to be able to express cycles present in $\mathcal{I}$) or if the role depth of C is bounded by some $d \in \mathbb{N}$, and these are then denoted as $\varXi^{\mathcal{I}}$ or $\varXi^{\mathcal{I}_d}$, respectively. These mappings $\cdot^{\mathcal{I}} \colon \wp(\Delta^{\mathcal{I}}) \to \mathcal{EL}^{\perp}_{\mathsf{gfp}}(\varSigma)$ and $\cdot^{\mathcal{I}_d} \colon \wp(\Delta^{\mathcal{I}}) \to \mathcal{EL}^{\perp}_{d}(\varSigma)$ are the adjoints of the respective extension functions $\cdot^{\mathcal{I}} \colon \mathcal{EL}^{\perp}_{\mathsf{gfp}}(\varSigma) \to \wp(\Delta^{\mathcal{I}})$ and $\cdot^{\mathcal{I}} \colon \mathcal{EL}^{\perp}_{d}(\varSigma) \to \wp(\Delta^{\mathcal{I}})$, and the pair of both constitutes a *Galois connection*, cf. [6, Lemma 4.1] and [5, Lemmas 4.3 and 4.4], respectively.

As a variant of these two approaches, the author presented in [16] a method for constructing canonical bases relative to an existing TBox. If $\mathcal{I}$ is an interpretation and $\mathcal{B}$ is a TBox such that $\mathcal{I} \models \mathcal{B}$, then a *concept inclusion base* for $\mathcal{I}$ *relative* to $\mathcal{B}$ is a TBox $\mathcal{T}$ such that, for each CI $C \sqsubseteq D$, it holds true that $C \sqsubseteq_{\mathcal{I}} D$ if, and only if, $C \sqsubseteq_{\mathcal{T} \cup \mathcal{B}} D$. The corresponding *canonical base* is denoted as $\mathsf{Can}(\mathcal{I}, \mathcal{B})$, cf. [16, Theorem 1].

So far, the complexity of computing CI bases in the description logic $\mathcal{EL}^{\perp}$ has not been determined. Using simple arguments, one could only infer that the canonical base $\mathsf{Can}(\mathcal{I})$ can be computed in double exponential time with respect to the cardinality of the domain $\Delta^{\mathcal{I}}$. However, since we want to determine the computational complexity of the task of constructing CI bases in the probabilistic description logic $\mathsf{Prob}^{>}\mathcal{EL}^{\perp}$, which we will describe and prove in the next section and which we will build on top of means for computing such bases in $\mathcal{EL}^{\perp}$, we cite a recent answer from the author to this open question in the following proposition.

[22, **Proposition 2**]. *For each finitely representable interpretation $\mathcal{I}$, its canonical base $\mathsf{Can}(\mathcal{I})$ can be computed in deterministic exponential time with respect to the cardinality of the domain $\Delta^{\mathcal{I}}$. Furthermore, there are finitely representable interpretations $\mathcal{I}$ for which a concept inclusion base cannot be encoded in polynomial space w.r.t. $|\Delta^{\mathcal{I}}|$.*

It is not hard to adapt this result to the role-depth-bounded case; one can show that computing $\mathsf{Can}(\mathcal{I}, d)$ can be done in deterministic exponential time w.r.t. $|\Delta^{\mathcal{I}}|$ and d.

5   Axiomatization of Concept Inclusions in $\mathsf{Prob}^{>}_{n} \mathcal{EL}^{\perp}$

In this section, we shall develop an effective method for axiomatizing $\mathsf{Prob}^{>}_{n} \mathcal{EL}^{\perp}$ concept inclusions which are valid in a given finitely representable probabilistic interpretation. After defining the appropriate notion of a *concept inclusion base*, we show how this problem can be tackled using the aforementioned existing results on computing concept inclusion bases in $\mathcal{EL}^{\perp}$ from Sect. 4. More specifically, we devise an extension of the given signature by finitely many probability restrictions $\mathsf{d} > p. C$ that are treated as additional concept names, and we define so-called *scalings* $\mathcal{I}_n$ of the input probabilistic interpretation $\mathcal{I}$ which are (single-world) interpretations that suitably interpret these new concept names and, furthermore, such that there is a correspondence between $\mathsf{Prob}^{>}_{n} \mathcal{EL}^{\perp}$ CIs valid in $\mathcal{I}$ and CIs valid in $\mathcal{I}_n$. This very correspondence makes it possible to utilize the above mentioned techniques for axiomatizing CIs in $\mathcal{EL}^{\perp}$.

Definition 2. *A $\mathsf{Prob}^{>}_{n} \mathcal{EL}^{\perp}$ concept inclusion base for a probabilistic interpretation $\mathcal{I}$ is a $\mathsf{Prob}^{>}_{n} \mathcal{EL}^{\perp}$ terminological box $\mathcal{T}$ which is sound for $\mathcal{I}$, that is, $C \sqsubseteq_{\mathcal{T}} D$ implies $C \sqsubseteq_{\mathcal{I}} D$ for each $\mathsf{Prob}^{>}_{n} \mathcal{EL}^{\perp}$ concept inclusion $C \sqsubseteq D$,[5] and complete for $\mathcal{I}$, that is, $C \sqsubseteq_{\mathcal{I}} D$ only if $C \sqsubseteq_{\mathcal{T}} D$ for any $\mathsf{Prob}^{>}_{n} \mathcal{EL}^{\perp}$ concept inclusion $C \sqsubseteq D$.*

The following definition is to be read inductively, that is, initially some objects are defined for the probability depth $n = 0$, and if the objects are defined for the probability depth n, then these are used to define the next objects for the probability depth $n + 1$.

A first important step is to significantly reduce the possibilities of concept descriptions occurring as a filler in the probability restrictions, that is, of fillers

---

[5] Of course, soundness is equivalent to $\mathcal{I} \models \mathcal{T}$.

C in expressions $\mathsf{d} \gtrless p.\, C$. As it turns out, it suffices to consider only those fillers that are model-based most specific concept descriptions of some suitable *scaling* of the given probabilistic interpretation $\mathcal{I}$. We shall demonstrate that there are only finitely many such fillers—provided that the given probabilistic interpretation $\mathcal{I}$ is finitely representable.

As next step, we restrict the probability bounds p occurring in probability restrictions $\mathsf{d} \gtrless p.\, C$. Apparently, it is sufficient to consider only those values p that can occur when evaluating the extension of $\mathsf{Prob}_{n+1}^{\gtrless}\mathcal{EL}^{\perp}$ concept descriptions in $\mathcal{I}$, which, obviously, are the values $\mathbb{P}^{\mathcal{I}}\{\delta \in C^{\mathcal{I}}\}$ for any $\delta \in \Delta^{\mathcal{I}}$ and any $C \in \mathsf{Prob}_{n}^{\gtrless}\mathcal{EL}^{\perp}(\Sigma)$. In the sequel of this section we will see that there are only finitely many such probability bounds if $\mathcal{I}$ is finitely representable.

Having found a finite number of representatives for probability bounds as well as a finite number of fillers to be used in probability restrictions for each probability depth n, we now show that we can treat these finitely many concept descriptions as concept names of a signature Γ_n extending Σ in a way such that any $\mathsf{Prob}_{n}^{\gtrless}\mathcal{EL}^{\perp}$ concept inclusion is valid in $\mathcal{I}$ if, and only if, that concept inclusion projected onto the extended signature Γ_n is valid in a suitable *scaling* of $\mathcal{I}$ that interprets Γ_n.

Definition 3. *Fix some probabilistic interpretation $\mathcal{I}$ over a signature Σ. Then, we define the following objects Γ_n, $\mathcal{I}_n$, and $P_{\mathcal{I},n}$ by simultaneous induction over $n \in \mathbb{N}$.*

1. *The nth signature Γ_n is inductively defined as follows. We set $(\Gamma_0)_\mathsf{C} := \Sigma_\mathsf{C}$ and $(\Gamma_0)_\mathsf{R} := \Sigma_\mathsf{R}$. The subsequent signatures are then obtained in the following way.[6]*

$$(\Gamma_{n+1})_\mathsf{C} := (\Gamma_n)_\mathsf{C} \cup \left\{ \mathsf{d} \geq p.\, X^{\mathcal{I}_n} \,\middle|\, \begin{array}{l} p \in P_{\mathcal{I},n} \setminus \{0\},\ X \subseteq \Delta^{\mathcal{I}} \times \Omega^{\mathcal{I}}, \\ \text{and } \perp \neq_{\emptyset} X^{\mathcal{I}_n} \neq_{\emptyset} \top \end{array} \right\}$$

$$(\Gamma_{n+1})_\mathsf{R} := \Sigma_\mathsf{R}$$

2. *The nth scaling of $\mathcal{I}$ is defined as the interpretation $\mathcal{I}_n$ over Γ_n that has the following components.*

$$\Delta^{\mathcal{I}_n} := \Delta^{\mathcal{I}} \times \Omega^{\mathcal{I}}$$

$$\cdot^{\mathcal{I}_n} : \begin{cases} A \mapsto \{ (\delta, \omega) \mid \delta \in A^{\mathcal{I}(\omega)} \} & \text{for each } A \in (\Gamma_n)_\mathsf{C} \\ r \mapsto \{ ((\delta, \omega), (\epsilon, \omega)) \mid (\delta, \epsilon) \in r^{\mathcal{I}(\omega)} \} & \text{for each } r \in (\Gamma_n)_\mathsf{R} \end{cases}$$

3. *The nth set $P_{\mathcal{I},n}$ of probability values for $\mathcal{I}$ is given as follows.*

$$P_{\mathcal{I},n} := \{ \mathbb{P}^{\mathcal{I}}\{\delta \in C^{\mathcal{I}}\} \mid \delta \in \Delta^{\mathcal{I}} \text{ and } C \in \mathsf{Prob}_{n}^{\gtrless}\mathcal{EL}^{\perp}(\Sigma) \}$$

Furthermore, for each $p \in [0,1)$, we define $(p)_{\mathcal{I},n}^{+}$ as the next value in $P_{\mathcal{I},n}$ above p, that is, we set

$$(p)_{\mathcal{I},n}^{+} := \bigwedge \{ q \mid q \in P_{\mathcal{I},n} \text{ and } q > p \}.$$

---

[6] The mapping $\cdot^{\mathcal{I}}: \wp(\Delta^{\mathcal{I}}) \to \mathcal{EL}^{\perp}(\Sigma)$ for some (non-probabilistic) interpretation $\mathcal{I}$ has been introduced in Sect. 4.

Of course, we have that $\{0,1\} \subseteq P_{\mathcal{I},n}$ for each $n \in \mathbb{N}$. Note that $\mathcal{I}_{n+1}$ extends $\mathcal{I}_n$ by also interpreting the additional concept names in $(\Gamma_{n+1})_\mathsf{C} \setminus (\Gamma_n)_\mathsf{C}$, that is, the restriction $\mathcal{I}_{n+1}{\restriction}_{\Gamma_n}$ equals $\mathcal{I}_n$. Similarly, $\mathcal{I}_n{\restriction}_{\Gamma_m}$ and $\mathcal{I}_m$ are equal if $m \le n$.

As explained earlier, it suffices to only consider fillers in probabilistic restrictions that are model-based most specific concept descriptions. More specifically, the following holds true.

Lemma 4. *Consider a probabilistic interpretation $\mathcal{I}$ and a concept description* $\mathsf{d} \geqslant p.\, C$ *such that* $C \in \mathcal{EL}^\perp(\Gamma_n)$ *for some* $n \in \mathbb{N}$*. Then, the concept equivalence* $\mathsf{d} \geqslant p.\, C \equiv \mathsf{d} \geqslant p.\, C^{\mathcal{I}_n \mathcal{I}_n}$ *is valid in $\mathcal{I}$.*

The above lemma does not hold true for arbitrary fillers C, but only for fillers that can (syntactically) also be seen as $\mathcal{EL}^\perp$ concept descriptions over Γ_n. However, this does not cause any problems, since we can simply project any other filler onto this signature Γ_n. In particular, we define projections of arbitrary $\mathsf{Prob}_n^{\geqslant}\mathcal{EL}^\perp$ concept descriptions onto the signature Γ_n in the following manner.

Definition 5. *Fix some $n \in \mathbb{N}$ as well as a probabilistic interpretation $\mathcal{I}$. The nth projection $\pi_{\mathcal{I},n}(C)$ of a $\mathsf{Prob}_n^{\geqslant}\mathcal{EL}^\perp$ concept description C with respect to $\mathcal{I}$ is obtained from C by replacing subconcepts of the form $\mathsf{d} \geqslant p.\, D$ with suitable elements from $(\Gamma_n)_\mathsf{C}$ and, more specifically, we recursively define it as follows. We set $\pi_{\mathcal{I},0}(C) := C$ for each concept description $C \in \mathcal{EL}^\perp(\Sigma)$. The subsequent projections are then given in the following manner.*

$$\pi_{\mathcal{I},n+1}(A) := A \qquad\qquad\qquad \text{if } A \in \Sigma_\mathsf{C} \cup \{\perp, \top\}$$
$$\pi_{\mathcal{I},n+1}(C \sqcap D) := \pi_{\mathcal{I},n+1}(C) \sqcap \pi_{\mathcal{I},n+1}(D)$$
$$\pi_{\mathcal{I},n+1}(\exists r.\, C) := \exists r.\, \pi_{\mathcal{I},n+1}(C)$$

$$\pi_{\mathcal{I},n+1}(\mathsf{d} \geqslant p.\, C) := \begin{cases} \perp & \text{if } \geqslant p = {>}1 \\ \top & \text{else if } \geqslant p = {\geq}0 \\ \perp & \text{else if } (\pi_{\mathcal{I},n}(C))^{\mathcal{I}_{n+1}\mathcal{I}_{n+1}} \equiv_\emptyset \perp \\ \top & \text{else if } (\pi_{\mathcal{I},n}(C))^{\mathcal{I}_{n+1}\mathcal{I}_{n+1}} \equiv_\emptyset \top \\ \mathsf{d} \geq p.(\pi_{\mathcal{I},n}(C))^{\mathcal{I}_{n+1}\mathcal{I}_{n+1}} & \text{else if } \geqslant\, = \geq \text{ and } p \in P_{\mathcal{I},n+1} \\ \mathsf{d} \geq (p)^+_{\mathcal{I},n+1}.(\pi_{\mathcal{I},n}(C))^{\mathcal{I}_{n+1}\mathcal{I}_{n+1}} & \text{else} \end{cases}$$

Usually, projection mappings in mathematics are *idempotent*. It is easy to verify by induction over n that this also holds true for our projection mappings $\pi_{\mathcal{I},n}$ which we have just defined. This justifies the naming choice. Furthermore, we can show that the mappings $\pi_{\mathcal{I},n}$ are *intensive*, i.e., projecting some $\mathsf{Prob}_n^{\geqslant}\mathcal{EL}^\perp$ concept description C onto the nth signature Γ_n yields a more specific concept description, cf. the next lemma. Furthermore, the mappings $\pi_{\mathcal{I},n}$ are monotonic—a fact that can be proven by induction over n as well. As a corollary, it follows that each mapping $\pi_{\mathcal{I},n}$ is a *kernel operator*. However, please just take this as a side note, since we do not need the two additional properties of idempotency and monotonicity within this document.

Lemma 6. *Assume that $\mathcal{I}$ is a probabilistic interpretation, let $n \in \mathbb{N}$, and fix some $\mathsf{Prob}_n^{\geq}\mathcal{EL}^{\perp}$ concept description C. Then, it holds true that $\pi_{\mathcal{I},n}(C) \sqsubseteq_{\emptyset} C$.*

As a crucial observation regarding projections, we see that—within our given probabilistic interpretation $\mathcal{I}$—we do not have to distinguish between any $\mathsf{Prob}_n^{\geq}\mathcal{EL}^{\perp}$ concept description C and its nth projection $\pi_{\mathcal{I},n}(C)$, since the upcoming lemma shows that both always possess the same extension in each world of $\mathcal{I}$. Simply speaking, the signatures Γ_n contain enough building bricks to describe anything that happens within $\mathcal{I}$ up to a probability depth of n.

Lemma 7. *Assume that $\mathcal{I}$ is a probabilistic interpretation, let $n \in \mathbb{N}$, and consider some $\mathsf{Prob}_n^{\geq}\mathcal{EL}^{\perp}$ concept description C. Then, C and its nth projection $\pi_{\mathcal{I},n}(C)$ have the same extension in any world of $\mathcal{I}$.*

As a last important statement on the properties of the projection mappings, we now demonstrate that validity of some concept inclusion $C \sqsubseteq D$ with a probability depth not exceeding n is equivalent to validity of the projected concept inclusion $\pi_{\mathcal{I},n}(C) \sqsubseteq \pi_{\mathcal{I},n}(D)$ in the scaling $\mathcal{I}_n$. This is a key lemma for the upcoming construction of a concept inclusion base for $\mathcal{I}$.

Lemma 8. *Let $n \in \mathbb{N}$, and consider a probabilistic interpretation $\mathcal{I}$ as well as some $\mathsf{Prob}_n^{\geq}\mathcal{EL}^{\perp}$ concept inclusion $C \sqsubseteq D$. Then, $C \sqsubseteq D$ is valid in $\mathcal{I}$ if, and only if, the nth projected concept inclusion $\pi_{\mathcal{I},n}(C) \sqsubseteq \pi_{\mathcal{I},n}(D)$ is valid in the nth scaling $\mathcal{I}_n$.*

Now we go on to considering the sets $P_{\mathcal{I},n}$ of essential probability values. As we have already claimed, these sets are always finite—provided that the fixed probabilistic interpretation is finitely representable. In order to prove this, we need the following statement.

Lemma 9. *For each probabilistic interpretation $\mathcal{I}$ and any $n \in \mathbb{N}$, the following equation is satisfied.*

$$P_{\mathcal{I},n} = \{\, \mathbb{P}^{\mathcal{I}}\{\delta \in X^{\mathcal{I}_n \mathcal{I}}\} \mid \delta \in \Delta^{\mathcal{I}} \text{ and } X \subseteq \Delta^{\mathcal{I}} \times \Omega^{\mathcal{I}} \,\}$$

For most, if not all, practical use case we can argue that the given probabilistic interpretation $\mathcal{I}$ can be assumed as finitely representable. Utilizing some of our previous results then implies that each nth scaling of $\mathcal{I}$ is finitely representable as well. More specifically, the following is satisfied.

Corollary 10. *If $\mathcal{I}$ is a finitely representable probabilistic interpretation, then it holds true that, for each $n \in \mathbb{N}$, the subset $\Gamma_n \setminus \Sigma$ of the nth signature is finite, the nth scaling $\mathcal{I}_n$ is finite and has a finite active signature, and the nth set $P_{\mathcal{I},n}$ of probability values is finite and satisfies $P_{\mathcal{I},n} \subseteq \mathbb{Q}$.*

As already mentioned in Sects. 2 and 4, we want to make use of existing techniques that allow for axiomatizing interpretations in the description logic $\mathcal{EL}^{\perp}$. In order to do so, we need to be sure that the semantics of $\mathcal{EL}^{\perp}$ and its probabilistic sibling $\mathsf{Prob}^{\geq}\mathcal{EL}^{\perp}$ are not too different, or expressed alternatively, that there is a suitable correspondence between (non-probabilistic) entailment in $\mathcal{EL}^\perp$ and (probabilistic) entailment in $\mathsf{Prob}^>\mathcal{EL}^\perp$. A more sophisticated formulation is presented in the following lemma.

Lemma 11. *Let $\mathcal{T}$ be a $\mathsf{Prob}^>\mathcal{EL}^\perp$ TBox, and assume that $\mathcal{B}$ is a set that consists of tautological $\mathsf{Prob}^>\mathcal{EL}^\perp$ concept inclusions, i.e., $\emptyset \models \mathcal{B}$. If $C \sqsubseteq D$ is a $\mathsf{Prob}^>\mathcal{EL}^\perp$ concept inclusion that is entailed by $\mathcal{T} \cup \mathcal{B}$ with respect to non-probabilistic entailment, then $C \sqsubseteq D$ is also entailed by $\mathcal{T}$ with respect to probabilistic entailment.*

As final step, we show that each concept inclusion base of the probabilistic scaling $\mathcal{I}_n$ induces a $\mathsf{Prob}_n^>\mathcal{EL}^\perp$ concept inclusion base of $\mathcal{I}$. While soundness is easily verified, completeness follows from the fact that $C \sqsubseteq_\mathcal{T} \pi_{\mathcal{I},n}(C) \sqsubseteq_\mathcal{T} \pi_{\mathcal{I},n}(D) \sqsubseteq_\emptyset D$ holds true for every valid $\mathsf{Prob}_n^>\mathcal{EL}^\perp$ concept inclusion $C \sqsubseteq D$ of $\mathcal{I}$.

Theorem 12. *Fix a number $n \in \mathbb{N}$ and some finitely representable probabilistic interpretation $\mathcal{I}$. If $\mathcal{T}_n$ is a concept inclusion base for the nth scaling $\mathcal{I}_n$ with respect to some set $\mathcal{B}_n$ of tautological $\mathsf{Prob}_n^>\mathcal{EL}^\perp$ concept inclusions used as background knowledge, then the following terminological box $\mathcal{T}$ is a $\mathsf{Prob}_n^>\mathcal{EL}^\perp$ concept inclusion base for $\mathcal{I}$.*

$$\mathcal{T} := \mathcal{T}_n \cup \bigcup\{\mathcal{U}_{\mathcal{I},\ell} \mid \ell \in \{1,\dots,n\}\} \quad where$$
$$\mathcal{U}_{\mathcal{I},\ell} := \{\,\mathsf{d} > p.\, X^{\mathcal{I}_\ell \mathcal{I}_\ell} \sqsubseteq \mathsf{d} \geq (p)_{\mathcal{I},\ell}^+.\, X^{\mathcal{I}_\ell \mathcal{I}_\ell} \mid p \in P_{\mathcal{I},\ell} \setminus \{1\} \text{ and } X \subseteq \Delta^\mathcal{I} \times \Omega^\mathcal{I}\,\}$$

As already mentioned in Sect. 4 and according to [16], a suitable such concept inclusion base $\mathcal{T}_n$ for the nth scaling $\mathcal{I}_n$ with respect to background knowledge $\mathcal{B}_n$ exists and can be computed effectively, namely the canonical base $\mathsf{Can}(\mathcal{I}_n, \mathcal{B}_n)$. This enables us to immediately draw the following conclusion.

Corollary 13. *Let $\mathcal{I}$ be a finitely representable probabilistic interpretation, fix some $n \in \mathbb{N}$, and let $\mathcal{B}_n$ denote the set of all $\mathcal{EL}^\perp$ concept inclusions over Γ_n that are tautological with respect to probabilistic entailment, i.e., are valid in every probabilistic interpretation. Then, the canonical base for $\mathcal{I}$ and probability depth n that is defined as*

$$\mathsf{Can}(\mathcal{I}, n) := \mathsf{Can}(\mathcal{I}_n, \mathcal{B}_n) \cup \bigcup\{\mathcal{U}_{\mathcal{I},\ell} \mid \ell \in \{1,\dots,n\}\}$$

is a $\mathsf{Prob}_n^>\mathcal{EL}^\perp$ concept inclusion base for $\mathcal{I}$, and it can be computed effectively.

Eventually, we close our investigations with a complexity analysis of the problem of actually computing the canonical base $\mathsf{Can}(\mathcal{I}, n)$. As it turns out, this computation is—in terms of computational complexity—not more expensive than the corresponding axiomatization task in $\mathcal{EL}^\perp$, cf. [22, Proposition 2]. However, this result only holds true if we dispense with the pre-computation of the tautological background knowledge $\mathcal{B}_n$ at all, and instead consider

$\mathsf{Can}^*(\mathcal{I}, n) := \mathsf{Can}(\mathcal{I}_n) \cup \bigcup \{ \mathcal{U}_{\mathcal{I},\ell} \mid \ell \in \{1, \ldots, n\} \}$, which is still a $\mathsf{Prob}^{\geq}_n \mathcal{EL}^{\perp}$ concept inclusion base for $\mathcal{I}$ but, as a drawback, might contain tautological axioms. More details can be found in the technical report [21].

Proposition 14. *For any finitely representable probabilistic interpretation $\mathcal{I}$ and any $n \in \mathbb{N}$, the canonical base $\mathsf{Can}^*(\mathcal{I}, n)$ can be computed in deterministic time that is exponential in $|\Delta^{\mathcal{I}}| \cdot |\Omega^{\mathcal{I}}|$ and polynomial in n. Furthermore, there are finitely representable probabilistic interpretations $\mathcal{I}$ for which a concept inclusion base cannot be encoded in polynomial space with respect to $|\Delta^{\mathcal{I}}| \cdot |\Omega^{\mathcal{I}}| \cdot n$.*

6 Conclusion

We have devised an effective procedure for computing finite axiomatizations of observations that are represented as probabilistic interpretations. More specifically, we have shown how concept inclusion bases—TBoxes that are sound and complete for the input data set—can be constructed in the probabilistic description logic $\mathsf{Prob}^{\geq} \mathcal{EL}^{\perp}$. In a complexity analysis we found that we can always compute a canonical base in exponential time.

Future research is possible in various directions. One could extend the results to a more expressive probabilistic DL, e.g., to $\mathsf{Prob}^{\geq} \mathcal{M}$, or one could include upper probability bounds. Furthermore, for increasing the practicability of the approach, it could be investigated how the construction of a concept inclusion base can be made *incremental* or *interactive*. It might be the case that there already exists a TBox and there are new observations in form of a probabilistic interpretation; the goal is then to construct a TBox being a base for the CIs that are entailed by the existing knowledge as well as hold true in the new observations. While this would represent a *push* approach of learning, future research could tackle the *pull* approach as well, i.e., equip the procedure with expert interaction such that an exploration of partial observations is made possible.

Additionally, it is worth investigating whether the proposed approach could be optimized; for instance, one could check if equivalent results can be obtained with a subset of Γ_n or with another extended signature. Currently, it is also unknown whether, for each finitely representable probabilistic interpretation $\mathcal{I}$, there is some finite bound n on the probability depth such that each $\mathsf{Prob}^{\geq}_n \mathcal{EL}^{\perp}$ concept inclusion base for $\mathcal{I}$ is also sound and complete for *all* $\mathsf{Prob}^{\geq} \mathcal{EL}^{\perp}$ concept inclusions that are valid in $\mathcal{I}$—much like this is the case for the role depth in $\mathcal{EL}^{\perp}$.

Acknowledgments. The author gratefully thanks Franz Baader for drawing attention to the issue in [15], and furthermore thanks the reviewers for their constructive remarks.

References

1. Baader, F., Distel, F.: A finite basis for the set of $\mathcal{EL}$-implications holding in a finite model. In: Medina, R., Obiedkov, S. (eds.) ICFCA 2008. LNCS (LNAI), vol. 4933, pp. 46–61. Springer, Heidelberg (2008). https://doi.org/10.1007/978-3-540-78137-0_4

2. Baader, F., Horrocks, I., Lutz, C., Sattler, U.: An Introduction to Description Logic. Cambridge University Press, Cambridge (2017)
3. Bacchus, F.: Representing and reasoning with probabilistic knowledge. Ph.D. thesis, The University of Alberta, Edmonton, Alberta (1988)
4. Borchmann, D.: Learning terminological knowledge with high confidence from erroneous data. Doctoral thesis, Technische Universität Dresden, Dresden, Germany (2014)
5. Borchmann, D., Distel, F., Kriegel, F.: Axiomatisation of general concept inclusions from finite interpretations. J. Appl. Non-Class. Log. **26**(1), 1–46 (2016)
6. Distel, F.: Learning description logic knowledge bases from data using methods from formal concept analysis. Doctoral thesis, Technische Universität Dresden, Dresden, Germany (2011)
7. Ganter, B.: Two Basic Algorithms in Concept Analysis. FB4-Preprint 831, Technische Hochschule Darmstadt, Darmstadt, Germany (1984)
8. Ganter, B., Obiedkov, S.A.: Conceptual Exploration. Springer, Heidelberg (2016). https://doi.org/10.1007/978-3-662-49291-8
9. Ganter, B., Wille, R.: Formal Concept Analysis: Mathematical Foundations. Springer, Heidelberg (1999). https://doi.org/10.1007/978-3-642-59830-2
10. Guigues, J.L., Duquenne, V.: Famille minimale d'implications informatives résultant d'un tableau de données binaires. Mathématiques et Sciences Humaines **95**, 5–18 (1986)
11. Gutiérrez-Basulto, V., Jung, J.C., Lutz, C., Schröder, L.: Probabilistic description logics for subjective uncertainty. J. Artif. Intell. Res. **58**, 1–66 (2017)
12. Halpern, J.Y.: An analysis of first-order logics of probability. Artif. Intell. **46**(3), 311–350 (1990)
13. Heinsohn, J.: Probabilistic description logics. In: López de Mántaras, R., Poole, D. (eds.) UAI 1994: Proceedings of the Tenth Annual Conference on Uncertainty in Artificial Intelligence, Seattle, Washington, USA, 29–31 July 1994, pp. 311–318. Morgan Kaufmann (1994)
14. Jaeger, M.: Probabilistic reasoning in terminological logics. In: Doyle, J., Sandewall, E., Torasso, P. (eds.) Proceedings of the 4th International Conference on Principles of Knowledge Representation and Reasoning (KR 1994), Bonn, Germany, 24–27 May 1994, pp. 305–316. Morgan Kaufmann (1994)
15. Kriegel, F.: Axiomatization of general concept inclusions in probabilistic description logics. In: Hölldobler, S., Krötzsch, M., Peñaloza, R., Rudolph, S. (eds.) KI 2015. LNCS (LNAI), vol. 9324, pp. 124–136. Springer, Cham (2015). https://doi.org/10.1007/978-3-319-24489-1_10
16. Kriegel, F.: Incremental learning of TBoxes from interpretation sequences with methods of formal concept analysis. In: Calvanese, D., Konev, B. (eds.) Proceedings of the 28th International Workshop on Description Logics, Athens, Greece, 7–10 June 2015. CEUR Workshop Proceedings, vol. 1350. CEUR-WS.org (2015)
17. Kriegel, F.: Acquisition of terminological knowledge from social networks in description logic. In: Missaoui, R., Kuznetsov, S.O., Obiedkov, S. (eds.) Formal Concept Analysis of Social Networks. LNSN, pp. 97–142. Springer, Cham (2017). https://doi.org/10.1007/978-3-319-64167-6_5
18. Kriegel, F.: Implications over probabilistic attributes. In: Bertet, K., Borchmann, D., Cellier, P., Ferré, S. (eds.) ICFCA 2017. LNCS (LNAI), vol. 10308, pp. 168–183. Springer, Cham (2017). https://doi.org/10.1007/978-3-319-59271-8_11
19. Kriegel, F.: Probabilistic implication bases in FCA and probabilistic bases of GCIs in $\mathcal{EL}^\perp$. Int. J. Gen. Syst. **46**(5), 511–546 (2017)

20. Kriegel, F.: Acquisition of terminological knowledge in probabilistic description logic. In: Trollmann, F., Turhan, A.-Y. (eds.) KI 2018. LNCS (LNAI), vol. 11117, pp. 46–53. Springer, Cham (2018). https://doi.org/10.1007/978-3-030-00111-7_5

21. Kriegel, F.: Learning description logic axioms from discrete probability distributions over description graphs (extended version). LTCS-Report 18–12, Chair of Automata Theory, Institute of Theoretical Computer Science, Technische Universität Dresden, Dresden, Germany (2018). https://tu-dresden.de/inf/lat/reports# Kr-LTCS-18-12

22. Kriegel, F.: Most specific consequences in the description logic $\mathcal{EL}$. LTCS-Report 18–11, Chair of Automata Theory, Institute of Theoretical Computer Science, Technische Universität Dresden, Dresden, Germany (2018). https://tu-dresden. de/inf/lat/reports#Kr-LTCS-18-11, accepted for publication in Discrete Applied Mathematics

23. Lukasiewicz, T.: Expressive probabilistic description logics. Artif. Intell. **172**(6–7), 852–883 (2008)

24. Rudolph, S.: Relational exploration: combining description logics and formal concept analysis for knowledge specification. Doctoral thesis, Technische Universität Dresden, Dresden, Germany (2006)

Learning Ontologies with Epistemic Reasoning: The $\mathcal{EL}$ Case

Ana Ozaki$^{(\boxtimes)}$ and Nicolas Troquard

KRDB Research Centre, Free University of Bozen-Bolzano, Bolzano, Italy
{ana.ozaki,nicolas.troquard}@unibz.it

Abstract. We investigate the problem of learning description logic ontologies *from entailments* via queries, using epistemic reasoning. We introduce a new learning model consisting of *epistemic membership and example queries* and show that polynomial learnability in this model coincides with polynomial learnability in Angluin's exact learning model with membership and equivalence queries. We then instantiate our learning framework to $\mathcal{EL}$ and show some complexity results for an epistemic extension of $\mathcal{EL}$ where epistemic operators can be applied over the axioms. Finally, we transfer known results for $\mathcal{EL}$ ontologies and its fragments to our learning model based on epistemic reasoning.

Keywords: Exact learning · Epistemic logic · Description logic

1 Introduction

Description logics (DL) balance expressivity and complexity of reasoning, resulting in a family of formalisms which can capture conceptual knowledge in various domains [3].[1] One of the most popular ontology languages, featuring polynomial time complexity of reasoning tasks such as entailment, is $\mathcal{EL}$ [2], which allows conjunctions ($\sqcap$) and existential restrictions ($\exists$) in its concept expressions but disallows negations of concepts. The following example illustrates $\mathcal{EL}$ ontologies (Sect. 4) representing knowledge of experts in different domains.

Example 1. Ana knows about Brazilian music (BM) and Nicolas is an expert in French cuisine (FC). We can represent some parts of their knowledge as follows.

$\mathcal{O}_{\mathsf{Ana}}^{\mathsf{BM}} = \{\mathsf{BrazilianSinger}(\mathsf{Caetano}) \quad \mathcal{O}_{\mathsf{Nicolas}}^{\mathsf{FC}} = \{\mathsf{FrenchChef}(\mathsf{Soyer})$
$\mathsf{BossaNova} \sqsubseteq \mathsf{BrazilianMusicStyle} \quad \mathsf{Crepe} \sqsubseteq \exists\mathsf{contains}.\mathsf{Flour}$
$\mathsf{ViolaBuriti} \sqsubseteq \exists\mathsf{madeFrom}.\mathsf{Buriti}\} \quad \mathsf{Crepe} \sqcap \exists\mathsf{contains}.\mathsf{Sugar} \sqsubseteq \mathsf{Dessert}\}$

Naturally, domain experts—humans, or artificial entities with complex neural networks—cannot be expected to be able to easily transfer their knowledge. However, when specific questions about the domain are posed, e.g., 'is Bossa

---

[1] The technical report [17] is a more complete version of this paper.

© Springer Nature Switzerland AG 2019
F. Calimeri et al. (Eds.): JELIA 2019, LNAI 11468, pp. 418–433, 2019.
https://doi.org/10.1007/978-3-030-19570-0_27

Nova a Brazilian music style?', an expert in the domain of Brazilian music can accurately decide whether such statement holds or not. So the ontology representation of the knowledge of an expert, even though *not directly accessible*, can be learned via a trial and error process in which individuals or machines, generically called *agents*, communicate with each other, in order to learn from the other agents. We assume that the *target* domain of interest to be learned is represented by a logical theory formulated in an ontology language.

In computational learning theory, a classical communication protocol coming from the exact learning model [1] is based on questions of two types: *membership* and *equivalence* queries. In a learning from entailments setting [11], these questions can be described as follows. Membership queries correspond to asking whether a certain statement formulated as a logical sentence follows from the target. Equivalence queries correspond to asking whether a certain logical theory, called *hypothesis*, precisely describes the target. If there are wrong or missing statements in the hypothesis, a statement illustrating the imprecision should be returned to the agent playing the role of the *learner*.

Example 2. Assume Ana wants to learn about French cuisine. She asks Nicolas whether it follows from his knowledge that 'every crepe is a dessert', in symbols, 'does $\mathcal{O}^{FC}_{Nicolas} \models Crepe \sqsubseteq Dessert$?', which the answer in this case is 'no', since only those which contain sugar are considered desserts. To receive new statements about French cuisine from Nicolas, Ana needs to pose equivalence queries, in symbols 'does $\mathcal{O}^{FC}_{Ana} \equiv \mathcal{O}^{FC}_{Nicolas}$?'. Each time she poses this type of questions, her best interest is to tell him everything she knows about French cuisine.

One of the main difficulties in implementing this protocol in practice [16, p. 297] comes from the putative unreasonableness of equivalence queries. Whenever a learner poses an equivalence query, the expert playing the role of an *oracle* needs to evaluate the whole hypothesis and decide whether or not it is equivalent to the target. If not, then the oracle returns a statement in the logical difference between the hypothesis and the target. One way out of this difficulty is hinted to us by a simple observation: during interactive communication among agents, not only domain knowledge is exchanged and acquired but also second-order knowledge, which is the knowledge of what is known by the other agents.

Example 3. When Ana and Nicolas communicate, they know what they have already told to each other. If Ana tells Nicolas that 'Buriti is a Brazilian tree' (Nicolas now *knows* this statement, in symbols, $\mathbf{K}_{Nicolas}(Buriti \sqsubseteq BrazilianTree)$) and that 'Viola de Buriti is made from Buriti' ($\mathbf{K}_{Nicolas}(ViolaBuriti \sqsubseteq \exists madeFrom.Buriti)$) she does not need to tell him that 'Viola de Buriti is made from a Brazilian tree' (as it follows that $\mathbf{K}_{Nicolas}(ViolaBuriti \sqsubseteq \exists madeFrom.BrazilianTree)$, see Sect. 4).

In this paper, we thus propose a new and more realistic learning model. It is based on a protocol which takes into account what is known by the agents, either because a statement was explicitly communicated or because it is a logical consequence of previous statements given during their interaction. Our protocol

EPISTEMIC[MEM,EX] $\overset{\text{Th. 3}}{=}$ EXACT[MEM,EQ] $\overset{\text{[16] and [5]}}{\subset}$ PAC[MEM]

EPISTEMIC[EX] $\overset{\text{Th. 1 and Th. 2}}{\subset}$ EXACT[EQ] $\overset{\text{[1] and [5]}}{\subset}$ PAC

Fig. 1. Polynomial learnability. Each class denotes the set of frameworks that are polynomial query learnable in the corresponding learning model. MEM, EQ and EX stand for membership, equivalence, and example queries respectively.

is based on queries of two types. The first is an epistemic version of membership queries where the oracle 'remembers' those membership queries whose reply was 'yes'. We call the second type *example queries*. When asked an example query, the oracle answers a statement which follows from its knowledge but does not follow from its knowledge about what the learner knows. The oracle also 'remembers' that the statements given are now known by the learner.

The first contribution of this work is the introduction of the learning model based on epistemic reasoning, which we call *epistemic learning model*, and an analysis of its 'power' in comparison with the exact learning model (Fig. 1). The second is an instantiation to the $\mathcal{EL}$ ontology language, whose polynomial learnability has been investigated in the exact learning model [10,14,15].

In more details, the epistemic learning model is introduced in Sect. 2. We then establish in Sect. 3 that polynomial learnability is strictly harder in the epistemic model without (an epistemic version of) membership queries (Theorems 1 and 2). Nonetheless, it coincides with polynomial learnability in the exact learning model if both types of queries are allowed (Theorem 3). Since it is known that polynomial learnability in the exact learning model with only equivalence queries implies polynomial learnability in the classical probably approximately correct learning model (PAC) [1,18], it follows that polynomial learnability in the epistemic learning model with only example queries implies polynomial learnability in the PAC learning model. The same relationship holds for the case where we have (an epistemic version of) membership queries in the epistemic model and the PAC model also allows membership queries. We also show in Sect. 4 some complexity results for an epistemic extension of $\mathcal{EL}$, which we call $\mathcal{ELK}$. In particular, we show that satisfiability in $\mathcal{ELK}$, which includes Boolean combinations of $\mathcal{EL}$ axioms, does not increase the NP-completeness of propositional logic (Theorem 4). We then show that a fragment of $\mathcal{ELK}$ features PTIME complexity for the satisfiability and entailment problems (Theorem 5), as in $\mathcal{EL}$ [2]. Crucially, it captures the epistemic reasoning that the agent playing the role of the oracle needs to perform. Finally, in Sect. 5 we transfer known results [10,14] for $\mathcal{EL}$ in the exact learning model to the epistemic learning model.

2 Learning with Epistemic Reasoning

We first define the epistemic extension of a description logic $\mathcal{L}$, which is often a notation variant of a fragment of first-order logic or propositional logic. The epistemic extension of $\mathcal{L}$ allows expressions of the form 'agent i knows some axiom of $\mathcal{L}$'. We then use the epistemic extension of a logic to define a learning framework based on epistemic reasoning.

2.1 The Epistemic Extension of $\mathcal{L}$

In the following, we formalise the epistemic extension $\mathcal{LK}$ of a description logic $\mathcal{L}$. Our notation and definitions can be easily adapted to the case $\mathcal{L}$ is a (fragment of) first-order or propositional logic. Assume symbols of $\mathcal{L}$ are taken from pairwise disjoint and countably infinite sets of concept, role and individual names N_C, N_R and N_I, respectively. Let $\mathbf{A}$ be a set of agents. An $\mathcal{LK}$ axiom is an expression of the form: $\beta ::= \alpha \mid \mathbf{K}_i\beta$ where α is an $\mathcal{L}$ formula and $i \in \mathbf{A}$. $\mathcal{LK}$ formulas φ, ψ are expressions of the form: $\varphi ::= \beta \mid \neg\varphi \mid \varphi \wedge \psi$ where β is an $\mathcal{LK}$ axiom.

An $\mathcal{L}$ *interpretation* $\mathcal{I} = (\Delta^{\mathcal{I}}, \cdot^{\mathcal{I}})$ over a non-empty set $\Delta^{\mathcal{I}}$, called the *domain*, defines an *interpretation function* $\cdot^{\mathcal{I}}$ that maps each concept name $A \in N_C$ to a subset $A^{\mathcal{I}}$ of $\Delta^{\mathcal{I}}$, each role name $r \in N_R$ to a binary relation $r^{\mathcal{I}}$ on $\Delta^{\mathcal{I}}$, and each individual name $a \in N_I$ to an element $a^{\mathcal{I}} \in \Delta^{\mathcal{I}}$. The extension of the mapping $\cdot^{\mathcal{I}}$ from concept names to $\mathcal{L}$ complex concept expressions depends on the precise definition of $\mathcal{L}$. We write $\models_{\mathcal{L}}$ and $\equiv_{\mathcal{L}}$ to denote the entailment and equivalence relations for $\mathcal{L}$ formulas, respectively.

An $\mathcal{LK}$ interpretation $\mathfrak{I} = (\mathcal{W}, \{\mathcal{R}_i\}_{i\in\mathbf{A}})$ consists of a set $\mathcal{W}$ of $\mathcal{L}$ interpretations and a set of accessibility relations $\mathcal{R}_i$ on $\mathcal{W}$, one for each agent $i \in \mathbf{A}$. We assume that the relations $\mathcal{R}_i$ are equivalence relations. A pointed $\mathcal{LK}$ interpretation is a pair $(\mathfrak{I}, \mathcal{I})$ where $\mathfrak{I} = (\mathcal{W}, \{\mathcal{R}_i\}_{i\in\mathbf{A}})$ is an $\mathcal{LK}$ interpretation and $\mathcal{I}$ is an element of $\mathcal{W}$. The *entailment* relation $\models_{\mathcal{LK}}$ of an $\mathcal{LK}$ formula φ in $\mathfrak{I} = (\mathcal{W}, \{\mathcal{R}_i\}_{i\in\mathbf{A}})$ pointed at $\mathcal{I} \in \mathcal{W}$ is inductively defined (for simplicity, we may omit the subscript $_{\mathcal{LK}}$ from $\models_{\mathcal{LK}}$):

$$\mathfrak{I}, \mathcal{I} \models \alpha \text{ iff } \mathcal{I} \models_{\mathcal{L}} \alpha \qquad \mathfrak{I}, \mathcal{I} \models \phi \wedge \psi \text{ iff } \mathfrak{I}, \mathcal{I} \models \phi \text{ and } \mathfrak{I}, \mathcal{I} \models \psi$$
$$\mathfrak{I}, \mathcal{I} \models \neg\phi \text{ iff not } \mathfrak{I}, \mathcal{I} \models \phi \qquad \mathfrak{I}, \mathcal{I} \models \mathbf{K}_i\beta \text{ iff } \forall(\mathcal{I}, \mathcal{J}) \in \mathcal{R}_i, \mathcal{J} \models \beta.$$

An $\mathcal{LK}$ formula φ *entails* an $\mathcal{LK}$ formula ψ, written $\varphi \models \psi$, iff for all pointed $\mathcal{LK}$ interpretations $(\mathfrak{I}, \mathcal{I})$, $\mathfrak{I}, \mathcal{I} \models \varphi$ implies $\mathfrak{I}, \mathcal{I} \models \psi$. An $\mathcal{LK}$ formula φ is *equivalent* to an $\mathcal{LK}$ formula ψ, written $\varphi \equiv \psi$ (we may omit $_{\mathcal{LK}}$ from $\equiv_{\mathcal{LK}}$), iff $\varphi \models \psi$ and $\psi \models \varphi$. We use the notion of a set of formulas and the conjunction of its elements interchangeably. The *size* of a formula or an interpretation X, denoted $|X|$, is the length of the string that represents it, where concept, role and individual names and domain elements are considered to be of length 1.

2.2 A Learning Model Based on Epistemic Reasoning

We first adapt the exact learning model with membership and equivalence queries to a multi-agent setting. We then introduce the epistemic learning model in a multi-agent setting and provide complexity notions for these models.

We introduce basic notions for the definition of a learning framework and the learning problem via queries [1], adapted to a *learning from entailments* setting [11] with multiple agents. A *learning (from entailments) framework* $\mathfrak{F}$ is a pair (X, L), where X is a set of *examples* (also called *domain* or *instance space*), and L is a set of *formulas* of a description logic $\mathcal{L}$. We say that $x \in X$ is a *positive example* for $l \in L$ if $l \models_{\mathcal{L}} x$ and a *negative example* for l if $l \not\models_{\mathcal{L}} x$. A *counterexample* x for $l \in L$ and $h \in L$ is either a *positive example* for l such that $h \not\models_{\mathcal{L}} x$ or a *negative example* for l such that $h \models_{\mathcal{L}} x$. A *multi-agent learning framework* $\mathfrak{F}(\mathbf{A})$ is a set $\{\mathfrak{F}_i = (X_i, L_i) \mid i \in \mathbf{A}\}$ of learning frameworks.

We first provide a formal definition of the exact learning model, based on membership and equivalence queries, and then we introduce the epistemic learning model, with example and epistemic membership queries. Let $\mathfrak{F}(\mathbf{A})$ be a multi-agent learning framework. Each $i \in \mathbf{A}$ aims at learning a *target* formula $l_j \in L_j$ of a description logic $\mathcal{L}$ of each other agent $j \neq i \in \mathbf{A}$ by posing them queries.

Definition 1 (Membership query). *For every $i \in \mathbf{A}$ and every $l_i \in L_i$, let* $\mathsf{MEM}_{\mathfrak{F}(\mathbf{A}), l_i}$ *be an oracle that takes as input $x \in X_i$ and outputs 'yes' if $l_i \models_{\mathcal{L}} x$ and 'no' otherwise. A* membership query *to agent $i \in \mathbf{A}$ is a call to* $\mathsf{MEM}_{\mathfrak{F}(\mathbf{A}), l_i}$.

Definition 2 (Equivalence query). *For every $i \in \mathbf{A}$ and every $l_i \in L_i$, we denote by* $\mathsf{EQ}_{\mathfrak{F}(\mathbf{A}), l_i}$ *an oracle that takes as input a hypothesis formula of a description logic $h \in L_i$ and returns 'yes' if $h \equiv_{\mathcal{L}} l_i$ and a counterexample for l_i and h otherwise. An* equivalence query *to agent $i \in \mathbf{A}$ is a call to* $\mathsf{EQ}_{\mathfrak{F}(\mathbf{A}), l_i}$. *There is no assumption about which counterexample is returned by* $\mathsf{EQ}_{\mathfrak{F}(\mathbf{A}), l_i}$.

In this work, we introduce *example* queries, where an agent $i \in \mathbf{A}$ can ask an agent $j \in \mathbf{A}$ to only provide examples which are not logical consequences of what they have already communicated. Intuitively, if agent j returns x to agent i in a language $\mathcal{L}$ and $x \models_{\mathcal{L}} y$ then agent i knows y, in symbols, $\mathbf{K}_i y$. Since agent j returned this example to agent i, the axiom $\mathbf{K}_i y$ is part of the logical theory representing the knowledge of agent j, so agent j acquires knowledge of what is known by agent i as they communicate. We use example queries in combination with an epistemic version of membership queries, called $\mathbf{K}$-*membership* queries. Given $i \in \mathbf{A}$, assume that L_i is a set of formulas of the logic $\mathcal{L}$ and denote by $L_i^{\mathbf{K}}$ the set of all formulas in the epistemic extension of $\mathcal{L}$, which, by definition of $\mathcal{L}\mathcal{K}$, includes all $\mathcal{L}$ formulas. The target formula l_i is an element of L_i, however, the oracles for the example and $\mathbf{K}$-membership queries may add $\mathcal{L}\mathcal{K}$ formulas to l_i. We denote by l_i^{k+1} the result of updating l_i^k upon receiving the k-th query, where $l_i^1 = l_i$. At all times X_i is a set of examples in $\mathcal{L}$ (not in $\mathcal{L}\mathcal{K}$).

Definition 3 ($\mathbf{K}$-membership query). *For every $i \in \mathbf{A}$ and every $l_i^k \in L_i^{\mathbf{K}}$, let* $\mathsf{MEM}^{\mathbf{K}}_{\mathfrak{F}(\mathbf{A}), l_i^k}$ *be an oracle that takes as input $x \in X_i$ and $j \in \mathbf{A}$, and, if $l_i^1 \models_{\mathcal{L}} x$, it outputs 'yes' and define $l_i^{k+1} := l_i^k \wedge \mathbf{K}_j x$[2].*
Otherwise it returns 'no' and defines $l_i^{k+1} := l_i^k$. The k-th $\mathbf{K}$-membership query *to agent $i \in \mathbf{A}$ is a call to* $\mathsf{MEM}^{\mathbf{K}}_{\mathfrak{F}(\mathbf{A}), l_i^k}$.

---

[2] We may write l_i^k for the conjunction of its elements.

Definition 4 (Example query). *For every $i \in \mathbf{A}$ and every $l_i^k \in L_i^{\mathbf{K}}$, let* $\mathsf{EX}_{\mathfrak{F}(\mathbf{A}),l_i^k}$ *be an oracle that takes as input some $j \in \mathbf{A}$ and outputs $x \in X_i$ such that $l_i^1 \models_{\mathcal{L}} x$ but $l_i^k \not\models_{\mathcal{L}\mathcal{K}} \mathbf{K}_j x$ if such x exists; or 'you finished', otherwise.*

Upon returning $x \in X_i$ such that $l_i^1 \models_{\mathcal{L}} x$ the oracle $\mathsf{EX}_{\mathfrak{F}(\mathbf{A}),l_i^k}$ defines $l_i^{k+1} :=$ $l_i^k \wedge \mathbf{K}_j x$. The k-th example query to agent $i \in \mathbf{A}$ is a call to $\mathsf{EX}_{\mathfrak{F}(\mathbf{A}),l_i^k}$.

An *exact learning algorithm* A_i for $\mathfrak{F}_i \in \mathfrak{F}(\mathbf{A})$ is a deterministic algorithm that takes no input, is allowed to make queries to $\mathsf{MEM}_{\mathfrak{F}(\mathbf{A}),l_i}$ and $\mathsf{EQ}_{\mathfrak{F}(\mathbf{A}),l_i}$ (without knowing what the target l_i to be learned is), and eventually halts and outputs some $h \in L_i$ with $h \equiv_{\mathcal{L}} l_i$. An *epistemic learning algorithm* for $\mathfrak{F}_i \in \mathfrak{F}(\mathbf{A})$ is a deterministic algorithm that takes no input, is allowed to make queries to $\mathsf{MEM}^{\mathbf{K}}_{\mathfrak{F}(\mathbf{A}),l_i^k}$ and $\mathsf{EX}_{\mathfrak{F}(\mathbf{A}),l_i^k}$ (without knowing what the target l_i^1 to be learned is), and eventually halts after receiving 'you finished' from $\mathsf{EX}_{\mathfrak{F}(\mathbf{A}),l_i^k}$.

We say that $\mathfrak{F}(\mathbf{A})$ is *exactly learnable* if there is an exact learning algorithm A_i for each $\mathfrak{F}_i \in \mathfrak{F}(\mathbf{A})$ and that $\mathfrak{F}(\mathbf{A})$ is *polynomial query exactly learnable* if each $\mathfrak{F}_i \in \mathfrak{F}(\mathbf{A})$ is exactly learnable by an algorithm A_i such that at every step the sum of the sizes of the inputs to queries made by A_i up to that step is bounded by a polynomial $p(|l_i|, |x|)$, where l_i is the target and $x \in X_i$ is the largest example seen so far by A_i. $\mathfrak{F}(\mathbf{A})$ is *polynomial time exactly learnable* if each $\mathfrak{F}_i \in \mathfrak{F}(\mathbf{A})$ is exactly learnable by an algorithm A_i such that at every step (we count each call to an oracle as one step of computation) of computation the time used by A_i up to that step is bounded by a polynomial $p(|l_i|, |x|)$, where $l_i \in L_i$ is the target and $x \in X$ is the largest counterexample seen so far. We may also say that $\mathfrak{F}(\mathbf{A})$ is learnable in $O(|l_i|, |x|)$ many steps, following the same notion of polynomial time learnability, except that the number of steps is bounded by $O(|l_i|, |x|)$.

We say that $\mathfrak{F}(\mathbf{A})$ is *epistemically learnable* if there is an epistemic learning algorithm for each $\mathfrak{F}_i \in \mathfrak{F}(\mathbf{A})$. Polynomial query/time epistemic learnability is defined analogously, with $p(|l_i^1|, |x|)$ defined in terms of $|l_i^1|$ and $|x|$. Clearly, if a learning framework $\mathfrak{F}(\mathbf{A})$ is polynomial time exactly/epistemically learnable then it is also polynomial query exactly/epistemically learnable.

3 Epistemic and Exact Polynomial Learnability

In this section we confront polynomial query and polynomial time learnability in the exact and epistemic learning models. We start by considering the case where the learner is only allowed to pose one type of query. Clearly, polynomial (query/time) exact learnability with only membership queries coincides with polynomial epistemic learnability with only $\mathbf{K}$-membership queries. We now analyse polynomial learnability with equivalence queries only and example queries only. Our first result is that polynomial (query/time) learnability in the epistemic learning model implies polynomial learnability in exact learning model.

Theorem 1. *If a multi-agent learning framework is polynomial query (resp. time) epistemically learnable with only example queries then it is polynomial query (resp. time) exactly learnable with only equivalence queries.*

Proof. Assume $\mathfrak{F}(\mathbf{A})$ is polynomial query epistemically learnable with only example queries (the case of polynomial time epistemic learnability with only example queries can be similarly proved). For each $\mathfrak{F}_i \in \mathfrak{F}(\mathbf{A})$ there is an epistemic learning algorithm A_i for $\mathfrak{F}_i$ with polynomial query complexity which only asks example queries. To construct an exact learning algorithm A_i' for $\mathfrak{F}_i$ which only asks equivalence queries using A_i, we define auxiliary sets $s_i^{\mathcal{K}}(k)$ and $s_i^{\mathcal{L}}(k)$ which will keep the information returned by $\mathsf{EQ}_{\mathfrak{F}(\mathbf{A}),l_i}$ up to the k-th query posed by a fixed but arbitrary agent in $\mathbf{A} \setminus \{i\}$ and agent i. We define $s_i^{\mathcal{K}}(1) = \emptyset$ and $s_i^{\mathcal{L}}(1) = \emptyset$.

- Whenever A_i poses an example query to agent $i \in \mathbf{A}$ (assume it is the k-th query), A_i' calls the oracle $\mathsf{EQ}_{\mathfrak{F}(\mathbf{A}),l_i}$ with $s_i^{\mathcal{L}}(k)$ as input. The oracle either returns 'yes' if $s_i^{\mathcal{L}}$ is equivalent to l_i or it returns some counterexample for l_i and $s_i^{\mathcal{L}}(k)$ (we may write $s_i^{\mathcal{L}}(k)$ to denote $\bigwedge_{\beta \in s_i^{\mathcal{L}}(k)} \beta$). Then A_i' adds $\mathbf{K}_j x$ to $s_i^{\mathcal{K}}(k)$ and x to $s_i^{\mathcal{L}}(k)$.

If $\mathsf{EQ}_{\mathfrak{F}(\mathbf{A}),l_i}$ returns 'yes' then algorithm A_i' converts it into 'you finished', as expected by algorithm A_i. We now argue that, for all $x \in X_i$ and all $k \geq 0$ such that $l_i \models_{\mathcal{L}} x$, we have that x is a (positive) counterexample for l_i and $s_i^{\mathcal{L}}(k)$ iff $l_i \wedge s_i^{\mathcal{K}}(k) \not\models_{\mathcal{LK}} \mathbf{K}_j x$. By definition of $s_i^{\mathcal{K}}(k)$ and $s_i^{\mathcal{L}}(k)$ and since l_i does not contain $\mathcal{LK}$ axioms, for all $x \in X_i$ and all $k \geq 0$, we have that $l_i \wedge s_i^{\mathcal{K}}(k) \models_{\mathcal{LK}} \mathbf{K}_j x$ iff $s_i^{\mathcal{L}}(k) \models_{\mathcal{L}} x$. By definition and construction of $s_i^{\mathcal{L}}(k)$, it follows that $l_i \models_{\mathcal{L}} s_i^{\mathcal{L}}(k)$. So $s_i^{\mathcal{L}}(k) \not\models_{\mathcal{L}} x$ iff $l_i \wedge s_i^{\mathcal{K}}(k) \not\models_{\mathcal{LK}} \mathbf{K}_j x$. Hence $\mathsf{EQ}_{\mathfrak{F}(\mathbf{A}),l_i}$ can simulate $\mathsf{EX}_{\mathfrak{F}(\mathbf{A}),l_i^k}$, where k represents the number of calls to $\mathsf{EX}_{\mathfrak{F}(\mathbf{A}),l_i^k}$ posed so far by A_i. By definition of A_i, at every step, the sum of the sizes of the inputs to queries made by A_i up to that step is bounded by a polynomial $p(|l_i|, |x|)$, where l_i is the target and $x \in X_i$ is the largest counterexample seen so far by A_i. Then, for all $k \geq 0$, we have that $|s_i^{\mathcal{L}}(k)| \leq |s_i^{\mathcal{K}}(k)| \leq p(|l_i|, |x|)$. Since all responses to queries are as required by A_i, if A_i halts after polynomially many polynomial size queries, the same happens with A_i', which returns a hypothesis $s_i^{\mathcal{L}}(k)$ equivalent to the target l_i, for some $k \leq p(|l_i|, |x|)$. $\square$

The converse of Theorem 1 does not hold, as we show in the next theorem.

Theorem 2. *There is a multi-agent learning framework $\mathfrak{F}(\mathbf{A})$ such that $\mathfrak{F}(\mathbf{A})$ is polynomial time exactly learnable with only equivalence queries but not polynomial query (so, not polynomial time) epistemically learnable with only example queries.*

Proof. Consider the learning framework $\mathfrak{F} = (X, L)$ where X is the set of propositional formulas over the variables $\mathsf{Prop} = \{q, p, p_1^0, \ldots, p_n^0, p_1^1, \ldots, p_n^1\}$ and $L = \{\varphi \mid \varphi \in X, \varphi \equiv (p \rightarrow q)\}$ (where $\equiv$ denotes logical equivalence in propositional logic). So the target can only be a formula equivalent to $p \rightarrow q$. Now let

$\mathfrak{F}(\mathbf{A})$ be the set $\{\mathfrak{F}_i = (X, L) \mid i \in \mathbf{A}\}$, with all learning frameworks are equal to $\mathfrak{F}$ (this does not mean that the target is the same for all agents but that they are taken from the same set L). If L is a language which only contains propositional formulas equivalent to $p \to q$, an exact learning algorithm can learn the target with only one equivalence query, passing the hypothesis $\{p \to q\}$ as input. However, $\mathsf{EX}_{\mathfrak{F}(\mathbf{A}),\{p \to q\}}$ can return any of the exponentially many examples of the form $p \wedge (p_1^{\ell_1} \wedge \ldots \wedge p_n^{\ell_n}) \to q$, with $\ell_j \in \{0, 1\}$ and $j \in \{1, \ldots, n\}$. The example oracle can always provide an example which does not follow from its knowledge of what is known by the learner by taking a fresh binary sequence. Thus, there is no epistemic algorithm which can learn the target with polynomially many queries. □

Interestingly, if we consider both types of queries then polynomial exact learnability *coincides* with polynomial epistemic learnability.

Theorem 3. *Let $\mathfrak{F}(\mathbf{A})$ be a multi-agent learning framework. $\mathfrak{F}(\mathbf{A})$ is polynomial query (resp. time) exactly learnable if, and only if, $\mathfrak{F}(\mathbf{A})$ is polynomial query (resp. time) epistemically learnable.*

Proof. ($\Rightarrow$) In our proof we use polynomial query exact learnability, the argument for polynomial time exact learnability is analogous. Assume $\mathfrak{F}(\mathbf{A})$ is polynomial query exactly learnable. Then, for each $\mathfrak{F}_i \in \mathfrak{F}(\mathbf{A})$ there is an exact learning algorithm A_i for $\mathfrak{F}_i$. We construct an epistemic learning algorithm A_i' for $\mathfrak{F}_i$ using A_i as follows. Recall that we write l_i^k to denote the target l_i^k after the k-th query (Sect. 2.2).

- Whenever A_i poses a membership query to agent $i \in \mathbf{A}$ with $x \in X_i$ as input, A_i' calls $\mathsf{MEM}_{\mathfrak{F}(\mathbf{A}),l_i^k}^{\mathbf{K}}$ with x as input, where k represents the number of queries posed so far by A_i'.
- Whenever A_i poses an equivalence query to agent $i \in \mathbf{A}$ with a hypothesis h as input, we have that, for each $x \in h$, A_i' calls $\mathsf{MEM}_{\mathfrak{F}(\mathbf{A}),l_i^k}^{\mathbf{K}}$ with x as input (and k is incremented). Then, the algorithm calls the oracle $\mathsf{EX}_{\mathfrak{F}(\mathbf{A}),l_i^k}$.

$\mathsf{MEM}_{\mathfrak{F}(\mathbf{A}),l_i}^{\mathbf{K}}$ behaves as it is required by algorithm A_i to learn $\mathfrak{F}_i$. We show that whenever $\mathsf{EX}_{\mathfrak{F}(\mathbf{A}),l_i^k}$ returns some $x \in X_i$ we have that x is a counterexample for l_i^1 and h, where h is the input of the equivalence query posed by A_i. By definition of A_i, at every step, the sum of the sizes of the inputs to queries made by A_i up to that step is bounded by a polynomial $p(|l_i^1|, |x|)$, where l_i^1 is the target and $x \in X_i$ is the largest example seen so far by A_i. Let h^ℓ denote the input to the ℓ-th equivalence query posed by A_i. For all $\ell > 0$, we have that $|h^\ell| \leq p(|l_i^1|, |x|)$. The fact that x is a counterexample for l_i^1 and h^ℓ follows from the definition of A_i', which poses membership queries for each $x \in h^\ell$, ensuring that l_i^k is updated with $\mathbf{K}_j x$ after each query. Hence $\mathsf{EX}_{\mathfrak{F}(\mathbf{A}),l_i^k}$ returns counterexamples for l_i^1 and h^ℓ (if they exist), as $\mathsf{EQ}_{\mathfrak{F}(\mathbf{A}),l_i^1}$. Since A_i poses only polynomially many queries, ℓ is bounded by $p(|l_i^1|, |x|)$. So the sum of the sizes of the inputs to queries made by the epistemic learning algorithm A_i' simulating A_i is quadratic in $p(|l_i^1|, |x|)$.

All in all, since all responses to queries are as required by A_i, if A_i halts and outputs some $h \in L_i$ with $h \equiv_{\mathcal{L}} l_i^1$ (with h the input to the last equivalence query) after polynomially many polynomial size queries, we have that $\mathsf{EX}_{\mathfrak{F}(\mathbf{A}),l_i^1}$ is forced to return 'you finished' and so A_i' also halts after polynomially many polynomial size queries. The ($\Leftarrow$) direction is similar to the proof of Theorem 1, except that we now also have (**K**-)membership queries.   □

4   The Epistemic $\mathcal{EL}$ Description Logic

To instantiate the multi-agent epistemic learning problem to the $\mathcal{EL}$ case, in Sect. 5, we define and study in this section the epistemic extension of $\mathcal{EL}$, called $\mathcal{ELK}$. We present $\mathcal{EL}$ [3] in Sect. 4.1. $\mathcal{ELK}$ is the instantiation of $\mathcal{LK}$ presented in Sect. 2.1 with the logic $\mathcal{EL}$. We establish the complexity of the satisfiability problem for $\mathcal{ELK}$ in Sect. 4.2 and of one of its fragments in Sect. 4.3.

We showed in Sect. 3 that example queries give strictly less power to the learner than equivalence queries. We also argued, quite informally so far, that example queries are less demanding on the oracle than equivalence queries. Instead of deciding whether two ontologies are equivalent, and then providing a counterexample when it is not the case, the oracle only needs to reason about what they know about the knowledge of the learner. Yet, we did not say anything about the actual complexity of the epistemic reasoning involved in example queries. If reasoning about the knowledge of the learner is harder than evaluating the equivalence of two ontologies, then the advantage of example queries for the oracle would be moot. We show that indeed the epistemic reasoning that the oracle needs to perform is in PTIME (Theorem 5). So, the oracle's benefit from example queries over equivalence queries is a net benefit.

4.1 $\mathcal{EL}$: Syntax, Semantics, and Complexity

$\mathcal{EL}$ concepts C, D are expressions of the form: $C, D ::= \top \mid A \mid \exists r.C \mid C \sqcap D$ where $A \in \mathsf{N_C}$ and $r \in \mathsf{N_R}$. An *inclusion* is an expression of the form $C \sqsubseteq D$ where C, D are $\mathcal{EL}$ concept expressions; and an *assertion* is of the form $A(a)$ or $r(a, b)$ with $a, b \in \mathsf{N_I}$, $A \in \mathsf{N_C}$, and $r \in \mathsf{N_R}$. An $\mathcal{EL}$ *axiom* is an inclusion or an assertion. An $\mathcal{EL}$ *formula*[3] is an expression of the form $\alpha ::= \mathsf{a} \mid \neg \alpha \mid \alpha \wedge \alpha$ where a is an $\mathcal{EL}$ axiom. An $\mathcal{EL}$ literal is an $\mathcal{EL}$ axiom or its negation. The semantics of $\mathcal{EL}$ is given by $\mathcal{L}$ interpretations $\mathcal{I} = (\Delta^{\mathcal{I}}, \cdot^{\mathcal{I}})$ as defined in Sect. 2.1, considering $\mathcal{L} = \mathcal{EL}$. We extend the mapping $\cdot^{\mathcal{I}}$ for $\mathcal{EL}$ complex concept expressions as follows:

$$\top^{\mathcal{I}} := \Delta^{\mathcal{I}}, \qquad (C \sqcap D)^{\mathcal{I}} := C^{\mathcal{I}} \cap D^{\mathcal{I}},$$
$$(\exists r.C)^{\mathcal{I}} := \{d \in \Delta^{\mathcal{I}} \mid \exists e \in C^{\mathcal{I}} : (d, e) \in r^{\mathcal{I}}\}.$$

---

[3] Typically an $\mathcal{EL}$ *ontology* is a set of $\mathcal{EL}$ axioms [3], and can also be seen as a conjunction of positive $\mathcal{EL}$ axioms. Here we also consider $\mathcal{EL}$ *formulas*, where we allow negations and conjunctions over the axioms.

We now define the entailment relation $\models_{\mathcal{EL}}$ for $\mathcal{EL}$ formulas. Given an $\mathcal{EL}$ interpretation $\mathcal{I}$ and an $\mathcal{EL}$ axiom (which can be an inclusion or an assertion, as above) we define: $\mathcal{I} \models_{\mathcal{EL}} C \sqsubseteq D$ iff $C^{\mathcal{I}} \subseteq D^{\mathcal{I}}$; $\mathcal{I} \models_{\mathcal{EL}} A(a)$ iff $a^{\mathcal{I}} \in A^{\mathcal{I}}$; and $\mathcal{I} \models_{\mathcal{EL}} r(a,b)$ iff $(a^{\mathcal{I}}, b^{\mathcal{I}}) \in r^{\mathcal{I}}$. We inductively extend the relation $\models_{\mathcal{EL}}$ to $\mathcal{EL}$ formulas as in Sect. 2.1: $\mathcal{I} \models_{\mathcal{EL}} \varphi \wedge \psi$ iff $\mathcal{I} \models_{\mathcal{EL}} \varphi$ and $\mathcal{I} \models_{\mathcal{EL}} \psi$; and $\mathcal{I} \models_{\mathcal{EL}} \neg\varphi$ iff not $\mathcal{I} \models_{\mathcal{EL}} \varphi$. In our proofs, we use the following result.

Lemma 1. *Satisfiability of a conjunction of $\mathcal{EL}$ literals is* PTime-*complete* [6].

We establish in Sect. 4.2 that reasoning about $\mathcal{ELK}$ formulas is NP-complete, just like reasoning about $\mathcal{EL}$ formulas. We note that $\mathcal{EL}(\mathcal{K})$ formulas allow arbitrary Boolean combinations of $\mathcal{EL}(\mathcal{K})$ axioms, hence the contrast with the PTime complexity of entailment from an $\mathcal{EL}$ ontology [2]. In Sect. 4.3 we show that reasoning about $\mathcal{ELK}$ restricted to conjunctions of literals is in PTime.

4.2 Reasoning in $\mathcal{ELK}$

Here we study the complexity of the satisfiability problem in $\mathcal{ELK}$. Our combination of epistemic logic and description logic is orthogonal to the work by De Giacomo et al. [8]: while our epistemic operators are over $\mathcal{EL}$ formulas, the epistemic operators of the mentioned work are over concepts and roles. For instance, there, **K** FrenchChef denotes the concept of *known* French chefs. Here, $\mathcal{ELK}$ contains formulas such as $\mathbf{K}_i(\mathsf{FrenchChef}(\mathsf{Soyer})) \wedge \neg\mathbf{K}_i\mathbf{K}_j(\mathsf{Crepe} \sqsubseteq \exists\mathsf{contains.Egg})$ indicating that agent i knows that Soyer is a French chef, but i does not know that j knows that crepes contain egg.

From the definition of the language of $\mathcal{LK}$ in Sect. 2.1, remember that the language of $\mathcal{ELK}$ does not admit alternating modalities; E.g., $\mathbf{K}_i\neg\mathbf{K}_jA(a)$ is not a formula of $\mathcal{ELK}$. It is rather easy to see that if there were no such syntactic restrictions, the satisfiability problem would turn out to be PSPACE-complete. (We could reduce satisfiability and adapt the tableaus method of propositional $S5_n$ [12].) Instead, we establish that satisfiability in $\mathcal{ELK}$ is NP-complete.

The lower bound follows from NP-hardness for propositional logic. The following lemma is central for showing membership in NP. It is a consequence of the fact that $\mathcal{EL}$ and propositional logic have the polynomial size model property and that in $\mathcal{ELK}$ the satisfiability test can be separated into two independent tests: one for the DL dimension and one for the epistemic dimension (see [4,6]).

Lemma 2. $\mathcal{ELK}$ *enjoys the polynomial size model property.*

Since $\mathcal{ELK}$ formulas can be translated into first-order logic, for a fixed $\mathcal{ELK}$ formula φ, checking whether a polynomial size interpretation is a model of φ can be performed in NLogSpace. Thus, membership in NP is by the fact that, by Lemma 2, one can guess a polynomial size model (if one exists) and check that it is a model in NLogSpace $\subseteq$ PTime.

Theorem 4. *Satisfiability in $\mathcal{ELK}$ is* NP-*complete.*

4.3   Reasoning in Conjunctive $\mathcal{ELK}$

We conclude this section considering the satisfiability problem for *conjunctive* $\mathcal{ELK}$, defined as the fragment of $\mathcal{ELK}$ which only allows negations in front of $\mathcal{EL}$ axioms or in front of $\mathcal{ELK}$ axioms of the form $\mathbb{K}\alpha$, with α a conjunction of $\mathcal{EL}$ literals and $\mathbb{K}$ a non-empty sequence of epistemic operators. Formally, conjunctive $\mathcal{ELK}$ formulas φ are expressions of the form: $\varphi ::= \alpha \mid \beta \mid \neg\beta \mid \varphi \wedge \varphi$ with $\beta ::= \mathbf{K}_i\alpha \mid \mathbf{K}_i\beta$, and $\alpha ::= \mathsf{a} \mid \neg\mathsf{a} \mid \alpha \wedge \alpha$, where a is an $\mathcal{EL}$ axiom.

Algorithm 1. $SAT(\varphi)$, deciding the satisfiability of conjunctive $\mathcal{ELK}$ formulas

---

Input: A conjunctive $\mathcal{ELK}$ formula φ
Output: TRUE if φ is satisfiable, and FALSE otherwise
1: **if** $\omega_0 \wedge \bigwedge\{\omega \mid \mathbb{K}_\sigma\omega \in \varphi^\flat\}$ is not $\mathcal{EL}$ satisfiable **then**
2:    **return** FALSE
3: **end if**
4: **for** $\neg\mathbb{K}_\sigma\omega \in \varphi^\flat$ **do**
5:    $\psi = \top \wedge \bigwedge\{\omega' \mid \mathbb{K}_{\sigma'}\omega' \in \varphi^\flat$, and σ is a subword of $\sigma'\}$
6:    $MS = \{\psi \wedge \neg\beta \mid \beta$ is an $\mathcal{EL}$ literal in $\omega\}$
7:    **if** all conjunctions of $\mathcal{EL}$ literals in MS are not $\mathcal{EL}$ satisfiable **then**
8:       **return** FALSE
9:    **end if**
10: **end for**
11: **return** TRUE

To establish the complexity of reasoning in conjunctive $\mathcal{ELK}$, we use the following notation. For every non-empty sequence $\sigma = a_1 \ldots a_k \in \mathbf{A}^+$ of agents, we associate a sequence $\mathbb{K}_\sigma = \mathbf{K}_{a_1} \ldots \mathbf{K}_{a_k}$ of epistemic operators. We write $\beta \in \psi$ if β is a conjunct occurring in ψ. We say that $\sigma' \in \mathbf{A}^+$ is a *subword* of $\sigma \in \mathbf{A}^+$ when σ' is the result of removing zero or more elements from σ (at any position of the sequence). Given a conjunctive $\mathcal{ELK}$ formula

$$\varphi = \omega_0 \wedge \mathbb{K}_{\sigma_1}\omega_{\sigma_1} \wedge \ldots \wedge \mathbb{K}_{\sigma_n}\omega_{\sigma_n} \wedge \neg\mathbb{K}_{\sigma_{n+1}}\omega_{\sigma_{n+1}} \wedge \ldots \wedge \neg\mathbb{K}_{\sigma_m}\omega_{\sigma_m}$$

where $\sigma_i \in \mathbf{A}^+$, for every $1 \leq i \leq m$, and each ω_i, with $0 \leq i \leq m$, is a conjunction of $\mathcal{EL}$ literals, we denote by $\varphi^\flat$ the formula resulting from exhaustively substituting in φ every adjacent repetitions $a \ldots a$ of an agent a occurring in σ_i, $1 \leq i \leq m$, with a. (E.g., $a_1a_2a_2a_3a_2$ becomes $a_1a_2a_3a_2$.)

The following proposition is central to the correctness of Algorithm 1.

Proposition 1. *A conjunctive $\mathcal{ELK}$ formula φ is unsatisfiable iff at least one of the following properties holds:*

1. $\omega_0 \wedge \bigwedge\{\omega \mid \mathbb{K}_\sigma\omega \in \varphi^\flat\}$ *is not $\mathcal{EL}$ satisfiable;*
2. *there is $\neg\mathbb{K}_\sigma\omega \in \varphi^\flat$ such that $\neg\omega \wedge \bigwedge\{\omega' \mid \mathbb{K}_{\sigma'}\omega' \in \varphi^\flat$, and σ is a subword of $\sigma'\}$ is not $\mathcal{EL}$ satisfiable.*

Proof. For convenience, we introduce some additional notation. For every $\sigma = a_1 \ldots a_k \in \mathbf{A}^*$ we note $\mathcal{R}_\sigma = \mathcal{R}_{a_1} \circ \ldots \circ \mathcal{R}_{a_k}$ and $\mathbb{K}_\sigma = \mathbf{K}_{a_1} \ldots \mathbf{K}_{a_k}$. The empty sequence is noted ϵ, and we have $\mathcal{R}_\epsilon = Id$, where Id is the identity relation, and $\mathbb{K}_\epsilon \omega = \omega$.

The two following properties, which are instrumental in the proof of the proposition, are simple consequences of well-known properties of the modal system $S5$ [13, p. 58]. We state them without proof.

Claim. The following holds.

i. If φ^b is an $\mathcal{ELK}$ formula, φ and φ^b are equivalent.
ii. Let $(\mathcal{W}, \{\mathcal{R}_i\}_{i \in \mathbf{A}})$ be an $\mathcal{ELK}$ interpretation. For all $\sigma \in \mathbf{A}^*$ and $\sigma' \in \mathbf{A}^*$, if σ is a subword of σ' then $\mathcal{R}_\sigma \subseteq \mathcal{R}_{\sigma'}$.

We are ready to prove the proposition. Since, by Point (i) of the Claim, φ^b and φ are equisatisfiable (in fact equivalent), w.l.o.g., we prove it for φ^b.

($\Leftarrow$) Suppose (1) holds. Since $\mathcal{R}_i$ is reflexive for all $i \in \mathbf{A}$, every model satisfying φ^b must satisfy $\omega_0 \wedge \bigwedge \{\omega \mid \mathbb{K}_\sigma \omega \in \varphi^b\}$. Since it is not $\mathcal{EL}$ satisfiable, there cannot be an $\mathcal{ELK}$ interpretation satisfying φ^b either. Suppose (2) holds. For some $\neg \mathbb{K}_\sigma \omega \in \varphi^b$, we have that $\psi = \neg \omega \wedge \bigwedge \{\omega' \mid \mathbb{K}_{\sigma'} \omega' \in \varphi^b$, and σ is a subword of $\sigma'\}$ is not $\mathcal{EL}$ satisfiable. Suppose towards contradiction that there exist an $\mathcal{ELK}$ interpretation $\mathfrak{I} = (\mathcal{W}, \{\mathcal{R}_i\}_{i \in \mathbf{A}})$ and an $\mathcal{EL}$ interpretation $\mathcal{J} \in \mathcal{W}$ such that $\mathfrak{I}, \mathcal{J} \models \varphi^b$. It means that $\mathfrak{I}, \mathcal{J} \models \neg \mathbb{K}_\sigma \omega$, that is, there is an $\mathcal{EL}$ interpretation $\mathcal{J}'$ such that $(\mathcal{J}, \mathcal{J}') \in \mathcal{R}_\sigma$ and $\mathfrak{I}, \mathcal{J}' \models \neg \omega$. By Point (ii) of the Claim, for every $\mathbb{K}_{\sigma'} \omega' \in \varphi^b$, if σ is a subword of σ', then $\mathcal{R}_\sigma \subseteq \mathcal{R}_{\sigma'}$. Hence, $\mathfrak{I}, \mathcal{J}' \models \psi$, which is a contradiction as ψ is not $\mathcal{EL}$ satisfiable.

($\Rightarrow$) Assume that none of (1) and (2) hold. We must show that φ^b is satisfiable. It suffices to build an $\mathcal{ELK}$ interpretation $\mathfrak{I} = (\mathcal{W}, \{\mathcal{R}_i\}_{i \in \mathbf{A}})$ for φ^b. $\mathcal{W}$ contains an $\mathcal{EL}$ interpretation $\mathcal{J}_0$ satisfying $\omega_0 \wedge \bigwedge \{\omega \mid \mathbb{K}_\sigma \omega \in \varphi^b\}$. Such an interpretation exists because (1) does not hold. For each $\neg \mathbb{K}_\sigma \omega \subset \varphi^b$, where $\sigma = a_1 \ldots a_k$, $\mathcal{W}$ also contains an interpretation $\mathcal{J}_k^\sigma$ satisfying $\neg \omega \wedge \bigwedge \{\omega' \mid \mathbb{K}_{\sigma'} \omega' \in \varphi^b$, and σ is a subword of $\sigma'\}$. Such an interpretation exists because (2) does not hold. Still for each $\neg \mathbb{K}_\sigma \omega \in \varphi^b$, $\mathcal{W}$, where $\sigma = a_1 \ldots a_k$, for each $1 \leq i < k$, $\mathcal{W}$ also contains an interpretation $\mathcal{J}_i^\sigma$ satisfying $\bigwedge \{\omega' \mid \mathbb{K}_{\sigma'} \omega' \in \varphi^b$, and $a_1 \ldots a_i$ is a subword of $\sigma'\}$. Such interpretations exist because (1) does not hold. $\mathcal{W}$ does not contain any more $\mathcal{EL}$ interpretations. We turn to the construction of $\mathcal{R}$. For every $\neg \mathbb{K}_\sigma \omega \in \varphi^b$, where $\sigma = a_1 \ldots a_k$, for every $1 \leq i \leq k$, let $(\mathcal{J}_{i-1}^\sigma, \mathcal{J}_i^\sigma) \in \mathcal{R}'_{a_i}$, where $\mathcal{J}_0^\sigma = \mathcal{J}_0$. For every $i \in \mathbf{A}$, let $\mathcal{R}_i$ be the equivalence closure of $\mathcal{R}'_i$. It is routine to check that $\mathfrak{I}, \mathcal{J}_0 \models \varphi^b$.   □

Proposition 1 suggests that the satisfiability of conjunctive $\mathcal{ELK}$ formulas can be reduced to checking the satisfiability of a few conjunctions of $\mathcal{EL}$ literals. We are finally ready to prove the complexity of deciding whether a conjunctive $\mathcal{ELK}$ formula is satisfiable.

Theorem 5. *Satisfiability in conjunctive $\mathcal{ELK}$ is* PTime-*complete.*

Proof. Consider Algorithm 1. The conjunctive $\mathcal{ELK}$ formula φ is satisfiable iff $SAT(\varphi)$ returns TRUE. The correctness of the algorithm follows immediately from Proposition 1. It suffices to observe that Lines 5–9 check the unsatisfiability of an $\mathcal{EL}$ formula $\neg\omega \wedge \psi$ where ω and ψ are two of conjunctions of $\mathcal{EL}$ literals ($\neg\omega \wedge \psi$ is *not* a conjunction of $\mathcal{EL}$ literals, unless ω contains only one literal) by checking the unsatisfiability of as many conjunctions of $\mathcal{EL}$ literals $\neg\beta \wedge \psi$ as there are literals β in ω. A simple analysis shows that the algorithm runs in time polynomial in the size of φ, with a polynomial number of calls to a procedure for checking the unsatisfiability of conjunctions of $\mathcal{EL}$ literals. By Lemma 1, each of these checks can be done in polynomial time. Membership in PTIME follows.   □

Algorithm 2. Adaptation of the learning algorithm for $\mathcal{EL}_{\mathsf{lhs,rhs}}$ [10]

Input: An $\mathcal{EL}$ terminology $\mathcal{O}$ given to the oracle; $\Sigma_{\mathcal{O}}$ given to the learner
Output: An $\mathcal{EL}$ terminology $\mathcal{H}$ computed by the learner such that $\mathcal{O} \equiv_{\mathcal{EL}} \mathcal{H}$
1: $\mathcal{H} := \{\mathsf{a} \mid \mathsf{MEM}^{\mathsf{K}}_{\mathfrak{F},\mathcal{O}^k}(\mathsf{a}) = \text{'yes'}, \mathsf{a}$ is a $\Sigma_{\mathcal{O}}$-assertion or $\mathsf{a} = A \sqsubseteq B, A, B \in \Sigma_{\mathcal{O}}\}$
2: **while** $\mathsf{EX}_{\mathfrak{F},\mathcal{O}^k} \neq \text{'you finished'}$ **do**
3:     Let $C \sqsubseteq D$ be the returned positive example for $\mathcal{O}$
4:     Compute, with $\mathsf{MEM}^{\mathsf{K}}_{\mathfrak{F},\mathcal{O}^k}$, $C' \sqsubseteq D'$ such that C' or D' in $\Sigma_{\mathcal{O}} \cap \mathsf{N_C}$
5:     **if** $C' \in \Sigma_{\mathcal{O}} \cap \mathsf{N_C}$ **then**
6:         Compute with $\mathsf{MEM}^{\mathsf{K}}_{\mathfrak{F},\mathcal{O}^k}$ a right $\mathcal{O}$-essential a from $C' \sqsubseteq D' \sqcap \underset{C' \sqsubseteq F' \in \mathcal{H}}{\bigsqcap} F'$
7:     **else**
8:         Compute with $\mathsf{MEM}^{\mathsf{K}}_{\mathfrak{F},\mathcal{O}^k}$ a left $\mathcal{O}$-essential a from $C' \sqsubseteq D'$
9:     **end if**
10:     Add a to $\mathcal{H}$
11: **end while**
12: **return** $\mathcal{H}$

---

5   Learning $\mathcal{EL}$ with Epistemic Reasoning

It is known that $\mathcal{EL}$ ontologies are not polynomial query exactly learnable, while the fragments of $\mathcal{EL}$ restricting one of the sides of inclusions to be a concept name, namely $\mathcal{EL}_{\mathsf{lhs}}$ and $\mathcal{EL}_{\mathsf{rhs}}$, are exactly learnable in polynomial time [14]. In this section, we transfer results known for $\mathcal{EL}$ and its fragments to our learning model. Our results are for learning frameworks where the learning language is the same for all agents. That is, we deal with the special case of a multi-agent learning framework $\mathfrak{F}(\mathbf{A}) = \{\mathfrak{F}_i = (X_i, L_i) \mid i \in \mathbf{A}\}$ where all formulas in all L_i are from a DL $\mathcal{L}$, denoted $\mathfrak{F}(\mathcal{L}, \mathbf{A})$. Theorem 6 is a consequence of Theorem 3 and complexity results for $\mathcal{EL}$ and its fragments in the exact learning model [14].

Theorem 6. *The learning framework $\mathfrak{F}(\mathcal{EL}, \mathbf{A})$ is not polynomial query epistemically learnable. The learning frameworks $\mathfrak{F}(\mathcal{EL}_{\mathsf{lhs}}, \mathbf{A})$ and $\mathfrak{F}(\mathcal{EL}_{\mathsf{rhs}}, \mathbf{A})$ are polynomial time epistemically learnable.*

The hardness result for $\mathcal{EL}$ holds even for the fragment of $\mathcal{EL}$ ontologies defined as the union of $\mathcal{EL}_{\mathsf{lhs}}$ and $\mathcal{EL}_{\mathsf{rhs}}$, that is, in a named form where at least one of the sides of concept inclusions is a concept name, which we call $\mathcal{EL}_{\mathsf{lhs,rhs}}$.

An implementation of a learning algorithm for $\mathcal{EL}$ ontologies in this named form was presented by Duarte et al. [9,10]. The algorithm is exponential in the size of the vocabulary $\Sigma_{\mathcal{O}}$ of the ontology $\mathcal{O}$ (which is the set of concept/role and individual names occurring in $\mathcal{O}$) and the largest concept expression $C_{\mathcal{O}}{}^4$, but it is not exponential in the size of the whole ontology.

Theorem 3 is not directly applicable in this case, however, we observe that if the exact learning algorithm uses the epistemic learning model, then the outcome of each example query will be a counterexample, and so, the complexity result obtained with that algorithm is transferable to the epistemic setting. To see this, consider Algorithm 2, which is an adaptation of the exact learning algorithm for $\mathcal{EL}_{\mathsf{lhs,rhs}}$ [9,10]. Assume $\mathfrak{F}$ in Algorithm 2 is $\mathfrak{F}(\mathcal{EL}_{\mathsf{lhs,rhs}}, \mathbf{A})$. The number of $\Sigma_{\mathcal{O}}$-assertions (defined as assertions with only symbols from $\Sigma_{\mathcal{O}}$) is polynomial in the size of $\mathcal{O}$, so, in Line 1, Algorithm 2 identifies those that occur in $\mathcal{O}$ using **K**-membership queries. It follows that all examples returned by the oracle in the 'while' loop are concept inclusions. In each iteration of the 'while' loop, the algorithm uses the examples returned by the $\mathsf{EX}_{\mathfrak{F}(\mathcal{EL}_{\mathsf{lhs,rhs}},\mathbf{A}),\mathcal{O}^k}$ oracle to compute what is called 'left $\mathcal{O}$-essential' and 'right $\mathcal{O}$-essential' concept inclusions using **K**-membership queries, and then updates the hypothesis with such inclusions. We do not go into details of the algorithm, which is fully presented in the mentioned reference, but point out that it only adds to its hypothesis concept inclusions that follow from the target ontology $\mathcal{O}$.

Since we use **K**-membership queries, the oracle is aware of the knowledge obtained by the learner in this way and does not return examples which follow from such entailments. With an inductive argument on the number of iterations of the main loop of the algorithm one can show that, at each iteration, if the learner asks for an example query instead of an equivalence query, the outcome will indeed be a counterexample for $\mathcal{O}$ and $\mathcal{H}$. So the number of membership and equivalence queries is the same as the number of **K**-membership and example queries. Moreover, the hypothesis $\mathcal{H}$ computed by Algorithm 2 is equivalent to the target $\mathcal{O}$ (where $\mathcal{O} = \mathcal{O}^1$, so without epistemic axioms). Our next theorem formalises the fact that the number of queries performed by the exact learning algorithm has the same bound in the epistemic learning framework.

Theorem 7. $\mathfrak{F}(\mathcal{EL}_{\mathsf{lhs,rhs}}, \mathbf{A})$ *is epistemically learnable in* $O(|\Sigma_{\mathcal{O}}|^{\sharp_{\mathcal{O}}} \cdot (|C \sqsubseteq D|)^2)$ *many steps, where* $\sharp_{\mathcal{O}} = 2 \cdot |C_{\mathcal{O}}| \cdot |\Sigma_{\mathcal{O}}| + 2$, $C_{\mathcal{O}}$ *is the largest concept expression in* $\mathcal{O}$ *and* $C \sqsubseteq D$ *is the largest counterexample given by the oracle.*

6 Discussion

We introduced the epistemic learning model and investigated polynomial learnability in our model, establishing that it coincides with polynomial learnability in the exact learning model, and as a consequence, we can also transfer results in our model to the PAC learning model extended with membership queries.

---

[4] 'The largest' concept expression (and, later, counterexample) refers to the maximum of the sizes of counterexamples/concept expressions.

When the learner is only allowed to pose example queries, we showed that polynomial learnability in our model in strictly harder than in the exact learning model with only equivalence queries. This suggests that example queries are less demanding for the oracle than equivalence queries. We showed that, in the $\mathcal{EL}$ case, the epistemic reasoning that the oracle needs to perform features PTIME complexity. Our results complement previous research on polynomial learnability in the exact and PAC learning models [7], where the authors analyse models between the exact and PAC learning models, in a learning from interpretations setting. As future work, we plan to investigate whether the implementation for $\mathcal{EL}_{\mathsf{lhs,rhs}}$ [10] could benefit from our approach, where the oracle keeps track of the knowledge passed to the learner, instead of processing the hypothesis at each iteration.

References

1. Angluin, D.: Queries and concept learning. Mach. Learn. **2**(4), 319–342 (1988)
2. Baader, F., Brandt, S., Lutz, C.: Pushing the $\mathcal{EL}$ envelope. In: Kaelbling, L., Saffiotti, A. (eds.) Proceedings of the 19th International Joint Conference on Artificial Intelligence (IJCAI), pp. 364–369. Professional Book Center (2005)
3. Baader, F., Calvanese, D., McGuinness, D., Nardi, D., Patel-Schneider, P. (eds.): The Description Logic Handbook: Theory, Implementation, and Applications, 2nd edn. Cambridge University Press, Cambridge (2007)
4. Baader, F., Ghilardi, S., Lutz, C.: LTL over description logic axioms. ACM Trans. Comput. Logic **13**(3), 21:1–21:32 (2012)
5. Blum, A.L.: Separating distribution-free and mistake-bound learning models over the Boolean domain. SIAM J. Comput. **23**(5), 900–1000 (1994)
6. Borgwardt, S., Thost, V.: Temporal query answering in the description logic EL. In: Proceedings of the Twenty-Fourth International Joint Conference on Artificial Intelligence, IJCAI, pp. 2819–2825 (2015)
7. Bshouty, N.H., Jackson, J.C., Tamon, C.: Exploring learnability between exact and PAC. J. Comput. Syst. Sci. **70**(4), 471–484 (2005)
8. De Giacomo, G., Iocchi, L., Nardi, D., Rosati, R.: Moving a robot: the KR&R approach at work. In: Aiello, L.C., Doyle, J., Shapiro, S.C. (eds.) Proceedings of the Fifth International Conference on Principles of Knowledge Representation and Reasoning (KR), pp. 198–209. Morgan Kaufmann (1996)
9. Duarte, M.R.C., Konev, B., Ozaki, A.: Exact learning of EL ontologies. In: Proceedings of the 31st International Workshop on Description Logics co-located with 16th International Conference on Principles of Knowledge Representation and Reasoning (KR) (2018)
10. Duarte, M.R.C., Konev, B., Ozaki, A.: Exactlearner: a tool for exact learning of EL ontologies. In: Principles of Knowledge Representation and Reasoning: Proceedings of the Sixteenth International Conference, KR, pp. 409–414 (2018)
11. Frazier, M., Pitt, L.: Learning from entailment: an application to propositional Horn sentences. In: International Conference on Machine Learning, ICML, pp. 120–127 (1993)
12. Halpern, J.Y., Moses, Y.: A guide to completeness and complexity for modal logics of knowledge and belief. Artif. Intell. **54**(3), 319–379 (1992). https://doi.org/10.1016/0004-3702(92)90049-4

13. Hughes, G., Cresswell, M.: A New Introduction to Modal Logic. Routledge, London and New York (1996)
14. Konev, B., Lutz, C., Ozaki, A., Wolter, F.: Exact learning of lightweight description logic ontologies. J. Mach. Learn. Res. **18**(201), 1–63 (2018)
15. Konev, B., Ozaki, A., Wolter, F.: A model for learning description logic ontologies based on exact learning. In: Proceedings of the Thirtieth AAAI Conference on Artificial Intelligence, pp. 1008–1015 (2016)
16. Mohri, M., Rostamizadeh, A., Talwalkar, A.: Foundations of Machine Learning. The MIT Press, Cambridge (2012)
17. Ozaki, A., Troquard, N.: Learning ontologies with epistemic reasoning: the EL case. CoRR (2019). https://arxiv.org/abs/1902.03273
18. Valiant, L.G.: A theory of the learnable. Commun. ACM **27**(11), 1134–1142 (1984)

Counting Strategies for the Probabilistic Description Logic $\mathcal{ALC}^{\mathsf{ME}}$ Under the Principle of Maximum Entropy

Marco Wilhelm[1]([✉]) [ID], Gabriele Kern-Isberner[1] [ID], Andreas Ecke[2] [ID], and Franz Baader[2] [ID]

[1] Department of Computer Science, TU Dortmund, Dortmund, Germany
marco.wilhelm@tu-dortmund.de
[2] Department of Computer Science, TU Dresden, Dresden, Germany

Abstract. We present $\mathcal{ALC}^{\mathsf{ME}}$, a probabilistic variant of the Description Logic $\mathcal{ALC}$ that allows for representing and processing conditional statements of the form "if E holds, then F follows with probability p" under the principle of maximum entropy. Probabilities are understood as degrees of belief and formally interpreted by the aggregating semantics. We prove that both checking consistency and drawing inferences based on approximations of the maximum entropy distribution is possible in $\mathcal{ALC}^{\mathsf{ME}}$ in time polynomial in the domain size. A major problem for probabilistic reasoning from such conditional knowledge bases is to count models and individuals. To achieve our complexity results, we develop sophisticated counting strategies on interpretations aggregated with respect to the so-called conditional impacts of types, which refine their conditional structure.

Keywords: Probabilistic description logics · Aggregating semantics · Principle of maximum entropy · Domain-lifted inference

1 Introduction

Description Logics [1] are a well-investigated family of logic-based knowledge representation languages that are tailored towards representing *terminological* knowledge, i.e. knowledge about concepts, which can then be used to state *facts* about individuals and objects in a concrete situation. In many application domains, like medicine, knowledge is, however, not always certain, which motivates the development of extensions that can deal with uncertainty. In this paper, we present the *probabilistic Description Logic $\mathcal{ALC}^{\mathsf{ME}}$*, which allows to represent and process uncertain knowledge using conditional statements of the form "if E holds, then F follows with probability p". Probabilities are understood

This work was supported by the German Research Foundation (DFG) within the Research Unit FOR 1513 "Hybrid Reasoning for Intelligent Systems".

F. Calimeri et al. (Eds.): JELIA 2019, LNAI 11468, pp. 434–449, 2019.
https://doi.org/10.1007/978-3-030-19570-0_28

as degrees of belief based on the *aggregating semantics* [9]. This semantic generalizes the statistical interpretation of conditional probabilities by combining it with subjective probabilities based on probability distributions over possible worlds. Basically, in a fixed world $\mathcal{I}$, the conditional $(F|E)$ can be evaluated statistically by considering the number of individuals that verify the conditional (i.e., belong to E and F) and dividing this number by the number of individuals to which the conditional applies (i.e., the elements of E). In the aggregation semantics, this is not done independently for each world. Instead, one first sums up these numbers over all possible worlds, weighted with the probability of the respective world, both in the numerator and in the denominator, and only then divides the resulting sums by each other. The semantics obtained this way therefore mimics statistical probabilities from a subjective point of view. This is in contrast to other approaches for probabilistic Description Logics, which handle either subjective [10] or statistical probabilities [13], or are essentially classical terminologies over probabilistic databases [4].

Due to this combination of statistical and subjective probabilities, the models of $\mathcal{ALC}^{ME}$-knowledge bases are probability distributions over a set of interpretations that serve as possible worlds. In order to ensure that the possible worlds have the same scope and that counting elements with certain properties leads to well-defined natural numbers, we assume that all the interpretations have the same *fixed finite domain*. However, reasoning on all models of an $\mathcal{ALC}^{ME}$-knowledge base is not productive due to the vast number of such models. Thus, for reasoning purposes, we select among all models of the knowledge base the distinct model with *maximum entropy* [12]. This MaxEnt distribution is known to be the only model fulfilling some evident common sense principles that can be summarized by the main idea that "essentially similar problems should have essentially similar solutions" [11]. In general, however, the MaxEnt distribution is a real-valued function without a finite, closed-form representation. In fact, from a computational point of view, it is the solution of a nonlinear optimization problem, and thus approximations with values in the rational numbers must be used.

The main result shown in this paper is that all required computations can be done in time polynomial in the chosen domain size. First, we show that checking consistency of $\mathcal{ALC}^{ME}$-knowledge bases is possible in time polynomial in the domain size. A consistent $\mathcal{ALC}^{ME}$-knowledge base always has a MaxEnt model. Second, we prove that, once an approximation of this distribution is determined, inferences can be drawn exactly from this approximation, and these inferences can again be computed in time polynomial in the domain size. Investigating the complexity with respect to the domain size is a fundamental problem in probabilistic reasoning as the domain size is usually *the* crucial quantity in application domains. Inferences that can be drawn in time polynomial in the domain size are known as *domain-lifted inferences* [6]. The problem of drawing inferences in a domain-lifted manner is non-trivial since probability distributions are defined over possible worlds, the number of which is exponential in the domain size. Thus, our complexity results require sophisticated strategies of aggregating and counting interpretations. More precisely, we capture the fact that interpretations with the same *conditional structure* [8] have the same impact on the aggregating semantics and the MaxEnt distribution, and we refine the notion of conditional structures of interpretations to *conditional impacts* of *types* [14,15], which enables the use of efficient counting strategies.

The rest of the paper is organized as follows. In Sect. 2, we introduce syntax and semantic of the Description Logic $\mathcal{ALC}^{\mathsf{ME}}$. We prove that checking consistency and drawing inferences from approximations of the maximum entropy distribution are possible in $\mathcal{ALC}^{\mathsf{ME}}$ in time polynomial in the domain size in Sect. 5. For this, we first discuss how interpretations can be aggregated into equivalence classes based on conditional structures and types (Sect. 3), and then show how these equivalence classes and their cardinalities can be determined efficiently (Sect. 4).

2   The Description Logic $\mathcal{ALC}^{\mathsf{ME}}$

We present $\mathcal{ALC}^{\mathsf{ME}}$, a probabilistic conditional extension of the terminological part of the Description Logic $\mathcal{ALC}$. The semantics of $\mathcal{ALC}^{\mathsf{ME}}$ is based on the *aggregating semantics* [16] and the *principle of maximum entropy* [12].

Let $\mathcal{N}_C$ and $\mathcal{N}_R$ be disjoint finite sets of concept and role names, respectively. A *concept* is either a concept name or of the form

$$\top, \quad \bot, \quad \neg C, \quad C \sqcap D, \quad C \sqcup D, \quad \exists r.C, \quad \forall r.C,$$

where C and D are concepts and r is a role name. The set of all *subconcepts* of a concept C, i.e. the concepts C is built of, is denoted by $\mathsf{sub}(C)$.

An *interpretation* $\mathcal{I} = (\Delta^{\mathcal{I}}, \cdot^{\mathcal{I}})$ is a tuple consisting of a non-empty set $\Delta^{\mathcal{I}}$ called *domain* and an *interpretation function* $\cdot^{\mathcal{I}}$ that maps every $C \in \mathcal{N}_C$ to a subset $C^{\mathcal{I}} \subseteq \Delta^{\mathcal{I}}$ and every $r \in \mathcal{N}_R$ to a binary relation $r^{\mathcal{I}} \subseteq \Delta^{\mathcal{I}} \times \Delta^{\mathcal{I}}$. The interpretation of arbitrary concepts is recursively defined as

- $\top^{\mathcal{I}} = \Delta^{\mathcal{I}}$ and $\bot^{\mathcal{I}} = \emptyset$,
- $(\neg C)^{\mathcal{I}} = \Delta^{\mathcal{I}} \setminus C^{\mathcal{I}}$, $(C \sqcap D)^{\mathcal{I}} = C^{\mathcal{I}} \cap D^{\mathcal{I}}$, and $(C \sqcup D)^{\mathcal{I}} = C^{\mathcal{I}} \cap D^{\mathcal{I}}$,
- $(\exists r.C)^{\mathcal{I}} = \{a \in \Delta^{\mathcal{I}} \mid \exists b \in \Delta^{\mathcal{I}} : (a,b) \in r^{\mathcal{I}} \wedge b \in C^{\mathcal{I}}\}$, and
- $(\forall r.C)^{\mathcal{I}} = \{a \in \Delta^{\mathcal{I}} \mid \forall b \in \Delta^{\mathcal{I}} : (a,b) \in r^{\mathcal{I}} \to b \in C^{\mathcal{I}}\}$.

Let C, D, E, F be concepts and let $p \in [0,1]$. An expression of the form $C \sqsubseteq D$ is called a *concept inclusion*, and an expression of the form $(F|E)[p]$ is called a *(probabilistic) conditional*. For computational issues, we assume p to be a rational number. Concept inclusions $C \sqsubseteq D$ represent strict knowledge ("every individual that has property C must also have property D") while conditionals $(F|E)[p]$ act as uncertain beliefs ("if E holds for an individual, then F follows with probability p").

An interpretation $\mathcal{I}$ is a *model* of a concept inclusion, written $\mathcal{I} \models C \sqsubseteq D$, iff $C^{\mathcal{I}} \subseteq D^{\mathcal{I}}$. The semantics of conditionals is based on probability distributions over possible worlds. For this, we require a fixed finite domain $\Delta = \Delta^{\mathcal{I}}$ for all interpretations as part of the input. The interpretations serve as possible worlds, thus the fixed finite domain guarantees that all possible worlds have the same scope. We denote the set of all interpretations $\mathcal{I} = (\Delta, \cdot^{\mathcal{I}})$ with $\mathcal{I}^{\Delta}$ and the set of all probability distributions $\mathcal{P} : \mathcal{I}^{\Delta} \to [0, 1]$ with $\mathfrak{P}^{\Delta}$.

Definition 1 (Aggregating Semantics). *A probability distribution $\mathcal{P} \in \mathfrak{P}^{\Delta}$ is a (probabilistic) model of a concept inclusion $C \sqsubseteq D$, written $\mathcal{P} \models C \sqsubseteq D$, iff*

$$\mathcal{I} \not\models C \sqsubseteq D \quad \Rightarrow \quad \mathcal{P}(\mathcal{I}) = 0 \quad \forall \mathcal{I} \in \mathcal{I}^{\Delta},$$

and of a conditional $(F|E)[p]$, written $\mathcal{P} \models (F|E)[p]$, iff

$$\frac{\sum_{\mathcal{I} \in \mathcal{I}^{\Delta}} |E^{\mathcal{I}} \cap F^{\mathcal{I}}| \cdot \mathcal{P}(\mathcal{I})}{\sum_{\mathcal{I} \in \mathcal{I}^{\Delta}} |E^{\mathcal{I}}| \cdot \mathcal{P}(\mathcal{I})} = p. \tag{1}$$

Concept inclusions are interpreted as hard constraints in the obvious manner: if a concept inclusion does not hold in an interpretation $\mathcal{I}$, then $\mathcal{I}$ has probability zero. Whether a concept inclusion holds in $\mathcal{I}$ can be decided independently of the probability distribution. The interpretation of conditionals is an adaption of the *aggregating semantics* [16] and needs more explanation. The core idea is to capture the definition of conditional probabilities by a probability-weighted sum of the number of individuals b for which the conditional $(F|E)$ is *verified* (i.e., $b \in |E^{\mathcal{I}} \cap F^{\mathcal{I}}|$) divided by a probability-weighted sum of the number of individuals a for which the conditional is *applicable* (i.e., $a \in |E^{\mathcal{I}}|$). Hence, the aggregating semantics mimics statistical probabilities from a subjective point of view, and probabilities can be understood as degrees of belief in accordance with type 2 probabilities in the classification of Halpern [7].

The aggregating semantics constitutes the main difference to the approaches in [10] and [13]: while there is no probabilistic semantics for terminological knowledge in [10], conditionals are interpreted in [13] purely statistically by the relative frequencies $|E^{\mathcal{I}} \cap F^{\mathcal{I}}|/|E^{\mathcal{I}}|$ in every single interpretation $\mathcal{I}$.

A *knowledge base* $\mathcal{R} = (\mathcal{T}, \mathcal{C})$ consists of a finite set of concept inclusions $\mathcal{T}$ and a finite set of conditionals $\mathcal{C} = \{(F_1|E_1)[p_1], \ldots, (F_n|E_n)[p_n]\}$. Without loss of generality, we make the following assumptions:

1. Knowledge bases contain concepts that are built using the constructors negation ($\neg C$), conjunction ($C \sqcap D$), and existential restriction ($\exists r.C$) only. In addition, we disallow double negation. For the rest of the paper, whenever the negation of an already negated concept is mentioned, we mean the concept itself.
2. Concepts in existential restrictions $\exists r.C$ are concept names. Otherwise, replace C by a fresh concept name A and add $C \sqsubseteq A$ and $A \sqsubseteq C$ to $\mathcal{T}$.
3. Probabilities of conditionals $(F|E)[p] \in \mathcal{C}$ satisfy $0 < p < 1$. This is without loss of generality, because $(F|E)[1]$ and $E \sqsubseteq F$ as well as $(F|E)[p]$ and $(\neg F|E)[1 - p]$ (and hence $(F|E)[0]$ and $E \sqsubseteq \neg F$) are semantically equivalent.

We also require the notion of the *signature* of a knowledge base $\mathcal{R}$. In particular, we denote the set of all concept names that are mentioned in $\mathcal{R}$ with $\mathrm{sig}_C(\mathcal{R})$, and the set of all role names that are mentioned in $\mathcal{R}$ with $\mathrm{sig}_R(\mathcal{R})$.

A probability distribution $\mathcal{P} \in \mathfrak{P}^{\Delta}$ is a *model* of a knowledge base $\mathcal{R} = (\mathcal{T}, \mathcal{C})$, written $\mathcal{P} \models \mathcal{R}$, iff it is a model of every concept inclusion in $\mathcal{T}$ and of every conditional in $\mathcal{C}$. A knowledge base with at least one model is called *consistent*. Knowledge bases with $\mathcal{C} = \emptyset$ are equivalent to $\mathcal{ALC}$-TBoxes (cf. [3]) and allow for classical entailment. In particular, our probabilistic notion of consistency then coincides with the classical one.

Example 1. Consider the following knowledge of an agent. Every person that is generous certainly is wealthy. Otherwise, she would not have anything to spend. And every wealthy person most likely is successful in her career or has a generous patron. Of course, the latter is uncertain as, for example, persons could also become wealthy because of luck in a lottery, etc. Further, wealthy persons typically are not generous. We represent this knowledge by the concept inclusion

$$c_1 : \text{Generous} \sqsubseteq \text{Wealthy}$$

and the conditionals

$$r_1 : (\neg\text{Successful} \sqcap \neg\exists\text{patron.Generous}|\text{Wealthy})[0.1],$$
$$r_2 : (\neg\text{Generous}|\text{Wealthy})[0.8],$$

and consider the knowledge base $\mathcal{R}_W = (\{c_1\}, \{r_1, r_2\})$ later on. Note that r_1 is equivalent to the conditional $(\text{Successful} \sqcup \exists\text{patron.Generous}|\text{Wealthy})[0.9]$.

Consistent probabilistic knowledge bases typically have infinitely many models even for a fixed finite domain. Instead of reasoning w.r.t. all models, it is often more useful to reason w.r.t. a fixed model since reasoning based on the whole set of models leads to monotonic and often uninformative inferences. Any selected model $\mathcal{P}$ yields the inference relation

$$\mathcal{R} \models_{\mathcal{P}} \begin{cases} C \sqsubseteq D & \text{iff} \quad \mathcal{P} \models C \sqsubseteq D, \\ (F|E)[p] & \text{iff} \quad \mathcal{P} \models (F|E)[p]. \end{cases} \tag{2}$$

From a commonsense point of view, the *maximum entropy distribution* is the most appropriate choice of model [11]. For every consistent knowledge base, the maximum entropy distribution exists and is unique.

Definition 2 (Maximum Entropy Distribution). *Let $\mathcal{R}$ be a consistent knowledge base and Δ a fixed domain. The probability distribution*

$$\mathcal{P}_{\mathcal{R}}^{\mathsf{ME}} = \arg\max_{\substack{\mathcal{P} \in \mathfrak{P}^{\Delta} \\ \mathcal{P} \models \mathcal{R}}} - \sum_{\mathcal{I} \in \mathfrak{I}^{\Delta}} \mathcal{P}(\mathcal{I}) \cdot \log \mathcal{P}(\mathcal{I}) \tag{3}$$

is called the maximum entropy distribution *(also MaxEnt distribution) of $\mathcal{R}$. In (3), the convention $0 \cdot \log 0 = 0$ applies.*

Since it is the solution of a nonlinear optimization problem, the MaxEnt distribution can only be calculated approximately in general. This is typically done by solving the dual optimization problem (cf. [5]), which leads to

$$
\mathcal{P}_{\mathcal{R}}^{\mathsf{ME}}(\mathcal{I}) = \begin{cases} \alpha_0 \cdot \prod_{i=1}^{n} \alpha_i^{f_i(\mathcal{I})} & \mathcal{I} \models \mathcal{T}, \\ 0 & \text{otherwise}, \end{cases} \tag{4}
$$

where, for $i = 1, \ldots, n$, the index i refers to the i-th conditional $(F_i | E_i)[p_i]$ in $\mathcal{C}$, the feature function f_i is defined as $f_i(\mathcal{I}) = |E_i^{\mathcal{I}} \cap F_i^{\mathcal{I}}| - p_i \cdot |E_i^{\mathcal{I}}|$, α_0 is a normalizing constant, and the vector $\boldsymbol{\alpha}_{\mathcal{R}}^{\mathsf{ME}} = (\alpha_1, \ldots, \alpha_n) \in \mathbb{R}_{>0}^{n}$ is a solution of the system of equations

$$
\sum_{\substack{\mathcal{I} \in \mathfrak{I}^{\Delta} \\ \mathcal{I} \models \mathcal{T}}} f_i(\mathcal{I}) \cdot \prod_{j=1}^{n} \alpha_j^{f_j(\mathcal{I})} = 0, \qquad i = 1, \ldots, n. \tag{5}
$$

Given $\alpha_1, \ldots, \alpha_n$ and the feature functions, the normalization constant α_0 is defined as

$$
\alpha_0 = \left(\sum_{\substack{\mathcal{I} \in \mathfrak{I}^{\Delta} \\ \mathcal{I} \models \mathcal{T}}} \prod_{i=1}^{n} \alpha_i^{f_i(\mathcal{I})} \right)^{-1}. \tag{6}
$$

Its rôle is to ensure that a probability distribution is obtained, i.e., that summing up the probabilities of the elements of $\mathfrak{I}^{\Delta}$ yields 1.

The system (5) can, for instance, be solved using Newton's method. Here, we do not investigate this approximation process, but assume that an approximation $\boldsymbol{\beta} \in \mathbb{Q}_{>0}^{n}$ of $\boldsymbol{\alpha}_{\mathcal{R}}^{\mathsf{ME}}$ is given. Then, $\boldsymbol{\beta}$ defines an approximation of $\mathcal{P}_{\mathcal{R}}^{\mathsf{ME}}$ via

$$
\mathcal{P}_{\mathcal{R}}^{\boldsymbol{\beta}}(\mathcal{I}) = \begin{cases} \beta_0 \cdot \prod_{i=1}^{n} \beta_i^{f_i(\mathcal{I})} & \mathcal{I} \models \mathcal{T}, \\ 0 & \text{otherwise}, \end{cases} \tag{7}
$$

where β_0 is a normalizing constant that is defined analogously to (6). It is easy to see that $\mathcal{P}_{\mathcal{R}}^{\boldsymbol{\beta}}$ indeed is a probability distribution. In particular, $\mathcal{P}_{\mathcal{R}}^{\boldsymbol{\beta}}$ is an exact model of $\mathcal{T}$ and of $\mathcal{C}$ up to a deviation depending on the precision of the approximation $\boldsymbol{\beta}$.

3   Conditional Structures and Types for $\mathcal{ALC}^{\mathsf{ME}}$

All kinds of maximum entropy calculations involve sums over interpretations. As the number of interpretations is exponential in $|\Delta|$, evaluating these sums in the naïve way is intractable. In this section, we aggregate interpretations into equivalence classes such that equivalent interpretations have the same impact on the calculations (basically, they have the same MaxEnt probability), while the number of equivalence classes is bounded polynomially in $|\Delta|$.

The *conditional structure* $\sigma_\mathcal{R}(\mathcal{I})$ of an interpretation $\mathcal{I}$ with respect to a knowledge base $\mathcal{R} = (\mathcal{T}, \mathcal{C})$ is a formal representation of how often the conditionals in $\mathcal{C}$ are verified and falsified in $\mathcal{I}$ [8]. Mathematically, the conditional structure

$$\sigma_\mathcal{R}(\mathcal{I}) = \prod_{i=1}^{n} (\mathbf{a_i^+})^{|E_i^\mathcal{I} \cap F_i^\mathcal{I}|} \cdot (\mathbf{a_i^-})^{|E_i^\mathcal{I} \cap (\neg F_i)^\mathcal{I}|} \tag{8}$$

is an element of the free Abelian group that is generated by $\mathfrak{G} = \{\mathbf{a_i^\pm} \mid i = 1, \ldots, n, \pm \in \{+, -\}\}$. The elements in $\mathfrak{G}$ indicate whether the i-th conditional is verified $(\mathbf{a_i^+})$ or falsified $(\mathbf{a_i^-})$. The frequencies of verification and falsification in $\mathcal{I}$ are respectively indicated by the exponents of $\mathbf{a_i^+}$ and $\mathbf{a_i^-}$.

Example 2. Recall $\mathcal{R}_W$ from Example 1 and consider the interpretation $\mathcal{I}$ in which each $d \in \Delta$ is wealthy $(d \in \mathsf{Wealthy}^\mathcal{I})$, successful $(d \in \mathsf{Successful}^\mathcal{I})$, but not generous $(d \notin \mathsf{Generous}^\mathcal{I})$. Then, $\sigma_{\mathcal{R}_W}(\mathcal{I}) = (\mathbf{a_1^-})^{|\Delta|} \cdot (\mathbf{a_2^+})^{|\Delta|}$.

Conditional structures are important for maximum entropy reasoning as the MaxEnt distribution $\mathcal{P}_\mathcal{R}^{\mathsf{ME}}$ assigns the same probability to interpretations that are models of $\mathcal{T}$ and have the same conditional structure. The same holds for all approximations of $\mathcal{P}_\mathcal{R}^{\mathsf{ME}}$ defined by (7) since $\sigma_\mathcal{R}(\mathcal{I}) = \sigma_\mathcal{R}(\mathcal{I}')$ implies $f_i(\mathcal{I}) = f_i(\mathcal{I}')$ for all $i = 1, \ldots, n$. We now refine conditional structures with respect to the so-called conditional impacts of types.

Definition 3 (Type [2]). *Let $\mathcal{M}$ be a set of concepts such that for every concept $C \in \mathcal{M}$ its negation is also in $\mathcal{M}$ (modulo removal of double negation). A subset τ of $\mathcal{M}$ is a type for $\mathcal{M}$ iff*

- *for every $C \in \mathcal{M}$, either C or $\neg C$ belongs to τ, and*
- *for every $C \sqcap D \in \mathcal{M}$ it holds that $C \sqcap D \in \tau$ iff $C, D \in \tau$.*

The set of all types for $\mathcal{M}$ is denoted by $\mathfrak{T}(\mathcal{M})$.

In particular, we are interested in types for a knowledge base $\mathcal{R} = (\mathcal{T}, \mathcal{C})$, i.e. types for $\mathfrak{T}_\mathcal{R} = \mathfrak{T}(\mathcal{M}_\mathcal{R})$ where $\mathcal{M}_\mathcal{R}$ is the closure under negation of the set of subconcepts of concepts occurring in $\mathcal{R}$, i.e.,

$$\mathcal{M}_\mathcal{R}^+ = \bigcup_{C \sqsubseteq D \in \mathcal{T}} \left(\mathsf{sub}(C) \cup \mathsf{sub}(D) \right) \cup \bigcup_{(F|E)[p] \in \mathcal{C}} \left(\mathsf{sub}(E) \cup \mathsf{sub}(F) \right),$$

and $\mathcal{M}_\mathcal{R} = \mathcal{M}_\mathcal{R}^+ \cup \{\neg C \mid C \in \mathcal{M}_\mathcal{R}^+\}$.

Example 3. There are 16 different types for $\mathcal{R}_W$ from Example 1 (cf. Table 1).

A type τ can be understood as the concept C_τ that is the conjunction of all concepts in τ. If $\tau \neq \tau'$ are different types, then C_τ and $C_{\tau'}$ are disjoint, i.e. $C_\tau^\mathcal{I} \cap C_{\tau'}^\mathcal{I} = \emptyset$ for all $\mathcal{I} \in \mathfrak{I}^\Delta$. Every concept $D \in \mathcal{M}$ can be expressed as a disjunction of such disjoint type concepts [2]:

$$D \equiv \bigsqcup_{\substack{\tau \in \mathfrak{T}(\mathcal{M}) \\ D \in \tau}} C_\tau \quad \text{and} \quad |D^\mathcal{I}| = \sum_{\substack{\tau \in \mathfrak{T}(\mathcal{M}) \\ D \in \tau}} |C_\tau^\mathcal{I}|. \tag{9}$$

Table 1. Types, their conditional impacts w.r.t. the conditionals in $\mathcal{R}_W$ (cf. Example 1), and their satisfaction behavior w.r.t. the concept inclusion c_1 in $\mathcal{R}_W$. Concept and role names are abbreviated by their first letter.

τ	$\rho_{\mathcal{R}_W}(\tau)$	$\tau \models c_1$?
$\tau_1 = \{\ S,\ W,\ G,\ \exists p.G, \neg(\neg S \sqcap \neg \exists p.G)\}$	$a_1^- a_2^-$	Yes
$\tau_2 = \{\ S,\ W,\ G, \neg \exists p.G, \neg(\neg S \sqcap \neg \exists p.G)\}$	$a_1^- a_2^-$	Yes
$\tau_3 = \{\ S,\ W, \neg G,\ \exists p.G, \neg(\neg S \sqcap \neg \exists p.G)\}$	$a_1^- a_2^+$	Yes
$\tau_4 = \{\ S,\ W, \neg G, \neg \exists p.G, \neg(\neg S \sqcap \neg \exists p.G)\}$	$a_1^- a_2^+$	Yes
$\tau_5 = \{\ S, \neg W,\ G,\ \exists p.G, \neg(\neg S \sqcap \neg \exists p.G)\}$	1	No
$\tau_6 = \{\ S, \neg W,\ G, \neg \exists p.G, \neg(\neg S \sqcap \neg \exists p.G)\}$	1	No
$\tau_7 = \{\ S, \neg W, \neg G,\ \exists p.G, \neg(\neg S \sqcap \neg \exists p.G)\}$	1	Yes
$\tau_8 = \{\ S, \neg W, \neg G, \neg \exists p.G, \neg(\neg S \sqcap \neg \exists p.G)\}$	1	Yes
$\tau_9 = \{\neg S,\ W,\ G,\ \exists p.G, \neg(\neg S \sqcap \neg \exists p.G)\}$	$a_1^- a_2^-$	Yes
$\tau_{10} = \{\neg S,\ W,\ G, \neg \exists p.G, \neg(\neg S \sqcap \neg \exists p.G)\}$	$a_1^+ a_2^-$	Yes
$\tau_{11} = \{\neg S,\ W, \neg G,\ \exists p.G, \neg(\neg S \sqcap \neg \exists p.G)\}$	$a_1^- a_2^+$	Yes
$\tau_{12} = \{\neg S,\ W, \neg G, \neg \exists p.G, \neg(\neg S \sqcap \neg \exists p.G)\}$	$a_1^+ a_2^+$	Yes
$\tau_{13} = \{\neg S, \neg W,\ G,\ \exists p.G,\ (\neg S \sqcap \neg \exists p.G)\}$	1	No
$\tau_{14} = \{\neg S, \neg W,\ G, \neg \exists p.G,\quad \neg S \sqcap \neg \exists p.G\ \}$	1	No
$\tau_{15} = \{\neg S, \neg W, \neg G,\ \exists p.G,\quad \neg S \sqcap \neg \exists p.G\ \}$	1	Yes
$\tau_{16} = \{\neg S, \neg W, \neg G, \neg \exists p.G,\quad \neg S \sqcap \neg \exists p.G\ \}$	1	Yes

Additionally, the cardinalities $|C_\tau^{\mathcal{I}}|$ of all type concepts $\tau \in \mathfrak{T}(\mathcal{M})$ sum up to $|\Delta|$:

$$\bigsqcup_{\tau \in \mathfrak{T}(\mathcal{M})} C_\tau \equiv \top \quad \text{and} \quad \sum_{\tau \in \mathfrak{T}(\mathcal{M})} |C_\tau^{\mathcal{I}}| = |\Delta|. \tag{10}$$

To prove this, let $\mathcal{I} \in \mathfrak{I}^\Delta$ and consider $d \in \Delta$. If we define $\tau = \{D \in \mathcal{M} \mid d \in D^{\mathcal{I}}\}$, then it is easy to see that τ is a type and that $d \in C_\tau^{\mathcal{I}}$. This shows that $\bigcup_{\tau \in \mathfrak{T}(\mathcal{M})} C_\tau^{\mathcal{I}} \equiv \Delta$, and thus also $|\Delta| = \sum_{\tau \in \mathfrak{T}(\mathcal{M})} |C_\tau^{\mathcal{I}}|$ due to the fact that the type concepts are pairwise disjoint.

As a consequence of (10), types can be seen as characterizations of individuals through the concepts they belong to. Hence, we may say that an individual $d \in \Delta$ is of type τ in the interpretation $\mathcal{I} \in \mathfrak{I}^\Delta$ iff $d \in C_\tau^{\mathcal{I}}$, and two individuals are equivalent iff they are of the same type. With this, the conditional structure of interpretations (8) can be broken down to the *conditional impact* of types. We define the *conditional impact* of a type τ for a knowledge base $\mathcal{R}$ by

$$\rho_{\mathcal{R}}(\tau) = \prod_{i=1}^{n} \begin{cases} a_i^+ & \text{iff } E_i, F_i \in \tau \\ a_i^- & \text{iff } E_i, \neg F_i \in \tau \\ 1 & \text{iff } \neg E_i \in \tau \end{cases}.$$

Example 4. The conditional impacts of the types for $\mathcal{R}_W$ from Example 1 are shown in Table 1.

Analogously to the conditional impact of a type, we define the *feature*

$$f_i(\tau) = \begin{cases} 1 - p_i & \text{iff} \quad E_i, F_i \in \tau \\ -p_i & \text{iff} \quad E_i, \neg F_i \in \tau \\ 0 & \text{iff} \quad \neg E_i \in \tau \end{cases} \tag{11}$$

of τ for $i = 1, \ldots, n$.

Proposition 1. *Let $\mathcal{R} = (\mathcal{T}, \mathcal{C})$ be a knowledge base. Then, for all $\mathcal{I} \in \mathfrak{I}^\Delta$,*

1. $\sigma_\mathcal{R}(\mathcal{I}) = \prod_{\tau \in \mathfrak{T}_\mathcal{R}} \rho_\mathcal{R}(\tau)^{|C_\tau^\mathcal{I}|}$,
2. $f_i(\mathcal{I}) = \sum_{\tau \in \mathfrak{T}_\mathcal{R}} |C_\tau^\mathcal{I}| \cdot f_i(\tau)$ *for $i = 1, \ldots, n$.*

Proof. To see that 1. holds, note that we have

$$\sigma_\mathcal{R}(\mathcal{I}) = \prod_{i=1}^n (\mathbf{a_i^+})^{|E_i^\mathcal{I} \cap F_i^\mathcal{I}|} \cdot (\mathbf{a_i^-})^{|E_i^\mathcal{I} \cap (\neg F_i)^\mathcal{I}|}$$

$$= \prod_{i=1}^n (\mathbf{a_i^+})^{|(\sqcup_{\substack{\tau \in \mathfrak{T}_\mathcal{R} \\ E_i, F_i \in \tau}} C_\tau)^\mathcal{I}|} \cdot (\mathbf{a_i^-})^{|(\sqcup_{\substack{\tau \in \mathfrak{T}_\mathcal{R} \\ E_i, \neg F_i \in \tau}} C_\tau)^\mathcal{I}|}$$

$$= \prod_{i=1}^n (\mathbf{a_i^+})^{\sum_{\substack{\tau \in \mathfrak{T}_\mathcal{R} \\ E_i, F_i \in \tau}} |C_\tau^\mathcal{I}|} \cdot (\mathbf{a_i^-})^{\sum_{\substack{\tau \in \mathfrak{T}_\mathcal{R} \\ E_i, \neg F_i \in \tau}} |C_\tau^\mathcal{I}|}$$

$$= \prod_{i=1}^n \prod_{\tau \in \mathfrak{T}_\mathcal{R}} \begin{cases} (\mathbf{a_i^+})^{|C_\tau^\mathcal{I}|} & \text{iff} \quad E_i, F_i \in \tau \\ (\mathbf{a_i^-})^{|C_\tau^\mathcal{I}|} & \text{iff} \quad E_i, \neg F_i \in \tau \end{cases}$$

$$= \prod_{\tau \in \mathfrak{T}_\mathcal{R}} \rho_\mathcal{R}(\tau)^{|C_\tau^\mathcal{I}|}.$$

The equations in 2. can be shown using the same arguments. □

Proposition 1 advises one to consolidate interpretations with the same counts $|C_\tau^\mathcal{I}|$ for $\tau \in \mathfrak{T}_\mathcal{R}$ to equivalence classes. We define $\mathcal{I} \sim_\mathcal{R} \mathcal{I}'$ iff $|C_\tau^\mathcal{I}| = |C_\tau^{\mathcal{I}'}|$ for all $\tau \in \mathfrak{T}_\mathcal{R}$, and obtain the following corollary.

Corollary 1. *Let $\mathcal{R}$ be a knowledge base, and let $\mathcal{I}, \mathcal{I}' \in \mathfrak{I}^\Delta$ with $\mathcal{I} \sim_\mathcal{R} \mathcal{I}'$.*

1. *Then, $\sigma_\mathcal{R}(\mathcal{I}) = \sigma_\mathcal{R}(\mathcal{I}')$ and $f_i(\mathcal{I}) = f_i(\mathcal{I}')$ for $i = 1, \ldots, n$.*
2. *If $\mathcal{R}$ is consistent and additionally $\mathcal{I}$ and $\mathcal{I}'$ are models of $\mathcal{T}$, then*
   (a) $\mathcal{P}_\mathcal{R}^{\mathrm{ME}}(\mathcal{I}) = \mathcal{P}_\mathcal{R}^{\mathrm{ME}}(\mathcal{I}')$,
   (b) $\mathcal{P}_\mathcal{R}^\beta(\mathcal{I}) = \mathcal{P}_\mathcal{R}^\beta(\mathcal{I}')$ *for any approximation $\mathcal{P}_\mathcal{R}^\beta$ of $\mathcal{P}_\mathcal{R}^{\mathrm{ME}}$ defined by (7).*

We close this section with a rough estimation of the number of equivalence classes in $\mathfrak{I}^\Delta / \sim_\mathcal{R}$. These equivalence classes $[\mathcal{I}]_{\sim_\mathcal{R}}$ can differ in the numbers $|C_\tau^\mathcal{I}|$ for $\tau \in \mathfrak{T}_\mathcal{R}$, all of which can vary between zero and $|\Delta|$. Hence, $|\mathfrak{I}^\Delta / \sim_\mathcal{R}|$ is bounded by $(|\Delta| + 1)^{|\mathfrak{T}_\mathcal{R}|}$, which is polynomial in $|\Delta|$. Note that this bound is not sharp.

4 Counting Strategies for $\mathcal{ALC}^{\mathsf{ME}}$

We give combinatorial arguments that allow us to compute the equivalence classes in $\mathfrak{I}^{\Delta}/\sim_{\mathcal{R}}$ as well as their cardinalities in time polynomial in $|\Delta|$.

By definition, the equivalence classes $[\mathcal{I}]_{\sim_{\mathcal{R}}} \in \mathfrak{I}^{\Delta}/\sim_{\mathcal{R}}$ differ in the *number* of individuals from Δ that have the types $\tau \in \mathfrak{T}_{\mathcal{R}}$, i.e., that belong to $C_{\tau}^{\mathcal{I}}$. No other properties of these individuals are relevant. Hence, specifying all equivalence classes in $\mathfrak{I}^{\Delta}/\sim_{\mathcal{R}}$ is related to the combinatorial problem of classifying $|\Delta|$-many elements into $|\mathfrak{T}_{\mathcal{R}}|$-many categories. For the rest of the paper let $k = |\Delta|$, $\mathfrak{T}_{\mathcal{R}} = \{\tau_1, \ldots, \tau_m\}$, and $k_i = k(\tau_i) = |C_{\tau_i}^{\mathcal{I}}|$, if it is clear from the context which interpretation $\mathcal{I}$ is considered. Then, $[\mathcal{I}]_{\sim_{\mathcal{R}}}$ is in a one-to-one correspondence with the vector $\boldsymbol{k} = (k_1, \ldots, k_m) \in \mathbb{N}_0^m$, and we may define $[\mathcal{I}]_{\boldsymbol{k}}$ as the unique equivalence class corresponding to $\boldsymbol{k}$. Due to (10), for all $[\mathcal{I}]_{\boldsymbol{k}}$ we have that

$$\sum_{i=1}^{m} k_i = k \tag{12}$$

holds. However, not every vector $\boldsymbol{k} \in \mathbb{N}_0^m$ that satisfies (12) leads to an equivalence class in $\mathfrak{I}^{\Delta}/\sim_{\mathcal{R}}$. This is due to the fact that existential restrictions relate individuals to each other and may force the existence of further individuals of a certain type.

Example 5. Consider the knowledge base

$$\mathcal{R}_{smk} = (\emptyset, \{(\exists \mathsf{friend}.\mathsf{Smoker}|\mathsf{Smoker})[0.9]\}$$

stating that smokers typically have at least one friend that is a smoker, too. There are four types for $\mathcal{R}_{smk}$ (concept and role names are abbreviated by their first letter):

$$t_1 = \{ \ S, \exists f.S\}, \qquad\qquad t_2 = \{ \ S, \neg\exists f.S\},$$
$$t_3 = \{\neg S, \exists f.S\}, \qquad\qquad t_4 = \{\neg S, \neg\exists f.S\}.$$

If there is an individual of type t_3, i.e. a non-smoker who has a friend that smokes, then there must be a second person who is a smoker, i.e., an individual of type t_1 or t_2. Hence, $k_3 > 0$ enforces $k_1 + k_2 > 0$.

To deal with this phenomenon, we adopt the following definition from [2].

Definition 4. *Let τ be a type that contains an existential restriction $\exists r.A$, and let $\neg\exists r.B_1, \ldots, \neg\exists r.B_l$ be all the negated existential restrictions for the role r in τ. A type τ' satisfies $\exists r.A$ in τ iff $A, \neg B_1, \ldots, \neg B_l \in \tau'$.*

It is now easy to see that, for every type $\tau \in \mathfrak{T}_{\mathcal{R}}$ and for every existential restriction $\exists r.A \in \tau$,

$$k(\tau) = 0 \quad \text{or} \quad \sum_{\substack{\tau' \in \mathfrak{T}_{\mathcal{R}} \\ \tau' \text{ satisfies } \exists r.A \text{ in } \tau}} k(\tau') > 0 \tag{13}$$

must hold. Conversely, using ideas from [2], it is not hard to show that any vector $\boldsymbol{k}$ satisfying $\sum_{i=1}^{m} k_i = k$ and (13) is realized by an interpretation. Thus, we have

$$\mathfrak{I}^{\Delta}/\!\sim_{\mathcal{R}} = \{[\mathcal{I}]_{\boldsymbol{k}} \mid \boldsymbol{k} \in \mathbb{N}_0^m, \sum_{i=1}^{m} k_i = k, \text{ and (13) holds}\}. \tag{14}$$

Equation (14) allows us to enumerate the equivalence classes in $\mathfrak{I}^{\Delta}/\!\sim_{\mathcal{R}}$ in time polynomial in $|\Delta|$, as Condition (13) is independent of Δ and iterating through all $\boldsymbol{k} \in \mathbb{N}_0^m$ that satisfy $\sum_{i=1}^{m} k_i = k$ is possible in time polynomial in $|\Delta|$. Furthermore, note that we are interested in only those interpretations that satisfy all concept inclusions in $\mathcal{T}$. In these interpretations there must not exist an individual $d \in \Delta$ with $d \in C^{\mathcal{I}}$ and $d \notin D^{\mathcal{I}}$ for any $C \sqsubseteq D \in \mathcal{T}$. Due to (9) and (10), this constraint is equivalent to

$$C, \neg D \in \tau \quad \Rightarrow \quad k(\tau) = 0 \quad \forall \tau \in \mathfrak{T}_{\mathcal{R}}, \ C \sqsubseteq D \in \mathcal{T}. \tag{15}$$

We say that a type $\tau \in \mathfrak{T}_{\mathcal{R}}$ for which $C \in \tau$ implies $D \in \tau$ for all $C \sqsubseteq D \in \mathcal{T}$ *satisfies* $\mathcal{T}$, written $\tau \models \mathcal{T}$. Hence, (15) states that $k(\tau) > 0$ holds for only those types that satisfy $\mathcal{T}$. Consequently, the set of all equivalence classes of those interpretations that satisfy $\mathcal{T}$ is

$$\mathfrak{I}_{\mathcal{T}}^{\Delta}/\!\sim_{\mathcal{R}} = \{[\mathcal{I}]_{\boldsymbol{k}} \in \mathfrak{I}^{\Delta}/\!\sim_{\mathcal{R}} \mid (15) \text{ holds}\}$$

and can be determined in time polynomial in $|\Delta|$, too.

Example 6. Recall $\mathcal{R}_W$ from Example 1. All types $\tau \in \mathfrak{T}_{\mathcal{R}_W}$ satisfy $\mathcal{T}_W$ except for $\tau_5, \tau_6, \tau_{13}$, and τ_{14} (cf. Table 1).

It still remains to determine the cardinalities $|[\mathcal{I}]_{\boldsymbol{k}}|$. These cardinalities depend on two factors. First, the k individuals in Δ have to be allocated to the types for $\mathcal{R}$. This is the combinatorial problem of classifying elements into categories mentioned at the beginning of this section, and for which there are

$$\binom{k}{k_1, \ldots, k_m} = \frac{k!}{k_1! \cdots k_m!}$$

many possibilities if $k_i = |\tau_i|$ for every $\tau_i \in \mathfrak{T}_{\mathcal{R}}$. Put differently, one can also say that this is the task of specifying $C_{\tau}^{\mathcal{I}}$ for every $\tau \in \mathfrak{T}_{\mathcal{R}}$ when previously only the cardinalities $|C_{\tau}^{\mathcal{I}}|$ were known.

Second, once this allocation is given, the sets $C_{\tau}^{\mathcal{I}}$ for every $\tau \in \mathfrak{T}_{\mathcal{R}}$ still do not determine a unique interpretation. There remains some degree of freedom when picking a single interpretation from $[\mathcal{I}]_{\boldsymbol{k}}$. To see this, recall that an interpretation $\mathcal{I} \in \mathfrak{I}^{\Delta}$ is fully specified iff for all concept names $C \in \mathcal{N}_C$ and for all role names $r \in \mathcal{N}_R$ the sets $C^{\mathcal{I}}$ and $r^{\mathcal{I}}$ are fixed. As every concept name A that is mentioned in $\mathcal{R}$ also occurs in every single type for $\mathcal{R}$ as either A or $\neg A$, the sets $A^{\mathcal{I}}$ for these concept names are uniquely determined by the types. However, this does not hold for concept names that are not mentioned in $\mathcal{R}$. Actually, given a concept name in $\mathcal{N}_C \setminus \mathrm{sig}_C(\mathcal{R})$, one can choose freely for every individual in Δ whether it belongs to this concept name or not. There are $2^{k \cdot |\mathcal{N}_C \setminus \mathrm{sig}_C(\mathcal{R})|}$ possibilities of allocating the k individuals in Δ to the concepts in $\mathcal{N}_C \setminus \mathrm{sig}_C(\mathcal{R})$. Determining the degree of freedom that arises from role memberships is more difficult. Again, for the roles that are not mentioned in $\mathcal{R}$, there is free choice such that there are $2^{k^2 \cdot |\mathcal{N}_R \setminus \mathrm{sig}_R(\mathcal{R})|}$ possible combinations of allocating k^2 many tuples of individuals to them. For the membership to roles that are mentioned in $\mathcal{R}$, we first define the degree of freedom of a role and discuss it afterwards.

Definition 5. *Let $\mathcal{R} = (\mathcal{T}, \mathcal{C})$ be a knowledge base, and let $\tau \in \mathfrak{T}_\mathcal{R}$ be a type. Further let $\exists r.A_1, \ldots, \exists r.A_l$ be all the existential restrictions and let $\neg \exists r.B_1, \ldots, \neg \exists r.B_h$ be all the negated existential restrictions for the role r in τ. We define the degree of freedom of r in τ with respect to $[\mathcal{I}]_k \in \mathfrak{I}^\Delta / \sim_\mathcal{R}$ as*

$$\phi_k(\tau, r) = \left(\sum_{\mathfrak{I} \subseteq \{1, \ldots, l\}} (-1)^{|\mathfrak{I}|} \cdot \prod_{\substack{j=1, \ldots, m, \\ \neg B_1, \ldots, \neg B_h \in \tau_j, \\ \neg A_i \in \tau_j \ \forall i \in \mathfrak{I}}} 2^{k_j} \right)^{k(\tau)}. \tag{16}$$

Definition 5 is a generalization of Definition 4 that takes counting aspects into account by making use of the well-known inclusion-exclusion principle. In this way, it keeps track of which individual guarantees that a certain existential restriction holds. To understand the good behavior of Definition 5, assume that there is *no* positive existential restriction $\exists r.A$ for r in τ. Then, for every $d \in A_\tau^\mathcal{I}$ and for every individual d' in any $A_{\tau'}^\mathcal{I}$ with $\neg B_1, \ldots, \neg B_h \in \tau'$, whether $(d, d') \in r^\mathcal{I}$ or not can be chosen freely, which results in the factor $(2^{k(\tau')})^{k(\tau)}$ in $\phi_k(\tau, r)$. Now, assume there is one (positive) existential restriction $\exists r.A$ in τ. For individuals $d' \in \tau'$ with τ' such that $\neg A, \neg B_1, \ldots, \neg B_h \in \tau'$, again the belonging of (d, d') to $r^\mathcal{I}$ is optional. However, there must be at least one individual d'' among the individuals of a type τ'' with $A, \neg B_1, \ldots, \neg B_h \in \tau''$ such that $(d, d'') \in r^\mathcal{I}$. This results in the degree of freedom

$$\phi_k(\tau, r) = \left(\prod_{\substack{\tau' \in \mathfrak{T}_\mathcal{R} \\ \neg B_1, \ldots, \neg B_h \in \tau'}} 2^{k(\tau')} - \prod_{\substack{\tau' \in \mathfrak{T}_\mathcal{R} \\ \neg B_1, \ldots, \neg B_h, \neg A \in \tau'}} 2^{k(\tau')} \right)^{k(\tau)}$$

$$= \left(\left(\prod_{\substack{\tau' \in \mathfrak{T}_\mathcal{R} \\ \neg B_1, \ldots, \neg B_h, \neg A \in \tau'}} 2^{k(\tau')} \right) \cdot \left(\prod_{\substack{\tau' \in \mathfrak{T}_\mathcal{R} \\ \neg B_1, \ldots, \neg B_h, A \in \tau'}} 2^{k(\tau')} - 1 \right) \right)^{k(\tau)}.$$

If there are more than one (positive) existential restrictions, then all of them could be satisfied by the same tuple of individuals. Alternatively, there may exist several tuples of individuals each satisfying only some of the restrictions. Then, a combination of tuples is needed to satisfy all of the existential restrictions. This makes the application of the inclusion-exclusion principle necessary.

Altogether, for every $[\mathcal{I}]_k \in \mathfrak{I}^\Delta/\!\sim_\mathcal{R}$, one has

$$|[\mathcal{I}]_k| = \binom{k}{k_1,\ldots,k_m} \cdot \left(\prod_{j=1}^{m} \prod_{r \in \mathrm{sig}_R(\mathcal{R})} \phi_k(\tau_j, r) \right)$$
$$\cdot\, 2^{(|\mathcal{N}_C \setminus \mathrm{sig}_C(\mathcal{R})|)\cdot k} \cdot 2^{(|\mathcal{N}_R \setminus \mathrm{sig}_R(\mathcal{R})|)\cdot k^2}, \qquad (17)$$

which can be calculated in time polynomial in $|\Delta|$.

5   Consistency Check and Drawing Inferences in $\mathcal{ALC}^{\mathsf{ME}}$

We build upon the results from Sects. 3 and 4 and prove that both checking consistency and drawing inferences from approximations of the MaxEnt distribution is possible in $\mathcal{ALC}^{\mathsf{ME}}$ in time polynomial in $|\Delta|$.

Proposition 2. *Let $\mathcal{R}$ be a knowledge base and Δ a finite domain. Then, consistency of $\mathcal{R}$ in a probabilistic model with domain Δ can be checked in time polynomial in $|\Delta|$.*

Proof. The knowledge base $\mathcal{R} = (\mathcal{T}, \mathcal{C})$ is consistent iff there is a probability distribution $\mathcal{P} \in \mathfrak{P}^\Delta$ such that $\mathcal{I} \not\models \mathcal{T}$ implies $\mathcal{P}(\mathcal{I}) = 0$ for all $\mathcal{I} \in \mathfrak{I}^\Delta$, and

$$\frac{\sum_{\mathcal{I} \in \mathfrak{I}^\Delta} |E_i^\mathcal{I} \cap F_i^\mathcal{I}| \cdot \mathcal{P}(\mathcal{I})}{\sum_{\mathcal{I} \in \mathfrak{I}^\Delta} |E_i^\mathcal{I}| \cdot \mathcal{P}(\mathcal{I})} = p_i, \quad i = 1, \ldots, n.$$

Alternatively, $\mathcal{R}$ is consistent iff the MaxEnt distribution $\mathcal{P}_\mathcal{R}^{\mathsf{ME}}$ exists. Hence, it is legitimate to limit the search space to any subset of $\mathfrak{P}^\Delta$ that contains $\mathcal{P}_\mathcal{R}^{\mathsf{ME}}$ when searching for a model of $\mathcal{R}$. Thus, it is sufficient to search for a model of $\mathcal{R}$ that satisfies $\mathcal{P}(\mathcal{I}) = \mathcal{P}(\mathcal{I}')$ if $\mathcal{I} \sim_\mathcal{R} \mathcal{I}'$ and $\mathcal{I}, \mathcal{I}' \models \mathcal{T}$, like $\mathcal{P}_\mathcal{R}^{\mathsf{ME}}$ does. In other words, it is sufficient to find a probability distribution $\mathcal{P} : \mathfrak{I}_\mathcal{T}^\Delta/\!\sim_\mathcal{R} \to [0,1]$ that satisfies

$$\frac{\sum_{[\mathcal{I}]_k \in \mathfrak{I}_\mathcal{T}^\Delta/\sim_\mathcal{R}} \left(\sum_{\substack{\tau \in \mathfrak{T}_\mathcal{R} \\ E_i, F_i \tau}} k(\tau) \right) \cdot \mathcal{P}([\mathcal{I}]_k)}{\sum_{[\mathcal{I}]_k \in \mathfrak{I}_\mathcal{T}^\Delta/\sim_\mathcal{R}} \left(\sum_{\substack{\tau \in \mathfrak{T}_\mathcal{R} \\ E_i \tau}} k(\tau) \right) \cdot \mathcal{P}([\mathcal{I}]_k)} = p_i, \quad i = 1, \ldots, n. \qquad (18)$$

Then, $\mathcal{P}$ can be extended to a probability distribution on $\mathfrak{I}^\Delta$ and thereby to a model of $\mathcal{R}$ by defining for all $\mathcal{I} \in \mathfrak{I}^\Delta$

$$\mathcal{P}(\mathcal{I}) = \begin{cases} \mathcal{P}([\mathcal{I}]_k) \cdot (|[\mathcal{I}]_k|)^{-1} & [\mathcal{I}]_k \in \mathfrak{I}_\mathcal{T}^\Delta/\!\sim_\mathcal{R} \\ 0 & \text{otherwise.} \end{cases}$$

The equations in (18) and the conditions $0 \leq \mathcal{P}([\mathcal{I}]_k) \leq 1$ for all $[\mathcal{I}]_k \in \mathfrak{I}_\mathcal{T}^\Delta/\!\sim_\mathcal{R}$ can easily be transformed into a system of linear inequalities with integer coefficients. Both the number of inequalities and the number of variables of this system is in $\mathcal{O}(|\mathfrak{I}_\mathcal{T}^\Delta/\!\sim_\mathcal{R}|)$ and, hence, polynomially bounded in $|\Delta|$. It follows, that satisfiability of this system can be decided in time polynomial in $|\Delta|$. $\square$

Proposition 3. *Let $\mathcal{R}$ be a consistent knowledge base, $\beta \in \mathbb{Q}_{>0}^n$, and let C, D, E, F be concepts.*

1. *Calculating the probability p for which $\mathcal{P}_{\mathcal{R}}^{\beta} \models (F|E)[p]$ holds, and*
2. *deciding whether $\mathcal{P}_{\mathcal{R}}^{\beta} \models C \sqsubseteq D$ holds*

is possible in time polynomial in $|\Delta|$.

Proof. As $\mathcal{P}_{\mathcal{R}}^{\beta} \models C \sqsubseteq D$ iff $\mathcal{P}_{\mathcal{R}}^{\beta} \models (D|C)[1]$, the second statement of the proposition follows from the first. To prove the first statement, we write $p_i = \frac{s_i}{t_i}$ with $s_i, t_i \in \mathbb{N}_{>0}$ for $i = 1, \ldots, n$, and $q = (F|E)[p]$. Then,

$$p = \frac{\sum_{\substack{\mathcal{I} \in \mathcal{J}^{\Delta} \\ \mathcal{I} \models \mathcal{T}}} |E^{\mathcal{I}} \cap F^{\mathcal{I}}| \cdot \mathcal{P}_{\mathcal{R}}^{\beta}(\mathcal{I})}{\sum_{\substack{\mathcal{I} \in \mathcal{J}^{\Delta} \\ \mathcal{I} \models \mathcal{T}}} |E^{\mathcal{I}}| \cdot \mathcal{P}_{\mathcal{R}}^{\beta}(\mathcal{I})} = \frac{\sum_{\substack{\mathcal{I} \in \mathcal{J}^{\Delta} \\ \mathcal{I} \models \mathcal{T}}} |E^{\mathcal{I}} \cap F^{\mathcal{I}}| \cdot \beta_0 \cdot \prod_{i=1}^{n} \beta_i^{f_i(\mathcal{I})}}{\sum_{\substack{\mathcal{I} \in \mathcal{J}^{\Delta} \\ \mathcal{I} \models \mathcal{T}}} |E^{\mathcal{I}}| \cdot \beta_0 \cdot \prod_{i=1}^{n} \beta_i^{f_i(\mathcal{I})}}$$

$$= \frac{\sum_{\substack{\mathcal{I} \in \mathcal{J}^{\Delta} \\ \mathcal{I} \models \mathcal{T}}} |E^{\mathcal{I}} \cap F^{\mathcal{I}}| \cdot \prod_{i=1}^{n} \beta_i^{|E^{\mathcal{I}} \cap F^{\mathcal{I}}| - \frac{s_i}{t_i} \cdot |E^{\mathcal{I}}|}}{\sum_{\substack{\mathcal{I} \in \mathcal{J}^{\Delta} \\ \mathcal{I} \models \mathcal{T}}} |E^{\mathcal{I}}| \cdot \prod_{i=1}^{n} \beta_i^{|E^{\mathcal{I}} \cap F^{\mathcal{I}}| - \frac{s_i}{t_i} \cdot |E^{\mathcal{I}}|}}$$

$$= \frac{\sum_{\substack{\mathcal{I} \in \mathcal{J}^{\Delta} \\ \mathcal{I} \models \mathcal{T}}} |E^{\mathcal{I}} \cap F^{\mathcal{I}}| \cdot \prod_{i=1}^{n} \beta_i^{t_i \cdot |E^{\mathcal{I}} \cap F^{\mathcal{I}}| - s_i \cdot |E^{\mathcal{I}}| + s_i \cdot |\Delta|}}{\sum_{\substack{\mathcal{I} \in \mathcal{J}^{\Delta} \\ \mathcal{I} \models \mathcal{T}}} |E^{\mathcal{I}}| \cdot \prod_{i=1}^{n} \beta_i^{t_i \cdot |E^{\mathcal{I}} \cap F^{\mathcal{I}}| - s_i \cdot |E^{\mathcal{I}}| + s_i \cdot |\Delta|}}. \qquad (19)$$

Note that

$$t_i \cdot |E_i^{\mathcal{T}} \cap F_i^{\mathcal{T}}| - s_i \cdot |E_i^{\mathcal{I}}| + s_i \cdot |\Delta| \geq 0 \qquad \forall \mathcal{I} \in \mathcal{J}^{\Delta}, \, i = 1, \ldots, n.$$

Hence, the last fraction in (19) mentions sums over products of integers ($|E^{\mathcal{I}} \cap F^{\mathcal{I}}|$ and $|E^{\mathcal{I}}|$, respectively) and rational numbers (β_i) with integer exponents only and can be computed exactly.

It remains to show that (19) can be calculated in time polynomial in $|\Delta|$. To prove this, we aggregate interpretations into equivalence classes as discussed in Sect. 3. However, we have to modify the set of types the equivalence classes are based on since the query conditional q may mention additional subconcepts that are not considered by the types in $\mathfrak{T}_{\mathcal{R}}$. Let $\mathcal{M}_q^+ = \{C \mid C \in \mathrm{sub}(E) \cup \mathrm{sub}(F)\}$, $\mathcal{M}_q = \mathcal{M}_q^+ \cup \{\neg C \mid C \in \mathcal{M}_q^+\}$, and $\mathfrak{T}_{\mathcal{R}}^q = \mathfrak{T}(\mathcal{M}_{\mathcal{R}} \cup \mathcal{M}_q)$. For interpretations $\mathcal{I}, \mathcal{I}' \in \mathcal{J}^{\Delta}$, we define the equivalence relation $\mathcal{I} \sim_{\mathcal{R}}^q \mathcal{I}'$ iff $C_{\tau}^{\mathcal{I}} = C_{\tau}^{\mathcal{I}'}$ for all $\tau \in \mathfrak{T}_{\mathcal{R}}^q$ in analogy to $\sim_{\mathcal{R}}$. Every type $\tau \in \mathfrak{T}_{\mathcal{R}}^q$ is a refinement of a unique type $\tau' \in \mathfrak{T}_{\mathcal{R}}$, i.e. $\tau' \subseteq \tau$, and we may define $\rho_{\mathcal{R}}(\tau') = \rho_{\mathcal{R}}(\tau)$. In plain words, τ' inherits its conditional impact from τ. Accordingly, we define $f_i(\tau') = f_i(\tau)$ for $i = 1, \ldots, n$. Then Proposition 1 as well as Corollary 1 still hold when replacing the underlying set of types $\mathfrak{T}_{\mathcal{R}}$ by $\mathfrak{T}_{\mathcal{R}}^q$. Also, the counting strategies and the complexity results for $\mathcal{J}^{\Delta} / \sim_{\mathcal{R}}^q$ are the same as for $\mathcal{J}^{\Delta} / \sim_{\mathcal{R}}$. Hence, (19) can be simplified to

$$p = \frac{\sum_{[\mathcal{I}]_k \in \mathfrak{I}\frac{\Delta}{\mathcal{T}}/\sim_{\mathcal{R}}^q} k_i^+ \cdot \prod_{i=1}^n \beta_i^{t_i \cdot k_i^+ - s_i \cdot k_i^o + s_i \cdot |\Delta|}}{\sum_{\substack{\mathcal{I} \in \mathfrak{I}^\Delta \\ \mathcal{I} \models \mathcal{T}}} k_i^o \cdot \prod_{i=1}^n \beta_i^{t_i \cdot k_i^+ - s_i \cdot k_i^o + s_i \cdot |\Delta|}}$$

where $k_i^+ = \sum_{\substack{\tau \in \mathfrak{T}_{\mathcal{R}}^q \\ E_i, F_i \in \tau}} k(\tau)$ and $k_i^o = \sum_{\substack{\tau \in \mathfrak{T}_{\mathcal{R}}^q \\ E_i \in \tau}} k(\tau)$. This fraction can clearly be calculated in time polynomial in $|\Delta|$.   □

Proposition 3 states that inferences in $\mathcal{P}_{\mathcal{R}}^\beta$ are domain-lifted (cf. [6]). Hence, the message of Proposition 3 is that the crucial part of drawing inferences at maximum entropy from $\mathcal{R}$ according to (2) is the approximation of $\mathcal{P}_{\mathcal{R}}^{ME}$ by $\mathcal{P}_{\mathcal{R}}^\beta$. Once this approximation is given, all further calculations can be performed *exactly* without additional inaccuracies and in time polynomial in $|\Delta|$.

6   Conclusion and Future Work

We have presented $\mathcal{ALC}^{ME}$, a probabilistic variant of the Description Logic $\mathcal{ALC}$, which allows one to express uncertain knowledge by probabilistic conditional statements of the form "if E holds, then F is true with probability p". Probabilities are understood as degrees of beliefs and a reasoner's belief state is established by the principle of maximum entropy based on the aggregating semantics. We have proved that both checking consistency and drawing inferences from approximations of the maximum entropy distribution is possible in $\mathcal{ALC}^{ME}$ in time polynomial in the domain size $|\Delta|$.

In future work, we want to investigate, on the one hand, complexity results for approximate inference at maximum entropy in $\mathcal{ALC}^{ME}$. For this, we need error estimations and complexity results for calculating approximations $\mathcal{P}_{\mathcal{R}}^\beta$ of the maximum entropy distribution $\mathcal{P}_{\mathcal{R}}^{ME}$ in addition to the results presented here. Note that the size of the equation system that is generated as input for the methods used to approximate $\mathcal{P}_{\mathcal{R}}^{ME}$ by $\mathcal{P}_{\mathcal{R}}^\beta$ (cf. (5)) can be bounded polynomially in $|\Delta|$, using the same counting strategies as presented in Sect. 4.

On the other hand, we want to extend our complexity results to more general $\mathcal{ALC}^{ME}$-knowledge bases containing also assertional knowledge, and to Description Logics that are more expressive than $\mathcal{ALC}$.

Finally, we intend to make a more fine-grained complexity analysis that investigates the complexity of reasoning not only w.r.t. the domain size, but also in terms of the size of the knowledge base.

References

1. Baader, F., Calvanese, D., McGuinness, D.L., Nardi, D., Patel-Schneider, P.F. (eds.): The Description Logic Handbook: Theory, Implementation, and Applications. Cambridge University Press, Cambridge (2003)

2. Baader, F., Ecke, A.: Extending the description logic ALC with more expressive cardinality constraints on concepts. In: Proceedings of the 3rd Global Conference on Artificial Intelligence (GCAI), pp. 6–19. EasyChair (2017)
3. Baader, F., Horrocks, I., Sattler, U.: Description logics. In: van Harmelen, F., Lifschitz, V., Porter, B. (eds.) Handbook of Knowledge Representation. Elsevier, Amsterdam (2007)
4. Baader, F., Koopmann, P., Turhan, A.-Y.: Using ontologies to query probabilistic numerical data. In: Dixon, C., Finger, M. (eds.) FroCoS 2017. LNCS (LNAI), vol. 10483, pp. 77–94. Springer, Cham (2017). https://doi.org/10.1007/978-3-319-66167-4_5
5. Boyd, S., Vandenberghe, L.: Convex Optimization. Cambridge University Press, Cambridge (2004)
6. Van den Broeck, G., Taghipour, N., Meert, W., Davis, J., De Raedt, L.: Lifted probabilistic inference by first-order knowledge compilation. In: Proceedings of the 22th International Joint Conference on Artificial Intelligence (IJCAI), pp. 2178–2185. AAAI Press (2011)
7. Halpern, J.Y.: An analysis of first-order logics of probability. Artif. Intell. **46**(3), 311–350 (1990)
8. Kern-Isberner, G.: Conditionals in Nonmonotonic Reasoning and Belief Revision. Springer, Heidelberg (2001). https://doi.org/10.1007/3-540-44600-1
9. Kern-Isberner, G., Thimm, M.: Novel semantical approaches to relational probabilistic conditionals. In: Proceedings of the 12th International Conference on the Principles of Knowledge Representation and Reasoning (KR), pp. 382–392. AAAI Press (2010)
10. Lutz, C., Schröder, L.: Probabilistic description logics for subjective uncertainty. In: Proceedings of the 12th International Conference on Principles of Knowledge Representation and Reasoning (KR), pp. 393–403. AAAI Press (2010)
11. Paris, J.B.: Common sense and maximum entropy. Synthese **117**(1), 75–93 (1999)
12. Paris, J.B.: The Uncertain Reasoner's Companion: A Mathematical Perspective. Cambridge University Press, Cambridge (2006)
13. Peñaloza, R., Potyka, N.: Towards statistical reasoning in description logics over finite domains. In: Moral, S., Pivert, O., Sánchez, D., Marín, N. (eds.) SUM 2017. LNCS (LNAI), vol. 10564, pp. 280–294. Springer, Cham (2017). https://doi.org/10.1007/978-3-319-67582-4_20
14. Pratt, V.R.: Models of program logics. In: Proceedings of the 20th Annual Symposium on Foundations of Computer Science (FOCS), pp. 115–122. IEEE Computer Society (1979)
15. Rudolph, S., Krötzsch, M., Hitzler, P.: Type-elimination-based reasoning for the description logic SHIQbs using decision diagrams and disjunctive datalog. Logical Methods Comput. Sci. **8**(1), 38 (2012)
16. Thimm, M., Kern-Isberner, G.: On probabilistic inference in relational conditional logics. Logic J. IGPL **20**(5), 872–908 (2012)

Logic Programming

Memory-Saving Evaluation Plans for Datalog

Carlo Allocca[2], Roberta Costabile[1], Alessio Fiorentino[1],
Simona Perri[1], and Jessica Zangari[1](✉)

[1] Department of Mathematics and Computer Science,
University of Calabria, Rende, Italy
{r.costabile,fiorentino,perri,zangari}@mat.unical.it
[2] Samsung Research, Staines-upon-Thames, UK
c.allocca@samsung.com

Abstract. Ontology-based query answering (OBQA), without any doubt, represents one of the fundamental reasoning services in Semantic Web applications. Specifically, OBQA is the task of evaluating a (conjunctive) query over a knowledge base (KB) consisting of an extensional dataset paired with an ontology. A number of effective practical approaches proposed in the literature rewrite the query and the ontology into an equivalent Datalog program. In case of very large datasets, however, classical approaches for evaluating such programs tend to be memory consuming, and may even slow down the computation. In this paper, we explain how to compute a memory-saving evaluation plan consisting of an optimal indexing schema for the dataset together with a suitable body-ordering for each Datalog rule. To evaluate the quality of our approach, we compare our plans with the classical approach used by DLV over widely used ontological benchmarks. The results confirm the memory usage can be significantly reduced without paying any cost in efficiency.

Keywords: Datalog · Query answering · Ontologies · Query-plan · Data indexing

1 Introduction

Ontological reasoning services represent fundamental features in the development of the Semantic Web. Among them, scientists are focusing their attention on so-called *ontology-based query answering*, OBQA [6–8, 10, 25], for short,

This work has been partially supported by Samsung under project "Enhancing the DLV system for large-scale ontology reasoning", by MISE under project "S2BDW" (F/050389/01-03/X32)-"Horizon2020" PON I&C2014-20, by Regione Calabria under project "DLV LargeScale" (CUP J28C17000220006) - POR Calabria 2014-20, and by the European Union's Horizon 2020 research and innovation programme under the Marie Skodowska-Curie grant agreement No. 690974 for the project "MIREL: MIning and REasoning with Legal texts".

F. Calimeri et al. (Eds.): JELIA 2019, LNAI 11468, pp. 453–461, 2019.
https://doi.org/10.1007/978-3-030-19570-0_29

454   C. Allocca et al.

where a Boolean query has to be evaluated against a *logical theory* (*knowledge base*) consisting of an extensional *database* paired with an *ontology*. A number of effective practical approaches proposed in the literature rewrite the query and the ontology into an equivalent Datalog program [16]. *DLV* [19] is an in-memory system for the evaluation of logic programs (Datalog programs possibly extended with disjunction, negation, aggregate functions, constraints, arithmetic operators, and many more constructs) can be successfully used in such a context. More precisely, *DLV* is a reasoner for Answer Set Programming (ASP) [9,14,15,17,22,24], a declarative programming paradigm evolved from logic programming, deductive databases, knowledge representation, and nonmonotonic reasoning, with several applications in Artificial Intelligence [1–5,20,21,26,27]. Its sub-system *I-DLV* [12,13] is endowed with explicit means for interoperability with external databases and incorporates a number of ad-hoc techniques for handling advanced database applications, such as magic-sets, indexing and join-orderings that make *DLV* a full-fledged deductive database system. However, in case of very large datasets, internal deductive database optimizations like those used in *DLV* can be extremely memory consuming as they require to compute extra information on the data for fine-tuning the heuristics or, in general, for optimizing execution times. For instance, *DLV* uses a join ordering policy that before instantiating a rule, reorders its body for enabling efficient join evaluations; it acts on the basis of statistics over the extensions of involved predicates that may require a considerable amount of memory. Moreover, *DLV* adopts ad-hoc indexed structures (i.e. indices) over predicate extensions: indices are computed on demand according to the positions of literals in the rule and their bindings. Hence, the indexing schema of each rule, i.e. the set of indices adopted to instantiate it, is chosen according to the body ordering strategy and created indices are strictly related to the way in which literals are rearranged. This ensures fast evaluation at the expense of higher memory consumption. Thus, when memory is an issue, parsimonious strategies that minimize the index occupation, without paying in efficiency, are preferable. In this paper, we explain how to compute a memory-saving evaluation plan for a Datalog program $\mathcal{P}$, consisting of an optimal indexing schema for the dataset together with a suitable body-ordering for each rule in $\mathcal{P}$. The approach makes use of ASP program for computing such plan before the actual evaluation of $\mathcal{P}$, in a pre-processing phase, and then forces *DLV* computation to follow the plan. This can be done by adding annotations in the Datalog program [12], i.e. explicit directions on the internal computation process of *DLV* specifying ordering/indexing criteria that override default strategies. In order to assess the effectiveness of the approach for ontology-based query answering, we conduct an experimental evaluation over popular ontological benchmarks widely used for testing both capabilities and performance of OBQA systems. We compared performance in terms of time and memory usage of *DLV* when the classical computation is performed, and when computation is driven by the planner. Results confirm that the planner reduces memory usage without worsening times.

2   An ASP-Based Evaluation Planner

In its computational process, for optimizing the evaluation of each rule, DLV on demand determines body orderings and indices, according to strategies taking into account only local information for the rule at hand. More in details, before instantiating a rule $r \in \mathcal{P}$, DLV reorders the body literals on the basis of some join-ordering heuristics [12]; then, according to the chosen ordering, it determines and creates needed indices. However, when memory consumption must be limited, an approach based on a global view over all rules, allowing for a more parsimonious creation of indices, is preferable.

In this section, we describe our approach for computing a *memory-saving evaluation plan* for a set $\mathcal{P}$ of positive Datalog rules to be evaluated over an extensional dataset $\mathcal{D}$. We define an evaluation plan of $\mathcal{P}$ as an indexing schema over $\mathcal{P} \cup \mathcal{D}$ together with a suitable body-ordering for each rule of $\mathcal{P}$. An indexing schema consists of the set of indices adopted to instantiate all rules in $\mathcal{P}$ over $\mathcal{D}$. Our approach makes use of an ASP program for computing a memory-saving evaluation plan $\mathcal{E}$ of $\mathcal{P}$ in a pre-processing phase; then $\mathcal{P}$ is annotated with directions that force DLV computation to follow $\mathcal{E}$ when evaluating $\mathcal{P}$.

In the following, after a formal definition of *memory-saving evaluation plan*, we describe the ASP code devised in order to compute such plans. For space reasons, we assume the reader is familiar with the ASP language and computation. For a complete reference to ASP, we refer the reader to [11].

2.1   Evaluation Plans

Let $\mathcal{P}$ be a set of positive Datalog rules with non-empty body and let $\mathcal{D}$ be a database. We indicate with $\text{pred}(\mathcal{P} \cup \mathcal{D})$ the set of all predicates occurring in $\mathcal{P} \cup \mathcal{D}$ and with $\text{rel}(p)$ the set $\{\alpha \in \mathcal{D} : \text{pred}(\alpha) = p\}$ of the elements of $\mathcal{D}$ sharing the predicate name p. We write $p[i]$ to indicate the i-th argument of the predicate p. In the following we provide some formal definitions in order to introduce the notion of *optimal evaluation plan*.

Definition 1. *Let r be a rule in $\mathcal{P}$ and $B(r)$ be the set of the atoms appearing in the body of r. Let F_a be a (possibly empty) subset of atoms in $B(r)$ and F_p be a subset of $\{1, \cdots, |B(r)|\}$. A position assignment on r is a one-to-one map $p_r : F_a \rightarrow F_p$. A pair (α, p) such that $p_r(\alpha) = p$ is called a fixed position w.r.t. p_r. An ordering on r is a bijective function $pos(r, \cdot) : B(r) \rightarrow \{1, \cdots, |B(r)|\}$. Having fixed a position assignment p_r on r, we define a p_r-ordering on r as an ordering on r such that $pos(r, \alpha) = p_r(\alpha)$ for each $\alpha \in F_a$.*

The definition above presents a body ordering as a rearrangement of the literals in the body, but notably, allows for having a certain number of atoms in the body in some prefixed positions. This is because, according to the knowledge of the domain at hand, if one is aware that a particular choice for the orderings is convenient, the planner can be driven so that only plans complying with this choice are identified.

Definition 2. *Let $U := \{p[i] : p \in pred(\mathcal{P} \cup \mathcal{D}), 1 \le i \le a(p)\}$, where $a(p)$ represents the arity of the predicate p. An indexing schema $\mathcal{S}$ over $\mathcal{P} \cup \mathcal{D}$ is a subset of U. Given a subset $I \subseteq U$, we say that $\mathcal{S}$ fixes I if $I \subseteq \mathcal{S}$.*

Intuitively, an indexing schema is a subset of the arguments of all predicates in $pred(\mathcal{P} \cup \mathcal{D})$. Furthermore, similarly to the definition of ordering that may allow for fixed positions, we give the possibility to fix also a set of indices.

With a rule $r \in \mathcal{P}$ we can associate a hypergraph $H(r) = (V, E)$ whose vertex set V is the set of all terms appearing in $B(r)$ and the edges in E are the term sets of each atom in $B(r)$. Given a rule r of $\mathcal{P}$, a *connected component* of r is a set of atoms in $B(r)$ that define a connected component in $H(r)$.

Let us introduce now the notions of *separation* between two connected components and *well ordering* of a component of a rule.

Definition 3. *Let r be a rule of $\mathcal{P}$ and $pos(r, \cdot)$ be an ordering on r. Two connected components C_1 and C_2 of r are separated w.r.t. $pos(r, \cdot)$ if $\max\{pos(r, \alpha) : \alpha \in C_1\} < \min\{pos(r, \beta) : \beta \in C_2\}$ or vice versa.*

Definition 4. *Let r be a rule of $\mathcal{P}$, $\mathcal{S}$ be an indexing schema and $pos(r, \cdot)$ be an ordering on r. A connected component C of r is well ordered w.r.t. $\mathcal{S}$ and $pos(r, \cdot)$ if, assuming $m = \min\{pos(r, \alpha) : \alpha \in C\}$, for each $\beta \in C$ with $pos(r, \beta) = j$ and $j > m$, it holds that there exists an argument of β belonging to $\mathcal{S}$ which is either a constant or a variable occurring in an atom $\gamma \in C$, with $pos(r, \gamma) < j$.*

The notion of separation among connected components is needed for identifying, within rule bodies, clusters of literals that do not share variables. The idea is that the ordering computed by the planner should keep separated these clusters in order to avoid, as much as possible, the computation of Cartesian products during the instantiation; at the same time, literals within the clusters are properly rearranged in order to comply with the selected indexing schema, thus avoiding the creation of further indices.

Next, we provide the *admissibility* property which, in turn, characterizes the evaluation plans.

Definition 5. *Given a rule $r \in \mathcal{P}$ and an indexing schema $\mathcal{S}$, we say that an ordering $pos(r, \cdot)$ is admissible w.r.t. $\mathcal{S}$ if the connected components of r are well ordered (w.r.t. $pos(r, \cdot)$ and $\mathcal{S}$) and mutually separated (w.r.t. $pos(r, \cdot)$).*

We define below an optimal evaluation plan.

Definition 6. *Let (i) $\{p_r ; r \in \mathcal{P}\}$ be a given set of position assignment, and (ii) I be a given subset of $\{p[i] : p \in pred(\mathcal{P} \cup \mathcal{D}), 1 \le i \le a(p)\}$. An evaluation plan $\mathcal{E}$ of $\mathcal{P}$ consists of an indexing schema $\mathcal{S}$ that fixes I together with a p_r-ordering of each rule r of $\mathcal{P}$ being admissible w.r.t. $\mathcal{S}$. We say that $\mathcal{P}$ enjoys an efficient evaluation if it is associated to an evaluation plan. Assuming $c(p, i)$ is the cost of building an index over $p[i]$, we say that an evaluation plan is optimal if the overall cost $\sum_{p[i] \in \mathcal{S}} c(p, i)$ is minimal.*

Note that the definition of optimal plan presupposes the knowledge of $c(p, i)$ values. Such costs can be estimated via heuristics or actually computed, depending on the application domain at hand.

2.2   Computing Evaluation Plans via ASP

We provide next an ASP program for computing optimal evaluation plans for $\mathcal{P}$. The program is based on the classical "Guess/Check/Optimize" paradigm and combines: (i) *choice and disjunctive rules* to guess an indexing schema $\mathcal{S}$ over $\mathcal{P} \cup \mathcal{D}$ and, for each rule r in $\mathcal{P}$, an ordering $\mathrm{ord}(r, \cdot)$; (ii) *strong constraints* to guarantee, for each rule r, the admissibility of $\mathrm{ord}(r, \cdot)$ w.r.t. $\mathcal{S}$; (iii) *weak constraints* to find out, among all the evaluation plans of $\mathcal{P}$, the one with the lowest memory consumption.

The program takes as input a set of facts representing $\mathcal{P}$ and the dataset $\mathcal{D}$. In particular, each rule of $\mathcal{P}$ is represented by means of facts of the form:

```
rule(RuleId,Description,NumberOfBodyAtoms).
headAtom(RuleId,Atom,PredName).
bodyAtom(RuleId,Atom,PredName).
sameVariable(RuleId,Atom1,Arg1,Atom2,Arg2).
constant(RuleId,Atom,Arg).
relation(PredicateName,Arity).
```

Facts over predicate **rule** associate each rule r to an identifier and provide $|B(r)|$. The sets $B(r)$ and $H(r)$, for each r, are represented by **bodyAtom** and **headAtom** predicates respectively. The predicate **sameVariable** provides the common variables related to any pair of atoms appearing in r, whereas **constant** states that a constant term occurs in the argument of an atom of r. The database $\mathcal{D}$ is represented by means of facts over predicate **relation**. Furthermore, according to the formal definitions of Sect. 2.1, an optimal plan is defined on the basis of the cost $c(p, i)$ of building an index over $\mathrm{rel}(p)$ on its i-th attribute, and possibly fixing some positions for the ordering, and some indices. Such information are given in input to the ASP planner by means of facts of the form:

```
index(PredicateName,Arg,MemoryConsumption).
fixedPosition(RuleId,Atom,Pos).
fixedIndex(PredicateName,Arg).
```

The ASP program computing the plans is rather long and involved, thus, we report here only some key parts; the full program is available on the online web page https://www.mat.unical.it/perri/planner.zip.

The following rule guesses an indexing schema $\mathcal{S}$ for $\mathcal{P}$. Notably, the arguments to be indexed are chosen among a restricted set of arguments, called indexable, in order to keep the search space smaller. For instance arguments that are not involved in joins are not indexable.

```
{setIndex(PredName,Arg)}:-indexable(PredName,Arg).
```

Beside this choice rule, the guess part contains also a number of disjunctive rules for guessing the ordering. The following constraint checks one of the conditions of admissibility for evaluation plans. In particular, it checks that connected components are separated.

```
:-pos(Atom1,RuleId,Pos1),pos(Atom2,RuleId,Pos2),
  sameComponent(RuleId,Atom1,Atom2),pos(Atom3,RuleId,Pos3),
  not sameComponent(RuleId,Atom1,Atom3),Pos1<Pos3,Pos3<Pos2.
```

Here, the predicate pos represents the position of a body atom in a rule, while the predicate sameComponent identifies connected components. The checking part contains a number of further constraints, some ensuring that the other admissibility conditions are respected and some verifying that guessed plans are correctly determined. Eventually, the following weak constraint constitutes the optimize part and is used for minimizing the memory consumption.

```
:~setIndex(X,Y),index(X,Y,Cost). [Cost@1, X,Y,Cost]
```

3   Experimental Evaluation

Hereafter we report the results of an experimental activity carried out to assess the effectiveness of using the ASP-based evaluation planner. Our experimental analysis relies on three benchmarks: LUBM, Stock Exchange and Vicodi. LUBM (Lehigh University BenchMark) is one of the most popular ontologies for testing both capabilities and performance of OBQA systems. LUBM has been specifically developed to facilitate the evaluation of Semantic Web reasoners in a standard and systematic way. In fact, the benchmark is intended to evaluate performance of those reasoners with respect to extensional queries over large data sets that refer to a single realistic ontology. The LUBM benchmark consists of a university domain OWL 2 ontology with customizable and repeatable synthetic data and a set of 14 input SPARQL queries. We used the standard LUBM data generator to produce three datasets consisting of 500, 1000 and 4000 universities. Stock Exchange and Vicodi are two real world ontologies widely used in literature for the evaluation of query rewriting systems [23]. For each of these two ontologies, we considered 5 queries and we used the SyGENiA generator [18] to produce five datasets having from 1,000 to 40,0000 tuples and a number of individuals varying from 100 to 4,000.

Experiments have been performed on a NUMA machine equipped with two 2.8 GHz AMD Opteron 6320 processors and 128 GB RAM. Unlimited time and memory were granted to running processes. Benchmarks and executables used for the experiments are available at https://www.mat.unical.it/perri/planner.zip.

First of all, since DLV makes use magic sets for evaluating these programs, we precomputed (running DLV) the magic rewritings for each query, so that plans can be computed over the rewritten programs. Then, two different executions have been performed: (i) a classical execution of DLV which, given as input the so generated encodings, chooses body orderings and indexing strategies with its default policies, and (ii) an execution driven by the planner in which DLV is forced to follow the precomputed evaluation plan that decided body orderings and indices in order to reduce memory consumption. These constraints have been defined via DLV annotations, that represent specific means for specifying

Table 1. Effectiveness of the ASP-based evaluation planner. Time are in seconds, memory in MB.

Query	No planner		Planner		
	Time	Memory	Time	Memory	Planning time
LUBM					
q01	1738.34	16887.97	1210.12	16891.87	0
q02	1880.47	18607.13	1335.18	17127.20	0.07
q03	1773.22	17474.40	1185.46	16891.77	0.01
q04	5944.26	41770.97	1574.18	33237.33	0.13
q05	1714.40	28217.20	1320.03	18483.63	0.08
q06	1511.81	20319.40	1549.19	19034.50	0.04
q07	2684.68	31848.20	1309.80	20910.20	0.09
q08	1970.73	32287.87	1346.23	22393.43	0.11
q09	1635.46	21632.13	1586.10	21616.00	0.07
q10	2034.92	31503.53	1306.76	20558.07	0.08
q11	1175.12	16892.27	1158.14	16889.50	0
q12	1462.17	22252.30	1287.47	18345.27	0.11
q13	1610.07	29931.10	1301.00	18378.77	0.08
q14	1210.43	16888.23	1178.08	16890.07	0.04
Stock exchange					
q01	0.83	11.98	0.82	11.72	0
q02	1.10	23.48	1.21	20.70	0.02
q03	2.06	39.64	2.39	37.04	0.03
q04	1.31	29.04	1.32	25.26	0.04
q05	2.35	46.40	2.57	41.28	0.09
Vicodi					
q01	0.83	9.88	0.83	10.04	0.01
q02	0.93	20.56	0.83	11.34	0.01
q03	0.82	11.38	0.78	10.16	0.02
q04	0.70	12.88	0.70	9.62	0.02
q05	0.78	12.54	0.83	12.82	0.08

preferences over its internal computational process [12]. Furthermore, in this latter execution scenario, as input for the planner we used the effective costs in memory for holding all possible indices and we choose an ordering policy which fixes magic literals in the last position; for LUBM these heuristic values have been extracted over the dataset featuring 100 universities, while for both Stock Exchange and Vicodi we relied the greatest generated dataset. Table 1 shows performance in terms of average running time and memory usage of *DLV* over all considered datasets when the classical computation is performed (columns 2 and 3) and when computation is driven by the planner (columns 4 and 5). In the 6th column, we reported the time spent to compute the optimal plan. As it can be seen, we obtained an average saving on memory of 16%, 9% and 15% on LUBM, Stock Exchange and Vicodi, respectively, with peaks among 30–45% in cases of queries 5, 7, 10, 13 of LUBM and query 2 of Vicodi. No significant increase of computation time is observable. In some cases, we obtained also some improvements in terms of time. This can be explained considering that indices selected by the planner, being, on the overall, less memory expensive are more efficiently computable.

4   Conclusion

In this work we introduced a memory-saving evaluation planner for Datalog programs. The planner has been conceived to be applied to ontology-based query answering contexts, where often, in case of large datasets, standard approaches are not convenient/applicable due to memory consumption. It relies on an ASP program that computes the plan, intended as an indexing schema for the dataset together with a body-ordering for each rule in the program. The computed plan minimizes the overall cost (in term of memory consumption) of indices; moreover, the usage of the plan with the *DLV* system allows to further reduce memory usage since some expensive internal optimizations of *DLV* can be disabled. Results of the experiments conducted on popular ontological benchmarks confirm the effectiveness of the approach. Future work concerns the development of a pre-processing tool for the automatic integration of the planner into *DLV*, as well as the experimental evaluation in further domains.

References

1. Adrian, W.T., Manna, M., Leone, N., Amendola, G., Adrian, M.: Entity set expansion from the web via ASP. In: ICLP (Technical Communications). OASICS, vol. 58, pp. 1:1–1:5. Schloss Dagstuhl - Leibniz-Zentrum fuer Informatik (2017)
2. Amendola, G.: Preliminary results on modeling interdependent scheduling games via answer set programming. In: Proceedings of RCRA. CEUR-WS.org (2018, to appear)
3. Amendola, G.: Solving the stable roommates problem using incoherent answer set programs. In: Proceedings of RCRA. CEUR-WS.org (2018, to appear)
4. Amendola, G., Dodaro, C., Leone, N., Ricca, F.: On the application of answer set programming to the conference paper assignment problem. In: Adorni, G., Cagnoni, S., Gori, M., Maratea, M. (eds.) AI*IA 2016. LNCS (LNAI), vol. 10037, pp. 164–178. Springer, Cham (2016). https://doi.org/10.1007/978-3-319-49130-1_13
5. Amendola, G., Greco, G., Leone, N., Veltri, P.: Modeling and reasoning about NTU games via answer set programming. In: IJCAI, pp. 38–45 (2016)
6. Amendola, G., Leone, N., Manna, M.: Finite model reasoning over existential rules. TPLP **17**(5–6), 726–743 (2017)

7. Amendola, G., Leone, N., Manna, M.: Finite controllability of conjunctive query answering with existential : Two steps forward. In: IJCAI, pp. 5189–5193 (2018)
8. Amendola, G., Leone, N., Manna, M., Veltri, P.: Enhancing existential rules by closed-world variables. In: IJCAI, pp. 1676–1682 (2018)
9. Brewka, G., Eiter, T., Truszczynski, M.: Answer set programming at a glance. Commun. ACM **54**(12), 92–103 (2011)
10. Calì, A., Gottlob, G., Lukasiewicz, T.: Tractable query answering over ontologies with datalog+/-. In: Proceedings of DL 2009 (2009)
11. Calimeri, F., et al.: ASP-core-2: Input language format (2012). https://www.mat.unical.it/aspcomp2013/files/ASP-CORE-2.03b.pdf
12. Calimeri, F., Fuscà, D., Perri, S., Zangari, J.: I-DLV: the new intelligent grounder of DLV. Intelligenza Artificiale **11**(1), 5–20 (2017)
13. Calimeri, F., Perri, S., Zangari, J.: Optimizing answer set computation via heuristic-based decomposition. In: TPLP, pp. 1–26 (2019)
14. Eiter, T., Faber, W., Leone, N., Pfeifer, G.: Declarative problem-solving using the DLV system. In: Minker, J. (ed.) Logic-Based Artificial Intelligence. SECS, vol. 597, pp. 79–103. Springer, Boston (2000). https://doi.org/10.1007/978-1-4615-1567-8_4
15. Eiter, T., Ianni, G., Krennwallner, T.: Answer set programming: a primer. In: Tessaris, S., et al. (eds.) Reasoning Web 2009. LNCS, vol. 5689, pp. 40–110. Springer, Heidelberg (2009). https://doi.org/10.1007/978-3-642-03754-2_2
16. Eiter, T., Ortiz, M., Simkus, M., Tran, T., Xiao, G.: Query rewriting for Horn-SHIQ plus rules. In: Proceedings of AAAI (2012)
17. Gelfond, M., Lifschitz, V.: Classical negation in logic programs and disjunctive databases. New Gener. Comput. **9**(3/4), 365–385 (1991)
18. Grau, B.C., Motik, B., Stoilos, G., Horrocks, I.: Completeness guarantees for incomplete ontology reasoners: theory and practice. J. Artif. Intell. Res. **43**, 419–476 (2012)
19. Leone, N., et al.: The DLV system for knowledge representation and reasoning. ACM Trans. Comput. Logic **7**(3), 499–562 (2006)
20. Manna, M., Ricca, F., Terracina, G.: Consistent query answering via ASP from different perspectives: theory and practice. TPLP **13**(2), 227–252 (2013)
21. Manna, M., Ricca, F., Terracina, G.: Taming primary key violations to query large inconsistent data via ASP. TPLP **15**(4–5), 696–710 (2015)
22. Marek, V.W., Truszczyński, M.: Stable models and an alternative logic programming paradigm. In: Apt, K.R., Marek, V.W., Truszczyński, M., Warren, D.S. (eds.) The Logic Programming Paradigm - A 25-Year Perspective. AI, pp. 375–398. Springer, Heidelberg (1999). https://doi.org/10.1007/978-3-642-60085-2_17
23. Mora, J., Corcho, O.: Towards a systematic benchmarking of ontology-based query rewriting systems. In: Alani, H., et al. (eds.) ISWC 2013. LNCS, vol. 8219, pp. 376–391. Springer, Heidelberg (2013). https://doi.org/10.1007/978-3-642-41338-4_24
24. Niemelä, I.: Logic programming with stable model semantics as constraint programming paradigm. Ann. Math. Artif. Intell. **25**(3–4), 241–273 (1999)
25. Ortiz, M.: Ontology based query answering: the story so far. In: AMW. CEUR Workshop Proceedings, vol. 1087. CEUR-WS.org (2013)
26. Ricca, F., et al.: A logic-based system for e-tourism. Fundam. Inform. **105**(1–2), 35–55 (2010)
27. Ricca, F., et al.: Team-building with answer set programming in the Gioia-Tauro seaport. TPLP **12**(3), 361–381 (2012)

Chain Answer Sets for Logic Programs
with Generalized Atoms

Mario Alviano[1] and Wolfgang Faber[2](✉)

[1] University of Calabria, Rende, Italy
`alviano@mat.unical.it`
[2] Alpen-Adria-Universität Klagenfurt, Klagenfurt, Austria
`wf@wfaber.com`

Abstract. Answer Set Programming (ASP) has seen several extensions
by generalizing the notion of atom used in these programs, for example dl-atoms, aggregate atoms, HEX atoms, generalized quantifiers, and
abstract constraints, referred to collectively as generalized atoms in this
paper. The idea common to all of these constructs is that their satisfaction depends on the truth values of a set of (non-generalized) atoms,
rather than the truth value of a single (non-generalized) atom. In a previous work, it was argued that for some of the more intricate generalized
atoms, the previously suggested semantics provide unintuitive results,
and an alternative semantics called supportedly stable was suggested.
Unfortunately, this semantics had a few issues on its own and also did not
have a particularly natural definition. In this paper, we present a family
of semantics called Chain Answer Sets, which has a simple, but somewhat unusual definition. We show several properties of the new semantics, including the computational complexity of the associated reasoning
tasks.

1 Introduction

The basic language of Answer Set Programming (ASP) relies on Datalog with
negation in rule bodies and possibly disjunction in rule heads. When actually
using the language for representing practical knowledge, it became apparent
that generalizations of the basic language are necessary for usability. Among the
suggested extensions are aggregate atoms (similar to aggregations in database
queries) [8,15,19,20] and atoms that rely on external truth valuations [7,9–12].
These extensions are characterized by the fact that deciding the truth values of
the new kinds of atoms depends on the truth values of a set of traditional atoms
rather than a single traditional atom. We will refer to such atoms as *generalized
atoms*, which cover also several other extensions such as abstract constraints,
generalized quantifiers, and HEX atoms.

Concerning semantics for programs containing generalized atoms, there have
been several different proposals. All of these appear to coincide for programs

---

This paper is an extended version of [5].

© Springer Nature Switzerland AG 2019
F. Calimeri et al. (Eds.): JELIA 2019, LNAI 11468, pp. 462–478, 2019.
https://doi.org/10.1007/978-3-030-19570-0_30

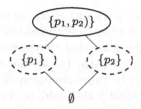

Fig. 1. Interpretations, supported (solid) and unsupported models (dashed) of the prisoners' dilemma example, where p_1 and p_2 are the propositions "the first player confesses" and "the second player confesses", respectively.

that do not contain generalized atoms in recursive definitions. The two main semantics that emerged as standards are the PSP semantics [21,22,24], and the FLP semantics [13,14] (the latter coinciding with Ferraris stable models [16] for the language considered in this paper). In [3] it was shown that the semantics coincide up to convex generalized atoms. It was already established earlier that each PSP answer set is also an FLP answer set, but not vice versa. So for programs containing non-convex generalized atoms, some FLP answer sets are not PSP answer sets. In particular, there are programs that have FLP answer sets but no PSP answer sets. In [4] it was argued that the FLP semantics is still too restrictive, and an attempt to improve the situation was made, defining the supportedly stable or SFLP (supportedly FLP) semantics. However, while SFLP solves some issues, it also introduces new ones.

Let us first review the reason why FLP is too restrictive. Consider a coordination game that is remotely inspired by the prisoners' dilemma. There are two players, each of which has the option to confess or defect. Let us also assume that both players have a fixed strategy already, which however still depends on the choice of the other player as well. In particular, each player will confess exactly if both players choose the same option, that is, if both players confess or both defect. This situation can be represented using two propositional atoms for "the first player confesses" and "the second player confesses", which must be derived true when "both players choose the same option", a composed proposition encoded by a generalized atom. A program encoding this scenario will not permit any answer set under the FLP, PSP, or any other semantics that we are aware of, except for SFLP. Also the more recent well-justified FLP [23] selects among the FLP answer sets and hence will have no answer set for this program either.

We point out that this is peculiar, as the scenario in which both players confess is a reasonable one; indeed, even a simple inflationary operator would result in this solution: starting from the empty set, the generalized atom associated with "both players choose the same option" is true; therefore, the atoms associated with "the first player confesses" and "the second player confesses" are derived true on the first application of the operator, which is also its fixpoint.

Looking at the reason why this is not an FLP answer set, we observe that it has two countermodels that prevent it from being an answer set, one in which only the first player confesses, and another one in which only the second player confesses (see Fig. 1). Both of these countermodels are models in the classical sense, but they are weak in the sense that they are not supported, meaning that there is no rule justifying their truth. In [4], the attempt to rectify this was by requiring countermodels to be supported as well (yielding SFLP), but it has clear weaknesses, most prominently that adding "tautological" rules like $p \leftarrow p$ can change the semantics of the program.

In this paper, we first define an even stronger version of this semantics, called Chain Answer Set Semantics (CHAS), which requires that countermodels are themselves answer sets of the reduct program. While at first sight it resolves the issues of SFLP, it turns out that it does not guarantee supportedness, prompting us to define two more variants, Chain Answer Set Semantics with Support (CHASS) and Supported Chain Answer Set Semantics (SCHAS), which require support in two different ways. We provide a complete analysis of the relationships among these semantics, as illustrated in Fig. 2, and show that deciding the existence of CHAS, CHASS, and SCHAS is PSPACE-complete, well above the complexity for deciding the existence of SFLP, FLP, PSP, and all other existing semantics known to us. Given the results, we believe that Chain Answer Set Semantics with Support (CHASS) is a good candidate for being the intended semantics for the class of programs considered in this paper.

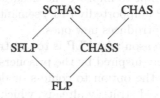

Fig. 2. Hasse diagram of subset-containment relationships between sets of answer sets (all containments are strict; FLP ⊂ SFLP proved in [4]).

2   Background

In this section we present the notation used in this paper and present the FLP semantics [13,14]. To ease the presentation, we will directly describe a propositional language here. This can be easily extended to the more usual ASP notations of programs involving variables, which stand for their ground versions (that are equivalent to a propositional program).

2.1   Notation

Let $\mathcal{B}$ be a countable set of *propositional atoms*. A *generalized atom* A on $\mathcal{B}$ is a pair (D_A, f_A), where $D_A \subseteq \mathcal{B}$ is the *domain* of A, and f_A is a mapping from

2^{D_A} to Boolean truth values $\{\mathbf{T}, \mathbf{F}\}$. To ease the presentation, we assume that the domain of each generalized atom is a finite set.

Example 1. Let p_1 represent the proposition "the first player confesses", and p_2 represent the proposition "the second player confesses." A generalized atom A representing the composed proposition "both players choose the same option" is such that $D_A = \{p_1, p_2\}$, $f_A(\{\}) = f_A(\{p_1, p_2\}) = \mathbf{T}$, and $f_A(\{p_1\}) = f_A(\{p_2\}) = \mathbf{F}$.

A general rule r is of the following form:

$$H(r) \leftarrow B(r) \tag{1}$$

where $H(r)$ is a disjunction $a_1 \vee \cdots \vee a_n$ $(n \geq 0)$ of propositional atoms in $\mathcal{B}$ referred to as the head of r, and $B(r)$ is a generalized atom on $\mathcal{B}$ called the body of r. For convenience, $H(r)$ is sometimes considered a set of propositional atoms. A general program P is a set of general rules. Let $At(P)$ denote the set of propositional atoms occurring in P.

It should be noted that this is a very abstract notation, aiming to be general enough to encompass many concrete languages. Languages adopted in practical systems will feature concrete syntax in place of generalized atoms, for example aggregate atoms or dl-atoms. In the sequel, we will at times also use more concrete notation in examples to ease reading. We will also frequently omit the term "general" when referring to general rules and general programs for simplicity.

2.2   FLP Semantics

An *interpretation* I is a subset of $\mathcal{B}$. I is a *model* for a generalized atom A, denoted $I \models A$, if $f_A(I \cap D_A) = \mathbf{T}$. Otherwise, if $f_A(I \cap D_A) = \mathbf{F}$, I is not a model of A, denoted $I \not\models A$. I is a model of a rule r of the form (1), denoted $I \models r$, if $H(r) \cap I \neq \emptyset$ whenever $I \models B(r)$. I is a model of a program P, denoted $I \models P$, if $I \models r$ for every rule $r \in P$.

Note that the fact that rule bodies are forced to be a single generalized atom is not really a limitation, and will ease the presentation of the results in the paper. In fact, a single generalized atom is sufficient for modeling conjunctions, default negation, aggregates and similar constructs.

Example 2. A conjunction $p_1 \wedge \cdots \wedge p_n$ of $n \geq 1$ propositional atoms is equivalently represented by a generalized atom A such that $D_A = \{p_1, \ldots, p_n\}$, and $f_A(B) = \mathbf{T}$ if and only if $B = \{p_1, \ldots, p_n\}$.

A conjunction $p_1, \ldots, p_m, {\sim}p_{m+1}, \ldots, {\sim}p_n$ of literals, where $n \geq m \geq 0$, $p_1, \ldots, p_n$ are propositional atoms and $\sim$ denotes *negation as failure*, is equivalently represented by a generalized atom A such that $D_A = \{p_1, \ldots, p_n\}$, and $f_A(B) = \mathbf{T}$ if and only if $\{p_1, \ldots, p_m\} \subseteq B$ and $B \cap \{p_{m+1}, \ldots, p_n\} = \emptyset$.

An aggregate $COUNT(\{p_1, \ldots, p_n\}) \neq k$, where $n \geq k \geq 0$, and $p_1, \ldots, p_n$ are propositional atoms, is equivalently represented by a generalized atom A such that $D_A = \{p_1, \ldots, p_n\}$, and $f_A(B) = \mathbf{T}$ if and only if $|B \cap D_A| \neq k$.

In the following, when convenient, we will represent generalized atoms as conjunctions of literals or aggregate atoms. Subsets of $\mathcal{B}$ mapped to true by such generalized atoms will be those satisfying the associated conjunction.

Example 3. Consider the following rules:

$$r_1: \ a \leftarrow COUNT(\{a,b\}) \neq 1 \qquad r_2: \ b \leftarrow COUNT(\{a,b\}) \neq 1$$

The following two programs show issues with FLP and later SFLP.

$$P_1 := \{r_1; r_2\} \qquad P_2 := \{r_1; r_2; a \leftarrow a\}$$

Note that if a and b are replaced by p_1 and p_2, the aggregate $COUNT(\{a,b\}) \neq 1$ is equivalent to the generalized atom A from Example 1, and therefore program P_1 encodes the coordination game depicted in the introduction.

We now describe the FLP semantics, introduced and analyzed in [13,14].

Definition 1 (FLP Reduct). *The FLP reduct P^I of a program P with respect to an interpretation I is defined as the set $\{r \in P \mid I \models B(r)\}$.*

Definition 2 (FLP Answer Sets). *An interpretation I is an FLP answer set of a program P if $I \models P$ and for each $J \subset I$ it holds that $J \not\models P^I$. Let $FLP(P)$ denote the set of FLP answer sets of P.*

Example 4. Consider the programs from Example 3:

- The models of P_1 are $\{a\}$, $\{b\}$ and $\{a,b\}$, none of which is an FLP answer set. Indeed, $P_1^{\{a\}} = P_1^{\{b\}} = \emptyset$, which have the trivial model $\emptyset$, which is of course a subset of $\{a\}$ and $\{b\}$. On the other hand $P_1^{\{a,b\}} = P_1$, and so $\{a\} \models P_1^{\{a,b\}}$, where $\{a\} \subset \{a,b\}$. We will discuss in the next section why this is a questionable situation.
- P_2 has the same models as P_1 and also no FLP answer set.

2.3   SFLP Semantics

Let us now review the SFLP semantics of [4]. As noted in the introduction, the fact that P_1 has no FLP answer sets is striking. If we first assume that both a and b are false (interpretation $\emptyset$), and then apply a generalization of the well-known one-step derivability operator, we obtain truth of both a and b (interpretation $\{a,b\}$). Applying this operator once more again yields the same interpretation, a fix-point. Interpretation $\{a,b\}$ is also a supported model, that is, for all true atoms there exists a rule in which this atom is the only true head atom, and in which the body is true.

It is instructive to examine why this seemingly robust model is not an FLP answer set. Its reduct is equal to the original program, $P_1^{\{a,b\}} = P_1$. There are therefore two models of P_1, $\{a\}$ and $\{b\}$, that are subsets of $\{a,b\}$ and therefore inhibit $\{a,b\}$ from being an FLP answer set. The problem is that, contrary to

$\{a, b\}$, these two models are rather weak, in the sense that they are not supported. Indeed, when considering $\{a\}$, there is no rule in P_1 such that a is the only true atom in the rule head and the body is true in $\{a\}$: The only available rule with a in the head has a false body. The situation for $\{b\}$ is symmetric.

SFLP stipulates that one should only consider supported models for finding inhibitors of answer sets. In other words, one does not need to worry about unsupported models of the reduct, even if they are subsets of the candidate. First, define supported models.

Definition 3 (Supportedness). *A model I of a program P is supported if for each $a \in I$ there is a rule $r \in P$ such that $I \cap H(r) = \{a\}$ and $I \models B(r)$. In this case we will write $I \models_s P$.*

Example 5. Continuing Example 4, program P_1 has one supported model, namely $\{a, b\}$. The model $\{a\}$ of P_1 is not supported because the body of the rule with a in the head has a false body with respect to $\{a\}$. For a symmetric argument, model $\{b\}$ of P_1 is not supported either. The supported models of P_2 are $\{a\}$ and $\{a, b\}$.

Now let us recall SFLP answer sets from [4].

Definition 4 (SFLP Answer Sets). *An interpretation I is an SFLP answer set of a program P if $I \models_s P$ and for each $J \subset I$ it holds that $J \not\models_s P^I$. Let $SFLP(P)$ denote the set of SFLP answer sets of P.*

Example 6. Consider again the programs from Example 3.

- Recall that P_1 has only one supported model, namely $\{a, b\}$, and $P_1^{\{a,b\}} = P_1$, but $\emptyset \not\models_s P_1^{\{a,b\}}$, $\{a\} \not\models_s P_1^{\{a,b\}}$, and $\{b\} \not\models_s P_1^{\{a,b\}}$, therefore no proper subset of $\{a, b\}$ is a supported model. Hence, it is an SFLP answer set.
- Finally, P_2 has no SFLP answer set. $\{a\}$ and $\{a, b\}$ are supported models. $P_2^{\{a,b\}} = P_2$, so $\{a\}$ prevents $\{a, b\}$ from being an SFLP answer set. $P_2^{\{a\}} = \{a \leftarrow a\}$, so $\emptyset \models P_2^{\{a\}}$ and so trivially also $\emptyset \models_s P_2^{\{a\}}$, preventing also $\{a\}$ from being an SFLP answer set.

3 Chain Answer Set Semantics

Considering P_1 and P_2 of the previous section, it is clear that SFLP answer sets have a problem. Adding a tautological rule, which should intuitively not have any effect, causes an SFLP answer set to be invalidated. In [4] we had suggested to consider "stronger notions of supportedness" for countermodels to possibly overcome this. We next try this with a radical step: requiring countermodels to be answer sets of the reduct.

Definition 5 (Chain Answer Sets). *An interpretation I is a Chain Answer Set of a program P if $I \models P$ and no $J \subset I$ is a Chain Answer Set of P^I. Let $CHAS(P)$ denote the set of Chain Answer Sets of P.*

Example 7. Reconsider the programs from Example 3.

- We get $CHAS(P_1) = \{\{a,b\}\}$. Indeed, for $\{a,b\}$ we have $\{a,b\} \models P_1$ and $P_1^{\{a,b\}} = P_1$. None of the subsets of $\{a,b\}$ ($\{a\}$, $\{b\}$, $\emptyset$) is in $CHAS(P_1^{\{a,b\}})$. $\emptyset \not\models P_1$, as the body of both rules is true, but their heads are false. Further, while $\{a\} \models P_1$ and $\{b\} \models P_1$, we observe that the bodies of both rules are false for these interpretations, so $P_1^{\{a\}} = P_1^{\{b\}} = \emptyset$, of which $\emptyset$ (a subset of both $\{a\}$ and $\{b\}$) is a trivial answer set. So $\{a\} \notin CHAS(P_1^{\{a,b\}})$ and $\{b\} \notin CHAS(P_1^{\{a,b\}})$.

- P_2 has the same three models $\{a\}$, $\{b\}$, $\{a,b\}$. $P_2^{\{a\}} = \{a \leftarrow a\}$, so of course $\emptyset \models P_2^{\{a\}}$, so $\{a\} \notin CHAS(P_2)$. $P_2^{\{b\}} = \emptyset$, so of course again $\emptyset \models P_2^{\{b\}}$, so $\{b\} \notin CHAS(P_2)$. $P_2^{\{a,b\}} = P_2$, so we have already established that no subset of $\{a,b\}$ is in $CHAS(P_2^{\{a,b\}})$, and hence $CHAS(P_2) = \{\{a,b\}\}$.

3.1   Supportedness, Anti-chain Property, Relationship to FLP

Chain Answer Sets are not necessarily supported, as the following example shows.

Example 8. Consider $P_3 = \{r_\alpha; r_\beta\}$, where

$$r_\alpha : a \leftarrow COUNT(\{a,b\}) \neq 1 \qquad r_\beta : b \leftarrow COUNT(\{a,b\}) < 2.$$

We have $\{a,b\} \models P_3$, and $P_3^{\{a,b\}} = \{r_\alpha\}$ consists only of the first rule. Again, $\emptyset \not\models P_3^{\{a,b\}}$, so $\emptyset \notin CHAS(P_3^{\{a,b\}})$. While $\{a\} \models P_3^{\{a,b\}}$ and $\{b\} \models P_3^{\{a,b\}}$, $P_3^{\{a,b\}\{a\}}$ and $P_3^{\{a,b\}\{b\}}$ are both empty, hence $\emptyset$ is a Chain Answer Set of both, and thus $\{a\} \notin CHAS(P_3^{\{a,b\}})$ and $\{b\} \notin CHAS(P_3^{\{a,b\}})$, which in turn implies $\{a,b\} \in CHAS(P_3)$.

However, $\{a,b\} \not\models_s P_3$, as for b, while $\{a,b\} \cap H(r_\beta) = \{b\}$, clearly $\{a,b\} \not\models B(r_\beta)$.

The same example shows that Chain Answer Sets do not guarantee the anti-chain property (that for any program, no Chain Answer Set is a subset of another Chain Answer Set).

Example 9. Reconsider P_3 from Example 8 and let us determine $CHAS(P_3)$. In Example 8 we have already shown that $\{a,b\} \in CHAS(P_3)$. Clearly, $\emptyset \not\models P_3$ and $\{a\} \not\models P_3$, therefore $\emptyset \notin CHAS(P_3)$ and $\{a\} \notin CHAS(P_3)$.

For the remaining interpretation $\{b\}$, we observe $\{b\} \models P_3$, and $P_3^{\{b\}}$ consists only of the second rule. But then $\emptyset \not\models P_3^{\{b\}}$, so $\emptyset \notin CHAS(P_3^{\{b\}})$, and $\{b\} \in CHAS(P_3)$.

We therefore obtain $CHAS(P_3) = \{\{b\}, \{a,b\}\}$, showing that Chain Answer Sets do not guarantee the anti-chain property.

The fact that the definition of Chain Answer Sets does not guarantee supportedness is quite disappointing. The absence of the anti-chain property is also not nice, but seems better motivated (also SFLP does not guarantee the anti-chain property), as we shall discuss in Sect. 6.

As suggested by the programs of Example 3, FLP answer sets are Chain Answer Sets, but the inverse does not necessarily hold.

Proposition 1. *For any program P, $FLP(P) \subseteq CHAS(P)$.*

Proof. By Definition 2, if $I \in FLP(P)$ then $I \models P$ and for each $J \subset I$ it holds that $J \not\models P^I$. But then no such J can be in $CHAS(P^I)$, and hence according to Definition 5, $I \in CHAS(P)$.   □

There are programs for which the inclusion is proper, as witnessed by P_1 and P_2 of Example 3.

Concerning the relationship to SFLP, the examples considered so far may suggest that SFLP answer sets are Chain Answer Sets as well, but we will show in the next section that this is not the case. As witnessed by P_2 of Example 3, there are programs that have Chain Answer Sets that are not SFLP answer sets.

4   Integrating Support with Chain Answer Sets

Since in the previous section we have seen that CHAS can be unsupported models, we now proceed with explicitly requiring support. We see two basic options, one is requiring support both for the answer set and countermodels (SCHAS), the other one is to require support for the answer set only (CHASS).

Definition 6 (Supported Chain Answer Sets). *An interpretation I is a Supported Chain Answer Set of a program P if $I \models_s P$ and no $J \subset I$ is a Supported Chain Answer Set of P^I. Let $SCHAS(P)$ denote the set of Supported Chain Answer Sets of P.*

Definition 7 (Chain Answer Sets with Support). *An interpretation I is a Chain Answer Set with Support of a program P if $I \models_s P$ and no $J \subset I$ is a Chain Answer Set of P^I. Let $CHASS(P)$ denote the set of Chain Answer Sets with Support of P.*

While at the first glance these two concepts appear to be very similar or even equivalent, it turns out that they are not. But let us first briefly revisit P_1 and P_2 of Example 3.

Example 10. Reconsider P_1 and P_2 of Example 3. Since $CHAS(P_1) = CHAS(P_2) = \{\{a, b\}\}$, and $\{a, b\} \models_s P_1$ and $\{a, b\} \models_s P_2$, it follows that $CHASS(P_1) = CHASS(P_2) = \{\{a, b\}\}$.

Concerning SCHAS, $\{a, b\}$ is the only supported model for P_1, and $P_1^{\{a,b\}} = P_1$, so none of its subsets is in $SCHAS(P_1^{\{a,b\}} = P_1)$, hence $SCHAS(P_1) = \{\{a, b\}\}$. For P_2, both $\{a\}$ and $\{a, b\}$ are supported models. Here, $P_2^{\{a\}} = \{a \leftarrow a\}$, so $\emptyset \models_s P_2^{\{a\}}$, hence $\emptyset \in SCHAS(P_2^{\{a\}})$ and $\{a\} \notin SCHAS(P_2)$. Also here $P_2^{\{a,b\}} = P_2$, so neither $\emptyset$ nor $\{b\}$ are in $SCHAS(P_2^{\{a,b\}} = P_2)$ as they are not models, and we have just shown $\{a\} \notin SCHAS(P_2^{\{a,b\}} = P_2)$, so $SCHAS(P_2) = \{\{a,b\}\}$.

From this we can immediately read off a few counterexamples for set inclusion.

Proposition 2. *There is a program P (for example P_2 of Example 3) such that all of the following hold:*

$$CHAS(P) \nsubseteq FLP(P) \qquad CHAS(P) \nsubseteq SFLP(P)$$
$$SCHAS(P) \nsubseteq FLP(P) \qquad SCHAS(P) \nsubseteq SFLP(P)$$
$$CHASS(P) \nsubseteq FLP(P) \qquad CHASS(P) \nsubseteq SFLP(P)$$

Now let us turn to P_3 from Example 8, for which CHASS and SCHAS eliminate the anomaly of CHAS by definition.

Example 11. Reconsider P_3 of Example 8. The only supported model of P_3 is $\{b\}$. $P_3^{\{b\}} = \{r_\beta\}$, and $\emptyset \not\models P_3^{\{b\}}$, so $\emptyset \notin CHAS(P_3^{\{b\}})$ and $\emptyset \notin SCHAS(P_3^{\{b\}})$, therefore $CHASS(P_3) = SCHAS(P_3) = \{\{b\}\}$.

These examples might lead one to think that CHASS and SCHAS might be equivalent. However, this is not the case, as the following example shows.

Example 12. Consider $P_4 = \{r_I; r_{II}; r_{III}\}$, where

$$r_I : a \leftarrow a, b, c \qquad r_{II} : b \leftarrow [a \vee \sim b] \qquad r_{III} : c \leftarrow a, b, c$$

We first observe that the only supported model of P_4 is $\{a, b, c\}$, while $\{b\}$, $\{a, b\}$, $\{b, c\}$ are additional unsupported models. The reduct $P_4^{\{a,b,c\}}$ is equal to P_4, so it immediately follows that $SFLP(P_4) = SCHAS(P_4) = \{\{a,b,c\}\}$ and that $\{a,b,c\} \notin FLP(P_4))$. The reducts $P_4^{\{b\}}$ and $P_4^{\{b,c\}}$ are both empty, so $\emptyset$ is a (supported) model and hence also CHAS of both, so $\{b\} \notin CHAS(P_4)$ and $\{b,c\} \notin CHAS(P_4)$. But $P_4^{\{a,b\}} = \{r_{II}\}$, and among the subsets of $\{a,b\}$, only $\{b\}$ is a model of $P_4^{\{a,b\}}$. But since $(P_4^{\{a,b\}})^{\{b\}}$ is empty, $\emptyset \in CHAS((P_4^{\{a,b\}})^{\{b\}})$, hence $\{b\} \notin CHAS(P_4^{\{a,b\}})$ and therefore $\{a,b\} \in CHAS(P_4)$. Since $P_4^{\{a,b,c\}} = P_4$, this also shows that $\{a,b,c\} \notin CHAS(P_4)$ and $\{a,b,c\} \notin CHASS(P_4)$. We therefore get $CHAS(P_4) = \{\{a,b\}\}$ and $CHASS(P_4) = \emptyset$, as $\{a,b,c\}$ is the only supported model of P_4.

In total we have $FLP(P_4) = \emptyset$, $SFLP(P_4) = \{\{a,b,c\}\}$, $CHAS(P_4) = \{\{a,b\}\}$, $CHASS(P_4) = \emptyset$, $SCHAS(P_4) = \{\{a,b,c\}\}$.

Looking at P_4, we would argue that it should not have any answer sets, as starting from everything false, one would derive b from r_{II}, which immediately annihilates the reason for b to be true, and there is no reason for a or c to become true.

From Example 12 we directly obtain a number of counterexamples for set inclusion.

Proposition 3. *There is a program P (for example P_4 of Example 12) such that all of the following hold:*

$$SFLP(P) \nsubseteq CHAS(P) \quad CHAS(P) \nsubseteq SFLP(P)$$
$$SCHAS(P) \nsubseteq CHAS(P) \quad CHAS(P) \nsubseteq SCHAS(P)$$
$$SFLP(P) \nsubseteq CHASS(P)$$
$$CHAS(P) \nsubseteq CHASS(P)$$
$$SCHAS(P) \nsubseteq CHASS(P)$$

Let us consider one more example.

Example 13. Consider $P_5 = \{r_a; r_b\}$, where

$$r_a : \ a \leftarrow COUNT(\{a, b\}) > 0 \qquad r_b : \ b \leftarrow COUNT(\{a, b\}) \neq 1$$

P_5 has two models, $\{a\}$ and $\{a, b\}$, both supported. $P_5^{\{a,b\}} = P_5$ and $P_5^{\{a\}} = \{r_a\}$. $\emptyset \models P_5^{\{a\}}$, so $\{a\}$ is not in any of $FLP(P_5)$, $SFLP(P_5)$, $CHAS(P_5)$, $CHASS(P_5)$, or $SCHAS(P_5)$. From this, it easily follows that $FLP(P_5) = \emptyset$, $SFLP(P_5) = \emptyset$, $CHAS(P_5) = \{\{a,b\}\}$, $CHASS(P_5) = \{\{a,b\}\}$, and $SCHAS(P_5) = \{\{a,b\}\}$.

From Example 13 we directly obtain some more counterexamples for set inclusion.

Table 1. Chain Answer Sets and (S)FLP answer sets of example programs, where A is the generalized atom $COUNT(\{a,b\}) \neq 1$, B is $COUNT(\{a,b\}) < 2$, and C is $COUNT(\{a,b\}) > 0$.

	Rules		Models	FLP	SFLP	CHAS	SCHAS	CHASS
P_1	$a \leftarrow A$	$b \leftarrow A$	$\{a\}, \{b\}, \{a,b\}$	—	$\{a,b\}$	$\{a,b\}$	$\{a,b\}$	$\{a,b\}$
P_2	$a \leftarrow A$	$b \leftarrow A$	$\{a\}, \{b\}, \{a,b\}$	—	—	$\{a,b\}$	$\{a,b\}$	$\{a,b\}$
	$a \leftarrow a$							
P_3	$a \leftarrow A$	$b \leftarrow B$	$\{b\}, \{a,b\}$	$\{b\}$	$\{b\}$	$\{b\}, \{a,b\}$	$\{b\}$	$\{b\}$
P_4	$a \leftarrow a,b,c$		$\{b\}, \{a,b\},$	—	$\{a,b,c\}$	$\{a,b\}$	$\{a,b,c\}$	—
	$b \leftarrow [a \vee \sim b]$							
	$c \leftarrow a,b,c$		$\{b,c\}, \{a,b,c\}$					
P_5	$a \leftarrow C$	$b \leftarrow A$	$\{a\}, \{a,b\}$	—	—	$\{a,b\}$	$\{a,b\}$	$\{a,b\}$

Proposition 4. *There is a program P (for example P_5 of Example 13) such that all of the following hold:*

$$CHASS(P) \nsubseteq SFLP(P)$$
$$SCHAS(P) \nsubseteq SFLP(P)$$

Some set inclusions do hold, however, and a few are quite easy to prove.

Proposition 5. $\forall P : FLP(P) \subseteq CHASS(P)$

Proof. From Theorem 1 in [4] ($\forall P : FLP(P) \subseteq SFLP(P)$) it follows that if $M \in FLP(P)$ then $M \models_s P$, Moreover, if $M \in FLP(P)$ then $\forall I \subsetneq M : I \not\models P^M$ and hence $\forall I \subsetneq M : I \notin CHAS(P^M)$.

Proposition 6. $\forall P : CHASS(P) \subseteq CHAS(P)$

Proof. By definition, for $M \in CHASS(P)$ we have $M \models_s P$ and $\forall I \subsetneq M : I \notin CHAS(P^M)$, therefore also $M \models P$, hence $M \in CHAS(P)$.

Proposition 7. $\forall P : SFLP(P) \subseteq SCHAS(P)$

Proof. From the definition, $M \in SFLP(P)$ if and only if $M \models_s P$ and $\forall I \subsetneq M : I \not\models_s P^M$. The latter implies $\forall I \subsetneq M : I \notin SCHAS(P^M)$ and hence $M \in SCHAS(P)$.

For completing the relationships in Fig. 2, we only miss one result, whose proof is a bit more involved.

Theorem 1. $\forall P : CHASS(P) \subseteq SCHAS(P)$

Proof. Given any program P, we show by induction on interpretations that $\forall M : M \in CHASS(P) \Rightarrow M \in SCHAS(P)$.

Base case ($M = \emptyset$): $\emptyset \in CHASS(P) \Leftrightarrow \emptyset \models_s P \Leftrightarrow \emptyset \in SCHAS(P)$ as $\forall I \subsetneq \emptyset : J \notin CHAS(P^{\emptyset})$ and $\forall I \subsetneq \emptyset : J \notin SCHAS(P^{\emptyset})$ are trivially true.

Let us now assume $M \supsetneq \emptyset$, with the hypothesis that $\forall I \subsetneq M : I \in CHASS(P) \Rightarrow I \in SCHAS(P)$. $M \in CHASS(P) \Leftrightarrow M \models_s P \wedge \forall I \subsetneq M : I \notin CHAS(P^M)$. By Proposition 6 this implies $M \models_s P \wedge \forall I \subsetneq M : I \notin CHASS(P^M)$. Using the hypothesis, this implies $M \models_s P \wedge \forall I \subsetneq M : I \notin SCHAS(P^M)$, hence $M \in SCHAS(P)$.

Looking at Table 1 and coming back to the argument that P_4 really should have no answer sets at all, we would argue that $CHASS$ is the only semantics that handles all our examples as desired, and it is therefore our candidate for the intended semantics for general programs. Also looking at Fig. 2, it seems to sit in a "sweet spot" among the other semantics, allowing for more answer sets than FLP, but not too many (as $CHAS$ and $SCHAS$) and different ones than the ill-fated $SFLP$.

5   Computational Complexity

In this section we assume that all generalized atoms are polynomial time computable, that is, given an interpretation I and a generalized atom (D_A, f_A), the computation of $f_A(I \cap D_A)$ takes time $O(|D_A|)$. Our aim is to show that for the new semantics checking the existence of an answer set of a given program is PSPACE-complete.

As for the membership, we can show that checking the existence of chain answer set for a program P belong to the complexity class Σ_n^P, where n is $|At(P)|$. The following lemma is functional to the membership result.

Lemma 1. *Let I be a set of atoms, and P be a program. Checking the existence of $J \subset I$ such that $J \in X(P)$ belongs to $\Sigma_{|I|-1}^P$, for $X \in \{CHAS, CHASS, SCHAS\}$.*

Proof. By induction on $n \geq 1$. For $n = 1$, the only candidate is $\emptyset$, and can be checked in polynomial time. As for the general case, if $X = CHAS$, then we can guess $J \subset I$ such that $J \models P$ and check whether there is no $K \subset J$ such that $K \in CHAS(P^J)$; since $|J| < |I|$, the induction hypothesis tells us that the latter check can be done in $\Pi_{|J|}^P$. Similarly, if $X = CHASS$, then we can guess $J \subset I$ such that $J \models_s P$ and check (in $\Pi_{|J|}^P$) whether there is no $K \subset J$ such that $K \in CHAS(P^J)$. Finally, if $X = SCHAS$, then we can guess $J \subset I$ such that $J \models_s P$ and check whether there is no $K \subset J$ such that $K \in SCHAS(P^J)$; since $|J| < |I|$, the induction hypothesis tells us that the latter check can be done in $\Pi_{|J|}^P$. $\qed$

Theorem 2. *Let P be a program, and n be $|At(P)|$. Checking $X(P) \neq \emptyset$ belongs to Σ_n^P, for $X \in \{CHAS, CHASS, SCHAS\}$.*

Proof. From Lemma 1 by noting that any $I \in X(P)$ is such that $I \subseteq At(P)$. $\qed$

As for the hardness, we show a reduction from *Quantified Boolean Formula* (QBF) validity. Let ψ be

$$\nexists \overline{x_1} \cdots \nexists \overline{x_m}\ \phi(\overline{x_0}, \ldots, \overline{x_m}) \qquad (2)$$

($m \geq 1$), where ϕ is quantifier-free, and $\overline{x_i}$ ($i \in [0..m]$) are distinct sets of variables; specifically, $\overline{x_0}$ are the free variables of ψ. For a given assignment $\nu_{\overline{x_0}}$ for the variables in $\overline{x_0}$, checking $\nu_{\overline{x_0}}(\psi) = 1$ is PSPACE-complete.

We define the following program $pr(\psi)$:

$$
\begin{aligned}
x_i^t \vee x_i^f &\leftarrow & \forall i \in [0..m], x_i \in \overline{x_i} \\
x_i^t &\leftarrow sat_i & \forall i \in [1..m], x_i \in \overline{x_i} \\
x_i^f &\leftarrow sat_i & \forall i \in [1..m], x_i \in \overline{x_i} \\
sat_i &\leftarrow [sat_{i-1} \vee \sim sat_i] & \forall i \in [1..m] \\
sat_m &\leftarrow (D_\phi, f_\phi) &
\end{aligned}
$$

where (D_ϕ, f_ϕ) is a generalized atom with domain $D_\phi := \{x_i^t, x_i^f \mid i \in [0..m], x_i \in \overline{x_i}\} \cup \{sat_i \mid i \in [0..m]\}$, and such that $f_\phi(I) = \mathbf{T}$ if and only if some of the following conditions are satisfied: (i) $sat_i \in I$ and $|\{x_i^t, x_i^f\} \cap I| \neq 1$ for some $i \in [0..m]$ and $x_i \in \overline{x_i}$; (ii) $|\{x_i^t, x_i^f\} \cap I| = 1$ for all $i \in [0..m]$ and $x_i \in \overline{x_i}$, and let ν_I be such that $\nu_I(x_i)$ is 1 if $x_i^t \in I$, and 0 otherwise; then, $\nu_I(\phi) = 0$.

Moreover, we define the following mapping $int(\psi, \nu_{\overline{x_0}})$ from assignments for $\overline{x_0}$ to interpretations:

$$\{x_0^t \mid x_0 \in \overline{x_0}, \nu(x_0) = 1\} \cup$$
$$\{x_0^f \mid x_0 \in \overline{x_0}, \nu(x_0) = 0\} \cup$$
$$\{x_i^t, x_i^f \mid i \in [1..m], x_i \in \overline{x_i}\}$$
$$\{sat_i \mid i \in [1..m]\}.$$

We can establish the following link between countermodels.

Lemma 2. *If* $m \geq 2$, *then for any* $J \subset int(\psi, \nu_{\overline{x_0}})$, $J \in X(pr(\psi)^{int(\psi, \nu_{\overline{x_0}})})$ *if and only if* $J \in X(pr(\sharp\overline{x_2} \cdots \sharp\overline{x_m}\ \phi))$, *for* $X \in \{CHAS, SCHAS\}$.

Proof. Since $sat_0 \notin int(\psi, \nu_{\overline{x_0}})$ and $sat_1 \in int(\psi, \nu_{\overline{x_0}})$ by construction, $sat_1 \leftarrow [sat_0 \vee {\sim}sat_1]$ is not in the reduct $pr(\psi)^{int(\psi, \nu_{\overline{x_0}})}$, which is therefore equal to the program $pr(\sharp\overline{x_2} \cdots \sharp\overline{x_m}\ \phi) \cup \{x_1^\alpha \leftarrow sat_1 \mid x_1 \in \overline{x_1}, \alpha \in \{t, f\}\}$. Note that $J \subset int(\psi, \nu_{\overline{x_0}})$ implies $sat_1 \notin J$, and therefore $(pr(\psi)^{int(\psi, \nu_{\overline{x_0}})})^J = pr(\sharp\overline{x_2} \cdots \sharp\overline{x_m}\ \phi)^J$, from which the claim follows. □

We can now establish the link between QBF validity and existence of answer sets.

Lemma 3. *For any* ψ *and* $\nu_{\overline{x_0}}$, $\nu_{\overline{x_0}}(\psi) = 1$ *if and only if* $int(\psi, \nu_{\overline{x_0}}) \in X(pr(\psi))$, *for* $X \in \{CHAS, CHASS, SCHAS\}$.

Proof. Let ψ be $\sharp\overline{x_1} \cdots \sharp\overline{x_m}\ \phi(\overline{x_0}, \ldots, \overline{x_m})$, and let us use induction on m. The base case for $m = 1$ is as follows.

($\Rightarrow$) Let $\nu_{\overline{x_0}}(\psi)$ be 1. Hence, there is no $\nu_{\overline{x_1}}$ such that $\nu_{\overline{x_0}} \circ \nu_{\overline{x_0}}(\phi) = 1$. It turns out that sat_1 must belong to any answer set in $X(pr(\psi^I))$, from which we have that $I \in X(pr(\psi))$.

($\Leftarrow$) Let $\nu_{\overline{x_0}}(\psi)$ be 0. Hence, there is $\nu_{\overline{x_1}}$ such that $\nu_{\overline{x_0}} \circ \nu_{\overline{x_1}}(\phi) = 1$. Let J be $int(\psi, \nu_{\overline{x_0}} \circ \nu_{\overline{x_1}})$. Thus, $J \subset I$ by construction, and J belongs to $CHAS(pr(\psi)^I)$ and $SCHAS(pr(\psi)^I)$. Hence, $I \notin X(pr(\psi))$.

As for the general case, let us assume the claim for some $m \geq 1$ and consider the case $m + 1$. Let I be $int(\psi, \nu_{\overline{x_0}})$.

($\Rightarrow$) Let $\nu_{\overline{x_0}}(\psi)$ be 1. Assume, by contradiction, that $I \notin X(pr(\psi))$. If $X \in \{CHAS, SCHAS\}$, then there is $J \subset I$ such that $J \in X(pr(\psi)^I)$. By Lemma 2, $J \in X(pr(\sharp\overline{x_2} \cdots \sharp\overline{x_m}\ \phi))$. Hence, we can apply the induction hypothesis: Let $\nu_{\overline{x_1}}(x_1)$ be 1 if $x_1^t \in J$, and 0 otherwise, for all $x_1 \in \overline{x_1}$; $\nu_{\overline{x_0}} \circ \nu_{\overline{x_1}}(\sharp\overline{x_2} \cdots \sharp\overline{x_m}\ \phi) = 1$, a contradiction. As for the remaining case, that is, $X = CHASS$, there is $J \subset I$ such that $J \in CHAS(pr(\psi)^I)$, and Lemma 2 implies $J \in CHAS(pr(\sharp\overline{x_2} \cdots \sharp\overline{x_m}\ \phi))$; hence, also in this case we have a contradiction.

($\Leftarrow$) Let $\nu_{\overline{x_0}}(\psi)$ be 0. Hence, there is $\nu_{\overline{x_1}}$ such that $\nu_{\overline{x_0}} \circ \nu_{\overline{x_1}}(\sharp\overline{x_2} \cdots \sharp\overline{x_m}\ \phi) = 1$. Let J be $int(\psi, \nu_{\overline{x_0}} \circ \nu_{\overline{x_1}})$. Thus, $J \subset I$ by construction. If $X \in \{CHAS, SCHAS\}$, by combining the induction hypothesis and Lemma 2 we have that $J \in X(pr(\psi)^I)$; that is, $I \notin X(pr(\psi))$. As for the remaining, that is, $X = CHASS$, we have just shown that $J \in CHAS(pr(\psi)^I)$, and therefore $I \notin CHASS(pr(\psi))$ holds. □

Moreover, any answer set of $pr(\psi)$ must be the image of some assignment.

Lemma 4. $I \in X(pr(\psi))$ *implies the existence of* $\nu_{\overline{x_0}}$ *such that* $int(\psi, \nu_{\overline{x_0}}) = I$, *for* $X \in \{CHAS, CHASS, SCHAS\}$.

Theorem 3. *Let* P *be a program, and* $X \in \{CHAS, CHASS, SCHAS\}$. *Checking* $X(P) \neq \emptyset$ *is PSPACE-complete.*

Proof. Theorem 2 gives membership. Lemma 3 and 4 give hardness.   □

6 Conclusion and Discussion

In this paper, we have first motivated why existing semantics for logic programs with generalized atoms do not seem satisfactory for all programs. An existing proposal to amend the issues, SFLP answer sets, introduces unintuitive results while fixing the highlighted issues. In this paper, we presented another attempt at defining semantics that repair the issues, named Chain Answer Sets (CHAS). The definition of CHAS looks a bit striking at first, as it refers to the defined concept itself. It is however well-defined, as the definition descends along the subset relation (even if for infinite Herbrand bases this may cause practical problems for computation).

However, it turns out that also CHAS has some peculiar properties. Most importantly, Chain Answer Sets are not necessarily supported, which is quite problematic. We then introduced two more attempts by explicitly requiring supportedness, in one case only for the answer sets (CHASS), in the other also for the countermodels (SCHAS). All versions of Chain Answer Sets (and SFLP) also do not guarantee the anti-chain property, which seems to be more of a feature than a problem, as general programs may stabilize in different ways.

Looking at Table 1, and especially at P_1 of Example 3 and P_4 of Example 12, we would argue that CHASS is the only semantics that assigns a reasonable semantics to all programs. It seems to be a good balance between extending FLP (by avoiding bogus countermodels) and overcompensating the extension in ways like SFLP, CHAS, and SCHAS do.

An interesting property is that for all versions of Chain Answer Sets the answer set existence problem is PSPACE-complete. This result suggests that the problem is most likely computationally more complex than for all the other existing semantics (being located on at most the second level of the polynomial hierarchy), and that implementations are likewise most likely to be more resource-intensive as well. However, also this might be a feature and could open an avenue for modelling more complex problems.

As future work, implementing reasoners supporting the new semantics would be of interest, for example by compiling the new semantics to FLP, so to use current ASP solvers such as DLV [6], CMODELS [18], CLASP [17], and WASP [1,2]. For Chain Answer Sets, this would lead to excessive space requirements, though, so for these a simple one-shot transformation is not likely to be viable. An application area would be systems that loosely couple OWL ontologies with rule bases, for instance by means of HEX programs.

That written, there seems to be a lack of applications involving non-convex generalized atoms that appear nonrecursively. We have experimented with a few simple domains stemming from game theory (as outlined in the introduction), but we are not aware of many other attempts. Our intuition is that such programs would be written in several domains that describe features with feedback loops, which applies to many so-called complex systems, which include models of biochemical systems.

Acknowledgments. Mario Alviano was partially supported by the European Union's Horizon 2020 research and innovation programme under the Marie Skodowska-Curie grant agreement No. 690974 for the project "MIREL: MIning and REasoning with Legal texts", by the POR CALABRIA FESR 2014–2020 projects "DLV Large Scale" (CUP J28C17000220006) and "Explora Process" (CUP J88C17000140006), by the EU H2020 PON I&C 2014–2020 project "S2BDW" (CUP B28I17000250008), and by GNCS-INdAM. Wolfgang Faber was partially supported by the S&T Cooperation CZ 05/2019 "Identifying Undoable Actions and Events in Automated Planning by Means of Answer Set Programming".

References

1. Alviano, M., Dodaro, C., Faber, W., Leone, N., Ricca, F.: WASP: a native ASP solver based on constraint learning. In: Cabalar, P., Son, T.C. (eds.) LPNMR 2013. LNCS (LNAI), vol. 8148, pp. 54–66. Springer, Heidelberg (2013). https://doi.org/10.1007/978-3-642-40564-8_6
2. Alviano, M., Dodaro, C., Ricca, F.: Anytime computation of cautious consequences in answer set programming. TPLP **14**(4–5), 755–770 (2014). https://doi.org/10.1017/S1471068414000325
3. Alviano, M., Faber, W.: The complexity boundary of answer set programming with generalized atoms under the FLP semantics. In: Cabalar, P., Son, T.C. (eds.) LPNMR 2013. LNCS (LNAI), vol. 8148, pp. 67–72. Springer, Heidelberg (2013). https://doi.org/10.1007/978-3-642-40564-8_7
4. Alviano, M., Faber, W.: Supportedly stable answer sets for logic programs with generalized atoms. In: ten Cate, B., Mileo, A. (eds.) RR 2015. LNCS, vol. 9209, pp. 30–44. Springer, Cham (2015). https://doi.org/10.1007/978-3-319-22002-4_4
5. Alviano, M., Faber, W.: Chain answer sets for logic programs with generalized atoms - how not to fix a semantic problem. In: Proceedings of the Second Workshop on Answer Set Programming and Other Computing Paradigms (TAASP 2018) (2018)
6. Alviano, M., Faber, W., Leone, N., Perri, S., Pfeifer, G., Terracina, G.: The disjunctive datalog system DLV. In: de Moor, O., Gottlob, G., Furche, T., Sellers, A. (eds.) Datalog 2.0 2010. LNCS, vol. 6702, pp. 282–301. Springer, Heidelberg (2011). https://doi.org/10.1007/978-3-642-24206-9_17
7. Calimeri, F., Cozza, S., Ianni, G.: External sources of knowledge and value invention in logic programming. Ann. Math. Artif. Intell. **50**(3–4), 333–361 (2007)

8. Dell'Armi, T., Faber, W., Ielpa, G., Leone, N., Pfeifer, G.: Aggregate functions in disjunctive logic programming: semantics, complexity, and implementation in DLV. In: Proceedings of the 18th International Joint Conference on Artificial Intelligence, IJCAI 2003, pp. 847–852. Morgan Kaufmann Publishers, Acapulco, August 2003
9. Eiter, T., Fink, M., Ianni, G., Krennwallner, T., Redl, C., Schüller, P.: A model building framework for answer set programming with external computations. TPLP **16**(4), 418–464 (2016). https://doi.org/10.1017/S1471068415000113
10. Eiter, T., Ianni, G., Lukasiewicz, T., Schindlauer, R., Tompits, H.: Combining answer set programming with description logics for the semantic web. Artif. Intell. **172**(12–13), 1495–1539 (2008). https://doi.org/10.1016/j.artint.2008.04.002
11. Eiter, T., Ianni, G., Schindlauer, R., Tompits, H.: A uniform integration of higher-order reasoning and external evaluations in answer set programming. In: International Joint Conference on Artificial Intelligence, IJCAI 2005, Edinburgh, UK, pp. 90–96, August 2005
12. Eiter, T., Lukasiewicz, T., Schindlauer, R., Tompits, H.: Combining answer set programming with description logics for the semantic web. In: Principles of Knowledge Representation and Reasoning: Proceedings of the Ninth International Conference (KR 2004), Whistler, Canada, pp. 141–151 (2004). Extended Report RR-1843-03-13. Institut für Informationssysteme, TU Wien (2003)
13. Faber, W., Leone, N., Pfeifer, G.: Recursive aggregates in disjunctive logic programs: semantics and complexity. In: Alferes, J.J., Leite, J. (eds.) JELIA 2004. LNCS (LNAI), vol. 3229, pp. 200–212. Springer, Heidelberg (2004). https://doi.org/10.1007/978-3-540-30227-8_19
14. Faber, W., Leone, N., Pfeifer, G.: Semantics and complexity of recursive aggregates in answer set programming. Artif. Intell. **175**(1), 278–298 (2011). https://doi.org/10.1016/j.artint.2010.04.002. Special Issue: John McCarthy's Legacy
15. Faber, W., Pfeifer, G., Leone, N., Dell'Armi, T., Ielpa, G.: Design and implementation of aggregate functions in the DLV system. Theory Practice Logic Program. **8**(5–6), 545–580 (2008). https://doi.org/10.1017/S1471068408003323
16. Ferraris, P.: Logic programs with propositional connectives and aggregates. ACM Trans. Comput. Log. **12**(4), 25 (2011). https://doi.org/10.1145/1970398.1970401
17. Gebser, M., Kaufmann, B., Schaub, T.: Conflict-driven answer set solving: from theory to practice. Artif. Intell. **187**, 52–89 (2012)
18. Lierler, Y., Maratea, M.: Cmodels-2: SAT-based answer set solver enhanced to non-tight programs. In: Lifschitz, V., Niemelä, I. (eds.) LPNMR 2004. LNCS (LNAI), vol. 2923, pp. 346–350. Springer, Heidelberg (2003). https://doi.org/10.1007/978-3-540-24609-1_32
19. Niemelä, I., Simons, P.: Extending the Smodels system with cardinality and weight constraints. In: Minker, J. (ed.) Logic-Based Artificial Intelligence, pp. 491–521. Kluwer Academic Publishers, Dordrecht (2000). citeseer.ist.psu.edu/niemel00extending.html
20. Niemelä, I., Simons, P., Soininen, T.: Stable model semantics of weight constraint rules. In: Gelfond, M., Leone, N., Pfeifer, G. (eds.) LPNMR 1999. LNCS (LNAI), vol. 1730, pp. 317–331. Springer, Heidelberg (1999). https://doi.org/10.1007/3-540-46767-X_23
21. Pelov, N.: Semantics of logic programs with aggregates. Ph.D. thesis, Katholieke Universiteit Leuven, Leuven, Belgium, April 2004
22. Pelov, N., Denecker, M., Bruynooghe, M.: Well-founded and stable semantics of logic programs with aggregates. Theory Practice Logic Program. **7**(3), 301–353 (2007)

23. Shen, Y., et al.: FLP answer set semantics without circular justifications for general logic programs. Artif. Intell. **213**, 1–41 (2014). https://doi.org/10.1016/j.artint.2014.05.001
24. Son, T.C., Pontelli, E.: A constructive semantic characterization of aggregates in ASP. Theory Practice Logic Program. **7**, 355–375 (2007)

Algorithm Selection for Paracoherent Answer Set Computation

Giovanni Amendola[1](✉) ⓘ, Carmine Dodaro[2] ⓘ, Wolfgang Faber[3] ⓘ,
Luca Pulina[4] ⓘ, and Francesco Ricca[1] ⓘ

[1] University of Calabria, Rende, Italy
{amendola,ricca}@mat.unical.it
[2] University of Genoa, Genoa, Italy
dodaro@dibris.unige.it
[3] University of Klagenfurt, Klagenfurt, Austria
wf@wfaber.com
[4] University of Sassari, Sassari, Italy
lpulina@uniss.it

Abstract. Answer Set Programming (ASP) is a well-established AI formalism rooted in nonmonotonic reasoning. Paracoherent semantics for ASP have been proposed to derive useful conclusions also in the absence of answer sets caused by cyclic default negation. Recently, several different algorithms have been proposed to implement them, but no algorithm is always preferable to the others in all instances. In this paper, we apply algorithm selection techniques to devise a more efficient paracoherent answer set solver combining existing algorithms. The effectiveness of the approach is demonstrated empirically running our system on existing benchmarks.

1 Introduction

Answer Set Programming (ASP) [20,21] is a powerful rule-based language for knowledge representation and reasoning that has been developed in the field of logic programming and nonmonotonic reasoning. ASP is based on the stable model (or answer set) semantics introduced in [28], and became a mainstream formalism of logic-based AI [4,26]. To solve a computational problem with ASP, one has to model it by a logic program such that its answer sets correspond to solutions; then the solutions are computed in practice by running an answer set system [21]. ASP solving technology has become mature [8,12,17,27,33,38]; and allowed for the development of practical applications in several areas [1], such as Artificial Intelligence [11,16,18,29,30], Bioinformatics [24], Databases [34,35], Game Theory [6,15], Information Extraction [2], E-learning [25].

However, a logic program may admit no answer sets due to cyclic default negation. In this case, it is not possible to draw any conclusion, even if this is not intended. To draw meaningful conclusions also from incoherent programs, paracoherent semantics based on answer sets have been proposed [13,14,40]. The

© Springer Nature Switzerland AG 2019
F. Calimeri et al. (Eds.): JELIA 2019, LNAI 11468, pp. 479–489, 2019.
https://doi.org/10.1007/978-3-030-19570-0_31

term paracoherent has been chosen to highlight both similarities and differences to paraconsistent semantics: their goal is similar, but the latter addresses classical logical contradictions, while the former addresses contradictions due to cyclic negation. Practical applications of these paracoherent semantics hinge on the availability of efficient algorithms and implementations. There is a vast potential of applications [7,13], the most immediate one being debugging of ASP, but also applications in diagnosis, planning, and reasoning about actions are conceivable. The concrete use of these paracoherent semantics depends on the availability of efficient implementations. This observation motivated the recent development of efficient evaluation techniques, including several algorithms and their implementation [9,10]. However, there is no algorithm that is always preferable to the others in all instances.

This observation can be turned into an advantage by applying algorithm selection techniques, which allow to select automatically the most promising algorithm for the instance at hand [39]. Algorithm selection techniques proved to be particularly effective when applied to ASP solvers [19,31,32,37]. Actually, ASP solvers based on these techniques have been dominating the last four editions of the ASP competition [27].

In this paper, we follow this approach and experiment with the application of algorithm selection techniques to devise a more efficient paracoherent answer set solver. The effectiveness of the approach is demonstrated empirically running our system on benchmarks from ASP competitions that have been already employed for assessing paracoherent ASP implementations [9,10].

2   Preliminaries

We start with recalling some basic notions of answer set semantics [21], paracoherent semantics [13], extended externally supported atoms [10] and the evaluation algorithms from [9].

2.1   Syntax of ASP

Given a propositional signature Σ, a *(disjunctive) rule r* is of the form

$$a_1 \vee \cdots \vee a_l \leftarrow b_1, ..., b_m, not\ c_1, ..., not\ c_n, \qquad (1)$$

where all a_i, b_j, and c_k are atoms (from Σ); $l, m, n \geq 0$, and $l + m + n > 0$; *not* represents *negation-as-failure* (sometimes also called default negation). The set $H(r) = \{a_1, ..., a_l\}$ is the *head* of r, while $B^+(r) = \{b_1, ..., b_m\}$ and $B^-(r) = \{c_1, \ldots, c_n\}$ are the *positive* and the *negative body* of r, respectively; the *body of r* is $B(r) = B^+(r) \cup B^-(r)$. We denote by $At(r) = H(r) \cup B(r)$ the set of all atoms occurring in r. A rule r is a *fact*, if $B(r) = \emptyset$ (we then omit $\leftarrow$); a *constraint*, if $H(r) = \emptyset$. Each constraint c is seen as shorthand for a rule r_c having in the head a fresh atom γ (not occurring elsewhere in the program) (i.e., $H(r_c) = \{\gamma\}$) and for the body $B^+(r_c) = B^+(c)$ and $B^-(r_c) = B^-(c) \cup \{\gamma\}$. A rule is *normal*, if

$|H(r)| \leq 1$ and *positive*, if $B^-(r) = \emptyset$. A *(disjunctive logic) program* P is a finite set of rules. P is called *normal* [resp. *positive*] if each $r \in P$ is normal [resp. positive]. We set $At(P) = \bigcup_{r \in P} At(r)$, that is the set of all atoms in P. In the following, we will also use *choice rules* [41] of the form $\{a\}$, where $a \in \Sigma$. A choice rule $\{a\}$ can be viewed as a syntactic shortcut for the rule $a \vee a_F$, where a_F is a fresh new atom not appearing elsewhere in the program, meaning that the atom a can be set to true.

2.2   Standard Semantics

Any set $I \subseteq \Sigma$ is an *interpretation*; it is a *model* of a program P (denoted $I \models P$) if and only if for each rule $r \in P$, $I \cap H(r) \neq \emptyset$ if $B^+(r) \subseteq I$ and $B^-(r) \cap I = \emptyset$ (denoted $I \models r$). A model M of P is *minimal*, if no model $M' \subset M$ of P exists. We denote by $MM(P)$ the set of all minimal models of P and by $AS(P)$ the set of all *answer sets (or stable models)* of P, i.e., the set of all interpretations I such that $I \in MM(P^I)$, where P^I is the *Gelfond-Lifschitz reduct* [28] of P w.r.t. I, i.e., the set of rules $a_1 \vee \dots \vee a_l \leftarrow b_1, \dots, b_m$, obtained from rules $r \in P$ of form (1), such that $B^-(r) \cap I = \emptyset$. We say that a program P is *coherent*, if it admits some answer set, otherwise, it is *incoherent* [5].

Now, we recall the notion of *weak constraint* [22]. A weak constraint ω is of the form $\leadsto b_1, \dots, b_m,\ not\, c_1, \dots,\ not\, c_n$. Given a program P and a set of weak constraints W, a constraint $\omega \in W$ is violated by an interpretation I if all positive atoms in ω are true, and all negated atoms are false w.r.t. I. An *optimum answer set* for $P \sqcup W$ is an answer set of P that minimizes the number of the violated weak constraints.

2.3   Paracoherent Semantics

Semi-stable semantics was introduced in [40]. Consider an extended signature $\Sigma^\kappa = \Sigma \cup \{Ka \mid a \in \Sigma\}$. Intuitively, Ka can be read as a is believed to hold. Semantically, we resort to subsets of Σ^κ as interpretations I^κ and the truth values false $\perp$, believed true **bt**, and true **t**. The truth value assigned by I^κ to an atom a is defined by $I^\kappa(a) = \mathbf{t}$, if $a \in I^\kappa$; $I^\kappa(a) = \mathbf{bt}$, if $Ka \in I^\kappa$ and $a \notin I^\kappa$; and $I^\kappa(a) = \perp$, otherwise.

Definition 1 (Epistemic κ-transformation P^κ). *Let P be a program. Then its epistemic κ-transformation is defined as the program P^κ obtained from P by replacing each rule r of the form (1) in P, such that $B^-(r) \neq \emptyset$, with:*

$$\lambda_{r,1} \vee \dots \vee \lambda_{r,l} \vee K c_1 \vee \dots \vee K c_n \leftarrow b_1, \dots, b_m \qquad (2)$$

$$a_i \leftarrow \lambda_{r,i} \qquad (3)$$

$$\leftarrow \lambda_{r,i}, c_j \qquad (4)$$

$$\lambda_{r,i} \leftarrow a_i, \lambda_{r,k} \qquad (5)$$

for $1 \leq i, k \leq l$ and $1 \leq j \leq n$, where the $\lambda_{r,i}, \lambda_{r,k}$ are fresh atoms.

For every interpretation I^κ over $\Sigma' \supseteq \Sigma^\kappa$, let $\mathcal{G}(I^\kappa) = \{Ka \in I^\kappa \mid a \notin I^\kappa\}$ denote the atoms believed true but not assigned true, also referred to as the gap of I^κ. Given a set $\mathcal{F}$ of interpretations over Σ', an interpretation $I^\kappa \in \mathcal{F}$ is *maximal canonical in* $\mathcal{F}$, if no $J^\kappa \in \mathcal{F}$ exists such that $\mathcal{G}(I^\kappa) \supset \mathcal{G}(J^\kappa)$. By $mc(\mathcal{F})$ we denote the set of maximal canonical interpretations in $\mathcal{F}$. Semi-stable models are then defined as *maximal canonical* interpretations among the answer sets of P^κ. More recently, in [10] it was identified an alternative transformation to P^κ, named the *externally supported program* of P, where a believed true atom is interpreted as an externally supported atom.

Definition 2 (Externally supported program P^s). *Let P be a program. Then its externally supported program is defined as the program P^s formed by*

$$a_1 \vee \ldots \vee a_l \leftarrow b_1, \ldots, b_m, not\, c_1, \ldots, not\, c_n, not\, Kc_1, \ldots, not\, Kc_n, \quad (6)$$
$$\{Ka\}, \quad (7)$$

for each rule r of the form (1) in P, and for each $Ka \in \Sigma^\kappa$, respectively.

This transformation leads to define the *minimal externally supported semantics* that is equivalent in spirit to the semi-stable semantics. More specifically, given a semi-stable model, there is a minimal externally supported model that has the same true and false atoms, and the same gap; and vice versa.

Semi-equilibrium Semantics. It was introduced in [13] to avoid some anomalies in semi-stable model semantics. Semi-equilibrium ones may be computed as maximal canonical answer sets of an extension of the epistemic κ-transformation.

Definition 3 (Epistemic HT-transformation P^{HT}). *Let P be a program over Σ. Then its epistemic HT-transformation P^{HT} is defined as the union of P^κ with the set of rules:*

$$Ka \leftarrow a, \quad (8)$$
$$Ka_1 \vee \ldots \vee Ka_l \vee Kc_1 \vee \ldots \vee Kc_n \leftarrow Kb_1, \ldots, Kb_m, \quad (9)$$

for $a \in \Sigma$, respectively for every rule $r \in P$ of the form (1).

Semi-equilibrium models are then defined as maximal canonical interpretations among the answer sets of P^{HT}. Amendola et al. [10] have defined an alternative transformation to P^{HT}, named *externally extended supported program*.

Definition 4 (Externally extended supported program P^{es}). *Let P be a program over Σ. Then its externally extended supported program P^{es} is defined as the union of P^s with the set of rules:*

$$Ka_1 \vee \ldots \vee Ka_l \vee Kc_1 \vee \ldots \vee Kc_n \leftarrow$$
$$Kb_1, \ldots, Kb_m, not\, a_1, \ldots, not\, a_l, not\, c_1, \ldots, not\, c_n. \quad (10)$$

for each rule $r \in P$ of the form (1).

This transformation leads to define the *minimal externally extended supported semantics* that is equivalent in spirit to the semi-equilibrium semantics. More specifically, given a semi-equilibrium model, there is a minimal externally extended supported model that has the same true and false atoms, and the same gap; and vice versa (for more details see [10]). In the following, we refer to semi-stable or semi-equilibrium models as *paracoherent answer sets*.

2.4 Evaluation Algorithms

In this section we list the state of the art algorithms to compute one paracoherent answer set, and the development of we refer the reader to [9] for more details.

First of all, we define the program $\Pi = P^{\chi} \cup P_g$, where P_g contains the following rules that capture the notion of gap: $gap(Ka) \leftarrow Ka, not\,a \,\forall a \in At(P)$, and P^{χ} denotes one of the transformations P^{κ}, P^{HT}, P^s, and P^{es}. By $gap(X)$ we denote the set of atoms in X over the predicate gap. An answer set M of Π is a paracoherent answer set of P^{χ}, if, and only if, there exists no answer set M_1 of Π such that $gap(M_1) \subset gap(M)$. In this way, the computation of a paracoherent answer set is reduced to find an answer set M of Π that is subset-minimal w.r.t. to atoms over the predicate gap. In the following, without loss of generality we assume that Π admits at least one paracoherent answer set. In fact, by properties of semi-stable and semi-equilibrium models, this kind of programs admit always a paracoherent answer set [13]. The minimization of $gap(X)$ was implemented using the following five strategies:

Guess&Check (G&C). It enumerates answer sets of Π, until one that is gap minimal is found, i.e., a candidate answer set is discarded by running a check that searches for one having a smaller gap.

Minimize. First searching for an answer set M of Π, and then checks whether it is gap-minimal, by adding a constraint enforcing that at least one atom in the gap of M should be false. This is repeated *on the same candidate answer set* until no answer sets can be found.

Split. First computes an answer set M of Π and creates a set C of gap atoms that are included in M. Then it checks for each atom in the gap of M whether it can be removed from the set to obtain a better solution.

Based on Opt. Intuitively, given the set of gap atoms A, the branching heuristic of the solver is forced to select *not p* for $p \in A$, before any other unassigned literal. When all atoms in A are assigned, standard stable model search procedure is applied without further modifications to the branching heuristic. Whenever a stable model is found, it is guaranteed to be minimal with respect to the set of objective atoms as in the algorithm *opt* of [23].

Based on Weak Constraints. The gap minimality can be obtained adding to Π the following set of weak constraints, say W: $\leadsto gap(Ka)$; $\forall a \in At(P)$. The answer set of the extended program is then an answer set of Π such that a minimal number of weak constraints in W is violated; therefore, it is also subset minimal with respect to the gap atoms, and so, it is a paracoherent answer set of P.

3   Classification Models and Experiments

In this work we leverage on an algorithm selection framework for attempting to select the best algorithm among the ones reported in the previous section.

Table 1. Selected instances from the ASP Competition 2017. In the first column we report the domain name, in the second the number of instances in each domain.

Domain	Instances
GraphColouring	42
KnightTourWithHoles	26
MinimalDiagnosis	64
QualitativeSpatialReasoning	76
StableMarriage	1
Visit-all	5

Table 2. Results of the considered paracoherent answer set solvers (computation of semi-stable models). The table is organized as follows. The first column shows the instance domain name, the remaining ones the considered algorithms. Each of latter columns is divided into two cells, one ("#") for the total amount of solved instances and one ("T") for the average CPU time (in seconds) on solved instances.

Domain	G&C		Minimize		Split		Pref		Weak		ME$_{SS}$		VBS	
	#	T	#	T	#	T	#	T	#	T	#	T	#	T
GraphCol	0	–	0	–	42	0.20	0	–	0	–	42	0.20	42	0.20
KnightTour	0	–	0	–	3	437.84	2	148.77	1	25.95	5	322.21	5	322.21
MinDiagn	64	243.56	64	59.20	64	67.77	64	70.42	64	204.49	64	66.95	64	53.24
QSR	28	216.22	45	298.47	46	181.59	55	243.40	38	315.49	57	230.71	59	222.15
StableMarr	0	–	0	–	0	–	0	–	0	–	0	–	0	–
Visit-all	5	52.27	5	110.00	5	0.66	5	19.58	5	20.69	5	0.66	5	0.66
Total	97	225.81	114	155.88	160	87.60	126	145.16	108	233.39	173	105.49	175	103.64

In our case, this selection is possible because we represent a ground ASP program as a set of *features*, i.e., numeric values representing particular characteristics of a given instance. The selection is automated by modeling the algorithm selection problem as a *multinomial classification* problem, where is given a set of patterns, i.e., input vectors $X = \{\underline{x}_1, \dots \underline{x}_k\}$ with $\underline{x}_i \in \mathbb{R}^n$, and a corresponding set of labels, i.e., output values $Y \in \{1, \ldots, m\}$, where Y is composed of values representing the m classes of the multinomial classification problem.

In our model, the m classes are m systems implementing the algorithms previously described. We think of the labels as generated by some unknown function $f : \mathbb{R}^n \to \{1, \ldots, m\}$ applied to the patterns, i.e., $f(\underline{x}_i) = y_i$ for $i \in \{1, \ldots, k\}$ and $y_i \in \{1, \ldots, m\}$. Given a set of patterns X and a corresponding set of labels Y, the task of a multinomial classifier c is to extrapolate f given X and Y, i.e., construct c from X and Y so that when we are given some $\underline{x}^\star \in X$ we should ensure that $c(\underline{x}^\star)$ is equal to $f(\underline{x}^\star)$. This task is called *training*, and the pair (X, Y) is called the *training set*.

In order to implement the framework mentioned above and apply it in our case, the first step consists in designing a set of (cheap-to-compute) features that are significant for classifying the instances. To do that, as a starting point we considered the set used in the multi-engine solver ME-ASP and we extended it with features that can be relevant for this application. In detail:

- **Problem size features:** number of rules r, number of atoms a, ratios r/a, $(r/a)^2$, $(r/a)^3$ and ratios reciprocal a/r, $(a/r)^2$ and $(a/r)^3$;
- **Balance features:** fraction of unary, binary and ternary rules;
- **"Proximity to horn" features:** fraction of horn rules;
- **ASP specific features:** number of true and disjunctive facts, fraction of normal rules and constraints c, number of choice rules, number of aggregates and number of weak constraints.
- **Paracoherent ASP specific features:** number of atoms to minimize (i.e., atoms over the predicate gap), number of negative literals, number of combinations of these with problem size features.

This final choice of features, together with some of their combinations, amounts to a total of 49 features. Note that the number of atoms to minimize and number of negative literals are strongly related to the size of the search space for the minimization algorithms. Indeed, the presence (and thus the number) of negative literals affects both indirectly (since paracoherent answer sets are caused by odd negative ciclyes) and directly (since the program produced by applying the techniques from [10] introduces many additional negative literals) the computation of paracoherent answer sets in all the proposed algorithms.

In order to train the classifiers, we have to select a pool of instances for training purpose. In particular, from the last ASP competition we selected a total amount of 214 instances comprised of the domains listed in Table 1. We selected all the incoherent instances that do not feature in the encoding neither *aggregates*, nor *choice rules*, nor *weak constraints*, since such features are not currently supported by the paracoherent semantics [13]. Note that we consider the same benchmarks used in [9,10].

Concerning the choice of a multinomial classifier algorithm, we considered a classifier able to deal with numerical features and multinomial class labels (the solvers). According to the study on multi-engine ASP solving [36,37], we selected k-*Nearest-Neighbor*, NN in the following. NN is a classifier yielding the label of the training instance which is closer to the given test instance, whereby closeness is evaluated using some proximity measure, e.g., Euclidean distance, and training instances are stored in order to have fast look-up, see, e.g., [3].

To deal with the proper algorithm selection related to the two semantics, we built two different classification models and we implement them in two different tools. In the following, ME_{SE} and ME_{SS} will denote the system related to the computation of semi-stable and semi-equilibrium models, respectively, and in Tables 2 and 3 we report the related results.

Table 3. Results of the considered paracoherent answer set solvers (computation of semi-equilibrium models). The table is organized like Table 2.

Domain	G&C		Minimize		Split		Pref		Weak		ME_{SE}		VBS	
	#	T	#	T	#	T	#	T	#	T	#	T	#	T
GraphCol	0	–	0	–	42	1.06	0	–	0	–	42	1.06	42	1.06
KnightTour	0	–	0	–	3	49.71	2	83.97	2	129.76	4	73.27	5	63.41
MinDiagn	0	–	8	809.64	8	908.01	58	74.74	58	214.94	58	74.74	58	74.74
QSR	0	–	0	–	0	–	0	–	0	–	0	–	0	–
StableMarr	0	–	0	–	0	–	0	–	0	–	0	–	0	–
Visit-all	5	29.21	5	40.19	5	1.67	5	22.89	5	17.47	5	2.32	5	1.60
Total	5	29.21	13	513.70	58	128.73	65	71.04	65	197.12	109	43.36	110	42.77

ME_{SS} and ME_{SE} have been compared with the algorithms used, as well as with the Virtual Best Solver (VBS), i.e., considering a problem instance, the oracle that always fares the best among available solvers. To do that, for the proposed systems we report the cumulative results of a *stratified 10-times 10-fold cross validation*. Given a training set (X, Y), we partition X in subsets X_i with $i \in \{1, \ldots 10\}$ such that $X = \bigcup_{i=1}^{10} X_i$ and $X_i \cap X_j = \emptyset$ whenever $i \neq j$; we then train $c_{(i)}$ on the patterns $X_{(i)} = X \setminus X_i$ and corresponding labels $Y_{(i)}$. We repeat the process 10 times, to yield 10 different c and we obtain the global performance. The considered value of k in the NN algorithm was 1.

Looking at the tables, we can see that, in general, the proposed systems are able to solve more instances with respect to their components, and their performance is very close to the one reported for the VBS.

Concerning Table 2, ME_{SS} returned a bad prediction only for 2 instances out of 76 in the QualitativeSpatialReasoning (QSR), while considering the remaining domains, it replicates the performance of VBS with the exception of what happened in MinimalDiagnosis (MinDiag), where we report for ME_{SS} an average CPU time about 20% higher than the time reported for the VBS.

Finally, looking at Table 3, we report that ME_{SE} emulates the behaviour of the VBS in all domains but KnightTourWithHoles and Visit-all. Considering the former, it was able to solve 1 instance less, while in the case of the latter, the predicted solver was slightly slower than the best one.

4   Conclusion

In this paper we studied whether it is possible to take advantage of algorithm selection techniques based on classification algorithms to select the best algorithm for computing paracoherent answer sets. The conducted experiments provided an empirical positive answer to this question. We want to emphasise here that the selection of appropriate features is not an easy task, in general. Among the set of all possible features, one has to select a suitable subset of them to maximise the performance of the classifier. This requires deep knowledge of standard ASP, paracoherent semantics, and machine learning techniques, so it might have an impact of on other researchers that have to deal with similar problems.

Acknowledgments. This work has been supported by the European Union's Horizon 2020 research and innovation programme under the Marie Skodowska-Curie grant agreement No. 690974 for the project "MIREL: MIning and REasoning with Legal texts".

References

1. Adrian, W.T., et al.: The ASP system DLV: advancements and applications. KI **32**(2–3), 177–179 (2018)
2. Adrian, W.T., Manna, M., Leone, N., Amendola, G., Adrian, M.: Entity set expansion from the web via ASP. In: ICLP (Technical Communications). OASICS, vol. 58, pp. 1:1–1:5. Schloss Dagstuhl - Leibniz-Zentrum fuer Informatik (2017)
3. Aha, D., Kibler, D., Albert, M.: Instance-based learning algorithms. Mach. Learn. **6**(1), 37–66 (1991)
4. Alviano, M., Amendola, G., Peñaloza, R.: Minimal undefinedness for fuzzy answer sets. In: AAAI 2017, pp. 3694–3700 (2017)
5. Amendola, G.: Dealing with incoherence in ASP: split semi-equilibrium semantics. In: DWAI@AI*IA. CEUR Workshop Proceedings, vol. 1334, pp. 23–32 (2014)
6. Amendola, G.: Preliminary results on modeling interdependent scheduling games via answer set programming. In: RiCeRcA@AI*IA. CEUR Workshop Proceedings, vol. 2272. CEUR-WS.org (2018)
7. Amendola, G.: Solving the stable roommates problem using incoherent answer set programs. In: RiCeRcA@AI*IA. CEUR Workshop Proceedings, vol. 2272 (2018)
8. Amendola, G.: Towards quantified answer set programming. In: RCRA@FLoC. CEUR Workshop Proceedings, vol. 2271. CEUR-WS.org (2018)
9. Amendola, G., Dodaro, C., Faber, W., Leone, N., Ricca, F.: On the computation of paracoherent answer sets. In: AAAI, pp. 1034–1040 (2017)
10. Amendola, G., Dodaro, C., Faber, W., Ricca, F.: Externally supported models for efficient computation of paracoherent answer sets. In: AAAI 2018, pp. 1034–1040 (2018)
11. Amendola, G., Dodaro, C., Leone, N., Ricca, F.: On the application of answer set programming to the conference paper assignment problem. In: Adorni, G., Cagnoni, S., Gori, M., Maratea, M. (eds.) AI*IA 2016. LNCS (LNAI), vol. 10037, pp. 164–178. Springer, Cham (2016). https://doi.org/10.1007/978-3-319-49130-1_13

12. Amendola, G., Dodaro, C., Ricca, F.: ASPQ: an ASP-based 2QBF solver. In: QBF@SAT. CEUR Workshop Proceedings, vol. 1719, pp. 49–54 (2016)
13. Amendola, G., Eiter, T., Fink, M., Leone, N., Moura, J.: Semi-equilibrium models for paracoherent answer set programs. Artif. Intell. **234**, 219–271 (2016)
14. Amendola, G., Eiter, T., Leone, N.: Modular paracoherent answer sets. In: Fermé, E., Leite, J. (eds.) JELIA 2014. LNCS (LNAI), vol. 8761, pp. 457–471. Springer, Cham (2014). https://doi.org/10.1007/978-3-319-11558-0_32
15. Amendola, G., Greco, G., Leone, N., Veltri, P.: Modeling and reasoning about NTU games via answer set programming. In: IJCAI 2016, pp. 38–45 (2016)
16. Amendola, G., Ricca, F., Truszczynski, M.: Generating hard random Boolean formulas and disjunctive logic programs. In: IJCAI, pp. 532–538 (2017)
17. Amendola, G., Ricca, F., Truszczynski, M.: A generator of hard 2QBF formulas and ASP programs. In: KR. AAAI Press (2018)
18. Amendola, G., Ricca, F., Truszczynski, M.: Random models of very hard 2QBF and disjunctive programs: an overview. In: ICTCS. CEUR Workshop Proceedings, CEUR-WS.org (2018)
19. Balduccini, M.: Learning and using domain-specific heuristics in ASP solvers. AICOM **24**(2), 147–164 (2011)
20. Bonatti, P., Calimeri, F., Leone, N., Ricca, F.: Answer set programming. In: Dovier, A., Pontelli, E. (eds.) A 25-Year Perspective on Logic Programming. LNCS, vol. 6125, pp. 159–182. Springer, Heidelberg (2010). https://doi.org/10.1007/978-3-642-14309-0_8
21. Brewka, G., Eiter, T., Truszczynski, M.: Answer set programming at a glance. Commun. ACM **54**(12), 92–103 (2011)
22. Buccafurri, F., Leone, N., Rullo, P.: Enhancing disjunctive datalog by constraints. IEEE Trans. Knowl. Data Eng. **12**(5), 845–860 (2000)
23. Di Rosa, E., Giunchiglia, E., Maratea, M.: Solving satisfiability problems with preferences. Constraints **15**(4), 485–515 (2010)
24. Erdem, E., Öztok, U.: Generating explanations for biomedical queries. TPLP **15**(1), 35–78 (2015). https://doi.org/10.1017/S1471068413000598
25. Garro, A., Palopoli, L., Ricca, F.: Exploiting agents in e-learning and skills management context. AI Commun. **19**(2), 137–154 (2006)
26. Gebser, M., Leone, N., Maratea, M., Perri, S., Ricca, F., Schaub, T.: Evaluation techniques and systems for answer set programming: a survey. In: IJCAI, pp. 5450–5456 (2018)
27. Gebser, M., Maratea, M., Ricca, F.: The sixth answer set programming competition. J. Artif. Intell. Res. **60**, 41–95 (2017)
28. Gelfond, M., Lifschitz, V.: Classical negation in logic programs and disjunctive databases. New Gener. Comput. **9**(3/4), 365–386 (1991)
29. Grasso, G., Iiritano, S., Leone, N., Lio, V., Ricca, F., Scalise, F.: An ASP-based system for team-building in the gioia-tauro seaport. In: Carro, M., Peña, R. (eds.) PADL 2010. LNCS, vol. 5937, pp. 40–42. Springer, Heidelberg (2010). https://doi.org/10.1007/978-3-642-11503-5_5
30. Grasso, G., Iiritano, S., Leone, N., Ricca, F.: Some DLV applications for knowledge management. In: Erdem, E., Lin, F., Schaub, T. (eds.) LPNMR 2009. LNCS (LNAI), vol. 5753, pp. 591–597. Springer, Heidelberg (2009). https://doi.org/10.1007/978-3-642-04238-6_63
31. Hoos, H., Kaminski, R., Schaub, T., Schneider, M.T.: ASPeed: ASP-based solver scheduling. In: Technical Communications of ICLP 2012. LIPIcs, vol. 17, pp. 176–187 (2012)

32. Hoos, H., Lindauer, M.T., Schaub, T.: Claspfolio 2: advances in algorithm selection for answer set programming. TPLP **14**(4–5), 569–585 (2014)
33. Lierler, Y., Maratea, M., Ricca, F.: Systems, engineering environments, and competitions. AI Mag. **37**(3), 45–52 (2016)
34. Manna, M., Ricca, F., Terracina, G.: Consistent query answering via ASP from different perspectives: theory and practice. TPLP **13**(2), 227–252 (2013)
35. Manna, M., Ricca, F., Terracina, G.: Taming primary key violations to query large inconsistent data via ASP. TPLP **15**(4–5), 696–710 (2015)
36. Maratea, M., Pulina, L., Ricca, F.: Applying machine learning techniques to ASP solving. In: Technical Communications of ICLP 2012. LIPIcs, vol. 17, pp. 37–48 (2012)
37. Maratea, M., Pulina, L., Ricca, F.: A multi-engine approach to answer-set programming. TPLP **14**(6), 841–868 (2014)
38. Maratea, M., Ricca, F., Faber, W., Leone, N.: Look-back techniques and heuristics in DLV: implementation, evaluation, and comparison to QBF solvers. J. Algorithms **63**(1–3), 70–89 (2008)
39. Rice, J.R.: The algorithm selection problem. Adv. Comput. **15**, 65–118 (1976)
40. Sakama, C., Inoue, K.: Paraconsistent stable semantics for extended disjunctive programs. J. Log. Comput. **5**(3), 265–285 (1995)
41. Simons, P., Niemelä, I., Soininen, T.: Extending and implementing the stable model semantics. Artif. Intell. **138**(1–2), 181–234 (2002)

Extending Bell Numbers
for Parsimonious Chase Estimation

Giovanni Amendola[iD] and Cinzia Marte[(✉)][iD]

University of Calabria, Rende, Italy
{amendola,marte}@mat.unical.it

Abstract. Ontology-Based Query Answering (OBQA) consists in querying databases by taking ontological knowledge into account. We focus on a logical framework based on existential rules or tuple generating dependencies (TGDs), also known as Datalog$^{\pm}$, which collects the basic decidable classes of TGDs, and generalizes several ontology specification languages, such as Description Logics. A fundamental notion to find certain answers to a query is the chase. This tool has been widely used to deal with different problems in databases, as it has the fundamental property of constructing a universal model. Recently, the so-called "parsimonious" chase procedure has been introduced. For some classes, it is sound and complete, and the termination is always guaranteed. However, no precise bound has been provided so far. To this end, we exploit the Bell number definition to count the exact maximal number of atoms generating by the parsimonious chase procedure.

Keywords: OBQA · Existential rules · Parsimonious chase · Bell numbers

1 Introduction

Ontology-Based Query Answering (OBQA) consists in querying databases by taking ontological knowledge into account. It is a fascinating research topic deeply studied not only in database theory [1,12], but also in artificial intelligence [5,6,10] and in logic [2,3,11]. Moreover, OBQA is strictly related to others important application areas such as data integration [20], data exchange [8], and consistent query answering [22,23]. In particular, OBQA is the problem of answering a query q against a logical theory consisting of an extensional database D paired with an ontology Σ. The goal is to find certain answers to q, i.e. the query must be true in every possible model of the theory [7,19]. Here, we focus on ontologies expressed via existential rules, also known as tuple generating dependencies (TGDs) or datalog$^{\exists}$ rules. They are at the core of Datalog$^{\pm}$ [13], an emerging family of ontology languages, which collects the basic decidable classes of TGDs, and generalizes several ontology specification languages such as Description Logics (DLs) [9]. Indeed, datalog$^{\exists}$ generalizes the well-known language Datalog [15] with existential quantification in the head.

© Springer Nature Switzerland AG 2019
F. Calimeri et al. (Eds.): JELIA 2019, LNAI 11468, pp. 490–497, 2019.
https://doi.org/10.1007/978-3-030-19570-0_32

OBQA can be reduced to the problem of answering q over a universal model U that can be homomorphically embedded into every other model of the logical theory. A way to compute a universal model is to employ the so called chase procedure. Starting from D, the chase "repairs" violations of rules by repeatedly adding new atoms–introducing fresh values, called nulls, whenever required by an existential variable–until a fixed point satisfying all rules is reached. Therefore, in the classical setting, the chase is sound and complete. But, unfortunately, the chase does not always terminates [16,17].

Recently, in [21] a new class of datalog$^\exists$ ontologies, called Shy, has been singled out for existential rules. It enjoys a new semantic property called *parsimony* and results in a powerful and decidable class that combines positive aspects of different Datalog$^\pm$ classes [4]. The parsimony property is based on the *parsimonious chase* (pchase) procedure that repairs violations of rules only if the (inferred) head atom can not be homomorphically mapped to any atom previously produced. For some classes of Datalog$^\pm$, the parsimony property is sound and complete with respect to atomic query answering. Moreover, the termination of the pchase is always guaranteed, and computational complexity has been studied [21]. However, to understand the nature of the pchase procedure, we need to understand what kind of atoms belong to the pchase. This has as side effect and it is strictly related to count the number of atoms generated by the pchase. An immediate consequence of this better understanding of the chase leads to re-prove computational complexity results, as we improve the upper bounds previously identified in [21]. Indeed, these are very large, as they are aimed at demonstrating computational complexity, and not how many atoms can be produced by the chase.

In this paper, to the best of our knowledge, we present the first study in OBQA that goes on this direction by providing an exact upper bound for the pchase. To this end, we exploit the notion of "equality type" defined in [18], which we show to be strictly related to the form of non-isomorphic atoms of a given predicate. Then, by exploiting the notion of Bell numbers, counting the number of distinct partitions of a finite set, we compute an upper bound for the number of atoms generating by the pchase procedure. Finally, we show that there exists a family of ontologies for which the pchase can produce exactly the upper bound previously computed, so that it corresponds to the maximal number of atoms effectively generated by the pchase procedure.

2 Preliminaries

Throughout this paper we use the following notation. Let $\Delta = \Delta_C \cup \Delta_N \cup \Delta_V$ the domain of the *terms*, consisting of the union of the three countably infinite domains of *constants*, *nulls* and *variables*, respectively. We write φ to denote a null; X a variable; $\underline{a}$ an atom, that is an expression of the form $p(\mathbf{t})$, where $p = pred(\underline{a})$ is a predicate, $\mathbf{t} = t_1, \ldots, t_k$ is a *tuple* of terms, $k = arity(\underline{a})$ is the arity of $\underline{a}$ or p, and $\underline{a}[i]$ is the i-th term of $\underline{a}$. Moreover, $const(\underline{a})$ (resp., $vars(\underline{a})$) is the set of constants (resp., variables) occurring in $\underline{a}$. The set of predicates is denoted by $\mathcal{R}$. Let $T \subseteq \Delta$ a nonempty subset, then the set of all atoms that can be formed with predicates of $\mathcal{R}$ and terms from T is denoted by $base(T)$. Moreover, any subset of $base(\Delta_C \cup \Delta_N)$ constitutes an *instance* I, and whenever $I \subseteq base(\Delta_C)$, then it is also called *database*. A *substitution* is a total mapping $s : \Delta \rightarrow \Delta$. Let χ_1 and χ_2 be two structures containing atoms. An *homomorphism* $h : \chi_1 \rightarrow \chi_2$ is a substitution such that: (i) if $c \in \Delta_C$, then $h(c) = c$; (ii) if $\varphi \in \Delta_N$, then $h(\varphi) \in \Delta_C \cup \Delta_N$; (iii) $h(\chi_1)$ is a substructure of χ_2. An *existential rule* r is a logical implication of the form $\forall \mathbf{X} \forall \mathbf{Y} (\exists \mathbf{Z}\ \underline{a}(\mathbf{X}, \mathbf{Z}) \leftarrow \phi(\mathbf{X}, \mathbf{Y}))$, where $\mathbf{X}$, $\mathbf{Y}$, and $\mathbf{Z}$ denote sets of variables; $head(r) = \underline{a}(\mathbf{X}, \mathbf{Z})$, while $body(r) = \phi(\mathbf{X}, \mathbf{Y})$ is a conjunction of atoms and can also be empty. We define a datalog$^\exists$ program P as a finite set of existential rules, called ontology and denoted by $dep(P)$ (*dependencies* of P), paired with a database instance, denoted by $data(P)$. Moreover, $pred(P)$ (resp., $const(P)$) represents the set of predicates (resp., constants) occurring in (P) and $arity(P)$ is the maximum arity over $pred(P)$.

Given an instance I, we say that a rule r *is satisfied by* I if whenever there is a homomorphism $h : body(r) \rightarrow I$, there is a homomorphism $h' \supset h|_{vars(body(r))}$ s.t. $h' : head(r) \rightarrow I$. An instance I is a *model* of a program P if each rule of $dep(P)$ is satisfied by I, and $data(P) \subseteq I$. A *firing homomorphism* for r and I is any homomorphism $h : body(r) \rightarrow I$ s.t. $h = h|_{vars(body(r))}$. The *fire* of r via h produces the atom $fire(r, h) = \sigma(h(head(r)))$, where $\sigma = \sigma|_{vars(h(head(r)))}$ (i.e., it replaces each existential variable of r with a different fresh null). Given a firing homomorphism h for a rule r and an instance I, we say that the pair $\langle r, h \rangle$ satisfies the *parsimonious fire condition* w.r.t. an instance $I' \supseteq I$ if there is no homomorphism from $\{h(head(r))\}$ to I'. Finally, given a datalog$^\exists$ program P, the *parsimonious chase* (pchase) of P ($pchase(P)$) is constructed as follows. We start from $I' = data(P)$ and create a copy of it in I. Then, for each r in $dep(P)$, for each unspent firing homomorphism h for the pair $\langle r, I \rangle$ we add the $fire(r, h)$ to I' if $\langle r, h \rangle$ satisfies the parsimonious fire condition w.r.t. I'. If $I \neq I'$, we create a new copy of I' and repeat the previous steps. Otherwise, we return I.

3   Parsimonious Chase Estimation

In this section, we introduce some basic notions that will help us to find a tight upper bound for the pchase. We highlight a main property of the pchase, based on isomorphic atoms, a crucial notion in several Datalog$^\pm$ classes [14].

Theorem 1. *Given a program P, $pchase(P)$ does not contain isomorphic atoms.*

Proof. Assume, by contradiction, that there are two isomorphic atoms $\underline{a}$ and $\underline{a}'$ in $pchase(P)$. Thus, there is a homomorphism h from $\{\underline{a}\}$ to $\{\underline{a}'\}$ s.t. h^{-1} is a homomorphism from $\{\underline{a}'\}$ to $\{\underline{a}\}$. W.l.o.g. assume that $\underline{a} \in I$, for some I generated during the pchase procedure. As $\underline{a}' \in pchase(P)$, then there is a rule r, an instance $I' \supseteq I$, and an unspent firing homomorphism h' for $\langle r, I' \rangle$, s.t. $fire(r, h') = \underline{a}'$, against the fact that $h^{-1} \circ \sigma$ is a homomorphism from

$\{h'(head(r))\}$ to I'. Indeed, $(h^{-1} \circ \sigma)(h'(head(r))) = h^{-1}(\sigma(h'(head(r)))) = h^{-1}(fire(r, h')) = h^{-1}(\underline{a}') = \underline{a} \in I \subseteq I'$. $\qquad\square$

To provide a precise upper bound for the number of steps execute by the pchase, we introduce the concept of *type* that is equivalent to the notion of equality type defined in [18].

Definition 1 (Type). *Let m be a positive integer, S an arbitrary partition of $\{1, \ldots, m\}$, C a set with $|C| \leq |S|$, and $f : C \to S$ an injective map. We define the type of S, C and f as the family of sets $T(S, C, f) = \{s \cup f^{-1}(s) \mid s \in S\}$.*

Example 1. Let $m = 6$, $C = \{c_1, c_2\}$, and let $S = \{\{1, 2\}, \{3, 6\}, \{4\}, \{5\}\}$ be a partition of $\{1, \ldots, 6\}$. Consider the injective map $f : C \to S$ such that $f(c_1) = \{3, 6\}$ and $f(c_2) = \{5\}$. Then, $T(S, C, f) = \{\{1, 2\}, \{3, 6, c_1\}, \{4\}, \{5, c_2\}\}$.

Fixed an integer m, our aim is to count the number of all possible types that can be generated from any partition of the set $\{1, \ldots, m\}$, by varying C on a superset D of a fixed size d. In order to do this, we resort to the Bell number B_n, that is the number of ways to partition a set of n labeled elements.

Theorem 2. *Let $m \in \mathbb{N}$, D a finite set of size $d > 0$, and B_n the n-th Bell number. Hence, the number of all possible types generated from all the partitions of the set $\{1, \ldots, m\}$ and all subsets of D is given by $\gamma_m^d = \sum_{h=0}^{m} \binom{m}{h} d^h B_{m-h}$.*

Proof Sketch. Recall that, given two sets A and B with $|A| = \alpha \leq |B| = \beta$, the number of injective maps from A to B is $\frac{\beta!}{(\beta-\alpha)!}$. Then, fixed a partition S of $\{1, ..., m\}$ with $|S| = s$, the number of injective maps from any subset $C \subseteq D$ to S, with $|C| = c \leq s$, is $\frac{s!}{(s-c)!}$, while the number of subsets of size c is $\binom{d}{c}$. Thus, the number of all possible types for the fixed partition S is $\sum_{c=0}^{min\{s,d\}} \binom{d}{c} \cdot \frac{s!}{(s-c)!}$. Hence, the number of types generated from all the partitions of the set $\{1, \ldots, m\}$ and all subsets of D is given by $\sum_{s=1}^{m} S(m, s) \cdot \sum_{c=0}^{min\{s,d\}} \binom{d}{c} \cdot \frac{s!}{(s-c)!}$, where $S(m, s)$ is the Stirling number counting the number of partitions of size s on m elements. It can be shown that it is equivalent to γ_m^d. $\qquad\square$

Taking advantage of the notion of type, we can provide a new representation of an arbitrary atom.

Definition 2 (Atom Type). *Given an atom $\underline{a} = p(t)$ of arity m, we define the type of the atom $\underline{a}$ as $T_{\underline{a}} = T(S, C, f)$, where $C = const(\underline{a})$; $S = \{\{n \mid \underline{a}[n] = t_i\} \mid i = 1, \ldots, m\}$; and $f : C \to S$ such that $f(c) = \{n \mid \underline{a}[n] = c\}$.*

Hence, the type of an atom $\underline{a}$ has the form $T_{\underline{a}} = \{\sigma(t_1), \ldots, \sigma(t_m)\}$, where σ is such that $\sigma(t_i) = \{n \mid n \in \{1, \ldots, m\} \wedge \underline{a}[n] = t_i\} \cup \{t_i\}$ if t_i is a constant, and $\sigma(t_i) = \{n \mid n \in \{1, \ldots, m\} \wedge \underline{a}[n] = t_i\}$ otherwise. Intuitively, the type of an atom is formed by the sets of positions where a term occurs, by highlighting positions where constants occur.

Example 2. Let $\underline{a} = p_1(\varphi_1, \varphi_3, \varphi_2, \varphi_1)$ and $\underline{b} = p_2(c, \varphi_1, d, c, \varphi_2, \varphi_2, \varphi_1)$. Then, $T_{\underline{a}} = \{\{1,4\}, \{2\}, \{3\}\}$ and $T_{\underline{b}} = \{\{1,4,c\}, \{2,7\}, \{3,d\}, \{5,6\}\}$.

Theorem 3. *Let $\underline{a} = p(t_1, \ldots, t_k)$ and $\underline{a}' = p(t'_1, \ldots, t'_k)$ be two atoms. Then, $\underline{a}$ and $\underline{a}'$ are isomorphic if, and only if, $pred(\underline{a}) = pred(\underline{a}')$ and $T_{\underline{a}} = T_{\underline{a}'}$.*

Proof. Let us consider two atoms $\underline{a}$ and $\underline{a}'$. If $pred(\underline{a}) \neq pred(\underline{a}')$ or $arity(\underline{a}) \neq arity(\underline{a}')$, then of course can not exists an isomorphism between them. Hence, we can take for granted that the two atoms have same predicate and arity. [$\Rightarrow$] Assume that there is an isomorphism between $\underline{a}$ and $\underline{a}'$, i.e., there is a homomorphism $h : \{\underline{a}\} \rightarrow \{\underline{a}'\}$ s.t. $h(t_i) = t'_i$, $i = 1, \ldots, k$ and s.t. $h^{-1} : \{\underline{a}'\} \rightarrow \{\underline{a}\}$ is a homomorphism. Let $T_{\underline{a}} = \{\sigma(t_1), \ldots, \sigma(t_k)\}$ and $T_{\underline{a}'} = \{\sigma'(t_1), \ldots, \sigma'(t_k)\}$. We claim that $\sigma(t_i) = \sigma(t'_i)$, for $i = 1, \ldots, k$. Assume that $\sigma(t_i) \subseteq \sigma(t'_i)$, and let $n \in \sigma(t_i) \cap \mathbb{N}$, so that $\underline{a}[n] = t_i$. Therefore, we have that $t'_i = h(t_i) = h(\underline{a}[n]) = h(\underline{a})[n] = \underline{a}'[n]$. Hence, $n \in \sigma(t'_i)$. Moreover, if $n = c$ is a constant, by definition of homomorphism, we have $c \in \sigma(t_i) \Rightarrow t_i = c \Rightarrow t'_i = h(t_i) = t_i = c \Rightarrow c \in \sigma(t'_i)$. The reverse inclusion can be easily proved by replacing h by h^{-1}. [$\Leftarrow$] Let us assume that $T_{\underline{a}} = T_{\underline{a}'}$. Let $h : \{\underline{a}\} \rightarrow \{\underline{a}'\}$ be s.t. $h(t_i) = t'_i$. First, we prove that h is a homomorphism. Let $t_i = c$ be a constant. Suppose that $c \in \sigma(t_i)$, then by assumption $c \in \sigma(t'_i)$, hence $t'_i = c$. It remains to be shown that h is also injective. Let $t'_i = t'_j$. Then, $\sigma(t'_i) = \sigma(t'_j) \Rightarrow \sigma(t_i) = \sigma(t_j) \Rightarrow t_i = t_j$. □

Now, we are able to provide an upper bound for the maximum number of atoms generating by the pchase procedure.

Theorem 4. *Let P be a program with $arity(P) = w$, $|const(P)| = d$, and l_m the number of predicates in $pred(P)$ of arity m. Then, $|pchase(P)| \leq \sum_{m=0}^{w} l_m \gamma_m^d$.*

Proof. By Theorems 2 and 3, the total number of non isomorphic atoms over $pred(P)$ and $const(P) \cup \Delta_N$ is given by $\sum_{m=0}^{w} l_m \gamma_m^d$. Moreover, by Theorem 1, we know that $pchase(P)$ does not contain isomorphic atoms. Hence, $|pchase(P)| \leq \sum_{m=0}^{w} l_m \gamma_m^d$. □

Let Γ_w^d be the upper bound in Theorem 4. To show that it is also tight, we introduce an ordering on types that will allow us to build a program with a sequence of firing homomorphisms generating a pchase of size exactly Γ_w^d.

Definition 3 (Type ordering). *Let $T = \mathcal{T}(S, C, f)$ and $T' = \mathcal{T}(S', C', f')$. Then, T precedes T', if (i) $|C| < |C'|$, or (ii) $|C| = |C'|$ and $|S| > |S'|$.*

Intuitively, such a program should have a rule for each possible atom tag, whenever constants are allowed in the rules. Otherwise, we need a predicate to collect all constants of the database. To better understand our idea, we give an example of such a program before we provide the formal result.

Example 3. Let C be a finite set of constant, and P be a program such that $data(P) = \{t(c_1), t(c_2)\}$, and $dep(P)$ is given by

$$\exists X, Y, Z p(X, Y, Z) \qquad \exists X, Y p(Z, X, Y) \leftarrow t(Z) \qquad \exists X p(X, Y, Z) \leftarrow t(Y), t(Z)$$
$$\exists X, Y p(X, X, Y) \qquad \exists X, Y p(X, Z, Y) \leftarrow t(Z) \qquad \exists X p(Y, X, Z) \leftarrow t(Y), t(Z)$$
$$\exists X, Y p(X, Y, X) \qquad \boldsymbol{\exists X, Y p(X, Y, Z) \leftarrow t(Z)} \qquad \exists X p(Y, Z, X) \leftarrow t(Y), t(Z)$$
$$\exists X, Y p(X, Y, Y) \qquad \exists X p(X, X, Y) \leftarrow t(Y) \qquad p(X, Y, Z) \leftarrow t(X), t(Y), t(Z)$$
$$\exists X p(X, X, X) \qquad \exists X p(X, Y, X) \leftarrow t(Y)$$
$$\exists X p(Y, X, X) \leftarrow t(Y) \qquad \exists X t(X)$$

We build $pchase(P)$ by starting from rules in the first column from top to bottom. For each rule r in this ordering, we consider all firing homomorphism h for r. E.g., the rule in bold produces the atoms $\{p(\varphi_1, \varphi_2, c_1), p(\varphi_3, \varphi_4, c_2)\}$. Thus, the number of atoms with predicate p generated by the pchase will be $37 = \gamma_3^2$, and $|pchase(P)| = 40 = \gamma_3^2 + \gamma_1^2$.

Theorem 5. *Let w be a positive integer, D a set of constants of size d, and Γ_w^d as above. Then, there is a family P_w of programs s.t. $|pchase(P_w)| = \Gamma_w^d$.*

Proof Sketch. We build a program P_w having two predicates p (of arity w) and t (of arity 1). We set $data(P_w) = \{t(c) \mid c \in D\}$, and define $dep(P_w)$ as follows. Given a partition $S_i = \{\Lambda_1, \ldots, \Lambda_n\}$ of w, where $n = |S_i|$, we construct a rule r_i with an empty body, by adding $X_1, \ldots, X_n$ existential variables so that $\Lambda_j = \{k \mid p[k] = X_j, \ k \in [w]\}$. Now, fixed a rule r_i with $n > 1$ existential variables, we produce $n - 1$ blocks of rules as follows. We translate j existential variables into universal ones, by adding j atoms over predicate t in the body. Hence, we construct $\binom{n}{j}$ rules. Then, we add the rules $p(X_1, \ldots, X_w) = t(X_1), \ldots, t(X_w)$, and $\exists X t(X)$. Finally, we remove all rules having in the head more than one repeated universal variable. To prove that $|pchase(P_w)| = \Gamma_w^d$, we provide a sequence of $\Gamma_w^d - d$ firing homomorphisms. To each rule r in $dep(P_w)$ we associate uniquely an atom $g(head(r))$, where g maps existential variables to fresh nulls, and universal variables to a fixed constant. The type ordering on the atoms gives an ordering on the rules, and so to the sequence of firing homomorphisms. $\square$

4   Discussion and Future Work

In this work, we identified the maximal number of distinct atoms generable by the pchase procedure. In particular, γ_m^d improves the bound given in [21], that is $(d + m)^m$. In particular, $d^m \leq \gamma_m^d \leq (d + m)^m$. Since in the OBQA context, normally, d is much bigger than m, it could seem that the effort to find such a precise upper bound can be useless for practical purposes. However, this is not the case, as shown in the paper. Indeed, the search for a precise upper bound led to identify the fundamental notions of type and type ordering that highlighted some qualitative characteristics of the pchase. Moreover, there could be other contexts where m is much bigger than d (think for example to scenarios where tuples encode strings over a certain alphabet, as in complexity proofs based on Turing Machine simulation). In this cases, our bound represents a concrete improvement. As future work, we plan to extend the pchase condition to rules with a complex head, and to compute the maximal number of distinct atoms generable in this case. Then, we will try to analyze the orderings of fire homomorphisms in the generation of the pchase to understand if we can identify a sort of best ordering that minimizes the number of atoms produced. Finally, we will try to apply this methodology to give exact estimations of others chase versions.

Acknowledgments. This work has been partially supported by the European Union's Horizon 2020 research and innovation programme under the Marie Skodowska-Curie grant agreement No. 690974 for the project "MIREL: MIning and REasoning with Legal texts".

References

1. Alviano, M., Pieris, A.: Default negation for non-guarded existential rules. In: Proc of PODS (2015)
2. Amendola, G., Leone, N., Manna, M.: Finite model reasoning over existential rules. TPLP **17**(5–6), 726–743 (2017)
3. Amendola, G., Leone, N., Manna, M.: Querying finite or arbitrary models? No matter! existential rules may rely on both once again (discussion paper). In: SEBD, CEUR Workshop Proceedings, vol. 2037, p. 218. CEUR-WS.org (2017)
4. Amendola, G., Leone, N., Manna, M.: Finite controllability of conjunctive query answering with existential rules: two steps forward. In: IJCAI, pp. 5189–5193. ijcai.org (2018)
5. Amendola, G., Leone, N., Manna, M., Veltri, P.: Reasoning on anonymity in datalog+/-. In: ICLP (Technical Communications), OASICS, vol. 58, pp. 3:1–3:5. Schloss Dagstuhl - Leibniz-Zentrum fuer Informatik (2017)
6. Amendola, G., Leone, N., Manna, M., Veltri, P.: Enhancing existential rules by closed-world variables. In: IJCAI, pp. 1676–1682. ijcai.org (2018)
7. Amendola, G., Libkin, L.: Explainable certain answers. In: IJCAI, pp. 1683–1690. ijcai.org (2018)
8. Arenas, M., Barceló, P., Libkin, L., Murlak, F.: Foundations of Data Exchange. Cambridge University Press, Cambridge (2014)
9. Baader, F., Calvanese, D., McGuinness, D.L., Nardi, D., Patel-Schneider, P.F. (eds.): The Description Logic Handbook. Cambridge University Press, Cambridge (2003)
10. Baget, J., Leclère, M., Mugnier, M., Salvat, E.: On rules with existential variables: walking the decidability line. Artif. Intell. **175**(9–10), 1620–1654 (2011)
11. Bárány, V., Gottlob, G., Otto, M.: Querying the guarded fragment. LMCS **10**(2) (2014)
12. Bourhis, P., Manna, M., Morak, M., Pieris, A.: Guarded-based disjunctive tuple-generating dependencies. ACM TODS **41**(4), 27 (2016)
13. Calì, A., Gottlob, G., Lukasiewicz, T.: Datalog$^\pm$: a unified approach to ontologies and integrity constraints. In: Proceedings of ICDT (2009)
14. Calì, A., Gottlob, G., Lukasiewicz, T.: A general datalog-based framework for tractable query answering over ontologies. In: PODS, pp. 77–86. ACM (2009)
15. Ceri, S., Gottlob, G., Tanca, L.: What you always wanted to know about datalog (and never dared to ask). IEEE Trans. Knowl. Data Eng. **1**(1), 146–166 (1989)
16. Deutsch, A., Nash, A., Remmel, J.B.: The chase revisited. In: Proceedings of PODS (2008)

17. Fagin, R., Kolaitis, P.G., Miller, R.J., Popa, L.: Data exchange: semantics and query answering. TCS **336**(1), 89–124 (2005)
18. Gottlob, G., Orsi, G., Pieris, A.: Ontological queries: rewriting and optimization. In: ICDE, pp. 2–13. IEEE Computer Society (2011)
19. Imielinski, T., Lipski, W.: Incomplete information in relational databases. J. ACM **31**(4), 761–791 (1984)
20. Lenzerini, M.: Data integration: a theoretical perspective. In: PODS, pp. 233–246. ACM (2002)
21. Leone, N., Manna, M., Terracina, G., Veltri, P.: Efficiently computable Datalog$^{\exists}$ programs. In: Proceedings of KR (2012)
22. Manna, M., Ricca, F., Terracina, G.: Consistent query answering via ASP from different perspectives: theory and practice. TPLP **13**(2), 227–252 (2013)
23. Manna, M., Ricca, F., Terracina, G.: Taming primary key violations to query large inconsistent data via ASP. TPLP **15**(4–5), 696–710 (2015)

The Weak Completion Semantics Can Model Inferences of Individual Human Reasoners

Christian Breu[ID], Axel Ind[ID], Julia Mertesdorf[ID], and Marco Ragni[✉][ID]

Cognitive Computation Lab, Technische Fakultät, Universität Freiburg,
Georges-Köhler-Allee 52, 79110 Freiburg, Germany
christian.breu@mars.uni-freiburg.de, axeltind@gmail.com,
{mertesdj,ragni}@informatik.uni-freiburg.de

Abstract. The weak completion semantics (WCS) based on three-valued Łukasiewicz logic has been demonstrated to be an adequate model for general human reasoning in a variety of different domains. Among the many experimental paradigms in cognitive psychology, the Wason Selection Task (WST) is a core problem with more than 200 publications demonstrating key factors of the systematic deviation of human reasoning from classical logic. Previous attempts were able to model general response patterns, but not the individual responses of participants. This paper provides a novel generalization of the weak completion semantics by using two additional principles, abduction and contraposition: This extension can model the four canonical cases of the WST for the Abstract, Everyday, and Deontic problem domain. Finally, a quantitative comparison between the WCS predictions of the extended model and the individual participants' responses in the three problem domains is performed. It demonstrates the power of the WCS to adequately model human reasoning on an individual human reasoner level.

Keywords: Logic programming · Weak completion semantics · Łukasiewicz logic · Non-monotonic logic · WST · Cognitive modelling

1 Introduction

The Wason Selection Task (WST) is one of the most commonly studied problems in cognitive psychology [6]. It provides a simple example of the disparity between human logical selection and logically valid conclusions. The task contains (at least) three logically identical problems, called the Abstract, Everyday, and Deontic cases. Despite their logical equivalence, subjects are more likely to derive the classical logic solution in the Everyday and Deontic cases than in

Supported by the DFG within grants RA 1934/3-1 and RA 1934/4-1.
Authors appear alphabetically.

© Springer Nature Switzerland AG 2019
F. Calimeri et al. (Eds.): JELIA 2019, LNAI 11468, pp. 498–508, 2019.
https://doi.org/10.1007/978-3-030-19570-0_33

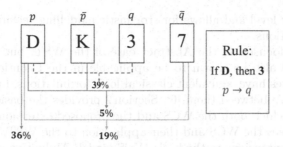

Fig. 1. The four cards D, K, 3, and 7 participants are presented with to check if the rule X holds "If a card has a D on one side it has a 3 on the other side". The percentages show, how many reasoners select the respective card combinations (see, [6]).

the Abstract case. Thus, the WST provides an illustration of the unsuitability of classical logic for cognitive modelling. The task is also of interest because it shows the human tendency to interpret logically equivalent data differently based on contextual knowledge of the problem domain [6]. In the abstract formulation of the task, a participant is shown four cards (Fig. 1) and learns that every card has a number on one side and a letter on the other side. The participant is asked to decide for each card if it needs to be turned over to test the conditional: *'If a card has a D on one side, it has a 3 on the other side.'*[1] The conditional of the WST translates into the proposition: $3 \leftarrow D$. Using propositional logic it is easy to derive the two cards that would contradict this conditional. If the card D did not have a 3 on its other side, the proposition would be shown to be false (*modus ponens*). Similarly, if card 7 was shown to have a D on the other side, the proposition would be violated (*modus tollens*). Thus, the two cards that should be turned over are D and 7. Despite the validity of its conclusions, propositional logic provides a poor model for the human conclusions drawn for the WST [6]. In reality, humans tend overwhelmingly to choose the cards D, or D and 3 (see Table in Sect. 5). These seemingly illogical choices are the reason for the significance of the task in cognitive modelling. A variety of cognitive modelling frameworks have been applied to the task in order to formalize the disparity between logical deduction and experimental reality [6].

The Weak Completion Semantics (WCS) has been shown to provide a suitable cognitive model for predictive modelling in many human reasoning domains, such as reasoning with conditionals [2] and syllogistic reasoning [1] among others. Furthermore, the WCS were successfully applied to model the WST [6], as shown by [3] (see the Experiment in [3]). The previous WCS model was, however, limited to explaining which cards are selected by the whole experimental group. This paper proposes and introduces two extensions to the existing WCS framework in order to facilitate WST modelling on an individual reasoner level. This represents for the first time that the WST has been modelled on an individual

---

[1] Note for a better readability, the cards are referred to by their face value. Specifically: $D \leftrightarrow p$, $\bar{p} \leftrightarrow K$, $q \leftrightarrow 3$, $\bar{q} \leftrightarrow 7$.

human reasoner level and allows for stochastic modelling techniques to predict individual selections.

This paper focuses on the Abstract case of the WST, but the approaches we propose will also be shown to be applicable in the Deontic and Everyday cases. These cases have equivalent classical logic formulations, but human selections vary widely between them [6]. Section 2 provides the basic mathematical concepts upon which both the WCS and the proposed extensions are modelled. Section 3 discusses the WCS and their application to the WST. Section 4 introduces two new extensions to the basic WCS model: Abduction and Contraposition. Section 5 provides the logical conclusion each extension draws to the task and a probabilistic testing procedure to evaluate the strength of the derived conclusion. Finally, the paper concludes with a discussion of the suitability of the extended WCS model for modelling the WST.

2   Mathematical Preliminaries

We expect the reader to be familiar with some logic and logic programming. We introduce the necessary definitions upon which the WCS is built and follow the notation in [3]. A *logic program* $\mathcal{P}$ is a finite set of clauses of the form

$$A \leftarrow A_1 \wedge \cdots \wedge A_k \wedge \neg B_1 \wedge \cdots \wedge \neg B_l \tag{1}$$

with propositional atoms A_i for $1 \leq i \leq k$ and B_j for $1 \leq j \leq l$. There are two distinct atoms $\top$ and $\bot$, where $A \leftarrow \top$ represents that A is true and $A \leftarrow \bot$ that A is false. The first type of clauses are called positive facts and the latter type negative facts. The propositional atom A in the clause above is called the *head* and $A_1 \wedge \cdots \wedge A_k \wedge \neg B_1 \wedge \cdots \wedge \neg B_l$ the *body* of the clause. We consider only cases where the bodies of clauses are not empty. An atom A is called *defined* in a logic program $\mathcal{P}$, if there is a clause with head A; otherwise it is *undefined*. An *interpretation* I is a mapping from formulae to one of the three truth values $\top, \bot, \mathsf{U}$, with $\top$ being *true*, $\bot$ being *false* and U being *unknown*. The truth value of a given formula under a given interpretation is determined by the Łukasiewicz interpretation. We write following [3] an interpretation as a pair $I = \langle I^\top, I^\bot \rangle$ of disjoint sets of atoms where $I^\top$ is the set of all atoms that are mapped by I to $\top$ and $I^\bot$ is the set of all atoms that are mapped by I to $\bot$. Please note that atoms mapped to U are neither in $I^\top$ nor in $I^\bot$. A *model* of a formula F is an interpretation I such that $I(F) = \top$. Table 1 shows the truth tables for the operators NOT, AND, OR, Implication and Equivalence of the three-valued Łukasiewicz logic. The least model of a given logic program is the model where positive and negative information is minimized: suppose that $I = \langle I^\top, I^\bot \rangle$ is a model of $\mathcal{P}$. The *least model* l of a logic program $\mathcal{P}$ is a model for which for all other models $J = \langle J^\top, J^\bot \rangle$ of $\mathcal{P}$ holds that $I^\top \subseteq J^\top$ and $I^\bot \subseteq J^\bot$. The weak completion transformation (wc L) [4] for a given logic program $\mathcal{P}$ is:

1. Disjunct all clauses with the same head, i.e., replace
$A \leftarrow body_1, \ldots, A \leftarrow body_l$ by the disjunction $A \leftarrow body_1 \vee \ldots \vee body_l$.
2. Replace all occurrences of $\leftarrow$ by $\leftrightarrow$.[2]

Table 1. Truth-tables for logical operators for the Łukasiewicz logic (cp. [3]).

F	$\neg F$	$\wedge$	T	U	⊥	$\vee$	T	U	⊥	$\leftarrow_L$	T	U	⊥	$\leftrightarrow_L$	T	U	⊥
T	⊥	T	T	U	⊥	T	T	T	T	T	T	T	T	T	T	U	⊥
⊥	T	U	U	U	⊥	U	T	U	U	U	U	T	T	U	U	T	U
U	U	⊥	⊥	⊥	⊥	⊥	T	U	⊥	⊥	⊥	U	T	⊥	⊥	U	T

The least model can be computed as the least fixed point of an appropriate semantic operator for logic programs, which was proposed by Stenning and Lambalgen in [7]. Let I be an interpretation in $\Phi_P(I) = \langle J^\top, J^\perp \rangle$, where

$$J^\top = \{A \mid \text{ there exists } A \leftarrow body \in P \text{ with } I(body) = \top\},$$
$$J^\perp = \{A \mid \text{ there exists } A \leftarrow body \in P \text{ and}$$
$$\text{for all } A \leftarrow body \in P \text{ we find } I(body) = \perp\}.$$

Hölldobler and Kencana Ramli [4] showed that the least fixed point of Φ_P is identical to the least model of the weak completion of P (lm wc P). It is started by the empty interpretation $I = \langle \emptyset, \emptyset \rangle$, lm wc P and iterating Φ_P and the model intersection property holds for weakly completed programs [4] which guarantees the existence of least models.

In the following paragraph, we will define backward reasoning in the context of the WCS [3], which is called abduction and represents the opposing process to forward reasoning and deduction. Abduction is applied in order to find an appropriate explanation $\mathcal{E}$ for an observation O, which consists of a non-empty set of literals. For explanations, the set of abducibles $\mathcal{A}_P$ with regards to the logic program P is considered, where

$$\mathcal{A}_P = \{A \leftarrow \top \mid A \text{ is undefined or } \neg A \text{ is assumed in } P\}$$
$$\cup \{A \leftarrow \perp \mid A \text{ is undefined in } P\}$$

Moreover, *integrity constraints* (IC) can be considered when searching for explanations. These are expressions of the form $U \leftarrow body$, where $body$ denotes a conjunction of literals and U the unknown, according to the three-valued Łukasiewiczs logic. An integrity constraint is mapped to True by an Interpretation I if all literals in the body are either mapped to False or Unknown: $I(body) \subseteq \{\perp, U\}$. Given a finite set of integrity constrains IC and an Interpretation I, IC is satisfied by I if all clauses that are contained in IC are mapped

---

[2] Human reasoners can assume a biconditional interpretation of a conditional [6].

to True under I. The complete abductive framework $\langle \mathcal{P}, IC, \mathcal{A}_\mathcal{P}, \models_{wcs} \rangle$ for modelling abduction consists of a logic program $\mathcal{P}$, a finite set of abducibles $\mathcal{A}_\mathcal{P}$ with regards to $\mathcal{P}$, a finite set of integrity constraints IC and an entailment relation $\models_{wcs}$. An observation $O = \{o_1, o_2, \ldots, o_n\}$ is explained by an explanation $\mathcal{E} \subseteq \mathcal{A}$ given $\mathcal{P}$ and IC if and only if $\mathcal{P} \cup \mathcal{E} \models_{wcs} o_1 \wedge o_2 \wedge \ldots \wedge o_n$ and $\mathcal{P} \cup \mathcal{E} \models_{wcs} IC$. As in the case of computing least models, minimal explanations are preferred, meaning there exists no other explanation $\mathcal{E}'$ for O such that $\mathcal{E}' \subset \mathcal{E}$.

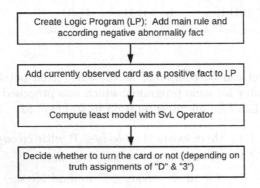

Fig. 2. The basic model for WCS prediction in the WST.

3   Modelling the WST with the WCS

The WST can be modelled under the Weak Completion Semantics. As in [3], conditionals can be represented by licenses for implications by adding a negated abnormality-predicate to the body of the implication. The rule of the WST $3 \leftarrow D$ can be transformed to $3 \leftarrow D \wedge \neg ab_1$, meaning that D implies 3, provided that nothing abnormal is known. After creating a new an empty logic program, the transformed rule $3 \leftarrow D \wedge \neg ab_1$ is added. Since nothing abnormal is known at this point, the fact $ab_1 \leftarrow \perp$ is added. After creating the basic logic program, the implementation needs to consider each of the four cards individually and decide, whether the card should be turned over. Since subjects directly observe a card with a letter or a number in front of them, they know that this letter or number is True, so the according atom encoding that letter or number has to hold in the logic program. This can be established by adding a positive fact of the form $card \leftarrow \top$ with regards to the currently observed card to the logic program. The next step is to apply the semantic operator (also called the SvL operator) which was introduced by Stenning and Lambalgen [7]. The result is the *least model* of the weak completion of the logic program, incorporating two lists, one list containing all positive and one containing all negative atoms. Depending on the computed atom assignments, a function deciding whether the currently observed card should be turned over or not can determine the result for the current card. A card is turned over, iff the given rule $3 \leftarrow D$ evaluates to $\top$ in the least model. The intuition behind this decision function is that if the main rule of the WST should hold (according to the conclusion of the reasoner with regards to the observed card), the reasoner verifies whether the rule actually holds by turning the observed card. We evaluate this rule with regular, two-valued logic to prevent turning the card when both atoms of the rule, D and 3, are unknown. When nothing about either of the atoms is known for the current card, there can be no information derived by turning it, which would be the case if the three-valued Łukasiewicz Logic were used instead. The process of observing a card, adding the according positive fact to the logic program, computing the least model and deciding whether to turn the card, is repeated for all remaining cards. The first step of creating the logic program and adding the main rule $3 \leftarrow D \wedge \neg ab_1$ and fact $ab_1 \leftarrow \bot$ is only done once for every simulated subject. The flowchart in Fig. 2 illustrates the problem solving process.

Example of the Basic Model. In the following, we provide an example to depict the problem solving process under the WCS as described in the previous section. The current observed card in this example is the card D. In the first step, the given rule of the WST, encoded as a license for an implication, is added to the logic program together with the according negative abnormality-fact: $\mathcal{P} = \{3 \leftarrow D \wedge \neg ab_1, ab_1 \leftarrow \bot\}$. Since the currently observed card is card D, the fact $D \leftarrow \top$ is added to $\mathcal{P}$, hence: $\mathcal{P} = \{3 \leftarrow D \wedge \neg ab_1, ab_1 \leftarrow \bot, D \leftarrow \top\}$. After adding all necessary rules and facts to the logic program, the semantic operator is applied. In the first iteration, D is set to $\top$ and ab_1 is set to $\bot$. In the next iteration, 3 is set to $\top$ since the body of the rule $3 \leftarrow D \wedge \neg ab_1$ evaluates to $\top$ as a result of the first iteration. No new truth assignments follow after this iteration, so the resulting least model of the logic program is: $\langle \{3, D\}, \{ab_1\} \rangle$. The model will then proceed with the turn-decision-function. The initial given rule $3 \leftarrow D$ evaluates to $\top$. Therefore, the card D is turned.

4   Extending the WCS for the Individual Case

Using only the basic model we introduced in the previous section, our model would always conclude that D should be turned, which corresponds to the canonical case p. However, this is not sufficient to model the WST for individual reasoners, as there is no variation in the results and none of the other three canonical cases can be derived. Therefore, this paper introduces two extensions to model the WST more precisely. These extensions can be enabled or disabled for each subject. The question of which extensions to enable will be discussed later.

Applying Abduction. When observing card 3, we generate the following logic program before applying the semantic operator:

$$\mathcal{P} = \{3 \leftarrow D \wedge \neg ab_1, ab_1 \leftarrow \bot, 3 \leftarrow \top\}$$

Whilst computing the least model, atom D cannot be assigned $\top$ or $\bot$ since D does not occur in the head of any rule, so the decision-turn-function will always derive not to turn card 3 since nothing is known about D. However, people might come to the conclusion that D has to be $\top$ in order for 3 to be $\top$ which results in turning 3. This thinking-process can be accurately modelled by abduction, which was explained in Sect. 2 in more detail. Applying abduction as a result of misinterpreting the given implication as an equivalence might be one of the major reasons many people chose the cards D and 3 in the abstract problem domain. This new extension of the basic model allows deriving the canonical case pq. If abduction is enabled for a subject, then our model will try to apply it to every observed card. However, only certain facts can be used as observations in the abductive framework and only if one such fact exists, an explanation can be found and with that, change the decision whether the observed card is turned or not. In order for a fact to be considered as an observation, the atom in the head of this fact needs to be in the head of another rule, which is not a fact. That means, abduction is only applicable for card 3, since then the fact $3 \leftarrow \top$ is added to the logic program and atom 3 is also the head of the rule $3 \leftarrow D \wedge \neg ab$. For all other cards, the abduction process will stop after not finding a fact which can be used as an observation. When an observation is found, an appropriate explanation needs to be computed. An explanation consists of a (sub)set of the *abducibles*. If a (sub)set of the abducibles, together with the logic program, leads to a least model which includes the atom in the observation-fact as a true atom, then this (sub)set of abducibles is an explanation for the observation. To compute the explanation, the observation-fact is first deleted from the logic program. Afterwards, the implementation computes the set of abducibles. All atoms, that are either undefined in the logic program or that are assumed to be False, are used as the heads of the abducibles. In case the atom is undefined, a positive and negative fact with the atom as its head is added to the list of abducibles. If the atom is assumed to be False, only a positive fact is added. After computing the abducibles, the implementation iterates trough the set of abducibles, adding one of the facts, computing the least model with this additional fact and checking whether the atom in the observation-fact is True in the resulting least model. If no fitting explanation is found, the implementation will iterate trough the abducibles again, this time adding two abducible-facts to the logic program before calculating the least model again. If a (sub)set of the abducibles is found which leads to a least model comprising the atom in the observation fact as a true atom, then this (sub)set is our explanation. The least model of the logic program conjoined with the computed explanation is our new least model. The turn-decision-function is executed on the atom assignment according to the new least model and derives a different conclusion for card 3.

Abduction Example. As abduction is only applicable for card 3, the following example illustrates the problem solving process for observing card 3. The first step, like in the example above, comprises adding the rule of the WST with the negated abnormality predicate in the body and the according negative abnormality fact to the logic program.

$$\mathcal{P} = \{3 \leftarrow D \wedge \neg ab_1, ab_1 \leftarrow \bot\}$$

Next, the currently observed card 3 is added to the logic program.

$$\mathcal{P} = \{3 \leftarrow D \wedge \neg ab_1, ab_1 \leftarrow \bot, 3 \leftarrow \top\}$$

Iterating the Semantic Operator leads to the least model: $\langle\{3\}, \{ab_1\}\rangle$. The atom 3 of the positive fact $3 \leftarrow \top$ is also head of the rule $3 \leftarrow D \wedge \neg ab_1$. Therefore, this fact can be used as an observation. The set of abducibles is $\{ab_1 \leftarrow \top, D \leftarrow \top, D \leftarrow \bot\}$ since atom D was undefined and ab_1 was assumed to be $\bot$ in the logic program. The only explanation for the observation is $\{D \leftarrow \top\}$. Adding this fact to the logic program, we obtain:

$$\mathcal{P} = \{3 \leftarrow D \wedge \neg ab_1, ab_1 \leftarrow \bot, 3 \leftarrow \top, D \leftarrow \top\}$$

The new computed least model is: $\langle\{3, D\}, \{ab_1\}\rangle$. With this atom assignment, the main rule $3 \leftarrow D$ evaluates to $\top$, since both D and 3 are True in the least model. Therefore, the card 3 is turned.

Contraposition. By adding more rules to the logic program, we can introduce new mechanisms to decide whether a card should be turned or not. Adding the contraposition rule $\neg D \leftarrow 7$ to the logic program allows our model to apply *modus tollens*. Since there is a restriction on logic programs, that no negated atoms are allowed in the heads of the rules, we transform the contraposition rule according to a common approach in logic programming (see, [1]): Adding the rules $D' \leftarrow 7$ and $D \leftarrow \neg D'$ encodes the contraposition rule while avoiding negated atoms in the rule heads. Furthermore, as in the case of the given main rule $3 \leftarrow D$, an according negated abnormality predicate is added to the body of the rule. Nothing abnormal is known in the usual case, so an according negative abnormality fact is added as well. The set of new rules is: $\{D' \leftarrow 7 \wedge \neg ab_2, D \leftarrow \neg D', ab_2 \leftarrow \bot\}$. Applying our second extension, adding the contraposition rule to the logic program after the first step of our basic model (Fig. 2), the implementation is now able to derive the canonical case $p\bar{q}$, which corresponds to the correct solution of the WST.

Contraposition Example. The next example shows the problem solving process with the Contraposition-extension for card 7. The initial logic program contains the given rule of the WST and the matching abnormality fact, like in the examples before.

$$\mathcal{P} = \{3 \leftarrow D \wedge \neg ab_1, ab_1 \leftarrow \bot\}$$

The newly introduced step adds Contraposition in the form of the two rules and the corresponding abnormality fact, as explained above.

$$\mathcal{P} = \{3 \leftarrow D \wedge \neg ab_1, D' \leftarrow 7 \wedge \neg ab_2, D \leftarrow \neg D', ab_1 \leftarrow \bot, ab_2 \leftarrow \bot\}$$

In the third step, the model adds the observed card 7 to the logic program.

$$\mathcal{P} = \{3 \leftarrow D \wedge \neg ab_1, D' \leftarrow 7 \wedge \neg ab_2, D \leftarrow \neg D', ab_1 \leftarrow \bot, ab_2 \leftarrow \bot, 7 \leftarrow \top\}$$

Iterating the semantic operator sets ab_1 to $\bot$, ab_2 to $\bot$ and 7 to $\top$ in the first iteration. In the next iteration, D' is set to $\top$ since $7 \wedge \neg ab_2$ evaluates to $\top$ after the first iteration. The third iteration sets D to $\bot$, since $\neg D'$ is $\bot$ due to the last iteration. Finally, atom 3 is set to $\bot$ as well, since the body of the rule $3 \leftarrow D \wedge \neg ab_1$ evaluates to $\bot$ with atom D being $\bot$. The least model is:

$$\langle \{7, D'\}, \{D, 3, ab_1, ab_2\} \rangle$$

Since both D and 3 are $\bot$ in the least model, the turn-decision-function is evaluated to $\top$ and card 7 is turned.

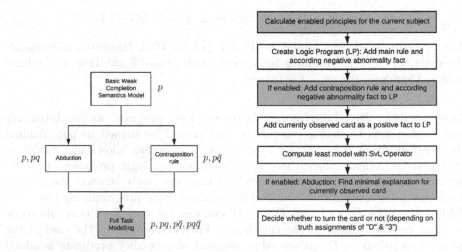

(a) Extension for individual patterns   (b) Flowchart of the extended model

Fig. 3. Both extensions combined (Color figure online)

Combining the Extensions. Above, we introduced two new extensions to model the WST in a more accurate manner. The Abduction extension allowed us to turn card q. The Contraposition extension allows us to model the classical logic solution to the WST, $p\bar{q}$. By applying both extensions, the last canonical case, $pq\bar{q}$, can be derived. The extended model is now able to derive all four canonical cases (see Fig. 3a) by selective application of the extensions. The steps in this combined model are shown in Fig. 3b. White blocks depict the basic WCS model and green blocks illustrate the two new extensions.

5   Results, Conclusion, and Future Work

In the absence of the two extensions only the canonical case $\{D\}$ is derivable (Sect. 3). As shown in Sect. 4, applying the Abduction and Contraposition extensions in conjunction with the basic WCS model allows the derivation of the other three cases[3]. Cases derived by the combined model of the WST under the assumption that all abnormalities are set to $\perp$.

	Abduction = True	Abduction = False
Contraposition = True	$\{D, 3, 7\}$	$\{D, 7\}$
Contraposition = False	$\{D, 3\}$	$\{D\}$

Following the procedure in Fig. 3a, the parameters combinations required to model all four canonical cases on the WST in our framework are shown in the table above. In order to test how accurately our model is capable of predicting individual responses to the Abstract, Everyday, and Deontic cases of the task, a stochastic model that pseudo-randomly determined the probability of applying Abduction and/or Contraposition rules was generated. These probabilities were optimized using the COBYLA numerical optimization tool [5]. The following table shows a comparison between the generated results against those achieved in reality and indicates that all three cases are closely approximated by the extended model.

	$\{D\}$	$\{D, 3\}$	$\{D, 3, 7\}$	$\{D, 7\}$	p(Abduction)	p(Contraposition)
Abstract	39/**36**	37/**39**	12/**5**	13/**19**	0.475	0.256
Everyday	29/**23**	31/**37**	21/**11**	20/**29**	0.49	0.424
Deontic	19/**13**	4/**19**	12/**4**	65/**64**	0.151	0.785

The above table shows the predicted answers and empirical results (in bold) of the WST and predicted probabilities of applying each extension to the WCS Framework to model the aggregated results of each WST case. This paper has served to show the suitability of the proposed extensions to the WCS for cognitive modeling of the WST. It has been demonstrated that all four canonical cases of the task can be accurately modelled at the level of individual reasoners in each of the three experimental cases (Abstract, Social and Deontic). The value of this work is two-fold. First, it has provided a novel framework for modelling the individual-level results of a problem that has previously been primarily concerned with approximating the properties of groups as whole. Second, it has shown that using suitable stochastic modelling techniques, it is possible to estimate group responses by considering multiple instances of the individual reasoner. It has been shown to approximate experimental, quantitative data over multiple trials when properly optimized. Exact interpretation of the value of such parameter data in cross-validation with other cognitive modelling tasks, and the possible addition of other well-founded logical extensions is a topic for future work.

---

[3] For the purposes of this experiment, only results relating to the four canonical cases ($\{D\}$, $\{D, 3\}$, $\{D, 3, 7\}$, $\{D, 7\}$) are presented. Other possible combinations were found to be quite rare and are not considered relevant to the task.

References

1. Costa, A., Dietz, E.A., Hölldobler, S., Ragni, M.: Syllogistic reasoning under the weak completion semantics. In: Bridging@ IJCAI, pp. 5–19 (2016)
2. Dietz, E.-A., Hölldobler, S.: A new computational logic approach to reason with conditionals. In: Calimeri, F., Ianni, G., Truszczynski, M. (eds.) LPNMR 2015. LNCS, vol. 9345, pp. 265–278. Springer, Cham (2015). https://doi.org/10.1007/978-3-319-23264-5_23
3. Dietz, E.A., Hölldobler, S., Ragni, M.: A computational logic approach to the abstract and the social case of the selection task. In: Proceedings of the 11th International Symposium on Logical Formalizations of Commonsense Reasoning, COMMONSENSE (2013)
4. Hölldobler, S., Kencana Ramli, C.D.P.: Logics and networks for human reasoning. In: Alippi, C., Polycarpou, M., Panayiotou, C., Ellinas, G. (eds.) ICANN 2009. LNCS, vol. 5769, pp. 85–94. Springer, Heidelberg (2009). https://doi.org/10.1007/978-3-642-04277-5_9
5. Powell, M.J.: A direct search optimization method that models the objective and constraint functions by linear interpolation. In: Gomez, S., Hennart, J.P. (eds.) Advances in Optimization and Numerical Analysis. MAIA, vol. 275, pp. 51–67. Springer, Dordrecht (1994). https://doi.org/10.1007/978-94-015-8330-5_4
6. Ragni, M., Kola, I., Johnson-Laird, P.N.: On selecting evidence to test hypotheses: a theory of selection tasks. Psychol. Bull. **144**(8), 779–796 (2018)
7. Stenning, K., Van Lambalgen, M.: Human Reasoning and Cognitive Science. MIT Press, Cambridge (2008)

Lower Bound Founded Logic of Here-and-There

Pedro Cabalar[1] ⓘ, Jorge Fandinno[2] ⓘ, Torsten Schaub[3](✉) ⓘ,
and Sebastian Schellhorn[3] ⓘ

[1] University of Corunna, A Coruña, Spain
[2] University of Toulouse, Toulouse, France
[3] University of Potsdam, Potsdam, Germany
torsten@cs.uni-potsdam.de

Abstract. A distinguishing feature of Answer Set Programming is that
all atoms belonging to a stable model must be founded. That is, an atom
must not only be true but provably true. This can be made precise by
means of the constructive logic of Here-and-There, whose equilibrium
models correspond to stable models. One way of looking at foundedness
is to regard Boolean truth values as ordered by letting *true* be greater
than *false*. Then, each Boolean variable takes the smallest truth value
that can be proven for it. This idea was generalized by Aziz to ordered
domains and applied to constraint satisfaction problems. As before, the
idea is that a, say integer, variable gets only assigned to the smallest
integer that can be justified. In this paper, we present a logical reconstruction of Aziz' idea in the setting of the logic of Here-and-There.
More precisely, we start by defining the logic of Here-and-There with
lower bound founded variables along with its equilibrium models and
elaborate upon its formal properties. Finally, we compare our approach
with related ones and sketch future work.

1 Motivation

A distinguishing feature of Answer Set Programming (ASP; [5]) is that all atoms
belonging to a stable model must be *founded*. That is, an atom must not only be
true but provably true. This can be made precise by means of the constructive
logic of Here-and-There (HT; [17]), whose equilibrium models correspond to stable models [23]. One way of looking at foundedness is to regard Boolean truth
values as ordered by letting *true* be greater than *false*. Then, each Boolean variable takes the smallest truth value that can be proven for it. Thus, in analogy to
[20,25] foundedness in ASP can be understood by minimizing values of Boolean
variables. This idea was generalized in [1] to ordered domains and applied to
constraint satisfaction problems. As before, the idea is that a, say integer, variable gets only assigned to the smallest integer that can be justified. In fact, ASP
follows the rationality principle, which says that we shall only believe in things,
we are forced to [15]. While this principle amounts to foundedness in the propositional case, there are at least two views of statements such as $x \geq 42$. First,

© Springer Nature Switzerland AG 2019
F. Calimeri et al. (Eds.): JELIA 2019, LNAI 11468, pp. 509–525, 2019.
https://doi.org/10.1007/978-3-030-19570-0_34

we may accept any value greater or equal than 42 for x. Second, we may only consider value 42 for x, unless there is a reason for a greater value. Arguably, the latter corresponds to the idea of foundedness in ASP.

The ASP literature contains several approaches dealing with atoms containing variables over non-Boolean domains [7,8,18] but these approaches do not comply with foundedness in our sense. For instance, approaches to Constraint ASP (CASP) like [7] only allow for atoms with variables over non-Boolean domains in the body of a rule. Thus, these atoms and the values of non-Boolean variables cannot be founded in terms of ASP.

Approaches like [8,18] focus on foundedness on an atom level and allow for almost any kind of atoms in heads and bodies. They match the view of the rationality principle that accepts any value satisfying a statement like $x \geq 42$. This permits assignments over non-Boolean domains to be founded but the variables are not necessarily assigned to the smallest value that can be justified. The following examples point out the difference of the two views of the rationality principle. Moreover, we show that taking any value satisfying a statement as a rational choice together with separate minimization will not yield foundedness in terms of ASP. Consider the rules

$$x \geq 0 \qquad\qquad y \geq 0 \qquad\qquad x \geq 42 \leftarrow y < 42 \qquad\qquad (1)$$

The approach presented in [8] produces the following result. The first two rules alone would generate any arbitrary pair of positive values for x and y, but the last rule further restricts $x \geq 42$ when the choice for y satisfies $y < 42$. It is clear that this last rule causes the range of x to depend on the value of y. Unfortunately, this dependence disappears if we try to minimize variable values a posteriori by imposing a Pareto minimality criterion on the solutions. If we do so, we get a first minimal solution with $y \mapsto 0$ and $x \mapsto 42$ which somehow captures the expected intuition: we first decide the minimal value of y (which does not depend on x) assigning 0 to y and then apply the third rule to conclude $x \geq 42$ obtaining the minimal value 42 for x. However, among the solutions of (1), we also get those in which we chose $y \geq 42$, so the third rule is not applicable and $x \geq 0$. Therefore, we get a second Pareto-minimal solution with $y \mapsto 42$ and $x \mapsto 0$ that seems counter intuitive: as y does not depend on x there seems to be no reason to assign a minimal value other than 0 to y. To show that separate minimization on solutions does not always yield all (and possibly more) solutions as expected by foundedness, consider the rules

$$x \geq 1 \qquad\qquad x \geq 42 \leftarrow \neg(x \leq 1) \qquad\qquad (2)$$

In this case, depending on whether we assume $\neg(x \leq 1)$ or not, we may get two founded solutions. By assuming $x \leq 1$, the second rule is disabled and the first rule $x \geq 1$ determines the founded minimal value 1 for x, still compatible with the assumption $x \leq 1$. If, on the contrary, we assume $\neg(x \leq 1)$, then the second rule imposes $x \geq 42$ determining the minimal value 42 for x that, again, confirms the assumption $\neg(x \leq 1)$. In other words, we expect two founded solutions with $x \mapsto 1$ and $x \mapsto 42$, respectively. In contrast, if we first apply [8] and then a

Pareto minimization, we lose the solution with $x \mapsto 42$. This is because when assuming $x \leq 1$, we get $x \geq 1$ as before, and the only compatible solution assigns 1 to x, whereas if we assume $\neg(x \leq 1)$, we obtain infinitely many values $x \geq 42$ compatible with the assumption. The solutions are then $x \mapsto 1$ plus the infinite sequence $x \mapsto 42$, $x \mapsto 43$ and so on. Thus, the unique Pareto minimal solution assigns 1 to x.

On the other hand, Aziz' original approach to foundedness [1] has some counter intuitive behavior. In this approach, $p \leftarrow \neg p$ alone yields a solution with p, unlike in traditional ASP. In view of this, we present in the following a logical reconstruction of Aziz' idea of foundedness in the setting of the logic of Here-and-There. More precisely, we start by defining the logic of *Here-and-There with lower bound founded variables* (HT$_{LB}$ for short) along with its equilibrium models.[1] We elaborate upon the formal properties of HT$_{LB}$ like persistence, negation and strong equivalence.[2] Furthermore, we point out the relation of HT$_{LB}$ to HT, and show that our approach can alternatively be captured via a Ferraris-style definition of stable models [11] adapted to our setting. Finally, we compare our approach with related work and point out the benefits of HT$_{LB}$.

2   Background

Let $\mathcal{A}$ be a set of propositional atoms. A formula φ is a combination of atoms by logical connectives $\bot$, $\wedge$, $\vee$, and $\leftarrow$. As usual, we define $\top \stackrel{\text{def}}{=} \bot \rightarrow \bot$ and $\neg\varphi \stackrel{\text{def}}{=} \varphi \rightarrow \bot$. A theory is a set of formulas.

We denote an interpretation over $\mathcal{A}$ by $I \subseteq \mathcal{A}$ and an HT-interpretation over $\mathcal{A}$ by $\langle H, T \rangle$ where $H \subseteq T \subseteq \mathcal{A}$ are interpretations. Since we want to abstract from the specific form of atoms, we rely upon denotations for fixing their semantics. A *denotation* of atoms in $\mathcal{A}$ is a function $\llbracket \cdot \rrbracket_\mathcal{A} : \mathcal{A} \rightarrow 2^{2^\mathcal{A}}$ mapping atoms in $\mathcal{A}$ to sets of interpretations over $\mathcal{A}$. Accordingly, $\llbracket p \rrbracket_\mathcal{A} \stackrel{\text{def}}{=} \{I \mid p \in I\}$ represents the set of interpretations where atom p holds.

With it, we next define satisfaction of formulas in HT.

Definition 1. *Let $\langle H, T \rangle$ be an HT-interpretation over $\mathcal{A}$ and φ a propositional formula over $\mathcal{A}$. Then, $\langle H, T \rangle$ satisfies φ, written $\langle H, T \rangle \models \varphi$, if the following conditions hold:*

1. $\langle H, T \rangle \not\models \bot$
2. $\langle H, T \rangle \models p$ iff $H \in \llbracket p \rrbracket_\mathcal{A}$ for propositional atom $p \in \mathcal{A}$
3. $\langle H, T \rangle \models \varphi_1 \wedge \varphi_2$ iff $\langle H, T \rangle \models \varphi_1$ and $\langle H, T \rangle \models \varphi_2$
4. $\langle H, T \rangle \models \varphi_1 \vee \varphi_2$ iff $\langle H, T \rangle \models \varphi_1$ or $\langle H, T \rangle \models \varphi_2$
5. $\langle H, T \rangle \models \varphi_1 \rightarrow \varphi_2$ iff $\langle I, T \rangle \not\models \varphi_1$ or $\langle I, T \rangle \models \varphi_2$ for both $I \in \{H, T\}$

As usual, we call $\langle H, T \rangle$ an HT-model of a theory Γ, if $\langle H, T \rangle \models \varphi$ for all φ in Γ. The usual definition of HT satisfaction (cf. [23]) is obtained by replacing Condition 2 above by

---

[1] Upper bound founded variables are treated analogously.

[2] We provide an extended version including all proofs at: www.cs.uni-potsdam.de/~seschell/JELIA19-paper-proofs.pdf.

2'. $\langle H, T \rangle \models p$ iff $p \in H$ for propositional atom $p \in \mathcal{A}$

It is easy to see that both definitions of HT satisfaction coincide.

Proposition 1. *Let $\langle H, T \rangle$ be an HT-interpretation and φ a formula over $\mathcal{A}$. Then, $\langle H, T \rangle \models \varphi$ iff $\langle H, T \rangle \models \varphi$ by replacing Condition 2 by 2'.*

As usual, an equilibrium model of a theory Γ is a (total) HT-interpretation $\langle T, T \rangle$ such that $\langle T, T \rangle \models \Gamma$ and there is no $H \subset T$ such that $\langle H, T \rangle \models \Gamma$. Then, T is also called a stable model of Γ.

Let us recall some characteristic properties of HT. For HT-interpretations $\langle H, T \rangle$ and $\langle T, T \rangle$ and formula φ over $\mathcal{A}$ both $\langle H, T \rangle \models \varphi$ implies $\langle T, T \rangle \models \varphi$ (*persistence*) and $\langle H, T \rangle \models \varphi \to \bot$ iff $\langle T, T \rangle \not\models \varphi$ (*negation*) holds. Furthermore, $\Gamma_1 \cup \Gamma$ and $\Gamma_2 \cup \Gamma$ have the same stable models for theories Γ_1 and Γ_2 and any theory Γ over $\mathcal{A}$ iff Γ_1 and Γ_2 have the same HT-models (*strong equivalence*).

3   Lower Bound Founded Logic of Here-and-There

In what follows, we introduce the logic of Here-and-There with lower bound founded variables, short HT_{LB}, and elaborate on its formal properties.

3.1 HT_{LB} Properties

The language of HT_{LB} is defined over a set of atoms $\mathcal{A}_{\mathcal{X}}$ comprising variables, $\mathcal{X}$, and constants over an ordered domain $(\mathcal{D}, \succeq)$. For simplicity, we assume that each element of $\mathcal{D}$ is uniquely represented by a constant and abuse notation by using elements from $\mathcal{D}$ to refer to constants. Similarly, we identify $\succeq$ with its syntactic representative. The specific syntax of atoms is left open but assumed to refer to elements of $\mathcal{X}$ and $\mathcal{D}$. The only requirement is that we assume that an atom depends on a subset of variables in $\mathcal{X}$. An atom can be understood to hold or not once all variables in it are substituted by domain elements. Clearly, variables not occurring in an atom are understood as irrelevant for its evaluation. Examples of ordered domains are $(\{0, 1, 2, 3\}, \geq)$ and $(\mathbb{Z}, \geq)$, respectively; corresponding atoms are $x = y$ and $x \geq 42$. An example of a formula is '$y < 42 \land \neg(x = y) \to x \geq 42$'. We let $vars(\varphi) \subseteq \mathcal{X}$ be the set of variables and $atoms(\varphi) \subseteq \mathcal{A}_{\mathcal{X}}$ the atoms occurring in a formula φ.

For capturing partiality, we introduce a special domain element u, standing for *undefined*, and extend $(\mathcal{D}, \succeq)$ to $(\mathcal{D}_u, \succeq_u)$ where $\mathcal{D}_u \stackrel{\text{def}}{=} \mathcal{D} \cup \{u\}$ and $\succeq_u \stackrel{\text{def}}{=} \succeq \cup \{(c, u) \mid c \in \mathcal{D}_u\}$. With it, we define a (partial) *valuation* over $\mathcal{X}, \mathcal{D}$ as a function $v : \mathcal{X} \to \mathcal{D}_u$ mapping each variable to a domain value or undefined. For comparing valuations by set-based means, we alternatively represent them by subsets of $\mathcal{X} \times \mathcal{D}$. Basically, any function v is a set of pairs (x, c) such that $v(x) = c$ for $c \in \mathcal{D}$. In addition, we view a pair (x, c) as $x \succeq c$ and add its downward closure $(x \downarrow c) \stackrel{\text{def}}{=} \{(x, d) \mid c, d \in \mathcal{D}, c \succeq d\}$. Given this, a valuation v

is represented by the set $\bigcup_{v(x)=c,x\in\mathcal{X}}(x\downarrow c).$[3] As an example, consider variables x and y over domain $(\{0,1,2,3\},\geq)$. The valuation $v = \{x \mapsto 2, y \mapsto 0\}$ can be represented by $v = (x \downarrow 2) \cup (y \downarrow 0) = \{(x,0),(x,1),(x,2),(y,0)\}$. Then, $v' = \{x \mapsto 1, y \mapsto u\}$, viz. $\{(x,0),(x,1)\}$ in set notation, can be regarded as "smaller" than v because $v' \subseteq v$. The comparison of two valuations v and v' by set-inclusion $\subseteq$ amounts to a twofold comparison. That is, v and v' are compared regarding the occurrence of variables and their particular values wrt $\succeq$. We let $\mathfrak{V}_{\mathcal{X},\mathcal{D}}$ stand for the set of valuations over $\mathcal{X}$ and $\mathcal{D}$.

We define the satisfaction of formulas over $\mathcal{A}_{\mathcal{X}}$ wrt *atom denotations* over $\mathcal{X},\mathcal{D}$, which are functions $[\![\cdot]\!]_{\mathcal{X},\mathcal{D}} : \mathcal{A}_{\mathcal{X}} \to 2^{\mathfrak{V}_{\mathcal{X},\mathcal{D}}}$ mapping atoms to sets of valuations. Let a be an atom of $\mathcal{A}_{\mathcal{X}}$ and $[\![a]\!]_{\mathcal{X},\mathcal{D}}$ its denotation. Then, $[\![a]\!]_{\mathcal{X},\mathcal{D}}$ is the set of valuations making a true. Since a depends on variables $vars(a) \subseteq \mathcal{X}$, we have for each $v \in [\![a]\!]_{\mathcal{X},\mathcal{D}}$ and valuation v' with $v(x) = v'(x)$ for $x \in vars(a)$ that $v' \in [\![a]\!]_{\mathcal{X},\mathcal{D}}$. Intuitively, values of $\mathcal{X} \setminus vars(a)$ may vary freely without changing the membership of a valuation to $[\![a]\!]_{\mathcal{X},\mathcal{D}}$. For simplicity, we drop indices $\mathcal{X},\mathcal{D}$ whenever clear from context.

For instance, interpreting the atoms $x \geq 42$, $42 \geq 0$ and $0 \geq 42$ over $(\mathbb{Z},\geq)$ yields the following denotations:

$$[\![x \geq 42]\!] \stackrel{\text{def}}{=} \{v \mid v(x) \geq 42\} \qquad [\![42 \geq 0]\!] \stackrel{\text{def}}{=} \mathfrak{V} \qquad [\![0 \geq 42]\!] \stackrel{\text{def}}{=} \emptyset.$$

$[\![x \geq 42]\!]$ is the set of valuations assigning x to values greater or equal than 42 and all variables in $\mathcal{X} \setminus \{x\}$ take any value in $\mathcal{D}_u$, eg $(x \downarrow 45)$ and $(x \downarrow 45) \cup (y \downarrow 0)$ for $y \in \mathcal{X} \setminus \{x\}$ are possible valuations. Interestingly, atoms like $x \succeq x$ with $[\![x \succeq x]\!] = \{v \mid v(x) \neq u\}$ force variables to be defined over $\mathcal{D}$ per definition of $\succeq$. A valuation v is *defined* for a set of variables $\mathcal{Y} \subseteq \mathcal{X}$ if $v(x) \neq u$ for all $x \in \mathcal{Y}$.

We define an HT_{LB}-valuation over $\mathcal{X},\mathcal{D}$ as a pair $\langle h,t\rangle$ of valuations over $\mathcal{X},\mathcal{D}$ with $h \subseteq t$. We define satisfaction of formulas in HT_{LB} as follows.

Definition 2. *Let $\langle h,t\rangle$ be an HT_{LB}-valuation over $\mathcal{X},\mathcal{D}$ and φ be a formula over $\mathcal{A}_{\mathcal{X}}$. Then, $\langle h,t\rangle$ satisfies φ, written $\langle h,t\rangle \models \varphi$, if the following holds:*

1. $\langle h,t\rangle \not\models \bot$
2. $\langle h,t\rangle \models a$ *iff* $v \in [\![a]\!]_{\mathcal{X},\mathcal{D}}$ *for atom* $a \in \mathcal{A}_{\mathcal{X}}$ *and for both* $v \in \{h,t\}$
3. $\langle h,t\rangle \models \varphi_1 \wedge \varphi_2$ *iff* $\langle h,t\rangle \models \varphi_1$ *and* $\langle h,t\rangle \models \varphi_2$
4. $\langle h,t\rangle \models \varphi_1 \vee \varphi_2$ *iff* $\langle h,t\rangle \models \varphi_1$ *or* $\langle h,t\rangle \models \varphi_2$
5. $\langle h,t\rangle \models \varphi_1 \to \varphi_2$ *iff* $\langle v,t\rangle \not\models \varphi_1$ *or* $\langle v,t\rangle \models \varphi_2$ *for both* $v \in \{h,t\}$

As usual, we call $\langle h,t\rangle$ an HT_{LB}-model of a theory Γ, if $\langle h,t\rangle \models \varphi$ for all φ in Γ. For a simple example, consider the theory containing atom $x \geq 42$ only. Then, every HT_{LB}-valuation $\langle h,t\rangle$ with $h,t \in [\![x \geq 42]\!]$ is an HT_{LB}-model of $x \geq 42$. Note that, different to HT, satisfaction of atoms in HT_{LB} forces satisfaction in both h and t, instead of h only. We discuss this in detail below when comparing to a Ferraris-like stable model semantics.

Our first result shows that the characteristic properties of persistence and negation hold as well when basing satisfaction on valuations and denotations.

---

[3] Note that $(x \downarrow u) = \emptyset$, since $u \notin \mathcal{D}$.

Proposition 2. *Let $\langle h, t \rangle$ and $\langle t, t \rangle$ be HT_{LB}-valuations over $\mathcal{X}, \mathcal{D}$, and φ be a formula over $\mathcal{A}_{\mathcal{X}}$. Then,*

1. $\langle h, t \rangle \models \varphi$ implies $\langle t, t \rangle \models \varphi$, and
2. $\langle h, t \rangle \models \varphi \to \bot$ iff $\langle t, t \rangle \not\models \varphi$.

Persistence implies that all atoms satisfied by $\langle h, t \rangle$ are also satisfied by $\langle t, t \rangle$. To make this precise, let $At(\langle h, t \rangle) \stackrel{\text{def}}{=} \{ a \in \mathcal{A}_{\mathcal{X}} \mid h \in [\![\, a \,]\!] \text{ and } t \in [\![\, a \,]\!] \}$ be the set of atoms satisfied by $\langle h, t \rangle$.

Corollary 1. *Let $\langle h, t \rangle$ and $\langle t, t \rangle$ be HT_{LB}-valuations over $\mathcal{X}, \mathcal{D}$. Then, $At(\langle h, t \rangle) \subseteq At(\langle t, t \rangle)$.*

Finally, we define an equilibrium model in HT_{LB}.

Definition 3. *An HT_{LB}-valuation $\langle t, t \rangle$ over $\mathcal{X}, \mathcal{D}$ is an HT_{LB}-equilibrium model of a theory Γ iff $\langle t, t \rangle \models \Gamma$ and there is no $h \subset t$ such that $\langle h, t \rangle \models \Gamma$.*

We refer to an HT_{LB}-equilibrium model $\langle t, t \rangle$ of Γ as an HT_{LB}-stable model t of Γ. Let us reconsider the theory containing atom $x \geq 42$ only. Then, $t = (x \downarrow 42)$ is an HT_{LB}-stable model of $x \geq 42$, since $t \in [\![\, x \geq 42 \,]\!]$ and there is no $h \subset t$ with $h \in [\![\, x \geq 42 \,]\!]$. In contrast, neither HT_{LB}-model $\langle t', t' \rangle$ with $t' = (x \downarrow 42) \cup (y \downarrow 0)$ nor $\langle t'', t'' \rangle$ with $t'' = (x \downarrow 53)$ are HT_{LB}-stable models since t is a proper subset of both and $\langle t, t' \rangle \models x \geq 42$ as well as $\langle t, t'' \rangle \models x \geq 42$ holds. Hence, HT_{LB}-stable models make sure that each variable is assigned to its smallest founded value.

Note that HT_{LB}-equilibrium models induce the non-monotonic counterpart of the monotonic logic of HT_{LB}. Following well-known patterns, we show that HT_{LB} allows us to decide strong equivalence wrt HT_{LB}-equilibrium models.

Proposition 3 (Strong Equivalence). *Let Γ_1, Γ_2 and Γ be theories over $\mathcal{A}_{\mathcal{X}}$.*
Then, theories $\Gamma_1 \cup \Gamma$ and $\Gamma_2 \cup \Gamma$ have the same HT_{LB}-stable models for every theory Γ iff Γ_1 and Γ_2 have the same HT_{LB}-models.

The idea is to prove the only if direction via contraposition, and the if direction by proving its direct implication. The contraposition assumes that there exists an HT_{LB}-valuation that satisfies Γ_1 but not Γ_2 which implies that the stable models of $\Gamma_1 \cup \Gamma$ and $\Gamma_2 \cup \Gamma$ do not coincide. There are two cases to construct Γ in a way that $\Gamma_1 \cup \Gamma$ has a stable model which is not a stable model of $\Gamma_2 \cup \Gamma$ and the other way around. Consider an example to illustrate the idea of the construction of Γ. Let $h = (x \downarrow 0)$ and $t = (x \downarrow 2) \cup (y \downarrow 0)$ be HT_{LB}-valuation over $\{x, y\}, \{0, 1, 2, 3\}$ with $\langle h, t \rangle \models \Gamma_1$ and $\langle h, t \rangle \not\models \Gamma_2$. For the first case, assume that $\langle t, t \rangle \not\models \Gamma_2$. Since t cannot be a model of $\Gamma_2 \cup \Gamma$ by assumption, we construct Γ in a way that t is a stable model of $\Gamma_1 \cup \Gamma$. Hence, let $\Gamma = \{ z \succeq c \mid (z, c) \in t \} = \{ x \succeq 0, x \succeq 1, x \succeq 2, y \succeq 0 \}$ be the theory with the only stable model t. By persistence of $\langle h, t \rangle$ wrt Γ_1 and construction of Γ, we get that t is a stable model of $\Gamma_1 \cup \Gamma$ but not of $\Gamma_2 \cup \Gamma$. For the second case, we assume $\langle t, t \rangle \models \Gamma_2$. Now, we construct Γ in a way that

t is a stable model of $\Gamma_2 \cup \Gamma$ but not of $\Gamma_1 \cup \Gamma$. By assumption, we have that $\langle h, t \rangle \models \Gamma_1$ and $\langle h, t \rangle \not\models \Gamma_2$ as well as $\langle t, t \rangle \models \Gamma_2$, thus we want to have $\langle h, t \rangle$ and $\langle v, v' \rangle$ with $t \subseteq v \subseteq v'$ as the only models of Γ. Hence, let $\Gamma = \Gamma' \cup \Gamma''$ with $\Gamma' = \{z \succeq c \mid (z, c) \in h\} = \{x \succeq 0\}$ be the theory satisfied by everything greater or equal than h, and $\Gamma'' = \{z \succeq t(z) \to z' \succeq t(z'),\ z \succeq c \to z \succeq t(z) \mid (z, c), (z, t(z)), (z', t(z')) \in t \setminus h, z \neq z'\} = \{x \succeq 2 \to y \succeq 0,\ y \succeq 0 \to x \succeq 2,\ x \succeq 1 \to x \succeq 2,\ x \succeq 2 \to x \succeq 2\}$ the theory deriving values of t for each v'' with $h \subset v'' \subset t$. Since $\langle h, t \rangle \not\models \Gamma_2$ and by construction of Γ, we get that t is a stable model of $\Gamma_2 \cup \Gamma$ but not of $\Gamma_1 \cup \Gamma$.

The following result shows that a formula $a \leftarrow \neg a$ has no stable model if a cannot be derived by some other formula.

Proposition 4. *Let Γ be a theory over $\mathcal{A}_\mathcal{X}$ containing a formula of form $a \leftarrow \neg a$ and for each HT_{LB}-stable model v of $\Gamma \setminus \{a \leftarrow \neg a\}$ over $\mathcal{X}, \mathcal{D}$ we have that $\langle v, v \rangle \not\models a$.*
Then, Γ has no HT_{LB}-stable model.

This proposition may seem to be trivial but we show in Sect. 4 that Aziz' original approach does not satisfy this property.

3.2 Negation in HT$_{LB}$

In the following, we elaborate on complements of atoms and their relation to negation, since $\mathcal{A}_\mathcal{X}$ may contain atoms like $x \geq 42$ and $x < 42$. Intuitively, the complement of an atom holds whenever the atom itself does not hold. This can be easily expressed by using atom denotations. More formally, the complement $\overline{a}$ of atom a is defined by its denotation $[\![\,\overline{a}\,]\!]_{\mathcal{X}, \mathcal{D}} \overset{\text{def}}{=} 2^{\mathfrak{V}_{\mathcal{X}, \mathcal{D}}} \setminus [\![\,a\,]\!]_{\mathcal{X}, \mathcal{D}}$.

To illustrate that the simple complement of an atom is insufficient to yield something similar to strong negation let us take a closer look at propositional atoms in HT$_{LB}$. For mimicking Boolean truth values, we consider the domain $(\{\mathbf{t}, \mathbf{f}\}, \{\mathbf{t} \succeq \mathbf{f}\})$. Then, the denotation of propositional atoms in HT$_{LB}$ can be defined as follows: $[\![\,p = \mathbf{t}\,]\!]_{\mathcal{A}, \{\mathbf{t}, \mathbf{f}\}} \overset{\text{def}}{=} \{v \mid v(p) = \mathbf{t}\}$ and $[\![\,p = \mathbf{f}\,]\!]_{\mathcal{A}, \{\mathbf{t}, \mathbf{f}\}} \overset{\text{def}}{=} \{v \mid v(p) = \mathbf{f}\}$. Note that $p = \mathbf{t}$ and $p = \mathbf{f}$ are regarded as strong negations of each other, as in the standard case [16]; their weak negations are given by $\neg(p = \mathbf{t})$ and $\neg(p = \mathbf{f})$, respectively. For instance, the complement $\overline{p = \mathbf{t}}$ is characterized by denotation $[\![\,\overline{p = \mathbf{t}}\,]\!]_{\mathcal{A}, \{\mathbf{t}, \mathbf{f}\}} = 2^{\mathfrak{V}_{\mathcal{A}, \{\mathbf{t}, \mathbf{f}\}}} \setminus [\![\,p = \mathbf{t}\,]\!]_{\mathcal{A}, \{\mathbf{t}, \mathbf{f}\}} = \{v \mid v(p) \neq \mathbf{t}\}$. However, this complement allows for valuations v with $v(p) = \boldsymbol{u}$ which are not in $[\![\,p = \mathbf{f}\,]\!]_{\mathcal{A}, \{\mathbf{t}, \mathbf{f}\}}$.

Let us define another complement to exclude assigning undefined to variables of an atom. First, we define a denotation $[\![\,a\,]\!]_{\mathcal{X}, \mathcal{D}}$ of an atom a as *strict* if each $v \in [\![\,a\,]\!]_{\mathcal{X}, \mathcal{D}}$ is defined for $vars(a)$. Then, we characterize the strict complement $\overline{a}^s$ of atom a by the strict denotation $[\![\,\overline{a}^s\,]\!]_{\mathcal{X}, \mathcal{D}} \overset{\text{def}}{=} 2^{\mathfrak{V}_{\mathcal{X}, \mathcal{D}}} \setminus ([\![\,a\,]\!]_{\mathcal{X}, \mathcal{D}} \cup \{v \mid v(x) = \boldsymbol{u} \text{ for some } x \in vars(a)\})$. Informally, the strict complement of an atom holds whenever all variables are defined and the atom itself does not hold. That is, atoms $p = \mathbf{f}$ and $p = \mathbf{t}$ are strict complements of each other.

More generally, an atom with a strict denotation and its strict complement can be regarded as being strongly negated to each other. For instance, consider atom $x \geq 42$ and its strict denotation $[\![\, x \geq 42\,]\!]_{\mathcal{X},\mathcal{D}} = \{v \mid v(x) \geq 42\}$. Then, its strict complement $\overline{x \geq 42}^{\,s}$ is defined by $[\![\, \overline{x \geq 42}^{\,s}\,]\!]_{\mathcal{X},\mathcal{D}} = \{v \mid \boldsymbol{u} \neq v(x) < 42\}$. As in the Boolean case, the strict complement $\overline{x \geq 42}^{\,s}$ can be seen as the strong negation of $x \geq 42$.

For making the relation of complements and negation precise, we define *entailment*: A theory Γ over $\mathcal{A}_{\mathcal{X}}$ entails a formula φ over $\mathcal{A}_{\mathcal{X}}$, written $\Gamma \models \varphi$, if all HT$_{\text{LB}}$-models of Γ are HT$_{\text{LB}}$-models of φ. Then, we have the following result.

Proposition 5. *Let a be an atom over $\mathcal{A}_{\mathcal{X}}$, and $\overline{a}$ and $\overline{a}^{\,s}$ its complement and its strict complement over $\mathcal{A}_{\mathcal{X}}$, respectively.*
Then, $\{\overline{a}^{\,s}\} \models \overline{a}$ and $\{\overline{a}\} \models \neg a$.

This implies that the strict complement $\overline{a}^{\,s}$ of an atom a implies its negation $\neg a$, just as strong negation implies weak negation in the standard case [23]. To illustrate that in general the negation of an atom does not entail its complement, viz $\{\neg a\} \not\models \overline{a}$, consider atom $x \leq 42$ with strict denotation $[\![\, x \leq 42\,]\!]_{\mathcal{X},\mathcal{D}} = \{v \mid \boldsymbol{u} \neq v(x) \leq 42\}$. Then, its complement $\overline{x \leq 42}$ is defined by $[\![\, \overline{x \leq 42}\,]\!]_{\mathcal{X},\mathcal{D}} = 2^{\mathfrak{V}_{\mathcal{X},\mathcal{D}}} \setminus [\![\, x \leq 42\,]\!]_{\mathcal{X},\mathcal{D}} = \{v \mid v(x) = \boldsymbol{u} \text{ or } v(x) > 42\}$. For valuations $h = (x \downarrow 42)$ and $t = (x \downarrow 50)$, we have $\langle h, t \rangle \models \neg(x \leq 42)$ since $(x \downarrow 50) \notin [\![\, x \leq 42\,]\!]_{\mathcal{X},\mathcal{D}}$. In contrast, $\langle h, t \rangle \not\models \overline{x \leq 42}$, since $(x \downarrow 42) \notin [\![\, \overline{x \leq 42}\,]\!]_{\mathcal{X},\mathcal{D}}$. Thus, the complement $\overline{a}$ can be seen as a kind of negation in between strong and weak negation.

3.3   HT$_{\text{LB}}$ versus HT

Analogously to [8], we next show that HT can be seen as a special case of HT$_{\text{LB}}$.

Note that both types of denotations $[\![\, p\,]\!]_{\mathcal{A}}$ in HT and $[\![\, p = \mathbf{t}\,]\!]_{\mathcal{A},\{\mathbf{t}\}}$ in HT$_{\text{LB}}$ of a propositional atom p collect interpretations and valuations assigning true to p. To begin with, we define a transformation τ relating each propositional atom p with corresponding atom $p = \mathbf{t}$ by $\tau(p) \stackrel{\text{def}}{=} p = \mathbf{t}$. Let Γ be a propositional theory, then $\tau(\Gamma)$ is obtained by substituting each $p \in atoms(\Gamma)$ by $\tau(p)$. Moreover, we extend τ to interpretations I by $\tau(I) \stackrel{\text{def}}{=} \{(p, \mathbf{t}) \mid p \in I\}$ to obtain a corresponding valuation over $\mathcal{A}, \{\mathbf{t}\}$. The next proposition establishes that HT can be seen as a special case of HT$_{\text{LB}}$.

Proposition 6. *Let Γ be a theory over propositional atoms $\mathcal{A}$ and $\langle H, T \rangle$ an HT-interpretation over $\mathcal{A}$. Let $\tau(\Gamma)$ be a theory over atoms $\{p = \mathbf{t} \mid p \in \mathcal{A}\}$ and $\langle \tau(H), \tau(T) \rangle$ an HT$_{LB}$-valuation over $\mathcal{A}, \{\mathbf{t}\}$.*
Then, $\langle H, T \rangle \models \Gamma$ iff $\langle \tau(H), \tau(T) \rangle \models \tau(\Gamma)$.

This can be generalized to any arbitrary singleton domain $\{d\}$ and corresponding atoms $p = d$ and the relationship still holds.

We obtain the following result relating HT$_{\text{LB}}$ and HT:

Proposition 7. *Let Γ be a theory over $\mathcal{A}_{\mathcal{X}}$ and $\langle h, t \rangle$ an HT$_{LB}$-model of Γ over $\mathcal{X}, \mathcal{D}$.*
Then, $\langle At(\langle h, t \rangle), At(\langle t, t \rangle) \rangle$ is an HT-model of Γ over $\mathcal{A}_{\mathcal{X}}$.

That is, the collected atoms satisfied by an HT_{LB}-model of Γ can be seen as an HT-model of Γ by interpreting $\mathcal{A}_\mathcal{X}$ as propositional atoms. For instance, consider the theory containing only atom $x \neq y$ and its denotation $[\![x \neq y]\!] \stackrel{\text{def}}{=} \{ v \mid \boldsymbol{u} \neq v(x) \neq v(y) \neq \boldsymbol{u} \}$. Let $h = (x \downarrow 0) \cup (y \downarrow 4)$ and $t = (x \downarrow 0) \cup (y \downarrow 42)$ be valuations and hence $At(\langle h, t \rangle) = At(\langle t, t \rangle) = \{ x \neq y \}$ interpretations. Then, $\langle h, t \rangle \models x \neq y$ in HT_{LB} and $\langle At(\langle h, t \rangle), At(\langle t, t \rangle) \rangle \models x \neq y$ in HT.

Furthermore, we relate tautologies in HT and HT_{LB}.

Proposition 8. *Let φ be a tautology in HT over $\mathcal{A}$ and φ' a formula over $\mathcal{A}_\mathcal{X}$ obtained by replacing each atom in φ by an atom of $\mathcal{A}_\mathcal{X}$.*

Then, φ' is a tautology in HT_{LB}.

That is, tautologies in HT are independent of the form of atoms. For example, consider the well known tautology $p \to p$ over $\mathcal{A}$. Then, $x \geq 42 \to x \geq 42$ over $\mathcal{A}_\mathcal{X}$ is a tautology as well. Note that the other direction of the implication does not hold, since $x \geq 42 \to y \geq 42$ over $\mathcal{A}_\mathcal{X}$ with domain $\{42\}$ is a tautology, but $p \to q$ over $\mathcal{A}$ is not.

3.4 HT_{LB}-stable versus Ferraris-style stable models

As mentioned, in Definition 2 satisfaction of atoms differs from HT by forcing satisfaction in both h and t, instead of h only. This is necessary to guarantee persistence in HT_{LB}. To see this, consider an HT_{LB}-valuation $\langle h, t \rangle$ satisfying atom a in $\mathcal{A}_\mathcal{X}$. Hence, by persistence, HT_{LB}-valuation $\langle t, t \rangle$ satisfies a as well. However, this does not necessarily mean that HT_{LB}-valuations $\langle v, t \rangle$ with $h \subset v \subset t$ satisfy a. For instance, consider atom $x \neq 42$ with $[\![x \neq 42]\!] \stackrel{\text{def}}{=} \{ v \mid \boldsymbol{u} \neq v(x) \neq 42 \}$ and valuations $h = (x \downarrow 0)$ and $t = (x \downarrow 53)$. Then, $\langle h, t \rangle \models x \neq 42$ and $\langle t, t \rangle \models x \neq 42$, but $\langle v, t \rangle \not\models x \neq 42$ for $v = (x \downarrow 42)$ with $h \subset v \subset t$.

A question that arises now is whether HT_{LB} behaves in accord with stable models semantics. To this end, we give straightforward definitions of classical satisfaction and the reduct by Ferraris [11] in our setting and show that equilibrium models correspond to stable models according to the resulting Ferraris-like stable model semantics.

We define the counterpart of classical satisfaction as follows.

Definition 4. *Let t be a valuation over $\mathcal{X}, \mathcal{D}$ and φ a formula over $\mathcal{A}_\mathcal{X}$. Then, t satisfies φ, written $t \models_{cl} \varphi$, if the following holds:*

1. $t \not\models_{cl} \bot$
2. $t \models_{cl} a$ iff $t \in [\![a]\!]_{\mathcal{X},\mathcal{D}}$ for atom $a \in \mathcal{A}_\mathcal{X}$
3. $t \models_{cl} \varphi_1 \wedge \varphi_2$ iff $t \models_{cl} \varphi_1$ and $t \models_{cl} \varphi_2$
4. $t \models_{cl} \varphi_1 \vee \varphi_2$ iff $t \models_{cl} \varphi_1$ or $t \models_{cl} \varphi_2$
5. $t \models_{cl} \varphi_1 \to \varphi_2$ iff $t \not\models_{cl} \varphi_1$ or $t \models_{cl} \varphi_2$.

We call t a classical model of a theory Γ, if $t \models_{cl} \varphi$ for all φ in Γ.

Then, we define a Ferraris-like reduct for formulas over $\mathcal{A}_\mathcal{X}$ as follows.

Definition 5. *Let φ be a formula over $\mathcal{A}_{\mathcal{X}}$ and t a valuation over $\mathcal{X}, \mathcal{D}$. Then, the reduct of φ wrt t, written φ^t, is defined as*

$$\varphi^t \stackrel{\text{def}}{=} \begin{cases} \bot & \text{if } t \not\models_{cl} \varphi \\ a & \text{if } t \models_{cl} \varphi \text{ and } \varphi = a \text{ is an atom in } \mathcal{A}_{\mathcal{X}} \\ \varphi_1{}^t \otimes \varphi_2{}^t & \text{if } t \models_{cl} \varphi \text{ and } \varphi = (\varphi_1 \otimes \varphi_2) \text{ for } \otimes \in \{\wedge, \vee, \rightarrow\} \end{cases}$$

For theory Γ and HT$_{LB}$-valuation t, we define $\Gamma^t \stackrel{\text{def}}{=} \{\varphi^t \mid \varphi \in \Gamma\}$. Note that in case of propositional formulas our reduct corresponds to Ferraris' original [11].

With it, we define a Ferraris-like stable model as expected.

Definition 6. *A valuation t over $\mathcal{X}, \mathcal{D}$ is a Ferraris-like stable model of theory Γ over $\mathcal{A}_{\mathcal{X}}$ iff $t \models_{cl} \Gamma^t$ and there is no $h \subset t$ such that $h \models_{cl} \Gamma^t$.*

In analogy to the standard case [11], the next proposition shows that models in HT$_{LB}$ can be alternatively characterized in the style of Ferraris:

Proposition 9. *Let $\langle h, t \rangle$ be an HT$_{LB}$-valuation over $\mathcal{X}, \mathcal{D}$ and Γ a theory over $\mathcal{A}_{\mathcal{X}}$.*
Then, $h \models_{cl} \Gamma^t$ iff $\langle h, t \rangle \models \Gamma$.

As a special case, we obtain that every HT$_{LB}$-stable model corresponds to a Ferraris-like stable model and vice versa.

Corollary 2. *Let t be a valuation over $\mathcal{X}, \mathcal{D}$ and Γ a theory over $\mathcal{A}_{\mathcal{X}}$.*
Then, t is an HT$_{LB}$-stable model of Γ iff t is a Ferraris-like stable model of Γ.

The last two results show that our logic follows well known patterns wrt different representations of stable models.

3.5 Modeling with Bound Founded Programs

In what follows, we define logic programs over linear constraint atoms to illustrate the modeling capabilities of HT$_{LB}$ on an example.

We define *linear constraint atoms* over the integers $(\mathbb{Z}, \geq)$ as

$$\sum_{i=1}^{m} w_i x_i \prec k$$

where $w_i, k \in \mathbb{Z}$ are constants, $x_i \in \mathcal{X}$ are distinct variables, and $\prec \in \{\geq, \leq, \neq, =\}^4$ is a binary relation. The denotation of a linear constraint atom is given by $[\![\sum_{i=1}^{m} w_i x_i \prec k]\!] \stackrel{\text{def}}{=} \{v \mid \sum_{i=1}^{m} w_i v(x_i) \prec k, \ v(x_i) \neq \boldsymbol{u}\}$. We denote the set of linear constraint atoms over variables $\mathcal{X}$ and domain $(\mathbb{Z}, \geq)$ by $\mathcal{L}_{\mathcal{X}}$.

---

[4] As usual, $w_1 x_1, + \cdots + w_n x_n < k$ and $w_1 x_1, + \cdots + w_n x_n > k$ can be expressed by $w_1 x_1, + \cdots + w_n x_n \leq k - 1$ and $w_1 x_1, + \cdots + w_n x_n \geq k + 1$, respectively.

A linear constraint atom a and its negation $\neg a$ over $\mathcal{L}_\chi$ are called literals. A *rule* is a formula over $\mathcal{L}_\chi$ of form

$$a_1 \vee \cdots \vee a_n \leftarrow l_1 \wedge \cdots \wedge l_{n'} \tag{3}$$

where a_i is a linear constraint atom for $1 \leq i \leq n$ and l_j is a literal for $1 \leq j \leq n'$. A *logic program* is a theory over $\mathcal{L}_\chi$ of rules of form (3).

As an example, consider the dependency of the revolutions per minute (rpm) of the engine of our car to its maximal range. The maximal range of a car decreases with higher rpm; we need more fuel when choosing a smaller gear which increases the rpm assuming the same conditions like speed. For simplicity, we do not model gears, fuel or speed. Assume that our car needs at least 2000 rpm. Moreover, we know that our car has a range of at least 100 km. If we go by less than 4000 rpm, then our range is at least 200 km. Then, the following program P models the dependency of rpm and range without explicitly using negation or minimization:

$$\text{rpm} \geq 2000$$
$$\text{range} \geq 100$$
$$\text{range} \geq 200 \leftarrow \text{rpm} < 4000$$

The HT_{LB}-stable model of P is (range $\downarrow$ 200) $\cup$ (rpm $\downarrow$ 2000), since 2000 is the minimal value satisfying rpm $\geq$ 2000 and thus rpm $<$ 4000 holds and yields range $\geq$ 200. For instance, if we extend P by the new statement rpm $\geq$ 4000, then we get the HT_{LB}-stable model (range $\downarrow$ 100) $\cup$ (rpm $\downarrow$ 4000), since the minimal value derived by rpm $\geq$ 4000 does not produce range $\geq$ 200 any more. Thus, 100 is the minimal value for range derived by range $\geq$ 100. Intuitively, it makes no sense to go by higher rpm and thus decrease the range if one is not forced to.

This example behaves similar to the example in (1). The intuition is to minimize the value of rpm first since it does not depend on range. Afterwards, we derive the minimal value of range out of the obtained consequences. Note that this example can also be modeled by other approaches like [1,8], but those may not provide the same intuitive modeling to achieve a bound founded semantics or behave counter intuitive on some well known modeling techniques like integrity constraints. For instance, the approach of [8] yields solutions for P consisting of any arbitrary pair of values with rpm $\geq$ 2000 and range $\geq$ 100 where range is further restricted to values greater or equal to 200 if the choice of rpm is smaller than 4000. To achieve the same bound founded intuition as in HT_{LB} with approaches like [8] we need to rewrite the rpm example in a less intuitive way. This is similar to representing formula $p \leftarrow q$ under stable models semantics in propositional logic.

4   Related Work

We start by comparing our approach to Aziz' Bound Founded ASP (BFASP; [1]). Both aim at generalizing foundedness to ordered domains. In BFASP, an arbitrary formula is called constraint and a rule is defined as a pair of a constraint and a variable called head. The constraint needs to be increasing wrt its head variable. Informally, a constraint is increasing in a variable if the constraint is monotonic in this variable. Note that increasing is defined on constraints instead of atoms. For an example, the constraint $x \leq 42$ is not increasing in x, but the constraint $x \leq 42 \leftarrow y < 0$ is increasing in x over domain $\mathbb{N}$. Stable models are defined in BFASP via a reduct depending on the monotonicity of constraints wrt their variables and by applying a fix point operation.

Both, BFASP and $\mathrm{HT_{LB}}$ assign variables to their smallest domain value by default. Interestingly, they differ in their understanding of smallest domain values. In $\mathrm{HT_{LB}}$, the smallest domain value is always the value 'undefined' to capture partiality, whereas in BFASP partiality is not considered if undefined is not explicitly part of the domain.

The value of a head variable is derived by the constraint even if it contains no implication. For instance, consider rule $(x + y \geq 42, x)$ over $\mathbb{N}$ in BFASP. Then, BFASP yields one stable model with $x \mapsto 42$ and $y \mapsto 0$. By default the value of y is 0, since y appears nowhere as a head. The value of x is derived from the value of $42 - y$. In contrast, $\mathrm{HT_{LB}}$ results in 43 stable models from $(x \downarrow 0) \cup (y \downarrow 42)$ to $(x \downarrow 42) \cup (y \downarrow 0)$ for theory $\{x + y \geq 42\}$. In $\mathrm{HT_{LB}}$, the variables of an (head) atom are treated in an equal way instead of an implicatory way by declaring one of them as head.

As already mentioned, BFASP does not satisfy Proposition 4. Rule $p \leftarrow \neg p$ has no stable model in ASP and $\mathrm{HT_{LB}}$, but BFASP yields a stable model containing p, since the BFASP reduct never replaces head variables and produces the rule as is and yields p as the minimal (and only) model of the rule. This means that BFASP provides a bound founded semantics but behaves unexpectedly on rules representing integrity constraints.

Next, we compare $\mathrm{HT_{LB}}$ to the logic of HT with constraints ($\mathrm{HT_C}$; [8]). First, note that both are based on HT and capture theories over (constraint) atoms in a non-monotonic setting and can thus express default values. The difference is that $\mathrm{HT_C}$ follows the rationality principle by accepting any value satisfying an atom and thus foundedness is focused on atom level. Unlike this, foundedness in $\mathrm{HT_{LB}}$ is focused on variable level by following the rationality principle in accepting minimal values only. The latter is achieved by additionally comparing models wrt the values assigned to variables to determine equilibrium models. For instance, reconsider the fact $x \geq 42$ over $\{x\}, \mathbb{N}$ and valuations v and v' with $v(x) = 42$ and $v'(x) = 43$. Then, in $\mathrm{HT_C}$ we have $v \neq v'$, whereas in $\mathrm{HT_{LB}}$ we have $v \subset v'$. Hence, v and v' are solutions in $\mathrm{HT_C}$ but only v is a solution in $\mathrm{HT_{LB}}$. The theories in (1) and (2) show that the semantics of $\mathrm{HT_{LB}}$ cannot be obtained by adding separate minimization to $\mathrm{HT_C}$.

On the other hand, both $\mathrm{HT_{LB}}$ and $\mathrm{HT_C}$ define atomic satisfaction in terms of atom denotations. A difference is that in $\mathrm{HT_C}$ denotations need to be closed. Informally, a denotation is (upwards) *closed* if it is closed under the superset relation. For $\mathrm{HT_{LB}}$, this cannot be maintained, due to the additional comparison of valuations regarding values. The closure of denotations is significant to satisfy persistence in HT_C. In contrast, in HT_{LB} persistence is established by forcing atomic satisfaction in both h and t, instead of h only as in HT_C. The corresponding benefit is that this allows us to consider denotations of atoms in HT_{LB} which are not allowed in HT_C, like $x \doteq y$ with $[\![x \doteq y]\!] \overset{\text{def}}{=} \{v \mid v(x) = v(y)\}$ which is not closed in HT_C.

The integration of non-Boolean variables into ASP is also studied in ASP modulo Theories [2–4, 6, 7, 10, 13, 14, 18, 19, 21, 22]. The common idea of these hybrid approaches is to integrate monotone theories, like constraint or linear programming, into the non-monotonic setting of ASP. Similar to HT_C, foundedness is only achieved at the atomic level—if at all. In fact, many approaches avoid this entirely by limiting the occurrence of theory atoms to rule bodies.

Finally, logic programs with linear constraints under HT_{LB}'s semantics amount to a non-monotonic counterpart of Integer Linear Programming (ILP; [24]). As a matter of fact, the monotonicity of ILP makes it hard to model default values and recursive concepts like reachability. It will be interesting future work to see whether HT_{LB} can provide a non-monotonic alternative to ILP.

5 Conclusion

We presented a logical reconstruction of the idea of foundedness over ordered domains in the setting of the logic of Here-and-There. We have shown that important properties like persistence, negation and strong equivalence hold in our approach. Also, we showed that HT is a special case of HT_{LB}, and that HT_{LB}-stable models correspond to stable models according to a Ferraris'-like stable model semantics. We instantiated HT_{LB} with linear constraints to illustrate its modeling capabilities by means of an example representing the dependency of the rpm of a car and its range. Finally, we compared our approach to related work to point out that foundedness is a non-trivial key feature of HT_{LB}. Although HT_{LB} and BFASP share the same motivation, they differ in their treatment of partiality. Furthermore, we indicated that HT_{LB} can be seen as a non-monotonic counterpart of monotonic theories such as ILP.

Interestingly, HT_{LB} offers a new view of aggregates under Ferraris' semantics as atoms. In fact, sum aggregates are related to linear constraint atoms in HT_{LB}. As we will show in a follow-up work, aggregates under Ferraris' semantics [12] can be represented by atoms in HT_{LB}. This is interesting since then aggregates are no longer an extension of an existing approach, but rather an integral atomic parts of HT_{LB}. Hence, results shown in this work also apply to aggregates (under Ferraris' semantics) and provide a way to elaborate upon properties and relationships to other conceptions of aggregates. The view on aggregates as atoms provided by HT_{LB} may thus help us to better understand the differences among various aggregate semantics.

Appendix of Proofs

Proof of Proposition 2. It is enough to prove the proposition for the base case, since the rest follows directly by structural induction for each formula over $\mathcal{A_X}$. Let $\langle h, t \rangle$ an HT_LB-valuation over $\mathcal{X}, \mathcal{D}$ and a atom of $\mathcal{A_X}$.

First, we prove persistence, represented by *1* of the proposition. We have

$$\langle h, t \rangle \models a \Leftrightarrow h \in [\![a]\!] \text{ and } t \in [\![a]\!] \Rightarrow t \in [\![a]\!] \Leftrightarrow \langle t, t \rangle \models a$$

Subsequently, we prove negation, represented by *2* of the proposition. We have

$$
\begin{aligned}
&\langle h, t \rangle \models a \to \bot \\
&\Leftrightarrow ((\langle h, t \rangle \models \bot \text{ or } \langle h, t \rangle \not\models a) \text{ and } ((\langle t, t \rangle \models \bot \text{ or } \langle t, t \rangle \not\models a) \\
&\Leftrightarrow \langle h, t \rangle \not\models a \text{ and } \langle t, t \rangle \not\models a \\
&\Leftrightarrow (h \notin [\![a]\!] \text{ or } t \notin [\![a]\!]) \text{ and } (t \notin [\![a]\!]) \\
&\Leftrightarrow \langle t, t \rangle \not\models a \qquad\qquad\qquad\qquad\qquad \square
\end{aligned}
$$

Proof of Proposition 4. We analyze what is needed to satisfy rule r of form $a \leftarrow \neg a$ and then derive from the fact that $\langle v, v \rangle \not\models a$ for each HT_LB-stable model v of $\Gamma \setminus \{a \leftarrow \neg a\}$ over $\mathcal{X}, \mathcal{D}$, that there exists no stable model for Γ.

Note that the following holds

$$
\begin{aligned}
&\langle h, t \rangle \models a \leftarrow \neg a \\
&\Leftrightarrow (\langle h, t \rangle \models a \text{ or } \langle h, t \rangle \not\models \neg a) \text{ and } (\langle t, t \rangle \models a \text{ or } \langle t, t \rangle \not\models \neg a) \\
&\Leftrightarrow (\langle h, t \rangle \models a \text{ or } \langle t, t \rangle \models a) \text{ and } (\langle t, t \rangle \models a) \\
&\Leftrightarrow t \in [\![a]\!]
\end{aligned}
$$

This implies that $\langle v, v \cup \{a\} \rangle \models \Gamma$ for each stable model v of $\Gamma \setminus \{a \leftarrow \neg a\}$. Furthermore, note that $v \subset v \cup \{a\}$, since $\langle v, v \rangle \not\models a$. Hence, Γ has no HT_LB-stable model. $\qquad \square$

Proof of Proposition 5. Let a be an atom over $\mathcal{A_X}$, and $\overline{a}$ and $\overline{a}^s$ its complement and its strict complement over $\mathcal{A_X}$, respectively.

First, we prove $\overline{a}^s \models \overline{a}$. For any HT_LB-valuation $\langle h, t \rangle$ over $\mathcal{X}, \mathcal{D}$ we have

$$
\begin{aligned}
&\langle h, t \rangle \models \overline{a}^s \\
&\Leftrightarrow h \in [\![\overline{a}^s]\!] \text{ and } t \in [\![\overline{a}^s]\!] \text{ with } [\![\overline{a}^s]\!] = 2^{\mathcal{V}} \setminus ([\![a]\!] \cup \{v \mid v(x) = \boldsymbol{u} \text{ for some } x \in vars(a)\}) \\
&\Rightarrow h \in 2^{\mathcal{V}} \setminus [\![a]\!] \text{ and } t \in 2^{\mathcal{V}} \setminus [\![a]\!] \\
&\Leftrightarrow \langle h, t \rangle \models \overline{a}
\end{aligned}
$$

Secondly, we prove $\overline{a} \models \neg a$. For any HT_{LB}-valuation $\langle h, t \rangle$ over $\mathcal{X}, \mathcal{D}$ we have

$$\langle h, t \rangle \models \overline{a}$$
$$\Leftrightarrow h \in [\![\, \overline{a} \,]\!] \text{ and } t \in [\![\, \overline{a} \,]\!] \text{ with } [\![\, \overline{a} \,]\!] = 2^{\mathcal{D}} \setminus [\![\, a \,]\!]$$
$$\Leftrightarrow h \notin [\![\, a \,]\!] \text{ and } t \notin [\![\, a \,]\!]$$
$$\Rightarrow t \notin [\![\, a \,]\!]$$
$$\overset{\text{Proposition 2}}{\Leftrightarrow} \langle h, t \rangle \models \neg a$$

$\square$

Proof of Proposition 6. It is enough to prove the proposition for the base case, since the rest follows directly by structural induction for each theory over Λ.

Let Γ be a theory over propositional atoms $\mathcal{A}$ and $\langle H, T \rangle$ an HT-interpretation over $\mathcal{A}$. Let $\tau(\Gamma)$ be a theory over atoms $\{p = \mathbf{t} \mid p \in \mathcal{A}\}$ and $\langle \tau(H), \tau(T) \rangle$ an HT_{LB}-valuation over $\mathcal{A}, \{\mathbf{t}\}$. Then we have

$$\langle H, T \rangle \models p$$
$$\Leftrightarrow H \in [\![\, p \,]\!]_{\mathcal{A}}$$
$$\overset{H \subseteq T}{\Leftrightarrow} H \in [\![\, p \,]\!]_{\mathcal{A}} \text{ and } T \in [\![\, p \,]\!]_{\mathcal{A}}$$
$$\Leftrightarrow \tau(H) \in [\![\, p = \mathbf{t} \,]\!]_{\mathcal{A},\{\mathbf{t}\}} \text{ and } \tau(T) \in [\![\, p = \mathbf{t} \,]\!]_{\mathcal{A},\{\mathbf{t}\}}$$
$$\Leftrightarrow \langle \tau(H), \tau(T) \rangle \models p = \mathbf{t}$$

$\square$

Proof of Proposition 7. It is enough to prove the proposition for the base case, since the rest follows directly by structural induction for each theory over $\mathcal{A}_{\mathcal{X}}$.

First, note that the pair $\langle H, T \rangle$ over $\mathcal{A}_{\mathcal{X}}$ with $H = At(\langle h, t \rangle)$ and $T = At(\langle t, t \rangle)$ is a well formed HT-interpretation, since $H \subseteq T$ holds by $h \subseteq t$ and Proposition 1. Then we have

$$\langle h, t \rangle \models a$$
$$\Leftrightarrow h \in [\![\, a \,]\!]_{\mathcal{X},\mathcal{D}} \text{ and } t \in [\![\, a \,]\!]_{\mathcal{X},\mathcal{D}}$$
$$\Rightarrow H \in [\![\, a \,]\!]_{\mathcal{A}_{\mathcal{X}}} \text{ and } T \in [\![\, a \,]\!]_{\mathcal{A}_{\mathcal{X}}}$$
$$\Rightarrow \langle H, T \rangle \models a$$

$\square$

Proof of Proposition 9. It is enough to prove the proposition for the base case, since the rest follows directly by structural induction for each theory over $\mathcal{A}_{\mathcal{X}}$.

Let Γ be a theory over $\mathcal{A}_{\mathcal{X}}$ and $\langle h, t \rangle$ an HT$_{LB}$-valuation over $\mathcal{X}, \mathcal{D}$. Then, we have

$$h \models_{cl} a^t$$
$$\Leftrightarrow h \models_{cl} a \text{ and } t \models_{cl} a$$
$$\Leftrightarrow h \in [\![\, a\,]\!] \text{ and } t \in [\![\, a\,]\!]$$
$$\Leftrightarrow \langle h, t \rangle \models a$$

$\square$

References

1. Aziz, R.: Answer set programming: founded bounds and model counting. Ph.D. thesis, University of Melbourne (2015)
2. Balduccini, M.: Representing constraint satisfaction problems in answer set programming. In: Faber, W., Lee, J. (eds.) Proceedings of the Second Workshop on Answer Set Programming and Other Computing Paradigms (ASPOCP 2009), pp. 16–30 (2009)
3. Banbara, M., et al.: aspartame: solving constraint satisfaction problems with answer set programming. In: Calimeri, F., Ianni, G., Truszczynski, M. (eds.) LPNMR 2015. LNCS (LNAI), vol. 9345, pp. 112–126. Springer, Cham (2015). https://doi.org/10.1007/978-3-319-23264-5_10
4. Banbara, M., Kaufmann, B., Ostrowski, M., Schaub, T.: Clingcon: the next generation. Theory Pract. Log. Program. **17**(4), 408–461 (2017)
5. Baral, C.: Knowledge Representation, Reasoning and Declarative Problem Solving. Cambridge University Press, Cambridge (2003)
6. Bartholomew, M., Lee, J.: System aspmt2smt: computing ASPMT theories by SMT solvers. In: Fermé, E., Leite, J. (eds.) JELIA 2014. LNCS (LNAI), vol. 8761, pp. 529–542. Springer, Cham (2014). https://doi.org/10.1007/978-3-319-11558-0_37
7. Baselice, S., Bonatti, P.A., Gelfond, M.: Towards an integration of answer set and constraint solving. In: Gabbrielli, M., Gupta, G. (eds.) ICLP 2005. LNCS, vol. 3668, pp. 52–66. Springer, Heidelberg (2005). https://doi.org/10.1007/11562931_7
8. Cabalar, P., Kaminski, R., Ostrowski, M., Schaub, T.: An ASP semantics for default reasoning with constraints. In: Kambhampati, R. (ed.) Proceedings of the Twenty-fifth International Joint Conference on Artificial Intelligence (IJCAI 2016), pp. 1015–1021. IJCAI/AAAI Press (2016)
9. Carro, M., King, A. (eds.): Technical Communications of the Thirty-second International Conference on Logic Programming (ICLP 2016), vol. 52. Open Access Series in Informatics (OASIcs) (2016)
10. Drescher, C., Walsh, T.: A translational approach to constraint answer set solving. Theory Pract. Log. Program. **10**(4–6), 465–480 (2010)
11. Ferraris, P.: Answer sets for propositional theories. In: Baral, C., Greco, G., Leone, N., Terracina, G. (eds.) LPNMR 2005. LNCS (LNAI), vol. 3662, pp. 119–131. Springer, Heidelberg (2005). https://doi.org/10.1007/11546207_10
12. Ferraris, P.: Logic programs with propositional connectives and aggregates. ACM Trans. Comput. Log. **12**(4), 25 (2011)
13. Gebser, M., Kaminski, R., Kaufmann, B., Ostrowski, M., Schaub, T., Wanko, P.: Theory solving made easy with clingo 5. In: Carro, M., King, A. (eds.) [9], pp. 2:1–2:15 (2016)

14. Gebser, M., Ostrowski, M., Schaub, T.: Constraint answer set solving. In: Hill, P.M., Warren, D.S. (eds.) ICLP 2009. LNCS, vol. 5649, pp. 235–249. Springer, Heidelberg (2009). https://doi.org/10.1007/978-3-642-02846-5_22

15. Gelfond, M., Kahl, Y.: Knowledge Representation, Reasoning, and the Design of Intelligent Agents: The Answer-Set Programming Approach. Cambridge University Press, Cambridge (2014)

16. Gelfond, M., Lifschitz, V.: Logic programs with classical negation. In: Warren, D., Szeredi, P. (eds.) Proceedings of the Seventh International Conference on Logic Programming (ICLP 1990), pp. 579–597. MIT Press (1990)

17. Heyting, A.: Die formalen Regeln der intuitionistischen Logik. In: Sitzungsberichte der Preussischen Akademie der Wissenschaften, p. 42–56. Deutsche Akademie der Wissenschaften zu Berlin (1930). Reprint in Logik-Texte: Kommentierte Auswahl zur Geschichte der Modernen Logik, Akademie-Verlag (1986)

18. Janhunen, T., Kaminski, R., Ostrowski, M., Schaub, T., Schellhorn, S., Wanko, P.: Clingo goes linear constraints over reals and integers. Theory Pract. Log. Program. 17(5–6), 872–888 (2017)

19. Janhunen, T., Liu, G., Niemelä, I.: Tight integration of non-ground answer set programming and satisfiability modulo theories. In: Cabalar, P., Mitchell, D., Pearce, D., Ternovska, E. (eds.) Proceedings of the First Workshop on Grounding and Transformation for Theories with Variables (GTTV 2011), pp. 1–13 (2011)

20. Leone, N., Rullo, P., Scarcello, F.: Disjunctive stable models: unfounded sets, fixpoint semantics, and computation. Inf. Comput. 135(2), 69–112 (1997)

21. Lierler, Y., Susman, B.: SMT-based constraint answer set solver EZSMT (system description). In: Carro, M., King, A. (eds.) [9], pp. 1:1–1:15 (2016)

22. Liu, G., Janhunen, T., Niemelä, I.: Answer set programming via mixed integer programming. In: Brewka, G., Eiter, T., McIlraith, S. (eds.) Proceedings of the Thirteenth International Conference on Principles of Knowledge Representation and Reasoning (KR 2012), pp. 32–42. AAAI Press (2012)

23. Pearce, D.: Equilibrium logic. Ann. Math. Artif. Intell. 47(1–2), 3–41 (2006)

24. Schrijver, A.: Theory of linear and integer programming. Discrete mathematics and optimization. Wiley, Hoboken (1999)

25. Van Gelder, A., Ross, K., Schlipf, J.: The well-founded semantics for general logic programs. J. ACM 38(3), 620–650 (1991)

A Logic-Based Question Answering System for Cultural Heritage

Bernardo Cuteri$^{(\boxtimes)}$ (ID), Kristian Reale (ID), and Francesco Ricca (ID)

Department of Mathematics and Computer Science,
University of Calabria, Rende, Italy
{cuteri,reale,ricca}@mat.unical.it

Abstract. Question Answering (QA) systems attempt to find direct answers to user questions posed in natural language. This work presents a QA system for the closed domain of Cultural Heritage. Our solution gradually transforms input questions into queries that are executed on a CIDOC-compliant ontological knowledge base. Questions are processed by means of a rule-based syntactic classification module running an Answer Set Programming system. The proposed solution is being integrated into a fully-fledged commercial system developed within the PIUCULTURA project, funded by the Italian Ministry for Economic Development.

Keywords: Question Answering · Answer Set Programming ·
Cultural heritage

1 Introduction

Question Answering (QA) attempts to find answers to the most (human) common form of expressing an information need: natural language questions. Historically, QA is classified either as Open Domain QA when there is no restriction on the domain of the questions; and closed domain QA when questions are bound to a specific domain [2]. In open domain QA, most systems are based on a combination of Information Retrieval (IR) and Natural Language Processing (NLP) techniques [30]. Such techniques are applied to a large corpus of documents. They first attempt to retrieve the best documents to look into for the answer, then selecting the paragraphs which are more likely to bear the desired answer and finally processing the extracted paragraphs by means of NLP. IR techniques have proven to be successful at locating relevant documents to user queries into large collections [10], but the effort of looking for a specific desired information into such documents is left to the user. A QA system, in addition, provides direct answers to users questions. In closed domain QA, the questions are posed on the entities of a well-defined specific domain of discourse. This additional hypothesis makes possible to exploit more specific techniques that are tailored to the domain of interest. Importantly, in closed domain QA, one can likely resort to *structured* (or *semi-structured*) knowledge sources, that are rich in details, and

F. Calimeri et al. (Eds.): JELIA 2019, LNAI 11468, pp. 526–541, 2019.
https://doi.org/10.1007/978-3-030-19570-0_35

contain precise, trustable, certified and identifiable data. Moreover, the structure and the vocabulary used in user questions is more limited and specific.

In this work, we present a closed domain QA system tailored to the cultural heritage domain, which has been developed within the PIUCULTURA project. The PIUCULTURA project, funded by the Italian Ministry for Economic Development, has the goal of devising a multi-paradigm platform that facilitates the fruition of cultural heritage sites in Italy. The QA system described in this work is one of the core components of the platform, that answers to the need of providing a more natural way of obtaining information from the system.

It is worth noting that a system working on the domain of Cultural Heritage can benefit from many existing structured data sources that adhere to international standards. One of the most successful standards is the CIDOC Conceptual Reference Model [19]. CIDOC-crm provides a common semantic framework for the mapping of cultural heritage information and has been already adopted as a base interchange format by museums, libraries, online data collections and archives all over the world [19,20]. For this reason, CIDOC-crm has been identified as the knowledge reference model for PIUCULTURA. Thus, our Question Answering prototype is applicable to query both general (e.g., online data collections) and specific (e.g., museums databases) CIDOC-compliant knowledge sources.

Our QA approach can be described as a waterfall-like process in which a user question is first processed from a syntactic point of view and then from a semantic point of view. Syntactic processing is based on the concept of *template*. A template represents a category of syntactically homogeneous sentence patterns. Templates are encoded in terms of Answer Set Programming (ASP) [14,15,25] rules. ASP is a well-established formalism for nonmonotonic reasoning, and combines a comparatively high knowledge-modeling power with a robust solving technology [23,35]. For these reasons ASP has become an established logic-based programming paradigm with successful applications to complex problems in Artificial Intelligence [3,5–8,26], Databases [37,38], Game Theory [4,9] and more. By using ASP we can work in a declarative fashion and avoid implementing (and re-engineering) the template matching procedure from scratch every time a new set of templates is added to the system. The semantic processing is instead based on the concept of *intent*. By intent we mean the purpose (i.e., the intent) of the question: two questions can belong to two disjoint syntactic categories but have the same intent and vice versa. To give an example: *who created Guernica?* and *who is the author of Guernica?* have a quite different syntactic structure, but have the same intent, i.e., *know who made the work Guernica*. On the other hand, if we consider *who created Guernica?* and *who restored Guernica?* we can say that they are syntactically similar (or homogeneous), but semantically different: the purpose of the two questions is different. Semantic disambiguation, in which intents are mapped to a set of predefined queries on the knowledge base, is done by resorting to the multilingual BabelNet [41] dictionary. Finally, the result of the execution of the query on the knowledge base is converted into a natural language form by using a simple expansion metalanguage.

In the remainder of this paper, we first briefly recall the ASP language, then we provide a more detailed overview of the problem we have approached; next, we present all the components of our QA system, focusing on the details of the ASP-based component. Finally, after presenting an experiment that assesses the performance of the template matching on a real-world knowledge base, we draw the conclusion of the paper.

2   Answer Set Programming

In this section, we briefly overview Answer Set Programming (ASP) [15,25], which is a declarative programming paradigm proposed in the area of non-monotonic reasoning and logic programming. Syntactically, a *rule* r is of the form:

$$a_1 | \ldots | a_n \coloncolon- b_1, \cdots, b_k, \text{ not } b_{k+1}, \cdots, \text{ not } b_m.$$

where $a_1, \ldots, a_n, b_1, \ldots, b_m$ are atoms. The disjunction of atoms $a_1, \ldots, a_n$ is the *head* of r, while the conjunction of literals $b_1, \ldots, b_k, \text{not } b_{k+1}, \ldots, \text{not } b_m$ is the *body* of r, where a literal is either an atom (positive literal) l or its negation not l (negative literal). Atoms might contain constants, variables and function symbols. A rule r is *safe* if each variable appearing in r appears also in some positive body literal of r^1. A rule with empty body ($m = k = 0$) is called *fact*. An *ASP program* P is a finite set of safe rules. The meaning of an ASP program is defined in terms of its *answer sets* (or stable models) [25]. Roughly, an answer set A is a minimal set of variable-free atoms that are interpreted to be true, satisfies all the rules of the program (i.e., at least one atom in the head is in A whenever all positive literals in the body are in A, and no atom occurring in a negative literal is in A) and is also stable w.r.t the definition of Gelfond-Lifschitz [25]. For example, the following ASP solves the well-known 3-Colorability problem on graphs.

```
color(red,X) | color(yellow, X) | color(blue,X) :- node(X).
:- color(C,X), col(C,Y), edge(X,Y).
```

The input to the program is given as a set of facts containing node(x) for each node x, and edge(x, y) for each edge (x, y) of the input graph. Intuitively, the rules can be read as follows: color node X either in red, yellow, or blue, and ensure that no adjacent node have the same colors.

Hereafter, we assume the reader is familiar with ASP and refer to [12,21, 22,24] for complementary introductory material on the topic.

3   Overview of the Problem

The goal of our approach is to answer questions on cultural heritage facts stored in a repository modeled according to a standard model of this domain. In particular, the target knowledge base model of the project is the CIDOC conceptual reference model [19]. The CIDOC-crm is a standardized maintained model

---

[1] The safety is in the folklore of logic-based languages [12].

that has been designed as a common language for the exchange and sharing of data on cultural heritage without loss of meaning, supporting the implementation of local data transformation algorithms towards this model. This standard has been adopted worldwide by a growing number of institutions and provides a more trustable, structured and complete source w.r.t. freely available (often unstructured and non-certified) web resources. Indeed, museums and institutions typically have structured sources in which they store information about their artifacts that can be mapped to CIDOC-crm rather easily (actually, this was one of the main goals of the promoters of CIDOC-crm). On the other hand, the availability of documentary sources is limited. If we take into consideration freely available documentary sources such as Wikipedia, we realize that the percentage coverage of works and authors is low. For example, a museum like the British Museum has about 8 million artifacts (made available in CIDOC-compliant format) while on Wikipedia there are in total about 500 thousand articles about works of art from all over the world. The CIDOC-crm is periodically released in RDFs format [16], thus our Question Answering system has to answer questions by finding the information required on an RDF knowledge base that follows the CIDOC-crm model. The reference query language of RDF is SPARQL [29]. So, in basic terms, the Question Answering system has to map natural language questions into SPARQL queries and produce answers in natural language from query results. A requirement of the project was to target the Italian language, together with the more diffused English language. We ended up devising and implementing an approach that can deal with both languages and can be easily adapted also to handle other languages.

4   ASP-based System for Question Answering

In this section we present step-by-step our question answering system for cultural heritage. The entire QA process is exemplified in Fig. 1, which shows the interaction among the various modules of the system. In particular, the question answering process is split into the following phases:

1. **Question NL Processing**: The input question is transformed into a three-level syntactic representation;
2. **Template Matching**: The representation is categorized by a template system that is implemented by means of logical rules;
3. **Intent Determination**: The identified template is mapped to an intent, where the intent identifies precisely the intent (or purpose) of the question;
4. **Query Generation**: An intent becomes a query on the knowledge base;
5. **Query Execution**: The Query is executed on the knowledge base;
6. **Answer Generation**: The result produced by the query is transformed into a natural language answer.

Splitting the QA process into distinct phases allowed us to implement a system by connecting loosely-coupled modules dedicated to each phase. In this way we also achieved better maintainability, and extensibility. In the following sections, we analyze in detail the 6 phases just listed.

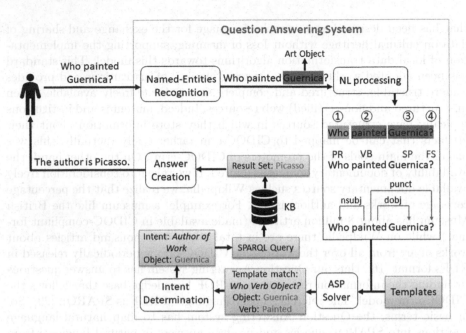

Fig. 1. Scenario of interaction with the Question Answering System

4.1 Question NL Processing

The NL processing phase deals with building a formal and therefore tractable representation of the input question. The question is decomposed and analyzed by highlighting both the atomic components that compose it, and the morphological properties of the components and the relationships that bind them. In particular, in this phase we perform the following NLP steps: (*i*) Named entities recognition; (*ii*) Tokenization and Part-of-speech tagging; and, (*iii*) Dependency parsing.

Named Entities Recognition. The recognition of named entities is an NLP task that deals with the identification and categorization of the entities that appear in a text. The named entities are portions of text that identify the names of people, organizations, places or other elements that are referenced by a proper name. For example, in the phrase *Michelangelo has painted the Last Judgment*, we can recognize two entities: *Michelangelo*, that could belong to a *Person* category, and *the Last Judgment* that could belong to an *Artwork* category. When the entities of the text have been recognized, they can be replaced with placeholders that are easier to manage in the subsequent stages of processing of natural language. For example, it is possible to replace long and decomposed names with atomic names (that is, composed of a single word) that are more easily handled during tokenization, Parts-of-speech tagging, and Dependency Parsing.

In our implementation we use CRF++ [31] that implements a supervised model based on conditional random fields that are probabilistic models for segmenting and labeling sequence data [32]. To train the CRF model, we generated a training set built from a database of 57 question patterns built from a database of possible questions provided by a partner of the PIUCULTURA project. Question patterns were specified by using a metalanguage and are expansible into a set of training questions. An example of question patterns is the following:

```
who {painted,created} [the work,the artwork] <W>.
```

The pattern is expanded by using, for each expansion, exactly one word from curly brackets sets, at most one word from square brackets set, and one available values from a predefined entities set identified with the id in angle brackets. The above pattern can generate four times the number of elements in the dictionary of words used to expand the placeholder <W>. So, if W = {Guernica, the Rosetta Stone, the Monalisa}, the resulting patterns expansion are 18 of the form:

```
who painted Guernica.
who created Guernica.
who painted the work Guernica.
. . .
```

The expansion of patterns has been down-sampled (i.e., we selected a subset) randomly by using a fixed maximum number of instances for each question pattern (set to 20 in our experiments).

After applying Named Entities Recognition (NER) the entities recognized in the text are replaced by placeholders that are easier to be processed by the subsequent NLP phases. At the end of the NLP phase, placeholders are then replaced back by the original entities of the text.

Tokenization and Parts-Of-Speech Tagging. Tokenization consists of splitting text into words (called tokens). A token is an indivisible unit of text. Tokens are separated by spaces or punctuation marks. In Italian, as in other western languages, the tokenization phase turns out to be rather simple, as these languages place quite clear word demarcations. In fact, the approaches used for natural language tokenization are based on simple regular expressions. Tokenization is the first phase of lexical analysis and creates the input for the next Part-of-Speech Tagging phase.

The part-of-speech tagging phase assigns to each word the corresponding part of the speech. Common examples of parts-of-speech are adjectives, nouns, pronouns, verbs, or articles. The part-of-speech assignment is typically implemented with supervised statistical methods. There are, for several languages, large manually annotated corpora that can be used as training sets to train a statistical system. Among the best performing approaches are those based on Maximum Entropy [6]. The set of possible parts of the speech (called tag-set) is not fixed, and above all, it can present substantial differences depending on the language taken into consideration. For Italian, a reference tag-set is the Tanl tag-set,[2] that was adopted in our system.

For tokenization and POS-tagging we used the Apache OpenNLP library[3] with pretrained models.[4]

Dependency Parsing. Dependency Parsing is the identification of lexical dependencies of the words of a text according to a grammar of dependencies. The dependency grammar (DG) is a class of syntactic theories that are all based on the dependency relationship (as opposed to the circumscription relation). Dependency is the notion that linguistic units, e.g., words, are connected to one another by directed connections (or dependencies). A dependency is determined by the relationship between a word (a head) and its dependencies. The methods for extracting grammar dependencies are typically supervised and use a reference tag-set and a standard input representation format known as the CoNLL standard developed and updated within the CoNLL scientific conference (Conference on Computational Natural Language Learning). In our implementation we used MaltParser[5] that is a system for data-driven dependency parsing [42].

4.2 Template Matching

Once the NLP phases are completed we perform one of the core phases of the system, that is the template matching phase. Template matching is in charge of classifying question from the syntactic point of view and extract the question terms that are needed to instantiate the query for retrieving the answer. Basically, a template represents a category of syntactically homogeneous questions. In our system, templates are encoded in terms of ASP rules. By using ASP we can work in a declarative fashion and avoid implementing the template matching procedure from scratch.

To this end, the output of the NLP phase is modeled by using ASP facts that constitute the input of the template matching module. In particular, words are indexed by their position in the sentence and they are associated with their morphological feature by using facts of the following forms:

```
word(pst,wrd).      pos(pst,pos_tag).      gr(pst1,pst2,rel_tag).
```

the first kind of fact associates position of words (`pst`) in a sentence to the word itself (`wrd`); the second associates words (`pst`) with their POS tags (`pos_tag`), and the latter models grammatical relations (a.k.a. typed dependencies) specifying the type of grammatical relation (`rel_tag`) holding among pair of words (`pst1,pst2`). The possible tags and relations terms are constants representing the labels produced by the NLP tools mentioned in the previous subsection.

---

[2] http://medialab.di.unipi.it/wiki/Tanl_POS_Tagset.
[3] https://opennlp.apache.org.
[4] https://github.com/aciapetti/opennlp-italian-models.
[5] http://www.maltparser.org/.

Consider, for example, the question *who painted Guernica?*, the output of the NLP phase would result in the following facts (cfr., Fig. 1 for a graphical representation of this NLP output).

```
word(1, "who"), word(2, "painted").
word(3, "Guernica"). word(4, "?").
pos(1, pr), pos(2, vb). pos(3, np). pos(4, f).
gr(2, 1, nsubj), gr(2, 3, dobj). gr(2, 4, punct).
```

We denote with F_Q the set of facts produced by the application of mentioned NLP phases and transformations to an input question Q.

In the template matching phase, questions are matched against question templates. Templates identify categories of questions that are uniform from the syntactic point of view and we express them in the form of ASP rules.

Definition 1. *A template rule R is a rule having in the head an ASP atom of the form*

$$template(ID, terms\_K(V_1, \ldots, V_K), W)$$

where template is a constant predicate name (that is the same for all templates), ID is an ASP constant that identifies the template, K is an integer that we call template arity, $V_1, \ldots, V_K$ are ASP variables and W is an integer that defines the template rule weight.

Basically, each template rule models a condition under which we identified a possible syntactic question pattern for a template. The function $terms\_K$ conveniently groups the terms that are extracted from the match. Finally the weight is numerical value that expresses the importance of a pattern. By using weights one can freely express preferences among patterns; for instance in our implementation we set this number to the size of the body to favour more specific templates rules over more generic ones. An example of template rule that matches questions of the form *who action object?* is the following:

```
template(who_action_object, terms_2(V, O), 8) :-
word (1, "who"),
word(2, V), word(3, O), word(4, "?"),
pos(1, pr), pos(2, vb), pos(3, np), pos(4, f),
gr(2, 1, nsubj), gr(2, 3, dobj), gr(2, 4, punct).
```

In the example, *who_action_object* is a constant that identifies the template, while $terms(V, W)$ is a function symbol that allows extracting the terms of the input question, respectively the verb V and the object O. The weight of the template rule is 8, which corresponds to the body size as described above.

Definition 2. *A template T is a set of template rules having the same ID and arity.*

Basically, a template collects a number of possible syntactic patterns (one per template rule), roughly corresponding to different ways of formulating a kind of question.

Definition 3. *A template matching program P is an ASP program that contains at least one template, and the following rule, defining the best matches (i.e., the ones with highest weight):*

```
bestMatch(T,R) :- template(T,R,M), #max{W: template(_,_,W)} = M.
```

Definition 4. *Given a template matching program P and the set of facts F_Q coming from the NLP phase w.r.t. a question Q, we say that (T, R) is a best match for Q iff bestMatch$(T, R) \in A$ where A is the answer set of $F_Q \cup P$. In such case, T identifies a best matching template and R defines the terms extracted from the match.*

Note that, it was by design that one can retrieve more than one best match, to give more freedom to the design of the interaction with the user. Pragmatically, in the first prototypical implementation, we simply select the first best-match assuming that all best-matches represent the question equally good.

Question templates are intended to be defined by the application designer, which is a reasonable choice in applications like the one we considered, where the number of templates to produce is limited. Nonetheless, to assist the definition of templates we developed a graphical user interface. Such interface helps the user at building template rules by working and generalizing examples, and does not require any previous knowledge of ASP or specific knowledge of NLP tools. The template editing interface is not described in this paper for space reasons.

In our prototype, we used DLV [33] as the ASP solver that computes the answer sets (thus the best matches) of the template matching phase, and the DLV Wrapper library [43] to programmatically manage DLV invocations from Java code.

The intent determination process is based on the lexical expansion of question terms extracted in the template matching phase.

4.3   Intent Determination

The identification of a question by templates is typically not sufficient to identify its intent or purpose. For example, *who painted Guernica?* and *who killed Caesar?* have a very similar syntactic structure and may fall into the same template, but they have two different purposes. The intent determination process is based on the lexical expansion of question terms extracted in the template matching phase and has the role of identifying what the question asks (i.e., its intent), starting from the result of the template matching phase. In other words, it disambiguates the intent of questions that fall into the same syntactic category (and that therefore have a match on the same template). In the previous example, painting is *hyponym* (i.e., a specific instance) of creating and this fact allows us to understand that the intent is to determine the creator of a work, while killing does not have such relationships and we should, therefore, instantiate a different intent. In the same way, *who painted Guernica?*, *who made Guernica?* or *who created Guernica?* are all questions that can be correctly mapped with a single template and can be correctly recognized by the same intent thanks to the fact that all three verbs are hyponyms or synonyms of the verb *create*. Words semantic relations can be obtained by using dedicated dictionaries, like wordnet [39] or BabelNet [41]. In our system we used BabelNet and we implemented the intent determination module in Java and used the BabelNet API library for accessing word relations. In particular, intent determination is implemented as a series of Java conditional checks (possibly nested) on word relations. Such conditional checks are expressed as a question term Q, a word relation R and a target word T. The BabelNet service receives such triple and returns true/false depending on whether Q is in relation R w.r.t. T, R is either synonymy, hyponymy or hyperonymy. Algorithm 1 presents a pseudo-code of the intent determination process for the *who_action_object* template with one verb and one object as terms.

The implementation of intent determination is done by the designer as template definition. Our system implements a set of intents that were identified during the analysis by a partner of the project.

Note that intent determination could also be easily encoded by means of ASP rules, which would have allowed having a single ASP program for handling both template matching and intent determination. However, the access to external dictionaries was not efficient in practice, and we decided to go for a straight implementation with imperative code.

Algorithm 1. Determine intent for who_action_object template

Input: matched terms: verb, object
Output: intent of question
1: **if** inDictionary(verb, "synonym", "created") **then**
2:     **return** AUTHOR_OF_WORK
3: **end if**
4: **if** inDictionary(verb, "synonym", "found") **then**
5:     **return** FOUNDER_OF_WORK
6: **end if**
7: **if** inDictionary(verb, "synonym", "married") **then**
8:     **return** SPOUSE_OF_PERSON
9: **end if**
10: **if** inDictionary(verb, "hyponym", "created") **then**
11:     **return** AUTHOR_OF_WORK
12: **end if**
13: ...
14: **return** $FAIL$

4.4 Query Execution

The intents identified in the previous phase are mapped one to one with template queries, called prepared statements in programming jargon. In the Query Execution phase, the query template corresponding to the identified event is filled with the slots with terms extracted from the template matching phase and executed over the knowledge base. The CIDOC-crm specification is, by definition, an RDF knowledge base [16], thus we implemented the queries corresponding to intents in the SPARQL language [29]. The problem of programmatically running a query on an RDF knowledge base is a problem for which there are already several solutions. Among the many, we mention Apache Jena for Java and Rasqal for C/C++. In our prototype, we store our data and run our queries using Apache Jena, as programmatic query API, and Virtuoso Open-Source Edition as knowledge base service.

4.5   Answer Generation

Finally, the latest phase of a typical user interaction with the QA system is the so-called Answer Generation. In this phase, the results produced by the execution of the query on the knowledge base are transformed into a natural language answer that is finally returned to the user. To implement this phase we have designed answer templates that are in some ways similar to the one seen for generating the test set for the NER phase. In this case, the idea is to have natural language patterns with parameterized slots that are filled according to the question intent and the terms extracted from the database. These answer templates can be expressed in a compact way through a metalanguage that allows expressing sentences with variations according to the subjects of question or answer. The example below presents a possible answer template for questions concerning the materials of a work.

```
The material{s:s}[R] of <Q> {s:is,p:are}[R] <R>.
```

The curly brackets denote a sequence of variants and the square brackets denote the term (or terms) with respect to which the block preceding it refers: R stands for answer (or response) and Q stands for question. A variant consists of a property and a value separated by a colon symbol. The block delimited by the braces is replaced by the value of the variant appropriate to the term enclosed between square brackets that follows the block. The determination of the appropriate variant can be implemented within the system using, for example, a dictionary of terms. In the example, the s variant is for singular forms and the p variant is for plural forms. The variants may possibly be extended into more complex types (possibly organized in hierarchies) and take into consideration other characteristics of the terms of answer and question extracted from appropriate dictionaries of terms or explicitly represented in the knowledge base. Finally, the $\langle Q \rangle$ tag is replaced by the question terms and the $\langle R \rangle$ tag from the answer terms. So, suppose we want to apply the answer template from the previous example to the fact that the Rosetta Stone is made of granodiorite we would get the answer: *The material of the Rosetta Stone is granodiorite.*

5   System Performance on Real-World Data

In this section, we report on the results of an experimental analysis conducted to assess the performance of the system, and in particular, we have checked whether

Table 1. Template matching time (average times on a sample of 167 questions)

Number of templates	20	30	40	50	60
Average matching time (milliseconds)	30	30	31	33	34

it scales well w.r.t the number of template rules present in a use case developed in the PIUCULTURA project.

We devised 60 template rules, which are able to handle basic question forms and types for the cultural heritage domain distributed in 20 different intents (e.g., authors, materials, dimensions, techniques of artworks, dates/locations of birth and death of artists, and so on). The queries have been executed on a dump of the *British Museum*[6] Knowledge-Base that consists of more than 200 million RDF triples. The hardware used is an Intel i7-7700HQ CPU with 16 GB of ram running a Linux operating system. The knowledge base was handled by Virtuoso ver. 7.2.4, connected to our system with JENA ver. 3.6.0. The ASP system we have used is DLV build BEN/Dec 17 2012.

The average execution times of the template matching phase measured on a sample of 167 questions and on an increasing number of template rules are reported in Table 1. Execution times are in the order of some milliseconds and seems to scale well w.r.t the number of templates. The DLV system performs well on the template programs we have implemented, which by design fall in the stratified [12] syntactic subclass of ASP, which is computationally cheap and efficiently handled by the ASP system we employ [33,34]. For what concerns the other phases of the QA system, we report that, on the same sample of 167 questions, the NL phase average execution time is of 30 ms and is at most 50 ms, the intent determination phase average execution time is of 50 ms and is at most 580 ms and the average query execution time is of 8 ms and is at most 32 ms. Overall the system presents good execution times, which are acceptable for a real-time QA system.

6   Related Work

This work is mostly related to other approaches and forms of QA. Most QA systems in the literature are concerned with retrieving answers from collections of documents, or on the Web, also thanks to the work developed in the context of the Text Retrieval Conference (TREC) that popularized and promoted this form of QA [46]. Systems that fall in this category are mainly based on information retrieval techniques. The most prominent differences to our approach are that we are collecting data from a structured knowledge base, instead of text collections.

For what concerns closed-domain QA, early examples are Baseball [28] and Lunar [47], they were essentially natural language interfaces to relational databases. Lunar allowed asking geologist questions about rocks, while Baseball

---

[6] http://www.britishmuseum.org/.

answered questions about data collected from a baseball season. AquaLog [36] is an ontology-portable Question Answering system that tries to map input questions into linguistic triples and then into ontology triples by mainly using similarity services. In our approach, there is no triple representation of questions and we implemented an intent layer that separates the NL and the ontology world. The intent layer allows implementing intents in actions/queries that are not SPARQL queries. Our approach is less general to be ported to other ontologies, but we provide more control to the developer to create precise NL-to-ontology mappings.

WEBCOOP [13] is a QA system for the tourism domain and implements a cooperative QA on unstructured data. WEBCOOP works on text collections instead of a structured knowledge base. In [44] input questions are transformed into SPARQL templates that mirror the internal structure of the question and are then filled with question terms. As for AcquaLog, the system is domain-independent and in contrast to AcquaLog, they capture questions that are not fully represented by triple clauses, but also those that need filtering and aggregations functions to be handled. Again, our approach is less general and less automatic, but also more controllable and less dependent on the data representation formalism that can vary independently from the question templates.

There are some systems that approach questions by transforming them into logic forms so as to be able to perform reasoning tasks [11,27,40], both in open and closed domains. This is particularly useful for difficult questions that need advanced reasoning capabilities to be answered. Our approach also uses logic, but for the different task of expressing question patterns matching input questions. Also related is NL2KR [45], that is a system that attempts to create direct translations from NL to knowledge representation languages. It takes examples of sentences and their translations together with a base lexicon, and constructs a translation system from NL to the desired target language.

7 Conclusion

In this work, we tackled the problem of Question Answering in the Cultural Heritage domain. The presented solution transforms input questions into SPARQL queries that are executed on an ontological knowledge base. It integrates in a non-trivial original way state-of-the-art NLP tools and models in a modular architecture, featuring a template matching module based on ASP. The system is designed for fast integration of new question forms (by adding templates) and new question intents (by adding intents) and it suits the need of closed domains that are characterized by a limited number of intents and question forms. We have instantiated our approach to answer questions posed in the Italian language to a CIDOC-compliant knowledge base, and we presented an assessment experiment that shows that the presented approach provides a performance acceptable for implementing a real-time QA system. The proposed solution is being integrated into a fully-fledged commercial system developed within the PIUCUL-TURA project, funded by the Italian Ministry for Economic Development.

As for future works, it would be interesting to: compare and possibly integrate the presented approach with other techniques for question answering, as the ones only based on machine learning; investigate the possible efficiency enhancements that can be obtained using a compiler for logic programs [17,18]; enhance the entity recognition by integrating the techniques of [1].

Acknowledgments. This work was partially supported by the Italian Ministry of Economic Development under project "PIUCultura (Paradigmi Innovativi per l'Utilizzo della Cultura)" n.F/020016/01-02/X27.

References

1. Adrian, W.T., Manna, M., Leone, N., Amendola, G., Adrian, M.: Entity set expansion from the web via ASP. In: ICLP (Technical Communications), OASICS, vol. 58, pp. 1:1–1:5. Schloss Dagstuhl - Leibniz-Zentrum fuer Informatik (2017)
2. Allam, A.M.N., Haggag, M.H.: The question answering systems: a survey. Int. J. Res. Rev. Inf. Sci. (IJRRIS) **2**(3), 211–221 (2012)
3. Alviano, M., Amendola, G., Peñaloza, R.: Minimal undefinedness for fuzzy answer sets. In: AAAI, pp. 3694–3700. AAAI Press (2017)
4. Amendola, G.: Preliminary results on modeling interdependent scheduling games via answer set programming. In: RiCeRcA@AI*IA, CEUR Workshop Proceedings, vol. 2272. CEUR-WS.org (2018)
5. Amendola, G.: Solving the stable roommates problem using incoherent answer set programs. In: RiCeRcA@AI*IA, CEUR Workshop Proceedings, vol. 2272. CEUR-WS.org (2018)
6. Amendola, G., Dodaro, C., Leone, N., Ricca, F.: On the application of answer set programming to the conference paper assignment problem. In: Adorni, G., Cagnoni, S., Gori, M., Maratea, M. (eds.) AI*IA 2016. LNCS (LNAI), vol. 10037, pp. 164–178. Springer, Cham (2016). https://doi.org/10.1007/978-3-319-49130-1_13
7. Amendola, G., Eiter, T., Fink, M., Leone, N., Moura, J.: Semi-equilibrium models for paracoherent answer set programs. Artif. Intell. **234**, 219–271 (2016)
8. Amendola, G., Eiter, T., Leone, N.: Modular paracoherent answer sets. In: Fermé, E., Leite, J. (eds.) JELIA 2014. LNCS (LNAI), vol. 8761, pp. 457–471. Springer, Cham (2014). https://doi.org/10.1007/978-3-319-11558-0_32
9. Amendola, G., Greco, G., Leone, N., Veltri, P.: Modeling and reasoning about NTU games via answer set programming. In: IJCAI 2016, pp. 38–45 (2016)
10. Baeza-Yates, R., Ribeiro-Neto, B., et al.: Modern Information Retrieval, vol. 463. ACM Press, New York (1999)
11. Balduccini, M., Baral, C., Lierler, Y.: Knowledge representation and question answering. Found. Artif. Intell. **3**, 779–819 (2008)
12. Baral, C.: Knowledge Representation: Reasoning and Declarative Problem Solving. Cambridge University Press, Cambridge (2010)
13. Benamara, F.: Cooperative question answering in restricted domains: the WEB-COOP experiment. In: Proceedings of the Conference on Question Answering in Restricted Domains (2004)
14. Bonatti, P., Calimeri, F., Leone, N., Ricca, F.: Answer set programming. In: Dovier, A., Pontelli, E. (eds.) A 25-Year Perspective on Logic Programming. LNCS, vol. 6125, pp. 159–182. Springer, Heidelberg (2010). https://doi.org/10.1007/978-3-642-14309-0_8

15. Brewka, G., Eiter, T., Truszczyński, M.: Answer set programming at a glance. Commun. ACM **54**(12), 92–103 (2011)
16. Consortium, W.W.W., et al.: RDF 1.1 concepts and abstract syntax (2014)
17. Cuteri, B., Ricca, F.: A compiler for stratified datalog programs: preliminary results. In: SEBD, CEUR Workshop Proceedings, vol. 2037, p. 158. CEUR-WS.org (2017)
18. Cuteri, B., Rosis, A.F.D., Ricca, F.: lp2cpp: a tool for compiling stratified logic programs. In: Esposito, F., Basili, R., Ferilli, S., Lisi, F. (eds.) AI*IA. LNCS, vol. 10640, pp. 200–212. Springer, Cham (2017). https://doi.org/10.1007/978-3-319-70169-1_15
19. Doerr, M.: The CIDOC conceptual reference module: an ontological approach to semantic interoperability of metadata. AI Mag. **24**(3), 75 (2003)
20. Doerr, M., Gradmann, S., Hennicke, S., Isaac, A., Meghini, C., Van de Sompel, H.: The Europeana data model (EDM). In: World Library and Information Congress: 76th IFLA General Conference and Assembly, pp. 10–15 (2010)
21. Eiter, T., Ianni, G., Krennwallner, T.: Answer set programming: a primer. In: Tessaris, T., et al. (eds.) Reasoning Web 2009. LNCS, vol. 5689, pp. 40–110. Springer, Heidelberg (2009). https://doi.org/10.1007/978-3-642-03754-2_2
22. Gebser, M., Kaminski, R., Kaufmann, B., Schaub, T.: Answer Set Solving in Practice. Synthesis Lectures on Artificial Intelligence and Machine Learning. Morgan & Claypool Publishers, San Rafael (2012)
23. Gebser, M., Leone, N., Maratea, M., Perri, S., Ricca, F., Schaub, T.: Evaluation techniques and systems for answer set programming: a survey. In: IJCAI, pp. 5450–5456. ijcai.org (2018)
24. Gelfond, M., Kahl, Y.: Knowledge Representation, Reasoning, and the Design of Intelligent Agents: The Answer-set Programming Approach. Cambridge University Press, Cambridge (2014)
25. Gelfond, M., Lifschitz, V.: Classical negation in logic programs and disjunctive databases. New Gener. Comput. **9**(3–4), 365–385 (1991)
26. Grasso, G., Iiritano, S., Leone, N., Ricca, F.: Some DLV applications for knowledge management. In: Erdem, E., Lin, F., Schaub, T. (eds.) LPNMR 2009. LNCS (LNAI), vol. 5753, pp. 591–597. Springer, Heidelberg (2009). https://doi.org/10.1007/978-3-642-04238-6_63
27. Green, C.: Theorem proving by resolution as a basis for question-answering systems. Mach. Intell. **4**, 183–205 (1969)
28. Green Jr, B.F., Wolf, A.K., Chomsky, C., Laughery, K.: Baseball: an automatic question-answerer. In: Western Joint IRE-AIEE-ACM Computer Conference, Papers Presented at 9–11 May 1961, pp. 219–224. ACM (1961)
29. Harris, S., Seaborne, A., Prud'hommeaux, E.: SPARQL 1.1 query language. W3C Recommendation 21(10) (2013)
30. Hirschman, L., Gaizauskas, R.: Natural language question answering: the view from here. Nat. Lang. Eng. **7**(4), 275–300 (2001)
31. Kudo, T.: CRF++ (2013). http://crfpp.sourceforge.net/
32. Lafferty, J., McCallum, A., Pereira, F.C.: Conditional random fields: probabilistic models for segmenting and labeling sequence data (2001)
33. Leone, N., et al.: The DLV system for knowledge representation and reasoning. ACM Trans. Comput. Logic (TOCL) **7**(3), 499–562 (2006)
34. Liang, S., Fodor, P., Wan, H., Kifer, M.: OpenRuleBench: an analysis of the performance of rule engines. In: WWW, pp. 601–610. ACM (2009)
35. Lierler, Y., Maratea, M., Ricca, F.: Systems, engineering environments, and competitions. AI Mag. **37**(3), 45–52 (2016)

36. Lopez, V., Pasin, M., Motta, E.: AquaLog: an ontology-portable question answering system for the semantic web. In: Gómez-Pérez, A., Euzenat, J. (eds.) ESWC 2005. LNCS, vol. 3532, pp. 546–562. Springer, Heidelberg (2005). https://doi.org/10. 1007/11431053_37
37. Manna, M., Ricca, F., Terracina, G.: Consistent query answering via ASP from different perspectives: theory and practice. TPLP **13**(2), 227–252 (2013)
38. Manna, M., Ricca, F., Terracina, G.: Taming primary key violations to query large inconsistent data via ASP. TPLP **15**(4–5), 696–710 (2015)
39. Miller, G.: WordNet: An Electronic Lexical Database. MIT Press, Cambridge (1998)
40. Moldovan, D., Clark, C., Harabagiu, S., Maiorano, S.: COGEX: a logic prover for question answering. In: Proceedings of the 2003 Conference of the North American Chapter of the Association for Computational Linguistics on Human Language Technology, vol. 1, pp. 87–93. Association for Computational Linguistics (2003)
41. Navigli, R., Ponzetto, S.P.: Babelnet: the automatic construction, evaluation and application of a wide-coverage multilingual semantic network. Artif. Intell. **193**, 217–250 (2012)
42. Nivre, J., et al.: MaltParser: a language-independent system for data-driven dependency parsing. Nat. Lang. Eng. **13**(2), 95–135 (2007)
43. Ricca, F.: A Java wrapper for DLV. In: Answer Set Programming, CEUR Workshop Proceedings, vol. 78. CEUR-WS.org (2003)
44. Unger, C., Bühmann, L., Lehmann, J., Ngonga Ngomo, A.C., Gerber, D., Cimiano, P.: Template-based question answering over RDF data. In: Proceedings of the 21st International Conference on World Wide Web, pp. 639–648. ACM (2012)
45. Vo, N.H., Mitra, A., Baral, C.: The NL2KR platform for building natural language translation systems. In: ACL (1), pp. 899–908. The Association for Computer Linguistics (2015)
46. Voorhees, E.M., Dang, H.T.: Overview of the TREC 2003 question answering track. In: TREC, vol. 2003, pp. 54–68 (2003)
47. Woods, W.A.: Semantics and quantification in natural language question answering. In: Advances in Computers, vol. 17, pp. 1–87. Elsevier (1978)

Characterising Relativised Strong Equivalence with Projection for Non-ground Answer-Set Programs

Tobias Geibinger[1]([envelope])[iD] and Hans Tompits[2][iD]

[1] Christian Doppler Laboratory for Artificial Intelligence and Optimization for Planning and Scheduling, Databases and Artificial Intelligence Group, Institute of Logic and Computation, Technische Universität Wien, Favoritenstraße 9-11, 1040 Vienna, Austria
tgeibing@dbai.tuwien.ac.at
[2] Knowledge-Based Systems Group, Institute of Logic and Computation, Technische Universität Wien, Favoritenstraße 9-11, 1040 Vienna, Austria
tompits@kr.tuwien.ac.at

Abstract. Starting with the seminal work on strong equivalence by Lifschitz, Pearce, and Valverde, many different advanced notions of program equivalence have been studied in the area of answer-set programming (ASP). In particular, *relativised strong equivalence with projection* has been introduced as a generalisation of strong equivalence by parameterising, on the one hand, the alphabet of the context programs used for checking program equivalence as well as, on the other hand, allowing the filtering of auxiliary atoms. Like many other advanced equivalence notions, it was introduced originally for propositional programs, along with model-theoretic concepts providing characterisations when equivalence between two programs hold. In this paper, we extend these concepts and characterisations to the general case of non-ground programs.

Keywords: Answer-set programming · Program equivalence · Model-theoretic characterisations

1 Introduction

The notion of *equivalence* is fundamental in programming and logic and lies at the heart of computability theory, as deciding whether two Turing machines compute the same function is well-known to be undecidable in general. While in classical logic (as well as in many others), the equivalence of two formulas in the sense of that they both possess the same models yields a replacement theorem which allows to interchange equivalent formulas in theories resulting in

This work was partially supported by the Austrian Federal Ministry for Digital and Economic Affairs and the National Foundation for Research, Technology, and Development.

F. Calimeri et al. (Eds.): JELIA 2019, LNAI 11468, pp. 542–558, 2019.
https://doi.org/10.1007/978-3-030-19570-0_36

equivalent theories, such a property does not hold in answer-set programming (ASP) or nonmonotonic logics in general. That is, although even if P and Q have the same answer sets, it may hold that $P \cup R$ and $Q \cup R$ do not have the same answer sets, for some programs P, Q, and R.

Starting with the seminal work on *strong equivalence* by Lifschitz, Pearce, and Valverde [12], which yields a replacement property essentially by definition, as two programs P and Q are strongly equivalent if $P \cup R$ and $Q \cup R$ have the same answer sets, for any program R (referred to as a *context program*), many different notions of program equivalence have been studied in ASP. Notably, *uniform equivalence* [2], which restricts the condition of strong equivalence in that the context programs contain facts only, and relativised notions thereof [18] which specifies the admitted alphabet of the context programs.

However, both notions do not take standard programming techniques like the use of local predicates into account, which may occur in subprograms but which are ignored in the final computation. Thus, these notions do not admit the *projection* of answer sets to a set of designated output letters. This led to the definition of *relativised strong equivalence with projection* [4] as well as of *relativised uniform equivalence with projection* [13,14]. More specifically, for two programs P and Q and sets A and B of atoms, P and Q are strongly equivalent relative to A projected to B if, for any context program R defined over A, the collection of all sets of form $I \cap B$, where I is an answer set of $P \cup R$, coincides with the collection of all sets of form $J \cap B$, where J is an answer set of $Q \cup R$, and relativised uniform equivalence with projection is defined similarly with R containing facts over A only. These and analogously defined fine-grained equivalence notions are relevant for different programming aspects like modular programming [11] and program simplification [1, 16].

Both relativised strong equivalence with projection [4] as well as without projection [18] have been analysed for propositional programs only so far. In this paper, we consider the general case of *non-ground programs* and study these notions by lifting the corresponding definitions and characterisations to the non-ground case. In particular, we give a model-based characterisation for relativised strong equivalence in terms of *RSE-models* ("relativised SE-models"). That is, two programs are strongly equivalent relative to an alphabet A iff they have the same RSE-models relative to A. Afterwards, we generalise the notion of a *spoiler* whose existence disproves program correspondence in the sense of relativised strong equivalence with projection. Then, we introduce a model-based characterisation for relativised strong equivalence with projection in terms of *certificates*. More specifically, two programs P and Q are strongly equivalent relative to A with projection to B (where A and B are alphabets) iff P and Q have the same minimal (A, B)-certificates. Finally, we discuss some computability issues of the introduced non-ground equivalence notions.

2 Preliminaries

2.1 Logic Programs

Logic programs are defined over a vocabulary $V = (\mathbb{P}, \mathbb{D})$, where $\mathbb{P}$ is a set of *predicates* and $\mathbb{D}$ is a set of *constants* (also referred to as the *domain* of V). Each predicate in $\mathbb{P}$ has an *arity* $n \geq 0$. We also assume a set $\mathcal{A}$ of *variables*.

An *atom* is defined as $p(t_1, \ldots, t_n)$, where $p \in \mathbb{P}$ and $t_i \in \mathbb{D} \cup \mathcal{A}$, for $1 \leq i \leq n$. We call an atom *ground* if no variable occurs in it.

The set of all ground atoms of a vocabulary V is called the *Herbrand base* of V, denoted by HB_V. For a set $P \subseteq \mathbb{P}$ of predicates and a set $C \subseteq \mathbb{D}$ of constants, the set of all ground atoms constructed by replacing the variables in P with constants of C is denoted by $HB_{P,C}$.

A (*disjunctive*) *rule*, r, is an ordered pair of form

$$a_1 \vee \cdots \vee a_n \leftarrow b_1, \ldots, b_k, not\ b_{k+1}, \ldots, not\ b_m, \qquad (1)$$

where $a_1, \ldots, a_n, b_1, \ldots, b_m$ are atoms, $n, m, k \geq 0$, and $n + m > 0$. Furthermore, "*not*" denotes *default negation*. The left-hand side of r is the *head* and the right-hand side is the *body* of r. We accordingly define the sets $H(r) = \{a_1, \ldots, a_n\}$ and $B(r) = \{b_1, \ldots, b_k, not\ b_{k+1}, \ldots, not\ b_m\}$, as well as $B^+(r) = \{b_1, \ldots, b_k\}$ and $B^-(r) = \{b_{k+1}, \ldots, b_m\}$.

A rule r of form (1) is called (i) a *fact*, if $m = 0$ and $n = 1$; (ii) *unary*, if $n = 1$ and $k = m \leq 1$; (iii) *safe*, if each variable occurring in $H(r) \cup B^-(r)$ also occurs in $B^+(r)$; and (iv) *ground*, if all atoms in r are ground.

A *program* is a set of safe rules. We call a program ground if all of its rules are ground. For a program P, we define $H(P) = \bigcup_{r \in P} H(r)$ and $B(P) = \bigcup_{r \in P} B(r)$. Furthermore, for any program P, a predicate symbol $p \notin H(P)$ is *extensional* (in P), and *intensional* otherwise.

The set of all constants appearing in a program P is called the *Herbrand universe* of P, symbolically HU_P. If no constant appears in P, then HU_P contains an arbitrary constant. Furthermore, the set of all predicates of P is denoted by $\mathcal{A}_P$. We define $HB_P := HB_{\mathcal{A}_P, HU_P}$ and $HB_{P,C} := HB_{\mathcal{A}_P, C}$.

Given a rule r and a set C of constants, we define $grd(r, C)$ as the set of all rules generated by replacing all variables of r with elements of C. For any program P, the *grounding of P with respect to C* is given by $grd(P, C) := \bigcup_{r \in P} grd(r, C)$. If P is a ground program, then $P = grd(P, C)$ for any C.

A set of ground atoms is called an *interpretation*. Following the answer-set semantics for logic programs as defined by Gelfond and Lifschitz [8], a ground rule r is *satisfied* by an interpretation I, denoted by $I \models r$, iff $H(r) \cap I \neq \emptyset$ whenever $B^+(r) \subseteq I$ and $B^-(r) \cap I = \emptyset$. For a ground program P, $I \models P$ iff each $r \in P$ is satisfied by I. The *Gelfond-Lifschitz reduct* [7] of a ground program P with respect to the interpretation I is given by

$$P^I := \{H(r) \leftarrow B^+(r) \mid r \in P,\ I \cap B^-(r) = \emptyset\}.$$

An interpretation I is an *answer set* of a non-ground program P iff I is a subset-minimal set satisfying $grd(P, HU_P)^I$. An alternate definition of answer sets is given the following way: An interpretation I is an answer set of a non-ground program P iff $I \models grd(P, HU_P)$ and $J \not\models grd(P, HU_P)^I$ for any $J \subset I$. We define $AS(P)$ as the set of all answer sets of P. Note that safety of rules ensures that if $I \in AS(P)$ then $I \subseteq HB_P$.

By $\mathcal{P}_\mathcal{V}^A$, we denote the set of all programs over $\mathcal{V}$ that contain only predicates of A. Similarly, by $\mathcal{F}_\mathcal{V}^A$ we denote the set of all sets of facts over $\mathcal{V}$ that consist only of predicates of A. If $A = \mathbb{P}$, we write $\mathcal{P}_\mathcal{V}$ and $\mathcal{F}_\mathcal{V}$.

2.2   Notions of Equivalence

In this work, we deal with a generalisation of *strong equivalence* [12] allowing for a parameterisation along two dimensions: one for specifying the alphabet of the context programs which are used in the definition of strong equivalence, and one for filtering the compared output, i.e., the answer sets, in terms of a specified set of predicates (which can be seen as the "output atoms" one is interested in).

Strong equivalence was originally introduced for propositional programs by Lifschitz, Pearce, and Valverde [12] and subsequently studied for the non-ground case by Eiter, Fink, Tompits, and Woltran [3].

Formally, two programs P and Q are *strongly equivalent* iff $AS(P \cup R) = AS(Q \cup R)$, for any program R (we generally refer to such an R as a *context program*). Weaker forms of equivalence are *ordinary equivalence*, which holds between P and Q iff $AS(P) = AS(Q)$, and *uniform equivalence* [2], which holds between P and Q iff $AS(P \cup F) = AS(Q \cup F)$, for any set F of facts. Obviously, strong equivalence implies uniform equivalence, which in turn implies ordinary equivalence, but in general not vice versa. As shown by Lifschitz, Pearce, and Valverde [12], strong equivalence corresponds to equivalence in Heyting's *logic of here-and-there* [10], which is equivalent to Gödel's three valued logic [9], when programs are interpreted as logical formulas.

An alternative characterisation of strong equivalence in the propositional case in terms of so-called *SE-models* was introduced by Turner [17], which has subsequently been extended to non-ground programs by Eiter, Fink, Tompits, and Woltran [3] as follows: Let $\mathcal{V} = (\mathbb{P}, \mathbb{D})$ be a vocabulary, P a program over $\mathcal{V}$, $C \subseteq \mathbb{D}$, and $X, Y \subseteq HB_{\mathbb{P}, C}$ sets of ground atoms. Then, an *SE-interpretation* is a triple $(X, Y)_C$ such that $X \subseteq Y$. Furthermore, $(X, Y)_C$ is an *SE-model* of P iff $Y \models grd(P, C)$ and $X \models grd(P, C)^Y$. The set of all SE-models of P is denoted by $SE(P)$. As shown by Eiter, Fink, Tompits, and Woltran [3], generalising Turner's corresponding result for propositional programs [17], two (non-ground) logic programs P and Q are strongly equivalent iff $SE(P) = SE(Q)$.

The following notation is convenient for our purposes: For an interpretation Y, we define $Y|_A := Y \cap A$ and, for an SE-interpretation $(I, J)_C$, we define $(I, J)_C|_A := (I|_A, J|_A)_C$, where A is a set. Furthermore, we define $S|_A := \{Y|_A \mid Y \in S\}$, where A again is a set and S is a set of interpretations or of SE-interpretations.

The generalised form of strong equivalence admitting parameterisation along two dimensions we deal with in this paper for non-ground programs was introduced in the propositional case by Eiter, Tompits, and Woltran [4] as follows: Let

P and Q be propositional programs, and A and B sets of propositional atoms. Then, P and Q are *strongly equivalent relative to A under projection to B* iff $AS(P \cup R)|_B = AS(Q \cup R)|_B$, for each program R containing only atoms from A. If B coincides with the set of all propositional atoms (effectively, performing no projection), then strong equivalence relative to A under projection to B is referred to as *strong equivalence relative to A* simpliciter, which was studied prior to the work of Eiter, Tompits, and Woltran [4] by Woltran [18]. Similar notions for uniform equivalence have also been studied by Oetsch, Tompits, and Woltran [14] for the propositional case and by Oetsch and Tompits [13] for the general non-ground case.

Further generalised notions of equivalence are *hyperequivalence* [19], studied for propositional programs only thus far, which is relativised strong equivalence where for the context programs the head and body atoms are parameterised separately, and the following notions coming from the realm of datalog: Suppose P and Q are (non-ground) programs, and ε is the set of all their extensional predicates. Then, P and Q are *query equivalent* with respect to a predicate p iff, for any set $F \in \mathcal{F}_{\mathcal{V}}^{\varepsilon}$ of facts, $AS(P \cup F)|_{HB_{\{p\},\mathbb{D}}} = AS(Q \cup F)|_{HB_{\{p\},\mathbb{D}}}$. Furthermore, P and Q are *program equivalent* iff $AS(P \cup F) = AS(Q \cup F)$, for any set of facts $F \in \mathcal{F}_{\mathcal{V}}^{\varepsilon}$.

3   Program Correspondence

We now define our central notions of equivalence, lifting the concept of relativised strong equivalence with projection to the non-ground case. We start with some additional auxiliary notation, which will be used throughout this paper.

For interpretations Y and X, we use $Y \equiv_{\mathcal{V}}^{A} X$ to stand for $Y|_{HB_{A,\mathbb{D}}} = X|_{HB_{A,\mathbb{D}}}$, where $\mathcal{V} = (\mathbb{P}, \mathbb{D})$ and $A \subseteq \mathbb{P}$. Furthermore, we write $Y \sqsubseteq_{\mathcal{V}}^{B} X$ as a shorthand for $Y|_{HB_{B,\mathbb{D}}} \subseteq X|_{HB_{B,\mathbb{D}}}$.

Our central equivalence notion is defined as follows, generalising its propositional pendants as introduced by Eiter, Tompits, and Woltran [4] and Woltran [18]:

Definition 1. *Let P and Q be logic programs over $\mathcal{V} = (\mathbb{P}, \mathbb{D})$ and let $A, B \subseteq \mathbb{P}$ be sets of predicates. Then, P and Q are strongly equivalent relative to A under projection to B if $AS(P \cup R) \equiv_{\mathcal{V}}^{B} AS(Q \cup R)$, for any program $R \in \mathcal{P}_{\mathcal{V}}^{A}$. If $B = \mathbb{P}$, then P and Q are simply called strongly equivalent relative to A.*

It is convenient to weaken equivalence in order to express it in terms of two set-inclusion relations:

Definition 2. *Under the conditions of Definition 1, we write $P \models_{A,\mathcal{V}}^{B} Q$ if $AS(P \cup R) \sqsubseteq_{\mathcal{V}}^{B} AS(Q \cup R)$, for any program $R \in \mathcal{P}_{\mathcal{V}}^{A}$.*

If $B = \mathbb{P}$, then $P \models_{A,\mathcal{V}}^{B} Q$ is abbreviated by $P \models_{A,\mathcal{V}} Q$, and if $\mathcal{V}$ is clear from the context, we may drop $\mathcal{V}$ from $\models_{A,\mathcal{V}}^{B}$ and simply write $\models_{A}^{B}$.

We therefore have the following relation:

Theorem 1. *For all programs P and Q over $V = (\mathbb{P}, \mathbb{D})$ and each $A, B \subseteq \mathbb{P}$, P and Q are strongly equivalent relative to A under projection to B iff both $P \models^B_{A,V} Q$ and $Q \models^B_{A,V} P$ hold.*

Eiter, Tompits, and Woltran [4] introduced the notion of a *correspondence frame* in order to have a general framework for expressing different forms of equivalence in a uniform manner, which was subsequently extended to the non-ground case by Oetsch and Tompits [13]. Like all other notions of equivalence studied in the literature, relativised strong equivalence with projection, as well as the relation defined in Definition 2, can also be expressed in terms of this framework and we will make use of this fact later on.

Following Oetsch and Tompits [13], by a *correspondence frame*, or simply a *frame*, F, we understand a triple $(V, \mathcal{C}, \rho)$, where V is a vocabulary, $\mathcal{C} \subseteq \mathcal{P}_V$, called the *context class* of F, and $\rho \subseteq 2^{2^{HB_V}} \times 2^{2^{HB_V}}$. For every program P, Q over V, we say that P and Q are *F-corresponding*, symbolically $P \simeq_F Q$, iff, for all $R \in \mathcal{C}$, $(AS(P \cup R), AS(Q \cup R)) \in \rho$.

A *correspondence problem*, Π, over a vocabulary V is a tuple $(P, Q, \mathcal{C}, \rho)$, where P and Q are programs over V and $(V, \mathcal{C}, \rho)$ is a frame. We say that $(P, Q, \mathcal{C}, \rho)$ *holds* iff $P \simeq_{(V,\mathcal{C},\rho)} Q$. Furthermore, a correspondence problem of the form $(P, Q, \mathcal{P}^A_V, \sqsubseteq^B_V)$ is called an *inclusion problem* whilst one of the form $(P, Q, \mathcal{P}^A_V, \equiv^B_V)$ an *equivalence problem*. Clearly, $(P, Q, \mathcal{P}^A_V, \equiv^B_V)$ holds iff iff $(P, Q, \mathcal{P}^A_V, \sqsubseteq^B_V)$ and $(Q, P, \mathcal{P}^A_V, \sqsubseteq^B_V)$ jointly hold.

We then obtain the following straightforward characterisations:

Theorem 2. *Let P and Q be programs over $V = (\mathbb{P}, \mathbb{D})$ and $A, B \subseteq \mathbb{P}$ be sets of predicates.*
Then:

(i) P and Q are strongly equivalent relative to A under projection to B iff the equivalence problem $(P, Q, \mathcal{P}^A_V, \equiv^B_V)$ holds.
(ii) P and Q are strongly equivalent relative to A iff $(P, Q, \mathcal{P}^A_V, =)$ holds.
(iii) $P \models^B_{A,V} Q$ iff $(P, Q, \mathcal{P}^A_V, \sqsubseteq^B_V)$ holds.

As for other equivalence notions, they can be expressed as follows: Let P and Q be programs over $V = (\mathbb{P}, \mathbb{D})$ and ε the set of all their extensional predicates. Then, P and Q are

- (ordinarily) equivalent iff $(P, Q, \{\emptyset\}, =)$ holds,
- uniformly equivalent iff $(P, Q, \mathcal{F}_V, =)$ holds,
- strongly equivalent iff $(P, Q, \mathcal{P}_V, =)$ holds,
- query equivalent with respect to p iff $(P, Q, \mathcal{F}^\varepsilon_V, \equiv^{\{p\}}_V)$ holds, and
- program equivalent iff $(P, Q, \mathcal{F}^\varepsilon_V, =)$ holds.

Furthermore, defining P and Q to be *hyperequivalent with respect to* $\langle H, B \rangle$ (thus, extending this notion from the propositional case), where $H, B \subseteq \mathbb{P}$, iff $AS(P \cup R) = AS(Q \cup R)$, for any program $R \in \mathcal{P}^{\langle H, B \rangle}_V$, where $\mathcal{P}^{\langle H, B \rangle}_V$ is the set of all $P \in \mathcal{P}_V$ such that $\bigcup_{r \in P} H(r) \subseteq HB_{H,\mathbb{D}}$ and $\bigcup_{r \in P} B(r) \subseteq HB_{B,\mathbb{D}}$, where $V = (\mathbb{P}, \mathbb{D})$. It holds that P and Q are hyperequivalent with respect to $\langle H, B \rangle$ iff $(P, Q, \mathcal{P}^{\langle H, B \rangle}_V, =)$ holds.

4   Characterising Relativised Strong Equivalence Without Projection

We now provide semantic characterisations of relativised strong equivalence. The case of adding projection will be dealt with in the next section.

We start with the following lemma which is needed subsequently and which is a slight adaption of a similar characterisation by Eiter et al. [3].

Lemma 1. *Let P be a program over $\mathcal{V} = (\mathbb{P}, \mathbb{D})$, $C, C' \subseteq \mathbb{D}$ sets of constants such that $C \subseteq C'$, and $Y \subseteq HB_{P,C}$. Then, $Y \models grd(P, C)$ iff $Y \models grd(P, C')$.*

Next, we lift a lemma from the propositional case [18] which lays the groundwork for the following model-based characterisations of relativised strong equivalence.

Lemma 2. *For programs P and Q over a vocabulary $\mathcal{V} = (\mathbb{P}, \mathbb{D})$ and a set $A \subseteq \mathbb{P}$ of predicates, the following conditions are equivalent:*

(i) $AS(P \cup R) \not\subseteq AS(Q \cup R)$, for some program $R \in \mathcal{P}_{\mathcal{V}}^{A}$;
(ii) there exists a unary program $U \in \mathcal{P}_{\mathcal{V}}^{A}$ such that $AS(P \cup U) \not\subseteq AS(Q \cup U)$;
(iii) there exists an interpretation $Y \subseteq (HB_{P,C_P} \cap HB_{Q,C_Q})$ and sets $HU_P \subseteq C_P \subseteq \mathbb{D}$ and $HU_Q \subseteq C_Q \subseteq \mathbb{D}$ of constants such that:
  (a) $Y \models grd(P, C_P)$,
  (b) for each $Y' \subset Y$ with $Y' \equiv_{\mathcal{V}}^{A} Y$, $Y' \not\models grd(P, C_P)^{Y}$ holds, and
  (c) $Y \models grd(Q, C_Q)$ implies the existence of an $X \subset Y$ such that $X \models grd(Q, C_Q)^{Y}$ and for each $X' \subset Y$ with $X' \equiv_{\mathcal{V}}^{A} X$, $X' \not\models grd(P, C_P)^{Y}$ holds.

The proof of this lemma is somewhat technical and follows the general argumentation of the one for the propositional case (for a full proof, cf. the thesis of the first author [6]).

Following Woltran's [18] model-theoretic approach for relativised strong equivalence of propositional programs, we now introduce a similar characterisation in the non-ground setting.

Definition 3. *Let $\mathcal{V} = (\mathbb{P}, \mathbb{D})$ be a vocabulary, $C \subseteq \mathbb{D}$ a set of constants, P a logic program over $\mathcal{V}$, and $X, Y \subseteq HB_{P,C}$ interpretations. Furthermore, let $A \subseteq \mathbb{P}$ be a set of predicates.*
  Then:

(i) $(X, Y)_C$ is an RSE-interpretation of P relative to A if either $X = Y$ or $X \subset Y|_{HB_{A,C}}$.
(ii) An RSE-interpretation $(X, Y)_C$ of P relative to A is an RSE-model of P relative to A if
  (a) $Y \models grd(P, C)$,
  (b) for all $Y' \subset Y$ with $Y' \equiv_{\mathcal{V}}^{A} Y$, $Y' \not\models grd(P, C)^{Y}$, and
  (c) $X \subset Y$ implies the existence of an $X' \subseteq Y$ with $X' \equiv_{\mathcal{V}}^{A} X$ such that $X' \models grd(P, C)^{Y}$.

The set of all RSE-models of P relative to A is denoted by $RSE^A(P)$.[1]

From here on we might drop the explicit mentioning of the set A an RSE-model is relative to, if it is clear from the context.

The next lemma is an adaption of the one given by Eiter et al. [3] and follows directly from Lemma 1.

Lemma 3. *Let P be a program, $C, C' \subseteq \mathbb{D}$ sets of constants such that $C \subseteq C'$, and $X \subseteq Y \subseteq HB_{P,C}$. Then, $(X,Y)_C \in RSE^A(P)$ iff $(X,Y)_{C'} \in RSE^A(P)$.*

Now that we have laid down the necessary groundwork, we can introduce the main theorem of this chapter.

Theorem 3. *Two logic programs P and Q are strongly equivalent relative to A iff $RSE^A(P) = RSE^A(Q)$.*

Proof. The proof proceeds analogously to the propositional case as laid down by Woltran [18].

First, suppose P and Q are not strongly equivalent relative to A. Without loss of generality, according to Lemma 2, there has to be some $Y \subseteq (HB_{P,C_P} \cap HB_{Q,C_Q})$ and sets of constants $C_P \supseteq HU_P$ and $C_Q \supseteq HU_Q$ such that

(α) $Y \models grd(P, C_P)$,
(β) for each $Y' \subset Y$ with $Y' \equiv_{\mathcal{V}}^A Y$, $Y' \not\models grd(P, C_P)^Y$ holds, and
(γ) $Y \models grd(Q, C_Q)$ implies the existence of an $X \subset Y$ such that $X \models grd(Q, C_Q)^Y$ and for each $X' \subset Y$ with $X' \equiv_{\mathcal{V}}^A X$, $X' \not\models grd(P, C_P)^Y$ holds.

What we now want to show is that there exists at least one RSE-model which is in $SE^A(P)$ but not in $SE^A(Q)$ or vice versa.

Set $C_{P \cup Q} := C_P \cup C_Q$. By Definition 3, $(Y,Y)_{C_{P \cup Q}}$ is an RSE-model of P relative to A iff

(i) $Y \models grd(P, C_{P \cup Q})$; and
(ii) $Y' \not\models grd(P, C_{P \cup Q})^Y$, for each $Y' \subset Y$ with $Y' \equiv_{\mathcal{V}}^A Y$.

We know from (α) that $Y \models grd(P, C_P)$ holds and since $C_P \subseteq C_{P \cup Q}$, (i) holds by Lemma 1. From (β) we know that $Y' \not\models grd(P, C_P)^Y$ holds for each $Y' \subset Y$ with $Y' \equiv_{\mathcal{V}}^A Y$. Again by Lemma 1, we obtain $Y' \not\models grd(P, C_{P \cup Q})^Y$ and therefore (ii) holds. Hence $(Y,Y)_{C_{P \cup Q}}$ is an RSE-model of P.

Condition (γ) gives us three cases we need to explore, viz. either

(1) $Y \not\models grd(Q, C_Q)$;
(2) $Y \models grd(Q, C_Q)$ and $X \equiv_{\mathcal{V}}^A Y$; or
(3) $Y \models grd(Q, C_Q)$ and $(X \cap HB_{A,\mathbb{D}}) \subset (Y \cap HB_{A,\mathbb{D}})$.

---

[1] Woltran called his structures *A-SE-interpretations* and *A-SE-models*, respectively, and denoted the set of *A*-SE-models of a program by $SE^A(P)$.

If (1), then $(Y,Y)_{C_{P\cup Q}}$ cannot be an RSE-model of Q, since by Lemma 1 and $C_Q \subseteq C_{P\cup Q}$, $Y \not\models grd(Q, C_Q)$ implies $Y \not\models grd(Q, C_{P\cup Q})$.

If (2), then, according to (γ), $X \subset Y$ and $X \models grd(Q, C_Q)^Y$, which, by Lemma 1, implies $X \models grd(Q, C_{P\cup Q})^Y$. Thus, condition (b) of item (ii) of Definition 3 is violated (just set $X = Y'$). Hence, $(Y,Y)_{P\cup Q}$ is not an RSE-model of Q.

If (3), then $(X \cap HB_{A,\mathbb{D}}, Y)_{C_{P\cup Q}}$ satisfies conditions (a), (b), and (c) of item (ii) of Definition 3 and is therefore an RSE-model of Q. But, by condition (γ), for every Z with $(Z \cap HB_{A,\mathbb{D}}) = (X \cap HB_{A,\mathbb{D}})$, $Z \not\models grd(P, C_P)^Y$ holds and, by Lemma 1, $Z \not\models grd(P, C_{P\cup Q})^Y$ holds. This means that condition (c) of item (iii) of Definition 3 cannot be fulfilled and thus $((X \cap HB_{A,\mathbb{D}}), Y)_{C_{P\cup Q}}$ is not an RSE-Model of P.

Now we proceed with the other direction of the theorem. Suppose $(Z,Y)_C$ is an RSE-model of P relative to A but not of Q. By Definition 3, $C \subseteq \mathbb{D}$ and thus, according to Lemma 3, $(Z,Y)_{\mathbb{D}} \in SE^A(P)$ and $(Z,Y)_{\mathbb{D}} \notin SE^A(Q)$. Since $HU_{P\cup Q} \subseteq \mathbb{D}$ obviously holds, we obtain $(Z,Y)_{HU_{P\cup Q}} \in SE^A(P)$ and $(Z,Y)_{HU_{P\cup Q}} \notin SE^A(Q)$ by applying Lemma 3. Now consider $C_{P\cup Q} \supseteq HU_{P\cup Q}$. Again by Lemma 3, $(Z,Y)_{C_{P\cup Q}} \in SE^A(P)$ and $(Z,Y)_{C_{P\cup Q}} \notin SE^A(Q)$ hold.

If $Z = Y$, then, from Definition 3, it follows that $Y \models grd(P, C_{P\cup Q})$ and, for each $Y' \subset Y$ with $Y' \equiv_\mathcal{V}^A Y$, $Y' \not\models grd(P, C_{P\cup Q})$. Thus, (a) and (b) of item (iii) from Lemma 2 hold. Since (Y,Y) is not an RSE-model of Q we get by Definition 3 that either $Y \not\models grd(Q, C_{P\cup Q})$ or there is an $Y' \subset Y$ with $Y' \equiv_\mathcal{V}^A Y$ such that $Y' \models grd(Q, C_{P\cup Q})$. In the case of $Y \not\models grd(Q, C_{P\cup Q})$, condition (c) of item (iii) of Lemma 2 is obviously satisfied. Otherwise, if $Y \models grd(Q, C_{P\cup Q})$, condition (c) of item (iii) is satisfied by setting $X = Y'$. Hence, P and Q are not strongly equivalent relative to A.

If $Z \neq Y$, then whenever $(Z,Y)_{C_{P\cup Q}}$ is an RSE-model of P, $(Y,Y)_{C_{P\cup Q}}$ is an RSE-model as well. The case with $(Y,Y)_{C_{P\cup Q}}$ not being an RSE-model of Q was shown above, so we only need to prove the case with $(Y,Y)_{C_{P\cup Q}}$ being an RSE-model of Q. Supposing this, we get that $Y \models grd(Q, C_{P\cup Q})$ and, for each $Y' \subset Y$ with $Y' \equiv_\mathcal{V}^A Y$, $Y' \not\models grd(Q, C_{P\cup Q})^Y$. Obviously, conditions (a) and (b) of item (iii) from Lemma 2 are satisfied for Y and Q. Since $(Z,Y)_{C_{P\cup Q}}$ is not an RSE-model of Q we get the following from (b) of item (ii) of Definition 3: for each $(X' \cap HB_{A,\mathbb{D}}) = Z$, $X' \not\models grd(Q, C_{P\cup Q})^Y$. Also, because $(Z,Y)_{C_{P\cup Q}}$ is an RSE-model of P, there is an $X'' \subset Y$ with $(X'' \cap HB_{A,\mathbb{D}}) = Z$ such that $X'' \models grd(Q, C_{P\cup Q})^Y$ (condition (c) of item (ii) of Definition 3). Those two observations imply that condition (c) of item (iii) of Lemma 2 is satisfied for Y and Q and therefore P and Q are not strongly equivalent relative to A. $\square$

Example 1. Consider the program M consisting of the following rules:

$$accepted(x) \leftarrow applicant(x), not\ rejected(x),$$
$$rejected(x) \leftarrow applicant(x), not\ accepted(x),$$
$$applicant(x) \leftarrow person(x), not\ hired(x),$$
$$person(jane) \leftarrow ,$$
$$person(bob) \leftarrow .$$

Furthermore, consider the following subprograms of M:

$$P = \{accepted(x) \leftarrow applicant(x), not\ rejected(x),$$
$$rejected(x) \leftarrow applicant(x), not\ accepted(x)\};$$

$$R = \{applicant(x) \leftarrow person(x), not\ hired(x),$$
$$person(jane) \leftarrow ,$$
$$person(bob) \leftarrow \}.$$

Obviously, $M = P \cup R$.

Now, assume we want to replace the subprogram P with $Q = \{accepted(x) \vee rejected(x) \leftarrow applicant(x)\}$.

We use the following shorthands: $ap(\cdot)$ for $applicant(\cdot)$, $ac(\cdot)$ for $accepted(\cdot)$, $re(\cdot)$ for $rejected(\cdot)$, $hi(\cdot)$ for $hired(\cdot)$, j for $jane$, and b for bob. Furthermore, we have the vocabulary $\mathcal{V} = (\mathbb{D}, \mathbb{P})$, where $\mathbb{D} = \{jane, bob\}$ and $\mathbb{P} = \{applicant(\cdot), accepted(\cdot), rejected(\cdot), person(\cdot), hired(\cdot)\}$.

From $AS(P) = AS(Q) = \emptyset$ it obviously follows that P and Q are ordinarily equivalent, but they are not strongly equivalent because $(X, Y)_C$, for $X = \{ap(j), ap(b)\}$, $Y = \{ap(j), ap(b), ac(j), ac(b), re(j), re(b)\}$, and $C = \{j, b\}$, is an SE-model of P but not of Q.

Let us now take a look at their RSE-models relative to $A = \{ap(\cdot), pe(\cdot), hi(\cdot)\}$. Then, we have that $RSE^A(P) = RSE^A(Q)$ and thus we can replace P with Q in M as $AS(P \cup R) = AS(Q \cup R)$.   □

5   Characterising Relativised Strong Equivalence with Projection

In order to introduce model-theoretic characterisations for strong equivalence with projection, we first have to introduce a structure which disproves the equivalence. This concept was introduced by Eiter et al. [4] for the ground case.

We start with some basic definitions and properties.

Eiter et al. [4] define a useful property for sets of SE-models. The following definition is a generalisation of that property.

Definition 4. *A set S of $(R)SE$-interpretations is* complete, *if $(X, Y)_C \in S$ implies both $(Y, Y)_C \in S$ as well as $(X, Z)_C \in S$, for any $Z \supseteq Y$ with $(Z, Z)_C \in S$.*

It can be shown that the set $RSE(P)$ of a program P is always complete [4].

Furthermore, we introduce the following definition.

Definition 5. *A set S of $(R)SE$-interpretations is called* over C *if for each $(X, Y)_{C'} \in S$, $C' = C$.*

That definition enables us to restrict a set of SE-models to a particular set of grounding constants. Think of a complete set of SE-models S over C. Then, the grounding of a program P with respect to C is semantically given by S.

In order to show the relationship between our structures and correspondence problems we need some auxiliary results. Those results are adapted from the previously established propositional case [4].

Definition 6. *For a set S of $(R)SE$-interpretations, a vocabulary $\mathcal{V}$, and an interpretation Y, the set $\sigma_{Y,\mathcal{V}}^A(S)$ is given by $\{(X,Z)_C \in S \mid Z \equiv_{\mathcal{V}}^A Y\}$.*

The next proposition is not really a lifting to the non-ground setting because reconstructing a non-ground program from a set of SE-models is not trivial. Our generalised approach takes a complete set of SE-models over a certain set of constants and computes a ground program which is semantically equal to the original non-ground program for the given constants. Nonetheless, the construction of the program is very similar to the one given by Eiter et al. [4].

Proposition 1. *Let $\mathcal{V} = (\mathbb{P},\mathbb{D})$ be a vocabulary, $A \subseteq \mathbb{P}$ a set of predicates, $C \subseteq \mathbb{D}$ a set of constants, and S a complete set of SE-models over C. Then, there exists a program $P_{S,A,C} \in \mathcal{P}_{\mathcal{V}}^A$ such that $SE(P_{S,A,C}) \equiv_{\mathcal{V}}^A S$.*

Proof (Sketch). Consider the program

$$P_{S,A,C} = \{\leftarrow Y, not(HB_{A,\mathbb{D}} \setminus Y) \mid Y \subseteq HB_{A,\mathbb{D}}, (Y,Y)_C \notin S|_{HB_{A,\mathbb{D}}}\} \cup$$
$$\{\textstyle\bigvee_{a \in (Y \setminus X)} a \leftarrow X, not(HB_{A,\mathbb{D}} \setminus Y) \mid X \subset Y, (Y,Y)_C \in S|_{HB_{A,\mathbb{D}}},$$
$$(X,Y)_C \notin S|_{HB_{A,\mathbb{D}}}\}.$$

It can be shown that $S \equiv_{\mathcal{V}}^A SE(P_{S,A,C})$ for any complete set S of SE-models over C. □

Now we come to the generalisation of a *spoiler*. This structure was introduced by Eiter et al. [4] in the propositional case and its existence for a certain inclusion problem *disproves* the correspondence.

Let us call an SE-interpretation $(I,J)_C$ *total* if $I = J$ and *non-total* otherwise. A set S of SE-interpretations is non-total if for each total $(J,J)_C \in S$ there exists a non-total $(I,J)_C \in S$.

Definition 7. *Let P and Q be programs over $\mathcal{V} = (\mathbb{P},\mathbb{D})$, $Y \subseteq HB_{P,C}$ an interpretation, $C \subseteq \mathbb{D}$ a set of constants, and $S \subseteq \sigma_{Y,\mathcal{V}}^{A \cup B}(RSE^A(Q))$. Then, the pair $(Y,S)_C$ is a spoiler for the correspondence problem $\Pi = (P,Q,\mathcal{P}_{\mathcal{V}}^A, \sqsubseteq_{\mathcal{V}}^B)$ iff*

(i) $(Y,Y)_C \in RSE^A(P)$,
(ii) for each $(Z,Z)_C \in S$, some non-total $(X,Z)_C \in S$ exists,
(iii) $(Z,Z)_C \in S$ iff $(Z,Z)_C \in \sigma_{Y,\mathcal{V}}^{A \cup B}(RSE^A(Q))$, and
(iv) $(X,Z)_C \in S$ implies $(X,Y)_C \notin RSE^A(P)$.

Intuitively, the interpretation Y in a spoiler $(Y,S)_C$ is an answer set of $P \cup R$ but not of $Q \cup R$, where R is semantically given by S.

The following theorem forms the link between correspondence problems and spoilers.

Theorem 4. *Let P and Q be programs over $\mathcal{V} = (\mathbb{P},\mathbb{D})$, and $A, B \subseteq \mathbb{P}$ sets of predicates. Then, $P \models_{A,\mathcal{V}}^B Q$ iff there is no spoiler for $(P,Q,\mathcal{P}_{\mathcal{V}}^A, \sqsubseteq_{\mathcal{V}}^B)$.*

Example 2. Let us again consider the programs from Example 1:

$$P = \{ accepted(x) \leftarrow applicant(x), not\ rejected(x),$$
$$rejected(x) \leftarrow applicant(x), not\ accepted(x),$$
$$applicant(x) \leftarrow person(x), not\ hired(x),$$
$$person(jane) \leftarrow ,$$
$$person(bob) \leftarrow \}.$$

$$Q = \{ accepted(x) \lor rejected(x) \leftarrow applicant(x),$$
$$applicant(x) \leftarrow person(x), not\ hired(x),$$
$$person(jane) \leftarrow ,$$
$$person(bob) \leftarrow \}.$$

Furthermore, consider the sets $A = B = \{accepted(\cdot), rejected(\cdot)\}$. The correspondence problem $\Pi = (Q, P, \mathcal{P}_{\mathcal{V}}^A, \sqsubseteq_{\mathcal{V}}^B)$ does not hold because there exists a spoiler $(Y, S)_C$ for Π, where $Y = \{ ac(j), re(j), ap(j), pe(j), ac(b), re(b), ap(b), pe(b)\}$, and S is given by

$$S = \{ (\emptyset, \{ap(j), ap(b), re(j), ac(j), re(b), ac(b)\}),$$
$$(\{ac(j)\}, \{ap(j), ap(b), re(j), ac(j), re(b), ac(b)\}),$$
$$(\{ac(b)\}, \{ap(j), ap(b), re(j), ac(j), re(b), ac(b)\}),$$
$$(\{re(j)\}, \{ap(j), ap(b), re(j), ac(j), re(b), ac(b)\}),$$
$$(\{re(b)\}, \{ap(j), ap(b), re(j), ac(j), re(b), ac(b)\}),$$
$$(\{ac(j), re(j)\}, \{ap(j), ap(b), re(j), ac(j), re(b), ac(b)\}),$$
$$(\{ac(b), re(b)\}, \{ap(j), ap(b), re(j), ac(j), re(b), ac(b)\}),$$
$$(\{ap(j), ap(b), re(j), ac(j), re(b), ac(b)\},$$
$$\{ap(j), ap(b), re(j), ac(j), re(b), ac(b)\}) \},$$

with $C = \{j, b\}$.   ⊓

An intermediate consequence of the theorem above is the next result:

Corollary 1. *Let* $\Pi = (P, Q, \mathcal{P}_{\mathcal{V}}^A, \equiv_{\mathcal{V}}^B)$ *be an equivalence problem. Then,* Π *holds iff neither* $(P, Q, \mathcal{P}_{\mathcal{V}}^A, \sqsubseteq_{\mathcal{V}}^B)$ *nor* $(Q, P, \mathcal{P}_{\mathcal{V}}^A, \sqsubseteq_{\mathcal{V}}^B)$ *has a spoiler.*

Now that we have introduced structures which disprove correspondence, we can next introduce one that does the opposite. These concepts were again already introduced for the propositional setting [4].

Definition 8. *Let* P *be a program over a vocabulary* $\mathcal{V} = (\mathbb{P}, \mathbb{D})$, *and* $A, B \in \mathbb{P}$ *sets of predicates. Then, a triple* $(\mathcal{X}, Y)_C$, *where* $Y \subseteq HB_{A \cup B, C}$ *and* $C \subseteq \mathbb{D}$, *is an* (A, B)-*certificate of* P *iff there exists a* Z *such that*

(i) $(Z, Z)_C \in RSE^A(P)$,
(ii) $Z \equiv_{\mathcal{V}}^{A \cup B} Y$, *and*
(iii) $\mathcal{X} = \{X \mid (X, Z)_C \in RSE^A(P), X \subset Z\}$.

An (A, B)-*certificate* $(\mathcal{X}, Y)_C$ *of a program* P *is minimal iff, for any* (A, B)-*certificate* $(\mathcal{Z}, Y)_C$ *of* P, $\mathcal{Z} \subseteq \mathcal{X}$ *implies* $\mathcal{Z} = \mathcal{X}$.

The following lemma links certificates to program correspondence and can be shown using spoilers.

Lemma 4. $P \models^B_{A,\lor} Q$ *iff for each* (A,B)*-certificate* $(\mathcal{X},Y)_C$ *of* P *there is an* (A,B)*-certificate* $(\mathcal{X}',Y)_C$ *of* Q *such that* $\mathcal{X}' \subseteq \mathcal{X}$.

Now, the corresponding theorem follows quite naturally.

Theorem 5. *Two programs* P *and* Q *are strongly equivalent relative to* A *with projection to* B *iff* P *and* Q *have the same minimal* (A,B)*-certificates.*

Proof. We start by showing that if the equivalence problem $\Pi = (P,Q,\mathcal{P}^A_\lor,\equiv^B_\lor)$ holds, then the minimal (A,B)-certificates of P and Q coincide. Since Π holds, it follows that $\Pi' = (P,Q,\mathcal{P}^A_\lor,\sqsubseteq^B_\lor)$ and $\Pi'' = (Q,P,\mathcal{P}^A_\lor,\sqsubseteq^B_\lor)$ both hold. Suppose that $(\mathcal{X},Y)_C$ is a minimal (A,B)-certificate of P. By Lemma 4 and since Π' holds, there has to be an (A,B)-certificate $(\mathcal{X}',Y)_C$ of Q such that $\mathcal{X}' \subseteq \mathcal{X}$. Towards a contradiction, suppose that $(\mathcal{X}',Y)_C$ is not minimal. Thus, there has to be an (A,B)-certificate $(\mathcal{Z},Y)_C$ of Q such that $\mathcal{Z} \subset \mathcal{X}'$. Now, again by Lemma 4 and since Π'' holds, there has to be an (A,B)-certificate $(\mathcal{Z}',Y)_C$ of P such that $\mathcal{Z}' \subseteq \mathcal{Z}$. But since $\mathcal{Z}' \subset \mathcal{X}' \subseteq \mathcal{X}$ obviously implies $\mathcal{Z}' \subset \mathcal{X}$, that would mean $(\mathcal{X},Y)_C$ is not a minimal (A,B)-certificate of P. Hence, we have a contradiction and $(\mathcal{X}',Y)_C$ is a minimal (A,B)-certificate of Q.

Now, with the same reasoning, the latter implies, again by Lemma 4, that there is some $\mathcal{X}'' \subseteq \mathcal{X}'$ such that $(\mathcal{X}'',Y)_C$ is a minimal (A,B)-certificate of P. But $(\mathcal{X},Y)_C$ is a minimal (A,B)-certificate of P, and hence $\mathcal{X}'' = \mathcal{X}$ and thus $\mathcal{X}' = \mathcal{X}$. Consequently, $(\mathcal{X},Y)_C$ is a minimal (A,B)-certificate of Q. So, each minimal (A,B)-certificate of P is also a minimal (A,B)-certificate of Q. By analogous arguments we have that the other inclusion also holds, hence the minimal (A,B)-certificates of P and Q coincide.

For the other direction of the theorem, suppose towards a contradiction that it does not hold. So, the minimal (A,B)-certificates of P and Q coincide but the equivalence problem $\Pi = (P,Q,\mathcal{P}^A_\lor,\equiv^B_\lor)$ does not hold. Without loss of generality, suppose $(P,Q,\mathcal{P}^A_\lor,\sqsubseteq^B_\lor)$ does not hold (the case with $(Q,P,\mathcal{P}^A_\lor,\sqsubseteq^B_\lor)$ is analogous). Then, by Lemma 4, there is an (A,B)-certificate $(\mathcal{X},Y)_C$ of P such that for each (A,B)-certificate $(\mathcal{X}',Y)_C$ of Q, $\mathcal{X}' \not\subseteq \mathcal{X}$ holds. If $(\mathcal{X},Y)_C$ is minimal we immediately have a contradiction since then it would also be an (A,B)-certificate of Q and clearly $\mathcal{X} \subseteq \mathcal{X}$. On the other hand, if $(\mathcal{X},Y)_C$ is not minimal then there has to be an (A,B)-certificate $(\mathcal{Z},Y)_C$ with $\mathcal{Z} \subset \mathcal{X}$. But then $(\mathcal{Z},Y)_C$ is also an (A,B)-certificate of Q and since $\mathcal{Z} \subset \mathcal{X}$ holds we again have a contradiction. $\qquad\square$

Example 3. Consider the subprograms from Example 1:

$$P = \{accepted(x) \leftarrow applicant(x), not\ rejected(x),$$
$$rejected(x) \leftarrow applicant(x), not\ accepted(x)\}.$$

$$Q = \{accepted(x) \lor rejected(x) \leftarrow applicant(x)\}.$$

Furthermore, consider the sets $A = \{ap(\cdot),pe(\cdot),hi(\cdot)\}$ and $B = \{ac(\cdot),re(\cdot)\}$. Then, the minimal (A,B)-certificates of both programs are given by the following set:

$$\{(\emptyset, \emptyset)_{\{j,b\}}, (\{\emptyset\}, \{ap(b), ac(b)\})_{\{j,b\}}, (\{\emptyset\}, \{ap(j), re(j)\})_{\{j,b\}},$$
$$(\{\emptyset\}, \{ap(j), ac(j)\})_{\{j,b\}}, (\{\emptyset\}, \{ap(b), re(b)\})_{\{j,b\}},$$
$$(\{\emptyset, \{ap(j)\}, \{ap(b)\}\}, \{ap(j), ap(b), ac(j), ac(b)\})_{\{j,b\}},$$
$$(\{\emptyset, \{ap(j)\}, \{ap(b)\}\}, \{ap(j), ap(b), re(j), re(b)\})_{\{j,b\}},$$
$$(\{\emptyset, \{ap(j)\}, \{ap(b)\}\}, \{ap(j), ap(b), ac(b), re(j)\})_{\{j,b\}},$$
$$(\emptyset, \emptyset)_{\{j\}}, (\{\emptyset\}, \{ap(j), ac(j)\})_{\{j\}}, (\{\emptyset\}, \{ap(j), re(j)\})_{\{j\}},$$
$$(\emptyset, \emptyset)_{\{b\}}, (\{\emptyset\}, \{ap(b), ac(b)\})_{\{b\}}, (\{\emptyset\}, \{ap(b), re(b)\})_{\{b\}}\}.$$

Therefore, according to Theorem 5, we get that P and Q are strongly equivalent relative to A with projection to B. $\qquad\square$

Another structure disproving correspondence is that of a *counterexample* [4], which follows more or less naturally from the definition of relativised strong equivalence.

Definition 9. *Let P and Q be programs over $\mathcal{V} = (\mathbb{P}, \mathbb{D})$, $R \in \mathcal{P}_\mathcal{V}^A$ a program, and $M \in AS(P \cup R)$ an answer set. Then, the pair (R, M) is a* counterexample *for the correspondence problem $\Pi = (P, Q, \mathcal{P}_\mathcal{V}^A, \sqsubseteq_\mathcal{V}^B)$ iff*

(i) $M \in AS(P \cup R)$,
(ii) $M|_{HB_{B,\mathbb{D}}} \notin AS(Q \cup R)|_{HB_{B,\mathbb{D}}}$, and
(iii) $AS(P \cup R) \not\sqsubseteq_\mathcal{V}^B AS(Q \cup R)$.

The following theorem shows the connection between spoilers and counterexamples and follows directly from Theorem 4, Proposition 1, and Definition 7.

Theorem 6. *Suppose $(Y, S)_C$ is a spoiler with $S \neq \emptyset$. Then, $(P_{S,A,C}, Y)$ is a counterexample for $\Pi = (P, Q, \mathcal{P}_\mathcal{V}^A, \sqsubseteq_\mathcal{V}^B)$, where $P_{S,A,C}$ is defined as in Proposition 1.*

Example 4. Recall the spoiler $(Y, S)_C$ and the correspondence problem $\Pi = (Q, P, \mathcal{P}_\mathcal{V}^A, \sqsubseteq_\mathcal{V}^B)$ from Example 2. Let $P_{S,A,C}$ be the program constructed as described in Proposition 1. Appending $P_{S,A,C}$ to the programs P and Q, we obtain the answer sets $AS(P \cup P_{S,A,C}) = \emptyset$ and $AS(Q \cup P_{S,A,C}) = \{\{ap(j), ap(b), ac(j), re(j), ac(b), re(b)\}\}$. Obviously, $Y \in AS(Q \cup P_{S,A,C})$ and $Y|_{HB_{B,\mathbb{D}}} \notin AS(P \cup P_{S,A,C})|_{HB_{B,\mathbb{D}}}$ both hold. Therefore, $(P_{S,A,C}, Y)$ is a counterexample for Π. $\qquad\square$

6   Computability Issues

We now discuss computability aspects of different instances of the correspondence framework.

We start with uniform equivalence. Eiter, Fink, Tompits, and Woltran [3] showed that while uniform equivalence in the non-ground case is decidable for finite domains, it is undecidable in general. Since uniform equivalence is an instance of the framework, we get the following result:

Proposition 2. *The problem of determining whether a given correspondence problem of form $(P, Q, \mathcal{F}_\mathcal{V}, =)$ over some vocabulary $\mathcal{V}$ is co-NEXPTIME^{NP}-complete for finite domains and undecidable in general.*

When Oetsch and Tompits [13] generalised the correspondence framework of Eiter et al. [4], they also lifted a refinement of uniform equivalence to the non-ground case. That refinement can be seen as *relativised uniform equivalence with projection*. They showed that checking this notion is decidable for finite domains, but the known undecidability of query equivalence immediately yields the following result:

Proposition 3. *The problem of determining whether a given correspondence problem of form $(P, Q, \mathcal{F}_\mathcal{V}^A, \equiv_\mathcal{V}^B)$ over some vocabulary $\mathcal{V}$ holds is co-NEXPTIME$^{\Sigma_2^P}$-complete for finite domains and undecidable in general.*

Eiter et al. [3] showed that, in contrast to uniform equivalence, strong equivalence is decidable even for infinite domains:

Proposition 4. *The problem of determining whether a given correspondence problem of form $(P, Q, \mathcal{P}_\mathcal{V}, =)$ over some vocabulary $\mathcal{V}$ is co-NEXPTIME-complete for finite domains and in general.*

As for relativised strong equivalence, Oetsch and Tompits [13] obtained:

Proposition 5. *The problem of determining whether a given correspondence problem of form $(P, Q, \mathcal{P}_\mathcal{V}^A, \equiv_\mathcal{V}^B)$ over some vocabulary $\mathcal{V}$ holds is co-NEXPTIME$^{\Sigma_3^P}$-complete for finite domains and undecidable in general.*

This stems from the undecidability of program equivalence and the following fact [13]:

Proposition 6. *Let P and Q be programs over $\mathcal{V}$ and ε the set of all their extensional predicates, then $(P, Q, \mathcal{F}_\mathcal{V}^\varepsilon, =)$ holds iff $(P, Q, \mathcal{P}_\mathcal{V}^\varepsilon, =)$ holds.*

The undecidability of relativised strong equivalence with projection is particularly interesting, because Oetsch et al. [13] showed that adding projection to unrelativised strong equivalence adds no significant complexity and unrelativised strong equivalence is decidable. In fact, we can even express unrelativised strong equivalence as the following correspondence problem.

Theorem 7. *Two programs P and Q over $\mathcal{V} = (\mathbb{P}, \mathbb{D})$ are strongly equivalent iff the equivalence problem $(P, Q, \mathcal{P}_\mathcal{V}^\mathbb{P}, =)$ holds.*

So, a correspondence frame of form $(P, Q, \mathcal{P}_\mathcal{V}^A, =)$ is decidable when $A = \mathbb{P}$ but is known to be undecidable in the case of $A = \varepsilon$. The exact lower bound on A for the decidability of such correspondence problems would be an interesting topic for future work.

The general undecideability of relativised strong equivalence with projection is of course rather bad news for its practical applications. For example, the elimination of disjunctions in programs as described by Pührer et al. [16] for the propositional case is most likely undecidable as well.

7   Conclusion

We generalised the concepts of relativised strong equivalence and relativised strong equivalence with projection to the non-ground setting by lifting the existing semantic characterisations for the propositional case to the non-ground setting and discussed some computability aspects.

There are multiple topics left for future work. For example, similarly to Oetsch and Tompits [13], we plan to provide an axiomatisation of our model-theoretic characterisations in terms of second-order logic. It would be interesting to investigate whenever or not there exist certain classes of programs were such a translation to second-order logic collapses to a first-order formula. Furthermore, studying the connection between those axiomatisations and the generalised answer-set semantics introduced by Ferraris et al. [5] would also be an interesting point, since their approach is actually based on second-order logic.

Work can also be done in the context of equilibrium logic and hyperequivalence. Equilibirium logic was recently generalised for a subset of first-order logic by Pearce and Valverde [15]. An interesting task would be the introduction of relativised strong equivalence with projection to the so-called *quantified equilibrium logic*. As for hyperequivalence, so far it only exists in the realm of ground programs. A lifting of its concepts to the non-ground setting—analogous to this work—would be a worthwhile endeavour.

References

1. Eiter, T., Fink, M., Tompits, H., Woltran, S.: Simplifying logic programs under uniform and strong equivalence. In: Lifschitz, V., Niemelä, I. (eds.) LPNMR 2004. LNCS (LNAI), vol. 2923, pp. 87–99. Springer, Heidelberg (2003). https://doi.org/10.1007/978-3-540-24609-1_10
2. Eiter, T., Fink, M.: Uniform equivalence of logic programs under the stable model semantics. In: Palamidessi, C. (ed.) ICLP 2003. LNCS, vol. 2916, pp. 224–238. Springer, Heidelberg (2003). https://doi.org/10.1007/978-3-540-24599-5_16
3. Eiter, T., Fink, M., Tompits, H., Woltran, S.: Strong and uniform equivalence in answer-set programming: Characterizations and complexity results for the non-ground case. In: Proceedings of the 20th National Conference on Artificial Intelligence (AAAI 2005), pp. 695–700. AAAI Press (2005)
4. Eiter, T., Tompits, H., Woltran, S.: On solution correspondences in answer set programming. In: Proceedings of the 19th International Joint Conference on Artificial Intelligence (IJCAI 2005), pp. 97–102. Professional Book (2005)
5. Ferraris, P., Lee, J., Lifschitz, V.: Stable models and circumscription. Artif. Intel. **175**(1), 236–263 (2011)
6. Geibinger, T.: Characterising relativised strong equivalence with projection for non-ground logic programs. Bachelor's thesis, Technische Universität Wien, Institute of Logic and Computation, E193–03 (2018)
7. Gelfond, M., Lifschitz, V.: The stable model semantics for logic programming. In: Proceedings of the 5th International Conference and Symposium on Logic Programming (ICLP/SLP 1988), pp. 1070–1080. MIT Press (1988)
8. Gelfond, M., Lifschitz, V.: Classical negation in logic programs and disjunctive databases. New Gener. Comput. **9**, 365–385 (1991)

9. Gödel, K.: Zum intuitionistischen Aussagenkalkül. Anzeiger der Akademie der Wissenschaften in Wien, pp. 65–66 (1932)
10. Heyting, A.: Die formalen Regeln der intuitionistischen Logik. Sitzungsberichte der Preußischen Akademie der Wissenschaften. Physikalisch-mathematische Klasse, pp. 42–56 (1930)
11. Janhunen, T., Oikarinen, E., Tompits, H., Woltran, S.: Modularity aspects of disjunctive stable models. J. Artif. Intel. Res. **35**, 813–857 (2009)
12. Lifschitz, V., Pearce, D., Valverde, A.: Strongly equivalent logic programs. ACM Trans. Comput. Logic **2**, 526–541 (2001)
13. Oetsch, J., Tompits, H.: Program correspondence under the answer-set semantics: the non-ground case. In: Garcia de la Banda, M., Pontelli, E. (eds.) ICLP 2008. LNCS, vol. 5366, pp. 591–605. Springer, Heidelberg (2008). https://doi.org/10.1007/978-3-540-89982-2_49
14. Oetsch, J., Tompits, H., Woltran, S.: Facts do not cease to exist because they are ignored: relativised uniform equivalence with answer-set projection. In: Proceedings of the 22nd National Conference on Artificial Intelligence (AAAI 2007), pp. 458–464. AAAI Press (2007)
15. Pearce, D., Valverde, A.: Quantified equilibrium logic and foundations for answer set programs. In: Garcia de la Banda, M., Pontelli, E. (eds.) ICLP 2008. LNCS, vol. 5366, pp. 546–560. Springer, Heidelberg (2008). https://doi.org/10.1007/978-3-540-89982-2_46
16. Pührer, J., Tompits, H.: Casting away disjunction and negation under a generalisation of strong equivalence with projection. In: Erdem, E., Lin, F., Schaub, T. (eds.) LPNMR 2009. LNCS (LNAI), vol. 5753, pp. 264–276. Springer, Heidelberg (2009). https://doi.org/10.1007/978-3-642-04238-6_23
17. Turner, H.: Strong equivalence made easy: Nested expressions and weight constraints. Theory Pract. Logic Prog. **3**, 602–622 (2003)
18. Woltran, S.: Characterizations for relativized notions of equivalence in answer set programming. In: Alferes, J.J., Leite, J. (eds.) JELIA 2004. LNCS (LNAI), vol. 3229, pp. 161–173. Springer, Heidelberg (2004). https://doi.org/10.1007/978-3-540-30227-8_16
19. Woltran, S.: A common view on strong, uniform, and other notions of equivalence in answer-set programming. Theory Pract. Logic Prog. **8**, 217–234 (2008)

Uhura: An Authoring Tool for Specifying Answer-Set Programs Using Controlled Natural Language

Tobias Kain$^{(\boxtimes)}$ and Hans Tompits

Institute of Logic and Computation, Knowledge-Based Systems Group,
Technische Universität Wien, Favoritenstraße 9-11, 1040 Vienna, Austria
{kain,tompits}@kr.tuwien.ac.at

Abstract. In this paper, we present the tool Uhura for developing answer-set programs by means of specifying problem descriptions in a controlled natural language which then are translated into answer-set programming (ASP) rules. The tool is aimed for supporting users not familiar with answer-set programming—or logic-based approaches in general—for developing programs. Uhura is based on a new controlled natural language called L^U, which is in turn an adaption of $PENG^{ASP}$, a controlled natural language employed in the PENG ASP system, developed by Guy and Schwitter, for solving computational problems by translating $PENG^{ASP}$ statements into answer-set programs. In contrast to $PENG^{ASP}$, L^U allows for a more natural translation into ASP rules and provides also a broader set of pre-defined sentence patterns. Uhura is implemented in Java and employs DLV as backend answer-set solver.

Keywords: Answer-set programming · Program development · Controlled natural language

1 Introduction

In the past couple of years, *answer-set programming* (ASP), i.e., logic programming under the answer-set semantics [15], has evolved into a viable approach for declarative problem solving. Although applications in many diverse fields using ASP have been developed, ASP is rarely used by developers who do not work in an academic environment. This is attributable, among other things, to a lack of support tools designed for ASP novices, although work on integrated development environments for ASP [2,9], as well as methods for debugging and testing answer-set programs are available [5,10,16,20,25]. Especially those who have never before used any logical programming languages have a hard time getting acquainted with ASP.

In this paper, we present a tool which addresses this issue. Our tool, Uhura, supports ASP novices as well as professional ASP developers in developing answer-set programs by providing an editor in which a problem description can

© Springer Nature Switzerland AG 2019
F. Calimeri et al. (Eds.): JELIA 2019, LNAI 11468, pp. 559–575, 2019.
https://doi.org/10.1007/978-3-030-19570-0_37

be specified by means of a *controlled natural language* (CNL) which is then translated into an answer-set program which is displayed vis-à-vis the CNL specification. The obtained ASP code can be executed using the solver DLV [23] and the computed answer sets can accordingly be displayed in a tab of Uhura as well. Uhura employs the ASP-Core-2 [3] syntax, which is supported by DLV as well as other ASP solvers. The name of our tool derives from the fictional Star Trek character Lieutenant Nyota Uhura, who serves as communication officer at the Starship Enterprise, because our tool and Lt. Uhura have somewhat similar tasks, viz. acting as a facilitator between a familiar and an unfamiliar language.

The CNL employed in Uhura, called L^U, is a novel CNL which is based on $PENG^{ASP}$ [30], a CNL whose primary purpose is to be a CNL which can unambiguously be translated into ASP. However, compared to $PENG^{ASP}$, the translation of L^U sentences into ASP is more direct and L^U offers a broader set of predefined sentence patterns. Following Kuhn [22], a CNL is a constructed language resembling a natural language but being more restrictive concerning lexicon, syntax, and/or semantics while preserving most of its natural properties. In effect, it is essentially a formal language and is often used as a bridge between a highly ambiguous natural language and a less human-readable formal language.

The idea of building a tool for translating a problem description expressed in a (controlled) natural language into an answer-set program is not a new one. For example, the system based on $PENG^{ASP}$ [17,18], as well as LOGICIA [24] and BioQuery-ASP [6,7] are systems that translate a CNL into ASP in order to achieve various goals. Furthermore, there is also an approach [8] to translate answer sets in more human-readable form based on a CNL using the ASP annotation language Lana [4].

However, what makes our approach unique is that the aim of Uhura is not only to translate CNL sentences into ASP rules but to perform the translation in such a way that the user can learn how to write answer-set programs. To increase the learning progress, we decided to design L^U in such a way that correspondence between the CNL sentences and the ASP rules is clearly evident. While most of the other available tools primarily focus on solving the described problem, the goal of translating a CNL problem description into an intuitive-to-read answer-set program comes at the expense of expressibility. Moreover, our tool does not aim for an optimised translation (concerning time resources). Uhura can also help to improve the communication between those people who provide the required knowledge to solve a certain problem (i.e., the domain experts) and those who put the knowledge into code (i.e., the knowledge engineers), since the domain expert can read and understand the CNL sentences the knowledge engineer has provided.

Our paper is organised as follows: Sect. 2 provides background information about answer-set programming and $PENG^{ASP}$, the CNL our language is based upon. Section 3 gives an overview of the system Uhura, including a description of a typical workflow in Uhura, details about L^U, the CNL underlying our system, and some implementational details. The paper concludes with Sect. 4, containing a discussion on related approaches and future work.

2 Preliminaries

2.1 Answer-Set Semantics

We assume the reader familiar with the basic elements of answer-set programming (ASP) [1,12,13]. To briefly recapitulate the relevant elements of ASP, by an *answer-set program* (or *program* for short) we understand a set of rules of form

$$a_1 \vee \cdots \vee a_m \; :- \; b_1, \ldots, b_k, \text{not } b_{k+1}, \ldots, \text{not } b_n, \tag{1}$$

where $a_1, \ldots, a_m$ and $b_1, \ldots, b_n$ are *literals* over a first-order vocabulary, i.e., atoms possibly preceded by the *strong negation* symbol "$-$", "$\vee$" denotes *disjunction*, and "not" stands for *default negation*. The intuitive meaning of rule (1) is that if $b_1, \ldots, b_k$ are derivable and $b_{k+1}, \ldots, b_n$ are *not* derivable, then at least one of $a_1, \ldots, a_m$ is asserted.

We refer to $a_1 \vee \cdots \vee a_m$ as the *head* of (1) and $b_1, \ldots, b_k, \text{not } b_{k+1}, \ldots, \text{not } b_n$ as the *body*. The latter in turn is subdivided into the *positive* and the *negative* body, given by $b_1, \ldots, b_k$ and $\text{not } b_{k+1}, \ldots, \text{not } b_n$, respectively.

Both the head and the body of a rule might be empty. In the former case, the resulting rule is referred to as a *fact*, whilst in the latter case, the rule is called a *constraint*.

The semantics of a program, P, is given in terms of *answer sets*, which are defined as minimal models of the usual *Gelfond-Lifschitz reduct* [14,15]. Prominent solvers for computing answer sets are, e.g., clasp [26] and DLV [23]. We also employ the aggregate function *#count* as used in DLV for counting elements satisfying certain properties.

2.2 The Controlled Natural Language PENG^{ASP}

The controlled natural language (CNL) underlying Uhura, L^{U}, is based on the CNL PENG^{ASP} [30], which itself is based on PENG Light [29] which in turn is the

Table 1. Word categories of PENG^{ASP}.

Word category	Example
PNoun (proper noun)	Vienna, Roberta, Spock
CNoun (common noun)	person, animal, university
Adjective	female, male, mortal
Verb	do, work, play
OrdNumber (order number)	first, second, third
CardRest (cardinality restriction)	exactly, at most, at least

Table 2. Simple sentences of PENG^{ASP}.

Pattern	Example
PNoun is a *CNoun*.	Roberta is a person.
PNoun is *Adjective*.	Roberta is female.
There is a *CNoun*.	There is a job.
A *CNoun* is *Adjective*.	A person is female.
A *OrdNumber CNoun* is a *CNoun* of a *OrdNumber CNoun*.	A first person is a husband of a second person.
A *CNoun Verb* a *CNoun* as *PNoun*.	A person holds a job as nurse.
CardRest CNoun Verb a *CNoun*.	Exactly one person holds a job.
A *CNoun Verb CardRest CNoun*.	A person holds exactly two jobs.

successor of PENG [28], a computer-oriented controlled natural language similar to Attempto Controlled English [11]. The goal of PENG Light is to provide a CNL that can be translated unambiguously into first-order logic. In contrast to its predecessor, PENG Light can be processed by a bidirectional grammar, meaning that first-order translations of sentences expressed in PENG Light can be used to create answers to these sentences. In what follows, we give a brief overview about PENG^{ASP}.

Like PENG Light, PENG^{ASP} differentiates between *simple* and *complex sentences*. Simple sentences are built on six word categories, which are given in Table 1 along with corresponding examples. A simple sentence, then, is one of the eight patterns depicted in Table 2 (similar to Table 1, each pattern is adjoined by a corresponding example). Depending on the application, more sentence patterns and word categories can be added.

Note that not all simple sentences listed in Table 2 can be translated immediately into ASP. Indeed, only the first two sentences of Table 2 are factual statements, meaning that they can be translated into an ASP rule. All the other simple sentences contained in Table 2 can only be used as part of a complex sentence, which are defined in PENG^{ASP} as follows:

If *SimpleSentence1* {and *SimpleSentenceN*} then *SimpleSentenceM*. (2)

Exclude that *SimpleSentence1* {and that *SimpleSentenceN*}.   (3)

Here, "{...}" means that the argument surrounded by the curly brackets can be used 0 to n times, where $n \in \mathbb{N}$.

A sentence that fulfills pattern (2) corresponds to an ASP rule which has a non-empty head and a non-empty body. On the other hand, a sentence that matches pattern (3) corresponds to an ASP constraint.

For illustration of the translation of PENG^{ASP} into ASP, consider the following two complex sentences and their respective ASP representations (for a detailed description of the translation process, cf. Schwitter [30]):

- "If a person holds a job as teacher then the person is educated":

$$educated(X) :- person(X), job(teacher), hold(X, teacher). \qquad (4)$$

- "Exclude that Roberta is female and that Roberta is a man":

$$:- female(roberta), man(roberta). \qquad (5)$$

Sentence (4) shows that PENG^{ASP} allows that the simple sentences which are part of a complex sentence can depend on each other. Therefore, it is not possible in general to translate the simple sentences of a complex sentence individually.

3   The System Uhura

Uhura is a tool for translating a problem definition expressed in the CNL L^{U} (to be detailed below) into an answer-set program. The development of Uhura was driven by the motivation to provide a system which supports ASP novices doing their first steps in answer-set programming. By specifying a problem in a language similar to English, but influenced by the syntax of ASP, users can learn how to express domain knowledge declaratively. As well, Uhura makes it possible to directly see how domain knowledge is translated into ASP rules, by observing the generated ASP rules from the specified CNL sentences. Indeed, Uhura converts CNL sentences in such a way that the user recognises which sentence is translated into which ASP rule(s). Our aim was also to keep the ASP rules as natural as possible, meaning that the resulting answer-set program should be easy to understand by developers unexperienced in ASP.

Uhura, as well as its source code, is available for download at: https://github.com/TobiasKain/uhura.

In what follows, we first describe a typical workflow when using Uhura. Afterwards, we give details about L^{U}, the CNL underlying Uhura. Finally, we briefly discuss aspects of the implementation of Uhura.

3.1   Workflow in Uhura

The Jobs Puzzle. To demonstrate how a typical workflow in Uhura looks like and how the system works, we use the following puzzle:

1. There are four people: Roberta, Thelma, Steve, and Pete.
2. Among them, they hold eight different jobs.
3. Each holds exactly two jobs.
4. The jobs are chef, guard, nurse, clerk, police officer (gender not implied), teacher, actor, and boxer.
5. The job of nurse is held by a male.

6. The husband of the chef is the clerk.
7. Roberta is not a boxer.
8. Pete has no education past the ninth grade.
9. Roberta, the chef, and the police officer went golfing together.

This puzzle is the so-called *jobs puzzle*, which was first introduced in 1984 along with other puzzles designed for automated reasoning [31].

The goal of this puzzle is to find out which person holds which jobs. Clearly, the solution to this puzzle cannot be found only by analysing the explicit information stated in the puzzle. Instead, we have to extract the implicit information of the puzzle and use this knowledge together with the explicit information to solve the puzzle.

Controlled Natural Language Problem Description. In order to solve the jobs puzzle using Uhura, the user has to phrase the implicit and explicit knowledge of the puzzle in the controlled natural language L^U, which is similar to $PENG^{ASP}$. However, compared to $PENG^{ASP}$, the controlled natural language we are working with comprises slightly different sentence patterns from those in $PENG^{ASP}$ as well as additional ones. Furthermore, Uhura also allows to define individual sentence patterns. We give more details about L^U below; a full description of the language can be found in the thesis of the first author [21].

The first sentence of the jobs puzzle states that our problem domain contains four different people. We express this fact by using the pattern

$$PNoun \text{ is a } CNoun.$$

In our case, we instantiate *PNoun*, referring to a proper noun, with *Roberta*, *Thelma*, *Steve*, and *Pete*, and *CNoun* (common noun) with *person*, obtaining the following sentences:

Roberta is a person. Thelma is a person. Steve is a person. Pete is a person.

Furthermore, we have to express that a person cannot be both male and female simultaneously. This means we drop all solutions which contain both genders for some person. We do this by using the following pattern:

Exclude that *SimpleSentence* {and that *SimpleSentence*}.

Since we want that this constraint is applied to every person in our problem domain, we use a variable instead of proper nouns.

Exclude that person X is male and that person X is female.

Next, we guess all the possible solution candidates. In order to do that, we use the following sentence pattern:

If *SimpleSentence* {and *SimpleSentence*} then *SimpleSentence*.

To guess whether a person holds a specific job or not, we use a disjunctive sentence:

If there is a person X and there is a job Y then person X holds job Y or person X does not hold job Y.

The second sentence of the jobs puzzle tells us that our problem domain includes eight different jobs and that every job is held by exactly one person. To formulate this, we use the following pattern as part of a constraint:

CNoun Variable Verb (more/less) than *Number CNoun Variable.*

Since we want to express that a job is held by *exactly* one person, we have to use this pattern twice:

Exclude that there is a job Y and that person X holds more than one job Y.
Exclude that there is a job Y and that person X holds less than one job Y.

The third sentence of the job puzzle states that each person holds exactly two jobs. As before, we use the cardinality pattern twice to formulate this statement:

Exclude that there is a person X and that person X holds more than two jobs Y.
Exclude that there is a person X and that person X holds less than two jobs Y.

The next sentence of the jobs puzzle enumerates all jobs our problem domain refers to. We formulate these facts using the same pattern we applied to phrase the first sentence:

Chef is a job. Guard is a job. Nurse is a job. Clerk is a job.
Police officer is a job. Teacher is a job. Actor is a job. Boxer is a job.

Chef, guard, nurse, clerk, police officer, teacher, and boxer are gender neutral jobs, meaning that they can be held by both genders. However, the job of an actor can only be done by a male, since a female actor is called an actress.

Furthermore, due to the fifth sentence of the jobs puzzle, we know that the job of a nurse is held by a male:

If a person X holds a job as actor then person X is male.
If a person X holds a job as nurse then person X is male.

According to the sixth sentence of the jobs puzzle, the husband of the chef is the clerk:

If a person X holds a job as chef and a person Y holds a job as clerk then person Y is a husband of person X.

The previous sentence implies that the clerk is male since he is the husband of another person and that the chef is female since she has a husband:

If a person X is a husband of a person Y then person X is male.
If a person X is a husband of a person Y then person Y is female.

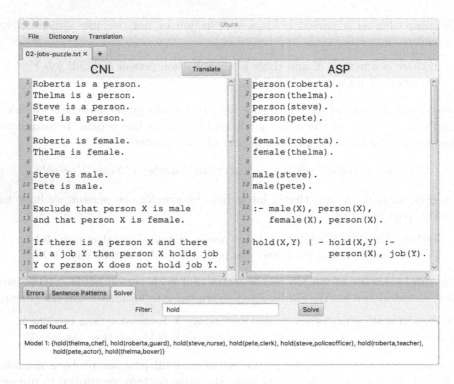

Fig. 1. The user interface of Uhura for the jobs puzzle.

Since the seventh sentence of the jobs puzzle states that Roberta is not a boxer, we exclude all solutions which claim that Roberta is a boxer:

Exclude that Roberta holds a job as boxer.

The eighth sentence of the jobs puzzle specifies that Pete is not educated past the ninth grade. Therefore, we drop all solutions that assert that Pete is educated past the ninth grade:[1]

Exclude that Pete is educated.

Furthermore, we can assume that a person has to be educated past the ninth grade to hold a job as a nurse, police officer, or teacher:

If a person X holds a job as nurse then person X is educated.
If a person X holds a job as police officer then person X is educated.
If a person X holds a job as teacher then person X is educated.

The last sentence of the jobs puzzle contains the implicit information that Roberta is neither a chef nor a police officer. Furthermore, this sentence also

---

[1] Here, and henceforth, in CNL sentences, we simply write "educated" to refer to the property of being educated past the ninth grade.

```
person(roberta).
person(thelma).
person(steve).
person(pete).

female(roberta).
female(thelma).
male(steve).
male(pete).

:- male(X), person(X), female(X), person(X).

hold(X,Y) | -hold(X,Y) :- person(X), job(Y).

:- job(Y), #count{X : hold(X,Y)} > 1.
:- job(Y), #count{X : hold(X,Y)} < 1.
:- person(X), #count{Y : hold(X,Y)} > 2.
:- person(X), #count{Y : hold(X,Y)} < 2.

job(chef).
job(guard).
job(nurse).
job(clerk).
job(policeofficer).
job(teacher).
job(actor).
job(boxer).

male(X)  :- hold(X,actor), person(X), job(actor).
male(X)  :- hold(X,nurse), person(X), job(nurse).
husband(Y,X) :- hold(X,chef), person(X), job(chef),
                hold(Y,clerk), person(Y), job(clerk).
male(X)  :- husband(X,Y), person(X), person(Y).
female(Y) :- husband(X,Y), person(X), person(Y).
educated(X) :- hold(X,nurse), person(X), job(nurse).
educated(X) :- hold(X,policeofficer), person(X),
               job(policeofficer).
educated(X) :- hold(X,teacher), person(X), job(teacher).

:- hold(roberta,boxer), job(boxer).
:- educated(pete).
:- hold(roberta,chef), job(chef).
:- hold(roberta,policeofficer), job(policeofficer).
:- hold(X,chef), person(X), job(chef), hold(X,policeofficer),
   person(X), job(policeofficer).
```

Fig. 2. ASP translation of the jobs puzzle L^U specification.

implies that the person who works as a chef and the person who works as a police officer are two different individuals:

> Exclude that Roberta holds a job as chef.
> Exclude that Roberta holds a job as police officer.
> Exclude that a person X holds a job as chef and that person X
> holds a job as police officer.

Composing the CNL Problem Description Using Uhura. As the previous discussion illustrates, the user has to work precisely to extract all the implicit information contained in the puzzle. Especially for inexperienced users, the task of extracting such implicit information is arguably one of the most demanding tasks in this context. Now, to support the user as good as possible during the process of composing the problem description, our tool provides a separate text field where the user writes down the domain knowledge (see Fig. 1). Alternatively, our tool also allows importing text files composed in a different text editor.

Since remembering all the different sentence patterns is unrewarding, the user can look them up by switching in the lower tab pane to the tab called *Sentence Patterns*.

In case the user enters a sentence that does not match any pattern, Uhura responds with an error message that explains where exactly in the sentence an error occurred. For example, assume the user types in the sentence "Roberta is not a lovely". Then, the system responds with the following error message, which tells the user which sentence pattern was detected and which word caused the error:

```
Error in sentence "Roberta is not a lovely.":
     "lovely" is not a common noun.
     (detected sentence-pattern: 'PNoun is [not] a CNoun.')
```

ASP Translation and Solving. Once the user clicks the *Translation* button, the system starts translating the entered CNL problem description into ASP rules. The answer-set program resulting from translating the CNL problem description for the jobs puzzle given above is depicted in Fig. 2. Note that the syntax used by Uhura is the ASP-Core-2 syntax, which is supported by DLV as well as other ASP solvers.

As can be seen in Fig. 1, the result of the translation process is displayed in the text editor next to the CNL problem description. Also, the (single) solution of the problem is shown in the *Solver* tab of the editor, which is situated in the bottom bar. Since the goal of the jobs puzzle is to find out which person holds which job, we are only interested in the predicate *hold* and therefore the resulting model is filtered by this predicate.

3.2   The Controlled Natural Language L^U of Uhura

We now describe the CNL of Uhura, L^U, in more detail.

Table 3. Word categories supported by L^U.

Word category	Example
PNoun (Proper Noun)	Vienna, Roberta, Spock
CNoun (Common Noun)	person, animal, university
Adjective	female, male, mortal
Verb	do, work, play
Variable	X, Y, Z
Preposition	at, to, in
Number	one, two, three

Table 4. Examples of default sentences which are supported by L^U.

Sentence	Translation
Birds normally fly.	$fly(X) :- bird(X), not -fly(X)$
Dogs normally do not fly.	$-fly(X) :- dog(X), not fly(X)$
Birds normally are beautiful.	$beautiful(X) :- bird(X), not -beautiful(X)$
Birds normally are not ugly.	$-ugly(X) :- bird(X), not ugly(X)$
Students normally are afraid of exams.	$afraid\_of(X, exam) :- student(X),$ $not -afraid\_of(X, exam)$
Students normally are not afraid of homework.	$-afraid\_of(X, homework) :- student(X),$ $not\ afraid\_of(X, homework)$

To begin with, the word categories of L^U, which are slightly different from PENG^{ASP}, are given in Table 3. Furthermore, L^U comprises, besides simple and complex sentences, also some other groups of sentence patterns. The set of sentence patterns supported by L^U comprises:

- *simple sentences* (divided into *factual simple sentences* and *non-factual simple sentences*),
- *complex sentences*,
- *default sentences*, and
- *categorical propositions*.

Another difference between L^U and PENG^{ASP} is that L^U does not allow cross references between the simple sentences used in a complex sentence. Therefore, simple sentences can be translated individually, which makes it easier to translate sentences expressed in L^U. A full listing of all sentence patterns of L^U, along with their ASP translations, can be found in the thesis of the first author [21]; here, we describe only some key aspects.

Simple Sentences. The group of simple sentences is divided into *factual simple sentences* and *non-factual simple sentences*. The difference between those two

Table 5. Examples of categorical propositions which are supported by L^{U}.

Sentence	Translation
All humans are mortal.	$mortal(X) \ :- \ human(X)$
No humans are perfect.	$-perfect(X) \ :- \ human(X)$
Some humans are bad.	$:- \ \#count\{X : human(X), bad(X)\} = 0$
Some humans are not bad.	$:- \ \#count\{X : human(X), not \ bad(X)\} = 0$

sentence types is that factual simple sentences can be directly transformed into an ASP rule, where, on the other hand, non-factual simple sentences can only be used as part of complex sentences.

For example, the factual simple sentence "Roberta is a person" can be directly transformed into the fact:

$$person(roberta) \ :- \ .$$

On the other hand, a non-factual simple sentence like "X is a person" cannot be directly transformed into an meaningful ASP rule. However, this non-factual simple sentence can be used, e.g., as part of a conditional sentence like "If X is a person then X is mortal", which can be translated into the ASP rule:

$$mortal(X) \ :- \ person(X).$$

The reason why L^{U} separates the group of simple sentences is because of the following complex sentence, which also serves as a factual simple sentence:

$$FactualSimpleSentence \ \{ \ or \ FactualSimpleSentence\}. \qquad (6)$$

Complex Sentences. L^{U} supports the same complex sentences that are defined by $\mathsf{PENG}^{\mathsf{ASP}}$, as well as complex sentences of form (6). A sentence of the latter form, like, e.g., "Roberta is a person or Roberta is a dog", can either be used as a factual simple sentence, which leads to the translation

$$person(roberta) \lor dog(roberta) \ :- \ ,$$

or as part of a complex sentence, like, e.g.:

If Roberta is mortal then Roberta is a person or Roberta is a dog.

This, in turn, corresponds to the ASP rule

$$person(roberta) \lor dog(roberta) \ :- \ mortal(X).$$

Default Sentences. *Default sentences* are used to describe circumstances that hold *typically*. L^{U} supports the following three default sentences as well as their negations:

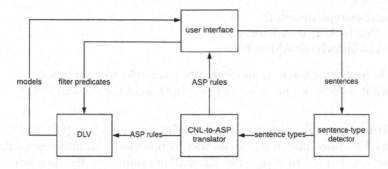

Fig. 3. The system architecture of Uhura.

- *CNoun* normally *Verb*.
- *CNoun* normally not *Verb*.
- *CNoun* normally are *Adjective*.
- *CNoun* normally are not *Adjective*.
- *CNoun* normally are *Adjective Preposition CNoun*.
- *CNoun* normally are not *Adjective Preposition CNoun*.

Table 4 shows an example sentence for each sentence pattern as well as its ASP translation.

Categorical Propositions. L^U also supports the four categorical propositions as used in Aristotle's system of syllogisms:

- All *A* are *B*.
- No *A* are *B*.
- Some *A* are *B*.
- Some *A* are not *B*.

An *A* has to be replaced by a *CNoun* and a *B* either by a *CNoun* or an *Adjective*. Table 5 illustrates each categorical proposition along with its translation. Note that the last two propositions (referred to as *particular statements* in the terminology of the syllogistic) employ the count aggregate of DLV.

3.3 Implementation

Uhura is implemented in Java. One of the main reasons why we chose Java is the availability of DLVWrapper [27], which is a Java library that provides all the functionalities of DLV. Another reason why we decided to implement our tool using Java is that we want to keep the option to integrate our tool into SeaLion [2], which is an integrated development environment for ASP.

Basically, Uhura consists of four different components:

- the user interface,

- a sentence-type detector,
- the CNL-to-ASP translator, and
- DLV (as underlying ASP solver).

Figure 3 shows how these components are connected to each other.

In what follows, we provide brief descriptions of these components.

User Interface. To design and create the user interface (UI) of Uhura, we used JavaFX. Since one of our goals was to provide an intuitive graphical user interface, we decided to design the UI of Uhura similar to the user interfaces of popular IDEs, like, e.g., IntelliJ, Eclipse, or VisualStudio.

Sentence-Type Detector. Once the user has typed in a sentence and clicked the *Translate* button, the sentence-type detector tries to find out which sentence pattern the entered sentence fulfills. Therefore, the sentence-type detector contains for each sentence pattern a regular expression ("regex") pattern. For example, the regex pattern of the sentence pattern "*PNoun* is a *CNoun*" is defined as follows:

$$.* \text{ is(n't } | \text{ not } | \text{)(a|an) }.*\backslash\backslash.\$.$$

Note that also the negated sentence pattern ("*PNoun* is not a *CNoun.*") matches this regex pattern. Furthermore, note that there is no space between the two alternations because the options of the first alternation (i.e., "(n't | not |)") end with a space.

To find out of which type the entered sentence is, the sentence-type detector sequentially checks if the sentence matches one of the regex patterns. In case a match is found, the sentence-type detector initiates the CNL-to-ASP translation of the sentence.

CNL-to-ASP Translator. The CNL-to-ASP translator is the heart of Uhura. It is responsible for translating the CNL sentences entered by the user into ASP rules. The basic idea of the CNL-to-ASP translator is to filter out the key words of a sentence and remove those words that are not used to put together the ASP rule. The CNL-to-ASP translator also checks if the words are of the correct category (e.g., *PNoun, CNoun*, adjective, verb, etc.). To do so, the translator makes use of the Stanford Parser[2], a natural-language parser that uses statistical data to parse sentences. In case a word is of a different type than expected, an exception is thrown, which tells the sentence-type detector to try if the sentence matches one of the remaining sentence patterns.

4   Conclusion and Discussion

In this paper, we presented the tool Uhura for translating sentences expressed in a controlled natural language into an answer-set program. Rather than aiming for

---

[2] https://nlp.stanford.edu/software/lex-parser.html.

a maximally expressive CNL and optimised ASP encodings, our goal was to have a system which helps users inexperienced in ASP or logical formalisms in general for developing programs by specifying problems in a language which is close to a natural one. Therefore, we introduced a new CNL, called L^U, which allows the user to unambiguously specify a problem. Furthermore, L^U is designed in such a way that the correspondence between the CNL sentences and the resulting ASP rules is clearly evident.

The idea of building a tool for translating a problem description expressed in a (controlled) natural language into an answer-set program is not a new one. For example, Schwitter and Guy presented a web-based predictive editor for PENG^{ASP} [17,18]. The editor suggests for every word that is typed in a selection of words from which the user can choose. Thus, sentences entered by the user are always valid PENG^{ASP} sentences. Compared to Uhura, this system can handle more complicated sentences but its focus lies more on problem solving rather than on obtaining natural-looking ASP encodings.

Furthermore, Baral and Mitra [24] developed the system LOGICIA for solving logic grid puzzles. To solve those puzzles, LOGICIA translates the puzzles, described in natural language, into ASP which is then solved by an answer-set solver. The system automatically learns how to translate the information given by the puzzle description. Obviously, the aim of LOGICIA differs from the goal of Uhura quite strongly. While our tool focuses on generating answer-set programs that can be easily understood by developers inexperienced in ASP, LOGICIA deals with translating sentences expressed in natural language. To do so, this tool represents answer-set rules in a more complicated and unintuitive way.

Other approaches in the context of ASP using CNLs is the BioQuery-ASP system [6,7] for expressing biomedical queries over predefined ontologies and translating them into ASP. Moreover, Min and Tompits [8] provided an approach to translate answer sets into natural language which is also based on a CNL using the annotation language Lana [4] for ASP.

As regards future work, one possibility would be to incorporate the approach mentioned last into Uhura such that not only the programs can be specified in a natural-language-looking way, but also the output of the programs, i.e., the answer sets.

Another possible enhancement of Uhura would be to integrate the system into SeaLion [2], which is an integrated development environment for answer-set programming. In this case, the only unit that has to be changed is the user interface. Furthermore, this integration would also allow providing a second ASP solver to solve the answer-set programs generated by Uhura since SeaLion supports two answer-set solvers, viz. DLV and clingo.

Another promising future work would be to use Uhura for specifying test cases for software projects. In particular, based on previous work [6,19], in which ASP is used to specify sequence-covering arrays, the idea would be to use Uhura to allow the user to specify a sequence-covering array in the controlled natural language offered by our system and then to translate this definition into ASP.

References

1. Baral, C.: Knowledge Representation, Reasoning and Declarative Problem Solving. Cambridge University Press, Cambridge (2003)
2. Busoniu, P., Oetsch, J., Pührer, J., Skocovsky, P., Tompits, H.: SeaLion: An Eclipse-based IDE for answer-set programming with advanced debugging support. Theory Pract. Log. Program. **13**(4–5), 657–673 (2013)
3. Calimeri, F., et al.: ASP-Core-2: Input language format. ASP Standardization Working Group (2012)
4. De Vos, M., Kisa, D.G., Oetsch, J., Pührer, J., Tompits, H.: Annotating answer-set programs in Lana. Theory Pract. Log. Program. **12**(4–5), 619–637 (2012)
5. Dodaro, C., Gasteiger, P., Musitsch, B., Ricca, F., Shchekotykhin, K.: Interactive debugging of non-ground ASP programs. In: Calimeri, F., Ianni, G., Truszczynski, M. (eds.) LPNMR 2015. LNCS (LNAI), vol. 9345, pp. 279–293. Springer, Cham (2015). https://doi.org/10.1007/978-3-319-23264-5_24
6. Erdem, E., Erdogan, H., Öztok, U.: BioQuery-ASP: Querying biomedical ontologies using answer set programming. In: Proceedings of the 5th International RuleML2011@BRF Challenge. CEUR Workshop Proceedings, vol. 799. CEUR-WS.org (2011)
7. Erdem, E., Öztok, U.: Generating explanations for biomedical queries. Theory Pract. Log. Program. **15**(1), 35–78 (2015)
8. Fang, M., Tompits, H.: An approach for representing answer sets in natural language. In: Seipel, D., Hanus, M., Abreu, S. (eds.) WFLP/WLP/INAP 2017. LNCS (LNAI), vol. 10997, pp. 115–131. Springer, Cham (2018). https://doi.org/10.1007/978-3-030-00801-7_8
9. Febbraro, O., Reale, K., Ricca, F.: ASPIDE: Integrated development environment for answer set programming. In: Delgrande, J.P., Faber, W. (eds.) LPNMR 2011. LNCS (LNAI), vol. 6645, pp. 317–330. Springer, Heidelberg (2011). https://doi.org/10.1007/978-3-642-20895-9_37
10. Febbraro, O., Leone, N., Reale, K., Ricca, F.: Unit testing in *ASPIDE*. In: Tompits, H., et al. (eds.) INAP/WLP 2011. LNCS (LNAI), vol. 7773, pp. 345–364. Springer, Heidelberg (2013). https://doi.org/10.1007/978-3-642-41524-1_21
11. Fuchs, N.E., Schwitter, R.: Attempto Controlled English (ACE). In: Proceedings of the First International Workshop on Controlled Language Applications (CLAW 1996). University of Leuven (1996)
12. Gebser, M., Kaminski, R., Kaufmann, B., Schaub, T.: Answer Set Solving in Practice. Synthesis Lectures on Artificial Intelligence and Machine Learning, Morgan & Claypool Publishers (2012)
13. Gelfond, M., Kahl, Y.: Knowledge Representation, Reasoning, and the Design of Intelligent Agents: The Answer-Set Programming Approach. Cambridge University Press, Cambridge (2014)
14. Gelfond, M., Lifschitz, V.: The stable model semantics for logic programming. In: Proceedings of the 5th International Conference and Symposium on Logic Programming (ICLP/SLP), pp. 1070–1080. MIT Press (1988)
15. Gelfond, M., Lifschitz, V.: Classical negation in logic programs and disjunctive databases. New Gener. Comput. **9**, 365–385 (1991)
16. Greßler, A., Oetsch, J., Tompits, H.: Harvey: A system for random testing in ASP. In: Balduccini, M., Janhunen, T. (eds.) LPNMR 2017. LNCS (LNAI), vol. 10377, pp. 229–235. Springer, Cham (2017). https://doi.org/10.1007/978-3-319-61660-5_21

17. Guy, S., Schwitter, R.: Architecture of a web-based predictive editor for controlled natural language processing. In: Davis, B., Kaljurand, K., Kuhn, T. (eds.) CNL 2014. LNCS (LNAI), vol. 8625, pp. 167–178. Springer, Cham (2014). https://doi.org/10.1007/978-3-319-10223-8_16

18. Guy, S.C., Schwitter, R.: The PENG^{ASP} system: Architecture, language and authoring tool. Lang. Resour. Eval. **51**(1), 67–92 (2017)

19. Irlinger, M.: Combinatorial testing using answer-set programming. Bachelor's thesis, Technische Universität Wien, Institute of Information Systems, E184/3 (2017)

20. Janhunen, T., Niemelä, I., Oetsch, J., Pührer, J., Tompits, H.: On testing answer-set programs. In: Proceedings of the 19th European Conference on Artificial Intelligence (ECAI 2010), pp. 951–956. IOS Press (2010)

21. Kain, T.: Uhura: an authoring tool for translating controlled natural language into answer-set programs. Bachelor's thesis, Technische Universität Wien, Institute of Information Systems, E184/3 (2017)

22. Kuhn, T.: A survey and classification of controlled natural languages. Comput. Linguist. **40**(1), 121–170 (2014)

23. Leone, et al.: The DLV system for knowledge representation and reasoning. ACM Trans. Comput. Log. **7**(3), 499–562 (2006)

24. Mitra, A., Baral, C.: Learning to automatically solve logic grid puzzles. In: Proceedings of the 2015 Conference on Empirical Methods in Natural Language Processing (EMNLP 2015), pp. 1023–1033. The Association for Computational Linguistics (2015)

25. Oetsch, J., Pührer, J., Tompits, H.: Stepwise debugging of answer-set programs. Theory Pract. Log. Program. **18**(1), 30–80 (2018)

26. Potassco. http://potassco.sourceforge.net

27. Ricca, F.: The DLV Java wrapper. In: Proceedings of the 8th Joint Conference on Declarative Programming (AGP 2003), pp. 263–274 (2003)

28. Schwitter, R.: English as a formal specification language. In: Proceedings of the 13th International Workshop on Database and Expert Systems Applications (DEXA 2002), pp. 220–232. IEEE (2002)

29. Schwitter, R.: Working for two: A bidirectional grammar for a controlled natural language. In: Wobcke, W., Zhang, M. (eds.) AI 2008. LNCS (LNAI), vol. 5360, pp. 168–179. Springer, Heidelberg (2008). https://doi.org/10.1007/978-3-540-89378-3_17

30. Schwitter, R.: The jobs puzzle: Taking on the challenge via controlled natural language processing. Theory Pract. Log. Program. **13**(4–5), 487–501 (2013)

31. Wos, L., Overbeck, R., Lusk, E., Boyle, J.: Automated reasoning: Introduction and applications. Prentice Hall Inc., Upper Saddle River (1984)

Abstraction for Non-ground Answer Set Programs

Zeynep G. Saribatur, Peter Schüller$^{(\boxtimes)}$, and Thomas Eiter

Institute of Logic and Computation, TU Wien, Vienna, Austria
{zeynep,ps}@kr.tuwien.ac.at

Abstract. We address the issue of abstraction, a widely used notion to simplify problems, in the context of Answer Set Programming (ASP), which is a highly expressive formalism and a convenient tool for declarative problem solving. We introduce a method to automatically abstract non-ground ASP programs given an abstraction over the domain, which ensures that each original answer set is mapped to some abstract answer set. We discuss abstraction possibilities on several examples and show the use of abstraction to gain insight into problem instances, e.g., domain details irrelevant for problem solving; this makes abstraction attractive for getting to the essence of the problem. We also provide a tool implementing automatic abstraction from an input program.

1 Introduction

Abstraction is an approach that is widely used in Computer Science and AI to simplify problems [2,8,14,16,23]. By omitting details, scenarios are reduced to ones that are easier to deal with and to understand; in fact, abstraction is ubiquitous in building models of reality, which approximate the latter to meet specific application purposes. Surprisingly, abstraction has not been considered much in the context of nonmonotonic knowledge representation and reasoning, and specifically not in Answer Set Programming (ASP) [7]. Simplification methods such as equivalence-based rewriting [12,26], partial evaluation [6,21], or forgetting [24], have been extensively studied. However, they strive for preserving the semantics, while abstraction may change it and lead to an over-approximation of the models (answer sets) of a program, in a modified language.

Recently, such an approach was presented in [29] that omits atoms from an ASP program, similar in spirit to abstraction in planning problems [18]. The approach is propositional in nature and does not account for the fact that in ASP, non-ground rules talk about a domain of discourse; e.g., a rule

$$col(X, r) \leftarrow node(X),\, not\ col(X, g),\, not\ col(X, b).$$

may express that node X must be red if it is neither green nor blue; or the rule

$$\{moveToTable(B, A, T)\} \leftarrow on(B, B_1, T),\, free(B, T)$$

© Springer Nature Switzerland AG 2019
F. Calimeri et al. (Eds.): JELIA 2019, LNAI 11468, pp. 576–592, 2019.
https://doi.org/10.1007/978-3-030-19570-0_38

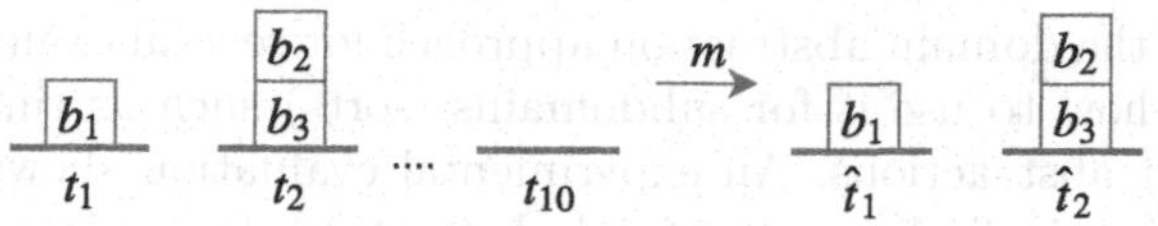

Fig. 1. Initial state of a blocksworld with multiple tables (concrete $\overset{m}{\rightarrow}$ abstract).

that the block B on top of a stack may at time T be moved to a table area A. For the (non)existence of an answer set, the precise set of elements (nodes resp. blocks and areas) may not matter, but rather how certain elements are related; for that, some elements may be abstracted into single elements. Then, a coloring of the abstracted graph, if one exists, may be refined to the original graph; if not, the latter is not colorable. Similarly, a plan for a blocksworld problem with abstract areas may be turned into a concrete one by instantiating them.

Example 1. *Figure 1 depicts a generalized blocks world with multiple tables. The (natural) encoding (cf. Appendix A[1]) contains the actions moveToT(B, Ta, T) and moveToB(B, B', T) that denote moving block B onto table Ta and onto block B', resp., at time T. Initially, blocks can be located anywhere; the goal is to pile them up at a picked table, say t_1. An abstraction that distinguishes table t_1 and clusters all other tables, leads to a concrete abstract answer set containing* moveToT$(b_2, \hat{t}_2, 0)$, moveToT$(b_3, \hat{t}_1, 1)$, moveToB$(b_2, b_3, 2)$, moveToB$(b_1, b_2, 3)$.

The abstraction shows that, for solving the problem, it is essential to distinguish the picked table from all others and that the number of tables is irrelevant.

Although lots of advanced solving techniques are available for ASP, the support for program analysis, especially in singling out relevant objects, is scarce. It is unexplored how, for a non-ground ASP program Π, given an abstraction over its domain, a suitable abstract program Π' can be automatically constructed and evaluated. We tackle this issue and make the following contributions.

- We introduce the notion of domain abstraction for ASP programs. For that, an abstraction of domain elements for a program Π is supplied with an abstract program Π' so that each answer set of Π maps to an abstract answer set of Π'.
- We provide a method to automatically construct such an abstract program Π'. It works modularly on the syntactic level, by constructing for each rule abstract rules with a similar structure, where uncertainty caused by the abstracted domain is carefully respected.
- We show how abstract answer sets can be computed and further processed. This includes a concreteness check, with possible output of an answer set of the original program, and a refinement strategy to deal with spurious answer sets using local search. The whole approach is implemented in a tool that provides automatic abstraction from an input program.

---

[1] http://www.kr.tuwien.ac.at/staff/zeynep/pub/jelia/SSE19appendix.pdf.

- We consider the domain abstraction approach for several examples, where we also discuss how to use it for subdomains (sorts) such as time, and how to compose sort abstractions. An experimental evaluation shows the potential of the approach in finding non-trivial abstractions for various applications.

2   Domain Abstraction for ASP

ASP. We adopt as a function-free first order language, in which a logic program Π is a finite set of rules r of the form $\alpha \leftarrow B(r)$ where α is an atom and the body $B(r) = l_1, \ldots, l_n$ is a set of positive and negative literals l_i of the form β or $not\ \beta$, respectively, where β is an atom and not is default negation; $B^+(r)$ and $B^-(r)$ are the sets of all positive resp. negative literals in $B(r)$. A rule r is a *constraint* if α is falsity ($\perp$, then omitted). A rule r resp. program Π is ground, if it is variable-free, and r is a *fact* if moreover $n = 0$. Rules r with variables stand for the sets $grd(r)$ of their ground instances, and semantically Π induces a set $AS(\Pi)$ of stable models (or answer sets) [15] which are Herbrand models (i.e., sets I of ground atoms) of Π justified by the rules, in that I is a $\subseteq$-minimal model of $f\Pi^I = \{r \in grd(\Pi) \mid I \models B(r)\}$ [11], where $grd(\Pi) = \bigcup_{r \in \Pi} grd(r)$. A program Π is *unsatisfiable*, if $AS(\Pi) = \emptyset$. A common syntactic extension are *choice rules* of the form $\{\alpha\} \leftarrow B$, which stands for the rules $\alpha \leftarrow B, not\ \alpha'$ and $\alpha' \leftarrow B, not\ \alpha$, where α' is a fresh atom.

To illustrate various challenges of abstraction we use the following example.

Example 2 (Running example). *Consider the following example program Π with domain predicate $int/1$ for an integer domain $D = \{0, \ldots, 5\}$.*

$$c(X) \leftarrow not\ d(X), X < 5, int(X). \tag{1}$$
$$d(X) \leftarrow not\ c(X), int(X). \tag{2}$$
$$b(X, Y) \leftarrow a(X), d(Y), int(X), int(Y). \tag{3}$$
$$e(X) \leftarrow c(X), a(Y), X \leq Y, int(X), int(Y). \tag{4}$$
$$\leftarrow b(X, Y), e(X), int(X), int(Y). \tag{5}$$

We furthermore have facts $a(1)$, $a(3)$, $int(0), \ldots, int(5)$.

Abstraction. A generic notion of abstraction is as follows.

Definition 1. *Given ground programs Π and Π' on sets $\mathcal{A}$ and $\mathcal{A}'$ of atoms, respectively, where $|\mathcal{A}| \geq |\mathcal{A}'|$, Π' is an* abstraction *of Π, if a mapping $m: \mathcal{A} \rightarrow \mathcal{A}'$ exists s.t. for each $I \in AS(\Pi)$, $I' = \{m(a) \mid a \in I\}$ is an answer set of Π'.*

We refer to m as an *abstraction mapping*. This notion aims at the grounding (propositional) view of programs. In this paper, we take a first-order view in which $\mathcal{A}$ is the Herbrand base of Π, which results from the available predicate symbols and the constants symbols (the domain D of discourse, i.e., the Herbrand universe), which are by default those occurring in Π. *Domain abstraction* induces abstraction mappings in which constants are merged.

Definition 2. *Given a domain D of Π, a* domain (abstraction) mapping *is a function $m : D \to \widehat{D}$ for a set $\widehat{D}$ (the* abstracted domain*) with $|\widehat{D}| \leq |D|$.*

Thus, a domain mapping divides D into *clusters* of elements $\{d \in D \mid m(d) = \hat{d}\}$, where $\hat{d} \in \widehat{D}$, seen as equal; if unambiguous, we also write $\hat{d}$ for its cluster $m^{-1}(\hat{d})$.

Example 3 (ctd). *A possible abstraction mapping for Π with $\widehat{D}_1 = \{k_1, k_2, k_3\}$ clusters $1, 2, 3$ to the element k_1 and 4 and 5 to singleton clusters, i.e., $m_1 = \{\{1, 2, 3\}/k_1, \{4\}/k_2, \{5\}/k_3\}$. A naive mapping is $m_2 = \{\{1, .., 5\}/k\}$ with $\widehat{D}_2 = \{k\}$.*

Each domain mapping m naturally extends to ground atoms $a = p(v_1, \ldots, v_n)$ by $m(a) = p(m(v_1), \ldots, m(v_n))$. To obtain for a program Π and a Herbrand base $\mathcal{A}$, an induced abstraction mapping $m : \mathcal{A} \to \mathcal{A}'$ where $\mathcal{A}' = m(\mathcal{A}) = \{m(a) \mid a \in \mathcal{A}\}$, we need a program Π' as in Definition 1. However, simply applying m to Π does not work. Moreover, we want domain abstraction for non-ground Π that results in a non-ground Π'. Building a suitable Π' turns out to be challenging and needs to solve several issues, which we gradually address in the next section.

3   Towards an Abstract Program

Handling Built-ins and (In)equalities. Original rules may rely on certain *built-in relations* involving variables, such as $<, \leq$ in (1) and (4), or $=$ and $\neq$. The idea is to lift the rules by lifting these relations and dealing with the uncertainty caused by the domain clustering.

Example 4 (ctd). *We abstract from Π using m_2. The rule (3) has no built-in relation and thus it is lifted with no change:*

$$b(X, Y) \leftarrow a(X), d(Y), \widehat{int}(X), \widehat{int}(Y);$$

however, lifting rule (4) simply to

$$e(X) \leftarrow c(X), a(Y), X \leq Y, \widehat{int}(X), \widehat{int}(Y).$$

does not work, as $X \leq Y$ behaves differently over the cluster k. As $k \leq k$, whenever $c(k)$ and $a(k)$ holds the lifted rule derives $e(k)$. This applies, e.g., to the abstraction of $I = \{a(1), a(3), c(4), d(0), \ldots, d(3)\}$, where (4) derives no e-atom as $4 \not\leq 3$ and $4 \not\leq 1$. However, I is an answer set of Π and must not be lost in the abstraction. Thus, when a cluster causes uncertainties over built-ins, we permit $e(k)$ to be false even if $c(k)$ and $a(k)$ holds by creating instead the following rule:

$$\{e(X)\} \leftarrow c(X), a(Y), X \leq Y, \widehat{int}(X), \widehat{int}(Y).$$

Negation. A naive abstraction approach is to turn all rule heads into choices. However, negative literals or certain built-ins (e.g., $\neq, <$) may cause a loss of original answer sets in the abstraction.

Example 5 (ctd). *We change in* (4) *the symbol* $\leq$ *to* $\neq$ *and consider*

$$\{e(X)\} \leftarrow c(X), a(Y), X \neq Y, \widehat{int}(X), \widehat{int}(Y).$$

As $k = k$, *the abstract body is never satisfied and* $e(k)$ *is never derived. However,* Π *has answer sets containing* $c(2)$, $a(3)$, *and thus also* $e(2)$, *as* $2 \neq 3$; *they are all lost. Adding a choice rule with a flipped relation,* $X = Y$, *catches such cases.*

Similarly, let us change $a(Y)$ *in* (4) *to* $not\ a(Y)$. *When the rule is lifted to*

$$\{e(X)\} \leftarrow c(X), not\ a(Y), X \leq Y, \widehat{int}(X), \widehat{int}(Y),$$

$e(k)$ *is not derived as* $a(k)$ *holds and originally* a *holds only for 1 and 3. Thus, original answer sets* I *may contain* $e(2)$ *or* $e(4)$ *but they are lost in the abstraction. Such cases are caught by additional rules with reversed negation for* $a(Y)$:

$$\{e(X)\} \leftarrow c(X), a(Y), X \leq Y, \widehat{int}(X), \widehat{int}(Y).$$

Constraints. Naively lifting the constraints to the abstract rules would result in losing answer sets for the non-singleton domain clusters. For example, if the constraint (5) is lifted with no change, then $b(k,k)$ and $e(k)$ would never occur in the abstract answer sets, while in the original program, answer sets can contain $b(x_1, y)$ and $c(x_2)$ as long as $x_1 \neq x_2$.

In conclusion, only creating choices is not enough to preserve all original answer sets; we need a fine-grained systematic approach to deal with uncertainties.

3.1   Lifted Built-in Relations

As shown before, built-in relations need special treatment, and so do multiple usages of a variable in a rule. To unify both issues, we focus on rules of form

$$r : l \leftarrow B(r), \Gamma_{rel}(r)$$

where the variables in $B(r)$ are standardized apart and Γ_{rel} consists of built-in atoms that constrain the variables in $B(r)$. E.g., the rule (3) has $\Gamma_{rel}(r) = \top$ while the rule (5) must be standardized apart into $\leftarrow b(X,Y), e(X_1), \Gamma_{rel}$ with $\Gamma_{rel} = (X = X_1)$.

Uncertainty is caused by relation restrictions over non-singleton clusters (i.e., $|\hat{d}| > 1$) or by negative literals mapped to non-singleton abstract literals. For simplicity, we first focus on binary built-ins, e.g., $=, <, \leq, \neq$, and a $\Gamma_{rel}(r)$ of the form $rel(X, c)$ or $rel(X, Y)$. When the relation rel is lifted to the abstract domain, the following cases τ_I–τ_{IV} for $rel(\hat{d}_1, \hat{d}_2)$ occur in a mapping:

$$\tau_I^{rel}(\hat{d}_1, \hat{d}_2): \quad rel(\hat{d}_1, \hat{d}_2) \wedge \forall x_1 \in \hat{d}_1, \forall x_2 \in \hat{d}_2.\ rel(x_1, x_2)$$
$$\tau_{II}^{rel}(\hat{d}_1, \hat{d}_2): \quad \neg rel(\hat{d}_1, \hat{d}_2) \wedge \forall x_1 \in \hat{d}_1, \forall x_2 \in \hat{d}_2.\ \neg rel(x_1, x_2)$$
$$\tau_{III}^{rel}(\hat{d}_1, \hat{d}_2): \quad rel(\hat{d}_1, \hat{d}_2) \wedge \exists x_1 \in \hat{d}_1, \exists x_2 \in \hat{d}_2.\ \neg rel(x_1, x_2)$$
$$\tau_{IV}^{rel}(\hat{d}_1, \hat{d}_2): \quad \neg rel(\hat{d}_1, \hat{d}_2) \wedge \exists x_1 \in \hat{d}_1, \exists x_2 \in \hat{d}_2.\ rel(x_1, x_2)$$

If $rel(\hat{d}_1, \hat{d}_2)$ holds for some $\hat{d}_1, \hat{d}_2 \in \hat{D}$, type III is more common in domain abstractions with clusters, while type I occurs for singleton mappings (i.e., $|\hat{d}_1| = |\hat{d}_2| = 1$) or for relations such as $\neq, <$.

Example 6. *Consider a mapping* $m = \{\{1\}/k_1, \{2,3\}/k_2, \{4,5\}/k_3\}$. *For the relation* "=", $k_1 = k_1$ *holds and for any* $x_1, x_2 \in k_1 = \{1\}$, $x_1 = x_2$ *holds and type I applies. In contrast,* $k_2 = k_2$ *holds while* $2, 3 \in k_2$ *and* $2 \neq 3$; *so type III applies. Further,* $k_2 < k_3$ *holds and for any* $x \in k_2 = \{2,3\}$ *and* $y \in k_3 = \{4,5\}$, *we have* $x < y$ *and so type I applies.*

If $rel(\hat{d}_1, \hat{d}_2)$ does not hold for some $\hat{d}_1, \hat{d}_2 \in \hat{D}$, type II is common, e.g., $=, \leq$, whereas type IV may occur for $\neq, <$.

Example 7 (ctd). *Reconsider m. Then* $k_2 \neq k_2$ *does not hold while* $k_2 = \{2,3\}$ *has different elements* $2 \neq 3$ *(type IV). Moreover,* $k_1 = k_2$ *does not hold in* $\hat{D}$ *nor does* $x = y$ *for every* $x \in k_1 = \{1\}$ *and* $y \in k_2 = \{2,3\}$ *(type II).*

For an abstraction m, we let $\mathcal{T}_m$ be the set of all atoms $\tau_\iota^{rel}(\hat{d}_1, \hat{d}_2)$ where $\iota \in \{\mathrm{I}, \ldots, \mathrm{IV}\}$ is the type of the built-in instance $rel(\hat{d}_1, \hat{d}_2)$ for m; note that $\mathcal{T}_m$ is easily computed.

4   Abstract Program Construction

By our analysis, the basic idea to construct an abstract program for a program Π with a domain mapping m is as follows. We either just abstract each atom in a rule, or in case of uncertainty due to domain abstraction, we guess rule heads to catch possible cases, or we treat negated literals by shifting their polarity depending on the abstract domain clusters.

For ease of presentation, we first consider programs Π with rules having (i) at most one negative body literal which shares an argument with the relation, (ii) a single, binary built-in literal and (iii) no cyclic dependencies between non-ground atoms. For any rule r and $* \in \{+, -\}$, let the set $S_{rel}^*(r) = \{l_j \in B^*(r) \mid arg(l_j) \cap \{t_1, t_2\} \neq \emptyset\}$ be the positive and negative body literals, respectively, that share an argument with $rel(t_1, t_2)$. By assumption (i), we have $B^-(r) \subseteq S_{rel}^*(r)$.

Definition 3. *Given a rule* $r : l \leftarrow B(r), rel(t_1, t_2)$ *as above and a domain mapping* m, *the set* r^m *contains the following rules:*

(a) $m(l) \leftarrow m(B(r)), rel(\hat{t}_1, \hat{t}_2), \tau_{\mathrm{I}}^{rel}(\hat{t}_1, \hat{t}_2)$.
(b) $\{m(l)\} \leftarrow m(B(r)), rel(\hat{t}_1, \hat{t}_2), \tau_{\mathrm{III}}^{rel}(\hat{t}_1, \hat{t}_2)$.
(c) $\{m(l)\} \leftarrow m(B(r)), \overline{rel}(\hat{t}_1, \hat{t}_2), \tau_{\mathrm{IV}}^{rel}(\hat{t}_1, \hat{t}_2)$.
(d) *For* $l_i \in S_{rel}^-(r)$:
    (i) $\{m(l)\} \leftarrow m(B_{l_i}^{sh}(r)), rel(\hat{t}_1, \hat{t}_2), \tau_{\mathrm{III}}^{rel}(\hat{t}_1, \hat{t}_2)$.
    (ii) $\{m(l)\} \leftarrow m(B_{l_i}^{sh}(r)), \overline{rel}(\hat{t}_1, \hat{t}_2), \tau_{\mathrm{IV}}^{rel}(\hat{t}_1, \hat{t}_2)$.
    (iii) $\{m(l)\} \leftarrow m(B_{l_i}^{sh}(r)), rel(\hat{t}_1, \hat{t}_2), isCluster(l_i)$.

where $B_{l_i}^{sh}(r) = B^+(r) \cup \{l_i\}$, *not* $B^-(r) \backslash \{l_i\}$, $\overline{rel}$ *denotes the complement of rel, and for* $j \in \{1, 2\}$, *if* t_j *is a constant then* $\hat{t}_j = m(t_j)$, *else* $\hat{t}_j = t_j$, *i.e., variables are not mapped. The auxiliary atom* $isCluster(l_i)$ *holds true if a variable from* $arg(l_i)$ *is mapped to a non-singleton cluster.*

In step (a), the case of having no uncertainty due to abstraction is applied. Steps (b) and (c) are for the cases of uncertainty. The head becomes a choice, and for case IV, we flip the relation, $\overline{rel}$, to catch the case of the relation holding true (which is causing the uncertainty). Constraints (e.g., (5)) are omitted in the cases with uncertainty (i.e., all steps except (a)).

Example 8 (ctd). *Consider Example 2 with domain mapping* $m = \{\{1\}/k_1, \{2,3\}/k_2, \{4,5\}/k_3\}$. *In rule* (4), *the relation* $X \leq Y$ *has* $S_{\leq}^{+}(r) = \{c(X), a(Y)\}$. *We have* $\tau_{\mathrm{I}}^{\leq}(x,y)$ *true for* $(x,y) \in \{(k_1,k_1),\ (k_1,k_2),\ (k_1,k_3),\ (k_2,k_3)\}$, *and* $\tau_{\mathrm{III}}^{\leq}(x,y)$ *true for* $(x,y) \in \{(k_2,k_2),\ (k_3,k_3)\}$, *and only type* II *for all other tuples* (x,y). *The abstract rules for* (4) *are:*

$$e(X) \leftarrow c(X), a(Y), X \leq Y, \tau_{\mathrm{I}}^{\leq}(X,Y), \widehat{int}(X), \widehat{int}(Y).$$
$$\{e(X)\} \leftarrow c(X), a(Y), X \leq Y, \tau_{\mathrm{III}}^{\leq}(X,Y), \widehat{int}(X), \widehat{int}(Y).$$

In step (d) of Definition 3, $rel(t_1, t_2)$ shares arguments with a negative body literal. We grasp the uncertainty arising from negation by adding rules where the related literal is shifted to the positive body via $B_{l_i}^{sh}(r)$. (d-iii) shifts the negative literal only if it shares arguments mapped to a non-singleton cluster.

Example 9 (ctd). *Rule* (1) *has a negative literal,* $not\ d(X)$, *and the relation* $X < 5$ *with shared argument* X. *When it is lifted to* $X < k_3$, *it has* $\tau_{\mathrm{II}}^{<}(a,b)$ *true for* $(a,b) \in \{(k_3,k_1),\ (k_3,k_2)\}$, $\tau_{\mathrm{IV}}^{<}(k_3,k_3)$, *and type* I *for all other tuples* (a,b).
By case (1), *it is abstracted without change for* τ_{I} *abstract values, while for* τ_{IV} *specially treated rules are added:*

$$c(X) \leftarrow not\ d(X), X < k_3, \tau_{\mathrm{I}}^{<}(X, k_3), \widehat{int}(X).$$
$$\{c(X)\} \leftarrow not\ d(X), X \geq k_3, \tau_{\mathrm{IV}}^{<}(X, k_3), \widehat{int}(X).$$
$$\{c(X)\} \leftarrow d(X), X \geq k_3, \tau_{\mathrm{IV}}^{<}(X, k_3), \widehat{int}(X).$$
$$\{c(X)\} \leftarrow d(X), X < k_3, isCluster(d(X)), \widehat{int}(X).$$

The abstract program is now as follows.

Definition 4. *Given a program* Π *as above and a domain abstraction* m, *the abstract program for* m *consists of the rules*

$$\Pi^m = \bigcup_{r:\ l \leftarrow B(r), rel(t_1,t_2) \in \Pi} r^m \cup \{x. \mid x \in \mathcal{T}_m\} \cup \{m(p(\mathbf{c})). \mid p(\mathbf{c}). \in \Pi\}.$$

Notably, the construction of Π^m is modular, rule by rule.

Theorem 1. *Let* m *be a domain mapping of a program* Π *under the above assumptions* (i)–(iii). *Then for every* $I \in AS(\Pi)$, $m(I) \cup \mathcal{T}_m \in AS(\Pi^m)$.

Proof (sketch). The rules added in steps (a)-(b) are to ensure that $m(I)$ is a model of Π^m, as either the original rule is kept or it is changed to a choice rule. Steps (c)-(d) serve to catch the cases that may violate the minimality of the model due to a negative literal or a relation over non-singleton clusters.

Abstract Program (General Case). We now describe how to remove the restrictions (i)–(iii) on programs from above.

(i) Multiple Negative Literals. If rule r has $|B^-(r)|>1$, we shift each negative literal that either (a) shares an argument with the abstracted relation rel, or (b) shares arguments mapped to a non-singleton cluster. Thus, instead of having $B_l^{sh}(r)$ for one literal, we consider the shifting of multiple literals at a time $B_L^{sh}(r)=B^+(r) \cup L, \text{not } B^-(r) \backslash L$, and all combinations of (non-)shifting of the literals in $L \in B^-(r)$.

(ii) Multiple Relation Literals. A simple approach to handle a built-in part $\Gamma_{rel} = rel(t_{1,1}, t_{2,1}), .. , rel(t_{1,k}, t_{2,k})$, $k>1$, is to view it as literal of an $2k$-ary built-in $rel'(X_{1,1}, X_{2,1}, .. , X_{1,k}, X_{2,k})$. The abstract version of such rel' and the cases I-IV are lifted from x_1, x_2 to $x_1, .. , x_n$. E.g., for $\Gamma_{rel} = (X_1{=}X_2, X_3{=}X_4)$, we use a new relation $rel'(X_1, X_2, X_3, X_4)$. For abstract values $\hat{d}_1, .. , \hat{d}_4$ s.t. $\hat{d}_1 = \hat{d}_2 \wedge \hat{d}_3 = \hat{d}_4$ holds, we have type τ_I if all $\hat{d}_i$ are singleton clusters and τ_{III} if some $\hat{d}_i$ is non-singleton; otherwise (i.e., $\overline{rel}'(\hat{d}_1, \hat{d}_2, \hat{d}_3, \hat{d}_4)$ holds) type τ_{II} applies.

(iii) Cyclic Dependencies. Rules which are involved in a cyclic dependency containing at least one negation between two literals need special consideration.

Example 10. *Consider the rules* (1)–(2) *(Example 2) and the mapping* $\{\{1, .. ,5\}/k\}$. *The abstract rules for them are*

$$\{c(X)\} \leftarrow not\ d(X), X \geq k, \tau_{IV}^{\lessgtr}(X, k), \widehat{int}(X).$$

$$\{c(X)\} \leftarrow d(X), X \geq k, \tau_{IV}^{\lessgtr}(X, k), \widehat{int}(X). \tag{6}$$

$$\{c(X)\} \leftarrow d(X), X < k, isCluster(d(X)), \widehat{int}(X). \tag{7}$$

$$\{d(X)\} \leftarrow c(X), \widehat{int}(X) \tag{8}$$

in addition to the abstracted rules due to step (a). While $\{c(k), d(k)\}$ *is a model of the rules, it is not minimal and hence not an answer set. However, the original rules have "choice" answer sets with c- and d-atoms, e.g.,* $I = \{c(0), d(1), c(2), d(3), c(4), d(5)\}$; *they are lost by the abstraction.*

To resolve this, we preprocess the program Π and mark atoms involved in a negative cyclic dependency. Then, in step (3) of Definition 3, we modify $B_{l_i}^{sh}(r)$ to eliminate marked literals l_i instead of shifting their polarity. For example, we eliminate $d(X)$ and $c(X)$ from the bodies of abstract rules (6)–(8).

Let Π^m denote the program obtained from a general program Π with the generalized abstraction procedure. Then:

Theorem 2. *Let m be a domain mapping of a program Π. Then for every $I \in AS(\Pi)$, $\hat{I} = m(I) \cup \mathcal{T}_m$ is an answer set of Π^m.*

Proof (sketch). For (i) and (iii), shifting the polarity of each negative literal related with a non-singleton cluster and omitting the ones that are involved in a negative cycle with the head of the rule ensures that the minimality is preserved. The approach in (ii) is a simple combination of the relations.

Over-approximation. The abstraction yields in general an over-approximation of the answer sets of a program. This motivates the following notion.

Definition 5. *An abstract answer set $\widehat{I} \in AS(\Pi^m)$ is* concrete, *if $\widehat{I} = m(I) \cup \mathcal{T}_m$ for an $I \in AS(\Pi)$, else it is* spurious.

A spurious abstract answer set has no corresponding concrete answer set. (Non-)existing spurious answer sets allow us to infer properties of the original program.

Proposition 3. *For any program Π,*

(i) $AS(\Pi^{m_{id}}) = \{I \cup \mathcal{T}_{m_{id}} \mid I \in AS(\Pi)\}$ for identity $m_{id} = \{\{x\}/x \mid x \in D\}$.
(ii) $AS(\Pi^m) = \emptyset$ implies that $AS(\Pi) = \emptyset$.
(iii) $AS(\Pi) = \emptyset$ iff some Π^m has only spurious answer sets.

Checking spuriousness has the following complexity.

Theorem 4. *Given a program Π, a domain mapping m and an abstract answer set $\widehat{I} \in AS(\Pi^m)$, deciding whether $\widehat{I}$ is not spurious is **NEXP**-complete in general and Σ_2^p-complete for bounded predicate arities.*

That is, the worst case complexity is the one of answer set existence for non-ground programs; the two problems can be reduced to each other in polynomial time. However, it drops to Σ_2^p if the domain size $|D|$ is polynomial in the abstracted domain size $|\widehat{D}|$; e.g., if each abstract cluster is small (and multiple clusters exist). As for testing faithfulness, we note the following result:

Theorem 5. *Given a program Π and a domain mapping m, deciding whether Π^m is faithful, i.e., has no spurious answer set, is co-**NEXP**$^{\mathbf{NP}}$-complete in general and Π_3^p-complete for bounded predicate arities (i.e., by a constant).*

Membership is shown by a guess & check algorithm resorting to answer set existence, and hardness by encoding the evaluation of suitable second-order formulas.

5   Abstract Answer Set Computation

After constructing the abstract program Π^m, we can run an ASP solver to obtain abstract answer sets $\widehat{I}$ for the program Π with the mapping m. We then need to check its concreteness, which can be done as follows.

Concreteness Check. Let $Q_{\widehat{I}}^m$ be the following constraints:

$$\bot \leftarrow \{\alpha \mid m(\alpha) = \hat{\alpha}\} \leq 0. \quad \hat{\alpha} \in \widehat{I} \setminus \mathcal{T}_m \tag{9}$$

$$\bot \leftarrow \alpha. \quad \hat{\alpha} \notin \widehat{I} \setminus \mathcal{T}_m, m(\alpha) = \hat{\alpha} \tag{10}$$

Here (9) ensures that a witnessing answer set I of Π contains for every non-τ_ι, abstract atom in $\widehat{I}$ some atom that is mapped to it. The constraint (10) ensures that I has no atom that is mapped to an abstract atom not in $\widehat{I}$. We then obtain:

Proposition 6. $\hat{I}$ *is spurious iff* $\Pi \cup Q_{\hat{I}}^m$ *is unsatisfiable.*

Refining Abstractions. After checking an abstract answer set, one can either continue finding other abstract answer sets and check their correctness, or *refine* the abstraction to reach an abstraction where less spurious answer sets occur.

Definition 6. *Given a domain mapping* $m : D \rightarrow D'$, *a mapping* $m' : D \rightarrow D''$ *is a* refinement *of* m *if for all* $x \in D$, $m'^{-1}(m'(x)) \subseteq m^{-1}(m(x))$.

Refinement is on dividing the abstract clusters to a finer grained domain. As an example, mapping $m' = \{\{1\}/k_1, \{2\}/k_{2,1}, \{3\}/k_{2,2}, \{4,5\}/k_3\}$ is a refinement of mapping $m = \{\{1\}/k_1, \{2,3\}/k_2, \{4,5\}/k_3\}$.

5.1 Implementation

We have implemented the workflow described above in a tool[2] that uses Python and Clingo 5 [13]. We next discuss practical implementation issues.

Concreteness Check and Debugging. We use a non-ground version of $Q_{\hat{I}}^m$:

$$\bot \leftarrow in(\hat{\alpha}), \{\alpha : map(X_1, \hat{X}_1), \dots, map(X_k, \hat{X}_k)\} \leq 0.$$
$$\bot \leftarrow \alpha, not\ in(\hat{\alpha}), map(X_1, \hat{X}_1), \dots, map(X_k, \hat{X}_k)$$

where $\alpha = p(X_1, ..., X_k)$ and $\hat{\alpha} = p(\hat{X}_1, ..., \hat{X}_k)$, and $map(X_i, \hat{X}_i)$ expresses the abstract mapping, with the set of facts $\{in(\hat{\alpha}). \mid \hat{\alpha} \in \hat{I}\}$.

If an abstract answer set $\hat{I}$ is spurious, $\Pi \cup Q_{\hat{I}}^m$ is unsatisfiable; this gives us no information on the reason of spuriousness. To overcome this, we add abnormality atoms, ab, in the rules of Π that contain arguments from the domain. This approach is inspired from [5] that introduces *tagging* atoms to the rules. We use a simplified encoding by disregarding loop formulas (cf. Appendix B); thus, we deal with tight programs only. E.g., in Example 2 rule (3) is converted to

$$b(X, Y) \leftarrow a(X), d(Y), int(X), int(Y), not\ ab(r3, X, Y).$$

and new rules for a guess over ab at a cost for its existence in the answer set are added. This extended program, Π_{ab}, gives us the possibility to catch the rules that need to be deactivated in order to keep satisfiability while checking the concreteness of an abstract answer set $\hat{I}$, in case it is spurious.

Refinement Search. We run a basic search among all possible refinements of a given initial abstraction (by default, the mapping $m = \{D/k_1\}$) until an abstraction that gives a concrete answer set is reached. For a refinement m' of m, we check the first abstract answer set, $\hat{I}$, of $\Pi^{m'}$, using Π_{ab}, i.e., $\Pi_{ab} \cup Q_{\hat{I}}^{m'}$, to see if $\hat{I}$ is concrete. We then choose the answer set with the smallest number of ab atoms in it; we call this number the *cost* of the refinement m'. Then, we

---

[2] http://www.kr.tuwien.ac.at/research/systems/abstraction/.

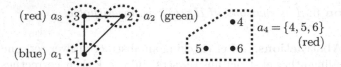

Fig. 2. Graph 3-coloring instance and abstract solution

perform a local distance-based search, where the distance between an abstraction and its refinement is the difference in the number of abstract clusters. We pick the refinement with the least cost as the new abstraction until cost 0 is achieved.

Further Features. In our implementation, *strong negated literals* $\neg \alpha$ are encoded, at a preprocessing step, as *neg_α* and constraints of form $\leftarrow \alpha, neg\_\alpha$ are added to the encoding. *Choice rules* are treated specially by ensuring that the abstraction is done on the body, and the choice over the head is kept. We *precompute the deterministic part* of a program (i.e., not involved in unstratified negation resp. guesses) and encode it as facts which are then lifted without introducing (unnecessary) nondeterminism.

6   Applications

Applications usually contain *sorts* that form subdomains of the Herbrand universe. For example, blocksworld contains sorts for blocks and time while in scheduling there are sorts of tasks and time or in coloring there are sorts for nodes and colors. We define an abstraction over a sort as follows.

Definition 7. *An abstraction is limited to a sort $D_i \subseteq D$, if all elements $x \in D \setminus D_i$ form singleton clusters $\{x\}/x$.*

For practical purposes, sorts can use overlapping elements of the domain, provided that all occurrences of the sort are guarded by domain predicates.

We next show our abstraction method on examples.

Example 11. *Consider the following 3-coloring encoding:*

$$col(X_1, r) \leftarrow not\ col(X_1, g), not\ col(X_2, b), X_1 = X_2.$$
$$col(X_1, g) \leftarrow not\ col(X_1, r), not\ col(X_2, b), X_1 = X_2.$$
$$col(X_1, b) \leftarrow not\ col(X_1, g), not\ col(X_2, r), X_1 = X_2.$$
$$hasEdgeTo(X, C) \leftarrow edge(X, Y_1), color(Y_2, C), Y_1 = Y_2.$$
$$\leftarrow hasEdgeTo(X_1, C), col(X_2, C), X_1 = X_2.$$
$$\leftarrow node(X), not\ colored(X).$$
$$colored(X) \leftarrow col(X, C), node(X).$$

and the graph with 6 nodes in Fig. 2. The abstraction $\{\{1\}/a_1, \{2\}/a_2, \{3\}/a_3, \{4,5,6\}/a_4\}$, which distinguishes the nodes in the clique 1-2-3 and clusters all others, has only concrete abstract answer sets, one of them is $\hat{I} = \{col(a_1, b), col(a_2, g), col(a_3, r), col(a_4, r)\}$ where the nodes 4,5,6 clustered to a_4 are red.

Abstraction over Time. In ASP, it is customary to represent time by an additional argument in atoms. Abstraction over time is handled equivalently as for other domains. This can be useful e.g. in scheduling for abstracting time intervals where 'nothing changes' in a schedule into single time points. Moreover, time is an ordered domain which must be respected by the refinements, e.g., by splitting intervals.

Example 12. *Consider the disjunctive scheduling problem of [1]: given tasks I with fixed duration D ($task(I, D)$), earliest start time S ($est(I, S)$), latest end time E ($let(I, E)$), and disjunctive constraints ($disj(I, I')$) for tasks that cannot overlap, assign to each task a start time such that all constraints are satisfied. We use the provided encoding (with variables standardized apart) and precomputed deterministic part of the program. For an instance $\{task(a, 7), est(a, 1), let(a, 8),$ $task(b, 5), est(b, 3), let(b, 10), task(c, 2), est(c, 8), let(c, 10), disj(a, c), disj(b, c)\}$, we reach from $\{\{1, \ldots, 10\}/k\}$ the abstraction $\{\{4, \ldots, 7\}/k_1, \{9, 10\}/k_2\}$ where only two abstract answer sets exist, and a concrete one is easily identified; it yields a solution $time(a, 1)$, $time(b, 3)$, $time(c, 8)$.*

Abstraction over Multiple Sorts. While time is important in scheduling and planning, abstracting only over time may not suffice for planning as spurious abstract answer sets with an incorrect order of action execution may occur. This can be countered by additional abstraction over other sorts in the agent domain, which allows for more abstract instances of actions that abstract from the concrete order of application as shown in Example 13 below. It is particularly desirable that the individual abstractions fulfill the following property.

Definition 8. *For a program Π and domain D, subdomains $D_1, \ldots, D_n \subseteq D$ are independent, if no rel-atom in Π shares arguments from D_i and D_j, $1 \leq i < j \leq n$.*

For independent sorts, abstractions can be composed.

Proposition 7. *For domain mappings m_1 and m_2 over independent domains D_1 and D_2, $(\Pi^{m_2})^{m_1} = (\Pi^{m_1})^{m_2}$.*

This property readily extends to multiple sorts. Note that sorts in the problems above mentioned are often independent; e.g., blocks, tables and time in Example 1. However, if block number i can not be put on table number j if $i = j$, then the above property can not hold.

Abstraction over time and the agent domain allows us to obtain abstract plans representing sequences of concrete actions.

Example 13. *Consider the blocksworld problem with a single table in Fig. 3. The encoding of Example 1 is modified for a single table (table argument omitted from moveToT/onT). The encoding gets standardized apart according to the block sort and the time sort.*

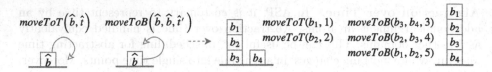

Fig. 3. Abstract and concrete plan of Example 13

Suppose further rules realize a policy that first puts all blocks on the table and piles them up in a second phase. (heads of form 1{...} choose at least one element and can here be treated like explained before):

$existsOnBlock(T) \leftarrow onB(B, B_1, T).$

$allOnTable(T) \leftarrow not\ existsOnBlock(T), time(T).$

$atPhase2(T_1) \leftarrow allOnTable(T), T < T_1.$

$1\{moveToT(B, T) : onB(B, B_1, T)\} \leftarrow T < t_{max}, not\ atPhase2(T), not\ allOnTable(T).$

$1\{moveToB(B, B_1, T) : onT(B, T), block(B_1)\} \leftarrow T < t_{max}, allOnTable(T).$

$1\{moveToB(B, B_1, T) : onT(B, T), onB(B_1, B_2, T)\} \leftarrow T < t_{max}, atPhase2(T).$

Given the initial state $\{onT(b_4, 1), onT(b_3, 1), onB(b_2, b_3, 1), onB(b_1, b_2, 1)\}$ and the time domain $\{1, \ldots, 6\}$, we abstract using the block mapping $\{\{b_1, \ldots, b_4\}/\hat{b}\}$ and the time mapping $\{\{1, 2\}/\hat{t}, \{3, \ldots, 6\}/\hat{t}'\}$. The constructed abstract program has 8 answer sets, including $\{onB(\hat{b}, \hat{b}, \hat{t}), onT(\hat{b}, \hat{t}), moveToT(\hat{b}, \hat{t}), onB(\hat{b}, \hat{b}, \hat{t}'),$ $onT(\hat{b}, \hat{t}'), moveToB(\hat{b}, \hat{b}, \hat{t}')\}$ which contains the abstract actions $moveToT(\hat{b}, \hat{t})$ and $moveToB(\hat{b}, \hat{t}')$ (see Fig. 3).

7   Experiments

To see whether our approach automatically finds non-trivial domain abstractions that yield concrete answer sets, we conducted several experiments.

3-Coloring. We randomly generated 20 graphs on 10 nodes with edge probability $0.1, 0.2, \ldots, 0.5$ each; out of the 100 graphs, 74 were 3-colorable. We evaluated the abstraction m reached from the initial single-cluster abstraction, by checking whether the corresponding abstract program has spurious answer sets (if not, m is *faithful*). In addition, we considered a *projected* notion of concreteness that limits the checking to a set of relevant atoms. E.g., only the colors of nodes 1-3 may be relevant, and an abstraction that assigns colors to them may be sufficient. Table 1 shows the collected results. The left side shows the average number of steps needed until a concrete answer was found, and the average of the resulting abstract domain sizes. The right side shows the percentage of the observed properties of the resulting abstractions. Trivial abstraction (*id*) corresponds to the case where the abstraction is refined back to the original domain. Observe that faithful and non-trivial abstractions were achieved, which shows the potential of the approach in singling out relevant objects. In case of projection, the trivial abstraction is reached (in 9 steps) much less than in the full case;

Table 1. Experimental results for 3-coloring (above) and scheduling (below).

	full	projected		full	projected
number of steps	7.65	5.25	trivial abstractions (id)	47%	6%
abs domain size	8.65	6.19	faithful & non-trivial abs.	27%	43%
faithful abs domain size	7.42	6.32	non-faithful abstraction	26%	51%

	$t = 10$:	v1	v2	$t = 20$:	v1	v2	$t = 30$:	v1	v2
number of steps		7.25	3.7		14.6	5.2		22.6	7.4
abs domain size		8.25	8.6		15.6	13.9		23.6	20

moreover, more non-trivial faithful abstractions are reached, which is beneficial. Furthermore, 80% of the non-colorable graphs were revealed by non-trivial full abstractions, and 77% under projection; hence, abstraction may be useful to catch and explain unsolvability.

Disjunctive Scheduling. For each $t \in \{10, 20, 30\}$, we generated 20 instances with 5 tasks over time $\{1, \ldots, t\}$. Table 1 shows the collected results. For the refinement search, we considered besides the one from above (v1) another one that looks at the domain elements in the ab atoms and guides the refinement either to not map these elements to the same cluster or to map them into single-ton clusters (v2). Observe that in v2 the number of steps to obtain a solution is greatly reduced which moreover has fewer clusters (except for $t = 10$ as creating singleton clusters quickly ends up with the trivial abstraction). The results show that with larger domains, the effect of the abstraction can be seen much better, e.g., the average abstract domain size reached for $t = 30$ is 66.6% (=20/30) of the original domain, while for $t = 10$, it shrinks to 86%. Note that with more sophisticated refinement methods, better abstractions can be reached.

Multi-table Blocksworld. We considered varying numbers of blocks and tables, starting with 5 each. Faithful abstractions readily resulted by 1-step refinements which separated the chosen table from the rest. However, as the abstraction is syntactic, other encodings may need more steps (e.g., bad auxiliary rules causing choices/spuriousness).

8 Conclusion

Related Work. Apart from simplification approaches to ASP we mentioned earlier, abstraction has been studied in logic programming [9]. However, the focus was on the use of abstract interpretations and termination analysis, and stable semantics was not addressed. In planning, plan refinement [22,28] uses abstract plans computed in an abstract space to find a concrete plan, while abstraction-based heuristics [10,17] use the costs of abstract solutions to guide the plan search. Pattern databases [10] project the state space to a set of variables (a 'pattern'), while merge & shrink abstraction [17] starts with a suite of single projections, and then computes an abstraction by merging them and shrinking. In [19], abstraction for numeric planning problems by reduction to classical planning is studied. Recently, the same authors used abstraction for problems that contain quantifiable objects [20], e.g., some number of packages to deliver to points A and B, to find generalized plans by abstracting away from the quantification that works for multiple instances of the problem. For this, they build a quantified planning problem by identifying sets of indistinguishable objects using reformulation techniques [27] to reduce symmetry, and then use an algorithm to compute a general policy. With our method, abstracting over the packages and time is possible as done in Example 13. It constructs an abstract program which contains a generalized plan (among possible spurious ones) for all instances of the problem. Furthermore, if the package delivery problem is extended with having a choice of points to pass through when moving from A to B, then abstracting over the points passed to reach B from A is possible with our method. Such a constraint is not representable by [20] due to the quantifiability conditions. Nevertheless, our method has the orthogonal potential drawback of producing spurious answers.

Abstraction was also studied for agent verification in situation calculus action theory [2] and multi-agent systems against specifications in epistemic logic [25] and temporal logic [3]. Lomuscio and Michaliszyn [25] present an automated predicate abstraction method in 3-valued semantics, and interpolant-based refinement [4]. All these works are quite different from ours; they address specific applications and are based on different (monotonic) logic formalisms.

Outlook. This seminal work has room for improvement, especially in the search for a refinement, where different heuristics may be employed. It can also be made more sophisticated by using domain-specific knowledge. Furthermore, the current quality assessment of refinements can be advanced by considering more than one abstract answer set or making the largest cluster size a parameter in determining the refinement quality. Predicate abstraction would be an interesting extension of this work. Our aim was not to increase reasoning efficiency, but this is an interesting future direction that needs significant follow-up work.

Acknowledgements. This work has been supported by Austrian Science Fund (FWF) project W1255-N23 and Austrian Federal Ministry of Transport Innovation and Technology (BMVIT) project 861263 (DynaCon).

References

1. ASPCOMP-11: Third (open) answer set programming competition: Disjunctive scheduling (2011). www.mat.unical.it/aspcomp2011
2. Banihashemi, B., De Giacomo, G., Lespérance, Y.: Abstraction in situation calculus action theories. In: Proceedings of AAAI, pp. 1048–1055 (2017)
3. Belardinelli, F., Lomuscio, A.: Abstraction-based verification of infinite-state reactive modules. In: Proceedings of ECAI, pp. 725–733 (2016)
4. Belardinelli, F., Lomuscio, A., Michaliszyn, J.: Agent-based refinement for predicate abstraction of multi-agent systems. In: ECAI, pp. 286–294 (2016)

5. Brain, M., Gebser, M., Pührer, J., Schaub, T., Tompits, H., Woltran, S.: Debugging ASP programs by means of ASP. In: Baral, C., Brewka, G., Schlipf, J. (eds.) LPNMR 2007. LNCS (LNAI), vol. 4483, pp. 31–43. Springer, Heidelberg (2007). https://doi.org/10.1007/978-3-540-72200-7_5
6. Brass, S., Dix, J.: Characterizations of the disjunctive stable semantics by partial evaluation. J. Log. Program. **32**(3), 207–228 (1997)
7. Brewka, G., Eiter, T., Truszczyński, M.: Answer set programming at a glance. Commun. ACM **54**(12), 92–103 (2011)
8. Clarke, E.M., Grumberg, O., Long, D.E.: Model checking and abstraction. ACM TOPLAS **16**, 1512–1542 (1994)
9. Cousot, P., Cousot, R.: Abstract interpretation and application to logic programs. J. Log. Program. **13**(2), 103–179 (1992)
10. Edelkamp, S.: Planning with pattern databases. In: Sixth European Conference on Planning (2001)
11. Faber, W., Leone, N., Pfeifer, G.: Recursive aggregates in disjunctive logic programs: semantics and complexity. In: Alferes, J.J., Leite, J. (eds.) JELIA 2004. LNCS (LNAI), vol. 3229, pp. 200–212. Springer, Heidelberg (2004). https://doi.org/10.1007/978-3-540-30227-8_19
12. Gebser, M., Kaminski, R., Kaufmann, B., Ostrowski, M., Schaub, T., Thiele, S.: Engineering an incremental ASP solver. In: Garcia de la Banda, M., Pontelli, E. (eds.) ICLP 2008. LNCS, vol. 5366, pp. 190–205. Springer, Heidelberg (2008). https://doi.org/10.1007/978-3-540-89982-2_23
13. Gebser, M., Kaufmann, B., Kaminski, R., Ostrowski, M., Schaub, T., Schneider, M.: Potassco: the potsdam answer set solving collection. AI Commun. **24**(2), 107–124 (2011)
14. Geißer, F., Keller, T., Mattmüller, R.: Abstractions for planning with state-dependent action costs. In: ICAPS, pp. 140–148 (2016)
15. Gelfond, M., Lifschitz, V.: The stable model semantics for logic programming. In: ICLP/SLP, pp. 1070–1080 (1988)
16. Giunchiglia, F., Walsh, T.: A theory of abstraction. AIJ **57**(2 3), 323 389 (1992)
17. Helmert, M., Haslum, P., Hoffmann, J., Nissim, R.: Merge-and-shrink abstraction: a method for generating lower bounds in factored state spaces. JACM **61**(3), 16 (2014)
18. Hoffmann, J., Sabharwal, A., Domshlak, C.: Friends or Foes? An AI planning perspective on abstraction and search. In: ICAPS, pp. 294–303 (2006)
19. Illanes, L., McIlraith, S.A.: Numeric planning via search space abstraction. In: Proceedings of KnowProS@IJCAI (2016)
20. Illanes, L., McIlraith, S.A.: Generalized planning via abstraction: arbitrary numbers of objects. In: AAAI (2019)
21. Janhunen, T., Niemelä, I., Seipel, D., Simons, P., You, J.H.: Unfolding partiality and disjunctions in stable model semantics. ACM TOCL **7**(1), 1–37 (2006)
22. Knoblock, C.A.: Automatically generating abstractions for planning. Artif. Intell. **68**(2), 243–302 (1994)
23. Kouvaros, P., Lomuscio, A.: A counter abstraction technique for the verification of robot swarms. In: Proceedings of AAAI (2015)
24. Leite, J.: A bird's-eye view of forgetting in answer-set programming. In: Balduccini, M., Janhunen, T. (eds.) LPNMR 2017. LNCS (LNAI), vol. 10377, pp. 10–22. Springer, Cham (2017). https://doi.org/10.1007/978-3-319-61660-5_2
25. Lomuscio, A., Michaliszyn, J.: Verification of multi-agent systems via predicate abstraction against ATLK specifications. In: Proceedings of AAMAS, pp. 662–670 (2016)

26. Pearce, D.: Simplifying logic programs under answer set semantics. In: Demoen, B., Lifschitz, V. (eds.) ICLP 2004. LNCS, vol. 3132, pp. 210–224. Springer, Heidelberg (2004). https://doi.org/10.1007/978-3-540-27775-0_15
27. Riddle, P., Douglas, J., Barley, M., Franco, S.: Improving performance by reformulating PDDL into a bagged representation. In: HSDIP@ICAPS, pp. 28–36 (2016)
28. Sacerdoti, E.D.: Planning in a hierarchy of abstraction spaces. Artif. Intell. 5(2), 115–135 (1974)
29. Saribatur, Z.G., Eiter, T.: Omission-based abstraction for answer set programs. In: Proceedings of KR, pp. 42–51 (2018)

The Hexlite Solver
Lightweight and Efficient Evaluation of HEX Programs

Peter Schüller$^{(\boxtimes)}$ (iD)

Institut für Logic and Computation, Knowledge-Based Systems Group,
Technische Universität Wien, Vienna, Austria
ps@kr.tuwien.ac.at

Abstract. HEXLITE is a lightweight solver for the HEX formalism which
integrates Answer Set Programming (ASP) with external computations.
The main goal of HEXLITE is efficiency and simplicity, both in implementation as well as in installation of the system. We define the Pragmatic
HEX Fragment which permits to partition external computations into
two kinds: those that can be evaluated during the program instantiation phase, and those that need to be evaluated during the answer set
search phase. HEXLITE is written in PYTHON and suitable for evaluating
this fragment with external computations that are realized in PYTHON.
Most performance-critical tasks are delegated to the PYTHON module of
CLINGO. We demonstrate that the Pragmatic HEX Fragment is sufficient
for many use cases and that it permits HEXLITE to have superior performance compared to the DLVHEX system in relevant application scenarios.

1 Introduction

The HEX formalism [8] facilitates the combination of logic programming and
external computations in other programming paradigms, and facilitates the integration of logical reasoning with diverse other reasoning methods such as motion
planning [20], description logics [14], or sub-symbolic reasoning [17].

Differently from externals in GRINGO and the PYTHON interface of CLINGO,
the HEX formalism provides uniform and generic syntax and semantics for external computations that influence (a) the instantiation of the program (by performing value invention), and (b) the solving process (by computing truth values
relative to interpretations).

Computing HEX semantics requires the evaluation of external computations
both during grounding and during search, in an interleaved fashion. The main
solver implementation for the HEX formalism is the DLVHEX system [13]. While
DLVHEX implements the full HEX language, it performs a lot of analysis and
preprocessing to be able to deal with all eventualities of combinations of external
computations, which makes it unnecessarily slow in several relevant application
scenarios.

In order to obtain performance when evaluating HEX programs, we here
present a new HEX solver that is lightweight and efficient, at the cost of handling
only a fragment of HEX, which is sufficient for many applications.

F. Calimeri et al. (Eds.): JELIA 2019, LNAI 11468, pp. 593–607, 2019.
https://doi.org/10.1007/978-3-030-19570-0_39

In this work, we make the following contributions.

- We define the Pragmatic HEX Fragment (PHF) that permits to separate external computations into those that can be evaluated completely during instantiation and those that can be evaluated completely during search. We show several application scenarios where the PHF is sufficient.
- We describe and provide the HEXLITE solver that provides lightweight and efficient evaluation machinery for the PHF. The solver is implemented in PYTHON and uses the CLINGO PYTHON API as a backend for ASP grounding and search. HEXLITE rewrites both classes of external atoms in different ways before passing the rules to CLINGO for evaluation. As a main benefit of this architecture, HEXLITE supports the full ASP input language of CLINGO without the need for dedicated code that supports weak constraints, choice rules, aggregates, expansion terms, and builtin arithmetics.
- We experimentally compare the HEXLITE solver with DLVHEX on two application scenarios that gave rise to the development of HEXLITE: cost-based abduction [30] and RDF processing [18]. Our experiments show, that HEXLITE performs better than DLVHEX in these applications. As HEXLITE uses the same PYTHON API as DLVHEX, we use the same plugin with both solvers, which makes the comparison very realistic.

HEXLITE can be installed via CONDA or PIP and is available as open source.[1]

2   Preliminaries

We give syntax and semantics of the HEX formalism [8,16] which generalizes logic programs under answer set semantics [24] with external computations.

2.1   HEX Syntax

Let $\mathcal{C}$, $\mathcal{X}$, and $\mathcal{G}$ be mutually disjoint sets whose elements are called *constant names*, *variable names*, and *external predicate names*, respectively. Usually, elements from $\mathcal{X}$ and $\mathcal{C}$ are denoted with first letter in upper case and lower case, respectively; while elements from $\mathcal{G}$ are prefixed with ' & '. Elements from $\mathcal{C} \cup \mathcal{X}$ are called *terms*. An (ordinary) *atom* is a tuple $p(Y_1, \ldots, Y_n)$ where $p \in \mathcal{C}$ is a predicate name and $Y_1, \ldots, Y_n$ are terms and $n \geq 0$ is the *arity* of the atom. An atom is *ground* if all its terms are constants. An *external atom* is of the form $\&g[Y_1, \ldots, Y_n](X_1, \ldots, X_m)$, where $Y_1, \ldots, Y_n$ and $X_1, \ldots, X_m$ are two lists of terms, called *input* and *output* lists, respectively, and $\&g \in \mathcal{G}$ is an external predicate name. We assume that input and output lists have fixed lengths $in(\&g) = n$ and $out(\&g) = m$. With each term Y_i in the input list, $1 \leq i \leq n$, we associate a type $t_i \in \{\mathbf{cons}\} \cup \mathbb{N}$. We call the term *constant input* iff $t_i = \mathbf{cons}$, otherwise we call it *predicate input of arity* t_i.

---

[1] https://github.com/hexhex/hexlite.

A *rule* r is of the form $\alpha_1 \vee \cdots \vee \alpha_k \leftarrow \beta_1, \ldots, \beta_n, not\ \beta_{n+1}, \ldots, not\ \beta_m$ with $m, k \geq 0$ where all α_i are atoms and all β_j are either atoms or external atoms. We let $H(r) = \{\alpha_1, \ldots, \alpha_k\}$ and $B(r) = B^+(r) \cup B^-(r)$, where $B^+(r) = \{\beta_1, \ldots, \beta_n\}$ and $B^-(r) = \{\beta_{n+1}, \ldots, \beta_m\}$. A rule r is a *constraint* if $H(r) = \emptyset$; a *fact* if $B(r) = \emptyset$ and $H(r) \neq \emptyset$; and *nondisjunctive* if $|H(r)| \leq 1$. We call r *ordinary* if it contains only ordinary atoms.

A *HEX program* is a finite set P of rules. We call a program P *ordinary* (resp., *nondisjunctive*) if all its rules are ordinary (resp., nondisjunctive). Note that we here assume that programs have no *higher-order* atoms (i.e., atoms of the form $Y_0(Y_1, \ldots, Y_n)$ where $Y_0 \in \mathcal{X}$) because HEX-programs with higher-order atoms can easily be rewritten to HEX-programs without higher-order atoms [8].

A comprehensive introduction to HEX is given in [18].

2.2 Semantics

Given a rule r, the grounding $grnd(r)$ of r is obtained by systematically replacing all variables with constants from $\mathcal{C}$. Given a HEX-program P, the *Herbrand base* HB_P of P is the set of all possible ground versions of atoms and external atoms occurring in P obtained by replacing variables with constants from $\mathcal{C}$. The grounding $grnd(P)$ of P is given by $grnd(P) = \bigcup_{r \in P} grnd(r)$. Importantly, the set of constants $\mathcal{C}$ that is used for grounding a program is only partially given by the program itself: in HEX, external computations may introduce new constants that are relevant for the semantics of the program.

Extensional Semantics [8,16] of external atoms are defined as follows: we associate a $(n+1)$-ary extensional evaluation function $F_{\&g}$ with every external predicate name $\&g \in \mathcal{G}$. Given an interpretation $I \subseteq HB_P$ and a ground input tuple $(x_1, \ldots, x_m)$, $F_{\&g}(I, y_1, \ldots, y_n)$ returns a set of ground output tuples $(x_1, \ldots, x_m)$. The external computation is *restricted* to depend (a) for constant inputs, i.e., $t_i = $ cons, only on the constant value of y_i; and (b) for predicate inputs, i.e., $t_i \in \mathbb{N}$, only on the extension of predicate y_i of arity t_i in I.[2]

An interpretation $I \subseteq HB_P$ is a *model* of an atom a, denoted $I \models a$ if a is an ordinary atom and $a \in I$. I is a model of a ground external atom $a = \&g[y_1, \ldots, y_n](x_1, \ldots, x_m)$ if $(x_1, \ldots, x_m) \in F_{\&g}(I, y_1, \ldots, y_n)$. Given a ground rule r, $I \models H(r)$ if $I \models a$ for some $a \in H(r)$; $I \models B(r)$ if $I \models a$ for all $a \in B^+(r)$ and $I \not\models a$ for all $a \in B^-(r)$; and $I \models r$ if $I \models H(r)$ whenever $I \models B(r)$. Given a HEX-program P, $I \models P$ if $I \models r$ for all $r \in grnd(P)$; the *FLP-reduct* [21] of P with respect to $I \subseteq HB_P$, denoted fP^I, is the set of all $r \in grnd(P)$ such that $I \models B(r)$; $I \subseteq HB_P$ is an *answer set* of P if I is a minimal model of fP^I, and we denote by $\mathcal{AS}(P)$ the set of all answer sets of P.

3 The Pragmatic HEX Fragment (PHF)

We next define a fragment of HEX that permits to separate external computations into two classes: grounding-relevant and solving-relevant.

---

[2] Formally, this is the set $\{y_i(v_1, \ldots, v_{t_i}) \in I\}$.

Definition 1. *A* HEX-*program P is in the Pragmatic* HEX *Fragment (PHF) iff each external atom of the form* $\&g[Y_1,\ldots,Y_n](X_1,\ldots,X_m)$ *with type signature* $t_1,\ldots,t_n$ *satisfies one of the following conditions:*

(G) $t_i = \mathbf{cons}$ *for all* i, $1 \leq i \leq n$*; or*
(S) $m = 0$ *and there is at least one type* t_i, $1 \leq i \leq n$, *such that* $t_i \in \mathbb{N}$.

Type (G). External atoms that satisfy condition (G) can be *evaluated during instantiation* of program P because their computation does not depend on I. These external computations can perform value invention: they can produce constants in the output tuple $X_1,\ldots,X_m$ that do not exist in P. In particular, output terms can recursively define input terms of the same external atom.

Example 1. We can use an external atom of the form $\&rdf[U](S,P,O)$ of type (G) to accesses a RDF [26] triple stores [18]. The function $F_{\&rdf}(I,U)$ returns all tuples (S,P,O) that are obtained from the RDF graph accessible at URI U. Intuitively, this external computation imports the RDF graph into the HEX program and provides all its constants to the instantiation process. The computation does not depend on I and returns arbitrary strings (value invention).

Type (S). External atoms that satisfy condition (S) have an empty output tuple and can therefore not produce any output apart from their own truth value. This makes it possible to instantiate rules that contain such external atoms, without performing the associated external computation; the external computation needs to be performed only *during the answer set search* phase, when the interpretation I is available.

Example 2. We can use external atoms of the form $\&transitive[p]()$ of type (S), with $t_1 = 2$ the arity of predicate p, to verify whether $p/2$ is transitive in the interpretation [30]. The function $F_{\&transitive}(I,p)$ returns the empty tuple if the extension of p in I is a transitive relation. Otherwise, it returns no tuple.

External atoms of type (S) have the possibility to create nogoods that relate the truth value of the ground external atom with parts of I that are relevant for computing that truth value. This feature, which also exists in DLVHEX, can be used for increasing evaluation performance by guiding the solver towards answer set candidates that are compatible with external computation results.

3.1 Properties

Clearly, the two classes (G) and (S) of external atoms are mutually exclusive. Those external atoms of type (G) that have no output terms (i.e., $m = 0$) could be evaluated during the solving process because their evaluation is not necessary for instantiating the ground program. However, we found it useful to evaluate (and therefore eliminate) as many external atoms as possible already during program instantiation.

Moreover, there are external atoms that fall neither into class (G) nor into class (S), for example an external atom $\&sum[pred](X)$ that has one predicate input *pred* of arity 1 and realizes a summation aggregate with extensional evaluation function $F_{\&sum}(I, pred) := \{(X)\}$ where $X = \Sigma\{x \mid p(x) \in I\}$.

External atoms of type (G) can be evaluated (and eliminated) during instantiation of the program as shown in the following proposition.

Proposition 1. *Given a ground* HEX*-program P in PHF, an equivalent program P′ can be produced by (1) omitting rules that contain an external atom a of type (G) where (i) a is in a positive literal and $\emptyset \not\models a$; or (ii) a is in a negative literal and $\emptyset \models a$; and (2) omitting all other external atoms of type (G).*

Proof (sketch). A ground external atom a of type (G) has only constant input, therefore $I \models a$ is independent from the value of I. Hence, rules where (1) applies can never obtain a satisfied body due to a while rules where (2) applies can never obtain a non-satisfied body due to a.

External atoms of type (S) can be handled the same way as in DLVHEX [8, 13], therefore we here do not provide formal results about them.[3]

External atoms outside the PHF fragment can be processed with Liberal Safety [10]: it permits automatic verification of finite instantiation of a HEX program in the presence of cyclic dependencies among external atoms that perform value invention, depend on the answer set candidate, and have certain (semantic) properties. Opposed to the methodology of Liberal Safety, HEXLITE delegates finiteness of instantiation to the programmer (as also done, e.g., by GRINGO).

3.2   Amenable Application Scenarios

External computations of type (S) can pass nogoods to the solver that describe how their truth value depends on the interpretation.

Constraint Answer Set Programming (CASP) [27] has been realized in HEX [29] using one external atom &*check* of type (S). Application scenarios in [29] use external atoms of type (G) for SQL querying: &*sql*[*Query*](*AnswerTuple*), where *Query* can be a fixed string or defined using external atoms. High-level *planning for robotics* has been interleaved with low-level motion planning using HEX [20], where external atoms for motion planning are either of type (S) or of type (G) and there is no value invention. HEX-programs with *existential quantification* (HEX$^\exists$) [9] as well as HEX-programs with function symbols use only external atoms of type (G) to perform tasks related to Skolemization, similar to what is presented in Sect. 5.1. The MCS-IE system for *explaining inconsistency in Multi-Context Systems* [4] is implemented in HEX and uses only external atoms of type (S). Two further application scenarios are *abduction* and *RDF processing*, shown in detail in Sects. 5.1 and 5.2.

---

[3] DLVHEX replaces them with an ordinary replacement atom, guesses truth of replacement atoms with extra rules, and accepts only answer set candidates I where guessed truth values correspond with external computations wrt. I, see Sect. 4.

4 Hexlite Solver Design and Architecture

Principles. The design of HEXLITE followed several guiding principles.

- Delegation: delegate as much as possible to the backend solver (currently CLINGO).
- Separation: deal with external atoms either during grounding or during solving in order to avoid multiple grounding passes.
- Programmer Responsibility: delegate the responsibility for finite instantiation to the programmer (as in GRINGO).

Delegation reduces computational overhead and duplication of code that already exists in the ASP backend. As the main consequence of this principle, HEXLITE performs no safety check and no syntax check, not even thorough parsing of the input. Instead, a shallow representation of the input program is created. This representation is sufficient for rewriting rules and external atoms for subsequent evaluation. As a consequence of Delegation, unsafe variables are detected only by GRINGO because safety checking is not required for HEXLITE rewriting. A second consequence of Delegation is, that HEXLITE has no internal representation of the current answer set candidate; instead, the CLASP PYTHON API is used to directly access the (partial) model within CLASP. Moreover, optimization is handled transparently within CLASP.

Separation is the basis for defining the PHF and contributes to the small implementation of HEXLITE, because evaluation follows the common structure of ASP solvers with external atoms that are relevant either for grounding or for solving. (Currently, HEXLITE is implemented using 3,300 lines of PYTHON code, which includes the shallow parser, FLP checker, and code comments.) A HEX program can be split into Evaluation Units, i.e., non-ground program modules that never mutually depend on one another [8]. While DLVHEX interleaves grounding and search over multiple Evaluation Units, HEXLITE always uses a single Evaluation Unit.

Programmer Responsibility is a principle from GRINGO: the burden of ensuring a finite instantiation is put on the programmer and not verified by preprocessing. This is the opposite of the philosophy followed in the DLVHEX solver where various safety notions such as Domain Expansion Safety and Liberal Domain Expansion Safety [11] are defined and also checked by the solver, depending on properties of external computations. The upside of not checking this in the solver is decreased preprocessing effort, the downside is that HEXLITE (just like GRINGO) will not complain about the program '$p(0) \leftarrow . \; p(s(X)) \leftarrow p(X).$' but starts to instantiate it and will exhaust the available memory due to its infinite instantiation. In HEX programs, external computations can cause infinite instantiation, but the programmer of external computations might take specific measures to prevent infinite instantiation (as shown in Sect. 5.1). Therefore, delegating responsibility to the user instead of performing costly verifications can be an advantage.

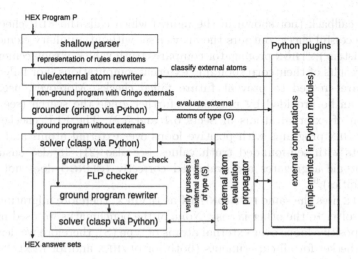

Fig. 1. Architecture of the HEXLITE system and its interaction with the CLINGO Python library and plugins for external computations.

Architecture. Figure 1 shows the architecture of HEXLITE. The input program P is analyzed with a *shallow parser*, followed by the rewriter module that rewrites only those parts of rules that contain external atoms. The *rewriter* accesses external computations for obtaining their type and creates the following GRINGO-compatible rules for each rule $r \in P$.

(i) a rule r' where each external atom a of the form $\&g[Y_1,...,Y_n](X_1,...,X_m)$
  (a) is replaced by a GRINGO external of the form $(X_1,...,X_m) = @g(Y_1,...,Y_n)$ if a is of type (G);
  (b) is replaced by a *replacement atom* of the form $c_{\&g}(Y_1,...,Y_n)$ if a is of type (S); and[4]
(ii) for each replacement atom created in (b) above a rule r'' of the form

$$e_{\&g}(Y_1,\ldots,Y_n) \vee \overline{e}_{\&g}(Y_1,\ldots,Y_n) \leftarrow B'$$

where $B' = \{\beta \in B(r) \mid \beta$ shares variables with $Y_1,\ldots,Y_n\}$.

(DLVHEX uses a similar rewriting, see [15,19].) After rewriting, GRINGO is used for instantiating the rewritten program with a PYTHON context that evalutes external computations of the form $(X_1,\ldots,X_m) = @g(Y_1,\ldots,Y_n)$ by assigning the tuple $(X_1,\ldots,X_m)$ all values returned by the external computation. The resulting ordinary ground program is passed to a CLASP instance that has been prepared with (i) a custom PYTHON propagator,[5] (ii) a ground program observer that collects the ground program for usage in the FLP checker, and (iii) an

---

[4] In that case $m = 0$ so the replacement atom does not include $X_1,\ldots,X_m$.
[5] A propagator is a program module that interfaces with the search process of CLASP and can (a) infer truth values and (b) add ground clauses based on a partial model.

on_model callback (not shown in the figure) which calls the FLP checker and, after a successful check, outputs the answer set without auxiliary elements.

The custom PYTHON propagator compares truth values of replacement atoms with the results of their corresponding external computations. For failed checks, nogoods are created to prevent future failed checks. Moreover, user-defined nogoods can be provided by plugins to further guide the search (see also the description of external atoms in Sects. 5.1 and 5.2). The FLP checker is necessary for HEX programs with positive loops over external atoms and prevents answer sets with self-founded truth values, see also [21]. It also ensures that non-monotonic aggregates are evaluated correctly (CLINGO does not support FLP semantics).[6]

HEXLITE uses the same PYTHON API as DLVHEX, therefore migrating plugins from one solver to the other is easy. None of the benchmarks we used in evaluations has positive loops over external atoms of type (S), therefore we deactivated the FLP checker for all experiments (both for DLVHEX and for HEXLITE).

5 Experimental Evaluation

For experimental evaluation of HEXLITE, we tried it out with two application domains: variants of cost-based abduction [30] and the RDF plugin [18].

We choose these domains because they both contain both types of external atoms, and because they were part of the inspiration for developing HEXLITE.

5.1 Cost-Based Abduction Benchmark

Cost-based abduction consists of 50 instances over the ACCEL natural language story understanding benchmark [28]. The full benchmark is available online.[7,8] ACCEL uses two external predicates: &invent for flexible Skolemization, and &transitive as described in Example 2 for ensuring transitivity of a guessed relation over many elements.

External predicate &invent is used for ensuring finite instantiation in the presence of existential variables in rule heads.[9] Given a rule R with an existential variable B in the head and universal variables $A_1, \ldots, A_k$ in the body, instead of replacing B with Skolem term $s(A_1,...,A_k)$ we add $\&invent[R, c_B, A_1,...,A_k](B)$ to the rule body and define $F_{\&invent}$ such that a finite set of values for B is

---

[6] The FLP check implemented in HEXLITE is described in Proposition 1 in [8]. The FLP check can be deactivated if it is not required (this is another example of Programmer Responsibility). The custom PYTHON propagator is re-used in the FLP checker.

[7] https://bitbucket.org/knowlp/asp-fo-abduction.

[8] To permit a fairer comparison, we used only objective functions CARD and COH (DLVHEX is incompatible with objective function WA) and we removed all facts of the form comment(...). which served only an informational purpose (DLVHEX is significantly slower if these facts are included).

[9] This generalizes the termination mechanism for reasoning as it was implemented in the original ACCEL reasoner [28].

invented, independent from cycles in the program. For our evaluation, we used two variants of this benchmark:

SK/P^1 *variant.* Value invention is blocked if at least one parent term is invented: $F_{\&invent^{P1}}(I, R, V, A_1, \ldots, A_k)$ returns the tuple $(s(R, V, A_1, \ldots, A_k))$ if no A_i, $1 \leq i \leq k$ is of the form $s(\cdots)$, otherwise it returns no tuple.

SK/G^1 *variant.* Value invention is blocked if at least one parent term was invented by the same ground external predicate: $F_{\&invent^{G1}}(I, R, V, A_1, \ldots, A_k)$ returns the tuple $(s(R, V, A_1, \ldots, A_k))$ if no A_i, $1 \leq i \leq k$ has a sub-term of the form $s(R, V, \cdots)$, otherwise it returns no tuple.

Intuitively, SK/P^1 invents only values that have non-invented *parents*, and SK/G^1 invents only a single *generation* of values in each rule. This method of ensuring finite instantiation is orthogonal to guarding domains predicates that ensure a finite chase in Datalog with existential quantifiers [5]: value invention is forced to be finite independent from the structure of the program. For details and examples of the finite instantiation property, we refer to Sect. 4.1 in [30].

External predicate *&transitive* appears in a single constraint of the form $\leftarrow not \ \&transitive[eq]()$. Each time this external computation evaluates to false, it creates nogoods that provide the reason for intransitivity (i.e., a triple of literals $eq(A, B)$, $eq(B, C)$, $\neg eq(A, C)$) to the solver to assist the search for a transitive relation. For more details see Sect. 4.2 in [30].

Importantly, $F_{\&invent}$ does not use I and therefore external atoms of the form $\&invent[\cdots](\cdots)$ are of type (G). Moreover, external predicate *&transitive* produces no values in output tuples (i.e., $m = 0$) and it has type $t_1 = 2$ (it uses the extension of a binary predicate p) therefore it is of type (S).

5.2 RDF Benchmark

The RDF plugin realizes the RDF triple external atom as described in Example 1. We here extend the original application [18] with a second external atom of type (S). We experiment with the COLINDA [31] knowledge graph which contains 150,000 triples about conferences.[10] We perform the following three reasoning problems.

Import. We simply import all triples using the program

$explore("\ldots/colinda.rdf") \leftarrow .$

$triple\_at(S, P, O) \leftarrow \&rdf[What](S, P, O), explore(What).$

which yields a single answer set with around 150,000 atoms.

Vegas. We are interested in names of all conferences in Las Vegas. The program

$explore("\ldots/colinda.rdf") \leftarrow . \quad location("http://sws.geonames.org/3635260/") \leftarrow .$

$conference(Conf) \leftarrow explore(G), location(Loc),$

$\quad \&rdf[G](Conf, "http://swrc.ontoware.org/ontology\#location", Loc).$

---

[10] Dataset retrieved from https://old.datahub.io/dataset/colinda.

$title(\,Title) \leftarrow explore(\,G), conference(\,Conf),$

    $\&rdf[G](\,Conf, "http://swrc.ontoware.org/ontology\#eventTitle", Title).$

yields a single answer set with 330 atoms, 164 of them containing the titles conferences in COLINDA that took place in Las Vegas (encoded as ID 3635260).

Marathon. This is an optimization problem where we are interested in making a conference marathon for visiting the maximum possible number of cities in France over two weeks. This is encoded in the following HEX program.

$explore(".\,.\,./colinda.rdf") \leftarrow .\quad country("France") \leftarrow .$

$location(Loc) \leftarrow explore(\,G), country(\,C),$

    $\&rdf[G](Loc, "http://www.geonames.org/ontology\#countryName", C).$

$conference(\,Conf, Loc) \leftarrow explore(\,G), location(Loc),$

    $\&rdf[G](\,Conf, "http://swrc.ontoware.org/ontology\#location", Loc).$

$in(\,Conf) \vee out(\,Conf) \leftarrow conference(\,Conf, Loc).$

$covered(Loc) \leftarrow conference(\,Conf, Loc), in(\,Conf).$

$\leftarrow\sim location(Loc), not\ covered(Loc).\quad [1, Loc]$

$date(Date) \leftarrow explore(\,G), in(\,Conf),$

    $\&rdf[G](\,Conf, "http://swrc.ontoware.org/ontology\#startDate", Date).$

$\leftarrow not\ \&dates\_span\_days[date, 14].$

This encoding represents locations in France in *location*, conferences and their locations (if in France) in *conference*, and performs a guess (*in*) selecting relevant conferences. Those conferences that are selected define which location is covered. We maximize coverage by incurring a cost of 1 for each location that is not covered by means of the weak constraint ($\leftarrow\sim$). Furthermore, we extract dates of covered conferences in *date* and use an external atom to indicate whether the dates lie within a 14 day period.

Function $F_{\&dates\_span\_days}(I, p, d)$ is defined to return an empty tuple iff all dates X with $p(X) \in I$ are within d days of one another. The external computation of *dates_span_days* guides the search by providing nogoods for all pairs of dates (X, X') with $p(X), p(X') \in I$ and more than d days between X and X'.

Evaluating this program yields an answer set with 29 locations and 404 conferences in France, and an optimal selection of 6 conferences (in 6 distinct cities) which start between the 12th and the 23rd of March 2012.

5.3   Experimental Setup

We performed experiments on a computer with an Intel(R) i5-3450 CPU with 4 cores and 16 GB RAM running Linux. For the Abduction Benchmark we limited memory consumption to 5 GB and execution time to 300 s (5 min). For the RDF Benchmark we limited execution time to 1800 s (30 min). We never executed more than 2 runs in parallel and we used non-parallel computation mode

Table 1. RDF benchmark: results of evaluating DLVHEX and HEXLITE on the COLINDA conference knowledge graph.

Problem	Engine	Time (s)	Space (MB)	Result	External computations		
					Calls (#)	Time (s)	Learned (#)
Import	DLVHEX	1,800	4,321	TO	1	19	0
	HEXLITE	31	254	OK	1	25	0
Vegas	DLVHEX	185	987	OK	2	38	0
	HEXLITE	20	191	OK	1	17	0
Marathon	DLVHEX	1,127	2,462	OK	2,543	58	29,860
	HEXLITE	28	199	OK	777	23	21,322

for solver settings. Time limits and reported times are CPU times. To make the comparison fair, we used the same PYTHON plugin for DLVHEX and HEXLITE (the plugin API of HEXLITE is compatible with the one of DLVHEX, including the API for learning nogoods in external computations). We used the latest version of DLVHEX[11] and the latest version of HEXLITE.[12]

5.4   Results

We will write TO (resp., MO) to indicate that the time (resp., memory) limit was exceeded.

Figure 2 shows cactus plots of the experiments on the abduction benchmark. For evaluation time (instantiation and search), for SK/P^1, HEXLITE solves each instance within at most 14 s while DLVHEX fails to solves 20 instances (8 times TO and 12 times MO). For SK/G^1, HEXLITE fails to solve 32 instances because of TO and DLVHEX fails to solve 72 instances (46 times TO and 26 times MO). HEXLITE solves all instances that DLVHEX manages to solve within the timeout. The corresponding plots of external computation times show, that DLVHEX calls the external computations more often than HEXLITE to solve the same instances. The plots of memory consumption show, that memory consumption of DLVHEX rises steeper than the one of HEXLITE. Overall, HEXLITE shows a much better performance than DLVHEX on the abduction benchmark, and the difference between the solvers is more striking for SK/G^1 variant.

Table 1 shows results of running the RDF benchmark using DLVHEX and HEXLITE. Interestingly, the only timeout happens for Import where the whole set of RDF triples is represented in the answer set. DLVHEX cannot compute the result within 30 min. For Vegas, where many triples can be ignored, both DLVHEX and HEXLITE are more efficient than for Import, however DLVHEX requires 3 min while HEXLITE requires 20 s to perform this (deterministic) computation. The search/optimization problem Marathon shows a big gap between DLVHEX and

---

[11] We used git hash 5a1ee06d from `git@github.com:hexhex/core.git` because the stable version 2.5.0 performed significantly worse.
[12] Git hash d0e7896eb from `git@github.com:hexhex/hexlite.git`.

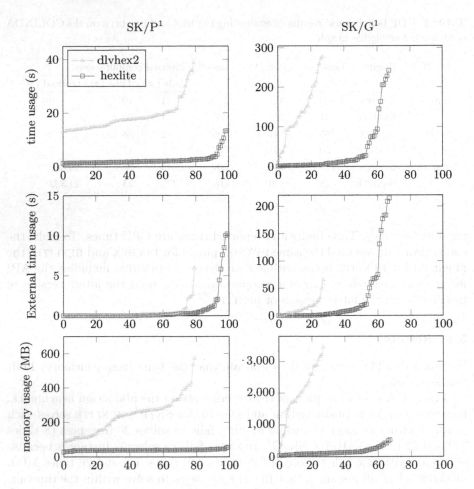

Fig. 2. Abduction benchmark: cactus plots for evaluation time, external computation time, and memory usage with two different value invention limits (SK/P^1 and SK/G^1).

HEXLITE, both in terms of time and space. In particular, HEXLITE performs fewer external atom calls and requires learning of fewer nogoods from the external computation in order to find an optimal answer set and prove its optimality. This can be explained by the lightweight usage of the CLINGO optimization feature in HEXLITE, while DLVHEX performs a lot of bookkeeping and additional computation to perform optimization.

6   Discussion and Conclusion

Our experiments show, that HEXLITE has better performance than DLVHEX in two real-world applications of HEX which are both in the Pragmatic HEX Fragment. Clearly, not all HEX programs are in PHF and some problems will be difficult to convert into PHF. Nevertheless, wherever HEXLITE can be applied it can be a faster alternative to DLVHEX that is also easier to install as it is fully implemented in PYTHON. In cases where the program contains only external atoms of type (S) and there is a loop over at least one such external atom in the program, the FLP check becomes mandatory and the DLVHEX system will most likely have a better performance than HEXLITE because of its more advanced method for performing the FLP check [12]. If only external atoms of type (G) exist, HEXLITE will most likely perform better than DLVHEX.

There are several reasons for the better performance of HEXLITE compared with DLVHEX. Firstly, HEXLITE can remove many external atoms during grounding and they will not even be seen by the solver, while DLVHEX creates guesses for all external atoms, even those that do not depend on the interpretation, and needs to verify their truth during the solving. This eliminates a lot of potential for backend solver preprocessing in DLVHEX. Secondly, HEXLITE passes all optimization tasks to the CLINGO solver backend and just checks during propagation whether the current assignment is in itself consistent (all interpretations are checked against external atom semantics, non-partial interpretations are additionally checked against the FLP property). Opposed to that, DLVHEX performs a lot of internal bookkeeping related to optimization and maintains its own representation of the interpretation and its own cost representation for answer sets, which causes significant memory and computation overhead.

Performance issues of DLVHEX were the original reason that the tool for cost-based abduction described in [30] is formalized using the HEX formalism but implemented using a custom reasoner based on CLINGO. With HEXLITE, this implementation could be realized with less effort and without a dedicated algorithm just by using HEXLITE and implementations of two external computations.

HEXLITE uses many aspects of the CLINGO API, however it does not use CLINGO Externals [23] which are truth values given 'from the outside' to the solving process. Instead, the HEX notion of external computation is in a tight interaction with the answer set candidate and the results of other external computations, and during HEX evaluation, truth values of externals might be reconsidered before finding an answer set. What we do use in the FLP checker are CLASP 'assumptions' to communicate the answer set candidate to the FLP checker (which uses a single rewriting of the ground program for checking the FLP property of all potential answer sets).

Related to this work is a study on lazy instantiation of constraints and an alternative usage of propagators instead of constraints [7] using the WASP solver [1,2]. In the future, WASP could be integrated into HEXLITE as an alternative to the CLINGO backend, the PYTHON API of WASP could be used to deal with external atoms of type (S). The new DLV grounder and its externals [6] could be integrated to handle external atoms of type (G).

We are glad that a study on Inductive Logic Programming [25] was successfully realized using HEXLITE. A (pragmatic) fragment of the ACTHEX extension of HEX [3,22] based on HEXLITE is available in the HEXLITE Git repository.

Acknowledgements. We are grateful to Stefano Germano, Tobias Kaminski, Christoph Redl, Antonius Weinzierl and the anonymous reviewers for feedback about the HEXLITE system and this manuscript. This work has received funding from the Austrian Federal Ministry of Transport, Innovation and Technology (BMVIT) under grant agreement 861263 (DynaCon), and from the European Union's Horizon 2020 research and innovation programme under grant agreement 825619 (AI4EU).

References

1. Alviano, M., Dodaro, C., Faber, W., Leone, N., Ricca, F.: WASP: a native ASP solver based on constraint learning. In: Cabalar, P., Son, T.C. (eds.) LPNMR 2013. LNCS (LNAI), vol. 8148, pp. 54–66. Springer, Heidelberg (2013). https://doi.org/10.1007/978-3-642-40564-8_6

2. Alviano, M., Dodaro, C., Leone, N., Ricca, F.: Advances in WASP. In: Calimeri, F., Ianni, G., Truszczynski, M. (eds.) LPNMR 2015. LNCS (LNAI), vol. 9345, pp. 40–54. Springer, Cham (2015). https://doi.org/10.1007/978-3-319-23264-5_5

3. Basol, S., Erdem, O., Fink, M., Ianni, G.: HEX programs with action atoms. In: LIPIcs-Leibniz International Proceedings in Informatics, vol. 7. Schloss Dagstuhl-Leibniz-Zentrum fuer Informatik (2010)

4. Bögl, M., Eiter, T., Fink, M., Schüller, P.: The MCS-IE system for explaining inconsistency in multi-context systems. In: Janhunen, T., Niemelä, I. (eds.) JELIA 2010. LNCS (LNAI), vol. 6341, pp. 356–359. Springer, Heidelberg (2010). https://doi.org/10.1007/978-3-642-15675-5_31

5. Calì, A., Gottlob, G., Kifer, M.: Taming the infinite chase: query answering under expressive relational constraints. J. Artif. Intell. Res. **48**, 115–174 (2013)

6. Calimeri, F., Fuscà, D., Perri, S., Zangari, J.: External computations and interoperability in the new DLV grounder. In: Esposito, F., Basili, R., Ferilli, S., Lisi, F. (eds.) AI*IA 2017. LNCS, vol. 10640, pp. 172–185. Springer, Cham (2017). https://doi.org/10.1007/978-3-319-70169-1_13

7. Cuteri, B., Dodaro, C., Ricca, F., Schüller, P.: Constraints, lazy constraints, or propagators in ASP solving: an empirical analysis. Theory Pract. Log. Program. **17**(5–6), 780–799 (2017)

8. Eiter, T., Fink, M., Ianni, G., Krennwallner, T., Redl, C., Schüller, P.: A model building framework for answer set programming with external computations. Theory Pract. Log. Program. **16**(4), 418–464 (2016)

9. Eiter, T., Fink, M., Krennwallner, T., Redl, C.: HEX-programs with existential quantification. In: Workshop on Logic Programming, pp. 99–117 (2013)

10. Eiter, T., Fink, M., Krennwallner, T., Redl, C.: Liberal safety for answer set programs with external sources. In: AAAI Conference on Artificial Intelligence, pp. 267–275 (2013)

11. Eiter, T., Fink, M., Krennwallner, T., Redl, C.: Domain expansion for ASP-programs with external sources. Artif. Intell. **233**, 84–121 (2016)

12. Eiter, T., Fink, M., Krennwallner, T., Redl, C., Schüller, P.: Efficient HEX-program evaluation based on unfounded sets. J. Artif. Intell. Res. **49**, 269–321 (2014)

13. Eiter, T., et al.: The DLVHEX system. KI - Künstliche Intelligenz **32**(2), 187–189 (2018). http://www.kr.tuwien.ac.at/research/systems/dlvhex/

14. Eiter, T., Ianni, G., Lukasiewicz, T., Schindlauer, R., Tompits, H.: Combining answer set programming with description logics for the semantic web. Artif. Intell. **172**(12–13), 1495–1539 (2008)

15. Eiter, T., Ianni, G., Schindlauer, R., Tompits, H.: A uniform integration of higher-order reasoning and external evaluations in answer-set programming. In: International Joint Conference on Artificial Intelligence (IJCAI), pp. 90–96 (2005)

16. Eiter, T., Ianni, G., Schindlauer, R., Tompits, H.: Effective integration of declarative rules with external evaluations for semantic-web reasoning. In: Sure, Y., Domingue, J. (eds.) ESWC 2006. LNCS, vol. 4011, pp. 273–287. Springer, Heidelberg (2006). https://doi.org/10.1007/11762256_22

17. Eiter, T., Kaminski, T.: Exploiting contextual knowledge for hybrid classification of visual objects. In: Michael, L., Kakas, A. (eds.) JELIA 2016. LNCS (LNAI), vol. 10021, pp. 223–239. Springer, Cham (2016). https://doi.org/10.1007/978-3-319-48758-8_15

18. Eiter, T., Kaminski, T., Redl, C., Schüller, P., Weinzierl, A.: Answer set programming with external source access. In: Ianni, G., et al. (eds.) Reasoning Web 2017. LNCS, vol. 10370, pp. 204–275. Springer, Cham (2017). https://doi.org/10.1007/978-3-319-61033-7_7

19. Eiter, T., Kaminski, T., Redl, C., Weinzierl, A.: Exploiting partial assignments for efficient evaluation of answer set programs with external source access. J. Artif. Intell. Res. **62**, 665–727 (2018)

20. Erdem, E., Patoglu, V., Schüller, P.: A systematic analysis of levels of integration between low-level reasoning and task planning. AI Commun. **29**(2), 319–349 (2016)

21. Faber, W., Pfeifer, G., Leone, N.: Semantics and complexity of recursive aggregates in answer set programming. Artif. Intell. **175**(1), 278–298 (2011)

22. Fink, M., Germano, S., Ianni, G., Redl, C., Schüller, P.: ActHEX: implementing HEX programs with action atoms. In: Cabalar, P., Son, T.C. (eds.) LPNMR 2013. LNCS (LNAI), vol. 8148, pp. 317–322. Springer, Heidelberg (2013). https://doi.org/10.1007/978-3-642-40564-8_31

23. Gebser, M., Kaminski, R., Kaufmann, B., Schaub, T.: Multi-shot ASP solving with clingo. Theory Practi. Log. Program. **19**, 1–56 (2018)

24. Gelfond, M., Lifschitz, V.: Classical negation in logic programs and deductive databases. New Gener. Comput. **9**, 365–385 (1991)

25. Kaminski, T., Eiter, T., Inoue, K.: Exploiting answer set programming with external sources for meta-interpretive learning. Theory Pract. Log. Program. **18**(3–4), 571–588 (2018)

26. Lassila, O., Swick, R.: Resource description framework (RDF) model and syntax specification (1999). www.w3.org/TR/1999/REC-rdf-syntax-19990222

27. Lierler, Y.: Relating constraint answer set programming languages and algorithms. Artif. Intell. **207**, 1–22 (2014)

28. Ng, H.T., Mooney, R.J.: Abductive plan recognition and diagnosis: a comprehensive empirical evaluation. In: Knowledge Representation and Reasoning (KR), pp. 499–508 (1992)

29. Rosis, A.D., Eiter, T., Redl, C., Ricca, F.: Constraint answer set programming based on HEX-programs. In: Proceedings of Workshop on Answer Set Programming and Other Computing Paradigms (ASPOCP) (2015)

30. Schüller, P.: Modeling variations of first-order Horn abduction in answer set programming. Fundamenta Informaticae **149**(1–2), 159–207 (2016)

31. Softic, S.: Conference Linked Data (COLINDA), version 1.0, last updated 30 July 2016. 149020 triples. http://www.colinda.org

Epistemic Answer Set Programming

Ezgi Iraz Su[1,2(✉)] (iD)

[1] Department of Computer Engineering, Istinye University, Istanbul, Turkey
Ezgi-Iraz.Su@irit.fr
[2] IRIT, University of Toulouse, Toulouse, France

Abstract. This paper introduces a new epistemic extension of answer set programming (ASP) called *epistemic ASP* (E-ASP). Then, it compares E-ASP with existing approaches, showing the advantages and the novelties of the new semantics and discusses which formalisms provide more intuitive results: compared to Gelfond's epistemic specifications (ES), E-ASP defines a simpler, but sufficiently strong language. Its *epistemic view* semantics is a natural and more standard generalisation of ASP's original answer set semantics, so it allows for ASP's previous language extensions. Moreover, compared to all semantics proposals in the literature, epistemic view semantics facilitates understanding of the intuitive meaning of epistemic logic programs and solves unintended results discussed in the literature, especially for epistemic logic programs including constraints.

Keywords: Answer set programming · Epistemic specifications · Modal logic S5 · Stable models · Answer sets · World views · Autoepistemic equilibrium models

1 Introduction

Logic programming (LP) [21] unifies different areas of computation by exploiting the greater generality of logic. Answer set programming (ASP) [13,14,24,25] is an approach to declarative programming, and it relates LP to declarative problem solving by *answer sets*—consistent sets A of literals[1] in which $p \notin A$ or $\sim p \notin A$. In a sense, they are *partial* valuations. Some researchers prefer to call them *3-valued.* For instance, empty valuation assigns neither *true* nor *false* to a propositional variable p, leaving it *undetermined*, which is characterised by *negation as failure* (NAF) [6,7] in ASP. Answer set semantics [10] of ASP has

---

I want to thank Andreas Herzig, Luis Fariñas del Cerro, Michael Gelfond, Patrick Thor Kahl, Thomas Eiter, Yi-Dong Shen, Pedro Cabalar, and Jorge Fandinno for their research related to this paper and the anonymous reviewers for their valued comments on the drafts of this work.

[1] In ASP, a literal is a propositional variable p or a *strongly-negated* propositional variable $\sim p$.

© Springer Nature Switzerland AG 2019
F. Calimeri et al. (Eds.): JELIA 2019, LNAI 11468, pp. 608–626, 2019.
https://doi.org/10.1007/978-3-030-19570-0_40

provided a correct interpretation of NAF and related ASP to nonmonotonic reasoning [28,32]. ASP is currently central to various approaches in nonmonotonic reasoning with a wide range of applications in science and technology.

Despite its successes, ASP has some drawbacks. Among others, ASP is not powerful enough to correctly represent incomplete information, exactly in situations where there are multiple answer sets of an ASP program because NAF performs locally (separately in each answer set) and cannot reason about over a whole range of answer sets. Since 1991, a considerable amount of ASP research has focused on the problem of incomplete information [3,5,8,9,11,17–20,22,29–31,33–39], none of which however resulted in a fully satisfactory semantics. We attack the same problem in order to overcome the obstacles of the previous approaches towards a solution.

The first approach of this line of research is Gelfond's *epistemic specifications* (ES) [8]: he extended a special form of ASP called disjunctive logic programming [14] by epistemic operators, able to quantify over *belief set* (which is, in structure, analogous to an answer set) collections. The interpretation of this new language is in terms of a *world view*—a maximal collection of belief sets about a world reflected by an epistemic logic program Π. Hence, a world view is a kind of 3-valued S5 model (set of valuations). Similar to the answer set semantics, the world view semantics is also reduct-based. However, different from the reduct definition of the former where we only eliminate NAF, here the goal is, in principle, to remove epistemic modal operators. Thus, the reduct $\Pi^{\mathcal{A}}$ of an epistemic logic program Π w.r.t. a world view candidate $\mathcal{A}$ is an ASP program which may include NAF as well. In both semantics, the selection of these special models from among all models of a program is in two steps (plus a fixed point check): first, we compute the reduct of a program by a candidate model (a valuation or a set of valuations, depending on the context); second, we construct the collection $\mathcal{A}$ of all answer sets of this reduct. If the candidate model which is a (possibly empty) set of literals in ASP, is an element of $\mathcal{A}$, then we call it an *answer set*. In ES, if the candidate model (which is similar to $\mathcal{A}$ in structure) equals $\mathcal{A}$, then we call it a *world view* of the original program. Thus, the ultimate decision follows a sort of fixed point construction.

Since Gelfond's first version [8], several semantics proposals have been suggested for ES. The majority are reduct-based world view semantics: while some offer a slightly different refinement of the preceding approach [9,11,17–20] in order to correct unintended results, some others propose significantly different definitions of reducts and world views [29,30]. There is also another kind of approach, inspired by the Kripke semantics of modal logics over a more general language [5,34]. The rest [4,33,35] are based on an epistemic extension of equilibrium model approach [26,27]. As [35] embeds Gelfond's obsolete previous version [9], it is out of our consideration. [4] contains a refinement of [33], and [4] is somewhat successful in providing intuitive results. To sum up, the (to a certain extent) successful approaches of the day are [4,20,29].

In this paper, we propose a novel epistemic extension of ASP called *epistemic ASP* (E-ASP), which has a modest, but neat syntax character, compared to Gelfond's ES. However, our language is expressive enough to formulate all motivating examples of ES. The semantics of this new language is given by *epistemic views*, which are, in structure, similar to world views. The main advantage of our approach over previous semantics is its simplicity and similarity to answer set semantics of ASP. Moreover, it performs well both with cyclic and acyclic programs, giving intuitive results. Especially, it offers a solution to the recent constraint problem discussed in the literature [3,19].

The paper is organised as follows. The first 3 sections present related work: Sect. 2 recalls ES and its world view semantics. Section 3 introduces autoepistemic equilibrium models as an alternative to world views. Section 4 defines epistemic negation, with which suggests a new reduct and world view definition. Section 5 includes the main contribution of this paper, where we introduce E-ASP. We propose epistemic view semantics and compare our results with those of [4,19,29]. Section 6 recalls epistemic splitting property by Cabalar et al. Section 7 concludes the paper with future work plan.

2 Epistemic Specifications (ES) and Its World View Semantics

We here recall the recent versions of Gelfond's ES, suggested by Kahl et al. [18–20].

2.1 The Language of ES ($\mathcal{L}_{ES}$)

The language $\mathcal{L}_{ES}$ extends that of ASP [1] by the modalities K ('known') and M ('may be true'). Literals of $\mathcal{L}_{ES}$ are divided into four kinds: *objective literals (l), extended objective literals (L), subjective literals (g)* and *extended subjective literals (G)*.

l	L	g	G
p $\mid$ $\sim p$	l $\mid$ not l	K l $\mid$ M l	g $\mid$ not g

where p ranges over a set $\mathbb{P}$ of propositional variables[2]. $\mathcal{L}_{ES}$ has two negations; strong negation $\sim$ and NAF (aka, default negation) not: not φ is read "φ is false by default".

A *rule* is a logical statement of the form '*head $\leftarrow$ body*'. In particular, a rule ρ of ES has the structure 'l_1 or ... or l_m $\leftarrow$ $e_1, \ldots, e_n$' in which $body(\rho)$ viz. '$e_1, \ldots, e_n$' is made up of arbitrary ES literals whereas $head(\rho)$ viz. 'l_1 or ... or l_m' is composed of only objective literals. When $m = 0$, we suppose $head(\rho)$ to be $\perp$ and call the rule ρ a *constraint*. When $n = 0$, we suppose $body(\rho)$ to be $\top$ and call the rule ρ a *fact*.

---

[2] The use of variables in ES is understood as abbreviations for the collection of their ground instances. Thus, for simplicity, we restrict here the language $\mathcal{L}_{ES}$ to the propositional case.

An *epistemic logic program* is a finite collection of the rules of ES. Here is Gelfond's *eligibility* program Π_G, motivating us for the need of modal operators in ASP[3]:

$$\Pi_G = \Big\{ e \leftarrow h \mid e \leftarrow f, m \mid \sim e \leftarrow \sim h, \sim f \mid h \text{ or } f \leftarrow \mid i \leftarrow \text{not K} e, \text{not K} \sim e \quad (1)$$

in which h stands for *highGPA*; f for *fairGPA*; e for *eligible*; m for *minority*; i for *interview*. The first three rules of Π_G indicate the college rules to decide eligibility for scholarship. When we consider these rules with a database, consisting of a disjunctive information given by the fact 'h or f' for a specific student, note that NAF alone is not sufficient anymore to formalise the statement "*a student whose eligibility is not determined by the college rules should be interviewed*". The correct representation is given by using modalities, able to quantify over belief sets, viz. '$i \leftarrow \text{not K} e, \text{not K} \sim e$'.

2.2 The Semantics of ES

Let $\mathcal{A}$ be a non-empty collection of consistent sets of objective literals, and let $A \in \mathcal{A}$. Satisfaction of literals is defined by: for an objective literal l and a subjective literal g,

$\mathcal{A}, A \models_{\text{ES}} l$ if $l \in A$;

$\mathcal{A}, A \models_{\text{ES}} \text{K} l$ if $l \in A$ for every $A \in \mathcal{A}$;

$\mathcal{A}, A \models_{\text{ES}} \text{M} l$ if $l \in A$ for some $A \in \mathcal{A}$;

$\mathcal{A}, A \models_{\text{ES}} \text{not } l$ if $l \notin A$.

$\mathcal{A}, A \models_{\text{ES}} \text{not } g$ if $\mathcal{A} \not\models_{\text{ES}} g$.

Note that satisfaction of an objective literal l is independent of $\mathcal{A}$, while satisfaction of a subjective literal g is independent of A. Thus, we sometimes write $\mathcal{A} \models_{\text{ES}} g$ or $A \models_{\text{ES}} l$. Then, satisfaction of an epistemic logic program Π is defined by: for every rule $\rho \in \Pi$,

$$\mathcal{A}, A \models_{\text{ES}} \rho \quad \text{viz.} \quad \text{"} \mathcal{A}, A \models_{\text{ES}} body(\rho) \text{ implies } \mathcal{A}, A \models_{\text{ES}} head(\rho)\text{"}.$$

Finally, given an epistemic logic program Π, whether $\mathcal{A}$ is a world view of Π is decided as follows: we first compute the reduct $\Pi^{\mathcal{A}} = \{ \rho^{\mathcal{A}} : \rho \in \Pi \}$ of Π with respect to $\mathcal{A}$, in which we eliminate K and M according to Table 1. Then, $\mathcal{A}$ is a *world view* of Π (w.r.t. [18]) if $\mathcal{A} = \text{AS}(\Pi^{\mathcal{A}})$ where $\text{AS}(\Pi^{\mathcal{A}})$ denotes the set of all answer sets of $\Pi^{\mathcal{A}}$.

For example, the only world view of Π_G (see (1)) is $\{\{h, e, i\}, \{f, i\}\}$. Table 2 contains more examples with focus on disjunctive information, among which the ones emphasising the necessity for a refinement of Gelfond's versions [8,9,11] are given in bold.

Then, Kahl extended his version [18] to allow for expressions, formed from objective literals being preceded by a sequence of not's and a modal operator (K or M). Major forms of such expressions are included in Tables 3, 4 and 5, together with the equivalence relations they are involved in.

---

[3] We use '|' (a bit informally) to separate the rules of a program in this paper.

Table 1. Kahl's definition of reduct

literal G	if $\mathcal{A} \models_{ES} G$	if $\mathcal{A} \not\models_{ES} G$
$K\,l$	replace by l	replace by $\perp$
$M\,l$	replace by $\top$	replace by not not l
not $K\,l$	replace by $\top$	replace by not l
not $M\,l$	replace by not l	replace by $\perp$

Table 2. Epistemic logic programs and their world views

epistemic logic program Π	world views	
p or $q \leftarrow$	$\{\{p\},\{q\}\}$	
$p \leftarrow$ not $K\,p$	no world view	
$p \leftarrow K\,p$	$\{\emptyset\}$	(in [8,9] : $\{\emptyset\}$ and $\{\{p\}\}$)
$p \leftarrow M\,p$	$\{\{p\}\}$	(in [8,9,11] : $\{\emptyset\}$ and $\{\{p\}\}$)
$q \leftarrow$ **not** $Kp \mid p \leftarrow$ **not** q	$\{\{q\}\}$	(in [8,9,11] : $\{\{p\}\}$ and $\{\{q\}\}$)
$p \leftarrow$ not $Kq \mid q \leftarrow$ not Kp	$\{\{p\}\}$ and $\{\{q\}\}$	
p or $q \leftarrow \mid p \leftarrow M\,q$	$\{\{p\}\}$	(in [8,9,11] : no world view)
p or $q \leftarrow \mid p \leftarrow$ not $K\,q$	$\{\{p\}\}$	
p or $q \leftarrow \mid r \leftarrow K\,p$	$\{\{p\},\{q\}\}$	
p or $q \leftarrow \mid p \leftarrow K\,q$	$\{\{p\},\{q\}\}$	
p or $q \leftarrow \mid p \leftarrow$ not $M\,q$	$\{\{p\},\{q\}\}$	

Table 3. Equivalence relations of multiply negated literals by NAF

exp_1	exp_2	Comment
not l	not not not l	an odd number of not $\equiv$ not
not not l	not not not not l	an even number (> 0) of not $\equiv$ not not

Table 4. Equivalence relations of extended subjective literals

exp_1	exp_2	Comment
$K\,l$	not M not l	
$M\,l$	not K not l	K and M are dual:
not $K\,l$	M not l	they can be expressed interchangeably.
not $M\,l$	K not l	

Table 5. Equivalences with modal operators and double not

exp_1	exp_2	exp_3	Comment
$K\,l$	K not not l	not not $K\,l$	NAF behaves classically here:
$M\,l$	M not not l	not not $M\,l$	double 'not' vanishes.

Soon after, [4] pointed at another program, $\Pi = \{p \leftarrow \mathsf{M}\,q, \mathsf{not}\,q \mid q \leftarrow \mathsf{M}\,p, \mathsf{not}\,p$ giving unintended world views under Kahl's refined version. Indeed, [18] proposes two world views $\{\emptyset\}$ and $\{\{p\}, \{q\}\}$, of which the former seems to be unintended. Following this example, Kahl et al. [20] came up with another update to address the issue, with semantics supporting only the latter: inspired by [29] (see Sect. 4), they first define

$$\mathrm{Ep}(\Pi) = \{G \ : \ G = \mathsf{not}\,\mathsf{K}\,L \text{ for some extended objective literal } L \text{ and } G$$
$$\text{appears in } \Pi\}.$$

Note that the set $\mathrm{Ep}(\Pi)$ checks all extended subjective literals occurring in Π and by using the equivalences between $\mathsf{notnotK}\,p$ and $\mathsf{K}\,p$, as well as $\mathsf{notKnot}p$ and $\mathsf{M}\,p$, picks the forms $\mathsf{not}\,\mathsf{K}\,L$ (for an extended objective literal L) in their structure. To illustrate this set, consider the program $\Gamma = \{t \leftarrow \mathsf{K}\,p, \mathsf{M}\,q, \mathsf{notK}\,r, \mathsf{notM}\,s\}$. Thus, $\mathrm{Ep}(\Gamma) = \{\mathsf{notK}\,p, \mathsf{notKnot}q, \mathsf{notK}\,r, \mathsf{notKnot}s\}$. Then, they take the subset $\Phi_{\mathcal{A}} = \{G \in \mathrm{Ep}(\Pi) \ : \ \mathcal{A} \models_{\mathsf{ES}} G\}$ w.r.t. a candidate model $\mathcal{A}$. Finally, $\mathcal{A}$ is a world view of Π if:

$$\mathcal{A} = \mathrm{AS}(\Pi^{\mathcal{A}}), \text{ and there is no } \mathcal{A}' \text{ such that } \mathcal{A}' = \mathrm{AS}(\Pi^{\mathcal{A}'}) \text{ and } \Phi_{\mathcal{A}'} \supset \Phi_{\mathcal{A}}.$$

On the one hand, as mentioned in [3,19], researchers have now discovered another problem: different from their effect on answer sets in ASP[4], in ES inserting a constraint into a program may now bring out completely new world views. The reason is because here constraints show their effect on its belief sets rather than a world view as a whole. So, not only Kahl's all versions, but also [4,29] suffer from new counterintuitive results produced over acyclic programs while they are trying to obtain the intuitive understanding of the behaviour of cycles. Interestingly, only in Gelfond's first version [8,9], and its generalisation [34] by Truszczyński, constraints function to rule out world views, violating that constraint (as desired). To sum up, as a negative outcome of added complexity, the recent semantics approaches seem to have lost this property. On the other hand, as argued in [29], Kahl's reduct definition offers a complex program transformation, lacking an intuitive explanation for the replacement of subjective literals.

Let us terminate our discussion with two examples: $\Pi_1 = \{p \leftarrow \mathsf{K}\,p \mid p \leftarrow \mathsf{not}\,\mathsf{K}\,p$ and $\Pi_2 = \{p \leftarrow \mathsf{M}\,p \mid p \leftarrow \mathsf{not}\,\mathsf{M}\,p$. As Kahl obtains no world view for Π_1, he gets a unique world view $\{\{p\}\}$ for Π_2. However, the body parts of these programs produce a tautology (see the equivalence relations given in Table 5), so it is strange to see two different solutions according to his semantics approach, but not $\{\{p\}\}$ only for both.

---

[4] In ASP, constraints show their effect on programs by eliminating or keeping their answer sets.

3   Fariñas et al.'s Approach: Autoepistemic Equilibrium Models

In 2015, Fariñas et al. [4] proposed the *autoepistemic equilibrium models* (AEEMs) approach as an alternative semantics for ES. This section briefly recalls their approach.

3.1   Epistemic Here-and-There Logic (**EHT**) and Its Equilibrium Models

EHT extends the logic of here-and-there (HT) [15] by (nondual) epistemic modal operators K and $\hat{K}$, of which K is the same as K in ES, but [4] never explains the meaning and reading of $\hat{K}$. Note that as shown later via an example, the modal operator M in ES is translated to $\neg K \neg$ in EHT. An EHT model is a collection of HT models. It can also be described as a refinement of S5 models (sets of valuations) [2] in which valuations are replaced by HT models. Formally, an *EHT model* is an ordered pair $\langle \mathcal{T}, \hbar \rangle$ in which

- $\mathcal{T} \subseteq 2^{\mathbb{P}}$ is a nonempty set of valuations (i.e., a classical S5 model);
- $\hbar : \mathcal{T} \to 2^{\mathbb{P}}$ is a map, assigning to each *there*-world $T \in \mathcal{T}$ a *here*-world $\hbar(T) \subseteq T$.

Epistemic equilibrium models (EEMs) of a formula $\varphi \in \mathcal{L}_{\mathsf{EHT}}$ are then defined as particular S5 models satisfying a minimality condition [4] (similar to that of [27])[5]:

$$\mathrm{EEM}(\varphi) = \left\{ \mathcal{T} \subseteq 2^{\mathbb{P}} : \mathcal{T}, \mathcal{T} \models_{\mathsf{s5}} \varphi \text{ and there is no } h \neq id \text{ such that } \langle \mathcal{T}, \hbar \rangle, \mathcal{T} \models_{\mathsf{EHT}} \varphi \right\}.$$

A typical ES program Π is translated into an EHT theory Π^* via a map $(.)^*$ as in:

$$\Pi = \left\{ p \text{ or } \sim q \leftarrow \mathsf{M} r, \text{not } s \mid q \leftarrow \text{not } \mathsf{K} p \right.$$

$$\Pi^* = \left((\neg \mathsf{K} \neg r \wedge \neg s) \to (p \vee \tilde{q}) \right) \wedge \left(\neg \mathsf{K} p \to q \right) \wedge \neg (q \wedge \tilde{q}).$$

The EEM approach fails to give intuitive results, especially in the presence of disjunction. Gelfond's example Π_G (see (1)) immediately supports this fact (see Table 6 for more examples): Π_G has a unique world view $\{\{h, e, i\}, \{f, i\}\}$, but Π_G^* has three EEMs: $\mathcal{T}_1 = \{\{h, e, i\}, \{f, i\}\}$, $\mathcal{T}_2 = \{\{h, e\}\}$ and $\mathcal{T}_3 = \{\{f, i\}\}$, among which $\mathcal{T}_2$ is unintended. To overcome this problem, [4] uses a *selection process* over EEMs and proposes *autoepistemic equilibrium models* (AEEMs)[6].

---

[5] For the truth conditions of EHT, you can refer to [4].

[6] However, as in Kahl's approach, adding a constraint into a program may also give here unexpected results. For instance, take the eligibility program Π_G and a constraint $\leftarrow i$. Then, the resulting EHT theory $\Pi_G^* \cup \{\neg i\}$ has a unique AEEM $\mathcal{T}_2 = \{\{h, e\}\}$, instead of having no AEEM.

The AEEM approach can handle a more general language, but its way of choosing intuitive models is highly complex: the AEEM semantics depends on two orderings, set inclusion $\subseteq$ and a preference ordering $\leq_\varphi$, which function simultaneously. So, it is possible in principle that two EEMs can eliminate each other w.r.t. their different orderings. To spell it out, it could happen that $\mathcal{T}_1 \subset \mathcal{T}_2$, but also $\mathcal{T}_2 <_\varphi \mathcal{T}_1$ for $\mathcal{T}_1, \mathcal{T}_2 \in \text{EEM}(\varphi)$. For instance, let $\varphi = p \vee r \vee \mathsf{K}\,(p \vee q)$. Then, $\text{EEM}(\varphi) = \{\{\{p\}\}, \{\{r\}\}, \{\{q\}\}, \{\{p\}, \{q\}\}, \{\{p\}, \{r\}\}\}$, among which there are two satisfying the condition above: $\{\{p\}, \{q\}\} <_\varphi \{\{p\}\}$ and $\{\{p\}\} \subset \{\{p\}, \{q\}\}$. Fortunately, in this case, $\text{AEEM}(\varphi) = \{\{\{p\}, \{r\}\}\}$ since $\{\{p\}\} \subset \{\{p\}, \{r\}\}$ and $\{\{p\}, \{q\}\} <_\varphi \{\{p\}, \{r\}\}$. One immediate question is if $\{\{p\}, \{q\}\}$ is indeed unintended. Briefly, this approach may be suffering from such a clash in the selection process although none has been found so far.

4   Shen and Eiter's Approach: Epistemic Negation

In 2016, Shen et al. [29,30] proposed a new semantics for ES. The idea is to use $\mathsf{not\,K}$ (which they call *epistemic negation*) to minimise knowledge in the set of all belief sets. Given an epistemic logic program Π and a nonempty collection $\mathcal{A} \subseteq 2^\mathbb{P}$ of consistent sets of objective literals, let $\text{Ep}(\Pi)$ (see Sect. 2.2) be the set of all epistemic negations appearing in Π, and let $\Phi \subseteq \text{Ep}(\Pi)$ be its subset (which they call a *guess*). Let $\Phi_\mathcal{A} = \{G \in \text{Ep}(\Pi) : \mathcal{A} \models G\}$ be the set of all epistemic negations in Π, satisfied by $\mathcal{A}$. Then, we transform Π into an epistemic reduct Π^Φ w.r.t. Φ by replacing every $\mathsf{not\,K}\,L \in \Phi$ with $\top$ and every $\mathsf{not\,K}\,L \in \text{Ep}(\Pi) \setminus \Phi$ with $\mathsf{not}\,L$. Finally, $\mathcal{A}$ is a world view of Π if

1. $\mathcal{A} = \text{AS}(\Pi^\Phi) = \{A : A \text{ is an answer set of } \Pi^\Phi\}$;
2. $\Phi_\mathcal{A}$ agrees with Φ, i.e., $\Phi_\mathcal{A} = \Phi$;
3. Φ is maximal, i.e., there is no bigger guess $\Phi' \supset \Phi$ such that $\mathcal{A}' = \text{AS}(\Pi^{\Phi'})$ and $\Phi_{\mathcal{A}'} = \Phi'$ for some nonempty collection $\mathcal{A}'$ of consistent sets of objective literals.

Let us illustrate their approach by an important application and motivation of ES: *Closed World Assumption* (CWA), which says that *"p is assumed to be false if there is no evidence to the contrary"* and is expressed in ASP by $\sim p \leftarrow \mathsf{not}\,p$[7]. However, it is formalised more adequately in ES as $\sim p \leftarrow \mathsf{not\,M}\,p$ by [12] or $\sim p \leftarrow \mathsf{not\,K}\,p$ by [29]. For instance, let $\Pi = \{\widetilde{p} \leftarrow \mathsf{not\,K}\,p \mid \bot \leftarrow p, \widetilde{p}\}$. Then, take the guess $\Phi = \{\mathsf{not\,K}\,p\}$. Thus, $\Pi^\Phi = \{\widetilde{p} \leftarrow \top \mid \bot \leftarrow p, \widetilde{p}\}$. Clearly, $\text{AS}(\Pi^\Phi) = \{\{\widetilde{p}\}\}$ and $\{\{\widetilde{p}\}\} \models_{\text{ES}} \Phi$. Since Φ is the maximal guess possible (see item 3 above), $\{\{\widetilde{p}\}\}$ is the unique world view of Π.

---

[7] However, this formalisation was then discovered to cause problems [12]. Consider $\Pi = \{p \text{ or } q \mid \sim p \leftarrow \mathsf{not}\,p\}$. Then, $\text{AS}(\Pi) = \{\{p\}, \{q, \sim p\}\}$, and it answers the query $\sim p$? unknown (as it does not appear in both answer sets) while p is undetermined. This result is unintended.

5 Our Approach: Epistemic ASP (E-ASP) and Its Epistemic Views

This section introduces an epistemic extension of ASP called *epistemic ASP*. We begin with a discussion on our motivation and the main differences with other approaches.

5.1 Motivation and Novelty

The problem of incomplete information in ASP still matters after more than two decades of research on the subject. Despite their successes, the approaches [4,20,29] are not fully satisfactory, and some of their seemingly intuitive results are still under discussion.

Compared to Kahl's language [18], we introduce a simpler language. We propose a modest syntax character, allowing only one epistemic operator K. However, different from ES, K may also appear in the head of a rule. We find our language strong enough to solve the problem of incomplete information in ASP because most of the critical examples in the literature, including Gelfond's Π_G (1) and the new formalisation of CWA, use notK only to solve the quantification problem. Note that Kahl and others use also M as dual of K. Besides, we more naturally extend the syntax of ASP through the same structure of program rules, allowing not to appear only in front of literals. Note that Kahl and others use it in a literal formation as notK, notKnot, Knot etc.

The semantics of the new language is via an *epistemic view*, which is a straightforward generalisation of the answer set notion in ASP. Different from world view semantics, our semantics approach exploits a two-fold computation procedure, by splitting the program into two levels: we first look for if the candidate model, which is involved in the reduction process, is a maximal minimal model of the first level. Our reduct definition is oriented to eliminate NAF in a similar way with that of ASP. Existing reduct definitions simplify the program by removing subjective literals in the form of Kl, Ml, $notKl$ and $notMl$ (but, not '$notl$') for an objective literal l. So, our reduct is always a positive program containing no NAF in it. The minimality condition is understood in the sense of set inclusion. It is given by checking the minimality of each set making up the (biggest possible) collection. This is similar to the method, searching for answer sets. Second, we check if such minimal models of the first level are compatible with the second level, composed of only the constraints of the main program. So, we aim to solve the recent constraint problem discussed in Sect. 2.2. We find the semantics approaches of [18,29] a bit nonstandard: first, is it a right attitude to eliminate the "positive" constructs in the form of Kl and Ml especially while world views of ES are given as kind of S5 models? Second, why do we force each valuation in such S5 models to be an answer set of the resulting program? In ES, we ask the query to the collection as a whole rather than its elements separately. At least, there is something going wrong in these approaches as always a new unintended model is being discovered, and then the reduction definitions have to be changed. To end with, our semantics approach can also be more smoothly adapted to E-ASP programs with NAF in the head [16] and to E-ASP programs with nested expressions [23], also including subjective literal $K\,l$.

5.2   The Language of Epistemic ASP ($\mathcal{L}_{\text{E-ASP}}$)

Literals (λ) of $\mathcal{L}_{\text{E-ASP}}$ are of two types: *objective literals (l)* and *subjective literals (g)*.

l		g	
p	$\sim p$	$K\,p$	$K\sim p$

in which $p \in \mathbb{P}$, and $\sim$ denotes strong negation. $K\,l$ is read "*l* is known". Different from ES, we do not allow NAF to appear in a literal formation. However, NAF can precede any literal λ in the body of a rule, and $\text{not}\,\lambda$ means that: *there is no evidence for λ, and so, the query λ? is undetermined.* Again, different from ES, we allow $K\,l$ to appear in the head of a rule. Thus, an E-ASP program is defined as a finite collection of rules

$$\lambda_1 \text{ or } \ldots \text{ or } \lambda_k \leftarrow \lambda_{k+1}, \ldots, \lambda_m, \text{not } \lambda_{m+1}, \ldots, \text{not } \lambda_n$$

in which λ_i's are arbitrary (objective or subjective) literals. When we restrict λ_i's to objective literals, the resulting program is a disjunctive logic program [14]. Hence, E-ASP rules are conservative extensions of ASP's disjunctive rules. As we follow the same structure, extensions to richer languages are straightforward via the main ASP track.

5.3   The Semantics of Epistemic ASP

The semantics of E-ASP is given by an *epistemic view*. Similar to a world view, it is a nonempty collection of consistent sets of objective literals. What we substantially differ is how we pick such intuitive models from among all models of an epistemic program. Let Π be an E-ASP program. We first split Π into two disjoint parts. The set of all constraints $r_c \in \Pi$ constitutes the upper layer ('*top*'), symbolised by $\overline{\Pi}$. This is the part of the program where we decide the ultimate epistemic views of Π through the process: *refute, accept* or *reorganise*. The rest, i.e., the set $\Pi \setminus \overline{\Pi}$ forms the lower layer ('*bottom*'), where we determine the collections of possible belief sets. We denote it by $\underline{\Pi}$.

Example 1. Given a program

$$\Sigma = \left\{ p \leftarrow \text{not } \sim q \mid \sim q \leftarrow \text{not } p \mid r \leftarrow \text{not } K\,p \mid \leftarrow \text{not } r \right. \tag{2}$$

we have $\underline{\Sigma} = \left\{ p \leftarrow \text{not } \sim q \mid \sim q \leftarrow \text{not } p \mid r \leftarrow \text{not } K\,p \right.$ and $\overline{\Sigma} = \left\{ \leftarrow \text{not } r \right.$

We start by computing the epistemic views of $\underline{\Pi}$, each of which are then involved in an evaluation process carried out in $\overline{\Pi}$. However, if $\underline{\Pi} = \emptyset$, then $\text{EV}(\Pi) = \text{EV}(\overline{\Pi})$, where $\text{EV}(\Pi)$ denotes the set of all epistemic views of Π. In this case, the epistemic view of the program is either $\{\emptyset\}$ or none. For instance, $\mathrm{EV}(\{\leftarrow p\}) = \{\{\emptyset\}\}$. Recall that $\leftarrow p$ has a unique answer set, namely $\emptyset$. If $\mathrm{EV}(\underline{\Pi}) = \emptyset$, then $\mathrm{EV}(\Pi) = \emptyset$. When $\overline{\Pi} = \emptyset$, $\mathrm{EV}(\Pi) = \mathrm{EV}(\underline{\Pi})$.

Our reduct based semantics is oriented to eliminate only NAF as in ASP. Remember that NAF appears as part of a construct $\mathbf{not}\,\lambda$ in an E-ASP program in which λ is an arbitrary literal. We here follow a "guess-and-check" method: let $\mathcal{A}$ be a nonempty collection of consistent sets of objective literals, and let $A \in \mathcal{A}$. Then, $\langle \mathcal{A}, A \rangle$ is a sort of pointed (3-valued) S5 model with A being the *actual* world. In an explicit representation, we simply underline the actual world A in a collection $\mathcal{A}$. The partial valuation of A assigns *true* to p if $p \in A$ and *false* if $\sim p \in A$ (*undefined* otherwise). The reduct $\underline{\Pi}^{\langle \mathcal{A}, A \rangle}$ of $\underline{\Pi}$ w.r.t. $\langle \mathcal{A}, A \rangle$ is given by replacing every occurrence of $\mathbf{not}\,\lambda$ with[8]

R.1 $\perp$ if $\mathcal{A}, A \models_{\text{E-ASP}} \lambda$ (simply, for $\lambda = l$ if $A \models_{\text{E-ASP}} l$; for $\lambda = \mathsf{K}\,l$ if $\mathcal{A} \models_{\text{E-ASP}} \mathsf{K}\,l$);

R.2 $\top$ if $\mathcal{A}, A \not\models_{\text{E-ASP}} \lambda$ (simply, for $\lambda = l$ if $A \not\models_{\text{E-ASP}} l$; for $\lambda = \mathsf{K}\,l$ if $\mathcal{A} \not\models_{\text{E-ASP}} \mathsf{K}\,l$).

Example 2. Given a pointed model $\{\underline{\{p\}}, \{\sim q\}\}$, consider (2) above. Then, $\underline{\Sigma}^{\{\underline{\{p\}},\{\sim q\}\}} = \{p \leftarrow \top \mid \sim q \leftarrow \perp \mid r \leftarrow \top$ since $\{p\} \not\models_{\text{E-ASP}} \sim q$, $\{p\} \models_{\text{E-ASP}} p$ and $\{\{p\}, \{\sim q\}\} \not\models_{\text{E-ASP}} \mathsf{K}\,p$. Now, we replace $\mathbf{not}\,\mathsf{K}\,p$ by $\mathsf{K}\,p$ and $\mathbf{not}\,r$ by $\mathbf{not}\,\mathsf{K}\,r$ in Σ and call the resulting program Γ:

$$\Gamma = \Big\{ p \leftarrow \mathbf{not}\,\sim q \mid \sim q \leftarrow \mathbf{not}\,p \mid r \leftarrow \mathsf{K}\,p \mid \leftarrow \mathbf{not}\,\mathsf{K}\,r. \tag{3}$$

Then, $\underline{\Gamma}^{\{\underline{\{p\}},\{\sim q\}\}} = \{p \leftarrow \perp \mid \sim q \leftarrow \top \mid r \leftarrow \mathsf{K}\,p$ since $\{\sim q\} \models_{\text{E-ASP}} \sim q$, but $\{\sim q\} \not\models_{\text{E-ASP}} p$.

Thus, our reduct definition simplifies a program, removing only NAF w.r.t. R.1 and R.2.

First of all, we introduce a *truth-minimality* criterion, based on set inclusion over each set A making up a collection $\mathcal{A}$: let $\mathbb{O}\text{-}Lit$ be the set of all objective literals of $\mathcal{L}_{\text{E-ASP}}$, and let $\mathbf{s} : \mathcal{A} \to 2^{\mathbb{O}\text{-}Lit}$ be a (subset) map such that $\mathbf{s}(A) \subseteq A$ for every $A \in \mathcal{A}$. (When $\mathbf{s}$ equals the identity map id, we obtain $\mathcal{A}$ itself.) Then, a *weakening* of $\mathcal{A}$ at a point $A \in \mathcal{A}$ is identified with $\langle \mathbf{s}[\mathcal{A}], \mathbf{s}(A) \rangle$ such that $\mathbf{s} \neq id$ and $\mathbf{s}|_{\mathcal{A} \setminus \{A\}} = id$, by which we take a strict subset of $A \in \mathcal{A}$ and do not modify the rest. We say that $\langle \mathbf{s}[\mathcal{A}], \mathbf{s}(A) \rangle$ is *weaker* than $\langle \mathcal{A}, A \rangle$ and denote it by $\langle \mathbf{s}[\mathcal{A}], \mathbf{s}(A) \rangle \lhd \langle \mathcal{A}, A \rangle$. For example, the weakenings of $\{\underline{\{p, \sim q\}}, \{r\}\}$ are $\{\underline{\{p\}}, \{r\}\}$, $\{\underline{\{\sim q\}}, \{r\}\}$ and $\{\underline{\emptyset}, \{r\}\}$. Finally, we define a nonmonotonic satisfaction relation $\models^*$ for pointed (three-valued) S5 models: $\mathcal{A}, A \models^* \Pi$ if and only if

$$\mathcal{A}, A \models_{\text{E-ASP}} \Pi \text{ and } \mathbf{s}[\mathcal{A}], \mathbf{s}(A) \not\models_{\text{E-ASP}} \Pi \text{ for every } \mathbf{s} \text{ viz. } \langle \mathbf{s}[\mathcal{A}], \mathbf{s}(A) \rangle \lhd \langle \mathcal{A}, A \rangle$$

where the latter condition says that none of the weakenings of $\langle \mathcal{A}, A \rangle$ is a model of Π.

---

[8] The satisfaction relation $\models_{\text{E-ASP}}$ of E-ASP is the same as the relation $\models_{\text{ES}}$ (see Sect. 2.2).

Definition 1. *Let $\mathcal{A} \subseteq 2^{\mathcal{O}\text{-}Lit}$ be a nonempty set of consistent sets of objective literals. Then, $\mathcal{A}$ is a minimal model of Π if $\mathcal{A}, A \models^* \Pi^{\langle \mathcal{A}, A \rangle}$ for every $A \in \mathcal{A}$.*

Example 3. $\{\{p\}, \{\sim q\}\}$ is a minimal model of $\underline{\Gamma}$ (3): $\underline{\Gamma}^{\{\{p\}, \{\sim q\}\}} = \{p \leftarrow \ | \ r \leftarrow \mathsf{K}p$ and $\{\{p\}, \{\sim q\}\} \models_{\text{E-ASP}} \underline{\Gamma}^{\{\{p\}, \{\sim q\}\}}$ while its weakening $\{\emptyset, \{\sim q\}\}$ refutes it. Likewise, $\underline{\Gamma}^{\{\{p\}, \{\sim q\}\}} = \{\sim q \leftarrow \ | \ r \leftarrow \mathsf{K}p$ and $\{\{p\}, \{\sim q\}\} \models_{\text{E-ASP}} \underline{\Gamma}^{\{\{p\}, \{\sim q\}\}}$ while its only weakening $\{\{p\}, \emptyset\}$ does not satisfy it. Clearly, $\{\{p, r\}\}$ and $\{\{\sim q\}\}$ are the other minimal models of $\underline{\Gamma}$. Similarly, $\{\{p, r\}, \{\sim q, r\}\}$ is a minimal model of $\underline{\Sigma}$ (2): indeed, $\underline{\Sigma}^{\{\{p,r\}, \{\sim q,r\}\}} = \{p \leftarrow \ | \ r \leftarrow$ and it is obvious that $\{\{p, r\}, \{\sim q, r\}\}$ satisfies it while all its weakenings refute it. We also have $\underline{\Sigma}^{\{\{p,r\}, \{\sim q,r\}\}} = \{\sim q \leftarrow \ | \ r \leftarrow$ and $\{\{p, r\} \{\sim q, r\}\} \models_{\text{E-ASP}} \underline{\Sigma}^{\{\{p,r\}, \{\sim q,r\}\}}$ while any of its weakenings violates it. The other two minimal models of $\underline{\Sigma}$ are $\{\{\sim q, r\}\}$ and $\{\{p\}\}$. In each program, the last two minimal models (i.e., the singleton models[9]) are unintended.

As seen above, minimality of truth does not always guarantee intuitive results. Therefore, we will now introduce a criterion to choose intended models among all such minimal models. Given an E-ASP program Π, we first define a Π-indexed partial preorder (denoted by $\preceq_\Pi$) over three-valued S5 models by: $\mathcal{A} \preceq_\Pi \mathcal{A}'$ if and only if

$$\mathcal{A} \cup \mathcal{A}', A \models_{\text{E-ASP}} \Pi \text{ for all } A \in \mathcal{A} \text{ implies } \mathcal{A} \cup \mathcal{A}', A' \models_{\text{E-ASP}} \Pi \text{ for all } A' \in \mathcal{A}'. \tag{4}$$

The strict version of $\preceq_\Pi$ is given as usual: $\mathcal{A} \prec_\Pi \mathcal{A}'$ iff $\mathcal{A} \preceq_\Pi \mathcal{A}'$ and $\mathcal{A}' \npreceq_\Pi \mathcal{A}$. If $\mathcal{A} \preceq_\Pi \mathcal{A}'$ and $\mathcal{A}' \preceq_\Pi \mathcal{A}$, then $\mathcal{A}$ is *equivalent* to $\mathcal{A}'$ w.r.t. $\preceq_\Pi$ (denoted by $\mathcal{A} \approx_\Pi \mathcal{A}'$).

Example 4. The program $\Upsilon = \{p \text{ or } q \ | \ p \leftarrow \mathsf{notK}q$ has two minimal models: $\{\{p\}\}$ and $\{\{q\}\}$, among which $\{\{q\}\} \prec_\Upsilon \{\{p\}\}$ since $\{\{p\}, \{q\}\} \models_{\text{E-ASP}} \Upsilon$, but $\{\{p\}, \{q\}\} \not\models_{\text{E-ASP}} \Upsilon$.

Definition 2. *$\mathcal{A} \subseteq 2^{\mathcal{O}\text{-}Lit}$ is an* epistemic view *of a "constraint-free" program Π if*

1. *$\mathcal{A}$ is a minimal model of Π;*
2. *there is no minimal model $\mathcal{A}'$ of Π such that $\mathcal{A} \prec_\Pi \mathcal{A}'$;*

---

[9] Singleton minimal models of a program Π are sometimes source of a problem in capturing intuitive results: for a singleton set, $\mathsf{K}p$ and p are of no difference, as well as $\mathsf{notK}p$ and $\mathsf{not}p$. Thus, an E-ASP program performs like an ASP program, and we may obtain "unjustified" minimal models. For instance, in $\underline{\Sigma}$, if we replace notK with not, the resulting ASP program has the answer sets $\{p\}$ and $\{\sim q, r\}$. Note that $\{\{p\}\}$ and $\{\{\sim q, r\}\}$ are minimal models of $\underline{\Sigma}$. We get a similar result if we change $\mathsf{K}p$ with p in $\underline{\Gamma}$. Thus, singleton sets do not allow us to quantify over all possible beliefs. In order to overcome this obstacle, we need to check the behaviour of singletons in an interplay with other minimal models by using an ordering.

Example 4, cont. Thus, $\mathrm{EV}(\Upsilon) = \{\{\{p\}\}\}$. Let $\Lambda = \{p \leftarrow \mathrm{not}\, q \mid q \leftarrow \mathrm{not}\mathsf{K}\, p$. Clearly, $\{\{p\}\}$ and $\{\{q\}\}$ are the only minimal models of Λ. Recall that for singletons, Λ behaves as an ASP program $\Lambda' = \{p \leftarrow \mathrm{not}q \mid q \leftarrow \mathrm{not}p$ and Λ' has 2 answer sets $\{p\}$ and $\{q\}$. So, again we cannot quantify over all beliefs. Indeed, $\{\{p\}, \{q\}\} \not\models_{\text{E-ASP}} \Lambda$, but $\{\{p\}, \{q\}\} \models_{\text{E-ASP}} \Lambda$. Thus, we have $\{\{p\}\} \prec_\Lambda \{\{q\}\}$. Consequently, $\mathrm{EV}(\Lambda) = \{\{\{q\}\}\}$.

Example 5. We have seen that $\varSigma$ (2) and $\varGamma$ (3) have 3 minimal models. Among these, we have the order, $\{\{p\}\} \prec_\varSigma \{\{\sim q, r\}\} \approx_\varSigma \{\{p, r\}, \{\sim q, r\}\}$ and $\{\{\sim q\}\} \approx_\varGamma \{\{p, r\}\} \approx_\varGamma \{\{p\}, \{\sim q\}\}$. So, the ordering $\preceq_\Pi$ is not strong enough to rule out all unintended models. When this is the case, we need to apply a third condition to compare equivalent models w.r.t. $\preceq_\Pi$.

We now introduce a *knowledge-minimising* condition: Let $\mathbb{L}(.)$ represent the set of objective literals occurring in any syntactic construct (head, body, etc). We first consider the set $\mathcal{H}_\Pi = \bigcup_{r \in \Pi} \mathbb{L}(head(r))$ of all objective literals occurring in the head parts of a program Π. For example, $\mathcal{H}_{\underline{\varSigma}} = \mathcal{H}_\varSigma = \mathcal{H}_\varGamma = \mathcal{H}_{\underline{\varGamma}} = \{p, \sim q, r\}$ (see (2) and (3)). Note that belief sets A's of an epistemic view $\mathcal{A}$ of Π can only contain literals from $\mathcal{H}_\Pi$[10]. Inspired by [29] (but, in a different way), we define the set of all *unknowns* among the literals in $\mathcal{H}_\Pi$ w.r.t. $\mathcal{A}$ and denote it by $\varPhi_{\mathcal{A}}^\Pi = \{l \in \mathcal{H}_\Pi : \mathcal{A} \models_{\text{E-ASP}} \mathrm{not}\,\mathsf{K}\, l\}$.

Definition 2, cont.

3. $\varPhi_{\mathcal{A}}^\Pi$ is maximal, i.e., there is no minimal model $\mathcal{A}'$ of Π such that $\varPhi_{\mathcal{A}}^\Pi \subset \varPhi_{\mathcal{A}'}^\Pi$.

Intuitively, item 3 means $\mathcal{A}$ to answer maximum possible head-literals *undetermined*.

Example 5, cont. If we reconsider the above $\preceq_\varSigma$-equivalent and $\preceq_\varGamma$-equivalent minimal models, then we see that $\{p, \sim q\} = \varPhi_{\{\{p,r\}, \{\sim q,r\}\}}^{\varSigma} \supset \varPhi_{\{\{\sim q,r\}\}}^{\varSigma} = \{p\}$. As a result, $\mathrm{EV}(\varSigma) = \{\{\{p, r\}, \{\sim q, r\}\}\}$. Similarly, $\varPhi_{\{\{p\}, \{\sim q\}\}}^{\varGamma} = \{p, \sim q, r\}$, $\varPhi_{\{\{\sim q\}\}}^{\varGamma} = \{p, r\}$ and $\varPhi_{\{\{p,r\}\}}^{\varGamma} = \{\sim q\}$. Then, we have: $\varPhi_{\{\{p\}, \{\sim q\}\}}^{\varGamma} \supset \varPhi_{\{\{\sim q\}\}}^{\varGamma}$ and $\varPhi_{\{\{p\}, \{\sim q\}\}}^{\varGamma} \supset \varPhi_{\{\{p,r\}\}}^{\varGamma}$. Thus, $\mathrm{EV}(\varGamma) = \{\{\{p\}, \{\sim q\}\}\}$.

Remark 1. Note that there is also an order between the orders of item 2 and item 3: we only use item 3 over minimal models of Π that are maximal, but equivalent w.r.t. $\preceq_\Pi$.

Example 6. We now consider Gelfond's program Π_G (1): Π_G has 3 minimal models, namely $\mathcal{A}_1 = \{\{f, i\}\}$, $\mathcal{A}_2 = \{\{h, e\}\}$ and $\mathcal{A}_3 = \{\{f, i\}, \{h, e, i\}\}$, among which $\mathcal{A}_2 \prec_\Pi \mathcal{A}_3 \approx_\Pi \mathcal{A}_1$. Thus, we need to check the unknowns of $\mathcal{A}_3$ and $\mathcal{A}_1$. Since $\{e, \sim e, h, f\} = \varPhi_{\mathcal{A}_3}^{\Pi_G} \supset \varPhi_{\mathcal{A}_1}^{\Pi_G} = \{e, \sim e, h\}$, we have $\mathrm{EV}(\Pi_G) = \{\mathcal{A}_3\}$. However, we may not always compare maximal $\preceq_\Pi$-equivalent minimal models: let $\varOmega = \{p \leftarrow \mathrm{not}\mathsf{K}\, q \mid q \leftarrow \mathrm{not}\mathsf{K}\, p$. $\varOmega$ has two minimal models $\{\{p\}\}$ and $\{\{q\}\}$ such that

---

[10] Fact [in ASP]: if $A \in \mathrm{AS}(\Pi)$, then every $l \in A$ belongs to the head of one of the rules in Π.

$\{\{p\}\} \approx_{\Omega} \{\{q\}\}$ since $\{\{p\}, \{q\}\} \not\models_{\text{E-ASP}} \Omega$ and $\{\{p\}, \{q\}\} \not\models_{\text{E-ASP}} \Omega$. Moreover, $\Phi^{\Omega}_{\{\{p\}\}} = \{q\}$ and $\Phi^{\Omega}_{\{\{q\}\}} = \{p\}$. As a result, $\text{EV}(\Omega) = \{\{\{p\}\}, \{\{q\}\}\}$.

When a program Π contains constraints, i.e, $\overline{\Pi} \neq \emptyset$, we first compute $\text{EV}(\overline{\Pi})$ as explained above. Then, we evaluate each $\mathcal{A} \in \text{EV}(\overline{\Pi})$ w.r.t. their behaviour on $\overline{\Pi}$: take $\varphi = \bigvee_{r_c \in \overline{\Pi}} body(r_c)$. For every $A \in \mathcal{A}$, if $\mathcal{A}, A \not\models_{\text{E-ASP}} \varphi$, then we *accept* $\mathcal{A}$ and call it $\mathcal{A}_{accept}$; else if $\mathcal{A}, A \models_{\text{E-ASP}} \varphi$, then we *eliminate* $\mathcal{A}$ and call it $\mathcal{A}_{refute}$. Finally, we reorganise the rest in such a way that we take the biggest possible subset $\mathcal{A}_{new} \subseteq \mathcal{A}$ such that $\mathcal{A}_{new}$ is still a minimal model of $\overline{\Pi}$ and $\mathcal{A}_{new}, A \not\models_{\text{E-ASP}} \varphi$, for every $A \in \mathcal{A}_{new}$. As a result, $\text{EV}(\Pi)$ is the collection of all $\mathcal{A}_{accept}$'s and $\mathcal{A}_{new}$'s. Note that when $\overline{\Pi}$ exclusively contains the constraints composed of only (negated) subjective literals, we either refute or accept the epistemic views of $\overline{\Pi}$.

Example 5, cont. We have seen that $\text{EV}(\Sigma) = \{\{\{p, r\}, \{\sim q, r\}\}\}$ and $\text{EV}(\Gamma) = \{\{\{p\}, \{\sim q\}\}\}$. As $\{\{p\}, \{\sim q\}\}$ violates $\leftarrow \text{not} Kr$, it fails to be the epistemic view of the program Γ (*refute!*). Hence, $\text{EV}(\Gamma) = \emptyset$. However, as $\{\{p, r\}, \{\sim q, r\}\} \models_{\text{E-ASP}} r$, it satisfies $\leftarrow \text{not} r$, and so, it passes the test (*accept!*). Thus, $\text{EV}(\Sigma) = \{\{\{p, r\}, \{\sim q, r\}\}\}$.

Example 7. Let $\Delta = \{p \text{ or } q \leftarrow \ | \ r \text{ or } s \leftarrow \text{not} Kp \ | \ \leftarrow r$. It is easy to see that

$$\text{EV}(\Delta) = \{\{\{p, r\}, \{q, r\}, \{p, s\}, \{q, s\}\}\}.$$

Then, since $\{\{p, r\}, \{q, r\}, \{p, s\}, \{q, s\}\} \models_{\text{E-ASP}} r$, we have to remove the actual worlds $\{p, r\}$ and $\{q, r\}$, resulting in a new collection $\{\{p, s\}, \{q, s\}\}$ (*reorganise!*). As a result, $\text{EV}(\Delta) = \{\{\{p, s\}, \{q, s\}\}\}$. However, while $\text{EV}(\Delta \cup \{\leftarrow Ks\}) = \text{EV}(\Delta)$, $\text{EV}(\Delta \cup \{\leftarrow Ks\}) = \emptyset$.

Example 8. Let $\Psi_1 = \{\leftarrow Kp, \text{not} q\}$ and $\Psi_2 = \{\leftarrow \text{not} Kp\}$ be the one rule (constraint) E-ASP programs. As mentioned above, the only candidate epistemic view is $\{\emptyset\}$ for Ψ_1 and Ψ_2. Since $\{\emptyset\} \not\models_{\text{E-ASP}} q$ and $\{\emptyset\} \not\models_{\text{E-ASP}} Kp$, we have $\Psi_1^{\{\emptyset\}} = \{\leftarrow Kp, \top\}$ and $\Psi_2^{\{\emptyset\}} = \{\leftarrow \top\}$. Clearly, $\text{EV}(\Psi_1) = \{\{\emptyset\}\}$ and $\text{EV}(\Psi_2) = \emptyset$.

5.4   Comparison of Epistemic Views with World Views and AEEMs

We here compare epistemic views with world views and AEEMs over some examples. Table 6 illustrates all these approaches. Overall, epistemic views of an E-ASP program perform well, aligning with its world views and AEEMs. However, one striking advantage of our method over existing semantics is its reasonable behaviour with programs including constraints: we have seen that $\text{EV}(\Gamma) = \{\{\{p\}, \{\sim q\}\}\}$ and $\text{EV}(\Gamma) = \emptyset$. However, while Γ has a unique world view (AEEM) $\{\{p\}, \{\sim q\}\}$, when we add a constraint $\leftarrow \text{not} Kr$ into Γ, the resulting program Γ has another world view (AEEM) $\{\{p, r\}\}$, violating the above property (see the last two examples of Table 6 as well).

To end with, Shen et al. [29] discuss that Pearce's equilibrium semantics suffers from circular justifications and relatedly claim that [4] inherits the same

Table 6. World views by both [20] and [29], AEEMs (bold), and epistemic views (bold)

program Π	world views	EEMs of Π^*	epistemic views
p or $q \leftarrow$	$\{\{p\},\{q\}\}$	$\{\{p\}\} \subset \{\{p\},\{q\}\}$ $\{\{q\}\} \subset \{\{p\},\{q\}\}$ $\{\{p\}\} \approx_{\Pi^*} \{\{q\}\} \approx_{\Pi^*} \{\{p\},\{q\}\}$	$\{\{p\},\{q\}\}$ minimal models (mm): $\{\{p\}\}$, $\{\{q\}\}$ and $\{\{p\},\{q\}\}$
p or $q \leftarrow$ $p \leftarrow Kq$	$\{\{p\},\{q\}\}$	$\{\{p\}\} \subset \{\{p\},\{q\}\}$ $\{\{p\}\} \approx_{\Pi^*} \{\{p\},\{q\}\}$	$\{\{p\},\{q\}\}$ mm: $\{\{p\}\}$ and $\{\{p\},\{q\}\}$
p or $q \leftarrow$ $p \leftarrow$ not Kq	$\{\{p\}\}$	$\{\{q\}\} <_{\Pi^*} \{\{p\}\}$ (incomparable w.r.t. $\subseteq$)	$\{\{p\}\}$ mm: $\{\{p\}\}$
CWA: p or $q\leftarrow$ $\bar{p}\leftarrow$not$K\,p$ $\perp\leftarrow p,\bar{p}$	$\{\{q,\bar{p}\}\}$	$\{\{p\}\} <_{\Pi^*} \{\{q,\bar{p}\}\}$ (incomparable w.r.t. $\subseteq$)	$\{\{q,\bar{p}\}\}$ mm: $\{\{p\}\}$ and $\{\{q,\bar{p}\}\}$
p or $q \leftarrow$ $r \leftarrow Kp$	$\{\{p\},\{q\}\}$	$\{\{p,r\}\} <_{\Pi^*} \{\{p\},\{q\}\}$ $\{\{q\}\} \subset \{\{p\},\{q\}\}$ $\{\{q\}\} \approx_{\Pi^*} \{\{p\},\{q\}\}$	$\{\{p\},\{q\}\}$ mm: $\{\{q\}\}$, $\{\{p,r\}\}$, and $\{\{p\},\{q\}\}$
$p \leftarrow$ q or $r \leftarrow Kp$	$\{\{p,q\},\{p,r\}\}$	$\{\{p,q\}\} \subset \{\{p,q\},\{p,r\}\}$ $\{\{p,r\}\} \subset \{\{p,q\},\{p,r\}\}$ $\{\{p,q\}\}\approx_{\Pi^*}\{\{p,r\}\}\approx_{\Pi^*}\{\{p,q\},\{p,r\}\}$	$\{\{p,q\},\{p,r\}\}$ mm: $\{\{p,r\}\}$, $\{\{p,q\}\}$, and $\{\{p,q\},\{p,r\}\}$
$p \leftarrow Kp$	$\{\emptyset\}$	$\{\emptyset\}$	$\{\emptyset\}$
$p \leftarrow Kp$ $p \leftarrow$ not Kp	none	none	none no minimal models
$p \leftarrow Kq$ $q \leftarrow Kp$	$\{\emptyset\}$	$\{\emptyset\}$	$\{\emptyset\}$ mm: $\{\emptyset\}$
$p \leftarrow q$ $q \leftarrow Kp$	$\{\emptyset\}$	$\{\emptyset\}$	$\{\emptyset\}$ mm: $\{\emptyset\}$
$p \leftarrow$ not q $q \leftarrow$ not Kp	$\{\{q\}\}$	$\{\{p\}\} <_{\Pi^*} \{\{q\}\}$ (incomparable w.r.t. $\subseteq$)	$\{\{q\}\}$ mm: $\{\{p\}\}$ and $\{\{q\}\}$
$p \leftarrow$ not Kq $q \leftarrow$ not Kp	$\{\{p\}\}$ and $\{\{q\}\}$	$\{\{p\}\}$ and $\{\{q\}\}$ (incomparable w.r.t. $\subseteq$ and $\leq_{\Pi^*}$)	$\{\{p\}\}$ and $\{\{q\}\}$ mm: $\{\{p\}\}$ and $\{\{q\}\}$
p or $q\leftarrow$ $\leftarrow$ not Kp	$\{\{p\}\}$	$\{\{p\}\}$	none no minimal models
p or $q\leftarrow$ $r \leftarrow$ not Kq $\leftarrow p$	$\{\{q\}\}$	$\{\{q\}\}$	none no minimal models

circularity, leading to some undesired results. One supporting example is $\Pi = \{p \leftarrow \text{not}Kp \mid p \leftarrow p$. [29] argues that Π has no AEEMs, but in fact, $\{\{p\}\}$ is expected to be its unique world view since $\text{not}Kp \vee p$ constitutes a tautology. However, for $\{\{p\}\}$, this formula is of no difference than $\text{not}p \vee p$ and it is hard to believe that the latter is a tautology. Our approach agrees with [4]: since $\{\{p\}\} \not\models_{\text{E-ASP}} \text{not}K\,p$, we have $\Pi^{\{\{p\}\}} = \{p \leftarrow \perp \mid p \leftarrow p$. Clearly, $\{\emptyset\}$ is the unique minimal model of $\Pi^{\{\{p\}\}}$. Thus, $\text{EV}(\Pi) = \emptyset$. Moreover, the first rule of Π intuitively says that *if there is no evidence for* Kp, *then* p *is always true*, so as already agreed by most of the approaches in the literature, this rule does not have a world view in ES. The second rule is just a tautology, giving no information. Under these conditions, Π cannot have a world view in ES.

6 Splitting Epistemic Logic Programs

Cabalar et al. [3] have recently established a formal property called *epistemic splitting*, with which they test if a semantics proposal of ES has a reasonable behaviour when subjective literals are stratified. The idea is to separate a program Π into two disjoint subprograms (if possible), *top* and *bottom*, among which top questions bottom via its subjective literals, and bottom never refers to head literals of top. If splitting is the case w.r.t. a set of literals U, then we calculate world views of Π in four steps: first we compute the world views $\mathcal{A}_b$ of bottom; second for each $\mathcal{A}_b$, we take kind of partial reduct $\Pi_U^{\mathcal{A}_b}$ by replacing subjective literals (whose literals are included in U) of top with their truth values in $\mathcal{A}_b$; third we find the world views $\mathcal{A}_t$ of $\Pi_U^{\mathcal{A}_b}$, and end with a solution $\langle \mathcal{A}_b, \mathcal{A}_t \rangle$ for Π; finally we concatenate the elements of $\mathcal{A}_b$ and $\mathcal{A}_t$, and result in new world views $\mathcal{A}_b \sqcup \mathcal{A}_t = \{A_b \cup A_t \ : \ A_b \in \mathcal{A}_b \text{ and } A_t \in \mathcal{A}_t\}$, answering the queried information.

All proposed semantics trials in the literature fail to satisfy this candidate property, but Gelfond's first version [8], which suffers most, among others, the counterintuitive behaviour of cyclic programs. (Recall that [8] computes two world views $\{\emptyset\}$ and $\{\{p\}\}$ for both $p \leftarrow \mathsf{K}p$ and $p \leftarrow \mathsf{M}p$. For the former rule, while $\{\{p\}\}$ is counterintuitive, for the latter, $\{\emptyset\}$ is counterintuitive, which has been justified by almost all semantics proposals in the literature.) The other semantics that passes epistemic splitting test is Truszczyński's approach [34]. (Remember that [34] produces a world view $\{\emptyset\}$ for the program $p \leftarrow p, \mathsf{not}\,p$, which departs it even from ASP.) Our approach is also compatible with epistemic splitting property because first, in a splittable program we can always put all (and only) constraints composed of just (negated) subjective literals into topmost layer since they are headless, and they do not contain objective literal conjuncts, and the rest of the constraints will appear in the below layers; second, we can compute the epistemic views of the lower layers as defined in Sect. 2.2 by dividing each layer into two parts where constraints are located at the top; finally, we evaluate the final epistemic views according to the truth values of topmost subjective literals conjuncts in the candidate world view by keeping or eliminating candidate epistemic views.

Example 9. We can split Γ (see (3)) into 3 layers: $L_0 = \{p \leftarrow \mathsf{not}{\sim}q \mid {\sim}q \leftarrow \mathsf{not}\,p, L_1 = \{r \leftarrow \mathsf{K}p$ and $L_2 = \{ \leftarrow \mathsf{not}\mathsf{K}r$. Then, $\mathsf{EV}(L_0) = \{\{\{p\}, \{{\sim}q\}\}\}$ and $\mathsf{EV}(L_1^{\{\{p\}, \{{\sim}q\}\}}) = \mathsf{EV}(r \leftarrow \bot) = \{\{\emptyset\}\}$. Next, $\mathsf{EV}(L_0 \cup L_1) = \{\{\{p\}, \{{\sim}q\}\}\}$. Finally, since $\mathsf{EV}(L_2^{\{\{p\}, \{{\sim}q\}\}}) = \mathsf{EV}(\leftarrow \top) = \emptyset$, we have $\mathsf{EV}(\Gamma) = \emptyset$.

7 Conclusion

In this paper, we propose a neat and more standard epistemic extension of ASP (E-ASP). E-ASP is a strong rival to existing approaches in the sense that: we introduce a simpler and more intuitive semantics, which will be better suited for knowledge representation, and the design of intelligent agents. The new reduct definition, which is similar to that of ASP, will hopefully lead to an efficient implementation of an E-ASP program solver, allowing the new language to be of more practical use. We will search first if ASP technology can be exploited to compute epistemic views. E-ASP provides a solid framework for further language extensions of ASP. Therefore, we also plan to adapt previous language extensions of ASP to E-ASP. Finally, we would like to propose a new epistemic extension of equilibrium logic, embedding E-ASP as well.

References

1. Baral, C., Gelfond, M.: Logic programming and knowledge representation. J. Log. Program. **19**, 73–148 (1994)
2. Blackburn, P., de Rijke, M., Venema, Y.: Modal Logic. Cambridge Tracts in Theoretical Computer Science. Cambridge University Press, Cambridge (2001)
3. Cabalar, P., Fandinno, J., Fariñas del Cerro, L.: Splitting epistemic logic programs. In: Proceedings of the 17th International Workshop on Nonmonotonic Reasoning, NMR 2018, Tempe, Arizona, USA, 27–29 October 2018 (2018)
4. Fariñas del Cerro, L., Herzig, A., Su, E.I.: Epistemic equilibrium logic. In: Yang, Q., Wooldridge, M. (eds.) Proceedings of the 24th International Joint Conference on Artificial Intelligence, pp. 2964–2970. AAAI Press (2015). http://ijcai.org/papers15/Abstracts/IJCAI15-419.html
5. Chen, J.: The generalized logic of only knowing (GOL) that covers the notion of epistemic specifications. J. Log. Comput. **7**(2), 159–174 (1997)
6. Clark, K.L.: Negation as failure. In: Gallaire, H., Minker, J. (eds.) Logic and Data Bases, Symposium on Logic and Data Bases, Centre d'études et de recherches de Toulouse, France. Advances in Data Base Theory, pp. 293–322. Plemum Press, New York (1977)
7. Gabbay, D.M.: What is negation as failure? In: Artikis, A., Craven, R., Kesim Çiçekli, N., Sadighi, B., Stathis, K. (eds.) Logic Programs, Norms and Action. LNCS (LNAI), vol. 7360, pp. 52–78. Springer, Heidelberg (2012). https://doi.org/10.1007/978-3-642-29414-3_5
8. Gelfond, M.: Strong introspection. In: Dean, T.L., McKeown, K. (eds.) Proceedings of the 9th National Conference on Artificial Intelligence, Anaheim, CA, USA, 14–19 July 1991, vol, 1, pp. 386–391. AAAI Press/The MIT Press (1991)
9. Gelfond, M.: Logic programming and reasoning with incomplete information. Ann. Math. Artif. Intell. **12**(1–2), 89–116 (1994)
10. Gelfond, M.: Answer sets. In: Handbook of Knowledge Representation, vol. 1, p. 285 (2008)
11. Gelfond, M.: New semantics for epistemic specifications. In: Delgrande, J.P., Faber, W. (eds.) LPNMR 2011. LNCS (LNAI), vol. 6645, pp. 260–265. Springer, Heidelberg (2011). https://doi.org/10.1007/978-3-642-20895-9_29
12. Gelfond, M.: New definition of epistemic specifications. In: KR Seminar. Texas Tech University, 28 April 2011. (talk)
13. Gelfond, M., Lifschitz, V.: The stable model semantics for logic programming. In: Kowalski, R.A., Bowen, K.A. (eds.) Logic Programming, Proceedings of the Fifth International Conference and Symposium, Seattle, Washington, USA, 15–19 August 1988, vol. 2, pp. 1070–1080. MIT Press (1988)

14. Gelfond, M., Lifschitz, V.: Classical negation in logic programs and disjunctive databases. New Gener. Comput. **9**(3/4), 365–386 (1991)
15. Heyting, A.: Die formalen Regeln der intuitionistischen Logik. Sitzungsber. Preuss. Akad. Wiss. **42–71**, 158–169 (1930)
16. Inoue, K., Sakama, C.: Negation as failure in the head. J. Log. Program. **35**(1), 39–78 (1998)
17. Kahl, P., Watson, R., Balai, E., Gelfond, M., Zhang, Y.: The language of epistemic specifications (refined) including a prototype solver. J. Log. Comput. (2015)
18. Kahl, P.T.: Refining the semantics for epistemic logic programs. Ph.D. thesis, Texas Tech University, Department of Computer Science, Lubblock, TX, USA, May 2014
19. Kahl, P.T., Leclerc, A.P.: Epistemic logic programs with world view constraints. In: Palù, A.D., Tarau, P., Saeedloei, N., Fodor, P. (eds.) Technical Communications of the 34th International Conference on Logic Programming, ICLP 2018, Oxford, United Kingdom, 14–17 July 2018. OpenAccess Series in Informatics OASICS, vol. 64, pp. 1:1–1:17. Schloss Dagstuhl - Leibniz-Zentrum fuer Informatik (2018). https://doi.org/10.4230/OASIcs.ICLP.2018.1
20. Kahl, P.T., Leclerc, A.P., Son, T.C.: A parallel memory-efficient epistemic logic program solver: harder, better, faster. CoRR abs/1608.06910 (2016). http://arxiv.org/abs/1608.06910
21. Kowalski, R.A.: Logic programming. In: Siekmann, J.H. (ed.) Computational Logic, Handbook of the History of Logic, vol. 9, pp. 523–569. Elsevier (2014). https://doi.org/10.1016/B978-0-444-51624-4.50012-5
22. Leclerc, A.P., Kahl, P.T.: A survey of advances in epistemic logic program solvers. abs/1809.07141 (2018). http://arxiv.org/abs/1809.07141. (Also in the Proceedings of the 11th International Workshop on Answer Set Programming and other Computer Paradigms, ASPOCP 2018, Oxford, UK, 18 July 2018)
23. Lifschitz, V., Tang, L.R., Turner, H.: Nested expressions in logic programs. Ann. Math. Artif. Intell. **25**(3–4), 369–389 (1999)
24. Marek, V.W., Truszczynski, M.: Stable models and an alternative logic programming paradigm. CoRR cs.LO/9809032 (1998). http://arxiv.org/abs/cs.LO/9809032
25. Niemelä, I.: Logic programs with stable model semantics as a constraint programming paradigm. Ann. Math. Artif. Intell. **25**(3–4), 241–273 (1999). https://doi.org/10.1023/A:1018930122475
26. Pearce, D.: A new logical characterisation of stable models and answer sets. In: Dix, J., Pereira, L.M., Przymusinski, T.C. (eds.) NMELP 1996. LNCS, vol. 1216, pp. 57–70. Springer, Heidelberg (1997). https://doi.org/10.1007/BFb0023801
27. Pearce, D.: Equilibrium logic. Ann. Math. Artif. Intell. **47**(1–2), 3–41 (2006)
28. Przymusinski, T.C.: On the relationship between logic programming and nonmonotonic reasoning. In: Shrobe, H.E., Mitchell, T.M., Smith, R.G. (eds.) Proceedings of the 7th National Conference on Artificial Intelligence, St. Paul, MN, USA, 21–26 August 1988, pp. 444–448. AAAI Press/The MIT Press (1988). http://www.aaai.org/Library/AAAI/1988/aaai88-078.php
29. Shen, Y., Eiter, T.: Evaluating epistemic negation in answer set programming. Artif. Intell. **237**, 115–135 (2016). https://doi.org/10.1016/j.artint.2016.04.004
30. Shen, Y., Eiter, T.: Evaluating epistemic negation in answer set programming (extended abstract). In: Sierra, C. (ed.) Proceedings of the 26th International Joint Conference on Artificial Intelligence, IJCAI 2017, Melbourne, Australia, 19–25 August 2017, pp. 5060–5064. ijcai.org (2017). https://doi.org/10.24963/ijcai.2017/722

31. Son, T.C., Le, T., Kahl, P.T., Leclerc, A.P.: On computing world views of epistemic logic programs. In: Proceedings of the 26th International Joint Conference on Artificial Intelligence, IJCAI 2017, Melbourne, Australia, 19–25 August 2017, pp. 1269–1275 (2017). https://doi.org/10.24963/ijcai.2017/176
32. Stalnaker, R.: What is a nonmonotonic consequence relation? Fundam. Inform. **21**(1/2), 7–21 (1994)
33. Su, E.I.: Extensions of equilibrium logic by modal concepts. (Extensions de la logique d'équilibre par des concepts modaux). Ph.D. thesis, Institut de Recherche en Informatique de Toulouse, France (2015). https://tel.archives-ouvertes.fr/tel-01636791
34. Truszczyński, M.: Revisiting epistemic specifications. In: Balduccini, M., Son, T.C. (eds.) Logic Programming, Knowledge Representation, and Nonmonotonic Reasoning. LNCS (LNAI), vol. 6565, pp. 315–333. Springer, Heidelberg (2011). https://doi.org/10.1007/978-3-642-20832-4_20
35. Wang, K., Zhang, Y.: Nested epistemic logic programs. In: Baral, C., Greco, G., Leone, N., Terracina, G. (eds.) LPNMR 2005. LNCS (LNAI), vol. 3662, pp. 279–290. Springer, Heidelberg (2005). https://doi.org/10.1007/11546207_22
36. Watson, R.: A splitting set theorem for epistemic specifications. CoRR cs.AI/0003038 (2000). http://arxiv.org/abs/cs.AI/0003038
37. Zhang, Y.: Updating epistemic logic programs. J. Log. Comput. **19**(2), 405–423 (2009). https://doi.org/10.1093/logcom/exn100
38. Zhang, Y., Zhang, Y.: Epistemic specifications and conformant planning. In: Barták, R., McCluskey, T.L., Pontelli, E. (eds.) Proceedings of the 2017 Workshop on Knowledge-Based Techniques for Problem Solving and Reasoning (KnowProS 2017) (2017)
39. Zhang, Z.: Introspecting preferences in answer set programming. In: Palù, A.D., Tarau, P., Saeedloei, N., Fodor, P. (eds.) Technical Communications of the 34th International Conference on Logic Programming, ICLP 2018, 14–17 July 2018, Oxford, United Kingdom. OASICS, vol. 64, pp. 3:1–3:13. Schloss Dagstuhl - Leibniz-Zentrum fuer Informatik (2018). https://doi.org/10.4230/OASIcs.ICLP.2018.3

Modal and Default Logic

A Logic of Objective and Subjective Oughts

Aldo Iván Ramírez Abarca[(✉)] and Jan Broersen

Utrecht University, 3512 JK Utrecht, The Netherlands
{a.i.ramirezabarca,J.M.broersen}@uu.nl

Abstract. The relation between agentive action, knowledge, and obligation is central to the understanding of responsibility – a main topic in Artificial Intelligence. Based on the view that an appropriate formalization of said relation would contribute to the development of ethical AI, we point out the main characteristics of a logic for objective and subjective oughts that was recently introduced in the literature. This logic extends the traditional stit paradigm with deontic and epistemic operators, and provides a semantics that deals with Horty's puzzles for knowledge and obligation. We provide an axiomatization for this logic, and address its soundness and completeness with respect to a class of relevant models.

1 Introduction

AI developers face a big challenge in creating systems that are expected to make ethically charged decisions. The field of machine ethics has seen a quick growth in recent years, and questions regarding *responsibility* of autonomous agents are very important. In our opinion, these questions can be categorized in two main trends: (1) *conceptual* questions that deal with the ontology and essential components of the notion of responsibility, and (2) *technical* questions concerning the implementation of such notion in AI. This work attempts to make a contribution in the *technical* category. We take part in a very specific line of research, where proof systems of deontic logic are intended to help in the testing of ethical behavior of AI through theorem proving [2,4,10]. That being said, answers to the technical kind of questions typically presuppose a particular choice of philosophical standpoint against questions of the first kind, the conceptual one. Our philosophical standpoint comes from John Horty's framework of act utilitarian stit logic [9], extended with epistemic relations. As such, we make explicit the goal of the present paper: to provide well-behaved formalizations of 3 essential components of responsibility of intelligent systems: *agentive action*, *knowledge*, and *obligation*.

According to [2], having an *expressive deontic logic with practical relevance* and an efficient algorithm for proving theorem-hood is highly applicable in the construction of logic-based ethical robots.[1] To support this statement, Arkoudas

---

[1] See [11] for an overview of the advantages and disadvantages of doing machine ethics via theorem proving.

© Springer Nature Switzerland AG 2019
F. Calimeri et al. (Eds.): JELIA 2019, LNAI 11468, pp. 629–641, 2019.
https://doi.org/10.1007/978-3-030-19570-0_41

et al. present in [2] a natural deduction calculus for a logic of ought-to-do that
was developed by Horty in [9] and axiomatised by Murakami in [10]. With an
interactive theorem proving system named ATHENA, they illustrate the fact that
we can mechanize deontic logic to do machine ethics.

The starting point of our work comes from a recent interest in enhancing both
the expressivity and practical relevance of Horty's stit theory of ought-to-do in
order to deal with situations in which agents' *knowledge* becomes significant.
Inspired by 3 puzzles for knowledge-dependent obligations that pose a problem
for merely extending his initial logic with epistemic operators, Horty presents in
[7] a novel semantics for *epistemic oughts* based on *action types*. Although the
approach is substantial, it comes with 3 disadvantages: (1) it diverges from his
work in [9], (2) there are semantic constraints that limit the expressivity of the
models, and (3) the use of action types precludes an efficient axiomatization.[2]

With similar motivations as Horty, the extended abstract [6] proposes an
alternative logic – where the main idea is to distinguish objective from subjective
obligations – that allegedly mitigates the disadvantages mentioned above. The
authors claim that this logic is simpler, more naturally connected to Horty's work
in [9], and axiomatizable. Being very brief, [6] only deals with the conceptual
benefits of the proposal, and the proof of soundness and completeness of the
logic's proof system is only mentioned. Here, we recover the definition of this
logic, address its benefits, and show that its proof system is indeed sound and
complete with respect to a class of relevant models. We do this hoping that the
results will give some background to new developments in the mechanization of
deontic logic for ethical AI, in the aforementioned tradition of [2,4].

The paper is structured as follows. After a short presentation of stit and its
applications in the modeling of action, knowledge, and obligation, we go through
Horty's puzzles. We mention his solution to them and justify the claim that his
approach with action types comes with disadvantages. Afterwards, we present
the logic developed by [6], show how it solves Horty's puzzles, and deal with its
axiomatizability.[3]

2   Action, Knowledge, and Obligation in Stit

We want to consider oughts from the perspective that an agent should be excused
for having failed at an obligation if it lacks the necessary knowledge to perform
a required task (*doctors ought to stop the bleeding of the patient, but if they do
not know how to, they should be excused*). A typical framework for expressing
statements that involve knowledge for required tasks as a component of responsibility is stit logic [3]. Stit logic was created to formalize the concept of *action*,
so it naturally lent itself to the study of *obligation* [9] and of *knowingly doing*
[5], all important elements in the notion of responsibility. For a comprehensive

---

[2] We will justify all these claims in the second section of this paper, after introducing
the 3 puzzles and addressing Horty's solution.

[3] The proof of completeness is dense and technical, so the full proofs of each statement
are provided in the extended version of the present work [1].

review of the interaction of these 3 concepts in the literature, we refer the reader to [12].

The 3 puzzles of Horty that we mentioned in the introduction are actually very good illustrations of how stit deals with action, knowledge, and obligation, but in order to tackle them we need to recover basic definitions of the paradigm known as *act utilitarian stit logic*. In this paradigm, *obligation* stems from a dominance ordering over the set of available actions. The idea is that the effects of the best actions in the ordering – the so-called *optimal* actions – are the obligations of a given agent at a given moment. We proceed to introduce the basic aspects of an extension of act utilitarian stit logic with epistemic modalities, and leave its examples to the section where we present Horty's puzzles.

Definition 1 (Syntax). *Given a finite set Ags of agent names, a countable set of propositions P such that $p \in P$ and $\alpha \in Ags$, the grammar for the formal language $\mathcal{L}_{KO}$ is given by:*

$$\varphi := p \mid \neg\varphi \mid \varphi \wedge \psi \mid \Box\varphi \mid [\alpha]\varphi \mid K_\alpha\varphi \mid \odot[\alpha]\varphi$$

$\Box\varphi$ is meant to express the 'historical necessity' of φ ($\Diamond\varphi$ abbreviates $\neg\Box\neg\varphi$). $[\alpha]\varphi$ stands for 'agent α sees to it that φ'. K_α is the epistemic operator for α. Finally, $\odot[\alpha]\varphi$ is meant to represent that α ought to see to it that φ.

As for the semantics, the structures in which we evaluate formulas of the language $\mathcal{L}_{KO}$ are based on what we call *epistemic act utilitarian branching time frames*.

Definition 2 (Branching time (BT) frames). *A finite-choice epistemic act utilitarian BT-frame is a tuple $\langle T, \sqsubset, \mathbf{Choice}, \{\sim_\alpha\}_{\alpha\in Ags}, \mathbf{Value}\rangle$ such that:*

- *T is a non-empty set of moments and $\sqsubset$ is a strict partial ordering on T satisfying 'no backward branching'. Each maximal $\sqsubset$-chain is called a history, which represents a way in which time might evolve. H denotes the set of all histories, and for each $m \in T$, $H_m := \{h \in H; m \in h\}$. Tuples $\langle m, h\rangle$ are called situations iff $m \in T$, $h \in H$, and $m \in h$. $\mathbf{Choice}$ is a function that maps each agent α and moment m to a finite partition $\mathbf{Choice}_\alpha^m$ of H_m, where the cells of such a partition represent α's available actions at m. $\mathbf{Choice}$ satisfies two constraints:*
  - *(NC) or 'no choice between undivided histories'. - For all $h, h' \in H_m$, if $m' \in h \cap h'$ for some $m' \sqsupset m$, then $h \in L$ iff $h' \in L$ for every $L \in \mathbf{Choice}_\alpha^m$.*
  - *(IA) or 'independence of agency'. - A function s on Ags is called a selection function at m if it assigns to each α a member of $\mathbf{Choice}_\alpha^m$. If we denote by $\mathbf{Select}^m$ the set of all selection functions at m, then we have that for every $m \in T$ and $s \in \mathbf{Select}^m$, $\bigcap_{\alpha\in Ags} s(\alpha) \neq \emptyset$ (see [3] for a discussion of the property).*
- *For $\alpha \in Ags$, $\sim_\alpha$ is the epistemic indistinguishability equivalence relation for agent α.*
- *$\mathbf{Value}$ is a deontic function that assigns to each history $h \in H$ a real number, representing the utility of h.*

As mentioned before, the idea is that obligations come from the optimal actions for a given agent. The optimality of such actions is relative to a dominance ordering of the actions, and this ordering is given by the value of the histories in those actions – itself provided by **Value**. In order to present the semantics for formulas involving the ought-to-do operator, we therefore need some previous definitions. For $\alpha \in Ags$ and $m_* \in T$, we define a dominance ordering $\preceq$ on $\mathbf{Choice}_\alpha^{m_*}$ such that for $L, L' \in \mathbf{Choice}_\alpha^{m_*}$, $L \preceq L'$ iff $\mathbf{Value}(h) \leq \mathbf{Value}(h')$ for every $h \in L, h' \in L'$. We write $L \prec L'$ iff $L \preceq L'$ and $L' \npreceq L$. The optimal set of actions, then, is taken as $\mathbf{Optimal}_\alpha^{m_*} := \{L \in \mathbf{Choice}_\alpha^{m_*}$; there is no $L' \in \mathbf{Choice}_\alpha^{m_*}$ such that $L \prec L'\}$. As is customary, the models and the semantics for the formulas are defined by adding a valuation function to the frames of Definition 2:

Definition 3. *A BT-model $\mathcal{M}$ consists of the tuple that results from adding a valuation function $\mathcal{V}$ to a BT-frame, where $\mathcal{V} : P \to 2^{T \times H}$ assigns to each atomic proposition a set of moment-history pairs. Relative to a model $\mathcal{M}$, the semantics for the formulas of $\mathcal{L}_{KO}$ is defined recursively by the following truth conditions, evaluated at a given situation $\langle m, h \rangle$:*

$$\langle m, h \rangle \models p \qquad \textit{iff} \quad \langle m, h \rangle \in \mathcal{V}(p)$$
$$\langle m, h \rangle \models \neg\varphi \qquad \textit{iff} \quad \langle m, h \rangle \not\models \varphi$$
$$\langle m, h \rangle \models \varphi \wedge \psi \quad \textit{iff} \quad \langle m, h \rangle \models \varphi \textit{ and } \langle m, h \rangle \models \psi$$
$$\langle m, h \rangle \models \Box\varphi \qquad \textit{iff} \quad \forall h' \in H_m, \langle m, h' \rangle \models \varphi$$
$$\langle m, h \rangle \models [\alpha]\varphi \qquad \textit{iff} \quad \forall h' \in \mathbf{Choice}_\alpha^m(h), \langle m, h' \rangle \models \varphi$$
$$\langle m, h \rangle \models K_\alpha\varphi \qquad \textit{iff} \quad \forall\langle m', h' \rangle \textit{ s.t. } \langle m, h \rangle \sim_\alpha \langle m', h' \rangle, \langle m', h' \rangle \models \varphi$$
$$\langle m, h \rangle \models \odot[\alpha]\varphi \quad \textit{iff} \quad \forall L \in \mathbf{Optimal}_\alpha^m, h' \in L \textit{ implies that } \langle m, h' \rangle \models \varphi.$$

Satisfiability, validity on a frame, and general validity are defined as usual. We write $|\varphi|^m$ to refer to the set $\{h \in H_m; \mathcal{M}, \langle m, h \rangle \models \varphi\}$.

2.1 Horty's Puzzles

The 3 puzzles that we have mentioned since the beginning of the paper, and that pose a problem for formalizing epistemic oughts just with the epistemic extension of act utilitarian logic, can be summarized as follows.

Example 1. Agent β places a coin on top of a table – either heads up or tails up – but hides it from agent α. Agent α can bet that the coin is heads up, that it is tails up, or it can refrain from betting. If α bets and chooses correctly, it wins €10. If it chooses incorrectly, it does not win anything, and if it refrains from betting, it wins €5.

The stit diagram that represents *Horty's interpretation* of the situation is included in Fig. 1. In this diagram, we take H to denote the proposition 'β places the coin heads up', T to denote 'β places the coin tails up', BH to denote 'α bets heads', BT to denote 'α bets tails', and G to denote 'α gambles'. In moment m_1, β places the coin on top of the table, so that its available actions

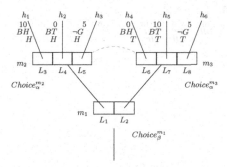

Fig. 1. Coin problem #1

are labeled by L_1 (placing the coin heads up) and L_2 (placing the coin tails up). At moments m_2 and m_3, it is α's turn to act, and the available actions are clear from the picture. The blue dotted line represents the epistemic class of α: since β is hiding the coin, α cannot distinguish whether it is at moment m_2 or m_3.[4] For such an interpretation regarding the epistemic structure of the agent, a problem ensues due to the fact that for every $i \in \{2,3\}$ and $h \in H_{m_i}$, we have that $\langle m_i, h \rangle \models K_\alpha \odot [\alpha]G$. This means that α knows that it ought to gamble, even if this is a 'risky' move that could result in a payoff of 0. In this sense, we could say that the agent's knowledge of what is optimal would lead it into taking a chance and gambling.

Example 2. With the same scheme as in the previous example, if α bets and chooses correctly, it wins €10. If it refrains from betting, it *also* wins €10. If it bets incorrectly, it does not win anything.

Intuitively, α ought to refrain from gambling in this scenario, for refraining implies that it would win by the same amount as when betting correctly but without engaging in an action that could possibly fail. In this case, the problem is that for every $i \in \{2,3\}$ and $h \in H_{m_i}$, we have that $\langle m_i, h \rangle \not\models K_\alpha \odot [\alpha]\neg G$: α does not know that it ought to refrain from gambling. Figure 2 includes the stit diagram for this scenario.

Example 3. With the same scheme as in the previous examples, if α bets and chooses correctly, it wins €10. If it bets incorrectly or refrains from betting, it does not win anything.

The problem here is that for every $i \in \{2,3\}$ and $h \in H_{m_i}$, $\langle m_i, h \rangle \models K_\alpha \odot [\alpha]W$, where W is the proposition that stands for 'α wins'. This means that α knows that it ought to win at any given situation, but such knowledge is not *action-guiding*, meaning that it will not provide α with a choice to make.

---

[4] Notice that Horty's formalization also yields that in none of the situations will α knowingly perform any of the available actions: it cannot epistemically distinguish between the situations in which it is 'betting heads', 'betting tails', or 'refraining'.

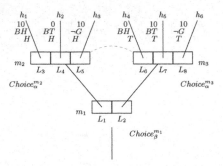

Fig. 2. Coin problem #2

Though the agent knowingly ought to win, it cannot knowingly do so – it simply does not have the means due to a lack of knowledge. Thus, Kant's principle of 'ought implies can' is not satisfied ($\langle m_i, h \rangle \not\models K_\alpha \odot [\alpha]W \to \Diamond K_\alpha [\alpha]W$). Figure 3 includes the stit diagram for this scenario.

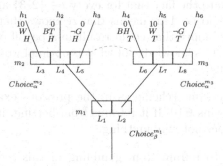

Fig. 3. Coin problem #3

Horty solves these 3 puzzles by introducing both syntactic and semantic addenda to epistemic act utilitarian stit logic. He extends the language with an operator [... kstit] to encode the concept of *ex interim* knowledge (or knowingly doing). The semantics for formulas involving this operator uses *action types*, with the premise that actions of the same *type* may lead to different outcomes in different moments (see [8]). Unfortunately, the introduction of the new operator and of types comes with two unfavorable semantic constraints:

1. In order for [... kstit] to be an **S5** operator, the epistemic relations must ensue not between moment-history pairs but between moments. The problem with this condition is that it limits the class of models to those in which

knowledge is moment-dependent (agents will not be able to know that they perform a given action),[5]

2. Indistinguishable moments must offer the same available types. The problem with this constraint is that it cannot be characterized syntactically without producing an infinite axiomatization. This is due to the fact that performing a certain action type can only be expressed syntactically with propositional constants (again, see [8] for the details).[6]

As a solution to the stated puzzles, Horty's approach is successful. However, [6] claims that we can also be successful without using action types. The benefits of the framework presented in [6], then, include technical characterizability of the constraints imposed on the structures – which is important for axiomatization – semantic simplicity, and enhanced expressivity. In the following section, all these claims will be substantiated.

3   A Logic of Objective and Subjective Oughts

[6] proposes to disambiguate two senses of ought-to-do in order to produce a system that solves Horty's puzzles, avoids action types, and is axiomatizable. The two senses are an *objective* one, which coincides with Horty's act utilitarian ought-to-do, and a *subjective* one, which arises from the epistemically best candidates in the set of available actions for a given agent. By 'epistemically best' we mean those actions that are undominated not only in the actual moment but whose all epistemic equivalents across different indistinguishable situations are also undominated.

Essentially, we are talking about an extension of the language in Definition 1 with a new operator $\odot_S[\alpha]$, meant to build up formulas that would express what α subjectively ought to do. As for the semantics of this new operator, it involves a dominance ordering as well, but one different to that which is used for objective ought-to-do's. In order to define this subjective dominance ordering, [6] introduces a new semantic concept known as *epistemic clusters*, which are nothing more than a given action's epistemic equivalents in situations that are indistinguishable to the actual one. Formally, we have that for $\alpha \in Ags$, $m_*, m \in T$, and $L \subseteq H_{m_*}$, L's *epistemic cluster* at m is the set

$$[L]_\alpha^m := \{h \in H_m; \exists h_* \in L \text{ s.t. } \langle m_*, h_* \rangle \sim_\alpha \langle m, h \rangle\}.$$

As a convention, we write $m \sim_\alpha m'$ if there exist $h \in H_m$, $h' \in H_{m'}$ such that $\langle m, h \rangle \sim_\alpha \langle m', h' \rangle$. The notion of epistemic clusters is used to define a subjective dominance ordering $\preceq_s$ on $\mathbf{Choice}_\alpha^{m_*}$ by the following rule: for $L, L' \in \mathbf{Choice}_\alpha^{m_*}$, $L \preceq_s L'$ iff for every m such that $m_* \sim_\alpha m$, $\mathbf{Value}(h) \leq \mathbf{Value}(h')$ for every $h \in [L]_\alpha^m$, $h' \in [L']_\alpha^m$. Just as in the case of objective ought-to-do's, this ordering allows us to define a subjectively optimal set of actions

---

[5] Horty's models satisfy the following constraint: if $\langle m, h \rangle \sim_\alpha \langle m', h' \rangle$ then $\langle m, h' \rangle \sim_\alpha \langle m', h'' \rangle$ for every $h' \in H_m$, $h'' \in H_{m'}$.

[6] It is an open problem to determine whether there is a finite axiomatization of Horty's logic of epistemic action and obligation if the types were also included in the object language.

$\mathbf{S} - \mathbf{optimal}_\alpha^{m_*} := \{L \in \mathbf{Choice}_\alpha^{m_*}; \text{ there is no } L' \in \mathbf{Choice}_\alpha^{m_*} \text{ s. t. } L \prec_s L'\}$, where we write $L \prec_s L'$ iff $L \preceq_s L'$ and $L' \npreceq_s L$. The idea, then, is that something will be a subjective obligation of a given agent at a given moment if it is an effect of all the subjectively optimal actions of that agent at that moment.

As established in [6], the models in which to evaluate the formulas of the extended language need to satisfy extra constraints in order to capture an appropriate interaction of action, knowledge, and subjective obligation. By this we mean to say that in these models (a) agents should be able to knowingly do the same things across epistemically indistinguishable states, (b) the subjective ought-to-do must conform to Kant's directive of 'ought implies can' in its epistemic version of 'subjectively ought-to-do implies ability of knowingly doing', and (c) if something is a subjective ought-to-do of a given agent, then the agent should know that that is the case. Therefore, we focus on models that fulfill the following requirements, which will grant the conditions mentioned above (as can be seen from the proof of soundness):

- (OAC) For every situation $\langle m_*, h_* \rangle$, if $\langle m_*, h_* \rangle \sim_\alpha \langle m, h \rangle$ for some $\langle m, h \rangle$, then $\langle m_*, h'_* \rangle \sim_\alpha \langle m, h \rangle$ for every $h'_* \in \mathbf{Choice}_\alpha^{m_*}(h_*)$. We refer to this constraint as the 'own action condition', since it implies that agents do not know more than what they perform. Because of this constraint, the knowledge that we are formalizing here is of a very particular kind: to know something is just the same as to knowingly do it.
- (Unif − H) For every situation $\langle m_*, h_* \rangle$, if $\langle m_*, h_* \rangle \sim_\alpha \langle m, h \rangle$ for some $\langle m, h \rangle$, then for every $h'_* \in H_{m_*}$, there exists $h' \in H_m$ such that $\langle m_*, h'_* \rangle \sim_\alpha \langle m, h' \rangle$. Combined with (OAC), this constraint is meant to capture a notion of uniformity of strategies, where epistemically indistinguishable situations should offer similar actions for the agent to choose upon. We call this condition 'uniformity of historical possibility'.

In finite-choice epistemic act utilitarian BT-models that satisfy these two constraints, then, the semantics for the formulas involving $\odot_S[\alpha]$ is defined as expected:

$$\langle m, h \rangle \models \odot_S[\alpha]\varphi \text{ iff } \forall L \in \mathbf{S} - \mathbf{optimal}_\alpha^m, \forall m' \text{ s.t. } m \sim_\alpha m', [L]_\alpha^{m'} \subseteq |\varphi|^{m'}.$$

3.1 Solution to Horty's Puzzles

The semantics for subjective ought-to-do's offers solutions to natural interpretations of Horty's puzzles, in which the assumption that the coin is hidden from the betting agent is captured by taking $\sim_\alpha$ to be defined by the following information sets: $\{\langle m_2, h_1 \rangle, \langle m_3, h_4 \rangle\}$, in which α bets heads; $\{\langle m_2, h_2 \rangle, \langle m_3, h_5 \rangle\}$, in which α bets tails; and $\{\langle m_2, h_3 \rangle, \langle m_3, h_6 \rangle\}$, in which α refrains from betting.

For Example 1, the problem is solved because although $\langle m_i, h_i \rangle \models K_\alpha \odot [\alpha]G$, we consider this as the knowledge of an *objective* ought-to-do. *Subjectively* speaking, we do not obtain that α knows that it ought to gamble: $\langle m_i, h_i \rangle \not\models \odot_S[\alpha]G$ and thus $\langle m_i, h_i \rangle \not\models K_\alpha \odot_S [\alpha]G$. This can be seen by noticing that $\mathbf{S - Optimal}_\alpha^{m_2} = \{L_3, L_4, L_5\}$ and $\mathbf{S - Optimal}_\alpha^{m_3} = \{L_6, L_7, L_8\}$. Figure 4 provides a stit diagram for this scenario.

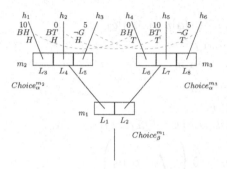

Fig. 4. Coin problem #1, revisited

In Example 2, the problem is solved because $\langle m_i, h_i \rangle \models \odot_S[\alpha]\neg G$ and $\langle m_i, h_i \rangle \models K_\alpha \odot_S [\alpha]\neg G$ (notice that $\mathbf{S - Optimal}_\alpha^{m_2} = \{L_5\}$ and $\mathbf{S - Optimal}_\alpha^{m_3} = \{L_8\}$).

For Example 3, the problem is solved because we obtain that $\langle m_i, h_i \rangle \not\models \odot_S[\alpha]W$, which in turn implies that $\langle m_i, h_i \rangle \not\models K_\alpha \odot_S [\alpha]W$ (notice that $\mathbf{S - Optimal}_\alpha^{m_2} = \{L_3, L_4, L_5\}$ and $\mathbf{S - Optimal}_\alpha^{m_3} = \{L_6, L_7, L_8\}$). Therefore, although α knows that it objectively ought to win, it is not the case that it subjectively ought to win.

When comparing these solutions to Horty's, it is important to point out that the formalization we are using is different from his, for it presupposes that the indistinguishability relation for agent α ensues between *situations*. Regardless of such difference, the solution is virtually the same: for Example 1, Horty gets that for every $h \in H_{m_2}$ $\langle m_2, h \rangle \not\models \odot[\alpha \ \text{kstit}]G$. For Example 2, he gets that for every $h \in H_{m_2}$ $\langle m_2, h \rangle \models \odot[\alpha \ \text{kstit}]\neg G$, and for Example 3, he gets that for every $h \in H_{m_2}$ $\langle m_2, h \rangle \not\models \odot[\alpha \ \text{kstit}]W$. Therefore, we can see that the notion of $\odot_S[\alpha]$ works as an analog of $\odot[... \ \text{kstit}]$.

4   Axiomatization and Some Logical Properties

In this section, we introduce a proof system for the logic presented, address its soundness and completeness results, and mention a few interesting properties of it.

Definition 4 (Proof system). *Let Λ be the proof system defined by the following axioms and rules of inference:*
(Axioms)

- *All classical tautologies from propositional logic.*
- *The **S5** axiom schemata for $\Box$, $[\alpha]$, K_α,[7]*
- *The following axiom schemata for the interactions of formulas with the given operators:*

$$\odot[\alpha](p \to q) \to (\odot[\alpha]p \to \odot[\alpha]q) \tag{A1}$$

$$\Box p \to [\alpha]p \wedge \odot[\alpha]p \tag{A2}$$

$$\Box \odot [\alpha]p \vee \Box\neg \odot [\alpha]p \tag{A3}$$

$$\odot[\alpha]p \to \odot[\alpha]([\alpha]p) \tag{A4}$$

$$\odot[\alpha]p \to \Diamond[\alpha]p \tag{Oic}$$

For $n \geq 1$ and pairwise different $\alpha_1, \ldots, \alpha_n$,

$$\bigwedge_{1\leq k\leq n} \Diamond[\alpha_i]p_i \to \Diamond\left(\bigwedge_{1\leq k\leq n} [\alpha_i]p_i\right) \tag{IA}$$

$$\odot_S[\alpha](p \to q) \to (\odot_S[\alpha]p \to \odot_S[\alpha]q) \tag{A5}$$

$$\odot_S[\alpha]p \to \odot_S[\alpha](K_\alpha p) \tag{A6}$$

$$K_\alpha p \to [\alpha]p \tag{OAC}$$

$$\Diamond K_\alpha p \to K_\alpha\Diamond p \tag{Unif-H}$$

$$K_\alpha\Box p \to \odot_S[\alpha]p \tag{s.N}$$

$$\odot_S[\alpha]p \to \Diamond K_\alpha p \tag{s.Oic}$$

$$\odot_S[\alpha]p \to K_\alpha\Box\odot_S[\alpha]p \tag{Cl}$$

(Rules of inference)

- *Modus Ponens, Substitution, and Necessitation for the modal operators.*

Schema (IA) encodes 'independence of agency'. (OAC) encodes the 'own action condition'. $(Unif-H)$ encodes the 'uniformity of historical possibility' constraint. (Oic) and $(s.Oic)$ concern the objective, resp. subjective, versions of Kant's directive of 'ought implies can'. $(s.N)$ (standing for 'subjective necessity') captures that all that is historically necessary at epistemically indistinguishable situations must be a subjective obligation, and (Cl) (standing for 'closure') characterizes a property that says that if one subjectively ought to do something, then one knows that is settled.

The axiom system Λ turns out to be sound and complete with respect to the class of epistemic act utilitarian *bi-valued* BT-models. Such models are more general than the ones introduced in Definition 3. Instead of only one value function, there are two: one for the objective ought-to-do's, and the other

---

[7] The **S5** axiom schemata are standard from modal logic, and we include their names here just for coherence. They are (K), (T), (4), and (5).

for the subjective ones.[8] These models, then, are of the form $\langle T, \sqsubset, \mathbf{Choice},$ $\{\sim_\alpha\}_{\alpha \in Ags}, \mathbf{Value}_O, \mathbf{Value}_S\rangle$. As such, the models in Definition 3 are particular instances of bi-valued models, in which both value functions assign the same value to each history of the tree.

Furthermore, our soundness and completeness results presuppose a logic of ought-to-do that deals with the 'sure-thing principle', according to which the ranking of the available actions of a given agent should take into consideration what all the other agents choose concurrently. For a given agent, the action profiles of the other agents are seen as the possible states in which the agent will act (see [9], Chapter 4, subsection 4.1.2). We implement Horty's approach for dealing with the 'sure-thing principle' in the logic that we axiomatize, and this means that the semantics that we use is in fact a generalization of the one introduced before. In order to address such a generalization and the soundness and completeness results, we need further definitions:

For $m \in T$ and $\beta \in Ags$, we define

$$\mathbf{State}_\beta^m = \{S \subseteq H_m; S = \bigcap_{\alpha \in Ags - \{\beta\}} s(\alpha), \text{ where } s \in \mathbf{Select}^m\}.$$

With this notion of states, we redefine the dominance orderings so that the actions are measured taking into consideration the states which those actions are facing. For $\alpha \in Ags$ and $m_* \in T$, we first define a general ordering $\leq$ on $\mathcal{P}(H_{m_*})$ such that for $X, Y \subseteq H_{m_*}$, $X \leq Y$ iff $\mathbf{Value}_O(h) \leq \mathbf{Value}_O(h')$ for every $h \in X, h' \in Y$. The objective dominance ordering $\preceq$ is now defined such that for $L, L' \in \mathbf{Choice}_\alpha^{m_*}$, $L \preceq L'$ iff $\forall S \in \mathbf{State}_\alpha^{m_*}, L \cap S \leq L' \cap S$. As for the subjective ought-to-do's, we first define a general ordering $\leq_s$ on $\mathcal{P}(H_{m_*})$ such that for $X, Y \subseteq H_{m_*}$, $X \leq_s Y$ iff $\mathbf{Value}_S(h) \leq_s \mathbf{Value}_S(h')$ forall $h \in X, h' \in Y$. The subjective dominance ordering $\preceq_s$ is then defined such that for $L, L' \subseteq H_{m_*}$, $L \preceq_s L'$ iff $\forall m$ such that $m_* \sim_\alpha m, \forall S \in \mathbf{State}_\alpha^m, [L]_\alpha^m \cap S \leq_s [L']_\alpha^m \cap S$.

---

[8] This extension is extremely useful for the proof of completeness, but neither its conceptual reach nor its philosophical implications has been a subject of our investigation as of yet. There are more than a few reasons to entertain skepticism about this technical decision, since it is not grounded philosophically. To have two deontic functions instead of one lends itself to potentially having different values for histories according to whether their utility is objective or subjective. However, we must observe that the notions of objective and subjective utility are not what drives the disambiguation of ought-to-do into objective and subjective obligations. What drives it is the epistemic structure of a given agent. Therefore, the use of two value functions should not be taken as essential for the proposal of the logic presented here. Moreover, the soundness result works for models in which there is only one deontic function, and the solution to Horty's puzzles does not rely on there being two. On a related note, we make explicit that the focus of this work was to develop well-behaved semantics for subjective ought-to-do's in the stit tradition, so that if we presented a language with only the subjective-ought operator and not the objective one, as well as with the operators for knowledge, action, and historical necessity, then our proof of completeness would in fact be enough to show completeness of this fragment with respect to the class of single-valued epistemic act utilitarian BT-models.

With these definitions, we adapt the semantics for the formulas involving ought-to-do operators, making the logic strong enough to deal with the 'sure-thing principle': we set $\langle m, h \rangle \models \odot[\alpha]\varphi$ iff for every $L \in \mathbf{Choice}_\alpha^m$ such that $\langle m, h_L \rangle \not\models \varphi$ for some $h_L \in L$, there exists $L' \in \mathbf{Choice}_\alpha^m$ such that $L \prec L'$ and if $L'' = L$ or $L' \preceq L''$, then $\langle m, h' \rangle \models \varphi$ for every $h' \in L''$. Similarly, we set $\langle m, h \rangle \models \odot_s[\alpha]\varphi$ iff for every $L \in \mathbf{Choice}_\alpha^m$ such that $\langle m', h_L \rangle \not\models \varphi$ for some $h_L \in [L]_\alpha^{m'}$ ($m \sim_\alpha m'$), there exists $L' \in \mathbf{Choice}_\alpha^m$ such that $L \prec_s L'$ and if $L'' = L'$ or $L' \preceq_s L''$, then for every m'' such that $m \sim_\alpha m''$, $\langle m'', h'' \rangle \models \varphi$ for every $h'' \in [L'']_\alpha^{m''}$.

4.1 Soundness

Proposition 1. *The system Λ is sound with respect to the class of epistemic act utilitarian bi-valued BT-models.*

Proof. Standard. See [1] for details.

4.2 Completeness

For reasons of space, we can only summarize the proof here, leaving the full detailed exposition in [1]. The proof of completeness of Λ with respect to the class of epistemic act utilitarian bi-valued BT-models is a two-step process. First, we introduce relational structures called Kripke-estit models for evaluating the formulas of the language $\mathcal{L}_{\mathsf{KO}}$ under a semantics that mirrors the semantics of Definition 3, and prove completeness of Λ with respect to these structures via the technique of canonical models. Secondly, we provide a truth-preserving correspondence between Kripke-estit models and certain epistemic act utilitarian bi-valued BT-models, so that completeness with respect to Kripke-estit models grants it with respect to bi-valued BT-models. Essential to the success of the technique of canonical models is to prove the so-called *existence* and *truth* lemmas just as in modal logic. In the case of this particular proof system, these lemmas are quite involved, and the reader is encouraged to go over them in [1], which offers enough room to address all their features carefully and with precision. In our opinion, the results of soundness and completeness are significant, all the more because we want to provide some theoretical foundations to the idea – explored by [2] – that we can actually do machine ethics via theorem-proving (or model-checking).

To end on a slightly less technical note, we finish this section by addressing some interesting properties concerning interactions of certain operators in the logic presented:

$$\not\models \odot[\alpha]\varphi \rightarrow \Diamond K_\alpha[\alpha]\varphi.$$

'*It is not the case that if the agent objectively ought to do something, then it can knowingly do it.*' Our solution to Example 3 poses a counterexample, because $\langle m_2, h_1 \rangle$ is such that $\langle m_2, h_1 \rangle \models \odot[\alpha]W$, but $\langle m_2, h_1 \rangle \not\models \Diamond K_\alpha[\alpha]W$, as witnessed by the facts that $\langle m_2, h_2 \rangle \not\models [\alpha]W$ and that $\langle m_3, h_4 \rangle \not\models [\alpha]W$.

$$\not\models \odot_s[\alpha]\varphi \rightarrow \odot[\alpha]\varphi.$$

'It is not the case that if the agent subjectively ought to do something, then it objectively ought to do it.' Our solution to Example 2 poses a counterexample, because $\langle m_2, h_1 \rangle$ is such that $\langle m_2, h_1 \rangle \models \odot_S[\alpha]\neg G$, but $\langle m_2, h_1 \rangle \not\models \odot[\alpha]\neg G$.

$$\not\models \odot[\alpha]\varphi \rightarrow \odot_S[\alpha]\varphi.$$

'It is not the case that if the agent objectively ought to do something, then it subjectively ought to do it.' Our solution to Example 3 poses a counterexample, because $\langle m_2, h_1 \rangle$ is such that $\langle m_2, h_1 \rangle \models \odot[\alpha]W$, but $\langle m_2, h_1 \rangle \not\models \odot_S[\alpha]W$.

5 Conclusion

This work deals with important questions in the modeling of agency, knowledge, and obligation. Formal depictions of such concepts are likely to be useful when it comes to doing machine ethics based on deontic logic and its mechanization. The approach discussed and analyzed here is based on a stit logic of utilitarian 'ought-to-do' enriched with epistemic relations. We argue that to solve certain problems in the treatment of knowledge and obligations within stit – namely Horty's puzzles – one possibility is to distinguish between objective and subjective versions of the ought-to-do modality. Moreover, we show that this possibility comes with formal advantages such as simplicity of semantics and axiomatizability.

References

1. Abarca, A.I.R., Broersen, J.: A logic of objective and subjective oughts (full paper with proofs). CoRR abs/1903.10577 (2019). https://arxiv.org/abs/1903.10577
2. Arkoudas, K., Bringsjord, S., Bello, P.: Toward ethical robots via mechanized deontic logic. In: AAAI Fall Symposium on Machine Ethics, pp. 17–23 (2005)
3. Belnap, N., Perloff, M., Xu, M.: Facing the Future: Agents and Choices in Our Indeterminist World. Oxford University Press, Oxford (2001)
4. Bringsjord, S., Arkoudas, K., Bello, P.: Toward a general logicist methodology for engineering ethically correct robots. IEEE Intell. Syst. 21(4), 38–44 (2006)
5. Broersen, J.: Deontic epistemic stit logic distinguishing modes of mens rea. J. Appl. Log. 9(2), 137–152 (2011)
6. Broersen, J., Ramírez Abarca, A.I.: Formalising oughts and practical knowledge without resorting to action types. In: Proceedings of the 17th International Conference on Autonomous Agents and MultiAgent Systems, pp. 1877–1879. International Foundation for Autonomous Agents and Multiagent Systems (2018)
7. Horty, J.: Epistemic oughts in stit semantics (2018)
8. Horty, J., Pacuit, E.: Action types in stit semantics. Rev. Symb. Log. 10, 617–637 (2017)
9. Horty, J.F.: Agency and Deontic Logic. Oxford University Press, Oxford (2001)
10. Murakami, Y.: Utilitarian deontic logic. In: AiML-2004: Advances in Modal Logic, vol. 287 (2004)
11. Pereira, L.M., Saptawijaya, A., et al.: Programming Machine Ethics, vol. 26. Springer, Cham (2016). https://doi.org/10.1007/978-3-319-29354-7
12. Xu, M.: Combinations of stit with ought and know. J. Philos. Log. 44(6), 851–877 (2015). https://doi.org/10.1007/s10992-015-9365-7

On the Complexity of Graded Modal Logics with Converse

Bartosz Bednarczyk$^{(\boxtimes)}$ (iD), Emanuel Kieroński$^{(\boxtimes)}$ (iD), and Piotr Witkowski$^{(\boxtimes)}$ (iD)

Institute of Computer Science, University of Wrocław, Wrocław, Poland
{Bartosz.Bednarczyk,Emanuel.Kieronski,Piotr.Witkowski}@cs.uni.wroc.pl

Abstract. A complete classification of the complexity of the local and global satisfiability problems for graded modal language over traditional classes of frames has already been established. By "traditional" classes of frames we mean those characterized by any positive combination of reflexivity, seriality, symmetry, transitivity, and the Euclidean property. In this paper we fill the gaps remaining in an analogous classification of the graded modal language with graded converse modalities. In particular, we show its NExpTime-completeness over the class of Euclidean frames, demonstrating this way that over this class the considered language is harder than the language without graded modalities or without converse modalities. We also consider its variation disallowing graded converse modalities, but still admitting basic converse modalities. Our most important result for this variation is confirming an earlier conjecture that it is decidable over transitive frames. This contrasts with the undecidability of the language with graded converse modalities.

1 Introduction

Since many years modal logic has been an active topic in many academic disciplines, including philosophy, mathematics, linguistics, and computer science. Regarding applications in computer science, e.g., in knowledge representation or verification, some important variations are those involving graded and converse modalities. In this paper, we investigate their computational complexity.

By *a modal logic* we will mean a pair $(\mathcal{L}, \mathcal{F})$, represented usually as $\mathcal{F}(\mathcal{L}^*)$, where $\mathcal{L}$ is a *modal language*, $\mathcal{F}$ is a *class of frames*, and $\mathcal{L}^*$ is a short symbolic representation of $\mathcal{L}$ (see the next paragraph), characterizing the *modalities* of $\mathcal{L}$.

While we are mostly interested in languages with graded and converse modalities, to set the scene we need to mention languages without them. Overall, the following five languages are relevant: the basic *one-way modal language* ($\mathcal{L}^* = \Diamond$) containing only one, *forward*, modality $\Diamond$; *graded one-way modal language* ($\mathcal{L}^* = \Diamond_{\geq}$) extending the previous one by *graded* forward modalities, $\Diamond_{\geq n}$, for all $n \in \mathbb{N}$; *two-way modal language* ($\mathcal{L}^* = \Diamond, \Diamond$) containing basic forward modality and the *converse* modality $\Diamond$; *graded two-way modal language* ($\mathcal{L}^* = \Diamond_{\geq}, \Diamond_{\geq}$) containing the forward modality, the converse modality and their graded versions $\Diamond_{\geq n}$, $\Diamond_{\geq n}$, for all $n \in \mathbb{N}$; and, additionally, a restriction of

© Springer Nature Switzerland AG 2019
F. Calimeri et al. (Eds.): JELIA 2019, LNAI 11468, pp. 642–658, 2019.
https://doi.org/10.1007/978-3-030-19570-0_42

the latter without graded converse modalities, but with basic converse modality ($\mathcal{L}^* = \Diamond_\geq, \diamond$).

The meaning of graded modalities is natural: $\Diamond_{\geq n}\varphi$ means "φ is true at no fewer than n successors of the current world", and $\diamond_{\geq}\varphi$ means "φ is true at no fewer than n predecessors of the current world". We also recall that $\Diamond\varphi$ means "φ is true at some successor of the current world" and $\diamond\varphi$—"φ is true at some predecessor of the current world". Thus, e.g., $\Diamond$ is simply $\Diamond_{\geq 1}$.

Our aim is to classify the complexity of the local ("in a world") and global ("in all worlds") satisfiability problems for all the logics obtained by combining any of the above languages with any class of frames from the so-called modal cube, that is a class of frames characterized by any positive combination of reflexivity (T), seriality (D), symmetry (B), transitivity (4), and the Euclidean property (5). See Fig. 1 for a visualization of the modal cube. Nodes of the depicted graph correspond to classes of frames and are labelled by letters denoting the above-mentioned properties, with S used in S4 and S5 for some historical reasons to denote reflexivity, and K denoting the class of all frames. Note that the modal cube contains only 15 classes, since some different combinations of the relevant properties lead to identical classes, e.g., seriality implies reflexivity, symmetry and transitivity imply the Euclideaness, and so on. A lot of work has been already done. The cases of basic one-way language and graded one-way language are completely understood. See Fig. 1. The results for the former can be established using some standard techniques, see, e.g., [3] and the classical paper [9]. The local satisfiability of the latter is systematically analysed in [7], with complexities turning out to lie between NP and NExpTime. As for its global satisfiability, some of the results follow from [7], some are given in [15], and the other can be easily obtained using again some standard techniques. In the case of non-graded two-way modal language, over most relevant classes of frames, tight complexity

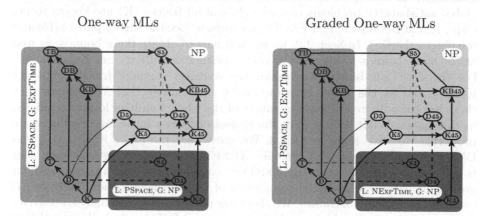

Fig. 1. Complexity of one-way modal logics. All bounds are tight. If local and global satisfiability differ in complexity then "L:" indicates the local and "G:"—the global satisfiability.

Two-way MLs   Graded Two-Way MLs

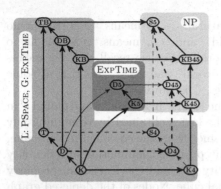 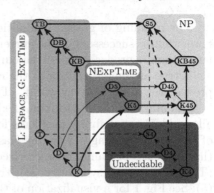

Fig. 2. Complexities of two-way modal logics. All bounds are tight.

bounds for local and global satisfiability are also known. However, according to the survey part of [15], for global satisfiability of the logics of transitive frames, K4($\Diamond, \diamondsuit$), S4($\Diamond, \diamondsuit$), D4($\Diamond, \diamondsuit$), which is known to be in EXPTIME (due to [5] or due to a translation to description logic SI, whose satisfiability is in EXPTIME [14]), the corresponding lower bound is missing. In the literature we were also not able find a tight lower bound for the logics of Euclidean frames, K5($\Diamond, \diamondsuit$), D5($\Diamond, \diamondsuit$). We provide both missing bounds in the full version of this paper [2], obtaining them by reductions from the acceptance problem for polynomially space bounded alternating Turing machines.[1] See the left part of Fig. 2 for a complete complexity map in this case.

Let us now turn our attention to the most expressive two-way graded modal language with both graded forward and graded converse modalities. Its local and global satisfiability problems over the class of all frames (K) are known to be, resp., PSPACE-complete and EXPTIME-complete (see the survey part of [15] and references therein). In Sect. 2.2, we explain how to obtain these bounds, as well as the same bounds in all cases involving neither transitivity nor Euclideaness. For the EXPTIME-bound, we employ the so-called *standard translation*. Over K4, D4 and S4 the logics turn out to be undecidable [15]. We remark that these are the only undecidable members of the whole family of logics considered in this paper. What remains are the classes of frames involving the Euclidean property. We solve them in Sect. 3. We prove that the logics K5($\Diamond_{\geq}, \diamondsuit_{\geq}$) and D5($\Diamond_{\geq}, \diamondsuit_{\geq}$) are locally and globally NEXPTIME-complete. Interestingly, this is a higher complexity than the EXPTIME-complexity of the language without graded modalities [5] and NP-complexity of the language without converse [7] over the same classes of frames. We also show that, when additionally transitivity is required, that is, for the logics K45($\Diamond_{\geq}, \diamondsuit_{\geq}$) and D45($\Diamond_{\geq}, \diamondsuit_{\geq}$), the complexity drops down to NP.

---

[1] As explained to the first author by Emil Jeřábek, the latter bound can be alternatively proved by a reduction from TB, whose EXPTIME-hardness follows from [4].

Finally, we consider the above-mentioned intermediate language $(\Diamondtail, \Diamond_{\geq})$ in which we can count the successors, we have the basic converse modality, but we cannot count the predecessors. Our main result here, presented in Sect. 4, is the decidability of the corresponding logics of transitive frames K4, D4 and S4. The result is obtained by showing the finite model property of the logics. This way we confirm a conjecture stated in [8] (an analogous conjecture was also formulated in the description logic setting [6,15]). The logics of the remaining classes of frames retain their complexities from the graded two-way case.

Due to a large number of papers in which the complexity bounds from Figs. 1 and 2 are scattered, we have not referenced all of them in this introduction. A reader willing to find an appropriate reference is asked to use an online tool prepared by the first author (http://bartoszbednarczyk.com/mlnavigator). For missing proofs see [2].

Related formalisms. Graded modalities are examples of *counting quantifiers* which are present in various formalisms. In particular, counting quantifiers were introduced for first-order logic: $\exists^{\geq n} x \varphi$ means: "at least n elements x satisfy φ". The satisfiability problem for some fragments of first-order logic with counting quantifiers was shown to be decidable. In particular, the two-variable fragment is NExpTime-complete [11], the two-variable guarded fragment is ExpTime-complete [12], and the one-variable fragment is NP-complete [13]. Counting quantifiers are also present, in the form of the so-called *number restrictions*, in some description logics, DLs. As some standard DLs embed modal logics, some results on DLs with number restrictions may be used to infer upper bounds on the complexity of some graded modal logics.

2 Preliminaries

2.1 Languages, Kripke Structures and Satisfiability

Let us fix a countably infinite set Π of *propositional variables*. The *language* of graded two-way modal logic is defined inductively as the smallest set of formulas containing Π, closed under Boolean connectives and, for any formula φ, containing $\Diamond_{\geq n} \varphi$ and $\Diamondtail_{\geq n} \varphi$, for all $n \in \mathbb{N}$. Given a formula φ, we denote its *length* by $|\varphi|$, and measure it as the number of symbols required to write φ, with numbers in subscripts $\geq n$ encoded in binary.

The basic modality $\Diamond$ can be defined in terms of graded modalities: $\Diamond \varphi := \Diamond_{\geq 1} \varphi$. Analogously, for the converse modality: $\Diamondtail := \Diamondtail_{\geq 1}$. Keeping this in mind, we may treat all languages mentioned in the introduction as fragments of the above defined graded two-way modal language. We remark that we may also introduce modalities $\Diamond_{\leq n} \varphi := \neg \Diamond_{\geq n+1} \varphi$, $\Diamondtail_{\leq n} \varphi := \neg \Diamondtail_{\geq n+1} \varphi$, $\Box \varphi := \neg \Diamond \neg \varphi$ and $\boxtail \varphi := \neg \Diamondtail \neg \varphi$.

The semantics is defined with respect to Kripke structures, that is, structures over the relational signature with unary predicates Π and a binary predicate R, represented as triples $\mathfrak{A} = \langle W, R, V \rangle$, where W is the universe, R is a binary relation on W, and V is a function $V : \Pi \to \mathcal{P}(W)$, called a *valuation*. The *satisfaction relation* is defined inductively as follows:

- $\mathfrak{A}, w \models p$ iff $w \in V(p)$, for $p \in \Pi$,
- $\mathfrak{A}, w \models \neg\varphi$ iff $\mathfrak{A}, w \not\models \varphi$ and similarly for the other Boolean connectives,
- $\mathfrak{A}, w \models \Diamond_{\geq n}\varphi$ iff there is at least n worlds $v \in W$ such that $\langle w, v \rangle \in R$ and $\mathfrak{A}, v \models \varphi$,
- $\mathfrak{A}, w \models \Diamondbar_{\geq n}\varphi$ iff there is at least n worlds $v \in W$ such that $\langle v, w \rangle \in R$ and $\mathfrak{A}, v \models \varphi$,

Given a structure $\mathfrak{A} = \langle W, R, V \rangle$ as above, we call the pair $\langle W, R \rangle$ its *frame*. For a class of frames $\mathcal{F}$, we define the local (global) satisfiability problem of a modal language $\mathcal{L}$ over $\mathcal{F}$ as follows. Given a formula φ of $\mathcal{L}$ verify if φ is satisfied at some world (all worlds) w of some structure $\mathfrak{A}$ whose frame belongs to $\mathcal{F}$. As said in the introduction, we are interested in all classes of frames characterized by any positive combination of reflexivity (T), seriality (D), symmetry (B), transitivity (4), and the Euclidean property (5).

2.2   Standard Translation

Modal logic can be seen as a fragment of first-order logic via the so-called *standard translation* (see, e.g., [3]). Here we present its variation suited for graded and converse modalities. We define functions $\mathbf{st}_z$ for $z \in \{x, y\}$. Let φ be a graded two-way modal logic formula. Below we explicitly show the definition of $\mathbf{st}_x$. The definition of $\mathbf{st}_y$ is symmetric.

$$\mathbf{st}_x(p) = p(x) \text{ for } p \in \Pi \tag{1}$$

$$\mathbf{st}_x(\varphi \wedge \psi) = \mathbf{st}_x(\varphi) \wedge \mathbf{st}_x(\psi) \text{ similarly for } \neg, \vee, \text{ etc.} \tag{2}$$

$$\mathbf{st}_x(\Diamond_{\geq C}\varphi) = \exists_{\geq C}.y(R(x, y) \wedge \mathbf{st}_y(\varphi)) \tag{3}$$

$$\mathbf{st}_x(\Diamondbar_{\geq C}\varphi) = \exists_{\geq C}.y(R(y, x) \wedge \mathbf{st}_y(\varphi)) \tag{4}$$

We note here that the obtained formula lies in the guarded two-variable fragment with counting quantifiers, GC^2, whose satisfiability is ExpTime-complete [12]. It is not difficult to see that φ is locally (globally) satisfiable iff $\exists x \mathbf{st}_x(\varphi)$ $(\forall x \mathbf{st}_x(\varphi))$ is satisfiable.

Since symmetry, seriality and reflexivity are trivially definable in GC^2, the standard translation can be used to provide a generic upper bound for the logics over all classes of frames from the modal cube involving neither transitivity nor Euclideaness. The global satisfiability for basic language $\Diamond$ is already ExpTime-hard [10] hence the following theorem holds.

Theorem 1. *The global satisfiability problem for $\mathcal{L}(\Diamond_{\geq}, \Diamondbar_{\geq})$ where $\mathcal{L}$ is any class of frames from the modal cube involving neither transitivity nor Euclideaness, is ExpTime-complete.*

In the case of local satisfiability, the complexity boils down to PSpace. For two-way graded language over K, D and T, we can adapt an existing tableaux algorithm by Tobies [14], yielding a tight PSpace bound. If the class of frames is symmetric, then the forward and converse modalities coincide and thus we may just apply the result for graded one-way language stated in [7]. Thus:

Theorem 2. *The local satisfiability problem for $\mathcal{L}(\Diamond_\geq, \diamondsuit_\geq)$, where $\mathcal{L}$ is any class of frames from the modal cube involving neither transitivity nor Euclideaness, is PSpace-complete.*

3 Euclidean Frames: Counting Successors and Predecessors

In this section, we consider the two-way graded modal language over frames from the modal cube satisfying the Euclidean property. We demonstrate an exponential gap (NExpTime vs NP) between the logics of Euclidean frames K5, D5 and the logics of transitive Euclidean frames K45, D45.

We note that for the two remaining Euclidean classes of frames, i.e., KB45 and S5, whose frames are additionally supposed to be symmetric, the obtained logics may be seen as one-way and thus their NP-completeness follows immediately from [7].

3.1 The Shape of Euclidean Frames

We begin by describing the shape of frames under consideration. Let $\mathfrak{A} = \langle W, R, V \rangle$ be a Kripke structure. A world $w \in W$ is called a *lantern* if $\langle w', w \rangle \notin R$, for every $w' \in W$. We say that lantern $l \in W$ *illuminates* world $w \in W$ if $\langle l, w \rangle \in R$. We say that l *illuminates a set of worlds* $I \subseteq W$ if l illuminates every world $w \in I$. We say that $w_1, w_2 \in W$ are *R-equivalent* (or simply *equivalent* if R is known from a context), if both $\langle w_1, w_2 \rangle \in R$ and $\langle w_2, w_1 \rangle \in R$. The *R-clique* for w_1 in $\mathfrak{A}$ is the set $Q_{\mathfrak{A}}(w_1) \subseteq W$ consisting of w_1 and all worlds R-equivalent to w_1. A world $w \in W$ is *reflexive* if $\langle w, w \rangle \in R$. We say that $\mathfrak{A}$ is *R-connected* if $\langle W, R \cup R^{-1} \rangle$ is a connected graph. By $L_{\mathfrak{A}}$ we denote the set of all lanterns in $\mathfrak{A}$. By $Q_{\mathfrak{A}}$ we denote $W \setminus L_{\mathfrak{A}}$. See Fig. 3.

Lemma 1. *Let $\mathfrak{A}$ be an R-connected structure over a Euclidean frame $\langle W, R \rangle$. All worlds in $Q_{\mathfrak{A}}$ are reflexive and $Q_{\mathfrak{A}}$ is an R-clique.*

Before we start proving complexity results for some more specific classes, we observe that global and local satisfiability are reducible to each other over any class involving Euclideaness. It follows from the fact that, as it usually happens for modal logics, we can restrict attention to R-connected frames and over such frames we can define a *universal modality* **U**. Recall that $\mathbf{U}\varphi$ is true at a world w of a Kripke structure $\mathfrak{A}$ if and only if φ is true at all worlds of $\mathfrak{A}$. Once we understand how connected Euclidean structures look like, it is not hard to see that the universal modality can be defined by setting $\mathbf{U}\varphi := \Box\Box\boxminus\varphi$ and to prove the following lemma:

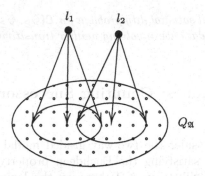

Fig. 3. A Euclidean structure $\mathfrak{A}$ with $L_{\mathfrak{A}} = \{l_1, l_2\}$

Lemma 2. *The universal modality* **U** *is definable in two-way modal language over connected Euclidean frames. Thus, for logics* $(\mathcal{L}, \mathcal{F})$, *where* $\mathcal{L}$ *contains the two-way modal language and* $\mathcal{F}$ *involves Euclideaness, the local and global satisfiability problems are polynomially interreducible.*

3.2   The Upper Bound for Graded Two-Way K5 and D5

Theorem 3. *The local and global satisfiability problems for* $K5(\Diamond_{\geq}, \Diamondleft_{\geq})$ *and* $D5(\Diamond_{\geq}, \Diamondleft_{\geq})$ *are in* NEXPTIME.

Proof. We start with the case of the class of all Euclidean frames K5. We translate a given modal formula φ to the two-variable logic with counting C^2, in which both graded modalities and the shape of connected Euclidean structures, as defined in Lemma 1, can be expressed. Since satisfiability of C^2 is in NEXP-TIME [12], we obtain the desired conclusion. Recall the standard translation **st** from Sect. 2.2. Let $lantern(\cdot)$ be a new unary predicate and define $\varphi_{\mathbf{tr}}$ as

$$\mathbf{st}_x(\varphi) \wedge \forall x \forall y. \, (\neg lantern(x) \wedge \neg lantern(y) \rightarrow R(x,y)) \wedge (lantern(y) \rightarrow \neg R(x,y)).$$

Since $\mathbf{st}_x(\varphi)$ belongs to GC^2, $\varphi_{\mathbf{tr}}$ belongs to C^2 (but not to GC^2), Moreover, it features one free variable x. Let $\mathfrak{B}$ be a Kripke structure over a Euclidean frame. Expand $\mathfrak{B}$ to a structure $\mathfrak{B}^+$ by setting $lantern^{\mathfrak{B}^+} = \{w \in \mathfrak{B} \mid w \in L_{\mathfrak{B}}\}$. Taking into account Lemma 1 a structural induction on φ easily establishes the following condition

$$\mathfrak{B}, w_0 \models \varphi \text{ if and only if } \mathfrak{B}^+ \models \varphi_{\mathbf{tr}}[w_0/x] \text{ for every world } w_0 \in B.$$

Thus, a $K5(\Diamond_{\geq}, \Diamondleft_{\geq})$ formula φ is locally satisfiable if and only if C^2 formula $\exists_{\geq 1} x. \varphi_{\mathbf{tr}}$ is satisfiable, yielding a NEXPTIME algorithm for $K5(\Diamond_{\geq}, \Diamondleft_{\geq})$ local satisfiability. Membership of global satisfiability in NEXPTIME is implied by Lemma 2.

For the case of serial Euclidean frames, D5, it suffices to supplement the C^2 formula defined in the case of K5 with a conjunct $\exists x. (\neg lantern(x))$ expressing seriality. Correctness follows then from the simple observation that a Euclidean frame is serial if and only if it contains at least one non-lantern world (recall that all these worlds are reflexive).

3.3   Lower Bounds for Two-Way Graded K5 and D5

We now show a matching NEXPTIME-lower bound for the logics from the previous section. We concentrate on local satisfiability, but by Lemma 2 the results will hold also for global satisfiability. Actually, we obtain a stronger result, namely, we show that the two-way graded modal logics K5 and D5 remain NEXPTIME-hard even if counting in one-way (either backward or forward) is forbidden. In particular, we show hardness of the logics $K5(\Diamond_\geq, \Diamond\!\!\!\!\diagdown)$ and $D5(\Diamond_\geq, \Diamond\!\!\!\!\diagdown)$. We recall that this gives a higher complexity than the EXPTIME-complexity of language $\Diamond, \Diamond\!\!\!\!\diagdown$ [5] and NP-complexity of language $\Diamond_\geq$ [7] over the same classes of frames. As a corollary, any adaptation of the translation to GF^2 from [5] fails when counting is allowed, unless EXPTIME=NEXPTIME.

For proving our hardness result, we employ the *torus tiling problem*, where the goal is to decide whether there is a solution of tilings of an exponential torus.

Definition 1 (5.16 from [1]). *A torus tiling problem* $\mathcal{P}$ *is a tuple* $(\mathcal{T}, \mathcal{H}, \mathcal{V})$, *where* $\mathcal{T}$ *is a finite set of tile types and* $\mathcal{H}, \mathcal{V} \subseteq \mathcal{T} \times \mathcal{T}$ *represent the horizontal and vertical matching conditions. Let* $\mathcal{P}$ *be a tilling problem and* $c = t_0, t_1, \ldots, t_{n-1} \in \mathcal{T}^n$ *an initial condition. A mapping* $\tau : \{0, 1, \ldots, 2^n - 1\} \times \{0, 1, \ldots, 2^n - 1\} \rightarrow \mathcal{T}$ *is a solution for* $\mathcal{P}$ *and* c *if and only if, for all* $i, j < 2^n$, *the following holds* $(\tau(i,j), \tau(i \oplus_{2^n} 1, j)) \in \mathcal{H}, (\tau(i,j), \tau(i, j \oplus_{2^n} 1)) \in \mathcal{V}$ *and* $\tau(0, i) = t_i$ *for all* $i < n$, *where* $\oplus_i$ *denotes addition modulo* i. *It is well-known that there exists a* NEXPTIME-*complete torus tiling problem.*

Outline of the Proof. The proof is based on a polynomial time reduction from torus tiling problem as in Definition 1. Henceforward we assume that a NEXPTIME-complete torus tiling problem $\mathcal{P} = (\mathcal{T}, \mathcal{H}, \mathcal{V})$ is fixed. Let $c = t_0, t_1, \ldots, t_{n-1} \in \mathcal{T}^n$ be its initial condition. We write a formula which is (locally) satisfiable iff $(\mathcal{P}, c)$ has a solution. Each cell of the torus carries a *position* $(H, V) \in \{0, 1, \ldots, 2^n - 1\} \times \{0, 1, \ldots, 2^n - 1\}$, encoded in binary in a natural way by means of propositional letters $v_0, v_1, \ldots, v_{n-1}$ and $h_0, h_1, \ldots, h_{n-1}$, with h_0 and v_0 denoting the least significant bits. In the reduction, a single cell of the torus corresponds to a unique *inner*, i.e., non-lantern, world. Since there are exactly $2^n \cdot 2^n$ cells, we enforce that also the total number of inner worlds is equal to $2^n \cdot 2^n$. We make use of graded modalities to specify that every inner world has exactly $2^n \cdot 2^n$ successors. We stress here that this is the only place where we employ counting. Thus the proof works in the case where graded converse modalities are disallowed (but the basic converse modality will be necessary). Alternatively we could equivalently write that every inner world have exactly $2^n \cdot 2^n$ inner predecessors, and obtain hardness of the language with graded converse modalities, but without graded forward modalities.

Once we enforced a proper size of our torus, we must be sure that two distinct inner worlds carry different positions. We do it in two steps. We first write that a world with position $(0,0)$ occurs in a model. For the second step, we assume that the grid is chessboard-like, i.e., all elements are coloured black or white in the same way as a chessboard is. Then, we say that every world is illuminated by four lanterns, where each of them propagates $\oplus_{2^n} 1$ relation on the proper axis (from a black node to a white one and vice versa). Finally, having the torus prepared we encode a solution for a given tiling by simply labelling each inner world with some tile letter t and ensure (from the vantage point of lanterns) that any two horizontal or vertical neighbours do not violate the tiling constraints.

Encoding the Exponential Torus. Our goal is now to define a formula describing the exponential torus. The shape of the formula is following:

$$\varphi_{\text{torus}} \overset{\text{def}}{=} \varphi_{\text{firstCell}} \wedge \mathbf{U}\left(\varphi_{\text{partition}} \wedge \varphi_{\text{chessboard}} \wedge \varphi_{\text{torusSize}} \wedge \varphi_{\text{succ}}\right)$$

where $\mathbf{U}$ is the universal modality as in Lemma 2. The formula is going to say that: (i) the current world has position $(0,0)$; (ii) every world is either a lantern or an inner world; (iii) the torus is chessboard-like, i.e., its cells are coloured *black* and *white* exactly as a real chessboard is; (iv) the overall size of the torus is equal to $2^n \cdot 2^n$; (v) each world of the torus has a proper vertical and a proper horizontal successor. The first four properties are straightforward to define:

$$\varphi_{\text{firstCell}} \overset{\text{def}}{=} inner \wedge white \wedge \bigwedge_{i=0}^{n-1} (\neg v_i \wedge \neg h_i)$$

$$\varphi_{\text{partition}} \overset{\text{def}}{=} (lantern \leftrightarrow \neg inner) \wedge (lantern \leftrightarrow \neg \Diamond \top)$$

$$\varphi_{\text{chessboard}} \overset{\text{def}}{=} (white \leftrightarrow \neg black) \wedge (white \leftrightarrow (v_0 \leftrightarrow h_0))$$

$$\varphi_{\text{torusSize}} \overset{\text{def}}{=} inner \rightarrow \Diamond_{=2^n \cdot 2^n} \top$$

The formula $\varphi_{\text{torusSize}}$ is valid, since the set of all inner worlds form a clique. The obtained formulae are of polynomial length since the number $2^n \cdot 2^n$ is encoded in binary.

What remains is to define φ_{succ}. For this, for every inner world we ensure that there exists a proper lantern responsible for establishing the appropriate successor relation. There will be four different types of such lanterns, denoted by propositional symbols: vbw, hbw, vwb, hwb. The intuition is the following: the first letter h or v indicates whether a lantern is responsible for H or V relation. The last two letters say whether a successor relation will be established between black and white worlds, or in the opposite way.

$$\varphi_{\text{succ}} \overset{\text{def}}{=} (lantern \rightarrow \bigvee_{\heartsuit \in \{vbw, hbw, vwb, hwb\}} (\heartsuit \wedge \varphi_\heartsuit)) \wedge$$

$$(inner \rightarrow \bigwedge_{\heartsuit \in \{vbw, hbw, vwb, hwb\}} \Diamond(lantern \wedge \varphi_\heartsuit))$$

Here we present φ_{vbw} only. The remaining formulas can be constructed in an analogous way and are explicitly shown in [2]. The formula below, intended to be interpreted at a lantern, consists of three parts: (i) the black and the white worlds illuminated by a lantern are pseudo-unique, i.e., all white (respectively, black) worlds illuminated by the same lantern carry the same position; uniqueness will follow later from $\varphi_{torusSize}$; (ii) all black worlds illuminated by a lantern have the same H-position as all white worlds illuminated by this lantern; (iii) if V_w (respectively, V_b) encodes a V-position of the white (respectively, black) worlds illuminated by a lantern, then $V_w = V_b \oplus_{2^n} 1$. Put $\varphi_{vbw} \overset{\text{def}}{=} \varphi_{pseudoUniqueness} \wedge \varphi_{equalH} \wedge \varphi_{V_w = V_b \oplus_{2^n} 1}$. The definitions of the first and the second part of φ_{vbw} are simple:

$$\varphi_{pseudoUniqueness} \overset{\text{def}}{=} \bigwedge_{c \in \{white, black\}} \bigwedge_{p \in \{v, h\}} \bigwedge_{i=0}^{n-1} \Diamond(c \wedge p_i) \rightarrow \Box(c \wedge p_i)$$

$$\varphi_{equalH} \overset{\text{def}}{=} \bigwedge_{i=0}^{n-1} \Diamond(black \wedge h_i) \leftrightarrow \Diamond(white \wedge h_i)$$

Finally, we need to encode the $\oplus_{2^n}$-operation as formula $\varphi_{V_w = V_b \oplus_{2^n} 1}$, but it is a standard implementation of binary addition. The following lemma says that the formula φ_{torus} indeed defines a proper torus. Its proof is routine.

Lemma 3. *Assume that the the formula φ_{torus} is locally satisfied at a world w of a Euclidean structure $\mathfrak{A} = \langle W, R, V \rangle$. Then, set $Q_{\mathfrak{A}}(w)$, i.e., the R-clique for w, contains exactly $2^n \cdot 2^n$ elements and each of them carries a different position (H, V), i.e., there are no two worlds v, v' satisfying exactly the same h_i- and v_i-predicates.*

Having defined a proper torus, it is quite easy to encode a solution to the torus tiling problem $\mathcal{P}$ with the initial condition c. Each inner node will be labelled with a single tile from $\mathcal{T}$ and using appropriate lanterns we enforce that two neighbouring worlds do not violate tiling rules $\mathcal{H}$ and $\mathcal{V}$. The whole process is again routine. Note that our intended modals are serial. Thus, the result holds also for the logic D5.

Theorem 4. *The local and global satisfiability problems for $K5(\Diamond_{\geq}, \Diamond)$ and $D5(\Diamond_{\geq}, \Diamond)$ are $\mathrm{NExpTime}$-hard.*

Together with Theorem 3 this gives:

Theorem 5. *The local and global satisfiability problems for logics $K5(\Diamond_{\geq}, \Diamond)$, $K5(\Diamond_{\geq}, \Diamond_{\geq})$, $D5(\Diamond_{\geq}, \Diamond)$ and $D5(\Diamond_{\geq}, \Diamond_{\geq})$ are $\mathrm{NExpTime}$-complete.*

3.4   Transitive Euclidean Frames

It turns out that the logics of transitive Euclidean frames have lower computational complexity. This is due to the following lemma.

Lemma 4. *Let $\mathfrak{A}$ be an R-connected structure over a transitive Euclidean frame $\langle W, R \rangle$. Then, every world $l \in L_{\mathfrak{A}}$ illuminates $Q_{\mathfrak{A}}$.*

A first-order formula stating that all non-lanterns are R-successors of all lanterns requires only two variables. Thus, as an immediate conclusion from Lemma 4, we can extend translation developed in the previous section to handle logic $K45(\Diamond_{\geq}, \Diamonddownright_{\geq})$, and obtain NEXPTIME upper bound for satisfiability problem. In fact, the shape of transitive Euclidean structures is so simple that two variable logic is no longer necessary. Below we translate $K45(\Diamond_{\geq}, \Diamonddownright_{\geq})$ and $D45(\Diamond_{\geq}, \Diamonddownright_{\geq})$ to one-variable logic C^1, which is NP-complete [13].

Theorem 6. *The local and global satisfiability problems for $K45(\Diamond_{\geq}, \Diamonddownright_{\geq})$ and $D45(\Diamond_{\geq}, \Diamonddownright_{\geq})$ are in NP.*

Proof. The proof is similar in spirit to the proof of Lemma 3 in [7]. Let $lantern(\cdot)$ be a new unary predicate. We first define translation function **tr** that, given a $K45(\Diamond_{\geq}, \Diamonddownright_{\geq})$ formula φ, produces an equisatisfiable C^1 formula $\mathbf{tr}(\varphi)$. We assume that all counting subscripts φ are non-zero.

$$\mathbf{tr}(p) = p(x) \text{ for all } p \in \Pi \tag{5}$$

$$\mathbf{tr}(\varphi \wedge \psi) = \mathbf{tr}(\varphi) \wedge \mathbf{tr}(\psi) \text{ similarly for } \neg, \vee, \text{ etc.} \tag{6}$$

$$\mathbf{tr}(\Diamond_{\geq C}\varphi) = \exists_{\geq C}.x(\neg lantern(x) \wedge \mathbf{tr}(\varphi)) \tag{7}$$

$$\mathbf{tr}(\Diamond_{\leq C}\varphi) = \exists_{\leq C}.x(\neg lantern(x) \wedge \mathbf{tr}(\varphi)) \tag{8}$$

$$\mathbf{tr}(\Diamonddownright_{\geq C}\varphi) = \neg lantern(x) \wedge \exists_{\geq C}.x(\mathbf{tr}(\varphi)) \tag{9}$$

$$\mathbf{tr}(\Diamonddownright_{\leq C}\varphi) = lantern(x) \vee \exists_{\leq C}.x(\mathbf{tr}(\varphi)) \tag{10}$$

Observe that $\mathbf{tr}(\varphi)$ is linear in the size of φ. Let $\mathfrak{B}$ be a Kripke structure over a transitive Euclidean frame. Expand $\mathfrak{B}$ to a structure $\mathfrak{B}^+$ by setting $lantern^{\mathfrak{B}^+} = \{w \in \mathfrak{B} \mid w \in L_{\mathfrak{B}}\}$. Taking into account Lemma 1 and Lemma 4, a structural induction on φ easily establishes the following condition

$$\mathfrak{B}, w_0 \models \varphi \text{ if and only if } \mathfrak{B}^+ \models \mathbf{tr}(\varphi)[w_0/x] \text{ for every world } w_0.$$

Thus, a $K45(\Diamond_{\geq}, \Diamonddownright_{\geq})$ formula φ is locally satisfiable if and only if C^1 formula $\exists_{\geq 1}.x(\mathbf{tr}(x))$ is satisfiable, yielding an NP algorithm for $K45(\Diamond_{\geq}, \Diamonddownright_{\geq})$ satisfiability. The algorithm for $D45(\Diamond_{\geq}, \Diamonddownright_{\geq})$ is obtained by just a slight update to the one given above. It suffices to supplement the C^1 formula defined in the case of $K45$ with a conjunct $\exists x.(\neg lantern(x))$ expressing seriality (cf. the proof of Theorem 3).

4 Transitive Frames: Counting Successors, Accessing Predecessors

In this section, we consider the language $\Diamond_\geq, \overleftarrow{\Diamond}$, that is the modal language in which we can count the successors, but cannot count the predecessors, having at our disposal only the basic converse modality. Over all classes of frames involving neither transitivity nor Euclideaness local satisfiability is PSPACE-complete and global satisfiability is ExpTime-complete, as the tight lower and upper bounds can be transferred from, resp., the one-way non-graded language $\Diamond$ and the full two-way graded language. Over the classes of Euclidean frames K5 and D5, both problems are NExpTime-complete, as proved in Theorem 3. Over the classes of transitive Euclidean frames KB45, K45, D45, and S5 the problems are NP-complete, as the lower bound transfers from the language $\Diamond$, and the upper bound from the full two-way graded language (Theorem 6). So, over all the above-discussed classes of frames the complexities of $\Diamond_\geq, \overleftarrow{\Diamond}$ and $\Diamond_\geq, \overleftarrow{\Diamond}_\geq$ coincide. What is left are the classes of transitive frames K4, D4, and S4.

Recall that, in contrast to their one-way counterparts, the two-way graded logics of transitive frames $K4(\Diamond_\geq, \overleftarrow{\Diamond}_\geq)$, $D4(\Diamond_\geq, \overleftarrow{\Diamond}_\geq)$, and $S4(\Diamond_\geq, \overleftarrow{\Diamond}_\geq)$ are undecidable [15]. Several papers [8][15][6] conjectured that decidability may possibly be regained if the restricted language $\Diamond_\geq, \overleftarrow{\Diamond}$ is considered. Here we confirm this conjecture, demonstrating the finite model property for the obtained logics. We remark that we do not obtain tight complexity bounds in this case: The decision procedure arising is non-elementary, and the best lower bound is NExpTime.

In Lemma 5.5 from [15], it is shown that over the class of transitive structures global satisfiability and local satisfiability problems for the considered language are polynomially equivalent. The same can be easily shown when, additionally, reflexivity or seriality of structures are required. Thus, while below we explicitly deal with global satisfiability our results apply also to local satisfiability.

Let us concentrate on the class K4 of all transitive frames. The finite model construction we are going to present is the most complicated part of this paper. It begins similarly to the exponential model construction in the case of local satisfiability of $K4(\Diamond_\geq)$ from [7]: we introduce a Scott-type normal form (Lemma 5), and then generalize two pieces of model surgery used there (Lemma 6) to our setting: starting from any model, we first obtain a model with short *paths of cliques* and then we decrease the size of the cliques. Some adaptations of the constructions from [7] are necessary to properly deal with the converse modality. Having a model with short paths of cliques and small cliques, we develop some new machinery of *clique profiles* and *clique types* allowing us to decrease the overall size of the structure.

Lemma 5. *Given a formula φ of the language $(\Diamond_{\geq}, \diamondsuit)$, we can compute in polynomial time a formula ψ of the form*

$$\eta \wedge \bigwedge_{1 \leq i \leq l} (p_i \to \Diamond_{\geq C_i} \pi_i) \wedge \bigwedge_{1 \leq i \leq m} (q_i \to \Diamond_{\leq D_i} \chi_i) \wedge$$

$$\bigwedge_{1 \leq i \leq l'} (p'_i \to \diamondsuit \pi'_i) \wedge \bigwedge_{1 \leq i \leq m'} (q'_i \to \boxminus \neg \chi'_i) \tag{11}$$

where p_i, q_i, p'_i, q'_i are propositional variables, C_i, D_i are natural numbers, and η and π_i, χ_i, π'_i, χ'_i are propositional formulas, such that φ and ψ are globally satisfiable over exactly the same transitive frames.

Proof. A routine renaming process (cf. [7]).

Let us introduce some helpful terminology, copying it mostly from [7]. Let $\mathfrak{A} = \langle W, R, V \rangle$ be a transitive structure, and $w_1, w_2 \in W$. We say that w_2 is an R-*successor* of w_1 if $\langle w_1, w_2 \rangle \in R$; w_2 is a *strict R-successor* of w_1 if $\langle w_1, w_2 \rangle \in R$, but $\langle w_2, w_1 \rangle \notin R$; w_2 is a *direct R-successor* of w_1 if w_2 is a strict R-successor of w_1 and, for every $w \in W$ such that $\langle w_1, w \rangle \in R$ and $\langle w, w_2 \rangle \in R$ we have either $w \in Q_{\mathfrak{A}}(w_1)$ or $w \in Q_{\mathfrak{A}}(w_2)$. Recall that $Q_{\mathfrak{A}}(w)$ denotes the R-clique for w in $\mathfrak{A}$.

The *depth* of a structure $\mathfrak{A}$ is the maximum over all $k \geq 0$ for which there exists worlds $w_0, \ldots, w_k \in W$ such that w_i is a strict R-successor of w_{i-1} for every $1 \leq i \leq k$, or ∞ if no such a maximum exists. The *breadth* of $\mathfrak{A}$ is the maximum over all $k \geq 0$ for which there exists worlds $w, w_1, \ldots, w_k$ such that w_i is a direct R-successor of w for every $1 \leq i \leq k$, and the sets $Q_{\mathfrak{A}}(w_1), \ldots Q_{\mathfrak{A}}(w_k)$ are disjoint, or ∞ if no such a maximum exists. The *width* of $\mathfrak{A}$ is the smallest k such that $k \geq |Q_{\mathfrak{A}}(w)|$ for all $w \in W$, or ∞ if no such k exists.

Lemma 6. *Let φ be a normal form formula. If φ is globally satisfied in a transitive model $\mathfrak{A}$ then it is globally satisfied in a transitive model $\mathfrak{A}'$ with depth $d' \leq (\sum_{i=1}^{m} D_i) + m + m' + 1$ and width $c' \leq (\sum_{i=1}^{l} C_i) + l' + 1$.*

The above lemma can be proved by a construction being a minor modification of Stages 1 and 4 of the construction from the proof of Lemma 6 in [7], where the language without backward modalities is considered. Our adaptation just additionally takes care of backward witnesses and is rather straightforward. We remark here that also Stage 2 of the above mentioned construction could be adapted, giving a better bound on the depth of $\mathfrak{A}'$. We omit it here since such an improvement would not be crucial for our purposes. Stage 3 cannot be directly adapted.

To describe our next step, we need a few more definitions. Given a world w of a structure $\mathfrak{A}$, we define its *depth* as the maximum over all $k \geq 0$ for which there exist worlds $w = w_0, \ldots, w_k \in W$ such that w_i is a strict R-successor of w_{i-1} for every $1 \leq i \leq k$, or as ∞ if no such a maximum exists. For an R-clique Q we define its *depth* as the depth of w for any $w \in Q$; this definition is sound since for all $w_1 \in Q_{\mathfrak{A}}(w)$ the depth of w is equal to the depth of w_1.

From this point, we will mostly work on the level of cliques rather than individual worlds. We may view any structure $\mathfrak{A}$ as a partially ordered set of cliques. We write $\langle Q_1, Q_2 \rangle \in R$, and say that a clique Q_1 *sends* an edge to a clique Q_2 (or that Q_2 *receives* an edge from Q_1) if $\langle w_1, w_2 \rangle \in R$ for any (equivalently: for all) $w_1 \in Q_1$, $w_2 \in Q_2$.

A 1-type of a world w in $\mathfrak{A}$ is the set of all propositional variables p such that $\mathfrak{A} \models p$. We sometimes identify a 1-type with the conjunction of all its elements and negations of variables it does not contain. Given a natural number k, a structure $\mathfrak{A}$ and a clique Q in this structure $\mathfrak{A}$, we define a k-*profile* of Q (called just a *profile* if k is clear from the context) in $\mathfrak{A}$ as the tuple $prof_{\mathfrak{A}}^k(Q) = (\mathcal{H}, \mathcal{A}, \mathcal{B})$, where $\mathcal{H}$ is the multiset of 1-types in which the number of copies of each 1-type α equals $\min(k, |\{w \in Q : \mathfrak{A}, w \models \alpha\}|)$, $\mathcal{A}$ is the multiset of 1-types in which the number of copies of each 1-type α equals $\min(k, |\{w : \mathfrak{A}, w \models \alpha \text{ and } w \text{ is a strict } R\text{-successor of a world from } Q\}|)$, and $\mathcal{B}$ is the set of 1-types of worlds for which a world from Q is its strict R-successor. Intuitively, $\mathcal{H}$ counts (up to k) realizations of 1-types *(H)ere* in Q, $\mathcal{A}$ counts (up to k) realizations 1-types *(A)bove* Q, and $\mathcal{B}$ says which 1-types appear *(B)elow* Q. Usually, given a normal form φ as in equation (11), we will be interested in M_φ-profiles of cliques, where $M_\varphi = \max(\{C_i\}_{i=1}^l \cup \{D_i + 1\}_{i=1}^m)$. Note that, given the M_φ-profiles of all cliques in a structure we are able to determine whether this structure is a global model of φ. The following observation is straightforward.

Lemma 7. *If* $\mathfrak{A} \models \varphi$ *for a normal form* φ, *and if in a structure* $\mathfrak{A}'$ *the* M_φ-*profile of every clique is equal to the* M_φ-*profile of some clique from* $\mathfrak{A}$, *then* $\mathfrak{A}' \models \varphi$.

We now prove the finite model property.

Lemma 8. *Let* φ *be a normal form formula. If* φ *is globally satisfied in a transitive model* $\mathfrak{A}$ *then it is globally satisfied in a finite transitive model* $\mathfrak{A}'$.

We assume that φ is as in (11). By Lemma 6, we may assume that $\mathfrak{A} = \langle W, R, V \rangle$ has depth $d \leq (\sum_{i=1}^m D_i) + m + m' + 1$ and width $c \leq (\sum_{i=1}^l C_i) + l' + 1$. Note that $\mathfrak{A}$ may be infinite due to possibly infinite breadth.

Let us split W into sets $U_0, \ldots, U_d$ with U_i consisting of all elements of W of depth i in $\mathfrak{A}$ (equivalently speaking: being the union of all cliques of depth i in $\mathfrak{A}$). They are called *layers*. Note that cliques from U_i may send R-edges only to cliques from U_j with $j < i$.

We now inductively define a sequence of models $\mathfrak{A} = \mathfrak{A}_{-1}, \mathfrak{A}_0, \ldots, \mathfrak{A}_d = \mathfrak{A}'$, $\mathfrak{A}_i = \langle W_i, R_i, V_i \rangle$ such that

- $W_i = U_0' \cup \ldots \cup U_i' \cup U_{i+1} \cup \ldots \cup U_d$, where each U_i' is a finite union of some cliques from U_i,
- $V_i = V \restriction W_i$,
- $\mathfrak{A}_i \restriction (U_0' \cup \ldots \cup U_i') = \mathfrak{A}_{i-1} \restriction (U_0' \cup \ldots \cup U_i')$,
- $\mathfrak{A}_i \restriction (U_0' \cup \ldots \cup U_{i-1}' \cup U_{i+1} \cup \ldots \cup U_d) = \mathfrak{A}_{i-1} \restriction (U_0' \cup \ldots \cup U_{i-1}' \cup U_{i+1} \cup \ldots \cup U_d)$
- in particular: $\mathfrak{A}_i \restriction (U_{i+1} \cup \ldots \cup U_d) = \mathfrak{A} \restriction (U_{i+1} \cup \ldots \cup U_d)$.

We obtain $\mathfrak{A}_i$ from $\mathfrak{A}_{i-1}$ by distinguishing a fragment U_i' of U_i, removing $U_i \setminus U_i'$ and adding some edges from $U_{i+1} \cup \ldots \cup U_d$ to U_i'; all the other edges remain untouched. We do it carefully, to avoid modifications of the profiles of the surviving cliques. Let us describe the process of constructing $\mathfrak{A}_i$ in details.

Assume $i \geq 0$. We first distinguish a finite subset U_i' of U_i. We define a *clique type* of every clique Q from U_i in $\mathfrak{A}_{i-1}$ as a triple $(\mathcal{H}, \mathcal{B}, S)$, where $\mathcal{H}$ and $\mathcal{B}$ are as in $prof_{\mathfrak{A}_{i-1}}^{M_\varphi}(Q)$ and S is the subset of cliques from $U_0' \cup \ldots \cup U_{i-1}'$, consisting of those cliques to which Q sends an R_{i-1}-edge (note that if $i = 0$, then this subset is empty). We stress that during the construction of $\mathfrak{A}_i$, the clique types of cliques are always computed in $\mathfrak{A}_{i-1}$.

For every clique type β realized in U_i, we mark M_φ cliques of this type, or all such cliques if there are less than M_φ of them. Let U_i' be the union of the marked cliques. We fix some arbitrary numbering of the marked cliques.

Now we define the relation R_i. As said before, for any pair of cliques Q_1, Q_2 both of which are contained in $U_0' \cup \ldots \cup U_{i-1}' \cup U_{i+1} \cup \ldots \cup U_d$ or in $U_0' \cup \ldots \cup U_i'$, we set $\langle Q_1, Q_2 \rangle \in R_i$ iff $\langle Q_1, Q_2 \rangle \in R_{i-1}$. It remains to define the R_i-edges from $U_{i+1} \cup \ldots \cup U_d$ to U_i'. For every clique Q from $U_{i+1} \cup \ldots \cup U_d$ and every clique type β realized in U_i', let $f(\beta)$ be the number of R_{i-1}-edges sent by Q to cliques of type β in U_i, if this number is not greater than M_φ, or, otherwise, let $f(\beta) = M_\varphi$. Let $f'(\beta)$ be the number of R_{i-1}-edges sent by Q to cliques of type β in U_i' (recall that this number is not greater than M_φ). We take all R_{i-1}-edges sent by Q to cliques of type β in U_i' to R_i. We send in $\mathfrak{A}_i$ $f(\beta) - f'(\beta)$ additional R_i-edges from Q to cliques of type β in U_i' using cliques to which Q does not send R_{i-1}-edges with minimal numbers in the fixed numbering. By the choice of U_i', we have enough such cliques in U_i'. We finish the construction of $\mathfrak{A}_i$ by removing all cliques from $U_i \setminus U_i'$.

Claim 7. *Each of the $\mathfrak{A}_i$ is a transitive structure.*

Claim 8. *The M_φ-profiles of every clique in $\mathfrak{A}_i$ is the same as its M_φ-profiles in $\mathfrak{A}$.*

The above claim and Lemma 7 imply that $\mathfrak{A}' = \mathfrak{A}_d$ is indeed a model of φ. As each of the U_i' contains a finite number of cliques and each of the cliques is finite, we get that $\mathfrak{A}'$ is finite. Let us estimate its size. To U_0' we take at most M_φ realizations of every clique type from U_0. M_φ is bounded exponentially, and the number of possible clique types in U_0 is bounded doubly exponentially in $|\varphi|$ (note that such cliques do not send any edges). Then, to construct U_i' we consider clique types distinguished, in particular, by the sets of cliques from $U_0' \cup \ldots U_{i-1}'$ to which a given clique sends edges. Thus, the number of cliques in U_i' may become exponentially larger than the number of cliques in U_{i-1}'. Thus, we can only estimate the number of cliques in our eventual finite model by a tower of exponents of height d (recall that our bound on d is exponential in $|\varphi|$, though a polynomial bound would not be difficult to obtain).

A careful inspection shows that our constructions respect reflexivity and seriality. Thus:

Theorem 9. *The logics* K4($\Diamond_{\geq}, \Diamond$), D4($\Diamond_{\geq}, \Diamond$), S4($\Diamond_{\geq}, \Diamond$) *have the finite model property. Their local and global satisfiability problems are decidable.*

Acknowledgements. We thank Evgeny Zolin for providing us a comprehensive list of gaps in the classification of the complexity of graded modal logics and for sharing with us his tikz files with modal cubes. We also thank Emil Jeřábek for his explanations concerning K5($\Diamond, \Diamond$). B.B. is supported by the Polish Ministry of Science and Higher Education program "Diamentowy Grant" no. DI2017 006447. E.K. and P.W. are supported by Polish National Science Centre grant no. 2016/21/B/ST6/01444.

References

1. Baader, F., Horrocks, I., Lutz, C., Sattler, U.: An Introduction to Description Logic. Cambridge University Press, Cambridge (2017). https://doi.org/10.1017/9781139025355
2. Bednarczyk, B., Kieronski, E., Witkowski, P.: On the complexity of graded modal logics with converse. CoRR abs/1812.04413 (2018). http://arxiv.org/abs/1812.04413
3. Blackburn, P., de Rijke, M., Venema, Y.: Modal Logic. Cambridge University Press, New York (2001). https://doi.org/10.1017/CBO9781107050884
4. Chen, C.-C., Lin, I.-P.: The complexity of propositional modal theories and the complexity of consistency of propositional modal theories. In: Nerode, A., Matiyasevich, Y.V. (eds.) LFCS 1994. LNCS, vol. 813, pp. 69–80. Springer, Heidelberg (1994). https://doi.org/10.1007/3-540-58140-5_8
5. Demri, S., de Nivelle, H.: Deciding regular grammar logics with converse through first-order logic. J. Logic Lang. Inf. **14**(3), 289–329 (2005). https://doi.org/10.1007/s10849-005-5788-9
6. Gutiérrez-Basulto, V., Ibáñez-García, Y.A., Jung, J.C.: Number restrictions on transitive roles in description logics with nominals. In: Proceedings of the Thirty-First AAAI Conference on Artificial Intelligence, San Francisco, California, USA, 4–9 February 2017, pp. 1121–1127 (2017)
7. Kazakov, Y., Pratt-Hartmann, I.: A note on the complexity of the satisfiability problem for graded modal logics. In: Proceedings of the 24th Annual IEEE Symposium on Logic in Computer Science, LICS 2009, Los Angeles, CA, USA, 11–14 August 2009, pp. 407–416 (2009). https://doi.org/10.1109/LICS.2009.17
8. Kazakov, Y., Sattler, U., Zolin, E.: How many legs do I have? Non-simple roles in number restrictions revisited. In: 2007 Proceedings of 14th International Conference on Logic for Programming, Artificial Intelligence, and Reasoning, LPAR 2007, Yerevan, Armenia, 15–19 October, pp. 303–317 (2007). https://doi.org/10.1007/978-3-540-75560-9_23
9. Ladner, R.E.: The computational complexity of provability in systems of modal propositional logic. SIAM J. Comput. **6**(3), 467–480 (1977). https://doi.org/10.1137/0206033
10. Blackburn, P., van Benthem, J.: Handbook of Modal Logic, chapter Modal Logic: A Semantic Perspective, pp. 255–325. Elsevier (2006)
11. Pratt-Hartmann, I.: Complexity of the two-variable fragment with counting quantifiers. J. Logic Lang. Inf. **14**(3), 369–395 (2005). https://doi.org/10.1007/s10849-005-5791-1

12. Pratt-Hartmann, I.: Complexity of the guarded two-variable fragment with counting quantifiers. J. Log. Comput. **17**(1), 133–155 (2007). https://doi.org/10.1093/logcom/exl034

13. Pratt-Hartmann, I.: On the computational complexity of the numerically definite syllogistic and related logics. Bull. Symbolic Logic **14**(1), 1–28 (2008). https://doi.org/10.2178/bsl/1208358842

14. Tobies, S.: PSPACE reasoning for graded modal logics. J. Log. Comput. **11**(1), 85–106 (2001). https://doi.org/10.1093/logcom/11.1.85

15. Zolin, E.: Undecidability of the transitive graded modal logic with converse. J. Log. Comput. **27**(5), 1399–1420 (2017). https://doi.org/10.1093/logcom/exw026

The Dynamic Logic of Policies
and Contingent Planning

Thomas Bolander[1] , Thorsten Engesser[3] , Andreas Herzig[2]([⊠]) ,
Robert Mattmüller[3] , and Bernhard Nebel[3]

[1] DTU Compute, Technical University of Denmark, Lyngby, Denmark
tobo@dtu.dk
[2] IRIT, CNRS, University of Toulouse, Toulouse, France
herzig@irit.fr
[3] Faculty of Engineering, University of Freiburg, Freiburg im Breisgau, Germany
{engesser,mattmuel,nebel}@cs.uni-freiburg.de

Abstract. In classical deterministic planning, solutions to planning
tasks are simply sequences of actions, but that is not sufficient for contingent plans in non-deterministic environments. Contingent plans are often
expressed through policies that map states to actions. An alternative is to
specify contingent plans as programs, e.g. in the syntax of Propositional
Dynamic Logic (PDL). PDL is a logic for reasoning about programs with
sequential composition, test and non-deterministic choice. However, as
we show in the paper, none of the existing PDL modalities directly captures the notion of a solution to a planning task under non-determinism.
We add a new modality to star-free PDL correctly capturing this notion.
We prove the appropriateness of the new modality by showing how to
translate back and forth between policies and PDL programs under the
new modality. More precisely, we show how a policy solution to a planning task gives rise to a program solution expressed via the new modality,
and vice versa. We also provide an axiomatisation of our PDL extension
through reduction axioms into standard star-free PDL.

1 Introduction

Several authors have investigated how Propositional Dynamic Logic PDL can
account for conformant planning [2,5,11,12]. We here push this program further
and investigate how contingent planning can be captured in PDL. We argue
that the standard PDL operators $[\pi]$ and $\langle \pi \rangle$ of necessity and possibility are
not well-suited to account for conditional plans and introduce a third modal
operator $([\pi])\gamma$, read "π is strong for γ". Such an operator was already proposed
for conformant planning in some of the above papers. Just as these proposals,
$([a])\varphi$ will be equivalent to $\langle a \rangle \top \wedge [a]\varphi$ for atomic actions a. More generally, for
sequences of atomic actions $a_1; \dots; a_n$ we have

$$([a_1; \dots; a_n])\varphi \leftrightarrow (\langle a_1 \rangle \top \wedge [a_1](\cdots(\langle a_n \rangle \top \wedge [a_n]\varphi)\cdots)).$$

F. Calimeri et al. (Eds.): JELIA 2019, LNAI 11468, pp. 659–674, 2019.
https://doi.org/10.1007/978-3-030-19570-0_43

We here go beyond sequential compositions and integrate nondeterministic composition and test. We show that this accounts for contingent planning, in the sense that there is a policy solving a contingent planning task $\langle S, \gamma, \mathcal{M}_{\mathsf{Act}} \rangle$ with initial states S, goal formula γ and set of actions Act if and only if there is a program π such that $\mathcal{M}_{\mathsf{Act}}, S \Vdash (\![\pi]\!)\gamma$, where $\mathcal{M}_{\mathsf{Act}}$ is the PDL Kripke model that captures the semantics of the actions Act.

The paper is organised as follows. In the next section we briefly recall PDL and define planning tasks and their sequential solutions. In Sect. 3 we define policies and contingent planning. In Sect. 4 we extend PDL by the new operator $(\![\cdot]\!)$. In Sect. 5 we associate to every program a policy and, the other way round, we associate to every policy a program in Sect. 6.

2   Background: PDL and Sequential Plans

Propositional Dynamic Logic (PDL) is a modal logic that can immediately capture at least some forms of planning. Let us detail this for the case of sequential plans under full observability. We start by a brief introduction of star-free PDL; the reader is referred to [8,9] for more details.

Let Prp denote a finite set of propositional variables and Act a finite set of actions. A *Kripke model* $\mathcal{M}_{\mathsf{Act}} = \langle W, \{R_a\}_{a \in \mathsf{Act}}, V \rangle$ then consists of a set W of states (alias possible worlds), each action $a \in \mathsf{Act}$ is modelled by a binary relation R_a on W, and $V : W \longrightarrow 2^{\mathsf{Prp}}$ is a valuation associating to every state the propositional variables that are true there. Given a state $s \in W$, the possible outcomes of executing a at s is the set of states $R_a(s) = \{t \in W \mid \langle s, t \rangle \in R_a\}$. When $R_a(s) \neq \emptyset$ we say that a *is applicable at* s.

A set of states $S \subseteq W$ is called *valuation determined* if for all distinct $s, t \in S$ we have $V(s) \neq V(t)$. So S is valuation determined if all states in S are distinguishable via their valuation. In automated planning, the set of states of a planning domain is often just taken to be a subset of 2^{Prp}, and hence the set of all states is trivially valuation determined. However, in PDL, models are rarely restricted to only allow one state per valuation, so we will not make that restriction here either. However, to ensure a match between PDL programs and policies, we need at least to make the following weaker assumption.

We will assume all Kripke models to be *locally valuation determined*: For all actions $a \in \mathsf{Act}$ and all states $s \in W$, $R_a(s)$ is valuation determined. This requirement ensures that distinct outcomes of nondeterministic actions are necessarily distinguishable via their valuations. This requirement is necessary to guarantee that every policy can be translated into a corresponding program. Policies are going to be defined as relations between states and actions. A policy could for instance contain $\langle s, a \rangle, \langle t_1, b \rangle, \langle t_2, c \rangle$, assigning action a to state s, action b to state t_1 and action c to state t_2. Suppose $R_a(s) = \{t_1, t_2\}$. Then the policy specifies to execute a in s, and depending on the outcome, do either b or c. If the two possible outcomes t_1 and t_2 of a are not distinguishable by their valuation, there might not exist a formula distinguishing them, and hence there can be no PDL program representing the policy.

Any model $\mathcal{M}_{\mathsf{Act}}$ can be unravelled to a bisimilar, and hence modally equivalent, *tree model* [6,9]. It follows that we can assume all our Kripke models to be *acyclic*. We recall that a PDL Kripke model is cyclic if there is a natural number $n \geq 1$ and sequence of states $\langle s_0, s_1, \ldots, s_n \rangle$ such that $s_0 = s_n$ and for every $k \geq 1$, $\langle s_{k-1}, s_k \rangle \in R_{a_k}$ for some a_k. Unravelling a locally valuation determined model will of course give a model that is also locally valuation determined.

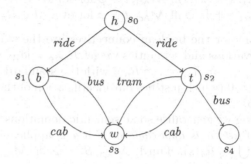

Fig. 1. A Kripke model.

Example 1. Consider the Kripke model given in Fig. 1. The story goes as follows: Initially, we are at home (h) and our goal is to get to work (w). We can get a lift by a friend who, depending on the traffic situation, will either drop us off at the train station (t) or the nearby bus station (b). We can then continue via multiple means of transportation, including the tram, the bus or a cab. At the bus station, taking the tram is not possible. Also, while we can take a bus from the train station, it will not get us to work.

Kripke models can interpret formulas and programs of PDL. We recall that the syntax of these is defined by the grammar

$$\varphi ::= p \mid \neg\varphi \mid \varphi \wedge \varphi \mid \langle\pi\rangle\varphi \mid [\pi]\varphi$$
$$\pi ::= a \mid \pi;\pi \mid \pi\cup\pi \mid \varphi?$$

where a ranges over Act and p over the set of atomic propositions Prp. We use the standard abbreviations; in particular, the programs $\mathtt{skip}$ and $\mathtt{fail}$ respectively abbreviate $\top?$ and $\bot?$. Furthermore, we use the notation $\bigcup_{x \in X} \pi_x$ for finite nondeterministic compositions, understanding that the latter equals $\mathtt{fail}$ when X is empty. A *sequential program* is a PDL program of the form $a_1; \ldots; a_n$, for $n \geq 0$. By convention, when $n = 0$ we identify such a program with $\mathtt{skip}$.

Example 2. Intuitively, in Example 1, the programs $\pi_1 = ride; (tram \cup cab)$ and $\pi_2 = ride; ((b?; bus) \cup (t?; tram))$ successfully get us to work. Note that in π_1, after the application of *ride*, it becomes clear from the applicability of the actions whether the action *cab* has to be taken or whether we can choose either of *tram* or *cab*. In contrast, the program π_2 relies on tests to ensure that we make a good choice and, in particular, don't take the bus from the train station.

The interpretation of formulas and programs is defined by mutual recursion as follows:

$$R_{\pi_1;\pi_2} = R_{\pi_1} \circ R_{\pi_2}$$
$$R_{\pi_1 \cup \pi_2} = R_{\pi_1} \cup R_{\pi_2}$$
$$R_{\varphi?} = \{\langle s,s \rangle \mid \mathcal{M}_{\mathsf{Act}}, s \Vdash \varphi\}$$
$$\mathcal{M}_{\mathsf{Act}}, s \Vdash p \text{ iff } p \in V(s)$$
$$\mathcal{M}_{\mathsf{Act}}, s \Vdash \langle \pi \rangle \varphi \text{ iff } \mathcal{M}_{\mathsf{Act}}, t \Vdash \varphi \text{ for some } t \in R_\pi(s)$$
$$\mathcal{M}_{\mathsf{Act}}, s \Vdash [\pi]\varphi \text{ iff } \mathcal{M}_{\mathsf{Act}}, t \Vdash \varphi \text{ for every } t \in R_\pi(s)$$

The truth conditions for the boolean connectives are the standard ones. From the provided abbrevations and semantics we get $R_{\mathtt{skip}} = \mathsf{id}_W = \{\langle s,s \rangle \mid s \in W\}$, $R_{\mathtt{fail}} = \emptyset$, and $R_{a_1;\dots;a_n} = R_{a_1} \circ \dots \circ R_{a_n}$, with the standard convention that it equals id_W when $n = 0$ (which justifies our identification of the empty sequential program with $\mathtt{skip}$).

Before proceeding we generalise some semantic definitions from states to sets of states $S \subseteq W$. First, a *is applicable at* S if a is applicable at every $s \in S$. Second, $R_a(S) = \bigcup_{s \in S} R_a(s)$. Third, $\mathcal{M}_{\mathsf{Act}}, S \Vdash \varphi$ iff $\mathcal{M}_{\mathsf{Act}}, s \Vdash \varphi$ for every $s \in S$. So $\mathcal{M}_{\mathsf{Act}}, \emptyset \Vdash \varphi$ for all φ, and we can rewrite the last truth condition of the semantics more compactly as: $\mathcal{M}_{\mathsf{Act}}, s \Vdash [\pi]\varphi$ iff $\mathcal{M}_{\mathsf{Act}}, R_\pi(s) \Vdash \varphi$.

A *planning task* is given by a triple $\langle S, \gamma, \mathcal{M}_{\mathsf{Act}} \rangle$ with a valuation determined set of initial states $S \subseteq W$, goal formula γ of PDL and set of actions Act whose semantics is given by the Kripke model $\mathcal{M}_{\mathsf{Act}}$. Traditionally, planning tasks have a single initial state, but generalising to arbitrary (valuation determined) sets makes the technicalities in the following cleaner. A sequential program $a_1; \dots; a_n$, alias a sequential plan, is a *solution* of $\langle S, \gamma, \mathcal{M}_{\mathsf{Act}} \rangle$ if and only if

- $n = 0$ implies $\mathcal{M}_{\mathsf{Act}}, S \Vdash \gamma$;
- $n > 0$ implies a_1 is applicable at S and $a_2; \dots; a_n$ is a solution of $\langle R_{a_1}(S), \gamma, \mathcal{M}_{\mathsf{Act}} \rangle$.

Sequential solutions of planning tasks can immediately be characterised in PDL when all actions are deterministic, i.e., when every $R_a(s)$ is either empty or a singleton: then the sequential plan $a_1; \dots; a_n$ is a solution of $\langle S, \gamma, \mathcal{M}_{\mathsf{Act}} \rangle$ iff $\mathcal{M}_{\mathsf{Act}}, S \Vdash \langle a_1; \dots; a_n \rangle \gamma$. Things are less straightforward when actions can be nondeterministic. We follow [1,2,5,12] and introduce a third modal operator $([a_1; \dots; a_n])$ (noted $[\![a_1; \dots; a_n]\!]$ in [1] and $((a_1; \dots; a_n))$ in [2,5]) whose semantics is defined recursively by:

$$\mathcal{M}_{\mathsf{Act}}, s \Vdash ([\mathtt{skip}])\varphi \quad \text{iff} \quad \mathcal{M}_{\mathsf{Act}}, s \Vdash \varphi$$
$$\mathcal{M}_{\mathsf{Act}}, s \Vdash ([a; \pi])\varphi \quad \text{iff} \quad a \text{ is applicable at } s \text{ and } \mathcal{M}_{\mathsf{Act}}, R_a(s) \Vdash ([\pi])\varphi$$

So $([a_1; \dots; a_n])\varphi$ is equivalent to $\langle a_1 \rangle \top \wedge [a_1](\cdots(\langle a_n \rangle \top \wedge [a_n]\varphi)\cdots)$. It was established by several authors, e.g. [2,5,12], that $a_1; \dots; a_n$ is a solution of $\langle S, \gamma, \mathcal{M}_{\mathsf{Act}} \rangle$ iff $\mathcal{M}_{\mathsf{Act}}, S \Vdash ([a_1; \dots; a_n])\gamma$.

In the rest of the paper we are going to extend the argument of this new modal operator to arbitrary star-free PDL programs. We are going to show that these programs capture policies, which means that our framework accounts for contingent planning.

3   Policies and Strong Solutions to Planning Tasks

Policies relate states to actions and provide the solution concept for contingent planning. We here introduce a slight generalisation of strong policies as defined in [4]. Note that we have assumed our models $\mathcal{M}_{\mathsf{Act}}$ to be acyclic, and hence our policies will also automatically be acyclic, consistent with the notion of a strong policy in [4].

Given a model $\mathcal{M}_{\mathsf{Act}}$, a *policy* (called state-action table in [4]) is a relation $\Lambda \subseteq W \times (\mathsf{Act} \cup \{\mathsf{stop}\})$. It is *defined* at a set of states $S \subseteq W$ if for every $s \in S$ there is an $x \in \mathsf{Act} \cup \{\mathsf{stop}\}$ such that $\langle s, x \rangle \in \Lambda$. It is *strongly executable* if for every $s \in W$ and $a \in \mathsf{Act}$, $\langle s, a \rangle \in \Lambda$ implies a is applicable at s and Λ is defined at $R_a(s)$. Note that our policies can be nondeterministic, since Λ is any relation between states and actions (instead of a partial function from states to actions). So we can for instance have $\langle s, a \rangle, \langle s, b \rangle \in \Lambda$, which means that the policy specifies two actions a and b in s that nature will choose nondeterministically between.

The special symbol stop is a 'license to stop': the elements of the set

$$\mathsf{Stop}(\Lambda) = \{t \in W \mid \langle t, \mathsf{stop} \rangle \in \Lambda\}$$

are the checkpoints of Λ where we are going to evaluate whether the goal is fulfilled. Such an entity is not a standard ingredient of polices, but makes sense in a nondeterministic setting: we can have policies such as $\Lambda = \{\langle s, \mathsf{stop}\rangle, \langle s, a\rangle\}$ which at s specifies a nondeterministic choice by nature between stoping to act (terminating policy execution) and performing action a. If the model $\mathcal{M}_{\mathsf{Act}}$ is such that some goal γ is true at s and at every outcome state $R_a(s)$, then we are entitled to say that Λ guarantees γ.

Given a finite policy Λ, the *depth* of Λ from a set of states $S \subseteq W$ is recursively defined by

$$\mathsf{d}(\Lambda, S) = \begin{cases} 0 & \text{if } \Lambda \setminus (S \times \{\mathsf{stop}\}) = \emptyset \\ 1 + \mathsf{d}(\Lambda, \bigcup_{\langle s,a \rangle \in \Lambda \setminus (S \times \{\mathsf{stop}\})} R_a(s)) & \text{otherwise} \end{cases}$$

So when $\mathsf{d}(\Lambda, S) = 0$, the only elements of Λ are of the form $\langle s, \mathsf{stop} \rangle$. The function $\mathsf{d}(\Lambda, S)$ is well-defined because Λ is finite and $\mathcal{M}_{\mathsf{Act}}$ is acyclic.

Example 3. Consider the following policies for the model from Example 1:

$$\Lambda_1 = \{\langle s_0, ride\rangle, \langle s_1, cab\rangle, \langle s_2, tram\rangle, \langle s_2, cab\rangle, \langle s_3, \mathsf{stop}\rangle\}$$
$$\Lambda_2 = \{\langle s_0, ride\rangle, \langle s_1, bus\rangle, \langle s_2, tram\rangle, \langle s_3, \mathsf{stop}\rangle\}$$

Both policies are acyclic, finite, strongly executable, and have a depth of 2 from $\{s_0\}$. More importantly, we can see that following these policies will always lead us to the goal w. Also, Λ_1 and Λ_2 intuitively correspond to the programs π_1 and π_2 from Example 2. Note that Λ_1 is a nondeterministic policy, which allows us to take either the tram or the cab from s_2.

In the following, we will define what it means for a policy to solve a planning task. Later, we will also define the correspondence between policies and programs.

Definition 1. *A policy Λ is a strong solution of a planning task $\langle S, \gamma, \mathcal{M}_{\mathsf{Act}} \rangle$ iff all of the following hold:*

1. *Λ is finite and strongly executable;*
2. *Λ is defined at S;*
3. *$\mathcal{M}_{\mathsf{Act}}, \mathsf{Stop}(\Lambda) \Vdash \gamma$.*

Lemma 1. *The policy $S \times \{\mathsf{stop}\}$ is a strong solution of a planning task $\langle S, \gamma, \mathcal{M}_{\mathsf{Act}} \rangle$ iff $\mathcal{M}_{\mathsf{Act}}, S \Vdash \gamma$.*

Proof. The policy $S \times \{\mathsf{stop}\}$ is strongly executable, and is defined at S. It is also finite, since the set S of initial states of any planning task is valuation determined, and hence finite (there is only a finite set of propositional variables and hence only a finite set of possible valuations).

Lemma 2. *If Λ is a strong solution of a planning task $\langle S, \gamma, \mathcal{M}_{\mathsf{Act}} \rangle$ then Λ is a strong solution of $\langle R_a(s), \gamma, \mathcal{M}_{\mathsf{Act}} \rangle$ for every $s \in S$ and $\langle s, a \rangle \in \Lambda$.*

Proof. Let Λ be a strong solution of $\langle S, \gamma, \mathcal{M}_{\mathsf{Act}} \rangle$ and $\langle s, a \rangle \in \Lambda$ for some $s \in S$. In order to establish that Λ is a strong solution of $\langle R_a(s), \gamma, \mathcal{M}_{\mathsf{Act}} \rangle$ it is enough to prove that Λ is defined at $R_a(s)$. This holds because Λ is strongly executable.

Lemma 3. *Suppose Λ_1 and Λ_2 are both strong solutions of the planning task $\langle S, \gamma, \mathcal{M}_{\mathsf{Act}} \rangle$. Then $\Lambda_1 \cup \Lambda_2$ is also a strong solution of $\langle S, \gamma, \mathcal{M}_{\mathsf{Act}} \rangle$.*

Proof. Condition 1 of Definition 1: We need to prove finiteness and strong executability. $\Lambda_1 \cup \Lambda_2$ is clearly finite, as both Λ_1 and Λ_2 are. For strong executability, note that if $\langle s, a \rangle \in \Lambda_1 \cup \Lambda_2$ then $\langle s, a \rangle \in \Lambda_i$ for $i = 1$ or $i = 2$. Strong executability of Λ_i implies that $R_a(s)$ is non-empty and Λ_i is defined at $R_a(s)$. Therefore $\Lambda_1 \cup \Lambda_2$ is defined at $R_a(s)$, too. Condition 2: If Λ_1 is defined at S, then any extension of Λ_1 is also defined at S, including $\Lambda_1 \cup \Lambda_2$. Condition 3: If $\mathcal{M}_{\mathsf{Act}}, \mathsf{Stop}(\Lambda_1) \Vdash \gamma$ and $\mathcal{M}_{\mathsf{Act}}, \mathsf{Stop}(\Lambda_2) \Vdash \gamma$ then $\mathcal{M}_{\mathsf{Act}}, \mathsf{Stop}(\Lambda_1) \cup \mathsf{Stop}(\Lambda_2) \Vdash \gamma$, and $\mathsf{Stop}(\Lambda_1) \cup \mathsf{Stop}(\Lambda_2) = \mathsf{Stop}(\Lambda_1 \cup \Lambda_2)$.

Lemma 4. *Suppose Λ_1 is a strong solution of $\langle S_1, \gamma, \mathcal{M}_{\mathsf{Act}} \rangle$ and Λ_2 is a strong solution of $\langle S_2, \gamma, \mathcal{M}_{\mathsf{Act}} \rangle$. Then $\Lambda_1 \cup \Lambda_2$ is a strong solution of $\langle S_1 \cup S_2, \gamma, \mathcal{M}_{\mathsf{Act}} \rangle$.*

Proof. Condition 1: As in the proof of the previous lemma. Condition 2: $\Lambda_1 \cup \Lambda_2$ is clearly defined at $S_1 \cup S_2$. Condition 3: $\mathcal{M}_{\mathsf{Act}}, \mathsf{Stop}(\Lambda_1 \cup \Lambda_2) \Vdash \gamma$ just as in the proof of the previous lemma.

The policy $\Lambda^{-\mathsf{stop}}$ is obtained from Λ by deleting all licenses to stop: $\Lambda^{-\mathsf{stop}} = \Lambda \setminus (W \times \{\mathsf{stop}\})$. This definition is useful to combine policies sequentially.

Lemma 5. *Suppose Λ_1 is finite, strongly executable and defined at S, and suppose Λ_2 is a strong solution of $\langle \mathsf{Stop}(\Lambda_1), \gamma, \mathcal{M}_{\mathsf{Act}} \rangle$. Then $\Lambda_1^{-\mathsf{stop}} \cup \Lambda_2$ is a strong solution of $\langle S, \gamma, \mathcal{M}_{\mathsf{Act}} \rangle$.*

Proof. Condition 1: $\Lambda_1^{-\text{stop}} \cup \Lambda_2$ is clearly finite. Let us show that it is also strongly executable. Suppose $\langle s, a \rangle \in \Lambda_1^{-\text{stop}} \cup \Lambda_2$. If $\langle s, a \rangle \in \Lambda_2$ then, as Λ_2 is strongly executable, a is applicable at s and Λ_2 is defined at $R_a(s)$, and so is $\Lambda_1^{-\text{stop}} \cup \Lambda_2$. Otherwise, if $\langle s, a \rangle \in \Lambda_1^{-\text{stop}}$ then, as Λ_1 is strongly executable, a is applicable at s and Λ_1 is defined at $R_a(s)$. The latter means that for every $t \in R_a(s)$ there is an $x_t \in \text{Act} \cup \{\text{stop}\}$ such that $\langle t, x_t \rangle \in \Lambda_1$. We distinguish two cases: (1) when $x_t \in \text{Act}$ then $\langle t, x_t \rangle \in \Lambda_1^{-\text{stop}}$, and so $\Lambda_1^{-\text{stop}} \cup \Lambda_2$ is defined at t; (2) when $x_t = \text{stop}$ then $t \in \text{Stop}(\Lambda_1)$, and as Λ_2 is defined at $\text{Stop}(\Lambda_1)$ we have that $\Lambda_1^{-\text{stop}} \cup \Lambda_2$ is defined at t. It follows that $\Lambda_1^{-\text{stop}} \cup \Lambda_2$ is defined at $R_a(s)$.

Condition 2: let us show that $\Lambda_1^{-\text{stop}} \cup \Lambda_2$ is defined at S. Let $s \in S$ be chosen arbitrarily. As Λ_1 is defined at S, either there is an $a \in \text{Act}$ such that $\langle s, a \rangle \in \Lambda_1$, and hence $\langle s, a \rangle \in \Lambda_1^{-\text{stop}} \cup \Lambda_2$, as required. Otherwise, $\langle s, \text{stop} \rangle \in \Lambda_1$. This implies $s \in \text{Stop}(\Lambda_1)$, and since Λ_2 applies to $\text{Stop}(\Lambda_1)$, there must exist an $x \in \text{Act} \cup \{\text{stop}\}$ such that $\langle s, x \rangle \in \Lambda_2$, implying $\langle s, x \rangle \in \Lambda_1^{-\text{stop}} \cup \Lambda_2$, as required.

Condition 3: As $\text{Stop}(\Lambda_1^{-\text{stop}} \cup \Lambda_2) = \text{Stop}(\Lambda_2)$ and Λ_2 is a strong solution of $\langle \text{Stop}(\Lambda_1), \gamma, \mathcal{M}_{\text{Act}} \rangle$, we must have $\mathcal{M}_{\text{Act}}, \text{Stop}(\Lambda_1^{-\text{stop}} \cup \Lambda_2) \Vdash \gamma$.

The above lemmas basically show that union and sequential composition of two policies preserve strong solutions.

The sequential policy associated to a sequential program $a_1; \ldots; a_n$ and a set of states $S \subseteq W$ is

$$
\text{SPol}(a_1; \ldots; a_n, S) = \begin{cases} \emptyset & \text{if } n = 0 \\ (S \times \{a_1\}) \cup \text{SPol}(a_2; \ldots; a_n, R_{a_1}(S)) & \text{otherwise} \end{cases}
$$

It is then straightforward to prove that the sequential program $a_1; \ldots; a_n$ is a solution of the planning task $\langle S, \gamma, \mathcal{M}_{\text{Act}} \rangle$ if and only if the policy $\text{SPol}(a_1; \ldots; a_n, S)$ is a strong solution of $\langle S, \gamma, \mathcal{M}_{\text{Act}} \rangle$. The other way round, it is clearly not the case that any policy can be mapped to a sequential program. For example, consider the policy Λ_2 from Example 3. This policy assigns the action *bus* to s_1 and *tram* to s_2. Since the action *ride* executed in s_0 can either result in s_1 or s_2, the policy specifies distinct actions depending on the outcome of *ride*. This policy can hence not be represented as a sequential program, as after the execution of *ride*, the choice of action to follow is conditional on the outcome of *ride*. This is also why the PDL program π_2 of Example 2 corresponding to Λ_2 includes tests on the outcome of *ride*: $\pi_2 = \textit{ride}; ((b?; \textit{bus}) \cup (t?; \textit{tram}))$.

4   Extending PDL by the Modal Operator $([\pi])$

As announced, we extend the language of PDL by a third modal operator on programs $([\pi])$. The interpretation of $([\pi])$ is defined inductively:

$$
\begin{aligned}
\mathcal{M}_{\text{Act}}, s \Vdash ([a])\varphi \quad &\text{iff } a \text{ is applicable at } s \text{ and } \mathcal{M}_{\text{Act}}, R_a(s) \Vdash \varphi \\
\mathcal{M}_{\text{Act}}, s \Vdash ([\pi_1; \pi_2])\varphi \quad &\text{iff } \mathcal{M}_{\text{Act}}, s \Vdash ([\pi_1])([\pi_2])\varphi \\
\mathcal{M}_{\text{Act}}, s \Vdash ([\pi_1 \cup \pi_2])\varphi \quad &\text{iff } \mathcal{M}_{\text{Act}}, s \Vdash (([\pi_1])\top \vee ([\pi_2])\top) \wedge \\
&\qquad\qquad (([\pi_1])\top \rightarrow ([\pi_1])\varphi) \wedge \\
&\qquad\qquad (([\pi_2])\top \rightarrow ([\pi_2])\varphi) \\
\mathcal{M}_{\text{Act}}, s \Vdash ([\psi?])\varphi \quad &\text{iff } \mathcal{M}_{\text{Act}}, s \Vdash \psi \text{ and } \mathcal{M}_{\text{Act}}, s \Vdash \varphi
\end{aligned}
$$

Satisfiability and validity are defined in the standard way. For example, the equivalence $([\pi])\varphi \leftrightarrow ([\pi; \varphi?])\top$ is easily seen to be valid. Furthermore, it can be checked that the equivalences $([a])\varphi \leftrightarrow \langle a \rangle \top \wedge [a]\varphi$ and $([a])\top \leftrightarrow \langle a \rangle \top$ are valid. These equivalences however do not generalise to arbitrary programs.

For the model from Example 1, one can easily verify that $\mathcal{M}_{\mathsf{Act}}, s_0 \Vdash ([\pi_1])w$ and $\mathcal{M}_{\mathsf{Act}}, s_0 \Vdash ([\pi_2])w$.

Remark 1. Programs that are equivalent in PDL are no longer necessarily equivalent under the new modality. To witness, consider the programs *ride* and $(ride; b?) \cup (ride; \neg b?)$, which have the same interpretation in PDL. In our running example, *ride* is applicable at s_0 and nondeterministically produces either b or $\neg b$. Thus $\mathcal{M}_{\mathsf{Act}}, s_0 \Vdash ([ride])\top$, while $\mathcal{M}_{\mathsf{Act}}, s_0 \nVdash ([(ride; b?) \cup (ride; \neg b?)])\top$ because $\mathcal{M}_{\mathsf{Act}}, s_0 \nVdash ([ride; b?])\top$ and $\mathcal{M}_{\mathsf{Act}}, s_0 \nVdash ([ride; \neg b?])\top$.

Remark 2. Our semantics has two kinds of nondeterminism. The nondeterminism of atomic programs is *demonic*: it is the environment who chooses for example the outcome of the nondeterministic *ride* action. The nondeterminism of the choice-operator $\cup$ has an *angelic* component: while all applicable actions have to be successful, it is not required that all actions are applicable. Let us illustrate this by a couple of examples.

The choice operator necessarily has to be given a semantics that has such an angelic flavour if we want to account for nondeterministic policies. In our running example, the policy $\Lambda_3 = \{\langle s_2, tram \rangle, \langle s_2, cab \rangle, \langle s_3, \mathsf{stop} \rangle\}$ is a strong solution of the planning problem of getting from the train station to work. So $\mathcal{M}_{\mathsf{Act}}, s_2 \Vdash ([tram])w \wedge ([cab])w$. The only reasonable description of Λ as a PDL program is $tram \cup cab$, and indeed, $\mathcal{M}_{\mathsf{Act}}, s \Vdash ([tram \cup cab])w$. Now let us contrast this with states s_1 and s_2 where $\mathcal{M}_{\mathsf{Act}}, s_1 \Vdash b \wedge ([bus])w$ and $\mathcal{M}_{\mathsf{Act}}, s_2 \Vdash \neg b \wedge ([tram])w$. The policy $\Lambda_4 = \{\langle s_1, bus \rangle, \langle s_2, tram \rangle, \langle s_3, \mathsf{stop} \rangle\}$ is a strong solution of the planning problem $\langle \{s_1, s_2\}, w, \mathcal{M}_{\mathsf{Act}} \rangle$. The only reasonable description of Λ_4 seems to be the PDL counterpart of the conditional program "if b then *bus* else *tram*", namely $(b?; bus) \cup (\neg b?; tram)$; and indeed, we have $\mathcal{M}_{\mathsf{Act}}, \{s_1, s_2\} \Vdash ([(b?; bus) \cup (\neg b?; tram)])w$.

Note that we cannot have a purely angelic semantics where $\cup$ is interpreted as disjunction, that is, where $([a_1 \cup a_2])\varphi \leftrightarrow (([a_1])\varphi \vee ([a_2])\varphi)$. To see this, first note that we have $\mathcal{M}_{\mathsf{Act}}, s_2 \Vdash ([tram])w \wedge ([bus])\top \wedge ([bus])\neg w$. A purely angelic semantics would hence give us $\mathcal{M}_{\mathsf{Act}}, s_2 \Vdash ([tram \cup bus])w$, something we would not like to assert: the agent does not have a free choice between *tram* and *bus* to guarantee w (if taking the bus, the agent will not end up at the workplace). Contrast with the fact that $\mathcal{M}_{\mathsf{Act}}, s_1 \Vdash ([bus])w \wedge \neg([tram])\top$. According to our semantics, we actually get $\mathcal{M}_{\mathsf{Act}}, s_1 \Vdash ([bus \cup tram])w$. This is OK, since *tram* is not even applicable at s_1, so the only possible execution of $bus \cup tram$ in s_1 is to execute *bus*. One can think of $\cup$ as giving a demonic nondeterministic choice where nature chooses which action will be executed, but only among the applicable ones. From the perspective of the acting agent, we can think of it as the agent choosing an arbitrary action, but again only among the applicable ones.

An axiomatisation of the validities of our language is obtained by adding the following to the axiomatisation of PDL:

$$[\![a]\!]\varphi \leftrightarrow \langle a \rangle \top \wedge [a]\varphi \tag{Atom}$$

$$[\![\pi_1; \pi_2]\!]\varphi \leftrightarrow [\![\pi_1]\!][\![\pi_2]\!]\varphi \tag{Seq}$$

$$[\![\pi_1 \cup \pi_2]\!]\varphi \leftrightarrow ([\![\pi_1]\!]\top \vee [\![\pi_2]\!]\top) \wedge ([\![\pi_1]\!]\top \rightarrow [\![\pi_1]\!]\varphi) \wedge ([\![\pi_2]\!]\top \rightarrow [\![\pi_2]\!]\varphi) \tag{NDet}$$

$$[\![\psi?]\!]\varphi \leftrightarrow \psi \wedge \varphi \tag{Test}$$

The first four axioms are reduction axioms for program operators. They can be used from the left to the right to eliminate complex programs, applying the rule of replacement of equivalents (that can be derived without the rule of equivalents for $[\![\pi]\!]$) to subformulas that are not in the scope of any $[\![\pi]\!]$. This results in formulas where all programs are of the form a.

Soundness of our axioms can be proved straightforwardly, given that the axioms closely match the truth conditions for $[\![\pi]\!]$. Completeness of the axiomatisation can be proved by eliminating all $[\![\pi]\!]$ from formulas via the above reduction axioms. If all $[\![\pi]\!]$ are eliminated from a formula, what remains is a formula in the language of standard PDL whose satisfiability can be checked by solvers for PDL [7,10]. It follows that satisfiability and validity in our augmented PDL are both decidable.

We note that

$$[\![\pi_1 \cup \pi_2]\!]\varphi \leftrightarrow ([\![\pi_1]\!]\varphi \wedge [\![\pi_2]\!]\varphi) \vee ([\![\pi_1]\!]\varphi \wedge \neg [\![\pi_2]\!]\top) \vee (\neg [\![\pi_1]\!]\top \wedge [\![\pi_2]\!]\varphi)$$

is a propositionally equivalent formulation of the axiom for nondeterministic composition. In the rest of the section we provide some properties of our logic.

The modal operator $[\![\pi]\!]$ has almost all the properties of a normal modal operator: it satisfies the rule of monotony and the axiom of conjunction, and therefore also the K-axiom [3]. However, the rule of necessitation does not preserve validity.

Proposition 1. *The following rule of monotony for $[\![\pi]\!]$ is derivable:*

$$if\ \varphi \rightarrow \varphi'\ then\ [\![\pi]\!]\varphi \rightarrow [\![\pi]\!]\varphi' \tag{RM$_{[\![.]\!]}$}$$

Proof. By induction on the form of π. We only give the case of nondeterministic composition. Suppose $\varphi \rightarrow \varphi'$. $[\![\pi_1 \cup \pi_2]\!]\varphi$ is logically equivalent to

$$([\![\pi_1]\!]\top \vee [\![\pi_2]\!]\top) \wedge ([\![\pi_1]\!]\top \rightarrow [\![\pi_1]\!]\varphi) \wedge ([\![\pi_2]\!]\top \rightarrow [\![\pi_2]\!]\varphi).$$

Applying to the latter the induction hypothesis that $\varphi \rightarrow \varphi'$ implies $[\![\pi_1]\!]\varphi \rightarrow [\![\pi_1]\!]\varphi'$ and $[\![\pi_2]\!]\varphi \rightarrow [\![\pi_2]\!]\varphi'$ (twice), we obtain

$$[\![\pi_1 \cup \pi_2]\!]\varphi \rightarrow ([\![\pi_1]\!]\top \vee [\![\pi_2]\!]\top) \wedge ([\![\pi_1]\!]\top \rightarrow [\![\pi_1]\!]\varphi') \wedge ([\![\pi_2]\!]\top \rightarrow [\![\pi_2]\!]\varphi'),$$

which is equivalent to $[\![\pi_1 \cup \pi_2]\!]\varphi \rightarrow [\![\pi_1 \cup \pi_2]\!]\varphi'$.

Given that we have rules of equivalence for the other PDL connectives, it follows from the above that the rule of replacement of equivalents is derivable. Note that the theorem $([\pi])\varphi \rightarrow ([\pi])\top$ directly follows from $RM_{([\cdot])}$.

Proposition 2. *The following axiom of conjunction is a theorem:*

$$(([\pi])\varphi \wedge ([\pi])\varphi') \rightarrow ([\pi])(\varphi \wedge \varphi') \qquad\qquad (C_{([\cdot])})$$

Proof. The proof is by induction on the form of the program. The base cases use axioms Atom and Test and PDL theorems. The induction step uses the above rule of monotony $RM_{([\cdot])}$. For sequential composition we have:

1. $(([\pi_1])([\pi_2])\varphi \wedge ([\pi_1])([\pi_2])\varphi') \rightarrow ([\pi_1])(([\pi_2])\varphi \wedge ([\pi_2])\varphi')$ (by IH)
2. $(([\pi_2])\varphi \wedge ([\pi_2])\varphi') \rightarrow ([\pi_2])(\varphi \wedge \varphi')$ (by IH)
3. $([\pi_1])(([\pi_2])\varphi \wedge ([\pi_2])\varphi') \rightarrow ([\pi_1])([\pi_2])(\varphi \wedge \varphi')$ (from 2 by $RM_{([\cdot])}$)
4. $(([\pi_1])([\pi_2])\varphi \wedge ([\pi_1])([\pi_2])\varphi') \rightarrow ([\pi_1])([\pi_2])(\varphi \wedge \varphi')$ (from 1 and 3)
5. $(([\pi_1;\pi_2])\varphi \wedge ([\pi_1;\pi_2])\varphi') \rightarrow ([\pi_1;\pi_2])(\varphi \wedge \varphi')$ (from 4 by Axiom Seq)

The case of nondeterministic composition is similar but a bit lengthy due to the size of Axiom NDet.

The equivalence $(([\pi])\varphi \wedge ([\pi])\varphi') \leftrightarrow ([\pi])(\varphi \wedge \varphi')$ can be proved from Axiom $C_{([\cdot])}$ and the derived inference rule $RM_{([\cdot])}$.

Altogether, it looks like $([\cdot])$ is a normal modal operator. However, the rule of necessitation 'from φ infer $([\pi])\varphi$' fails to preserve validity. Indeed, $([\pi])\top$ fails to be valid. To see this, consider a model where R_a is empty: then $\langle a \rangle \top$ is false at any state s, and therefore $([a])\top$ is false everywhere, too. This is as it should be: if $\langle a \rangle \top$ was valid then any action a would be applicable. Worse, validity of $\langle \pi \rangle \top$ for any program π would mean that e.g. the 'fail' program $\perp$? would be applicable.

The following theorems can be proved by induction on the form of programs, except item (7).

Proposition 3. *The following are theorems.*

$$([\pi])\perp \leftrightarrow \perp \qquad\qquad (1)$$
$$([\pi])\varphi \rightarrow \langle \pi \rangle \varphi \qquad\qquad (2)$$
$$[\pi]\varphi \wedge ([\pi])\top \rightarrow ([\pi])\varphi \qquad\qquad (3)$$
$$([\pi \cup \perp?])\varphi \leftrightarrow ([\pi])\varphi \qquad\qquad (4)$$
$$([\pi_1 \cup \pi_2])\top \leftrightarrow (([\pi_1])\top \vee ([\pi_2])\top) \qquad\qquad (5)$$
$$([(\pi_1;\pi_2) \cup (\pi_1;\pi_2')])\varphi \rightarrow ([\pi_1;(\pi_2 \cup \pi_2')])\varphi \qquad\qquad (6)$$
$$([\psi_1? \cup \psi_2?])\varphi \leftrightarrow (\psi_1 \vee \psi_2) \wedge \varphi \qquad\qquad (7)$$

None of the implications in Proposition 3 can be extended into equivalences. To see this for item (2), it suffices to consider a nondeterministic atomic action a with two possible outcomes p and $\neg p$: then $\langle a \rangle p$ holds but $([a])p$ does not. For item (3), this follows from the falsifiability of $([\pi])\varphi \rightarrow [\pi]\varphi$. To see this, consider the program $\pi = p? \cup (a; \neg p?)$ and a model $\mathcal{M}_{\mathsf{Act}}$ with a state s where p is true and where a nondeterministically produces outcome p or $\neg p$. Then $\mathcal{M}_{\mathsf{Act}}, s \Vdash (\![\pi]\!)p$, in particular because $\mathcal{M}_{\mathsf{Act}}, s \Vdash \neg(\![a; \neg p?]\!)\top$. On the other hand, $\mathcal{M}_{\mathsf{Act}}, s \nVdash [\pi]p$ because $\mathcal{M}_{\mathsf{Act}}, s \nVdash [a; \neg p?]p$. For item (6), this can be seen from from the example that we have given in Remark 1.

5   From Programs to Policies

In this section we associate a policy to a given program. Recall that models $\mathcal{M}_{\mathsf{Act}}$ are assumed to be acyclic (without loss of generality). We recursively associate to every program π and set of states S a policy $\mathsf{Pol}(\pi, S)$ as follows:

- If $\mathcal{M}_{\mathsf{Act}}, S \nVdash (\![\pi]\!)\top$ then $\mathsf{Pol}(\pi, S) = \emptyset$;
- If $\mathcal{M}_{\mathsf{Act}}, S \Vdash (\![\pi]\!)\top$ then, depending on the form of π:

$$\mathsf{Pol}(\psi?, S) = S \times \{\mathsf{stop}\}$$

$$\mathsf{Pol}(a, S) = (S \times \{a\}) \cup (R_a(S) \times \{\mathsf{stop}\})$$

$$\mathsf{Pol}(\pi_1; \pi_2, S) = (\mathsf{Pol}(\pi_1, S))^{-\mathsf{stop}} \cup \mathsf{Pol}(\pi_2, \mathsf{Stop}(\mathsf{Pol}(\pi_1, S)))$$

$$\mathsf{Pol}(\pi_1 \cup \pi_2, S) = \bigcup_{s \in S} (\mathsf{Pol}(\pi_1, \{s\}) \cup \mathsf{Pol}(\pi_2, \{s\}))$$

Example 4. Suppose $\mathcal{M}_{\mathsf{Act}}$ is such that $R_{a_1} = \{\langle s_1, t_1 \rangle\}$ and $R_{a_2} = \{\langle s_2, t_2 \rangle\}$. Then $\mathsf{Pol}(a_1 \cup a_2, \{s_1, s_2\}) = \{\langle s_1, a_1 \rangle, \langle s_2, a_2 \rangle, \langle t_1, \mathsf{stop} \rangle, \langle t_2, \mathsf{stop} \rangle\}$. This justifies the case of nondeterministic composition: $\mathsf{Pol}(a_1 \cup a_2, \{s_1, s_2\})$ would be empty had we defined $\mathsf{Pol}(\pi_1 \cup \pi_2, S)$ as $\mathsf{Pol}(\pi_2, S) \cup \mathsf{Pol}(\pi_2, S)$ (plus $\mathsf{Pol}(a, S)$ as empty if a is inapplicable at some $s \in S$).

Example 5. Suppose $\mathcal{M}_{\mathsf{Act}}$ is the model from our running example (Fig. 1). For the program $h?$ we have $\mathsf{Pol}(h?, \{s_0\}) = \{\langle s_0, \mathsf{stop} \rangle\}$. Consider the program $ride; b?$. Then $\mathcal{M}_{\mathsf{Act}}, s_0 \nVdash (\![ride; b?]\!)\top$, and therefore $\mathsf{Pol}(ride; b?, \{s_0\}) = \emptyset$. Consider the program $\pi = h? \cup (ride; b?)$. Then $\mathcal{M}_{\mathsf{Act}}, s_0 \Vdash (\![h?]\!)\top$ and $\mathcal{M}_{\mathsf{Act}}, s_0 \nVdash (\![ride; b?]\!)\top$, and therefore $\mathsf{Pol}(\pi, \{s_0\}) = \{\langle s_0, \mathsf{stop} \rangle\}$.

While $R_\pi(S)$ contains $\mathsf{Stop}(\mathsf{Pol}(\pi, S))$ for every set of states S (the proof is by induction on the form of π), the converse fails to hold. This can be seen from the above example: s_1 is not in $\mathsf{Stop}(\mathsf{Pol}(\pi, S))$, although it is in $R_{ride}(s)$.

Example 6. For the model from our running example and the program consisting of the single action $ride$, we obtain the following policy:

$$\mathsf{Pol}(ride, \{s_0\}) = (\{s_0\} \times \{ride\}) \cup (\{s_1, s_2\} \times \{\mathsf{stop}\})$$
$$= \{\langle s_0, ride \rangle, \langle s_1, \mathsf{stop} \rangle, \langle s_2, \mathsf{stop} \rangle\}$$

For the program $\pi_1 = ride; (tram \cup cab)$ we then obtain the following policy:

$$\mathsf{Pol}(\pi_1, \{s_0\})$$
$$= \mathsf{Pol}(ride, \{s_0\})^{-\mathsf{stop}} \cup \mathsf{Pol}(tram \cup cab, \mathsf{Stop}(\mathsf{Pol}(ride, \{s_0\})))$$
$$= \{\langle s_0, ride\rangle\} \cup \mathsf{Pol}(tram \cup cab, \{s_1, s_2\})$$
$$= \{\langle s_0, ride\rangle\} \cup \bigcup\{\mathsf{Pol}(tram, \{s_1\}) \cup \mathsf{Pol}(cab, \{s_1\}),$$
$$\mathsf{Pol}(tram, \{s_2\}) \cup \mathsf{Pol}(cab, \{s_2\})\}$$
$$= \{\langle s_0, ride\rangle\} \cup \emptyset \cup \{\langle s_1, cab\rangle, \langle s_3, \mathsf{stop}\rangle\}$$
$$\cup \{\langle s_2, tram\rangle, \langle s_3, \mathsf{stop}\rangle\} \cup \{\langle s_2, cab\rangle, \langle s_3, \mathsf{stop}\rangle\}$$
$$= \{\langle s_0, ride\rangle, \langle s_1, cab\rangle, \langle s_2, tram\rangle, \langle s_2, cab\rangle, \langle s_3, \mathsf{stop}\rangle\} = \Lambda_1$$

This verifies that indeed Λ_1 is the policy corresponding to π_1 as claimed in Example 3.

Lemma 6. *Suppose S is finite. Then $\mathsf{Pol}(\pi, S)$ finite, and for every $a \in \mathsf{Act}$, $\langle s, a\rangle \in \mathsf{Pol}(\pi, S)$ implies that a is applicable at s.*

Proof. We can prove by induction on the form of π that for every $a \in \mathsf{Act}$, if $\langle s, a\rangle \in \mathsf{Pol}(\pi, S)$ then a is applicable at s. Now note that since models are assumed to be locally valuation determined, for every action a and state s, $R_a(s)$ must be finite. Finiteness of $\mathsf{Pol}(\pi, S)$ is then due to finiteness of S and to finiteness of every $R_a(s)$; the proof is by induction on the form of π.

The hypotheses of Lemma 6 are not enough to guarantee strong executability of $\mathsf{Pol}(\pi, S)$. Consider our model from Fig. 1 which clearly satisfies the hypotheses of Lemma 6. Here, $\mathsf{Pol}(ride; tram, \{s_0\})$ is empty because $\mathcal{M}_{\mathsf{Act}}, s_0 \not\Vdash (\![ride; tram]\!)\top$. The next result says that $\mathsf{Pol}(\pi, S)$ is strongly executable under the condition that $(\![\pi]\!)\gamma$ is true at S (for any γ, so in particular when γ is $\top$). It moreover says that then $\mathsf{Pol}(\pi, S)$ is defined at S and $\mathcal{M}_{\mathsf{Act}}, \mathsf{Stop}(\mathsf{Pol}(\pi, S)) \Vdash \gamma$.

Proposition 4. *Let $\langle S, \gamma, \mathcal{M}_{\mathsf{Act}}\rangle$ be a planning task and suppose $\mathcal{M}_{\mathsf{Act}}, S \Vdash (\![\pi]\!)\gamma$. Then $\mathsf{Pol}(\pi, S)$ is a strong solution of $\langle S, \gamma, \mathcal{M}_{\mathsf{Act}}\rangle$.*

Proof. Since $\langle S, \gamma, \mathcal{M}_{\mathsf{Act}}\rangle$ is a planning task, S is valuation determined, and hence finite. Thus, by Lemma 6, $\mathsf{Pol}(\pi, S)$ is finite, and $\langle s, a\rangle \in \mathsf{Pol}(\pi, S)$ implies that a is applicable at s for every $a \in \mathsf{Act}$. To show that $\mathsf{Pol}(\pi, S)$ is strongly executable it remains to show that $\langle s, a\rangle \in \mathsf{Pol}(\pi, S)$ implies that $\mathsf{Pol}(\pi, S)$ is defined at $R_a(s)$. Furthermore, we have to show that $\mathsf{Pol}(\pi, S)$ is defined at S and that $\mathcal{M}_{\mathsf{Act}}, \mathsf{Stop}(\mathsf{Pol}(\pi, S)) \Vdash \gamma$. We proceed by induction on the form of π.

$\mathcal{M}_{\mathsf{Act}}, S \Vdash (\![\psi?]\!)\gamma$ implies $\mathcal{M}_{\mathsf{Act}}, S \Vdash \psi$ and $\mathcal{M}_{\mathsf{Act}}, S \vDash \gamma$ by the truth condition for test. By Lemma 1, $\mathsf{Pol}(\psi?, S) = S \times \{\mathsf{stop}\}$ is a strong solution of $\langle S, \gamma, \mathcal{M}_{\mathsf{Act}}\rangle$.

$\mathcal{M}_{\mathsf{Act}}, S \Vdash (\![a]\!)\gamma$ implies $\mathcal{M}_{\mathsf{Act}}, R_a(S) \Vdash \gamma$. The policy $\mathsf{Pol}(a, S) = (S \times \{a\}) \cup (R_a(S) \times \{\mathsf{stop}\})$ is defined at S and at $R_a(S)$ (so due to the latter it is strongly executable). Hence $\mathsf{Pol}(a, S)$ is a strong solution of $\langle S, \gamma, \mathcal{M}_{\mathsf{Act}}\rangle$.

$\mathcal{M}_{\mathsf{Act}}, S \Vdash (\![\pi_1; \pi_2]\!)\gamma$ implies $\mathcal{M}_{\mathsf{Act}}, S \Vdash (\![\pi_1]\!)(\![\pi_2]\!)\gamma$. By induction hypothesis $\mathsf{Pol}(\pi_1, S)$ is a strong solution of $\langle S, (\![\pi_2]\!)\gamma, \mathcal{M}_{\mathsf{Act}}\rangle$. So $\mathcal{M}_{\mathsf{Act}}, \mathsf{Stop}(\mathsf{Pol}(\pi_1, S)) \Vdash$ $(\![\pi_2]\!)\gamma$. We apply the induction hypothesis again: $\mathsf{Pol}(\pi_2, \mathsf{Stop}(\mathsf{Pol}(\pi_1, S)))$ is a strong solution of the planning task $\langle \mathsf{Stop}(\mathsf{Pol}(\pi_1, S)), \gamma, \mathcal{M}_{\mathsf{Act}}\rangle$. Then

$$\mathsf{Pol}(\pi_1; \pi_2, S) = \left(\mathsf{Pol}(\pi_1, S)\right)^{-\mathsf{stop}} \cup \mathsf{Pol}(\pi_2, \mathsf{Stop}(\mathsf{Pol}(\pi_1, S)))$$

is a strong solution of $\langle S, \gamma, \mathcal{M}_{\mathsf{Act}}\rangle$ thanks to Lemma 5.

$\mathcal{M}_{\mathsf{Act}}, S \Vdash (\![\pi_1 \cup \pi_2]\!)\gamma$ implies that for every $s \in S$, one of the following holds:
1. $\mathcal{M}_{\mathsf{Act}}, s \Vdash (\![\pi_1]\!)\gamma$ and $\mathcal{M}_{\mathsf{Act}}, s \Vdash (\![\pi_2]\!)\gamma$;
2. $\mathcal{M}_{\mathsf{Act}}, s \Vdash (\![\pi_1]\!)\gamma$ and $\mathcal{M}_{\mathsf{Act}}, s \not\Vdash (\![\pi_2]\!)\top$;
3. $\mathcal{M}_{\mathsf{Act}}, s \not\Vdash (\![\pi_1]\!)\top$ and $\mathcal{M}_{\mathsf{Act}}, s \Vdash (\![\pi_2]\!)\gamma$.

Remember that by definition $\mathsf{Pol}(\pi_i, S)$ is empty if $\mathcal{M}_{\mathsf{Act}}, S \not\Vdash (\![\pi_i]\!)\top$. Therefore by the induction hypothesis one of the following holds:
1. $\mathsf{Pol}(\pi_1, \{s\})$ and $\mathsf{Pol}(\pi_2, \{s\})$ are both strong solutions of $\langle \{s\}, \gamma, \mathcal{M}_{\mathsf{Act}}\rangle$;
2. $\mathsf{Pol}(\pi_1, \{s\})$ is a strong solution of $\langle \{s\}, \gamma, \mathcal{M}_{\mathsf{Act}}\rangle$ and $\mathsf{Pol}(\pi_2, \{s\}) = \emptyset$;
3. $\mathsf{Pol}(\pi_1, \{s\}) = \emptyset$ and $\mathsf{Pol}(\pi_2, \{s\})$ is a strong solution of $\langle \{s\}, \gamma, \mathcal{M}_{\mathsf{Act}}\rangle$.

In each of these three cases we have that $\mathsf{Pol}(\pi_1, \{s\}) \cup \mathsf{Pol}(\pi_2, \{s\})$ is a strong solution of $\langle \{s\}, \gamma, \mathcal{M}_{\mathsf{Act}}\rangle$, where in the first case we apply Lemma 3. Finally, by Lemma 4 we conclude that $\mathsf{Pol}(\pi_1 \cup \pi_2, S) = \bigcup_{s \in S} \left(\mathsf{Pol}(\pi_1, \{s\}) \cup \mathsf{Pol}(\pi_2, \{s\})\right)$ is a strong solution of $\langle S, \gamma, \mathcal{M}_{\mathsf{Act}}\rangle$. This completes the proof.

We immediately get the following, given that by definition $\mathsf{Pol}(\pi, S)$ is empty when $\mathcal{M}_{\mathsf{Act}}, S \not\Vdash (\![\pi]\!)\gamma$.

Corollary 1. *Let $\langle S, \gamma, \mathcal{M}_{\mathsf{Act}}\rangle$ be a planning task. Then $\mathcal{M}_{\mathsf{Act}}, S \Vdash (\![\pi]\!)\gamma$ iff $\mathsf{Pol}(\pi, S)$ is a strong solution of $\langle S, \gamma, \mathcal{M}_{\mathsf{Act}}\rangle$.*

6 From Policies to Programs

In this section we associate a program to a given policy. Given a model $\mathcal{M}_{\mathsf{Act}} = \langle W, \{R_a\}_{a \in \mathsf{Act}}, V\rangle$, the *characteristic formula* of a state $s \in W$ is

$$\chi_s = \left(\bigwedge_{p \in V(s)} p\right) \wedge \left(\bigwedge_{p \notin V(s)} \neg p\right)$$

Such formulas will be tested in the program associated to a policy Λ in order to correctly capture the actions of Λ that apply at s. The crucial property is that χ_s is only true in states that have the same valuation as s, as is immediately seen from the definition of the χ_s.

The abbreviation $\mathsf{skipifstop}_\Lambda(s) = \bigcup_{\langle s, \mathsf{stop}\rangle \in \Lambda} \mathsf{skip}$ will be convenient: when $\langle s, \mathsf{stop}\rangle \in \Lambda$ then it is equivalent to skip; otherwise (by our convention of Sect. 2) it equals fail. Now we are ready to associate to every finite policy Λ and finite set of states S a program $\pi_{\Lambda, S}$ as follows:

$$\pi_{\Lambda, S} = \bigcup_{s \in S} \left(\chi_s?; \left(\mathsf{skipifstop}_\Lambda(s) \cup \bigcup_{a \mid \langle s, a\rangle \in \Lambda} (a; \pi_{\Lambda, R_a(s)})\right)\right)$$

The function $\pi_{\Lambda,S}$ is well-defined because Λ is finite and $\mathcal{M}_{\mathsf{Act}}$ is acyclic.

Proposition 5. *If Λ is a strong solution of the planning task $\langle S, \gamma, \mathcal{M}_{\mathsf{Act}} \rangle$ then $\mathcal{M}_{\mathsf{Act}}, S \Vdash (\![\pi_{\Lambda,S}]\!)\gamma$.*

Proof. By induction on the depth $\mathsf{d}(\Lambda, S)$ of the policy Λ from S. If $\mathsf{d}(\Lambda, S) = 0$ then there can be no $\langle a, s \rangle \in \Lambda$ for any $s \in S$, and for every s the subprogram $\bigcup_{a | \langle s,a \rangle \in \Lambda} (a; \pi_{\Lambda, R_a(s)})$ of $\mathsf{Pol}(\Lambda, S)$ is the $\mathtt{fail}$ program. Therefore $\pi_{\Lambda,S}$ is $\bigcup_{s \in S} (\chi_s?; (\mathsf{skipifstop}_\Lambda(s) \cup \mathtt{fail}))$, which is equivalent to $\bigcup_{s \in S} (\chi_s?; (\mathsf{skipifstop}_\Lambda(s)))$, by Proposition 3, item (4). Suppose Λ is a strong solution of $\langle S, \gamma, \mathcal{M}_{\mathsf{Act}} \rangle$. So γ is true at $\mathsf{Stop}(\Lambda) = S$ and Λ applies to S. The latter means that $\mathsf{skipifstop}_\Lambda(s)$ equals $\mathtt{skip}$ for every $s \in S$. Therefore the program $\pi_{\Lambda,S}$ equals $\bigcup_{s \in S} (\chi_s?; \mathtt{skip})$, which is equivalent to the program $\bigcup_{s \in S} \chi_s?$ (more precisely, we have $R_{\pi;\mathtt{skip}} = R_\pi \circ R_{\top?} = R_\pi$). By item (7) of Proposition 3, the formula $(\![\bigcup_{s \in S} \chi_s?]\!)\gamma$ is equivalent to $(\bigvee_{s \in S} \chi_s) \wedge \gamma$; and as $\mathcal{M}_{\mathsf{Act}}, S \Vdash \bigvee_{s \in S} \chi_s$, we have that $\mathcal{M}_{\mathsf{Act}}, S \Vdash (\![\bigcup_{s \in S} \chi_s?]\!)\gamma$. So we can conclude that $\mathcal{M}_{\mathsf{Act}}, S \Vdash (\![\pi_{\Lambda,S}]\!)\gamma$.

If $\mathsf{d}(\Lambda, S) \geq 1$ then suppose Λ is a strong solution of $\langle S, \gamma, \mathcal{M}_{\mathsf{Act}} \rangle$. Choose $s \in S$ arbitrarily. We then need to prove $\mathcal{M}_{\mathsf{Act}}, s \Vdash (\![\pi_{\Lambda,S}]\!)\gamma$. By Lemma 2, Λ is a strong solution of $\langle R_a(s), \gamma, \mathcal{M}_{\mathsf{Act}} \rangle$ for every $\langle s, a \rangle \in \Lambda$. Then by the induction hypothesis we have for every $\langle s, a \rangle \in \Lambda$

$$\mathcal{M}_{\mathsf{Act}}, R_a(s) \Vdash (\![\pi_{\Lambda, R_a(s)}]\!)\gamma,$$

i.e., as Λ applies to s, that for every a such that $\langle s, a \rangle \in \Lambda$:

$$\mathcal{M}_{\mathsf{Act}}, s \Vdash (\![a]\!)(\![\pi_{\Lambda, R_a(s)}]\!)\gamma.$$

Therefore,

$$\mathcal{M}_{\mathsf{Act}}, s \Vdash \bigwedge_{a | \langle s,a \rangle \in \Lambda} (\![a; \pi_{\Lambda, R_a(s)}]\!)\gamma,$$

which by the validity of Axiom NDet implies that

$$\mathcal{M}_{\mathsf{Act}}, s \Vdash (\![\bigcup_{a | \langle s,a \rangle \in \Lambda} (a; \pi_{\Lambda, R_a(s)})]\!)\gamma.$$

Furthermore, as Λ is a strong solution of $\langle S, \gamma, \mathcal{M}_{\mathsf{Act}} \rangle$ we have $\mathcal{M}_{\mathsf{Act}}, \mathsf{Stop}(\Lambda) \Vdash \gamma$ and hence,

$$\mathcal{M}_{\mathsf{Act}}, s \Vdash (\![\mathsf{skipifstop}_\Lambda(s)]\!)\gamma \vee \neg(\![\mathsf{skipifstop}_\Lambda(s)]\!)\top.$$

Due to the validity of Axiom NDet we can combine the last two lines and obtain

$$\mathcal{M}_{\mathsf{Act}}, s \Vdash (\![\mathsf{skipifstop}_\Lambda(s) \cup (\bigcup_{a | \langle s,a \rangle \in \Lambda} (a; \pi_{\Lambda, R_a(s)}))]\!)\gamma.$$

Since $\mathcal{M}_{\mathsf{Act}}, s \Vdash \chi_s$, we have:

$$\mathcal{M}_{\mathsf{Act}}, s \Vdash (\![\chi_s?]\!)(\![\mathsf{skipifstop}_\Lambda(s) \cup (\bigcup_{a | \langle s,a \rangle \in \Lambda} (a; \pi_{\Lambda, R_a(s)}))]\!)\gamma.$$

Using the validity of Axiom Seq, we then get:

$$\mathcal{M}_{\mathsf{Act}}, s \Vdash (\![\chi_s?; (\mathsf{skipifstop}_\varLambda(s) \cup (\bigcup_{a \mid \langle s,a \rangle \in \varLambda} (a; \pi_{\varLambda, R_a(s)})))]\!) \gamma.$$

Since the set S of initial states of any planning task is assumed to be valuation determined, we must have $\mathcal{M}_{\mathsf{Act}}, s \Vdash \neg \chi_t$ for every $t \in S \setminus \{s\}$. This implies $\mathcal{M}_{\mathsf{Act}}, s \Vdash \neg (\![\chi_t]\!) \top$, and hence:

$$\mathcal{M}_{\mathsf{Act}}, s \Vdash \neg (\![\chi_t?; (\mathsf{skipifstop}_\varLambda(t) \cup (\bigcup_{a \mid \langle t,a \rangle \in \varLambda} (a; \pi_{\varLambda, R_a(t)})))]\!) \top, \text{ for } t \in S \setminus \{s\}.$$

Applying Axiom NDet to the last two lines, we now get

$$\mathcal{M}_{\mathsf{Act}}, s \Vdash (\![\bigcup_{s \in S} (\chi_s?; (\mathsf{skipifstop}_\varLambda(s) \cup \bigcup_{a \mid \langle s,a \rangle \in \varLambda} (a; \pi_{\varLambda, R_u(s)})))]\!) \gamma.$$

In other words, $\mathcal{M}_{\mathsf{Act}}, s \Vdash (\![\pi_{\varLambda, S}]\!) \gamma$ as required.

Putting Propositions 4 and 5 together now finally gives us the following.

Corollary 2. *A planning task $\langle S, \gamma, \mathcal{M}_{\mathsf{Act}} \rangle$ has a strong solution iff there exists a star-free PDL program π such that $\mathcal{M}_{\mathsf{Act}}, S \Vdash (\![\pi]\!) \gamma$.*

This indicates that PDL with our new modality $(\![\cdot]\!)$ provides an appropriate linguistic and semantic framework to reason about policies.

References

1. Andersen, M.B., Bolander, T., Jensen, M.H.: Conditional epistemic planning. In: del Cerro, L.F., Herzig, A., Mengin, J. (eds.) JELIA 2012. LNCS (LNAI), vol. 7519, pp. 94–106. Springer, Heidelberg (2012). https://doi.org/10.1007/978-3-642-33353-8_8
2. Bolander, T., Engesser, T., Mattmüller, R., Nebel, B.: Better eager than lazy? How agent types impact the successfulness of implicit coordination. In: Proceedings of the 16th International Conference on Principles of Knowledge Representation and Reasoning (KR 2018). AAAI Press (2018)
3. Chellas, B.F.: Modal Logic: An Introduction. Cambridge University Press, Cambridge (1980)
4. Cimatti, A., Pistore, M., Roveri, M., Traverso, P.: Weak, strong, and strong cyclic planning via symbolic model checking. Artif. Intell. **147**(1–2), 35–84 (2003)
5. Engesser, T., Bolander, T., Mattmüller, R., Nebel, B.: Cooperative epistemic multi-agent planning for implicit coordination. In: Ghosh, S., Ramanujam, R. (eds.) Proceedings of the Ninth Workshop on Methods for Modalities, M4M. EPTCS, vol. 243, pp. 75–90 (2017)
6. Gabbay, D., Kurucz, A., Wolter, F., Zakharyaschev, M.: Many-Dimensional Modal Logics: Theory and Applications, Studies in Logic and the Foundations of Mathematics, vol. 148. Elsevier (2003)
7. Goré, R., Widmann, F.: An optimal on-the-fly tableau-based decision procedure for PDL-satisfiability. In: Schmidt, R.A. (ed.) CADE 2009. LNCS (LNAI), vol. 5663, pp. 437–452. Springer, Heidelberg (2009). https://doi.org/10.1007/978-3-642-02959-2_32

8. Harel, D.: Dynamic logic. In: Gabbay, D.M., Günthner, F. (eds.) Handbook of Philosophical Logic, vol. II, pp. 497–604. D. Reidel, Dordrecht (1984)
9. Harel, D., Kozen, D., Tiuryn, J.: Dynamic Logic. MIT Press, Cambridge (2000)
10. Hustadt, U., Schmidt, R.A.: A comparison of solvers for propositional dynamic logic. In: Schmidt, R.A., Schulz, S., Konev, B. (eds.) Proceedings of the 2nd Workshop on Practical Aspects of Automated Reasoning, PAAR-2010, Edinburgh, Scotland, UK, 14 July 2010. EPiC Series in Computing, vol. 9, pp. 63–73. EasyChair (2010)
11. Li, Y.: Knowing What to Do: A Logical Approach to Planning and Knowing How. Ph.D. thesis, University of Groningen (2017)
12. Yu, Q., Li, Y., Wang, Y.: More for free: a dynamic epistemic framework for conformant planning over transition systems. J. Logic Comput. **27**, 2383–2410 (2017)

Interpolation and Beth Definability in Default Logics

Valentin Cassano[1]([✉]), Raul Fervari[1], Carlos Areces[1], and Pablo F. Castro[2]

[1] CONICET and Universidad Nacional de Córdoba, Córdoba, Argentina
vcassano@famaf.unc.edu.ar
[2] CONICET and Universidad Nacional de Río Cuarto, Río Cuarto, Argentina

Abstract. We investigate interpolation and Beth definability in default logics. To this end, we start by defining a general framework which is sufficiently abstract to encompass most of the usual definitions of a default logic. In this framework a default logic $\mathscr{DL}$ is built on a base, monotonic, logic $\mathscr{L}$. We then investigate the question of when interpolation and Beth definability results transfer from $\mathscr{L}$ to $\mathscr{DL}$. This investigation needs suitable notions of interpolation and Beth definability for default logics. We show both positive and negative general results: depending on how $\mathscr{DL}$ is defined and of the kind of interpolation/Beth definability involved, the property might or might not transfer from $\mathscr{L}$ to $\mathscr{DL}$.

1 Introduction

Interpolation and Beth definability are recognized as important properties of the meta-theory of a logic (see, e.g., [19]). Interpolation goes back to the seminal work of Craig in [11] and is, in one form, the following result: suppose that $\varphi \vdash \psi$, there is ξ in the common language of φ and ψ s.t. $\varphi \vdash \xi$ and $\xi \vdash \psi$. In addition to its theoretical relevance, interpolation has also proven to be influential in applications in Computer Science, e.g., in the context of software specification [6,14,25,34], in the construction of Formal Ontologies [23], and in Model Checking [26]. Though interpolation stands as a property in its own right, its main importance lies in the fact that it can be used to prove a result known as Beth definability via a standard argument (see, e.g., [28]). Intuitively, Beth definability implies that the syntax of the language is powerful enough to define any notion that is semantically fixed in a model. This is commonly regarded as a sign of a well behaved logic, where syntax and semantics are in harmony. Interpolation and Beth definability have received a lot less attention in non-classical and, in particular, non-monotonic logics. With this as our motivation, we investigate interpolation and Beth definability in default logics, a sub-class of the field of Non-monotonic Logic.

We start by defining a general framework which is sufficiently abstract to encompass most of the usual default logics (e.g., those introduced in [13,24, 27,29]), generalizing ideas presented in [17,18]. We define a default logic $\mathscr{DL}$ on a base, monotonic, logic $\mathscr{L}$ satisfying some minimal requirements. Then, we

© Springer Nature Switzerland AG 2019
F. Calimeri et al. (Eds.): JELIA 2019, LNAI 11468, pp. 675–691, 2019.
https://doi.org/10.1007/978-3-030-19570-0_44

turn to the question of when interpolation and Beth definability results transfer from $\mathcal{L}$ to $\mathscr{D}\mathcal{L}$. As a result of the generality of our framework, we are able to prove far-reaching transfer results for a comprehensive class of default logics. We draw attention to the fact that interpolation and Beth definability for default logics need suitable definitions. When dealing with a non-monotonic logical consequence relation $\vdash$, it may not simply be possible to define interpolation as: if $\varphi \vdash \psi$, then there is ξ in the common language of φ and ψ s.t. $\varphi \vdash \xi$ and $\xi \vdash \psi$. For starters, since $\vdash$ is non-monotonic, it may not be transitive. Moreover, since consequence in most default logics is defined in terms of *default theories*, the notion of "common language", and the left and right hand sides of $\vdash$ should also be dealt with care. After discussing how to define interpolation and Beth definability in default logics, we show both positive and negative results. Depending on how $\mathscr{D}\mathcal{L}$ is defined and of which kind of interpolation/Beth definability property we study, the property might or might not transfer from $\mathcal{L}$ to $\mathscr{D}\mathcal{L}$. In particular, we show that the Strong Craig Interpolation Property (SCIP) always transfer from $\mathcal{L}$ to $\mathscr{D}\mathcal{L}$ (Proposition 6), while the Split Interpolation Property (SIP) fails for any traditional $\mathscr{D}\mathcal{L}$ based on $\mathcal{L}$ extending classical propositional logic (CPL), even though CPL has SIP (Proposition 7). Similarly, if $\mathcal{L}$ has SIP and $\mathscr{D}\mathcal{L}$ is stable under substitutions, then sceptical default consequence in $\mathscr{D}\mathcal{L}$ has a version of the Beth definability property (Proposition 8), while this property fails for credulous default consequence in traditional $\mathscr{D}\mathcal{L}$ based on $\mathcal{L}$ extending CPL (Proposition 9).

Structure. In Sect. 2 we provide a general definition of a default logic. We start by defining what we require of a base logic in Sect. 2.1. We introduce default logics in Sect. 2.2, and define traditional default logics in Sect. 2.3. In Sect. 2.4 we briefly discuss strongly saturated default logics – a class of well behaved default logics generalizing traditional default logics. Section 3 investigates interpolation and Beth definability. We introduce appropriate definitions in Sects. 3.1 and 3.3. Our main results are shown in Sects. 3.2 and 3.4. Section 4 concludes the paper discussing related work and providing pointers for future research.

2   What Is a Default Logic?

Default logics are a sub-class of non-monotonic logics. Different default logics have been introduced after the originating proposal in Reiter's seminal work [29]. These different default logics have in common the notion of a *default* and an *extension*. A default is a triple of formulas of a formal language, notation $\pi \overset{\rho}{\Rightarrow} \chi$, capturing a conditional, defeasible statement. An extension is a set of formulas making precise some constraints on π and ρ, enabling us to detach χ from $\pi \overset{\rho}{\Rightarrow} \chi$. Default logics differ from one another in the conditions enabling detaching a default. Defaults and extensions are basic ingredients in what is a default logic.

2.1 Preliminary Definitions

We define default logics over a *base logic*. In our setting, a base logic, or a *logic* for short, has two ingredients: a set of *formulas* and a *consequence* relation. Formulas are defined over a *language*, i.e., a triple $\mathscr{F} = \langle \mathscr{A}, \mathscr{L}, \mathscr{G} \rangle$ where: $\mathscr{A}$ is a set of non-logical symbols (the alphabet); $\mathscr{L}$ is a set of logical symbols with corresponding arities; and $\mathscr{G}$ are the rules of grammar. We also use $\mathscr{F}$ for the set of all formulas of a language $\mathscr{F}$. As usual, lowercase and uppercase Greek letters are variables for formulas and sets of formulas, resp. We restrict our attention to *propositional languages*, i.e., languages where $\mathscr{A}$ is a set of proposition symbols. We use p, q, r, etc., for proposition symbols. For any $\mathscr{F}$ and $\Phi \subseteq \mathscr{F}$, $\mathscr{A}(\Phi)$ is the *alphabet* of Φ, i.e., the set of proposition symbols appearing in formulas in Φ. We say that Φ is *defined on an alphabet* A if $\mathscr{A}(\Phi) \subseteq A$. We define $\mathscr{F}|_A = \{ \varphi \in \mathscr{F} \mid \mathscr{A}(\varphi) \subseteq A \}$. We use $S_q^p(\Phi)$ to indicate the result of substituting every appearance of p by q in every formula in Φ. A consequence relation $\vdash$ is a subset of $2^{\mathscr{F}} \times \mathscr{F}$ indicating what follows from what in a logic. We use $\Phi \vdash \varphi$ for $(\Phi, \varphi) \in \vdash$; and $\vdash \varphi$ if $\Phi = \emptyset$ (we omit brackets for singleton sets). We make no assumptions regarding whether $\vdash$ is defined syntactically or semantically. We do assume that $\vdash$ satisfies *reflexivity, monotonicity, cut*, and *structurality* (see, e.g., [16]). We make precise what a logic is in the next definition.

Definition 1 (Logic). *A logic is a tuple $\mathfrak{L} = \langle \mathscr{F}, \vdash \rangle$ where $\mathscr{F}$ is a language, and $\vdash \subseteq 2^{\mathscr{F}} \times \mathscr{F}$ is a consequence relation s.t. $\varphi \vdash \varphi$ (reflexivity); if $\Phi \vdash \varphi$ and $\Phi \subseteq \Phi'$, then $\Phi' \vdash \varphi$ (monotonicity); if $\Phi \vdash \varphi_i$ and $\Phi \cup \{ \varphi_i \mid i \in I \} \vdash \psi$, then $\Phi \vdash \psi$ (cut); and if $\Phi \vdash \varphi$, then $S_q^p(\Phi) \vdash S_q^p(\varphi)$ (structurality).*

For any logic $\mathfrak{L}$, we say that φ is a consequence of Φ iff $\Phi \vdash \varphi$. We define $\Phi^{\bullet} = \{ \varphi \mid \Phi \vdash \varphi \}$. The operator $(\ )^{\bullet}$ is a *closure operator*, i.e.: $\Phi \subseteq \Phi^{\bullet}$; if $\Phi \subseteq \Phi'$, then $\Phi^{\bullet} \subseteq \Phi'^{\bullet}$; and $\Phi^{\bullet} = \Phi^{\bullet\bullet}$. A set of sentences Φ is *consistent* if $\Phi^{\bullet} \subset \mathscr{F}$.

Definition 2. *An* implicative logic *is a logic whose logical symbols contain nullary symbols $\top$ (verum) and $\bot$ (falsum), and a binary symbol $\supset$ (implication); whose set $\mathscr{F}$ of formulas contains $\{ \top \supset \varphi, \varphi \supset \top, \bot \supset \varphi, \varphi \supset \bot, \varphi \supset \psi \}$; and whose consequence relation satisfies: $\top \in \Phi^{\bullet}$ iff $\bot \supset \bot \in \Phi^{\bullet}$ ($\top\bot$-def); $\varphi \in \Phi^{\bullet}$ iff $\top \supset \varphi \in \Phi^{\bullet}$ ($\top$-left-neutral); if $\{ \varphi \supset \phi, \phi \supset \psi \} \subseteq \Phi^{\bullet}$, $\varphi \supset \psi \in \Phi^{\bullet}$ ($\supset$-transitive); and if $\{ \varphi, \varphi \supset \psi \} \subseteq \Phi^{\bullet}$, $\psi \in \Phi^{\bullet}$ (modus ponens).*

Henceforth, by a logic, we mean an implicative logic. Implicative logics play a fundamental role in our treatment of interpolation and Beth definability.

Example 1. The following are some typical cases of logics: Classical Propositional Logic (CPL) [15]; Intuitionistic Propositional Logic (IPL) [33]; the class of Normal Modal Logics [7]; in particular, the Basic Modal Logic K with *local* consequence [7]; the Basic Modal Logic K with *global* logical consequence [7]; the Modal Logic $\mathsf{KAlt_1}$ [7]; the Standard Deontic Logic D [10, 35]; the Deontic Logic KDA [9]; the epistemic logic S5 [10, 21]; and the hybrid logic $\mathsf{H}(\mathsf{A}, \downarrow)$ [5] (which is equivalent to Classical First-Order Logic over the appropriate language).

2.2 Default Logics

We start with a general definition of a default logic.

Definition 3 (Default Logic). *A default logic is a pair $\mathscr{DL} = \langle \mathfrak{L}, \mathscr{E} \rangle$ where $\mathfrak{L}$ is a logic and $\mathscr{E} : (2^{\mathscr{F}} \times 2^{(\mathscr{F}^3)}) \rightarrow 2^{(2^{\mathscr{F}})}$ is a function s.t. for every $E \in \mathscr{E}(\Phi, \Delta)$, $E = (\Phi \cup \{\chi \mid (\pi, \rho, \chi) \in \Delta'\})^{\bullet}$ for some $\Delta' \subseteq \Delta$.*

$\mathscr{D} = \mathscr{F}^3$ is the set of all *defaults* of a default logic. $\pi \overset{\rho}{\Rightarrow} \chi$ is notation for $(\pi, \rho, \chi) \in \mathscr{D}$. A default theory Θ is a pair (Φ, Δ) where $\Phi \subseteq \mathscr{F}$ and $\Delta \subseteq \mathscr{D}$. If Θ is a default theory, Φ_{Θ} and Δ_{Θ} are the sets of formulas and defaults of Θ, resp. For a default theory Θ, $\mathscr{E}(\Theta)$ is its set of *extensions*. We associate with each default logic two notions of default consequence: *credulous*, and *sceptical*. Formally, φ is a credulous default consequence of a default theory Θ, notation $\Theta \mathrel{\vdash^{c}} \varphi$, iff $\varphi \in \bigcup \mathscr{E}(\Theta)$; in turn, φ is a sceptical default consequence of Θ, notation $\Theta \mathrel{\vdash^{s}} \varphi$, iff $\varphi \in \bigcap \mathscr{E}(\Theta)$. If $\mathscr{E}(\Theta) = \emptyset$, $\bigcup \mathscr{E}(\Theta) = \emptyset$ and $\bigcap \mathscr{E}(\Theta) = \mathscr{F}$ (see [32]). Define $\Theta^{c} = \{\varphi \mid \Theta \mathrel{\vdash^{c}} \varphi\}$ and $\Theta^{s} = \{\varphi \mid \Theta \mathrel{\vdash^{s}} \varphi\}$. We use $\vdash$ and Θ^{d} when there is no need to distinguish between $\vdash^{c}$ and $\vdash^{s}$, and Θ^{c} and Θ^{s}, resp.

The rest of this section illustrates how some of the most common properties of Default Logics fit into our definition. We say that a default logic $\mathscr{DL}$ *guarantees extensions* iff for all Θ, $\mathscr{E}(\Theta) \neq \emptyset$. Default logics that guarantee extensions are *supra-classical*, i.e., for all Θ, $(\Phi_{\Theta})^{\bullet} \subseteq \Theta^{d}$; and they satisfy $\Theta^{s} \subseteq \Theta^{c}$ for all Θ. These properties are not satisfied if extensions fail to exist, i.e., if there is Θ s.t. $\mathscr{E}(\Theta) = \emptyset$. Let Θ_1 and Θ_2 be default theories, define $\Theta_1 \sqsubseteq \Theta_2$ iff $\Phi_{\Theta_1} \subseteq \Phi_{\Theta_2}$ and $\Delta_{\Theta_1} \subseteq \Delta_{\Theta_2}$. We say that $\mathscr{DL}$ is *non-monotonic* iff there are Θ_1 and Θ_2 s.t. $\Theta_1 \sqsubseteq \Theta_2$ and $(\Theta_1)^{d} \not\subseteq (\Theta_2)^{d}$. We say that $\mathscr{DL}$ is *semi-monotonic* iff for any two Θ_1 and Θ_2 s.t. $\Theta_1 \sqsubseteq \Theta_2$, if $\Phi_{\Theta_1} = \Phi_{\Theta_2}$, then for all $E_1 \in \mathscr{E}(\Theta_1)$, there is $E_2 \in \mathscr{E}(\Theta_2)$ s.t. $E_1 \subseteq E_2$. Further, we say that $\mathscr{DL}$ is $\mathscr{E}$-*consistent* iff for all Θ, if Φ_{Θ} is $\mathfrak{L}$-consistent, then all $E \in \mathscr{E}(\Theta)$ are $\mathfrak{L}$-consistent. Non-monotonocity, semi-monotonicity, and $\mathscr{E}$-consistency do not follow from Definition 3. Moreover, they need not be satisfied by default logics (even if they guarantee extensions); they depend on the particularities of the definition of $\mathscr{E}$. We make no assumptions regarding whether an arbitrary default logic satisfies any of the properties above.

2.3 Traditional Default Logics

Definition 3 paints a general picture of what is a default logic. At the same time, it captures default logics that are, in a sense, "degenerate". E.g., we can define a default logic s.t. for all Θ, $\mathscr{E}(\Theta) = \{(\Phi_{\Theta})^{\bullet}\}$. This default logic ignores defaults, thus collapsing default reasoning into reasoning in the underlying logic, i.e., $\Theta^{c} = \Theta^{s} = (\Phi_{\Theta})^{\bullet}$ for all Θ. We call any default logic satisfying this condition *trivial*. Trivial default logics are extreme cases of little interest from a Default Logic perspective. In defining a default logic, we wish to provide a precise account of what does it mean to reason with defaults in a way such that reasoning in the underlying logic is extended non-monotonically. This is the purpose of *traditional* default logics. Traditional default logics encompass Reiter's seminal work on default logic [29] and some of its major variants, e.g., [13, 24, 27, 30], summarized in [2, 12]. We introduce what we mean by a traditional default logic in Definition 8 by building on, and generalizing, definitions and results presented in [17, 18].

We begin by taking a closer look at defaults. Typically, a default $\pi \overset{\rho}{\Rightarrow} \chi$ is intuitively read as: if π is *grounded* in what is known and ρ is *coherent* with what is known, then, *detach* χ and assume it tentatively as part of what is known. Extensions formalize the set of "known things", what is meant by grounded, coherent, and detached and assumed tentatively. How these concepts are formalized separate traditional default logics from each other, as different intuitions lead to different formalizations.

Henceforth, by *consistency* we mean $\mathfrak{L}$-consistency. Define, for all sets Δ, $\Delta^\Pi = \{\, \pi \mid \pi \overset{\rho}{\Rightarrow} \chi \in \Delta \,\}$, $\Delta^P = \{\, \rho \mid \pi \overset{\rho}{\Rightarrow} \chi \in \Delta \,\}$ and $\Delta^X = \{\, \chi \mid \pi \overset{\rho}{\Rightarrow} \chi \in \Delta \,\}$.

Definition 4 (Grounded). *Let Θ be a default theory, and $\Delta_1 \subseteq \Delta_2 \subseteq \Delta_\Theta$; we say that Δ_2 is grounded in Δ_1 iff $\Delta_2^\Pi \subseteq (\Phi_\Theta \cup \Delta_1^X)^\bullet$. In addition, for all $\Delta \subseteq \Delta_\Theta$, we say that Δ is a closed set iff $\Delta^\Pi \subseteq (\Phi_\Theta \cup \Delta^X)^\bullet$.*

Definition 4 captures a standard view on what does it mean for a set of defaults to be grounded. Intuitively, if we think of the sets Δ_1 and Δ_2 as defaults "already considered" and defaults "to be considered", resp., the view of grounded in Definition 4 permits only for the consequents of "already considered" defaults to be used to establish the prerequisites of "to be considered" defaults. Closed sets are sets of defaults whose prerequisites can be established from within the set.

Definition 5 (Coherence). *Let Θ be a default theory, and $\Delta_1 \subseteq \Delta_2 \subseteq \Delta_\Theta$; we say that Δ_2 is i-coherent w.r.t. Δ_1 iff:*

(1-coherent) for all $\delta_2 \in \Delta_2$, $(\Phi_\Theta \cup \Delta_1^X \cup \delta_2^P)^\bullet$ is consistent.
(2-coherent) for all $\delta_2 \in \Delta_2$, $(\Phi_\Theta \cup \Delta_2^X \cup \delta_2^P)^\bullet$ is consistent.
(3-coherent) $(\Phi_\Theta \cup \Delta_1^X \cup \Delta_2^P)^\bullet$ is consistent.
(4-coherent) $(\Phi_\Theta \cup \Delta_2^X \cup \Delta_2^P)^\bullet$ is consistent.

In addition, we say that Δ_2 is self i-coherent if it is i-coherent w.r.t. itself.

Proposition 1. *i-coherence implies 1-coherence, while 4-coherence implies i-coherence, for $1 \leq i \leq 4$. Further, self 1-coherence implies self 2-coherence; self 3-coherence implies self 4-coherence.*

A default $\pi \overset{\rho}{\Rightarrow} \chi \in \Delta$ is *normal* iff $\rho = \chi$. We use $\pi \Rightarrow \chi$ as notation for normal defaults. A default theory Θ is *normal* if all $\delta \in \Delta_\Theta$ are normal.

Proposition 2. *For normal default theories, the four notions of coherence introduced in Definition 5 are equivalent.*

Table 1. Coherence and detachment

Coherence	Detachment	Proponent	Reference
1-coherence	classical	Reiter	[29]
2-coherence	justified	Łukaszewicz	[24]
3-coherence	rational	Mikitiuk and Truszczynski	[27]
4-coherence	constrained	Delgrande, Jackson, and Schaub	[13,30]

Definition 5 captures four different views on what does it mean for a set of defaults to be coherent. The relation between these different views is made clear in Propositions 1 and 2. Again, if we think of the sets Δ_1 and Δ_2 as defaults "already considered" and defaults "to be considered", resp., 1-coherence and 2-coherence require the justifications of the defaults "to be considered" to be individually consistent w.r.t. the defaults "already considered". They differ from each other in whether or not the consequents of the defaults "to be considered" should be included in the consistency check. These takes on coherence correspond to Reiter [24,29] and to Łukaszewicz [24], resp. In turn, 3-coherence and 4-coherence require the justifications of the defaults "to be considered" to be jointly consistent; and differ from each other in whether or not the consequents of the defaults "to be considered" should be included in the consistency check. These takes on coherence correspond to Mikitiuk and Truszczynski [27], and to Delgrande, Jackson, and Schaub [13,30], resp. When there is no need to distinguish between the different types of coherence, we simply say that Δ_2 is *coherent* w.r.t. Δ_1.

Definition 6 (Detachment). *Let Θ be a default theory and $\Delta_1, \Delta_2 \subseteq \Delta_\Theta$; we say that Δ_2 is detached by Δ_1 if Δ_2 is grounded in, and coherent w.r.t., Δ_1. We say that δ is detached by Δ_1 if $\Delta_2 = \Delta_1 \cup \delta$ is detached by Δ_1.*

Intuitively, detachment can be thought of as a version of modus-ponens for defaults. Fixing a definition of coherence, we say that detachment is: *classical, justified, rational*, and *constrained*, according to Table 1.

Remark 1. Recall that every well-ordering $\prec$ is order-equivalent to exactly one ordinal number τ. Such an ordinal number τ is the order type of $\prec$. The precise definitions of these terms, and that of a limit ordinal, can be found in [32].

Definition 7. *Let Θ be a default theory; we say that $\Delta \subseteq \Delta_\Theta$ is regular if there is a well-ordering $\prec$ on Δ_Θ s.t. $\Delta = \mathsf{D}_\Theta^\prec(\tau)$, where τ is the order type of $\prec$, and for all ordinals ω s.t. $0 < \omega < \tau$, and all limit ordinals λ s.t. $\lambda \leq \tau$, $\mathsf{D}_\Theta^\prec$ is defined:*

$$\mathsf{D}_\Theta^\prec(0) = \emptyset$$

$$\mathsf{D}_\Theta^\prec(\omega + 1) = \begin{cases} \mathsf{D}_\Theta^\prec(\omega) \cup \delta & \text{if } \delta \in (\Delta \setminus \mathsf{D}_\Theta^\prec(\omega)) \text{ is detached by } \mathsf{D}_\Theta^\prec(\omega) \text{ and for all other} \\ & \delta' \in (\Delta \setminus \mathsf{D}_\Theta^\prec(\omega)), \text{ if } \delta' \text{ is detached by } \mathsf{D}_\Theta^\prec(\omega), \delta \prec \delta' \\ \mathsf{D}_\Theta^\prec(\omega) & \text{otherwise} \end{cases}$$

$$\mathsf{D}_\Theta^\prec(\lambda) = \bigcup \{ \mathsf{D}_\Theta^\prec(\omega) \mid \omega \leq \lambda \}$$

Again, Definition 7 encompasses four kinds of regularity. We say that a regular set of defaults is: *classical, justified, rational,* and *constrained*, depending on the definition of detachment it uses. Regularity captures a prescriptive view of how to cumulatively detach defaults in default theory. The function $D_\Theta^\prec$ is the closure under detachment of a set of defaults under the selection strategy defined by the well-ordering $\prec$, and is a standard definition of a function by *transfinite* recursion. Example 2 illustrates the need for transfiniteness.

Example 2. In some cases, we may wish to prove that our default logic is semi-monotonic. Suppose that extensions in a default logic $\mathscr{DL}$ are obtained through regular sets of defaults, and only those sets. This example shows that unless we allow for transfinite steps, we may fail to prove semi-monotonicity due to restrictions on the definition of $D_\Theta^\prec$. Let $\mathscr{DL}$ be an $\mathscr{E}$-consistent default logic built over $KAlt_1\Diamond^+$ (i.e., the modal logic where $\Diamond$ is interpreted over a weakly functional accessibility relation, and $\Diamond^+$ is its transitive closure, see, e.g., [7]). Let Θ_1 be a default theory s.t. $\Phi_{\Theta_1} = \{\Diamond\top\}$ and $\Delta_{\Theta_1} = \{\Diamond^i\top \Rightarrow \Diamond^{(i+1)}\top \mid i \geq 0\}$. Δ_{Θ_1} is regular for all kinds of detachment. Let $E_1 = (\Phi_{\Theta_1} \cup \Delta_{\Theta_1})^\bullet = \{\Diamond^i\top \mid i \geq 0\}^\bullet$. E_1 is satisfied in Kriple models in which every world has a successor. Let Θ_2 be s.t. $\Theta_1 \sqsubseteq \Theta_2$, $\Phi_{\Theta_1} = \Phi_{\Theta_2}$, and $\Delta_{\Theta_2} = \Delta_{\Theta_1} \cup \{\top \Rightarrow \Diamond^+\Box\bot\}$; the formula $\Diamond^+\Box\bot$ describes the existence of a world reachable in a finite number of steps through the accessibility relation, which has no successors. There is no well-ordering $\prec$ on Δ_{Θ_2} of order type ω_0 s.t. $E_1 \subseteq (\{\Diamond\top\} \cup (D_{\Theta_2}^\prec(\omega_0))^X)^\bullet$. To see why, note that any such $\prec$ on Δ_{Θ_2} contains $\top \Rightarrow \Diamond^+\Box\bot$ at some position n. Since $\top \Rightarrow \Diamond^+\Box\bot$ is detached by any $\Delta_2 \subseteq \Delta_{\Theta_2}$, $D_{\Theta_2}^\prec(\omega_0)$ detaches $\top \Rightarrow \Diamond^+\Box\bot$ in at most n steps. But as soon as $\top \Rightarrow \Diamond^+\Box\bot$ is detached no other default in Δ_{Θ_2} can be detached. Thus, for all $\prec$, $E_2 = (\{\Diamond\top\} \cup (D_{\Theta_2}^\prec(\omega_0))^X)^\bullet$ is satisfied in Kripke models consisting of chains of at most n worlds; and so $E_1 \not\subseteq E_2$. This establishes a failure of semi-monotonicity. By allowing transfinite steps, we can first detach all defaults in Δ_{Θ_1}, and then proceed to check whether or not $\top \Rightarrow \Diamond\Box\bot$ can be detached in a transfinite step. From this, we can recover semi-monotonicity.

Definition 8 (Traditional Default Logic). *We say that a default logic $\mathscr{DL}$ is traditional iff for all default theories Θ, $\mathscr{E}(\Theta)$ is the smallest set s.t. for all regular and self coherent subsets Δ of Δ_Θ, there is $E \in \mathscr{E}(\Theta)$ s.t. $E = (\Phi_\Theta \cup \Delta^X)^\bullet$.*

From Definition 8 it is possible to prove that traditional default logics encompass four distinct sub-classes of default logics. These classes are: classical default logics (classical regularity and 1-coherence); justified default logics (justified regularity and 2-coherence); rational default logics (rational regularity and 3-coherence); and constrained default Logics (constrained regularity and 4-coherence). This claim is made precise in Proposition 3.

Proposition 3. *Every traditional default logic is either a classical, a justified, a constrained, or a rational default logic, and vice-versa.*

It follows by construction, adapting the argument in [17,18], that *Classical Default Logic*, defined by Reiter in [29], is a classical default logic. The same is true, *mutatis mutandis*, for *Justified Default Logic*, defined by Łukaszewicz in [24], *Rational Default Logic*, defined by Mikitiuk and Truszczynski in [27], and *Constrained Default Logic*, defined by Delgrande, Jackson, and Schaub in [13].

2.4   Intermediate Default Logics

Definition 3 paints a very general picture of what is a default logic. In turn, Definition 8 captures default logics whose extensions are obtained in a very prescriptive way via regular set of defaults. The obvious question is whether there are some "interesting" default logics "stricter" than those in Definition 3 but "weaker" than those in Definition 8.

Definition 9. *Let $\mathscr{DL}$ be any default logic, and Θ be any default theory; we say that $\Delta \subseteq \Delta_\Theta$ is saturated iff for all $\Delta' \subseteq \Delta_\Theta$, if Δ' is detached by Δ, $\Delta' \subseteq \Delta$.*

Definition 10. *We say that a default logic $\mathscr{DL}$ is weakly saturated iff for all default theories Θ and all $E \in \mathscr{E}(\Theta)$, there exists a saturated $\Delta \subseteq \Delta_\Theta$ s.t. $E = (\Phi_\Theta \cup \Delta^X)^\bullet$. In addition, we say that $\mathscr{DL}$ is strongly saturated iff it is weakly saturated and for all default theories Θ and all saturated $\Delta \subseteq \Delta_\Theta$, if Δ is self coherent, then there is $E \in \mathscr{E}(\Theta)$ s.t. $E = (\Phi_\Theta \cup \Delta^X)^\bullet$.*

Proposition 4. *Every traditional default logic is strongly saturated.*

We can think of weakly saturated default logics as imposing an "upper bound" on extensions, i.e., anything that is not a saturated set of defaults cannot be an extension. On the other hand, strongly saturated default logics impose a "lower bound" on extensions, i.e., anything that is a saturated and self coherent set of defaults must be an extension. Strongly saturated default logics are an interesting generalization of traditional default logics for they simplify the proof of some results circumventing the prescriptive definition of extensions in Definition 8.

3   Interpolation and Beth Definability

As mentioned, interpolation and Beth definability are recognized as important properties of the meta-theory of a logic. Here, we investigate interpolation and Beth definability in Default Logics. More precisely, we investigate when results transfer from $\mathscr{L}$ to $\mathscr{DL}$. In order to accomplish this, we first need to formulate suitable notions of interpolation and Beth definability for a default logics.

3.1   Interpolation

There is no unifying definition of interpolation in the literature, see [22]. Instead, this property comes in many flavours. In what follows, we discuss some relevant formulations of interpolation. In this discussion we assume an arbitrary logic $\mathscr{L}$.

Let us start with the so-called *Craig Interpolation Property* (CIP).

Definition 11. *We say that consequence in $\mathfrak{L}$ has* CIP *iff whenever $\vdash \varphi \supset \psi$, there is ξ defined on $\mathscr{A}(\varphi) \cap \mathscr{A}(\psi)$ s.t. $\vdash \varphi \supset \xi$ and $\vdash \xi \supset \psi$.*

On certain occasions, in place for CIP, we may wish to have a stronger version.

Definition 12. *We say that consequence $\mathfrak{L}$ has the* Strong Craig Inteprolation Property (SCIP) *iff whenever $\Phi \vdash \varphi \supset \psi$, there is ξ defined on $\mathscr{A}(\Phi, \varphi) \cap \mathscr{A}(\psi)$ s.t. $\Phi \vdash \varphi \supset \xi$ and $\Phi \vdash \xi \supset \psi$.*

A rather different formulation of interpolation, used in the standard argument for *Beth Definability*, is the so-called *Split Interpolation Property* (SIP), see [31].

Definition 13. *We say that consequence $\mathfrak{L}$ has* SIP *iff for any Φ and φ defined on an alphabet A_1, and any Ψ and ψ defined on an alphabet A_2; if $\Phi \cup \Psi \vdash \varphi \supset \psi$, there is ξ defined on $A_1 \cap A_2$ s.t. $\Phi \vdash \varphi \supset \xi$ and $\Psi \vdash \xi \supset \psi$. The formula ξ is called a* split interpolant.

In general, CIP, SCIP, and SIP are not equivalent (having one does not imply having the others). Equivalence depends on the particularities of the logical connectives under consideration and on logical consequence satisfying properties such as compactness, deduction, etc. Logics known to have all three different versions of interpolation are, for example, CPL, IPL, and the modal logics K, S5 and H(A, ↓) with local and global consequence. For a discussion regarding equivalence of interpolation in these logics see [3,4]. We take a particular interest in SIP: as an interpolation result in its own right, given its widespread applicability, and as a step towards obtaining Beth definability in a standard way [28].

3.2   Interpolation in Default Logics

We explore what the natural formulations of CIP, SCIP, and SIP, look like for default consequence in default logics.

Definition 14. *We say that default consequence in a default logic $\mathscr{DL}$ has the* Default Craig Interpolation Property, *notation $\mathscr{D}$CIP, iff whenever $\vdash \varphi \supset \psi$, there is ξ defined on $\mathscr{A}(\varphi) \cap \mathscr{A}(\psi)$, s.t. $\vdash \varphi \supset \xi$ and $\vdash \xi \supset \psi$.*

Proposition 5. *For any default logic $\mathscr{DL} = \langle \mathfrak{L}, \mathscr{E} \rangle$; if consequence in $\mathfrak{L}$ has* CIP, *then, default consequence in $\mathscr{DL}$ has $\mathscr{D}$CIP.*

The proof of Proposition 5 is direct from the definition of a default logic and CIP for $\vdash$ in $\mathfrak{L}$. $\mathscr{D}$CIP is rather trivial as it involves only reasoning from empty default theories, thus reducing default consequences to consequences in the underlying logic. Let us consider the more interesting case of $\mathscr{D}$SCIP, the SCIP version of interpolation for Default Logics, which makes use of non-empty default theories.

Definition 15. *We say that default consequence in a default logic $\mathscr{DL}$ has the* Default Strong Craig Interpolation Property, *notation $\mathscr{D}$SCIP, iff whenever $\Theta \vdash \varphi \supset \psi$, there is ξ defined on $\mathscr{A}(\Theta, \varphi) \cap \mathscr{A}(\psi)$, s.t. $\Theta \vdash \varphi \supset \xi$ and $\Theta \vdash \xi \supset \psi$.*

Proposition 6. *For any default logic $\mathscr{DL} = \langle \mathfrak{L}, \mathscr{E} \rangle$; if consequence in $\mathfrak{L}$ has* SCIP, *then, default consequence in $\mathscr{DL}$ has $\mathscr{D}$SCIP.*

Proof (by cases). Let Θ be a default theory; if $\mathscr{E}(\Theta) = \emptyset$, $\Theta^c = \emptyset$ and $\Theta^s = \mathscr{F}$. The result follows trivially from these facts. If $\mathscr{E}(\Theta) \neq \emptyset$:

(c) Let $\Theta \vdash^c \varphi \supset \psi$; then, there is $E \in \mathscr{E}(\Theta)$ s.t. $E \vdash \varphi \supset \psi$. From SCIP, there is ξ defined on $\mathscr{A}(E, \varphi) \cap \mathscr{A}(\psi)$ s.t. $E \vdash \varphi \supset \xi$ and $E \vdash \xi \supset \psi$. So, $\Theta \vdash^c \varphi \supset \xi$ and $\Theta \vdash^c \xi \supset \psi$, with $\mathscr{A}(\xi) \subseteq \mathscr{A}(\Theta, \varphi) \cap \mathscr{A}(\psi)$.

(s) Let $\Theta \vdash^s \varphi \supset \psi$, and $\Gamma = \bigcap \mathscr{E}(\Theta)$; then, $\Gamma \vdash \varphi \supset \psi$. From SCIP, there is ξ defined on $\mathscr{A}(\Gamma, \varphi) \cap \mathscr{A}(\psi)$ s.t. $\Gamma \vdash \varphi \supset \xi$ and $\Gamma \vdash \xi \supset \psi$. Thus, $\Theta \vdash^s \varphi \supset \xi$ and $\Theta \vdash^s \xi \supset \psi$, with $\mathscr{A}(\xi) \subseteq \mathscr{A}(\Theta, \varphi) \cap \mathscr{A}(\psi)$.

The result follows from (c) and (s). $\qquad$

We now turn our attention to what does SIP look like for default consequence.

Remark 2. For default theories Θ_i, define $\Theta_1 \sqcup \Theta_2 = (\Phi_{\Theta_1} \cup \Phi_{\Theta_2}, \Delta_{\Theta_1} \cup \Delta_{\Theta_2})$.

Definition 16. *We say that default consequence in a default logic $\mathscr{DL}$ has the* Default Split Interpolation Property, *notation $\mathscr{D}$SIP, iff for all Θ_1 and φ defined on an alphabet A_1, and Θ_2 and ψ defined on an alphabet A_2, if $\Theta_1 \sqcup \Theta_2 \vdash \varphi \supset \psi$, there is ξ defined on $A_1 \cap A_2$, s.t. $\Theta_1 \vdash \varphi \supset \xi$ and $\Theta_2 \vdash \xi \supset \psi$.*

For $\mathscr{D}$SIP we obtain a negative result in the following form.

Proposition 7. *For any traditional default logic $\mathscr{DL}$ built on a logic extending* Classical Propositional Logic, *default consequence in $\mathscr{DL}$ does not have $\mathscr{D}$SIP.*

Proof. W.l.o.g. let $\mathfrak{L}$ be CPL, and $\Theta_1 = (\{p\}, \{p \Rightarrow q\})$ and $\Theta_2 = (\emptyset, \{q \Rightarrow r\})$, it follows that:

(1) for all $E_1 \in \mathscr{E}(\Theta_1)$, $E_1 = \{p, q\}^\bullet$.
(2) for all $E_2 \in \mathscr{E}(\Theta_2)$, $E_2 = \emptyset^\bullet$.
(3) for all $E \in \mathscr{E}(\Theta_1 \sqcup \Theta_2)$, $E_3 = \{p, q, r\}^\bullet$.

From (3), $\Theta_1 \sqcup \Theta_2 \vdash p \supset r$. Immediately, $p \in \mathscr{A}(\Theta_1)$, and $r \in \mathscr{A}(\Theta_2)$. Then, any formula ξ defined on $\mathscr{A}(\Theta_1) \cap \mathscr{A}(\Theta_2)$ is equivalent to $\top$, $\bot$, q, or $\neg q$. If we fix ξ to any of these formulas, either from (1), $\Theta_1 \not\vdash p \supset \xi$; or from (2), $\Theta_2 \not\vdash \xi \supset r$. $\qquad$

We explored some natural formulations of CIP, SCIP, and SIP for default consequence in a default logic. We have shown positive transfer results for $\mathscr{D}$CIP and $\mathscr{D}$SCIP. We highlight the generality of these results: not only they concern traditional logics, but all default logics. This level of generality, i.e., proofs depending on extensions and not their construction, is achieved thanks to the abstract presentation of what is a default logic. We have also shown a negative transfer result for $\mathscr{D}$SIP. In this case the counter-example is much more concrete, but still sufficiently general to cover all traditional default logics. Lack of $\mathscr{D}$SIP is a set back for Beth definability, as we are now pre-empted to use the standard argument for establishing the latter from the former [28]. Nonetheless, we show that Beth definability can still be obtained in some form for some default logics.

3.3   Definability

Beth definability is commonly regarded as a sign of a well behaved logic. We adapt our definition of this property from [22].

Definition 17. *Let $\mathfrak{L}$ be any logic, Φ be a set of formulas s.t. $\mathscr{A}(\Phi) \subseteq A$, and $q \notin A$; we say that consequence in $\mathfrak{L}$ has the* Beth Definability Property (BDP) *iff whenever*

$$\Phi \cup S_q^p(\Phi) \vdash p \supset q \quad and \quad \Phi \cup S_q^p(\Phi) \vdash q \supset p \tag{1}$$

there is ε defined on an alphabet $A_0 = A \setminus \{p\}$ s.t.

$$\Phi \vdash p \supset \varepsilon \quad and \quad \Phi \vdash \varepsilon \supset p \tag{2}$$

Equation (1) *expresses that Φ implicitly defines p; whereas Eq. (2) is the explicit definition of p from Φ.*

In general, BDP can be obtained from SIP through a standard argument [28]. Let us remark that failure of SIP does not necessarily imply failure of BDP. The latter property may still be obtained through other means.

3.4   Definability in Default Logics

Definition 18 introduces a natural formulation of Beth definability for default logics.

Definition 18. *Let $\mathscr{D}\mathfrak{L}$ be a default logic, Θ a default theory s.t. $\mathscr{A}(\Theta) \subseteq A$, and $q \notin A$; we say that default consequence in $\mathscr{D}\mathfrak{L}$ has the* Default Beth definability property $(\mathscr{D}\text{BDP})$ *iff whenever*

$$\Theta \sqcup S_q^p(\Theta) \vdash p \supset q \quad and \quad \Theta \sqcup S_q^p(\Theta) \vdash q \supset p \tag{3}$$

there is ε defined on an alphabet $A_0 = A \setminus \{p\}$ s.t.

$$\Theta \vdash p \supset \varepsilon \quad and \quad \Theta \vdash \varepsilon \supset p \tag{4}$$

Equation (3) *expresses that Θ implicitly defines p; whereas ε in Eq. (4) is the explicit definition of p from Θ.*

Proving Beth definability for default consequence in default logics requires some additional definitions and lemmas (the proofs of which are in Appendix A). First, it needs a condition on *stability*, see Definition 19. This condition states that the extensions of a default theory are in harmony with the extensions of its extended default theory under substitution.

Definition 19. *We say that a default logic $\mathscr{D}\mathfrak{L} = \langle \mathfrak{L}, \mathscr{E} \rangle$ is* stable *iff for all default theories Θ defined on an alphabet A, if $q \notin A$, it follows that for all $E \in \mathscr{E}(\Theta)$, there is $E' \in \mathscr{E}(\Theta \sqcup S_q^p(\Theta))$ s.t. $E' = (E \cup S_q^p(E))^\bullet$.*

Lemma 1 shows that the condition of being stable is rather natural, in the sense that it is satisfied by a non-trivial class of default logics, i.e., those that are strongly saturated and, in particular, by traditional default logics.

Lemma 1. *Any strongly saturated default logic $\mathscr{DL}$ is stable.*

Lemma 2 establishes that the notion coherence for the extensions of a given default theory is preserved if we augment the default theory by substitution.

Lemma 2. *Let $\mathscr{DL}$ be a default logic; for all default theories Θ and all $\Delta \subseteq \Delta_\Theta$, if Δ is self coherent in Θ, then, $\Delta \cup S_q^p(\Delta)$ is self coherent in $\Theta \sqcup S_q^p(\Theta)$.*

The following lemma, simplifies a key step in the proof of Proposition 8.

Lemma 3. *Let $\{\Phi_i \mid i \in I\}$ be a set of sets of formulas s.t. for all $i \in I$, $\mathscr{A}(\Phi_i) \subseteq A$ and $\Phi_i = \Phi_i{}^\bullet$; if consequence in $\mathfrak{L}$ has SIP, $q \notin A$, and $p \supset q \in \bigcap\{(\Phi_i \cup S_q^p(\Phi_i))^\bullet \mid i \in I\}$, then $p \supset q \in (\bigcap\{\Phi_i \mid i \in I\} \cup \bigcap\{S_q^p(\Phi_i) \mid i \in I\})^\bullet$.*

Proposition 8. *For any default logic $\mathscr{DL} = \langle \mathfrak{L}, \mathscr{E} \rangle$; if $\mathscr{DL}$ is stable and consequence in $\mathfrak{L}$ has SIP, then, sceptical default consequence in $\mathscr{DL}$ has $\mathscr{D}$BDP.*

Proof (by cases). Let Θ be any default theory defined on alphabet A, and $q \notin A$; if $\mathscr{E}(\Theta \sqcup S_q^p(\Theta)) = \emptyset$, the result holds trivially from the fact that $\mathscr{DL}$ is stable. Otherwise, i..e, if $\mathscr{E}(\Theta \sqcup S_q^p(\Theta)) \neq \emptyset$, let $\Theta \sqcup S_q^p(\Theta) \vdash^s p \supset q$; from the fact that $\mathscr{DL}$ is stable, $p \supset q \in \bigcap\{(E \cup S_q^p(E))^\bullet \mid E \in \mathscr{E}(\Theta)\}$. From Lemma 3, $p \supset q \in (\bigcap\{E \mid E \in \mathscr{E}(\Theta)\} \cup \bigcap\{S_q^p(E) \mid E \in \mathscr{E}(\Theta)\})^\bullet$. From SIP, there is ξ defined on $A \setminus \{p\}$ s.t. $p \supset \xi \in \bigcap\{E \mid E \in \mathscr{E}(\Theta)\}$ and (†) $\xi \supset q \in \bigcap\{S_q^p(E) \mid E \in \mathscr{E}(\Theta)\}$. Substituting p for q in (†) we obtain $\xi \supset p \in \bigcap\{E \mid E \in \mathscr{E}(\Theta)\}$. Therefore, there is ξ defined on $A \setminus \{p\}$ s.t. $\Theta \vdash^s p \supset \xi$ and $\Theta \vdash^s \xi \supset p$.

Corollary 1. *For all traditional default logics built on a logic $\mathfrak{L}$; if $\mathfrak{L}$ has SIP, then sceptical consequence has $\mathscr{D}$BDP.*

For credulous default consequence we obtain the following negative result.

Proposition 9. *For all traditional default logic $\mathscr{DL}$ built on a logic extending CPL, credulous default consequence in $\mathscr{DL}$ does not have $\mathscr{D}$SIP.*

Proof. W.l.o.g. let $\mathfrak{L}$ be CPL; consider a default theory $\Theta = (\emptyset, \{\delta_1, \delta_2\})$, where

$$\delta_1 = \top \overset{\neg p}{\Longrightarrow} [(\neg p \vee r) \wedge s] \qquad \delta_2 = s \overset{p}{\Longrightarrow} (p \wedge \neg r)$$

Trivially, we get $S_q^p(\Theta) = (\emptyset, \{\top \overset{\neg q}{\Longrightarrow} [(\neg q \vee r) \wedge s], s \overset{q}{\Longrightarrow} (q \wedge \neg r)\})$. Moreover:

(1) In classical, justified, constrained, and rational default logic on $\mathfrak{L}$, it follows that, $\mathscr{E}(\Theta \sqcup S_q^p(\Theta)) \supseteq \{(\Delta_i^X)^\bullet \mid i \in \{1, 2\}\}$ where: $\Delta_1 = \{\delta_1, S_q^p(\delta_2)\}$; and $\Delta_2 = \{S_q^p(\delta_1), \delta_2\}$.
(2) In justified, constrained, and rational default logic on $\mathfrak{L}$, it follows that, for all $E \in \mathscr{E}(\Theta)$, $E = (\{\delta_1\}^X)^\bullet$.
(3) In classical default logic on $\mathfrak{L}$, it follows that, $\mathscr{E}(\Theta) = \emptyset$.

Clearly, $q \notin \mathscr{A}(\Theta)$. From (1), $\Theta \sqcup S_q^p(\Theta) \vdash^c p \supset q$ and $\Theta \sqcup S_q^p(\Theta) \vdash^c q \supset p$. To see why, note that $(\Delta_1^X)^\bullet = \{[(\neg p \vee r) \wedge s], \neg r\}^\bullet$ and $(\Delta_2^X)^\bullet = \{[(\neg q \vee r) \wedge s], \neg r\}^\bullet$ are both in $\mathscr{E}(\Theta \sqcup S_q^p(\Theta))$. Immediately, $\{[(\neg p \vee r) \wedge s], \neg r\} \vdash p \supset q$, and also $\{[(\neg q \vee r) \wedge s], \neg r\} \vdash q \supset p$. In justified, constrained, and rational default logic on $\mathcal{L}$, there is no ξ defined on $\mathscr{A}(\Theta) \setminus \{p\}$ for which $\Theta \vdash^c p \supset \xi$ and $\Theta \vdash^c \xi \supset p$. To see why, note from (2) that every $E \in \mathscr{E}(\Theta)$ is equal to $\{(\neg p \vee r) \wedge s\}^\bullet$. Let E be any such extension, it is easy to see that there are models $\mathfrak{M}_1$ and $\mathfrak{M}_2$ of E s.t. $\mathfrak{M}_1 \Vdash p$ and $\mathfrak{M}_1 \Vdash \neg p$. This establishes failure of $\mathscr{D}$BDP for justified, constrained, and rational default logic on $\mathcal{L}$. In classical default logic on $\mathcal{L}$, there is no ξ defined on $\mathscr{A}(\Theta) \setminus \{p\}$ for which $\Theta \vdash^c p \supset \xi$ and $\Theta \vdash^c \xi \supset p$ simply because $\mathscr{E}(\Theta) = \emptyset$. This establishes failure of $\mathscr{D}$BDP for classical default logic on $\mathcal{L}$. In summary, the default theory Θ defined above exhibits a counter-example for $\mathscr{D}$BDP for credulous default consequence in any traditional default logic built on a logic extending CPL.

Even though $\mathscr{D}$SIP fails for default logics, we showed that under certain conditions, $\mathscr{D}$BDP can be still obtained for the sceptical default consequence.

4   Final Remarks

Interpolation and Beth definability are recognized as important properties of the meta-theory of a logic. However, few authors have explored these properties in the field of Non-monotonic Logic, and in default logics in particular. A pioneering work in this area is [1]. Therein the author studies interpolation for circumscription, default logic, and logic programs with the stable models semantics. The version of interpolation presented in [1] is different from the ones investigated here, and is proven for sceptical default consequence in what we would call classical default logic over CPL (with finite vocabularies). The author also formulates a version of split interpolation and proves it for credulous consequence in the same context. However, the proof of this property requires the alphabet of the consequences of one default theory to be disjoint from the alphabet of the prerequisites and justifications of the defaults in other default theory. Thus the result applies to a restricted set of cases. In contrast, our results hold for a richer collection of default logics and generalize some of those introduced in [1]. Another interesting interpolation result in the field of Non-monotonic is [20]. This work studies interpolation in *equilibrium logic*; presenting a technique to obtain interpolation results by relying on the fact that the version of non-monotonic consequence in question can be defined via some minimally (axiomatically) defined models in some monotonic logic. This technique does not directly apply in default logics, since minimal sets of models of the base logics are not immediately connected to extensions. But this deserves a deeper investigation. We are, to the best of our knowledge, unaware of investigations of Beth definability in default logics.

We investigated interpolation and Beth definability in default logics. To this end, we started with a presentation of a general frawework for defining a default logic $\mathscr{D}\mathcal{L}$ from a basic monotonic logic $\mathcal{L}$. This framework covers well-known traditional default logics found in the literature, but encompasses a much richer family of default logics. Then, we defined suitable versions of interpolation and Beth definability for Default Logics, and studied their statuses. Given the generality of our definition of a default logic, the discussed results hold (or fail to hold) for several versions of default logics. In particular, we showed that CIP and SCIP (two versions of the so-called *Craig Interpolation Property*) transfers from $\mathfrak{L}$ to $\mathscr{D}\mathfrak{L}$, but Split Interpolation SIP fails for default logics extending CPL, even if $\mathfrak{L}$ has it. When considered as a step towards Beth definability, this negative result is a set back. However, we showed that the sceptical default consequence in a $\mathscr{D}\mathfrak{L}$ has Beth definability ($\mathscr{D}$BDP) if $\mathscr{D}\mathfrak{L}$ is stable (i.e., the extensions of a default theory are in harmony with those of its augmented default theory under substitution) and $\mathfrak{L}$ has SIP. Different is the case for credulous default consequence, in which $\mathscr{D}$BDP fails for any $\mathscr{D}\mathfrak{L}$ built on a logic extending CPL.

We view this work as a first step towards a better understanding of the meta-theory of default logics in general. As future work, it would be interesting to apply similar ideas to study proof calculi for default logics that are parameterized on the underlying logic. Moreover, it would be interesting to see whether the methods for constructing interpolants in the underlying proof calculi transfer to the default version (see e.g. [8]).

Ackowledgements. This work was partially supported by ANPCyT-PICTs-2017-1130 and 2016-0215, MinCyT Córdoba, SeCyT-UNC, the Laboratoire International Associé INFINIS and the European Union's Horizon 2020 research and innovation programme under the Marie Skodowska-Curie grant agreement No. 690974 for the project MIREL: MIning and REasoning with Legal texts.

A   Selected Proofs

Remark 3. Let $\mathfrak{L}$ be any logic, and Φ and Ψ be sets of sentences; we say that Ψ is a *conservative extension* of Φ, notation $\Psi \geq \Phi$, iff $\Phi^{\bullet} \subseteq \Psi^{\bullet}$ and $(\Psi^{\bullet}\!\restriction_{\mathscr{A}(\Phi)}) \subseteq \Phi^{\bullet}$.

Lemma 4. *Let $\mathfrak{L}$ be any logic, Φ be a set of sentences defined on an alphabet A, and $q \notin A$; if consequence in $\mathfrak{L}$ has SIP, $\Phi \cup S_q^p(\Phi) \geq \Phi$ and $\Phi \cup S_q^p(\Phi) \geq S_q^p(\Phi)$.*

Proof. Trivially, $\Phi^{\bullet} \subseteq (\Phi \cup S_q^p(\Phi))^{\bullet}$. In turn, let $\varphi \in (\Phi \cup S_q^p(\Phi))^{\bullet}\!\restriction_{\mathscr{A}(\Phi)}$; then, $\Phi \cup S_q^p(\Phi) \vdash \varphi$, alt., $\Phi \cup S_q^p(\Phi) \vdash \top \supset \varphi$. From SIP, there is ε defined on $A \setminus \{p\}$ s.t. $S_q^p(\Phi) \vdash \top \supset \varepsilon$ and $\Phi \vdash \varepsilon \supset \varphi$. Since $q \notin \mathscr{A}(\Phi, \varepsilon)$, $S_p^q(S_q^p(\Phi)) \vdash S_p^q(\top \supset \varepsilon)$ results in $\Phi \vdash \top \supset \varepsilon$. Then, $\Phi \vdash \top \supset \varepsilon$ and $\Phi \vdash \varepsilon \supset \varphi$; and so, $\Phi \vdash \top \supset \varphi$, alt., $\Phi \vdash \varphi$. Therefore, $(\Phi \cup S_q^p(\Phi))^{\bullet}\!\restriction_{\mathscr{A}(\Phi)} \subseteq \Phi^{\bullet}$.

Lemma 1. *Any strongly saturated default logic $\mathscr{D}\mathfrak{L}$ is stable.*

Proof. Let Θ be a default theory defined on an alphabet A, and and $q \notin A$. In addition, let $E \in \mathscr{E}(\Theta)$ be s.t. $E = (\Phi_\Theta \cup \Delta^{\mathsf{X}})^{\bullet}$ for some $\Delta \subseteq \Delta_\Theta$. Since $\mathscr{D}\mathfrak{L}$ is strongly saturated, Δ is saturated in Θ. The result follows immediately if $\Delta \cup S_q^p(\Delta)$ is saturated in $\Theta \sqcup S_q^p(\Theta)$; as $E' = (\Phi_\Theta \cup S_q^p(\Phi_\Theta) \cup (\Delta \cup S_q^p(\Delta))^{\mathsf{X}})^{\bullet}$ is our extension. The proof proceeds by contradiction. Let $\Delta \cup S_q^p(\Delta)$ be not saturated in $\Theta \sqcup S_q^p(\Theta)$; w.l.o.g. there is a default $\delta \notin \Delta \cup S_q^p(\Delta)$ s.t. δ is detached by $\Delta \cup S_q^p(\Delta)$. Clearly, $\delta \in \Delta_\Theta$ or $\delta = S_q^p(\delta')$ for some $\delta' \in \Delta_\Theta$. If $\delta \in \Delta_\Theta$, from Lemma 4, δ is detached by Δ; and so Δ is not saturated. This yields a contradiction. If $\delta = S_q^p(\delta')$ for some $\delta' \in \Delta_\Theta$, from Lemma 4, $S_q^p(\delta')$ is detached by $S_q^p(\Delta)$; and so $S_q^p(\Delta)$ is not saturated. But by substitution, δ' is detached by Δ, and so Δ is not saturated. This also yields a contradiction. Thus, $\Delta \cup S_q^p(\Delta)$ is saturated in $\Theta \sqcup S_q^p(\Theta)$.

Lemma 2. *Let $\mathscr{DL}$ be a default logic; for all default theories Θ and all $\Delta \subseteq \Delta_\Theta$, if Δ is self coherent in Θ, then, $\Delta \cup S_q^p(\Delta)$ is self coherent in $\Theta \sqcup S_q^p(\Theta)$.*

Proof. Similar to that of Lemma 1.

Lemma 3. *Let $\{\Phi_i \mid i \in I\}$ be a set of sets of formulas s.t. for all $i \in I$, $\mathscr{A}(\Phi_i) \subseteq A$ and $\Phi_i = \Phi_i^\bullet$; if consequence in $\mathfrak{L}$ has SIP, $q \notin A$, and $p \supset q \in \bigcap\{(\Phi_i \cup S_q^p(\Phi_i))^\bullet \mid i \in I\}$, then $p \supset q \in (\bigcap\{\Phi_i \mid i \in I\} \cup \bigcap\{S_q^p(\Phi_i) \mid i \in I\})^\bullet$.*

Proof (by contradiction). Let us assume that $p \supset q \in \bigcap\{(\Phi_i \cup S_q^p(\Phi_i))^\bullet \mid i \in I\}$; by definition, it follows that all $(*)$ $\Phi_i \cup S_q^p(\Phi_i) \vdash p \supset q$. At the same time, let $p \supset q \notin (\bigcap\{\Phi_i \mid i \in I\} \cup \bigcap\{S_q^p(\Phi_i) \mid i \in I\})^\bullet$; then, for all ξ defined on $A \setminus \{p\}$, either $(\dagger)$ $p \supset \xi \notin \bigcap\{\Phi_i \mid i \in I\}$ or $(\ddagger)$ $\xi \supset q \notin \bigcap\{S_q^p(\Phi_i) \mid i \in I\}$. From $(\dagger)$, there is $\Phi_i \nvdash p \supset \xi$; and from Lemma 4, $(\S)$ $\Phi_i \cup S_q^p(\Phi_i) \nvdash p \supset \xi$. But $(\S)$ leads to a contradiction; since from $(*)$ $\Phi_i \cup S_q^p(\Phi_i) \vdash p \supset q$, by SIP, there is in fact ξ defined on $A \setminus \{p\}$ s.t. $\Phi_i \cup S_q^p(\Phi_i) \vdash p \supset \xi$! Similarly, we obtain a contradiction from $(\ddagger)$. Thus, $p \supset q \in (\bigcap\{\Phi_i \mid i \in I\} \cup \bigcap\{S_q^p(\Phi_i) \mid i \in I\})^\bullet$.

References

1. Amir, E.: Interpolation theorems for nonmonotonic reasoning systems. In: Flesca, S., Greco, S., Ianni, G., Leone, N. (eds.) JELIA 2002. LNCS (LNAI), vol. 2424, pp. 233–244. Springer, Heidelberg (2002). https://doi.org/10.1007/3-540-45757-7_20
2. Antoniou, G., Wang, K.: Default logic. In: Gabbay, D., Woods, J. (eds.) The Many Valued and Nonmonotonic Turn in Logic. Handbook of the History of Logic, vol. 8, pp. 517–555. North-Holland (2007)
3. Areces, C., Blackburn, P., Marx, M.: Hybrid logics: characterization, interpolation and complexity. J. Symb. Logic 66(3), 977–1010 (2001)
4. Areces, C., de Rijke, M.: Interpolation and bisimulation in temporal logic. In: Workshop on Logic, Language, Information and Computation (WoLLIC 1998), pp. 15–21 (1998)
5. Areces, C., ten Cate, B.: Hybrid logics. In: Blackburn, P., van Benthem, J., Wolter, F. (eds.) Handbook of Modal Logic, pp. 821–868. Elsevier (2006)
6. Bicarregui, J., Dimitrakos, T., Gabbay, D., Maibaum, T.: Interpolation in practical formal development. Logic J. IGPL 9(2), 231–244 (2001)
7. Blackburn, P., de Rijke, M., Venema, Y.: Modal Logic. Cambridge University Press, Cambridge (2001)
8. Blackburn, P., Marx, M.: Constructive interpolation in hybrid logic. J. Symb. Logic 68(2), 463–480 (2003)

9. Cassano, V., Areces, C., Castro, P.: Reasoning about prescription and description using prioritized default rules. In: Barthe, G., Sutcliffe, G., Veanes, M. (eds.) 22nd International Conference on Logic for Programming, Artificial Intelligence and Reasoning (LPAR-22). EPiC Series in Computing, vol. 57, pp. 196–213. EasyChair (2018)
10. Chellas, B.: Modal Logic: An Introduction. Cambridge University Press, Cambridge (1980)
11. Craig, W.: Three uses of the Herbrand-Gentzen theorem in relating model theory and proof theory. J. Symb. Logic **22**, 269–285 (1957)
12. Delgrande, J., Schaub, T.: Expressing default logic variants in default logic. J. Logic Comput. **15**(5), 593–621 (2005)
13. Delgrande, J., Schaub, T., Jackson, W.: Alternative approaches to default logic. Artif. Intell. **70**(1–2), 167–237 (1994)
14. Diaconescu, R., Goguen, J., Stefaneas, P.: Logical support for modularisation. Papers Presented at the 2nd Annual Workshop on Logical Environments, pp. 83–130. Cambridge University Press, Cambridge (1993)
15. Enderton, H.: A Mathematical Introduction to Logic, 2nd edn. Academic Press, Cambridge (2001)
16. Font, J.: Abstract Algebraic Logic. An Introductory Textbook, 1st edn. College Publications (2016)
17. Froidevaux, C., Mengin, J.: A framework for default logics. In: Pearce, D., Wagner, G. (eds.) JELIA 1992. LNCS, vol. 633, pp. 154–173. Springer, Heidelberg (1992). https://doi.org/10.1007/BFb0023427
18. Froidevaux, C., Mengin, J.: Default logics: a unified view. Comput. Intell. **10**, 331–369 (1994)
19. Gabbay, D., Maksimova, L.: Interpolation and Definability: Modal and Intuitionistic Logic. Oxford University Press, Oxford (2005)
20. Gabbay, D., Pearce, D., Valverde, A.: Interpolable formulas in equilibrium logic and answer set programming. J. Artif. Intell. Res. **42**, 917–943 (2011)
21. Hintikka, J.: Knowledge and Belief. Cornell University Press, Ithaca (1962)
22. Hoogland, E.: Definability and Interpolation. Ph.D. thesis, Institute for Logic, Language and Computation Universiteit van Amsterdam (2001)
23. Kontchakov, R., Wolter, F., Zakharyaschev, M.: Can you tell the difference between DL-Lite ontologies? In: 11th International Conference on Principles of Knowledge Representation and Reasoning (KR 2008), pp. 285–295. AAAI Press (2008)
24. Łukaszewicz, W.: Considerations on default logic: an alternative approach. Comput. Intell. **4**, 1–16 (1988)
25. Maibaum, T., Sadler, M.: Axiomatizing specification theory. In: 3rd Workshop on Theory and Applications of ADTs (WADT 1984). Informatik-Fachberichte, vol. 116, pp. 171–177. Springer, Heidelberg (1984)
26. McMillan, K.L.: Applications of craig interpolants in model checking. In: Halbwachs, N., Zuck, L.D. (eds.) TACAS 2005. LNCS, vol. 3440, pp. 1–12. Springer, Heidelberg (2005). https://doi.org/10.1007/978-3-540-31980-1_1
27. Mikitiuk, A., Truszczynski, M.: Constrained and rational default logics. In: 14th International Joint Conference on Artificial Intelligence (IJCAI 1995), pp. 1509–1517 (1995)
28. Parikh, R.: Beth definability, interpolation and language splitting. Synthese **179**(2), 211–221 (2011)
29. Reiter, R.: A logic for default reasoning. AI **13**(1–2), 81–132 (1980)
30. Schaub, T.: On constrained default theories. In: 11th European Conference on Artificial Intelligence (ECAI 1992), pp. 304–308 (1992)

31. Shoenfield, J.: Mathematical Logic. Addison-Wesley, Boston (1967)
32. Suppes, P.: Axiomatic Set Theory. Dover Books on Mathematics. Dover Publications, Mineola (1972)
33. van Dalen, D.: Logic and structure, 5th edn. Springer, Heidelberg (2004). https://doi.org/10.1007/978-3-540-85108-0
34. Veloso, P., Maibaum, T.: On the modularization theorem for logical specifications. Inf. Process. Lett. **53**(5), 287–293 (1995)
35. Von Wright, G.H.: Deontic logic. Mind **60**, 1–15 (1951)

Axiomatising Logics with Separating Conjunction and Modalities

Stéphane Demri[1], Raul Fervari[2(✉)], and Alessio Mansutti[1]

[1] LSV, CNRS, ENS Paris-Saclay, Université Paris-Saclay, Cachan, France
[2] CONICET and Universidad Nacional de Córdoba, Córdoba, Argentina
fervari@famaf.unc.edu.ar

Abstract. Modal separation logics are formalisms that combine modal operators to reason locally, with separating connectives that allow to perform global updates on the models. In this work, we design Hilbert-style proof systems for the modal separation logics $\mathrm{MSL}(*, \langle \neq \rangle)$ and $\mathrm{MSL}(*, \Diamond)$, where $*$ is the separating conjunction, $\Diamond$ is the standard modal operator and $\langle \neq \rangle$ is the difference modality. The calculi only use the logical languages at hand (no external features such as labels) and take advantage of new normal forms and of their axiomatisation.

1 Introduction

Separation Logics with Epistemic Flavour. Modal logic [7,8] is a family of languages extending propositional logic with operators to describe and reason about different modes of truth. Such operators are usually called modalities. For instance, this family includes deontic (for permissions and obligations), epistemic (to reason about knowledge) and temporal modalities. On the other hand, separation logic [29,30] is a family of assertion languages originally conceived to perform Hoare-style verification [26] of programs with mutable data structures. The key components of separation logic are its non-classical connectives, that allow us to reason about updates of the models. For example, the formula $\phi * \psi$ uses the *separating conjunction* $*$, which requires to split a model into two disjoint pieces, one satisfying ϕ and the other one satisfying ψ. Over the last years, several approaches combining modal and separation logics have appeared. In most cases, the modal and the separation dimensions are orthogonal (see e.g. [9,12,13]), allowing us to design decision procedures by combinations of procedures from each dimension. However, recently, combinations of such operators interpreted over the same structures have been considered, see e.g. [17,18]. In this way, the underlying modal relational structure can be seen as a model from separation logic: states can be seen as memory locations, and edges can be seen as links between these locations.

These efforts on combining separation and modal logics witness the numerous attempts to use separation logic in different contexts. When interpreted on sets, separation logic can be used to model some particular phenomena in belief revision [25]. It can be combined with modalities from epistemic logic to capture

F. Calimeri et al. (Eds.): JELIA 2019, LNAI 11468, pp. 692–708, 2019.
https://doi.org/10.1007/978-3-030-19570-0_45

reachable states (see the epistemic logic for resources introduced in [13]). Epistemic separation logic [15], where models have equivalence relations representing possible worlds, has been extended in [14] with public announcements. Lastly, in [28] operators from temporal and separation logics are combined, allowing to express both temporal and spatial conditions in search control knowledge for AI planning (see also [10]). From a logical perspective, modal operators to perform updates on a relational model can be seen as weaker versions or variants of separating connectives, since they all have similar effects: updating the model (by adding, removing or changing some feature of the model) while evaluating a formula. For example, consider the sabotage modal logic SML introduced in [34] (see [24] for application in formal learning theory). SML is an extension of the basic modal language with a so-called sabotage operator which deletes one arrow of the model when it is evaluated. This operator can be seen as a weak version of the separating conjunction that separates only one edge from the rest of the model (see [18] for details). Other examples of dynamic logics used to describe graph evolution in games can be found in [3,33] (see also [16]).

Due to their ability to perform updates on a relational model, designing proof methods for such logics is known to be a non-trivial task. As a matter of fact, no proof system without features external from the logical language is known for the above-mentioned logics. For instance, there exist tableaux-based procedures to check satisfiability of sabotage logics [2,4] but model updates are handled with labels. Moreover, the rules in these calculi are quite complex, and they are far from providing a good understanding of the logics. On the other hand, there are no Hilbert-style calculi, as it is extremely challenging to axiomatise these logics that do not satisfy the uniform substitution rule (see e.g. [3]).

Our Motivations. We pursue a research program about modal separation logics to better understand the computational complexity of their decision problems and to design proof systems, such as Hilbert-style calculi. These calculi have clearly an historical value but also provide essential means to grasp what are the core validities and rules of the logical formalisms, see a recent illustration in [1]. It should be noted that not all modal separation logics admit finite axiomatisation, see e.g. [18], and sometimes, the axiomatisation of abstract separation logics requires the need for external features such as nominals or labels, see e.g. [11, 27]. In this work, we adopt a puristic approach to design Hilbert-style proof systems for the very logical language without any external help. In the context of modal separation logics, this is a requirement that happens to be rewarding for understanding their expressive power, considering that such logics freely mix modal operators and separating connectives having global effects.

Our Contribution. We design sound and complete Hilbert-style proof systems for the modal separation logics $\mathrm{MSL}(*, \Diamond)$ and $\mathrm{MSL}(*, \langle \neq \rangle)$ [18], where $*$ is the separating conjunction, $\Diamond$ is the standard modal operator and $\langle \neq \rangle$ is the difference modality. In both cases, we provide a syntactical treatment to the semantical abstractions used to decide such logics in [18], leading to NP-completeness. Each formula is shown equivalent to a Boolean combination of *core formulae*: simple formulae of the logic expressing elementary properties about the models.

More precisely, each elementary property consists of a *"modal part"* (describing partially the structure of the model), and a *"size part"* (related to the number of edges). Thus, we show how to introduce axioms to transform every formula into a Boolean combination of core formulae, together with axioms to deal with these simple formulae. This result borrows some ideas from the Gaifman's Theorem in first-order logic [21], which states that every first-order sentence is logically equivalent to a Boolean combination of so-called local formulae. A similar strategy is also followed for axiomatising dynamic epistemic logics [35–37] with the introduction of *reduction axioms*. In this technique, it is essential to translate each formula containing a dynamic operator into a formula without it, by using provably equivalent formulae. Then, completeness follows from the completeness of the system for the 'basic' language (see also a similar approach for the linear μ-calculus in [20]). In our case, another difficulty arises as we also have to design an axiomatisation for such Boolean combinations. The proof system for $\mathrm{MSL}(*, \Diamond)$ (Sect. 3) uses partially the standard machinery for modal logic, but it is a bit different from the axiomatisation for the modal logic Alt_1, i.e., the modal logic over deterministic frames, characterised by the axiom $\Diamond p \Rightarrow \Box p$ (see e.g. [5]). For $\mathrm{MSL}(*, \langle \neq \rangle)$ (Sect. 4), the modal part extends results from [32] to infinite models (a peculiarity of modal separation logics as the set of locations is infinite). These constructions give us an exact characterisation of the properties that can be expressed on each logic. Moreover, it is also remarkable to have axiomatisations for these two NP-complete logics, since the full logic MSL (including the separating implication) is not (finitely) axiomatisable [18].

2   Preliminaries About Modal Separation Logics

We briefly recall the definition of the modal separation logic $\mathrm{MSL}(*, \Diamond, \langle \neq \rangle)$ introduced in [18]. Let $\mathrm{PROP} = \{p, q, \dots\}$ be a countably infinite set of propositional symbols. Formulae of the logic $\mathrm{MSL}(*, \Diamond, \langle \neq \rangle)$ are defined by the grammar:

$$\phi ::= \top \mid p \mid \mathtt{emp} \mid \neg\phi \mid \phi \vee \phi \mid \Diamond\phi \mid \langle \neq \rangle\phi \mid \phi * \phi,$$

where $p \in \mathrm{PROP}$ (as usual $\bot \stackrel{\mathrm{def}}{=} \neg\top$). A *model* is a tuple $\mathfrak{M} = \langle \mathbb{N}, \mathfrak{R}, \mathfrak{V} \rangle$ such that

- the set of *locations* is the set of natural numbers $\mathbb{N}$,
- $\mathfrak{R} \subseteq \mathbb{N} \times \mathbb{N}$ is finite and weakly functional (a.k.a. deterministic, i.e. $(\mathfrak{l}, \mathfrak{l}') \in \mathfrak{R}$ and $(\mathfrak{l}, \mathfrak{l}'') \in \mathfrak{R}$ imply $\mathfrak{l}' = \mathfrak{l}''$) and,
- $\mathfrak{V} : \mathrm{PROP} \to \mathcal{P}(\mathbb{N})$ is a valuation.

In the rest of the document, by 'functional', we mean 'weakly functional'. Since separation logics are interpreted on structures representing heaps [6], this explains why in the models, the domain is $\mathbb{N}$ (an infinite set of *locations*), and the accessibility relation is finite and functional (formal relationships with separation logics can be found in [18, Sect. 2.2]). The models $\mathfrak{M}_1 = \langle \mathbb{N}, \mathfrak{R}_1, \mathfrak{V} \rangle$ and $\mathfrak{M}_2 = \langle \mathbb{N}, \mathfrak{R}_2, \mathfrak{V} \rangle$ are *disjoint* if $\mathfrak{R}_1 \cap \mathfrak{R}_2 = \emptyset$; when this holds, $\mathfrak{M}_1 \uplus \mathfrak{M}_2$

denotes the model corresponding to the disjoint union of $\mathfrak{M}_1$ and $\mathfrak{M}_2$. Given $\mathfrak{M} = \langle N, \mathfrak{R}, \mathfrak{V} \rangle$ and $\mathfrak{l} \in N$, the satisfaction relation $\models$ is defined below (we omit standard clauses for Boolean connectives):

$$\mathfrak{M}, \mathfrak{l} \models p \quad \overset{\text{def}}{\Leftrightarrow} \quad \mathfrak{l} \in \mathfrak{V}(p) \qquad \mathfrak{M}, \mathfrak{l} \models \text{emp} \quad \overset{\text{def}}{\Leftrightarrow} \quad \mathfrak{R} = \emptyset$$

$$\mathfrak{M}, \mathfrak{l} \models \Diamond\phi \quad \overset{\text{def}}{\Leftrightarrow} \quad \mathfrak{M}, \mathfrak{l}' \models \phi, \text{ for some } \mathfrak{l}' \in N \text{ such that } (\mathfrak{l}, \mathfrak{l}') \in \mathfrak{R}$$

$$\mathfrak{M}, \mathfrak{l} \models \langle\neq\rangle\phi \quad \overset{\text{def}}{\Leftrightarrow} \quad \mathfrak{M}, \mathfrak{l}' \models \phi, \text{ for some } \mathfrak{l}' \in N \text{ such that } \mathfrak{l}' \neq \mathfrak{l}$$

$$\mathfrak{M}, \mathfrak{l} \models \phi_1 * \phi_2 \quad \overset{\text{def}}{\Leftrightarrow} \quad \langle N, \mathfrak{R}_1, \mathfrak{V} \rangle, \mathfrak{l} \models \phi_1 \text{ and } \langle N, \mathfrak{R}_2, \mathfrak{V} \rangle, \mathfrak{l} \models \phi_2,$$
$$\text{for some partition } \{\mathfrak{R}_1, \mathfrak{R}_2\} \text{ of } \mathfrak{R}.$$

The semantics for the modal operators and the separating connectives is the standard one, see e.g. [7,30]. The restriction of $\text{MSL}(*, \Diamond, \langle\neq\rangle)$ without the modal operator $\Diamond$ (resp. $\langle\neq\rangle$) is denoted by $\text{MSL}(*, \langle\neq\rangle)$ (resp. $\text{MSL}(*, \Diamond)$). It is established in [18] that the satisfiability problems for $\text{MSL}(*, \Diamond)$ and $\text{MSL}(*, \langle\neq\rangle)$ are NP-complete whereas the problem for $\text{MSL}(*, \langle\neq\rangle, \Diamond)$ is TOWER-complete[1].

To illustrate the expressive power of $\text{MSL}(*, \Diamond)$, let us define loop_1, which states that the model consists of a single reflexive edge at the evaluation point:

$$\neg\text{emp} \wedge \neg(\neg\text{emp} * \neg\text{emp}) \wedge \Diamond\Diamond\top.$$

Moreover, it is possible to define the formula loop_2, that interpreted on a location $\mathfrak{l}$, states that the model contains exactly a loop of length 2 visiting $\mathfrak{l}$:

$$(\neg\text{emp} * \neg\text{emp}) \wedge \neg(\neg\text{emp} * \neg\text{emp} * \neg\text{emp}) \wedge \Diamond\Diamond\Diamond\top \wedge$$

$$\neg(\neg\text{emp} * \Diamond\Diamond\Diamond\top) \wedge \neg\Diamond(\neg\text{emp} * \Diamond\Diamond\Diamond\top).$$

Notice that $*$ is associative. Obviously, these properties cannot be expressed in the modal logic Alt_1.

So, in this paper, we aim at providing Hilbert style axiomatisations for $\text{MSL}(*, \Diamond)$ and $\text{MSL}(*, \langle\neq\rangle)$, which amounts to characterise syntactically the set of valid formulae by means of a proof system. By contrast, the complexity results from [18] are obtained semantically, without any proof-theoretical analysis.

3   Axiomatising $\text{MSL}(*, \Diamond)$ with Core Formulae

In this section, we define a proof system for $\text{MSL}(*, \Diamond)$, namely $\mathcal{H}\text{MSL}(*, \Diamond)$. To do so, we introduce a set of *core formulae* that are simple formulae capturing essential properties. As shown later on, every $\text{MSL}(*, \Diamond)$ formula is logically equivalent to a Boolean combination of core formulae. However, as every core formula is shown to be an $\text{MSL}(*, \Diamond)$ formula, we can derive an axiomatisation of $\text{MSL}(*, \Diamond)$ by axiomatising Boolean combinations of core formulae. So, we define three sets of axioms and inference rules: (1) those dedicated to the propositional logic of core formulae, (2) those that, given a Boolean combination of

---

[1] The class TOWER [31] is the class of problems of time complexity bounded by a tower of exponentials, whose height is an elementary function of the input.

core formulae ϕ, allow to derive a Boolean combination of core formulae that is equivalent to $\Diamond\phi$ (a property called herein $\Diamond$-elimination, see Lemma 6), and (3) those that, given two Boolean combinations of core formulae ϕ_1, ϕ_2, allow to derive a Boolean combination of core formulae that is equivalent to $\phi_1 * \phi_2$ (a property called herein *-elimination, see Lemma 9).

Core Formulae for MSL $(*, \Diamond)$. Core formulae are divided into two families: a set of *size formulae* that express properties about the size of the model (i.e. the number of edges) and a set of *graph formulae* describing the shape of the model that is observable from the current location. As the relation $\Re$ in models is weakly functional, the number of distinct shapes is limited, ranging from lasso shapes to segments with dead-end.

Let us introduce expressions of the form $\texttt{size} \geq \beta$ that hold true whenever $\Re$ has at least β elements (the symbol β always refers to a natural number throughout the paper). A *size literal* is a formula of the form $\texttt{size} \geq \beta$ or $\neg\texttt{size} \geq \beta$. Every Boolean combination of size literals is a *size formula*. We also use $\texttt{size} = \beta$ as an abbreviation for $\texttt{size} \geq \beta \wedge \neg\texttt{size} \geq \beta+1$. At this stage, it is worth noting that $\texttt{size} \geq \beta$ should be understood as a built-in atomic formula enriching the logical language for MSL$(*, \Diamond)$. However, as it will quickly appear below, $\texttt{size} \geq \beta$ can be characterised with a formula of MSL$(*, \Diamond)$ and later on in the document, such occurrences of $\texttt{size} \geq \beta$ should be understood as mere abbreviations. The same distinction applies to the graph formulae defined below.

Graph formulae describe the shape of a portion of the model, partly inspired from the semantical notion of abstract frame from [18, Sect. 4.1] but with constraints on propositional variables. Formally, every graph formula is an expression derived from the non-terminal $\mathcal{G}$ of the grammar below:

$$\ell := \top \mid \bot \mid p \mid \neg p \qquad Q := \ell \mid Q \wedge Q \qquad \mathcal{G} := |Q,...,Q\rangle \mid |Q,...,Q] \mid |Q,...,\overleftarrow{Q},...,Q|,$$

where $p \in \text{PROP}$, and $\mathcal{G}$ must contain at least one conjunction Q. By slightly abusing the standard terminology, expressions of the form ℓ are called *literals*. A conjunction Q is *contradictory* whenever $\bot$ occurs in Q or there is some p such that both p and $\neg p$ occur in Q. Note that Q is contradictory iff Q is unsatisfiable. By convention, contradictory conjunctions are denoted by $Q^\perp$. A graph formula is *contradictory* if at least one of its conjunctions is contradictory. Note also that the semantics for graph formulae shall guarantee that a graph formula is contradictory iff it is unsatisfiable.

Since we are working on weakly functional and finite relations, graph formulae represent paths satisfying a conjunction of literals Q at each position. A formula of the form $|Q_1,...,Q_n\rangle$ expresses that there exists a path of length n in which all the locations are distinct of each other, and we do not know whether it continues after. The formula $|Q_1,...,Q_n]$ states that there is a path of length $n-1$, all the locations are distinct, and the last location has no successor. Finally, the formula of the form $|Q_1,...,\overleftarrow{Q_i},...,Q_n|$ expresses that there is a path of size $n-1$ with all distinct locations, and there is a loop from the location in position n and the one in the position i (lasso shape). Sometimes, we write $|Q_1,...,Q_n?$ to refer to graph formulae of any kind. Furthermore, we write $|Q,...,Q'?_{(n)}$ to express that the last argument Q' of the corresponding graph formula is at position n. For example, $|\top,...,\top]_{(5)}$ stands for $|\top,\top,\top,\top,\top]$. Lastly, we write $\sharp(|Q_1,...,Q_n?)$ to denote the *graph size* of $|Q_1,...,Q_n?$ defined as follows:

$$\sharp(|Q_1,...,Q_n\rangle) \overset{\text{def}}{=} n \qquad \sharp(|Q_1,...,Q_n]) \overset{\text{def}}{=} n-1 \qquad \sharp(|Q_1,...,\overset{\curvearrowright}{Q_i},...,Q_n|) \overset{\text{def}}{=} n.$$

Given $\mathfrak{M} = \langle \mathbb{N}, \mathfrak{R}, \mathfrak{V} \rangle$ and $\mathfrak{l} \in \mathbb{N}$, the relation $\models$ is extended to core formulae:

$\mathfrak{M}, \mathfrak{l} \models \mathtt{size} \geq \beta \qquad \overset{\text{def}}{\Leftrightarrow} \quad \mathrm{card}(\mathfrak{R}) \geq \beta$

$\mathfrak{M}, \mathfrak{l} \models |Q_1,...,Q_n\rangle \qquad \overset{\text{def}}{\Leftrightarrow} \quad$ there are distinct $\mathfrak{l}_1,...,\mathfrak{l}_{n+1}$ s.t. $\mathfrak{l}=\mathfrak{l}_1\mathfrak{R}\mathfrak{l}_2\mathfrak{R}...\mathfrak{R}\mathfrak{l}_{n+1}$, and for all $j \in [1,n]$, $\mathfrak{M}, \mathfrak{l}_j \models Q_j$

$\mathfrak{M}, \mathfrak{l} \models |Q_1,...,Q_n] \qquad \overset{\text{def}}{\Leftrightarrow} \quad$ there are distinct $\mathfrak{l}_1,...,\mathfrak{l}_n$ s.t. $\mathfrak{l}=\mathfrak{l}_1\mathfrak{R}\mathfrak{l}_2\mathfrak{R}...\mathfrak{R}\mathfrak{l}_n$, $\mathfrak{R}(\mathfrak{l}_n) = \emptyset$ and for each $j \in [1,n]$, $\mathfrak{M}, \mathfrak{l}_j \models Q_j$

$\mathfrak{M}, \mathfrak{l} \models |Q_1,...,\overset{\curvearrowright}{Q_i},...,Q_n| \quad \overset{\text{def}}{\Leftrightarrow} \quad$ there are distinct $\mathfrak{l}_1,...,\mathfrak{l}_n$ s.t. $\mathfrak{l}=\mathfrak{l}_1\mathfrak{R}\mathfrak{l}_2\mathfrak{R}...\mathfrak{l}_n\mathfrak{R}\mathfrak{l}_i$ and for all $j \in [1,n]$, $\mathfrak{M}, \mathfrak{l}_j \models Q_j$.

Below, we establish that every core formula has a logically equivalent counterpart in $\mathrm{MSL}(*,\Diamond)$ (Lemma 1). This is an essential property as these formulae are the building blocks of the axiomatisation of $\mathrm{MSL}(*,\Diamond)$. Consequently, we obtain that our axioms are only made of $\mathrm{MSL}(*,\Diamond)$ formulae, with no need for external properties or extra machinery such as nominals or labels.

For every core formula ψ, we define its *extension* $\mathrm{ext}(\psi)$ in $\mathrm{MSL}(*,\Diamond)$.

- $\mathrm{ext}(\mathtt{size} \geq 0) \overset{\text{def}}{=} \top$ and $\mathrm{ext}(\mathtt{size} \geq \beta) \overset{\text{def}}{=} \overbrace{\neg\mathtt{emp} * \cdots * \neg\mathtt{emp}}^{\beta \text{ times}}$ for $\beta > 0$.

- $\mathrm{ext}(|Q]) \overset{\text{def}}{=} Q \wedge \neg\Diamond\top$. For $n \geq 2$, $\mathrm{ext}(|Q_1,Q_2,...,Q_n]) \overset{\text{def}}{=} Q_1 \wedge \Diamond\mathrm{ext}(|Q_2,...,Q_n])$.

- $\mathrm{ext}(|Q_1,...,Q_n\rangle) \overset{\text{def}}{=} \mathrm{ext}(|Q_1,...,Q_n,\top]) * \top$.

- $\mathrm{ext}(|\overset{\curvearrowright}{Q_1},...,Q_n|)$ is defined as the formula

$$\top * (\mathrm{ext}(\mathtt{size} = n) \wedge \Diamond^{n+1}\top \wedge (\mathrm{ext}(|Q_1,...,Q_n]) * \top) \wedge \neg\Diamond(\mathrm{ext}(\mathtt{size} = 1) * \Diamond^n\top))$$

where $\Diamond^0\phi \overset{\text{def}}{=} \phi$ and $\Diamond^{i+1}\phi \overset{\text{def}}{=} \Diamond\Diamond^i\phi$. For $i > 1$, $\mathrm{ext}(|Q_1,...,\overset{\curvearrowright}{Q_i},...,Q_n|)$ is

$$\top * \big(\mathrm{ext}(\mathtt{size} = n) \wedge \Diamond^{n+1}\top \wedge (\mathrm{ext}(|Q_1,...,Q_n]) * \top) \wedge$$
$$\Diamond^{i-1}(\mathrm{ext}(\mathtt{size} = i-1) * \mathrm{ext}(|\overset{\curvearrowright}{\top},...,\top]_{(n-i+1)})))\big).$$

Lemma 1. *All the core formulae ψ are logically equivalent to $\mathrm{ext}(\psi)$.*

From now on, for any occurrence of a core formula ψ, including occurrences in the axioms or inference rules, we mean the formula $\mathrm{ext}(\psi)$ so that their provisory status of built-in atomic formula is upgraded to a permanent abbreviation.

Hilbert-style Proof System for $\mathrm{MSL}(*,\Diamond)$. To obtain an axiomatisation of $\mathrm{MSL}(*,\Diamond)$, we start by introducing the proof system $\mathcal{H}_c$ dedicated to Boolean combinations of core formulae. As $\mathrm{MSL}(*,\Diamond)$ includes the propositional logic, $\mathcal{H}_c$ and all the subsequent proof systems contain the axiom schemas and modus ponens for the propositional calculus. Throughout the paper we use standard notations about Hilbert-style proof systems. To simplify, sometimes we will abuse the terminology and use 'axiom' instead of 'axiom schema'. The axioms whose name is of the form $\mathbf{G}_i^?$ (resp. $\mathbf{S}_i^?$) handle graph formulae (resp. size formulae). We start with the axioms for $\texttt{size} \geq \beta$, its interactions with graph formulae and one axiom schema for inconsistent graph formulae.

Axioms for size formulae and for inconsistent graph formulae
(S$_1^c$) $\texttt{size} \geq 0$ **(G$_1^c$)** $\|Q_1,...,Q_n? \Rightarrow \texttt{size} \geq \sharp(\|Q_1,...,Q_n?)$
(S$_2^c$) $\texttt{size} \geq \beta+1 \Rightarrow \texttt{size} \geq \beta$ **(G$_2^c$)** $\neg\|..., Q^\perp,...?$

The meaning of these axioms is straightforward. For instance, the axiom (S$_2^c$) states that if the accessibility relation of a model has at least $\beta+1$ elements, then it has at least β elements. The axiom (G$_1^c$) states that if a model satisfies a graph formula $\mathcal{G}$ then its accessibility relation cannot have less elements than its graph size. We complete the definition of $\mathcal{H}_c$ with two families of axioms, involving graph formulae. The first family (with the axioms from (G$_3^c$) to (G$_{13}^c$) concerns conjunctions of graph formulae. In particular, given two graph formulae, these axioms allow us to derive an equivalent graph formula. Similarly, the second family (with the axioms from (G$_{14}^c$) to (G$_{16}^c$)) concerns the negation of a graph formula. With these axioms, every negation of a graph formula is shown equivalent to a disjunction of graph formulae. Let us begin with the first family.

Axioms for conjunction of graph formulae
(G$_3^c$) $\neg(\|\dots]_{(n)} \wedge \|\overleftarrow{\dots}\|_{(m)})$ **(G$_5^c$)** $\neg(\|\dots\rangle_{(n)} \wedge \|\overleftarrow{\dots}\|_{(m)})$ with $n \geq m$
(G$_4^c$) $\neg(\|\dots\rangle_{(n)} \wedge \|\dots]_{(m)})$ with $n \geq m$ **(G$_6^c$)** $\neg(\|\dots]_{(n)} \wedge \|\dots]_{(m)})$ with $n \neq m$
(G$_7^c$) $\|Q_1,...,Q_n\rangle \wedge \|Q_1',...,Q_m'\rangle \Leftrightarrow \|Q_1 \wedge Q_1',...,Q_n \wedge Q_n', Q_{n+1}',...,Q_m'\rangle$ with $n \leq m$,
(G$_8^c$) $\|Q_1,...,Q_n\rangle \wedge \|Q_1',...,Q_m'] \Leftrightarrow \|Q_1 \wedge Q_1',...,Q_n \wedge Q_n', Q_{n+1}',...,Q_m']$ with $n < m$,
(G$_9^c$) $\|Q_1,...,Q_n] \wedge \|Q_1',...,Q_n'] \Leftrightarrow \|Q_1 \wedge Q_1',...,Q_n \wedge Q_n']$
(G$_{10}^c$) $\neg(\|Q_1,...,\overleftarrow{Q_i},...,Q_n] \wedge \|Q_1',...,\overleftarrow{Q_j'},...,Q_m'])$ with $n \neq m$ or $i \neq j$
(G$_{11}^c$) $\|Q_1,...,\overleftarrow{Q_i},...,Q_n] \wedge \|Q_1',...,\overleftarrow{Q_i'},...,Q_n'] \Leftrightarrow \|Q_1 \wedge Q_1',...,\overleftarrow{Q_i \wedge Q_i'},...,Q_n \wedge Q_n']$
(G$_{12}^c$) if $n < i \leq m$,
$\|Q_1,...,Q_n\rangle \wedge \|Q_1',...,\overleftarrow{Q_i'},...,Q_m'] \Leftrightarrow \|Q_1 \wedge Q_1',...,Q_n \wedge Q_n', Q_{n+1}',...,\overleftarrow{Q_i'},...,Q_m']$
(G$_{13}^c$) if $i \leq n < m$,
$\|Q_1,...,Q_n\rangle \wedge \|Q_1',...,\overleftarrow{Q_i'},...,Q_m'] \Leftrightarrow \|Q_1 \wedge Q_1',...,\overleftarrow{Q_i \wedge Q_i'},...,Q_n \wedge Q_n', Q_{n+1}',...,Q_m']$

Thanks to these axioms, any conjunction of two graph formulae is valid only if it express properties that can be found together in a single model. For instance, $\|\dots]_{(n)} \wedge \|\overleftarrow{\dots}\|_{(m)}$ is clearly contradictory (see the axiom (G$_3^c$)), as the existence of a loop contradicts the fact that there is a dead-end (i.e. a location without successors). To ease the readability of the axioms for negation, we first define some auxiliary formulae.

$$\rho_n \stackrel{\text{def}}{=} \|\top,...,\top\rangle_{(n)} \qquad \tau_n \stackrel{\text{def}}{=} \bigvee_{i \in [1,n]} \|\top,...,\top]_{(i)} \qquad \lambda_n \stackrel{\text{def}}{=} \bigvee_{\substack{i \in [1,n] \\ j \in [1,i]}} \|\top,...,\overleftarrow{\top},...,\top\|_{(i)}^{j} \quad (i)$$

In λ_n, the index j below $\top$ indicates that the loop begins at the j-th position. We introduce the involution $\overline{(.)}$ on literals so that for every $p \in \mathrm{PROP}$, $\overline{p} \overset{\text{def}}{=} \neg p$, $\overline{\neg p} \overset{\text{def}}{=} p$, $\overline{\top} \overset{\text{def}}{=} \bot$ and $\overline{\bot} \overset{\text{def}}{=} \top$. This development is needed since graph formulae do not admit doubly negated literals. We write $\ell \in Q$ to denote that ℓ is a literal occurring in Q with the same polarity. So, $\neg p$ appearing in Q does not imply $p \in Q$. The axioms for dealing with negation are defined as follows.

Axioms for negation of graph formulae

$(\mathbf{G_{14}^c})$ $\neg|Q_1,...,Q_n\rangle \Leftrightarrow \lambda_n \vee \tau_n \vee \bigvee_{\substack{i\in[1,n]\\ \ell\in Q_i}} |\top,...,\underset{i}{\overline{\ell}},...,\top\rangle_{(n)}$

$(\mathbf{G_{15}^c})$ $\neg|Q_1,...,Q_n] \Leftrightarrow \rho_n \vee \tau_{n-1} \vee \lambda_n \vee \bigvee_{\substack{i\in[1,n]\\ \ell\in Q_i}} |\top,...,\underset{i}{\overline{\ell}},...,\top]_{(n)}$

$(\mathbf{G_{16}^c})$ $\neg|Q_1,...,\overline{Q_i},...,Q_n| \Leftrightarrow \rho_n \vee \tau_n \vee \lambda_{n-1} \vee \bigvee_{\substack{i\in[1,n-1]\\ \ell\in Q_i}} |\top,...,\underset{i}{\overline{\ell}},...,\top\rangle_{(n-1)}$

$\qquad\qquad\qquad \vee \bigvee_{k\in[1,n]\backslash\{i\}} |\top,...,\underset{k}{\overset{\frown}{\top}},...,\top|_{(n)} \vee \bigvee_{\ell\in Q_n} |\top,...,\underset{i}{\top},...,\overline{\ell}|_{(n)}$

These axioms characterise the shape of the accessibility relation when one particular shape is excluded. For example, if $\mathfrak{M}, \mathfrak{l} \models \neg|\top,\top,\top]$, then the path starting from $\mathfrak{l}$ is of length 0, 1 or greater than 2. When it is of length 2 (equal to $\sharp(|\top,\top,\top]))$, it has a lasso shape. These cases are captured by the axiom $(\mathbf{G_{15}^c})$.

Lemma 2. *Every axiom in $\mathcal{H}_c$ is valid for $MSL(*, \Diamond)$.*

To show the completeness of $\mathcal{H}_c$, we exploit its ability to eliminate negations and conjunctions of graph formulae. This is enough to show that every Boolean combination of core formulae is equivalent to a disjunction of formulae of the form either $\mathcal{G} \wedge \mathtt{size} \geq \beta$ or $\mathcal{G} \wedge \mathtt{size} \geq \beta \wedge \neg\mathtt{size} \geq \beta'$, where $\mathcal{G}$ is a graph formula. Such formulae are called *elementary shapes*.

Lemma 3. *Let ϕ be a Boolean combination of core formulae. There is a disjunction of elementary shapes ψ such that $\vdash_{\mathcal{H}_c} \phi \Leftrightarrow \psi$.*

By Lemma 2, the formulae ϕ and ψ in Lemma 3 are logically equivalent. We prove that $\mathcal{H}_c$ is complete for the restricted case of elementary shapes.

Lemma 4. *Let ϕ be an elementary shape. ϕ is satisfiable iff $\nvdash_{\mathcal{H}_c} \neg\phi$.*

From this result, we can establish the completeness of $\mathcal{H}_c$ with respect to Boolean combinations of core formulae. This is an essential step to get a complete proof system for $MSL(*, \Diamond)$ (its definition is to be completed in the rest of Sect. 3).

Theorem 1. *A Boolean combination of core formulae ϕ is valid iff $\vdash_{\mathcal{H}_c} \phi$.*

Proof. Let ϕ be a Boolean combination of core formulae. By Lemma 2, $\vdash_{\mathcal{H}_c} \phi$ implies that ϕ is valid. Conversely, let us assume that ϕ is valid and *ad absurdum*, let us suppose that $\nvdash_{\mathcal{H}_c} \phi$. By propositional calculus, there exists a formula ϕ' in conjunctive normal form (CNF) such that the "literals" are core formulae or their negations, and $\vdash_{\mathcal{H}_c} \phi \Leftrightarrow \phi'$. As $\nvdash_{\mathcal{H}_c} \phi$, there is a conjunct of ϕ', say ψ, such that $\nvdash_{\mathcal{H}_c} \psi$. As ϕ' is valid, this implies that ψ is valid too. By Lemma 3, $\vdash_{\mathcal{H}_c} \neg\psi \Leftrightarrow (\varphi_1 \vee \cdots \vee \varphi_n)$ where $\varphi_1 \vee \cdots \vee \varphi_n$ is a disjunction of elementary shapes and therefore $(\varphi_1 \vee \cdots \vee \varphi_n)$ is unsatisfiable. Consequently, for all $i \in [1, n]$, the formula φ_i is unsatisfiable and by Lemma 4, we get that $\vdash_{\mathcal{H}_c} \neg\varphi_i$. By propositional reasoning, we get $\vdash_{\mathcal{H}_c} \neg\varphi_1 \wedge \cdots \wedge \neg\varphi_n$ and again by propositional reasoning using $\vdash_{\mathcal{H}_c} \neg\psi \Leftrightarrow (\varphi_1 \vee \cdots \vee \varphi_n)$, we obtain $\vdash_{\mathcal{H}_c} \psi$, which leads to a contradiction. $\qquad\square$

$\Diamond$-**elimination.** We enrich $\mathcal{H}_c$ by adding axioms and one inference rule that handle $\Diamond$, leading to the extended proof system $\mathcal{H}_c(\Diamond)$ dedicated to the set of formulae obtained by closing core formulae under Boolean connectives and $\Diamond$.

Axioms and inference rule for $\mathcal{H}_c(\Diamond)$
($\Diamond$DISTR) $\Diamond(\phi \vee \psi) \Leftrightarrow \Diamond(\phi) \vee \Diamond(\psi)$ **(G$_{17}^{\Diamond}$)** $\Diamond(\lfloor Q_1,...,Q_n \rfloor) \Leftrightarrow \lfloor \top, Q_1,...,Q_n \rfloor$
(S$_3^{\Diamond}$) $\Diamond(\phi \wedge \mathcal{S}) \Leftrightarrow \Diamond(\phi) \wedge \mathcal{S}$ where $\mathcal{S}$ is a size formula,
(G$_{18}^{\Diamond}$) $\Diamond(\lfloor Q_1,\ldots,Q_n \rangle) \Leftrightarrow \lfloor \overline{\top}, Q_1,...,Q_n \rfloor \vee \lfloor \top, Q_1,...,Q_n \rangle$
(G$_{19}^{\Diamond}$) $\Diamond(\lfloor Q_1,...,\overline{Q_i},...,Q_n \rfloor) \Leftrightarrow \lfloor \top, Q_1,...,\overline{Q_i},...,Q_n \rfloor$ with $i \geq 2$,
(G$_{20}^{\Diamond}$) $\Diamond(\lfloor \overline{Q_1},...,Q_{n-1},Q_n \rfloor) \Leftrightarrow \lfloor \overline{Q_n}, Q_1,...,Q_{n-1} \rfloor \vee \lfloor \top, \overline{Q_1},...,Q_{n-1},Q_n \rfloor$
Regularity rule: $\dfrac{\phi \Rightarrow \psi}{\Diamond\phi \Rightarrow \Diamond\psi}$

Lemma 5. *Axioms and rules in $\mathcal{H}_c(\Diamond)$ are valid for MSL$(*, \Diamond)$.*

These axioms give us some insight about the interplay between separating and modal connectives. In the case of size formulae, there is no interplay at all (see the axiom **(S$_3^{\Diamond}$)**). Indeed, every condition in a formula ψ about the size of the accessibility relation $\mathfrak{R}$ carries on independently of the structure of $\mathfrak{R}$ described by ψ through modalities. However, there are interplays with respect to loops (see e.g. the axiom **(G$_{18}^{\Diamond}$)**) and recall that $\mathsf{ext}(\lfloor Q_1,...,\overline{Q_i},...,Q_n \rfloor)$ uses $*$).

Lemma 6. *Let ϕ be a Boolean combination of core formulae. There is a Boolean combination of core formulae ψ such that $\vdash_{\mathcal{H}_c(\Diamond)} \Diamond\phi \Leftrightarrow \psi$.*

By Lemma 5, the formulae $\Diamond\phi$ and ψ in Lemma 6 are logically equivalent.

$*$-**elimination.** Finally, we enrich $\mathcal{H}_c$ by adding axioms and one inference rule for the separating conjunction. We denote the resulting proof system by $\mathcal{H}_c(*)$.

Axioms and inference rule for $\mathcal{H}_c(*)$

(COM) $(\phi * \psi) \Leftrightarrow (\psi * \phi)$	**(*DISTR)** $(\phi_1 \vee \phi_2) * \psi \Leftrightarrow (\phi_1 * \psi) \vee (\phi_2 * \psi)$
(ASSOC) $(\phi * \psi) * \varphi \Leftrightarrow \phi * (\psi * \varphi)$	$(\mathbf{G_{22}^*})$ $\neg(\mathcal{G}_1 * \mathcal{G}_2)$ with $\sharp(\mathcal{G}_1) \times \sharp(\mathcal{G}_2) \geq 1$
$(\perp)$ $\neg(\perp * \phi)$ (with $\perp \overset{\text{def}}{=} \neg \texttt{size} \geq 0$)	$(\mathbf{G_{23}^*})$ $\lvert Q_1, ..., Q_n \rangle * \phi \Rightarrow \lvert Q_1, ..., Q_n \rangle$
$(\mathbf{S_4^*})$ $\phi \Leftrightarrow (\phi * \neg \texttt{size} \geq 1)$	$(\mathbf{G_{24}^*})$ $\lvert Q_1, ..., \overleftarrow{Q_i}, ..., Q_n \rceil * \phi \Rightarrow \lvert Q_1, ..., \overleftarrow{Q_i}, ..., Q_n \rceil$

$(\mathbf{S_5^*})$ $\texttt{size} \geq \beta_1 + \beta_2 \Rightarrow \texttt{size} = \beta_1 * \texttt{size} \geq \beta_2$

$(\mathbf{S_6^*})$ $\neg \texttt{size} \geq \beta_1 * \neg \texttt{size} \geq \beta_2 \Rightarrow \neg \texttt{size} \geq (\beta_1 + \beta_2) \doteq 1$ $\qquad (\alpha_1 \doteq \alpha_2 \overset{\text{def}}{=} \max(0, \alpha_1 - \alpha_2))$

$(\mathbf{G_{25}^*})$ $\lvert Q_1, ..., Q_n \rceil * \texttt{size} \geq 1 \Rightarrow \lvert Q_1, ..., Q_n \rceil \vee \lvert Q_1, ..., Q_n \rangle \vee \bigvee_{i \in [1,n]} \lvert Q_1, ..., \overleftarrow{Q_i}, ..., Q_n \rceil$

$(\mathbf{G_{26}^*})$ $(\lvert Q_1 \wedge Q, ..., Q_n ? \wedge \phi) * \psi \Leftrightarrow (\lvert Q_1, ..., Q_n ? \wedge \phi) * (\lvert Q \rceil \wedge \psi)$

$(\mathbf{G_{27}^*})$ $\lvert Q_1, ..., Q_n ? \wedge \texttt{size} \geq \beta \Rightarrow (\lvert Q_1, ..., Q_n ? \wedge \texttt{size} = \beta) * \top$ with $\beta \geq \sharp(\lvert Q_1, ..., Q_n ?)$

$(\mathbf{G_{28}^*})$ $\lvert Q_1, ..., Q_n \rangle \wedge \texttt{size} \geq \beta + n \Rightarrow (\lvert Q_1, ..., Q_n \rceil \wedge \texttt{size} \geq (\beta + n) \doteq 1) * \texttt{size} = 1$

$(\mathbf{G_{29}^*})$ $\lvert Q_1, ..., \overleftarrow{Q_i}, ..., Q_n \rceil \wedge \texttt{size} \geq \beta + n \Rightarrow (\lvert Q_1, ..., Q_n \rceil \wedge \texttt{size} \geq (\beta + n) - 1) * \texttt{size} = 1$

*-introduction rule: $\dfrac{\phi \Rightarrow \varphi}{\phi * \psi \Rightarrow \varphi * \psi}$

The first property to check is the soundness of $\mathcal{H}_c(*)$.

Lemma 7. *Axioms and rules in $\mathcal{H}_c(*)$ are valid for $MSL(*, \Diamond)$.*

Forthcoming Lemma 9 states that the separating conjunction $\phi * \psi$ of two Boolean combinations of core formulae is equivalent in $\mathcal{H}_c(*)$ to some Boolean combination of core formulae φ, and therefore by Lemma 7, $\phi * \psi$ is also logically equivalent to φ. Thanks to the axioms **(COM)** and **(*DISTR)**, the *-introduction rule and propositional reasoning, the satisfaction of such a property amounts to check it in the restricted case of elementary shapes (see Lemma 8).

With the formula $\lvert Q_1, ..., Q_n \overline{\rangle\rceil}$ we denote a formula of the form either $\lvert Q_1, ..., Q_n \rangle$ or $\lvert Q_1, ..., \overleftarrow{Q_i}, ..., Q_n \rceil$ (this excludes graph formulae of the form $\lvert Q_1, ..., Q_n \rceil$). In the table below, the occurrences of $\lvert Q_1, ..., Q_n \overline{\rangle\rceil}$ on the left and on the right of every double implication are for the same form, i.e. either both $\lvert Q_1, ..., Q_n \rangle$ or both $\lvert Q_1, ..., \overleftarrow{Q_i}, ..., Q_n \rceil$ (where the position i is the same). Moreover, $0 \leq \beta_1 < \beta_1'$ and $0 \leq \beta_2 < \beta_2'$. Finally, we write φ_n to denote

$\varphi_n \overset{\text{def}}{=} (\lvert Q_1 \wedge Q, ..., Q_n \rceil \vee \lvert Q_1 \wedge Q, ..., Q_n \rangle \vee \bigvee_{i \in [1,n]} \lvert Q_1 \wedge Q, ..., \overleftarrow{Q_i}, ..., Q_n \rceil) \wedge \texttt{size} \geq \beta_1 + \beta_2 + 1$.

Derivable formulae about separating conjunctions of elementary shapes

- $(\lvert Q_1, ..., Q_n \overline{\rangle\rceil} \wedge \texttt{size} \geq \beta_1) * (\lvert Q \rceil \wedge \texttt{size} \geq \beta_2) \Leftrightarrow \lvert Q_1 \wedge Q, ..., Q_n \overline{\rangle\rceil} \wedge \texttt{size} \geq \beta_1 + \beta_2$
- $(\lvert Q_1, ..., Q_n \overline{\rangle\rceil} \wedge \texttt{size} \geq \beta_1 \wedge \neg \texttt{size} \geq \beta_1') * (\lvert Q \rceil \wedge \texttt{size} \geq \beta_2)$

  $\Leftrightarrow \lvert Q_1 \wedge Q, ..., Q_n \overline{\rangle\rceil} \wedge \texttt{size} \geq \beta_1 + \beta_2$
- $(\lvert Q_1, ..., Q_n \overline{\rangle\rceil} \wedge \texttt{size} \geq \beta_1) * (\lvert Q \rceil \wedge \texttt{size} \geq \beta_2 \wedge \neg \texttt{size} \geq \beta_2')$

  $\Leftrightarrow \lvert Q_1 \wedge Q, ..., Q_n \overline{\rangle\rceil} \wedge \texttt{size} \geq \beta_1 + \beta_2$
- $(\lvert Q_1, ..., Q_n \overline{\rangle\rceil} \wedge \texttt{size} \geq \beta_1 \wedge \neg \texttt{size} \geq \beta_1') * (\lvert Q \rceil \wedge \texttt{size} \geq \beta_2 \wedge \neg \texttt{size} \geq \beta_2')$

  $\Leftrightarrow \lvert Q_1 \wedge Q, ..., Q_n \overline{\rangle\rceil} \wedge \texttt{size} \geq \beta_1 + \beta_2 \wedge \neg \texttt{size} \geq (\beta_1' + \beta_2') \doteq 1$
- $(\lvert Q_1, ..., Q_n \rceil \wedge \texttt{size} \geq \beta_1) * (\lvert Q \rceil \wedge \neg \texttt{size} \geq 1) \Leftrightarrow \lvert Q_1 \wedge Q, ..., Q_n \rceil \wedge \texttt{size} \geq \beta_1$

- $(\lfloor Q_1,...,Q_n \rfloor \wedge \texttt{size} \geq \beta_1 \wedge \neg\texttt{size} \geq \beta_2) * (\lfloor Q \rfloor \wedge \neg\texttt{size} \geq 1)$
  $\Leftrightarrow \lfloor Q_1 \wedge Q,...,Q_n \rfloor \wedge \texttt{size} \geq \beta_1 \wedge \neg\texttt{size} \geq \beta_2$
- $(\lfloor Q_1,...,Q_n \rfloor \wedge \texttt{size} \geq \beta_1) * (\lfloor Q \rfloor \wedge \texttt{size} \geq \beta_2{+}1) \Leftrightarrow \varphi_n$
- $(\lfloor Q_1,...,Q_n \rfloor \wedge \texttt{size} \geq \beta_1 \wedge \neg\texttt{size} \geq \beta_1') * (\lfloor Q \rfloor \wedge \texttt{size} \geq \beta_2{+}1) \Leftrightarrow \varphi_n$
- $(\lfloor Q_1,...,Q_n \rfloor \wedge \texttt{size} \geq \beta_1) * (\lfloor Q \rfloor \wedge \texttt{size} \geq \beta_2{+}1 \wedge \neg\texttt{size} \geq \beta_2') \Leftrightarrow \varphi_n$
- $(\lfloor Q_1,...,Q_n \rfloor \wedge \texttt{size} \geq \beta_1 \wedge \neg\texttt{size} \geq \beta_1') * (\lfloor Q \rfloor \wedge \texttt{size} \geq \beta_2{+}1 \wedge \neg\texttt{size} \geq \beta_2') \Leftrightarrow$
  $\varphi_n \wedge \neg\texttt{size} \geq \beta_1'{+}\beta_2'{\dot{-}}1$

Once Lemma 8 is shown, forthcoming Lemma 9 can be easily shown.

Lemma 8. *The formulae listed in the table above are derivable in $\mathcal{H}_c(*)$ assuming that for any elementary shape ψ of the form either $\mathcal{G} \wedge \texttt{size} \geq \beta$ or $\mathcal{G} \wedge \texttt{size} \geq \beta \wedge \neg\texttt{size} \geq \beta'$, we have $\sharp(\mathcal{G}) \leq \beta$, $\beta < \beta'$ and $\nvdash_{\mathcal{H}_c} \neg\psi$.*

From Lemmata 7 and 9, we get the main result about $*$-elimination.

Lemma 9. *Let ϕ, ψ be Boolean combinations of core formulae. There is a Boolean combination of core formulae φ such that $\vdash_{\mathcal{H}_c(*)} (\phi * \psi) \Leftrightarrow \varphi$.*

In the proof of Lemma 9, if $\vdash_{\mathcal{H}_c(*)} \neg\phi$ or $\vdash_{\mathcal{H}_c(*)} \neg\psi$, the axiom ($\perp$) is then used. Otherwise, the proof amounts to prove the statement for elementary shapes only, which corresponds to Lemma 8. Let $\mathcal{H}\text{MSL}(*, \Diamond)$ be the Hilbert-style proof system defined as the union of the axioms and inference rules from $\mathcal{H}_c(\Diamond)$ and $\mathcal{H}_c(*)$ (with the intersection $\mathcal{H}_c$) augmented with the axiom below:

$$(\mathbf{G}_{30}) \quad p \Leftrightarrow (\lfloor p \rfloor \vee \lfloor p \rfloor \vee \lfloor \overset{\leftarrow}{p} \rfloor) \text{ with } p \in \text{PROP}.$$

Theorem 2. *$\mathcal{H}\text{MSL}(*, \Diamond)$ is sound and complete for $\text{MSL}(*, \Diamond)$.*

Proof. (sketch) We need to show that (1) the axiom $(\mathbf{G}_{30})$ is valid for $\text{MSL}(*, \Diamond)$ (easy), (2) to show that all the axioms and inference rules of $\mathcal{H}\text{MSL}(*, \Diamond)$ are valid for $\text{MSL}(*, \Diamond)$ and (3) to prove that $\vdash_{\mathcal{H}\text{MSL}(*, \Diamond)} \phi$ for every valid formula ϕ.

The proof of (2) is a consequence of (1), Lemma 5 and Lemma 7. However, one needs to notice that the validity of the axiom schemas and inference rules can be deduced from the proofs of Lemma 5 and Lemma 7, even though in $\mathcal{H}\text{MSL}(*, \Diamond)$, the metavariables ϕ, ψ and φ used in the axioms and inference rules from $\mathcal{H}_c(\Diamond)$ and $\mathcal{H}_c(*)$, can be safely instantiated by any formula in $\text{MSL}(*, \Diamond)$.

The proof of (3) consists in showing that there is a Boolean combination of core formulae ψ such that $\vdash_{\mathcal{H}\text{MSL}(*, \Diamond)} \phi \Leftrightarrow \psi$ (ϕ and ψ are logically equivalent by (2)). For instance, $\texttt{loop}_1$ from Sect. 2 is logically equivalent to $\neg\texttt{size} \geq 2 \wedge \lfloor \overset{\leftarrow}{\top} \rfloor$, whereas $\texttt{loop}_2$ is logically equivalent to $\neg\texttt{size} \geq 3 \wedge \lfloor \overset{\leftarrow}{\top}, \top \rfloor$. These equivalences can be derived in $\mathcal{H}\text{MSL}(*, \Diamond)$. So, ψ is valid and by Theorem 1, we get $\vdash_{\mathcal{H}_c} \psi$ and therefore $\vdash_{\mathcal{H}\text{MSL}(*, \Diamond)} \psi$. By propositional reasoning, we conclude that $\vdash_{\mathcal{H}\text{MSL}(*, \Diamond)} \phi$. It remains to prove that ψ exists. The proof is by structural induction using Lemma 6, Lemma 9 and the axiom $(\mathbf{G}_{30})$. $\square$

4   Hilbert-Style Proof System for MSL$(*, \langle \neq \rangle)$

In this section, we present a proof system for MSL$(*, \langle \neq \rangle)$ by using previous developments from Sect. 3 as well as by adapting to infinite models the proof method in [32] for axiomatising the logic of elsewhere ML$(\langle \neq \rangle)$. The NP upper bound proof for MSL$(*, \langle \neq \rangle)$ satisfiability in [18] takes advantage of an abstraction accounting only for the number of edges in the model (up to a value depending linearly on the size of the input formula) and whether given a propositional valuation (restricted to the propositional variables occurring in the input formula), there are none, one or two locations satisfying it. The developments below propose a syntactic characterisation for MSL$(*, \langle \neq \rangle)$ validity that also witnesses that the interplay between the number of edges and the constraints on the valuations is very weak. Below, a *pure separation formula* is understood as a formula in MSL$(*, \langle \neq \rangle)$ with no occurrences of $\langle \neq \rangle$ and propositional symbols, and a *pure modal formula* is understood as a formula with no occurrences of $*$ and emp. We denote these families as MSL$(*)$ and MSL$(\langle \neq \rangle)$, respectively.

We design the system $\mathcal{H}$MSL$(*, \langle \neq \rangle)$ for MSL$(*, \langle \neq \rangle)$ by the union of the system $\mathcal{H}$MSL$(\langle \neq \rangle)$ for MSL$(\langle \neq \rangle)$, of the system $\mathcal{H}$MSL$(*)$ for MSL$(*)$, plus the new axioms $(\langle \neq \rangle \mathbf{SEP})$ and $(*\mathbf{SEP})$.

Axiomatising ML$(\langle \neq \rangle)$ on MSL Models. We introduce $\mathcal{H}$MSL$(\langle \neq \rangle)$ for axiomatising the logic MSL$(\langle \neq \rangle)$, that is designed by augmenting the Hilbert-style system for the logic of elsewhere ML$(\langle \neq \rangle)$ from [32] by an axiom expressing that MSL$(\langle \neq \rangle)$ models have an infinite number of locations (namely $(\mathbf{INF})$). For instance, the formula $\langle U \rangle (p \wedge [\neq] \neg p) \wedge \langle U \rangle (\neg p \wedge [\neq] p)$, where $[\neq] \phi \stackrel{\text{def}}{=} \neg \langle \neq \rangle \neg \phi$ and $\langle U \rangle \phi \stackrel{\text{def}}{=} \phi \vee \langle \neq \rangle \phi$, is satisfiable in some ML$(\langle \neq \rangle)$ model with two locations exactly whereas it is unsatisfiable for MSL$(\langle \neq \rangle)$. As usual, the axiom schemas and modus ponens for propositional calculus are part of $\mathcal{H}$MSL$(\langle \neq \rangle)$.

Axioms and inference rule for $\mathcal{H}$MSL$(\langle \neq \rangle)$

$(\mathbf{K})$ $[\neq](\phi \Rightarrow \psi) \Rightarrow ([\neq]\phi \Rightarrow [\neq]\psi)$

$(\mathbf{B})$ $\phi \Rightarrow [\neq]\langle \neq \rangle \phi$ $(\mathbf{ALIO})$ $\phi \Rightarrow ([\neq]\phi \Rightarrow [\neq][\neq]\phi)$

$(\mathbf{INF})$ $\bigvee_{X \subseteq \{p_1, \ldots, p_n\}} \langle U \rangle (\psi_X \wedge \langle \neq \rangle \psi_X)$ for every $\{p_1, \ldots, p_n\} \subseteq_{\text{fin}}$ PROP,
where ψ_X stands for $(\bigwedge_{p \in X} p) \wedge (\bigwedge_{p \in (\{p_1, \ldots, p_n\} \setminus X)} \neg p)$.

Necessitation rule: $\dfrac{\phi}{[\neq]\phi}$

In $\mathcal{H}$MSL$(\langle \neq \rangle)$, the axiom $(\mathbf{K})$ and the necessitation rule are standard for normal modal logics, whereas the axiom $(\mathbf{B})$ (resp. $(\mathbf{ALIO})$) takes care of the symmetry (resp. the aliotransitivity) of the difference relation. As the MSL$(\langle \neq \rangle)$ models are necessarily infinite (by contrast to the models for the logic of elsewhere), we add the axiom $(\mathbf{INF})$.

Lemma 10. *Axioms and rules in $\mathcal{H}$MSL$(\langle \neq \rangle)$ are valid for MSL$(\langle \neq \rangle)$.*

An MSL$(\langle \neq \rangle)$ model $\mathfrak{M} = \langle \mathbb{N}, \mathfrak{R}, \mathfrak{V} \rangle$ can be understood as the ML$(\langle \neq \rangle)$ model $\langle \mathbb{N}, \neq, \mathfrak{V} \rangle$ since the language MSL$(\langle \neq \rangle)$ does not require to use of $\mathfrak{R}$ to evaluate formulae. So, in the sequel, we assume that the models for $ML(\langle\neq\rangle)$ are of the form $\langle\mathfrak{W}, \neq, \mathfrak{V}\rangle$, whereas those for $MSL(\langle\neq\rangle)$ are the restrictions with $\mathfrak{W} = \mathbb{N}$.

Lemma 11. $\mathcal{H}MSL(\langle\neq\rangle)$ *is sound and complete for* $MSL(\langle\neq\rangle)$.

The completeness of $\mathcal{H}MSL(\langle\neq\rangle)$ is shown by adapting the completeness proof from [32] and by taking advantage of the infinity axiom **(INF)**.

Axiomatising MSL($*$). We present the Hilbert-style system $\mathcal{H}MSL(*)$ for the logic $MSL(*)$. It is designed as a fragment of the Hilbert-style system $\mathcal{H}MSL(*, \Diamond)$ from Sect. 3 by simplifying the axioms and by keeping only what is needed for $MSL(*)$.

Axioms and inference rules for $\mathcal{H}MSL(*)$

(COM) $(\phi * \psi) \Leftrightarrow (\psi * \phi)$

($*$DISTR) $(\phi_1 \vee \phi_2) * \psi \Leftrightarrow (\phi_1 * \psi) \vee (\phi_2 * \psi)$ **($\bot$)** $\neg(\bot * \phi)$

(ASSOC) $(\phi * \psi) * \varphi \Leftrightarrow \phi * (\psi * \varphi)$ **(S_1^c)** $\texttt{size} \geq 0$

(S_4^*) $\phi \Leftrightarrow (\phi * \neg\texttt{size} \geq 1)$ **(S_2^c)** $\texttt{size} \geq \beta+1 \Rightarrow \texttt{size} \geq \beta$

(S_5^*) $\texttt{size} \geq \beta_1+\beta_2 \Rightarrow \texttt{size} = \beta_1 * \texttt{size} \geq \beta_2$

(S_6^*) $\neg\texttt{size} \geq \beta_1 * \neg\texttt{size} \geq \beta_2 \Rightarrow \neg\texttt{size} \geq (\beta_1+\beta_2) \dotminus 1$ $(\alpha_1 \dotminus \alpha_2 \stackrel{\text{def}}{=} \max(0, \alpha_1 - \alpha_2))$

$*$-introduction rule: $\dfrac{\phi \Rightarrow \varphi}{\phi * \psi \Rightarrow \varphi * \psi}$

As $MSL(*)$ is a fragment of both $MSL(*, \Diamond)$ and $MSL(*, \langle\neq\rangle)$, it should not come as a surprise that all the axioms above were already introduced in Sect. 3. Before proving completeness, we establish a few results about $\mathcal{H}MSL(*)$ that can be shown along the lines of Sect. 3 but drastic simplifications apply.

Lemma 12. *Axioms and rules in* $\mathcal{H}MSL(*)$ *are valid for* $MSL(*)$.

This is a consequence of the correctness for $\mathcal{H}MSL(*, \Diamond)$ (see Sect. 3), as derivability in $\mathcal{H}MSL(*)$ implies derivability in $\mathcal{H}MSL(*, \Diamond)$.

Lemma 13. *Given* ϕ *in* $MSL(*)$, $\vdash_{\mathcal{H}MSL(*)} \phi \Leftrightarrow \psi$ *for some size formula* ψ.

Proving completeness is now by an easy verification.

Lemma 14. $\mathcal{H}MSL(*)$ *is sound and complete for* $MSL(*)$.

Proof. (sketch) Soundness is from Lemma 12. It remains to establish completeness. Let ϕ be a formula that is valid for $MSL(*)$. First, notice that the following property holds: if $\vdash_{\mathcal{H}MSL(*)} \phi \Leftrightarrow \phi'$, then $\vdash_{\mathcal{H}MSL(*)} \psi[\phi]_\rho \Leftrightarrow \psi[\phi']_\rho$, where the formula $\psi[\phi]_\rho$ stands for the formula obtained from ψ by replacing the formula at the occurrence ρ by the formula ϕ.

By Lemma 13, it is easy to show that there is a size formula ϕ' in CNF such that $\vdash_{\mathcal{H}MSL(*)} \phi \Leftrightarrow \phi'$ in $\mathcal{H}MSL(*)$ and each conjunct of ϕ' contains at most 2 size literals, and they are of distinct polarity. By Lemma 12, ϕ' is also $MSL(*)$ valid and therefore each conjunct is valid. If a conjunct is of the form $\texttt{size} \geq \beta$, then $\beta = 0$ as $\texttt{size} \geq \beta$ should be valid. As $\texttt{size} \geq 0 = \top$, we have $\vdash_{\mathcal{H}\mathrm{MSL}(*)}$ `size` ≥ 0. No conjunct can be of the form $\neg(\mathtt{size} \geq \beta)$ as no formula of the form $\neg(\mathtt{size} \geq \beta)$ is valid. If a conjunct is of the form $\mathtt{size} \geq \beta \vee \neg(\mathtt{size} \geq \beta')$, then $\beta' \geq \beta$ as $\mathtt{size} \geq \beta \vee \neg(\mathtt{size} \geq \beta')$ is required to be valid. By propositional reasoning and by using $(\beta' - \beta)$ times the axiom $(\mathbf{S}_2^{\varsigma})$, we can conclude that $\vdash_{\mathcal{H}\mathrm{MSL}(*)} (\mathtt{size} \geq \beta') \Rightarrow (\mathtt{size} \geq \beta)$ and therefore $\vdash_{\mathcal{H}\mathrm{MSL}(*)}$ $\mathtt{size} \geq \beta \vee \neg(\mathtt{size} \geq \beta')$ by propositional reasoning. Hence, $\vdash_{\mathcal{H}\mathrm{MSL}(*)} \phi'$, and since $\vdash_{\mathcal{H}\mathrm{MSL}(*)} \phi \Leftrightarrow \phi'$, by propositional reasoning, we also get $\vdash_{\mathcal{H}\mathrm{MSL}(*)} \phi$. $\square$

Putting All Together: Axiomatising MSL$(*, \langle \neq \rangle)$. It is now time to define the Hilbert-style proof system $\mathcal{H}\mathrm{MSL}(*, \langle \neq \rangle)$ obtained from the calculus containing the axioms and rules from $\mathcal{H}\mathrm{MSL}(*)$ and $\mathcal{H}\mathrm{MSL}(\langle \neq \rangle)$. We need however to introduce two more axioms, stating that pure separation formulae can be separated from pure modal formulae. Notice that this property has some similarities with the separation theorem for Past LTL from [23].

Separation axioms
$(\langle \neq \rangle \mathbf{SEP})$ $\langle \neq \rangle (\phi \wedge \psi) \Leftrightarrow (\langle \neq \rangle \phi) \wedge \psi$ where ψ is a pure separation formula
$(*\mathbf{SEP})$ $\phi * (\phi' \wedge \psi) \Leftrightarrow (\phi * \phi') \wedge \psi$ where ψ is a pure modal formula

Lemma 15. *Axioms and rules in $\mathcal{H}\mathrm{MSL}(*, \langle \neq \rangle)$ are valid for $\mathrm{MSL}(*, \langle \neq \rangle)$.*

Completeness of $\mathcal{H}\mathrm{MSL}(*, \langle \neq \rangle)$ takes advantage of the resp. completeness of $\mathcal{H}\mathrm{MSL}(\langle \neq \rangle)$ and $\mathcal{H}\mathrm{MSL}(*)$, and the fact that for all pure modal (resp. separation) formulae ϕ_M (resp. ϕ_S), $\phi_M \vee \phi_S$ is valid iff ϕ_M is valid or ϕ_S is valid.

Theorem 3. $\mathcal{H}\mathrm{MSL}(*, \langle \neq \rangle)$ *is sound and complete for $\mathrm{MSL}(*, \langle \neq \rangle)$.*

Proof. (sketch) Soundness is from Lemma 15. Let us establish completeness. Let ϕ be valid for $\mathrm{MSL}(*, \langle \neq \rangle)$. By using the axioms $(\langle \neq \rangle \mathbf{SEP})$ and $(*\mathbf{SEP})$, one can show that there is a formula ϕ' such that $\vdash_{\mathcal{H}\mathrm{MSL}(*, \langle \neq \rangle)} \phi \Leftrightarrow \phi'$ and ϕ' is a Boolean combination of formulae from $\mathrm{MSL}(*) \cup \mathrm{MSL}(\langle \neq \rangle)$. By the validity of the axioms and inference rules (Lemma 15), we have that ϕ' is $\mathrm{MSL}(*, \langle \neq \rangle)$ valid as well. By propositional reasoning in $\mathcal{H}\mathrm{MSL}(*, \langle \neq \rangle)$, there is ϕ'' in CNF such that $\vdash_{\mathcal{H}\mathrm{MSL}(*, \langle \neq \rangle)} \phi' \Leftrightarrow \phi''$ and ϕ'' is a conjunction of disjunctions of the form $\phi_M \vee \phi_S$ where ϕ_M is a pure modal formula and ϕ_S is a pure separation formula. Again, by the validity of the axioms and inference rules, each disjunction $\phi_M \vee \phi_S$ is valid in $\mathrm{MSL}(*, \langle \neq \rangle)$.

Now, one can show that $\phi_M \vee \phi_S$ is valid iff ϕ_M is valid for $\mathrm{MSL}(\langle \neq \rangle)$ or ϕ_S is valid for $\mathrm{MSL}(*)$. By completeness of $\mathcal{H}\mathrm{MSL}(\langle \neq \rangle)$ and $\mathcal{H}\mathrm{MSL}(*)$, we get that $\phi_M \vee \phi_S$ is valid iff $\vdash_{\mathcal{H}\mathrm{MSL}(\langle \neq \rangle)} \phi_M$ or $\vdash_{\mathcal{H}\mathrm{MSL}(*)} \phi_S$. This is sufficient to conclude that $\vdash_{\mathcal{H}\mathrm{MSL}(*, \langle \neq \rangle)} \phi_M \vee \phi_S$. Consequently, for each disjunct $\phi_M \vee \phi_S$ of ϕ'', we have $\vdash_{\mathcal{H}\mathrm{MSL}(*, \langle \neq \rangle)} \phi_M \vee \phi_S$ and therefore by propositional reasoning, we get that $\vdash_{\mathcal{H}\mathrm{MSL}(*, \langle \neq \rangle)} \phi''$. As $\vdash_{\mathcal{H}\mathrm{MSL}(*, \langle \neq \rangle)} \phi \Leftrightarrow \phi'$ and $\vdash_{\mathcal{H}\mathrm{MSL}(*, \langle \neq \rangle)} \phi' \Leftrightarrow \phi''$, we get that $\vdash_{\mathcal{H}\mathrm{MSL}(*, \langle \neq \rangle)} \phi$. Therefore, $\mathcal{H}\mathrm{MSL}(*, \langle \neq \rangle)$ is complete. $\square$

5   Concluding Remarks

We provided an axiomatisation for the logics $\mathrm{MSL}(*, \Diamond)$ and $\mathrm{MSL}(*, \langle \neq \rangle)$, despite the well-known difficulties to axiomatise logics equipped with operators that update the models in the evaluation process. Such operators are ubiquitous in theoretical computer science and in knowledge representation areas, and we hope that our calculi shed some new light on their expressive power. For the axiomatisation of $\mathrm{MSL}(*, \Diamond)$ we had to identify the core properties that can be expressed in the logic, partially following the semantical analysis from [18]. We also had to express them in the language with the so-called core formulae. Implicitly, the axiomatisation is divided into two parts: axioms and rules to transform any formula of $\mathrm{MSL}(*, \Diamond)$ into a Boolean combination of core formulae and the axiomatisation of these Boolean combinations. For the axiomatisation of $\mathrm{MSL}(*, \langle \neq \rangle)$, we use a similar approach, except that we had to adapt the axiomatisation of the logic of elsewhere from [32] to infinite models and to implement syntactically a separation principle satisfied by $\mathrm{MSL}(*, \langle \neq \rangle)$. It is worth noting that the completeness of $\mathcal{H}\mathrm{MSL}(*, \Diamond)$ and $\mathcal{H}\mathrm{MSL}(*, \langle \neq \rangle)$ does not imply their strong completeness, as $\mathrm{MSL}(*)$ is not compact. Let us consider $X_\infty = \{\texttt{size} \geq \beta \mid \beta \in \mathbb{N}\}$. Indeed, for both logics, X_∞ is unsatisfiable, since MSL models have finite accessibility relations. Strong completeness would imply that $\bot$ could be derived from X_∞. As all rules are finitary, then there is a finite subset $X \subseteq X_\infty$ such that $X \vdash \bot$, or equivalently $\vdash \bigvee_{\psi \in X} \neg \psi$. This leads to a contradiction by the correctness of $\mathcal{H}\mathrm{MSL}(*, \Diamond)$ and $\mathcal{H}\mathrm{MSL}(*, \langle \neq \rangle)$. The same argument can be used for other finitary proof systems, with the same set X_∞.

As part of future work, we aim at Hilbert-style axiomatisations for separation logics having a notion of core formulae (see e.g. [19,22]), or for very expressive modal separation logics such as $\mathrm{MSL}(*, \langle \neq \rangle, \Diamond)$. Additionally, the expressivity characterisation provided by core formulae appears to be handy not only as the basic ingredient for the axiomatisations, but also for studying other problems, such as the implementation of proof methods, or the analysis of meta-theoretical properties of the logics.

Ackowledgements. This work was partially supported by ANPCyT-PICTs-2017-1130 and 2016-0215, MinCyT Córdoba, SeCyT-UNC, the Laboratoire International Associé INFINIS and the Centre National de la Recherche Scientifique (CNRS).

References

1. Areces, C., Fervari, R.: Hilbert-style axiomatization for hybrid XPath with data. In: Michael, L., Kakas, A. (eds.) JELIA 2016. LNCS (LNAI), vol. 10021, pp. 34–48. Springer, Cham (2016). https://doi.org/10.1007/978-3-319-48758-8_3
2. Areces, C., Fervari, R., Hoffmann, G.: Tableaux for relation-changing modal logics. In: Fontaine, P., Ringeissen, C., Schmidt, R.A. (eds.) FroCoS 2013. LNCS (LNAI), vol. 8152, pp. 263–278. Springer, Heidelberg (2013). https://doi.org/10.1007/978-3-642-40885-4_19
3. Areces, C., Fervari, R., Hoffmann, G.: Relation-changing modal operators. Logic J. IGPL **23**(4), 601–627 (2015)

4. Aucher, G., van Benthem, J., Grossi, D.: Modal logics of sabotage revisited. JLC **28**(2), 269–303 (2018)
5. Balbiani, Ph., Tinchev,T.: Unification in modal logic Alt$_1$. In: AiML 2016, pp. 117–134. College Publications (2016)
6. Berdine, Josh, Calcagno, Cristiano, O'Hearn, Peter W.: A Decidable Fragment of Separation Logic. In: Lodaya, Kamal, Mahajan, Meena (eds.) FSTTCS 2004. LNCS, vol. 3328, pp. 97–109. Springer, Heidelberg (2004). https://doi.org/10.1007/978-3-540-30538-5_9
7. Blackburn, P., de Rijke, M., Venema, Y.: Modal Logic, Cambridge University Press (2001)
8. Blackburn, P., van Benthem, J.F., Wolter, F. (eds.): Handbook of Modal Logic. Elsevier (2006)
9. Boudou, J.: Decidable logics with associative binary modalities. In: LIPIcs CSL 2017, vol. 82, pp. 1–15. Schloss Dagstuhl - Leibniz-Zentrum fuer Informatik (2017)
10. Brochenin, R., Demri, S., Lozes, E.: Reasoning about sequences of memory states. Ann. Pure Appl. Logic **161**(3), 305–323 (2009)
11. Brotherston, J., Villard, J.: Parametric completeness for separation theories. In: POPL 2014, pp. 453–464. ACM (2014)
12. Calvanese, D., Kotek, T., Šimkus, M., Veith, H., Zuleger, F.: Shape and content. In: Albert, E., Sekerinski, E. (eds.) IFM 2014. LNCS, vol. 8739, pp. 3–17. Springer, Cham (2014). https://doi.org/10.1007/978-3-319-10181-1_1
13. Courtault, J.-R., Galmiche, D.: A modal separation logic for resource dynamics. JLC **28**(4), 733–778 (2018)
14. Courtault, J.-R., van Ditmarsch, H., Galmiche, D.: A public announcement separation logic. Math. Struct. Comput. Sci. (2019, to appear)
15. Courtault, J.-R., van Ditmarsch, H., Galmiche, D.: An epistemic separation logic. In: de Paiva, V., de Queiroz, R., Moss, L.S., Leivant, D., de Oliveira, A.G. (eds.) WoLLIC 2015. LNCS, vol. 9160, pp. 156–173. Springer, Heidelberg (2015). https://doi.org/10.1007/978-3-662-47709-0_12
16. Dawar, A., Gardner, P., Ghelli, G.: Expressiveness and complexity of graph logic. IC **205**(3), 263–310 (2007)
17. Demri, S., Deters, M.: Two-variable separation logic and its inner circle. ToCL **2**(16), 15:1–15:36 (2015)
18. Demri, S., Fervari, R.: On the complexity of modal separation logics. In: AiML 2018, pp. 179–198. College Publications (2018)
19. Demri, S., Lozes, É., Mansutti, A.: The effects of adding reachability predicates in propositional separation logic. In: Baier, C., Dal Lago, U. (eds.) FoSSaCS 2018. LNCS, vol. 10803, pp. 476–493. Springer, Cham (2018). https://doi.org/10.1007/978-3-319-89366-2_26
20. Doumane, A.: Constructive completeness for the linear-time μ-calculus. In: LICS 2017, pp. 1–12. IEEE Computer Society (2017)
21. Ebbinghaus, H.D., Flum, J.: Finite Model Theory. Perspectives in Mathematical Logic. Springer, Heidelberg (1999). https://doi.org/10.1007/978-3-662-03182-7
22. Echenim, M., Iosif, R., Peltier, N.: On the expressive completeness of Bernays-Schönfinkel-Ramsey separation logic. Technical report arXiv:1802.00195, arXiv:cs.LO, February 2018. To appear in FOSSACS 2019
23. Gabbay, D.: The declarative past and imperative future. In: Banieqbal, B., Barringer, H., Pnueli, A. (eds.) Temporal Logic in Specification. LNCS, vol. 398, pp. 409–448. Springer, Heidelberg (1989). https://doi.org/10.1007/3-540-51803-7_36

24. Gierasimczuk, N., Kurzen, L., Velázquez-Quesada, F.R.: Learning and teaching as a game: a sabotage approach. In: He, X., Horty, J., Pacuit, E. (eds.) LORI 2009. LNCS (LNAI), vol. 5834, pp. 119–132. Springer, Heidelberg (2009). https://doi.org/10.1007/978-3-642-04893-7_10

25. Herzig, A.: A simple separation logic. In: Libkin, L., Kohlenbach, U., de Queiroz, R. (eds.) WoLLIC 2013. LNCS, vol. 8071, pp. 168–178. Springer, Heidelberg (2013). https://doi.org/10.1007/978-3-642-39992-3_16

26. Hoare, C.A.R.: An axiomatic basis for computer programming. Commun. ACM **12**(10), 576–580 (1969)

27. Hou, Z., Clouston, R., Goré, R., Tiu, A.: Modular labelled sequent calculi for abstract separation logics. ToCL **19**(2), 13:1–13:35 (2018)

28. Lu, X., Tian, C., Duan, Z.: Temporalising separation logic for planning with search control knowledge. In: IJCAI 2017, pp. 1167–1173 (2017)

29. Pym, D., Spring, J., O'Hearn, P.W.: Why separation logic works. In: Philosophy and Technology, pp. 1–34 (2018). https://doi.org/10.1007/s13347-018-0312-8

30. Reynolds, J.C.: Separation logic: a logic for shared mutable data structures. In: LICS 2002, pp. 55–74. IEEE (2002)

31. Schmitz, S.: Complexity hierarchies beyond elementary. ACM Trans. Comput. Theor. **8**(1), 3:1–3:36 (2016)

32. Segerberg, K.: A note on the logic of elsewhere. Theoria **47**, 183–187 (1981)

33. Shoham, Y., Leyton-Brown, K.: Multiagent Systems: Algorithmic, Game-Theoretic, and Logical Foundations. Cambridge University Press, New York (2008)

34. Benthem, J.: An essay on sabotage and obstruction. In: Hutter, D., Stephan, W. (eds.) Mechanizing Mathematical Reasoning. LNCS (LNAI), vol. 2605, pp. 268–276. Springer, Heidelberg (2005). https://doi.org/10.1007/978-3-540-32254-2_16

35. van Benthem, J.: Logical Dynamics of Information and Interaction. Cambridge University Press (2011)

36. van Ditmarsch, H., van der Hoek, W., Kooi, B.: Dynamic Epistemic Logic. Synthese Library Series, vol. 337. Springer, Dordrecht (2008). https://doi.org/10.1007/978-1-4020-5839-4

37. Wang, Y., Cao, Q.: On axiomatizations of public announcement logic. Synthese **190**(Supplement-1), 103–134 (2013)

Nested Sequents for the Logic
of Conditional Belief

Marianna Girlando[1,2(✉)] (iD), Björn Lellmann[3] (iD), and Nicola Olivetti[1] (iD)

[1] Aix Marseille University, Université de Toulon, CNRS, LIS, Marseille, France
{marianna.girlando,nicola.olivetti}@univ-amu.fr
[2] University of Helsinki, Helsinki, Finland
[3] Technische Universität Wien, Vienna, Austria
lellmann@logic.at

Abstract. The logic of conditional belief, called Conditional Doxastic Logic (CDL), was proposed by Board, Baltag and Smets to model revisable belief and knowledge in a multi-agent setting. We present a proof system for CDL in the form of a nested sequent calculus. To the best of our knowledge, ours is the first internal and standard calculus for this logic. We take as primitive a multi-agent version of the "comparative plausibility operator", as in Lewis' counterfactual logic. The calculus is analytic and provides a decision procedure for CDL. As a by-product we also obtain a nested sequent calculus for multi-agent modal logic $S5_i$.

Keywords: Nested sequent calculus · Conditional doxastic logic · Belief revision · Multi-agent epistemic logic

1 Introduction

Knowledge and belief are the most important propositional attitudes to reason about epistemic interaction among agents. Conditional Doxastic Logic (CDL) was proposed by Board [4] and Baltag and Smets [1–3] for modelling both belief and knowledge in a multi-agent setting (see also [14]). Differently from knowledge, the essential feature of beliefs is that they are *revisable* whenever the agent learns new information. To capture the revisable nature of beliefs, CDL contains the conditional belief operator $Bel_i(C|B)$, the meaning of which is that agent i would believe C in case she learnt B. Both unconditional beliefs and knowledge can be defined in CDL: Bel_iB (agent i believes B) as $Bel_i(B|\top)$, K_iB (agent i knows B) as $Bel_i(\bot|\neg B)$, the latter meaning that i considers impossible (inconsistent) to learn $\neg B$. We also consider the comparative plausibility operator $A \preccurlyeq_i B$, whose reading is that the agent i considers A to be at least as plausible as B. This operator, introduced by Lewis for (single-agent) counterfactual logics is interdefinable with the conditional belief operator; thereby also simple belief and knowledge can be defined directly in terms of it.

This work was partially supported by the Project TICAMORE ANR-16-CE91-0002-01 and by WWTF project MA 16-28.

F. Calimeri et al. (Eds.): JELIA 2019, LNAI 11468, pp. 709–725, 2019.
https://doi.org/10.1007/978-3-030-19570-0_46

The logic of conditional belief has been significantly employed in game theory [17], and it has been used as the basic formalism to study further dynamic extensions of epistemic logics, determined by several kinds of epistemic/doxastic actions. Not surprisingly, the axiomatization of the operator Bel in CDL internalises the well-known AGM postulates of belief revision.

The difference between the conditional belief operator $Bel_i(B|A)$ and the simple belief operator $Bel_i(A \rightarrow B)$ is illustrated by the following (modified) example from [17]. Let agent i believe that Jones is a coward, $Bel_i\,C(j)$. We want to express that if the agent is to learn that Jones has been sent to battle, $S(j)$, he would no longer believe that he is a coward (since only brave men are sent to battle). Using the simple belief operator would yield a contradiction, because $\neg Bel_i(S(j) \rightarrow C(j))$ implies $\neg Bel_i C(j)$. However, if we express it as $\neg Bel_i(C(j)|S(j))$, we retain consistency, since $\neg Bel_i C(j)$ cannot be derived (this is verified, e.g., using the calculus below). As a second example, consider a variant of the three-wise-men puzzle, where agent i initially believes that she has a white hat, $Bel_i W_i$. However, if i were to learn that agent j knows the colour of the hat j herself wears, she would change her beliefs and be convinced that she is wearing a black hat instead: $Bel_i(B_i|K_j(W_j \wedge B_j))$. The two formulas are consistent (assuming $\neg(B_i \wedge W_i)$) as the operator is non-monotonic: $Bel_i(C|A)$ does not entail $Bel_i(C|A \wedge B)$.

The original semantics of CDL is defined in terms of *Plausibility Models*, i.e., standard epistemic models, where each agent is further equipped with a "comparative plausibility" relation between worlds used to evaluate her (conditional) beliefs. However, following [8,9], an alternative semantics is given in terms of *multi-agent neighbourhood models*, which are essentially a multi-agent version of Lewis' sphere models for counterfactual logics [10]. In particular, the semantics of CDL coincides with a multi-agent version of Lewis' logic VTA. Proof-theoretically the logic CDL has not been studied much, the only existing calculus for it being the labelled sequent calculus based on this neighbourhood semantics from [9].

Here we propose the first *internal calculus* for CDL, meaning that the syntactic structures employed in the calculus (nested sequents) have a direct formula translation. Since CDL admits two rather different semantics, the internal calculus presents the advantage of being *independent* of the choice of the semantics, differently from what happens with a labelled proof system.

Similarly to the calculi for Lewis' conditional logics in [7], our calculus $\mathcal{N}_{\mathsf{CDL}}$ takes as primitive the comparative plausibility operator, albeit in its multi-agent version $A \preccurlyeq_i B$. In order to obtain an internal calculus for CDL, the simple hypersequent structure used to capture Lewis' logics in [7], is no longer adequate. To keep track of the "locality" of information for each agent, and to account for beliefs of an agent occurring within the beliefs of another, we use a *nested* structure, which is not necessary in the single-agent case. The calculus $\mathcal{N}_{\mathsf{CDL}}$ is analytic and provides a decision procedure for CDL. Its completeness is proved semantically by extracting a finite countermodel from failed proof search. As mentioned, the epistemic operator K_i is defined in CDL, and it corresponds to the knowledge operator of multi-agent S5$_i$. Hence, "specialising" the rules of $\mathcal{N}_{\text{CDL}}$ to the K_i fragment we obtain a natural *nested sequent calculus* for S5$_i$.

2 Multi-agent Conditional Logic CDL

The language of CDL extends propositional logic with operators for (conditional) belief, knowledge, and comparative plausibility, all labelled with an agent.

Definition 1. *Let $\mathcal{A}$ be a set of agents, and let i be an agent. Formulas of CDL are generated as follows, for P propositional variable:*

$$\mathcal{F}_{\text{CDL}} \ni A ::= P \mid \bot \mid \top \mid A \to A \mid A \preccurlyeq_i A \mid Bel_i(A|A)$$

A conditional belief formula $Bel_i(C|B)$ is read "agent i believes C, given B". The meaning of a formula $A \preccurlyeq_i B$ is that agent i considers A at least as plausible as B. The operators of Bel_i and $\preccurlyeq_i$ are interdefinable:

$$Bel_i(B|A) \equiv (\bot \preccurlyeq_i A) \vee \neg((A \wedge \neg B) \preccurlyeq (A \wedge B))$$
$$A \preccurlyeq_i B \equiv Bel_i(\bot|A \vee B) \vee \neg Bel_i(\neg A|A \vee B)$$

Intuitively, an agent conditionally believes B given A whenever she considers A impossible or she considers $A \wedge \neg B$ to be less plausible than $A \wedge B$. Unconditional belief and knowledge can then be defined by these operators as follows[1]:

$$Bel_iA :- Bel_i(A|\top) \qquad Bel_iA := \neg(\neg A \preccurlyeq_i \top) \quad \text{(belief)}$$
$$K_iA := Bel_i(\bot|\neg A) \qquad K_iA := \bot \preccurlyeq_i \neg A \quad \text{(knowledge)}$$

An axiomatization of CDL is given by the following axioms and rules [3,4]:

(0) Axiomatization of classical propositional logic
(1) If $\vdash B$, then $\vdash Bel_i(B|A)$
(2) If $\vdash A \leftrightarrow B$, then $\vdash Bel_i(C|A) \leftrightarrow Bel_i(C|B)$
(3) $(Bel_i(B|A) \wedge Bel_i(B \to C|A)) \to Bel_i(C|A)$
(4) $Bel_i(A|A)$
(5) $Bel_i(B|A) \to (Bel_i(C|A \wedge B) \leftrightarrow Bel_i(C|A))$
(6) $\neg Bel_i(\neg B|A) \to (Bel_i(C|A \wedge B) \leftrightarrow Bel_i(B \to C|A))$
(7) $Bel_i(B|A) \to Bel_i(Bel_i(B|A)|C)$
(8) $\neg Bel_i(B|A) \to Bel_i(\neg Bel_i(B|A)|C)$
(9) $A \to \neg Bel_i(\bot|A)$

These axioms represent an "internalised" version of the AGM belief revision postulates in a multi-agent setting, e.g., axioms 5 and 6 encode the Minimal Change Principle[2] An alternative axiomatization of CDL taking $\preccurlyeq_i$ as primitive

---

[1] An equivalent definition of the simple belief operator is the following: $Bel_iA := \neg(\neg A \preccurlyeq_i A)$ [10]. We choose a simpler formulation in terms of $\top$, also from [10].
[2] Refer to [4,9] for a detailed correspondence.

essentially amounts to a multi-agent version of Lewis' counterfactual logic system $\mathbb{V}\mathbb{T}\mathbb{A}$ [7] and contains in addition to classical propositional logic the following:

(CPR) $\dfrac{\vdash B \to A}{\vdash A \preccurlyeq_i B}$ (CPA) $(A \preccurlyeq_i A \vee B) \vee (B \preccurlyeq_i A \vee B)$

(TR) $(A \preccurlyeq_i B) \wedge (B \preccurlyeq_i C) \to (A \preccurlyeq_i C)$ (CO) $(A \preccurlyeq_i B) \vee (B \preccurlyeq_i A)$

(N) $\neg(\bot \preccurlyeq_i \top)$ (T) $(\bot \preccurlyeq_i \neg A) \to A$

(A$_1$) $(A \preccurlyeq_i B) \to (\bot \preccurlyeq_i \neg(A \preccurlyeq_i B))$ (A$_2$) $\neg(A \preccurlyeq_i B) \to (\bot \preccurlyeq_i (A \preccurlyeq_i B))$

The original semantics of CDL is given in terms of plausibility models; the alternative semantics in terms of neighbourhood models from [9] is as follows.

Definition 2. *Let $\mathcal{A}$ be a set of agents; a multi-agent neighbourhood model has the form $\mathcal{M} = \langle W, \{N_i\}_{i \in \mathcal{A}}, [\![\ ]\!] \rangle$ where W is a non empty set of worlds, $[\![\ ]\!] : Atm \to \mathcal{P}(W)$ is the evaluation for atomic formulas and for each $i \in \mathcal{A}$, $N_i : W \to \mathcal{P}(\mathcal{P}(W))$ is a neighbourhood function, satisfying:*

- *Non-emptiness: For all $\alpha \in N_i(x)$, $\alpha \neq \emptyset$*
- *Nesting: For all $\alpha, \beta \in N_i(x)$, $\alpha \subseteq \beta$ or $\beta \subseteq \alpha$*
- *Total reflexivity: There exists $\alpha \in N_i(x)$ such that $x \in \alpha$*
- *Local absoluteness: If $\alpha \in N_i(x)$ and $y \in \alpha$ then $N_i(x) = N_i(y)$*

The truth conditions for Boolean combinations of formulas are standard; the remaining ones use the *local forcing* notation introduced in [12], i.e., $\alpha \Vdash^\forall A$ iff for all $y \in \alpha$ we have $y \Vdash A$, and $\alpha \Vdash^\exists A$ iff there exists $y \in \alpha$ such that $y \Vdash A$:

$x \Vdash Bel_i(B|A)$ iff for all $\alpha \in N_i(x)$ it holds that $\alpha \Vdash^\forall \neg A$ or there exists $\beta \in N_i(x)$ such that $\beta \Vdash^\exists A$ and $\beta \Vdash^\forall A \to B$

$x \Vdash A \preccurlyeq_i B$ iff for all $\beta \in N_i(x)$ if $\beta \Vdash^\exists B$ then $\beta \Vdash^\exists A$

$x \Vdash Bel_i B$ iff there exists $\beta \in N_i(x)$ such that $\beta \Vdash^\forall B$

$x \Vdash K_i B$ iff for all $\beta \in N_i(x)$ it holds that $\beta \Vdash^\forall B$

A formula A is *valid* in $\mathcal{M}$ if for all $w \in W$, $w \Vdash A$. A formula A is *valid* if A is valid in every multi-agent neighbourhood model.

3   Nested Sequent Calculus $\mathcal{N}_{\mathsf{CDL}}$

In this section we present a sequent for CDL. The calculus is based on the structure of *nested sequents* (e.g., [5,16]), adjusted to the multiagent setting and extended with the mechanism to handle comparative plausibility formulas using *conditional blocks* from [6,13] as follows.

Definition 3. *A multi-agent conditional block for agent i is a syntactic structure $i: (A_1 \ldots A_n \lhd_i B)$, interpreted as: $(A_1 \vee \cdots \vee A_n) \preccurlyeq_i B$. A multi-agent nested sequent (short: nested sequent) S is a structure*

$$S = \Gamma \Rightarrow \Delta, [G_1]^{i_1}, \ldots, [G_n]^{i_n}$$

where $i_1, \ldots, i_n \in \mathcal{A}$, Γ is a multiset of formulas, and Δ is a multiset of formulas and multi-agent conditional blocks, and each $G_1, \ldots, G_n$ is a nested sequent.

Intuitively, a nested sequent is a finite labelled directed tree with nodes labelled with sequents $\Gamma \Rightarrow \Delta$, where Δ also contains multi-agent conditional blocks, and edges labelled with agents. We call the nodes with their sequent label the *components* of the nested sequent. Thus each G_j represents an immediate subtree of the tree with root S. The *formula interpretation* is given by:

$$(\Gamma \Rightarrow \Delta, (\Sigma_1 \vartriangleleft_i C_1), \ldots, (\Sigma_k \vartriangleleft_j C_k), [G_1]^{i_1}, \ldots, [G_n]^{i_n})^{int} :=$$

$$\bigwedge \Gamma \to \bigvee \Delta \vee \bigvee_{1 \leqslant s \leqslant k} ((\bigvee \Sigma_s) \preccurlyeq_i C_s) \vee K_{i_1} (G_1)^{int} \vee \cdots \vee K_{i_n} (G_n)^{int}$$

for $K_i A = \bot \preccurlyeq_i \neg A$. We sometimes include nested successors into the succedent of a sequent, denoted with superscript $*$. E.g., for $\Gamma \Rightarrow \Delta, [G]^i$ we also write $\Gamma \Rightarrow \Delta^*$. For a multiset Δ, we write $\mathsf{set}(\Delta)$ for its *underlying set*, i.e., its carrier.

To operate with nested sequents, we use the notion of *context*, denoting a nested sequent with a unique "hole", to be filled with another nested sequent.

Definition 4. *We define a* context $G\{\ \}$ *as:*

- $G\{\ \} = \Gamma \Rightarrow \Delta^*, \{\ \}$ *is a context;*
- *if* $F\{\ \}$ *is a context, then* $G\{\ \} = \Gamma \Rightarrow \Delta^*, [F\{\ \}]^i$ *is a context.*

The result of filling a context $G\{\ \}$ *with a nested sequent* $\Gamma \Rightarrow \Delta^*$ *then is denoted as* $G\{\Gamma \Rightarrow \Delta^*\}$ *and defined via:*

- *If* $G\{\ \} = \Sigma \Rightarrow \Pi^*, \{\ \}$, *then* $G\{\Gamma \Rightarrow \Delta^*\} = \Gamma, \Sigma \Rightarrow \Delta^*, \Pi^*$;
- *If* $G\{\ \} = \Sigma \Rightarrow \Pi^*, [F\{\ \}]^i$ *then* $G\{\Gamma \Rightarrow \Delta^*\} = \Sigma \Rightarrow \Pi^*, [F\{\Gamma \Rightarrow \Delta^*\}]^i$.

The rules of the multi-agent nested sequent calculus $\mathcal{N}_{\mathsf{CDL}}$ are given in Fig. 1. They are formulated in the cumulative version, repeating all formulas and blocks of the conclusion in the premisses. This is used for proving completeness, but of course could be avoided at the cost of explicit contraction rules.

As in nested calculi, each nested sequent can be thought as encoding the formulas relative to one world of the model. Since our neighbourhood models are multi-agent, each nested sequent has associated a label for an agent.

More in detail, rule $\mathsf{R} \preccurlyeq$ introduces backwards a conditional block, and rule $\mathsf{L} \preccurlyeq$ (read upwards) combines a the true plausibility formula in the antecedent of a sequent with a with the false conditional block in the consequent by means of a case analysis. With the com rule, two blocks communicate with one another. This rule can be thought as a syntactic equivalent of the nesting condition over neighbourhoods, with each conditional block encoding the comparative plausibility formulas relative to one neighbourhood of the model. The jump rule creates a new nested sequent in correspondence to a conditional block, with the same agent label. Rule T accounts for the condition of total reflexivity of the neighbourhood function, and the transfer rules are needed to express local absoluteness: due to this condition comparative plausibility formulas are evaluated in the same way at all the worlds accessible for the same agent - and thus, these formulas are allowed to "pass" between nested sequents with the same agent label. Finally, the rules of conditional belief make use of the definition of $Bel_i(B|A)$ in terms of the comparative plausibility operator given in the previous section. For instance, rule $\mathsf{Bel_L}$ read backwards states that if $Bel_i(B|A)$ is true, either A is impossible (left premiss) or $A \wedge \neg B$ is strictly less plausible than A (right premiss).

Initial sequents $G\{p, \Gamma \Rightarrow \Delta, p\}$ $G\{\bot, \Gamma \Rightarrow \Delta\}$

Propositional rules

$$\dfrac{G\{A \rightarrow B, B, \Gamma \Rightarrow \Delta\} \quad G\{A \rightarrow B, \Gamma \Rightarrow \Delta, A\}}{G\{A \rightarrow B, \Gamma \Rightarrow \Delta\}} \; \mathsf{L}\!\rightarrow \qquad \dfrac{G\{A, \Gamma \Rightarrow \Delta, A \rightarrow B, B\}}{G\{\Gamma \Rightarrow \Delta, A \rightarrow B\}} \; \mathsf{R}\!\rightarrow$$

Rules for comparative plausibility and conditional blocks

$$\dfrac{G\{\Gamma \Rightarrow \Delta, A \preccurlyeq_i B, (A \lhd_i B)\}}{G\{\Gamma \Rightarrow \Delta, A \preccurlyeq_i B\}} \; \mathsf{R}\!\preccurlyeq$$

$$\dfrac{G\{A \preccurlyeq_i B, \Gamma \Rightarrow \Delta, (\Sigma \lhd_i C), (\Sigma \lhd_i A)\} \quad G\{A \preccurlyeq_i B, \Gamma \Rightarrow \Delta, (B, \Sigma \lhd_i C), (\Sigma \lhd_i C)\}}{G\{A \preccurlyeq_i B, \Gamma \Rightarrow \Delta, (\Sigma \lhd_i C)\}} \; \mathsf{L}\!\preccurlyeq$$

$$\dfrac{G\{\Gamma \Rightarrow \Delta, (\Sigma \lhd_i C), [C \Rightarrow \Sigma]^i\}}{G\{\Gamma \Rightarrow \Delta, (\Sigma \lhd_i C)\}} \; \mathsf{jump}$$

$$\dfrac{\{\Gamma \Rightarrow \Delta, (\Sigma_1, \Sigma_2 \lhd_i A), (\Sigma_1 \lhd_i A), (\Sigma_2 \lhd_i B)\} \quad G\{\Gamma \Rightarrow \Delta, (\Sigma_1 \lhd_i A), (\Sigma_2 \lhd_i B), (\Sigma_1, \Sigma_2 \lhd_i B)\}}{G\{\Gamma \Rightarrow \Delta, (\Sigma_1 \lhd_i A), (\Sigma_2 \lhd_i B)\}} \; \mathsf{com}$$

$$\dfrac{G\{A \preccurlyeq_i B, \Gamma \Rightarrow \Delta, (\bot \lhd_i A)\} \quad G\{A \preccurlyeq_i B, \Gamma \Rightarrow \Delta, B\}}{G\{A \preccurlyeq_i B, \Gamma \Rightarrow \Delta\}} \; \mathsf{T}$$

Transfer rules

$$\dfrac{G\{A \preccurlyeq_i B, \Gamma \Rightarrow \Delta, [A \preccurlyeq_i B, \Sigma \Rightarrow \Pi]^i\}}{G\{A \preccurlyeq_i B, \Gamma \Rightarrow \Delta, [\Sigma \Rightarrow \Pi]^i\}} \; \mathsf{Tr_1} \qquad \dfrac{G\{A \preccurlyeq_i B, \Gamma \Rightarrow \Delta, [A \preccurlyeq_i B, \Sigma \Rightarrow \Pi]^i\}}{G\{\Gamma \Rightarrow \Delta, [A \preccurlyeq_i B, \Sigma \Rightarrow \Pi]^i\}} \; \mathsf{Tr_2}$$

$$\dfrac{G\{\Gamma \Rightarrow \Delta, (\Lambda \lhd_i C), [\Sigma \Rightarrow \Pi, (\Lambda \lhd_i C)]^i\}}{G\{\Gamma \Rightarrow \Delta, (\Lambda \lhd_i C), [\Sigma \Rightarrow \Pi]^i\}} \; \mathsf{Tr_3} \qquad \dfrac{G\{\Gamma \Rightarrow \Delta, (\Lambda \lhd_i C), [\Sigma \Rightarrow \Pi, (\Lambda \lhd_i C)]^i\}}{G\{\Gamma \Rightarrow \Delta, [\Sigma \Rightarrow \Pi, (\Lambda \lhd_i C)]^i\}} \; \mathsf{Tr_4}$$

Rules for conditional belief

$$\dfrac{G\{(A \wedge \neg B) \preccurlyeq_i A, \Gamma \Rightarrow \Delta, (\bot \lhd_i A)\}}{G\{\Gamma \Rightarrow \Delta, Bel_i(B|A)\}} \; \mathsf{Bel_R}$$

$$\dfrac{G\{\bot \preccurlyeq_i A, Bel_i(B|A), \Gamma \Rightarrow \Delta\} \quad G\{Bel_i(B|A), \Gamma \Rightarrow \Delta, (A \wedge \neg B \lhd_i A)\}}{G\{Bel_i(B|A), \Gamma \Rightarrow \Delta\}} \; \mathsf{Bel_L}$$

Fig. 1. Nested calculus $\mathcal{N}_{\mathsf{CDL}}$

Theorem 1 (Soundness). *If G is derivable in $\mathcal{N}_{\mathsf{CDL}}$ then $(G)^{int}$ is valid.*

Proof. By induction on the derivation height, showing that if the premiss of a rule is valid, so is its conclusion. By means of example we show jump, T and $\mathsf{Tr_1}$.

Suppose the premiss of jump is valid, and its conclusion is not. Thus, there exists a model such that $\mathcal{M}, x \Vdash F$ for all $F \in \Gamma$ and $\mathcal{M}, x \nVdash H$ for all $H \in \Delta$. Since $x \nVdash (\Sigma \lhd C)$, there exists $\alpha \in N_i(x)$ such that $\alpha \Vdash^\exists C$ and $\alpha \nVdash^\exists (A_1 \vee \cdots \vee A_n)$, for $\Sigma = A_1, \ldots, A_n$. Then there exists $y \in \alpha$ such that $\mathcal{M}, y \Vdash C$ and $\mathcal{M}, y \nVdash (A_1 \vee \cdots \vee A_n)$. However, from the previous conditions and validity of the premiss we have that for all $k \in \bigcup N_i(x)$ either $\mathcal{M}, k \nVdash C$ or $\mathcal{M}, k \Vdash A_s$, for some $A_s \in \Sigma$, contradicting the latter statement.

As for T, suppose the premisses of the rule are valid, while the conclusion is not. Thus, there is a model $\mathcal{M}, x \Vdash A \preccurlyeq_i B$, such that for all $F \in \Gamma$, $H \in \Delta$, $\mathcal{M}, x \Vdash F$ and $\mathcal{M}, x \nVdash H$. From $\mathcal{M}, x \Vdash A \preccurlyeq_i B$ we have for all $\alpha \in N_i(x)$, if $\alpha \Vdash^\exists B$, then $\alpha \Vdash^\exists A$. As for the premisses, it must hold that $\mathcal{M}, x \Vdash \bot \preccurlyeq_i A$, and thus that $(*)$ for all $\alpha \in N_i(x)$, $\alpha \nVdash^\exists A$ and $\mathcal{M}, x \Vdash B$. By total reflexivity, there is a $\beta \in N_i(x)$ such that $x \in \beta$. Thus, $\beta \Vdash^\exists B$, whence $\beta \Vdash^\exists A$, which contradicts $(*)$.

Similarly, suppose the premiss of Tr$_1$ is valid, while the conclusion is not. Then there is a model such that $\mathcal{M}, x \Vdash A \preccurlyeq_i B$, and for all $F \in \Gamma$, $H \in \Delta$, $\mathcal{M}, x \Vdash F$ and $\mathcal{M}, x \nVdash H$. Moreover, we have that there exists $y \in \bigcup N_i(x)$ such that $\mathcal{M}, y \Vdash S$ for all $S \in \Sigma$, and $\mathcal{M}, y \nVdash P$, for all $P \in \Pi$. From all these conditions, and from the fact that the premiss of Tr$_1$ are assumed to be valid, we obtain in particular that $(\star)$ $\mathcal{M}, y \nVdash A \preccurlyeq_i B$. However, by local absoluteness we have $N_i(x) = N_i(y)$; thus $\mathcal{M}, x \Vdash A \preccurlyeq_i B$, against $(\star)$. $\qquad\square$

Lemma 1. *The rules of weakening and contraction are admissible in* $\mathcal{N}_{\mathsf{CDL}}$*:*

$$\frac{G\{\Gamma \Rightarrow \Delta^*\}}{G\{\Gamma, \Sigma \Rightarrow \Delta^*, \Pi^*\}} \; \mathsf{W} \qquad \frac{G\{\Gamma, A, A \Rightarrow \Delta^*\}}{G\{\Gamma, A \Rightarrow \Delta^*\}} \; \mathsf{C}_L \qquad \frac{G\{\Gamma \Rightarrow \Delta^*, A, A\}}{G\{\Gamma \Rightarrow \Delta^*, A\}} \; \mathsf{C}_R$$

Proof. Standard, by induction on the depth of the derivation. $\qquad\square$

Remark 1. The rules for simple belief and knowledge can be explicitly defined as follows:

$$\frac{G\{\Gamma \Rightarrow \Delta, (\neg A \lessdot_i \top)\}}{G\{Bel_i\, A, \Gamma \Rightarrow \Delta\}} \; \mathsf{B}_L \qquad \frac{G\{\neg A \preccurlyeq_i \top, \Gamma \Rightarrow \Delta\}}{G\{\Gamma \Rightarrow \Delta, Bel_i\, A\}} \; \mathsf{B}_R$$

$$\frac{G\{K_i A, \Gamma \Rightarrow \Delta, (\neg A, \Sigma \lessdot_i C)\}}{G\{K_i A, \Gamma \Rightarrow \Delta, (\Sigma \lessdot_i C)\}} \; \mathsf{K}_L \qquad \frac{G\{\Gamma \Rightarrow \Delta, (\bot \lessdot_i A)\}}{G\{\Gamma \Rightarrow \Delta, K_i A\}} \; \mathsf{K}_R$$

Example 1. A derivation of $K_i A \rightarrow Bel_i\ (\neg Bel_j(\bot|A))$ is shown in Fig. 2, with rule R$\neg$ derivable from R $\rightarrow$, recalling $\neg A = A \rightarrow \bot$. We omit repetitions of the principal formulas in the premisses.

4   Completeness of $\mathcal{N}_{\mathsf{CDL}}$

To prove completeness of $\mathcal{N}_{\mathsf{CDL}}$, we show how to construct a countermodel from failed proof-search. For this, we first introduce the notion of saturated sequent (Definition 7), i.e., an unprovable sequent to which all the rules have been non-redundantly applied. Then, we build a countermodel for the sequent placed at the root of the derivation from the information contained in the saturated sequent.

Intuitively, we can consider a saturated sequent S as a labelled tree, where each node is a nested component S_j of S. Each world of a countermodel for S corresponds to a node of the tree, and the world falsifying S as a whole is the node placed at the root of the tree.

In countermodel construction we have to take care of the following: (a) for each agent i and world S_j define a system of neighbourhoods $N_i(S_j)$; and (b)

$$
\dfrac{
\dfrac{
\dfrac{
\dfrac{
\dfrac{
\dfrac{
Bel_j(\perp|A) \preccurlyeq_i K_iA \Rightarrow [\perp \preccurlyeq_i A, Bel_j(\perp|A), A \Rightarrow \perp, A]^i
}{
Bel_j(\perp|A) \preccurlyeq_i K_iA \Rightarrow [\perp \preccurlyeq_i A, Bel_j(\perp|A) \Rightarrow \neg A, \perp, A]^i
}\,\text{R}\neg \quad (2)
}{
Bel_j(\perp|A) \preccurlyeq_i K_iA \Rightarrow [\perp \preccurlyeq_i A, Bel_j(\perp|A) \Rightarrow \neg A, \perp]^i
}\,\text{T} \quad (1)
}{
Bel_j(\perp|A) \preccurlyeq_i K_iA \Rightarrow [Bel_j(\perp|A) \Rightarrow \neg A, \perp]^i
}\,\text{Bel}_\text{L}
}{
Bel_j(\perp|A) \preccurlyeq_i K_iA \Rightarrow (\neg A, \perp \lessdot_i Bel_j(\perp|A))
}\,\text{jump}
}{
Bel_j(\perp|A) \preccurlyeq_i K_iA \Rightarrow (\perp \lessdot_i Bel_j(\perp|A)) \qquad \cdots \Rightarrow \top
}\,\text{K}_\text{L} \ \ \text{T}
}{
Bel_j(\perp|A) \preccurlyeq_i K_iA \Rightarrow
}
$$

$$
\dfrac{
\dfrac{
Bel_j(\perp|A) \preccurlyeq_i K_iA \Rightarrow
}{
K_iA \Rightarrow Bel_i(\neg Bel_j(\perp|A))
}\,\text{B}_\text{R}
}{
\Rightarrow K_iA \rightarrow Bel_i(\neg Bel_j(\perp|A))
}\,\text{R}\rightarrow
$$

The derivations of sequents (1) and (2) respectively are:

$$
\dfrac{
\cdots \Rightarrow [\cdots \Rightarrow \neg A, \perp, [A \Rightarrow A]^j]^i \quad \cdots \Rightarrow [\cdots \Rightarrow \neg A, \perp, [A \Rightarrow \top]^j]^i
}{
\dfrac{
Bel_j(\perp|A) \preccurlyeq_i K_iA \Rightarrow [Bel_j(\perp|A) \Rightarrow \neg A, \perp, [A \Rightarrow A \wedge \top]^j]^i
}{
Bel_j(\perp|A) \preccurlyeq_i K_iA \Rightarrow [Bel_j(\perp|A) \Rightarrow \neg A, \perp, (A \wedge \top \lessdot_j A)]^i
}\,\text{jump}
}\,\text{R}\wedge
$$

$$
\dfrac{
Bel_j(\perp|A) \preccurlyeq_i K_iA \Rightarrow [Bel_j(\perp|A) \Rightarrow \neg A, \perp, [\perp \Rightarrow \perp]^j]^i
}{
Bel_j(\perp|A) \preccurlyeq_i K_iA \Rightarrow [Bel_j(\perp|A) \Rightarrow \neg A, \perp, (\perp \lessdot_j \perp)]^i
}\,\text{jump}
$$

Fig. 2. Derivation of the formula $K_iA \rightarrow Bel_i(\neg Bel_j(\perp|A))$.

verify that the condition of local absoluteness holds in the model. Concerning (a), the neighbourhoods $N_i(S_j)$ will be determined by the blocks $(\varSigma \lessdot_i C)$ contained in the consequent of S_j. As for (b), we need our models to satisfy the following property. Let $\mathcal{M}$ be an arbitrary model, x, y two worlds in the model, and $R_i(x,y)$ the relation defined as $y \in \bigcup N_i(x)$. By local absoluteness it follows that R_i is an equivalence relation[3] and from $R_i(x,y)$ follows $N_i(y) = N_i(x)$. The syntactic counterpart of R_i is the equivalence relation $\sim_i$ between two components S_j and S_k of S, one of which might be S itself (Definition 6). This relation holds whenever S_j and S_k are related by an i-path in the tree associated with S. Lemma 2 proves that if $S_j \sim_i S_k$ then the two nested sequents contain the same blocks. This suffices to ensure that $N_i(S_j) = N_i(S_k)$.

Let us come back to (a). To define the set $N_i(S_j)$ for a world S_j, we consider the blocks $(\varSigma \lessdot_i C)$ occurring in the consequent of S_j. However since the rules are cumulative, S_j may contain two blocks $(A_1, A_2 \lessdot_i C)$ and $(A_1, A_2, A_3 \lessdot_i C)$. In this case the former block can be disregarded, as it is included in the latter. Thus, only "maximal" blocks (Definition 8) are relevant in order to define $N_i(S_j)$. It turns out that maximal blocks of a saturated sequent are ordered by set inclusion, due to the com rule. Moreover, each maximal block $(\varSigma \lessdot_i C)$ occurring in S_j is supposed to be false in world S_j. This means that S_j has associated a "witnessing" world S_k where C is true and all formulas in

---

[3] Refer to next section on S5_i.

Σ are false. This world/component is such that $S_j \sim_i S_k$, and its existence is guaranteed by saturation with respect to jump. Thus, the neighbourhoods $N_i(S_j)$ are determined by the maximal blocks and their witnessing worlds. The following example should illustrate the construction.

Example 2. For p_i, r, s, t, u, distinct atomic formulas, let:

$$\Pi = (p_1 \lhd_i r), (p_1 \lhd_i s), (p_1, p_2 \lhd_i t), (p_1, p_2, p_3 \lhd_i u)$$

$$S = c \Rightarrow \Pi, [r \Rightarrow p_1, \Pi]^i, [s \Rightarrow p_1, \Pi]^i, [t \Rightarrow p_1, p_2, \Pi]^i, [u \Rightarrow p_1, p_2, p_3, \Pi]^i$$

The four components of S are numbered as S_1, S_2, S_3, S_4 respectively (so that $S_1 = [r \Rightarrow p_1, \Pi]^i$ etc.). Sequent S is saturated according to Definition 7. Moreover, observe that the blocks in Π are ordered by set inclusion, and that each block has an associated witnessing world: $(p_1 \lhd_i r)$ is associated to S_1, $(p_1 \lhd_i s)$ to S_2, $(p_1, p_2 \lhd_i t)$ to S_3 and $(p_1, p_2, p_3 \lhd_i u)$ to S_4. In the countermodel, $W = \{S, S_1, S_2, S_3, S_4\}$. The system of neighbourhoods $N_i(S)$ is determined by putting in the *smallest* neighbourhood the worlds corresponding to the *largest* block, and so on.

$$N_i(S) = \{\{S_4\}, \{S_4, S_3\}, \{S_4, S_3, S_2, S_1\}, \{S_4, S_3, S_2, S_1, S\}\}$$

This ensures that if a neighbourhood α falsifies a block $(\Sigma \lhd_i C)$, i.e., $\alpha \Vdash^\exists C$ and $\alpha \not\Vdash^\exists \bigvee \Sigma$, then any larger neighbourhood falsifies the block as well. The inclusion of S in the largest sphere is needed to ensure total reflexivity. Since the worlds are related by $\sim_i$, we have that $N_i(S_j) = N_i(S)$. Finally, the evaluation function assigns to atoms the worlds / nested component containing the atoms in the antecedent. Thus, $[\![u]\!] = \{S_4\}, [\![t]\!] = \{S_3\}, [\![u]\!] = \{S_2\}, [\![r]\!] = \{S_1\}, [\![c]\!] = \{S\}$. It can be easily seen that would S falsifies sequent S : for instance, in case of block $(p_1, p_2 \lhd_i t)$, we have $\{S4, S3\} \Vdash^\exists t$ but $\{S4, S3\} \not\Vdash^\exists p_1 \vee p_2$.

Definition 5. *Let S_1 and S_2 be two nested sequents. We say that S_2 occurs in S_1, in symbols $S_2 \tilde{\in} S_1$ if $S_1 = S_2$ or $S_1 = \Gamma \Rightarrow \Delta^*, [S_3]^i$ for some i and $S_2 \tilde{\in} S_3$.*

Viewing nested sequents as labelled trees, we thus have $S_2 \tilde{\in} S_1$ if S_2 is a subtree of S_1. We denote by the symbol $\in$ occurrence of a formula A or conditional block $(\Sigma \lhd_i A)$ in a multiset Γ of formulas and conditional blocks.

Definition 6. *Let S be a nested sequent. For every agent i the relation $\sim_i$ on the nested sequents occurring in S is the equivalence relation generated by the relation $\sim_i^1$ given by: $S_1 \sim_i^1 S_2$ iff $S_1 = \Gamma \Rightarrow \Delta, [S_2]^i$.*

Intuitively, we have $S_1 \sim_i S_2$ if $S_1 = S_2$ or the two components are linked with an i-path . Next, recall that $\mathsf{set}(\Delta)$ is the set underlying the multiset Δ.

Definition 7. *Let $S = \Gamma \Rightarrow \Delta, [G_1]^{i_1}, \ldots [G_n]^{i_n}$ be a nested sequent. We say that S is* locally saturated *if it satisfies the following conditions.*

1. *(init)* $\Gamma \cap \Delta = \emptyset$ *and* $\perp \notin \Gamma$;
2. $(\mathsf{L} \to)$ *If* $A \to B \in \Gamma$ *then* $A \in \Delta$ *or* $B \in \Gamma$;
3. $(\mathsf{R} \to)$ *If* $A \to B \in \Delta$ *then* $A \in \Gamma$ *and* $B \in \Delta$;
4. $(\mathsf{R} \preccurlyeq)$ *If* $A \preccurlyeq_i B \in \Delta$ *then there exists a conditional block* $(A \lhd_i B) \in \Delta$;
5. $(\mathsf{L} \preccurlyeq)$ *If* $A \preccurlyeq_i B \in \Gamma$ *and* $(\Sigma \lhd_i C) \in \Delta$, *then there is a* $(\Sigma' \lhd_i C) \in \Delta$ *with* $\mathsf{set}(\Sigma, B) = \mathsf{set}(\Sigma')$ *or* $(\Sigma \lhd_i A) \in \Delta$;
6. *(com)* *If* $(\Sigma_1 \lhd_i A)$ *and* $(\Sigma_2 \lhd_i B) \in \Delta$, *then for some* Π *with* $\mathsf{set}(\Sigma_1, \Sigma_2) \subseteq \mathsf{set}(\Pi)$ *we have* $(\Pi \lhd_i A) \in \Delta$ *or* $(\Pi \lhd_i B) \in \Delta$.
7. (T) *If* $A \preccurlyeq_i B \in \Delta$ *then either* $(\perp \lhd_i A) \in \Delta$ *or* $B \in \Delta$;

We denote by $\mathsf{Block}_i(S)$ *the set of conditional blocks in* Δ *labelled with* i. *Moreover, we say that* S *is* saturated *if the following conditions hold for every* $S_1 \tilde{\in} S$:

- S_1 *is locally saturated;*
- *(jump) If* $S_1 = \Gamma \Rightarrow \Delta^*, (\Sigma \lhd_i C)$, *then there is a* $S_2 \sim_i S_1$ *with* $S_2 = \Phi \Rightarrow \Omega^*, [\Psi, C \Rightarrow \Sigma, \Xi^*]^i$;
- *(Transfer rules) If* $S_1 = \Gamma \Rightarrow \Delta^*, [\Sigma \Rightarrow \Pi^*]^i$, *then* $\mathsf{Block}_i(S_1) = \mathsf{Block}_i(\Sigma \Rightarrow \Pi^*)$ *and for every formula* $A \preccurlyeq_i B$ *we have* $A \preccurlyeq_i B \in \Gamma$ *iff* $A \preccurlyeq_i B \in \Sigma$;

Lemma 2. *If* S_1 *and* S_2 *are saturated and* $S_1 \sim_i S_2$, *then* $\mathsf{Block}_i(S_1) = \mathsf{Block}_i(S_2)$.

Proof. By induction on the length of the i-path between S_1 and S_2, using the saturation condition for the transfer rules in the base case. $\square$

We define a naive backwards proof-search strategy for $\mathcal{N}_{\mathsf{CDL}}$ as follows: Apply the rules bottom-up to the nested sequent unless the saturation condition associated to the particular application of the rule is already satisfied. If the sequent is saturated and not an initial sequent, return it, otherwise return "derivable".

Lemma 3. *Let* S *be a nested sequent. Then proof search under the strategy above terminates and yields a derivation or a saturated nested sequent.*

Proof. For termination, we first bound the number of the nested sequents occurring in the proof search. Let n be the *size* of S, i.e., the number of symbols occurring in it. Note that the premisses of the rules contain at least one formula occurrence more than the conclusion. Since according to the proof-search strategy rules are not applied if the nested sequent already satisfies the corresponding saturation condition, no formula or block is added twice. Since S contains at most n many formulas, at most $2^n \cdot n$ many different conditional blocks and $2^n \cdot 2^n$ many sequents consisting only of formulas can be obtained without repetition. Hence at most $2^{2^n \cdot n} \cdot 2^{2n}$ many different sequents consisting of formulas and blocks occur in the proof search. To bound the maximal depth of a nested sequent (seen as a tree) occurring in the proof search, we consider a branch in such a nested sequent and divide it into *blocks*, taking two components S_1 and S_2 in the branch to be in the same block if for some agent i we have $S_1 \sim_i S_2$. Since the maximal nesting depth of comparative plausibility formulas in S is n, the number of alternations between agents in such a formula is at most

n. Every application of the jump rule produces a new component such that the maximal nesting depth of formulas in this component is strictly smaller than that of the component from which it was created. Moreover the transfer rules only transfer comparative plausibility formulas and blocks across nesting operators for the same agent. Hence every branch of every nested sequent occurring in the proof search contains at most n many non-trivial blocks in addition to those of S. Thus the maximal depth of a nested sequent occurring in the proof search is the number of possible sequents times the maximal number of blocks in a branch, i.e., $2^{2^n \cdot n} \cdot 2^{2n} \cdot 2n = \mathcal{O}(2^{2^n})$. Since the branching of the nested sequents themselves (seen as trees) is caused by applications of the jump rule, by the saturation conditions the branching of a nested sequent is bounded by the number of formula-formula sequents, i.e., 2^{2n}. Hence the number of components of a nested sequent occurring in the proof search is $\mathcal{O}((2^{2^n})^{2^{2n}})$. Further, each of these components contains one of at most $\mathcal{O}(2^{2^n})$ many sequents. Hence the total number of nested sequents which might occur in the proof search is finite. Together with the fact that in every step of the proof search at least one new occurrence of a formula is added, this means that the algorithm terminates.

It is straightforward to construct a derivation if the procedure returns "derivable". Suppose that it does not yield a derivation. Since the algorithm terminates, it yields a nested sequent S. But this nested sequent must satisfy the saturation conditions for every rule, since otherwise it would be possible to apply the corresponding rule and the procedure would not have terminated.   □

We then construct a countermodel from a saturated nested sequent. While the worlds of the model will be the components of the nested sequents, for defining the neighbourhood function we consider the "largest" blocks in the components:

Definition 8. *For a nested sequent S, a conditional block $(\Sigma \lhd_i C) \subset \mathsf{Block}_i(S)$ is* maximal *if there is no block $(\Sigma' \lhd_i C) \in \mathsf{Block}_i(S)$ with $\mathsf{set}(\Sigma) \subsetneq \mathsf{set}(\Sigma')$. We write* $\mathsf{MaxBlock}_i(S)$ *for the set of maximal blocks in* $\mathsf{Block}_i(S)$.

Remark 2. A maximal conditional block is the "largest" (containing most formulas in the antecedent) of all the blocks in $\mathsf{Block}_i(S)$ with the same consequent. Thus, all maximal blocks have a different consequent. If S is saturated, the antecedents of the conditional blocks in $\mathsf{MaxBlock}_i(S)$ can be ordered w.r.t. set inclusion, such that $\mathsf{set}(\Sigma_1) \subset \mathsf{set}(\Sigma_2) \subset \cdots \subset \mathsf{set}(\Sigma_k)$, for k the number of maximal conditional blocks. Note that there could be maximal blocks sharing the same antecedent, e.g., as a consequence of saturation with respect to Tr_3, Tr_4 or com, this latter applied to two different pairs of conditional blocks.

Given a saturated nested sequent S as above, the construction of the countermodel $\mathcal{M}_{\mathcal{N}} = \langle W, \{N_i\}_{i \in \mathcal{A}}, [\![\,]\!] \rangle$ proceeds as follows.

- $W := \{S_j \mid S_j \tilde{\in} S\}$;
- $[\![p]\!] := \{S_j \in W \mid p \in \Phi_j\}$.

To define the neighbourhood functions, observe that by the condition of absoluteness, this must be the same for all worlds seen by the same agent. Thus, for all nested sequents S_m with $S_m \sim_i S_j$, we define a single neighbourhood function $N_i(S_j) = N_i(S_m)$. In order to do so, we consider the maximal blocks occurring in S_j, knowing by Lemma 2 that if $S_j \sim_i S_m$ then $\mathsf{Block}_i(S_j) = \mathsf{Block}_i(S_m)$, and hence $\mathsf{MaxBlock}_i(S_j) = \mathsf{MaxBlock}_i(S_m)$. Suppose the set $\mathsf{MaxBlock}_i(S_j)$ contains $n_1 + n_2 + \cdots + n_k$ maximal conditional blocks, with exactly k different sets $\mathsf{set}(\Sigma_1) \subset \mathsf{set}(\Sigma_2) \subset \cdots \subset \mathsf{set}(\Sigma_k)$:

$$
\begin{array}{ccc}
(\Sigma_1 \lhd_i C_1^1) & ,\ldots, & (\Sigma_1 \lhd_i C_{n_1}^1) \\
(\Sigma_2 \lhd_i C_1^2) & ,\ldots, & (\Sigma_2 \lhd_i C_{n_2}^2) \\
\vdots & & \vdots \\
(\Sigma_k \lhd_i C_1^k) & ,\ldots, & (\Sigma_k \lhd_i C_{n_k}^k)
\end{array}
$$

So for each $z \leqslant k$ there are n_z different blocks $(\Sigma_z \lhd_i C_1^z), \ldots, (\Sigma_z \lhd_i C_{n_z}^z)$ with the same antecedent. By the saturation condition for jump, for all Σ_z, C_w^z with $w \in \{1, \ldots, n_z\}$, there is a $S_{z,w} = \Phi_{z,w} \Rightarrow \Omega_{z,w} \tilde{\in} S$ with $S_j \sim_i S_{z,w}$, $C_w^z \in \Phi_{z,w}$ and $\Sigma_z \subseteq \Omega_{z,w}$. Let $W_i^{S_j} = \{S_z \mid S_z \sim_i S_j\}$. Now define $N_i(S_j)$ as follows:

$$N_i(S_j) := \{\{S_{k,1}, \ldots, S_{k,n_k}\}, \{S_{k,1}, \ldots, S_{k,n_k}, S_{k-1,1}, \ldots, S_{k-1,n_{k-1}}\}, \cdots,$$

$$\{S_{k,1}, \ldots, S_{k,n_k}, S_{k-1,1}, \ldots, S_{k-1,n_{k-1}}, \ldots S_{1,1}, \ldots, S_{1,n_1}\}, W_i^{S_j}\}$$

I.e., we add into the same neighbourhood the worlds associated to blocks sharing the same antecedent. The so defined $\mathcal{M_N}$ is a model for CDL: it satisfies the properties of non-emptiness, nesting and local absoluteness (immediate from the definition). Total reflexivity follows from the fact that for all S_j, $W_i^{S_j} \in N_i(S_j)$.

Lemma 4. *Let S be a saturated nested sequent and $S_j = \Phi_j \Rightarrow \Omega_j^*$ a nested sequent with $S_j \sim_i S$. Let $\mathcal{M_N}$ be the model as just defined. Let $\mathsf{MaxBlock}_i(S_j) = (\Sigma_1 \lhd_i C_1^1), \ldots, (\Sigma_1 \lhd_i C_{n_1}^1), \ldots, (\Sigma_k \lhd_i C_1^k), \ldots, (\Sigma_k \lhd_i C_{n_k}^k)$. For A a formula and $(\Sigma \lhd_i C)$ a conditional block the following hold:*

1. *If $A \in \Phi_j$ then $\mathcal{M_N}, S_j \Vdash A$;*
2. *If $A \in \Omega_j^*$ then $\mathcal{M_N}, S_j \not\Vdash A$;*
3. *If $(\Sigma \lhd_i C) \in \Omega_j^*$ then $\mathcal{M_N}, S_j \not\Vdash (\bigvee_{B \in \Sigma} B \preccurlyeq_i C)$.*

Proof. We prove statements 1 and 2 by induction on the complexity of A, showing only the case of comparative plausibility formulas. The proof of statement 3 uses the proof of 2. As for 1, suppose $A \preccurlyeq_i B \in \Phi_j$. We have to show that $\mathcal{M_N}, S_j \Vdash A \preccurlyeq_i B$, i.e. that for all the $\alpha \in N_i(S_j)$ we have $\alpha \not\Vdash^\exists B$ or $\alpha \Vdash^\exists A$. First, suppose $\alpha \neq W_i^{S_j}$. Then, $\alpha = \{S_{k,1}, \ldots, S_{k,n_k}, \ldots, S_{t,1}, \ldots, S_{t,n_t}\}$, for some $t \leqslant k$. For $z \leqslant k$ and $w \in \{1, \ldots, n_z\}$, each $S_{z,w}$ comes from a maximal conditional block $(\Sigma_z \lhd_i C_w^z)$, and denotes a nested sequent $\Phi_{z,w} \Rightarrow \Omega_{z,w}$ occurring in W with $C_w^z \in \Phi_{z,w}$ and $\Sigma_z \subseteq \Omega_{z,w}$. By saturation condition $\mathsf{L} \preccurlyeq$, either $B \in \Sigma_t$ or $A = C_q^t$, for some $q \in \{t, \ldots, n_t\}$. In the former case, by $\mathsf{set}(\Sigma_t) \subset \mathsf{set}(\Sigma_{t+1}) \subset \cdots \subset \mathsf{set}(\Sigma_k)$ and by inductive hypothesis, we have that for all $S_{z,w}$, with $z \leqslant k$ and $w \in \{1, \ldots, n_z\}$, $\mathcal{M_N}, S_{z,w} \not\Vdash B$; thus, $\alpha \not\Vdash^\exists B$. Otherwise, let $A = C_q^t$, for some $q \in \{1, \ldots, n_t\}$. Then, $S_{t,q} = A, \Phi_{t,q}' \Rightarrow \Omega_{t,q}$. By inductive hypothesis and since $S_{t,q} \in \alpha$ we get $\alpha \Vdash^\exists A$.

If $\alpha = W_i^{S_j}$, we have to prove that $W_i^{S_j} \not\Vdash^\exists B$ or $W_i^{S_j} \Vdash^\exists A$. Let $W_i^{S_j} = \{S_1, \ldots, S_t\}$. By the saturation conditions for Tr_1 and Tr_2 we have $A \preccurlyeq_i B \in \Phi_q$, for all $q \leqslant t$. By saturation condition T, either there exists some S_q with $(\bot \lhd_i A) \in \mathsf{Block}_i(S_q)$, or for all S_q we have $B \in \Omega_q$. In the former case, by saturation condition jump, to S_q is associated a nested sequent $S_{q'} = A, \Phi_{q'} \Rightarrow \Omega_{q'}$. It holds that $S_q \sim_i^1 S_{q'}$, and thus $S_{q'} \in W_i^{S_j}$. By inductive hypothesis, $\mathcal{M}, S_{q'} \Vdash A$, and $W_i^{S_j} \Vdash^\exists A$. Otherwise, we have that for all S_q, $B \in \Omega_q$. By inductive hypothesis $\mathcal{M}, S_q \not\Vdash B$, and thus $W_i^{S_j} \not\Vdash^\exists B$.

As for 2, suppose $A \preccurlyeq_i B \in \Omega_j$. We have to prove that $\mathcal{M}_N, S_j \not\Vdash A \preccurlyeq B$, i.e., that there is an $\alpha \in N_i(S_j)$ with $\alpha \Vdash^\exists B$ and $\alpha \Vdash^\exists B$ and $\alpha \not\Vdash^\exists A$. From the definition of $N_i(S_j)$, and with $z \leqslant k$ and $w \in \{1, \ldots, n_z\}$, we have that to each $S_{z,w}$ occurring in $\bigcup N_i(S_j)$ is associated a sequent $C_w^z, \Phi_{z,w} \Rightarrow \Omega_{z,w}, \Sigma_z$, coming from a maximal conditional block $(\Sigma_z \lhd_i C_w^z)$. Thus, by saturation for $\mathsf{R} \preccurlyeq$ there exists $z \leqslant k$ and $w \in \{1, \ldots, n_z\}$ such that $B = C_w^z$ and $A \in \Sigma_z$. Let us consider the world $S_{z,w}$ associated to this nested sequent, and the sphere to which $S_{z,w}$ belongs: $\alpha = \{S_{k,1}, \ldots S_{k,n_k} \ldots, S_{z,1}, \ldots, S_{z,n_z}\}$. By inductive hypothesis, $\mathcal{M}_N \Vdash B$, and thus $\alpha \Vdash^\exists B$. Moreover, since $\mathsf{set}(\Sigma_z) \subset \mathsf{set}(\Sigma_{z+1}) \subset \cdots \subset \mathsf{set}(\Sigma_k)$ and by inductive hypothesis, it holds that for all $S_{l,q}$, for $l \in \{z, \ldots, k\}$ and $q \in \{1, \ldots, n_l\}$, $S_{l,q} \not\Vdash A$. Since no worlds in α validate A, $\alpha \not\Vdash^\exists A$. $\square$

Corollary 1. *Let $S = \Gamma \Rightarrow \Delta, [G_1]^{i_1}, \ldots, [G_n]^{i_n}$ be a saturated nested sequent and $\mathcal{M}_N$ a model as defined above. Then, for all $S_j \in W$ it holds that $\mathcal{M}_N, S_j \not\Vdash (S_j)^{int}$, and $\mathcal{M}_N, S \not\Vdash (S)^{int}$.* $\square$

Completeness of $\mathcal{N}_{\mathsf{CDL}}$ follows immediately: by Lemma 3, backwards proof search terminates, yielding a derivation or a saturated sequent. In the former case the formula is derivable; in the latter case, we obtain a countermodel using Corollary 1. Moreover, the completeness proof constructs a *finite* countermodel from a saturated sequent, and thereby also shows the finite model property of the logic.

Theorem 2 (Completeness). *Every valid formula is derivable in $\mathcal{N}_{\mathsf{CDL}}$.* $\square$

Example 3. We construct the countermodel $\mathcal{M}$ for the underivable sequent $\Rightarrow Bel_i(P \to Q) \to Bel_i(Q|P)$. By backwards applications of $\mathcal{N}_{\mathsf{CDL}}$ rules we obtain the following saturated sequent, where we assume $\preccurlyeq_i$ binds stronger than $\wedge$:

$$S = P \wedge \neg Q \preccurlyeq_i P, \mathsf{Block}_i(S) \Rightarrow [P \Rightarrow Q, \mathsf{Block}_i(S)]^i, [\mathsf{T} \Rightarrow P, \mathsf{Block}_i(S)]^i$$

where $\mathsf{Block}_i(S) = (\bot \lhd_i P \wedge \neg Q), (P \wedge \neg Q, P, \bot \lhd_i \mathsf{T})$. Let $S_1 = P \Rightarrow Q, \mathsf{Block}_i(S)$ and $S_2 = \mathsf{T} \Rightarrow P, \mathsf{Block}_i(S)$. Then, $W = W_i^S = \{S, S_1, S_2\}$, and $S \sim_i S_1 \sim_i S_2$. Sequent S_1 and S_2 are obtained by jump respectively from the former and latter conditional block in $\mathsf{Block}_i(S)$. Since $\{\bot\} \subset \{P \wedge \neg Q, P, \bot\}$ we have that $N_i(S) = N_i(S_1) = N_i(S_2) = \{\{S_2\}, \{S_2, S_1\}, W_i^S\}$. By definition, P is true only at world S_2, and Q is false at all the worlds. It holds that (i) $\mathcal{M}, S \Vdash Bel_i(P \to Q)$, i.e., that there exists an $\alpha \in N_i(S)$ such that $\alpha \Vdash^\forall P \to Q$. Neighbourhood $\{S_2\}$ satisfies the condition. It also holds that

(ii) $\mathcal{M}, S \not\Vdash Bel_i(Q|P)$, i.e., that there exists an $\alpha \in N_i(S)$ such that $\alpha \Vdash^{\exists} P$ and that for all $\beta \in N_i(S)$ it holds that $\beta \Vdash^{\exists} P \wedge \neg Q$. The former condition is satisfied by the neighbourhood $\{S_2, S_1\}$, and all neighbourhoods satisfy the latter condition. Since (i) and (ii) hold for all the worlds in the model, $\mathcal{M}$ is a countermodel for the sequent.

Initial sequents and propositional rules - same as $\mathcal{N}_{\mathsf{CDL}}$

Modal rules

$$\frac{G\{\Gamma \Rightarrow \Delta, [\Rightarrow A]^i\}}{G\{\Gamma \Rightarrow \Delta, K_i A\}} \; \mathsf{K}_\mathsf{R}^{\square} \qquad \frac{G\{A, K_i A, \Gamma \Rightarrow \Delta\}}{G\{K_i A, \Gamma \Rightarrow \Delta\}} \; \mathsf{K}_\mathsf{T}^{\square}$$

$$\frac{G\{\Gamma, K_i A \Rightarrow \Delta, [K_i A, \Sigma \Rightarrow \Pi]^i\}}{G\{\Gamma, K_i A \Rightarrow \Delta, [\Sigma \Rightarrow \Pi]^i\}} \; \mathsf{Tr1}^{\square} \qquad \frac{G\{\Gamma, K_i A, \Rightarrow \Delta, [\Sigma, K_i A \Rightarrow \Pi]^i\}}{G\{\Gamma \Rightarrow \Delta, [\Sigma, K_i A \Rightarrow \Pi]^i\}} \; \mathsf{Tr2}^{\square}$$

Fig. 3. Rules of $\mathcal{N}_{\mathsf{S5}_i}$

5   Relationship with S5$_i$

As mentioned, the operator K_i can be defined by $K_i A = \bot \preccurlyeq_i \neg A$. If we adopt this definition, restrict the language to $\mathcal{F}_{\mathsf{S5}_i} = p \mid \bot \mid A \to B \mid K_i A$, and apply the rules of $\mathcal{N}_{\mathsf{CDL}}$ to these formulas (Remark 1), we obtain a nested sequent calculus for a multi-agent modal epistemic logic, where the knowledge operator corresponds to the $\square$ modality. The proof system, called $\mathcal{N}_{\mathsf{S5}_i}$, captures multi-agent logic S5$_i$.

Nested sequents of $\mathcal{N}_{\mathsf{S5}_i}$ are interpreted as $\mathcal{N}_{\mathsf{CDL}}$ nested sequents, with the difference that $\mathcal{N}_{\mathsf{S5}_i}$ does not need conditional blocks to capture the simpler semantics of S5$_i$. Observe that the rules of $\mathcal{N}_{\mathsf{S5}_i}$ are essentially the multi-agent versions of the standard nested sequent rules for single-agent S5 [5,11,16]. But while the nested sequent structure is an overkill for S5, it is necessary to capture S5$_i$. To the best of our knowledge, the only published sequent calculus for S5$_i$ is Poggiolesi's hypersequent calculus, which uses syntactic labels for the agents [15]. The connection between mono-agent CDL and S5 is known since [10]: As mentioned above, counterfactual logic $\mathbb{VTA}$ is the mono-agent system corresponding to CDL. But a Kripke-style accessibility relation R can be obtained from (mono-agent) neighbourhood models by setting $R(x, y)$ if and only if $y \in \bigcup N(x)$. For $\mathbb{VTA}$ this yields an equivalence relation, thus characterizing modal logic S5. The relation can be used to evaluate formulas KA, i.e., formulas $\bot \preccurlyeq \neg A^4$. For $A \in \mathcal{F}_{\mathsf{S5}_i}$, define $T(A) \in \mathcal{F}_{\mathsf{CDL}}$ to be the formula obtained by replacing every occurrence of $K_i A$ with $\bot \preccurlyeq_i \neg A$. The translation is lifted to nested sequents in the obvious way. By generalizing Lewis' argument to the multi-agent case, we obtain the following:

---

[4] Evaluating KA at a world x corresponds to evaluating $\bot \preccurlyeq \neg A$ in the *outer* neighbourhood of $N(x)$. For this reason, Lewis calls S5 the *outer* modal logic of $\mathbb{VTA}$.

Lemma 5. *If A is a theorem of* $S5_i$, *then* $T(A)$ *is a theorem of* CDL.

Completeness of the nested calculus for $S5_i$ seems to be unpublished, but considered folklore in the nested sequent community. Using the previous proposition, it can be obtained proof-theoretically from the completeness of $\mathcal{N}_{CDL}$.

Theorem 3. *The calculus* $\mathcal{N}_{S5_i}$ *is sound and complete w.r.t. modal logic* $S5_i$.

Proof (Sketch). Soundness can be proved directly (standard). For completeness, we only sketch the main argument. We claim that for a sequent $S = K_i A_1, \ldots, K_i A_n, \Gamma \Rightarrow \Delta, K_i B_1, \ldots, K_i B_m$, if there is a derivation of $T(S) = \bot \preccurlyeq_i \neg A_1, \ldots, \bot \preccurlyeq_i \neg A_n, \Gamma \Rightarrow \Delta, \bot \preccurlyeq_i \neg B_1, \ldots, \bot \preccurlyeq_i \neg B_m$ in $\mathcal{N}_{CDL}$, then there is a derivation of the original sequent S in $\mathcal{N}_{S5_i}$. If $T(S)$ is derivable in $\mathcal{N}_{CDL}$, then it must have been derived (modulo rule permutations) either by an application of T or by multiple applications of R $\preccurlyeq$, followed by applications of L $\preccurlyeq$ and com, and finally jump. In the former case, the first premiss of the application of T contains a block $(\bot \lhd_i \bot)$ and is derivable via jump, while the right premiss modulo propositional rules is just the premiss of $K_T^\square$. In the latter case, after (backwards) applications of R $\preccurlyeq$, we first reach the sequent:

$$\bot \preccurlyeq_i \neg A_1, \ldots, \bot \preccurlyeq_i \neg A_n, \Gamma \Rightarrow \Delta, (\bot \lhd_i \neg B_1), \ldots, (\bot \lhd_i \cdot B_m).$$

Similarly to the case of T, the left premiss in any (backwards) application of L $\preccurlyeq$ to a formula $\bot \preccurlyeq_i \neg A_\ell$ and a block $(\bot \lhd_i \neg B_k)$ is derivable, since it contains the conditional block $(\bot \lhd_i \bot)$. The other premiss of an application of L $\preccurlyeq$ is:

$$\bot \preccurlyeq_i \neg A_1, \ldots, \bot \preccurlyeq_i \neg A_n, \Gamma \Rightarrow \Delta, (A_j, \bot \lhd_i \neg B_1), \ldots, (\bot \lhd_i \neg B_m).$$

Exhaustive backwards applications of L $\preccurlyeq$ yield the sequent

$$\bot \preccurlyeq_i \neg A_1, \ldots, \bot \preccurlyeq_i \neg A_n, \Gamma \Rightarrow \Delta, (\Sigma \lhd_i \neg B_1), \ldots, (\Sigma \lhd_i B_m)$$

where all blocks have the same $\Sigma = \neg A_1, \ldots, \neg A_n$. Hence the rule of com is not really necessary: with applications of L $\preccurlyeq$ until saturation we obtain the same sequent as with mixed applications of L $\preccurlyeq$ and com. Finally, by applications of jump and of the rules for negation to the above sequent we reach the sequent

$$T(S^*) = \bot \preccurlyeq_i \neg A_1, \ldots, \bot \preccurlyeq_i \neg A_n, \Gamma \Rightarrow \Delta, [\Sigma \Rightarrow B_1]^i, \ldots, [\Sigma \Rightarrow B_m]^i.$$

The corresponding $\mathcal{N}_{S5_i}$ sequent S^* is the same sequent that can be obtained from $\Gamma, K_i A_1, \ldots, K_i A_n \Rightarrow \Delta, K_i B_1, \ldots, K_i B_m$ by applying first rule $K_R^\square$ to all $K_i B_1, \ldots, K_i B_m$ and then $Tr1^\square$ exhaustively on $K_i A_1, \ldots, K_i A_n$.

Thus, the nested calculus $\mathcal{N}_{S5_i}$ simulates by macro-steps $\mathcal{N}_{CDL}$ derivations in the restricted language $\mathcal{F}_{S5_i}$. Since the structure of conditional blocks is not needed, the rules of com, Tr_3 and Tr_4 become superfluous and have no corresponding rules in $\mathcal{N}_{S5_i}$. Rule $Tr2^\square$ simulates rule Tr_2.   □

6   Conclusions

We have presented the first internal calculus $\mathcal{N}_{CDL}$ for the multi-agent logic of conditional beliefs CDL. The calculus manipulates nested sequents, where the nesting is determined by nested beliefs of different agents. The calculus provides a decision procedure for the logic. Since CDL contains as a fragment multi-agent $S5_i$, by specialising the rules of $\mathcal{N}_{CDL}$ to that fragment we obtain a natural internal calculus for $S5_i$. CDL logic in itself can be extended to formalise the dynamics of beliefs induced by different kinds of announcements [1]. We plan to study how to extend our calculus to deal with the dynamic extension of CDL.

References

1. Baltag, A., Smets, S.: Conditional doxastic models: a qualitative approach to dynamic belief revision. Electron. Notes Theor. Comput. Sci. **165**, 5–21 (2006)
2. Baltag, A., Smets, S.: A qualitative theory of dynamic interactive belief revision. Log. Found. Game Decis. Theory (LOFT 7) **3**, 9–58 (2008)
3. Baltag, A., Smets, S., et al.: The logic of conditional doxastic actions. Texts Log. Games Spec. Issue New Perspect. Games Interact. **4**, 9–31 (2008)
4. Board, O.: Dynamic interactive epistemology. Games Econ. Behav. **49**(1), 49–80 (2004)
5. Brünnler, K.: Deep sequent systems for modal logic. Arch. Math. Log. **48**, 551–577 (2009)
6. Girlando, M., Lellmann, B., Olivetti, N., Pozzato, G.L.: Standard sequent calculi for Lewis' logics of counterfactuals. In: Michael, L., Kakas, A. (eds.) JELIA 2016. LNCS (LNAI), vol. 10021, pp. 272–287. Springer, Cham (2016). https://doi.org/10.1007/978-3-319-48758-8_18
7. Girlando, M., Lellmann, B., Olivetti, N., Pozzato, G.L.: Hypersequent calculi for Lewis' conditional logics with uniformity and reflexivity. In: Schmidt, R.A., Nalon, C. (eds.) TABLEAUX 2017. LNCS (LNAI), vol. 10501, pp. 131–148. Springer, Cham (2017). https://doi.org/10.1007/978-3-319-66902-1_8
8. Girlando, M., Negri, S., Olivetti, N., Risch, V.: The logic of conditional beliefs: neighbourhood semantics and sequent calculus. In: Advances in Modal Logic, pp. 322–341 (2016)
9. Girlando, M., Negri, S., Olivetti, N., Risch, V.: Conditional beliefs: from neighbourhood semantics to sequent calculus. Rev. Symb. Log. **11**(4), 736–779 (2018)
10. Lewis, D.K.: Counterfactuals. Blackwell, Oxford (1973)
11. Marin, S., Straßburger, L.: Label-free modular systems for classical and intuitionistic modal logics. In: Goré, R., Kooi, B.P., Kurucz, A. (eds.) AiML 10. pp. 387–406. College (2014)
12. Negri, S.: Proof theory for non-normal modal logics: the neighbourhood formalism and basic results. IFCoLog J. Log. Appl. **4**, 1241–1286 (2017)
13. Olivetti, N., Pozzato, G.L.: A standard internal calculus for Lewis' counterfactual logics. In: De Nivelle, H. (ed.) TABLEAUX 2015. LNCS (LNAI), vol. 9323, pp. 270–286. Springer, Cham (2015). https://doi.org/10.1007/978-3-319-24312-2_19
14. Pacuit, E.: Neighbourhood semantics for modal logics. Springer, Heidelberg (2017). https://doi.org/10.1007/978-3-319-67149-9
15. Poggiolesi, F.: A cut-free simple sequent calculus for modal logic S5. Rev. Symb. Log. **1**(1), 3–15 (2008)

16. Poggiolesi, F.: The method of tree-hypersequents for modal propositional logic. In: Makinson, D., Malinowski, J., Wansing, H. (eds.) Towards Mathematical Philosophy. TL, vol. 28, pp. 31–51. Springer, Dordrecht (2009). https://doi.org/10.1007/978-1-4020-9084-4_3

17. Stalnaker, R.: Belief revision in games: forward and backward induction 1. Math. Soc. Sci. **36**(1), 31–56 (1998)

Reasoning About Cognitive Attitudes in a Qualitative Setting

Emiliano Lorini[(✉)]

IRIT-CNRS, Toulouse University, Toulouse, France
lorini@irit.fr

Abstract. We present a general logical framework for reasoning about agents' cognitive attitudes of both epistemic type and motivational type. We provide a sound and complete axiomatization for our logic and we show that it allows us to express a variety of relevant concepts for qualitative decision theory including the concepts of knowledge, belief, strong belief, conditional belief, desire, strong desire, comparative desirability and choice.

1 Introduction

Since the seminal work of Hintikka on epistemic logic [17], of Von Wright on the logic of preference [28,29] and of Cohen and Levesque on the logic of intention [10], many formal logics for reasoning about cognitive attitudes of agents such as knowledge and belief [14], preference [6,21], desire [13], intention [19,27] and their combination [23,30] have been proposed. Generally speaking, these logics are nothing but formal models of rational agency relying on the idea that an agent endowed with cognitive attitudes makes decisions on the basis of what she believes and of what she desires or prefers.

The idea of describing rational agents in terms of their epistemic and motivational attitudes is something that these logics share with classical decision theory and game theory. Classical decision theory and game theory provide a quantitative account of individual and strategic decision-making by assuming that agents' beliefs and desires can be respectively modeled by subjective probabilities and utilities. Qualitative approaches to individual and strategic decision-making have been proposed in AI [7,12] to characterize criteria that a rational agent should adopt for making decisions when she cannot build a probability distribution over the set of possible events and her preference over the set of possible outcomes cannot be expressed by a utility function but only by a qualitative ordering over the outcomes. For example, going beyond expected utility maximization, qualitative criteria such as the maxmin principle (choose the action that will minimize potential loss) and the maxmax principle (choose the action that will maximize potential gain) have been studied and axiomatically characterized [8,9].

The aim of this paper is to present a rich logical framework for representing a variety of agents' cognitive attitudes in a multi-agent setting. In agreement with philosophical theories [18,22,25,26], our logic allows us to distinguish two

© Springer Nature Switzerland AG 2019
F. Calimeri et al. (Eds.): JELIA 2019, LNAI 11468, pp. 726–743, 2019.
https://doi.org/10.1007/978-3-030-19570-0_47

general categories of cognitive attitudes: *epistemic* attitudes, including belief and knowledge, and *motivational* ones, including desires and preferences. Moreover, in agreement with rational choice theory, it allows us to capture a notion of choice which depends on what an agent believes and desires as well as on the decision criterion she adopts.

The paper is organized as follows. In Sect. 2, we present the semantics and syntax of our logic, called Dynamic Logic of Cognitive Attitudes (DLCA). At the semantic level, it exploits two orderings that capture, respectively, an agent's comparative plausibility and comparative desirability over states. At the syntactic level, it uses program constructs of dynamic logic (sequential composition, non-deterministic choice, intersection, converse and test) to build complex cognitive attitudes from simple ones. Following [15,24], it also uses nominals in order to axiomatize intersection of programs. In Sect. 3, we illustrate the expressive power of our logic by using it to formalize a variety of cognitive attitudes of agents including knowledge, belief, strong belief, conditional belief, desire, strong desire, comparative desirability and choice. In Sect. 4, we present a sound and complete axiomatization for it. In Sect. 5 we conclude.

2 Dynamic Logic of Cognitive Attitudes

Let Atm be a countable infinite set of atomic propositions, let Nom be a countable infinite set of nominals disjoint from Atm and let Agt be a finite set of agents.

Definition 1 (Multi-agent cognitive model). *A multi-agent cognitive model (MCM) is a tuple* $M = (W, (\preceq_{i,P})_{i \in Agt}, (\preceq_{i,D})_{i \in Agt}, (\equiv_i)_{i \in Agt}, V)$ *where:*

- *W is a set of worlds or states;*
- *for every* $i \in Agt$, $\preceq_{i,P}$ *and* $\preceq_{i,D}$ *are preorders on W and* $\equiv_i$ *is an equivalence relation on W such that for all* $\tau \in \{P, D\}$ *and for all* $w, v \in W$:
  - **(C1)** $\preceq_{i,\tau} \subseteq \equiv_i$,
  - **(C2)** *if* $w \equiv_i v$ *then* $w \preceq_{i,\tau} v$ *or* $v \preceq_{i,\tau} w$;
- $V : W \longrightarrow 2^{Atm \cup Nom}$ *is a valuation function such that for all* $w, v \in W$:
  - **(C3)** $V_{Nom}(w) \neq \emptyset$,
  - **(C4)** *if* $V_{Nom}(w) \cap V_{Nom}(v) \neq \emptyset$ *then* $w = v$;
  where $V_{Nom}(w) = Nom \cap V(w)$.

$w \preceq_{i,P} v$ means that, according to agent i, v is at least as plausible as w, whereas $w \preceq_{i,D} v$ means that, according to agent i, v is at least as desirable as w. Finally, $w \equiv_i v$ means that w and v are indistinguishable for agent i. For every $w \in W$, $\equiv_i(w)$ is also called agent i's information set at state w. According to Constraint C1, an agent can only compare the plausibility (resp. desirability) of two states in her information set. According to Constraint C2, the plausibility (resp. desirability) of two states in an agent's information set are always comparable. Constraints C3 and C4 capture the two basic properties of nominals: every state is associated with at least one nominal and there are no different states associated with the same nominal.

We introduce the following modal language $\mathcal{L}_{DLCA}(Atm, Nom, Agt)$, or simply $\mathcal{L}_{DLCA}$, for the Dynamic Logic of Cognitive Attitudes DLCA:

$$\pi ::= \equiv_i | \preceq_{i,P} | \preceq_{i,D} | \preceq_{i,P}^{\sim} | \preceq_{i,D}^{\sim} | \pi;\pi' | \pi \cup \pi' | \pi \cap \pi' | -\pi | \varphi?$$
$$\varphi ::= p \mid x \mid \neg\varphi \mid \varphi \wedge \varphi' \mid [\pi]\varphi$$

where p ranges over Atm, x ranges over Nom and i ranges over Agt. The other Boolean constructions $\top$, $\bot$, $\vee$, $\rightarrow$ and $\leftrightarrow$ are defined from p, $\neg$ and $\wedge$ in the standard way.

Elements π are called *cognitive programs* or, more shortly, *programs*. The set of all programs is denoted by $\mathcal{P}(Atm, Nom, Agt)$, or simply, $\mathcal{P}$.

Cognitive programs correspond to the basic constructions of Propositional Dynamic Logic (PDL) [16]: atomic programs of type $\equiv_i$, $\preceq_{i,P}$, $\preceq_{i,D}$, $\preceq_{i,P}^{\sim}$ and $\preceq_{i,D}^{\sim}$, sequential composition (;), non-deterministic choice ($\cup$), intersection ($\cap$), converse ($^-$) and test (?). A given cognitive program π corresponds to a specific configuration of the agents' cognitive states including their epistemic states and their motivational states.

The formula $[\pi]\varphi$ has to be read "φ is true, according to the cognitive program π". As usual, we define $\langle\pi\rangle$ to be the dual operator of $[\pi]$, that is, $\langle\pi\rangle\varphi =_{def} \neg[\pi]\neg\varphi$.

The atomic program $\equiv_i$ represents the standard S5, partition-based and fully introspective notion of knowledge [2,14]. $[\equiv_i]\varphi$ has to be read "φ is true according to what agent i knows" or more simply "agent i knows that φ is true", which just means that "φ is true in all worlds that agent i envisages".

The atomic programs $\preceq_{i,P}$ and $\preceq_{i,D}$ capture, respectively, agent i's plausibility ordering and agent i's desirability ordering over facts. In particular, $[\preceq_{i,P}]\varphi$ has to be read "φ is true at all states that, according to agent i, are at least as plausible as the current one", while $[\preceq_{i,D}]\varphi$ has to be read "φ is true at all states that, according to agent i, are at least as desirable as the current one". The atomic programs $\preceq_{i,P}^{\sim}$ and $\preceq_{i,D}^{\sim}$ are the complements of the atomic programs $\preceq_{i,P}$ and $\preceq_{i,D}$, respectively. In particular, $[\preceq_{i,P}^{\sim}]\varphi$ has to be read "φ is true at all states that, according to agent i, are *not* at least as plausible as the current one", while $[\preceq_{i,D}^{\sim}]\varphi$ has to be read "φ is true at all states that, according to agent i, are *not* at least as desirable as the current one". The program constructs ;, $\cup$, $\cap$, $-$ and ? are used to define complex cognitive programs from the atomic cognitive programs. For example, the formula $[\preceq_{i,P} \cup \preceq_{i,D}]\varphi$ has to be read "φ is true at all states that, according to agent i, are either at least as plausible *or* at least as desirable as the current one", whereas the formula $[\preceq_{i,P} \cap \preceq_{i,D}]\varphi$ has to be read "φ is true at all states that, according to agent i, are at least as plausible *and* at least as desirable as the current one".

The following definition provides truth conditions for formulas in $\mathcal{L}_{DLCA}$:

Definition 2 (Truth conditions). *Let* $M = (W, (\preceq_{i,P})_{i \in Agt}, (\preceq_{i,D})_{i \in Agt}, (\equiv_i)_{i \in Agt}, V)$ *be a MCM and let* $w \in W$. *Then:*

$$M, w \models p \Longleftrightarrow p \in V(w)$$
$$M, w \models x \Longleftrightarrow x \in V(w)$$
$$M, w \models \neg\varphi \Longleftrightarrow M, w \not\models \varphi$$
$$M, w \models \varphi \wedge \psi \Longleftrightarrow M, w \models \varphi \text{ and } M, w \models \psi$$
$$M, w \models [\pi]\varphi \Longleftrightarrow \forall v \in W : \text{ if } wR_\pi v \text{ then } M, v \models \varphi$$

where the binary relation R_π *on* W *is inductively defined as follows, with* $\tau \in \{P, D\}$:

$$wR_{\equiv_i}v \text{ iff } w \equiv_i v$$
$$wR_{\preceq_{i,\tau}}v \text{ iff } w \preceq_{i,\tau} v$$
$$wR_{\preceq^\sim_{i,\tau}}v \text{ iff } w \equiv_i v \text{ and } w \not\preceq_{i,\tau} v$$
$$wR_{\pi;\pi'}v \text{ iff } \exists u \in W : wR_\pi u \text{ and } uR_{\pi'}v$$
$$wR_{\pi \cup \pi'}v \text{ iff } wR_\pi v \text{ or } wR_{\pi'}v$$
$$wR_{\pi \cap \pi'}v \text{ iff } wR_\pi v \text{ and } wR_{\pi'}v$$
$$wR_{-\pi}v \text{ iff } vR_\pi w$$
$$wR_{\varphi?}v \text{ iff } w = v \text{ and } M, w \models \varphi$$

For notational convenience, we use $wR_\pi v$ and $(w, v) \in R_\pi$ as interchangeable notations.

We can build a variety of cognitive programs capturing different types of plausibility and desirability relations between possible worlds. For instance, for every $\tau \in \{P, D\}$, we can define:

$$\succeq_{i,\tau} =_{def} - \preceq_{i,\tau}$$
$$\succ_{i,\tau} =_{def} \succeq_{i,\tau} \cap \preceq^\sim_{i,\tau}$$
$$\succeq^\sim_{i,\tau} =_{def} - \preceq^\sim_{i,\tau}$$
$$\prec_{i,\tau} =_{def} \preceq_{i,\tau} \cap \succeq^\sim_{i,\tau}$$
$$\approx_{i,\tau} =_{def} \preceq_{i,\tau} \cap \succeq_{i,\tau}$$

The five definitions denote respectively "at most as plausible (resp. desirable) as", "less plausible (resp. desirable) than", "not at most as plausible (resp. desirable) as", "more plausible (resp. desirable) than" and "equally plausible (resp. desirable) as".

For every formula φ in $\mathcal{L}_{DLCA}$ we say that φ is valid if and only if for every multi-agent cognitive model M and world w in M, we have $M, w \models \varphi$. Conversely, we say that φ is satisfiable if $\neg\varphi$ is not valid.

For a given multi-agent cognitive model $M = (W, (\preceq_{i,P})_{i \in Agt}, (\preceq_{i,D})_{i \in Agt}, (\equiv_i)_{i \in Agt}, N, V)$, we define $\|\varphi\|_M = \{v \in W : M, v \models \varphi\}$ to be the truth set of φ in M. Moreover, for every $w \in W$ and for every $i \in Agt$, we define $\|\varphi\|_{i,w,M} = \{v \in W : M, v \models \varphi \text{ and } w \equiv_i v\}$ to be the truth set of φ from i's point of view at state w in M.

730   E. Lorini

3 Formalization of Cognitive Attitudes

In this section, we show how the logic DLCA can be used to model the variety
of cognitive attitudes of agents that we have briefly discussed in Sect. 1.

3.1 Epistemic Attitudes

We start with the family of epistemic attitudes by defining a standard notion of
belief. We say that an agent believes that φ if and only if φ is true at all states
that the agent considers maximally plausible.

Definition 3 (Belief). *Let* $M = (W, (\preceq_{i,P})_{i \in Agt}, (\preceq_{i,D})_{i \in Agt}, (\equiv_i)_{i \in Agt}, V)$ *be
a MCM and let* $w \in W$. *We say that agent* i *believes that* φ *at* w, *denoted by*
$M, w \models \mathsf{B}_i\varphi$, *if and only if* $Best_{i,P}(w) \subseteq \|\varphi\|_M$ *where* $Best_{i,P}(w) = \{v \in W :
w \equiv_i v \text{ and } \forall u \in W, \text{ if } w \equiv_i u \text{ then } u \preceq_{i,P} v\}$.

As the following proposition highlights, the previous notion of belief is expressible
in the logic DLCA by means of the cognitive program $\equiv_i; [\prec_{i,P}]\bot?$.

Proposition 1. *Let* $M = (W, (\preceq_{i,P})_{i \in Agt}, (\preceq_{i,D})_{i \in Agt}, (\equiv_i)_{i \in Agt}, V)$ *be a MCM
and let* $w \in W$. *Then, we have*

$$M, w \models \mathsf{B}_i\varphi \text{ iff } M, w \models \big[\equiv_i; [\prec_{i,P}]\bot? \big]\varphi.$$

It is worth noting that the set $Best_{i,P}(w)$ in Definition 3 might be empty,
since it is not necessarily the case that the relation $\preceq_{i,P}$ is conversely well-
founded.[1] As a consequence, the belief operator B_i does not necessarily satisfy
Axiom D, i.e., the formula $\mathsf{B}_i\varphi \wedge \mathsf{B}_i\neg\varphi$ is satisfiable in the logic DLCA. More
details about these aspects will be given at the end of Sect. 4.

In the literature on epistemic logic [3], mere belief of Definition 3 is usually distinguished from strong belief. Specifically, we say that an agent strongly
believes that φ if and only if, according to agent i, all φ-worlds are strictly more
plausible than all $\neg\varphi$-worlds.

Definition 4 (Strong belief). *Let* $M = (W, (\preceq_{i,P})_{i \in Agt}, (\preceq_{i,D})_{i \in Agt},
(\equiv_i)_{i \in Agt}, V)$ *be a MCM and let* $w \in W$. *We say that agent* i *strongly believes
that* φ *at* w, *denoted by* $M, w \models \mathsf{SB}_i\varphi$, *if and only if* $\forall v \in \|\varphi\|_{i,w,M}$ *and* $\forall u \in
\|\neg\varphi\|_{i,w,M} : u \prec_{i,P} v$.

As the following proposition highlights, the previous notion of strong belief
is expressible in the logic DLCA by means of the cognitive program $\equiv_i; \varphi?; \preceq_{i,P}$.

Proposition 2. *Let* $M = (W, (\preceq_{i,P})_{i \in Agt}, (\preceq_{i,D})_{i \in Agt}, (\equiv_i)_{i \in Agt}, V)$ *be a MCM
and let* $w \in W$. *Then, we have*

$$M, w \models \mathsf{SB}_i\varphi \text{ iff } M, w \models \big[\equiv_i; \varphi?; \preceq_{i,P} \big]\varphi.$$

---

[1] This means that there could be a world v such that $w \equiv_i v$ and there is a $\preceq_{i,P}$-infinite
ascending chain from v.

Strong belief that φ implies belief that φ, if the agent envisages at least one state in which φ is true. This property is expressed by the following validity:

$$\models (\mathsf{SB}_i\varphi \wedge \langle\equiv_i\rangle\varphi) \to \mathsf{B}_i\varphi \tag{1}$$

Conditional belief is another notion which has been studied by epistemic logicians given its important role in belief dynamics [5]. We say that an agent believes that φ conditional on ψ, or she would believe that φ if she learnt that ψ, if and only if, according to agent i, all most plausible ψ-worlds are also φ-worlds.

Definition 5 (Conditional belief). *Let* $M = (W, (\preceq_{i,P})_{i\in Agt}, (\preceq_{i,D})_{i\in Agt}, (\equiv_i)_{i\in Agt}, V)$ *be a MCM and let* $w \in W$. *We say that agent* i *would believe that* φ *if she learnt that* ψ *at* w, *denoted by* $M, w \models \mathsf{B}_i(\psi, \varphi)$, *if and only if* $Best_{i,P}(\psi, w) \subseteq \|\varphi\|_M$, *where* $Best_{i,P}(\psi, w) = \{v \in \|\psi\|_{i,w,M} : \forall u \in \|\psi\|_{i,w,M}, u \preceq_{i,P} v\}$.

Note that $Best_{i,P}(\top, w) = Best_{i,P}(w)$.

As for belief and strong belief, we have a specific cognitive program $\equiv_i; (\psi \wedge [\prec_{i,P}]\neg\psi)$? corresponding to the belief that φ conditional on ψ, so that the latter can be represented in the language of the logic DLCA.

Proposition 3. *Let* $M = (W, (\preceq_{i,P})_{i\in Agt}, (\preceq_{i,D})_{i\in Agt}, (\equiv_i)_{i\in Agt}, V)$ *be a MCM and let* $w \in W$. *Then, we have*

$$M, w \models \mathsf{B}_i(\psi, \varphi) \text{ iff } M, w \models \lceil \equiv_i; (\psi \wedge [\prec_{i,P}]\neg\psi)?\rceil\varphi.$$

3.2 Motivational Attitudes

The first kind of motivational attitude we consider is desire. Following [13], we say that an agent desires that φ if and only if all states that the agent envisages at which φ is true is true are not minimally desirable for the agent. In other words, desiring that φ consists in having some degree of attraction for all situations in which φ is true.

Definition 6 (Desire). *Let* $M = (W, (\preceq_{i,P})_{i\in Agt}, (\preceq_{i,D})_{i\in Agt}, (\equiv_i)_{i\in Agt}, V)$ *be a MCM and let* $w \in W$. *We say that agent* i *desires that* φ *at* w, *denoted by* $M, w \models \mathsf{D}_i\varphi$, *if and only if* $Worst_{i,D}(w) \cap \|\varphi\|_M = \emptyset$, *where* $Worst_{i,D}(w) = \{v \in W : w \equiv_i v \text{ and } \forall u \in W, \text{ if } w \equiv_i u \text{ then } v \preceq_{i,D} u\}$.

As the following proposition highlights, the previous notion of desire is characterized by the cognitive program $\equiv_i; [\succ_{i,D}]\bot$?.

Proposition 4. *Let* $M = (W, (\preceq_{i,P})_{i\in Agt}, (\preceq_{i,D})_{i\in Agt}, (\equiv_i)_{i\in Agt}, V)$ *be a MCM and let* $w \in W$. *Then, we have*

$$M, w \models \mathsf{D}_i\varphi \text{ iff } M, w \models \lceil \equiv_i; [\succ_{i,D}]\bot?\rceil\neg\varphi.$$

Similarly to the set $Best_{i,P}(w)$ in Definition 3, the set $Worst_{i,D}(w)$ in Definition 6 might be empty, since it is not necessarily the case that the relation $\preceq_{i,D}$ is well-founded.[2] As a consequence, desires are not necessarily consistent, i.e., the formula $D_i\varphi \wedge D_i\neg\varphi$ is satisfiable in the logic DLCA. As emphasized by [13], this notion of desire satisfies the following property:

$$\models D_i\varphi \rightarrow D_i(\varphi \wedge \psi) \tag{2}$$

Indeed, if an agent has some degree of attraction for all situations in which φ is true then, clearly, it should have some degree of attraction for all situations in which $\varphi \wedge \psi$ is true, since all $\varphi \wedge \psi$-situations are also φ-situations. It is a property that this notion of desire shares with the *open reading* of the concept of permission studied in the area of deontic logic (see, e.g., [1,20]).[3]

One way of blocking this inference is by strengthening the notion of desire. We say that an agent strongly desires that φ if and only if, according to agent i, all φ-worlds are strictly more desirable than all $\neg\varphi$-worlds.

Definition 7 (Strong desire). *Let* $M = (W, (\preceq_{i,P})_{i \in Agt}, (\preceq_{i,D})_{i \in Agt}, (\equiv_i)_{i \in Agt}, V)$ *be a MCM and let* $w \in W$. *We say that agent* i *strongly desires that* φ *at* w, *denoted by* $M, w \models SD_i\varphi$, *if and only if* $\forall v \in ||\varphi||_{i,w,M}$ *and* $\forall u \in ||\neg\varphi||_{i,w,M} : u \prec_{i,D} v$.

As for desire, there exists a cognitive program which characterizes strong desire, namely, the program $\equiv_i; \varphi?; \preceq_{i,D}$.

Proposition 5. *Let* $M = (W, (\preceq_{i,P})_{i \in Agt}, (\preceq_{i,D})_{i \in Agt}, (\equiv_i)_{i \in Agt}, V)$ *be a MCM and let* $w \in W$. *Then, we have*

$$M, w \models SD_i\varphi \text{ iff } M, w \models [\ \equiv_i; \varphi?; \preceq_{i,D}\ ]\varphi.$$

We have that strong desire implies desire:

$$\models SD_i\varphi \rightarrow D_i\varphi \tag{3}$$

Differently from desiring, it is not necessarily the case that strongly desiring that φ implies strongly desiring that $\varphi \wedge \psi$, i.e., the formula $SD_i\varphi \wedge \neg SD_i(\varphi \wedge \psi)$ is satisfiable in the logic DLCA. Indeed, strongly desiring that φ is compatible with envisaging a situation in which $\varphi \wedge \psi$ holds and another situation in which $\varphi \wedge \neg\psi$ holds such that the first situation is less desirable than the second one.

---

[2] This means that there could be a world v such that $w \equiv_i v$ and there is a $\preceq_{i,D}$-infinite descending chain from v.

[3] According to deontic logicians, there are at least two candidate readings of the statement "φ is permitted": (i) every instance of φ is OK according to the normative regulation, and (ii) at least one instance of φ (but possibly not all) is OK according to the normative regulation. The former is the so-called *open reading* of permission.

3.3   From comparative desirability to choice

We consider two views about comparative statements between formulas of the form "the state of affairs φ is for agent i at least as desirable as the state of affairs ψ". According to the optimistic view, when assessing whether φ is at least as desirable as ψ, an agent focuses on the best φ-situations in comparison with the best ψ-situations. Specifically, an "optimistic" agent i considers φ at least as desirable as ψ if and only if, for every ψ-situation envisaged by i there exists a φ-situation envisaged by i such that the latter is at least as desirable as the former. According to the pessimistic view, she focuses on the worst φ-situations in comparison with the worst ψ-situations. Specifically, a "pessimistic" agent i considers φ at least as desirable as ψ if and only if, for every φ-situation envisaged by i there exists a ψ-situation envisaged by i such that the former is at least as desirable as the latter.

Let us first define comparative desirability according to the optimistic view.

Definition 8 (Comparative desirability: optimistic view). *Let* $M = (W, (\preceq_{i,P})_{i \in Agt}, (\preceq_{i,D})_{i \in Agt}, (\equiv_i)_{i \in Agt}, V)$ *be a MCM and let* $w \in W$. *We say that, according to agent* i's *optimistic assessment,* φ *is at least as desirable as* ψ *at* w, *denoted by* $M, w \models \mathsf{D}_i^{Opt}(\psi \preceq \varphi)$, *if and only if* $\forall u \in ||\psi||_{i,w,M}, \exists v \in ||\varphi||_{i,w,M} : u \preceq_{i,D} v$.

As the following proposition highlights, it is expressible in the language $\mathcal{L}_{\text{DLCA}}$.

Proposition 6. *Let* $M = (W, (\preceq_{i,P})_{i \in Agt}, (\preceq_{i,D})_{i \in Agt}, (\equiv_i)_{i \in Agt}, V)$ *be a MCM and let* $w \in W$. *Then, we have*

$$M, w \models \mathsf{D}_i^{Opt}(\psi \preceq \varphi) \text{ iff } M, w \models [\equiv_i; \psi?]\langle \preceq_{i,D} \rangle \varphi.$$

The following abbreviation defines *strict* comparative desirability according to the optimistic view:

$$\mathsf{D}_i^{Opt}(\psi \prec \varphi) =_{def} \mathsf{D}_i^{Opt}(\psi \preceq \varphi) \wedge \neg \mathsf{D}_i^{Opt}(\varphi \preceq \psi)$$

$\mathsf{D}_i^{Opt}(\psi \prec \varphi)$ has to be read "according to i's optimistic assessment, φ is more desirable than ψ".

Let us now define comparative desirability according to the pessimistic view.

Definition 9 (Comparative desirability: pessimistic view). *Let* $M = (W, (\preceq_{i,P})_{i \in Agt}, (\preceq_{i,D})_{i \in Agt}, (\equiv_i)_{i \in Agt}, V)$ *be a MCM and let* $w \in W$. *We say that, according to agent* i's *pessimistic assessment,* φ *is at least as desirable as* ψ *at* w, *denoted by* $M, w \models \mathsf{D}_i^{Pess}(\psi \preceq \varphi)$, *if and only if* $\forall v \in ||\varphi||_{i,w,M}, \exists u \in ||\psi||_{i,w,M} : u \preceq_{i,D} v$.

As for the optimistic view, the pessimistic view is also expressible in the language $\mathcal{L}_{\text{DLCA}}$.

Proposition 7. *Let* $M = (W, (\preceq_{i,P})_{i \in Agt}, (\preceq_{i,D})_{i \in Agt}, (\equiv_i)_{i \in Agt}, V)$ *be a MCM and let* $w \in W$. *Then, we have*

$$M, w \models \mathsf{D}_i^{Pess}(\psi \preceq \varphi) \text{ iff } M, w \models [\equiv_i; \varphi?]\langle \succeq_{i,D} \rangle \psi.$$

The following abbreviation defines *strict* comparative desirability according to the pessimistic view:

$$\mathsf{D}_i^{Pess}(\psi \prec \varphi) =_{def} \mathsf{D}_i^{Pess}(\psi \preceq \varphi) \wedge \neg \mathsf{D}_i^{Pess}(\varphi \preceq \psi)$$

$\mathsf{D}_i^{Pess}(\psi \prec \varphi)$ has to be read "according to i's pessimistic assessment, φ is more desirable than ψ".

The previous notion of (optimistic and pessimistic) comparative desirability does not depend on what the agent believes. This means that, in order to assess whether φ is at least as desirable as ψ, an agent also takes into account worlds that are implausible (or, more generally, not maximally plausible). *Realistic* comparative desirability requires that an agent compares two formulas φ and ψ only with respect to the set of most plausible states. This idea has been discussed in the area of qualitative decision theory by different authors [7–9].

The following definition introduces *realistic* comparative desirability according to the optimistic view.

Definition 10 (Realistic comparative desirability: optimistic view). *Let* $M = (W, (\preceq_{i,P})_{i \in Agt}, (\preceq_{i,D})_{i \in Agt}, (\equiv_i)_{i \in Agt}, V)$ *be a MCM and let* $w \in W$. *We say that, according to agent* i*'s optimistic assessment,* φ *is realistically at least as desirable as* ψ *at* w, *denoted by* $M, w \models \mathsf{RD}_i^{Opt}(\psi \preceq \varphi)$, *if and only if* $\forall u \in Best_{i,P}(w) \cap ||\psi||_{i,w,M}, \exists v \in Best_{i,P}(w) \cap ||\varphi||_{i,w,M} : u \preceq_{i,D} v$.

The idea is that an "optimistic" agent i considers φ *realistically* at least as desirable as ψ if and only if, for every ψ-situation in agent i's belief set there exists a φ-situation in agent i's belief set such that the latter is at least as desirable as the former.

The previous notion as well is expressible in the language $\mathcal{L}_{\mathrm{DLCA}}$.

Proposition 8. *Let* $M = (W, (\preceq_{i,P})_{i \in Agt}, (\preceq_{i,D})_{i \in Agt}, (\equiv_i)_{i \in Agt}, V)$ *be a MCM and let* $w \in W$. *Then, we have*

$$M, w \models \mathsf{RD}_i^{Opt}(\psi \preceq \varphi) \text{ iff } M, w \models [\equiv_i; [\prec_{i,P}]\bot?; \psi?]\langle \preceq_{i,D} \cap (\equiv_i; [\prec_{i,P}]\bot?)\rangle \varphi.$$

We define:

$$\mathsf{RD}_i^{Opt}(\psi \prec \varphi) =_{def} \mathsf{RD}_i^{Opt}(\psi \preceq \varphi) \wedge \neg \mathsf{RD}_i^{Opt}(\varphi \preceq \psi)$$

$\mathsf{RD}_i^{Opt}(\psi \prec \varphi)$ has to be read "according to agent i's optimistic assessment, φ is realistically more desirable than ψ".

The following definition introduces *realistic* comparative desirability according to the pessimistic view.

Definition 11 (Realistic comparative desirability: pessimistic view).
Let $M = (W, (\preceq_{i,P})_{i \in Agt}, (\preceq_{i,D})_{i \in Agt}, (\equiv_i)_{i \in Agt}, V)$ be a MCM and let $w \in W$. We say that, according to agent i's pessimistic assessment, φ is realistically at least as desirable as ψ at w, denoted by $M, w \models \mathsf{RD}_i^{Pess}(\psi \preceq \varphi)$, if and only if $\forall v \in Best_{i,P}(w) \cap ||\varphi||_{i,w,M}, \exists u \in Best_{i,P}(w) \cap ||\psi||_{i,w,M} : u \preceq_{i,D} v.$

The idea is that a "pessimistic" agent i considers φ *realistically* at least as desirable as ψ if and only if, for every φ-situation in agent i's belief set there exists a ψ-situation in agent i's belief set such that the former is at least as desirable as the latter.

It is also expressible in the language $\mathcal{L}_{\mathrm{DLCA}}$.

Proposition 9. *Let $M = (W, (\preceq_{i,P})_{i \in Agt}, (\preceq_{i,D})_{i \in Agt}, (\equiv_i)_{i \in Ayt}, V)$ be a MCM and let $w \in W$. Then, we have*

$$M, w \models \mathsf{RD}_i^{Pess}(\psi \preceq \varphi) \text{ iff } M, w \models [\equiv_i; [\prec_{i,P}]\bot?; \varphi?]\langle \succeq_{i,D} \cap(\equiv_i; [\prec_{i,P}]\bot?)\rangle\psi.$$

We define:

$$\mathsf{RD}_i^{Pess}(\psi \prec \varphi) =_{def} \mathsf{RD}_i^{Pess}(\psi \preceq \varphi) \wedge \neg \mathsf{RD}_i^{Pess}(\varphi \preceq \psi)$$

$\mathsf{RD}_i^{Pess}(\psi \prec \varphi)$ has to be read "according to agent i's pessimistic assessment, φ is realistically more desirable than ψ".

We conclude this section by defining two notions of choice: agent i's optimistic choice that φ, denoted by $\mathsf{C}_i^{Opt}\varphi$, and agent i's pessimistic choice that φ, denoted by $\mathsf{C}_i^{Pess}\varphi$.

$$\mathsf{C}_i^{Opt}\varphi =_{def} \mathsf{RD}_i^{Opt}(\neg\varphi \prec \varphi)$$
$$\mathsf{C}_i^{Pess}\varphi =_{def} \mathsf{RD}_i^{Pess}(\neg\varphi \prec \varphi)$$

According to these definitions, an optimistic (resp. pessimistic) agent should choose φ if and only if, according to her optimistic (resp. pessimistic) assessment, φ is realistically more desirable than $\neg\varphi$.

4 Axiomatization

In this section, we provide a sound and complete axiomatization for the logic DLCA. The first step consists in precisely defining this logic.

Definition 12. *We define* DLCA *to be the extension of classical propositional logic given by the following axioms and rules with* $\tau \in \{P, D\}$:

$$([\pi]\varphi \wedge [\pi](\varphi \to \psi)) \to [\pi]\psi \tag{$\mathbf{K}_\pi$}$$

$$[\equiv_i]\varphi \to \varphi \tag{$\mathbf{T}_{\equiv_i}$}$$

$$[\equiv_i]\varphi \to [\equiv_i][\equiv_i]\varphi \tag{$\mathbf{4}_{\equiv_i}$}$$

$$\neg[\equiv_i]\varphi \to [\equiv_i]\neg[\equiv_i]\varphi \tag{$\mathbf{5}_{\equiv_i}$}$$

$$[\preceq_{i,\tau}]\varphi \to \varphi \tag{$\mathbf{T}_{\preceq_{i,\tau}}$}$$

$$[\preceq_{i,\tau}]\varphi \to [\preceq_{i,\tau}][\preceq_{i,\tau}]\varphi \tag{$\mathbf{4}_{\preceq_{i,\tau}}$}$$

$$[\equiv_i]\varphi \to [\preceq_{i,\tau}]\varphi \tag{$\mathbf{Int}_{\preceq_{i,\tau},\equiv_i}$}$$

$$(\langle\equiv_i\rangle\varphi \wedge \langle\equiv_i\rangle\psi) \to (\langle\equiv_i\rangle(\varphi \wedge \langle\preceq_{i,\tau}\rangle\psi) \vee \langle\equiv_i\rangle(\psi \wedge \langle\preceq_{i,\tau}\rangle\varphi)) \tag{$\mathbf{Conn}_{\preceq_{i,\tau},\equiv_i}$}$$

$$[\pi;\pi']\varphi \leftrightarrow [\pi][\pi']\varphi \tag{$\mathbf{Red}_;$}$$

$$[\pi \cup \pi']\varphi \leftrightarrow ([\pi]\varphi \wedge [\pi']\varphi) \tag{$\mathbf{Red}_\cup$}$$

$$([\pi]\varphi \wedge [\pi']\psi) \to [\pi \cap \pi'](\varphi \wedge \psi) \tag{$\mathbf{Add1}_\cap$}$$

$$(\langle\pi\rangle x \wedge \langle\pi'\rangle x) \to \langle\pi \cap \pi'\rangle x \tag{$\mathbf{Add2}_\cap$}$$

$$\varphi \to [\pi]\langle-\pi\rangle\varphi \tag{$\mathbf{Conv1}_-$}$$

$$\varphi \to [-\pi]\langle\pi\rangle\varphi \tag{$\mathbf{Conv2}_-$}$$

$$([\preceq_{i,\tau}]\varphi \wedge [\preceq^\sim_{i,\tau}]\varphi) \leftrightarrow [\equiv_i]\varphi \tag{$\mathbf{Comp1}_\sim$}$$

$$\langle\preceq_{i,\tau}\rangle x \to [\preceq^\sim_{i,\tau}]\neg x \tag{$\mathbf{Comp2}_\sim$}$$

$$[?\varphi]\psi \to (\varphi \to \psi) \tag{$\mathbf{Red}_?$}$$

$$\langle\pi\rangle(x \wedge \varphi) \to [\pi'](x \to \varphi) \tag{$\mathbf{Most}_x$}$$

$$\frac{\varphi}{[\pi]\varphi} \tag{$\mathbf{Nec}_\pi$}$$

$$\frac{[\pi]\neg x \ for \ all \ x \in Num}{[\pi]\bot} \tag{$\mathbf{Cov}$}$$

For every $\varphi \in \mathcal{L}_{\mathrm{DLCA}}$, we write $\vdash \varphi$ to denote the fact that φ is a theorem of DLCA, i.e., there exists an at most countably infinite sequence $\psi_0, \psi_1, \ldots$ such that $\psi_0 = \varphi$ and for all $k \geq 0$, ψ_k is an instance of some axiom or ψ_k can be obtained from some later members of the sequence by an application of some inference rule.

The rest of this section is devoted to prove that the logic DLCA is sound and complete for the class of multi-agent cognitive models.

Soundness, namely checking that the axioms are valid and the rules of inferences preserve validity, is a routine exercise. Notice that the admissibility of the rule of inference **Cov** is guaranteed by the fact that the set of nominals *Nom* is infinite.

As for completeness, the proof is organized in several steps. We use techniques from dynamic logic and modal logic with names [15, 24].

In the rest of this section, we denote sets of formulas from $\mathcal{L}_{DLCA}$ by $\Sigma, \Sigma', \ldots$. Let $\varphi \in \mathcal{L}_{DLCA}$ and $\Sigma \subseteq \mathcal{L}_{DLCA}$, we define:

$$\Sigma + \varphi = \{\psi \in \mathcal{L}_{DLCA} : \varphi \to \psi \in \Sigma\}.$$

Let us start by defining the concepts of theory and maximal consistent theory.

Definition 13. *A set of formulas Σ is said to be a theory if it contains all theorems of DLCA and is closed under modus ponens and rule **Cov**. It is said to be a consistent theory if it is a theory and $\perp \notin \Sigma$. It is said to be a maximal consistent theory (MCT) if it is a consistent theory and, for each consistent theory Σ', we have that if $\Sigma \subseteq \Sigma'$ then $\Sigma = \Sigma'$.*

We have the following property for theories.

Proposition 10. *Let Σ be a theory and let $\varphi \in \mathcal{L}_{DLCA}$. Then, $\Sigma + \varphi$ is a theory. Moreover, if Σ is consistent then either $\Sigma + \varphi$ is consistent or $\Sigma + \neg\varphi$ is consistent.*

The following proposition highlights some standard properties of MCTs.

Proposition 11. *Let Σ be a MCT. Then, for all $\varphi, \psi \in \mathcal{L}_{DLCA}$:*

- $\varphi \in \Sigma$ *or* $\neg\varphi \in \Sigma$,
- $\varphi \vee \psi \in \Sigma$ *iff* $\varphi \in \Sigma$ *or* $\psi \in \Sigma$.

The following variant of the Lindenbaum's lemma is proved in the same way as [24, Lemma 4.15].

Lemma 1. *Let Σ be a consistent theory and let $\varphi \notin \Sigma$. Then, there exists a MCT Σ^+ such that $\Sigma \subseteq \Sigma^+$ and $\varphi \notin \Sigma^+$.*

The following lemma highlights a fundamental properties of MCTs.

Lemma 2. *Let Σ be a MCT. Then, there exists $x \in Num$ such $x \in \Sigma$.*

Let us now define the canonical model for our logic.

Definition 14. *The canonical model is the tuple $M^c = (W^c, (\preceq_{i,P}^c)_{i \in Agt}, (\preceq_{i,D}^c)_{i \in Agt}, (\equiv_i^c)_{i \in Agt}, V^c)$ such that:*

- W^c *is the set of all MCTs,*
- *for all $i \in Agt$, for all $\tau \in \{P, D\}$, for all $w, v \in W^c$, $w \preceq_{i,\tau}^c v$ iff, for all $\varphi \in \mathcal{L}_{DLCA}$, if $[\preceq_{i,\tau}]\varphi \in w$ then $\varphi \in v$,*
- *for all $i \in Agt$, for all $w, v \in W^c$, $w \equiv_i^c v$ iff, for all $\varphi \in \mathcal{L}_{DLCA}$, if $[\equiv_i]\varphi \in w$ then $\varphi \in v$,*
- *for all $w \in W^c$, $V^c(w) = (Atm \cup Nom) \cap w$.*

Let us now define the canonical relations for the complex programs π.

Definition 15. *Let* $M^c = (W^c, (\preceq_{i,P}^c)_{i \in Agt}, (\preceq_{i,D}^c)_{i \in Agt}, (\equiv_i^c)_{i \in Agt}, V^c)$ *be the canonical model. Then, for all* $\pi \in \mathcal{P}$ *and for all* $w, v \in W^c$:

$$wR_\pi^c v \text{ iff, for all } \varphi \in \mathcal{L}_{\text{DLCA}}, \text{ if } [\pi]\varphi \in w \text{ then } \varphi \in v.$$

The following Lemma 3 highlights one fundamental property of the canonical model.

Lemma 3. *Let* $M^c = (W^c, (\preceq_{i,P}^c)_{i \in Agt}, (\preceq_{i,D}^c)_{i \in Agt}, (\equiv_i^c)_{i \in Agt}, V^c)$ *be the canonical model. Then, for all* $\Sigma, \Sigma' \in W^c$, *for all* $\pi \in \mathcal{P}$ *and for all* $x \in Num$, *if* $x \in \Sigma, x \in \Sigma'$ *and* $\Sigma R_\pi^c \Sigma'$ *then* $\Sigma = \Sigma'$.

The next step consists in proving the following existence lemma.

Lemma 4. *Let* $M^c = (W^c, (\preceq_{i,P}^c)_{i \in Agt}, (\preceq_{i,D}^c)_{i \in Agt}, (\equiv_i^c)_{i \in Agt}, V^c)$ *be the canonical model, let* $w \in W^c$ *and let* $\langle \pi \rangle \varphi \in \mathcal{L}_{\text{DLCA}}$. *Then, if* $\langle \pi \rangle \varphi \in w$ *then there exists* $v \in W^c$ *such that* $wR_\pi^c v$ *and* $\varphi \in v$.

The following truth lemma is proved in the usual way by induction on the structure of φ thanks to Lemma 4.

Lemma 5. *Let* $M^c = (W^c, (\preceq_{i,P}^c)_{i \in Agt}, (\preceq_{i,D}^c)_{i \in Agt}, (\equiv_i^c)_{i \in Agt}, V^c)$ *be the canonical model, let* $w \in W^c$ *and let* $\varphi \in \mathcal{L}_{\text{DLCA}}$. *Then,* $M^c, w \models \varphi$ *iff* $\varphi \in w$.

The pre-final stage of the proof consists in introducing an alternative semantics for the language $\mathcal{L}_{\text{DLCA}}$ which turns out to be equivalent to the original semantics based on MCMs.

Definition 16 (Quasi multi-agent cognitive model). *A quasi multi-agent cognitive model (quasi-MCM) is a tuple* $M = (W, (\preceq_{i,P})_{i \in Agt}, (\preceq_{i,D})_{i \in Agt}, (\equiv_i)_{i \in Agt}, V)$ *where* $W, \preceq_{i,P}, \preceq_{i,D}, \equiv_i$ *and* V *are as in Definition 1 except that Constraint C4 is replaced by the following weaker constraint. For all* $w, v \in W$:

(C4*) *if* $V_{Nom}(w) \cap V_{Nom}(v) \neq \emptyset$ *and* $wR_\pi v$ *for some* $\pi \in \mathcal{P}$ *then* $w = v$.

By the generated submodel property, it is easy to show that the semantics in terms of MCMs and the semantics in terms of quasi-MCMs are equivalent with respect to the language $\mathcal{L}_{\text{DLCA}}$.

Proposition 12. *Let* $\varphi \in \mathcal{L}_{\text{DLCA}}$. *Then,* φ *is valid relative to the class of MCMs if and only if* φ *is valid relative to the class of quasi-MCMs.*

The following theorem highlights that the canonical model is indeed a structure of the right type.

Lemma 6. *The canonical model* M^c *is a quasi-MCM.*

Let us conclude the proof by supposing $\not\vdash \neg\varphi$. Therefore, by Lemma 1 and the fact that the set of DLCA-theorems is a consistent theory, there exists a MCT w such that $\neg\varphi \notin w$. Thus, by Proposition 11, we can find a MCT w such that $\varphi \in w$. By Lemma 5, the latter implies $M^c, w \models \varphi$ for some $w \in W^c$. Since, by Lemma 6, M^c is a quasi-MCM, it follows that φ is satisfiable relative to the class of quasi-MCMs. Therefore, by Proposition 12, φ is satisfiable relative to the class of MCMs.

We can finally state the main result of this section.

Theorem 1. *The logic* DLCA *is sound and complete for the class of multi-agent cognitive models.*

We conclude this section by discussing the properties of converse well-foundedness for the relation $\preceq_{i,P}$ and well-foundedness for the relation $\preceq_{i,D}$. As emphasized in Sect. 3, these properties are required to make agents' beliefs and desires consistent, namely, to guarantee that the formulas $\neg(\mathsf{B}_i\varphi \wedge \mathsf{B}_i\neg\varphi)$ and $\neg(\mathsf{D}_i\varphi \wedge \mathsf{D}_i\neg\varphi)$ become valid. It turns out that these properties can be easily added to our logical framework.

In particular, let us consider the class of multi-agent cognitive models whose relations $\preceq_{i,D}$ and $\preceq_{i,P}$ are, respectively, well-founded and conversely well-founded.

Furthermore, let us consider the following two axioms:

$$\langle\equiv_i\rangle\psi \rightarrow \langle\equiv_i\rangle(\psi \wedge [\prec_{i,P}]\neg\psi) \qquad\qquad (\mathbf{CWF}_{\preceq_{i,P}})$$

$$\langle\equiv_i\rangle\psi \rightarrow \langle\equiv_i\rangle(\psi \wedge [\succ_{i,D}]\neg\psi) \qquad\qquad (\mathbf{WF}_{\preceq_{i,D}})$$

Let us define DLCA^{wf} to be the extension of the logic DLCA of Definition 12 by these axioms. It is straightforward to verify that the logic DLCA^{wf} is sound for the class of multi-agent cognitive models whose relations $\preceq_{i,D}$ and $\preceq_{i,P}$ are, respectively, well-founded and conversely well-founded. We conjecture that we can easily adapt the proof of Theorem 1 to show that it is also complete.

5 Conclusion

We have presented a logical framework for modelling a rich variety of cognitive attitudes of both epistemic type and motivational type. We have provided a sound and complete axiomatization for our logic.

Directions of future research are manifold. The present paper is devoted to study the proof-theoretic aspects of the logic. In future work, we plan to investigate its computational aspects including decidability of its satisfiability problem and, at a later stage, complexity. In order to prove decidability, we expect to be able to use existing filtration techniques from modal logic. Following the literature on dynamic epistemic logic (DEL) [11], we also plan to study several dynamic extensions of our logic in order to capture a large variety of cognitive dynamics in a multi-agent setting. The latter includes belief change, desire change and choice change. We believe choice change is particularly interesting given the dependence of an agent's choices on her beliefs and desires, as illustrated in Sect. 3.3. Specifically, since an agent's choices depend on her plausibility and desirability orderings over possible worlds, if these orderings change, then the agent's choices may also change. In other words, choice change can be seen as derivative of belief change and desire change. Another research direction we plan to follow in the future is to connect the notion of choice formalized in Sect. 3.3 with a notion of action in the sense of STIT logic, the logic of "seeing to it that" by [4]. The interesting aspect of STIT is that agents' choices are explicit in its semantics and agents' actions are conceived as results of their choices.

Acknowledgments. This work was supported by the ANR project CoPains. I would like to thank Philippe Balbiani for his useful comments on its content.

A   Proofs

We provide a selection of the proofs for the results given in the paper.

A.1   Proof of Lemma 2

Proof. We prove the lemma by reductio ad absurdum. Let Σ be a MCT. Moreover, suppose that, for all $x \in Nom$, $x \notin \Sigma$. By Proposition 11, it follows that, for all $x \in Nom$, $\neg x \in \Sigma$.

By Axiom **Red?**, we have $\neg x \leftrightarrow [?\top]\neg x \in \Sigma$ for all $x \in Nom$. Thus, for all $x \in Nom$, $[?\top]\neg x \in \Sigma$. Hence, since Σ is closed under **Cov**, $[?\top]\bot \in \Sigma$. By Axiom **Red?**, the latter is equivalent to $\bot \in \Sigma$. The latter is contradiction with the fact that Σ is a MCT. $\qquad\square$

A.2   Proof of Lemma 3

Proof. Let us first prove that (i) if $x \in \Sigma$ and $\varphi \in \Sigma$ then $[\pi](x \to \varphi) \in \Sigma$. Suppose $x, \varphi \in \Sigma$. Thus, $x \land \varphi \in \Sigma$ since Σ is a MCT. Moreover, $(x \land \varphi) \to [\pi](x \to \varphi) \in \Sigma$, because of Axiom **Most$_x$**). Hence, $[\pi](x \to \varphi) \in \Sigma$.

Now let us prove by absurdum that (ii) if $x \in \Sigma, \Sigma'$ and $\Sigma R_\pi^c \Sigma'$ then $\Sigma = \Sigma'$. Suppose $x \in \Sigma, \Sigma'$, $\Sigma R_\pi^c \Sigma'$ and $\Sigma \neq \Sigma'$. The latter implies that there exists φ such that $\varphi \in \Sigma$ and $\varphi \notin \Sigma'$. By item (i) above, it follows that $[\pi](x \to \varphi) \in \Sigma$. Since $\Sigma R_\pi^c \Sigma'$, the latter implies that $x \to \varphi \in \Sigma'$. Since $x \in \Sigma'$, it follows that $\varphi \in \Sigma'$ which leads to a contradiction. $\qquad\square$

A.3   Proof of Lemma 4

Proof. Suppose w is a MCT and $\langle \pi \rangle \varphi \in w$. It follows that $[\pi]w = \{\psi : [\pi]\psi \in w\}$ is a consistent theory. Indeed, it is easy to check that $[\pi]w$ contains all theorems of DLCA, is closed under modus ponens and rule **Cov**. Let us prove that it is consistent by reductio ad absurdum. Suppose $\bot \in [\pi]w$. Thus, $[\pi]\bot \in w$. Hence,

$[\pi]\neg\varphi \in w$. Since $\langle\pi\rangle\varphi \in w$, $\bot \in w$. The latter contradicts the fact that w is a MCT. Let us distinguish two cases.

Case 1: $\varphi \in [\pi]w$. Thus, $\neg\varphi \notin [\pi]w$ since w is consistent. Thus, by Lemma 1, there exists MCT v such that $[\pi]w \subseteq v$, $\varphi \in v$ and $\neg\varphi \notin v$. By definition of R_π^c, $wR_\pi^c v$.

Case 2: $\varphi \notin [\pi]w$. By Proposition 10, $[\pi]w+\varphi$ is a theory since $[\pi]w$ is a theory. $[\pi]w+\varphi$ is consistent. Suppose it is not. Thus, $\varphi \to \bot \in [\pi]w$ and, consequently, $\neg\varphi \in [\pi]w$. Hence, $[\pi]\neg\varphi \in w$. It follows that $\bot \in w$, since $\langle\pi\rangle\varphi \in w$. But this contradicts the fact that w is a MCT. Thus, $[\pi]w + \varphi$ is a consistent theory. Moreover, $\varphi \in [\pi]w + \varphi$, $\neg\varphi \notin [\pi]w + \varphi$ and $[\pi]w \subseteq [\pi]w + \varphi$. By Lemma 1, there exists MCT v such that $[\pi]w \subseteq v$, $\varphi \in v$ and $\neg\varphi \notin v$. By definition of R_π^c, $wR_\pi^c v$. □

A.4 Proof of Lemma 6

Proof. The fact that M^c satisfies Constraints C3 and C4* follows from Lemmas 2 and 3. To prove that $\equiv_i$ is an equivalence relation that $\preceq_{i,D}^c$ and $\preceq_{i,D}^c$ are preorders and that M^c satisfies Constraints C1 and C2 is just a routine exercise. Indeed, Axioms $\mathbf{T}_{\equiv_i}$, $\mathbf{4}_{\equiv_i}$, $\mathbf{5}_{\equiv_i}$, $\mathbf{T}_{\preceq_{i,\tau}}$, $\mathbf{4}_{\preceq_{i,\tau}}$, $\mathbf{Int}_{\preceq_{i,\tau},\equiv_i}$ and $\mathbf{Conn}_{\preceq_{i,\tau},\equiv_i}$ are canonical for these semantic conditions.

To conclude, we need to prove that the following six conditions hold, for $i \in Agt$ and $\tau \in \{P, D\}$:

$$(w,v) \in R_{\preceq_{i,\tau}^\sim}^c \text{ iff } (w,v) \in R_{\equiv_i}^c \text{ and } (w,v) \notin R_{\preceq_{i,\tau}}^c$$

$$(w,v) \in R_{\pi;\pi'}^c \text{ iff } \exists u \in W^c : (w,u) \in R_\pi^c \text{ and } (u,v) \in R_{\pi'}^c$$

$$(w,v) \in R_{\pi\cup\pi'}^c \text{ iff } (w,v) \in R_\pi^c \text{ or } (w,v) \in R_{\pi'}^c$$

$$(w,v) \in R_{\pi\cap\pi'}^c \text{ iff } (w,v) \in R_\pi^c \text{ and } (w,v) \in R_{\pi'}^c$$

$$(w,v) \in R_{-\pi}^c \text{ iff } (v,w) \in R_\pi^c$$

$$wR_{\varphi?}^c v \text{ iff } w = v \text{ and } M^c, w \models \varphi$$

We only prove the second and fourth conditions which are the most difficult ones to prove.

Let us start with the proof of the second condition. The right-to-left direction is standard. We only prove the left-to-right direction. Suppose $(w,v) \in R_{\pi;\pi'}^c$. Let $[\pi]w = \{\psi : [\pi]\psi \in w\}$. Moreover, let $\langle\pi'\rangle v = \{\langle\pi'\rangle\psi : \psi \in v\}$. Finally, let $\langle\pi'\rangle\psi_1, \langle\pi'\rangle\psi_2, \ldots$ be an enumeration of the elements of $\langle\pi'\rangle v$. We define $\Sigma^1 = [\pi]w + \langle\pi'\rangle\psi_1$ and, for all $k > 1$, $\Sigma^k = \Sigma^{k-1} + \langle\pi'\rangle\psi_k$. By Proposition 10 and the fact that $[\pi]w$ is a theory, it can be shown that every Σ^k is a theory. Moreover, by induction on k, it can be shown that every Σ^k is consistent. Since $\Sigma^{k-1} \subseteq \Sigma^k$ for all $k > 1$, it follows that $\Sigma = \bigcup_{k>1} \Sigma^{k-1}$ is a consistent theory. By Lemma 1 and the definition of Σ, there exists $u \in W^c$ such that $\Sigma \subseteq u$, $(w,u) \in R_\pi^c$ and $(u,v) \in R_{\pi'}^c$.

Let us now prove the fourth condition. Suppose $(w,v) \in R_{\pi\cap\pi'}^c$. By Definition 15 and Proposition 11, it follows that, for all φ, if $\varphi \in v$ then $\langle\pi \cap \pi'\rangle\varphi \in w$.

The latter implies that for all φ, if $\varphi \in v$ then $\langle \pi \cap \pi' \rangle (\varphi \vee \bot) \in w$ since $\vdash \langle \pi \cap \pi' \rangle \varphi \rightarrow \langle \pi \cap \pi' \rangle (\varphi \vee \bot)$. By Axiom $\mathbf{K}_\pi$, it follows that, for all φ, if $\varphi \in v$ then $\langle \pi \rangle \varphi \vee \langle \pi' \rangle \bot \in w$. Thus, for all φ, if $\varphi \in v$ then $\langle \pi \rangle \varphi \in w$, since $\vdash (\langle \pi \rangle \varphi \vee \langle \pi' \rangle \bot) \rightarrow \langle \pi \rangle \varphi$. In a similar way, we can prove that, for all φ, if $\varphi \in v$ then $\langle \pi' \rangle \varphi \in w$. By Definition 15 and Proposition 11, it follows that $(w, v) \in R_\pi^c$ and $(w, v) \in R_{\pi'}^c$.

Now suppose $(w, v) \in R_\pi^c$ and $(w, v) \in R_{\pi'}^c$. Thus, by Definition 15 and Proposition 11, (i) for all φ, if $\varphi \in v$ then $\langle \pi \rangle \varphi \in w$ and $\langle \pi' \rangle \varphi \in w$. By Proposition 11 and Lemma 2, we have that (ii) there exists $x \in Num$ such that, for all φ, $\varphi \in v$ iff $x \wedge \varphi \in v$. Item (i) and item (ii) together imply that (iii) there exists $x \in Num$ such that, for all φ, if $\varphi \in v$ then $\langle \pi \rangle (x \wedge \varphi) \in w$ and $\langle \pi' \rangle (x \wedge \varphi) \in w$. We are going to prove the following theorem:

$$\vdash (\langle \pi \rangle (x \wedge \varphi) \wedge \langle \pi' \rangle (x \wedge \varphi)) \rightarrow \langle \pi \cap \pi' \rangle (x \wedge \varphi)$$

By Axiom $\mathbf{K}_\pi$, $\langle \pi \rangle (x \wedge \varphi) \wedge \langle \pi' \rangle (x \wedge \varphi)$ implies $\langle \pi \rangle x \wedge \langle \pi' \rangle x$. By Axiom $\mathbf{Add2}_\cap$, the latter implies $\langle \pi \cap \pi' \rangle x$. Moreover, by Axiom $\mathbf{Int}_{\preceq_{i,\tau},\equiv_i}$ and Axiom $\mathbf{Most}_x$), $\langle \pi \rangle (x \wedge \varphi)$ implies $[\equiv_\emptyset](x \rightarrow \varphi)$. By Axiom $\mathbf{Int}_{\preceq_{i,\tau},\equiv_i}$, the latter implies $[\pi \cap \pi'](x \rightarrow \varphi)$. By Axiom $\mathbf{K}_\pi$, $[\pi \cap \pi'](x \rightarrow \varphi)$ and $\langle \pi \cap \pi' \rangle x$ together imply $\langle \pi \cap \pi' \rangle (x \wedge \varphi)$. Thus, $\langle \pi \rangle (x \wedge \varphi) \wedge \langle \pi' \rangle (x \wedge \varphi)$ implies $\langle \pi \cap \pi' \rangle (x \wedge \varphi)$.

From previous item (iii) and the previous theorem it follows that there exists $x \in Num$ such that, for all φ, if $\varphi \in v$ then $\langle \pi \cap \pi' \rangle (x \wedge \varphi)$. The latter implies that, for all φ, if $\varphi \in v$ then $\langle \pi \cap \pi' \rangle \varphi$. The latter implies that $(w, v) \in R_{\pi \cap \pi'}^c$. $\square$

References

1. Anglberger, A.J., Gratzl, N., Roy, O.: Obligation, free choice, and the logic of weakest permissions. Rev. Symb. Log. **8**, 807–827 (2015)
2. Aumann, R.: Interactive epistemology I: knowledge. Int. J. Game Theory **28**(3), 263–300 (1999)
3. Baltag, A., Smets, S.: Talking your way into agreement: belief merge by persuasive communication. In: Proceedings of the Second Multi-Agent Logics, Languages, and Organisations Federated Workshops (MALLOW), volume 494 of CEUR Workshop Proceedings (2009)
4. Belnap, N., Perloff, M., Xu, M.: Facing the Future: Agents and Choices in Our Indeterminist World. Oxford University Press, Oxford (2001)
5. van Benthem, J.: Dynamic logic for belief revision. J. Appl. Non-Class. Log. **17**(2), 129–155 (2007)
6. van Benthem, J., Girard, P., Roy, O.: Everything else being equal: a modal logic for ceteris paribus preferences. J. Philos. Log. **38**, 83–125 (2009)
7. Boutilier, C.: Towards a logic for qualitative decision theory. In: Proceedings of International Conference on Principles of Knowledge Representation and Reasoning (KR 1994), pp. 75–86. AAAI Press (1994)
8. Brafman, R.I., Tennenholtz, M.: An axiomatic treatment of three qualitative decision criteria. J. ACM **47**(3), 452–482 (2000)
9. Brafman, R.I., Tennenholtz, M.: On the foundations of qualitative decision theory. In: Proceedings of the Thirteenth National Conference on Artificial Intelligence (AAAI 1996), pp. 1291–1296. AAAI Press (1996)

10. Cohen, P.R., Levesque, H.J.: Intention is choice with commitment. Artif. Intell. **42**, 213–261 (1990)
11. van Ditmarsch, H., van der Hoek, W., Kooi, B.: Dynamic Epistemic Logic. Synthese Library, vol. 337. Springer, Heidelberg (2007). https://doi.org/10.1007/978-1-4020-5839-4
12. Doyle, J., Thomason, R.: Background to qualitative decision theory. The AI Mag. **20**(2), 55–68 (1999)
13. Dubois, D., Lorini, E., Prade, H.: The strength of desires: a logical approach. Mind. Mach. **27**(1), 199–231 (2017)
14. Fagin, R., Halpern, J., Moses, Y., Vardi, M.: Reasoning About Knowledge. MIT Press, Cambridge (1995)
15. Gargov, G., Goranko, V.: Modal logic with names. J. Philoso. Log. **22**, 607–636 (1993)
16. Harel, D., Kozen, D., Tiuryn, J.: Dynamic Logic. MIT Press, Cambridge (2000)
17. Hintikka, J.: Knowledge and Belief: An Introduction to the Logic of the Two Notions. Cornell University Press, Ithaca (1962)
18. Humberstone, I.L.: Direction of fit. Mind **101**(401), 59–83 (1992)
19. Icard, T.F., Pacuit, E., Shoham, Y.: Joint revision of beliefs and intention. In: Proceedings of the Twelfth International Conference on Principles of Knowledge Representation and Reasoning (KR 2010), pp. 572–574. AAAI Press (2010)
20. Lewis, D.: A problem about permission. In: Saarinen, E., Hilpinen, R., Niiniluoto, I., Hintikka, M.P. (eds.) Essays in Honour of Jaakko Hintikka, vol. 124, pp. 163–175. Springer, Dordrecht (1979). https://doi.org/10.1007/978-94-009-9860-5_11
21. Liu, F.: Reasoning about Preference Dynamics. Springer, Heidelberg (2011). https://doi.org/10.1007/978-94-007-1344-4
22. Lorini, E.: Logics for games, emotions and institutions. If-CoLog J. Log. Appl. **4**(9), 3075–3113 (2017)
23. Meyer, J.J.Ch., van der Hoek, W., van Linder, B.: A logical approach to the dynamics of commitments. Artif. Intell. **113**(1–2), 1–40 (1999)
24. Passy, S., Tinchev, T.: An essay in combinatorial dynamic logic. Inf. Comput. **93**, 263–332 (1991)
25. Platts, M.: Ways of Meaning. Routledge and Kegan Paul, Abingdon (1979)
26. Searle, J.: Expression and Meaning. Cambridge University Press, Cambridge (1979)
27. Shoham, Y.: Logical theories of intention and the database perspective. J. Philos. Log. **38**(6), 633–647 (2009)
28. Von Wright, G.H.: The Logic of Preference. Edinburgh University Press, Edinburgh (1963)
29. Von Wright, G.H.: The logic of preference reconsidered. Theory Decis. **3**, 140–169 (1972)
30. Wooldridge, M.: Reasoning About Rational Agents. MIT Press, Cambridge (2000)

Computational Complexity of Core Fragments of Modal Logics T, K4, and S4

Przemysław Andrzej Wałęga[1,2(✉)]

[1] Department of Computer Science, University of Oxford, Oxford, UK
[2] Institute of Philosophy, University of Warsaw, Warsaw, Poland
p.a.walega@gmail.com

Abstract. We show that the satisfiability problem in core fragments of modal logics T, K4, and S4 in whose languages diamond modal operators are disallowed is NL-complete. Moreover, we provide deterministic procedures for satisfiability checking. We show that the above fragments correspond to certain core fragments of linear temporal logic, hence our results imply NL-completeness of the latter.

Keywords: Modal logic · Sub-propositional fragments ·
Computational complexity

1 Introduction

Modal logics are formal systems which enable us to talk about relational structures and have a wide range of applications [3]. In order to obtain modal languages of lower computational complexity a number of methods have been introduced, e.g., restricting the nesting depth of modal operators [8,11–13] or bounding the number of propositional variables [7]. In this paper we consider another, recently investigated, way of restricting syntax of a language which leads to *sub-propositional* fragments by [6,15]:

- limiting formulas to the *Horn*, *Krom*, or *core* forms (which are analogous as in the propositional calculus [9,10]), denoted by "*horn*", "*krom*", and "*core*", respectively, in the lower index of a fragment's symbol, and
- allowing only $\Box$ or only $\Diamond$ operators, which is denoted by "$\Box$" and "$\Diamond$", respectively, in the upper index of a fragment's symbol.

This method often results in fragments which have a good compromise between computational complexity and expressive power. Such fragments have been studied, e.g., in the case of linear temporal logic [1], temporal description logics [2], interval temporal logics [4,5], and, recently, normal modal logics **K**, **T**, **K4**, **S4**, and **S5** [6,15]. Recall that **K** is the basic modal logic which semantically corresponds to the class of relational structures with an arbitrary binary relation, whereas in **T**, **K4**, **S4**, and **S5** the relation is reflexive, transitive, a preorder (i.e., reflexive and transitive), and an equivalence, respectively. In this paper we

© Springer Nature Switzerland AG 2019
F. Calimeri et al. (Eds.): JELIA 2019, LNAI 11468, pp. 744–759, 2019.
https://doi.org/10.1007/978-3-030-19570-0_48

identify complexity of a logic with the computational complexity of the satisfiability problem of its formulas. It is well-known that the logics **K**, **T**, **K4**, and **S4** are PSPACE-complete, whereas **S5** is NP-complete [11]. A Hasse diagram for fragments of these logics together with the computational complexity results is depicted in Fig. 1, where an arrow indicates a syntactical extension of a given fragment.

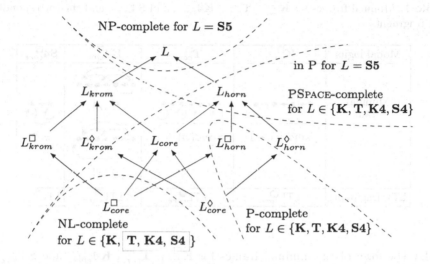

Fig. 1. Computational complexity map for sub-propositional fragments of normal modal logics, where results established in this paper are presented in a frame

In particular, it is known that $L_{horn}^{\square}$ is P-complete for $L \in \{\mathbf{K}, \mathbf{T}, \mathbf{K4}, \mathbf{S4}\}$ [6,15]. On the other hand, its fragment $L_{core}^{\square}$ is known to be NL-complete for $L = \mathbf{K}$ but its complexity for $L \in \{\mathbf{T}, \mathbf{K4}, \mathbf{S4}\}$ was not known. As stated in [15], it was only known that the problem is in P (by P-completeness of $L_{horn}^{\square}$ [6]), and NL-hard (by NL-completeness of the core fragment of classical propositional calculus [14]). The core fragment is particularly interesting since it is expressive enough to represent some basic constraints used in conceptual modelling, and hence, it has a potential for practical applications [2]. On the other hand, in most of the investigated cases (e.g., in linear temporal logic [1] and interval logics [4]) tight complexity bounds for the satisfiability problem in core fragments are usually unknown.

The main result of this paper is that $L_{core}^{\square}$ for $L \in \{\mathbf{T}, \mathbf{K4}, \mathbf{S4}\}$ is in NL, which implies NL-completeness of these fragments. In particular, we show that given an $L_{core}^{\square}$-formula φ, we can reduce the problem of checking its satisfiability in $\mathbf{S4}_{core}^{\square}$ to checking if φ is satisfiable in the *minimal frame* with 2 elements – see Table 1. In the case of $\mathbf{T}_{core}^{\square}$ the minimal frame is of size $md(\varphi) + 1$, where $md(\varphi)$ is the modal depth of φ, i.e., the maximum number of nested modal operators in φ. For $\mathbf{K4}_{core}^{\square}$ there are two types of minimal frames, both of size at most $|\varphi|$, where $|\varphi|$ is the length of φ. Next, we show that for a minimal frame of $\mathbf{T}_{core}^{\square}$, $\mathbf{K4}_{core}^{\square}$, and $\mathbf{S4}_{core}^{\square}$ we can construct the minimal model based on this frame, such that φ is satisfiable in the minimal frame if and only if it is satisfied in the the minimal model. As we show, the latter condition can be checked in NL, which implies that these fragments are in NL.

Table 1. Minimal frames for $\mathbf{K}_{core}^{\square}$, $\mathbf{T}_{core}^{\square}$, $\mathbf{K4}_{core}^{\square}$, and $\mathbf{S4}_{core}^{\square}$, and the corresponding LTL fragments

Modal logic:	$\mathbf{K}_{core}^{\square}$	$\mathbf{T}_{core}^{\square}$	$\mathbf{K4}_{core}^{\square}$	$\mathbf{S4}_{core}^{\square}$
Minimal frame:	$\bullet \to \bullet \to \bullet \to \bullet$ $\underbrace{\qquad}_{\leq md(\varphi)+1}$	$\bullet \to \bullet \to \bullet \to \bullet$ $\circlearrowleft\ \circlearrowleft\ \circlearrowleft\ \circlearrowleft$ $= md(\varphi)+1$	$\bullet \to \bullet \to \bullet \to \bullet$ $\leq |\varphi|$ $\bullet \to \bullet \to \bullet \to \bullet \circlearrowright$ $\underbrace{\qquad}_{\leq |\varphi|}$	$\bullet \to \bullet$ $\circlearrowleft\ \circlearrowleft$ $= 2$
LTL fragment:	$\mathsf{LTL}_{core}^{\bigcirc}$	$\mathsf{LTL}_{core}^{\bullet}$	$\mathsf{LTL}_{core}^{\square}$	$\mathsf{LTL}_{core}^{\blacksquare}$

By the form of the minimal frames for $\mathbf{K}_{core}^{\square}$, $\mathbf{T}_{core}^{\square}$, $\mathbf{K4}_{core}^{\square}$, and $\mathbf{S4}_{core}^{\square}$ it follows that these logics coincide with core fragments of linear temporal logic (LTL) with temporal modal operators $\bigcirc$ 'in the next time-point', $\bullet$ 'now and in the next time-point', $\square$ 'always in the future', and $\blacksquare$ 'now and always in the future', respectively. Our results imply that the above-mentioned fragments of LTL are NL-complete over time lines of arbitrary countable length. Slightly different fragments of LTL (with clauses preceded by the universal modality) have been classified according to their computational complexity over integers in [1], where it is shown that $\mathsf{LTL}_{core}^{\square}$ with clauses preceded by universal modalities is NL-complete over integers.

The paper is organized as follows. In Sect. 2 we define core fragments of normal modal logics and in Sect. 3 we recall results on minimal frames, which were established in [15]. In Sect. 4 we prove that $\mathbf{T}_{core}^{\square}$, $\mathbf{K4}_{core}^{\square}$, and $\mathbf{S4}_{core}^{\square}$ are in NL, and in Sect. 5 we construct deterministic algorithms for the satisfiability problem in these fragments. In Sect. 6 we describe implications of our results for the complexity of LTL -fragments and in Sect. 7 we conclude the paper.

2 Syntax and Semantics

We start by introducing syntax and semantics of core fragments of normal modal logics. Let formulas of the core fragment with box modal operator only (i.e., without diamonds), denoted by $\mathbf{L}_{core}^{\Box}$-formulas, be generated by the following abstract grammar:

$$\varphi := \lambda \mid \neg\lambda \mid \Box^s(\neg\lambda \vee \lambda) \mid \Box^s(\neg\lambda \vee \neg\lambda) \mid \varphi \wedge \varphi, \qquad (1)$$
$$\lambda := \top \mid p \mid \Box\lambda,$$

where for any $s \in \mathbb{N}$ ($\mathbb{N}$ is the set of all natural numbers including 0), $\Box^s\varphi$ stands for $\underbrace{\Box \ldots \Box}_{s \text{ times}}\varphi$ and $p \in \mathsf{PROP}$ for PROP a countable set of propositional variables.

A *Kripke frame* (a frame in short) is a pair $\mathfrak{F} = (W, R)$, where W is a non-empty set of *worlds* and $R \subseteq W \times W$ is an *accessibility relation*. A *model* based on a frame $\mathfrak{F}$ is a pair $\mathcal{M} = (\mathfrak{F}, V)$ (we will also write $\mathcal{M} = (W, R, V)$), where $V : \mathsf{PROP} \longrightarrow \mathcal{P}(W)$ is a *valuation* assigning a set of worlds to each propositional variable. The *satisfaction relation* $\models$ for a model $\mathcal{M} = (W, R, V)$ and a world $w \in W$ is defined inductively as follows:

$$
\begin{array}{lll}
\mathcal{M}, w \models \top & & \text{for all } w \in W; \\
\mathcal{M}, w \models p & \text{iff} & w \in V(p), \text{ for all } p \in \mathsf{PROP}; \\
\mathcal{M}, w \models \neg\varphi & \text{iff} & \mathcal{M}, w \not\models \varphi; \\
\mathcal{M}, w \models \varphi_1 \wedge \varphi_2 & \text{iff} & \mathcal{M}, w \models \varphi_1 \text{ and } \mathcal{M}, w \models \varphi_2; \\
\mathcal{M}, w \models \varphi_1 \vee \varphi_2 & \text{iff} & \mathcal{M}, w \models \varphi_1 \text{ or } \mathcal{M}, w \models \varphi_2; \\
\mathcal{M}, w \models \Box\varphi & \text{iff} & \mathcal{M}, w' \models \varphi \text{ for all } w' \text{ such that } R(w, w'),
\end{array}
$$

where φ, φ_1, and φ_2 are $\mathbf{L}_{core}^{\Box}$-formulas.

For convenience we introduce an equisatisfiable grammar for $\mathbf{L}_{core}^{\Box}$-formulas given by:

$$\varphi := \Box^s\lambda \mid \Box^s(p \rightarrow \lambda) \mid \Box^s(\lambda \rightarrow p) \mid \Box^s(p \wedge p \rightarrow \bot) \mid \varphi \wedge \varphi, \qquad (2)$$

where $s \in \mathbb{N}$, $p \in \mathsf{PROP}$, $\bot$ is an abbreviation for $\neg\top$, and $\varphi_1 \rightarrow \varphi_2$ is an abbreviation for $\neg\varphi_1 \vee \varphi_2$. We denote the set of all conjuncts in φ by $clauses(\varphi)$ and the set of all propositional variables occurring in φ by $\mathsf{PROP}(\varphi)$. The following result is obtained by a straight forward translation.

Proposition 1. *Any formula generated by (2) can be transformed in L into an equisatisfiable formula generated by (1), and vice versa.*

A formula φ is $\mathbf{T}$-*satisfiable* if it is satisfied in some model $\mathcal{M} = (W, R, V)$ in which R is reflexive. Analogously, φ is $\mathbf{K4}$-*satisfiable* if R is transitive and φ is $\mathbf{S4}$-*satisfiable* if R is transitive and reflexive.

3   Pre-linear Models

In this Section we will briefly recall results from [6] and [15] on minimal frames in $\mathbf{K}_{core}^{\Box}$, $\mathbf{K4}_{core}^{\Box}$, and $\mathbf{S4}_{core}^{\Box}$, which will be useful in further Sections. Following [6], we call a frame $\mathfrak{F} = (W, R)$ a *pre-linear* frame if W is countable (finite or infinite), i.e., $W = \{w_0, w_1, \ldots\}$ and $R = \{(w_{k-1}, w_k) \mid w_k \in W \text{ and } k \neq 0\}$ – see Fig. 2.

Moreover, for any $R \subseteq W \times W$, we denote by $R^\circlearrowright$ its reflexive closure, by $\vec{R}$ its transitive closure, and by R^* its transitive and reflexive closure. If (W, R) is a pre-linear frame, then $(W, R^\circlearrowright)$ is a *pre-linear reflexive* frame, $(W, \vec{R})$ is a strict linear order (asymmetric, transitive, and total relation) and (W, R^*) a non-strict linear order (reflexive, antisymmetric, transitive, and total relation). A model is pre-linear, reflexive pre-linear, strict linear, or non-strict linear if it is based, respectively, on a pre-linear, reflexive pre-linear, strict linear, or non-strict linear frame. As shown in [15], pre-linear models can be used to check satisfiability of an $\mathbf{L}_{core}^\square$-formula, as follows:

Theorem 2 ([15]). *The following statements hold for all $\mathbf{L}_{core}^\square$-formulas φ:*

  (i) *φ is $\mathbf{T}$-satisfiable if and only if it is satisfiable in the root of a pre-linear reflexive model of size at most $md(\varphi) + 1$;*
 (ii) *φ is $\mathbf{K4}$-satisfiable if and only if it is satisfiable in the root of a model $\mathcal{M}$ of size at most $|\varphi|$ such that (i) $\mathcal{M}$ is strict linear or (ii) $\mathcal{M}$ is strict linear and additionally its last world is in accessibility relation with itself;*
(iii) *φ is $\mathbf{S4}$-satisfiable if and only if it is satisfiable in the root of a non-strict linear model of size at most $|\varphi|$.*

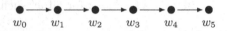

$$w_0 \quad w_1 \quad w_2 \quad w_3 \quad w_4 \quad w_5$$

Fig. 2. A pre-linear frame $\mathfrak{F} = (W, R)$, where $W = \{w_0, \ldots, w_5\}$ and an arrow from w_i to w_j denotes that $R(w_i, w_j)$

4   Computational Complexity

By $L_{core}^\square$-satisfiability, for $L \in \{\mathbf{T}, \mathbf{K4}, \mathbf{S4}\}$, we denote the problem of checking whether a given $\mathbf{L}_{core}^\square$-formula is L-satisfiable. It is known that $L_{core}^\square$-satisfiability for $L \in \{\mathbf{T}, \mathbf{K4}, \mathbf{S4}\}$ is NL-hard and in PTIME [6,15] but, to the best of our knowledge, the tight complexity bounds were unknown so far. In the following Subsections we will show that each of these problems is in NL, which implies that they are all NL-complete.

4.1   Core Fragment of T

The first result we will show is that $\mathbf{T}_{core}^\square$-satisfiability is in NL. By Theorem 2 in order to check whether an $\mathbf{L}_{core}^\square$-formula φ is $\mathbf{T}$-satisfiable it suffices to check if φ is satisfiable in the root of some pre-linear reflexive model of size at most $md(\varphi) + 1$. We will show that in order to check whether φ is satisfiable in some pre-linear reflexive model of size $D + 1$ it suffices to construct the minimal model of size $D + 1$, denoted by $\mathcal{M}_{D,\varphi}^{\mathbf{T}}$, and to check whether φ is satisfied there (Lemma 3). We show that $\mathcal{M}_{D,\varphi}^{\mathbf{T}}$ is monotonic in a sense that if a propositional variable holds in some world in $\mathcal{M}_{D,\varphi}^{\mathbf{T}}$, then this propositional variable holds in all ancestors of this world (Lemma 4). This property allows us to simplify rules used to construct the minimal model (Lemma 5) and to show that to check satisfiability of φ it suffices to verify whether φ is satisfied in the minimal model of size $md(\varphi) + 2$ (Corollary 6). Finally, we use the monotonicity property from Lemma 4 to show that checking whether φ is satisfied in the minimal model of size $md(\varphi)+2$ reduces to the reachability problem in a directed graph (Lemma 7), hence the former is in NL.

For an $\mathbf{L}_{core}^{\square}$-formula φ and $D \in \mathbb{N}$ we introduce the minimal pre-linear reflexive model of size $D + 1$ with respect to φ, $\mathcal{M}_{D,\varphi}^{\mathbf{T}} = (W, R, V)$, where (W, R) is the pre-linear reflexive frame of size $D+1$, i.e., $W = \{w_0, \dots, w_D\}$ and $R = \{(w_k, w_k) \mid k \leq D\} \cup \{(w_k, w_{k+1}) \mid k < D\}$. To define $V : \text{PROP} \longrightarrow \mathcal{P}(W)$ we start by setting $V_0 : \text{PROP} \longrightarrow \mathcal{P}(W)$ such that for all $p \in \text{PROP}$:

$$V_0(p) := \{w_k \in W \mid \square^s(\square^m p) \in clauses(\varphi) \text{ and } k \leq s+m\}. \tag{3}$$

For a function $f : \text{PROP} \longrightarrow \mathcal{P}(W)$, let $\mathsf{cl}(f)$ be the result of non-recursive application of the below rules to f:

($\mathsf{cl}_1\mathbf{T}$) If $\square^s(p_1 \to \square^m p_2) \in clauses(\varphi)$ and $w_k \in f(p_1)$ for some $k \leq s$, then add to $f(p_2)$ all w_l such that $k \leq l \leq k + m$;

($\mathsf{cl}_2\mathbf{T}$) If $\square^s(\square^m p_1 \to p_2) \in clauses(\varphi)$ and for some $k \leq s$ it holds that for all l such that $k \leq l \leq k + m$ we have $w_l \in f(p_1)$, then add w_k to $f(p_2)$,

where $k, l \leq D$. The rules ($\mathsf{cl}_1\mathbf{T}$) and ($\mathsf{cl}_2\mathbf{T}$) capture semantics of formulas of the forms $\square^s(p_1 \to \square^m p_2)$ and $\square^s(\square^m p_1 \to p_2)$, respectively. Define the sets, obtained by subsequent applications of cl to V_0 as follows:

$$\mathsf{cl}^0(V_0) := V_0; \qquad \mathsf{cl}^{n+1}(V_0) := \mathsf{cl}(\mathsf{cl}^n(V_0)).$$

Since W and $\text{PROP}(\varphi)$ are finite, there are only finitely many functions of the form $f : \text{PROP}(\varphi) \longrightarrow \mathcal{P}(W)$, and so cl has the fixed point. We define V as this fixed point. An example of $\mathcal{M}_{D,\varphi}^{\mathbf{T}}$ is presented in Fig. 3.

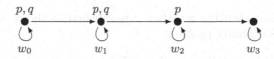

Fig. 3. The minimal model $\mathcal{M}_{D,\varphi}^{\mathbf{T}}$ for $D = 3$ and $\varphi = \square^2(p) \land \square^2(\square p \to q)$

By the construction of the minimal model we can show that the following result holds.

Lemma 3. *The following conditions are equivalent for all $\mathbf{L}_{core}^{\square}$-formulas φ:*

(1) φ *is satisfied in the root of some pre-linear reflexive model of size* $D + 1$;
(2) φ *is satisfied in the root of* $\mathcal{M}^{\mathbf{T}}_{D,\varphi}$.

Moreover, $\mathcal{M}^{\mathbf{T}}_{D,\varphi}$ is monotonic in the following sense.

Lemma 4. *For all* $p \in \mathsf{PROP}$ *and* $w_k \in W$, *if* $\mathcal{M}^{\mathbf{T}}_{D,\varphi}, w_k \models p$, *then we have* $\mathcal{M}^{\mathbf{T}}_{D,\varphi}, w_l \models p$ *for all* $l < k$.

This Lemma allows us to simplify construction of the minimal model by replacing $(\mathsf{cl}_1\mathbf{T})$ and $(\mathsf{cl}_2\mathbf{T})$ with the following rules:

$(\mathsf{cl}_1\mathbf{T}')$ If $\Box^s(p_1 \rightarrow \Box^m p_2) \in clauses(\varphi)$ and $w_k \in f(p_1)$ for some $k \leq s$, then
    add to $f(p_2)$ all w_l such that $l \leq k + m$;
$(\mathsf{cl}_2\mathbf{T}')$ If $\Box^s(\Box^m p_1 \rightarrow p_2) \in clauses(\varphi)$ and $w_k \in f(p_1)$, then:
   (i) if $k = D$, then for all $l \leq s$ add w_l to $f(p_2)$;
   (ii) if $k < D$, then for all $l \leq s$ such that $l \leq k - m$ add w_l to $f(p_2)$.

To see that $(\mathsf{cl}_2\mathbf{T})$ can be replaced with $(\mathsf{cl}_2\mathbf{T}')$ note that by Lemma 4 the model $\mathcal{M}^{\mathbf{T}}_{D,\varphi}$ is such that if $w_k \in V(p_1)$, then all its ancestors belong to $V(p_1)$. If p_1 is satisfied in all worlds, then a clause $\Box^s(\Box^m p_1 \rightarrow p_2)$ forces p_2 to be satisfied in worlds $w_0, \ldots, w_s$. If p_1 is satisfied in w_k for some $k < D$, then a clause $\Box^s(\Box^m p_1 \rightarrow p_2)$ forces p_2 to be satisfied in $\mathcal{M}^{\mathbf{T}}_{D,\varphi}$ in worlds $w_0, \ldots, w_l$ such that $l \leq s$ and $l \leq k - m$. As we will show afterwards, the new form of rules is essential to obtain the decision procedure in NL. We can also show that the following property holds:

Lemma 5. *Let* φ *be a* $\mathbf{L}^{\Box}_{core}$-*formula and* D *a positive natural number. If* φ *is satisfied in the root of* $\mathcal{M}^{\mathbf{T}}_{D,\varphi}$, *then* φ *is satisfied in the root of* $\mathcal{M}^{\mathbf{T}}_{D+1,\varphi}$.

As a result of Lemma 5, rather than checking whether φ is satisfied in the root of some pre-linear reflexive model of size at most $md(\varphi) + 1$, it suffices to check if φ is satisfied in the root of the pre-linear reflexive model of size exactly $md(\varphi) + 1$.

Corollary 6. *An* $\mathbf{L}^{\Box}_{core}$-*formula* φ *is* $\mathbf{T}^{\Box}_{core}$-*satisfiable if and only if* φ *is satisfied in the root of* $\mathcal{M}^{\mathbf{T}}_{md(\varphi)+1,\varphi}$.

Next, we show that checking whether φ is satisfied in the root of $\mathcal{M}^{\mathbf{T}}_{md(\varphi)+1,\varphi}$ reduces to the reachability problem.

Lemma 7. *Checking whether an* $\mathbf{L}^{\Box}_{core}$-*formula* φ *is satisfied in the root of* $\mathcal{M}^{\mathbf{T}}_{D,\varphi}$ *is in* NL.

Proof. We use the fact that NL= coNL [14] and introduce an NL procedure checking whether φ is not satisfied in the root of $\mathcal{M}^{\mathbf{T}}_{D,\varphi}$.

Note that all rules in φ which do not contain $\bot$ are satisfied in $\mathcal{M}^{\mathbf{T}}_{D,\varphi}$ by its construction. Hence, to check whether $\mathcal{M}^{\mathbf{T}}_{D,\varphi} w_0 \not\models \varphi$ it suffices to non-deterministically guess a rule $\Box^s(p_1 \wedge p_2 \rightarrow \bot)$ in φ and then verify that $\mathcal{M}^{\mathbf{T}}_{D,\varphi}, w_0 \not\models \Box^s(p_1 \wedge p_2 \rightarrow \bot)$. If $\mathcal{M}^{\mathbf{T}}_{D,\varphi}, w_0 \not\models \Box^s(p_1 \wedge p_2 \rightarrow \bot)$, then by

Lemma 4 we have $\mathcal{M}_{D,\varphi}^{\mathbf{T}}, w_0 \models p_1$ and $\mathcal{M}_{D,\varphi}^{\mathbf{T}}, w_0 \models p_2$. To check in NL whether this is the case we construct a directed graph $G = (Vert, E)$ such that:

$$Vert = \{start\} \cup \{(p, w) \mid p \in \mathsf{PROP}(\varphi) \text{ and } w \in W\};$$
$$E = \{(start, (p, w)) \mid w \in V_0(p)\}$$
$$\cup \{((p, w), (p', w')) \mid w \in f(p) \text{ implies } w' \in \mathsf{cl}(f)(p') \text{ by } (\mathsf{cl}_1 \mathbf{T}')\}$$
$$\cup \{((p, w), (p', w')) \mid w \in f(p) \text{ implies } w' \in \mathsf{cl}(f)(p') \text{ by } (\mathsf{cl}_2 \mathbf{T}')\}.$$

This graph (see Fig. 4), which we call an *application graph*, is of a polynomial size with respect to $|\varphi|$ and can be constructed in L.

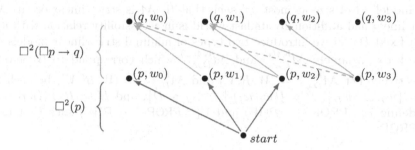

Fig. 4. An application graph for $\varphi = \Box^2(p) \wedge \Box^2(\Box p \to q)$ and $D = 3$, where curly brackets indicate clauses used to construct corresponding edges (one of the arrows is dashed only in order to make the figure more readable)

We claim that for all $p \in \mathsf{PROP}$ and $w \in W$ we have $\mathcal{M}_{D,\varphi}^{\mathbf{T}}, w \models p$ if and only if there is a path in G starting in *start* and ending in (p, w). Indeed, assume that there is a path in G from *start* to (p, w). Edges in E correspond to the construction of V_0 and applications of rules $(\mathsf{cl}_1 \mathbf{T}')$ and $(\mathsf{cl}_2 \mathbf{T}')$, hence $w \in V(p)$. For the other direction assume that $w \in V(p)$. Then, there is a sequence of applications of rules $(\mathsf{cl}_1 \mathbf{T}')$ and $(\mathsf{cl}_2 \mathbf{T}')$ to V_0 which results in adding w to $V(p)$. Importantly, the rules $(\mathsf{cl}_1 \mathbf{T}')$ and $(\mathsf{cl}_2 \mathbf{T}')$ are linear in a sense that each of them has only one precondition, so the above-mentioned sequence of applications can be represented as a path in G, starting in *start* and ending in (p, w).

We have reduced in L checking whether $\mathcal{M}_{D,\varphi}^{\mathbf{T}}, w \models p$ to checking if there is a path in a directed graph. The latter problem is well-known to be in NL [14], so the former is in NL as well. It follows that checking $\mathcal{M}_{D,\varphi}^{\mathbf{T}}, w_0 \models \varphi$ is in NL.

By Corollary 6 and Lemma 7 we obtain that $\mathbf{T}_{core}^{\Box}$-satisfiability is in NL, so the following result holds.

Theorem 8. $\mathbf{T}_{core}^{\Box}$*-satisfiability is* NL*-complete.*

4.2   Core Fragment of K4

Next, we consider $\mathbf{K4}_{core}^{\square}$-satisfiability and show that it is also in NL. The proof is similar to the one for $\mathbf{T}_{core}^{\square}$-satisfiability, however, there are some important differences. First, there are two types of minimal models (Lemma 9) and second, these models are monotonic but the direction of monotonicity is opposite to the direction of the monotonicity in minimal models for $\mathbf{T}$. In particular, if a propositional variable holds in a minimal model for $\mathbf{K4}$ in some world, then it holds in all descendants of this world (Lemma 11). This property also allows us to reduce the satisfiability problem to the graph reachability problem, which implies that $\mathbf{K4}_{core}^{\square}$-satisfiability is in NL (Theorem 12).

By Theorem 2 a $\mathbf{K4}_{core}^{\square}$-formula φ is satisfiable if it is satisfied in a root of a model $\mathcal{M}$ of size at most $|\varphi|$ such that (i) $\mathcal{M}$ is strict linear or (ii) $\mathcal{M}$ is strict linear and additionally its last world is in accessibility relation with itself. For a fixed $D \in \mathbb{N}$ we introduce two types of minimal strict linear models with respect to φ, namely $\mathcal{M}_{D,\varphi}^{\mathbf{K4}(i)}$ and $\mathcal{M}_{D,\varphi}^{\mathbf{K4}(ii)}$ which correspond to (i) and (ii), respectively. Let $\mathcal{M}_{D,\varphi}^{\mathbf{K4}(i)} = (W, R, V)$ and $\mathcal{M}_{D,\varphi}^{\mathbf{K4}(ii)} = (W, R', V')$ be such that $W = \{w_0, \dots, w_D\}$, $R = \{(w_i, w_j) \mid i < j \leq D\}$, and $R' = R \cup \{(w_D, w_D)\}$. We define $V_0 : \mathrm{PROP} \longrightarrow \mathcal{P}(W)$ and $V_0' : \mathrm{PROP} \longrightarrow \mathcal{P}(W)$ such that for all $p \in \mathrm{PROP}$:

$$V_0(p) := \{w_k \in W \mid \square^s(\square^m p) \in clauses(\varphi) \text{ and } k \geq s + m\}$$
$$\cup \{w_k \in W \mid \square^s(\square^m q \to p) \in clauses(\varphi), k \geq s, \text{ and } k + m > D\};$$
$$V_0'(p) := \{w_k \in W \mid \square^s(\square^m p) \in clauses(\varphi) \text{ and } k \geq s + m\}$$
$$\cup \{w_D \mid \square^s(\square^m p) \in clauses(\varphi) \text{ for all } s, m \in \mathbb{N}\}.$$

For a function $f : \mathrm{PROP} \longrightarrow \mathcal{P}(W)$, let $\mathsf{cl}_{(i)}(f)$ be the result of non-recursive application of the following rules to f:

(cl$_1$**K4**(i))   If $\square^s(p_1 \to \square^m p_2) \in clauses(\varphi)$ and $w_k \in f(p_1)$ for some $k \geq s$, then add to $f(p_2)$ all w_l such that $l \geq k + m$;

(cl$_2$**K4**(i))   If $\square^s(\square^m p_1 \to p_2) \in clauses(\varphi)$ and for some $k \geq s$ it holds that for all l with $l \geq k + m$ we have $w_l \in f(p_1)$, then add w_k to $f(p_2)$,

where $k, l \leq D$. Similarly, $\mathsf{cl}_{(ii)}(f)$ is the result of non-recursive application of the following rules to $f : \mathrm{PROP} \longrightarrow \mathcal{P}(W)$:

(cl$_1$**K4**(ii))   If $\square^s(p_1 \to \square^m p_2) \in clauses(\varphi)$ and $w_k \in f(p_1)$ for some $k \geq s$, then add to $f(p_2)$ the world w_D and all w_l such that $l \geq k + m$;

(cl$_2$**K4**(ii))   If $\square^s(\square^m p_1 \to p_2) \in clauses(\varphi)$, $w_D \in f(p_1)$, and for some $k \geq s$ it holds that for all l such that $l \geq k + m$ we have $w_l \in f(p_1)$, then add w_k to $f(p_2)$,

where $k, l \leq D$. We define:

$$\mathsf{cl}_{(x)}^0(V_0) := V_0; \qquad \mathsf{cl}_{(x)}^{n+1}(V_0) := \mathsf{cl}_{(x)}(\mathsf{cl}_{(x)}^n(V_0)).$$

Since W and $\mathsf{PROP}(\varphi)$ are finite, there is a fixed point of $\mathsf{cl}_{(x)}$ for $x \in \{i, ii\}$. Let V be the fixed point of $\mathsf{cl}_{(i)}$ and V' the fixed point of $\mathsf{cl}_{(ii)}$. The models $\mathcal{M}_{D,\varphi}^{\mathbf{K4}(i)}$ and $\mathcal{M}_{D,\varphi}^{\mathbf{K4}(ii)}$ satisfy the following properties.

Lemma 9. *The following hold for all* $\mathbf{L}_{core}^{\square}$*-formulas* φ *and all* $D \in \mathbb{N}$*:*

(1) $\mathcal{M}_{D,\varphi}^{\mathbf{K4}(i)}, w_0 \models \varphi$ *if an only if* φ *is satisfied in the root of a strict linear model of size* $D + 1$*;*

(2) $\mathcal{M}_{D,\varphi}^{\mathbf{K4}(ii)}, w_0 \models \varphi$ *if an only if* φ *is satisfied in the root of a strict linear model of size* $D + 1$ *with additional accessibility relation from the last world to itself.*

Corollary 10. *An* $\mathbf{L}_{core}^{\square}$*-formula* φ *is* $\mathbf{K4}_{core}^{\square}$*-satisfiable if an only if for some* $D \leq |\varphi| - 1$ *we have* $\mathcal{M}_{D,\varphi}^{\mathbf{K4}(i)}, w_0 \models \varphi$ *or* $\mathcal{M}_{D,\varphi}^{\mathbf{K4}(ii)}, w_0 \models \varphi$.

By the transitivity of the accessibility relation in $\mathbf{K4}$ we can show that both $\mathcal{M}_{D,\varphi}^{\mathbf{K4}(i)}$ and $\mathcal{M}_{D,\varphi}^{\mathbf{K4}(ii)}$ are monotonic in the following sense.

Lemma 11. *Let* φ *be an* $\mathbf{L}_{core}^{\square}$*-formula,* $D \in \mathbb{N}$*,* $p \in \mathsf{PROP}$*,* $x \in \{i, ii\}$*, and* $w_k \in W$ *such that* $w_k \neq w_0$*. If* $\mathcal{M}_{D,\varphi}^{\mathbf{K4}(x)}, w_k \models p$*, then* $\mathcal{M}_{D,\varphi}^{\mathbf{K4}(x)}, w_l \models p$ *for all* $w_l \in W$ *such that* $l > k$*.*

Therefore, each of $(\mathsf{cl}_2\mathbf{K4}(i))$ and $(\mathsf{cl}_2\mathbf{K4}(ii))$ can be replaced with the following rule:

$(\mathsf{cl}_2\mathbf{K4}')$ If $\square^s(\square^m p_1 \to p_2) \in clauses(\varphi)$, and $w_k \in f(p_1)$ for some $w_k \neq w_0$, then for any $l \geq k - m$ with $l \geq s$ add w_l to $f(p_2)$.

Theorem 12. $\mathbf{K4}_{core}^{\square}$*-satisfiability is* NL*-complete.*

Proof. Fix an $\mathbf{L}_{core}^{\square}$-formula φ and nondeterministically guess the natural number $D \leq |\varphi| - 1$ and the type of a model, i.e., $x \in \{i, ii\}$. By Corollary 10 the formula φ is $\mathbf{K4}_{core}^{\square}$-satisfiable if and only if $\mathcal{M}_{D,\varphi}^{\mathbf{K4}(i)}, w_0 \models \varphi$ or $\mathcal{M}_{D,\varphi}^{\mathbf{K4}(ii)}, w_0 \models \varphi$. Both of the latter conditions reduce to reachability in the application graph which we construct in an analogous way as in the proof of Lemma 7. It follows that the whole procedure is in NL. The matching lower bound is well-known.

4.3   Core Fragment of S4

In this Section we will study the satisfiability problem in $\mathbf{S4}_{core}^{\square}$. We will show that to check whether an $\mathbf{S4}_{core}^{\square}$-formula is satisfiable in a frame of size $D + 1$ it suffices to construct the minimal model $\mathcal{M}_{D,\varphi}^{\mathbf{S4}}$ and check whether the formula holds there (Lemma 13). Then, we show that if a propositional variable holds in a non-root world in a minimal model $\mathcal{M}_{D,\varphi}^{\mathbf{S4}}$, then it holds everywhere in this model (Lemma 14). Hence, for all $D > 1$ we can construct a surjective p-morphism from $\mathcal{M}_{D,\varphi}^{\mathbf{S4}}$ to $\mathcal{M}_{1,\varphi}^{\mathbf{S4}}$, so $\mathbf{S4}_{core}^{\square}$-satisfiability reduces to checking whether $\mathcal{M}_{1,\varphi}^{\mathbf{S4}}, w_0 \models \varphi$ (Corollary 15), which can be solved in NL (Theorem 16).

For a fixed $\mathbf{L}_{core}^{\square}$-formula φ, let $\mathcal{M}_{D,\varphi}^{\mathbf{S4}} = (W, R, V)$ be the minimal non-strict linear model of size $D + 1$, where (W, R) is the non-strict linear frame of size $D + 1$, i.e., $W = \{w_0, \ldots, w_D\}$ and $R = \{(w_i, w_j) \mid i \le j \le D\}$. We define $V_0 : \mathsf{PROP} \longrightarrow \mathcal{P}(W)$ such that for all $p \in \mathsf{PROP}$:

$$V_0(p) := \{w_0 \mid \square^0(\square^0 p) \in clauses(\varphi)\}$$
$$\cup \{w_0, \ldots, w_D \mid \square^s(\square^m p) \in clauses(\varphi) \text{ and } s + m > 0\}.$$

For a function $f : \mathsf{PROP} \longrightarrow \mathcal{P}(W)$, let $\mathsf{cl}(f)$ be the result of non-recursive application of the following rules to f:

($\mathsf{cl_1 S4}$) If $\square^0(p_1 \to p_2) \in clauses(\varphi)$ and $w_0 \in f(p_1)$, then add w_0 to $f(p_2)$;
($\mathsf{cl_2 S4}$) If $\square^s(p_1 \to p_2) \in clauses(\varphi)$ and $w \in f(p_1)$, then add w to $f(p_2)$;
($\mathsf{cl_3 S4}$) If $\square^0(p_1 \to \square^m p_2) \in clauses(\varphi)$ and $w_0 \in f(p_1)$, then $f(p_2) := W$;
($\mathsf{cl_4 S4}$) If $\square^s(p_1 \to \square^m p_2) \in clauses(\varphi)$ and $w_k \in f(p_1)$, add $w_k, \ldots, w_D$ to $f(p_2)$;
($\mathsf{cl_5 S4}$) If $\square^0(\square^m p_1 \to p_2) \in clauses(\varphi)$ and $f(p_1) = W$, then add w_0 to $f(p_2)$;
($\mathsf{cl_6 S4}$) If $\square^s(\square^m p_1 \to p_2) \in clauses(\varphi)$ and $w_k, \ldots, w_D \in f(p_1)$, then add w_k to $f(p_2)$,

where $m, s > 0$. We define the following sets, obtained by applying cl to V_0:

$$\mathsf{cl}^0(V_0) := V_0; \qquad \mathsf{cl}^{n+1}(V_0) := \mathsf{cl}(\mathsf{cl}^n(V_0)).$$

Let V be the fixed point of cl. For an example of $\mathcal{M}_{D,\varphi}^{\mathbf{S4}}$ see Fig. 5.

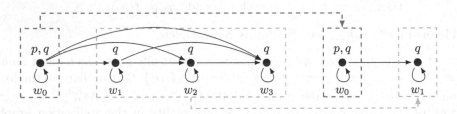

Fig. 5. The minimal models $\mathcal{M}_{3,\varphi}^{\mathbf{S4}}$ and $\mathcal{M}_{1,\varphi}^{\mathbf{S4}}$ for $\varphi = \square^0(p) \wedge \square^2(p \to \square q)$, where the p-morphism from $\mathcal{M}_{3,\varphi}^{\mathbf{S4}}$ to $\mathcal{M}_{1,\varphi}^{\mathbf{S4}}$ is indicated with dashed arrows

Lemma 13. *An $\mathbf{L}_{core}^{\square}$-formula is satisfied in the root of a non-strict linear model of size $D + 1$ if and only if φ is satisfied in the root of $\mathcal{M}_{D,\varphi}^{\mathbf{S4}}$.*

Furthermore, if a propositional variable is satisfied in $\mathcal{M}_{D,\varphi}^{\mathbf{S4}}$ in some $w_k \ne w_0$, then this variable is satisfied in all worlds of $\mathcal{M}_{D,\varphi}^{\mathbf{S4}}$.

Lemma 14. *Let φ be an $\mathbf{L}_{core}^{\square}$-formula, $D \in \mathbb{N}$, and $\mathcal{M}_{D,\varphi}^{\mathbf{S4}} = (W, R, V)$. For all $k \ge 1$ and $p \in \mathsf{PROP}$ if $\mathcal{M}_{D,\varphi}^{\mathbf{S4}}, w_k \models p$, then $\mathcal{M}_{D,\varphi}^{\mathbf{S4}}, w \models p$ for all $w \in W$.*

As a consequence of Lemma 14 and the form of the rules $(\mathsf{cl}_1\mathbf{S4})$–$(\mathsf{cl}_6\mathbf{S4})$ we can show that for all $D > 1$ there is a surjective p-morphism from $\mathcal{M}^{\mathbf{S4}}_{D,\varphi}$ to $\mathcal{M}^{\mathbf{S4}}_{1,\varphi}$ (for a description of p-morphisms see [3]). This surjective p-morphism maps the root of $\mathcal{M}^{\mathbf{S4}}_{D,\varphi}$ into the root of $\mathcal{M}^{\mathbf{S4}}_{1,\varphi}$ and all non-root worlds of $\mathcal{M}^{\mathbf{S4}}_{D,\varphi}$ into the non-root world of $\mathcal{M}^{\mathbf{S4}}_{1,\varphi}$ as depicted in Fig. 5. Then, by the existence of such a p-morphism, $\mathcal{M}^{\mathbf{S4}}_{D,\varphi}, w_0 \models \varphi$ implies $\mathcal{M}^{\mathbf{S4}}_{1,\varphi}, w_0 \models \varphi$. Moreover, by the form of the rules $(\mathsf{cl}_1\mathbf{S4})$–$(\mathsf{cl}_6\mathbf{S4})$ it is easy to show that $\mathcal{M}^{\mathbf{S4}}_{0,\varphi}, w_0 \models \varphi$ implies $\mathcal{M}^{\mathbf{S4}}_{1,\varphi}, w_0 \models \varphi$, hence:

Lemma 15. *An* $\mathbf{L}^{\square}_{core}$*-formula* φ *is* $\mathbf{S4}^{\square}_{core}$*-satisfiable if and only if it is satisfied in the root of* $\mathcal{M}^{\mathbf{S4}}_{1,\varphi}$.

It follows that to check if an $\mathbf{L}^{\square}_{core}$-formula is $\mathbf{S4}^{\square}_{core}$-satisfiable it is sufficient check whether $\mathcal{M}^{\mathbf{S4}}_{1,\varphi}, w_0 \models \varphi$. By Lemma 14 if $D > 0$, then the rules $(\mathsf{cl}_5\mathbf{S4})$ and $(\mathsf{cl}_6\mathbf{S4})$ can be replaced with the following:

$(\mathsf{cl}_5\mathbf{S4}')$ If $\square^0(\square^m p_1 \to p_2) \in clauses(\varphi)$ and $w_1 \in f(p_1)$, then add w_0 to $f(p_2)$;
$(\mathsf{cl}_6\mathbf{S4}')$ If $\square^s(\square^m p_1 \to p_2) \in clauses(\varphi)$ and $w_1 \in f(p_1)$, then $f(p_2) = W$,

where $s > 0$. Each of the rules $(\mathsf{cl}_1\mathbf{S4})$–$(\mathsf{cl}_4\mathbf{S4})$, $(\mathsf{cl}_5\mathbf{S4}')$, and $(\mathsf{cl}_6\mathbf{S4}')$ has only one precondition, so we can construct an application graph for $\mathcal{M}^{\mathbf{S4}}_{1,\varphi}$ analogously as in the proof of Lemma 7. Hence, $\mathbf{S4}^{\square}_{core}$-satisfiable reduces to reachability, so it is in NL.

Theorem 16. $\mathbf{S4}^{\square}_{core}$*-satisfiability is NL-complete.*

5   Algorithms

In the previous Section we have showed that the satisfiability problems for $\mathbf{T}^{\square}_{core}$, $\mathbf{K4}^{\square}_{core}$, and $\mathbf{S4}^{\square}_{core}$ are NL-complete. In the current Section, we present deterministic algorithms for solving these problems. The algorithms will construct a minimal model and check if the formula is satisfied in the root of this model.

The pseudocode for satisfiability checking in $\mathbf{T}^{\square}_{core}$ is depicted in Algorithm 1. For a given $\mathbf{L}^{\square}_{core}$-formula φ the algorithm constructs a set M of pairs of the form (w, p) such that $(w, p) \in M$ is to mean that in the minimal model $\mathcal{M}^{\mathbf{T}}_{md(\varphi),\varphi}$ the propositional variable p is satisfied in the world w. The construction is initialized in the Lines 1–2 by fixing the size D of the minimal model and adding to M elements corresponding to V_0 as defined in (3). Afterwards, in the Lines 3–7, the rules $(\mathsf{cl}_1\mathbf{T}')$ and $(\mathsf{cl}_2\mathbf{T}')$ are applied to M until a fixed point is reached (as we have discussed in the previous Section this procedure terminates). It remains to check in the Lines 8–9 whether some clause of the form $\square^s(p_1 \land p_2 \to \bot)$ occurring in φ raises a contradiction. If this is the case, the input formula is not $\mathbf{T}^{\square}_{core}$-satisfiable and the algorithm returns 'False', otherwise the formula is $\mathbf{T}^{\square}_{core}$-satisfiable and the algorithm returns 'True'.

The algorithms for checking $\mathbf{S4}^{\square}_{core}$- and $\mathbf{K4}^{\square}_{core}$-satisfiability are obtained by suitable modifications of Algorithm 1. The procedure for $\mathbf{S4}^{\square}_{core}$-satisfiability

---

Algorithm 1. Checking $\mathbf{T}_{core}^{\square}$-satisfiability

---

Input: an $\mathbf{L}_{core}^{\square}$-formula φ
Output: 'True' if φ is $\mathbf{T}$-satisfiable, 'False' otherwise
1: $D \leftarrow md(\varphi)$
2: $M \leftarrow \{(w, p) \mid w \in V_0(p)\}$
3: **while** something changes **do**
4:      $M' \leftarrow \emptyset$
5:      **for all** $c \in clauses(\varphi)$ **and** $(w_k, p_1) \in M$ **do**
6:          $M' \leftarrow M' \cup \{(w_l, p_2) \mid w_k \in f(p_1)$ implies $w_l \in f(p_2)$ by application
               of $(\mathsf{cl}_1 \mathbf{T}')$ or $(\mathsf{cl}_2 \mathbf{T}')$ to $c\}$
7:      $M \leftarrow M \cup M'$
8: **for all** $\square^s(p_1 \wedge p_2 \rightarrow \bot) \in clauses(\varphi)$ **do**
9:      **if** $(w_0, p_1) \in M$ **and** $(w_0, p_2) \in M$ **then**
10:         **return** False
11: **return** True

---

requires the following changes: (a) the Line 1 becomes "$D \leftarrow 1$" as the minimal model for $\mathbf{S4}_{core}^{\square}$ is of size 2, (b) in the Line 6 "$(\mathsf{cl}_1 \mathbf{T}')$ or $(\mathsf{cl}_2 \mathbf{T}')$" is replaced with "$(\mathsf{cl}_1 \mathbf{S4})$–$(\mathsf{cl}_4 \mathbf{S4})$ or $(\mathsf{cl}_5 \mathbf{S4}')$–$(\mathsf{cl}_6 \mathbf{S4}')$".

The algorithm for $\mathbf{K4}_{core}^{\square}$-satisfiability is more complex. For an $\mathbf{L}_{core}^{\square}$-formula φ it has to be checked for all $D \leq |\varphi| - 1$ and for all $x \in \{i, ii\}$ whether $\mathcal{M}_{D,\varphi}^{\mathbf{K4}(x)}, w_0 \models \varphi$. Hence, for a fixed $D \leq |\varphi| - 1$ and $x \in \{i, ii\}$ the following modifications of Algorithm 1 needs to be done: (a) the Line is 1 deleted because D is already fixed, (b) if $x = i$, then in the Line 6 "$(\mathsf{cl}_1 \mathbf{T}')$ or $(\mathsf{cl}_2 \mathbf{T}')$" is replaced with "$(\mathsf{cl}_1 \mathbf{K4}(i))$ or $(\mathsf{cl}_2 \mathbf{K4}')$", otherwise it is replaced with "$(\mathsf{cl}_1 \mathbf{K4}(ii))$ or $(\mathsf{cl}_2 \mathbf{K4}')$", (c) in the Line 9 all occurrences of "w_0" are replaced with "w_D".

The above described algorithms construct minimal models of a relevant type and check whether no clause of the form $\square^s(p_1 \wedge p_2 \rightarrow \bot)$ raises a contradiction. By Corollaries 6, 10, and 15, these procedures are sufficient for satisfiability checking.

6   Correspondence to Linear Temporal Logic

Since there is a close correspondence between the minimal models which we have introduced for checking $\mathbf{T}_{core}^{\square}$-, $\mathbf{K4}_{core}^{\square}$-, and $\mathbf{S4}_{core}^{\square}$-satisfiability with fragments of the linear temporal logic, our results transfer to the latter.

Let $\bigcirc$, $\bullet$, $\square$, and $\blacksquare$, be modal temporal operators whose intuitive reading is, respectively, 'in the next time-point', 'now and in the next time-point', 'always in the future', and 'now and always in the future'. For each $X \in \{\bigcirc, \bullet, \square, \blacksquare\}$ let LTL_{core}^X-formulas be generated by the following grammar:

$$\varphi_X := \lambda_X \mid \neg\lambda_X \mid \square^s(\neg\lambda_X \vee \lambda_X) \mid \square^s(\neg\lambda_X \vee \neg\lambda_X) \mid \varphi_X \wedge \varphi_X; \qquad (4)$$
$$\lambda_X := \top \mid p \mid X\lambda,$$

where $s \in \mathbb{N}$ and $p \in \mathsf{PROP}$.

As usual in linear temporal logic, LTL^X_{core}-formulas are interpreted over a linear order of time-points, namely an LTL-model is a tuple $\mathcal{M} = (T, <, V)$, where $(T, <)$ is a countable discrete and linear order of time-points and the valuation $V : \mathsf{PROP} \longrightarrow \mathcal{P}(T)$ assigns sets of time points to propositional variables. The satisfaction relation for a model $\mathcal{M}$ and a time point $t \in T$ is defined for temporal modal operators as follows:

$$
\begin{array}{llll}
\mathcal{M}, t \models \bigcirc\varphi & \text{iff} & \mathcal{M}, t' \models \varphi \text{ for } t' \text{ the immediate } <\text{-succesor of } t; \\
\mathcal{M}, t \models \bullet\varphi & \text{iff} & \mathcal{M}, t \models \varphi \wedge \bigcirc\varphi; \\
\mathcal{M}, t \models \Box\varphi & \text{iff} & \mathcal{M}, t' \models \varphi \text{ for all } t' \text{ such that } t < t'; \\
\mathcal{M}, t \models \blacksquare\varphi & \text{iff} & \mathcal{M}, t \models \varphi \wedge \Box\varphi,
\end{array}
$$

where $t' \in T$ and for other propositional connectives the satisfaction relation is defines as in normal modal logics. Let 0 be the smallest element in $(T, <)$. Then, an LTL-formula φ is satisfiable if there exists an LTL-model $\mathcal{M}$ such that $\mathcal{M}, 0 \models \varphi$.

To show how the fragments of LTL correspond to the fragments of normal modal logics we introduce a translation $\tau_X(\varphi)$ for $X \in \{\bigcirc, \bullet, \Box, \blacksquare\}$ and an $\mathbf{L}^\Box_{core}$-formula φ, such that $\tau_X(\varphi)$ is an LTL^X_{core}-formula obtained from φ by replacing each occurrence of "$\Box$" in φ with "X" except $\Box$'s proceeding clauses, which remain unchanged. Consider the following example:

$$
\varphi = \Box^2(p) \wedge \Box^2(\Box p \rightarrow q);
$$
$$
\tau(\varphi)_{\bigcirc} = \bigcirc^2(p) \wedge \Box^2(\bigcirc p \rightarrow q).
$$

Then, by the form of minimal models in $\mathbf{K}^\Box_{core}$, $\mathbf{T}^\Box_{core}$, $\mathbf{K4}^\Box_{core}$, and $\mathbf{S4}^\Box_{core}$ we obtain the following correspondence for all $\mathbf{L}^\Box_{core}$-formulas φ:

- φ is $\mathbf{K}^\Box_{core}$-satisfiable if an only if $\tau(\varphi)_{\bigcirc}$ is LTL-satisfiable;
- φ is $\mathbf{T}^\Box_{core}$-satisfiable if an only if $\tau(\varphi)_{\bullet}$ is LTL-satisfiable;
- φ is $\mathbf{K4}^\Box_{core}$-satisfiable if an only if $\varphi(\Box)$ is LTL-satisfiable;
- φ is $\mathbf{S4}^\Box_{core}$-satisfiable if an only if $\tau(\varphi)_{\blacksquare}$ is LTL-satisfiable.

It follows that satisfiability in LTL^X_{core} is NL-complete for all $X \in \{\bigcirc, \bullet, \Box, \blacksquare\}$. A similar result for $\mathsf{LTL}^\Box_{core}$ has been established in [1], where a slightly modified version of the grammar of $\mathsf{LTL}^\Box_{core}$-formulas was shown to be NL-complete over time lines coinciding with the standard ordering of integers. The modification was obtained by replacing "$\Box^s$" preceding clauses in the grammar (4) with the universal modality, stating that a formula holds in all time points.

7   Conclusions and Future Work

In the paper we have showed that the satisfiability problem in core fragments of normal modal logics $\mathbf{T}^\Box_{core}$, $\mathbf{K4}^\Box_{core}$, and $\mathbf{S4}^\Box_{core}$ are NL-complete. We have conducted the proofs by constructing minimal models and checking if the input formula is satisfiable in them. We have showed that for a given $\mathbf{L}_{core}^{\square}$-formula φ there is a single $\mathbf{T}_{core}^{\square}$ and a single $\mathbf{S4}_{core}^{\square}$ minimal model of sizes $md(\varphi) + 1$ and 2, respectively. These results enabled us to construct simple algorithms for satisfiability checking in $\mathbf{T}_{core}^{\square}$ and $\mathbf{S4}_{core}^{\square}$. In the case of $\mathbf{K4}_{core}^{\square}$ there are two types of minimal models which make the algorithm more complex.

Moreover, by the form of the minimal models we have showed a correspondence of the above fragments with core fragments of linear temporal logic. Therefore, our computational complexity results for $\mathbf{T}_{core}^{\square}$, $\mathbf{K4}_{core}^{\square}$, and $\mathbf{S4}_{core}^{\square}$ immediately transfer to the corresponding fragments of linear temporal logic.

The complexity map for sub-propositional fragments of normal modal logics still contains a number open problems – see Fig. 1. As a future work we plan to investigate the following questions:

- What is the complexity of $L_{core}^{\Diamond}$ for $L \in \{\mathbf{K.T}, \mathbf{K4}, \mathbf{S4}\}$? These fragments are known to be NL-hard and in P but no tight complexity bounds have been established for them so far;
- What is the computational complexity of core fragments in the basic interval logic, known as the logic of Halpern and Shoham? Is it possible to exploit our proof techniques in the case of interval logics?

Acknowledgments. This work is supported by the National Science Centre in Poland (NCN) grant 2016/23/N/HS1/02168 and by the Foundation for Polish Science (FNP).

References

1. Artale, A., Kontchakov, R., Ryzhikov, V., Zakharyaschev, M.: The complexity of clausal fragments of LTL. In: McMillan, K., Middeldorp, A., Voronkov, A. (eds.) LPAR 2013. LNCS, vol. 8312, pp. 35–52. Springer, Heidelberg (2013). https://doi.org/10.1007/978-3-642-45221-5_3
2. Artale, A., Kontchakov, R., Ryzhikov, V., Zakharyaschev, M.: A cookbook for temporal conceptual data modelling with description logics. ACM Trans. Comput. Logic (TOCL) 15(3), 25 (2014)
3. Blackburn, P., De Rijke, M., Venema, Y.: Modal Logic. Cambridge University Press, Cambridge (2002)
4. Bresolin, D., Kurucz, A., Muñoz-Velasco, E., Ryzhikov, V., Sciavicco, G., Zakharyaschev, M.: Horn fragments of the Halpern-Shoham interval temporal logic. ACM Trans. Comput. Logic (TOCL) 18(3), 22:1–22:39 (2017)
5. Bresolin, D., Muñoz-Velasco, E., Sciavicco, G.: Sub-propositional fragments of the interval temporal logic of Allen's relations. In: Fermé, E., Leite, J. (eds.) JELIA 2014. LNCS (LNAI), vol. 8761, pp. 122–136. Springer, Cham (2014). https://doi.org/10.1007/978-3-319-11558-0_9
6. Bresolin, D., Munoz-Velasco, E., Sciavicco, G.: On the complexity of fragments of Horn modal logics. In: 2016 23rd International Symposium on Temporal Representation and Reasoning (TIME), pp. 186–195. IEEE (2016)
7. Halpern, J.Y.: The effect of bounding the number of primitive propositions and the depth of nesting on the complexity of modal logic. Artif. Intell. 75(2), 361–372 (1995)

8. Halpern, J.Y., Moses, Y.: A guide to completeness and complexity for modal logics of knowledge and belief. Artif. Intell. **54**(3), 319–379 (1992)
9. Horn, A.: On sentences which are true of direct unions of algebras. J. Symbolic Logic **16**(1), 14–21 (1951)
10. Krom, M.R.: The decision problem for formulas in prenex conjunctive normal form with binary disjunctions. J. Symbolic Logic **35**(2), 210–216 (1970)
11. Ladner, R.E.: The computational complexity of provability in systems of modal propositional logic. SIAM J. Comput. **6**(3), 467–480 (1977)
12. Nguyen, L.A.: Constructing the least models for positive modal logic programs. Fundam. Inf. **42**(1), 29–60 (2000)
13. Nguyen, L.A.: On the complexity of fragments of modal logics. Adv. Modal Logic **5**, 318–330 (2004)
14. Papadimitriou, C.H.: Computational Complexity. Wiley, Hoboken (2003)
15. Sciavicco, G., Muñoz-Velasco, E., Bresolin, D.: On sub-propositional fragments of modal logic. Logical Methods. Comput. Sci. **14**, 1–35 (2018)

Temporal Logic

Axiomatic Systems and Topological Semantics for Intuitionistic Temporal Logic

Joseph Boudou[1], Martín Diéguez[2]([✉]) [iD], David Fernández-Duque[3] [iD], and Fabián Romero[1] [iD]

[1] IRIT, Toulouse University, Toulouse, France
{Joseph.Boudou, Fabian.Romero}@irit.fr
[2] LAB-STICC, CERV, ENIB, Brest, France
martin.dieguez@enib.fr
[3] Department of Mathematics, Ghent University, Ghent, Belgium
David.FernandezDuque@UGent.be

Abstract. The importance of intuitionistic temporal logics in Computer Science and Artificial Intelligence has become increasingly clear in the last few years. From the proof-theory point of view, intuitionistic temporal logics have made it possible to extend functional languages with new features via type theory, while from its semantical perspective several logics for reasoning about dynamical systems and several semantics for logic programming have their roots in this framework. In this paper we propose four axiomatic systems for intuitionistic linear temporal logic and show that each of these systems is sound for a class of structures based either on Kripke frames or on dynamic topological systems. Our topological semantics features a new interpretation for the 'henceforth' modality that is a natural intuitionistic variant of the classical one. Using the soundness results, we show that the four logics obtained from the axiomatic systems are distinct.

1 Introduction

Intuitionistic logic (IL) [24] enjoys a myriad of interpretations based on computation, information or topology, making it a natural framework to reason about dynamic processes in which these phenomena play a crucial role. Thus it should not be surprising that combinations of intuitionistic logic and linear temporal logic (LTL) [27] have been proposed for applications within several different contexts.

The first involves the Curry-Howard correspondence [17], which identifies intuitionistic proofs with the λ-terms of functional programming. Several extensions of the λ-calculus with operators from LTL have been proposed in order to introduce new features to functional languages: Davies [7,8] has suggested

Martín Diéguez is funded by the ANR-12-ASTR-0020 project STRATEGIC and the European COST Action CA17124.

adding a 'next' (○) operator to IL in order to define the type system λ°, which allows extending functional languages with *staged computation*[1] [13]. Davies and Pfenning [9] proposed the functional language Mini-ML$^\square$ which is supported by intuitionistic S4 and allows capturing complex forms of staged computation as well as runtime code generation. Yuse and Igarashi later extended λ° to $\lambda^\square$ [29] by incorporating the 'henceforth' operator (□), useful for modelling persistent code that can be executed at any subsequent state.

Alternately, intuitionistic temporal logics have been proposed as a tool for modelling semantically-given processes. Maier [23] observed that an intuitionistic temporal logic with 'henceforth' and 'eventually' (◊) could be used for reasoning about safety and liveness conditions in possibly-terminating reactive systems, and Fernández-Duque [14] has suggested that a logic with 'eventually' can be used to provide a decidable framework in which to reason about topological dynamics. In the areas of nonmonotonic reasoning, knowledge representation (KR), and artificial intelligence, intuitionistic and intermediate logics have played an important role within the successful answer set programming (ASP) [5] paradigm for practical KR, leading to several extensions of modal ASP [6] that are supported by intuitionistic-based modal logics like *temporal here and there* [3].

Despite interest in the above applications, there is a large gap to be filled regarding our understanding of the computational behaviour of intuitionistic temporal logics. We have successfuly employed semantical methods to show the decidability of the logic ITL^e defined by a natural class of Kripke frames [4] and shown that these semantics correspond to a natural calculus over the □-free fragment [12]. However, as we will see, in the presence of □, new validities arise which may be undesirable from the point of view of an extended Curry-Howard isomorphism. Thus our goal is to provide semantics for weaker axiomatically-defined intuitionistic temporal logics in order to provide tools for understanding their computational behaviour. We demonstrate the power of our semantics by separating several natural axiomatically-given calculi, which in particular answers in the negative a conjecture of Yuse and Igarashi [29] that the Gentzen-style and the Hilbert-style calculi presented there prove the same set of formulas.

There have already been some notable efforts towards a semantical study of intuitionistic temporal logics. Kojima and Igarashi [19] endowed Davies's logic with Kripke semantics and provided a complete deductive system. Bounded-time versions of logics with henceforth were later studied by Kamide and Wansing [18]. Both use semantics based on Simpson's bi-relational models for intuitionistic modal logic [28]. Since then, Balbiani and the authors have shown that temporal here-and-there is decidable and enjoys a natural axiomatization [3]. Topological semantics for intuitionistic modal and tense logics have also been studied by Davoren et al. [10,11], and Kremer suggested a topologically-defined intuitionistic variant of LTL with ○ and □ [21]. The decidability of Kremer's

---

[1] *Staged computation* is a technique that allows dividing the computation in order to exploit the early availability of some arguments.

logic remains open, but Fernández-Duque has shown that a similar logic with 'eventually' $\Diamond$ instead of $\Box$ is decidable [14].

In this paper we lay the groundwork for an axiomatic treatment of intuitionistic linear temporal logics. We will introduce a 'minimal' intuitionistic temporal logic, ITL^0, defined by adding standard axioms of LTL to intuitionistic modal logic. We also consider additional Fischer Servi axioms and a 'constant domain' axiom $\Box(p \lor q) \to \Box p \lor \Diamond q$. Combining these, we obtain four intuitionistic temporal logics, each of them sound for a class of structures: the two logics with the constant domain axiom are sound for the class of dynamic posets, and the Fischer Servi axioms correspond to backwards-confluence of the transition function.

The constant domain axiom is not derivable from the others, and to show this, we will consider topological semantics for intuitionistic temporal logic. As our axioms involve both $\Diamond$ and $\Box$, we would like to be able to interpret both tenses. Kremer [21] observed that his semantics for $\Box$ do not satisfy some key LTL validities, namely $\Box p \to \circ \Box p$, $\Box \circ p \to \circ \Box p$, and $\Box p \to \Box\Box p$. Consequently ITL^0 is not sound for this interpretation. In order to obtain models of ITL^0, we propose an alternative interpretation for $\Box$. Our approach is natural from an algebraic perspective, as we define the interpretation of $\Box\varphi$ via a greatest fixed point in the Heyting algebra of open sets. We will show that dynamic topological systems provide semantics for the logics without the constant domain axiom, from which we conclude the independence of the latter. Moreover, we show that the Fischer Servi axioms are valid for the class of *open* dynamical topological systems. The constant domain axiom shows that the $\{\Diamond, \Box\}$-logic of dynamic posets is different from that of dynamic topological systems. We show via an alternative axiom that the $\{\circ, \Box\}$-logics are also different.

LAYOUT. Section 2 introduces the syntax and the four axiomatic systems we propose for intuitionistic temporal logic. Section 3 reviews dynamic topological systems, which are used in Sect. 4 to provide semantics for our formal language. Section 5 shows that each of the four logics is sound for a class of dynamical systems. These soundness results are used in Sect. 6 to show that the four logics are pairwise distinct. Finally, Sect. 7 lists some open questions.

2   Syntax and Axiomatics

In this section we will introduce four natural intuitionistic temporal logics. All of the axioms have appeared either in the intuitionistic logic, the temporal logic, or the intuitionistic modal logic literature. They will be based on the language of linear temporal logic, as defined next.

Fix a countably infinite set $\mathbb{P}$ of *propositional variables*. The language $\mathcal{L}$ of intuitionistic (linear) temporal logic ITL is given by the grammar

$$\bot \mid p \mid \varphi \land \psi \mid \varphi \lor \psi \mid \varphi \to \psi \mid \circ\varphi \mid \Diamond\varphi \mid \Box\varphi,$$

where $p \in \mathbb{P}$. As usual, we use $\neg\varphi$ as a shorthand for $\varphi \to \bot$ and $\varphi \leftrightarrow \psi$ as a shorthand for $(\varphi \to \psi) \land (\psi \to \varphi)$. We read $\circ$ as 'next', $\Diamond$ as 'eventually', and

□ as 'henceforth'. Given any formula φ, we denote the set of subformulas of φ by sub(φ). The language $\mathcal{L}_\Diamond$ is defined as the sublanguage of $\mathcal{L}$ without the modality □. Similarly, $\mathcal{L}_\Box$ is the language without $\Diamond$.

We begin by establishing our basic axiomatization. It is obtained by adapting the standard axioms and inference rules of LTL [22], as well as their dual versions. To be precise, the logic ITL^0 is the least set of $\mathcal{L}$-formulas closed under the following rules and axioms.

(i) All intuitionistic tautologies.

(ii) $\neg \circ \bot$.

(iii) $\circ(\varphi \wedge \psi) \leftrightarrow (\circ\varphi \wedge \circ\psi)$;

(iv) $\circ(\varphi \vee \psi) \leftrightarrow (\circ\varphi \vee \circ\psi)$;

(v) $\circ(\varphi \to \psi) \to (\circ\varphi \to \circ\psi)$;

(vi) $\Box(\varphi \to \psi) \to (\Box\varphi \to \Box\psi)$;

(vii) $\Box(\varphi \to \psi) \to (\Diamond\varphi \to \Diamond\psi)$;

(viii) $\Box\varphi \to \varphi \wedge \circ\Box\varphi$;

(ix) $\varphi \vee \circ\Diamond\varphi \to \Diamond\varphi$;

(x) $\Box(\varphi \to \circ\varphi) \to (\varphi \to \Box\varphi)$;

(xi) $\Box(\circ\varphi \to \varphi) \to (\Diamond\varphi \to \varphi)$;

(xii) $\dfrac{\varphi \quad \varphi \to \psi}{\psi}$;

(xiii) $\dfrac{\varphi}{\circ\varphi}$.

Each axiom is either included in the axiomatization of Goldblatt [16, p. 87] or is a mild variant of one of them (e.g., a contrapositive); this is standard in intuitionistic modal logic, as such variants are needed to account for the independence of the basic connectives. We do not consider 'until' in this paper, but have studied its intuitionistic semantics in [2]. Modal intuitionistic logics often involve additional axioms, and in particular Fischer Servi [15] includes the schema

$$\text{FS}_\Diamond(\varphi, \psi) \stackrel{\text{def}}{=} (\Diamond\varphi \to \Box\psi) \to \Box(\varphi \to \psi).$$

Recalling that $\circ$ is self-dual, we also define

$$\text{FS}_\circ(\varphi, \psi) \stackrel{\text{def}}{=} (\circ\varphi \to \circ\psi) \to \circ(\varphi \to \psi).$$

Later we will show that these schemas lead to strictly stronger logics. Finally, we consider additional axioms reminiscent of constant domain axioms in first-order intuitionistic logic. As we will see, in the context of intuitionistic temporal logics, these axioms separate Kripke semantics from the more general topological semantics.

$$\text{CD}(\varphi, \psi) \stackrel{\text{def}}{=} \Box(\varphi \vee \psi) \to \Box\varphi \vee \Diamond\psi$$

$$\text{BI}(\varphi, \psi) \stackrel{\text{def}}{=} \Box(\varphi \vee \psi) \wedge \Box(\circ\psi \to \psi) \to \Box\varphi \vee \psi.$$

Here, CD stands for 'constant domain' and BI for 'backward induction'.

From a constructive perspective CD might not be desirable, as from $\Box(\varphi \vee \psi)$ one cannot in general extract an upper bound for a witness for $\Diamond\psi$.[2] The axiom BI is meant to be a $\Diamond$-free approximation to CD, as witnessed by the following.

---

[2] For example, if φ represents the 'active' states and ψ the 'halting' states of a program, then CD would require us to decide whether the program halts, which is not possible to do constructively.

Proposition 1. $\mathsf{ITL}^0 \vdash \mathrm{CD}(p,q) \to \mathrm{BI}(p,q)$.

Proof. We reason within ITL^0. Assume that (1) $\mathrm{CD}(p,q)$, (2) $\square(\circ q \to q)$, and (3) $\square(p \vee q)$. From (1) and (3) we obtain $\square p \vee \lozenge q$, which together with (2) and axiom (xi) gives us $\square p \vee q$, as needed.

With this, we define the following logics:

$$\mathsf{ITL}^{\mathsf{FS}} \equiv \mathsf{ITL}^0 + \mathrm{FS}_\circ + \mathrm{FS}_\lozenge, \qquad \mathsf{ITL}^{\mathsf{CD}} \equiv \mathsf{ITL}^0 + \mathrm{CD}, \qquad \mathsf{ITL}^1 \equiv \mathsf{ITL}^{\mathsf{FS}} + \mathsf{ITL}^{\mathsf{CD}}.$$

We are also interested in logics over sublanguages of $\mathcal{L}$. For any logic Λ defined above, let $\Lambda_\square$ be defined by restricting similarly all rules and axioms to $\mathcal{L}_\square$, except that when CD is an axiom of Λ, we add the axiom BI to $\Lambda_\square$. The logic $\mathsf{ITL}^0_\square$ is similar to a Hilbert calculus for the $\wedge, \vee$-free fragment considered by Yuse and Igarashi [29], although they do not include induction but include the axioms $\square\varphi \to \square\square\varphi$ and $\square \circ \varphi \leftrightarrow \circ\square\varphi$. It is not difficult to check that the latter are derivable from our basic axioms, and hence their logic is contained in $\mathsf{ITL}^0_\square$.

We also define $\Lambda_\lozenge$ be the logic obtained by restricting all rules and axioms to $\mathcal{L}_\lozenge$, and adding the rules $\frac{\varphi \to \psi}{\lozenge\varphi \to \lozenge\psi}$ and $\frac{\circ\varphi \to \varphi}{\lozenge\varphi \to \varphi}$. Note that these rules correspond to axioms (vii), (xi), respectively, but do not involve $\square$. In this paper we are mostly concerned with logics including 'henceforth', but $\square$-free logics are studied in detail in [12].

3   Dynamic Topological Systems

The four logics over $\mathcal{L}$ defined above are pairwise distinct. We will show this by introducing semantics for each of them. They will be based on dynamic topological systems (or dynamical systems for short), which, as was observed in [14], generalize their Kripke semantics [4]. Let us first recall the definition of a *topological space* [25]:

Definition 1. *A* topological space *is a pair* $(X, \mathcal{T})$, *where* X *is a set and* $\mathcal{T}$ *a family of subsets of* X *satisfying (a)* $\varnothing, X \in \mathcal{T}$; *(b) if* $U, V \in \mathcal{T}$ *then* $U \cap V \in \mathcal{T}$, *and (c) if* $\mathcal{O} \subseteq \mathcal{T}$ *then* $\bigcup \mathcal{O} \in \mathcal{T}$. *The elements of* $\mathcal{T}$ *are called* open sets.

If $x \in X$, a *neighbourhood* of x is an open set $U \subseteq X$ such that $x \in U$. Given a set $A \subseteq X$, its *interior*, denoted A°, is the largest open set contained in A. It is defined formally by

$$A^\circ = \bigcup \{U \in \mathcal{T} : U \subseteq A\}. \tag{1}$$

Dually, we define the closure $\overline{A}$ as $X \setminus (X \setminus A)^\circ$; this is the smallest closed set containing A.

If $(X, \mathcal{T})$ is a topological space, a function $S \colon X \to X$ is *continuous* if, whenever $U \subseteq X$ is open, it follows that $S^{-1}[U]$ is open. The function S is *open* if, whenever $V \subseteq X$ is open, then so is $S[V]$. An open, continuous function is an *interior map*, and a bijective interior map is a *homeomorphism*.

A dynamical system is then a topological space equipped with a continuous function:

Definition 2. *A dynamical (topological) system is a triple* $\mathcal{X} = (X, \mathcal{T}, S)$ *such that* $(X, \mathcal{T})$ *is a topological space and* $S \colon X \to X$ *is continuous. We say that* $\mathcal{X}$ *is invertible if* S *is a homeomorphism, i.e.,* S *is bijective and* S^{-1} *is also a continuous function, and open if* S *is an interior map.*

Topological spaces generalize posets in the following way. Let $\mathcal{F} = (W, \preccurlyeq)$ be a poset; that is, W is any set and $\preccurlyeq$ is a transitive, reflexive, antisymmetric relation on W. To see $\mathcal{F}$ as a topological space, define $\uparrow w = \{v : w \preccurlyeq v\}$. Then consider the topology $\mathcal{T}_{\preccurlyeq}$ on W given by setting $U \subseteq W$ to be open if and only if, whenever $w \in U$, we have $\uparrow w \subseteq U$. A topology of this form is a *up-set topology* [1]. The interior operator on such a topological space can be computed by

$$A^{\circ} = \{w \in W : \uparrow w \subseteq A\}; \tag{2}$$

i.e., w lies on the interior of A if whenever $v \succcurlyeq w$, it follows that $v \in A$.

Throughout this text we will often identify partial orders with their corresponding topologies, and many times do so tacitly. In particular, a dynamical system generated by a poset is called a *dynamic poset*. It will be useful to characterize the continuous and open functions on posets:

Lemma 1. *Consider a poset* $(W, \preccurlyeq)$ *and a function* $S \colon W \to W$. *Then,*

1. *S is continuous with respect to the up-set topology if and only if, whenever $w \preccurlyeq w'$, it follows that $S(w) \preccurlyeq S(w')$, and*
2. *S is open with respect to the up-set topology if whenever $S(w) \preccurlyeq v$, there is $w' \in W$ such that $w \preccurlyeq w'$ and $S(w') = v$.*

These are confluence properties common in multi-modal logics; open, continuous maps on a poset are called *persistent*.

(a) Continuity   (b) Openness

Fig. 1. On a dynamic poset the above diagrams can always be completed if S is continuous or open, respectively.

4   Semantics

In this section we will see how dynamical systems can be used to provide a natural intuitionistic semantics for the language of linear temporal logic.

Formulas are interpreted as open subspaces of a dynamical system. Each propositional variable p is assigned an open set $[\![p]\!]$, and then $[\![\cdot]\!]$ is defined recursively for more complex formulas according to the following:

Definition 3. *Given a dynamical system* $\mathcal{X} = (X, \mathcal{T}, S)$, *a valuation on* $\mathcal{X}$ *is a function* $[\![\cdot]\!] \colon \mathcal{L} \to \mathcal{T}$ *such that:*

$$[\![\bot]\!] = \varnothing \qquad\qquad\qquad [\![\circ\varphi]\!] = S^{-1}[\![\varphi]\!]$$
$$[\![\varphi \wedge \psi]\!] = [\![\varphi]\!] \cap [\![\psi]\!] \qquad\qquad [\![\Diamond\varphi]\!] = \bigcup_{n \geq 0} S^{-n}[\![\varphi]\!]$$
$$[\![\varphi \vee \psi]\!] = [\![\varphi]\!] \cup [\![\psi]\!]$$
$$[\![\varphi \to \psi]\!] = ((X \setminus [\![\varphi]\!]) \cup [\![\psi]\!])^{\circ} \qquad [\![\Box\varphi]\!] = \bigcup \left\{ U \in \mathcal{T} : S[U] \subseteq U \subseteq [\![\varphi]\!] \right\}$$

A tuple $\mathcal{M} = (X, \mathcal{T}, S, [\![\cdot]\!])$ *consisting of a dynamical system with a valuation is a* dynamic topological model, *and if* $\mathcal{T}$ *is generated by a partial order, we will say that* $\mathcal{M}$ *is a* dynamic poset model.

All of the semantic clauses are standard from either intuitionistic or temporal logic, with the exception of that for $\Box\varphi$, which we discuss in greater detail below. It is not hard to check by structural induction on φ that $[\![\varphi]\!]$ is uniquely defined given any assignment of the propositional variables to open sets, and that $[\![\varphi]\!]$ is always open. We define validity in the standard way, and with this introduce four additional semantically-defined logics, two of which were already studied by us in Boudou et al. [4].

Definition 4. *If* $\mathcal{M} = (X, \mathcal{T}, S, [\![\cdot]\!])$ *is any dynamic topological model and* $\varphi \in \mathcal{L}$ *is any formula, we write* $\mathcal{M} \models \varphi$ *if* $[\![\varphi]\!] = X$. *Similarly, if* $\mathcal{X} = (X, \mathcal{T}, S)$ *is a dynamical system, we write* $\mathcal{X} \models \varphi$ *if for any valuation* $[\![\cdot]\!]$ *on* $\mathcal{X}$, *we have that* $(\mathcal{X}, [\![\cdot]\!]) \models \varphi$. *Finally, if* Ω *is a class of structures, we write* $\Omega \models \varphi$ *if for every* $\mathcal{A} \in \Omega$, $\mathcal{A} \models \varphi$, *in which case we say that* φ *is* valid *on* Ω.

We denote the set of formulas valid over the class of all dynamical systems by ITL^{c}, *over the class of all dynamic posets by* ITL^{e}, *over the class of all persistent posets by* ITL^{p} *and over the class of all open dynamical systems by* ITL^{o}. *If* Λ *is one of these four logics we define* $\Lambda_{\Box} = \Lambda \cap \mathcal{L}_{\Box}$ *and* $\Lambda_{\Diamond} = \Lambda \cap \mathcal{L}_{\Diamond}$.

In practice, it is convenient to have a 'pointwise' characterization of the semantic clauses of Definition 3. For a model $\mathcal{M} = (X, \mathcal{T}, S, [\![\cdot]\!])$, $x \in X$ and $\varphi \in \mathcal{L}$, we write $\mathcal{M}, x \models \varphi$ if $x \in [\![\varphi]\!]$, and $\mathcal{M} \models \varphi$ if $[\![\varphi]\!] = X$. Then, in view of (1), given formulas φ and ψ, $\mathcal{M}, x \models \varphi \to \psi$ if and only if there is a neighbourhood U of x such that for all $y \in U$, if $\mathcal{M}, y \models \varphi$ then $\mathcal{M}, y \models \psi$; note that this is a special case of *neighbourhood semantics* [26].

Using (2), this can be simplified somewhat in the case that $\mathcal{T}$ is generated by a partial order $\preccurlyeq$:

Proposition 2. *If* $(X, \preccurlyeq, S, [\![\cdot]\!])$ *is a dynamic poset model,* $x \in X$, *and* φ, ψ *are formulas, then* $\mathcal{M}, x \models \varphi \to \psi$ *if and only if whenever* $y \succcurlyeq x$ *and* $\mathcal{M}, y \models \varphi$, *it follows that* $\mathcal{M}, y \models \psi$.

This is the standard relational interpretation of implication, and thus topological semantics are a generalization of the usual Kripke semantics. Now let us discuss the topological interpretation of 'henceforth', which is the main novelty in our semantics. In classical temporal logic, $[\![\Box\varphi]\!]$ is the largest set contained in $\llbracket \varphi \rrbracket$ which is closed under S. In our semantics, $\llbracket \Box \varphi \rrbracket$ is the greatest *open* set which is closed under S. From this perspective, our interpretation is the natural intuitionistic variant of the classical one. If $\mathcal{M}, x \models \Box \varphi$, this fact is witnessed by an open, S-invariant neighbourhood of x, where $U \subseteq X$ is *S-invariant* if $S[U] \subseteq U$.

Proposition 3. *If $(X, \mathcal{T}, S, \llbracket \cdot \rrbracket)$ is a dynamic topological model, $x \in X$, and φ is any formula, then $\mathcal{M}, x \models \Box \varphi$ if and only if there is an S-invariant neighbourhood U of x such that for all $y \in U$, $\mathcal{M}, y \models \varphi$.*

In fact, the open, S-invariant sets form a topology; that is, the family of S-invariant open sets is closed under finite intersections and arbitrary unions. This topology is coarser than $\mathcal{T}$, in the sense that every S-invariant open set is (tautologically) open. Thus $\Box$ can itself be seen as an interior operator based on a coarsening of $\mathcal{T}$, and $\llbracket \Box \varphi \rrbracket$ is always an S-invariant open set.

Example 1. As usual, the real number line is denoted by $\mathbb{R}$ and we assume that it is equipped with the standard topology, where $U \subseteq \mathbb{R}$ is open if and only if it is a union of intervals of the form (a, b). Consider a dynamical system based on $\mathbb{R}$ with $S \colon \mathbb{R} \to \mathbb{R}$ given by $S(x) = 2x$. We claim that for any model $\mathcal{M}$ based on $(\mathbb{R}, S)$ and any formula φ, $\mathcal{M}, 0 \models \Box \varphi$ if and only if $\mathcal{M} \models \varphi$.

To see this, note that one implication is obvious since $\mathbb{R}$ is open and S-invariant, so if $\llbracket \varphi \rrbracket = \mathbb{R}$ it follows that $\mathcal{M}, 0 \models \Box \varphi$. For the other implication, assume that $\mathcal{M}, 0 \models \Box \varphi$, so that there is an S-invariant, open $U \subseteq \llbracket \varphi \rrbracket$ with $0 \in U$. It follows from U being open that for some $\varepsilon > 0$, $(-\varepsilon, \varepsilon) \subseteq U$. Now, let $x \in \mathbb{R}$, and let n be large enough so that $|2^{-n} x| < \varepsilon$. Then, $2^{-n} x \in U$, and since U is S-invariant, $x = S^n(2^{-n} x) \in U$. Since x was arbitrary, $U = \mathbb{R}$, and it follows that $\mathcal{M} \models \varphi$.

On the other hand, suppose that $0 < a < x$ and $(a, \infty) \subseteq \llbracket \varphi \rrbracket$. Then, (a, ∞) is open and S-invariant, so it follows that $x \in \llbracket \Box \varphi \rrbracket$. Hence in this case we do not require that $\llbracket \varphi \rrbracket = \mathbb{R}$. Similarly, if $x < a < 0$ and $(-\infty, a) \subseteq \llbracket \varphi \rrbracket$, we readily obtain $x \in \llbracket \Box \varphi \rrbracket$.

As was the case for implication, our interpretation for $\Box$ becomes familiar when restricted to Kripke semantics.

Lemma 2. *Let $\mathcal{M} = (W, \preccurlyeq, S, \llbracket \cdot \rrbracket)$ be any dynamic poset model, $w \in W$ and $\varphi \in \mathcal{L}$. Then, the following are equivalent:*

(a) $\mathcal{M}, w \models \Box \varphi$; (b) $w \in \left(\bigcap_{n < \omega} S^{-n} \llbracket \varphi \rrbracket \right)^\circ$; (c) for all $n < \omega$, $\mathcal{M}, S^n(w) \models \varphi$.

Proof. First we prove that (a) implies (b). Assume that $\mathcal{M}, w \models \Box \varphi$, so that there is an S-invariant neighbourhood U of w with $U \subseteq \llbracket \varphi \rrbracket$. To see that $w \in \left(\bigcap_{n < \omega} S^{-n} \llbracket \varphi \rrbracket \right)^\circ$, we must show that if $v \succcurlyeq w$, then $v \in \bigcap_{n < \omega} S^{-n} \llbracket \varphi \rrbracket$. So fix such a v and $n < \omega$. Since U is S-invariant, $S^n(w) \in U$, and since $S^n(v) \succcurlyeq S^n(w)$ and U is open, $S^n(v) \in U$, as needed. Thus $v \in \bigcap_{n < \omega} S^{-n} \llbracket \varphi \rrbracket$, and since $v \succcurlyeq w$ was arbitrary, (b) holds.

That (b) implies (c) is immediate from

$$\left(\bigcap_{n<\omega} S^{-n}[\![\varphi]\!] \right)^{\circ} \subseteq \bigcap_{n<\omega} S^{-n}[\![\varphi]\!],$$

so it remains to show that (c) implies (a). Suppose that for all $n < \omega$, $\mathcal{M}, S^n(w) \models \varphi$, and let $U = \bigcup_{n<\omega} {\uparrow} S^n(w)$. That the set U is open follows from each ${\uparrow} S^n(w)$ being open and unions of opens being open. If $v \in U$, then $v \succcurlyeq S^n(w)$ for some $n < \omega$ and hence by upwards persistence, from $\mathcal{M}, S^n(w) \models \varphi$ we obtain $\mathcal{M}, v \models \varphi$; moreover, $S(v) \succcurlyeq S^{n+1}(w)$ so $S(v) \in U$. Since $v \in U$ was arbitrary, we conclude that U is S-invariant and $U \subseteq [\![\varphi]\!]$. Thus U witnesses that $\mathcal{M}, w \models \Box\varphi$.

Remark 1. Kremer [21] uses (b) as the definition of $[\![\Box\varphi]\!]$. However, as we mentioned in the introduction, even our minimal axiomatic system ITL^0 is not sound for such an interpretation over arbitrary dynamical systems.

5 Soundness

In this section we will show that the four logics we have considered are sound for semantics based on different classes of dynamic topological systems. First we show that our minimal logic is sound for the class of *all* dynamical systems. The following simple observation will be useful.

Lemma 3. *If $\mathcal{M} = (X, \mathcal{T}, S, [\![\cdot]\!])$ is any model and $\varphi, \psi \in \mathcal{L}$, then $\mathcal{M} \models \varphi \to \psi$ if and only if $[\![\varphi]\!] \subseteq [\![\psi]\!]$.*

Proof. If $[\![\varphi]\!] \subseteq [\![\psi]\!]$ then $(X \setminus [\![\varphi]\!]) \cup [\![\psi]\!] = X$, so $[\![\varphi \to \psi]\!] = ((X \setminus [\![\varphi]\!]) \cup [\![\psi]\!])^{\circ} = X^{\circ} = X$. Otherwise, there is $z \in [\![\varphi]\!]$ such that $z \notin [\![\psi]\!]$, so that $z \notin ((X \setminus [\![\varphi]\!]) \cup [\![\psi]\!])^{\circ}$, i.e. $z \notin [\![\varphi \to \psi]\!]$.

Theorem 1. ITL^0 *is sound for the class of dynamical systems; that is,* $\mathsf{ITL}^0 \subseteq \mathsf{ITL}^c$.

Proof. Let $\mathcal{M} = (X, \mathcal{T}, S, [\![\cdot]\!])$ be any dynamical topological model; we must check that all the axioms (i)–(xi) are valid on $\mathcal{M}$ and the rules (xii), (xiii), preserve validity. Note that all intuitionistic tautologies are valid due to the soundness for topological semantics [24]. Many of the other axioms can be checked routinely, so we focus only on those axioms involving the continuity of S or the semantics for $\Box$.

(v) Suppose that $x \in [\![\circ(\varphi \to \psi)]\!]$. Then, $S(x) \in [\![\varphi \to \psi]\!]$. Since S is continuous and $[\![\varphi \to \psi]\!]$ is open, $U = S^{-1}[\![\varphi \to \psi]\!]$ is a neighbourhood of x. Then, for $y \in U$, if $y \in [\![\circ\varphi]\!]$, it follows that $S(y) \in [\![\varphi]\!] \cap [\![\varphi \to \psi]\!]$, so that $S(y) \in [\![\psi]\!]$ and $y \in [\![\circ\psi]\!]$. Since $y \in U$ was arbitrary, $x \in [\![\circ\varphi \to \circ\psi]\!]$, thus $[\![\circ(\varphi \to \psi)]\!] \subseteq [\![\circ\varphi \to \circ\psi]\!]$, and by Lemma 3 (which we will henceforth use without mention), (v) is valid on $\mathcal{M}$.

(vi) Suppose that $x \in [\![\Box(\varphi \to \psi)]\!]$. Then, there is an S-invariant neighbourhood U of x such that $U \subseteq [\![\varphi \to \psi]\!]$. We claim that if $y \in U \cap [\![\Box\varphi]\!]$ it follows that $y \in [\![\Box\psi]\!]$, from which we obtain $x \in [\![\Box\varphi \to \Box\psi]\!]$, as needed. If $y \in U \cap [\![\Box\varphi]\!]$, let U' be an S-invariant neighbourhood of y such that $U' \subseteq [\![\varphi]\!]$, and define $V = U \cap U'$. Then, the set V is an S-invariant neighbourhood of y. Moreover, if $z \in V$, then $z \in U \subseteq [\![\varphi \to \psi]\!]$, while $z \in U' \subseteq [\![\varphi]\!]$, hence $z \in [\![\psi]\!]$. It follows that $V \subseteq [\![\psi]\!]$, and thus $y \in [\![\Box\psi]\!]$, as desired.

(vi) Observe that $[\![\Box(\varphi \to \psi)]\!]$ is an S-invariant open subset of $[\![\varphi \to \psi]\!]$. Similarly, $[\![\Box\varphi]\!]$ is an S-invariant open subset of $[\![\varphi]\!]$. Let

$$U = [\![\Box(\varphi \to \psi)]\!] \cap [\![\Box\varphi]\!].$$

Since U is open, it suffices to prove that $U \subseteq [\![\Box\psi]\!]$. Moreover, U is S-invariant, therefore it suffices to prove that $U \subseteq [\![\psi]\!]$, which is direct because $U \subseteq [\![\varphi \to \psi]\!] \cap [\![\varphi]\!]$ and $[\![\varphi \to \psi]\!] \subseteq (X \setminus [\![\varphi]\!]) \cup [\![\psi]\!]$.

(vii) As before, suppose that $x \in [\![\Box(\varphi \to \psi)]\!]$, and let U be an S-invariant neighbourhood of x such that $U \subseteq [\![\varphi \to \psi]\!]$. If $y \in U \cap [\![\Diamond\varphi]\!]$, then $S^n(y) \in [\![\varphi]\!]$ for some n; since U is S-invariant, $S^n(y) \in U$, hence $S^n(y) \in [\![\psi]\!]$ and $y \in [\![\Diamond\psi]\!]$. We conclude that $x \in [\![\Diamond\varphi \to \Diamond\psi]\!]$.

(viii) Suppose that $x \in [\![\Box\varphi]\!]$, and let $U \subseteq [\![\varphi]\!]$ be an S-invariant neighbourhood of x. Then, $x \in U$, so $x \in [\![\varphi]\!]$. Moreover, U is also an S-invariant neighbourhood of $S(x)$, so $S(x) \in [\![\Box\varphi]\!]$ and thus $x \in [\![\circ\Box\varphi]\!]$. We conclude that $x \in [\![\varphi \wedge \circ\Box\varphi]\!]$.

(x) Supppose that $x \in [\![\Box(\varphi \to \circ\varphi)]\!]$. If $x \in [\![\varphi]\!]$, then $U = [\![\varphi]\!] \cap [\![\Box(\varphi \to \circ\varphi)]\!]$ is open (by the intuitionistic semantics) and S-invariant, since if $y \in U$, from $y \in [\![\varphi \to \circ\varphi]\!]$ we obtain $S(y) \in [\![\varphi]\!]$. It follows that U is an S-invariant neighbourhood of x, so $x \in [\![\Box\varphi]\!]$.

(xi) Suppose that $x \in [\![\Box(\circ\varphi \to \varphi)]\!] \cap [\![\Diamond\varphi]\!]$. Let $U \subseteq [\![\circ\varphi \to \varphi]\!]$ be an S-invariant neighbourhood of x. Let n be least so that $S^n(x) \in [\![\varphi]\!]$; if $n > 0$, since U is S-invariant we see that $S^{n-1}(x) \in U \subseteq [\![\circ\varphi \to \varphi]\!]$, hence $S^{n-1}(x) \in [\![\varphi]\!]$, contradicting the minimality of n. Thus $n = 0$ and $x \in [\![\varphi]\!]$.

The additional axioms we have considered are valid over specific classes of dynamical systems. Specifically, the constant domain axiom is valid for the class of dynamic posets, while the Fischer Servi axioms are valid for the class of open systems. Let us begin by discussing the former in more detail.

Theorem 2. ITL^{CD} *and* ITL$_\Box^{\mathsf{CD}}$ *are sound for the class of dynamic posets; that is,* ITL$^{\mathsf{CD}} \subseteq$ ITL$^\mathsf{e}$ *and* ITL$_\Box^{\mathsf{CD}} \subseteq$ ITL$_\Box^\mathsf{e}$.

Proof. Let $\mathcal{M} = (X, \preccurlyeq, S, [\![\cdot]\!])$ be a dynamic poset model; in view of Theorem 1, it only remains to check that CD and BI are valid on $\mathcal{M}$. However, by Proposition 1, BI is a consequence of CD, so we only check the latter. Suppose that $x \in [\![\Box(\varphi \vee \psi)]\!]$, but $x \notin [\![\Box\varphi]\!]$. Then, in view of Lemma 2, for some $n \geq 0$, $S^n(x) \notin [\![\varphi]\!]$. It follows that $S^n(x) \in [\![\psi]\!]$, so that $x \in [\![\Diamond\psi]\!]$.

Note that the relational semantics are used in an essential way, since Lemma 2 is not available in the topological setting, and indeed we will show in Proposition 4 that these axioms are not topologically valid. But before that, let's turn our attention to the Fischer Servi axioms.

Theorem 3. $\mathsf{ITL}^{\mathsf{FS}} \subseteq \mathsf{ITL}^{\circ}$, *i.e.* $\mathsf{ITL}^{\mathsf{FS}}$ *is sound for the class of open dynamical systems.*

Proof. Let $\mathcal{M} = (X, \mathcal{T}, S, [\![\cdot]\!])$ be a dynamical topological model where S is an interior map. We check that axioms $\mathsf{FS}_{\circ}$ and $\mathsf{FS}_{\Diamond}$ are valid on $\mathcal{M}$.

($\mathsf{FS}_{\circ}$) Suppose that $x \in [\![\circ\varphi \to \circ\psi]\!]$, and let $U \subseteq [\![\circ\varphi \to \circ\psi]\!]$ be a neighbourhood of x. Since S is open, $V = S[U]$ is a neighbourhood of $S(x)$. Let $y \in V \cap [\![\varphi]\!]$, and choose $z \in U$ so that $y = S(z)$. Then, $z \in U \cap [\![\circ\varphi]\!]$, so that $z \in [\![\circ\psi]\!]$, i.e. $y \in [\![\psi]\!]$. Since $y \in V$ was arbitrary, $S(x) \in [\![\varphi \to \psi]\!]$, and $x \in [\![\circ(\varphi \to \psi)]\!]$.

($\mathsf{FS}_{\Diamond}$) Suppose that $x \in [\![\Diamond\varphi \to \Box\psi]\!]$, and let $U \subseteq [\![\Diamond\varphi \to \Box\psi]\!]$ be a neighbourhood of x. Set $V = \bigcup_{n<\omega} S^n[U]$; since S is open and unions of opens are open, V is open as well. Moreover, V is clearly S-invariant, as if $x \in V$, then $x \in S^n[U]$ for some $n \geq 0$, so that $S(x) \in S^{n+1}[U] \subseteq V$.

We claim that $V \subseteq [\![\varphi \to \psi]\!]$, from which we obtain a witness that $\mathcal{M}, x \models \Box(\varphi \to \psi)$. Suppose that $y \in V \cap [\![\varphi]\!]$. By the definition of V, $y = S^n(z)$ for some $n < \omega$ and some $z \in U$. Then, $z \in U \cap [\![\Diamond\varphi]\!]$, so that $z \in [\![\Box\psi]\!]$. From this we may choose an S-invariant neighbourhood $Z \subseteq [\![\psi]\!]$ of z. But $y = S^n(z) \in Z$ so that $y \in [\![\psi]\!]$, and since $y \in V$ was arbitrary we see that $V \subseteq [\![\varphi \to \psi]\!]$, as needed.

As an easy consequence, we mention the following combination of Theorems 2 and 3. Recall that dynamic posets with an interior map are also called *persistent*.

Corollary 1. ITL^1 *and* $\mathsf{ITL}^1_{\Box}$ *are sound for the class of persistent dynamic posets, that is,* $\mathsf{ITL}^1 \subseteq \mathsf{ITL}^{\mathsf{P}}$ *and* $\mathsf{ITL}^1_{\Box} \subseteq \mathsf{ITL}^{\mathsf{P}}_{\Box}$.

6 Independence

In this section we will use our soundness results to show that the four logics we have considered are pairwise distinct. First we note that the formulas CD and BI separate Kripke semantics from the general topological semantics.

Proposition 4. *The formulas* $\mathrm{CD}(p, q)$ *and* $\mathrm{BI}(p, q)$ *are not valid over the class of invertible dynamical systems based on* $\mathbb{R}$, *hence* $\mathsf{ITL}^{\mathsf{FS}} \not\vdash \mathrm{CD}(p, q)$ *and* $\mathsf{ITL}^{\mathsf{FS}} \not\vdash \mathrm{BI}(p, q)$.

Proof. Define a model $\mathcal{M}$ on $\mathbb{R}$, with $S(x) = 2x$, $[\![p]\!] = (-\infty, 1)$ and $[\![q]\!] = (0, \infty)$. Clearly $[\![p \vee q]\!] = \mathbb{R}$, so that $[\![\Box(p \vee q)]\!] = \mathbb{R}$ as well.

Let us see that $\mathcal{M}, 0 \not\models \mathrm{CD}(p, q)$. Since $\mathcal{M}, 0 \models \Box(p \vee q)$, it suffices to show that $\mathcal{M}, 0 \not\models \Box p \vee \Diamond q$. It is clear that $\mathcal{M}, 0 \not\models \Diamond q$ simply because $S^n(0) = 0 \notin [\![q]\!]$

for all n. Meanwhile, by Example 1, $\mathcal{M}, 0 \models \Box p$ if and only if $[\![p]\!] = \mathbb{R}$, which is not the case. We conclude that $\mathcal{M}, 0 \not\models \mathrm{CD}(p, q)$.

To see that $\mathcal{M}, 0 \not\models \mathrm{BI}(p, q)$ we proceed similarly, where the only new ingredient is the observation that $\mathcal{M}, 0 \models \Box(\circ q \to q)$. But this follows easily from the fact that if $\mathcal{M}, x \models \circ q$, then $x > 0$ so that $\mathcal{M}, x \models q$, hence $[\![\circ q \to q]\!] = \mathbb{R}$.

Proposition 5. *The formula* $\mathrm{BI}(p, q) \to \mathrm{CD}(p, q)$ *is not valid over the class of invertible dynamical systems based on* $\mathbb{R}$.

Proof. Consider a model $\mathcal{M}$ similar to that used in the proof of Proposition 4, except that $[\![q]\!] = \mathbb{R} \setminus [-1/2, 1/2]$. Then, $\Box(p \vee q) \to \Box p \vee \Diamond q$ fails at 0 (by essentially the same reasoning). However, it could easily be checked that $[\![\Box(\circ q \to q)]\!] = [\![q]\!]$. Hence $0 \in [\![\neg\Box(\circ q \to q)]\!]$, from which it readily follows that 0 satisfies

$$\Box(\circ q \to q) \to (\Box(p \vee q) \to \Box p \vee q).$$

Therefore $\mathrm{BI}(p, q)$ does not imply $\mathrm{CD}(p, q)$ over the class of invertible dynamical systems.

Note, however, that Proposition 5 does not necessarily imply that there are no formulas φ, ψ such that $\mathrm{BI}(\varphi, \psi) \to \mathrm{CD}(p, q)$ is derivable, and hence it is reasonable to use BI in place of CD to axiomatize $\Diamond$-free logics.

The Fischer Servi axioms are also not valid in general, as shown in Boudou et al. [2]. From this and the soundness of $\mathsf{ITL}^{\mathsf{FS}}$ (Theorem 3), we immediately obtain that they are not derivable in ITL^0.

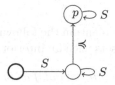

Fig. 2. A dynamic poset model falsifying both Fischer Servi axioms. Propositional variables that are true on a point are displayed; only one point satisfies p and no point satisfies q. It can readily be checked that $\mathrm{FS}_\circ(p, q)$ and $\mathrm{FS}_\Diamond(p, q)$ fail on the highlighted point on the left. Note that S is continuous but not open, as can easily be seen by comparing to Fig. 1.

Proposition 6. $\mathrm{FS}_\circ(p, q)$ *and* $\mathrm{FS}_\Diamond(p, q)$ *are not valid over the class of dynamic posets, hence* $\mathsf{ITL}^{\mathsf{CD}} \not\vdash \mathrm{FS}_\circ(p, q)$ *and* $\mathsf{ITL}^{\mathsf{CD}} \not\vdash \mathrm{FS}_\Diamond(p, q)$.

Proof. Let $\{p, q\}$ be a set of propositional variables and let us consider the model $\mathcal{M} = (W, \preccurlyeq, S, V)$ defined by (1) $W = \{w, v, u\}$; (2) $S(w) = v$, $S(v) = v$ and $S(u) = u$; (3) $v \preccurlyeq u$; (4) $V(p) = \{u\}$, and (5) $V(q) = \varnothing$ (see Fig. 2). Clearly, $\mathcal{M}, u \not\models p \to q$, so $\mathcal{M}, v \not\models p \to q$. By definition, $\mathcal{M}, w \not\models \circ(p \to q)$ and $\mathcal{M}, w \not\models \Box(p \to q)$; however, $\mathcal{M}, w \models \circ p \to \circ q$ and $\mathcal{M}, w \models \Diamond p \to \Box q$ since the negation of each antecedent holds, so $\mathcal{M}, w \not\models (\circ p \to \circ q) \to \circ(p \to q)$ and $\mathcal{M}, w \not\models (\Diamond p \to \Box q) \to \Box(p \to q)$.

Remark 2. As mentioned previously, Yuse and Igarashi [29] present a Hilbert-calculus which yields a sub-logic of $\mathsf{ITL}_\square^0$. They also present a Gentzen-style calculus and conjecture that their two calculi prove the same set of formulas. However, Kojima and Igarashi [19] show that the formula $\mathrm{FS}_\circ(p,q)$ is derivable in this Gentzen calculus. Thus Proposition 6 shows that the two calculi are not equivalent.

The above independence results are sufficient to see that each of our four syntactically-defined logics, as well as each of our four semantically-defined logics, are pairwise distinct.

Theorem 4. *The logics* ITL^0, $\mathsf{ITL}^{\mathsf{FS}}$, $\mathsf{ITL}^{\mathsf{CD}}$ *and* ITL^1 *are pairwise distinct, as are* $\mathsf{ITL}_\square^0$, $\mathsf{ITL}_\square^{\mathsf{FS}}$, $\mathsf{ITL}_\square^{\mathsf{CD}}$ *and* $\mathsf{ITL}_\square^1$. *Similarly,* ITL^c, ITL°, ITL^e *and* ITL^p *are pairwise distinct, as are* $\mathsf{ITL}_\square^c$, $\mathsf{ITL}_\square^\circ$, $\mathsf{ITL}_\square^e$ *and* $\mathsf{ITL}_\square^p$.

Proof. By Proposition 4 and the definition of $\mathsf{ITL}^{\mathsf{CD}}$, $\mathrm{CD}(p,q) \in \mathsf{ITL}^{\mathsf{CD}} \setminus \mathsf{ITL}^{\mathsf{FS}}$; similarly, by Proposition 6, $\mathrm{FS}_\circ(p,q) \in \mathsf{ITL}^{\mathsf{FS}} \setminus \mathsf{ITL}^{\mathsf{CD}}$. Thus $\mathsf{ITL}^{\mathsf{FS}}$ and $\mathsf{ITL}^{\mathsf{CD}}$ are incomparable, from which we conclude that ITL^0, which is contained in their intersection, is strictly smaller than either of them, while ITL^1, which contains their union, is strictly larger. The arguments for the logics over $\mathcal{L}_\square$ are analogous, except that CD is replaced with BI, as is the argument for semantically-defined logics.

7 Concluding Remarks

We have proposed a natural 'minimalist' intuitionistic temporal logic, ITL^0, along with possible extensions including Fischer Servi or constant domain axioms. We have seen that relational semantics validate the constant domain axiom, leading us to consider a wider class of models based on topological spaces, with a novel interpretation for 'henceforth' based on invariant neighbourhoods. With this, we have shown that the logics ITL^0, $\mathsf{ITL}^{\mathsf{CD}}$, $\mathsf{ITL}^{\mathsf{FS}}$ and ITL^1 are sound for the class of all dynamical systems, of all dynamical posets, of all open dynamical systems, and of all persistent dynamical posets, respectively, which we have used in order to prove that the logics are pairwise distinct. Of course this immediately raises the question of completeness, which we have not addressed. Specifically, the following are left open.

Question 1. Are the logics:

- ITL^0 and $\mathsf{ITL}_\square^0$ complete for the class of dynamical systems?
- $\mathsf{ITL}^{\mathsf{CD}}$ and $\mathsf{ITL}_\square^{\mathsf{CD}}$ complete for the class of dynamic posets?
- $\mathsf{ITL}^{\mathsf{FS}}$, $\mathsf{ITL}_\lozenge^{\mathsf{FS}}$ and $\mathsf{ITL}_\square^{\mathsf{FS}}$ complete for the class of open dynamical systems?
- ITL^1, $\mathsf{ITL}_\lozenge^1$ and $\mathsf{ITL}_\square^1$ complete for the class of persistent dynamic posets?

We already know that $\mathsf{ITL}_\lozenge^0$ is sound and complete for the class of dynamic posets [12]. However, the completeness of $\mathsf{ITL}_\lozenge^{\mathsf{FS}}$ and $\mathsf{ITL}_\lozenge^1$ is likely to be a more difficult problem than that of $\mathsf{ITL}_\lozenge^0$, as in these cases it is not even known if the set of valid formulas is computably enumerable, let alone decidable.

Question 2. Are any of the logics Λ, $\Lambda_\Diamond$, or $\Lambda_\Box$ with $\Lambda \in \{\mathsf{ITL^p}, \mathsf{ITL^o}\}$ decidable and/or computably enumerable?

In any of these cases a negative answer is possible, since that is the case for their classical counterparts [20] and these logics do not have the finite model property [4]. Nevertheless, the proofs of non-axiomatizability in the classical case do not carry over to the intuitionistic setting in an obvious way, and these remain challenging open problems.

References

1. Aleksandroff, P.: Diskrete räume. Matematicheskii Sbornik **2**(44), 501–518 (1937)
2. Balbiani, P., Boudou, J., Diéguez, M., Fernández-Duque, D.: Bisimulations for intuitionistic temporal logics. arXiv:1803.05078 (2018)
3. Balbiani, P., Diéguez, M.: Temporal here and there. In: Michael, L., Kakas, A. (eds.) JELIA 2016. LNCS (LNAI), vol. 10021, pp. 81–96. Springer, Cham (2016). https://doi.org/10.1007/978-3-319-48758-8_6
4. Boudou, J., Diéguez, M., Fernández-Duque, D.: A decidable intuitionistic temporal logic. In: 26th EACSL Annual Conference on Computer Science Logic (CSL), vol. 82, pp. 14:1–14:17 (2017)
5. Brewka, G., Eiter, T., Truszczyński, M.: Answer set programming at a glance. Commun. ACM **54**(12), 92–103 (2011)
6. Cabalar, P., Pérez Vega, G.: Temporal equilibrium logic: a first approach. In: Moreno Díaz, R., Pichler, F., Quesada Arencibia, A. (eds.) EUROCAST 2007. LNCS, vol. 4739, pp. 241–248. Springer, Heidelberg (2007). https://doi.org/10.1007/978-3-540-75867-9_31
7. Davies, R.: A temporal-logic approach to binding-time analysis. In: Proceedings, 11th Annual IEEE Symposium on Logic in Computer Science, New Brunswick, New Jersey, USA, 27–30 July, 1996, pp. 184–195 (1996)
8. Davies, R.: A temporal logic approach to binding-time analysis. J. ACM **64**, 1:1–1:45 (2017)
9. Davies, R., Pfenning, F.: A modal analysis of staged computation. J. ACM **48**(3), 555–604 (2001)
10. Davoren, J.M.: On intuitionistic modal and tense logics and their classical companion logics: topological semantics and bisimulations. Ann. Pure Appl. Logic **161**(3), 349–367 (2009)
11. Davoren, J.M., Coulthard, V., Moor, T., Goré, R., Nerode, A.: Topological semantics for intuitionistic modal logics, and spatial discretisation by A/D maps. In: Workshop on Intuitionistic Modal Logic and Applications (IMLA) (2002)
12. Diéguez, M., Fernández-Duque, D.: An intuitionistic axiomatization of 'eventually'. In: Advances in Modal Logic, vol. 12, pp. 199–218 (2018)
13. Ershov, A.P.: On the partial computation principle. Inf. Process. Lett. **6**(2), 38–41 (1977)
14. Fernández-Duque, D.: The intuitionistic temporal logic of dynamical systems. Logical Methods Comput. Sci. **14**(3), 1–35 (2018)
15. Fischer Servi, G.: Axiomatisations for some intuitionistic modal logics. In: Rendiconti del Seminario Matematico, vol. 42, pp. 179–194. Universitie Politecnico Torino (1984)

16. Goldblatt, R.: Logics of time and computation. In: Center for the Study of Language and Information, CSLI Lecture Notes, no. 7, 2nd edn. Stanford (1992)
17. Howard, W.A.: The formulas-as-types notion of construction. In: Seldin, J.P., Hindley, J.R. (eds.) To H. B. Curry: Essays on Combinatory Logic, Lambda Calculus, and Formalism, pp. 479–490. Academic Press (1980)
18. Kamide, N., Wansing, H.: Combining linear-time temporal logic with constructiveness and paraconsistency. J. Appl. Logic **8**(1), 33–61 (2010)
19. Kojima, K., Igarashi, A.: Constructive linear-time temporal logic: proof systems and Kripke semantics. Inf. Comput. **209**(12), 1491–1503 (2011)
20. Konev, B., Kontchakov, R., Wolter, F., Zakharyaschev, M.: On dynamic topological and metric logics. Stud. Logica **84**, 129–160 (2006)
21. Kremer, P.: A small counterexample in intuitionistic dynamic topological logic (2004). http://individual.utoronto.ca/philipkremer/onlinepapers/counterex.pdf
22. Lichtenstein, O., Pnueli, A.: Propositional temporal logics: decidability and completeness. Logic J. IGPL **8**(1), 55–85 (2000)
23. Maier, P.: Intuitionistic LTL and a new characterization of safety and liveness. In: Marcinkowski, J., Tarlecki, A. (eds.) CSL 2004. LNCS, vol. 3210, pp. 295–309. Springer, Heidelberg (2004). https://doi.org/10.1007/978-3-540-30124-0_24
24. Mints, G.: A Short Introduction to Intuitionistic Logic. University Series in Mathematics. Springer (2000). https://doi.org/10.1007/b115304
25. Munkres, J.R.: Topology. Featured Titles for Topology Series, Prentice Hall, Incorporated (2000)
26. Pacuit, E.: Neighborhood Semantics for Modal Logic. Springer, Heidelberg (2017). https://doi.org/10.1007/978-3-319-67149-9
27. Pnueli, A.: The temporal logic of programs. In: 18th Annual Symposium on Foundations of Computer Science (SFCS 1977), pp. 46–57 (1977)
28. Simpson, A.K.: The proof theory and semantics of intuitionistic modal logic. Ph.D. thesis, University of Edinburgh, UK (1994)
29. Yuse, Y., Igarashi, A.: A modal type system for multi-level generating extensions with persistent code. In: Proceedings of the 8th ACM SIGPLAN International Conference on Principles and Practice of Declarative Programming, PPDP 2006, pp. 201–212 (2006)

Interval Temporal Logic Decision Tree Learning

Andrea Brunello[2] , Guido Sciavicco[1(✉)] , and Ionel Eduard Stan[2]

[1] Department of Mathematics and Computer Science,
University of Ferrara, Ferrara, Italy
guido.sciavicco@unife.it
[2] Department of Mathematics, Computer Science, and Physics,
University of Udine, Udine, Italy
andrea.brunello@uniud.it, stan.ioneleduard@spes.uniud.it

Abstract. Decision trees are simple, yet powerful, classification models used to classify categorical and numerical data, and, despite their simplicity, they are commonly used in operations research and management, as well as in knowledge mining. From a logical point of view, a decision tree can be seen as a structured set of logical rules written in propositional logic. Since knowledge mining is rapidly evolving towards temporal knowledge mining, and since in many cases temporal information is best described by interval temporal logics, propositional logic decision trees may evolve towards interval temporal logic decision trees. In this paper, we define the problem of interval temporal logic decision tree learning, and propose a solution that generalizes classical decision tree learning.

Keywords: Decision trees · Interval temporal logics ·
Symbolic learning

1 Introduction

It is commonly recognized that modern decision trees are of primary importance among classification models [30]. They owe their popularity mainly to the fact that they can be trained and applied efficiently even on big datasets, and that they are easily interpretable, meaning that they are not only useful for prediction per se, but also for understanding the reasons behind the predictions. Interpretability is of extreme importance in domains in which understanding the classification process is as important as the accuracy of the classification itself, such in the case of production business systems or in the computer-aided medicine domain. A typical decision tree is constructed in a recursive manner, following the traditional *Top Down Induction of Decision Trees* (TDIDT) approach [26]: starting from the root, at each node the attribute that best partitions the training data, according to a predefined score, is chosen as a test to guide the partitioning of instances into child nodes. The process continues until a sufficiently high degree of purity (with respect to the target class), or a

F. Calimeri et al. (Eds.): JELIA 2019, LNAI 11468, pp. 778–793, 2019.
https://doi.org/10.1007/978-3-030-19570-0_50

minimum cardinality constraint (with respect to the number of instances reaching the node), is achieved in the generated partitions. This is the case of the well-known decision tree learning algorithm ID3 [26], which is the precursor of the commonly-used C4.5 [27]. A decision tree can be seen as a structured set of rules: every node of the tree can be thought of as a decision point, and, in this way, each branch becomes a conjunction of such conditional statements, that is, a *rule*, whose right-hand part is the class. A conditional statement may have many forms: it can be a yes/no statement (for binary categorical attributes), a categorical value statement (for non-binary categorical attributes), or a splitting value statement (for numerical attributes); the ariety of the resulting tree is two if all attributes are binary or numerical, or more, if there are categorical attributes with more than two categories. Each statement can be equivalently represented with *propositional letters*, so that a decision tree can be also seen as a structured set of *propositional logic* rules.

Temporal Classification: Static Solutions. Just focusing on the static aspects of data is not always adequate for classification; for example, in the medical domain, one may want to take into account which symptoms a patient was experiencing at the same time, or whether two symptoms were overlapping. That is, in some application domains, the temporal aspects of the information may be essential to an accurate prediction. Within static decision tree learning, temporal information may be aggregated in order to circumvent the absence of explicit tools for dealing with temporal information (for example, a patient can be labelled with a natural number describing how many times he/she has been running a fever during the observation period); the ability of a decision tree to perform a precise classification based on such processed data, however, strongly depends on how well data are prepared, and therefore on how well the underlying domain is understood. Alternatively, decision trees have been proposed that use *frequent patterns* [15,19,22] in nodes, considering the presence/absence of a frequent pattern as a categorical attribute [13,18]. Nevertheless, despite being the most common approach to (explicit) temporal data classification, frequent patterns in sequences or series have a limited expressive power, as they are characterized by being *existential* and by intrinsically representing temporal information with instantaneous events.

Our Approach: Interval Temporal Logic Decision Trees. A different approach to temporal classification is mining temporal logic formulas, and since temporal databases universally adopt an interval-based representation of time, the ideal choice to represent temporal information in data is *interval* temporal logic. The most representative propositional interval temporal logic is Halpern and Shoham's Modal Logic of Allen's Relations [20], also known as HS. Its language encompasses one modal operator for each interval-to-interval relation, such as *meets* or *before*, and the computational properties of HS and its fragments have been studied in the recent literature (see, e.g. [10–12]). The very high expressive power of HS, as well as its versatility, make HS the ideal candidate to serve as the basis of a temporal decision tree learning algorithm. Based on these premises, we propose in this paper a decision tree learning algorithm that produces HS-based trees. Our proposal, Temporal ID3, is a direct generalization of the ID3 algorithm [26], founded on the logical interpretation of tree nodes, and focuses on data representation and node generation; we borrow other aspects, such as splitting based on information gain and the overall learning process from the original algorithm. The accuracy of a decision tree and its resilience to over-fitting also depends on the stopping criterion and possible post-pruning operations, but we do not discuss these aspects here.

Existing Approaches to Temporal Logic Decision Trees. Learning temporal logic decision trees is an emerging field in the analysis of physical systems, and, among the most influential approaches, we mention learning of automata [3] and learning Signal Temporal Logic (STL) formulas [6,14,24,28]. In particular, STL is a point-based temporal logic with *until* that encompasses certain metric capabilities, and learning formulas of STL has been focused on both the fine tuning of the metric parameters of a predefined formula and the learning the innermost structure of a formula; among others, decision trees have been used to this end [8]. Compared with STL decision tree learning, our approach has the advantage of learning formulas written in a well-known, highly expressive interval-based temporal logic language; because of the nature of the underlying language and of the interval temporal logic models, certain application domains fit naturally into this approach. Moreover, since our solution generalizes the classical decision tree learning algorithm ID3, and, particularly, the notion of information gain, it is not limited to binary classification only. Moreover, in [7] a first-order framework for TDIDT is presented with the attempt to make such paradigm more attractive to inductive logic programming (ILP). Such a framework provides a sound basis for logical decision tree induction; in opposition, we employ the framework to represent *modal*, instead of first-order, relational data. Additionally, our approach should not be confused with [23], in which the term *interval* indicates an uncertain numerical value (e.g., *the patient has a fever of 38 Celsius* versus *the patient has a fever between 37.5 and 38.5 Celsius*), and in which an algorithm for inducing decision trees on such uncertain data is presented that is based on the so-called Kolmogorov-Smirnov criterion, but the data that are object of that study are not necessarily temporal, and the produced trees do not employ any temporal (logical) relation. In [4,29] and [21], the authors present two other approaches to a temporal generalization of decision tree learning. In the former, the authors provide a general method for building point-based temporal decision trees, but with no particular emphasis on any supporting formal language. In the latter, the constructed trees can be seen as real-time algorithms that have the ability to make decisions even if the entire description of the instance is not yet available. Finally, in [16], a generalization of the decision tree model is presented in which nodes are possibly labelled with a timestamp to indicate when a certain condition should be checked.

Summarizing, our approach is essentially different from those presented in the literature in several aspects. As a matter of fact, by giving a logical perspective to decision tree learning, we effectively generalize the learning model to a temporal one, instead of introducing a new paradigm. In this way, instances that present some temporal component are naturally seen as timelines, and, thanks to the expressive power provided by HS, our algorithm can learn a decision tree based on the temporal relations between values, instead of the static information carried by the values.

2   Preliminaries

Decision Trees. Decision tree induction is based on the following simple concepts [27]. Given a set of observable values $V = \{v_1, v_2, \ldots, v_n\}$, with associated probabilities $\Pi = \{\pi_1, \pi_2, \ldots, \pi_n\}$, the *information conveyed by Π* (or *entropy*), is defined as:

$$E(\Pi) = -\sum_{i=1}^{n} \pi_i \log(\pi_i).$$

Assume that a dataset $\mathcal{T}$ has n instances, each characterized by the attributes $A_1, \ldots, A_l$, and distributed over s classes $C_1, \ldots, C_s$. Each class C can be seen as the subset of $\mathcal{T}$ composed of precisely those instances classified as C, so that the information needed to identify the class of an element of $\mathcal{T}$ is:

$$Info(\mathcal{T}) = E(\{\frac{|C_1|}{|T|}, \frac{|C_2|}{|T|}, \ldots, \frac{|C_s|}{|T|}\}).$$

Intuitively, the entropy is inversely proportional to the purity degree of $\mathcal{T}$ with respect to the class values. *Splitting*, which is the main operation in decision tree learning, is performed over a specific attribute A. If A is categorical and its domain $Dom(A)$ consists of m distinct values, we can split $\mathcal{T}$ into $\mathcal{T}_1, \ldots, \mathcal{T}_m$, each $\mathcal{T}_i$ being characterized by A having precisely the value a_i (i.e., $A = a_i$). The information of a categorical split, therefore, is:

$$InfoCat(A, \mathcal{T}) = \sum_{i=1}^{m} (\frac{|T_i|}{|T|}) Info(\mathcal{T}_i).$$

If, on the other hand, A is numerical, then the set $\{a_1 < \ldots < a_m\}$ of *actual* values for A that are present in $\mathcal{T}$ gives rise to $m - 1$ possible splits, all of them binary, and the information conveyed by each possible split is, then, a function not only of the attribute but also of the chosen value:

$$InfoNum(A, a_i, \mathcal{T}) = (\frac{|T_1|}{|T|}) Info(\mathcal{T}_1) + (\frac{|T_2|}{|T|}) Info(\mathcal{T}_2),$$

where $\mathcal{T}_1$ (respectively, $\mathcal{T}_2$) encompasses all and only those instances with $A \leq a_i$ (respectively, $A > a_i$). The information conveyed by an attribute can be consequently defined as:

HS	Allen's relations	Graphical representation
$\langle A \rangle$	$[x,y]R_A[x',y'] \Leftrightarrow y = x'$	
$\langle L \rangle$	$[x,y]R_L[x',y'] \Leftrightarrow y < x'$	
$\langle B \rangle$	$[x,y]R_B[x',y'] \Leftrightarrow x = x', y' < y$	
$\langle E \rangle$	$[x,y]R_E[x',y'] \Leftrightarrow y = y', x < x'$	
$\langle D \rangle$	$[x,y]R_D[x',y'] \Leftrightarrow x < x', y' < y$	
$\langle O \rangle$	$[x,y]R_O[x',y'] \Leftrightarrow x < x' < y < y'$	

Fig. 1. Allen's interval relations and HS modalities.

$$InfoAtt(A,\mathcal{T}) = \begin{cases} InfoCat(A,\mathcal{T}) & \text{if } A \text{ is categorical,} \\ \min_{a_i \in Dom(A)} \{InfoNum(A,a_i,\mathcal{T})\} & \text{if } A \text{ is numerical,} \end{cases}$$

and the *information gain* brought by A is defined as:

$$Gain(A,\mathcal{T}) = Info(\mathcal{T}) - InfoAtt(A,\mathcal{T}).$$

The information gain, which can be also seen as the reduction of the expected entropy when the attribute A has been chosen, is used to drive the splitting process, that is, to decide over which attribute (and how) the next split is performed. The underlying principle to decision tree building consists of recursively splitting the dataset over the attribute that guarantees the greatest information gain until a certain stopping criterion is met. Each split can be seen as a propositional condition *if p then -, else -*. When splitting is performed over a numerical attribute, e.g., $A \leq a_i$, then the corresponding propositional statement is simply the condition itself (in our example, is a propositional letter $p_{A \leq a_i}$); when it is performed over a categorical attribute, e.g., $A = a_1$, $A = a_2$, ..., then each statement is a propositional statement (in our example, $p_{A=a_1}, p_{A=a_2}, \ldots$) on its own.

Interval Temporal Logic. Let $\mathbb{D} \subseteq \mathbb{N}$. In the *strict* interpretation, an *interval* over $\mathbb{D}$ is an ordered pair $[x,y]$, where $x,y \in \mathbb{D}$ and $x < y$, and we denote by $\mathbb{I}(\mathbb{D})$ the set of all intervals over $\mathbb{D}$. If we exclude the identity relation, there are 12 different Allen's relations between two intervals in a linear order [1]: the six relations R_A (adjacent to), R_L (later than), R_B (begins), R_E (ends), R_D (during), and R_O (overlaps), depicted in Fig. 1, and their inverses, that is, $R_{\overline{X}} = (R_X)^{-1}$, for each $X \in \mathcal{A}$, where $\mathcal{A} = \{A, L, B, E, D, O\}$. Halpern and Shoham's modal logic of temporal intervals (HS) is defined from a set of propositional letters $\mathcal{AP}$, and by associating a universal modality $[X]$ and an existential one $\langle X \rangle$ to each Allen's relation R_X. Formulas of HS are obtained by

$$\varphi ::= p \mid \neg\varphi \mid \varphi \vee \varphi \mid \langle X \rangle\varphi \mid \langle \overline{X} \rangle\varphi,$$

where $p \in \mathcal{AP}$ and $X \in \mathcal{A}$. The other Boolean connectives and the logical constants, e.g., $\rightarrow$ and $\top$, as well as the universal modalities $[X]$, can be defined in the standard way. For each $X \in \mathcal{A}$, the modality $\langle \overline{X} \rangle$ (corresponding to the inverse relation $R_{\overline{X}}$ of R_X) is said to be the *transpose* of the modalities $\langle X \rangle$, and vice versa. The semantics of HS formulas is given in terms of *timelines* $T = \langle \mathbb{I}(\mathbb{D}), V \rangle^1$, where $\mathbb{D}$ is a linear order and $V : \mathcal{AP} \rightarrow 2^{\mathbb{I}(\mathbb{D})}$ is a *valuation function* which assigns to each atomic proposition $p \in \mathcal{AP}$ the set of intervals $V(p)$ on which p holds. The *truth* of a formula φ on a given interval $[x, y]$ in an interval model T is defined by structural induction on formulas as follows:

$$T, [x, y] \Vdash p \quad \text{if } [x, y] \in V(p), \text{ for } p \in \mathcal{AP};$$
$$T, [x, y] \Vdash \neg \psi \quad \text{if } T, [x, y] \not\Vdash \psi;$$
$$T, [x, y] \Vdash \psi \vee \xi \text{ if } T, [x, y] \Vdash \psi \text{ or } T, [x, y] \Vdash \xi;$$
$$T, [x, y] \Vdash \langle X \rangle \psi \text{ if there is } [w, z] \text{ s.t } [x, y] R_X [w, z] \text{ and } T, [w, z] \Vdash \psi;$$
$$T, [x, y] \Vdash \langle \bar{X} \rangle \psi \text{ if there is } [w, z] \text{ s.t } [x, y] R_{\bar{X}} [w, z] \text{ and } T, [w, z] \Vdash \psi.$$

HS is a very general interval temporal language and its satisfiability problem is undecidable [20]. Our purpose here, however, is to study the problem of formula *induction* in the form of decision trees, and not of formula *deduction*, and therefore the computational properties of the satisfiability problem can be ignored at this stage.

3 Motivations

In this section, we present some realistic scenarios in which learning a temporal decision tree may be convenient, and, then, we discuss aspects of data preprocessing related to the temporal component.

Learning. There are several application domains in which learning a temporal decision tree may be useful. Consider, for example, a medical scenario in which we consider a dataset of classified patients, each one characterized by its medical history, as in Fig. 2, top. Assume, first, that we are interested in learning a *static* (propositional) classification model. The history of our patients, that is, the collection of all relevant pieces of information about tests, results, symptoms, and hospitalizations of the patient that occurred during the entire observation period, must be processed so that temporal information is subsumed in propositional letters. For instance, if some patient has been running a fever during the observation period, we may use a proposition $fever$, with positive values for those patient that have had fever, and negative values for the others (as in Fig. 2, bottom, left). Depending on the specific case, we may, instead, use the actual temperature of each patient, and a static decision tree learning system may split over $fever < t$, for some threshold temperature t, effectively introducing a new propositional letter, and therefore a binary split. Either way, the temporal information is lost in the preprocessing. For example, we can no longer

---
[1] We deliberately use the symbol T to indicate both a timeline and an instance in a dataset.

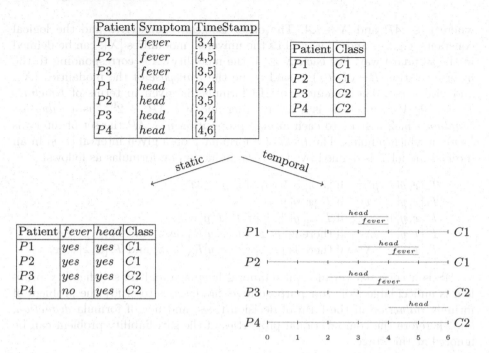

Fig. 2. Example of static and temporal treatment of information in the medical domain.

take into account whether *fever* occurred before, after, or while the patient was experiencing headache (*head*), which may be a relevant information for a classification model. By generating, instead, the timeline of each patient (as in Fig. 2, bottom, right), we keep all events and their relative qualitative relations. By learning a decision tree on a preprocessed dataset such as the one in Fig. 2 (bottom, left), we see that the attribute *head* has zero variance, and therefore zero predictive capabilities; then, we are forced to build a decision tree using attribute *fever* alone, which results in a classifier with 75% accuracy. On the contrary, by using the temporal information in the learning process, we are able to distinguish the two classes: *C*1 is characterized by presenting both *head* and *fever*, but not overlapping, and this classifier has, in this toy example, 100% accuracy. In this example, the term *accuracy* refers to the *training set accuracy* (we do not consider independent trainining and test data), that is, the ability of the classification system to discern among classes on the data used to train the system itself; it should not be confused with *test set accuracy*, which measures the real classification performances that can be expected on future, real-life examples.

Alternatively, consider a problem in the natural language processing domain. In this scenario, a timeline may represent a *conversation* between two individuals. It is known that, in automatic processing of conversations, it is sometimes interesting to label each interval of time with one or more *context*, that is, a particular topic that is being discussed [2,5,25], in order to discover the existence of unexpected or interesting temporal relations among them. Suppose, for example, that a certain company wants to analyze conversations between selling agents and potential customers: the agents contact the customers with the aim of selling a certain product, and it is known that certain contexts, such as the price of the product (*price*), its known advantages (*advantages*) over other products, and its possible minor defects (*disadvantages*) are interesting. Assume that each conversation has been previously classified between those that have been successful and those that ended without the product being acquired. Now, we want to learn a model able to predict such an outcome. By using only static information, nearly every conversation would be labelled with the three contexts, effectively hiding the underlying knowledge, if it exists. By keeping the relative temporal relations between contexts, instead, we may learn useful information, such as, for example, *if price and disadvantages are not discussed together, the conversation will be likely successful.*

Preprocessing. Observe, now, how switching from static to temporal information influences data preparation. First, in a context such as the one described in our first example, numerical attributes may become less interesting: for instance, the information on *how many times* a certain symptom occurred, or its *frequency*, are not needed anymore, considering that each occurrence is taken into account in the timeline. Moreover, since the focus is on attributes *relative temporal positions*, even categorical attributes may be ignored in some contexts: for instance, in our scenario, we may be interested in establishing the predictive value of the relative temporal position of *fever* and *head* regardless of the sex or age of the patient. It is also worth underlying that propositional attributes over intervals allow us to express a variety of situations, and sometimes propositional labelling may result in *gaining* information, instead of loosing it. Consider, again, the case of fever, and suppose that a certain patient is experiencing low fever in an interval $[x, y]$, say, a given day, and that during just one hour of that day, that is, over the interval $[w, z]$ strictly contained in $[x, y]$, he/she has an episode of high fever. A natural choice is to represent such a situation by labelling the interval $[x, y]$ with lo and its sub-interval $[w, z]$ with hi. On the other hand, representing the same pieces of information as three intervals $[x, w], [w, z], [z, y]$ respectively labelled with lo, hi, and lo, which would be the case with a point-based representation (or with an interval-based representation under the homogeneity assumption), would be unnatural, and it would entail hiding a potentially important information such as: *"the patient presented low fever during the entire day, except for a brief episode of high fever"*. Building on such considerations, our approach in the rest of this paper is based on propositional, non-numerical attributes only.

4   Learning Interval Temporal Logic Decision Trees

In this section we describe a generalization of the algorithm ID3 that is capable of learning a binary decision tree over a temporal dataset, as in the examples of the previous section; as in classical decision trees, every branch of a temporal decision tree can be read as a logical formula, but instead of classical propositional logic we use the temporal logic HS. To this end, we generalize the notion of information gain, while, at this stage, we do not discuss pre-pruning, post-pruning, and purity degree of a sub-tree [9,27].

Data Preparation and Presentation. We assume that the input dataset contains timelines as instances. For the sake of simplicity, we also assume that all timelines are based on the same finite domain $\mathbb{D}$ of length N (from 0 to $N-1$). The dataset $\mathcal{T}$ can be seen as an array of n structures; $\mathcal{T}[j]$ represents the j-th timeline of the dataset, and it can be thought of as an interval model. Given a dataset $\mathcal{T}$, we denote by $\mathcal{AP}$ the set of all propositional letters that occur in it.

Temporal Information. We are going to design the learning process based on the same principles of classical decision tree learning. This means that we need to define a notion of splitting as well as a notion of information conveyed by a split, and, to this end, we shall use the truth relation as defined in Sect. 2 applied to a timeline. Unlike the atemporal case, splits are not performed over attributes, but, instead, over propositional letters. Splitting is defined *relatively to an interval* $[x, y]$, and it can be local, if it is applied on $[x, y]$ itself, or temporal, in which case it depends on the existence of an interval $[z, t]$ related to $[x, y]$ and the particular relation R_X such that $[x, y]R_X[z, t]$ (or the other way around). A *local split* of $\mathcal{T}$ into $\mathcal{T}_1$ and $\mathcal{T}_2$, where $[x, y]$ is the *reference* interval of $\mathcal{T}$, and p is the propositional letter over which the split takes place is defined by:

$$\begin{aligned}\mathcal{T}_1 &= \{T \in \mathcal{T} \mid T, [x, y] \Vdash p\}, \\ \mathcal{T}_2 &= \{T \in \mathcal{T} \mid T, [x, y] \Vdash \neg p\}.\end{aligned} \tag{1}$$

On the contrary, a *temporal split*, in the same situation, over the temporal relation R_X, is defined by:

$$\begin{aligned}\mathcal{T}_1 &= \{T \in \mathcal{T} \mid T, [x, y] \Vdash \langle X \rangle p\}, \\ \mathcal{T}_2 &= \{T \in \mathcal{T} \mid T, [x, y] \Vdash [X] \neg p\}.\end{aligned} \tag{2}$$

Consequently, the *local information gain* of a propositional letter p is defined as:

$$LocalGain(p, \mathcal{T}) = Info(\mathcal{T}) - \left((\frac{|\mathcal{T}_1|}{|\mathcal{T}|})Info(\mathcal{T}_1) + (\frac{|\mathcal{T}_2|}{|\mathcal{T}|})Info(\mathcal{T}_2) \right),$$

where $\mathcal{T}_1$ and $\mathcal{T}_2$ are defined as in (1), while the *temporal information gain* of a propositional letter p is defined as:

$$TemporalGain(p, \mathcal{T}) = Info(\mathcal{T}) - \min_{X \in \mathcal{A}} \left\{ (\frac{|\mathcal{T}_1|}{|\mathcal{T}|})Info(\mathcal{T}_1) + (\frac{|\mathcal{T}_2|}{|\mathcal{T}|})Info(\mathcal{T}_2) \right\},$$

where $\mathcal{T}_1$ and $\mathcal{T}_2$ are defined as in (2) and depend on the relation R_X. Therefore, the information gain of a propositional letter becomes:

$$Gain(p, \mathcal{T}) = \max\{LocalGain(p, \mathcal{T}), TemporalGain(p, \mathcal{T})\},$$

and, at each step, we aim to find the letter that maximizes the gain.

```
proc FindBestUnanchoredSplit (T)
  gBest = 0
  for ([x, y] ∈ I(D))
    AssignReferenceInterval(T, [x, y])
    < X, p, g >= FindBestAnchoredSplit(T)
    if (g > gBest)
      then
        < XBest, pBest, gBest >=< X, p, g >
        [xBest, yBest] = [x, y]
    AssignReferenceInterval(T, [xBest, yBest])
  return  < XBest, pBest, gBest, [xBest, yBest] >
```

```
proc FindBestAnchoredSplit (T)
  gBest = 0
  for (p ∈ AP)
    < X, g >= Gain(p, T)
    if (g > gBest)
      then    < XBest, pBest, gBest >=< X, p, g >
  return  < XBest, pBest, gBest >
```

```
proc Temporal ID3 (T)
  c = CreateNode()
  Learn(T, c)
```

```
proc Learn (T, c)
  if NoStop(T)
    then
      if UnAnchored(T)
        then
          < X, p, g, [x, y] >= FindBestUnanchoredSplit(T)
          Label(c, [x, y])
        else   < X, p, g >= FindBestAnchoredSplit(T)
      (T1, T2) = Split(T, X, p)
      c1 = CreateLeftChild(c)
      c2 = CreateRightChild(c)
      Learn(T1, c1)
      Learn(T2, c2)
```

Fig. 3. The algorithm Temporal ID3.

The Algorithm. Let us analyze the code in Fig. 3. At the beginning, the timelines in T are not assigned any reference interval, and we say that the dataset is *unanchored*. The procedure *FindBestUnanchoredSplit* systematically explores every possible reference interval of an unanchored dataset, and, for each one of them, calls *FindBestAnchoredSplit*, which, in turn, tries every propositional letter (and, implicitly, every temporal relation) in the search of the best split. This procedure returns the best possible triple $<X, p, g>$, where X is an interval relation, if the best split is temporal, or it has no value, if the best split is local, p is a propositional letter, and g is the information gain. *Temporal ID3* first creates a root node, and then calls *Learn*. The latter, in turn, first checks possible stopping conditions, and then finds the best split into two datasets T_1 and T_2. Of these, the former is now *anchored* (to the reference interval returned by *FindBestUnanchoredSplit*), while the latter is still unanchored. During a recursive call, when T_1 is analyzed to find its best split, the procedure for this task will be *FindBestAnchoredSplit*, called directly, instead of passing through *FindBestUnanchoredSplit*. So, in our learning model, all splits are binary. Given a node, the 'lefthand' outgoing edge is labeled with the chosen $\langle X \rangle p$, or just p, when the

Patient	Symptom	TimeStamp
P1	fever	[0,2]
P2	fever	[1,3]
P3	head	[0,2]
P4	head	[1,3]

Patient	Class
P1	C1
P2	C1
P3	C2
P4	C2

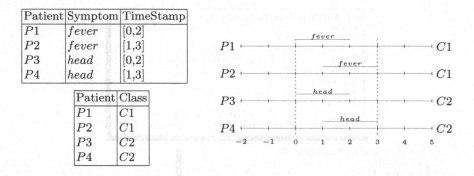

Fig. 4. Example of a problematic dataset.

split is local, whereas the corresponding 'righthand' edge is labeled with $[X]\neg p$ (or just $\neg p$); also, the node is labeled with a new reference interval if its corresponding dataset is unanchored. After a split, every $T \in \mathcal{T}_1$ (the existential dataset, which is now certainly anchored) is associated with a new *witnessing interval*: in fact, those instances satisfy $\langle X \rangle p$ on $[x, y]$, and, for each one of them, there is a possibly distinct witness. Witnesses are assigned by the function *Split*; while the witnessing interval of an instance may change during the process, its reference interval is set only once.

Consider, now, the function *AssignReferenceInterval* and the example shown in Fig. 4. As can be seen, neglecting the temporal dimension, one may classify the instances with just a single split based on the presence of the symptom fever (or headache). On the contrary, given the temporal dataset with domain $\mathbb{D} = \{0, 1, 2, 3\}$ it is not possible discriminate the classes within a single step. A natural solution consists of augmenting $\mathbb{D}$ in such a way to simulate the behaviour of an infinite domain model. In our example, it suffices to consider $\mathbb{D} = \{-2, -1, 0, 1, 2, 3, 4, 5\}$, so that a single split may be based on the rule: $\langle L \rangle fever \rightarrow C1$, otherwise $C2$ holding on $[-2, -1]$ (or, equivalently, its inverse formulation on $[4, 5]$). Thus, the function *AssignReferenceIntervals*, while searching all possible reference intervals, takes into consideration two extra points at each side of the domain. Although it is possible to obtain a similar result by adding less than four points (in our example, -2 and -1 suffice), this is no longer true if we include the possibility that Temporal ID3 is called on a *subset* of HS modalities, for example, for computational efficiency reasons. Adding four points, on the other hand, guarantees that the most discriminative split can always be found.

Analysis. We now analyze the computational complexity of Temporal ID3. To this end, we first compute the cost of finding the best splitting. Since the cardinality of the domain of each timeline is N, there are $O(N^2)$ possible intervals. This means that, fixed a propositional letter and a relation R_X, computing $\mathcal{T}_1$ and $\mathcal{T}_2$ costs $O(nN^2)$, where n is the number of timelines. Therefore, the cost of *FindBestAnchoredSplit* is obtained by multiplying the cost of a single (tentative) splitting by the number of propositional letters and the number of temporal relations (plus one, to take into account the local splitting), which sums up to $O(13nN^2|\mathcal{AP}|)$. The cost of *FindBestUnanchoredSplit* increases by a factor of N^2, as the **for** cycle ranges over all possible intervals, and therefore it becomes $O(13nN^4|\mathcal{AP}|)$. We can increase the efficiency of the implementation by suitably pre-compute the value of $\langle X \rangle p$ for each temporal relation, each propositional letter, and each interval, thus eliminating a factor of N^2 from both costs.

If we consider $\mathcal{AP}$ as fixed, and N as a constant, the cost of finding the best splitting becomes $O(n)$, and, under such (reasonable) assumption, we can analyze the complexity of an execution of *Learn* in terms of the number n of timelines. Two cases are particularly interesting. In the worst case, every binary split leads to a very unbalanced partition of the dataset, with $|\mathcal{T}_1| = 1$ and $|\mathcal{T}_2| = n - 1$ (or the other way around). The recurrence that describes such a situation is:

$$t(n) = t(n-1) + O(n),$$

which can be immediately solved to obtain $t(n) = O(n^2)$. However, computing the worst case has only a theoretical value; we can reasonably expect Temporal ID3 to behave like a randomized divide-and-conquer algorithm, and its computational complexity to tend towards the average case. In the average case, every binary split leads to a non-unbalanced partition, but we cannot foresee the relative cardinality of each side of the partition. Assuming that every partition is equally probable, the recurrence that describes this situation is:

$$t(n) = \frac{1}{n} \sum_{k=1}^{n} (t(k) + t(n-k)) + O(n).$$

We want to prove that $t(n) = O(n \log(n))$. To this end, we first prove a useful bound for the expression $\sum_{k=1}^{n} k \log(k)$, as follows:

$$\sum_{k=1}^{n} (k \log(k)) = \sum_{k=1}^{\lceil \frac{n}{2} \rceil - 1} (k \log(k)) + \sum_{k=\lceil \frac{n}{2} \rceil}^{n} (k \log(k))$$

$$\leq \sum_{k=1}^{\lceil \frac{n}{2} \rceil - 1} (k \log(\tfrac{n}{2})) + \sum_{k=\lceil \frac{n}{2} \rceil}^{n} (k \log(n))$$

$$= (\log(n) - 1) \sum_{k=1}^{\lceil \frac{n}{2} \rceil - 1} k + \log(n) \sum_{k=\lceil \frac{n}{2} \rceil}^{n} k$$

$$= \log(n) \sum_{k=1}^{n} k - \sum_{k=1}^{\lceil \frac{n}{2} \rceil - 1} k$$

$$\leq \tfrac{1}{2} \log(n) n(n+1) - \tfrac{1}{2} \tfrac{n}{2} (\tfrac{n}{2} + 1)$$

$$= \tfrac{1}{2} (n^2 \log(n) + n \log(n)) - \tfrac{1}{8} n^2 - \tfrac{1}{4} n.$$

Now, we prove, by induction, that $t(n) \leq a\,n \log(n) + b$ for some positive constants a, b, as follows:

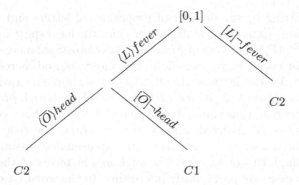

Fig. 5. A decision tree learned by Temporal ID3 on the example in Fig. 2.

$$t(n) = \frac{1}{n} \sum_{k=1}^{n} (t(k) + t(n-k)) + O(n)$$

$$= \frac{2}{n} \sum_{k=1}^{n} t(k) + O(n)$$

$$\leq \frac{2}{n} \sum_{k=1}^{n} (ak \log(k) + b) + O(n) \qquad \text{inductive hypothesis}$$

$$= \frac{2}{n} \sum_{k=1}^{n} (ak \log(k)) + \frac{2}{n} \sum_{k=1}^{n} b + O(n)$$

$$= \frac{2a}{n} \sum_{k=1}^{n} (k \log(k)) + 2b + O(n)$$

$$\leq \frac{2a}{n} (\frac{1}{2}(n^2 \log(n) + n \log(n)) - \frac{1}{8}n^2 - \frac{1}{4}n)$$

$$\quad + 2b + O(n) \qquad\qquad\qquad \text{proved above}$$

$$= an \log(n) + 2a \log(n) - \frac{an}{4} - \frac{a}{2}$$

$$\quad + 2b + O(n)$$

$$\leq an \log(n) + b. \qquad\qquad \text{if } \frac{an}{4} \geq 2a\log(n) - \frac{a}{2} + b + O(n).$$

Example of Execution. Consider our initial example of Fig. 2, with four time-lines distributed over two classes. Since this is a toy example, there are many different combination of intervals, relations, and propositional letters that give the same information gain. Figure 5 gives one possible outcome, which seems to indicate that, looking at the entire history, the class $C2$ is characterized by presenting headache and overlapping fever, or no fever at all.

There are several running parameters that can be modulated for an execution of Temporal ID3, and further analysis is required to understand how they influence the final result, and, particularly, the properties of the resulting classifier. The most important ones are: *(i)* how to behave in case of two splits with the same information gain; *(ii)* how to behave in case of more than one possible witness interval for a given timeline; *(iii)* how to behave in case of more than one optimal reference interval for a given unanchored temporal dataset. If we allow, in all such cases, a random choice, the resulting learning algorithm is not deterministic anymore, and different executions may result in different decision trees. This is a typical situation in machine learning (e.g., in algorithms such as *k-means clustering*, or *random forest*), that involves some experience in order to meaningfully assess the results.

5 Conclusions

Classical decision trees, which are a popular class of learning algorithms, are designed to interpret categorical and numerical attributes. In decision trees, every node can be seen as a propositional letter; therefore, a decision tree can be seen as a structured set of propositional logic rules, the right-hand part of which is a class. Since classifying based on the static aspects of data is not always adequate, and since decision tree learning cannot deal with temporal knowledge in an explicit manner, we considered the problem of learning a classification model capable to combine propositional knowledge with qualitative temporal information. Towards its solution, we showed how temporal data can be prepared in a optimal way for a temporal decision tree to be learned and presented a generalization of the classical decision tree learning algorithm ID3 that is able to split the dataset based on temporal, instead of static, information, using the well-known temporal logic HS. Future work include testing our method on real data, improving the capabilities of Temporal ID3 by enriching the underlying language, and studying the effect of different pruning and stopping conditions. Moreover, it would be interesting to study adapting ID3 to other logical languages, although this may require re-designing some key elements, such as the representation of temporal datasets, or the process that underlies the splitting algorithm.

Machine learning is generically focused on a non-logical approach to knowledge representation. However, when learning should take into account temporal aspects of data, a logical approach can be associated to classical methods, and besides decision tree learning, interval temporal logics has been already proposed as a possible tool, for example, for temporal rules extraction [17]. Focusing these approaches on fragments of interval temporal logics whose satisfiability problem is decidable (and tractable) may result into an integrated systems that pairs induction and deduction of formulas, intelligent elimination of redundant rules, and automatic verification of inducted knowledge against formal requirement. Also, using a logical approach in learning may require non-standard semantics for logical formulas (e.g., fuzzy semantics, or multi-valued propositional semantics); these, in turn, pose original and interesting questions on the theoretical side concerning the computational properties of the problems associated with these logics (i.e., satisfiability), generating, *de facto*, a cross-feeding effect on the two fields.

References

1. Allen, J.F.: Maintaining knowledge about temporal intervals. Commun. ACM **26**(11), 832–843 (1983)
2. Alluhaibi, R.: Simple interval temporal logic for natural language assertion descriptions. In: Proceedings of the 11th International Conference on Computational Semantics (IWCS), pp. 283–293 (2015)
3. Angluin, D.: Learning regular sets from queries and counterexamples. Inf. Comput. **75**(2), 87–106 (1987)
4. Antipov, S., Fomina, M.: A method for compiling general concepts with the use of temporal decision trees. Sci. Tech. Inf. Process. **38**(6), 409–419 (2011)
5. Baeza-Yates, R.: Challenges in the interaction of information retrieval and natural language processing. In: Gelbukh, A. (ed.) CICLing 2004. LNCS, vol. 2945, pp. 445–456. Springer, Heidelberg (2004). https://doi.org/10.1007/978-3-540-24630-5_55
6. Bartocci, E., Bortolussi, L., Sanguinetti, G.: Data-driven statistical learning of temporal logic properties. In: Legay, A., Bozga, M. (eds.) FORMATS 2014. LNCS, vol. 8711, pp. 23–37. Springer, Cham (2014). https://doi.org/10.1007/978-3-319-10512-3_3
7. Blockeel, H., De Raedt, L.: Top-down induction of first-order logical decision trees. Artif. Intell. **101**(1–2), 285–297 (1998)
8. Bombara, G., Vasile, C., Penedo, F., Yasuoka, H., Belta, C.: A decision tree approach to data classification using signal temporal logic. In: Proceedings of the 19th International Conference on Hybrid Systems: Computation and Control, pp. 1–10 (2016)
9. Breiman, L., Friedman, J., Olshen, R., Stone, C.: Classification and Regression Trees. Wadsworth and Brooks, Monterey (1984)
10. Bresolin, D., Della Monica, D., Goranko, V., Montanari, A., Sciavicco, G.: Metric propositional neighborhood logics on natural numbers. Softw. Syst. Model. **12**(2), 245–264 (2013)
11. Bresolin, D., Monica, D.D., Montanari, A., Sala, P., Sciavicco, G.: Interval temporal logics over strongly discrete linear orders: expressiveness and complexity. Theor. Comput. Sci. **560**, 269–291 (2014)
12. Bresolin, D., Sala, P., Sciavicco, G.: On begins, meets, and before. Int. J. Found. Comput. Sci. **23**(3), 559–583 (2012)
13. Brunello, A., Marzano, E., Montanari, A., Sciavicco, G.: J48S: a sequence classification approach to text analysis based on decision trees. In: Proceedings of the 24th International Conference on Information and Software Technologies (ICIST), pp. 240–256 (2018)
14. Bufo, S., Bartocci, E., Sanguinetti, G., Borelli, M., Lucangelo, U., Bortolussi, L.: Temporal logic based monitoring of assisted ventilation in intensive care patients. In: Margaria, T., Steffen, B. (eds.) ISoLA 2014. LNCS, vol. 8803, pp. 391–403. Springer, Heidelberg (2014). https://doi.org/10.1007/978-3-662-45231-8_30
15. Cheng, H., Yan, X., Han, J., Hsu, C.: Discriminative frequent pattern analysis for effective classification. In: Proceedings of the 23rd International Conference on Data Engineering (ICDE), pp. 716–725 (2007)
16. Console, L., Picardi, C., Dupré, D.: Temporal decision trees: model-based diagnosis of dynamic systems on-board. J. Artif. Intell. Res. **19**, 469–512 (2003)

17. Della Monica, D., de Frutos-Escrig, D., Montanari, A., Murano, A., Sciavicco, G.: Evaluation of temporal datasets via interval temporal logic model checking. In: Proceedings of the 24th International Symposium on Temporal Representation and Reasoning (TIME), pp. 11:1–11:18 (2017)

18. Fan, W., et al.: Direct mining of discriminative and essential frequent patterns via model-based search tree. In: Proceedings of the 14th ACM SIGKDD International Conference on Knowledge Discovery and Data Mining, pp. 230–238 (2008)

19. Fournier-Viger, P., Gomariz, A., Šebek, M., Hlosta, M.: VGEN: fast vertical mining of sequential generator patterns. In: Bellatreche, L., Mohania, M.K. (eds.) DaWaK 2014. LNCS, vol. 8646, pp. 476–488. Springer, Cham (2014). https://doi.org/10.1007/978-3-319-10160-6_42

20. Halpern, J., Shoham, Y.: A propositional modal logic of time intervals. J. ACM **38**(4), 935–962 (1991)

21. Karimi, K., Hamilton, H.J.: Temporal rules and temporal decision trees: a C4.5 approach. Technical report, CS-2001-02, Department of Computer Science, University of Regina (2001)

22. Lin, W., Orgun, M.A.: Temporal data mining using hidden periodicity analysis. In: Raś, Z.W., Ohsuga, S. (eds.) ISMIS 2000. LNCS (LNAI), vol. 1932, pp. 49–58. Springer, Heidelberg (2000). https://doi.org/10.1007/3-540-39963-1_6

23. Mballo, C., Diday, E.: Decision trees on interval valued variables. Symbolic Data Anal. **3**(1), 8–18 (2005)

24. Nguyen, L., Kapinski, J., Jin, X., Deshmukh, J., Butts, K., Johnson, T.: Abnormal data classification using time-frequency temporal logic. In: Proceedings of the 20th International Conference on Hybrid Systems: Computation and Control, pp. 237–242 (2017)

25. Pratt-Hartmann, I.: Temporal prepositions and their logic. Artif. Intell. **166**(1–2), 1–36 (2005)

26. Quinlan, J.: Induction of decision trees. Mach. Learn. **1**, 81–106 (1986)

27. Quinlan, J.: Simplifying decision trees. Int. J. Hum.-Comput. Stud. **51**(2), 497–510 (1999)

28. Rajan, A.: Automated requirements-based test case generation. SIGSOFT Softw. Eng. Notes **31**(6), 1–2 (2006)

29. Vagin, V., Morosin, O., Fomina, M., Antipov, S.: Temporal decision trees in diagnostics systems. In: 2018 International Conference on Advances in Big Data, Computing and Data Communication Systems (icABCD), pp. 1–10 (2018)

30. Witten, I., Frank, E., Hall, M., Pal, C.: Data Mining: Practical Machine Learning Tools and Techniques. Morgan Kaufmann, Burlington (2016)

Stable-Ordered Models for Propositional Theories with Order Operators

Johannes Oetsch[✉] and Juan-Carlos Nieves

Department of Computing Science, Umeå University, Umeå, Sweden
{joetsch,jcnieves}@cs.umu.se

Abstract. The stable-model semantics has been generalised from logic programs to arbitrary theories. We explore a further generalisation and consider sequences of atoms as models instead of sets. The language is extended by suitable order operators to access this additional information. We recently introduced an extension of classical logic by a single order operator with a temporal interpretation for activity reasoning. The logic envisaged here is a nonmonotonic version thereof. Our definition of what we call stable-ordered models is based on the stable-model semantics for theories due to Ferraris and Lifschitz with the necessary changes. Compared to related nonmonotonic versions of temporal logics, our approach is less costly as checking model existence remains at the second level of the polynomial hierarchy. We demonstrate versatile applications from activity reasoning, combinatorial testing, debugging concurrent programs, and digital forensics.

Keywords: Stable-model semantics · Temporal logic · Nonmonotonic reasoning · Knowledge representation

1 Introduction

Answer-set programming (ASP) is a problem solving paradigm with many AI applications [7]. It means that problems are encoded as logic programs so that the solutions correspond to the models of the programs [13,15]. The stable-model semantics for logic programs, introduced by Gelfond and Lifschitz [10], is the basis of ASP. It has been generalised to arbitrary theories by Pearce [17] using equilibrium logic. Ferraris and Lifschitz [8,9] came up with an alternative characterisation that is based on reducts which is more in the spirit of the original definition. We explore a further generalisation and consider sequences of atoms as models instead of sets. The language is extended by suitable order operators to access this additional information. The order of atoms can be interpreted in different ways: either temporal, e.g., the order in which goals or events are achieved, or in a more general sense as how objects of interest are arranged or permuted.

Besides curiosity, our motivation to study a new generalisation comes from *activity reasoning*, a topic that we studied in recent work [16]. There, we introduced a monotonic version of the logic we are envisioning here. Models in this

F. Calimeri et al. (Eds.): JELIA 2019, LNAI 11468, pp. 794–802, 2019.
https://doi.org/10.1007/978-3-030-19570-0_51

monotonic logic, dubbed *ordered models*, are sequences of atoms without repetition and the language is standard classical logic plus a single modal operator. Intuitively, a model represents in which order goals—viewed as atomic entities—are achieved. However, the monotonic semantics comes with the usual limitations for representing incomplete knowledge which is common in activity reasoning. Based on the temporal logic from previous work, we introduce a *nonmonotonic semantics for theories with order operators*. We use the reduct-based definition of stable models for theories from Ferraris and Lifschitz [8,9] with the necessary changes to define what we call *stable-ordered models*.

Related to this work is a nonmonotonic variant of linear-temporal logic (LTL) [18] based on infinite traces and equilibrium logic [1]. A version of this logic for finite traces has been introduced recently by Cabalar et al. [5]. Their approach is readily implementable via ASP but requires multi-shot solving, i.e., several calls to an ASP solver are necessary to compute a satisfying trace. This is in accordance with the complexity of satisfiability checking which is PSPACE hard. Also other approaches extend LTL for nonmonotonic reasoning and elaboration tolerant goal representations [2,3]. Our approach is different from all previous work as the idea to use a sequence of atoms as model is quite unique. The complexity of checking model existence remains at Σ_2^P which means a computational advantage over related work. Although our notion of stable-ordered model is less expressive than arbitrary traces of states, there are interesting applications where it suffices. We demonstrate this with examples from activity reasoning, combinatorial testing, fault detection for concurrent programs, and digital forensics.

2 Preliminaries

The logic we introduce in this paper is a nonmonotonic version of a monotonic temporal logic that we proposed in recent work in the context of activity reasoning [16]. Language $\mathcal{L}$ is determined by an infinite countable set $\mathcal{U}$ of atoms, Boolean connectives $\supset$, $\wedge$, $\vee$, $\bot$, and the modal operators $\circ$, $\Diamond$, and $\Box$, where $\circ$ means previously, $\Box$ stands for now and always in the past, and $\Diamond$ means now or at some time in the past.[1] A *formula* φ is defined by the grammar $\varphi ::= a \mid \bot \mid (\varphi_1 \supset \varphi_2) \mid (\varphi_1 \wedge \varphi_2) \mid (\varphi_1 \vee \varphi_2) \mid (\circ\varphi) \mid (\Diamond\varphi) \mid (\Box\varphi)$ where $a \in \mathcal{L}$ is an atom. Parentheses are omitted if no ambiguities arise.

A *theory* is a set of formulas. For an expression (formula or theory) e, $At(e)$ is the set of atoms occurring in e. We use $P = \langle a_1, \ldots, a_n \rangle$ to denote a finite sequence of elements. The *length* of P, denoted by $|P|$, is n. For two sequences P and Q, PQ is the concatenation of P and Q. We say that P is a *prefix* of Q and write $P \preceq Q$ iff $Q = PR$ for some sequence R. The empty sequence is denoted by ε. Note that the notion of prefix is reflexive. An *ordered model* M over $\mathcal{U}$ is a

---

[1] Note that $\circ$ was not part of the initial version of the logic to avoid unintended effects when used under the open-world assumption [16]. Also, note that we do not consider strong negation.

sequence of atoms from $\mathcal{U}$ without repetition. We write $M \models \varphi$ to denote that formula φ is *true* in M. Relation $\models$ is inductively defined as follows:

$M \not\models \bot$

$M \models a$ iff a occurs in M, for an atom $a \in \mathcal{U}$;

$M \models \varphi_1 \wedge \varphi_2$ iff $M \models \varphi_1$ and $M \models \varphi_2$;

$M \models \varphi_1 \vee \varphi_2$ iff $M \models \varphi_1$ or $M \models \varphi_2$;

$M \models \varphi_1 \supset \varphi_2$ iff $M \not\models \varphi_1$ or $M \models \varphi_2$;

$M \models \circ\varphi$ iff $M' \models \varphi$ for some $M' \preceq M$ with $|M| - |M'| = 1$;

$M \models \Diamond\varphi$ iff $M' \models \varphi$ for some $M' \preceq M$;

$M \models \Box\varphi$ iff $M' \models \varphi$ for each $M' \preceq M$.

For a theory T, $M \models T$ iff $M \models \varphi$ for each $\varphi \in T$. Also, entailment, equivalence, etc. are defined as in classical logic. We use the abbreviations $\neg\varphi := \varphi \supset \bot$ and $\top := \neg\bot$. To denote the initial state, we define $\mathbb{I} := \neg\circ\top$ which is only true in ε.

An ordered model $\langle a_1, \ldots, a_n \rangle$ can be understood as a compact representation of a sequence $s_0, \ldots, s_n$ of classical models that represent states of the world, where $s_0 = \emptyset$ and the only difference between any s_i and s_{i+1} is that atom a_{i+1} becomes true in s_{i+1}. Note that two properties that are reasonable to assume in the context of goal achievements are implicit in this representation: First, once an atom becomes true, i.e., a goal has been achieved, it remains true (*persistence*). Second, the same goal cannot be reached twice (*Heraclitus principle*). We refer the reader to previous work for details [16].

3 Stable-Ordered Models

The nonmonotonic semantics of language $\mathcal{L}$ that we define in this paper is an adaptation of the stable-model semantics due to Ferraris and Lifschitz [8,9] for propositional theories with the necessary changes. For a formula φ and an ordered model X over $At(\varphi)$, we define the *reduct* of φ with respect to X, φ^X in symbols, inductively as follows:

$$\bot^X = \bot$$

$$a^X = \begin{cases} a & \text{if } a \text{ is an atom and } X \models a \\ \bot & \text{otherwise} \end{cases}$$

$$(\varphi_1 \otimes \varphi_2)^X, \otimes \in \{\wedge, \vee, \supset\} = \begin{cases} \varphi_1^X \otimes \varphi_2^X & \text{if } X \models \varphi_1 \otimes \varphi_2 \\ \bot & \text{otherwise} \end{cases}$$

$$(\circ\varphi)^X = \begin{cases} \circ\varphi^Y & \text{if } Y \preceq X, |X| - |Y| = 1, \text{ and } Y \models \varphi \\ \bot & \text{otherwise} \end{cases}$$

$$(\Diamond\varphi)^X = \bigvee_{Y \in \{X' | X' \preceq X\}} \Diamond\varphi^Y$$

$$(\Box\varphi)^X = \bigwedge_{Y \in \{X' | X' \preceq X\}} \Box\varphi^Y$$

For a theory T, $T^X = \{\varphi^X \mid \varphi \in T\}$. An ordered model M over $At(T)$ is a *stable-ordered model* of T iff $M \models T^M$, and for each subsequence M' of M, $M' \models T^M$ implies $M' = M$. With other words, M is a subsequence-minimal ordered model of T^M. The stable-ordered models of a formula φ are the ones of the theory $\{\varphi\}$.

The definition of the reduct for the classical connectives is the one for propositional theories [8,9]. For the classical connectives and a formula φ, the context X is propagated to all direct subformulas of φ if a formula is true in X. Otherwise, φ is replaced by $\bot$. For the order operators, φ is evaluated not in X but in respective prefixes of X. An evaluation of $\Diamond\varphi$, resp., $\Box\varphi$, in X corresponds to the disjunction, resp., conjunction, of φ with respect to all prefixes of X. Note that such a disjunction or conjunction is equivalent to $\bot$ if the formula is false in X.

Consider $X = \langle a,b \rangle$ and $\varphi = \Diamond((a \wedge \neg b) \vee b) \wedge (a \supset b)$. The reduct of φ for X is

$$(\Diamond((a \wedge \neg b) \vee b))^X \wedge (a \supset b)^X$$
$$= \left(\Diamond((a \wedge \neg b) \vee b)^\varepsilon \vee \Diamond((a \wedge \neg b) \vee b)^{\langle a \rangle} \vee \Diamond((a \wedge \neg b) \vee b)^{\langle a,b \rangle} \right) \wedge \left(a^X \supset b^X \right)$$
$$= (\Diamond\bot \vee \Diamond a \vee \Diamond b) \wedge (a \supset b)$$
$$= (\Diamond a \vee \Diamond b) \wedge (a \supset b)$$

The single minimal ordered model of φ^X is $\langle b \rangle$, thus X is not stable. But this is reasonable: In the formation of the minimal ordered model of the reduct, subformula $\psi = \Diamond((a \wedge \neg b) \vee b)$ is not strong enough to force a (and subsequently b by $a \supset b$) when evaluated in context X as ψ can also be satisfied by $\langle b \rangle$. This is reflected by the disjunction in φ^X. It can be checked that the only stable-ordered model of φ is $\langle b \rangle$.

It holds that every stable-ordered model is also an ordered model:

Theorem 1. *For a formula $\varphi \in \mathcal{L}$ and ordered model X over $At(\varphi)$, $X \models \varphi$ iff $X \models \varphi^X$.*

Proof. For the if direction, assume that $X \not\models \varphi$. Then, $\varphi^X \equiv \bot$ and $X \not\models \varphi^X$ follows.

We show the only-if direction by induction on the structure of φ. If $\varphi = \bot$ or φ is atomic, $X \models \varphi$ implies $\varphi^X = \varphi$ and $X \models \varphi^X$ follows.

Otherwise, φ is of form $\varphi_1 \otimes \varphi_2$, $\otimes \in \{\wedge, \vee, \supset\}$, $\circ\varphi_1$, $\Diamond\varphi_1$, or $\Box\varphi_1$. The cases for the classical connectives are straight forward: For any $\otimes \in \{\wedge, \vee, \supset\}$, $\varphi^X = \varphi_1^X \otimes \varphi_2^X$. By induction, $X \models \varphi_1$ iff $X \models \varphi_1^X$ and $X \models \varphi_2$ iff $X \models \varphi_2^X$. Hence, $X \models \varphi_1 \otimes \varphi_2$ implies $X \models \varphi_1^X \otimes \varphi_2^X$, and $X \models \varphi^X$ follows.

Assume $\varphi = \circ\varphi_1$. $X \models \varphi$ implies that that there is a prefix X' of X with $|X| - |X'| = 1$ and $X' \models \varphi_1$. By the inductive hypothesis, $X' \models \varphi_1^{X'}$, and thus $X \models \circ\varphi_1^{X'}$. As $\varphi^X = \circ\varphi_1^{X'}$, $X \models \varphi^X$ follows.

Assume $\varphi = \Diamond\varphi_1$. $X \models \varphi$ implies that there is some prefix X' of X with $X' \models \varphi_1$. By induction, $X' \models \varphi_1^{X'}$. This implies that $X \models \Diamond\varphi_1^{X'}$. As $\Diamond\varphi_1^{X'}$ is a disjunct of φ^X by definition, we conclude with $X \models \varphi^X$.

Finally, assume $\varphi = \Box\varphi_1$. $X \models \varphi$ implies that each prefix X' of X satisfies φ_1 and, by induction, $\varphi_1^{X'}$. Hence, X satisfies $\Box\varphi_1^{X'}$ for each prefix X' of X, and consequently $X \models \varphi^X$. $\square$

Our logic indeed generalises the stable-model semantics as the stable models for theories without order operators correspond to its stable-ordered models and vice versa.

As stable model existence for disjunctive programs is a Σ_2^P-complete problem [6], Σ_2^P-hardness for deciding existence of a stable-ordered model for a formula follows. Deciding if an ordered model satisfies a formula in $\mathcal{L}$ can be done in polynomial time [16].[2] This implies that checking whether an ordered model is a subsequence-minimal model of a formula is in coNP. As we can compute the reduct φ^X in polynomial time, the following result follows:

Theorem 2. *Given a formula $\varphi \in \mathcal{L}$, the problem of deciding whether a stable-ordered model for φ exists is Σ_2^P-complete.*

4   Applications

We illustrate ASP with theories under the stable-ordered model semantics with problems involving knowledge representation, temporal reasoning, and combinatorial search.

Activity Reasoning. We studied *activity reasoning* based on achieving hierarchically structured goals in previous work [16]. A goal can depend on subgoals that need to be reached beforehand. An activity model is a formal description of goal hierarchies together with constraints, where the activities correspond to top-level goals. For illustration, consider the activity model for activities a and d involving the subgoals b, c, and e, where a requires b and c, d requires e, e requires c or f, and c cannot precede b. It can be formalised by the following $\mathcal{L}$ formulas:

$$a \supset \Diamond(\neg a \wedge (b \wedge c)) \tag{1}$$
$$d \supset \Diamond(\neg d \wedge e) \tag{2}$$
$$e \supset \Diamond(\neg e \wedge (c \vee f)) \tag{3}$$
$$\neg (b \wedge \Diamond(\neg b \wedge c)) \tag{4}$$

Formulas (1)–(3) represent the subgoal relation, and (4) is the constraint regarding the order of c and b. Assume we observe that c is already archived. We want to explain this observation in terms of the activity model. That is, does some activity entail the observation? We use the following formulas:

$$a \vee d \tag{5}$$
$$\neg\neg\Diamond(c \wedge \circ \mathbb{I}) \tag{6}$$

The single stable-ordered model of formulas (1)–(6) is $\langle c, e, d \rangle$. Only activity d can explain the observation as a can never be realised because of constraint (4).

---

[2] Although this result was formulated for $\mathcal{L}$ without $\circ$, it is applicable for $\mathcal{L}$ mutatis mutandis.

This is an example of abductive reasoning from the activities as hypotheses: Formula (5) nondeterministically selects either activity a or activity d and (6) enforces that the activity model derives the observation that c has already been archived.

Combinatorial Event-Sequence Testing. In many applications, faults are triggered by the order of events. Based on the fault model that the number of events relevant to a bug is typically low, Kuhn et al. introduced *sequence-covering arrays* (SCAs) as combinatorial designs to avoid the high costs of exercising all possible event sequences [11]. ASP for event-sequence testing has been studied in previous work [4]. Given a set E of events, an E-sequence is a permutation of the events in E. An SCA of strength t and size n is a set $\{e_1, \ldots, e_n\}$ of E-sequences such that each sequence of pairwise distinct atoms from E with length t is subsequence of some e_i, $1 \le i \le n$. We assume a fixed $t = 3$. Often, some sequences are not feasible, e.g., "paste" cannot happen before "copy". Let C be a set of binary constraints over E with $(a, b) \in C$ iff a must not precede b in any e_i. Define

$$P = \{(a, b, c) \in E^3 \mid a \ne b, b \ne c, a \ne c, (a, b) \notin C, (b, c) \notin C, \text{ and } (a, c) \notin C\}$$

The following $\mathcal{L}$ formulas with parameter n encode all SCAs of size n compatible with the constraints in C:

$$\bigwedge_{a \subset E, 0 < i \le n} a_i \tag{7}$$

$$\bigwedge_{(a,b) \subset C, 0 < i \le n} \neg(b_i \wedge \Diamond(\neg b_i \wedge a_i)) \tag{8}$$

$$\bigwedge_{(a,b,c) \in P} \bigvee_{0 < i \le n} (a_i \wedge \Diamond(\neg a_i \wedge b_i \wedge \Diamond(\neg b_i \wedge a_i))) \tag{9}$$

Formula (7) defines the test-input space in terms of sets of E-sequences. Index i means that event a_i belongs to e_i. Formula (8) is a constraint that enforces that there is no e_i where a precedes b if $(a, b) \in C$. Set P contains all triples of events that need to be covered, i.e., occur as a subsequence of some E-sequence. Finally, coverage of all elements of P is guaranteed by Formula (9).

Fault Detection in Concurrent Programs. Finding bugs in multi-threaded programs is notoriously hard due the vast number of possible thread interleavings. A program consists of threads $t_1, \ldots, t_m$ and a set E of shared variables. Each thread t_i is modelled by a sequence $\langle a_1^i, \ldots, a_{n_i}^i \rangle$ of read or write accesses to variables from E. A thread interleaving is a total order on all a_j^i such that the relative order within the threads is preserved. Based on the fault model that many bugs are caused by reading a variable that has been defined by the wrong writer, *define-use pairs* have been studied as coverage criterion to select interesting interleavings [12]. A define-use pair $(w, r)_v$ is a write and a read access to the same variable v. An interleaving covers $(w, r)_v$ iff w precedes r, and there is no write to v inbetween.

Let P be the set of define-use pairs. To obtain total coverage of P by a set of interleavings, we iterate the following steps until $P = \emptyset$:

(i) search for an interleaving I that covers some $p \in P$, and
(ii) remove all pairs covered by I from P.

The following $\mathcal{L}$ formulas can be used to search for an interleaving that covers a given define-use pair $q = (w, r)_v$ and to identify all additionally covered ones. Let W_v be the set of all write accesses to a variable v.

$$\bigwedge_{i=1}^{m} \left(a_1^i \wedge \bigwedge_{j=1}^{n_i-1} \left(a_{j+1}^i \wedge \Diamond(\neg a_{j+1}^i \wedge a_j^i) \right) \right) \tag{10}$$

$$\bigwedge_{(w,r)_v \in P} \left(\left(r \wedge \Diamond(\neg r \wedge w) \wedge \bigwedge_{a \in W_v \setminus \{w\}} \neg\Diamond(w \wedge a \wedge \neg r) \right) \supset c_{(w,r)_v} \right) \tag{11}$$

$$\neg\neg c_{(w,r)_v} \tag{12}$$

Formula (10) spans the search space of possible thread interleavings. Formula (11) derives $c_{(w,r)_v}$ if the define-use pair $(w, r)_v$ is covered. Finally, (12) is a constraint that prunes away all models where the specified define-use pair q is not covered.

Digital Forensics. A frequent problem in digital forensics is *file carving*, i.e., to recover fragmented files when file-table information is not available. Files are typically stored in terms of clusters but these clusters are not necessarily in order on a storage device. The problem of recovering multiple files from a set of clusters has been studied by Pal and Memon [14] as a k-vertex disjoint graph problem. The clusters are the vertices V of a graph $G = (V, E)$, some clusters are identified as headers $H \subseteq V$ or footers $F \subseteq V$, and $(a, b) \in E$ iff $a \notin F$, $b \notin H$, and the likelihood that b follows a—calculated by a suitable metric—is above a fixed threshold. We want to find k paths in G that start with a header and end in a footer such that each cluster appears in exactly one path. We can formalise this problem concisely as follows:

$$\bigwedge_{a \in V} a \tag{13}$$

$$\bigwedge_{(a,b) \in V^2 \setminus (E \cup (F \times H))} \neg\Diamond(b \wedge \circ(a \wedge \neg b) \wedge \neg\circ\circ a) \tag{14}$$

Formula (13) spans the search space in terms of permutations of all clusters. Paths where b follows a but $(a, b) \notin E$, unless a is a footer and b is a header, i.e., a new path starts, are excluded via (14). Each stable-ordered model of formulas (13)–(14) describes a solution to the specified k-vertex disjoint graph problem.

5   Discussion

Our idea of sequences of atoms as models naturally lends itself to reasoning about goal achievements when goals are seen as atomic entities and the order operators have a temporal interpretation. This is by design as our initial motivation comes from activity reasoning [16]. In fact, ordered models are a compact representation of LTL traces where in each step a single new atom becomes true. Also others dealt with nonmonotonic temporal logics based on LTL [1-3,5], but the idea of ordered models is quite unique and allows for a semantics closer to standard stable models. Notably, the complexity of deciding model existence remains in Σ_2^P. Although this is a distinctive advantage compared to aforementioned related work, the flip-side is reduced expressiveness. Yet, we demonstrate versatile applications from activity reasoning combinatorial testing, concurrent programming, and digital forensics. Although these problems can also be encoded in standard ASP, we think that dedicated order operators allow for more natural and concise problem encodings.

We expect that common results for theories under the stable-model semantics (strong equivalence, splitting sets, etc.) hold for theories under the stable-ordered model semantics as well but leave this for future work. Also, we plan to identify normal forms of theories that are closer to the familiar rule based syntax of logic programming and study translations into standard ASP so that existing solvers can be used for model generation.

References

1. Aguado, F., Cabalar, P., Diéguez, M., Pérez, G., Vidal, C.: Temporal equilibrium logic: a survey. J. Appl. Non-Class. Logics **23**(1-2), 2-24 (2013)
2. Baral, C., Zhao, J.: Non-monotonic temporal logics for goal specification. In: Proceedings of the 20th International Joint Conference on Artificial Intelligence (IJCAI 2007), pp. 236-242. AAAI Press (2007)
3. Baral, C., Zhao, J.: Non-monotonic temporal logics that facilitate elaboration tolerant revision of goals. In: Proceedings of the 23rd AAAI Conference on Artificial Intelligence (AAAI 2008), pp. 406-411. AAAI Press (2008)
4. Brain, M., et al.: Event-sequence testing using answer-set programming. Int. J. Adv. Softw. **5**(3 & 4), 237-251 (2012)
5. Cabalar, P., Kaminski, R., Schaub, T., Schuhmann, A.: Temporal answer set programming on finite traces. TPLP **18**(3-4), 406-420 (2018)
6. Eiter, T., Gottlob, G.: On the computational cost of disjunctive logic programming: propositional case. Ann. Math. Artif. Intell. **15**(3-4), 289-323 (1995)
7. Erdem, E., Gelfond, M., Leone, N.: Applications of answer set programming. AI Mag. **37**(3), 53-68 (2016)
8. Ferraris, P.: Answer sets for propositional theories. In: Baral, C., Greco, G., Leone, N., Terracina, G. (eds.) LPNMR 2005. LNCS (LNAI), vol. 3662, pp. 119-131. Springer, Heidelberg (2005). https://doi.org/10.1007/11546207_10
9. Ferraris, P., Lifschitz, V.: Mathematical foundations of answer set programming. In: We Will Show Them! Essays in Honour of Dov Gabbay, vol. 1, pp. 615-664. College Publications (2005)
10. Gelfond, M., Lifschitz, V.: The stable model semantics for logic programming. In: Proceedings of the 5th International Conference and Symposium on Logic Programming, pp. 1070-1080. MIT Press (1988)

11. Kuhn, D.R., Higdon, J.M., Lawrence, J., Kacker, R., Lei, Y.: Combinatorial methods for event sequence testing. In: Proceedings of the 5th IEEE International Conference on Software Testing, Verification and Validation (ICST 2012), pp. 601–609. IEEE Computer Society (2012)
12. Lu, S., Jiang, W., Zhou, Y.: A study of interleaving coverage criteria. In: Proceedings of the 6th joint meeting of the European Software Engineering Conference and the ACM SIGSOFT International Symposium on Foundations of Software Engineering, pp. 533–536. ACM (2007)
13. Marek, V.W., Truszczyński, M.: Stable models and an alternative logic programming paradigm. In: Apt, K.R., Marek, V.W., Truszczynski, M., Warren, D.S. (eds.) The Logic Programming Paradigm, pp. 375–398. Springer, Heidelberg (1999). https://doi.org/10.1007/978-3-642-60085-2_17
14. Memon, N.D., Pal, A.: Automated reassembly of file fragmented images using greedy algorithms. IEEE Trans. Image Process. **15**(2), 385–393 (2006)
15. Niemelä, I.: Logic programs with stable model semantics as a constraint programming paradigm. Ann. Math. Artif. Intell. **25**(3–4), 241–273 (1999)
16. Oetsch, J., Nieves, J.C.: A knowledge representation perspective on activity theory. arxiv eprint arXiv:1811.05815 (2018)
17. Pearce, D.: A new logical characterisation of stable models and answer sets. In: Dix, J., Pereira, L.M., Przymusinski, T.C. (eds.) NMELP 1996. LNCS, vol. 1216, pp. 57–70. Springer, Heidelberg (1997). https://doi.org/10.1007/BFb0023801
18. Pnueli, A.: The temporal logic of programs. In: Proceedings of the 18th IEEE Symposium on the Foundations of Computer Science (FOCS 1977), pp. 46–57. IEEE Computer Society Press (1977)

Cut-Free Calculi and Relational Semantics for Temporal STIT Logics

Kees van Berkel$^{(\boxtimes)}$ and Tim Lyon$^{(\boxtimes)}$

Institut für Logic and Computation, Technische Universität Wien, Vienna, Austria
{kees,lyon}@logic.at

Abstract. We present cut-free labelled sequent calculi for a central formalism in logics of agency: STIT logics with temporal operators. These include sequent systems for Ldm, Tstit and Xstit. All calculi presented possess essential structural properties such as contraction- and cut-admissibility. The labelled calculi G3Ldm and G3Tstit are shown sound and complete relative to irreflexive temporal frames. Additionally, we extend current results by showing that also Xstit can be characterized through relational frames, omitting the use of BT+AC frames.

Keywords: Labelled sequent calculi · Cut-free completeness ·
Temporal logic · Multi-agent STIT logic · Relational semantics

1 Introduction

Various autonomous machines are developed with the aim of performing particular human tasks. Human acting, however, is inevitably connected to legal and moral decision making—sometimes more than we think. Hence, such machines will eventually be found in difficult scenarios in which normatively acceptable actions must be generated [12]. What is more, these decisions can quickly turn into complex (technical) problems [13]. The above stresses the need for formal tools that allow for reasoning about agents, the choices they have, and the actions they are *able* and *allowed* to perform. Implementable logics of agency can play an important role in the development of such automated systems: they can provide explicit proofs that can be checked and which, more importantly, can be understood by humans (*e.g.* [1]). The present work takes a first step in this direction by providing cut-free sequent calculi for one of the central formalisms of agency: STIT logic with temporal operators.

The logic of STIT, which is an acronym for 'Seeing To It That', is a prominent modal framework for the formal analysis of multi-agent interaction and reasoning about choices.[1] In short, STIT logics contain modal formulae of the form $[i]\phi$, capturing the notion that "the agent i sees to it that the state of affairs

---

[1] For an introduction to STIT logic and a historical overview we refer to [3,4,16].

Work funded by the projects WWTF MA16-028, FWF I2982 and FWF W1255-N23.

F. Calimeri et al. (Eds.): JELIA 2019, LNAI 11468, pp. 803–819, 2019.
https://doi.org/10.1007/978-3-030-19570-0_52

ϕ is brought about". STIT logic knows many fruitful extensions and its recent application to legal theory, deontic reasoning, and epistemics shows that issues of agency are essentially tied to *temporal aspects* of choice: for example, consider issues in legal responsibility [18]; social commitment [17]; knowledge-based obligations [7]; agent-bound instrumentality [5]; and actions as events [28].

Unfortunately, nearly all available proof systems for STIT logics are Hilbert-style systems, which are known to be cumbersome for proof search and not suitable for proving metalogical properties of the intended formalisms. To this purpose, a renowned alternative proof framework is Gentzen's *sequent calculus* [11]. It allows one to construct proofs that decompose the formulae to be proven in a stepwise manner; making it an effective tool for proof search and a good candidate for automated deduction procedures. However, this framework is not strong enough to design cut-free analytic calculi for many modal logics of interest [20]; including STIT logic. In this work, we will treat several STIT logics through a more expressive extension of this formalism: Labelled Sequent Calculi [20, 26].

The aim of the present paper is to provide labelled calculi for several central *temporal* STIT logics: Ldm, Tstit and Xstit. To our knowledge, there have only been three attempts to capture STIT logics in alternative proof systems: in [1] a natural deduction system for a deontic STIT logic is proposed and in [24, 27] tableaux systems for multi-agent deliberative STIT logics are presented.

On the one hand, the novelty of the present contribution compared to previous works, is that all presented calculi (i) possess useful proof-theoretic properties such as contraction- and cut-admissibility and (ii) are modular and extend to several *temporal* STIT-logics, including both temporal operators and inherently temporal STIT-operators (in a multi-agent, as well as a group setting). In doing so, we answer an open question in [27] regarding the construction of a rule-based proof system for temporal extensions of Ldm. On the other hand, the investigation of STIT has been with an essential focus on its intuitive semantics: branching time structures, extended with histories as paths and agential choice-functions (BT+AC-frames). Recent work [2, 14, 17], however, shows that the basic atemporal STIT logic Ldm and its temporal extension Tstit are characterizable through simpler relational frames. The current work extends these results by showing that also the logic Xstit can be semantically characterized without using BT+AC structures.

In Sect. 2 we will introduce the base logic Ldm and its corresponding labelled calculus. Thereafter, in Sect. 3, we provide a cut-free calculus for the temporal STIT logic Tstit, introduced in [17], which exploits a temporal irreflexivity rule based on [10]. Last, in Sect. 4, we provide a labelled calculus for the inherently temporal STIT logic Xstit from [7,8]. Here we show that the *independence of agents* principle of STIT logic can be captured using *systems of rules* from [22]. We conclude and highlight some envisaged future work in Sect. 5.

2   The Logic Ldm

2.1   Axioms and Relational Semantics for Ldm

The basic STIT logic Ldm offers a framework for reasoning about individual agents realizing propositions via the choices available to them at particular moments in time. In the semantics of Ldm, each *moment* can be formalized as an equivalence class of *worlds*, where each world sits in a linear chain (referred to as a *history*) extending to the future and (possibly to) the past. Therefore, each world contained in a particular moment can be thought of as an alternative state of affairs that evolves along a different timeline. Moreover, for each agent, moments are further partitioned into equivalence classes, where each class represents a possible choice available to the agent for realizing a set of potential outcomes. Hence, if a proposition ϕ holds true in every world of a particular choice for an agent i, then we claim that "i sees to it that ϕ" (written formally as $[i]\phi$) at each world of that choice; *i.e.* i's committal to the choice ensures ϕ regardless of which world in the choice set is actual.

The above STIT operator $[i]$ is referred to as the *Chellas*-STIT (i.e. *cstit*) [4]. It is often distinguished from the *deliberative* STIT (i.e. *dstit*) which consists of *cstit* together with a negative condition: we say that "agent i deliberatively sees to it that ϕ" (written formally as $[i]^d$) when (i) "i sees to it that ϕ" and (ii) "ϕ is currently not settled true" [15,16]. The second condition ensures that the realization of ϕ *depends* on the choice made by the agent; *i.e.* ϕ might not have been case had the agent chosen to act differently. By making use of the *settledness* operator $\Box$, which is prefixed to a formula when the formula holds true at every world in a moment, *cstit* and *dstit* become inter-definable: namely, $[i]^d\phi$ *iff* $[i]\phi \wedge \neg\Box\phi$. As an example of a STIT formula, the formula $\Diamond[i]^d\phi$ must be interpreted as follows. at the current moment, agent i has a possible choice available that allows i to see to it that ϕ is guaranteed, and there is an alternative choice present to i that does not guarantee ϕ. In this paper, we introduce $\Box$ and $[i]$ as primitive and take $[i]^d$ as defined.

In this section, we make all of the aforementioned notions formally precise and provide a relational semantics for Ldm along with a corresponding cut-free labelled calculus. In Sect. 3, we will extend Ldm with temporal operators, obtaining the logic Tstit. Since both logics rely on the same semantics, we introduce their languages and semantics simultaneously, avoiding unnecessary repetition. Lastly, in what follows we give all formulae of the associated logics in negation normal form. This reduces the number of rules in the associated calculi and offers a simpler presentation of the proof theory. The languages for Ldm and Tstit are given below:

Definition 1 (The Languages $\mathcal{L}_{\mathsf{Ldm}}$ and $\mathcal{L}_{\mathsf{Tstit}}$). *Let $Ag = \{1, 2, ..., n\}$ be a finite set of agent labels and let $Var = \{p_1, p_2, p_3...\}$ be a countable set of propositional variables. The language $\mathcal{L}_{\mathsf{Ldm}}$ is given by the following BNF grammar:*

$$\phi ::= p \mid \overline{p} \mid \phi \wedge \phi \mid \phi \vee \phi \mid \Box\phi \mid \Diamond\phi \mid [i]\phi \mid \langle i\rangle\phi$$

The language $\mathcal{L}_{\mathsf{Tstit}}$ is defined accordingly:

$$\phi ::= p \mid \overline{p} \mid \phi \wedge \phi \mid \phi \vee \phi \mid \Box\phi \mid \Diamond\phi \mid [i]\phi \mid \langle i \rangle\phi \mid [Ag]\phi \mid \langle Ag \rangle\phi \mid \mathsf{G}\phi \mid \mathsf{F}\phi \mid \mathsf{H}\phi \mid \mathsf{P}\phi$$

where $i \in Ag$ and $p \in Var$.

The language $\mathcal{L}_{\mathsf{Tstit}}$ extends $\mathcal{L}_{\mathsf{Ldm}}$ through the incorporation of the tense modalities G, F, H, and P and the modalities $[Ag]$ and $\langle Ag \rangle$ for the grand coalition Ag of agents. G and F are duals and read, respectively, as 'always will be in the future' and 'somewhere in the future'. H are P are also dual and are interpreted, respectively, as 'always has been in the past' and 'somewhere in the past' (cf. [17,25]). The operator $[Ag]$ captures the notion that 'the grand coalition of agents sees to it that'. Note that the negation of a formula ϕ, written $\overline{\phi}$, is obtained in the usual way by replacing each operator with its dual, each positive propositional atom p with its negation $\overline{p}$, and each negative propositional atom $\overline{p}$ with its positive version p. We may therefore define $\phi \to \psi$ as $\overline{\phi} \vee \psi$, $\phi \leftrightarrow \psi$ as $\phi \to \psi \wedge \psi \to \phi$, $\top$ as $p \vee \overline{p}$, and $\bot$ as $p \wedge \overline{p}$. We will use these abbreviations throughout the paper.

At present, we are principally interested in Ldm and temporal frames: in particular, since Tstit will be introduced as the temporal extension of Ldm and, more generally, because the logic of STIT has an implicit temporal intuition underlying choice-making (*cf.* original branching-time frames employed for Ldm [4,15,16]). We will prove that Ldm is strongly complete with respect to these more elaborate *irreflexive* Temporal Kripke STIT frames.

Definition 2 (Relational Tstit Frames and Models [17]). *Let $\mathcal{R}_\alpha(w) :=$ $\{v \in W | (w,v) \in \mathcal{R}_\alpha\}$ for $\alpha \in \{\Box, Ag, \mathsf{G}, \mathsf{H}\} \cup Ag$. A relational Temporal STIT frame (Tstit-frame) is defined as a tuple $F = (W, \mathcal{R}_\Box, \{\mathcal{R}_i | i \in Ag\}, \mathcal{R}_{Ag}, \mathcal{R}_\mathsf{G}, \mathcal{R}_\mathsf{H})$ where W is a non-empty set of worlds $w, v, u...$ and:*

- *For all $i \in Ag$, $\mathcal{R}_\Box$, $\mathcal{R}_i$, $\mathcal{R}_{Ag} \subseteq W \times W$ are equivalence relations where:*
  - **(C1)** *For each i, $\mathcal{R}_i \subseteq \mathcal{R}_\Box$;*
  - **(C2)** *For all $u_1, ..., u_n \in W$, if $\mathcal{R}_\Box u_i u_j$ for all $1 \le i,j \le n$, then $\bigcap_i \mathcal{R}_i(u_i) \ne \emptyset$;*
  - **(C3)** *For all $w \in W$, $\mathcal{R}_{Ag}(w) = \bigcap_{i \in Ag} \mathcal{R}_i(w)$;*
- *$\mathcal{R}_\mathsf{G} \subseteq W \times W$ is a transitive and serial binary relation and $\mathcal{R}_\mathsf{H}$ is the converse of $\mathcal{R}_\mathsf{G}$, and the following conditions hold:*
  - **(C4)** *For all $w, u, v \in W$, if $\mathcal{R}_\mathsf{G} wu$ and $\mathcal{R}_\mathsf{G} wv$, then $\mathcal{R}_\mathsf{G} uv$, $u = v$, or $\mathcal{R}_\mathsf{G} vu$;*
  - **(C5)** *For all $w, u, v \in W$, if $\mathcal{R}_\mathsf{H} wu$ and $\mathcal{R}_\mathsf{H} wv$, then $\mathcal{R}_\mathsf{H} uv$, $u = v$, or $\mathcal{R}_\mathsf{H} vu$;*
  - **(C6)** *$\mathcal{R}_\mathsf{G} \circ \mathcal{R}_\Box \subseteq \mathcal{R}_{Ag} \circ \mathcal{R}_\mathsf{G}$; (Relation composition $\circ$ is defined as usual.)*
  - **(C7)** *For all $w, u \in W$, if $u \in \mathcal{R}_\Box(w)$, then $u \notin \mathcal{R}_\mathsf{G}(w)$.*

A Tstit-model is defined as a tuple $M = (F, V)$ where F is a Tstit-frame and V is a valuation function assigning propositional variables to subsets of W; that is, $V: Var \mapsto \mathcal{P}(W)$.

The property expressed in C2 corresponds to the familiar *independence of agents* principle of STIT logic, which states that if it is currently possible for each distinct agent to make a certain choice, then it is possible for all such choices to be made simultaneously. Condition C6 captures the STIT principle of *no choice between undivided histories*, which ensures that if two time-lines remain undivided at some future moment, then no agent can currently make a choice realizing one time-line without the other. (This principle is inexpressible in the atemporal language of the base logic Ldm.) For a philosophical discussion of these principles see [4]. Last, condition C7 ensures that the temporal frames under consideration are *irreflexive*, which means that the future is a strict future (excluding the present). For a discussion of the other frame properties we refer to [17].

Definition 3 (Semantics for $\mathcal{L}_{\mathsf{Ldm}}$ and $\mathcal{L}_{\mathsf{Tstit}}$). *Let M be a Tstit-model and let w be a world in its domain W. The satisfaction of a formula ϕ on M at w is inductively defined as follows (in clauses 1–14 we omit explicit mention of M):*

1. $w \models p$ iff $w \in V(p)$
2. $w \models \overline{p}$ iff $w \notin V(p)$
3. $w \models \phi \wedge \psi$ iff $w \models \phi$ and $w \models \psi$
4. $w \models \phi \vee \psi$ iff $w \models \phi$ or $w \models \psi$
5. $w \models \Box\phi$ iff $\forall u \in \mathcal{R}_\Box(w)$, $u \models \phi$
6. $w \models \Diamond\phi$ iff $\exists u \in \mathcal{R}_\Box(w)$, $u \models \phi$
7. $w \models [i]\phi$ iff $\forall u \in \mathcal{R}_i(w)$, $u \models \phi$

8. $w \models \langle i \rangle \phi$ iff $\exists u \in \mathcal{R}_i(w)$, $u \models \phi$
9. $w \models [Ag]\phi$ iff $\forall u \in \mathcal{R}_{Ag}(w)$, $u \models \phi$
10. $w \models \langle Ag \rangle \phi$ iff $\exists u \in \mathcal{R}_{Ag}(w)$, $u \models \phi$
11. $w \models \mathsf{G}\phi$ iff $\forall u \in \mathcal{R}_\mathsf{G}(w)$, $u \models \phi$
12. $w \models \mathsf{F}\phi$ iff $\exists u \in \mathcal{R}_\mathsf{G}(w)$, $u \models \phi$
13. $w \models \mathsf{H}\phi$ iff $\forall u \in \mathcal{R}_\mathsf{H}(w)$, $u \models \phi$
14. $w \models \mathsf{P}\phi$ iff $\exists u \in \mathcal{R}_\mathsf{H}(w)$, $u \models \phi$

A formula ϕ is globally true on M (i.e. $M \models \phi$) iff it is satisfied at every world w in the domain W of M. A formula ϕ is valid (i.e. $\models \phi$) iff it is globally true on every Tstit-model.

Definition 4 (The Logic Ldm [4]). *The Hilbert system of Ldm consists of the following axioms and inference rules:*

$$\phi \to (\psi \to \phi) \quad (\overline{\psi} \to \overline{\phi}) \to (\phi \to \psi) \quad (\phi \to (\psi \to \chi)) \to ((\phi \to \psi) \to (\phi \to \chi))$$

$$\Box\phi \to \phi \quad \Diamond\phi \to \Box\Diamond\phi \quad \Box(\phi \to \psi) \to (\Box\phi \to \Box\psi) \quad [i]\phi \to \phi \quad \langle i \rangle \phi \to [i]\langle i \rangle \phi$$

$$\Box\phi \vee \Diamond\overline{\phi} \quad [i]\phi \vee \langle i \rangle\overline{\phi} \quad \bigwedge_{i \in Ag} \Diamond[i]\phi_i \to \Diamond(\bigwedge_{i \in Ag}[i]\phi_i)$$

$$[i](\phi \to \psi) \to ([i]\phi \to [i]\psi) \quad \Box\phi \to [i]\phi \quad \frac{\phi}{\Box\phi} \quad \frac{\phi \qquad \phi \to \psi}{\psi}$$

A derivation of ϕ in Ldm from a set of premises Θ, is written as $\Theta \vdash_{\mathsf{Ldm}} \phi$. When Θ is the empty set, we refer to ϕ as a theorem and write $\vdash_{\mathsf{Ldm}} \phi$.

The axiomatization contains duality-axioms $\Box\phi \vee \Diamond\overline{\phi}$ and $[i]\phi \vee \langle i \rangle\overline{\phi}$ which ensure the usual interaction between the box and diamond modalities. Furthermore, the axiom $\bigwedge_{i \in Ag} \Diamond[i]\phi_i \to \Diamond(\bigwedge_{i \in Ag}[i]\phi_i)$ is the *independence of agents* (*IOA*) axiom.

Theorem 1 (Soundness [17]). *For any formula ϕ, if $\vdash_{\mathsf{Ldm}} \phi$, then $\models \phi$.*

Observe that all axioms of Ldm are within the Sahlqvist class. Therefore, we know that Ldm is already strongly complete relative to the simpler class of frames defined by the first-order properties corresponding to its axioms [6] (*cf.* [2,14] for alternative completeness proofs of Ldm relative to this class of relational frames). As mentioned previously, we are interested in Ldm relative to the more involved *temporal* frames. The usual canonical model construction from [6] cannot be applied to obtain completeness of Ldm in relation to Tstit-frames. This follows from the fact that the axioms of Ldm do not impose any temporal structure on the canonical model of Ldm, and hence, we are not ensured that the resulting model qualifies as a Tstit-model. Theorem 2 is therefore proved via an alternative canonical model construction. Since our main focus is sequent calculi for STIT logics, we omit the lengthy completeness proof here, and refer the interested reader to the appendix (available at http://arxiv.org/abs/1902.06632).

Theorem 2 (Completeness). *Any consistent set* $\Sigma \subset \mathcal{L}_{\mathsf{Ldm}}$ *is satisfiable.*

2.2   A Cut-Free Labelled Calculus for Ldm

We now provide a cut-free labelled calculus for Ldm, which can be seen as a simplification of the tableaux calculus in [27]. Labelled sequents Γ are defined through the following BNF grammar:

$$\Gamma ::= x : \phi \mid \Gamma, \Gamma \mid \mathcal{R}_\alpha xy, \Gamma$$

where x is from a countable set of labels $L = \{x, y, z, ...\}$, $\alpha \in \{\Box\} \cup Ag$, and $\phi \in \mathcal{L}_{\mathsf{Ldm}}$. Note that commas are used equivocally in the interpretation of a labelled sequent: representing (i) a conjunction when occurring between relational atoms, (ii) a disjunction when occurring between labelled formulae, and (iii) an implication when binding the multiset of relational atoms to the multiset of labelled formulae, which comprise a sequent. Last, we use the notation $\vdash_{G3X} x : \phi$ (for $\mathsf{X} \in \{\mathsf{Ldm}, \mathsf{Tstit}, \mathsf{Xstit}\}$) to denote here and later that the labelled formula $x : \phi$ is derivable in the calculus G3X.

The first order correspondents of all Ldm axioms are *geometric axioms*: that is, axioms of the form $\forall x_1...x_n((\phi_1 \wedge ... \wedge \phi_m) \rightarrow \exists y_1...y_k(\psi_1 \vee ... \vee \psi_l))$ where each ϕ_i is atomic and does not contain free occurrences of y_j (for $1 \leq j \leq k$), and each ψ_i is a conjunction $\chi_1 \wedge ... \wedge \chi_r$ of atomic formulae. The calculus G3Ldm is obtained by transforming all such correspondents into rules; *i.e. geometric rules*. (For further discussion on extracting rules from axioms we refer to [20,22].) Last, since our formulae are in negation normal form, we provide a one-sided version of the calculi introduced in [20]. This allows for a simpler formalism with fewer rules, but which is equivalent in expressivity.

Definition 5 (The Calculus G3Ldm).

$$\frac{}{\Gamma, w : p, w : \overline{p}} \text{ (id)} \qquad \frac{\Gamma, w : \phi \qquad \Gamma, w : \psi}{\Gamma, w : \phi \wedge \psi} \text{ (}\wedge\text{)} \qquad \frac{\Gamma, w : \phi, w : \psi}{\Gamma, w : \phi \vee \psi} \text{ (}\vee\text{)} \qquad \frac{\Gamma, \mathcal{R}_\Box wv, v : \phi}{\Gamma, w : \Box\phi} \text{ (}\Box\text{)}^*$$

$$\frac{\Gamma, \mathcal{R}_\Box wu, w : \Diamond\phi, u : \phi}{\Gamma, \mathcal{R}_\Box wu, w : \Diamond\phi} \text{ (}\Diamond\text{)} \qquad \frac{\Gamma, \mathcal{R}_i wv, v : \phi}{\Gamma, w : [i]\phi} \text{ (}[i]\text{)}^* \qquad \frac{\Gamma, \mathcal{R}_i wu, w : \langle i\rangle\phi, u : \phi}{\Gamma, \mathcal{R}_i wu, w : \langle i\rangle\phi} \text{ (}\langle i\rangle\text{)}$$

$$\frac{\mathcal{R}_\Box ww, \Gamma}{\Gamma} \ (\mathsf{refl}_\Box) \quad \frac{\mathcal{R}_i ww, \Gamma}{\Gamma} \ (\mathsf{refl}_{[i]}) \quad \frac{\mathcal{R}_\Box wu_1, ..., \mathcal{R}_\Box wu_n, \mathcal{R}_1 u_1 v, ..., \mathcal{R}_n u_n v, \Gamma}{\mathcal{R}_\Box wu_1, ..., \mathcal{R}_\Box wu_n, \Gamma} \ (\mathsf{IOA})^*$$

$$\frac{\mathcal{R}_\Box wu, \mathcal{R}_\Box wv, \mathcal{R}_\Box uv, \Gamma}{\mathcal{R}_\Box wu, \mathcal{R}_\Box wv, \Gamma} \ (\mathsf{eucl}_\Box) \quad \frac{\mathcal{R}_\Box wu, \mathcal{R}_i wu, \Gamma}{\mathcal{R}_i wu, \Gamma} \ (\mathsf{br}_{[i]}) \quad \frac{\mathcal{R}_i wu, \mathcal{R}_i wv, \mathcal{R}_i uv, \Gamma}{\mathcal{R}_i wu, \mathcal{R}_i wv, \Gamma} \ (\mathsf{eucl}_{[i]})$$

The '*' on the labels ($\Box$), ($[i]$), and (IOA) indicates an eigenvariable condition for this rule: i.e. the label v occurring in the premise of the rule cannot occur in the conclusion.

The rule (id) is an initial sequent and the rules ($\wedge$), ($\vee$), ($\Box$), ($\Diamond$), ($[i]$) and ($\langle i \rangle$) allow us to decompose connectives. Furthermore, as indicated by the relational atoms, the rules ($\mathsf{refl}_\Box$), ($\mathsf{refl}_{[i]}$), ($\mathsf{eucl}_\Box$), ($\mathsf{eucl}_{[i]}$), ($\mathsf{br}_{[i]}$) capture the behavior of the corresponding modal operators, and the rule (IOA) secures independence of agents in G3Ldm. In order to establish the intended soundness and completeness results, we need to formally interpret a labelled sequent relative to a given model. For the sake of brevity, we provide the semantics uniformly for all labelled sequent languages appearing in this paper:

Definition 6 (Interpretation, Satisfiability, Validity). *Let* X $\in$ {Ldm, Tstit, Xstit}. *Let* M *be a model for* X *with domain* W, L *the set of labels used in the labelled sequent language of* G3X, Γ *a sequent in* G3X *and let* $\mathcal{R}_\alpha$ *be a relation of* M. *(We have* $\mathcal{R}_\alpha \in \{\mathcal{R}_\Box, \mathcal{R}_i\}$ *for* X = Ldm, $\mathcal{R}_\alpha \in \{\mathcal{R}_\Box, \mathcal{R}_i, \mathcal{R}_{Ag}, \mathcal{R}_G, \check{\mathcal{R}}_G, \mathcal{R}_H\}$ *for* X = Tstit, *and* $\mathcal{R}_\alpha \in \{\mathcal{R}_\Box, \mathcal{R}_X, \mathcal{R}_A\}$, *for all* $A \subseteq Ag$, *when* X = Xstit. *We take* $\check{\mathcal{R}}_G$ *as the complement of the relation* $\mathcal{R}_G$.) *Last, let* I *be an interpretation function of* L *on* M *that maps labels to worlds; i.e.* $I: L \mapsto W$. *We say that,*

a sequent Γ *is satisfied in* M *with* I *iff for all relational atoms* $\mathcal{R}_\alpha xy$ *and equalities* $x = y$ *in* Γ, *if* $\mathcal{R}_\alpha x^I y^I$ *holds in* M, *then there must exist some* $z : \phi$ *in* Γ *such that* $M, z^I \models \phi$.

A sequent Γ *is valid iff it is satisfiable in any model* M *with any* I *of* L *on* M.

Theorem 3 (Soundness). *Every sequent derivable in* G3Ldm *is valid.*

Proof. By induction on the height of the given G3Ldm derivation. For initial sequents of the form $\Gamma, w{:}p, w{:}\overline{p}$ the claim is clear. The inductive step is argued by showing that each inference rule preserves validity (cf. Theorem 5.3 in [21]).

Lemma 1. *For all* $\phi \in \mathcal{L}_{\mathsf{Ldm}}$, *if* $\vdash_{\mathsf{Ldm}} \phi$, *then* $\vdash_{\mathsf{G3Ldm}} x : \phi$.

Proof. The derivation of each axiom and inference rule of Ldm, except for the IOA-axiom, is straightforward (See [20,23]). For readability, we only present the derivation of the IOA-axiom for two agents; the general case is similar:

$$\frac{\mathcal{R}_1 vu, \mathcal{R}_1 yv, \mathcal{R}_1 yu, ..., y : \langle 1\rangle\overline{\phi}_1, u : \overline{\phi}_1, u : \phi_1}{\frac{\mathcal{R}_1 vu, \mathcal{R}_1 yv, \mathcal{R}_i yu, ..., y : \langle 1\rangle\overline{\phi}_1, u : \phi_1}{\frac{\mathcal{R}_1 vu, \mathcal{R}_1 yv, ..., y : \langle 1\rangle\overline{\phi}_1, u : \phi_1}{\mathcal{R}_1 yv, ..., y : \langle 1\rangle\overline{\phi}_1, v : [1]\phi_1}}}$$

$$\frac{\mathcal{R}_2 vu, \mathcal{R}_2 zv, \mathcal{R}_i zw, ..., z : \langle 2\rangle\overline{\phi}_2, w : \overline{\phi}_2, w : \phi_2}{\frac{\mathcal{R}_2 vw, \mathcal{R}_2 zv, \mathcal{R}_2 zw, ..., z : \langle 2\rangle\overline{\phi}_2, w : \phi_2}{\frac{\mathcal{R}_2 vw, \mathcal{R}_2 zv, ..., z : \langle 2\rangle\overline{\phi}_2, w : \phi_2}{\mathcal{R}_2 zv, ..., z : \langle 2\rangle\overline{\phi}_2, v : [2]\phi_2}}}$$

$$\frac{\mathcal{R}_1 yv, \mathcal{R}_2 zv, \mathcal{R}_\square xy, \mathcal{R}_\square yv, \mathcal{R}_\square xv, \mathcal{R}_\square xz, y : \langle 1\rangle\overline{\phi}_1, z : \langle 2\rangle\overline{\phi}_2, x : \Diamond([1]\phi_1 \wedge [2]\phi_2), v : [1]\phi_1 \wedge [2]\phi_2}{\frac{\mathcal{R}_1 yv, \mathcal{R}_2 zv, \mathcal{R}_\square xy, \mathcal{R}_\square yv, \mathcal{R}_\square xv, \mathcal{R}_\square xz, y : \langle 1\rangle\overline{\phi}_1, z : \langle 2\rangle\overline{\phi}_2, x : \Diamond([1]\phi_1 \wedge [2]\phi_2)}{\frac{\mathcal{R}_1 yv, \mathcal{R}_2 zv, \mathcal{R}_\square xy, \mathcal{R}_\square yv, \mathcal{R}_\square xz, y : \langle 1\rangle\overline{\phi}_1, z : \langle 2\rangle\overline{\phi}_2, x : \Diamond([1]\phi_1 \wedge [2]\phi_2)}{\frac{\mathcal{R}_1 yv, \mathcal{R}_2 zv, \mathcal{R}_\square xy, \mathcal{R}_\square xz, y : \langle 1\rangle\overline{\phi}_1, z : \langle 2\rangle\overline{\phi}_2, x : \Diamond([1]\phi_1 \wedge [2]\phi_2)}{\frac{\mathcal{R}_\square xy, \mathcal{R}_\square xz, y : \langle 1\rangle\overline{\phi}_1, z : \langle 2\rangle\overline{\phi}_2, x : \Diamond([1]\phi_1 \wedge [2]\phi_2)}{\frac{x : \square\langle 1\rangle\overline{\phi}_1, x : \square\langle 2\rangle\overline{\phi}_2, x : \Diamond([1]\phi_1 \wedge [2]\phi_2)}{x : \square\langle 1\rangle\overline{\phi}_1 \vee \square\langle 2\rangle\overline{\phi}_2 \vee \Diamond([1]\phi_1 \wedge [2]\phi_2)}}}}}$$

The dashed lines in the above proof indicate the use of transitivity rules, which are derivable from the (refl$_{[i]}$), (eucl$_{[i]}$), (refl$_\square$), and (eucl$_\square$) rules (see [20]).

Theorem 4 (Completeness). *For all $\phi \in \mathcal{L}_{\mathsf{Ldm}}$, if $\models \phi$, then $\vdash_{\mathsf{G3Ldm}} x : \phi$.*

Proof. Follows from Theorem 2 and Lemma 1.

Due to the fact that all labelled sequent calculi given in this paper fit within the scheme presented in [20, 22], we obtain the subsequent theorem specifying their proof-theoretic properties:

Theorem 5. *Each calculus* G3X *with* X $\in$ {Ldm, Tstit, Xstit} *has the following properties:*

1. *All sequents of the form $\Gamma, x : \phi, x : \overline{\phi}$ are derivable in* G3X *with ϕ in the language $\mathcal{L}_X$;*
2. *All inference rules of* G3X *are height-preserving invertible;*
3. *Weakening, contraction, and variable-substitution are height-preserving admissible;*
4. *Cut is admissible.*

Proof. See [20] and [22] for details.

In order to maintain the admissibility of contraction, our calculi must satisfy the *closure condition* [20, 22]. That is, the calculi G3Ldm, G3Tstit and G3Xstit adhere to the following condition: For any *generalized geometric rule* in which a substitution of variables produces a duplication of relational atoms or equalities active in the rule, the instance of the rule with such duplicates contracted is added to the calculus. Since variable substitutions can only bring about a finite number of rule instances possessing duplications, the closure condition adds at most finitely many rules and is hence unproblematic. (Generalized geometric rules extend the class of geometric rules and can be extracted from generalized geometric axioms. In short, these are formulae of the form $GA_n = \forall x_1...x_n((\phi_1 \wedge ... \wedge \phi_m) \to (\exists y_1 \bigwedge GA_{k_1} \vee ... \vee \exists y_m \bigwedge GA_{k_m}))$, where each $\bigwedge GA_{k_j}$ (for $0 \leq k_1, \cdots, k_m < n$) stands for a conjunction of generalized geometric axioms, inductively constructed up to k_j-depth with the base case GA_0 being a geometric axiom. For a formal treatment of these axioms and rules see [22]).

3 The Logic Tstit

3.1 Axiomatization for Tstit

The logic Tstit extends the logic Ldm through the incorporation of tense modalities and the modality for the grand coalition of agents (see Definition 1). This additional expressivity allows for the application of Tstit in settings where one wishes to reason about the joint action of all agents, or the consequences of choices over time. The logic was originally proposed in [17] as a Hilbert system, in this section we provide a corresponding cut-free calculus.

Definition 7 (The Logic Tstit [17]). *The Hilbert system for the logic Tstit is defined as the logic Ldm extended with the following axioms and inference rules:*

$$[Ag]\phi \to \phi \qquad \langle Ag\rangle\phi \to [Ag]\langle Ag\rangle\phi \qquad \bigwedge_{1\le i\le n}[i]\phi_i \to [Ag]\bigwedge_{1\le i\le n}\phi_i \qquad \phi \to \mathsf{GP}\phi$$

$$\mathsf{FP}\phi \to \mathsf{P}\phi \vee \phi \vee \mathsf{F}\phi \qquad \mathsf{G}(\phi \to \psi) \to (\mathsf{G}\phi \to \mathsf{G}\psi) \qquad \phi \to \mathsf{HF}\phi \qquad \mathsf{PF}\phi \to \mathsf{P}\phi \vee \phi \vee \mathsf{F}\phi$$

$$\mathsf{H}(\phi \to \psi) \to (\mathsf{H}\phi \to \mathsf{H}\psi) \qquad \mathsf{G}\phi \to \mathsf{F}\phi \qquad \mathsf{FF}\phi \to \mathsf{F}\phi \qquad \mathsf{F}\Diamond\phi \to \langle Ag\rangle\mathsf{F}\phi \qquad [Ag]\phi \vee \langle Ag\rangle\overline{\phi}$$

$$\mathsf{G}\phi \vee \mathsf{F}\overline{\phi} \qquad \mathsf{H}\phi \vee \mathsf{P}\overline{\phi} \qquad \frac{\phi}{\mathsf{G}\phi} \qquad \frac{\phi}{\mathsf{H}\phi} \qquad \frac{(\Box\neg p \wedge \Box(\mathsf{G}p \wedge \mathsf{H}p)) \to \phi}{\phi} \ \textit{with } p \notin \phi$$

A derivation of ϕ in Tstit from a set of premises Θ, is written as $\Theta \vdash_{\mathsf{Tstit}} \phi$. When Θ is the empty set, we refer to ϕ as a theorem and write $\vdash_{\mathsf{Tstit}} \phi$.

Note that the axiom $\mathsf{F}\Diamond\phi \to \langle Ag\rangle\mathsf{F}\phi$ characterizes the *no choice between undivided histories* property (Definition 2, C6). Furthermore, the last inference rule, a variation of Gabbay's irreflexivity rule [10], characterizes the property of $\mathcal{R}_G$-irreflexivity (Definition 2, C7). For a discussion of all axioms and rules see [17].

Theorem 6 (Soundness and Completeness [17]). *For any formula $\phi \in \mathcal{L}_{\mathsf{Tstit}}$, $\vdash_{\mathsf{Tstit}} \phi$ iff $\models \phi$.*

3.2 A Cut-Free Labelled Calculus for Tstit

Let $L = \{x, y, z, ...\}$ be a countable set of labels. The language of G3Tstit is defined as follows:

$$\Gamma ::= x : \phi \mid \Gamma, \Gamma \mid \mathcal{R}_\alpha xy, \Gamma$$

where $x \in L$, $\phi \in \mathcal{L}_{\mathsf{Tstit}}$, and $\mathcal{R}_\alpha \in \{\mathcal{R}_\Box, \mathcal{R}_i, \mathcal{R}_{Ag}, \mathcal{R}_G, \check{\mathcal{R}}_G, \mathcal{R}_H\}$. On the basis of this language, we construct the calculus G3Tstit as an extension of G3Ldm.

Definition 8 (The Calculus G3Tstit). *The labelled calculus G3Tstit consists of all the rules of G3Ldm extended with the following set of rules:*

$$\frac{\mathcal{R}_H wu, \mathcal{R}_G uw, \Gamma}{\mathcal{R}_H wu, \Gamma} \ (\mathsf{conv_H}) \qquad \frac{\Gamma, \mathcal{R}_H wu, w : \mathsf{P}\phi, u : \phi}{\Gamma, \mathcal{R}_H wu, w : \mathsf{P}\phi} \ (\mathsf{P}) \qquad \frac{}{\mathcal{R}_G wu, \check{\mathcal{R}}_G wu, \Gamma} \ (\mathsf{comp_{G1}})$$

$$\frac{\Gamma, \mathcal{R}_G wv, v : \phi}{\Gamma, w : \mathsf{G}\phi} \ (\mathsf{G})^* \qquad \frac{\Gamma, \mathcal{R}_G wu, w : \mathsf{F}\phi, u : \phi}{\Gamma, \mathcal{R}_G wu, w : \mathsf{F}\phi} \ (\mathsf{F}) \qquad \frac{\mathcal{R}_G wu, \mathcal{R}_H uw, \Gamma}{\mathcal{R}_G wu, \Gamma} \ (\mathsf{conv}_\mathsf{G})$$

$$\frac{\Gamma, \mathcal{R}_{Ag} wu, w : \langle Ag \rangle \phi, u : \phi}{\Gamma, \mathcal{R}_{Ag} wu, w : \langle Ag \rangle \phi} \ (\langle \mathsf{Ag} \rangle) \qquad \frac{\mathcal{R}_{Ag} ww, \Gamma}{\Gamma} \ (\mathsf{refl}_{Ag}) \qquad \frac{w = w, \Gamma}{\Gamma} \ (\mathsf{refl}_=)$$

$$\frac{\mathcal{R}_G uv, \mathcal{R}_G wu, \mathcal{R}_G wv, \Gamma \qquad u = v, \mathcal{R}_G wu, \mathcal{R}_G wv, \Gamma \qquad \mathcal{R}_G vu, \mathcal{R}_G wu, \mathcal{R}_G wv, \Gamma}{\mathcal{R}_G wu, \mathcal{R}_G wv, \Gamma} \ (\mathsf{conn}_\mathsf{G})$$

$$\frac{\mathcal{R}_H uv, \mathcal{R}_H wu, \mathcal{R}_H wv, \Gamma \qquad u = v, \mathcal{R}_H wu, \mathcal{R}_H wv, \Gamma \qquad \mathcal{R}_H vu, \mathcal{R}_H wu, \mathcal{R}_H wv, \Gamma}{\mathcal{R}_H wu, \mathcal{R}_H wv, \Gamma} \ (\mathsf{conn}_\mathsf{H})$$

$$\frac{\mathcal{R}_G wu, \mathcal{R}_\square uz, \mathcal{R}_{Ag} wv, \mathcal{R}_G vz, \Gamma}{\mathcal{R}_G wu, \mathcal{R}_\square uz, \Gamma} \ (\mathsf{ncuh})^* \qquad \frac{\mathcal{R}_G wu, \Gamma \qquad \check{\mathcal{R}}_G wu, \Gamma}{\Gamma} \ (\mathsf{comp}_\mathsf{G2})$$

$$\frac{\mathcal{R}_G wu, \mathcal{R}_G uv, \mathcal{R}_G wv, \Gamma}{\mathcal{R}_G wu, \mathcal{R}_G uv, \Gamma} \ (\mathsf{trans}_\mathsf{G}) \qquad \frac{\mathcal{R}_{Ag} wu, \mathcal{R}_i wu, \Gamma}{\mathcal{R}_{Ag} wu, \Gamma} \ (\mathsf{agd}) \qquad \frac{\Gamma, \mathcal{R}_H wv, v : \phi}{\Gamma, w : \mathsf{H}\phi} \ (\mathsf{H})^*$$

$$\frac{\mathcal{R}_G wv, \Gamma}{\Gamma} \ (\mathsf{ser}_\mathsf{G})^* \qquad \frac{\mathcal{R}_{Ag} wu, \mathcal{R}_{Ag} wv, \mathcal{R}_{Ag} uv, \Gamma}{\mathcal{R}_{Ag} wu, \mathcal{R}_{Ag} wv, \Gamma} \ (\mathsf{eucl}_{Ag}) \qquad \frac{\mathcal{R}_\square wu, \check{\mathcal{R}}_G wu, \Gamma}{\mathcal{R}_\square wu, \Gamma} \ (\mathsf{irr}_\mathsf{G})$$

$$\frac{w = u, \Delta[w], \Delta[u], \Gamma}{w = u, \Delta[w], \Gamma} \ (\mathsf{sub}_=) \qquad \frac{w = u, w = v, u = v, \Gamma}{w = u, w = v, \Gamma} \ (\mathsf{eucl}_=) \qquad \frac{\Gamma, \mathcal{R}_{Ag} wv, v : A}{\Gamma, w : [Ag]A} \ ([\mathsf{Ag}])^*$$

For (H), ([Ag]), (G), (ncuh), *and* (ser$_\mathsf{G}$) *the '*$*$*' states that v must be an eigenvariable.*

We note that the rules (conv$_\mathsf{G}$) and (conv$_\mathsf{H}$) express the converse relation between $\mathcal{R}_\mathsf{G}$ and $\mathcal{R}_\mathsf{H}$, and the rules (agd), (conn$_\mathsf{G}$), (conn$_\mathsf{H}$), (ncuh) and $\{(\mathsf{irr}_\mathsf{G}), (\mathsf{comp}_\mathsf{G1}), (\mathsf{comp}_\mathsf{G2})\}$ correspond to conditions **(C3)–(C7)** of Definition 2, respectively. Furthermore, the notation $\Delta[u]$ in the substitution rule (sub$_=$) is used to express a collection of relational atoms and labelled formulae where all occurrences of the label w in $\Delta[w]$ have been replaced by occurrences of u. This notation uniformly captures all of the substitution rules given in [20].

Theorem 7 (Soundness). *Every sequent derivable in* G3Tstit *is valid.*

Proof. Similar to Theorem 3.

Unfortunately, with respect G3Tstit completeness, we cannot use the relatively simple strategy applied in proving G3Ldm completeness. This is because the irreflexivity rule (Definition 7) does not readily lend itself to derivation in G3Tstit. Here we prove G3Tstit completeness relative to irreflexive Tstit-frames by leveraging the methods presented in [21]. (NB. For this reason, we introduced $\check{\mathcal{R}}_\mathsf{G}$–the complement of $\mathcal{R}_\mathsf{G}$–directly into the language of the proof system).

Lemma 2. *Let Γ be a* G3Tstit*-sequent. Either, Γ is* G3Tstit*-derivable, or it has a* Tstit*-countermodel.*

Proof. We construct the *Reduction Tree* (**RT**) of a given sequent Γ, following the method of [21]. If **RT** is finite, all leaves are initial sequents that are conclusions of (id) or (comp$_{G1}$). If **RT** is infinite, by König's lemma, there exists an infinite branch: $\Gamma_0, \Gamma_1, ..., \Gamma_n,...$ (with $\Gamma_0 = \Gamma$). Let $\Gamma = \bigcup \Gamma_i$. We define a Tstit-model $M^* = (W, \mathcal{R}_\square, \{R_i | i \in Ag\}, \mathcal{R}_{Ag}, \mathcal{R}_G, \mathcal{R}_H, V)$ as follows: Let $x \sim_\Gamma y$ *iff* $x = y \in \Gamma$. (Usage of the rules (ref$_=$) and (eucl$_=$) in the infinite branch ensure $\sim_\Gamma$ is an equivalence relation.) Define W to consist of all equivalence classes $[x]$ of labels in Γ under $\sim_\Gamma$. For each $\mathcal{R}_\alpha x y \in \Gamma$ let $([x]_{\sim_\Gamma}, [y]_{\sim_\Gamma}) \in \mathcal{R}_\alpha$ (with $\mathcal{R}_\alpha \in \{\mathcal{R}_\square, \mathcal{R}_i, \mathcal{R}_{Ag}, \mathcal{R}_G, \check{\mathcal{R}}_G, \mathcal{R}_H\}$), and for each labelled propositional atom $x : p \in \Gamma$, let $[x]_{\sim_\Gamma} \notin V(p)$. It is a routine task to show that all relations and the valuation are well-defined. Last, let the interpretation $I : L \mapsto W$ map each label x to the class of labels $[x]_{\sim_\Gamma}$ containing x, and suppose I maps all other labels not in Γ arbitrarily. We show that: **(i)** M^* is a Tstit model, and **(ii)** M^* is a counter-model for Γ.

(i) First, we assume w.l.o.g. that $\Gamma \neq \emptyset$ because the empty sequent is not satisfied on any model. Thus, there must exist at least one label in Γ; i.e. $W \neq \emptyset$.

We argue that $\mathcal{R}_\square$ is an equivalence relation and omit the analogues proofs showing that $\mathcal{R}_i$ and $\mathcal{R}_{Ag}$ are equivalence relations. Suppose, for some Γ_n in the infinite branch there occurs a label x but $\mathcal{R}_\square xx \notin \Gamma_n$. By definition of **RT**, at some later stage Γ_{n+k} the rule (refl$_\square$) will be applied; hence, $\mathcal{R}_\square xx \in \Gamma$. The argument is similar for the (eucl$_\square$) rule. Properties **(C1)** and **(C2)** follow from the rules (br$_{[i]}$) and (IOA), respectively. Regarding **(C3)**, we only obtain $\mathcal{R}_{Ag} \subseteq \bigcap_{i \in Ag} \mathcal{R}_i$ in M^* via the (agd) rule. Using lemma 9 of [17], we can transform M^* into a model where (i) $\mathcal{R}_{Ag} = \bigcap_{i \in Ag} \mathcal{R}_i$ and where (ii) the model satisfies the same formulae.

We obtain that $\mathcal{R}_G$ is transitive and serial due to the (trans$_G$) and (ser$_G$) rules. $\mathcal{R}_H$ is the converse of $\mathcal{R}_G$ by (conv$_G$) and (conv$_H$). The properties **(C4)**, **(C5)** and **(C6)** follow from the rules (conn$_G$), (conn$_H$) and (ncuh), respectively.

(C7) follows from (irr$_G$), (comp$_{G1}$), and the equality rules: these rules ensure that (∗) if $[u]_{\sim_\Gamma} \in \mathcal{R}_\square([w]_{\sim_\Gamma})$, then $[u]_{\sim_\Gamma} \notin \mathcal{R}_G([w]_{\sim_\Gamma})$. In what follows, we abuse notation and use $[w]$ to denote equivocally the label w, as well as any other label v for which a chain of equalities between w and v occurs in the sequent. The claim (∗) is obtained accordingly: if both $\mathcal{R}_\square[w][u]$ and $\mathcal{R}_G[w][u]$ appear together in some sequent Γ_i, then higher up in the infinite branch, the equality rules will introduce relational atoms of the form $\mathcal{R}_\square w'u'$ and $\mathcal{R}_G w'u'$. Eventually, the rule (irr$_G$) will also be applied and, subsequently, the rule (comp$_{G1}$) will ensure that the reduction tree procedure halts for the given branch. Moreover, if $\mathcal{R}_G[w][w]$ occurs in a sequent Γ_i of **RT**, then higher up in the branch the equality rules will introduce a relational atom of the form $\mathcal{R}_G w'w'$. Eventually, (refl$_\square$) will be applied which adds $\mathcal{R}_\square w'w'$ to the branch containing Γ_i. Lastly, (irr$_G$) will be applied even higher up this branch, adding $\check{\mathcal{R}}_G w'w'$, which by (comp$_{G1}$) will halt the **RT**-procedure for that branch. Thus we may conclude: for any infinite branch of **RT** $\mathcal{R}_G ww$ will not occur for any label w; meaning that not only will M^* satisfy **(C7)**, its relation $\mathcal{R}_G$ will be irreflexive. Additionally, note that (comp$_{G2}$) will ensure that $\check{\mathcal{R}}_G$ is the complement of $\mathcal{R}_G$.

Lastly, as long as $[x]_{\sim_r} \notin V(p)$ when $x : p \in \Gamma$, all other labels can be mapped by V in any arbitrary manner. Thus, V is a valid valuation function.

(ii) By construction, M^* satisfies each relational atom in Γ, and therefore, satisfies each relational atom in Γ. By induction on the complexity of ϕ it is shown that for any formula $x : \phi \in \Gamma$ we have $M^*, [x]_{\sim_r} \not\models \phi$ (See [21] for details). Hence, Γ is falsified on M^* with I.

Theorem 8 (Completeness). *Every valid sequent is derivable in* G3Tstit.

Proof. Follows from Lemma 2.

4   The Logic Xstit

4.1   Axioms and Relational Semantics for Xstit

A common feature of the *cstit*- and *dstit*-operator is that they do not internally employ temporal structures. In this section, we consider the logic of Xstit which contains a non-instantaneous STIT-operator explicitly affecting next states. This logic, introduced in [7,8], has been motivated by the observation that affecting next states is a central aspect of agency in computer science. Moreover, extensions of the logic Xstit have been employed to investigate the concepts of purposeful and voluntary acts and their relation to different levels of legal culpability [7]. The logic was originally proposed for a two-dimensional semantics making reference to both states and histories; the latter defined as maximally linear ordered paths on a frame. In this section, we provide a semantics for Xstit that relies on relational frames, avoiding the use of complex two-dimensional indices (the possibility of which was already noted in [7]). We provide a labelled calculus G3Xstit for this logic and prove that it is sound and complete with respect to its relational characterization. Furthermore, by showing a correspondence between the original Hilbert system Xstit and the calculus G3Xstit we show that the language of Xstit does not allow us to distinguish between the two available semantics.

Definition 9 (The Language $\mathcal{L}_{\mathsf{Xstit}}$). *Let $Ag = \{1, 2, ..., n\}$ be a finite set of agent labels and let $Var = \{p_1, p_2, p_3...\}$ be a countable set of propositional variables. $\mathcal{L}_{\mathsf{Xstit}}$ is defined as follows:*

$$\phi ::= p \mid \overline{p} \mid \phi \wedge \phi \mid \phi \vee \phi \mid \Box\phi \mid \Diamond\phi \mid [A]^x\phi \mid \langle A \rangle^x\phi \mid [X]\phi \mid \langle X \rangle\phi$$

where $p \in Var$; and $A \subseteq Ag$ (with special cases $\emptyset$ and Ag).

The language uses the settledness operator $\Box$, a group-stit operator $[A]^x$, and the operator $[X]$ referring to the next state. Formulae of the form $[A]^x\phi$ must be read as 'group A effectively sees to it that in the next state ϕ holds'.

As mentioned previously, we provide a semantics for the logic Xstit based on relational frames. The conditions on these frames are obtained through a simple transformation of the two-dimensional frame properties presented in [7].

Definition 10 (Relational Xstit Frames and Models). *An* Xstit-*frame is defined to be a tuple* $F = (W, \mathcal{R}_\square, \mathcal{R}_X, \{\mathcal{R}_A | A \subseteq Ag\})$ *such that* $W \neq \emptyset$ *and:*

(D1) $\mathcal{R}_\square \subseteq W \times W$ *is an equivalence relation;*
(D2) $\mathcal{R}_X \subseteq W \times W$ *is serial and deterministic;*
(D3) $\mathcal{R}_A \subseteq W \times W$ *such that,*

  (i) $\mathcal{R}_\emptyset = \mathcal{R}_\square \circ \mathcal{R}_X$;
  (ii) $\mathcal{R}_{Ag} = \mathcal{R}_X \circ \mathcal{R}_\square$;
  (iii) $\mathcal{R}_A \subseteq \mathcal{R}_B$ *for* $\emptyset \subseteq B \subseteq A \subseteq Ag$;
  (iv) *For any* $B, A \subseteq Ag$ *(s.t.* $B \cap A = \emptyset$*) and* $\forall w_1, w_2, w_3, w_5, w_6 \in W$ *we have:* $(\mathcal{R}_\square w_1 w_2 \wedge \mathcal{R}_\square w_1 w_3) \rightarrow \exists w_4 (\mathcal{R}_\square w_1 w_4 \wedge (\mathcal{R}_A w_4 w_5 \rightarrow \mathcal{R}_A w_2 w_5) \wedge (\mathcal{R}_B w_4 w_6 \rightarrow \mathcal{R}_B w_3 w_6))$

A relational Xstit-*model is a tuple* $M = (F, V)$ *where* F *is an* Xstit-*frame and* V *a valuation function mapping propositional variables* $p_i \in Var$ *to subsets of* W; *i.e.* $V : Var \mapsto \mathcal{P}(W)$.

Condition (D3)-(iv) expresses the *independence of agents* principle for Xstit. From condition (D3)-(ii) we obtain that $\mathcal{R}_{Ag} \subseteq \mathcal{R}_X \circ \mathcal{R}_\square$, which ensures the principle of *no choice between undivided histories* (*cf.* Definition 2, C6). Furthermore, we stress that, following [7], the relation $\mathcal{R}_X$ is not explicitly defined as a *strict* next-relation; that is, the frame construction allows for reflexive worlds. For a discussion of all the frame properties we refer the reader to [7].

Definition 11 (Semantics of $\mathcal{L}_{\text{Xstit}}$). *To define the satisfaction of a formula* $\phi \in \mathcal{L}_{\text{Xstit}}$ *on* M *at* w, *we make use of clauses (1)–(6) from Definition 3, taking* M *to be an* Xstit-*model (but omitting explicit mention of* M *in the clauses), along with the following clauses (global truth and validity are defined as usual):*

7. $w \models [A]^x \phi$ *iff* $\forall u \in \mathcal{R}_A(w)$, $u \models \phi$;   9. $w \models \lfloor X \rfloor \phi$ *iff* $\forall u \in \mathcal{R}_X(w)$, $u \models \phi$;
8. $w \models \langle A \rangle^x \phi$ *iff* $\exists u \in \mathcal{R}_A(w)$, $u \models \phi$;   10. $w \models \langle X \rangle \phi$ *iff* $\exists u \in \mathcal{R}_X(w)$, $u \models \phi$.

Definition 12 (The Logic Xstit [7]). *The Hilbert system for* Xstit *consists of the axioms and rules below, where* $\phi, \psi \in \mathcal{L}_{\text{Xstit}}$, $A \subseteq Ag$ *and* $\alpha \in \{\square, [A]^x, [X]\}$:

$$\phi \rightarrow (\psi \rightarrow \phi) \quad (\overline{\psi} \rightarrow \overline{\phi}) \rightarrow (\phi \rightarrow \psi) \quad (\phi \rightarrow (\psi \rightarrow \chi)) \rightarrow ((\phi \rightarrow \psi) \rightarrow (\phi \rightarrow \chi))$$

$$\alpha(\phi \rightarrow \psi) \rightarrow (\alpha\phi \rightarrow \alpha\psi) \quad \square\phi \rightarrow \phi \quad \Diamond\phi \rightarrow \square\Diamond\phi \quad [A]^x\phi \rightarrow \langle A \rangle^x\phi \quad \langle X \rangle\phi \rightarrow [X]\phi$$

$$\square[X]\phi \leftrightarrow [\emptyset]^x\phi \quad [Ag]^x\phi \leftrightarrow [X]\square\phi \quad [A]^x\phi \rightarrow [B]^x\phi^{(\dagger)} \quad \square\phi \vee \Diamond\overline{\phi} \quad [A]^x\phi \vee \langle A \rangle^x\overline{\phi}$$

$$\Diamond[A]^x\phi \wedge \Diamond[B]^x\psi \rightarrow \Diamond([A]^x\phi \wedge [B]^x\psi)^{(\dagger\dagger)} \quad [X]\phi \vee \langle X \rangle\overline{\phi} \quad \frac{\phi \quad \phi \rightarrow \psi}{\psi} \quad \frac{\phi}{\alpha\phi}$$

where $(\dagger) A \subseteq B \subseteq Ag$; *and* $(\dagger\dagger) A \cap B = \emptyset$.

A derivation of ϕ in Xstit from Θ is written as $\Theta \vdash_{\text{Xstit}} \phi$. When Θ is the empty set, we refer to ϕ as a *theorem* and write $\vdash_{\text{Xstit}} \phi$.

We refer to $\Diamond[A]^x\phi \wedge \Diamond[B]^x\psi \to \Diamond([A]^x\phi \wedge [B]^x\psi)$ as the IOA^x-axiom. In contrast with the standard IOA-axiom, observe that IOA^x-axiom refers to the independence of isolated *groups* of agents with respect to *successor* states. For a natural language interpretation of the other axioms of Xstit we refer to [7].

Instead of proving completeness for the intended sequent calculus directly, we prove it first for the Hilbert calculus. This enables us to eventually conclude the equivalence of these two calculi with respect to the logic Xstit.

Theorem 9 (Completeness of Xstit). *For all $\phi \in \mathcal{L}_{\mathsf{Xstit}}$, if $\models \phi$, then $\vdash_{\mathsf{Xstit}} \phi$.*

Proof. As observed in [7], all axioms of Xstit are Sahlqvist formulae. Furthermore, the first-order correspondents of the Xstit axioms taken together define the class of frames from Definition 10. Applying Theorem 4.42 of [6], we obtain that the logic Xstit is complete relative to this class of frames.

4.2   A Cut-Free Labelled Calculus for Xstit

We provide a labelled calculus G3Xstit that is sound and complete relative to the relational frames of Definition 10. In order to convert the Xstit axiomatization into rules for the intended calculus, we first observe that every axiom of Xstit is a *geometric formula* with the exception of the IOA^x axiom. For the geometric formulae we can find corresponding geometric rules, following [20]. The first-order frame condition (D3)(iv) for IOA^x (Definition 10) is not a geometric formula; however, we observe that its components $\mathcal{R}_A w_4 w_5 \to \mathcal{R}_A w_2 w_5$ and $\mathcal{R}_B w_4 w_6 \to \mathcal{R}_B w_3 w_6$ in fact are. The IOA^x-condition is, thus, a *generalized geometric axiom* of type GA_1 and we may therefore find an equivalent system of rules, following [22].

We refer to the following system of rules $\langle(\mathsf{IOA-E}), \{(\mathsf{IOA-U_1}), (\mathsf{IOA-U_2})\}\rangle$ as the 'independence of agents' rule ($\mathsf{IOA_X}$). We may use the rule ($\mathsf{IOA-E}$) wherever throughout the course of a derivation, but if we use either ($\mathsf{IOA-U_1}$) or ($\mathsf{IOA-U_2}$), then we must (i) use the other ($\mathsf{IOA-U}_i$) rule (for $i \in \{1,2\}$) in a separate branch of the derivation and (ii) use the ($\mathsf{IOA-E}$) rule below both instances of ($\mathsf{IOA-U}_i$); *i.e.* the derivation is of the form represented below:

$$\frac{\mathcal{R}_A w_4 w_5, \mathcal{R}_A w_2 w_5, \Gamma}{\mathcal{R}_A w_4 w_5, \Gamma} \ (\mathsf{IOA-U_1}) \qquad \frac{\mathcal{R}_B w_4 w_6, \mathcal{R}_B w_3 w_6, \Gamma'}{\mathcal{R}_B w_4 w_6, \Gamma'} \ (\mathsf{IOA-U_2})$$

$$\vdots \qquad\qquad\qquad \vdots$$

$$\frac{R_\square w_1 w_2, R_\square w_1 w_3, R_\square w_1 w_4, \Gamma''}{R_\square w_1 w_2, R_\square w_1 w_3, \Gamma''} \ (\mathsf{IOA-E})^*$$

where (*) w_4 is an eigenvariable in the ($\mathsf{IOA-E}$) rule.

Definition 13 (The Calculus G3Xstit). *The labeled calculus G3Xstit consists of the rules* (id), $(\wedge)$, $(\vee)$, $(\mathsf{refl}_=)$, $(\mathsf{eucl}_=)$, $(\mathsf{sub}_=)$, $(\square)$, $(\Diamond)$, $(\mathsf{refl}_\square)$, *and* $(\mathsf{eucl}_\square)$ *from Definitions 5 and 8 extended with the* ($\mathsf{IOA_X}$)*-rule and the following:*

$$\frac{\Gamma, \mathcal{R}_A wv, v : \phi}{\Gamma, w : [A]^x \phi} \ ([A]^x)^* \qquad \frac{\Gamma, \mathcal{R}_A wu, w : \langle A \rangle^x \phi, u : \phi}{\Gamma, \mathcal{R}_A wu, w : \langle A \rangle^x \phi} \ (\langle A \rangle^x)$$

$$\frac{\Gamma, \mathcal{R}_X wv, w : \langle X \rangle \phi, v : \phi}{\Gamma, \mathcal{R}_X wvw : \langle X \rangle \phi} \ (\langle X \rangle) \qquad \frac{\mathcal{R}_\square wv, \mathcal{R}_X vu, \mathcal{R}_\emptyset wu, \Gamma}{\mathcal{R}_\square wv, \mathcal{R}_X vu, \Gamma} \ (\mathsf{Eff}\emptyset)$$

$$\frac{\mathcal{R}_A wv, \mathcal{R}_B wv, \Gamma}{\mathcal{R}_A wv, \Gamma} \ (\mathsf{C-Mon})^\dagger \qquad \frac{\mathcal{R}_X wv, \Gamma}{\Gamma} \ (\mathsf{ser}_X)^* \qquad \frac{v = u, \mathcal{R}_X wv, \mathcal{R}_X wu, \Gamma}{\mathcal{R}_X wv, \mathcal{R}_X wu, \Gamma} \ (\mathsf{det}_X)$$

$$\frac{\Gamma, \mathcal{R}_X wv, v : \phi}{\Gamma, w : [X] \phi} \ ([X])^* \qquad \frac{\mathcal{R}_\square wv, \mathcal{R}_X vu, \mathcal{R}_\emptyset wu, \Gamma}{\mathcal{R}_\emptyset wu, \Gamma} \ (\emptyset\mathsf{Eff})^*$$

$$\frac{\mathcal{R}_{Ag} wu, \mathcal{R}_X wv, \mathcal{R}_\square vu, \Gamma}{\mathcal{R}_X wv, \mathcal{R}_\square vu, \Gamma} \ (\mathsf{EffAg}) \qquad \frac{\mathcal{R}_{Ag} wu, \mathcal{R}_X wv, \mathcal{R}_\square vu, \Gamma}{\mathcal{R}_{Ag} wu, \Gamma} \ (\mathsf{AgEff})^*$$

where $(*)$ v is an eigenvariable; and $(\dagger)$ $B \subseteq A \subseteq Ag$.

Observe that the rules $\{(\emptyset\mathsf{Eff}), (\mathsf{Eff}\emptyset)\}, \{(\mathsf{AgEff}), (\mathsf{EffAg})\}, (\mathsf{C-Mon})$ and (IOA_X) of the labelled calculus G3Xstit capture the frame conditions (D3)$(i)-(iv)$ of Definition 10, respectively.[1]

Theorem 10 (Soundness). *Every sequent derivable in* G3Xstit *is valid.*

Proof. Similar to Theorem 3. Since all rules of G3Xstit are generalized geometric rules, we can apply the general soundness results of Theorem 6.3 of [22]. □

In order to prove completeness of G3Xstit relative to the logic Xstit, we employ the same strategy as for G3Ldm, by first proving that every formula derivable in Xstit is derivable in G3Xstit.

Lemma 3. *For all* $\phi \in \mathcal{L}_{\mathsf{Xstit}}$, *if* $\vdash_{\mathsf{Xstit}} \phi$, *then* $\vdash_{\mathsf{G3Xstit}} x : \phi$.

Proof. The derivation of each axiom and inference rule is straightforward (See [20]). The G3Xstit-derivation of the IOA^x-axiom can be obtained by applying the rule system (IOA_X) (see appendix at http://arxiv.org/abs/1902.06632). □

Corollary 1 (Completeness). *For all* $\phi \in \mathcal{L}_{\mathsf{Xstit}}$, *if* $\models \phi$, *then* $\vdash_{\mathsf{G3Xstit}} x : \phi$

Proof. Follows from Theorem 9 and Lemma 3. □

As another consequence, we obtain that the logic Xstit can be characterized without using two-dimensional frames employing histories, as applied in [7].

---

[1] In [22] it is shown that every generalized geometric formula can be captured through (a system of) rules, allowing for the construction of *analytic* calculi for the minimal modal logic K extended with any axioms from the Sahlqvist class. Since all axioms of Ldm and Xstit are Sahlqvist formulae, the results also apply to these logics.

5   Conclusion and Future Work

In this paper, we laid the proof-theoretic foundations for implementable logics of agency by providing calculi for one of its central formalisms: STIT logic. In particular, we developed cut-free labelled sequent calculi for three STIT logics: Ldm, Tstit and Xstit. Furthermore, by providing the cut-free calculus G3Tstit for temporal STIT logic we answered the open question from [27]. All labelled calculi presented in this work, are sound and cut-free complete relative to their classes of *temporal relational* frames. As a corollary to the latter, we extended prior results from [2,14,17] and provided a characterization of Xstit through relational frames.

We see two possible future extensions of the calculi provided in this paper: First, we aim to use these calculi to solve the decidability problems for Tstit and Xstit, which are currently open questions. Our approach will be proof-theoretic in nature and will consist of showing decidability via proof-search. To realize our goal, we plan on harnessing refinement (i.e. internalization) procedures, such as those in [9], to obtain variants of our labelled calculi that are more suitable for proof-search. Second, we aim to extend the current calculi to incorporate formal concepts that enable reasoning about normative choice-making, for example, those found in utilitarian deontic STIT [16,19] and legal theory [18].

Acknowledgments. The authors would like to thank their supervisor Agata Ciabattoni for her helpful comments.

References

1. Arkoudas, K., Bringsjord S., Bello, P.: Toward ethical robots via mechanized deontic logic. In: AAAI Fall Symposium on Machine Ethics, pp. 17–23 (2005)
2. Balbiani, P., Herzig, A., Troquard, N.: Alternative axiomatics and complexity of deliberative STIT theories. J. Philos. Logic **37**(4), 387–406 (2008)
3. Belnap, N., Perloff, M.: Seeing to it that: a canonical form for agentives. In: Kyburg, H.E., Loui, R.P., Carlson, G.N. (eds.) Knowledge Representation and Defeasible Reasoning, pp. 167–190. Springer, Dordrecht (1990). https://doi.org/10.1007/978-94-009-0553-5_7
4. Belnap, N., Perloff, M., Xu, M.: Facing the Future: Agents and Choices in Our Indeterminist World. Oxford University Press on Demand, Oxford (2001)
5. van Berkel, K., Pascucci, M.: Notions of instrumentality in agency logic. In: Miller, T., Oren, N., Sakurai, Y., Noda, I., Savarimuthu, B.T.R., Cao Son, T. (eds.) PRIMA 2018. LNCS (LNAI), vol. 11224, pp. 403–419. Springer, Cham (2018). https://doi.org/10.1007/978-3-030-03098-8_25
6. Blackburn, P., de Rijke, M., Venema, Y.: Modal Logic. Cambridge University Press, Cambridge (2001)
7. Broersen, J.: Deontic epistemic stit logic distinguishing modes of Mens Rea. J. Appl. Logic **9**(2), 137–152 (2011)
8. Broersen, J.: Making a start with the stit logic analysis of intentional action. J. Philos. Logic **40**(4), 499–530 (2011)
9. Ciabattoni, A., Lyon, T., Ramanayake, R., Tiu, A.: Mutual translations between nested and labelled calculi for tense logics (2019, unpublished)

10. Gabbay, D.M., Hodkinson, I., Reynolds, M.: Temporal Logic: Mathematical Foundations and Computational Aspects. Oxford University Press, Oxford (1994)
11. Gentzen, G.: Untersuchungen über das logische Schließen. Mathematische Zeitschrift **39**(3), 405–431 (1935)
12. Gerdes, J.C., Thornton, S.M.: Implementable ethics for autonomous vehicles. In: Maurer, M., Gerdes, J.C., Lenz, B., Winner, H. (eds.) Autonomes Fahren, pp. 87–102. Springer, Heidelberg (2015). https://doi.org/10.1007/978-3-662-45854-9_5
13. Goodall, N.J.: Machine ethics and automated vehicles. In: Meyer, G., Beiker, S. (eds.) Road Vehicle Automation. Lecture Notes in Mobility, pp. 93–102. Springer, Cham (2014). https://doi.org/10.1007/978-3-319-05990-7_9
14. Herzig, A., Schwarzentruber, F.: Properties of logics of individual and group agency. In: Advances in Modal Logic, vol. 7, pp. 133–149. College Publications (2008)
15. Horty, J.F., Belnap, N.: The deliberative stit: a study of action, omission, ability, and obligation. J. Philos. Logic **24**(6), 583–644 (1995)
16. Horty, J.: Agency and Deontic Logic. Oxford University Press, Oxford (2001)
17. Lorini, E.: Temporal STIT logic and its application to normative reasoning. J. Appl. Non-Class. Logics **23**(4), 372–399 (2013)
18. Lorini, E., Sartor, G.: Influence and responsibility: a logical analysis. In: Legal Knowledge and Information Systems, pp. 51–60. IOS Press (2015)
19. Murakami, Y.: Utilitarian deontic logic. In: Advances in Modal Logic, vol. 5, pp. 211–230. King's College Publications (2005)
20. Negri, S.: Proof analysis in modal logic. J. Philos. Logic **34**(5–6), 507–544 (2005)
21. Negri, S.: Kripke completeness revisited. In: Acts of Knowledge-History, Philosophy and Logic, pp. 247–282 (2009)
22. Negri, S.: Proof analysis beyond geometric theories: from rule systems to systems of rules. J. Logic Comput. **26**(2), 513–537 (2016)
23. Negri, S., von Plato, J.: Structural Proof Theory. Cambridge University Press, Cambridge (2001)
24. Olkhovikov, G., Wansing, H.: An axiomatic system and a tableau calculus for STIT imagination logic. J. Philos. Logic **47**(2), 259–279 (2018)
25. Prior, A.N.: Past, Present and Future. Clarendon Press, Oxford (1967)
26. Viganò, L.: Labelled Non-Classical Logics. Kluwer Academic Publishers (2000)
27. Wansing, H.: Tableaux for multi-agent deliberative-stit logic. In: Advances in Modal Logic, vol. 6, pp. 503–520. College Publications (2006)
28. Xu, M.: Actions as events. J. Philos. Logic **41**(4), 765–809 (2012)

Author Index

Printed in the United States
By Bookmasters